Penguin Books

**The Global 2000 Report
to the President**

The Global
2000 Report
to the President

Entering the Twenty-First Century

D1564363

## About the Cover

*The Global 2000 Report to
the President* presents a
picture that can be painted
only in broad strokes and with
a brush still in need of
additional bristles. It is,
however, the most complete
and consistent such picture
ever painted by the U.S.
Government. Many rapid and
undesirable developments
are foreseen if public policies
concerning population
stabilization, resource
conservation, and environmental protection remain unchanged over the coming
decades. Vigorous and determined new initiatives are
needed around the world.
These initiatives need to be
taken soon while the picture
is yet fluid and nations are still
preparing to enter the twenty-
first century.

# The Global
# 2000 Report
# to the President

Penguin Books

Penguin Books Ltd, Harmondsworth, Middlesex, England
Penguin Books, 625 Madison Avenue, New York, New York 10022, U.S.A.
Penguin Books Australia Ltd, Ringwood, Victoria, Australia
Penguin Books Canada Ltd, 2801 John Street, Markham, Ontario, Canada L3R 1B4
Penguin Books (N.Z.) Ltd, 182-190 Wairau Road, Auckland 10, New Zealand

First published in Great Britain by Allen Lane 1982
Published simultaneously in Penguin Books

Made and printed in Great Britain by
Butler and Tanner Ltd

# The Global 2000 Report to the President

## Entering the Twenty-First Century

A Report Prepared by the Council on Environmental Quality and the Department of State

Gerald O. Barney
Study Director

Volume One

## Letter of Transmittal

The President

Sir: In your Environmental Message to the Congress of May 23, 1977, you directed the Council on Environmental Quality and the Department of State, working with other federal agencies, to study the "probable changes in the world's population, natural resources, and environment through the end of the century." This endeavor was to serve as "the foundation of our longer-term planning."

The effort we then undertook to project present world trends and to establish a foundation for planning is now complete, and we are pleased to present our report to you. What emerges are not predictions but rather projections developed by U.S. Government agencies of what will happen to population, resources, and environment if present policies continue.

Our conclusions, summarized in the pages that follow, are disturbing. They indicate the potential for global problems of alarming proportions by the year 2000. Environmental, resource, and population stresses are intensifying and will increasingly determine the quality of human life on our planet. These stresses are already severe enough to deny many millions of people basic needs for food, shelter, health, and jobs, or any hope for betterment. At the same time, the earth's carrying capacity—the ability of biological systems to provide resources for human needs—is eroding. The trends reflected in the Global 2000 Study suggest strongly a progressive degradation and improverishment of the earth's natural resource base.

If these trends are to be altered and the problems diminished, vigorous, determined new initiatives will be required worldwide to meet human needs while protecting and restoring the earth's capacity to support life. Basic natural resources—farmlands, fisheries, forests, minerals, energy, air, and water—must be conserved and better managed. Changes in public policy are needed around the world before problems worsen and options for effective action are reduced.

A number of responses to global resource, environment, and population problems—responses only touched on in the Study—are underway. Heightened international concern is reflected in the "Megaconferences" convened by the United Nations during the last decade: Human Environment (1972), Population (1974), Food (1974), Human Settlements (1976), Water (1977), Desertification (1977), Science and Technology for Development (1979), and New and Renewable Sources of Energy, scheduled for August 1981 in Nairobi. The United States has contributed actively to these conferences, proposing and supporting remedial actions of which many are now being taken. We are also working with other nations bilaterally, building concern for population growth, natural resources, and environment into our foreign aid programs and cooperating with our immediate neighbors on common problems ranging from cleanup of air and water pollution to preservation of soils and development of new crops. Many nations around the world are adopting new approaches—replanting deforested areas, conserving energy, making family planning measures widely available, using natural predators and selective pesticides to protect crops instead of broadscale destructive application of chemicals.

Nonetheless, given the urgency, scope, and complexity of the challenges before us, the efforts now underway around the world fall far short of what is needed. An era of unprecedented global cooperation and commitment is essential.

The necessary changes go beyond the capability of any single nation. But our nation can itself take important and exemplary steps. Because of our preeminent position as a producer and consumer of food and energy, our efforts to conserve soil, farmlands, and energy resources are of global, as well as national, importance. We can avoid polluting our own environment, and we must take care that we do not degrade the global environment.

Beyond our borders we can expand our collaboration with both developed and developing nations in a spirit of generosity and justice. Hundreds of millions of the world's people are now trapped in a condition of abject poverty. People at the margin of existence must take cropland, grazing land, and fuel where they can find it, regardless of the effects upon the earth's resource base. Sustainable economic development, coupled with environmental protection, resource management, and family planning is essential. Equally important are better understanding and effective responses to such global problems as the buildup of carbon dioxide in the atmosphere and the threat of species loss on a massive scale.

Finally, to meet the challenges described in the Global 2000 Study our federal government requires a much stronger capability to project and analyze long-term trends. The Study clearly points to the need for improving the present foundation for long-term planning. On this foundation rest decisions that involve the future welfare of the Nation.

We wish to express our thanks to and our admiration for the Director of the Global 2000 Study, Dr. Gerald O. Barney and his staff. Their diligence, dedication, and ability to bring forth the best from a legion of contributors is much appreciated. Special thanks is also due to those of the Council on Environmental Quality and the Department of State who worked closely with the Study and to the 11 other agencies that contributed greatly to it.\* Without the detailed knowledge provided by these agencies' experts, the Global 2000 Study would have been impossible.

Respectfully,

THOMAS R. PICKERING
*Assistant Secretary, Oceans and*
*International Environmental*
*and Scientific Affairs,*
*Department of State*

GUS SPETH
*Chairman,*
*Council on Environmental*
*Quality*

\*The Federal agencies that cooperated with us in this effort were the Departments of Agriculture, Energy, and the Interior, the Agency for International Development, the Central Intelligence Agency, the Environmental Protection Agency, the Federal Emergency Management Agency, the National Aeronautics and Space Administration, the National Science Foundation, the National Oceanic and Atmospheric Administration, and the Office of Science and Technology Policy.

# Preface

Environmental problems do not stop at national boundaries. In the past decade, we and other nations have come to recognize the urgency of international efforts to protect our common environment.

As part of this process, I am directing the Council on Environmental Quality and the Department of State, working in cooperation with the Environmental Protection Agency, the National Science Foundation, the National Oceanic and Atmospheric Administration, and other appropriate agencies, to make a one-year study of the probable changes in the world's population, natural resources, and environment through the end of the century. This study will serve as the foundation of our longer-term planning.

President Carter issued this directive in his Environmental Message to the Congress on May 23, 1977. It marked the beginning of what became a three-year effort to discover the long-term implications of present world trends in population, natural resources, and the environment and to assess the Government's foundation for long-range planning.

Government concern with trends in population, resources, and environment is not new. Indeed, study of these issues by Federal commissions and planning boards extends back at least 70 years.[1] The earlier studies, however, tended to view each issue without relation to the others, to limit their inquiries to the borders of this nation and the short-term future, and to have relatively little effect on policy.[2] What is new in more recent studies is a growing awareness of the interdependence of population, resources, and environment. The Global 2000 Study is the first U.S. Government effort to look at all three issues from a long-term global perspective that recognizes their interrelationships and attempts to make connections among them.

The Global 2000 Study is reported in three volumes. This Summary is the first volume. Volume II, the Technical Report, presents the Study in further detail and is referenced extensively in this Summary. The third volume provides technical documentation on the Government's global models. All three volumes are available from the U.S. Government Printing Office.

# CONTENTS

## List of Tables

## List of Figures

All figures, unless otherwise noted, are from *The Global Report to the President: Entering the Twenty-First Century*, vol. 2, *Technical Report*, Washington: Government Printing Office, 1980.

# Major Findings and Conclusions

If present trends continue, the world in 2000 will be more crowded, more polluted, less stable ecologically, and more vulnerable to disruption than the world we live in now. Serious stresses involving population, resources, and environment are clearly visible ahead. Despite greater material output, the world's people will be poorer in many ways than they are today.

For hundreds of millions of the desperately poor, the outlook for food and other necessities of life will be no better. For many it will be worse. Barring revolutionary advances in technology, life for most people on earth will be more precarious in 2000 than it is now—unless the nations of the world act decisively to alter current trends.

This, in essence, is the picture emerging from the U.S. Government's projections of probable changes in world population, resources, and environment by the end of the century, as presented in the Global 2000 Study. They do not predict what will occur. Rather, they depict conditions that are likely to develop if there are no changes in public policies, institutions, or rates of technological advance, and if there are no wars or other major disruptions. A keener awareness of the nature of the current trends, however, may induce changes that will alter these trends and the projected outcome.

## Principal Findings

Rapid growth in world population will hardly have altered by 2000. The world's population will grow from 4 billion in 1975 to 6.35 billion in 2000, an increase of more than 50 percent. The rate of growth will slow only marginally, from 1.8 percent a year to 1.7 percent. In terms of sheer numbers, population will be growing faster in 2000 than it is today, with 100 million people added each year compared with 75 million in 1975. Ninety percent of this growth will occur in the poorest countries.

While the economies of the less developed countries (LDCs) are expected to grow at faster rates than those of the industrialized nations, the gross national product per capita in most LDCs remains low. The average gross national product per capita is projected to rise substantially in some LDCs (especially in Latin America), but in the great populous nations of South Asia it remains below $200 a year (in 1975 dollars). The large existing gap between the rich and poor nations widens.

World food production is projected to increase 90 percent over the 30 years from 1970 to 2000. This translates into a global per capita increase of

1

less than 15 percent over the same period. The bulk of that increase goes to countries that already have relatively high per capita food consumption. Meanwhile per capita consumption in South Asia, the Middle East, and the LDCs of Africa will scarcely improve or will actually decline below present inadequate levels. At the same time, real prices for food are expected to double.

Arable land will increase only 4 percent by 2000, so that most of the increased output of food will have to come from higher yields. Most of the elements that now contribute to higher yields—fertilizer, pesticides, power for irrigation, and fuel for machinery—depend heavily on oil and gas.

During the 1990s world oil production will approach geological estimates of maximum production capacity, even with rapidly increasing petroleum prices. The Study projects that the richer industrialized nations will be able to command enough oil and other commercial energy supplies to meet rising demands through 1990. With the expected price increases, many less developed countries will have increasing difficulties meeting energy needs. For the one-quarter of humankind that depends primarily on wood for fuel, the outlook is bleak. Needs for fuelwood will exceed available supplies by about 25 percent before the turn of the century.

While the world's finite fuel resources—coal, oil, gas, oil shale, tar sands, and uranium—are theoretically sufficient for centuries, they are not evenly distributed; they pose difficult economic and environmental problems; and they vary greatly in their amenability to exploitation and use.

Nonfuel mineral resources generally appear sufficient to meet projected demands through 2000, but further discoveries and investments will be needed to maintain reserves. In addition, production costs will increase with energy prices and may make some nonfuel mineral resources uneconomic. The quarter of the world's population that inhabits industrial countries will continue to absorb three-fourths of the world's mineral production.

Regional water shortages will become more severe. In the 1970–2000 period population growth alone will cause requirements for water to double in nearly half the world. Still greater increases would be needed to improve standards of living. In many LDCs, water supplies will become increasingly erratic by 2000 as a result of extensive deforestation. Development of new water supplies will become more costly virtually everywhere.

Significant losses of world forests will continue over the next 20 years as demand for forest products and fuelwood increases. Growing stocks of commercial-size timber are projected to decline 50 percent per capita. The world's forests are now disappearing at the rate of 18–20 million hectares a year (an area half the size of California), with most of the loss occurring in the humid tropical forests of Africa, Asia, and South America. The projections indicate that by 2000 some 40 percent of the remaining forest cover in LDCs will be gone.

Serious deterioration of agricultural soils will occur worldwide, due to erosion, loss of organic matter, desertification, salinization, alkalinization, and waterlogging. Already, an area of cropland and grassland approximately the size of Maine is becoming barren wasteland each year, and the spread of desert-like conditions is likely to accelerate.

Atmospheric concentrations of carbon dioxide and ozone-depleting chemicals are expected to increase at rates that could alter the world's climate and upper atmosphere significantly by 2050. Acid rain from increased combustion of fossil fuels (especially coal) threatens damage to lakes, soils, and crops. Radioactive and other hazardous materials present health and safety problems in increasing numbers of countries.

Extinctions of plant and animal species will increase dramatically. Hundreds of thousands of species—perhaps as many as 20 percent of all species on earth—will be irretrievably lost as their habitats vanish, especially in tropical forests.

The future depicted by the U.S. Government projections, briefly outlined above, may actually understate the impending problems. The methods available for carrying out the Study led to certain gaps and inconsistencies that tend to impart an optimistic bias. For example, most of the individual projections for the various sectors studied—food, minerals, energy, and so on—assume that sufficient capital, energy, water, and land will be available in each of these sectors to meet their needs, regardless of the competing needs of the other sectors. More consistent, better-integrated projections would produce a still more emphatic picture of intensifying stresses, as the world enters the twenty-first century.

## Conclusions

At present and projected growth rates, the world's population would reach 10 billion by 2030 and would approach 30 billion by the end of the twenty-first century. These levels correspond closely to estimates by the U.S. National Academy of Sciences of the maximum carrying capacity of the entire earth. Already the populations in sub-Saharan Africa and in the Himalayan hills of Asia have exceeded the carrying capacity of the immediate area, triggering an erosion of the land's capacity to support life. The resulting poverty and ill health have further complicated efforts to reduce fertility. Unless this circle of interlinked problems is broken soon, population growth in such areas will unfortunately be slowed for reasons other than declining birth rates. Hunger and disease will claim more babies and young children, and more of those surviving will be mentally and physically handicapped by childhood malnutrition.

Indeed, the problems of preserving the carrying capacity of the earth and sustaining the possibility of a decent life for the human beings that inhabit it are enormous and close upon us. Yet there is reason for hope. It must be emphasized that the Global 2000 Study's projections are based on the assumption that national policies regarding population stabilization, resource conservation, and environmental protection will remain essentially unchanged through the end of the century. But in fact, policies are beginning to change. In some areas, forests are being replanted after cutting. Some nations are taking steps to reduce soil losses and desertification. Interest in energy conservation is growing, and large sums are being invested in exploring alternatives to petroleum dependence. The need for family planning is slowly becoming better understood. Water supplies are being improved and waste treatment systems built. High-yield seeds are widely available and seed banks are being expanded. Some wildlands with their genetic resources are being protected. Natural predators and selective pesticides are being substituted for persistent and destructive pesticides.

Encouraging as these developments are, they are far from adequate to meet the global challenges projected in this Study. Vigorous, determined new initiatives are needed if worsening poverty and human suffering, environmental degradation, and international tension and conflicts are to be prevented. There are no quick fixes. The only solutions to the problems of population, resources, and environment are complex and long-term. These problems are inextricably linked to some of the most perplexing and persistent problems in the world—poverty, injustice, and social conflict. New and imaginative ideas—and a willingness to act on them—are essential.

The needed changes go far beyond the capability and responsibility of this or any other single nation. An era of unprecedented cooperation and commitment is essential. Yet there are opportunities—and a strong rationale —for the United States to provide leadership among nations. A high priority for this Nation must be a thorough assessment of its foreign and domestic policies relating to population, resources, and environment. The United States, possessing the world's largest economy, can expect its policies to have a significant influence on global trends. An equally important priority for the United States is to cooperate generously and justly with other nations—particularly in the areas of trade, investment, and assistance—in seeking solutions to the many problems that extend beyond our national boundaries. There are many unfulfilled opportunities to cooperate with other nations in efforts to relieve poverty and hunger, stabilize population, and enhance economic and environmental productivity. Further cooperation among nations is also needed to strengthen international mechanisms for protecting and utilizing the "global commons"—the oceans and atmosphere.

To meet the challenges described in this Study, the United States must improve its ability to identify emerging problems and assess alternative responses. In using and evaluting the Government's present capability for long-term global analysis, the Study found serious inconsistencies in the methods and assumptions employed by the various agencies in making their projections. The Study itself made a start toward resolving these inadequacies. It represents the Government's first attempt to produce an interrelated set of population, resource, and environmental projections, and it has brought forth the most consistent set of global projections yet achieved by U.S. agencies. Nevertheless, the projections still contain serious gaps and contradictions that must be corrected if the Government's analytic capability is to be improved. It must be acknowledged that at present the Federal agencies are not always capable of providing projections of the quality needed for long-term policy decisions.

While limited resources may be a contributing factor in some instances, the primary problem is lack of coordination. The U.S. Government needs a mechanism for continuous review of the assumptions and methods the Federal agencies use in their projection models and for assurance that the agencies' models are sound, consistent, and well documented. The improved analyses that could result would provide not only a clearer sense of emerging problems and opportunities, but also a better means for evaluating alternative responses, and a better basis for decisions of worldwide significance that the President, the Congress, and the Federal Government as a whole must make.

With its limitations and rough approximations, the Global 2000 Study may be seen as no more than a reconnaissance of the future; nonetheless its conclusions are reinforced by similar findings of other recent global studies that were examined in the course of the Global 2000 Study (see Appendix). All these studies are in general agreement on the nature of the problems and on the threats they pose to the future welfare of humankind. The available evidence leaves no doubt that the world—including this Nation—faces enormous, urgent, and complex problems in the decades immediately ahead. Prompt and vigorous changes in public policy around the world are needed to avoid or minimize these problems before they become unmanageable. Long lead times are required for effective action. If decisions are delayed until the problems become worse, options for effective action will be severely reduced.

# The Study in Brief

The President's directive establishing the Global 2000 Study called for a "study of the probable changes in the world's population, natural resources, and environment through the end of the century" and indicated that the Study as a whole was to "serve as the foundation of our longer-term planning."[3] The findings of the Study identify problems to which world attention must be directed. But because all study reports eventually become dated and less useful, the Study's findings alone cannot provide the foundation called for in the directive. The necessary foundation for longer-term planning lies not in study findings *per se*, but in the Government's continuing institutional capabilities—skilled personnel, data, and analytical models—for developing studies and analyses. Therefore, to meet the objectives stated in the President's directive, the Global 2000 Study was designed not only to assess probable changes in the world's population, natural resources, and environment, but also, through the study process itself, to identify and strengthen the Government's capability for longer-term planning and analysis.[4]

## Building the Study

The process chosen for the Global 2000 Study was to develop trend projections using, to the fullest extent possible, the long-term global data and models routinely employed by the Federal agencies. The process also included a detailed analysis of the Government's global modeling capabilities as well as a comparison of the Government's findings with those of other global analyses.

An executive group, established and co-chaired by the Council on Environmental Quality and the State Department, together with a team of designated agency coordinators, assisted in locating the agencies' experts, data, and analytical models. A number of Americans from outside Government and several people from other countries advised on the study structure. The agencies' expert met occasionally with some of these advisers to work out methods for coordinating data, models, and assumptions.

Overall, the Federal agencies have an impressive capability for long-term analyses of world trends in population, resources, and environment. Several agencies have extensive, richly detailed data bases and highly elaborate sectoral models. Collectively, the agencies' sectoral models and data constitute the Nation's present foundation for long-term planning and analysis.[5]

Currently, the principal limitation in the Government's long-term global analytical capability is that the models for various sectors were not designed to be used together in a consistent and interactive manner. The agencies' models were created at different times, using different methods, to meet different objectives. Little thought has been given to how the various sectoral models—and the institutions of which they are a part—can be related to each other to project a comprehensive, consistent image of the world. As a result, there has been little direct interaction among the agencies' sectoral models.[6]

With the Government's current models, the individual sectors addressed in the Global 2000 Study could be interrelated only by developing projections sequentially, that is, by using the results of some of the projections as inputs to others. Since population and gross national product (GNP) projections were required to estimate demand in the resource sector models, the population and GNP projections were developed first, in 1977. The resource projections followed in late 1977 and early 1978. All of the projections were linked to the environment projections, which were made during 1978 and 1979.[7]

The Global 2000 Study developed its projections in a way that furthered interactions, improved internal consistency, and generally strengthened the Government's global models. However, the effort to harmonize and integrate the Study's projections was only partially successful. Many internal contradictions and inconsistencies could not be resolved. Inconsistencies arose immediately from the fact that sequential projections are not as interactive as events in the real world, or as projections that could be achieved in an improved model. While the sequential process allowed some interaction among the model's sectors, it omitted the continuous influence that all the elements—population, resources, economic activity, environment—have upon each other. For example, the Global 2000 Study food projections assume that the catch from traditional fisheries will increase as fast as world population, while the fisheries projections indicate that this harvest will not increase over present levels on a sustainable basis. If it has been possible to link the fisheries and food projections, the expected fisheries contribution to the human food supply could have been realistically reflected in the food projections. This and other inconsistencies are discussed in detail in the Technical Report.[8]

Difficulties also arise from multiple allocation of resources. Most of the quantitative projections simply assume that resource needs in the sector they cover—needs for capital, energy, land, water, minerals—will be met. Since the needs for each sector are not clearly identified, they cannot be summed up and compared with estimates of what might be available. It is very likely that the same resources have been allocated to more than one sector.[9]

Equally significant, some of the Study's resource projections implicitly assume that the goods and services provided in the past by the earth's land, air, and water will continue to be available in larger and larger amounts, with no maintenance problems and no increase in costs. The Global 2000 Study projections for the environment cast serious doubt on these assumptions.[10]

Collectively, the inconsistencies and missing linkages that are unavoidable with the Government's current global models affect the Global 2000 projections in many ways. Analysis of the assumptions underlying the projections and comparisons with other global projections suggest that most of the Study's quantitative results understate the severity of potential problems the world will face as it prepares to enter the twenty-first century.[11]

The question naturally arises as to whether circumstances have changed significantly since the earliest projections were made in 1977. The answer is no. What changes have occurred generally support the projections and highlight the problems identified. The brief summaries of the projections (beginning on the next page) each conclude with comments on how the projections might be altered if redeveloped today.

The Global 2000 Study has three major underlying assumptions. First, the projections assume a general continuation around the world of present public policy relating to population stabilization, natural resource conservation, and environmental protection.* The projections thus point to the expected future if policies continue without significant changes.

The second major assumption relates to the effects of technological developments and of the market mechanism. The Study assumes that rapid rates of technological development and adoption will continue, and that the rate of development will be spurred on by efforts to deal with problems identified by this Study. Participating agencies were asked to use the technological assumptions they normally use in preparing long-term global projections. In general, the agencies assume a continuation of rapid rates of technological development and no serious social resistance to the adoption of new technologies. Agricultural technology, for example, is assumed to continue increasing crop yields as rapidly as during the past few decades, including the period of the Green Revolution (see Figure 1). The projections assume no revolutionary advances—such as immediate wide-scale availability of nuclear fusion for energy production—and no disastrous setbacks—such as serious new health risks from widely used contraceptives or an outbreak of plant disease severely affecting an important strain of grain. The projections all assume that price, operating through the market mechanism, will reduce demand whenever supply constraints are encountered.[12]

Third, the Study assumes that there will be no major disruptions of international trade as a result

*There are a few important exceptions to this rule. For example, the population projections anticipate shifts in public policy that will provide significantly increased access to family planning services. (See Chapter 14 of the Technical Report for further details.)

8

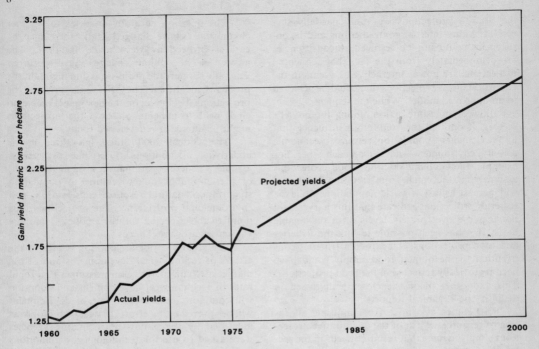

**Figure 1.** Historic and projected grain yields, 1960–2000. The food projections assume a continued rapid development and adoption of agricultural technology, much of it heavily dependent on fossil fuels.

of war, disturbance of the international monetary system, or political disruption. The findings of the Study do, however, point to increasing potential for international conflict and increasing stress on international financial arrangements. Should wars or a significant disturbance of the international monetary system occur, the projected trends would be altered in unpredictable ways.[13]

Because of the limitations outlined above, the Global 2000 Study is not the definitive study of future population, resource, and environment conditions. Nor is it intended to be a prediction. The Study does provide the most internally consistent and interrelated set of global projections available so far from the U.S. Government. Furthermore, its major findings are supported by a variety of nongovernmental global studies based on more highly interactive models that project similar trends through the year 2000 or beyond.[14]

## Population and Income

Population and income projections provided the starting point for the Study. These projections

were used wherever possible in the resource projections to estimate demand.

### Population

One of the most important findings of the Global 2000 Study is that enormous growth in the world's population will occur by 2000 under any of the wide range of assumptions considered in the Study. The world's population increases 55 percent from 4.1 billion people in 1975 to 6.35 billion by 2000, under the Study's medium-growth projections.* While there is some uncertainty in these numbers, even the lowest-growth population projection shows a 46 percent increase—to 5.9 billion people by the end of the century.[15]

Another important finding is that the rapid growth of the world's population will not slow appreciably. The rate of growth per year in 1975 was 1.8 percent; the projected rate for 2000 is 1.7 per-

*Most of the projections in the Technical Report—including the population projections—provide a high, medium, and low series. Generally, only the medium series are discussed in this Summary Report.

cent. Even under the lowest growth projected, the number of persons being added annually to the world's population will be significantly greater in 2000 than today.[16]

Most of the population growth (92 percent) will occur in the less developed countries rather than in the industrialized countries. Of the 6.35 billion people in the world in 2000, 5 billion will live in LDCs. The LDCs' share of the world's population increased from 66 percent in 1950 to 72 percent in 1975, and is expected to reach 79 percent by 2000. LDC population growth rates will drop slightly, from 2.2 percent a year in 1975 to 2 percent in 2000, compared with 0.7 percent and 0.5 percent in developed countries. In some LDCs,

growth rates will still be more than 3 percent a year in 2000. Table 1 summarizes the population projections. Figure 2 shows the distribution of the world's population in 1975 and 2000.[17]

Figure 3 shows the age structure of the population in less developed and industrialized nations for 1975 and 2000. While the structures shown for the industrialized nations become more column-shaped (characteristic of a mature and slowly growing population), the structures for the LDCs remain pyramid-shaped (characteristic of rapid growth). The LDC populations, predominantly young with their childbearing years ahead of them, have a built-in momentum for further growth. Because of this momentum, a world

**TABLE 1**
**Population Projections for World, Major Regions, and Selected Countries**

| | 1975 | 2000 | Percent Increase by 2000 | Average Annual Percent Increase | Percent of World Population in 2000 |
|---|---|---|---|---|---|
| | *millions* | | | | |
| World | 4,090 | 6,351 | 55 | 1.8 | 100 |
| More developed regions | 1,131 | 1,323 | 17 | 0.6 | 21 |
| Less developed regions | 2,959 | 5,028 | 70 | 2.1 | 79 |
| Major regions | | | | | |
| Africa | 399 | 814 | 104 | 2.9 | 13 |
| Asia and Oceania | 2,274 | 3,630 | 60 | 1.9 | 57 |
| Latin America | 325 | 637 | 96 | 2.7 | 10 |
| U.S.S.R. and Eastern Europe | 384 | 460 | 20 | 0.7 | 7 |
| North America, Western Europe, Japan, Australia, and New Zealand | 708 | 809 | 14 | 0.5 | 13 |
| Selected countries and regions | | | | | |
| People's Republic of China | 935 | 1,329 | 42 | 1.4 | 21 |
| India | 618 | 1,021 | 65 | 2.0 | 16 |
| Indonesia | 135 | 226 | 68 | 2.1 | 4 |
| Bangladesh | 79 | 159 | 100 | 2.8 | 2 |
| Pakistan | 71 | 149 | 111 | 3.0 | 2 |
| Philippines | 43 | 73 | 71 | 2.1 | 1 |
| Thailand | 42 | 75 | 77 | 2.3 | 1 |
| South Korea | 37 | 57 | 55 | 1.7 | 1 |
| Egypt | 37 | 65 | 77 | 2.3 | 1 |
| Nigeria | 63 | 135 | 114 | 3.0 | 2 |
| Brazil | 109 | 226 | 108 | 2.9 | 4 |
| Mexico | 60 | 131 | 119 | 3.1 | 2 |
| United States | 214 | 248 | 16 | 0.6 | 4 |
| U.S.S.R. | 254 | 309 | 21 | 0.8 | 5 |
| Japan | 112 | 133 | 19 | 0.7 | 2 |
| Eastern Europe | 130 | 152 | 17 | 0.6 | 2 |
| Western Europe | 344 | 378 | 10 | 0.4 | 6 |

*Source:* Global 2000 Technical Report, Table 2-10.

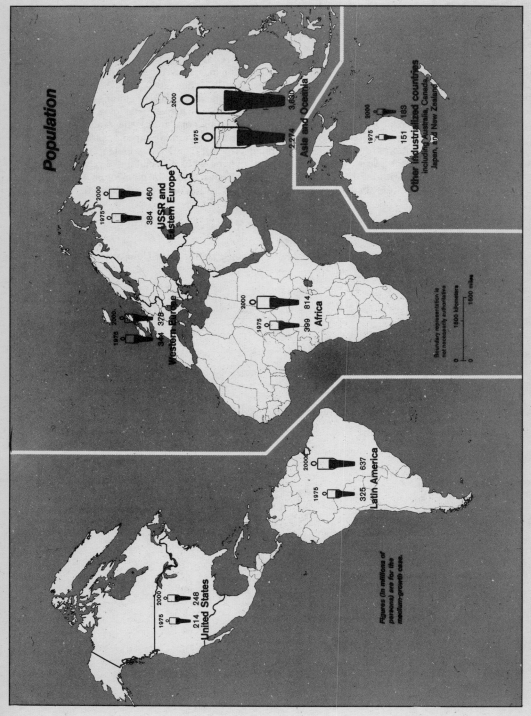

**Figure 2.** Distribution of the world's population, 1975 and 2000.

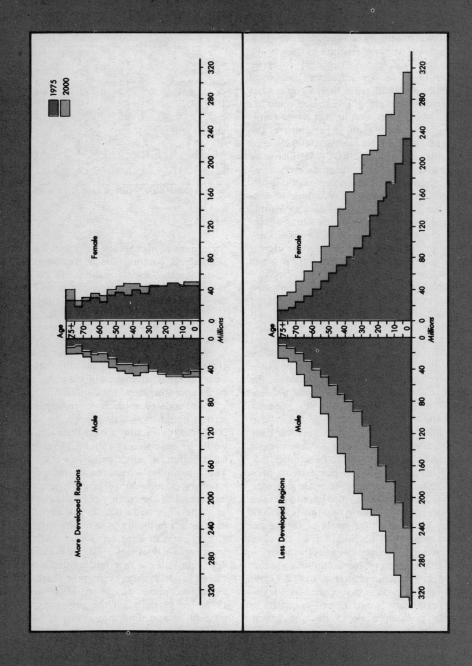

11

1975
2000

More Developed Regions

Female

Age
75+
-70
-60
-50
-40
-30
-20
-10
-0

Male

Millions
320  280  240  200  160  120  80  40  0  40  80  120  160  200  240  280  320

Less Developed Regions

Female

Age
75+
-70
-60
-50
-40
-30
-20
-10
-0

Male

Millions
320  280  240  200  160  120  80  40  0  40  80  120  160  200  240  280  320

Figure 3. Age-sex composition of the world's population, medium series, 1975 and 2000.

12

population of around 6 billion is a virtual certainty for 2000 even if fertility rates were somehow to drop quickly to replacement levels (assuming there are no disastrous wars, famine, or pestilence).[18]

The projected fertility rates and life expectancies, together with the age structure of the world's population, are extremely significant for later years since these factors influence how soon world population could cease to grow and what the ultimate stabilized global population could be. The Study's projections assume that world fertility rates will drop more than 20 percent over the 1975–2000 period, from an average of 4.3 children per fertile woman to 3.3. In LDCs, fertility rates are projected to drop 30 percent as a result of moderate progress in social and economic development and increased availability and use of contraceptive methods. The projections also assume that life expectancies at birth for the world will increase 11 percent, to 65.5 years, as a result of improved health. The projected increases in life expectancies and decreases in fertility rates produce roughly counterbalancing demographic effects.[19]

In addition to rapid population growth, the LDCs will experience dramatic movements of rural populations to cities and adjacent settlements. If present trends continue, many LDC cities will become almost inconceivably large and crowded. By 2000, Mexico City is projected to have more than 30 million people— roughly three times the present population of the New York metropolitan area. Calcutta will approach 20 million. Greater Bombay, Greater Cairo, Jakarta, and Seoul are all expected to be in the 15–20 million range, and 400 cities will have passed the million mark.[20] Table 2 shows present and projected populations for 12 LDC cities.

Rapid urban growth will put extreme pressures on sanitation, water supplies, health care, food, shelter, and jobs. LDCs will have to increase urban services approximately two-thirds by 2000 just to stay even with 1975 levels of service per capita. The majority of people in large LDC cities are likely to live in "uncontrolled settlements"— slums and shantytowns where sanitation and other public services are minimal at best. In many large cities—for example, Bombay, Calcutta, Mexico City, Rio de Janeiro, Seoul, Taipei—a quarter or more of the population already lives in uncontrolled settlements, and the trend is sharply upward. It is not certain whether the trends projected

### TABLE 2
### Estimates and Rough Projections of Selected Urban Agglomerations in Developing Countries

| | 1960 | 1970 | 1975 | 2000 |
|---|---|---|---|---|
| | *Millions of persons* | | | |
| Calcutta | 5.5 | 6.9 | 8.1 | 19.7 |
| Mexico City | 4.9 | 8.6 | 10.9 | 31.6 |
| Greater Bombay | 4.1 | 5.8 | 7.1 | 19.1 |
| Greater Cairo | 3.7 | 5.7 | 6.9 | 16.4 |
| Jakarta | 2.7 | 4.3 | 5.6 | 16.9 |
| Seoul | 2.4 | 5.4 | 7.3 | 18.7 |
| Delhi | 2.3 | 3.5 | 4.5 | 13.2 |
| Manila | 2.2 | 3.5 | 4.4 | 12.7 |
| Tehran | 1.9 | 3.4 | 4.4 | 13.8 |
| Karachi | 1.8 | 3.3 | 4.5 | 15.9 |
| Bogota | 1.7 | 2.6 | 3.4 | 9.5 |
| Lagos | 0.8 | 1.4 | 2.1 | 9.4 |

*Source*: Global 2000 Technical Report, Table 13–9.

for enormous increases in LDC urban populations will in fact continue for 20 years. In the years ahead, lack of food for the urban poor, lack of jobs, and increasing illness and misery may slow the growth of LDC cities and alter the trend.[21]

Difficult as urban conditions are, conditions in rural areas of many LDCs are generally worse. Food, water, health, and income problems are often most severe in outlying agricultural and grazing areas. In some areas rural-urban migration and rapid urban growth are being accelerated by deteriorating rural conditions.[22]

An updated medium-series population projection would show little change from the Global 2000 Study projections. World population in 2000 would be estimated at about 6.18 (as opposed to 6.35) billion, a reduction of less than 3 percent. The expectation would remain that, in absolute numbers, population will be growing more rapidly by the end of the century than today.[23]

The slight reduction in the population estimate is due primarily to new data suggesting that fertility rates in some areas have declined a little more rapidly than earlier estimates indicated. The new data indicate that fertility declines have occurred in some places even in the absence of overall socioeconomic progress.[24] Between 1970 and 1976, for example, in the presence of extreme poverty and malnutrition, fertility declines of 10–15 percent occurred in Indonesia and 15–20 percent in the poorest income classes in Brazil.[25]

## Income

Projected declines in fertility rates are based in part on anticipated social and economic progress, which is ultimately reflected in increased income. Income projections were not possible, and gross national product projections were used as surrogates. GNP, a rough and inadequate measure of social and economic welfare, is projected to increase worldwide by 145 percent over 25 years from 1975 to 2000. But because of population growth, per capita GNP increases much more slowly, from $1,500 in 1975 to $2,300 in 2000—an increase of 53 percent. For both the poorer and the richer countries, rates of growth in GNP are projected to decelerate after 1985.[26]

GNP growth is expected to be faster in LDCs (an average annual growth of 4.5 percent, or an approximate tripling over 25 years) than in developed regions (an average annual growth of 3.3 percent, or somewhat more than a doubling). However, the LDC growth in gross national product develops from a very low base, and population growth in the LDCs brings per capita increases in GNP down to very modest proportions. While parts of the LDC world, especially several countries in Latin America, are projected to improve significantly in per capita GNP by 2000, other countries will make little or no gains from their present low levels. India, Bangladesh, and Pakistan, for example, increase their per capita GNP by 31 percent, 8 percent, and 3 percent, respectively, but in all three countries GNP per capita remains below $200 (in 1975 dollars).[27] Figure 4 shows projected per capita gross national product by regions in 2000.

The present income disparities between the wealthiest and poorest nations are projected to widen. Assuming that present trends continue, the group of industrialized countries will have a per capita GNP of nearly $8,500 (in 1975 dollars) in 2000, and North America, Western Europe, Australia, New Zealand, and Japan will average more than $11,000. By contrast, per capita GNP in the LDCs will average less than $600. For every $1 increase in GNP per capita in the LDCs, a $20 increase is projected for the industrialized countries.[28] Table 3 and 4 summarize the GNP projections. The disparity between the developed countries and the less developed group is so marked that dramatically different rates of change would be needed to reduce the gap significantly by

the end of the century.* Disparities between the rich and poor of many LDCs are equally striking.

Updated GNP projections would indicate somewhat lower economic growth than shown in the Global 2000 projections. Projections for the member nations of the Organization for Economic Cooperation and Development (OECD) have been revised downward over the past 2–3 years because of the effects of increasing petroleum prices and because of anticipated measures to reduce inflation. In turn, depressed growth in the OECD economies is expected to lead to slowed growth in LDC economies. For example, in 1976 the World Bank projected that the industrialized nations' economies would expand at 4.9 percent annually over the 1980–85 period; by 1979 the Bank had revised these projections downward to 4.2 percent annually over the 1980–90 period. Similarly, between 1976 and 1979 Bank projections for LDC economies dropped from 6.3 percent (1980-85 period) to 5.6 percent (1980-90 period).[29]

## Resources

The Global 2000 Study resource projections are based to the fullest extent possible on the population and GNP projections presented previously. The resource projections cover food, fisheries, forests, nonfuel minerals, water, and energy.

### Food

The Global 2000 Study projects world food production to increase at an average annual rate of about 2.2 percent over the 1970–2000 period. This rate of increase is roughly equal to the record growth rates experienced during the 1950s, 1960s, and early 1970s, including the period of the so-called Green Revolution. Assuming no deterioration in climate or weather, food production is projected to be 90 percent higher in 2000 than in 1970.[30]

---

*The gap would be significantly smaller—in some cases it would be reduced by about one half—if the comparison were based on purchasing power considerations rather than exchange rates, but a large gap would remain. (See I. B. Kravis et al., *International Comparisons of Real Product and Purchasing Power*, Baltimore: Johns Hopkins University Press. 1978.)

14

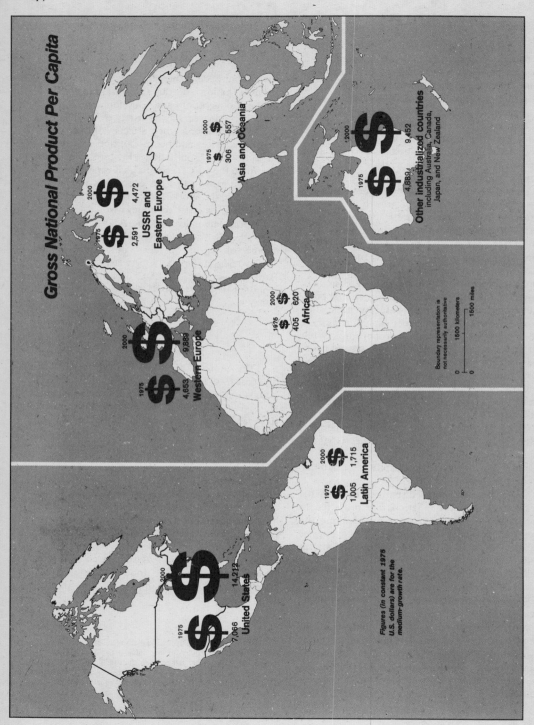

**Gross National Product Per Capita**

**United States**
1975 7,066
2000 14,212

**Latin America**
1975 1,005
2000 1,715

**Western Europe**
1975 4,653
2000 9,889

**Africa**
1975 405
2000 620

**USSR and Eastern Europe**
1975 2,591
2000 4,472

**Asia and Oceania**
1975 306
2000 557

**Other industrialized countries** including Australia, Canada, Japan, and New Zealand
1975 4,889
2000 9,452

Figures (in constant 1975 U.S. dollars) are for the medium-growth rate.

Boundary representation is not necessarily authoritative

0   1600 kilometers
0   1500 miles

**Figure 4.** Per capita gross national product, by regions, 1975 and 2000.

## TABLE 3

## GNP Estimates (1975) and Projections and Growth Rates (1985, 2000) by Major Regions and Selected Countries and Regions

*(Billions of constant 1975 dollars)*

| | 1975 GNP | 1975–85 Growth Rate | 1985 Projections[a] | 1985–2000 Growth Rate | 2000 Projections[a] |
|---|---|---|---|---|---|
| | | *percent* | | *percent* | |
| WORLD | 6,025 | 4.1 | 8,991 | 3.3 | 14,677 |
| More developed regions | 4,892 | 3.9 | 7,150 | 3.1 | 11,224 |
| Less developed regions | 1,133 | 5.0 | 1,841 | 4.3 | 3,452 |
| | | | | | |
| MAJOR REGIONS | | | | | |
| Africa | 162 | 5.2 | 268 | 4.3 | 505 |
| Asia and Oceania | 697 | 4.6 | 1,097 | 4.2 | 2,023 |
| Latin America[b] | 326 | 5.6 | 564 | 4.5 | 1,092 |
| U.S.S.R. and Eastern Europe | 996 | 3.3 | 1,371 | 2.8 | 2,060 |
| North America, Western Europe, Japan, Australia, and New Zealand | 3,844 | 4.0 | 5,691 | 3.1 | 8,996 |
| | | | | | |
| SELECTED COUNTRIES AND REGIONS[c] | | | | | |
| People's Republic of China | 286 | 3.8 | 413 | 3.8 | 718 |
| India | 92 | 3.6 | 131 | 2.8 | 198 |
| Indonesia | 24 | 6.4 | 45 | 5.4 | 99 |
| Bangladesh | 9 | 3.6 | 13 | 2.8 | 19 |
| Pakistan | 10 | 3.6 | 14 | 2.8 | 21 |
| | | | | | |
| Philippines | 16 | 5.6 | 27 | 4.4 | 52 |
| Thailand | 15 | 5.6 | 25 | 4.4 | 48 |
| South Korea | 19 | 5.6 | 32 | 4.4 | 61 |
| Egypt | 12 | 5.6 | 20 | 4.4 | 38 |
| Nigeria | 23 | 6.4 | 43 | 5.4 | 94 |
| | | | | | |
| Brazil | 108 | 5.6 | 185 | 4.4 | 353 |
| Mexico | 71 | 5.6 | 122 | 4.4 | 233 |
| United States[d] | 1,509 | 4.0 | 2,233 | 3.1 | 3,530 |
| U.S.S.R. | 666 | 3.3 | 917 | 2.8 | 1,377 |
| Japan | 495 | 4.0 | 733 | 3.1 | 1,158 |
| Eastern Europe (excluding U.S.S.R.) | 330 | 3.3 | 454 | 2.8 | 682 |
| Western Europe | 1,598 | 4.0 | 2,366 | 3.1 | 3,740 |

[a]Projected growth rates of gross national product were developed using complex computer simulation techniques described in Chapter 16 of the Global 2000 Technical Report. These projections represent the result of applying those projected growth rates to the 1975 GNP data presented in the 1976 World Bank Atlas. Projections shown here are for medium-growth rates.
[b]Includes Puerto Rico.

[c]In most cases, gross national income growth rates were projected for groups of countries rather than for individual countries. Thus the rates attributed to individual LDCs in this table are the growth rates applicable to the group with which that country was aggregated for making projections and do not take into account country specific characteristics.
[d]Does not include Puerto Rico.
*Source:* Global 2000 Technical Report, Table 3-3.

## TABLE 4
## Per Capita GNP Estimates (1975) and Projections and Growth Rates (1985, 2000) by Major Regions and Selected Countries and Regions

*(Constant 1975 U.S. dollars)*

| | 1975 | Average Annual Growth Rate, 1975–85 | 1985 Projections[a] | Average Annual Growth Rate, 1985–2000 | 2000 Projections[a] |
|---|---|---|---|---|---|
| | | *percent* | | *percent* | |
| WORLD | 1,473 | 2.3 | 1,841 | 1.5 | 2,311 |
| More developed countries | 4,325 | 3.2 | 5,901 | 2.5 | 8,485 |
| Less developed countries | 382 | 2.8 | 501 | 2.1 | 587 |
| MAJOR REGIONS | | | | | |
| Africa | 405 | 2.2 | 505 | 1.4 | 620 |
| Asia and Oceania | 306 | 2.7 | 398 | 2.3 | 557 |
| Latin America[b] | 1,005 | 2.6 | 1,304 | 1.8 | 1,715 |
| U.S.S.R. and Eastern Europe | 2,591 | 2.4 | 3,279 | 2.1 | 4,472 |
| North America, Western Europe, Japan, Australia, and New Zealand | 5,431 | 3.4 | 7,597 | 2.6 | 11,117 |
| SELECTED COUNTRIES AND REGIONS[c] | | | | | |
| People's Republic of China | 306 | 2.3 | 384 | 2.3 | 540 |
| India | 148 | 1.5 | 171 | 0.8 | 194 |
| Indonesia | 179 | 4.1 | 268 | 3.1 | 422 |
| Bangladesh | 111 | 0.6 | 118 | 0.1 | 120 |
| Pakistan | 138 | 0.4 | 144 | −0.1 | 142 |
| Philippines | 368 | 3.2 | 503 | 2.3 | 704 |
| Thailand | 343 | 3.0 | 460 | 2.2 | 633 |
| South Korea | 507 | 3.5 | 718 | 2.7 | 1,071 |
| Egypt | 313 | 2.9 | 416 | 2.2 | 578 |
| Nigeria | 367 | 3.3 | 507 | 2.2 | 698 |
| Brazil | 991 | 2.2 | 1,236 | 1.6 | 1,563 |
| Mexico | 1,188 | 2.0 | 1,454 | 1.3 | 1,775 |
| United States[d] | 7,066 | 3.3 | 9.756 | 2.5 | 14,212 |
| U.S.S.R. | 2,618 | 2.3 | 3,286 | 2.1 | 4,459 |
| Japan | 4,437 | 3.1 | 6,023 | 2.5 | 8,712 |
| Eastern Europe | 2,539 | 2.6 | 3,265 | 2.2 | 4,500 |
| Western Europe | 4,653 | 3.7 | 6,666 | 2.7 | 9,889 |

[a]The medium-series projections of gross national product and population presented in Tables 3-3 and 3-4 of the Global 2000 Technical Report were used to calculate the 1975, 1985, and 2000 per capita gross national product figures presented in this table.
[b]Includes Puerto Rico.
[c]In most cases, gross national product growth rates were projected for groups of countries rather than for individual countries. Thus, the rates attributed to individual LDCs in this table are the growth rates applicable to the group with which that country was aggregated for making projections and do not take into account country-specific characteristics.
[d]Does not include Puerto Rico.
*Source*: Global 2000 Technical Report, Table 3-5.

The projections indicate that most of the increase in food production will come from more intensive use of yield-enhancing, energy-intensive inputs and technologies such as fertilizer, pesticides, herbicides, and irrigation—in many cases with diminishing returns. Land under cultivation is projected to increase only 4 percent by 2000 because most good land is already being cultivated. In the early 1970s one hectare of arable land supported an average of 2.6 persons; by 2000 one hectare will have to support 4 persons. Because of this tightening land constraint, food production is not likely to increase fast enough to meet rising demands unless world agriculture becomes significantly more dependent on petroleum and petroleum-related inputs. Increased petroleum dependence also has implications for the cost of food production. After decades of generally falling prices, the real price of food is projected to increase 95 percent over the 1970–2000 period, in significant part as a result of increased petroleum dependence.[31] If energy prices in fact rise more rapidly than the projections anticipate, then the effect on food prices could be still more marked.

On the average, world food production is projected to increase more rapidly than world population, with average per capita consumption increasing about 15 percent between 1970 and 2000. Per capita consumption in the industrialized nations is projected to rise 21 percent from 1970 levels, with increases of from 40 to more than 50 percent in Japan, Eastern Europe, and the U.S.S.R., and 28 percent in the United States.* In the LDCs, however, rising food output will barely keep ahead of population growth.[32]

An increase of 9 percent in per capita food consumption is projected for the LDCs as a whole, but with enormous variations among regions and nations. The great populous countries of South Asia—expected to contain 1.3 billion people by 2000—improve hardly at all, nor do large areas of low-income North Africa and the Middle East. Per capita consumption in the sub-Saharan African LDCs will actually decline, according to the projections. The LDCs showing the greatest per capita growth (increases of about 25 percent) are concentrated in Latin America and East Asia.[33] Table 5 summarizes the projections for food production and consumption, and Table 6 and Figure 5 show per capita food consumption by regions.

The outlook for improved diets for the poorest people in the poorest LDCs is sobering. In the 1970s, consumption of calories in the LDCs averaged only 94 percent of the minimum requirements set by the U.N. Food and Agriculture Organization (FAO).† Moreover, income and

*"Consumption" statistics are based on the amount of food that leaves the farms and does not leave the country and therefore include transportation and processing losses. Projected increases in per capita consumption in countries like the United States, where average consumption is already at least nutritionally adequate, reflect increasing losses of food during transportation and processing and might also be accounted for by increased industrial demand for grain, especially for fermentation into fuels.

†The FAO standard indicates the *minimum* consumption that will allow normal activity and good health in adults and will permit children to reach normal body weight and intelligence in the absence of disease.

food distribution within individual LDCs is so skewed that national average caloric consumption generally must be 10–20 percent above minimum levels before the poorest are likely to be able to afford a diet that meets the FAO minimum standard. Latin America is the only major LDC region where average caloric consumption is projected to be 20 percent or more above the FAO minimum standard in the year 2000. In the other LDC regions—South, East, and Southeast Asia, poor areas of North Africa and the Middle East, and especially Central Africa, where a calamitous drop in food per capita is projected—the quantity of food available to the poorest groups of people will simply be insufficient to permit children to reach normal body weight and intelligence and to permit normal activity and good health in adults. Consumption in the LDCs of central Africa is projected to be more than 20 percent below the FAO minimum standard, assuming no recurrence of severe drought. In South Asia (primarily India, Pakistan, and Bangladesh), average caloric intake is projected to remain below the FAO minimum standard, although increasing slightly—from 12 percent below the FAO standard in the mid-1970s to about 3 percent below the standard in 2000. In East Asia, Southeast Asia, and affluent areas of North Africa and the Middle East, average per capita caloric intakes are projected to be 6-17 percent above FAO minimum requirement levels, but because the great majority of people in these regions are extremely poor, they will almost certainly continue to eat less than the minimum. The World Bank has estimated that the number of malnourished people in LDCs could rise from 400–600 million in the mid-1970s to 1.3 billion in 2000.[34]

The projected food situation has many implications for food assistance and trade. In the developing world, the need for imported food is expected to grow. The most prosperous LDCs will turn increasingly to the world commercial markets. In the poorest countries, which lack the wherewithal to buy food, requirements for international food assistance will expand. LDC exporters (especially Argentina and Thailand) are projected to enlarge food production for export because of their cost advantage over countries dependent on energy-intensive inputs. LDC grain-exporting countries, which accounted for only a little more than 10 percent of the world grain

## TABLE 5
### Grain Production, Consumption, and Trade, Actual and Projected, and Percent Increase in Total Food Production and Consumption

| | Grain (million metric tons) | | | Food (Percent increase over the 1970-2000 period) |
|---|---|---|---|---|
| | 1969–71 | 1973–75 | 2000 | |
| **Industrialized countries** | | | | |
| Production | 401.7 | 434.7 | 679.1 | 43.7 |
| Consumption | 374.3 | 374.6 | 610.8 | 47.4 |
| Trade | + 32.1 | + 61.6 | + 68.3 | |
| **United States** | | | | |
| Production | 208.7 | 228.7 | 402.0 | 78.5 |
| Consumption | 169.0 | 158.5 | 272.4 | 51.3 |
| Trade | + 39.9 | + 72.9 | + 129.6 | |
| **Other developed exporters** | | | | |
| Production | 58.6 | 61.2 | 106.1 | 55.6 |
| Consumption | 33.2 | 34.3 | 65.2 | 66.8 |
| Trade | + 28.4 | + 27.7 | + 40.9 | |
| **Western Europe** | | | | |
| Production | 121.7 | 132.9 | 153.0 | 14.6 |
| Consumption | 144.2 | 151.7 | 213.1 | 31.6 |
| Trade | − 21.8 | − 19.7 | − 60.1 | |
| **Japan** | | | | |
| Production | 12.7 | 11.9 | 18.0 | 31.5 |
| Consumption | 27.9 | 30.1 | 60.1 | 92.8 |
| Trade | − 14.4 | − 19.3 | − 42.1 | |
| **Centrally planned countries** | | | | |
| Production | 401.0 | 439.4 | 722.0 | 74.0 |
| Consumption | 406.6 | 472.4 | 758.5 | 79.9 |
| Trade | − 5.2 | − 24.0 | − 36.5 | |
| **Eastern Europe** | | | | |
| Production | 72.1 | 89.4 | 140.0 | 83.2 |
| Consumption | 78.7 | 97.7 | 151.5 | 81.7 |
| Trade | − 6.1 | − 7.8 | − 11.5 | |
| **U.S.S.R.** | | | | |
| Production | 165.0 | 179.3 | 290.0 | 72.7 |
| Consumption | 161.0 | 200.7 | 305.0 | 85.9 |
| Trade | + 3.9 | − 10.6 | − 15.0 | |
| **People's Republic of China** | | | | |
| Production | 163.9 | 176.9 | 292.0 | 69.0 |
| Consumption | 166.9 | 180.8 | 302.0 | 71.4 |
| Trade | − 3.0 | − 3.9 | − 10.0 | |

market in 1975, are projected to capture more than 20 percent of the market by 2000. The United States is expected to continue its role as the world's principal food exporter. Moreover, as the year 2000 approaches and more marginal, weather-sensitive lands are brought into production around the world, the United States is likely to become even more of a residual world supplier than today; that is, U.S. producers will be responding to widening, weather-related swings in world production and foreign demand.[35]

Revised and updated food projections would reflect reduced estimates of future yields, increased pressure on the agricultural resource base, and several changes in national food policies.

Farmers' costs of raising—and even maintaining—yields have increased rapidly in recent years. The costs of energy-intensive, yield-enhancing inputs—fertilizer, pesticides, and fuels—have risen very rapidly throughout the world, and where these inputs are heavily used, increased applications are bringing diminishing returns. In the United States, the real cost of producing food increased roughly 10 percent in both

## TABLE 5 (Cont.)

| | Grain (million metric tons) | | | Food (Percent increase over the 1970-2000 period) |
|---|---|---|---|---|
| | 1969–71 | 1973–75 | 2000 | |
| **Less developed countries** | | | | |
| Production | 306.5 | 328.7 | 740.6 | 147.7 |
| Consumption | 326.6 | 355.0 | 772.4 | 142.8 |
| Trade | −18.5 | −29.5 | −31.8 | |
| **Exporters[a]** | | | | |
| Production | 30.1 | 34.5 | 84.0 | 125.0 |
| Consumption | 18.4 | 21.5 | 36.0 | 58.0 |
| Trade | +11.3 | +13.1 | +48.0 | |
| **Importers[b]** | | | | |
| Production | 276.4 | 294.2 | 656.6 | 149.3 |
| Consumption | 308.2 | 333.5 | 736.4 | 148.9 |
| Trade | −29.8 | −42.6 | −79.8 | |
| **Latin America** | | | | |
| Production | 63.8 | 72.0 | 185.9 | 184.4 |
| Consumption | 61.2 | 71.2 | 166.0 | 165.3 |
| Trade | +3.2 | +0.2 | +19.9 | |
| **North Africa/Middle East** | | | | |
| Production | 38.9 | 42.4 | 89.0 | 157.8 |
| Consumption | 49.5 | 54.1 | 123.7 | 167.3 |
| Trade | −9.1 | −13.8 | −29.7 | |
| **Other African LDCs** | | | | |
| Production | 32.0 | 31.3 | 63.7 | 104.9 |
| Consumption | 33.0 | 33.8 | 63.0 | 96.4 |
| Trade | −1.0 | −2.4 | +0.7 | |
| **South Asia** | | | | |
| Production | 119.1 | 127.7 | 259.0 | 116.8 |
| Consumption | 125.3 | 135.1 | 275.7 | 119.4 |
| Trade | −6.2 | −9.3 | −16.7 | |
| **Southeast Asia** | | | | |
| Production | 22.8 | 21.4 | 65.0 | 210.0 |
| Consumption | 19.3 | 17.9 | 47.0 | 163.6 |
| Trade | +3.4 | +3.7 | +18.0 | |
| **East Asia** | | | | |
| Production | 29.9 | 34.0 | 73.0 | 155.3 |
| Consumption | 38.3 | 42.9 | 97.0 | 164.9 |
| Trade | −8.8 | −9.7 | −24.0 | |
| **World** | | | | |
| Production/Consumption | 1,108.0 | 1,202.0 | 2,141.7 | 91.0 |

*Note:* In grade figures, plus sign indicates export, minus sign indicates import.
[a]Argentina and Thailand.
[b]All others, including several countries that export in some scenarios (e.g., Brazil, Indonesia, and Colombia).
*Source:* Global 2000 Technical Report, Table 6-5.

1978 and 1979.[36] Other industrialized countries have experienced comparable production cost increases. Cost increases in the LDCs appear to be lower, but are still 2-3 times the annual increases of the 1960s and early 1970s. While there have been significant improvements recently in the yields of selected crops, the diminishing returns and rapidly rising costs of yield-enhancing inputs suggest that yields overall will increase more slowly than projected.

Since the food projections were made, there have been several important shifts in national food and agricultural policy concerns. In most industrialized countries, concern with protecting agricultural resources, especially soils, has increased as the resource implications of sustained

**TABLE 6**
**Per Capita Grain Production, Consumption, and Trade, Actual and Projected,**
**and Percent Increase in Per Capita Total Food Production and Consumption**

| | Grain (kilograms per capita) | | | Food (Percent increase over the 1970-2000 period) |
|---|---|---|---|---|
| | 1969–71 | 1973–75 | 2000 | |
| Industrialized countries | | | | |
| Production | 573.6 | 592.6 | 769.8 | 18.4 |
| Consumption | 534.4 | 510.7 | 692.4 | 21.2 |
| Trade | +45.8 | +84.0 | +77.4 | |
| United States | | | | |
| Production | 1,018.6 | 1,079.3 | 1,640.3 | 51.1 |
| Consumption | 824.9 | 748.0 | 1,111.5 | 28.3 |
| Trade | +194.7 | +344.0 | +528.8 | |
| Other developed exporters | | | | |
| Production | 1,015.6 | 917.0 | 915.6 | −11.3 |
| Consumption | 575.4 | 514.0 | 562.6 | −5.7 |
| Trade | +492.2 | +415.0 | +353.0 | |
| Western Europe | | | | |
| Production | 364.9 | 388.4 | 394.0 | 1.0 |
| Consumption | 432.4 | 443.3 | 548.8 | 15.5 |
| Trade | −65.4 | −57.6 | −154.8 | |
| Japan | | | | |
| Production | 121.7 | 108.5 | 135.4 | 6.1 |
| Consumption | 267.5 | 274.4 | 452.3 | 54.2 |
| Trade | −138.1 | −175.9 | −316.7 | |
| Centrally planned countries | | | | |
| Production | 356.1 | 368.0 | 451.1 | 29.6 |
| Consumption | 361.0 | 395.6 | 473.9 | 35.8 |
| Trade | −4.6 | −20.1 | −22.8 | |
| Eastern Europe | | | | |
| Production | 574.0 | 693.0 | 921.9 | 53.3 |
| Consumption | 626.6 | 757.4 | 997.6 | 52.1 |
| Trade | −48.6 | −60.5 | −75.8 | |
| U.S.S.R. | | | | |
| Production | 697.6 | 711.2 | 903.2 | 28.1 |
| Consumption | 663.1 | 796.1 | 949.9 | 41.4 |
| Trade | +16.1 | −42.0 | −46.7 | |
| People's Republic of China | | | | |
| Production | 216.3 | 217.6 | 259.0 | 17.4 |
| Consumption | 220.2 | 222.4 | 267.8 | 19.1 |
| Trade | −4.0 | −4.8 | −8.8 | |

production of record quantities of food here become more apparent. Debate on the 1981 U.S. farm bill, for example, will certainly include more consideration of "exporting top soil" than was foreseeable at the time the Global 2000 Study's food projections were made.[37] The heightened concern for protection of agricultural resources is leading to a search for policies that encourage improved resource management practices. Still further pressure on the resource base can be expected, however, due to rising industrial demand for grain, especially for fermentation into alcohol-based fuels. Accelerated erosion, loss of natural soil fertility and other deterioration of the agricultural resource base may have more effect in the coming years than is indicated in the Global 2000 food projections.

In the LDCs, many governments are attempting to accelerate investment in food production capacity. This policy emphasis offers important long-term benefits. Some LDC governments are intervening more frequently in domestic food markets to keep food prices low, but often at the cost of low rural incomes and slowed development

## TABLE 6 (Cont.)

| | Grain<br>(kilograms per capita) | | | Food<br>Percent increase<br>over the<br>1970–2000 period |
|---|---|---|---|---|
| | 1969–71 | 1973–75 | 2000 | |
| Less developed countries | | | | |
| Production | 176.7 | 168.7 | 197.1 | 10.8 |
| Consumption | 188.3 | 182.2 | 205.5 | 8.6 |
| Trade | −10.7 | −15.1 | −8.4 | |
| Exporters[a] | | | | |
| Production | 491.0 | 521.9 | 671.7 | 10.4 |
| Consumption | 300.1 | 325.3 | 287.8 | −22.6 |
| Trade | +184.3 | +198.2 | +383.9 | |
| Importers[b] | | | | |
| Production | 159.4 | 173.8 | 180.7 | 10.8 |
| Consumption | 177.7 | 193.6 | 202.7 | 10.8 |
| Trade | −17.2 | −24.1 | −21.9 | |
| Latin America | | | | |
| Production | 236.1 | 241.0 | 311.4 | 33.7 |
| Consumption | 226.5 | 238.3 | 278.1 | 25.1 |
| Trade | +11.8 | +2.7 | +33.3 | |
| North Africa/Middle East | | | | |
| Production | 217.1 | 214.6 | 222.5 | −1.8 |
| Consumption | 276.2 | 273.8 | 292.8 | 2.2 |
| Trade | −50.8 | −69.8 | −70.3 | |
| Other African LDCs | | | | |
| Production | 134.9 | 118.3 | 113.2 | −15.5 |
| Consumption | 139.1 | 127.7 | 112.0 | −19.1 |
| Trade | −4.2 | −9.1 | +1.2 | |
| South Asia | | | | |
| Production | 161.6 | 162.4 | 170.0 | 4.6 |
| Consumption | 170.0 | 171.8 | 181.0 | 5.8 |
| Trade | −8.4 | −11.8 | −11.0 | |
| Southeast Asia | | | | |
| Production | 244.7 | 214.5 | 316.5 | 35.9 |
| Consumption | 207.2 | 182.6 | 228.5 | 14.6 |
| Trade | +37.5 | +31.9 | +87.5 | |
| East Asia | | | | |
| Production | 137.3 | 136.0 | 163.5 | 22.8 |
| Consumption | 176.2 | 171.5 | 217.3 | 27.3 |
| Trade | −40.4 | −38.8 | −53.8 | |
| World | | | | |
| Production/Consumption | 311.5 | 313.6 | 343.2 | 14.5 |

*Note:* In trade figures, plus sign indicates export, minus sign indicates import.

[a]Argentina and Thailand.

[b]All others, including several countries that export in some scenarios (e.g., Brazil, Indonesia, and Colombia).

*Source:* Global 2000 Technical Report, Table 6-6.

of agricultural production capacity.[38]

Worldwide, the use of yield-enhancing inputs is likely to be less, and soil deterioration greater, than expected. As a result, revised food projections would show a tighter food future—somewhat less production and somewhat higher prices—than indicated in the Global 2000 projections.

## Fisheries

Fish is an important component of the world's diet and has sometimes been put forth as a possible partial solution to world food shortages. Unfortunately, the world harvest of fish is expected to rise little, if at all, by the year 2000.* The world catch of naturally produced fish leveled off in the 1970s at about 70 million metric tons a year

---

*The food projections assumed that the world fish catch would increase at essentially the same rate as population and are therefore likely to prove too optimistic on this point. (See Chapters 6, 14, and 18 of the Global 2000 Technical Report for further discussion of this point.)

22

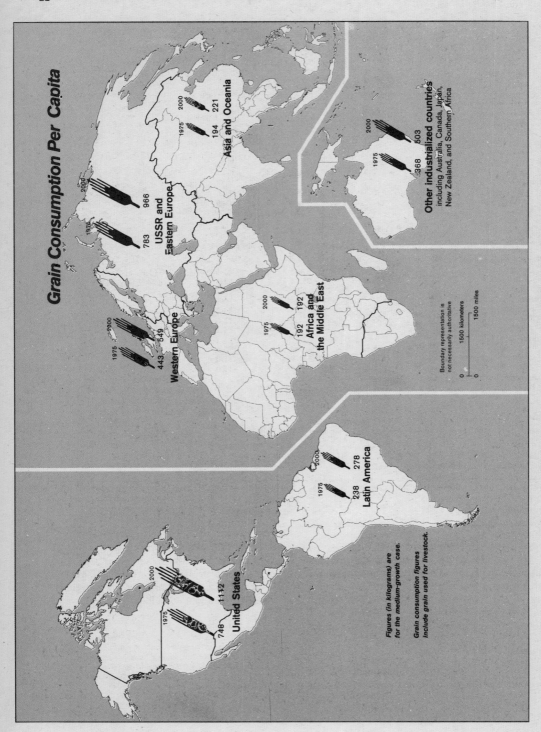

**Grain Consumption Per Capita**

USSR and
Eastern Europe
1975 783
2000 966

Asia and Oceania
1975 194
2000 221

Other industrialized countries
including Australia, Canada, Japan,
New Zealand, and Southern Africa
1975 368
2000 503

Western Europe
1975 443
2000 549

Africa and
the Middle East
1975 192
2000 192

United States
1975 748
2000 1132

Latin America
1975 238
2000 278

Boundary representation is
not necessarily authoritative

0          1500 kilometers
0          1500 miles

*Figures (in kilograms) are
for the medium-growth case.*

*Grain consumption figures
include grain used for livestock.*

**Figure 5.** Per capita grain consumption, by regions, 1975 and 2000.

(60 million metric tons for marine fisheries, 10 million metric tons for freshwater species). Harvests of traditional fisheries are not likely to increase on a sustained basis, and indeed to maintain them will take good management and improved protection of the marine environment. Some potential for greater harvests comes from aquaculture and from nontraditional marine species, such as Antarctic krill, that are little used at present for direct human consumption.[39]

Traditional freshwater and marine species might be augmented in some areas by means of aquaculture. The 1976 FAO World Conference on Aquaculture concluded that a five- to tenfold increase in production from aquaculture would be possible by 2000, given adequate financial and technical support. (Aquaculture contributed an estimated 6 million metric tons to the world's total catch in 1975.) However, limited investment and technical support, as well as increasing pollution of freshwater ponds and coastal water, are likely to be a serious impediment to such growth.[40]

While fish is not a solution to the world needs for calories, fish does provide an important source of protein. The 70 million metric tons caught and raised in 1975 is roughly equivalent to 14 million metric tons of protein, enough to supply 27 percent of the minimum protein requirements of 4 billion people. (Actually since more than one-third of the fish harvest is used for animal feed, not food for humans, the contribution of fish to human needs for protein is lower than these figures suggest.[41]) A harvest of about 115 million metric tons would be required to supply 27 percent of the protein needs of 6.35 billion people in 2000. Even assuming that the catch of marine and freshwater fish rises to the unlikely level of 100 million metric tons annually, and that yields from aquaculture double, rising to 12 million tons, the hypothetical total of 112 metric tons would not provide as much protein per capita as the catch of the mid-1970s. Thus, on a per capita basis, fish may well contribute less to the world's nutrition in 2000 than today.

Updated fisheries projections would show little change from the Global 2000 Study projections. FAO fisheries statistics are now available for 1978 and show a world catch of 72.4 million metric tons. (The FAO statistics for the 1970-78 period have been revised downward somewhat to reflect improved data on the catch of the People's Republic of China.) While there has been some slight recovery of the anchovy and menhaden fisheries, traditional species continue to show signs of heavy pressure. As indicated in the Global 2000 projections, the catch of nontraditional species is filling in to some extent. Perhaps the biggest change in updated fisheries projections would stem from a careful analysis of the effects of the large increase in oil prices that occurred in 1979. Scattered observations suggest that fishing fleets throughout the world are being adversely affected except where governments are keeping oil prices to fishing boats artificially low.[42]

## Forests

If present trends continue, both forest cover and growing stocks of commercial-size wood in the less developed regions (Latin America, Africa, Asia, and Oceania) will decline 40 percent by 2000. In the industrialized regions (Europe,

**TABLE 7**
**Estimates of World Forest Resources, 1978 and 2000**

| | Closed Forest[a] (millions of hectares) | | Growing Stock (billions cu m overbark) | |
|---|---|---|---|---|
| | 1978 | 2000 | 1978 | 2000 |
| U.S.S.R. | 785 | 775 | 79 | 77 |
| Europe | 140 | 150 | 15 | 13 |
| North America | 470 | 464 | 58 | 55 |
| Japan, Australia, New Zealand | 69 | 68 | 4 | 4 |
| Subtotal | 1,464 | 1,457 | 156 | 149 |
| Latin America | 550 | 329 | 94 | 54 |
| Africa | 188 | 150 | 39 | 31 |
| Asia and Pacific LDCs | 361 | 181 | 38 | 19 |
| Subtotal (LDCs) | 1,099 | 660 | 171 | 104 |
| Total (world) | 2,563 | 2,117 | 327 | 253 |

| | Growing Stock per Capita (cu m biomass) | |
|---|---|---|
| Industrial countries | 142 | 114 |
| LDCs | 57 | 21 |
| Global | 76 | 40 |

[a]Closed forests are relatively dense and productive forests. They are defined variously in different parts of the world. For further details, see Global 2000 Technical Report, footnote, p. 117.

*Source:* Global 2000 Technical Report, Table 13-29.

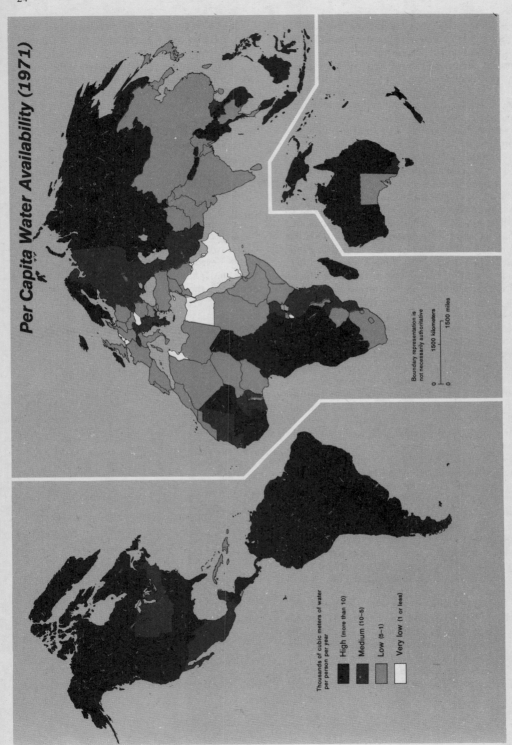

**Per Capita Water Availability (1971)**

Thousands of cubic meters of water per person per year

- High (more than 10)
- Medium (10–5)
- Low (5–1)
- Very low (1 or less)

Boundary representation is not necessarily authoritative

0  1500 kilometers
0  1500 miles

**Figure 6.** Per capita water availability, 1971.

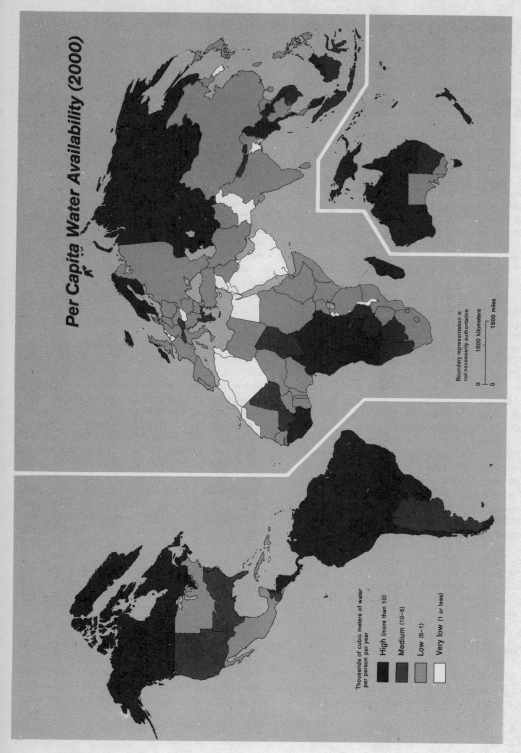

## Per Capita Water Availability (2000)

Thousands of cubic meters of water
per person per year

High (more than 10)

Medium (10–5)

Low (5–1)

Very low (1 or less)

Boundary representation is
not necessarily authoritative

0   1500 kilometers

0   1500 miles

**Figure 7.** Projected per capita water availability, 2000.

the U.S.S.R., North America, Japan, Australia, New Zealand) forests will decline only 0.5 percent and growing stock about 5 percent. Growing stock per capita is expected to decline 47 percent worldwide and 63 percent in LDCs.[43] Table 7 shows projected forest cover and growing stocks by region for 1978 and 2000.

Deforestation is projected to continue until about 2020, when the total world forest area will stabilize at about 1.8 billion hectares. Most of the loss will occur in the tropical forests of the developing world. About 1.45 billion hectares of forest in the industrialized nations has already stabilized and about 0.37 billion hectares of forest in the LDCs is physically or economically inaccessible. By 2020, virtually all of the physically accessible forest in the LDCs is expected to have been cut.[44]

The real prices of wood products—fuelwood, sawn lumber, wood panels, paper, wood-based chemicals, and so on—are expected to rise considerably as GNP (and thus also demand) rises and world supplies tighten. In the industrialized nations, the effects may be disruptive, but not catastrophic. In the less developed countries, however, 90 percent of wood consumption goes for cooking and heating, and wood is a necessity of life. Loss of woodlands will force people in many LDCs to pay steeply rising prices for fuelwood and charcoal or to spend much more effort collecting wood—or else to do without.[45]

Updated forest projections would present much the same picture as the Global 2000 Study projections. The rapid increase in the price of crude oil will probably limit the penetration of kerosene sales into areas now depending on fuelwood and dung and, as a result, demand for fuelwood may be somewhat higher than expected. Some replanting of cut tropical areas is occurring, but only at low rates similar to those assumed in the Global 2000 Study projections. Perhaps the most encouraging developments are those associated with heightened international awareness of the seriousness of current trends in world forests.[46]

## Water

The Global 2000 Study population, GNP, and resource projections all imply rapidly increasing demands for fresh water.[47] Increases of at least 200-300 percent in world water withdrawals are expected over the 1975-2000 period. By far the largest part of the increase is for irrigation. The United Nations has estimated that water needed for irrigation, which accounted for 70 percent of human uses of water in 1967, would double by 2000. Moreover, irrigation is a highly consumptive use, that is, much of the water withdrawn for this purpose is not available for immediate reuse because it evaporates, is transpired by plants, or becomes salinated.[48]

Regional water shortages and deterioration of water quality, already serious in many parts of the world, are likely to become worse by 2000. Estimates of per capita water availability for 1971 and 2000, based on population growth alone, *without allowance for other causes of increased demand,* are shown in Figures 6 and 7. As indicated in these maps, population growth alone will cause demands for water at least to double relative to 1971 in nearly half the countries of the world. Still greater increases would be needed to improve standards of living.[49]

Much of the increased demand for water will be in the LDCs of Africa, South Asia, the Middle East, and Latin America, where in many areas fresh water for human consumption and irrigation is already in short supply. Although the data are sketchy, it is known that several nations in these areas will be approaching their maximum developable water supply by 2000, and that it will be quite expensive to develop the water remaining. Moreover, many LDCs will also suffer destabilization of water supplies following extensive loss of forests. In the industrialized countries competition among different uses of water—for increasing food production, new energy systems (such as production of synthetic fuels from coal and shale), increasing power generation, expanding food production, and increasing needs of other industry—will aggravate water shortages in many areas.[50]

Updated water projections would present essentially the same picture. The only significant change that has occurred since the projections were developed is that the price of energy (especially oil) has increased markedly. Increased energy costs will adversely affect the economics of many water development projects, and may reduce the amount of water available for a variety of uses. Irrigation, which usually requires large amounts of energy for pumping, may be particularly affected.

## Nonfuel Minerals

The trends for nonfuel minerals, like those for the other resources considered in the Global 2000 Study, show steady increases in demand and consumption. The global demand for and consumption of most major nonfuel mineral commodities is projected to increase 3-5 percent annually, slightly more than doubling by 2000. Consumption of all major steelmaking mineral commodities is projected to increase at least 3 percent annually. Consumption of all mineral commodities for fertilizer production is projected to grow at more than 3 percent annually, with consumption of phosphate rock growing at 5.2 percent per year—the highest growth rate projected for any of the major nonfuel mineral commodities. The nonferrous metals show widely varying projected growth rates; the growth rate for aluminum, 4.3 percent per year, is the largest.[51]

The projections suggest that the LDC's share of nonfuel mineral use will increase only modestly. Over the 1971-75 period, Latin America, Africa, and Asia used 7 percent of the world's aluminum production, 9 percent of the copper, and 12 percent of the iron ore. The three-quarters of the world's population living in these regions in 2000 are projected to use only 8 percent of aluminum production, 13 percent of copper production, and 17 percent of iron ore production. The one-quarter of the world's population that inhabits industrial countries is projected to continue absorbing more than three-fourths of the world's nonfuel minerals production.[52] Figure 8 shows the geographic distribution of per capita consumption of nonfuel minerals for 1975 and 2000.

The projections point to no mineral exhaustion problems but, as indicated in Table 8, further discoveries and investments will be needed to maintain reserves and production of several mineral commodities at desirable levels. In most cases, however, the resource potential is still large (see Table 9), especially for low grade ores.[53]

Updated nonfuel minerals projections would need to give further attention to two factors affecting investment in mining. One is the shift over the past decade in investment in extraction and processing away from the developing countries toward industrialized countries (although this trend may now be reversing). The other factor is the rapid increase in energy prices. Production of many nonfuel minerals is highly energy-intensive, and the recent and projected increases in oil prices can be expected to slow the expansion of these mineral supplies.[54]

## Energy

The Global 2000 Study's energy projections show no early relief from the world's energy problems. The projections point out that petroleum production capacity is not increasing as rapidly as demand. Furthermore, the rate at which petroleum reserves are being added per unit of exploratory effort appears to be falling. Engineering and geological considerations suggest that world petroleum production will peak before the end of the century. Political and economic decisions in the OPEC countries could cause oil production to level off even before technological constraints come into play. A world transition away from petroleum dependence must take place, but there is still much uncertainty as to how this transition will occur. In the face of this uncertainty, it was not possible at the time the Global 2000 energy projections were made—late 1977—for the Department of Energy (DOE) to develop meaningful energy projections beyond 1990.[55] Updated DOE analyses, discussed at the end of this section, extend the global energy projections available from the U.S. Government to 1995.

DOE projections prepared for the Study show large increases in demand for all commercial sources over the 1975-90 period (see Table 10). World energy demand is projected to increase 58 percent, reaching 384 quads (quadrillion British thermal units) by 1990. Nuclear and hydro sources (primarily nuclear) increase most rapidly (226 percent by 1990), followed by oil (58 percent), natural gas (43 percent), and coal (13 percent). Oil is projected to remain the world's leading energy source, providing 46-47 percent of the world's total energy through 1990, assuming that the real price of oil on the international market increases 65 percent over the 1975-90 period. The energy projections indicate that there is considerable potential for reductions in energy consumption.[56]

Per capita energy consumption is projected to increase everywhere. The largest increase—72 percent over the 1975-90 period—is in industrialized countries other than the United States. The

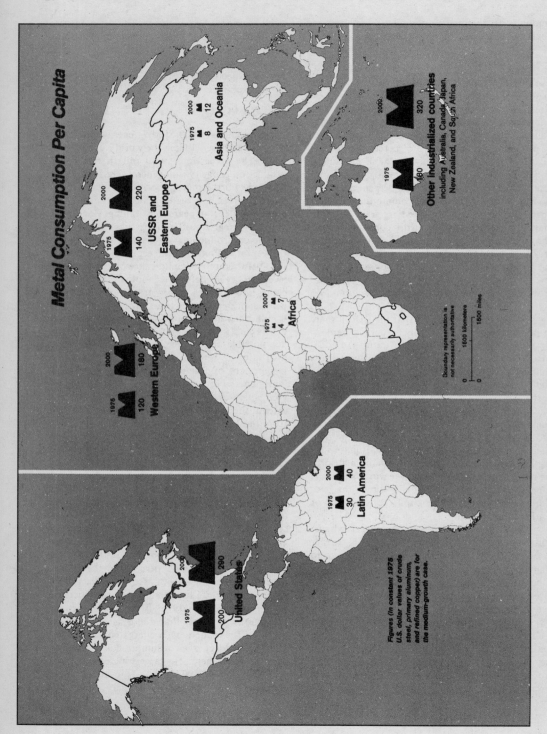

**Metal Consumption Per Capita**

United States
1975 200
2000 290

Latin America
1975 30
2000 40

Western Europe
1975 120
2000 180

USSR and Eastern Europe
1975 140
2000 220

Africa
1975 4
2000 7

Asia and Oceania
1975 8
2000 12

Other industrialized countries including Australia, Canada, Japan, New Zealand, and South Africa
1975 180
2000 320

*Figures (in constant 1975 U.S. dollar values of crude steel, primary aluminum, and refined copper) are for the medium-growth case.*

Boundary representation is not necessarily authoritative

0    1600 kilometers
0    1500 miles

**Figure 8.** Distribution of per capita consumption of nonfuel minerals, 1975 and 2000.

## TABLE 8
## Life Expectancies of 1976 World Reserves of Selected Mineral Commodities
## at Two Different Rates of Demand

| | 1976 Reserves | 1976 Primary Demand | Projected Demand Growth Rate | Life Expectancy in Years[a] | |
|---|---|---|---|---|---|
| | | | | Static at 1976 Level | Growing at Projected Rates |
| | | | *percent* | | |
| Fluorine (*million short tons*) | 37 | 2.1 | 4.58 | 18 | 13 |
| Silver (*million troy ounces*) | 6,100 | 305 | 2.33 | 20 | 17 |
| Zinc (*million short tons*) | 166 | 6.4 | 3.05 | 26 | 19 |
| Mercury (*thousand flasks*) | 5,210 | 239 | 0.50 | 22 | 21 |
| Sulfur (*million long tons*) | 1,700 | 50 | 3.16 | 34 | 23 |
| Lead (*million short tons*) | 136 | 3.7 | 3.14 | 37 | 25 |
| Tungsten (*million pounds*) | 4,200 | 81 | 3.26 | 52 | 31 |
| Tin (*thousand metric tons*) | 10,000 | 241 | 2.05 | 41 | 31 |
| Copper (*million short tons*) | 503 | 8.0 | 2.94 | 63 | 36 |
| Nickel (*million short tons*) | 60 | 0.7 | 2.94 | 86 | 43 |
| Platinum (*million troy ounces*) | 297 | 2.7 | 3.75 | 110 | 44 |
| Phosphate rock (*million metric tons*) | 25,732 | 107 | 5.17 | 240 | 51 |
| Manganese (*million short tons*) | 1,800 | 11.0 | 3.36 | 164 | 56 |
| Iron in ore (*billion short tons*) | 103 | 0.6 | 2.95 | 172 | 62 |
| Aluminum in bauxite (*million short tons*) | 5,610 | 18 | 4.29 | 312 | 63 |
| Chromium (*million short tons*) | 829 | 2.2 | 3.27 | 377 | 80 |
| Potash (*million short tons*) | 12,230 | 26 | 3.27 | 470 | 86 |

*Note:* Corresponding data for helium and industrial diamonds not available.
[a]Assumes no increase to 1976 reserves.
*Source:* After Global 2000 Technical Report, Table 12-4, but with updated and corrected entries. Updated reserves and demand data from U.S. Bureau of Mines, *Mineral Trends and Forecasts,* 1979. Projected demand growth rates are from Global 2000 Technical Report, Table 12-2.

smallest increase, 12 percent, is in the centrally planned economies of Eastern Europe. The percentage increases for the United States and for the LDCs are the same—27 percent—but actual per capita energy consumption is very different. By 2000, U.S. per capita energy consumption is projected to be about 422 million Btu (British thermal units) annually. In the LDCs, it will be only 14 million Btu, up from 11 million in 1975[57] (see Table 11 and Figure 9).

While prices for oil and other commercial energy sources are rising, fuelwood—the poor person's oil—is expected to become far less available than it is today. The FAO has estimated that the demand for fuelwood in LDCs will increase at 2.2 percent per year, leading to local fuelwood shortages in 1994 totaling 650 million cubic meters—approximately 25 percent of the projected need. Scarcities are now local but expanding. In the arid Sahel of Africa, fuelwood gathering has become a full-time job requiring in some places 360 person-days of work per household each year. When demand is concentrated in cities, surrounding areas have already become barren for considerable distances—50 to 100 kilometers in some places. Urban families, too far from collectible wood, spend 20 to 30 percent of their income on wood in some West African cities.[58]

The projected shortfall of fuelwood implies that fuel consumption for essential uses will be reduced, deforestation expanded, wood prices increased, and growing amounts of dung and crop residues shifted from the field to the cooking fire. No explicit projections of dung and crop residue combustion could be made for the Study, but it is known that a shift toward burning these organic materials is already well advanced in the Himalayan hills, in the treeless Ganges plain of India, in other parts of Asia, and in the Andean region of South America. The FAO reports that in 1970 India burned 68 million tons of cow dung and 39 million tons of vegetable waste, accounting for roughly a third of the nation's total noncommercial energy consumption that year. Worldwide, an estimated 150-400 million tons of dung are burned annually for fuel.[59]

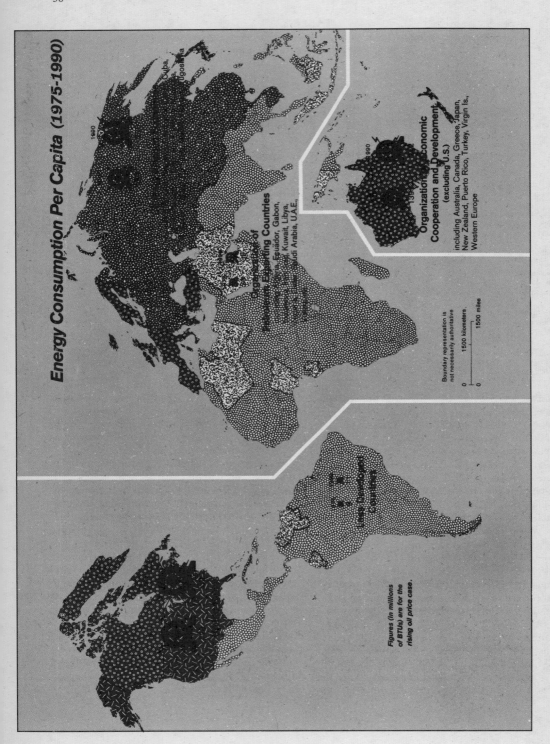

**Figure 9.** Energy consumption per capita, 1975–90.

## TABLE 9
### World Production and Reserves in 1977 (Estimated), Other Resources in 1973–77 (as Data Available), Resource Potential, and Resource Base of 17 Elements

*(Millions of metric tons)*

|  | Production | Reserves | Other Resources | Resource Potential (Recoverable) | Resource Base (Crustal Mass) |
|---|---|---|---|---|---|
| Aluminum | 17[a] | 5,200[a] | 2,800[a] | 3,519,000 | 1,990,000,000,000 |
| Iron | 495[b] | 93,100 | 143,000[c] | 2,035,000 | 1,392,000,000,000 |
| Potassium | 22 | 9,960 | 103,000 | n.a. | 408,000,000,000 |
| Manganese | 10[d] | 2,200 | 1,100[e] | 42,000 | 31,200,000,000 |
| Phosphorus | 14[f] | 3,400[f] | 12,000[f] | 51,000 | 28,800,000,000 |
| Fluorine | 2[g] | 72 | 270 | 20,000 | 10,800,000,000 |
| Sulfur | 52 | 1,700 | 3,800[h] | 51,000 | 9,600,000,000 |
| Chromium | 3[i] | 780[i] | 6,000[i] | 3,260 | 2,600,000,000 |
| Zinc | 6 | 159 | 4,000 | 3,400 | 2,250,000,000 |
| Nickel | 0.7 | 54 | 103[e] | 2,590 | 2,130,000,000 |
| Copper | 8 | 456 | 1,770[j] | 2,120 | 1,510,000,000 |
| Lead | 4 | 123 | 1,250 | 550 | 290,000,000 |
| Tin | 0.2 | 10 | 27 | 68 | 40,800,000 |
| Tungsten | 0.04 | 1.8 | 3.4 | 51 | 26,400,000 |
| Mercury | 0.008 | 0.2 | 0.4 | 3.4 | 2,100,000 |
| Silver | 0.010 | 0.2 | 0.5 | 2.8 | 1,800,000 |
| Platinum group[k] | 0.0002 | 0.02 | 0.05[l] | 1.2[m] | 1,100,000 |

[a]In bauxite, dry basis, assumed to average 21 percent recoverable aluminum.
[b]In ore and concentrates assumed to average 58 percent recoverable iron.
[c]In ore and concentrates assumed to average 26 percent recoverable iron.
[d]In ore and concentrates assumed to average 40 percent manganese.
[e]Excludes metal in deep-sea nodules and, in the case of nickel, unidentified resources.
[f]In phosphate rock ore and concentrates assumed to average 13 percent phosphorus.
[g]In fluorspar and phosphate rock ore and concentrates assumed to average 44 percent fluorine.

[h]Excludes unidentified sulfur resources, enormous quantities of sulfur in gypsum and anhydrite, and some 600 billion tons of sulfur in coal, oil shale, and in shale that is rich in organic matter.
[i]In ore and concentrates assumed to average 32 percent chromium.
[j]Includes 690 million tons in deep-sea nodules.
[k]Platinum, palladium, iridium, cesium, rhodium, and ruthenium.
[l]Approximate midpoint of estimated range of 0.03–0.06 million metric tons.
[m]Platinum only.

*Source:* Global 2000 Technical Report, Table 12-7.

## TABLE 10
### Global Primary[a] Energy Use, 1975 and 1990, by Energy Type

|  | 1975 | | 1990 | | Percent Increase (1975-90) | Average Annual Percent Increase |
|---|---|---|---|---|---|---|
|  | $10^{15}$ Btu | Percent of Total | $10^{15}$ Btu[b] | Percent of Total | | |
| Oil | 113 | 46 | 179 | 47 | 58 | 3.1 |
| Coal | 68 | 28 | 77 | 20 | 13 | 0.8 |
| Natural gas | 46 | 19 | 66 | 17 | 43 | 2.4 |
| Nuclear and hydro | 19 | 8[c] | 62 | 16[c] | 226 | 7.9 |
| Solar (other than conservation/ and hydro)[d] | — | — | — | — | — | — |
| Total | 246 | 100 | 384 | 100 | 56 | 3.0 |

[a]All of the nuclear and much of the coal primary (i.e., input) energy is used thermally to generate electricity. In the process, approximately two-thirds of the primary energy is lost as waste heat. The figures given here are primary energy.
[b]The conversions from the DOE projections in Table 10-8 were made as follows: *Oil* 84.8 × $10^6$ bbl/day × 365 days × 5.8 × $10^6$ Btu/bbl = 179 × $10^6$ Btu. *Coal:* 5,424 × $10^6$ short tons/yr × 14.1 × $10^6$ Btu/short ton [DOE figure for world average grade coal] = 77 × $10^{15}$ Btu. *Natural gas:* 64.4 × $10^{12}$ft³/yr ×

1,032 Btu/ft³ = 66 × $10^{15}$ Btu. *Nuclear and Hydro:* 6,009 × $10^{12}$ Wh [output]/yr × 3,412 Btu/Wh × 3 input Btu/output Btu = 62 × $10^{12}$ Btu.
[c]After deductions for lost (waste) heat (see note a), the corresponding figures for output energy are 2.7 percent in 1975 and 6.0 in 1990.
[d]The IIES projection model is able to include solar only as conservation or hydro.

*Source:* Global 2000 Technical Report, Table 13-32.

**TABLE 11**
**Per Capita Global Primary Energy Use, Annually, 1975 and 1990**

| | 1975 | | 1990 | | | |
|---|---|---|---|---|---|---|
| | $10^6$ Btu | Percent of World Average | $10^6$ Btu | Percent of World Average | Percent Increase (1975-90) | Average Annual Percent Increase |
| United States | 332 | 553 | 422 | 586 | 27 | 1.6 |
| Other industrialized countries | 136 | 227 | 234 | 325 | 72 | 3.6 |
| Less developed countries[a] | 11 | 18 | 14 | 19 | 27 | 1.6 |
| Centrally planned economies | 58 | 97 | 65 | 90 | 12 | 0.8 |
| World | 60 | 100 | 72 | 100 | 20 | 1.2 |

[a]Since population projections were not made separately for the OPEC countries, those countries have been included here in LDC category.
*Source:* Global 2000 Technical Report, Table 13-34.

Updated energy projections have been developed by the Department of Energy based on new price scenarios that include the rapid 1979 increase in the price of crude oil. The new price scenarios are not markedly different from the earlier estimates for the 1990s. The new medium-scenario price for 1995 is $40 per barrel (in 1979 dollars), which is about 10 percent higher than the $36 price (1979 dollars) implied by the earlier scenario. However, the prices for the early 1980s are almost 100 percent higher than those in the projections made by DOE in late 1977 for the Study.[60] The sudden large increase in oil prices of 1979 is likely to have a more disruptive effect on other sectors than would the gradual increase assumed in the Global 2000 Study projections.

DOE's new projections differ in several ways from those reported in this Study. Using the higher prices, additional data, and a modified model, DOE is now able to project supply and demand for an additional five years, to 1995. Demand is projected to be lower because of the higher prices and also because of reduced estimates of economic growth. Coal is projected to provide a somewhat larger share of the total energy supply. The nuclear projections for the OECD countries are lower, reflecting revised estimates of the speed at which new nuclear plants will be built. Updated estimates of OPEC maximum production are lower than earlier estimates, reflecting trends toward resource conservation by the OPEC nations. The higher oil prices will encourage the adoption of alternative fuels and technologies, including solar technology and conservation measures.[61]

## Environmental Consequences

The population, income, and resource projections all imply significant consequences for the quality of the world environment. Virtually every aspect of the earth's ecosystems and resource base will be affected.[62]

### Impacts on Agriculture

Perhaps the most serious environmental development will be an accelerating deterioration and loss of the resources essential for agriculture. This overall development includes soil erosion; loss of nutrients and compaction of soils; increasing salinization of both irrigated land and water used for irrigation; loss of high-quality cropland to urban development; crop damage due to increasing air and water pollution; extinction of local and wild crop strains needed by plant breeders for improving cultivated varieties; and more frequent and more severe regional water shortages—especially where energy and industrial developments compete for water supplies, or where forest losses are heavy and the earth can no longer absorb, store, and regulate the discharge of water.

Deterioration of soils is occurring rapidly in LDCs, with the spread of desert-like conditions in drier regions, and heavy erosion in more humid areas. Present global losses to desertification are estimated at around 6 million hectares a year (an area about the size of Maine), including 3.2 million hectares of rangeland, 2.5 million hectares of rainfed cropland, and 125 thousand hectares of irrigated farmland. Desertification does not necessarily mean the creation of Sahara-like sand deserts, but rather it includes a variety of ecological changes that destroy the cover of vegetation and fertile soil in the earth's drier regions, rendering the land useless for range or crops. Principal direct causes are overgrazing, destructive cropping practices, and use of woody plants for fuel.

At presently estimated rates of desertification, the world's desert areas (now some 800 million hectares) would expand almost 20 percent by 2000. But there is reason to expect that losses to desertification will accelerate, as increasing numbers of people in the world's drier regions put more pressures on the land to meet their needs for livestock range, cropland, and fuelwood. The United Nations has identified about 2 billion hectares of lands (Figure 10) where the risk of desertification is "high" or "very high." These lands at risk total about two and one-half times the area now classified as desert.

Although soil loss and deterioration are especially serious in many LDCs, they are also affecting agricultural prospects in industrialized nations. Present rates of soil loss in many industrialized nations cannot be sustained without serious implications for crop production. In the United States, for example, the Soil Conservation Service, looking at wind and water erosion of U.S. soils, has concluded that to sustain crop production indefinitely at even present levels, soil losses must be cut in half.

The outlook for making such gains in the United States and elsewhere is not good. The food and forestry projections imply increasing pressures on soils throughout the world. Losses due to improper irrigation, reduced fallow periods, cultivation of steep and marginal lands, and reduced vegetative cover can be expected to accelerate, especially in North and Central Africa, the humid and high-altitude portions of Latin America, and much of South Asia. In addition, the increased burning of dung and crop wastes for domestic fuel will deprive the soil of nutrients and degrade the soil's ability to hold moisture by reducing its organic content. For the world's poor, these organic materials are often the only source of the nutrients needed to maintain the productivity of farmlands. It is the poorest people—those least able to afford chemical fertilizers—who are being forced to burn their organic fertilizers. These

nutrients will be urgently needed for food production in the years ahead, since by 2000 the world's croplands will have to feed half again as many people as in 1975.[63] In the industrialized regions, increasing use of chemical fertilizers, high-yield plant varieties, irrigation water, and herbicides and pesticides have so far compensated for basic declines in soil conditions. However, heavy dependence on chemical fertilizers also leads to losses of soil organic matter, reducing the capacity of the soil to retain moisture.

Damage and loss of irrigated lands are especially significant because these lands have yields far above average. Furthermore, as the amount of arable land per capita declines over the next two decades, irrigated lands will be counted upon increasingly to raise per capita food availability. As of 1975, 230 million hectares—15 percent of the world's arable area—were being irrigated; an additional 50 million hectares are expected to be irrigated by 1990. Unfortunately there is great difficulty in maintaining the productivity of irrigated lands. About half of the world's irrigated land has already been damaged to some degree by salinity, alkalinity, and waterlogging, and much of the additional land expected to be irrigated by 1990 is highly vulnerable to irrigation-related damage.

Environmental problems of irrigation exist in industrialized countries (for example, in the San Joaquin Valley in California) as well as in LDCs (as in Pakistan, where three-quarters of the irrigated lands are damaged). It is possible, but slow and costly, to restore damaged lands. Prevention requires careful consideration of soils and attention to drainage, maintenance, and appropriate water-saving designs.

Loss of good cropland to urban encroachment is another problem affecting all countries. Cities and industries are often located on a nation's best agricultural land—rich, well-watered alluvial soils in gently sloping river valleys. In the industrialized countries that are members of the OECD, the amount of land devoted to urban uses has been increasing twice as fast as population. The limited data available for LDCs point to similar trends. In Egypt, for example, despite efforts to open new lands to agriculture, the total area of irrigated farmland has remained almost unchanged in the past two decades. As fast as additional acres are irrigated with water from the

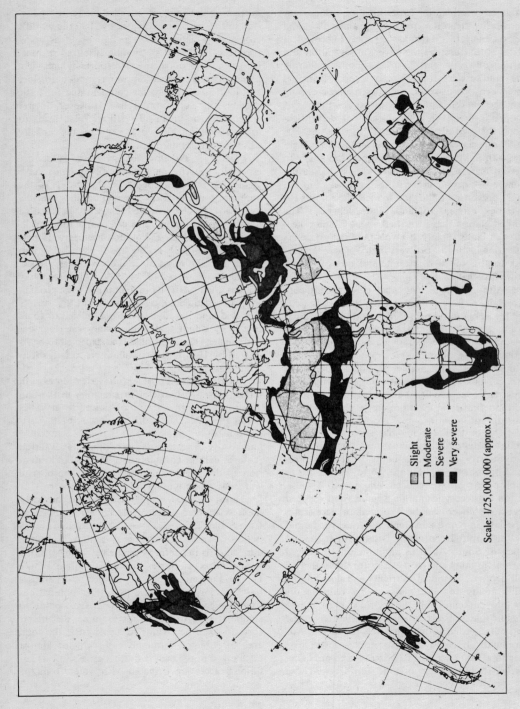

Scale: 1/25,000,000 (approx.)

Slight
Moderate
Severe
Very severe

**Figure 10.** Desertification map (*U.N. Desertification Conference, 1977*).

Aswan Dam, old producing lands on the Nile are converted to urban uses.

The rising yields assumed by the Global 2000 food projections depend on wider adoption of existing high-yield agricultural technology and on accelerating use of fertilizers, irrigation, pesticides, and herbicides. These yield-enhancing inputs, projected to more than double in use worldwide and to quadruple in LDCs, are heavily dependent on fossil fuels. Even now, a rapid escalation of fossil fuel prices or a sudden interruption of supply could severely disturb world agricultural production, raise food prices, and deprive larger numbers of people of adequate food. As agriculture becomes still more dependent on energy-intensive inputs, the potential for disruption will be even greater.

Accelerating use of pesticides is expected to raise crop yields quickly and substantially, especially in LDCs. Yet, many of these chemicals produce a wide range of serious environmental consequences, some of which adversely affect agricultural production. Destruction of pest predator populations and the increasing resistance of pests to heavily used pesticides have already proved to be significant agricultural problems. On California farms, for example, 17 of 25 major agricultural pests are now resistant to one or more types of pesticides, and the populations of pest predators have been severely reduced. Many millions of dollars in crop damage are now caused annually in California by resistant pests whose natural predators have been destroyed.

Crop yields are expected to be increased significantly by much wider use of high-yield strains of grains. Unfortunately, large monocultures of genetically identical crops pose increased risks of catastrophic loss from insect attacks or crop epidemics. The corn blight that struck the U.S. corn belt in 1970 provided a clear illustration of the vulnerability of genetically identical monocultures.

**Impacts on Water Resources**

The quality of the world's water resources is virtually certain to suffer from the changes taking place between now and the year 2000. Water pollution from heavy application of pesticides will cause increasing difficulties. In the industrialized countries, shifts from widespread use of long-lived chemicals such as DDT are now underway, but in the LDCs—where the largest increases in agricultural chemical use is projected—it is likely that the persistent pesticides will continue to be used. Pesticide use in LDCs is expected to at least quadruple over the 1975–2000 period (a sixfold increase is possible if recent rates of increase continue). Pollution from the persistent pesticides in irrigation canals, ponds, and rice paddies is already a worrisome problem. Farmers in some parts of Asia are reluctant to stock paddies and ponds because fish are being killed by pesticides. This means a serious loss of high-quality protein for the diets of rural families.

In addition to the potential impacts on soils discussed above, irrigation adversely affects water quality by adding salt to the water returning to streams and rivers. Downstream from extensive irrigation projects the water may become too saline for further use, unless expensive desalinization measures are undertaken. As the use of water for irrigation increases, water salinity problems are certain to increase as well.

Water pollution in LDCs is likely to worsen as the urban population soars and industry expands. Already the waters below many LDC cities are heavily polluted with sewage and wastes from pulp and paper mills, tanneries, slaughterhouses, oil refineries, and chemical plants.

River basin development that combines flood control, generation of electricity, and irrigation is likely to increase in many less developed regions, where most of the world's untapped hydropower potential lies. While providing many benefits, large-scale dams and irrigation projects can also cause highly adverse changes in both freshwater and coastal ecosystems, creating health problems (including schistosomiasis, river blindness, malaria), inundating valuable lands, and displacing populations. In addition, if erosion in the watersheds of these projects is not controlled, siltation and buildup of sediments may greatly reduce the useful life of the projects.

Virtually all of the Global 2000 Study's projections point to increasing destruction or pollution of coastal ecosystems, a resource on which the commercially important fisheries of the world depend heavily. It is estimated that 60-80 percent of commercially valuable marine fishery species use estuaries, salt marshes, or mangrove swamps for habitat at some point in their life cycle. Reef habitats also provide food and shelter for large numbers of fish and invertebrate species. Rapidly expanding cities and industry are likely to claim coastal wetland areas for development; and increasing coastal pollution from agriculture, industry, logging, water resources development, energy systems, and coastal communities is anticipated in many areas.

## Impacts of Forest Losses

The projected rapid, widespread loss of tropical forests will have severe adverse effects on water and other resources. Deforestation—especially in South Asia, the Amazon basin, and central Africa—will destabilize water flows, leading to siltation of streams, reservoirs behind hydroelectric dams, and irrigation works, to depletion of ground water, to intensified flooding, and to aggravated water shortages during dry periods. In South and Southeast Asia approximately one billion people live in heavily farmed alluvial basins and valleys that depend on forested mountain watersheds for their water. If present trends continue, forests in these regions will be reduced by about half in 2000, and erosion, siltation, and erratic streamflows will seriously affect food production.

In many tropical forests, the soils, land forms, temperatures, patterns of rainfall, and distribution of nutrients are in precarious balance. When these forests are disturbed by extensive cutting, neither trees nor productive grasses will grow again. Even in less fragile tropical forests, the great diversity of species is lost after extensive cutting.

## Impacts on the World's Atmosphere and Climate

Among the emerging environmental stresses are some that affect the chemical and physical nature of the atmosphere. Several are recognized as problems; others are more conjectural but nevertheless of concern.

Quantitative projections of urban air quality around the world are not possible with the data and models now available, but further pollution in LDCs and some industrial nations is virtually certain to occur under present policies and practices. In LDC cities, industrial growth projected for the next 20 years is likely to worsen air quality. Even now, observations in scattered LDC cities show levels of sulfur dioxide, particulates, nitrogen dioxide, and carbon monoxide far above levels considered safe by the World Health Organization. In some cities, such as Bombay and Caracas, recent rapid increases in the numbers of cars and trucks have aggravated air pollution.

Despite recent progress in reducing various types of air pollution in many industrialized countries, air quality there is likely to worsen as increased amounts of fossil fuels, especially coal, are burned. Emissions of sulfur and nitrogen oxides are particularly troubling because they combine with water vapor in the atmosphere to form acid rain or produce other acid deposition. In large areas of Norway, Sweden, southern Canada, and the eastern United States, the pH value of rainfall has dropped from 5.7 to below 4.5, well into the acidic range. Also, rainfall has almost certainly become more acid in parts of Germany, Eastern Europe, and the U.S.S.R., although available data are incomplete.

The effects of acid rain are not yet fully understood, but damage has already been observed in lakes, forests, soils, crops, nitrogen-fixing plants, and building materials. Damage to lakes has been studied most extensively. For example, of 1,500 lakes in southern Norway with a pH below 4.3, 70 percent had no fish. Similar damage has been observed in the Adirondack Mountains of New York and in parts of Canada. River fish are also severely affected. In the last 20 years, first salmon and then trout disappeared in many Norwegian rivers as acidity increased.

Another environmental problem related to the combustion of fossil fuels (and perhaps also to the global loss of forests and soil humus) is the increasing concentration of carbon dioxide in the earth's atmosphere. Rising $CO_2$ concentrations are of concern because of their potential for causing a warming of the earth. Scientific opinion differs on the possible consequences, but a widely held view is that highly disruptive effects on world agriculture could occur before the middle of the twenty-first century. The $CO_2$ content of the world's atmosphere has increased about 15 percent in the last century and by 2000 is expected to be nearly a third higher than preindustrial levels. If the projected rates of increase in fossil fuel combustion (about 2 percent per year) were to continue, a doubling of the $CO_2$ content of the atmosphere could be expected after the middle of the next century; and if deforestation substantially reduces tropical forests (as projected), a doubling of atmosphereic $CO_2$ could occur sooner. The result could be significant alterations of precipitation patterns around the world, and a 2°–3°C rise in temperatures in the middle latitudes of the earth. Agriculture and other human endeavors would have great difficulty in adapting to such large, rapid changes in climate. Even a 1°C increase in average global temperatures would make the earth's climate warmer than it has been any time in the last 1,000 years.

A carbon dioxide-induced temperature rise is expected to be 3 or 4 times greater at the poles than in the middle latitudes. An increase of 5°–10°C in polar temperatures could eventually lead to the melting of the Greenland and Antarctic ice caps and a gradual rise in sea level, forcing abandonment of many coastal cities.

Ozone is another major concern. The stratospheric ozone layer protects the earth from damaging ultraviolet light. However, the ozone layer is being threatened by chlorofluorocarbon emissions from aerosol cans and refrigeration equipment, by nitrous oxide ($N_2O$) emissions from the denitrification of both organic and inorganic nitrogen fertilizers, and possibly by the effects of high-altitude aircraft flights. Only the United States and a few other countries have made serious efforts to date to control the use of aerosol cans. Refrigerants and nitrogen fertilizers present even more difficult challenges. The most widely discussed effect of ozone depletion and the resulting increase in ultraviolet light is an increased incidence of skin cancer, but damage to food crops would also be significant and might actually prove to be the most serious ozone related problem.

## Impacts of Nuclear Energy

The problems presented by the projected production of increasing amounts of nuclear power are different from but no less serious than those related to fossil fuel combustion. The risk of radioactive contamination of the environment due to nuclear power reactor accidents will be increased, as will the potential for proliferation of nuclear weapons. No nation has yet conducted a demonstration program for the satisfactory disposal of radioactive wastes, and the amount of wastes is increasing rapidly. Several hundred thousand tons of highly radioactive spent nuclear fuel will be generated over the lifetimes of the nuclear plants likely to be constructed through the year 2000. In addition, nuclear power production will create millions of cubic meters of low-level radioactive wastes, and uranium mining and processing will lead to the production of hundreds of millions of tons of low-level radioactive tailings. It has not yet been demonstrated that all of these high- and low-level wastes from nuclear power production can be safely stored and disposed of without incident. Some of the by-products of reactors, it should be noted, have half-lives approximately five times as long as the period of recorded history.

## Species Extinctions

Finally, the world faces an urgent problem of loss of plant and animal genetic resources. An estimate prepared for the Global 2000 Study suggests that between half a million and 2 million species—15 to 20 percent of all species on earth—could be extinguished by 2000, mainly because of loss of wild habitat but also in part because of pollution. Extinction of species on this scale is without precedent in human history.[63]

One-half to two-thirds of the extinctions projected to occur by 2000 will result from the clearing or degradation of tropical forests. Insect, other invertebrate, and plant species—many of them unclassified and unexamined by scientists—will account for most of the losses. The potential value of this genetic reservoir is immense. If preserved and carefully managed, tropical forest species could be a sustainable source of new foods (especially nuts and fruits), pharmaceutical chemicals, natural predators of pests, building materials, speciality woods, fuel, and so on. Even careful husbandry of the remaining biotic resources of the tropics cannot compensate for the swift, massive losses that are to be expected if present trends continue.

Current trends also threaten freshwater and marine species. Physical alterations—damming, channelization, siltation—and pollution by salts, acid rain, pesticides, and other toxic chemicals are profoundly affecting freshwater ecosystems throughout the world. At present 274 freshwater vertebrate taxa are threatened with extinction, and by the year 2000 many may have been lost.

Some of the most important genetic losses will involve the extinction not of species but of subspecies and varieties of cereal grains. Four-fifths of the world's food supplies are derived from less than two dozen plant and animal species. Wild and local domestic strains are needed for breeding resistance to pests and pathogens into the high-yield varieties now widely used.

These varietal stocks are rapidly diminishing as marginal wild lands are brought into cultivation. Local domesticated varieties, often uniquely suited to local conditions, are also being lost as higher-yield varieties displace them. And the increasing practice of monoculture of a few strains—which makes crops more vulnerable to disease epidemics or plagues of pests—is occurring at the same time that the genetic resources to resist such disasters are being lost.

# Entering the Twenty-First Century

The preceding sections have presented individually the many projections made by U.S. Government agencies for the Global 2000 Study. How are these projections to be interpreted collectively? What do they imply about the world's entry into the twenty-first century?[64]

The world in 2000 will be different from the world today in important ways. There will be more people. For every two persons on the earth in 1975 there will be three in 2000. The number of poor will have increased. Four-fifths of the world's population will live in less developed countries. Furthermore, in terms of persons per year added to the world, population growth will be 40 percent *higher* in 2000 than in 1975.[65]

The gap between the richest and the poorest will have increased. By every measure of material welfare the study provides—per capita GNP and consumption of food, energy, and minerals—the gap will widen. For example, the gap between the GNP per capita in the LDCs and the industrialized countries is projected to grow from about $4,000 in 1975 to about $7,900 in 2000.[66] Great disparities within countries are also expected to continue.

There will be fewer resources to go around. While on a worldwide average there was about four-tenths of a hectare of arable land per person in 1975, there will be only about one-quarter hectare per person in 2000[67] (see Figure 11 below). By 2000 nearly 1,000 billion barrels of the world's total original petroleum resource of approximately 2,000 billion barrels will have been consumed. Over just the 1975-2000 period, the world's remaining petroleum resources per capita can be expected to decline by at least 50 percent.[68] Over the same period world per capita water supplies will decline by 35 percent because of greater population alone; increasing competing demands will put further pressure on available water supplies.[69] The world's per capita growing stock of wood is projected to be 47 percent lower in 2000 than in 1978[70].

The environment will have lost important life-supporting capabilities. By 2000, 40 percent of the forests still remaining in the LDCs in 1978 will have been razed.[71] The atmospheric concentration of carbon dioxide will be nearly one-third higher than preindustrial levels.[72] Soil erosion will have removed, on the average, several inches of soil from croplands all over the world. Desertification (including salinization) may have claimed a significant fraction of the world's rangeland and cropland. Over little more than two decades, 15-20 percent of the earth's total species of plants and animals will have become extinct—a loss of at least 500,000 species.[73]

Prices will be higher. The price of many of the most vital resources is projected to rise in real terms—that is, over and above inflation. In order to meet projected demand, a 100 percent increase in the real price of food will be required.[74] To keep energy demand in line with anticipated supplies, the real price of energy is assumed to rise more than 150 percent over the 1975-2000 period.[75] Supplies of water, agricultural land, forest products, and many traditional marine fish species are projected to decline relative to growing demand at current prices,[76] which suggests that real price rises will occur in these sectors too. Collectively, the projections suggest that resource-based inflationary pressures will continue and intensify, especially in nations that are poor in resources or are rapidly depleting their resources.

The world will be more vulnerable both to natural disaster and to disruptions from human causes. Most nations are likely to be still more dependent on foreign sources of energy in 2000 than they are today.[77] Food production will be more vulnerable to disruptions of fossil fuel energy supplies and to weather fluctuations as cultivation expands to more marginal areas. The loss of diverse germ plasm in local strains and wild progenitors of food crops, together with the increase of monoculture, could lead to greater risks

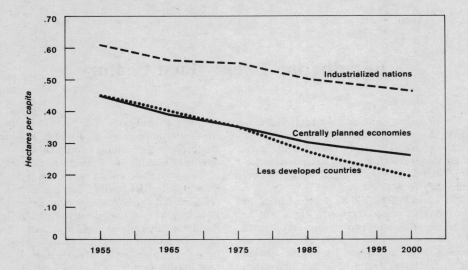

**Figure 11.** Arable land per capita, 1955, 1975, 2000.

of massive crop failures.[78] Larger numbers of people will be vulnerable to higher food prices or even famine when adverse weather occurs.[79] The world will be more vulnerable to the disruptive effects of war. The tensions that could lead to war will have multiplied. The potential for conflict over fresh water alone is underscored by the fact that out of 200 of the world's major river basins, 148 are shared by two countries and 52 are shared by three to ten countries. Long standing conflicts over shared rivers such as the Plata (Brazil, Argentina), Euphrates (Syria, Iraq), or Ganges (Bangladesh, India) could easily intensify.[80]

Finally, it must be emphasized that if public policy continues generally unchanged the world will be different as a result of lost opportunities. The adverse effects of many of the trends discussed in this Study will not be fully evident until 2000 or later; yet the actions that are necessary to change the trends cannot be postponed without foreclosing important options. The opportunity to stabilize the world's population below 10 billion, for example, is slipping away; Robert McNamara, President of the World Bank, has noted that for every decade of delay in reaching replacement fertility, the world's ultimately stabilized population will be about 11 percent greater.[81] Similar losses of opportunity accompany delayed perceptions or

action in other areas. If energy policies and decisions are based on yesterday's (or even today's) oil prices, the opportunity to wisely invest scarce capital resources will be lost as a consequence of undervaluing conservation and efficiency. If agricultural research continues to focus on increasing yields through practices that are highly energy-intensive, both energy resources and the time needed to develop alternative practices will be lost.

The full effects of rising concentrations of carbon dioxide, depletion of stratospheric ozone, deterioration of soils, increasing introduction of complex persistent toxic chemicals into the environment, and massive extinction of species may not occur until well after 2000. Yet once such global environmental problems are in motion they are very difficult to reverse. In fact, few if any of the problems addressed in the Global 2000 Study are amenable to quick technological or policy fixes; rather, they are inextricably mixed with the world's most perplexing social and economic problems.

Perhaps the most troubling problems are those in which population growth and poverty lead to serious long-term declines in the productivity of renewable natural resource systems. In some areas the capacity of renewable resource systems to support human populations is already being seriously damaged by efforts of present populations to meet desperate immediate needs, and the damage threatens to become worse.[82]

Examples of serious deterioration of the earth's most basic resources can already be found today in scattered places in all nations, including the industrialized countries and the better-endowed LDCs. For instance, erosion of agricultural soil and salinization of highly productive irrigated farmland is increasingly evident in the United States,[83] and extensive deforestation, with more or less permanent soil degradation, has occurred in Brazil, Venezuela, and Colombia.[84] But problems related to the decline of the earth's carrying capacity are most immediate, severe, and tragic in those regions of the earth containing the poorest LDCs.

Sub-Saharan Africa faces the problem of exhaustion of its resource base in an acute form. Many causes and effects have come together there to produce excessive demands on the environment, leading to expansion of the desert. Overgrazing, fuelwood gathering, and destructive cropping practices are the principal immediate causes of a series of transitions from open woodland, to scrub, to fragile semiarid range, to worthless weeds and bare earth. Matters are made worse when people are forced by scarcity of fuelwood to burn animal dung and crop wastes. The soil, deprived of organic matter, loses fertility and the ability to hold water—and the desert expands. In Bangladesh, Pakistan, and large parts of India, efforts by growing numbers of people to meet their basic needs are damaging the very cropland, pasture, forests, and water supplies on which they must depend for a livelihood.[85] To restore the lands and soils would require decades—if not centuries—*after* the existing pressures on the land have diminished. But the pressures are growing, not diminishing.

There are no quick or easy solutions, particularly in those regions where population pressure is already leading to a reduction of the carrying capacity of the land. In such regions a complex of social and economic factors (including very low incomes, inequitable land tenure, limited or no educational opportunities, a lack of non-agricultural jobs, and economic pressures toward higher fertility) underlies the decline in the land's carrying capacity. Furthermore, it is generally believed that social and economic conditions must improve before fertility levels will decline to replacement levels. Thus a vicious circle of causality may be at work. Environmental deterioration caused by large populations creates living conditions that make reductions in fertility difficult to achieve; all the while, continuing population growth increases further the pressures on the environment and land.[86]

The declines in carrying capacity already being observed in scattered areas around the world point to a phenomenon that could easily be much more widespread by 2000. In fact, the best evidence now available—even allowing for the many beneficial effects of technological developments and adoptions—suggests that by 2000 the world's human population may be within only a few generations of reaching the entire planet's carrying capacity.

The Global 2000 Study does not estimate the earth's carrying capacity, but it does provide a basis for evaluating an earlier estimate published in the U.S. National Academy of Sciences' report, *Resources and Man*. In this 1969 report, the Academy concluded that a world population of 10 billion ''is close to (if not above) the maximum that an *intensively managed* world might hope to support with some degree of comfort and individual choice.'' The Academy also concluded that even with the sacrifice of individual freedom and choice, and even with chronic near starvation for the great majority, the human population of the world is unlikely to ever exceed 30 billion.[87]

Nothing in the Global 2000 Study counters the Academy's conclusions. If anything, data gathered over the past decade suggest the Academy may have underestimated the extent of some problems, especially deforestation and the loss and deterioration of soils.[88]

At present and projected growth rates, the world's population would rapidly approach the Academy's figures. If the fertility and mortality rates projected for 2000 were to continue unchanged into the twenty-first century, the world's population would reach 10 billion by 2030. Thus anyone with a present life expectancy of an additional 50 years could expect to see the world population reach 10 billion. This same rate of growth would produce a population of nearly 30 billion before the end of the twenty-first century.[89]

Here it must be emphasized that, unlike most

of the Global 2000 Study projections, the population projections assume extensive policy changes and developments to reduce fertility rates. Without the assumed policy changes, the projected rate of population growth would be still more rapid.

Unfortunately population growth may be slowed for reasons other than declining birth rates. As the world's populations exceed and reduce the land's carrying capacity in widening areas, the trends of the last century or two toward improved health and longer life may come to a halt. Hunger and disease may claim more lives—especially lives of babies and young children. More of those surviving infancy may be mentally and physically handicapped by childhood malnutrition.

The time for action to prevent this outcome is running out. Unless nations collectively and individually take bold and imaginative steps toward improved social and economic conditions, reduced fertility, better management of resources, and protection of the environment, the world must expect a troubled entry into the twenty-first century.

# APPENDIX

## The Global 2000 Study Compared with
## Other Global Studies

In the course of the Global 2000 Study, the Government's several models (here referred to collectively as the "Government's global model") and their projections were compared with those of five other global studies.[90] The purpose was not only to compare the results of different projections, but also to see whether and how different assumptions and model structures may have led to different projections and findings.

The Global 2000 Study's principal findings are generally consistent with those of the five other global studies despite considerable differences in models and assumptions. On the whole, the other studies and their models lack the richness of detail that the Government's global model provides for the various individual sectors—food and agriculture, forests, water, energy, and so on. However, the linkages among the sectors in the other models are much more complete. Many apparent inconsistencies and contradictions in the Global 2000 projections are due to the weakness of the linkages among sectors of the Government's global model.

Another important difference is that the Government's projections stop at the year 2000 or before, while the other global studies project well into the twenty-first century. The most dramatic developments projected in the other studies—serious resource scarcities, population declines due to rising death rates, severe environmental deterioration—generally occur in the first half of the twenty-first century and thus cannot be compared with the Government's projections. Up to the turn of the century, all of the analyses, including the Government's, indicate more or less similar trends: continued economic growth in most areas, continued population growth everywhere, reduced energy growth, an increasingly tight and expensive food situation, increasing water problems, and growing environmental stress.

The most optimistic of the five models is the Latin American World Model. Instead of projecting future conditions on the basis of present policies and trends, this model asks: "How can global resources best be used to meet basic human needs for all people?" The model allocates labor and capital to maximize life expectancy. It assumes that personal consumption is sacrificed to maintain very high investment rates (25 percent of GNP per year), and it posits an egalitarian, nonexploitative, wisely managed world society that avoids pollution, soil depletion, and other forms of environmental degradation. Under these assumptions it finds that in little more than one generation basic human needs could be adequately satisfied in Latin America and in Africa. Thereafter, GNP would grow steadily and population growth would begin to stabilize.

But in Asia, even assuming these near-utopian social conditions and high rates of investment, the system collapses. The model projects an Asian food crisis beginning by 2010, as land runs out; food production cannot rise fast enough to keep up with population growth, and a vicious circle begins that leads to starvation and economic collapse by midcentury. The modelers suggest that an Asian food crisis could be avoided by such means as food imports from other areas with more cropland, better crop yields, and effective family planning policies. Nonetheless, it is striking that this model, which was designed to show that the fundamental constraints on human welfare were social, not physical, does project catastrophic food shortages in Asia due to land scarcity.

The World 2 and World 3 models, which were the basis of the 1972 Club of Rome report *The Limits to Growth,* give much attention to environmental factors—the only models in the group of five to do so. The World models, like the Global 2000 Study, considered trends in population, resources, and environment. However, these models are highly aggregated, looking at the world as a whole and omitting regional differences. In the cases that assume a continuation of present policies, the World 2 and 3 models project large global increases in food and income per capita until 2020, at which time either food scarcity or resource depletion would cause a downturn. The two models do suggest that major changes of policy can significantly alter these trends.

The World Integrated Model, a later effort sponsored by the Club of Rome, is much more detailed than the World 2 and 3 models in its treatment of regional differences, trade, economics, and shifts from one energy source to another, but it is less inclusive in its treatment of the environment. This complex model has been run under many different assumptions of conditions and policies. Almost invariably the runs project a long-term trend of steeply rising food prices. Under a wide range of policies and conditions the runs indicate massive famine in Asia and, to a lesser degree, in non-OPEC Africa, before the turn of the century.

The United Nations World Model found that to meet U.N. target rates for economic growth, developing countries would have to make great sacrifices in personal consumption, saving and investing at unprecedented rates. Personal consumption would not exceed 63 percent of income in any developing region, and none would have a level of private investment of less than 20 percent. To meet food requirements, global agricultural production would have to rise fourfold by 2000, with greater increases required in many places (500 percent, for example, in low-income Asia and Latin America).

The Model of International Relations in Agriculture (MOIRA) confines itself to agriculture; it takes into account the effects of agriculture policies but not those of environmental degradation. Its results are more optimistic than the Global 2000 projections: world food production more than doubles from 1975 to 2000, and per capita consumption rises 36 percent. Even so, because of unequal distribution, the number of people subsisting on two-thirds or less of the biological protein requirement rises from 350 million in 1975 to 740 million in 2000.

The Global 2000 Study conducted an experiment with two of the more integrated nongovernment models to answer the question: "How would projections from the Government's global model be different if the model were more integrated and included more linkages and feedback?" The linkages in the two nongovernment models were severed so that they bore some resemblance to the unconnected and inconsistent structure of the Government's global model. Chosen for the experiment were the World 3 model and the World Integrated Model.

In both models, severing the linkages led to distinctly more favorable outcomes. On the basis of results with World 3, the Global 2000 Study concluded that a more integrated Government model would project that:

- Increasing competition among agriculture, industry, and energy development for capital would lead to even higher resource cost inflation and significant decreases in real GNP growth (this assumes no major technological advances).
- The rising food prices and regional declines in food consumption per capita that are presently projected would be intensified by competition for capital and by degradation of the land.
- Slower GNP and agricultural growth would lead to higher death rates from widespread hunger—or from outright starvation—and to higher birth rates, with greater numbers of people trapped in absolute poverty.
- A decisive global downturn in incomes and food per capita would probably not take place until a decade or two after 2000 (this assumes no political disruptions).

When links in the World Integrated Model (WIM) were cut, outcomes again were more favorable. The results of the unlinked version were comparable to the Global 2000 quantitative projections for global GNP, population, grain production, fertilizer use, and energy use. But in the original integrated version of WIM, gross world product was 21 percent lower than in the unlinked version—$11.7 trillion instead of $14.8 trillion in 2000. In the linked version, world agricultural production rose 85 percent instead of 107 percent; grain available for human consumption rose less than 85 percent because some of the grain was fed to animals for increased meat production. Population rose only to 5.9 billion rather than 6.2 billion, in part because of widespread starvation (158 million deaths cumulatively by 2000) and in part because of lower birth rates in the industrialized countries. The effects of severing the linkages are much less in lightly populated regions with a wealth of natural resources, such as North America, than in regions under stress, where great numbers of people are living at the margin of existence. In North America, the difference in GNP per capita was about 5 percent; in South Asia, about 30 percent.

The inescapable conclusion is that the omission of linkages imparts an optimistic bias to the Global 2000 Study's (and the U.S. Government's) quantitative projections.[91] This appears to be particularly true of the GNP projections. The experiments with the World Integrated Model suggest that the Study's figure for gross world product in 2000 may be 15—20 percent too high.

# REFERENCES

1. *The Global 2000 Report to the President: Entering the Twenty-First Century,* vol. 2, *Technical Report,* Gerald O. Barney, Study Director, Washington: Government Printing Office, 1980, App. A.
2. Ibid.
3. Jimmy Carter, *The President's Environmental Program, 1977,* Washington: Government Printing Office, May 1977, p. M-11.
4. A more detailed discussion of the Global 2000 Study process is provided in *The Global 2000 Report to the President,* vol. 2, *Technical Report,* "Preface and Acknowledgments" and Ch. 1, "Introduction to the Projections."
5. *The Global 2000 Report to the President: Entering the Twenty-First Century,* vol. 2, Ch. 14–23; and *The Global 2000 Report to the President: Entering the Twenty-First Century,* vol. 3, *The Government's Global Model,* Gerald O. Barney, Study Director, Washington: Government Printing Office, 1980.

## NOTE

Unless otherwise indicated, the following chapter citations refer to the various chapters of *The Global 2000 Report to the President: Entering the Twenty-First Century,* vol. 2, *Technical Report;* Washington: Government Printing Office, 1980.

6. Ch. 13, 14, and 31.
7. Ch. 1.
8. "Closing the Loops," Ch. 13; Ch. 14.
9. Ibid.
10. Ch. 13, especially "Closing the Loops."
11. "Closing the Loops," Ch. 13; Ch. 14 and 31.
12. Ch. 1, 5, 14, and 23.
13. Ch. 1 and 14.
14. Ch. 30 and 31.
15. Ch. 2.
16. Ibid.
17. Ibid.
18. Ibid.
19. Ibid.; "Population Projections and the Environment," Ch. 13.
20. "Population Projections and the Environment." Ch. 13.
21. Ibid.; "Closing the Loops," Ch. 13.
22. Ibid.
23. *The Global 2000 Report to the President,* vol. 3, *The Government's Global Model,* Chapter on population models and the population projections update.
24. Ronald Freedman, "Theories of Fertility Decline: A Reappraisal," in Philip M. Hauser, ed., *World Population and Development,* Syracuse, N.Y.: Syracuse University Press, 1979; John C. Caldwell, "Toward a Restatement of Demographic Transition Theory," *Population and Development Review,* Sept./Dec., 1976.
25. For a discussion of Indonesia, see Freeman, op. cit.; for a discussion of Brazil, see "Demographic Projections Show Lower Birth Rate for the Poor" (in Portuguese), *VEJA,* Oct. 24, 1979, p. 139, citing the research of Elza Berquo of the Brazilian Analysis and Planning Center.
26. Ch. 3.
27. Ibid.
28. Ibid.
29. World Bank, *Prospects for Developing Countries, 1977–85,* Washington, Sept. 1976, Statistical Appendix, Table 1; World Bank, *World Development Report, 1979,* Washington, 1979, p. 13.
30. Ch. 6.
31. Ibid., "Food and Agriculture Projections and the Environment," Ch. 13.
32. Ch. 6.
33. Ibid.
34. "Food and Agriculture Projections and the Environment," Ch. 13.
35. Ch. 6.
36. U.S. Department of Agriculture, *Farm Income Statistics,* Washington: Economics, Statistics, and Cooperative Services, U.S.D.A., 1978 and 1979.
37. J. B. Penn, "The Food and Agriculture Policy Challenge of the 1980's," Washington: Economics, Statistics and Cooperative Service, U.S.D.A., Jan. 1980.
38. P. Osam, *Accelerating Foodgrain Production in Low-Income Food-Deficit Countries—Progress, Potentials and Paradoxes,* Hawaii: East-West Center, May 1978; J. Gravan, *The Calorie Energy Gap in Bangladesh, and Strategies for Reducing It,* Washington: International Food Policy Research Institute, Aug. 1977.
39. Ch. 7.
40. Ibid.; "The Projections and the Marine Environment" and "Water Projections and the Environment," Ch. 13.
41. Ch. 7.
42. Food and Agriculture Organization, *Fisheries Statistics Yearbook, 1978.* Rome, 1979; Richard Hennemuth, Deputy Director, Northeast Fisheries Center, National Oceanic and Atmospheric Administration, personal communication, 1980.
43. Ch. 8 and App. C.
44. Ibid.
45. Ibid.; "Population Projections and the Environment," "Forestry Projections and the Environment," and "Energy Projections and the Environment," Ch. 13.
46. Norman Myers, *The Sinking Ark,* New York: Pergamon Press, 1979; U.S. Department of State, *Proceedings of the U.S. Strategy Conference on Tropical Deforestation,* Washington, Oct. 1978.
47. See especially Ch. 2, 6, 9, 10, and 12.
48. Ch. 9.
49. Ibid.; "Water Projections and the Environment," Ch. 13.
50. Ch. 9 and 13.
51. Ch. 12.
52. Ibid.
53. Ibid.
54. Ibid.; "Nonfuel Minerals Projections and the Environment," Ch. 13.
55. Ch. 10; "Energy Projections and the Environment," Ch. 13.
56. Ibid.
57. Ibid.
58. Ch. 8; "Population Projections and the Environment," "Forestry Projections and the Environment," and "Energy Projections and the Environment," Ch. 13.
59. Ch. 8; "Forestry Projections and the Environment," "Energy Projections and the Environment," and "Clos-

ing the Loops," Ch. 13.

60. See the IEES Model Projections reported in "International Energy Assessment," in Energy Information Administration, *Annual Report to Congress, 1978,* vol. 3, Washington: Department of Energy, 1979, pp. 11–34; Energy Information Administration, *Annual Report to the Congress, 1979,* forthcoming.

61. See Energy Information Administration, *Annual Report, 1979,* op. cit.; John Pearson and Derriel Cato, personal communication, Mar. 13, 1980.

62. The discussion of "Environmental Consequences" that follows is based on Ch. 13.

63. Thomas E. Lovejoy, "A Projection of Species Extinctions," Ch. 13, pp. 328-31.

64. This section is based largely on material contained in "Closing the Loops," Ch. 13.

65. Ch. 2.

66. Ch. 3.

67. Ch. 6.

68. Ch. 10; "Energy Projections and the Environment," Ch. 13.

69. Ch. 9.

70. Ch. 8.

71. Ibid.; "Forestry Projections and the Environment," Ch. 13.

72. Ch. 4; "Climate Projections and the Environment," Ch. 13.

73. "Food and Agriculture Projections and the Environment," "Forestry Projections and the Environment," and "Closing the Loops," Ch. 13.

74. Ch. 6.

75. Extrapolating from Ch. 10, which assumes a 5 percent per year increase over the 1980–90 period.

76. Ch. 6–9.

77. Ch. 10 and 11.

78. Ch. 6; "Food and Agriculture Projections and the Environment," Ch. 13.

79. Ibid.; Ch. 4; "Climate Projections and the Environment," Ch. 13.

80. Ch. 9.

81. Robert S. McNamara, President, World Bank, "Address to the Board of Governors," Belgrade, Oct. 2, 1979, pp. 9, 10.

82. Ch. 13.

83. "Food and Agriculture Projections and the Environment," Ch. 13.

84. "Forestry Projections and the Environment," Ch. 13, and Peter Freeman, personal communication, 1980, based on field observations in 1973.

85. "Population Projections and the Environment," "Food and Agriculture Projections and the Environment," "Forestry Projections and the Environment," and "Water Projections and the Environment," Ch. 13.

86. "Population Projections and the Environment," and "Closing the Loops," Ch. 13; Erik Eckholm, *The Dispossessed of the Earth: Land Reform and Sustainable Development,* Washington: Worldwatch Institute, June 1979.

87. National Academy of Sciences, Committee on Resources and Man, *Resources and Man,* San Francisco: Freeman, 1969, p. 5; "Closing the Loops," Ch. 13.

88. "Closing the Loops," Ch. 13.

89. Projection by the U.S. Bureau of the Census communicated in a personal letter, Feb. 26, 1980, from Dr. Samuel Baum, Chief, International Demographic Data Center. This letter and projection are presented in vol. 3 of the *Global 2000 Report to the President,* Population section.

90. The discussion in this Appendix is based on the detailed analyses in Ch. 24–31 and on two papers by Jennifer Robinson (author of those chapters) presented at the International Conference on Modeling Related to Environment, sponsored by the Polish Academy of Sciences: "The Global 2000 Study: An Attempt to Increase Consistency in Government Forecasting" and "Treatment of the Environment in Global Models."

91. Further discussion of these and other potential biases in the Government's projections are provided in Ch. 14–23, and App. B.

# The Global 2000 Report to the President

## The Technical Report

A Report Prepared by
the Council on Environ-
mental Quality and the
Department of State

Gerald O. Barney
Study Director

Volume Two

# Preface and Acknowledgments

ON MAY 23, 1977, President Carter stated in his Environmental Message to the Congress:

> Environmental problems do not stop at national boundaries. In the past decade, we and other nations have come to recognize the urgency of international efforts to protect our common environment.
>
> As part of this process, I am directing the Council on Environmental Quality and the Department of State, working in cooperation with the Environmental Protection Agency, the National Science Foundation, the National Oceanic and Atmospheric Administration, and other appropriate agencies, to make a one-year study of the probable changes in the world's population, natural resources, and environment through the end of the century. This study will serve as the foundation of our longer-term planning.

*Entering the Twenty-first Century* is the interagency report prepared by the Global 2000 Study in response to President Carter's directive. The report comprises three volumes: (1) an interpretive report that summarizes the findings in nontechnical terms, (2) this technical report, which presents the projections and related analyses in greater detail, and (3) a volume of basic documentation on the models used in this Study.

The Study was supervised by an executive group cochaired originally by Charles Warren, Chairman of the Council on Environmental Quality, and Patsy Mink, Assistant Secretary of State for Oceans and International Environmental and Scientific Affairs. During the course of the study Mr. Warren was succeeded by Mr. Gus Speth, and Mrs. Mink by Mr. Thomas Pickering. The other executive group members and participating agencies are as follows:

ALVIN ALM (later C. WILLIAM FISCHER)
Assistant Secretary for Policy
Department of Energy

RICHARD C. ATKINSON
Director
National Science Foundation

BARBARA BLUM
Deputy Administrator
Environmental Protection Agency

RUPERT CUTLER
Assistant Secretary for Natural Resources and Environment
Department of Agriculture

JOAN DAVENPORT
Assistant Secretary for Energy and Minerals
Department of the Interior

RICHARD A. FRANK
Administrator
National Oceanic and Atmospheric Administration
Department of Commerce

ROBERT A. FROSCH
Administrator
National Aeronautics and Space Administration

JOHN J. GILLIGAN (later DOUGLAS BENNET)
Administrator
Agency for International Development
Department of State

JAMES LIVERMAN (later RUTH CLUSEN)
Assistant Secretary for Environment
Department of Energy

FRANK PRESS
Director
Office of Science and Technology Policy
Executive Office of the President

BARDYL R. TIRANA (later JOHN W. MACY)
Director, Federal Emergency Management Agency

STANSFIELD TURNER
Director
Central Intelligence Agency

Each executive group member designated a member of his or her staff to be a point of coordination for the Study. The coordinators are as follows:

WILLIAM ARON
Director, Office of Ecology and Environmental Conservation
National Oceanic and Atmospheric Administration
Department of Commerce

CARROLL BASTIAN (later ELINOR C. TERHUNE)
Division of Policy Research and Analysis
National Science Foundation

LINDSEY GRANT (later WM. ALSTON HAYNE)
Deputy Assistant Secretary for Environment and Population Affairs
Department of State

GORDON LAW
Science Advisor to the Secretary
Department of the Interior

CLIFFORD MCLEAN
Director, Program Analysis and Evaluation
Federal Emergency Management Agency

RICHARD MESERVE
Office of Science and Technology Policy
Executive Office of the President

JAMES R. MORRISON (later PITT THOME)
Director, Resource Observation Division
National Aeronautics and Space Administration

ROGER NAILL
Office of Analytical Services
Department of Energy

ALICE POPKIN (later LEWIS HUGHES
Associate Administrator for International Activities
Environmental Protection Agency

C. LEROY QUANCE
Economics, Statistics, and Cooperatives Service
Department of Agriculture

FRANK ROSSOMONDO
Chief, Environment and Resource Analysis Center
Central Intelligence Agency

PENNY SEVERNS (later JOHN WASIELEWSKI)
Special Assistant to the Administrator
Agency for International Development
Department of State

GEORGE SHEPHERD (later PETER HOUSE)
Office of The Assistant Secretary for Environment
Department of Energy

LEE M. TALBOT (later KATHERINE B. GILLMAN)
Assistant to the Chairman for International and Scientific Affairs
Council on Environmental Quality
Executive Office of the President

# Study Plan and Focus

President Carter's purpose in requesting this Study was to understand the long-term implications of present policies and programs and to establish a foundation for longer-range planning. Such a foundation cannot be established by merely publishing official projections. An assessment and a strengthening of the Government's current analytic capabilities is also needed.

Accordingly, it was decided early that the Global 2000 Study should exercise and employ the "present foundation" to the fullest extent possible. As a result the Study has been conducted almost exclusively with Government personnel and Government projection tools. Research and data from outside the Government were used only when needed capabilities and information within the Government were not available.

It was also decided that methodologies underlying the Study's projections should be carefully described. Therefore, Chapters 14 through 23 of this technical report contain an analysis—in relatively nontechnical terms—of every model and analytical tool used to project trends for this Study.

*Entering the Twenty-First Century* builds upon the work of a number of important Government-sponsored organizations that preceded it, including:

National Commission on Supplies and Shortages (1975)
Advisory Committee on National Growth Policy Processes (1975)
National Growth Reports Staff (1972)
Commission on Population Growth and the American Future (1972)
National Commission on Materials Policy (1970)
National Goals Research Staff (1969)
Public Land Law Review Commission (1965)
President's Commission on National Goals (1960)
Outdoor Recreation Resources Review Commission (1958)
President's Materials Policy ("Paley") Commission (1951)
National Resources Planning Board (1939)

The work of these organizations has contributed significantly to the Government's present foundation of tools for longer-range planning relating to population, resources, and environment, and one of the Study's first priorities was to review and assess the impact of this earlier work. The results of this historical review are summarized in Appendix A.

Perhaps the most striking feature of this review is the very existence of a 70-year record of Government concern with issues relating to population, resources, and environment—issues that are often thought of as new. There are, however, several genuinely new features emerging in the most recent studies, interdependence being perhaps the most important. The early studies view population, resources, and environment primarily as unrelated short-term, national (regional, or even local) topics. Only in the most recent studies does the interrelatedness of these three topics come increasingly into focus.

The present Study is the first Government study to address all three topics from a relatively long-term, global perspective. It also attempts to emphasize interconnections and feedback, but in this much remains to be done.

The basic plan for the Global 2000 Study was to identify the long-term global models* currently used by Government agencies and to establish a set of uniform assumptions so that these models and tools could be used by the agencies' projection experts as a single, internally consistent system. Since the models and tools used in this Study are the ones now employed by the agencies in their long-term global analyses, they reflect the present foundation for long-term planning. Collectively, therefore, these models and tools can be thought of as the Government's present "global model."

The elements of the Government's global model were not, of course, designed to be used together as an integrated whole. The constituent models were developed separately and at different times to serve the various projection needs of individual agencies. As a result, there are certain inconsistencies in the Government's overall global model. These inconsistencies and the individual constituent models are described and analyzed in Chapters 14 to 23. While some of the inconsistencies were eliminated during the Study, difficulties were encountered in linking the agencies' models together and in synthesizing the projections into a coherent whole.

A group of outside experts (listed in the acknowledgments) met with the agency experts and the Study staff to assist in synthesizing the projections. This group had many criticisms. Some of the problems noted were corrected; others could not be. Excerpts from the criticisms are included in Appendix B.

In spite of remaining weaknesses, the projections reported in Chapters 1 through 13 present an important and useful picture of the future. Assuming continued technological progress (but no departures from present public policy), the picture that emerges is one of only modest—if any—global increase in human welfare. In fact, there is real risk that population growth and environmental degradation may lead to a significant decrease in welfare in parts of the world by 2000. (See appendix C for examples of this phenomenon already being observed.) Furthermore unless present efforts to meet human expectations and basic human needs are modified between now and 2000, they may undermine biological capabilities to meet basic needs early in the 21st century. Finally, Chapter 31 suggests that the projections behind this picture would be still more sobering if it had been possible to correct the remaining inconsistencies in the analysis and to supply the missing linkages.

The projections were developed assuming no change in public policy.† Clearly policy changes will be made, and these changes will have important

---

* The agencies guided the selection of these models and tools. Emphasis was placed on models that are (1) long-term, (2) global, and (3) used.

† Exceptions to this rule wer made in the population projections and the projections of energy impacts on the environment. The population projections assumed that countries that do not already do so will make family planning services available to an appreciable portion of their populations during the 1975–2000 period, and that countries with family planning programs now in operation will extend coverage, particularly in rural areas. The projections of energy impacts on the environment assume that all countries will have implemented U.S. new-source emission-standards by 1985 at all energy-conversion facilities.

| SECTOR | PROJECTION CHAPTER | ANALYSIS CHAPTER |
|---|---|---|
| Population | 2 | 15 |
| Gross National Product | 3 | 16 |
| Climate | 4 | 17 |
| Technology | 5 | 23 |
| Food | 6 | 18 |
| Fisheries | 7 | 19 |
| Forestry | 8 | 19 |
| Water | 9 | 19 |
| Energy | 10 | 20 |
| Fuel Minerals | 11 | 21 |
| Nonfuel Minerals | 12 | 22 |
| Environment | 13 | 19 |

effects on long-term trends. Equally clearly, improved tools are needed to analyze and evaluate alternative policies if optimal choices to be made.

Since only one policy option—no policy change—was analyzed, the Study is not an adequate basis for detailed policy recommendations. Consequently, no detailed policy recommendations are made, but the chapters presenting the projections and those presenting the analysis of the projection tools (see the following table) unavoidably imply ways in which both the projections and the future might be improved.

The Study plan also called for the examination of alternative methodologies for projecting longer-term global trends on an integrated basis. Since the early 1970s, when the Club of Rome sponsored the first global model to examine longer-term trends involving population, resources and the environment, there have been several private-sector attempts to develop internally consistent global models from a variety of differing perspectives. At least five global models now exist. Chapters 24 to 31 examine these models and compare their results and structures with the Government's global model. Most of the non-Government global models contain many more feedback linkages than it has been possible to achieve in this Study with the agencies' models. Chapter 31 describes the results of experiments in which feedback linkages in two global models were cut to make these two models more closely resemble the linkages achieved by this Study among the agencies' models. Projections from these two global models are distinctly more optimistic when the feedback linkages are missing (as they are in the Government's global model) than when the linkages are present.

Finally, it should be stated that this is the first time the Government has attempted such a broad study, and difficulties in interagency coordination of analyses and assumptions were encountered on an enormous scale. Resolving of the inconsistencies received the first priority of attention, and, in spite of time extensions, other important (but less urgent) objectives thus proved to be unattainable. For example, there is an unevenness in style in the chapters of this volume. There is no indication of the uncertainty associated with most of the numbers reported, and in several places results are reported as, for example, "3.745816352," when what is really meant is "4, plus or minus 50 percent." It was intended originally to use metric units throughout followed by values in other units in parentheses; instead, the report contains a mixture of metric and other units. (To help the reader with the units problem, Appendix D provides an extensive set of conversion tables.) A consistent grouping of countries by region, with individual detail provided for a small set of representative countries, was desired, but current methodological differences underlying the agencies' projections made this impossible. In the time available, problems of this sort were simply unavoidable.

## Acknowledgments

Literally hundreds of people contributed in one way or another to this Study, and at different points each contribution was vitally important. Initially, the members of the executive group (listed earlier) made the project possible by establishing guidelines and providing the necessary budget.

The agency coordinators (also listed earlier) played a vital role throughout in helping to identify persons in their agencies who could provide data and analysis. Five persons—George M. Bennsky, Lindsey Grant, Dolores Gregory, Donald King, and Lee M. Talbot—played particularly important roles in the developed of the papers setting forth the initial concept of the Study.

The hardest work—the detailed preparation of the projections—was done by a group of experts, most of whom were already more than fully occupied with other work before this study came along, but somehow they managed to find time to complete their contributions to the study. These experts and their contributions are:

PROJECTIONS

| | | |
|---|---|---|
| Chapter 1 | Introduction | Gerald O. Barney |
| Chapter 2 | Population | Samuel Baum, Nancy B. Frank, Larry Heligman, Donald Bogue, Amy Tsui, Melanie Werkin McClintock, Patricia Baldi |
| Chapter 3 | Gross National Product | Gerald O. Barney, Nicholas G. Carter, Lachman Khemani |
| Chapter 4 | Climate | Russell Ambroziak |
| Chapter 5 | Technology | Pieter VanderWerf |
| Chapter 6 | Food | Patrick O'Brien |
| Chapter 7 | Fisheries | Richard Hennemuth, Charles Rockwood |
| Chapter 8 | Forestry | Bruce Ross-Sheriff |
| Chapter 9 | Water | John J. Boland, John Kammerer, Walter Langbein, James Jones, Peter Freeman, Alan C. More |
| Chapter 10 | Energy | John Pearson, Mark Rodekohr; Richard Ball, Gregory D'Alessio, Stephen Gage, Leonard Hamilton, Sam Morris, Gerald Rausa, Steve Resnek, Walter Sevian |

| Appendix A | Historic Analysis | Robert Cahn and Patricia L. Cahn |
| Appendix B | Advisory Views | Ned W. Dearborn (editor) |

The thoughtful and insightful writing done by Ned W. Dearborn, Jennifer Robinson, and Pieter VanderWerf of the Global 2000 Study staff, deserves special note and acknowledgment.

The Study benefited enormously from the active participation of two groups of expert advisers. One group consists of seven persons who have previously attempted integrated studies of population, resources, and the environment. They are:

ANNE CARTER
Brandeis University, Waltham, Mass.
NICHOLAS G. CARTER
World Bank, Washington, D.C.
ANNE EHRLICH
Stanford University, Stanford, Calif.
PETER J. HENRIOT
Center of Concern, Washington, D.C.

MIHAJLO MESAROVIC
Case Western Reserve University, Cleveland, Ohio
DOUGLAS N. ROSS
Joint Economic Committee, U.S. Congress, Washington D.C.
KENNETH E. F. WATT
University of California, Davis, Calif.

On two occasions these seven met for a total of three days with the agency experts to discuss ways of integrating and improving the projections. Their criticisms were often pointed but always constructive. Some of the problems and inconsistencies they noted could be resolved; others could not be. Excerpts from written criticisms submitted by this group are included in Appendix B.

The other group consists of more than one hundred individuals from academic institutions, public interest groups, business, labor, and foundations, who read and criticized the manuscripts. Their constructive—sometimes rather candid—comments were very helpful in identifying errors, weaknesses, and inconsistencies. Some of their comments are also included in Appendix B. The members of this group are listed at the end of the Acknowledgments.

Information regarding forestry and agricultural practices and trends in a score of countries in Africa, Asia, and Latin America was provided on very short notice by U.S. Embassy personnel in response to the Study's last-minute request for information not otherwise available. Their cabled responses, which were particularly helpful in making the environment projections presented in Chapter 13, are reproduced in Appendix C.

Assistance and consulting on particular topics was provided by George Bennsky, Edmond R. du Pont, Frank Pinto, Patrick Caddell, Daniel Tunstall, Nicolai Timenes, Bill Long, Donald King, James L. Holt, John H. DeYoung, Jr., Michael Field, David Overton, and Raphael Kasper.

Several persons made special contributions to the study. Story Shem, detailed from the Department of State, served as Special Assistant to the Study Director and provided the primary liaison between the Council on Environmental Quality and the Department of State. In addition, she contributed to the research and writing and found imaginative solutions to a seemingly endless array of institutional, financial and procedural difficulties. Jeffrey M. Maclure, a member of the Study's small central staff, contributed to the research and writing, and coordinated much of the final rewriting and editing. Frank Rossomondo often went out of his way to facilitate progress of the Study generally and to locate missing data and needed documents. George Bennsky, Delores Gregory, and Leonardo Neher were always available for valuable counsel and guidance. And Lee Talbot and Lindsey Grant were especially helpful throughout in guiding and shaping the Study. During the final phase of the Study Wm. Alston Hayne, Katherine B. Gillman, Lindsey Grant (then a consultant to the Department of State), and John M. Richardson Jr. contributed significantly to the reviewing and editing.

A great deal of credit goes to the persons who brought the pieces of the Study together in an attractive final form. Fred Howard edited the entire manuscript in an incredibly short time. The cartographic and graphic support effort was handled by Holly Byrne and Roy Abel of the CIA's Cartographic Division with consulting assistance from Lawrence Fahey. Charles D. Collison guided the manuscripts through the Government Printing Office under difficult circumstances. Louise Neely, Project Secretary, managed to remain calm and collected through seemingly endless pressures and illegible manuscript. But the job could not have been done without others, too, including Thomas J. Delaney, Lilia Barr, Linda Arnold, Bernice Carney, Alvin Edwards, Susan Reigeluth, Gavin Sanner, Marie Pfaff, Charles McKeown, Betty Ann Welch, Lachman Khemani, Nancy Boone, Judith Johnson, and Oriole Harris.

Finally, indirect—but very important—contributions by the Rockefeller Brothers Fund and the George Gund Foundation are acknowledged gratefully.

GERALD O. BARNEY
Study Director

## Informal Advisers to the Study

John Adams
Natural Resources Defense Council
New York, New York

Robert M. Avedon
Population Reference Bureau
Washington, D.C.

Russell Beaton
Willamette University
Salem, Oregon

Thomas Bender, Jr.
R.A.I.N.
Portland, Oregon

James Benson
Council on Economic Priorities
New York, New York

Norman E. Borlaug
International Maize in Wheat Improvement
Mexico City, Mexico

Daniel B. Botkin
Marine Biological Laboratory
Woods Hole, Massachusetts

Wallace Bowman
Library of Congress
Washington, D.C.

Shirley A. Briggs
Rachel Carson Trust
Washington, D.C.

David R. Brower
Friends of the Earth
San Francisco, California

Lester R. Brown
Worldwatch Institute
Washington, D.C.

Gerhart Bruckmann
International Institute for Applied Systems Analysis
Vienna, Austria

Reid A. Bryson
University of Wisconsin
Madison, Wisconsin

Nicholas G. Carter
World Bank
Washington, D.C.

Verne Chant
Canadian Association for the Club of Rome
Ottawa, Canada

Duane Chapman
Cornell University
Ithaca, New York

Anne W. Cheatham
Congressional Clearing House for the Future
U.S. Congress
Washington, D.C.

Wilson Clark
Governor's Office
Sacramento, California

Philander P. Claxton, Jr.
World Population Society
Washington, D.C.

Harlan Cleveland
Aspen Institute of Humanistic Studies
Aspen, Colorado

Joseph F. Coates
Office of Technology Assessment
U.S. Congress
Washington, D.C.

Vary Coates
George Washington University
Washington, D.C.

John N. Cole
Maine Times
Brunswick, Maine

Kent H. Collins
Charles F. Kettering Foundation
Dayton, Ohio

Earl Cook
College of Geoscience
Texas A & M. University
College Station, Texas

Chester L. Cooper
Institute for Energy Analysis
Washington, D.C.

Arthur Cordell
Science Council of Canada
Ontario, Canada

Robert W. Crosby
Department of Transportation
Washington, D.C.

Herman Daly
Louisiana State University
Baton Rouge, Louisiana

Richard H. Day
University of Southern California
Los Angeles, California

T. L. de Fayer
Department of the Environment
Ottawa, Canada

Henry L. Diamond
Bevendge, Fairbanks, and Diamond
Washington, D.C.

Charles J. DiBona
American Petroleum Institute
Washington, D.C.

Wouter Van Dieren
Foundation for Applied Ecology
Edam, The Netherlands

William M. Dietel
Rockefeller Brothers Foundation
New York, New York

Scott Donaldson
Command and Control Technical Center, Joint Chiefs of Staff
Washington, D.C.

Andrew J. Dougherty
National Defense University
Washington, D.C.

Henry L. Duncombe, Jr.
General Motors Corporation
New York, New York

Erik Eckholm
Worldwatch Institute
Washington, D.C.

Anne H. Ehrlich
Stanford University
Stanford, California

Kenneth R. Farrell
Department of Agriculture
Washington, D.C.

Frank Fenner
The Australian National University
Canberra, Australia

Andrew Ford
University of California
Los Alamos, New Mexico

Jay W. Forrester
Massachusetts Institute of Technology
Cambridge, Massachusetts

Irving S. Friedman
First National City Bank
New York, New York

William R. Gasser
Department of Agriculture
Washington, D.C.

Robert Gelbard
Department of State
Washington, D.C.

Theodore J. Gordon
The Futures Group
Gastonbury, Connecticut

James Grant
Overseas Development Council
Washington, D.C.

Reginald W. Griffith
Reginald Griffith Associates
Washington, D.C.

Walter Hahn
Congressional Research Service
Washington, D.C.

Robert Hamrin
Joint Economic Committee
U.S. Congress
Washington, D.C.

Bruce Hannon
Center for Advanced Computation
University of Illinois
Urbana, Illinois

Peter Harnick
Environmental Action
Washington, D.C.

Hazel Henderson
Princeton Center for Alternative Futures
Princeton, New Jersey

Peter J. Henriot
Center of Concern
Washington, D.C.

Ralph Hofmeister
World Bank
Washington, D.C.

John P. Holdren
Energy & Resources Program
University of California
Berkeley, California

Richard Hough
Agency for International Development
Washington, D.C.

Peter R. Huessy
The Environmental Fund
Washington, D.C.

Benjamin A. Jayne
Duke University
Durham, North Carolina

Philip L. Johnson
Oak Ridge Associated Universities
Oak Ridge, Tennessee

Edward G. Kaelber
College of the Atlantic
Bar Harbor, Maine

Lawrence R. Kegan
Population Crisis Committee
Washington, D.C.

Thomas L. Kimball
National Wildlife Federation
Washington, D.C.

Alexander King
International Federation of Institutes for
  Advanced Study
Stockholm, Sweden

Erasmus H. Kloman
National Academy of Public Administra-
  tion
Washington, D.C.

George R. Lamb
American Conservation Association
New York, New York

Donald Lesh
U.S. Association for the Club of Rome
Washington, D.C.

Hans Linnemann
Economisch En Sociaal Instituut
Vrije Universiteit Amsterdam
Amsterdam, The Netherlands

James S. Lipscomb
Gorden Gund Foundation
Cleveland, Ohio

Robert Lisensky
Willamette University
Salem, Oregon

Dennis Little
Congressional Research Service
Library of Congress
U.S. Congress
Washington, D.C.

Thomas V. Long II
Committee on Public Policy Studies
University of Chicago
Chicago, Illinois

Thomas E. Lovejoy
World Wildlife Foundation
Washington, D.C.

Gordon MacDonald
Mitre Corporation
McLean, Virginia

Thomas F. Malone
Holcomb Research Institute
Indianapolis, Indiana

John McHale
Center for Integrative Studies
University of Houston
Houston, Texas

Magda Cordell McHale
Center for Integrative Studies
University of Houston
Houston, Texas

George McRobie
Technology Development Group
London, England

Dennis Meadows
Dartmouth College
Hanover, New Hampshire

Donnella Meadows
Dartmouth College
Hanover, New Hampshire

Martha Mills
League of Women Voters Education
 Fund
Washington, D.C.

J. Murray Mitchell, Jr.
National Oceanic and Atmospheric
 Administration
Washington, D.C.

Roy Morgan
Zero Population Growth
Washington, D.C.

Norman Myers
Natural Resources Defense Council
Nairobi, Kenya

Sam Nilsson
International Federation of Institutes for
 Advanced Studies
Solna, Sweden

Ian C. T. Nisbet
Massachusetts Audubon Society
Lincoln, Massachusetts

Patrick F. Noonan
Nature Conservancy
Washington, D.C.

Patrick O'Dell
University of Texas
Dallas, Texas

Howard Odum
University of Florida
Gainesville, Florida

Lewis J. Perelman
Solar Energy Research Institute
Golden, Colorado

Russell Peterson
Office of Technology Assessment
Washington, D.C.

David Pimentel
Department of Entomology
Cornell University
Ithaca, New York

Dennis Pirages
Department of Government and Politics
University of Maryland
College Park, Maryland

Wilson Prichett, III
Environmental Fund
Washington, D.C.

J. A. Potworowski
Energy, Mines and Resources
Ottawa, Canada

Roger Revelle
Center for Population Studies
Harvard University
Cambridge, Massachusetts

Elliot Richardson
Department of State
Washington, D.C.

Ralph W. Richardson, Jr.
Rockefeller Foundation
New York, New York

Ronald G. Ridker
Resources for the Future
Washington, D.C.

Peter C. Roberts
Department of the Environment
London, England

Walter Orr Roberts
Aspen Institute for Humanistic Studies
Aspen, Colorado

William Robertson IV
National Academy of Sciences
Washington, D.C.

Archibald C. Rogers
RTKL Associates, Inc.
Baltimore, Maryland

Rafael M. Salas
UN Fund for Population Activities
United Nations
New York, New York

John E. Sawyer
Andrew W. Mellon Foundation
New York, New York

Lee Schipper
Royal Academy of Sciences
Stockholm, Sweden
and Lawrence Berkeley Laboratory
Berkeley, California

Peter Schwartz
Stanford Research Institute
Menlo Park, California

James Selvaggi
Department of Housing and Urban Development
Washington, D.C.

Arlie Shardt
Environmental Defense Fund
New York, New York

Manfred Siebker
S.C.I.E.N.C.E. S.P.R.L.
Brussels, Belgium

Joseph Smagorinsky
National Oceanic and Atmospheric Administration
Princeton, New Jersey

Anthony Wayne Smith
National Parks and Conservation Association
Washington, D.C.

Soedjatmoko
National Development Planning Agency
Jakarta, Indonesia

Robert B. Stecker
American Telephone and Telegraph Company
New York, New York

Robert Stein
International Institute for Environment and Development
Washington, D.C.

Thomas B. Stoel, Jr.
Natural Resources Defense Council
Washington, D.C.

Richard S. Takasaki
East-West Center
Honolulu, Hawaii

Joanna Underwood
INFORM
New York, New York

Carl Wahren
International Planned Parenthood Federation
London, England

Franklin Wallack
United Automobile, Aerospace and Agricultural Implement Workers of America
Washington, D.C.

Kenneth E. F. Watt
Department of Zoology
University of California
Davis, California

Edward Wenk, Jr.
Aerospace Research Lab
University of Washington
Seattle, Washington

N. Richard Werthamer
Exxon Research and Engineering Company
Florham Park, New Jersey

Walter Westman
Department of Geography
University of California
Los Angeles, California

Gilbert F. White
Institute of Behavioral Science
University of Colorado
Boulder, Colorado

Robert M. White
National Academy of Sciences
Washington, D.C.

Mason Willrich
The Rockefeller Foundation
New York, New York

Carroll L. Wilson
Massachusetts Institute of Technology
Cambridge, Massachusetts

Nathaniel Wollman
College of Arts and Sciences
University of New Mexico
Albuquerque, New Mexico

George Woodwell
Marine Biological Laboratory
Woods Hole, Massachusetts

Jane Yarn
Charles A. Lindbergh Fund
Atlanta, Georgia

George Zeidenstein
The Population Council
New York, New York

# CONTENTS

# Part II
# ANALYSIS OF PROJECTION TOOLS: THE GOVERNMENT'S GLOBAL MODEL

## Part III
## ANALYSIS OF PROJECTION TOOLS: OTHER GLOBAL MODELS

## Part IV
# COMPARISON OF RESULTS

# APPENDIXES

# LIST OF TABLES

# LIST OF FIGURES

# LIST OF MAPS

Part I

# The Projections

# 1 Introduction to the Projections

The President's 1977 Environmental Message required the Global 2000 Study to develop projections of trends in population, resources, and the environment for the entire world through the year 2000. There is nothing uniquely significant about the year 2000, however, and the projections reported in this volume are not intended to be precise estimates for particular years. They are, instead, broadly indicative of the direction in which major trends point.

Similarly, it must be stressed that the results of this study are projections, not forecasts. Forecasts are attempts to predict the future, which, of course, is influenced by public-policy decisions. In contrast, this study projects foreseeable trends *under the assumption that present policies and policy trends continue without major change.*\* In a sense, the projections are intended to be self-defeating, in that the basic purpose of the President's directive was to establish a foundation for longer-term planning—which in turn should lead to policy changes aimed at altering the projected trends.

A considerable amount of longer-range analysis and planning was already being conducted by various federal agencies prior to this study, but usually only in response to the planning requirements of the agencies' individual areas of responsibility. As a result, most longer-term government projections tend to focus on a single factor, directly relevant to the sponsoring agency's area of responsibility (for example, food or population), without adequate consideration of the interrelations and feedback involved in a world system in which population, resources, and the environment are all interacting variables.

As the President's directive establishing this study makes clear, however, the time has passed when population (or energy, or food, or clean air, or public health, or employment) can be considered in isolation. In establishing a foundation for longer-range analysis and planning, ways must be found to better understand the linkages and interactions among these important elements of the world system.

*As discussed in Chapter 14 and summarized in Table 14–2, some policy changes were nevertheless assumed in developing the projections.

## The Study Plan

The approach used in the Global 2000 Study was relatively simple. Each of the participating agencies was asked to make projections using the projection tools it currently employs in making long-term projections.\* The assignments were as follows:

| | |
|---|---|
| Population: | Bureau of the Census and Agency for International Development. |
| GNP: | Global 2000 Study staff, with assistance from the Agency for International Development, Central Intelligence Agency, and World Bank. |
| Climate: | National Oceanic and Atmospheric Administration, Department of Agriculture, National Defense University, and Central Intelligence Agency. |
| Technology: | The Global 2000 Study staff, with assistance from participating agencies. |

---

* Emphasis was placed on models that are (1) global, (2) long-term, and (3) used. The government has large numbers of other models, some of which include more feedback and interactions than the models used in this Study. The models chosen, however, are the global, long-term models most often used by the agencies in their long-term planning and analysis. Broad surveys that include other government models are provided in *A Guide to Models in Governmental Planning and Operations,* Office of Research and Development, Environmental Protection Agency, Washington, D.C., Aug. 1974, and in G. Fromm, W. L. Hamilton, and D. E. Hamilton, *Federally Supported Mathematical Models: Survey and Analysis,* National Science Foundation, Washington, D.C., June 1974. A discussion of the evolving role of models in government is provided by M. Greenberger, M. A. Crenson, and B. L. Crissey in their *Models in the Policy Process,* Russell Sage Foundation, New York, 1976, and in Congressional Research Service, *Computer Simulation Methods to Aid National Growth Policy,* prepared for the Subcommittee on Fisheries and Wildlife Conservation and the Environment, U.S. House of Representatives, Washington: Government Printing Office, 1975.

Food: Department of Agriculture.

Fisheries: National Oceanic and Atmospheric Administration and outside consultants.

Forestry: Central Intelligence Agency, with assistance from the Department of Agriculture, Department of State, and Agency for International Development.

Water: Department of the Interior, with assistance from outside consultants.

Fuel Minerals: Department of Energy, with assistance from the Bureau of Mines and the Geological Survey.

Nonfuel Minerals: The Global 2000 Study staff, with assistance from the Department of the Interior and outside consultants.

Energy: Department of Energy.

Environment: The Global 2000 Study staff, with assistance from the Environmental Protection Agency, Agency for International Development, and outside consultants.

This approach has had both advantages and disadvantages. It was a distinct advantage to be able to move ahead quickly, using previously developed tools. It was also an advantage to be able to test and evaluate the existing long-term analytical capabilities of the government. It was a disadvantage to use projection tools that do not lend themselves easily to the analysis of the many interactions among population, resources, and environment. It was also a disadvantage that these analytical tools require that the projections be undertaken sequentially. This last point needs explanation.

Future environmental trends depend in large measure on demands for resources (minerals, energy, food, water, etc.); therefore, the environmental trends cannot be projected and assessed until relevant resource projections have been completed. However, the demand for resources depends on the number of people and their income, as well as on policy, climate, and technology. In the real world (and in more interactive models) all of these variables evolve and interact continuously, but with the government's present

tools, the projections must be made independently and sequentially.

The sequential approach used in this study is illustrated in Figure 1—1. The first step is the establishment of policy assumptions (assumed constant in this study), followed by projections of population, GNP, technology, and climate. These assumptions and projections are necessary inputs to the resource projections in the second step. The resource projections, in turn, are needed for the environmental analysis. It is only through this sequential process that a measure of self-consistency, coherence, and interrelationship is obtainable with present government projection tools.

Many important linkages, however, cannot be established by this sequential process. In particular, the population and GNP projections that are made in the first step are based largely on extrapolations of past trends and are uninformed by interactive feedback from the resource and environmental projections. The resource and environmental analyses, however, project developments that may significantly influence GNP and population trends.

## The Projections

The agency experts were asked to produce a first draft of their projections in just six weeks, at which time they, the Global 2000 Study staff, and a small group of outside experts,* met for a weekend synthesis meeting. The purpose of the meeting was to improve the consistency of the projections and to begin—at least subjectively—to consider the implications of the resource and environmental projections for the independently derived projections of GNP and population. So unusual is this type of agency interaction that most of the agencies' long-term projection experts were until then not acquainted with each other.

A certain amount of difficulty was expected in this preliminary meeting, and, in fact, many inconsistencies were revealed. The experts then decided collectively how best to adjust and modify the projections to improve the internal consistency of the whole set. The final projections were prepared during the following two months.

It must be made clear, therefore, that the projections reported in this study are based on the

*Anne Carter, Brandeis University, Waltham, Mass.; Nicholas G. Carter, World Bank, Washington, D.C.; Anne Ehrlich, Stanford University, Stanford, Calif.; Peter Henriot, Center of Concern, Washington, D.C.; Mihajlo Mesarovic, Case Western Reserve University, Cleveland, Ohio; Douglas Ross, The Conference Board, New York City; and Kenneth E. F. Watt, University of California, Davis.

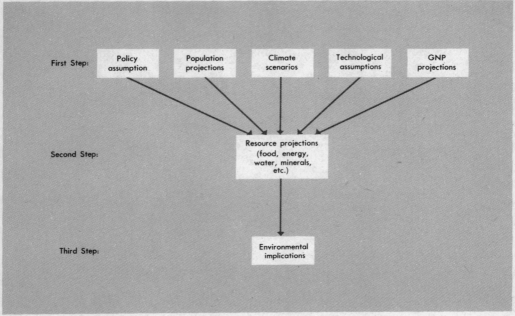

First Step:

Policy assumption

Population projections

Climate scenarios

Technological assumptions

GNP projections

Second Step:

Resource projections (food, energy, water, minerals, etc.)

Third Step:

Environmental implications

**Figure 1-1.** The process of projecting trends.

collective judgment of the agency experts who participated in the effort. To ensure internal consistency, several adjustments were required in individual agency projections. As a result, the projections may not agree completely with projections previously published by the participating agencies. Since the manuscript has not been subjected to formal interagency clearance procedures, the agencies are not responsible for any errors in fact or judgment that may have occurred.

One striking finding of this study is that, collectively, the executive agencies of the government are currently incapable of presenting the President with a mutually consistent set of projections of world trends in population, resources, and the environment. While the projections presented in the chapters that follow are probably the most internally consistent ever developed with the long-range, global models now used by the agencies, they are still plagued with inadequacies and inconsistencies.

While the analyses are admittedly imperfect, they are still highly useful. This is the first time that an effort has been made to apply—collectively and consistently—the global, long-range models used by the government. Careful attention

was given throughout to introducing as much feedback and interaction as possible. The resulting projections are certainly sufficient to indicate the general nature and direction of the trends. Furthermore, as discussed in Chapter 31, the inadequacies and inconsistencies that remain generally tend to make the projections more optimistic than they would be if it had been possible to eliminate the inadequacies and inconsistencies. The projections therefore establish a "best-case" analysis in that (given the assumptions of steady technological progress, but no public-policy changes) improved analysis is likely to assign more importance—rather than less—to future problems of population, resources, and environment.

Finally, analysis of the limitations and weaknesses in the models now in use (see Chapters 14 through 23) provides a basis for developing and introducing improved models. The issues are important. Population, resources, and environment are long-term, global, highly interrelated issues, not likely to disappear without further attention. Improved methods of analysis are needed to better understand the future implications of present decisions and policies. Given adquate coordination and the necessary resources, better models can be developed.

# 2  Population Projections

Population projections comprise one of the basic prerequisites for predicting and planning for future needs in such areas as food, energy, employment, community facilities, and social services. It would be ideal to have a single forecast of population on which there was general agreement. However, since the factors influencing population trends—fertility, mortality, migration—are not perfectly predictable, projections usually represent individual or collective judgments that differ greatly, even among experts. Indeed, there is often even disagreement about the data used as the base for projections.

Because of these inherent difficulties, population estimates are presented in this chapter in terms of an illustrative range, with a high and a low series, representing the highest and lowest population counts that may reasonably be expected to occur, and a medium series, representing reasonable expectations, given existing trends and present knowledge of the underlying factors.

Two sets of population projections are used in the Global 2000 Study: those made by the U.S. Bureau of the Census and those made by the Community and Family Study Center (CFSC) of the University of Chicago.

It was decided to include the CFSC projections along with the Census projections in order to illustrate how such estimates are affected by differences in basic assumptions about such factors as fertility rates. For instance, the Census Bureau's high, medium, and low projections of world population in the year 2000 are 14, 8, and 3 percent higher, respectively, than the corresponding CFSC projections.

Along with discrepancies between the base-year data used in the two sets of projections (population estimates, fertility rates and mortality rates for 1975), there are also significant differences in the way in which each group projected trends in fertility. Using a mathematical model, the CFSC arrived at significantly more optimistic projections of fertility rates in the year 2000. Differences between the two methodologies will be discussed further in Chapter 16.

The projections by both the Bureau of the Census and the Community and Family Study Center assume no migration; a final section in this chapter discusses probable developments in migration and their possible effects on the projections.

The terms used in the tables and the discussions in this chapter are defined as follows:

*Crude birth rate:* The number of births per 1,000 persons in one year (based on midyear population).

*Crude death rate:* The number of deaths per 1,000 persons in one year (based on midyear population).

*Growth rate:* The annual increase (or decrease) in the population resulting from a surplus of deficit of births over deaths and a surplus or deficit of migrants into or out of the country, expressed as a percentage of the base population.*

*Rate of natural increase:* The annual increase (or decrease) in the population resulting from a surplus or deficit of births over deaths, expressed as a percentage of the midyear population. The natural increase of the population does not include the migration of persons into or out of the country.

*Total fertility rate (TFR):* The average number of children that would be born per woman if all women lived to the end of their childbearing years and bore children according to a given set of age-specific fertility rates. It is five times the sum of the age-specific fertility rates, divided by 1,000.†

## Bureau of the Census Projections

The detailed Bureau of the Census projections are presented in Tables 2–10 through 2–14 at the end of this section. Tables 2–10 and 2–11 include estimates and projections for all three series (high, medium, and low) to provide an indication of the

---

*Average annual growth rates are computed using the compound growth formula $r = \ln(P_2/P_1)/t$.

†Population projections usually employ total fertility rate as a unit of measure rather than crude birth rate, in order to avoid methodological difficulties pertaining to age composition, sex ratios, and interaction between fertility and mortality.

range covered by the projections and to serve as a basis for comparison with the corresponding CFSC projections. Tables 2-12, 2-13, and 2-14 show only the medium range projections of population growth rates, mortality rates, and birth rates. Table 2-1 summarizes the salient data from the Census estimates and projections. The map on the following page illustrates the population changes projected in the medium case.

## Assumptions

*Fertility Assumptions.* The general assumptions that underlie the Census projections with regard to fertility are:

1. Less developed countries will continue to make moderate progress in social and economic development during the 1975-2000 period.

2. As less developed countries (LDCs) progress in social and economic development, the fertility level is expected to decline more or less continuously but with some temporary plateaus.

3. Almost all countries that do not already do so will make family planning services available to an appreciable portion of the population during the 1975-2000 period, and countries with present family planning programs will extend coverage, particularly in rural areas.

### TABLE 2-1

**Bureau of Census Estimates and Projections, Medium Series, Summary Data, 1975-2000**

(*Population in billions*)

| | Population | Percent of World Pop. | Annual Percent Growth[a] |
|---|---|---|---|
| 1975 World | 4.09 | — | |
| More developed regions | 1.13 | 28 | |
| Less developed regions | 2.96 | 72 | |
| 1980 World | 4.47 | — | 1.78 |
| More developed regions | 1.17 | 26 | 0.68 |
| Less developed regions | 3.30 | 74 | 2.18 |
| 1985 World | 4.88 | — | 1.77 |
| More developed regions | 1.21 | 25 | 0.70 |
| Less developed regions | 3.67 | 75 | 2.14 |
| 1990 World | 5.34 | — | 1.78 |
| More developed regions | 1.25 | 23 | 0.66 |
| Less developed regions | 4.09 | 77 | 2.14 |
| 1995 World | 5.83 | — | 1.77 |
| More developed regions | 1.29 | 22 | 0.59 |
| Less developed regions | 4.54 | 78 | 2.11 |
| 2000 World | 6.35 | — | 1.70 |
| More developed regions | 1.32 | 21 | 0.51 |
| Less developed regions | 5.03 | 79 | 2.02 |

[a]Annual percent growth for the preceding 5-year period.

4. Knowledge and methods of family limitation will become better known and will be better used among populations that wish to reduce fertility. Expansion of family limitation practices will expedite the process of fertility decline, and in countries where rapid social and economic progress and strong desires for smaller families coincide, fertility decline will be very rapid.

In making projections for each country or region, the Census Bureau adopted fertility levels for the year 2000 that represented in their judgment the "most likely" level, which corresponds to the level for the medium series. Specific fertility levels were also assumed for the purpose of the high and low series. Consideration was given to fertility assumptions made in existing projections prepared by national agencies or universities, based on the belief that demographers in the individual countries could be expected to have a special understanding of what are "reasonable" fertility levels to expect in the future of their own country.

For the more developed countries the fertility assumptions in existing official national projections were used with, in some instances, slight modification. The aggregates of Eastern and Western Europe were projected on the basis of fertility trends according to the U.N. medium series, with slight adjustment at the U.S. Bureau of the Census to take account of fertility data available since the U.N. projections were prepared. For the less developed countries the fertility assumptions were made on a judgmental basis by demographers who have worked with the demographic and related socioeconomic data for the individual countries over extended time periods. Specifically, no mathematical model of fertility change was used. However, in setting the target fertility levels and paths of fertility decline for the less developed countries, the demographers took into consideration the following major factors:

1. Current level of fertility.

2. Recent trends in fertility.

3. Current levels and recent trends in social and economic development.

4. Current status and approximate past impact of family planning and public health programs.

5. Government policy on population matters.

6. Recent fertility trends in countries with similar cultural, social, and economic conditions and prospects.

7. Expressed "desired" family size in the population.

8. Fertility assumptions made by international agencies, such as the U.N. and the World Bank.

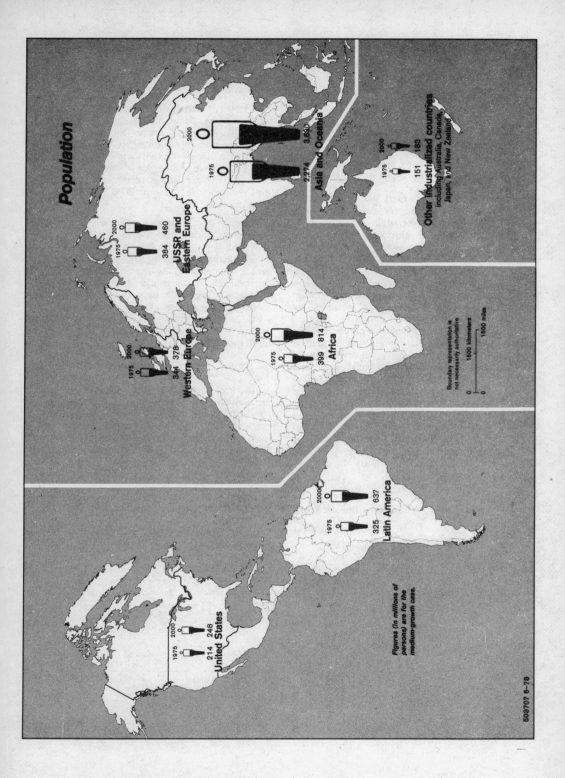

*Population*

Asia and Oceania
1975 2,274
2000 3,630

Other industrialized countries
including Australia, Canada,
Japan, and New Zealand
1975 151
2000 183

USSR and
Eastern Europe
1975 384
2000 460

Western Europe
1975 344
2000 378

Africa
1975 399
2000 814

Latin America
1975 325
2000 637

United States
1975 214
2000 248

Boundary representation is
not necessarily authoritative

0    1500 kilometers
0    1500 miles

*Figures (in millions of
persons) are for the
medium-growth case.*

503707 6-78

Furthermore, two general guidelines were adopted in setting the range of fertility levels in the year 2000.

1. The higher the level of fertility at the base date, the wider the range of assumed fertility levels in the year 2000.

2. The greater the uncertainty about current fertility levels and current trends, the greater the range of assumed fertility levels in the year 2000.

*Mortality Assumptions.* Only one specific mortality trend was assumed for each projection, except for the People's Republic of China. Estimates for mortality in the base year of the projections and for the projection period through 2000 are developed through the use of life table estimates. The life tables for the base year of the projections were usually compiled from a variety of sources, including vital registration data on deaths by age and sex (adjusted at times for underregistration) and survey or census data on deaths by age and sex during the preceding year (after appropriate evaluation and adjustment if necessary), or by analyzing age distributions of the population at one or more points in time and applying a variety of demographic techniques such as stable population analysis and use of model life tables. In a few countries, such as Nigeria, where little reliable information is available, "guesstimates" of the appropriate level of mortality and of the model life table pattern were made, always considering estimates that have been made by other institutions, such as the United Nations.

Projection of mortality, using the base year as the starting point, was generally done in one of two ways:

1. Either a target life expectancy at birth (and corresponding life table) was chosen for the year 2000 with life expectancies for the intervening years obtained by assuming a "reasonable pattern" of change of mortality; or

2. The pattern and degree of change in mortality from year to year was assumed with the eventual life expectancy in the year 2000 "falling out" of the process.

In either case, consideration was always given to the trends and levels shown in national projections and in projections by international organizations, and by considering the mortality trends in similar countries in the region that have already experienced the relevant portion of the mortality transition. Target life expectancies for the year 2000 were sometimes chosen, in fact, to be the same as those already achieved in "leading" countries, or previously assumed in national or U.N. projections.

## Total Population

All three Bureau of the Census estimates and projections of total world population are summarized in Table 2–2. The medium series is considered the population growth trend most likely to occur. The high and low series represent a "reasonable range" above and below the medium series.

### TABLE 2–2

### Census Bureau World Estimates and Projections

Population Size and Net Growth

| | Total Population (Millions) | | Net Growth 1975 to 2000 | | Average Annual Growth Rate (Percent) |
|---|---|---|---|---|---|
| | 1975 | 2000 | Millions | Percent | |
| Medium series | 4,090 | 6,351 | 2,261 | 55 | 1.8 |
| High series | 4,134 | 6,798 | 2,664 | 64 | 2.0 |
| Low series | 4,043 | 5,922 | 1,879 | 46 | 1.5 |

Vital Rates[a]

| | Crude Birth Rate (per 1,000) | | Crude Death Rate (per 1,000) | | Rate of Natural Increase (Percent) | |
|---|---|---|---|---|---|---|
| | 1975 | 2000 | 1975 | 2000 | 1975 | 2000 |
| Medium series | 30.4 | 25.6 | 12.3 | 9.1 | 1.8 | 1.6 |
| High series | 32.0 | 29.4 | 12.9 | 9.4 | 1.9 | 2.0 |
| Low series | 28.8 | 21.9 | 11.9 | 8.9 | 1.7 | 1.3 |

[a] Rates shown for 2000 refer to midyear 1999 to midyear 2000.

The medium series begins with a 1975 base population total of about 4.09 billion, a crude birth rate of 30 per 1,000, and a crude death rate of 12 per 1,000. The series implies declines of 16 percent in the crude birth rate and 26 percent in the crude death rate from 1975 to 2000, generating changes in the natural increase from 1.8 percent in 1975 to 1.6 percent in 2000. Net population growth during this whole 25-year period would add about 2.26 billion to the base population and produce an end-of-century world population total of about 6.35 billion.

The high series of world population projections begins with a 1975 base population of 4.13 billion, and the low series with a 1975 base population of 4.04 billion.* Using the 1975 base populations and, alternately, the high and low series trends of 1975–2000 vital rates, world population would increase in the high series by about 2.66 billion between 1975 and 2000 and would total about 6.8 billion by the end of the century; in the low series, world population would increase by about 1.88 billion between 1975 and 2000 and would total about 5.92 billion by the end of the century.

World population growth between 1950 and 1975 is estimated at about 1.56 billion, reflecting an average growth rate of about 1.9 percent per year. The latter may be compared to the medium, high, and low projections for 1975 to 2000 as follows:

|  | Net Growth (billions) | Average Annual Growth Rate (percent) |
|---|---|---|
| 1950 to 1975 estimates | 1.56 | 1.9 |
| 1975 to 2000 projections |  |  |
| Medium series | 2.26 | 1.8 |
| High series | 2.66 | 2.0 |
| Low series | 1.88 | 1.5 |

The medium projection series suggests that the population of the world may grow between 1975 and 2000 at a slightly lower annual rate than that observed from 1950 to 1975. The high and low series present alternative increase rates for 1975 to 2000. However, it should not be overlooked that irrespective of the medium, high, or low rates of growth during 1975 to 2000, all three projection series indicate a net addition to the world population total of an appreciably greater number of

*Nearly all of the differences between the 1975 estimates of world population in the medium, high, and low series are due to the use of the following alternate 1975 population estimates for the People's Republic of China: medium series, 935 million; high series, 978 million; low series, 889 million.

people during the period 1975–2000 (1.88–2.26 billion) than during the 1950–1975 period (1.56 billion).

*Contrasts Between More Developed and Less Developed Regions.* There are characteristic demographic differences between the populations of the more developed and less developed regions of the world (Table 2–3). For example, the estimated crude birth rate for the less developed regions in 1975 was more than double the estimated crude birth rate for the more developed regions; the estimated crude death rate for the less developed regions in 1975 was significantly higher than for the more developed regions; and the resulting rate of natural increase for the less developed regions in 1975 was two-thirds higher than for the more developed regions. These characteristic differences are expected to persist into the future, as indicated by the projected vital rate differences for the year 2000.

The medium series for the more developed regions begins with a 1975 base population total of about 1.13 billion, a crude birth rate of about 16 per 1,000, and a crude death rate of about 9.6 per 1,000. The series implies a slight change in the crude birth rate, increasing from 16 in 1975 to a peak of 17 by 1985, and thereafter declining to 15 by the year 2000, an increase in the crude death rate from 9.6 per 1,000 in 1975 to 10.4 per 1,000 in 2000 and an average annual growth rate of 0.6 percent. Net population growth during this entire 25-year period would add about 0.19 billion to the base population and produce an end-of-century population figure of 1.32 billion for the more developed regions.

The same 1975 base population estimate is used for the more developed regions in the high and low series as in the medium series. However, alternately high and low trends in vital rates are utilized for 1975 to 2000. Thus, the population of the developed regions in the year 2000 might be as high as 1.38 billion or as low as 1.27 billion.

The medium series for the less developed regions begins with a 1975 base population total of 2.96 billion, a crude birth rate of about 36 per 1,000, and a crude death rate of about 13 per 1,000. The series implies declines of 21 percent in the crude birth rate and 35 percent in the crude death rate during 1975 to 2000; these changes result in rates of natural increase of 2.2 percent in 1975 and 2.0 percent in 2000. Population growth during this 25-year period would add over 2 billion to the base population, producing an end-of-century population figure of about 5 billion for the less developed regions.

## TABLE 2–3

### More Developed Regions and Less Developed Regions—Census Bureau Estimates and Projections

Population Size and Net Growth

| | Total population (Millions) | | Net Growth 1975 to 2000 | | Average Annual Growth Rate (Percent) |
|---|---|---|---|---|---|
| | 1975 | 2000 | Millions | Percent | |
| More developed regions | | | | | |
| Medium series | 1,131 | 1,323 | 192 | 17 | 0.6 |
| High series | 1,131 | 1,377 | 246 | 22 | 0.8 |
| Low series | 1,131 | 1,274 | 143 | 13 | 0.5 |
| Less developed regions | | | | | |
| Medium series | 2,959 | 5,028 | 2,069 | 70 | 2.1 |
| High series | 3,003 | 5,420 | 2,417 | 80 | 2.4 |
| Low series | 2,912 | 4,648 | 1,736 | 60 | 1.9 |

Vital Rates[a]

| | Crude Birth Rate (per 1,000) | | Crude Death Rate (per 1,000) | | Rate of Natural Increase (Percent) | |
|---|---|---|---|---|---|---|
| | 1975 | 2000 | 1975 | 2000 | 1975 | 2000 |
| More developed regions | | | | | | |
| Medium series | 16.1 | 15.2 | 9.6 | 10.4 | 0.6 | 0.5 |
| High series | 16.1 | 17.4 | 9.6 | 10.1 | 0.6 | 0.7 |
| Low series | 16.1 | 13.0 | 9.6 | 10.7 | 0.6 | 0.2 |
| Less developed regions | | | | | | |
| Medium series | 35.9 | 28.4 | 13.4 | 8.7 | 2.2 | 2.0 |
| High series | 38.0 | 32.4 | 14.1 | 9.2 | 2.4 | 2.3 |
| Low series | 33.7 | 24.3 | 12.8 | 8.4 | 2.1 | 1.6 |

[a] Rates shown for 2000 refer to midyear 1999 to midyear 2000.

For the less developed regions, alternate high and low projections of population growth for the 1975 to 2000 period result in total population growth during the period of as high as 2.42 billion or as low as 1.74 billion.

Estimates of net population growth in the more developed and less developed regions between 1950 and 1975 may be compared to the projections for 1975 to 2000, as follows:

| | Net Growth (billions) | Average Annual Growth Rate (percent) |
|---|---|---|
| More developed regions | | |
| 1950 to 1975 | 0.27 | 1.1 |
| 1975 to 2000 | | |
| Medium series | 0.19 | 0.6 |
| High series | 0.25 | 0.8 |
| Low series | 0.14 | 0.5 |
| Less developed regions | | |
| 1950 to 1975 | 1.28 | 2.3 |
| 1975 to 2000 | | |
| Medium series | 2.07 | 2.1 |
| High series | 2.42 | 2.4 |
| Low series | 1.74 | 1.9 |

For the more developed regions, all three projection series in the present report indicate that population growth from 1975 to the end of the century would be lower than was the case between 1950 and 1975, in terms of both absolute increments and rates of growth.

For the less developed regions, the medium projection series suggests that the population may grow between 1975 and 2000 at a somewhat lower annual rate than that observed from 1950 to 1975. Regardless of the differences in the high, medium, and low series growth rates, however, all three projections indicate a net addition to the population of the less developed regions of an appreciably greater number of people during the 1975–2000 period (1.74 to 2.42 billion) than during the preceding 25-year period (1.28 billion).

The population of the less developed regions comprised about 72 percent of the world's population in 1975 and, according to the three projection series, will constitute 78–80 percent of the world's population in the year 2000. This dramatic increase is hardly surprising when one considers that the less developed regions would account for nine-tenths of world population growth according to the projections (see Fig. 2–1 for medium series projections). During the previous quarter century, less developed regions accounted for four-fifths of world population growth, and thereby increased

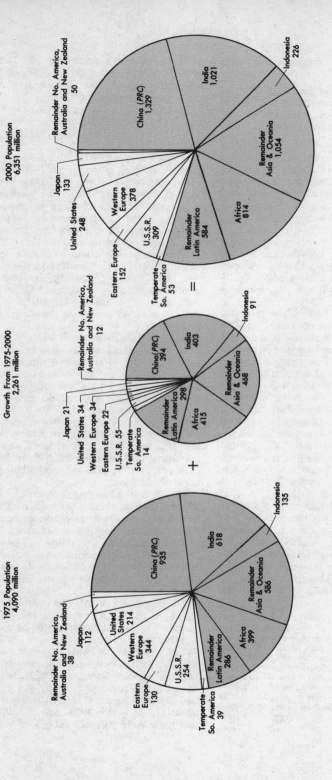

**Figure 2-1.** Twenty-five years of world population growth, medium series.

1975 Population
4,090 million

Growth From 1975-2000
2,261 million

2000 Population
6,351 million

China (PRC)
935

India
618

Indonesia
135

Remainder
Asia & Oceania
586

Africa
399

Remainder
Latin America
286

Temperate
So. America
39

U.S.S.R.
254

Eastern
Europe
130

Western
Europe
344

United States
214

Japan
112

Remainder No. America,
Australia and New Zealand
38

China (PRC)
394

India
403

Indonesia
91

Remainder
Asia & Oceania
468

Africa
415

Remainder
Latin America
298

Temperate
So. America
14

U.S.S.R.
55

Eastern Europe 22

Western Europe 34

United States 34

Japan 21

Remainder No. America,
Australia and New Zealand
12

China (PRC)
1,329

India
1,021

Indonesia
226

Remainder
Asia & Oceania
1,054

Africa
814

Remainder
Latin America
584

Temperate
So. America
53

U.S.S.R.
309

Eastern Europe
152

Western
Europe
378

United States
248

Japan
133

Remainder No. America,
Australia and New Zealand
50

+

=

Numerals are in million persons

☐ Industrialized countries

▨ Less Developed Countries

their share of world population from 66 percent in 1950 to 72 percent in 1975.

*Note:* Hereafter, the tables and discussions of the Bureau of the Census projections will pertain only to the medium series of estimates and projections unless otherwise specified.

*Changes in Selected Vital Rates and Total Population.* The data presented in this chapter refer to a projection period of 25 years, from 1975 to 2000. In terms of fundamental demographic change, this is a relatively short time period. Any profound modification (barring major calamities) of world population growth trends, including requisite changes in age composition, would require a much longer time to evolve. According to these projections, the population growth rates for the world as a whole and for the less developed regions in particular, will decline only slightly from 1975 to 2000, despite significant declines in fertility levels.

For the less developed regions the projected rate of natural increase declines from 1975 to 2000 by only 12 percent, despite a decline in the crude birth rate of 21 percent and a decline of 30 percent in the total fertility rate.* This projected decline of 12 percent notwithstanding, the resulting "lower" rate for 2000 of about 2.0 percent per year is still relatively high. For example, applied to the larger base population of 5.03 billion, it produces a much higher annual increment of total population in 2000 (99 million) than the 2.2 percent rate of natural increase produced in 1975 (67 million). In fact, an annual rate of natural increase of 2 percent, if continued after 2000, would double the population of the less developed regions in only 35 years.

For the more developed regions of the world, the projections indicate a decline from 1975 to 2000 of about one-fourth in the rate of natural increase, concurrently with a slight decline in the crude birth rate and a slight increase in the projected total fertility rate. However, the rate of natural increase for 2000 (about 0.5 percent per year) is quite low; it produces a lower annual

increment in total population in 2000 than in 1975 and, if continued after 2000, would require nearly 140 years to cause the population of the more developed regions to double.

*Major Regions.* The medium series of estimates and projections of population growth for the world's major regions from 1975 to 2000 are shown in Table 2–4.

Africa's population is characterized by high fertility and high mortality rates—a population of about 0.81 billion in the year 2000, a net increase of 0.42 billion over 1975. This increase would reflect a more than doubling of Africa's population in only 25 years and represents the most rapid population growth rate projected for any major world region during the period 1975 to 2000.

Moderately high crude birth and death rates characterize the less developed countries of the Asia and Oceania region. The projected population of these LDCs in 2000 is 3.63 billion, a net increase of 1.36 billion over 1975, or about 60 percent of world population growth projected for this period.

Fertility remains high in Latin America and crude death rates low. The projections indicate a total population of about 0.64 billion by the year 2000, a 96 percent increase over 1975. Latin America's projected percent increase is the second highest for any major world region.

The populations of the U.S.S.R. and Eastern Europe (including Albania and Yugoslavia) are characterized by relatively low fertility, mortality, and growth rates. The projections reveal a total population of 0.46 billion by 2000, or an increase of 20 percent over 1975—the second lowest of any major world region.

The industrialized North American countries, Western Europe, Japan, Australia, and New Zealand have completed their "demographic transition," and their populations are characterized by relatively low fertility, mortality, and growth rates. By the end of the century, their population will increase to about 0.81 billion, or 14 percent over 1975, by far the lowest percent increase of any major world region.

The percentage distribution of world population by major regions as estimated for 1975 and as projected in the medium series for 2000 are shown in Table 2–5.

The projections indicate that at the end of the century the less developed countries of Asia and Oceania will continue to have the highest percentage of world population of any major region by far—about 57.2 percent in 2000, as compared with about 55.6 percent in 1975. Also, by 2000 Africa's and Latin America's percentages of world popu-

---

*The difference between the 30 percent decline in the total fertility rate and the 21 percent decline in the crude birth rate from 1975 to 2000 can be explained as follows. About 6 percentage points of the difference is due to a larger proportion of women in the childbearing ages (15–49 years) in 2000 than in 1975. The rest of the difference is due to changes in the age patterns of fertility within the childbearing years. The difference between the 21 percent decline in the crude birth rate and the 12 percent decline in the rate of natural increase is due to the decrease in the crude death rate by a greater percentage than the decrease in the crude birth rate.

## TABLE 2–4

### Major Regions—Census Bureau Estimates and Projections

Population Size and Net Growth

| | Total Population (Millions) | | Net Growth 1975 to 2000 | | Average Annual Growth Rate (Percent) |
|---|---|---|---|---|---|
| | 1975 | 2000 | Millions | Percent | |
| World | 4,090 | 6,351 | 2,261 | 55 | 1.8 |
| Africa | 399 | 814 | 416 | 104 | 2.9 |
| Asia and Oceania [a] | 2,274 | 3,630 | 1,356 | 60 | 1.9 |
| Latin America | 325 | 637 | 312 | 96 | 2.7 |
| U.S.S.R. and Eastern Europe [b] | 384 | 460 | 76 | 20 | 0.7 |
| North America, Western Europe, [c] Japan, Australia, and New Zealand | 708 | 809 | 101 | 14 | 0.5 |

Vital Rates [d]

| | Crude Birth Rate (per 1,000) | | Crude Death Rate (per 1,000) | | Rate of Natural Increase (Percent) | |
|---|---|---|---|---|---|---|
| | 1975 | 2000 | 1975 | 2000 | 1975 | 2000 |
| World | 30.4 | 25.6 | 12.3 | 9.1 | 1.8 | 1.6 |
| Africa | 46.7 | 38.5 | 19.0 | 11.3 | 2.8 | 2.7 |
| Asia and Oceania [a] | 33.7 | 25.9 | 13.0 | 8.7 | 2.1 | 1.7 |
| Latin America | 37.2 | 28.7 | 8.9 | 5.7 | 2.8 | 2.3 |
| U.S.S.R. and Eastern Europe [b] | 17.7 | 15.9 | 9.7 | 10.5 | 0.8 | 0.5 |
| North America, Western Europe, [c] Japan, Australia, and New Zealand | 14.8 | 14.5 | 9.6 | 10.5 | 0.5 | 0.4 |

[a] Developing countries only, i.e., excluding Japan, Australia, and New Zealand.
[b] Eastern Europe includes Albania and Yugoslavia.
[c] Western Europe as used here comprises all of Europe except Eastern Europe, Albania, and Yugoslavia. The U.S.S.R. is also excluded.
[d] Rates shown for 2000 refer to midyear 1999 to midyear 2000.

## TABLE 2–5

### Percent Distribution of World Population by Major Region, Census Bureau Medium Series

| | 1975 | 2000 |
|---|---|---|
| Africa | 9.8 | 12.8 |
| Asia and Oceania [a] | 55.6 | 57.2 |
| Latin America | 7.9 | 10.0 |
| U.S.S.R. and Eastern Europe [b] | 9.4 | 7.3 |
| North America, Western Europe, [c] Japan, Australia, and New Zealand | 17.3 | 12.7 |

[a] Developing countries only, i.e., excluding Japan, Australia, and New Zealand.
[b] Eastern Europe includes Albania and Yugoslavia.
[c] Western Europe as used here comprises all of Europe except Eastern Europe, Albania, and Yugoslavia. The U.S.S.R. is also excluded.

lation will increase significantly, while the percentage of world population living in the U.S.S.R. and Eastern Europe will decline to about 7.3 percent, and the percentage living in the nonsocialist more developed countries of North America and Western Europe, as well as in Japan, Australia, and New Zealand, will decrease to less than 13 percent.

*15 Selected Countries.* Estimates and projections of population growth from 1975 to 2000 for the 15 selected countries are presented in Table 2–6.

The largest population increases indicated are for India and the People's Republic of China, each adding about 0.4 billion inhabitants between 1975 and 2000. The highest percentage increases, however, are projected for Mexico, Nigeria, Pakistan, Brazil, and Bangladesh, each of which shows an increase of 100 percent or more. The lowest percentage increases are projected for the United States, Japan, and the U.S.S.R. In the year 2000 the People's Republic of China would still be the world's most populous nation, comprising one-fifth of the world's population. The second most populous nation—India—would constitute about 16 percent of the world's population. The U.S.S.R. and the United States would remain the third and fourth most populous nations with about 5 percent and 4 percent, respectively, and Japan, which in 1975 was the sixth most populous of the 15 selected countries, would drop to 10th place with about 2 percent of the total world population.

## TABLE 2–6

**Population Size, Net Growth, and Percent of World Population of 15 Selected Countries, Census Bureau Medium Series**

| Country | Total Population (millions) | | Net Growth, 1975 to 2000 | | Average Annual Growth Rate (Percent) | Percent of World Population | |
|---|---|---|---|---|---|---|---|
| | 1975 | 2000 | Millions | Percent | | 1975 | 2000 |
| People's Republic of China | 935 | 1,329 | 394 | 42 | 1.4 | 22.9 | 20.9 |
| India | 618 | 1,021 | 402 | 65 | 2.0 | 15.1 | 16.1 |
| Indonesia | 135 | 226 | 91 | 68 | 2.1 | 3.3 | 3.6 |
| Bangladesh | 79 | 159 | 79 | 100 | 2.8 | 1.9 | 2.5 |
| Pakistan | 71 | 149 | 78 | 111 | 3.0 | 1.7 | 2.4 |
| Philippines | 43 | 73 | 30 | 71 | 2.2 | 1.0 | 1.2 |
| Thailand | 42 | 75 | 33 | 77 | 2.3 | 1.0 | 1.2 |
| South Korea | 37 | 57 | 20 | 55 | 1.7 | 0.9 | 0.9 |
| Egypt | 37 | 65 | 29 | 77 | 2.3 | 0.9 | 1.0 |
| Nigeria | 63 | 135 | 72 | 114 | 3.0 | 1.5 | 2.1 |
| Brazil | 109 | 226 | 117 | 108 | 2.9 | 2.7 | 3.6 |
| Mexico | 60 | 131 | 71 | 119 | 3.1 | 1.5 | 2.1 |
| United States | 214 | 248 | 35 | 16 | 0.6 | 5.2 | 3.9 |
| U.S.S.R. | 254 | 309 | 54 | 21 | 0.8 | 6.2 | 4.9 |
| Japan | 112 | 133 | 21 | 19 | 0.7 | 2.7 | 2.1 |

## Age Composition of the Population

*Broad Age Groups.* The age composition of the world and of the more developed and less developed regions in 1975 is summarized in Table 2–7 (medium series). The more developed regions had significantly higher percentages of population in the 15–64 age group and in the age group 65 and over, and a far lower percentage of population in the 0–14 group. For the world as a whole, the percentages of population in the various broad age groups were closer to the age composition percentages of the less developed regions, since over 72 percent of the world's population lived in the less developed regions in 1975.

## TABLE 2–7

**Broad Age Groups, by More Developed Regions and Less Developed Regions, 1975 and 2000 (Census Bureau)**

*(Population in millions)*

| | World | | More Dev. | | Less Dev. | |
|---|---|---|---|---|---|---|
| **1975:** | | | | | | |
| 0–14 yrs | 1,505 | 37 | 281 | 25 | 1,224 | 42 |
| 15–64 yrs | 2,368 | 58 | 731 | 65 | 1,637 | 55 |
| 65 & over | 217 | 5 | 119 | 10 | 98 | 3 |
| All ages | 4,090 | 100 | 1,131 | 100 | 2,959 | 100 |
| **2000:** | | | | | | |
| 0–14 yrs | 2,055 | 32 | 297 | 22 | 1,758 | 35 |
| 15–64 yrs | 3,906 | 62 | 859 | 65 | 3,047 | 61 |
| 65 & over | 390 | 6 | 167 | 13 | 223 | 4 |
| All ages | 6,351 | 100 | 1,323 | 100 | 5,028 | 100 |

As projected to 2000, the age composition of the population of the world's more developed regions would still be significantly different from that of the less developed regions, as can be seen from Figure 2–2. The age composition of the less developed regions would still be very similar to that of the world as a whole, since 80 percent of the world's population would be living in these regions by 2000.

In absolute figures, the 15–64 age group shows the largest projected increases from 1975 to 2000. The highest percentage increase over 1975, however, is shown by the 65 and over group, and the lowest by the 0–14 group.

For the five major world regions and the 15 selected countries, Table 2–8 shows the percent distribution of population by age in 1975 and in 2000 and the 1975–2000 percent increase in population by age.

*Functional Age Groups.* Table 2–9 presents a summary of projected changes from 1975 to 2000 in the population of certain functional age groups for the world, the more developed and less developed regions, the major regions, and 15 selected countries.

For the world as a whole, the projected percent increases in the school-age population are lower than the projected percent increases in total populations, but for Africa, Latin America, and many of the selected LDCs, the projected percent increases in school-age population are extremely high. For the less developed regions as a whole,

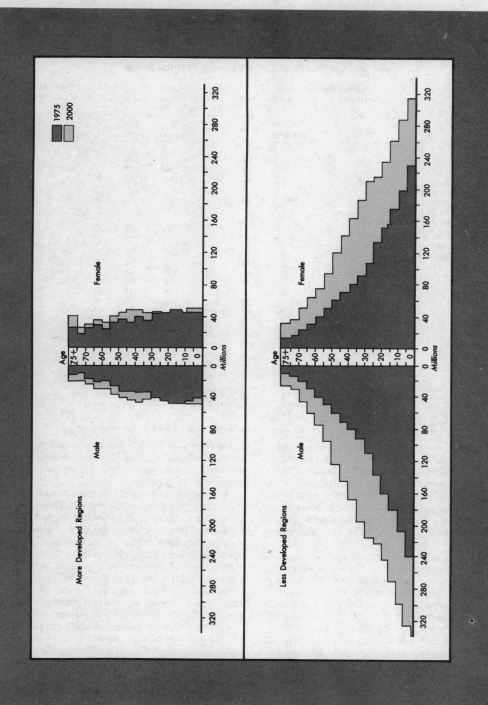

**Figure 2-2.** Age-sex composition of population, medium series, 1975 and 2000.

## TABLE 2–8

### Percent Distribution of Population, 1975 and 2000, and 1975–2000 Increase for Major Regions and Selected Countries, Census Bureau Medium Series

| | Percent Distribution of Total Population by Age in 1975 | | | Percent Increase of Population by Age, 1975 to 2000 | | | | Percent Distribution of Total Population by Age in 2000 | | |
|---|---|---|---|---|---|---|---|---|---|---|
| | 0–14 | 15–64 | 65 and over | 0–14 | 15–64 | 65 and over | All Ages | 0–14 | 15–64 | 65 and over |
| **Major regions** | | | | | | | | | | |
| Africa | 44 | 53 | 3 | 97 | 109 | 129 | 104 | 43 | 54 | 3 |
| Asia and Oceania[a] | 41 | 56 | 3 | 29 | 78 | 125 | 60 | 32 | 63 | 5 |
| Latin America | 42 | 54 | 4 | 73 | 112 | 124 | 96 | 38 | 58 | 4 |
| U.S.S.R. and Eastern Europe[b] | 25 | 65 | 10 | 10 | 19 | 49 | 20 | 23 | 65 | 12 |
| North America, Western Europe,[c] Japan, Australia, and New Zealand | 25 | 64 | 11 | 1 | 15 | 36 | 14 | 22 | 65 | 13 |
| **Selected countries** | | | | | | | | | | |
| People's Republic of China | 38 | 58 | 4 | 5 | 62 | 116 | 42 | 28 | 66 | 6 |
| India | 40 | 57 | 3 | 36 | 82 | 147 | 65 | 34 | 62 | 4 |
| Indonesia | 43 | 55 | 2 | 44 | 82 | 201 | 68 | 37 | 60 | 3 |
| Bangladesh | 46 | 51 | 3 | 79 | 120 | 85 | 100 | 41 | 56 | 3 |
| Pakistan | 46 | 51 | 3 | 84 | 133 | 124 | 111 | 40 | 57 | 3 |
| Philippines | 44 | 53 | 3 | 30 | 102 | 119 | 91 | 34 | 62 | 4 |
| Thailand | 43 | 54 | 3 | 45 | 99 | 135 | 77 | 35 | 61 | 4 |
| South Korea | 39 | 58 | 3 | 14 | 75 | 170 | 55 | 28 | 66 | 6 |
| Egypt | 41 | 56 | 3 | 54 | 91 | 136 | 77 | 35 | 60 | 5 |
| Nigeria | 45 | 53 | 2 | 115 | 111 | 159 | 114 | 45 | 52 | 3 |
| Brazil | 43 | 54 | 3 | 88 | 119 | 167 | 108 | 39 | 57 | 4 |
| Mexico | 48 | 49 | 3 | 88 | 150 | 109 | 119 | 41 | 56 | 3 |
| United States | 26 | 64 | 10 | 0 | 19 | 40 | 16 | 21 | 66 | 13 |
| U.S.S.R. | 26 | 65 | 9 | 11 | 20 | 59 | 21 | 23 | 65 | 12 |
| Japan | 24 | 68 | 8 | 2 | 16 | 108 | 19 | 20 | 66 | 14 |

[a] Developing countries only, i.e., excluding Japan, Australia, and New Zealand.
[b] Eastern Europe includes Albania and Yugoslavia.
[c] Western Europe as used here comprises all of Europe except Eastern Europe, Albania, and Yugoslavia. The U.S.S.R. is also excluded.

the projected net increase in the school-age population amounts to 0.36 billion (a 48 percent increase), an enormous increment in terms of maintaining or improving the quality of education. By comparison, in the more developed regions of the world, where nearly full enrollment has already been achieved, the projected increment for the school-age group is only 8 million (an increase of 4 percent).

The broad age group comprising persons 15–64 years of age corresponds approximately to a country's working-age (or main working-age) population. For the less developed regions, the projected 86 percent increase in this group is greater than the projected 70 percent increase in total population. Among the 15 selected countries, the largest projected percentage increases are for Mexico, Pakistan, Bangladesh, Brazil, and Nigeria. While such a large growth in working-age population represents a beneficial increase in the productive sector of the population, the net increment (about 1.41 billion persons) will create addi-

tional demands for training and employment. In more developed regions, the projected increment amounts to only about 0.13 billion persons (an increase of 18 percent).

As may be expected, the growth patterns for the female population in the reproductive ages will be similar to those of the working-age population. Thus, the projected increase of females in the reproductive ages in the less developed regions is about 85 percent from 1975 to 2000, as compared with about 13 percent in the more developed regions. Such rapid growth in the numbers of women in the fertile ages in the less developed regions will ensure an increase in the absolute number of births, even if fertility rates decline.

The highest percentage increases are projected for the age group 65 years and over in both less and more developed regions. Although the growth of this group is particularly rapid in the less developed regions (127 percent as shown in Table 2–8), it constitutes only about 6 percent of total 1975–2000 population increase for these regions.

## TABLE 2-9

### Changes in Functional Age Groups and Total Population, 1975–2000, for World, More Developed and Less Developed Regions, Major Regions, and Selected Countries, Census Bureau Medium Series

| | School-Age Population: 5-14 | | Working-Age Population: 15-64 | | Females of Reproductive Age: 15-49 | | Old-Age Population: 65 and over | | Total Population: All ages | |
|---|---|---|---|---|---|---|---|---|---|---|
| | Millions | Percent | Millions | Percent | Millions | Percent | Millions | Percent | Millions | Percent |
| World | 369 | 39 | 1,538 | 65 | 619 | 64 | 173 | 80 | 2,261 | 55 |
| More developed regions[a] | 8 | 4 | 128 | 18 | 37 | 13 | 49 | 41 | 192 | 17 |
| Less developed regions | 361 | 48 | 1,410 | 86 | 582 | 85 | 125 | 127 | 2,069 | 70 |
| **Major regions** | | | | | | | | | | |
| Africa | 110 | 105 | 231 | 109 | 99 | 108 | 15 | 129 | 416 | 104 |
| Asia and Oceania[b] | 184 | 32 | 994 | 78 | 405 | 76 | 96 | 125 | 1,356 | 60 |
| Latin America | 69 | 82 | 196 | 112 | 83 | 111 | 15 | 124 | 312 | 96 |
| U.S.S.R. and Eastern Europe[c] | 7 | 10 | 48 | 19 | 14 | 14 | 18 | 49 | 76 | 20 |
| Northern America, Western Europe,[d] Japan, Australia, and New Zealand | -1 | -1 | 70 | 15 | 19 | 11 | 29 | 36 | 101 | 14 |
| **Selected countries** | | | | | | | | | | |
| People's Republic of China | 9 | 4 | 334 | 62 | 133 | 59 | 43 | 116 | 394 | 42 |
| India | 61 | 39 | 286 | 82 | 114 | 80 | 27 | 147 | 402 | 65 |
| Indonesia | 18 | 52 | 61 | 82 | 26 | 79 | 5 | 200 | 91 | 68 |
| Bangladesh | 20 | 93 | 48 | 120 | 21 | 126 | 2 | 85 | 79 | 100 |
| Pakistan | 19 | 96 | 49 | 133 | 21 | 138 | 2 | 124 | 78 | 111 |
| Philippines | 4 | 30 | 23 | 102 | 10 | 96 | 2 | 119 | 30 | 71 |
| Thailand | 6 | 50 | 23 | 99 | 10 | 98 | 2 | 135 | 33 | 77 |
| South Korea | 1 | 14 | 16 | 76 | 6 | 68 | 2 | 170 | 20 | 55 |
| Egypt | 6 | 60 | 19 | 91 | 8 | 89 | 2 | 136 | 29 | 77 |
| Nigeria | 20 | 122 | 37 | 111 | 16 | 114 | 3 | 159 | 72 | 114 |
| Brazil | 28 | 103 | 70 | 119 | 30 | 116 | 6 | 167 | 117 | 108 |
| Mexico | 17 | 95 | 44 | 150 | 19 | 146 | 2 | 108 | 71 | 119 |
| United States | -1 | -2 | 26 | 19 | 9 | 17 | 9 | 40 | 35 | 16 |
| U.S.S.R. | 5 | 10 | 34 | 20 | 11 | 16 | 13 | 59 | 54 | 21 |
| Japan | 1 | 4 | 12 | 16 | 0 | 0 | 9 | 108 | 21 | 19 |

[a] Includes North America, Europe (including the U.S.S.R.), Australia, New Zealand, Japan, temperate South America (i.e., Argentina, Chile, Falkland Islands, and Uruguay).
[b] Developing countries only, i.e., excluding Japan, Australia, and New Zealand.
[c] Eastern Europe includes Albania and Yugoslavia.
[d] Western Europe as used here comprises all of Europe except Eastern Europe, Albania, and Yugoslavia. The U.S.S.R. is also excluded.

In the more developed regions, however, the increase of about 41 percent in the size of the old-age group is especially significant, since it comprises one-fourth of the total population increase for these regions.

## Summary

The Bureau of Census projections* presented in Tables 2–10 through 2–14 can be summarized briefly as follows:

World population totaled about 4.09 billion persons in 1975 and as projected in the Bureau of the Census medium series would increase by about 55 percent and number about 6.35 billion in 2000. This means that world population would

*A more detailed presentation of the Census projections is provided in U.S. Department of Commerce Bureau of the Census, *Illustrative Projections of World Populations to the 21st Century*, Washington: U.S. Government Printing Office, 1979.

grow between 1975 and 2000 at a slightly lower annual rate than between 1950 and 1975, but that an appreciably greater number of people would be added to the total world population during the 1975–2000 period than during the former period. The less developed regions would account for nine-tenths of the world population growth between 1975 and 2000. By 2000 these regions would comprise more than three-fourths of the world's population, reflecting notable projected population increases in Africa, Latin America, and the less developed countries of Asia and Oceania. As indicated in Table 2–1, the percentage of the world's population in the LDCs continues to increase, approaching 80 percent by 2000. The LDC growth rate declines from about 2.28 percent to 2.02 percent and by 2000 is the predominant influence in the world growth rate—which declines only slightly, from 1.78 percent in the 1975–80 period to 1.70 percent in the 1995–2000 period.

# BUREAU OF THE CENSUS PROJECTIONS

U.S. Bureau of the Census projections for total population, total fertility rates, population growth rates, crude death rates, and crude birth rates are presented in Tables 2–10 through 2–14. In each table:

*More developed regions* comprise Northern America, temperate South America, Europe, U.S.S.R., Japan, Australia, and New Zealand. All other regions of the world are classified as *less developed regions*.

*Asia and Oceania* excludes Japan, Australia, and New Zealand.

*Eastern Europe* includes Albania and Yugoslavia.

*Western Europe* comprises all of Europe except Eastern Europe (including the U.S.S.R.), Albania, and Yugoslavia.

## TABLE 2–10

**Census Bureau Projected Total Population for World, Major Regions, and Selected Countries**

*(In thousands)*

|  | 1975 | 1980 | 1985 | 1990 | 1995 | 2000 |
|---|---|---|---|---|---|---|
| | HIGH SERIES | | | | | |
| World | 4,134,049 | 4,548,928 | 5,012,753 | 5,544,671 | 6,143,076 | 6,797,504 |
| More developed regions | 1,130,989 | 1,173,831 | 1,224,157 | 1,276,131 | 1,327,400 | 1,377,258 |
| Less developed regions | 3,003,060 | 3,375,096 | 3,788,596 | 4,268,539 | 4,815,676 | 5,420,245 |
| Major Regions | | | | | | |
| Africa | 398,694 | 459,653 | 533,548 | 621,830 | 726,565 | 846,880 |
| Asia and Oceania | 2,318,028 | 2,580,123 | 2,861,277 | 3,185,185 | 3,551,394 | 3,951,198 |
| Latin America | 325,085 | 377,073 | 438,796 | 509,969 | 589,698 | 677,904 |
| U.S.S.R. and Eastern Europe | 384,336 | 402,262 | 422,289 | 441,660 | 460,433 | 479,518 |
| Northern America, Western Europe, Japan, Australia, and New Zealand | 707,906 | 729,817 | 756,842 | 786,028 | 814,987 | 842,003 |
| Selected Countries and Regions | | | | | | |
| People's Republic of China | 977,862 | 1,071,378 | 1,150,998 | 1,241,497 | 1,347,876 | 1,467,860 |
| India | 618,470 | 694,190 | 786,222 | 893,586 | 1,012,943 | 1,141,900 |
| Indonesia | 134,988 | 150,467 | 168,155 | 188,290 | 210,993 | 235,720 |
| Bangladesh | 79,411 | 92,319 | 107,565 | 125,171 | 144,862 | 166,185 |
| Pakistan | 70,974 | 83,261 | 98,078 | 115,339 | 134,777 | 156,083 |

## TABLE 2–10 (Cont.)

*(In thousands)*

| | 1975 | 1980 | 1985 | 1990 | 1995 | 2000 |
|---|---|---|---|---|---|---|
| **HIGH SERIES (cont.)** | | | | | | |
| Philippines | 43,029 | 49,063 | 55,545 | 62,697 | 70,771 | 79,773 |
| Thailand | 42,473 | 48,435 | 55,168 | 62,805 | 71,354 | 80,806 |
| South Korea | 36,895 | 40,946 | 45,507 | 50,663 | 56,087 | 61,535 |
| Egypt | 36,859 | 42,122 | 48,250 | 55,162 | 62,658 | 70,534 |
| Nigeria | 62,925 | 72,473 | 84,271 | 98,722 | 116,159 | 136,934 |
| Brazil | 108,882 | 128,235 | 151,309 | 177,977 | 207,995 | 241,436 |
| Mexico | 60,188 | 72,214 | 86,468 | 103,006 | 121,618 | 142,022 |
| United States | 213,540 | 222,395 | 234,841 | 248,034 | 259,823 | 270,174 |
| U.S.S.R. | 254,393 | 267,577 | 282,384 | 296,415 | 309,551 | 322,787 |
| Japan | 111,566 | 117,076 | 122,169 | 126,768 | 131,102 | 135,309 |
| Eastern Europe | 129,943 | 134,685 | 139,905 | 145,245 | 150,882 | 156,731 |
| Western Europe | 343,517 | 348,908 | 355,610 | 364,172 | 374,386 | 384,331 |
| **MEDIUM SERIES** | | | | | | |
| World | 4,090,133 | 4,470,380 | 4,884,743 | 5,340,419 | 5,833,887 | 6,351,070 |
| More developed regions | 1,130,989 | 1,169,863 | 1,211,772 | 1,252,233 | 1,289,712 | 1,322,824 |
| Less developed regions | 2,959,143 | 3,300,516 | 3,672,971 | 4,088,186 | 4,544,175 | 5,028,246 |
| **Major Regions** | | | | | | |
| Africa | 398,694 | 458,861 | 530,567 | 613,894 | 708,896 | 814,272 |
| Asia and Oceania | 2,274,471 | 2,508,490 | 2,754,505 | 3,025,189 | 3,320,192 | 3,630,195 |
| Latin America | 324,725 | 374,774 | 432,486 | 496,624 | 565,431 | 636,937 |
| U.S.S.R. and Eastern Europe | 384,336 | 400,789 | 418,080 | 433,672 | 447,658 | 460,471 |
| Northern America, Western Europe, Japan, Australia, and New Zealand | 707,906 | 727,466 | 749,105 | 771,041 | 791,710 | 809,195 |
| **Selected Countries and Regions** | | | | | | |
| People's Republic of China | 934,626 | 1,007,858 | 1,075,999 | 1,151,665 | 1,237,029 | 1,328,645 |
| India | 618,471 | 689,545 | 764,157 | 843,643 | 929,102 | 1,020,917 |
| Indonesia | 134,988 | 150,246 | 167,005 | 185,375 | 205,425 | 226,388 |
| Bangladesh | 79,411 | 92,186 | 106,892 | 123,202 | 140,666 | 158,724 |
| Pakistan | 70,974 | 83,145 | 97,512 | 113,754 | 131,296 | 149,464 |
| Philippines | 42,810 | 48,181 | 53,657 | 59,526 | 66,064 | 73,229 |
| Thailand | 42,420 | 48,101 | 54,307 | 61,051 | 68,056 | 75,238 |
| South Korea | 36,846 | 40,604 | 44,561 | 48,721 | 52,902 | 56,983 |
| Egypt | 36,859 | 42,046 | 47,739 | 53,648 | 59,477 | 65,380 |
| Nigeria | 62,925 | 72,469 | 84,215 | 98,439 | 115,261 | 134,680 |
| Brazil | 108,797 | 127,825 | 149,762 | 173,723 | 199,110 | 225,897 |
| Mexico | 59,913 | 71,136 | 84,016 | 98,555 | 114,450 | 131,320 |
| United States | 213,540 | 220,497 | 228,912 | 237,028 | 243,581 | 248,372 |
| U.S.S.R. | 254,393 | 266,304 | 278,973 | 290,235 | 300,020 | 308,893 |
| Japan | 111,566 | 116,962 | 121,741 | 125,870 | 129,574 | 132,951 |
| Eastern Europe | 129,943 | 134,485 | 139,107 | 143,437 | 147,638 | 151,578 |
| Western Europe | 343,517 | 348,733 | 354,878 | 362,306 | 370,702 | 378,222 |
| **LOW SERIES** | | | | | | |
| World | 4,043,444 | 4,384,420 | 4,753,612 | 5,140,162 | 5,533,442 | 5,921,745 |
| More developed regions | 1,130,989 | 1,166,263 | 1,200,970 | 1,231,408 | 1,256,351 | 1,274,174 |
| Less developed regions | 2,912,455 | 3,218,157 | 3,552,642 | 3,908,754 | 4,277,091 | 4,647,571 |
| **Major Regions** | | | | | | |
| Africa | 398,694 | 457,621 | 525,247 | 599,530 | 677,723 | 758,842 |
| Asia and Oceania | 2,228,443 | 2,431,561 | 2,650,767 | 2,882,418 | 3,121,231 | 3,359,092 |
| Latin America | 324,064 | 370,543 | 421,024 | 473,826 | 527,467 | 580,958 |
| U.S.S.R. and Eastern Europe | 384,336 | 399,321 | 413,884 | 425,712 | 434,955 | 441,680 |
| Northern America, Western Europe, Japan, Australia, and New Zealand | 707,906 | 725,374 | 742,689 | 758,677 | 772,066 | 781,174 |
| **Selected Countries and Regions** | | | | | | |
| People's Republic of China | 889,015 | 937,955 | 991,581 | 1,050,502 | 1,113,447 | 1,175,761 |
| India | 618,471 | 686,790 | 757,233 | 827,960 | 899,438 | 974,282 |

## TABLE 2–10 (Cont.)

*(In thousands)*

|  | 1975 | 1980 | 1985 | 1990 | 1995 | 2000 |
|---|---|---|---|---|---|---|
| | | LOW SERIES (cont.) | | | | |
| Indonesia | 134,988 | 149,831 | 164,983 | 180,321 | 195,349 | 209,125 |
| Bangladesh | 79,411 | 91,993 | 105,995 | 120,959 | 136,299 | 151,136 |
| Pakistan | 70,974 | 83,075 | 97,169 | 112,735 | 128,852 | 144,181 |
| Philippines | 42,630 | 47,462 | 52,031 | 56,682 | 61,635 | 66,786 |
| Thailand | 42,352 | 47,813 | 53,349 | 58,824 | 64,219 | 69,384 |
| South Korea | 36,677 | 39,990 | 43,372 | 46,918 | 50,390 | 53,550 |
| Egypt | 36,859 | 41,918 | 46,772 | 51,067 | 54,909 | 58,803 |
| Nigeria | 62,925 | 72,437 | 83,907 | 97,313 | 112,397 | 128,749 |
| Brazil | 108,524 | 126,508 | 146,582 | 168,100 | 190,688 | 213,838 |
| Mexico | 59,526 | 68,800 | 78,432 | 88,664 | 99,451 | 110,595 |
| United States | 213,540 | 219,078 | 224,962 | 229,919 | 233,078 | 234,328 |
| U.S.S.R. | 254,393 | 265,031 | 275,563 | 284,056 | 290,495 | 295,115 |
| Japan | 111,566 | 116,733 | 120,884 | 124,141 | 126,796 | 128,891 |
| Eastern Europe | 129,943 | 134,290 | 138,321 | 141,656 | 144,460 | 146,565 |
| Western Europe | 343,517 | 348,457 | 353,916 | 359,983 | 366,132 | 370,788 |

## TABLE 2–11

### Census Bureau Projected Total Fertility Rate[a] for World, Major Regions, and Selected Countries

|  | 1975 | 1980 | 1985 | 1990 | 1995 | 2000 |
|---|---|---|---|---|---|---|
| | | HIGH SERIES | | | | |
| World | 4.5299 | 4.2163 | 4.0892 | 4.0523 | 4.0037 | 3.9189 |
| More developed regions | 2.1505 | 2.3184 | 2.4060 | 2.4700 | 2.5408 | 2.6080 |
| Less developed regions | 5.5202 | 4.9494 | 4.6814 | 4.5493 | 4.4103 | 4.2417 |
| Major Regions | | | | | | |
| Africa | 6.3847 | 6.3826 | 6.3315 | 6.2211 | 6.0755 | 5.6424 |
| Asia and Oceania | 5.3501 | 4.6174 | 4.2917 | 4.1600 | 4.0175 | 3.8829 |
| Latin America | 5.3992 | 5.2939 | 5.1726 | 4.9912 | 4.7436 | 4.4952 |
| U.S.S.R. and Eastern Europe | 2.3687 | 2.4887 | 2.5284 | 2.5642 | 2.6178 | 2.6719 |
| Northern America, Western Europe, Japan, Australia, and New Zealand | 1.9703 | 2.1702 | 2.2987 | 2.3832 | 2.4577 | 2.5328 |
| Selected Countries and Regions | | | | | | |
| People's Republic of China | 5.1710 | 3.6565 | 3.0870 | 3.0750 | 3.0750 | 3.0750 |
| India | 5.3000 | 5.2099 | 5.1750 | 5.0500 | 4.8000 | 4.5000 |
| Indonesia | 5.3235 | 4.8805 | 4.6495 | 4.4490 | 4.2495 | 4.0000 |
| Bangladesh | 6.9999 | 6.8500 | 6.5500 | 6.1000 | 5.5600 | 5.0000 |
| Pakistan | 6.9000 | 6.6100 | 6.2700 | 5.8900 | 5.4500 | 5.0000 |
| Philippines | 5.3995 | 4.9005 | 4.4505 | 4.1000 | 3.8995 | 3.7995 |
| Thailand | 5.1675 | 4.7005 | 4.4000 | 4.2005 | 4.0000 | 3.9000 |
| South Korea | 3.9251 | 3.4000 | 3.2250 | 3.1249 | 3.1100 | 3.1000 |
| Egypt | 5.8190 | 5.8500 | 5.7000 | 5.4700 | 5.1000 | 4.6001 |
| Nigeria | 6.6999 | 6.7000 | 6.7000 | 6.6749 | 6.5499 | 6.3750 |
| Brazil | 5.7800 | 5.7255 | 5.6750 | 5.5755 | 5.3005 | 5.0000 |
| Mexico | 6.7005 | 6.4610 | 6.1600 | 5.7200 | 5.2600 | 4.7000 |
| United States | 1.7705 | 2.2160 | 2.4785 | 2.6335 | 2.6890 | 2.6965 |
| U.S.S.R. | 2.4055 | 2.5390 | 2.5690 | 2.6000 | 2.6305 | 2.6610 |
| Japan | 1.9245 | 2.1122 | 2.3000 | 2.3000 | 2.3000 | 2.3000 |
| Eastern Europe | 2.2699 | 2.3520 | 2.4340 | 2.5160 | 2.5980 | 2.6800 |
| Western Europe | 2.0219 | 2.0830 | 2.1540 | 2.2520 | 2.3380 | 2.4199 |
| | | MEDIUM SERIES | | | | |
| World | 4.2654 | 3.8571 | 3.6692 | 3.5456 | 3.4389 | 3.3098 |
| More developed regions | 2.1481 | 2.1714 | 2.1891 | 2.1921 | 2.2120 | 2.2272 |
| Less developed regions | 5.1473 | 4.5051 | 4.1862 | 3.9683 | 3.7789 | 3.5775 |

[a] The total fertility rate in a given year basically represents the average number of children each woman would have over her lifetime, assuming the age-specific fertility rates for that year applied to her lifetime.

## TABLE 2–11 (Cont.)

|  | 1975 | 1980 | 1985 | 1990 | 1995 | 2000 |
|---|---|---|---|---|---|---|
| MEDIUM SERIES (cont.) | | | | | | |
| **Major Regions** | | | | | | |
| Africa | 6.3524 | 6.2884 | 6.1263 | 5.8446 | 5.4979 | 5.0156 |
| Asia and Oceania | 4.8865 | 4.0835 | 3.7307 | 3.5315 | 3.3713 | 3.2238 |
| Latin America | 5.2679 | 5.0546 | 4.7661 | 4.4427 | 4.0520 | 3.6391 |
| U.S.S.R. and Eastern Europe | 2.3694 | 2.3513 | 2.3230 | 2.2920 | 2.2783 | 2.2659 |
| Northern America, Western Europe, Japan, Australia, and New Zealand | 1.9697 | 2.0175 | 2.0748 | 2.1051 | 2.1430 | 2.1751 |
| **Selected Countries and Regions** | | | | | | |
| People's Republic of China | 4.1280 | 2.8590 | 2.5690 | 2.5620 | 2.5620 | 2.5620 |
| India | 5.3000 | 4.6750 | 4.1749 | 3.8750 | 3.6500 | 3.4999 |
| Indonesia | 5.3235 | 4.7700 | 4.4205 | 4.1100 | 3.8400 | 3.5000 |
| Bangladesh | 6.9999 | 6.7400 | 6.2700 | 5.5900 | 4.9200 | 4.2500 |
| Pakistan | 6.9000 | 6.5100 | 6.0400 | 5.4999 | 4.8799 | 4.2500 |
| Philippines | 5.0705 | 4.3500 | 3.8495 | 3.4495 | 3.3000 | 3.1995 |
| Thailand | 5.0500 | 4.2500 | 3.9500 | 3.6000 | 3.3005 | 3.1000 |
| South Korea | 3.7889 | 3.1199 | 2.7800 | 2.5499 | 2.5200 | 2.5000 |
| Egypt | 5.8190 | 5.6500 | 5.2000 | 4.5500 | 3.9499 | 3.6000 |
| Nigeria | 6.7000 | 6.6800 | 6.6499 | 6.5250 | 6.2750 | 5.9000 |
| Brazil | 5.7255 | 5.6000 | 5.2755 | 4.9005 | 4.4000 | 3.9995 |
| Mexico | 6.3600 | 5.9605 | 5.4805 | 5.0005 | 4.4800 | 4.0005 |
| United States | 1.7705 | 1.8710 | 1.9940 | 2.0615 | 2.0900 | 2.0955 |
| U.S.S.R. | 2.4055 | 2.3740 | 2.3455 | 2.3170 | 2.2865 | 2.2575 |
| Japan | 1.9245 | 2.0622 | 2.2000 | 2.1667 | 2.1333 | 2.1000 |
| Eastern Europe | 2.2699 | 2.2699 | 2.2699 | 2.2699 | 2.2699 | 2.2699 |
| Western Europe | 2.0220 | 2.0520 | 2.0919 | 2.1340 | 2.1740 | 2.2070 |
| LOW SERIES | | | | | | |
| World | 3.9942 | 3.5261 | 3.3180 | 3.0877 | 2.9026 | 2.7546 |
| More developed regions | 2.1473 | 2.0363 | 2.0050 | 1.9429 | 1.9092 | 1.8694 |
| Less developed regions | 4.7647 | 4.0967 | 3.7747 | 3.4449 | 3.1796 | 2.9761 |
| **Major Regions** | | | | | | |
| Africa | 6.3146 | 6.1381 | 5.7409 | 5.1969 | 4.5308 | 4.0436 |
| Asia and Oceania | 4.4170 | 3.6382 | 3.3499 | 3.0668 | 2.8700 | 2.7163 |
| Latin America | 5.1030 | 4.6033 | 4.0976 | 3.6399 | 3.2144 | 2.8949 |
| U.S.S.R. and Eastern Europe | 2.3696 | 2.2162 | 2.1196 | 2.0219 | 1.9429 | 1.8620 |
| Northern America, Western Europe, Japan, Australia, and New Zealand | 1.9695 | 1.8774 | 1.8986 | 1.8653 | 1.8622 | 1.8559 |
| **Selected Countries and Regions** | | | | | | |
| People's Republic of China | 3.0830 | 2.0600 | 2.0500 | 2.0500 | 2.0500 | 2.0500 |
| India | 5.3000 | 4.5250 | 3.9500 | 3.4250 | 3.1500 | 3.0000 |
| Indonesia | 5.3235 | 4.5400 | 3.9995 | 3.4695 | 2.9700 | 2.4995 |
| Bangladesh | 6.9999 | 6.5800 | 5.9200 | 5.1100 | 4.2999 | 3.5000 |
| Pakistan | 6.9000 | 6.4500 | 5.9000 | 5.2300 | 4.4300 | 3.5000 |
| Philippines | 4.7995 | 3.8995 | 3.2505 | 2.8500 | 2.6000 | 2.5000 |
| Thailand | 4.9000 | 4.0000 | 3.4000 | 3.0000 | 2.6500 | 2.4000 |
| South Korea | 3.4099 | 2.6800 | 2.3200 | 2.1799 | 2.1300 | 2.1275 |
| Egypt | 5.8190 | 5.3000 | 4.2001 | 3.2500 | 2.7500 | 2.6000 |
| Nigeria | 6.6999 | 6.6500 | 6.4500 | 6.1300 | 5.5999 | 4.9999 |
| Brazil | 5.5500 | 5.2000 | 4.8005 | 4.4000 | 3.9750 | 3.5000 |
| Mexico | 5.9120 | 4.7600 | 4.0595 | 3.5695 | 3.2000 | 3.0000 |
| United States | 1.7705 | 1.6070 | 1.6975 | 1.6940 | 1.6935 | 1.6935 |
| U.S.S.R. | 2.4055 | 2.2120 | 2.1230 | 2.0335 | 1.9440 | 1.8540 |
| Japan | 1.9245 | 1.9622 | 2.0000 | 1.9333 | 1.8667 | 1.8000 |
| Eastern Europe | 2.2700 | 2.1900 | 2.1100 | 2.0300 | 1.9499 | 1.8700 |
| Western Europe | 2.0219 | 2.0039 | 2.0260 | 1.9850 | 1.9750 | 1.9590 |

## TABLE 2–12

**Census Bureau Projected Average Annual Population Growth Rates for World, Major Regions, and Selected Countries (Medium Series)**

|  | 1975 to 1980 | 1980 to 1985 | 1985 to 1990 | 1990 to 1995 | 1995 to 2000 |
|---|---|---|---|---|---|
| World | 1.8 | 1.8 | 1.8 | 1.8 | 1.7 |
| More developed regions | 0.7 | 0.7 | 0.7 | 0.6 | 0.5 |
| Less developed regions | 2.2 | 2.1 | 2.1 | 2.1 | 2.0 |
| Major Regions |  |  |  |  |  |
| Africa | 2.8 | 2.9 | 2.9 | 2.9 | 2.8 |
| Asia and Oceania | 2.0 | 1.9 | 1.9 | 1.9 | 1.8 |
| Latin America | 2.9 | 2.9 | 2.8 | 2.6 | 2.4 |
| U.S.S.R. and Eastern Europe | 0.8 | 0.8 | 0.7 | 0.6 | 0.6 |
| Northern America, Western Europe, Japan, Australia, and New Zealand | 0.5 | 0.6 | 0.6 | 0.5 | 0.4 |
| Selected Countries and Regions |  |  |  |  |  |
| People's Republic of China | 1.5 | 1.3 | 1.4 | 1.4 | 1.4 |
| India | 2.2 | 2.1 | 2.0 | 1.9 | 1.9 |
| Indonesia | 2.1 | 2.1 | 2.1 | 2.1 | 1.9 |
| Bangladesh | 3.0 | 3.0 | 2.8 | 2.7 | 2.4 |
| Pakistan | 3.2 | 3.2 | 3.1 | 2.9 | 2.6 |
| Philippines | 2.4 | 2.2 | 2.1 | 2.1 | 2.1 |
| Thailand | 2.5 | 2.4 | 2.3 | 2.2 | 2.0 |
| South Korea | 1.9 | 1.9 | 1.8 | 1.6 | 1.5 |
| Egypt | 2.6 | 2.5 | 2.3 | 2.1 | 1.9 |
| Nigeria | 2.8 | 3.0 | 3.1 | 3.2 | 3.1 |
| Brazil | 3.2 | 3.2 | 3.0 | 2.7 | 2.5 |
| Mexico | 3.4 | 3.3 | 3.2 | 3.0 | 2.7 |
| United States | 0.6 | 0.7 | 0.7 | 0.5 | 0.4 |
| U.S.S.R. | 0.9 | 0.9 | 0.8 | 0.7 | 0.6 |
| Japan | 0.9 | 0.8 | 0.7 | 0.6 | 0.5 |
| Eastern Europe | 0.7 | 0.7 | 0.6 | 0.6 | 0.5 |
| Western Europe | 0.3 | 0.3 | 0.4 | 0.5 | 0.4 |

## Community and Family Study Center Projections

The CFSC projections of population, fertility rates, death rates, and birth rates are shown in Tables 2–16 through 2–20 at the end of this section.

### Assumptions

*Fertility Assumptions.* The CFSC projections rest on the condition that fertility has considerably more potential for change in population growth and hence is more important than the other two components of population growth—migration and mortality. The "validity" of the population projections in this series depends then primarily upon assumptions made concerning fertility. In the case of the CFSC projections, these assumptions rest upon a theoretical base somewhat different from that employed by the Census Bureau and others. The basic premises underlying the CFSC argument are as follows:

1. Throughout the entire world, in developed and developing societies, the need to reduce the pace of population growth is being increasingly felt. This pressure is manifested both at the aggregate (governmental and policy) level and at the level of the family and the individual. Modernization is inherently inconsistent with high fertility, and high fertility is inherently inconsistent with most of the objectives and life goals sought by most peoples (literacy, health, a higher standard of living, better housing, basic luxury commodities, physical comfort). Even in nations where this set of pressures has not been officially recognized, they are present and mounting in individual families. Environmental, economic, and social factors will increase this pressure substantially during the remainder of this century.

2. The present pace of economic development and modernization will bring down fertility to the replacement level gradually through provision of facilities and gradual accumulation of knowledge and motivation. The pace will be somewhat faster than that followed by Europe and North America during the 19th and early 20th centuries because of improved communications and improved methods of contraception.

## TABLE 2–13

### Census Bureau Estimated and Projected Crude Death Rates for World, Major Regions, and Selected Countries (Medium Series)

| | Estimated 1975 | Projected July 1 to June 30 | | | | |
|---|---|---|---|---|---|---|
| | | 1979/80 | 1984/85 | 1989/90 | 1994/95 | 1999/2000 |
| World | 12.3 | 11.4 | 10.6 | 10.1 | 9.5 | 9.1 |
| More developed regions | 9.6 | 9.9 | 10.0 | 10.1 | 10.1 | 10.4 |
| Less developed regions | 13.4 | 11.9 | 10.8 | 10.0 | 9.4 | 8.7 |
| Major Regions | | | | | | |
| Africa | 19.0 | 17.7 | 16.0 | 14.3 | 12.8 | 11.3 |
| Asia and Oceania | 13.0 | 11.4 | 10.4 | 9.7 | 9.2 | 8.7 |
| Latin America | 8.9 | 8.0 | 7.2 | 6.6 | 6.1 | 5.7 |
| U.S.S.R. and Eastern Europe | 9.7 | 10.0 | 10.2 | 10.3 | 10.0 | 10.5 |
| Northern America, Western Europe, Japan, Australia, and New Zealand | 9.6 | 9.8 | 10.0 | 10.1 | 10.2 | 10.5 |
| Selected Countries and Regions | | | | | | |
| People's Republic of China | 9.8 | 8.3 | 7.9 | 7.9 | 8.1 | 8.3 |
| India | 14.4 | 12.7 | 11.1 | 10.1 | 9.2 | 8.4 |
| Indonesia | 18.2 | 16.1 | 14.3 | 12.7 | 11.3 | 10.2 |
| Bangladesh | 18.2 | 16.8 | 15.4 | 14.2 | 13.1 | 12.1 |
| Pakistan | 13.6 | 11.7 | 10.3 | 9.2 | 8.2 | 7.3 |
| Philippines | 10.1 | 9.3 | 8.4 | 7.4 | 6.4 | 6.1 |
| Thailand | 9.9 | 9.5 | 9.0 | 8.1 | 7.1 | 6.7 |
| South Korea | 6.2 | 5.8 | 5.6 | 5.4 | 5.7 | 6.0 |
| Egypt | 12.5 | 11.9 | 11.0 | 9.9 | 9.0 | 8.3 |
| Nigeria | 22.0 | 20.4 | 18.6 | 16.8 | 15.0 | 13.2 |
| Brazil | 8.3 | 7.3 | 6.5 | 6.0 | 5.7 | 5.7 |
| Mexico | 7.2 | 6.7 | 6.1 | 5.4 | 5.0 | 4.8 |
| United States | 8.9 | 9.3 | 9.6 | 9.8 | 10.1 | 10.3 |
| U.S.S.R. | 9.3 | 9.7 | 10.0 | 10.2 | 10.1 | 10.5 |
| Japan | 7.0 | 7.1 | 7.3 | 8.0 | 8.8 | 9.7 |
| Eastern Europe | 10.4 | 10.7 | 10.6 | 10.4 | 10.0 | 10.4 |
| Western Europe | 11.0 | 11.2 | 11.3 | 11.2 | 10.8 | 11.1 |

3. The pace of fertility decline is directly influenced by family planning programs, organized on a national or regional basis to provide information, motivation, and contraceptive services. The larger the per capita investment, the more wholehearted the official support, and the greater the accessibility to the entire public of these services, the more rapid will be the decline.

4. The pace of the decline of fertility will be that of a reverse S curve. When birth rates are high and family planning programs are in stages of establishment and gaining social acceptance, the pace will be slow. As birth rates sink to lower levels, the rate of decline will accelerate to a maximum when the crude birth rate is between 38 and 20 per 1,000 women. In this interval, the pace may be very rapid. When the crude birth rate reaches the lower 20s, complete saturation of contraception is being approached. Only young people still starting families and a residue of reactionary "late adopters" will remain to be convinced about the need for fertility decline. The decline continues, but at a decelerating rate.

5. Those countries which now have no family planning programs may be expected to begin at least weak (partial) programs within the very near future. Nations that presently have weak or moderate family planning programs may be expected to strengthen them substantially. By the end of the century, every nation on earth may be expected to have at least some kind of a substantial family planning effort (either public or private or both) and these programs may be expected to have a substantial impact in reducing fertility faster than otherwise would be the case.

Table 2–15 illustrates the impact on future birth rates of the factors identified above. The right-hand column of the table shows the estimated annual decline in crude birth rate that may be expected in the future on the basis of modernization alone, with no special efforts at providing family planning information and services. The downward trend anticipated then is almost linear, with a one-point decline in the crude birth rate every four or five years. Under this set of conditions, it would require about 135 years for a

## TABLE 2–14

**Census Bureau Estimated and Projected Crude Birth Rates for World, Major Regions, and Selected Countries (Medium Series)**

| | Estimated 1975 | Projected July 1 to June 30 | | | | |
|---|---|---|---|---|---|---|
| | | 1979/80 | 1984/85 | 1989/90 | 1994/95 | 1999/2000 |
| World | 30.4 | 29.0 | 28.5 | 27.9 | 27.0 | 25.6 |
| More developed regions | 16.1 | 16.8 | 17.0 | 16.4 | 15.7 | 15.2 |
| Less developed regions | 35.9 | 33.3 | 32.2 | 31.5 | 30.3 | 28.4 |
| Major Regions | | | | | | |
| Africa | 46.7 | 46.3 | 45.2 | 43.5 | 41.4 | 38.5 |
| Asia and Oceania | 33.7 | 30.2 | 29.1 | 28.5 | 27.6 | 25.9 |
| Latin America | 37.2 | 36.9 | 35.6 | 33.7 | 31.2 | 28.7 |
| U.S.S.R. and Eastern Europe | 17.7 | 18.6 | 18.3 | 17.1 | 16.1 | 15.9 |
| Northern America, Western Europe, Japan, Australia, and New Zealand | 14.8 | 15.4 | 15.9 | 15.7 | 15.1 | 14.5 |
| Selected Countries and Regions | | | | | | |
| People's Republic of China | 27.6 | 21.6 | 21.0 | 21.8 | 22.5 | 22.0 |
| India | 36.9 | 33.9 | 31.3 | 29.7 | 28.3 | 27.1 |
| Indonesia | 40.3 | 37.3 | 35.3 | 33.4 | 31.6 | 28.9 |
| Bangladesh | 47.9 | 46.7 | 44.7 | 41.9 | 38.8 | 35.2 |
| Pakistan | 44.6 | 43.7 | 42.0 | 39.3 | 35.8 | 32.1 |
| Philippines | 35.3 | 31.7 | 29.5 | 27.9 | 27.4 | 26.3 |
| Thailand | 35.8 | 34.0 | 33.2 | 30.8 | 28.1 | 26.2 |
| South Korea | 26.9 | 24.6 | 24.1 | 22.6 | 21.6 | 20.2 |
| Egypt | 38.9 | 38.1 | 35.8 | 32.1 | 28.5 | 26.9 |
| Nigeria | 49.4 | 49.5 | 49.3 | 48.4 | 46.5 | 44.1 |
| Brazil | 40.2 | 39.8 | 37.5 | 34.8 | 32.0 | 30.3 |
| Mexico | 42.0 | 40.7 | 38.9 | 36.7 | 34.0 | 31.3 |
| United States | 14.5 | 16.1 | 17.1 | 16.3 | 14.8 | 13.8 |
| U.S.S.R. | 18.1 | 19.1 | 18.9 | 17.4 | 16.4 | 16.1 |
| Japan | 17.0 | 15.9 | 14.9 | 14.2 | 14.4 | 14.4 |
| Eastern Europe | 17.0 | 17.6 | 17.2 | 16.3 | 15.6 | 15.5 |
| Western Europe | 13.8 | 14.3 | 15.1 | 15.5 | 15.4 | 14.7 |

population to make the demographic transition from a crude birth rate of 45 to the replacement level of about 15 per thousand.

## TABLE 2–15

**Census Bureau Annual Decline in Crude Birth Rate**

| Crude Birth Rate (per thousand) | Strength of Family Planning Effort | | | |
|---|---|---|---|---|
| | Strong | Moderate | Weak | None |
| 45 and over | .40 | .333 | .25 | .20 |
| 40–44 | .60 | .50 | .30 | .20 |
| 35–39 | .80 | .667 | .40 | .25 |
| 30–34 | 1.00 | .75 | .50 | .25 |
| 25–29 | 1.00 | .667 | .40 | .25 |
| 20–24 | .80 | .50 | .30 | .20 |
| 15–19 | .60 | .333 | .25 | .20 |
| 13–14 | .40 | .25 | .15 | .15 |
| 40–44 | 8.0 | 10.0 | 17.0 | .25 |
| 35–39 | 6.0 | 8.0 | 12.0 | .25 |
| 30–34 | 5.0 | 7.0 | 10.0 | .20 |
| 25–29 | 5.0 | 8.0 | 12.0 | .20 |
| 20–24 | 6.0 | 10.0 | 17.0 | .25 |
| 15–19 | 8.0 | 15.0 | 20.0 | .25 |
| Time required to decline from CBR = 45 to CBR = 15 | 38.0 | 58.0 | 88.0 | 135 |

The "Strong" column of Table 2–15 shows the annual decline in the crude birth rate that CFSC expects in the presence of a strong, well-financed, well-organized, and well-administered family planning program that reaches the entire population, both urban and rural, in a sustained way. Under these conditions, the CFSC estimated that the annual rates of decline would be two to four times those that would occur in the absence of a program.

This acceleration in the pace of decline, it is estimated, would be capable of bringing about a complete demographic transition from a crude birth rate of 45 to one of 15 within a span of about 38 years, or in about one-fourth the time that would be required in the absence of a family planning program.

The assumptions of Table 2–15 were translated into annual declines in birth rates for individual countries and regions of the world on the following basis:

1. Each country was classified into one of four categories, according to the level of its family

planning program effort: Strong, Moderate, Weak, or None.

2. *The high estimates* in the table assume that each country will maintain its present family planning status and will follow out the schedule of changes in the total fertility rate that would be expected under this set of assumptions.

3. *The medium projections* assume that the schedule of fertility declines shown in the table will occur, but in addition, the respective nations will strengthen their family planning programs as follows:

- Nations that presently have no family planning program will remain in that status for five years (until 1980) and then linearly trend toward a weak program by 1985. They will then trend toward a moderate family planning program by 1990 and a strong family planning program by the year 2000.
- Nations that presently have a weak family planning program will remain in that status until 1980 and then linearly trend toward a moderate program by 1990 and a strong program by the year 2000.
- Nations that presently have a moderate family planning program will remain in that status for five years and then trend toward a strong family planning program by 1990 and remain in that status until the year 2000.
- Nations that presently have strong family planning programs will remain in that status for the entire span of time.

4. *The low projections* assume a much greater family planning effort than for the medium projections. They assume that the respective nations will strengthen their family planning programs as follows:

- Nations that presently have no family planning programs will linearly trend toward a weak program by 1985, a moderate program by 1990, and a strong program by the year 1995.
- Nations that presently have a weak family planning program will trend linearly toward a moderate program by 1985 and toward a strong program by 1995. They will remain in that status until the year 2000.
- Nations that presently have a moderate family planning program will trend linearly toward a strong family planning program by 1980 and will remain in that status until 2000.
- Nations that presently have a strong family planning program will remain in that status for the entire span of time, but the efficacy of the program will improve linearly from its present 38 years for transition time to one-half that amount (to 19 years), equivalent to doubling the coefficients in the table for the strong program.

When carried out mechanically, some of these assumptions, especially the "low" projections, will call for birth rates that are exceedingly low. CFSC assumes that when crude birth rates (CBR) approach the replacement levels—CBR = 14, or TFR (total fertility rate per woman) 2.1—no further fertility decline will be experienced. The birth rates will be allowed to sink to a minimum level, and it is assumed that they will remain at this level for the remainder of the century. These minimum levels are:

For high projections, TFR = 2.0 (CBR about 14)

For medium projections, TFR = 1.9 (CBR about 13.5)

For low projections, TFR = 1.8 (CBR about 13).

Thus, the medium and low projections permit fertility to sink somewhat below replacement levels and remain there indefinitely.

Birth rates in the nations of Western Europe and North America are already below replacement levels, but CFSC anticipates that they will remain in this state for a period of 10 years and will then trend linearly toward replacement by the year 2000; for medium and low projections, the rates trend linearly toward 1900 and 1800 respectively. As these countries reach a stage of absolute zero growth, it is expected that systems of subsidies and other inducements will be launched that will seek to encourage fertility.

*Mortality Assumptions.* Throughout the world there is a slow but nevertheless steady increase in survivorship over mortality. That increase is greatest in LDCs where mortality rates have been high, and least in industrialized countries that have already pushed public health and medical technology almost to the limits of their life saving capability. The United Nations has made detailed and careful studies of trends in mortality decline and projected future declines in mortality, assuming that national and international efforts to provide health and medical care to the population continue. These projected declines have been carefully reviewed by the World Bank. It has been observed that in recent years the declines in mortality have not been as great as those anticipated by the U.N. in certain countries, especially those classified as "underdeveloped." The World Bank, with considerations of each nation's current income status, has therefore rescheduled the expected future mortality (survivorship) rates on a somewhat less optimistic basis. In most cases, these revisions have been reviewed with the U.N., and it is expected that future U.N. assumptions will also reflect the slower progress in mortality reduction encountered in recent years.

For the CFSC projections, the mortality assumptions of the World Bank were accepted without change.

The Community and Family Study Center estimates and projections are presented in Tables 2–16 through 2–20.

## COMMUNITY AND FAMILY STUDY CENTER PROJECTIONS

Community and Family Study Center (CFSC) projections for total population, total fertility rates, population growth rates, crude death rates, and crude birth rates are presented in Tables 2–16 through 2–20. In each table:

*Asia and Oceania* excludes Japan, Australia, and New Zealand.
*Eastern Europe* includes Albania and Yugoslavia.
*Western Europe* comprises all of Europe except Eastern Europe (including the U.S.S.R.), Albania, and Yugoslavia.

### TABLE 2–16

### CFSC Projected Total Population for World, Major Regions, and Selected Countries

(*In thousands*)

| | 1975 | 1980 | 1985 | 1990 | 1995 | 2000 |
|---|---|---|---|---|---|---|
| | | | HIGH SERIES | | | |
| World | 4,014,902 | 4,379,997 | 4,762,226 | 5,151,919 | 5,553,432 | 5,973,719 |
| Major Regions | | | | | | |
| Africa | 402,363 | 465,323 | 536,100 | 616,108 | 707,303 | 811,216 |
| Asia and Oceania | 2,201,322 | 2,417,633 | 2,641,232 | 2,865,626 | 3,092,772 | 3,325,036 |
| Latin America | 312,372 | 356,695 | 405,041 | 456,277 | 509,700 | 564,195 |
| U.S.S.R. and Eastern Europe | 384,408 | 401,934 | 419,237 | 434,386 | 446,964 | 458,467 |
| Northern America, Western Europe, Japan, Australia and New Zealand | 714,437 | 738,412 | 760,616 | 779,522 | 796,693 | 814,805 |
| Selected Countries and Regions | | | | | | |
| People's Republic of China | 896,806 | 952,133 | 1,002,270 | 1,048,207 | 1,092,397 | 1,138,447 |
| India | 607,375 | 675,841 | 747,010 | 821,080 | 895,715 | 967,732 |
| Indonesia | 130,496 | 144,184 | 157,569 | 170,888 | 183,481 | 194,387 |
| Bangladesh | 79,314 | 91,341 | 105,554 | 121,900 | 139,648 | 157,978 |
| Pakistan | 70,267 | 80,164 | 91,763 | 105,030 | 119,525 | 134,561 |
| Philippines | 41,821 | 47,823 | 54,136 | 60,674 | 67,185 | 73,348 |
| Thailand | 41,648 | 46,769 | 51,980 | 57,267 | 62,438 | 67,034 |
| South Korea | 35,274 | 38,129 | 40,990 | 43,790 | 46,393 | 48,748 |
| Egypt | 37,766 | 42,257 | 46,872 | 51,643 | 56,404 | 61,155 |
| Nigeria | 62,921 | 71,991 | 82,697 | 95,220 | 109,838 | 126,850 |
| Brazil | 106,997 | 122,502 | 138,878 | 156,010 | 173,565 | 191,148 |
| Mexico | 59,924 | 70,136 | 81,929 | 95,324 | 109,979 | 125,335 |
| United States | 216,625 | 224,242 | 231,693 | 237,673 | 242,599 | 247,714 |
| U.S.S.R. | 254,394 | 266,698 | 279,145 | 290,209 | 299,209 | 306,962 |
| Japan | 110,955 | 116,990 | 121,333 | 124,309 | 126,981 | 130,266 |
| Eastern Europe | 130,014 | 135,236 | 140,092 | 144,177 | 147,755 | 151,505 |
| Western Europe | 347,439 | 355,461 | 363,684 | 371,601 | 387,669 | 396,307 |
| | | | MEDIUM SERIES[a] | | | |
| World | 4,014,902 | 4,380,258 | 4,759,425 | 5,137,885 | 5,512,997 | 5,883,373 |
| Major Regions | | | | | | |
| Africa | 402,363 | 465,364 | 535,148 | 611,779 | 694,452 | 781,496 |
| Asia and Oceania | 2,201,322 | 2,417,830 | 2,639,989 | 2,858,619 | 3,072,769 | 3,281,203 |
| Latin America | 312,372 | 356,694 | 404,434 | 453,695 | 503,361 | 551,672 |
| U.S.S.R. and Eastern Europe | 384,408 | 401,934 | 419,225 | 434,340 | 446,532 | 456,934 |
| Northern America, Western Europe, Japan, Australia and New Zealand | 714,437 | 738,436 | 760,629 | 779,452 | 795,883 | 812,068 |

See footnotes on next page.

## TABLE 2–16 (Cont.)

*(In thousands)*

| | 1975 | 1980 | 1985 | 1990 | 1995 | 2000 |
|---|---|---|---|---|---|---|
| MEDIUM SERIES (cont.) | | | | | | |
| **Selected Countries and Regions** | | | | | | |
| People's Republic of China | 896,806 | 952,133 | 1,001,232 | 1,043,867 | 1,083,505 | 1,124,943 |
| India | 607,374 | 675,629 | 745,389 | 815,750 | 884,040 | 946,761 |
| Indonesia | 130,496 | 144,184 | 157,569 | 170,888 | 183,481 | 194,387 |
| Bangladesh | 79,314 | 91,305 | 105,308 | 121,156 | 137,909 | 154,442 |
| Pakistan | 70,267 | 80,125 | 91,417 | 103,848 | 116,842 | 129,566 |
| Philippines | 41,821 | 47,823 | 54,136 | 60,674 | 67,185 | 73,348 |
| Thailand | 41,648 | 46,769 | 51,980 | 57,267 | 62,438 | 67,034 |
| South Korea | 35,274 | 38,129 | 40,990 | 43,790 | 46,393 | 48,748 |
| Egypt | 37,766 | 42,257 | 46,809 | 51,344 | 55,669 | 59,698 |
| Nigeria | 62,921 | 71,977 | 82,459 | 94,361 | 107,476 | 121,451 |
| Brazil | 106,997 | 122,502 | 138,644 | 155,004 | 171,070 | 186,255 |
| Mexico | 59,924 | 70,101 | 81,662 | 94,409 | 107,856 | 121,261 |
| United States | 216,625 | 224,242 | 231,693 | 237,673 | 242,371 | 246,844 |
| U.S.S.R. | 254,394 | 266,698 | 279,145 | 290,209 | 298,948 | 305,932 |
| Japan | 110,955 | 116,990 | 121,333 | 124,309 | 126,879 | 129,823 |
| Eastern Europe | 130,014 | 135,236 | 140,080 | 144,131 | 147,584 | 151,004 |
| Western Europe | 347,439 | 355,485 | 363,697 | 371,351 | 378,944 | 386,147 |
| LOW SERIES | | | | | | |
| World | 4,014,902 | 4,378,932 | 4,448,622 | 5,102,327 | 5,437,410 | 5,752,309 |
| **Major Regions** | | | | | | |
| Africa | 402,363 | 465,364 | 534,732 | 610,662 | 689,594 | 770,168 |
| Asia and Oceania | 2,201,322 | 2,417,413 | 2,633,507 | 2,834,121 | 3,020,138 | 8,192,445 |
| Latin America | 312,872 | 356,291 | 402,572 | 448,914 | 493,386 | 533,369 |
| U.S.S.R. and Eastern Europe | 384,408 | 401,704 | 418,151 | 431,793 | 442,211 | 450,845 |
| Northern America, Western Europe, Japan, Australia and New Zealand | 714,437 | 738,160 | 759,660 | 777,437 | 792,081 | 805,482 |
| **Selected Countries and Regions** | | | | | | |
| People's Republic of China | 896,806 | 951,795 | 1,001,038 | 1,045,632 | 1,086,428 | 1,125,249 |
| India | 607,374 | 675,382 | 743,157 | 808,157 | 867,631 | 918,104 |
| Indonesia | 130,496 | 144,228 | 156,848 | 167,452 | 176,344 | 183,839 |
| Bangladesh | 79,314 | 91,289 | 105,109 | 120,368 | 135,716 | 149,478 |
| Pakistan | 70,267 | 80,115 | 91,217 | 103,036 | 114,852 | 125,556 |
| Philippines | 41,821 | 47,780 | 53,768 | 59,410 | 64,623 | 69,350 |
| Thailand | 41,648 | 46,734 | 51,700 | 56,262 | 60,465 | 64,272 |
| South Korea | 35,274 | 38,039 | 40,685 | 43,261 | 45,640 | 47,778 |
| Egypt | 37,766 | 42,235 | 46,641 | 50,809 | 54,540 | 57,735 |
| Nigeria | 62,921 | 71,975 | 82,398 | 94,106 | 106,774 | 119,830 |
| Brazil | 106,997 | 122,457 | 138,212 | 153,458 | 167,673 | 180,224 |
| Mexico | 59,924 | 70,093 | 81,485 | 93,672 | 106,008 | 117,508 |
| United States | 216,625 | 224,242 | 231,693 | 237,673 | 242,155 | 245,997 |
| U.S.S.R. | 254,394 | 266,536 | 278,365 | 288,311 | 295,740 | 301,563 |
| Japan | 110,955 | 116,906 | 121,101 | 123,938 | 126,301 | 128,863 |
| Eastern Europe | 130,014 | 135,168 | 139,786 | 143,482 | 146,471 | 149,282 |
| Western Europe | 347,439 | 355,307 | 363,010 | 370,017 | 376,228 | 381,870 |

* Projected fertility change to 1980 is slower in the medium series than in the high series, and as a result some country projections produce regional totals that are slightly higher than the medium series than in the high series.

## Migration

Both sets of population projections used in the Global 2000 Study assume no influence of migration. Migration, of course, produces no global change in population, but it certainly has regional, national and local implications.

Modern migration has taken on the characteristic of an ebb and flow that results from the technological and economic inequalities that exist between individual settlements. Today, countries are looking at the role migration plays in both urban growth and urban decay since most migration is, in fact, to urban areas. Internationally, individual nation states are beginning to look more seriously at migration flows as they feel the effects of either a rapidly expanding or a stabilizing population, resource scarcity, and economic slow-

## TABLE 2–17

### CFSC Estimated Total Fertility Rate[a] for World, Major Regions, and Selected Countries

|  | 1975 | | | 2000[b] | | |
|---|---|---|---|---|---|---|
|  | High | Medium | Low | High | Medium | Low |
| World | 3777 | 3777 | 3777 | 2241 | 1998 | 1800 |
| **Major Regions** | | | | | | |
| Africa | 5280 | 5280 | 5280 | 3763 | 3535 | 3246 |
| Asia and Oceania | 4201 | 4201 | 4201 | 2000 | 1900 | 1800 |
| Latin America | 4422 | 4422 | 4422 | 2547 | 2194 | 1829 |
| U.S.S.R. and Eastern Europe | 2485 | 2485 | 2485 | 2000 | 1900 | 1800 |
| Northern America, Western Europe, Japan, Australia, New Zealand | 2256 | 2256 | 2256 | 2000 | 1900 | 1800 |
| **Selected Countries** | | | | | | |
| China (PRC) | 3200 | 3200 | 3200 | 2000 | 1900 | 1800 |
| India | 5500 | 5500 | 5500 | 3206 | 2886 | 2471 |
| Indonesia | 5120 | 5120 | 5120 | 2333 | 2333 | 1899 |
| Bangladesh | 6575 | 6575 | 6575 | 4501 | 4085 | 3409 |
| Pakistan | 6265 | 6265 | 6265 | 4170 | 3583 | 3053 |
| Philippines | 5505 | 5505 | 5505 | 2526 | 2526 | 2037 |
| Thailand | 4850 | 4850 | 4850 | 2036 | 2036 | 1800 |
| South Korea | 3580 | 3580 | 3580 | 2000 | 1900 | 1800 |
| Egypt | 5210 | 5210 | 5210 | 2986 | 2596 | 2182 |
| Nigeria | 6699 | 6699 | 6699 | 5761 | 4790 | 4499 |
| Brazil | 5150 | 5150 | 5150 | 2937 | 2536 | 2122 |
| Mexico | 6133 | 6133 | 6133 | 3956 | 3429 | 2898 |
| United States | 1799 | 1799 | 1799 | 2000 | 1900 | 1800 |
| U.S.S.R. | 2417 | 2417 | 2417 | 2029 | 1900 | 1803 |
| Japan | 2159 | 2159 | 2159 | 2000 | 1900 | 1800 |
| Eastern Europe | 2034 | 2034 | 2034 | 2000 | 1900 | 1800 |
| Western Europe | 2205 | 2205 | 2205 | 2000 | 1900 | 1800 |

[a] The total fertility rate in a given year basically represents the average number of children each woman would have over her lifetime, assuming the age-specific fertility rates for that year applied to her lifetime.
[b] Regional estimates for 2000 were not based on aggregated projected fertility rules.

down. The developing countries are looking at how migration might relieve their developmental pressures, while the industrialized countries struggle to determine whether migration will exacerbate or relieve their current economic worries. Essentially, what concern there is for the migration issue is of an economic nature with little attention being given to the demographic, environmental, and resource consequences of continued large-scale migration.

The study of migration is at least as complex as the study of fertility and mortality. The latter are distinct biological processes that are relatively easy to distinguish and record. Migration is a less distinct process that can have several stages. For instance, a person may move first from his rural village to an urban area nearby. Failing to find the personal opportunities he expected, he crosses the border and enters a second country. After remain-ing there for a period of months or years, he may move again, either to a third destination or back to his country of origin.

The measurement of these movements within countries and across national boundaries is decidedly more difficult than the recording of births and deaths and at least as difficult as determining the cause of changes in the rates of fertility and mortality. Countries have become increasingly interested in the collection of immigration statistics as they have sought to control their growth through restrictive immigration policies, but the collection of emigration statistics is still limited in most areas of the world.

The measurement of migration is further complicated by definitional problems. The effect of migration on a sending or receiving country is sure to be different if a migrant is temporary rather than permanent. (The U.N. has defined a

## TABLE 2–18

### CFSC Projected Average Annual Population Growth Rates for World, Major Regions, and Selected Countries (Medium Series)

|  | 1975–79 | 1980–84 | 1985–89 | 1990–94 | 1995–99 |
|---|---|---|---|---|---|
| World | 1.82 | 1.73 | 1.59 | 1.46 | 1.34 |
| **Major Regions** | | | | | |
| Africa | 3.13 | 3.00 | 2.86 | 2.70 | 2.51 |
| Asia and Oceania | 1.97 | 1.84 | 1.66 | 1.50 | 1.36 |
| Latin America | 2.84 | 2.84 | 2.44 | 2.19 | 1.92 |
| U.S.S.R. and Eastern Europe | 0.91 | 0.86 | 0.72 | 0.56 | 0.47 |
| Northern America, Western Europe, Japan, Australia, and New Zealand | 0.67 | 0.60 | 0.49 | 0.42 | 0.41 |
| **Selected Countries and Regions** | | | | | |
| People's Republic of china | 1.24 | 1.07 | 0.85 | 0.74 | 0.74 |
| India | 2.18 | 2.03 | 1.82 | 1.61 | 1.38 |
| Indonesia | 2.05 | 1.83 | 1.59 | 1.35 | 1.10 |
| Bangladesh | 2.87 | 2.92 | 2.84 | 2.61 | 2.28 |
| Pakistan | 2.72 | 2.79 | 2.74 | 2.53 | 2.20 |
| Philippines | 2.75 | 2.55 | 2.31 | 2.04 | 1.77 |
| Thailand | 2.38 | 2.19 | 1.97 | 1.73 | 1.42 |
| South Korea | 1.57 | 1.46 | 1.33 | 1.16 | 1.00 |
| Egypt | 2.31 | 2.11 | 1.87 | 1.61 | 1.40 |
| Nigeria | 2.74 | 2.77 | 2.73 | 2.63 | 2.47 |
| Brazil | 2.78 | 2.56 | 2.26 | 1.98 | 1.72 |
| Mexico | 3.22 | 3.14 | 2.94 | 2.69 | 2.37 |
| United States | 0.69 | 0.65 | 0.51 | 0.39 | 0.36 |
| U.S.S.R. | 0.94 | 0.91 | 0.78 | 0.59 | 0.46 |
| Japan | 1.06 | 0.73 | 0.48 | 0.41 | 0.45 |
| Eastern Europe | 0.80 | 0.72 | 0.58 | 0.48 | 0.46 |
| Western Europe | 0.46 | 0.46 | 0.43 | 0.40 | 0.38 |

temporary or short-term immigrant as a nonresident intending to take up a remunerated occupation for one year or less.)

### Recent Trends

People began migrating from the then developed world to the less developed in massive numbers between 1840 and 1930. In the past 100 years, 25 million persons emigrated from Italy alone, a huge movement when compared with its present day population of 55 million. This trend of migration continued in pulses of varying strength through 1950 with the recipient nations developing and in some cases surpassing the countries of origin in their stage of development.

Since the end of World War II, the flow of migrants from the developed countries of northern Europe has slowed, and the historic pattern of migration from the less to the more developed countries has returned. The poorer countries around the Mediterranean and those of Latin America, Africa, and Asia are now supplying increasing numbers of migrants. Before attempting to predict future migration flows and their impact, a review of migration patterns since 1950 is in order.

*North America and Oceania.* The United States, Canada, Australia, and New Zealand have long been the principal countries of destination for European emigrants. According to the U.N. 1976 "Report on Monitoring Population Trends," the gross intake of immigrants by these four countries during 1950–74 amounted to more than 16 million, with net immigration totaling about 8.3 million in the United States, 2.2 million in Canada, 1.9 million in Australia, and 200,000 in New Zealand. But by the late 1960's Latin America had surpassed Europe as the region supplying the largest numbers of legal immigrants to the United States. In the 1970's, the proportion from Latin America stopped rising and in fact declined slightly. Similar reversals also took place in Canada, Australia, and New Zealand.

*Europe.* While international migration within Europe is not new, it has assumed a larger volume and taken on different patterns since the Second World War, particularly since the early 1960s. The increasing inflows from Turkey and North Africa and a high return rate among European emigrants appear to have led to a net immigration for the continent in the 1970–74 period before immigration

## TABLE 2–19

**CFSC Estimated and Projected Crude Death Rates for World, Major Regions, and Selected Countries**
**(Medium Series)**

|  | Estimated 1975[a] | Projected July 1 to June 30 | | | | |
|---|---|---|---|---|---|---|
|  |  | 1979/80 | 1984/85 | 1989/90 | 1994/95 | 1999/2000 |
| World | 11.2 | 10.56 | 9.71 | 9.06 | 8.61 | 8.25 |
| **Major Regions** |  |  |  |  |  |  |
| Africa | 18.9 | 16.03 | 14.50 | 13.35 | 12.30 | 11.29 |
| Asia and Oceania | 10.0 | 10.91 | 9.95 | 9.26 | 8.81 | 8.42 |
| Latin America | 8.8 | 7.86 | 7.12 | 6.54 | 6.14 | 5.73 |
| U.S.S.R. and Eastern Europe | 9.7 | 9.18 | 9.07 | 9.19 | 9.27 | 9.28 |
| Northern America, Western Europe, Japan, Australia and New Zealand | 9.0 | 9.30 | 9.63 | 9.98 | 10.18 | 10.22 |
| **Selected Countries and Regions** |  |  |  |  |  |  |
| People's Republic of China | 6.0 | 9.45 | 8.98 | 8.69 | 8.57 | 8.46 |
| India | 15.0 | 14.18 | 13.20 | 12.39 | 11.69 | 11.10 |
| Indonesia | 18.0 | 14.27 | 12.93 | 12.04 | 11.27 | 10.65 |
| Bangladesh | 20.0 | 16.90 | 15.34 | 13.84 | 12.12 | 10.73 |
| Pakistan | 15.0 | 14.32 | 13.05 | 11.96 | 10.99 | 9.92 |
| Philippines | 10.0 | 8.72 | 7.72 | 7.05 | 6.49 | 5.90 |
| Thailand | 9.0 | 7.85 | 7.23 | 6.58 | 6.39 | 6.07 |
| South Korea | 7.0 | 7.92 | 7.68 | 7.03 | 6.94 | 6.58 |
| Egypt | 12.0 | 13.02 | 11.45 | 10.56 | 9.39 | 8.69 |
| Nigeria | 23.0 | 20.59 | 18.77 | 17.06 | 15.21 | 13.44 |
| Brazil | 9.0 | 8.30 | 7.36 | 6.63 | 6.07 | 5.62 |
| Mexico | 7.0 | 7.87 | 6.96 | 6.01 | 5.29 | 4.67 |
| United States | 9.0 | 9.39 | 9.29 | 9.37 | 9.43 | 9.55 |
| U.S.S.R. | 9.0 | 8.63 | 8.63 | 8.84 | 9.07 | 9.14 |
| Japan | 6.0 | 7.01 | 7.35 | 7.98 | 8.40 | 9.04 |
| Eastern Europe | 9.7 | 10.03 | 10.09 | 10.45 | 10.73 | 10.72 |
| Western Europe | 9.1 | 10.88 | 10.81 | 10.88 | 10.80 | 10.54 |

[a] These figures were taken from Agency for International Development, *Estimated Population, Crude Birth and Crude Death Rate, and Rate of Natural Increase for Every Country and Region of the World*, 1975; they were not used as base numbers for these projections.

was slowed by the effect of the world energy crisis.

Compared to the rest of Europe, Southern Europe has had, until very recently, relatively high rates of natural population increase, resulting in an excess labor supply, and large numbers of migrants left the region in search of better opportunities. At first, they went mainly to overseas areas, but beginning in the late 1950s they went increasingly to the industrialized countries of Western and Northern Europe.

*Africa.* According to recent estimates of the International Labor Office, about 1.6 million persons from North African countries (mainly Algeria, Morocco and Tunisia) were living in Europe at the beginning of 1975. More than 90 percent of the Algerian migrants had gone to France. Emigration from Egypt, though increasing, has been on a smaller scale, with Australia, Canada, and the United States as the main destinations.

Migration within Africa, which tends to be mostly of an intraregional character, has greater significance than intercontinental migration. The main patterns of this migration were established during the period of colonial rule, and the general tendency of newly independent states, for either economic or political reasons, has been to reduce movements across national boundaries. The largest importer of African labor has been the Republic of South Africa, but this migration is of a temporary nature, most workers being restricted from bringing their families and from staying in South Africa for more than two years.

*Latin America.* The principal countries of immigration in Latin America are Argentina, Uruguay, Venezuela, and Brazil. The flow of immigrants to these countries from other Latin American countries and from Italy, Spain, and Portugal, heavy during the 1950s, was cut by more than half in the 1960s.

Little is known of the migration of Latin Americans to Europe. The statistics of Northern and Western European countries give no indication of significant numbers of migrants from Spanish-speaking Latin American countries. The countries of Southern Europe, which, owing to

## TABLE 2–20

### CFSC Estimated and Projected Crude Birth Rates for World, Major Regions, and Selected Countries (Medium Series)

| | Estimated 1975[a] | Projected July 1 to June 30 | | | | |
|---|---|---|---|---|---|---|
| | | 1979/80 | 1984/85 | 1989/90 | 1994/95 | 1999/2000 |
| World | 26.6 | 24.45 | 22.80 | 20.79 | 19.60 | 17.90 |
| Major Regions | | | | | | |
| Africa | 45.4 | 37.20 | 35.66 | 33.91 | 31.85 | 29.25 |
| Asia and Oceania | 27.0 | 25.09 | 23.07 | 20.53 | 19.24 | 17.29 |
| Latin America | 34.6 | 28.28 | 26.35 | 23.87 | 24.55 | 24.32 |
| U.S.S.R. and Eastern Europe | 18.0 | 17.15 | 15.64 | 13.79 | 13.54 | 13.40 |
| Northern America, Western Europe, Japan, Australia and New Zealand | 14.5 | 15.62 | 15.05 | 14.23 | 13.89 | 13.45 |
| Selected Countries and Regions | | | | | | |
| People's Republic of China | 26.0 | 20.09 | 18.28 | 15.96 | 16.10 | 15.82 |
| India | 35.0 | 34.51 | 32.08 | 29.41 | 26.64 | 23.41 |
| Indonesia | 38.0 | 32.74 | 29.99 | 27.26 | 24.32 | 20.55 |
| Bangladesh | 47.0 | 45.34 | 43.72 | 41.29 | 36.39 | 31.71 |
| Pakistan | 44.0 | 40.92 | 39.08 | 36.80 | 33.16 | 29.05 |
| Philippines | 35.0 | 34.46 | 31.61 | 28.61 | 25.60 | 21.73 |
| Thailand | 31.0 | 29.70 | 27.66 | 24.95 | 22.18 | 18.48 |
| South Korea | 24.0 | 22.56 | 21.66 | 19.09 | 17.63 | 15.75 |
| Egypt | 36.0 | 34.27 | 31.04 | 27.68 | 24.59 | 21.31 |
| Nigeria | 49.0 | 47.75 | 45.73 | 43.88 | 40.41 | 37.14 |
| Brazil | 37.0 | 34.20 | 30.95 | 27.57 | 24.48 | 21.11 |
| Mexico | 38.0 | 38.97 | 36.71 | 34.09 | 30.34 | 26.38 |
| United States | 15.0 | 14.14 | 14.68 | 14.32 | 13.40 | 12.80 |
| U.S.S.R. | 18.0 | 17.01 | 16.10 | 14.42 | 13.69 | 13.23 |
| Japan | 17.0 | 14.83 | 12.98 | 12.40 | 13.00 | 13.57 |
| Eastern Europe | 18.1 | 14.58 | 13.81 | 12.93 | 13.06 | 13.13 |
| Western Europe | 13.7 | 13.64 | 13.45 | 13.02 | 13.23 | 13.03 |

[a] These figures were taken from Agency for International Development, *Estimated Population, Crude Birth and Crude Death Rate, and Rate of Natural Increase for Every Country and Region of the World*, 1975; they were not used as base numbers for these projections.

cultural similarities, might have attracted such migrants, generally publish immigration data only for returning nationals.

Several new or intensified currents of emigration from Latin America since 1950 include a sharply rising trend of emigration from Spanish-speaking areas of the region to the United States, a substantial flow from the former British West Indies to Canada and the United States, as well as to the United Kingdom, and a flow of considerable significance in recent years from Surinam to the Netherlands.

Mexico and Cuba have sent the largest numbers of Latin American migrants to the United States. The estimated number of Cubans in the U.S. in 1974 equaled nearly 6 percent of the Cuban population. Three other Caribbean countries have equally large percentages of their population that have migrated to the U.S.: Jamaica (6 percent) and Trinidad and Tobago (5 percent each).

Migration between Latin American countries has taken on greater importance since 1950 with Argentina and Venezuela being the principal countries of immigration and Paraguay, Chile, Colombia, Bolivia, and El Salvador the principal countries of emigration. In contrast to previous trends, the bulk of the current migration is of an intracontinental nature.

*Asia.* Except in western South Asia, relatively little migration in the economic sense has occurred between Asian countries since 1950. In recent decades the largest international migration movements in Asia have been refugee movements.

One of the major Asian migration movements since 1960 has been the flow of Turkish workers to Western Europe. Workers sent abroad through the Turkish Ministry of Labor totaled 569,200 for 1960–71, and many others emigrated without going through official channels. The Federal Republic of Germany, the main receiving country for Turkish migrants, recorded 429,000 Turkish nationals in their May 1970 population census. Between 1970 and 1974 the number doubled, bringing the number of Turkish immigrants in Germany close to 1 million.

Another major Asian migration flow was the movement of Indians to the United Kingdom from 1950 to 1975, with more than 20,000 Indians

entering the U.K. each year during the 1960s. The
United States replaced the United Kingdom as
the leading country of destination for Indians by
the 1970s. Indian migration to Australia is also on
the rise.

Modern migration flows in western South Asia
are probably best described by the "push" and
"pull" principle which is in operation around the
globe today. Foreign workers have begun to flow
into oil-producing countries in western South Asia
and North Africa to fill the jobs created as a result
of the increased oil revenues of recent years.
Migration in this region has been stimulated by
existing disparities among the Arab States. Those
states that are rich in resources and have been
experiencing rapid economic growth lack qualified
manpower, while other countries in the region
lack resources but, have an abundance of manpower. Migrants to the resource-rich countries
have been mainly, but not exclusively, Arabs;
they have also been workers from more distant
countries such as Pakistan and, to a lesser extent,
India. By early 1976, according to press reports,
an estimated 50,000 Pakistanis were living in the
United Arab Emirates and around 30,000 in Kuwait.

Though it is impossible to predict the size,
composition and destination of future migration
flows it is safe to assume that international flows
will continue to function in response to global
technical and economic inequalities, but acceptance of these influxes will vary according to the
changing needs of the country in question. Already we see many areas of the world where the
size of the migration flow exceeds the perceived
needs and hospitality of the countries of destination. More people wish to enter the United States
than are allowed under current U.S. immigration
law, and migrants are entering outside the legal
immigration process.

Historical immigration flows were not thought
to have much impact on the population of receiving countries, since such countries were experiencing high birthrates, which reduced the contribution immigration made to their annual growth.
The major receiving countries today, however,
have low birthrates, which either stabilize or
reduce the native population. As a consequence,
immigration is accounting for a higher percentage
of their annual growth than ever before—a positive or negative phenomenon, depending on the
population goals of the receiving countries.

Neither internal nor international migration are
expected to have a direct effect on projected
trends in total world population growth. Even if
the fertility and mortality experiences of certain

types of migrants change from previous levels, the
average fertility and mortality experiences for all
migrants must significantly differ from pre-migra-
tion levels in order to have a noticeable affect on
the projections. The following discussion considers whether or not such changes are likely to
occur and the extent to which this may affect
world population growth.

## International Migration

International migration will have a direct effect
on the projected growth of countries and regions
in proportion to the net movement across boundaries. The total effect will be a combination of
these direct effects and the indirect effects of
fertility and mortality experiences within the migrant population.

International migration on a world scale is a
relatively unstudied aspect of population change,
due to the lack of complete and reliable measures
for most countries, particularly the LDCs. Thus,
any set of national and regional population projections on a global scale must either exclude consideration of international migration, as was done in
the Global 2000 Study projections, or selectively
include available data—the approach taken by the
United Nations in its 1977 study *World Population
Prospects as Assessed in 1973* (Population Studies
No. 60). The distribution of the world population
in 1975 is very similar for both the Global 2000
Study medium projections (without migration) and
the U.N. medium variant projection series (with
migration). The change in distribution implied by
each of the two studies for the years 1975 and
2000 is shown in Table 2–21.

*Individual Countries.* The change in the percentage of the world population represented by
any particular country will be somewhat affected
by the net growth in all countries or regions;
however, large changes will reflect differences in
the assumptions of growth within the country. If
the figures in Table 2–21 showing the change in
percent of world population 1975–2000 were
rounded to the nearest whole percent, only two
estimates of change—People's Republic of China
and Bangladesh—would differ between the two
projections. If rounded to the nearest tenth of a
percent, only two estimates of change—People's
Republic of China and India—would differ by
one-half of 1 percent or more. The significance of
this observation is that the largest differences
between the net change of selected countries, as
shown in the table, occur in cases where no
migration was assumed by the United Nations.

TABLE 2-21

**Comparison of Global 2000 Medium Series Projections Without Migration, and U.N. Medium Variant Projections With Migration, 1975 and 2000**

*(Population in millions)*

| Area[a] | 1975 Global 2000 Study Medium Series Population | 1975 Global 2000 Study Medium Series Percent of World Pop. | 1975 U.N. Medium Variant Series Population | 1975 U.N. Medium Variant Series Percent of World Pop. | 2000 Global 2000 Study Medium Series Population | 2000 Global 2000 Study Medium Series Percent of World Pop. | 2000 U.N. Medium Variant Series Population | 2000 U.N. Medium Variant Series Percent of World Pop. | Change in Percent of World Pop. Global 2000 Series | Change in Percent of World Pop. U.N. Medium Variant |
|---|---|---|---|---|---|---|---|---|---|---|
| World | 4,090 | 100.0 | 3,968 | 100.0 | 6,351 | 100.0 | 6,254 | 100.0 | — | — |
| More developed regions [b] | 1,131 | 27.7 | 1,132 | 28.5 | 1,323 | 20.8 | 1,360 | 21.8 | −6.82 | −6.77 |
| Less developed regions [b] | 2,959 | 72.4 | 2,836 | 71.5 | 5,028 | 79.2 | 4,894 | 78.3 | +6.82 | +6.77 |
| **Major Regions** | | | | | | | | | | |
| Africa [b] | 399 | 9.8 | 401 | 10.1 | 814 | 12.8 | 814 | 13.0 | +3.07 | +2.90 |
| Asia and Oceania [b] | 2,274 | 55.6 | 2,150 | 54.2 | 3,630 | 57.2 | 3,513 | 56.2 | +1.55 | +1.99 |
| Latin America [b] | 325 | 7.9 | 324 | 8.2 | 637 | 10.0 | 620 | 9.9 | +2.09 | +1.74 |
| U.S.S.R. and Eastern Europe | 384 | 9.4 | 385 | 9.7 | 460 | 7.3 | 466 | 7.5 | −2.15 | −2.25 |
| Northern America, Western Europe, Japan, Australia, and New Zealand [b] | 708 | 17.3 | 708 | 17.8 | 809 | 12.7 | 842 | 13.5 | −4.57 | −4.38 |
| **Selected Countries and Regions** | 3,282 | 80.2 | 3,176 | 80.1 | 4,867 | 76.6 | 4,761 | 76.1 | −3.61 | −3.93 |
| People's Republic of China | 935 | 22.9 | 839 | 21.1 | 1,329 | 20.9 | 1,148 | 18.4 | −1.93 | −2.79 |
| India | 618 | 15.1 | 613 | 15.5 | 1,021 | 16.1 | 1,059 | 16.9 | +0.95 | +1.49 |
| Indonesia | 135 | 3.3 | 136 | 3.4 | 226 | 3.6 | 238 | 3.8 | +0.26 | +0.37 |
| Bangladesh | 79 | 1.9 | 74 | 1.9 | 159 | 2.5 | 144 | 2.3 | +0.56 | +0.45 |
| Pakistan | 71 | 1.7 | 71 | 1.8 | 149 | 2.4 | 147 | 2.4 | +0.61 | +0.57 |
| Philippines | 43 | 1.1 | 44 | 1.1 | 73 | 1.2 | 90 | 1.4 | +0.10 | +0.31 |
| Thailand | 42 | 1.0 | 42 | 1.1 | 75 | 1.2 | 86 | 1.4 | +0.14 | +0.31 |
| South Korea | 37 | 0.9 | 35 | 0.9 | 57 | 0.9 | 53 | 0.9 | 0.00 | −0.02 |
| Egypt | 37 | 0.9 | 38 | 1.0 | 65 | 1.0 | 65 | 1.0 | +0.13 | +0.08 |
| Nigeria | 63 | 1.5 | 63 | 1.6 | 135 | 2.1 | 135 | 2.2 | +0.58 | +0.57 |
| Brazil | 107 | 2.67 | 110 | 2.8 | 226 | 3.6 | 213 | 3.4 | −0.90 | +0.63 |
| Mexico [b] | 60 | 1.5 | 59 | 1.5 | 131 | 2.1 | 132 | 2.1 | +0.61 | +0.62 |
| United States [b] | 214 | 5.2 | 214 | 5.4 | 248 | 3.9 | 264 | 4.2 | −1.31 | −1.16 |
| U.S.S.R. | 254 | 6.2 | 255 | 6.4 | 309 | 4.9 | 315 | 5.0 | −1.36 | −1.39 |
| Japan | 112 | 2.7 | 111 | 2.8 | 133 | 2.1 | 133 | 2.1 | −0.64 | −0.67 |
| Eastern Europe | 130 | 3.2 | 130 | 3.3 | 152 | 2.4 | 151 | 2.4 | −0.79 | −0.86 |
| Western Europe [b] | 344 | 8.4 | 343 | 8.7 | 378 | 6.0 | 388 | 6.2 | −2.44 | −2.44 |

Note: Figures may not add to totals due to rounding.

[a] "More developed regions" comprise Northern America, temperate South America, Europe, U.S.S.R., Japan, Australia, and New Zealand; all other regions are classified as "less developed." "Asia and Oceania" excludes Japan, Australia, and New Zealand. "Eastern Europe" includes Albania and Yugoslavia. "Western Europe" comprises all of Europe except Eastern Europe (including the U.S.S.R.), Albania, and Yugoslavia.

[b] Migration assumptions were made by the U.N. in regard to these regions and nations only; the others were assumed to have no migration.

Source: U.N. data are from *World Population Prospects as Assessed in 1973* (U.N. Population Studies No. 60), 1977, Table 28.

Thus, it is easy to see that the projected distribution of the world population by country in the year 2000 is likely to be more affected by the assumptions of fertility and mortality than by selectively including assumptions regarding international migration. This does not exclude the importance of projected migration trends for the future of individual countries; rather it illustrates the relative importance of such trends in determining global projections.

When international migration between specific countries is an important concern, such as between the United States and Mexico, a case study approach provides the best opportunity to characterize and assess the situation. This is particularly true when registered data or official estimates on migration are considered to be incomplete. In the case of the United States and Mexico, it is suspected that there are a significant number of illegal migrants in addition to the legal migrants; however, neither the U.S. Bureau of the Census nor the U.S. Immigration and Naturalization Service have enough hard data to officially estimate or project the illegal portion of this migration stream with any statistical accuracy. In addition, the United States does not statistically record emigration to other countries, which increases the subjectivity of performing any analysis of illegal international migration from census data and legal immigration statistics. Such problems are by no means unique to the U.S. data collection system, and the global proliferation of similarly incomplete data on international migration was the major consideration for not including migration assumptions for individual countries in the Global 2000 Study projections. The effect of including estimates of legal migration for the United States and Mexico is summarized in Table 2–22.

*Major Regions.* In table 2–21, it can be seen that international migration assumptions may have a noticeable effect on the projected distribution of the world population by major regions in the year 2000. In particular, the historically large net movement of North Africans to Western Europe and of Latin Americans to North America was taken into account in the U.N. projections and is reflected in the resulting regional population distribution in Table 2–21.

The largest regional difference between the Global 2000 Study and U.N. projections is in the percentage gain for the Asia and Oceania region. This difference is likely the result of differing fertility and mortality assumptions for the People's Republic of China and India, rather than of the few migration assumptions that the U.N. included for this region.

## TABLE 2–22

### Population Projections, Medium Series, for U.S. and Mexico, 1975–2000—No Migration vs. Estimated Net Migration

*(In thousands)*

|  | Global 2000 Study Est. without Migration | Other Estimates with Migration[a] | Percent Change (migration included) |
|---|---|---|---|
| **United States**[b] | | | |
| 1975 | 213,540 | 213,540 | — |
| 1980 | 220,497 | 222,159 | +0.75 |
| 1985 | 228,912 | 232,880 | +1.73 |
| 1990 | 237,028 | 243,513 | +2.74 |
| 1995 | 243,581 | 252,750 | +3.76 |
| 2000 | 248,372 | 260,378 | +4.83 |
| **Mexico**[c] | | | |
| 1975[d] | 59,913 | 59,562 | −0.59 |
| 1980 | 71,136 | 70,314 | −1.16 |
| 1985 | 84,016 | 82,626 | −1.65 |
| 1990 | 98,555 | 96,520 | −2.06 |
| 1995 | 114,450 | 111,706 | −2.40 |
| 2000 | 131,320 | 127,801 | −2.68 |

[a] Projected migration is based on assumed trends in legally registered immigrants and emigrants.
[b] Projections with migration are as reported in U.S. Bureau of the Census, "Projections of the Population of the United States: 1977 to 2050," *Current Population Reports,* Series P–25, No. 704, Washington, 1977, Table 8.
[c] Projections with migration are unpublished U.S. Bureau of the Census estimates.
[d] The 1975 populations differ as the result of assumed migration since the 1970 census. Although it was intended to include migration through 1975 in the base population for the Global 2000 Study projections, this was accidentally overlooked in the case of Mexico.

Examination of the statistics on migration between major regions (see the 1976 U.N. *Report on Monitoring Population Trends*) reveals similar data deficiencies as for individual countries. Furthermore, since regional migration tends to be economically motivated, the problem of projecting future trends in regional migration involves the related questions of trends in economic growth. Table 2–21 again illustrates that the relative difference in the projected distribution of the world population at the regional level is only slightly affected by the exclusion of the U.N. estimates of legal international migration. Illegal immigration, while of potential significance, is by its nature so poorly documented that it cannot be addressed here.

*Summary.* The fertility and mortality assumptions made for individual countries or groups of countries will be the major determinants of projected population levels in the year 2000, excluding extraordinary and unpredictable mass migration movements, such as those that occurred at the time of partition of Bangladesh and Pakistan. Since the net effect of predictable levels of international migration is relatively small, it is reasonable to conclude that any change in the fertility and mortality experience of international migrants will have a negligible effect on projections of global population growth.

**Internal Migration**

Internal migration, by definition, does not have a direct effect on the population size of a particular country at the time it occurs. Certain patterns of population redistribution within a country may, however, have a significant indirect effect on the fertility and mortality experience of the migrants and consequently affect the future level of population growth within that country. Among the patterns of redistribution most studied in this regard is that of urbanization.

"Urbanization" refers to an increase in the proportion of a given population living within and in close proximity to major urban centers. The impact of population redistribution from rural to urban areas has been studied in the context of numerous demographic and socioeconomic variables, but a concise understanding of this process and its importance in future trends of population growth has not yet emerged.

One of the most significant difficulties involved in studying urbanization is that of conceptualizing and measuring the process. Definitions of urban areas, particularly according to criteria other than size of population, are often unavailable in the published results of censuses and surveys and may change from one census or survey to the next in the same country. Even when reasonable data are available, there are many measures of urbanization that can be constructed and analyzed in relation to other demographic or socioeconomic variables.

The unified study and analysis of urbanization on a global scale is further complicated by the many socioeconomic and cultural variations in the urban setting. It is often difficult to justify applying observed relationships between measures of urbanization, fertility, and mortality from one country or region to another, particularly when comparing industrialized countries with less developed countries. There are also serious theoretical difficulties involved in projecting the impact of urbanization on future population growth. It is generally recognized that inverse relationship exists between the level of urbanization and the rate of urban growth, with LDCs currently having lower levels of urbanization and projecting substantial urban growth through the year 2000. It has also been said that the growth in urban population is largely a reflection of growth rates in total population. However, at least two opposing hypotheses can be proposed regarding global projections for population growth.

One is to assume that urbanization advances the level of economic growth and social development, and that progress in this direction will tend to induce a substantial decline in fertility and a noticeable decline in the net rate of natural increase as has been the case in many industrialized countries. The other relies less on the past experience of industrialized countries and views the present trend of rapid urbanization in LDCs as a new and different problem. It is possible to assume that continued LDC urbanization will be due more to a failure to restrain general population growth than to the success of economic development or modernization. From this point of view, one could project urban poverty as a persistent and possibly growing problem, with varying implications on the rate of population growth, depending on the assumed nature of such massive poverty, were it to occur.

Therefore, one of the recognized purposes for constructing alternative projections on future population growth is to account for equally possible, yet virtually unpredictable, variations in population growth without becoming futilely entangled in specific and complex assumptions. The assumption is that a set of complex assumptions would yield a range of future population projections no more useful or accurate than the standard low, medium, and high growth variants employed by the Bureau of the Census and the United Nations. This is likely to be and remain a valid assumption until our understanding of the relationships between demographic change and urbanization, between socioeconomic development and modernization, becomes more precise, and our ability to forecast changes in these related variables improves considerably.

*Summary.* There is little doubt that future levels and trends of internal migration will have a significant impact on the global population perspective in the year 2000, particularly in the less developed regions of the world. The trends in, and the effects of, internal migration are inherently more indicative of significant social and cultural change within a country than are the trends in, and effects of, international migration.

The above discussion has focused on urbanization, since present data indicate a global trend in this direction, but the fact remains that a trend in continued urbanization cannot be assumed with absolute certainty. It is not beyond reason to consider the potential effect of advancements in the science of agriculture and of programs for reform in land tenure. Perhaps the future economic development of less developed countries will result in the ruralization of their populations. For the present, however, it is reasonable to assume that internal migration will not likely affect world population growth beyond the low or high growth rate projections that surround the medium-growth series of the Global 2000 Study projections.

# 3  GNP Projections

All the methodologies used in making resource projections for the Global 2000 Study require projections of real gross national product (GNP) as inputs. It was therefore necessary to develop a set of real GNP projections (or assumptions) in order to provide a common frame of reference for other projections in the Global 2000 Study.*

GNP, however, should not be the starting point for long-term projections. It represents the total goods and services available to a society and is a consequence of all other developments in an economy, not a predetermined input. As an indicator of social and economic progress, it is now widely recognized as seriously inadequate. GNP components that are growing rapidly today in many countries are merely compensation for formerly "free" goods and services, such as pollution control, and for the increased security required by society in such vulnerable sites as airports, large buildings, and nuclear powerplants. Conversely, many economic activities that make significant contributions to social welfare are not included in gross national product. GNP data are particularly misleading in the case of less developed countries (LDCs) because the contributions of the "traditional" sector are not adequately represented.

Ideally, GNP and other indicators of social and economic health should be outputs of the analytical process, but since a properly integrated analytical system was not available, it was necessary in developing the other projections in this volume to use a few common guidelines—such as GNP—to achieve an approximation of consistency.

It must also be pointed out that long-range projections of GNP are extremely difficult to make, due to a lack of knowledge about all the variables involved. Projections for 2000 can differ by a factor of two or more simply as a result of slightly different assumptions about major components such as energy or population. The shorter

the time horizon, the more reliable the projections; projections of GNP (and GDP) are made routinely on a quarterly basis and for periods up to five years. Beyond five years, the few projections that do exist have been developed primarily as extrapolations of short-run projections.

No federal agency makes the GNP projections required for the Global 2000 Study. The Treasury and Commerce Departments and the CIA make short-term projections for selected countries. The Department of State uses data from other agencies but makes no projections itself. Its Agency for International Development (AID) formerly made GNP projections, but budget cuts have forced the Agency to rely for the present entirely on World Bank data for its projections.

The United Nations publishes GNP projections for the entire world, but the projections are often unreliable and based on optimistic hopes of the nations providing the data. However, the *World Bank Atlas: Population, per Capita Product, and Growth Rates*, published by the Bank in 1976, provides a complete and consistent set of GNP figures for the world in 1975, and these figures were used as a starting point for the Global 2000 Study projections. While some concern has arisen regarding the Study's use of 1975 as the base year, since 1975 growth was generally slower than in previous years, the World Bank has taken this characteristic of 1975 into account in its projections. Some development experts even contend that 1975 is closer to what is likely to become a normal year for the world than any other recent year.

A basic tool used by the World Bank for ensuring consistency among its GDP projections is the SIMLINK model, described in Chapter 16 of this volume. Unfortunately, SIMLINK generally projects to 1985 only, rather than to the year 2000. However, the 1977 report of the Workshop on Alternative Energy Strategies (WAES) judgmentally extended the SIMLINK projections to 2000 for all but the Soviet and Chinese block countries.† The World Bank staff recommended that the

---

*GNP is the most widely used economic indicator in the industrialized nations; in the LDCs GDP (gross domestic product) is more commonly used. Since the two indicators are almost identical for most LDCs, they are used interchangeably with regard to LDCs throughout this study.

†The WAES report was published in 1977 by McGraw-Hill as *Energy: Global Prospects 1985-2000*.

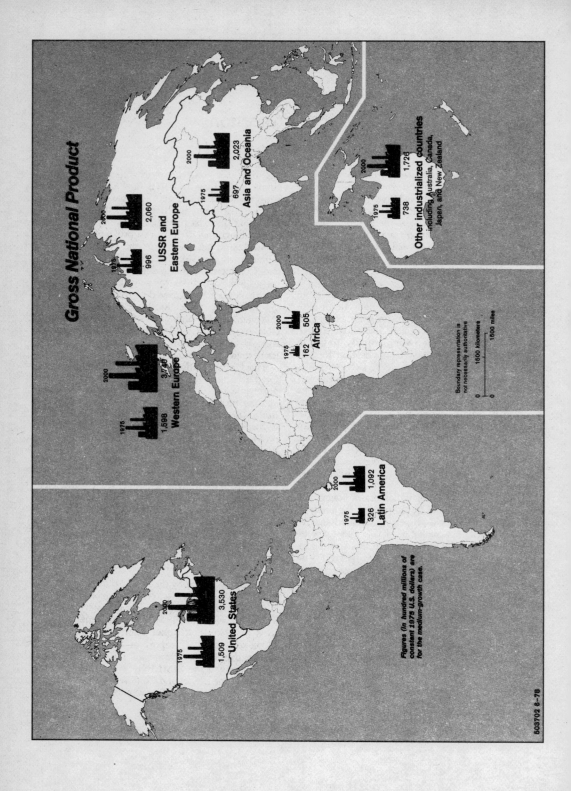

# Gross National Product

USSR and Eastern Europe
2000 2,060
1975 996

Asia and Oceania
2000 2,023
1975 697

Other industrialized countries
including Australia, Canada, Japan, and New Zealand
2000 1,726
1975 738

Western Europe
2000 3,720
1975 1,598

Africa
2000 505
1975 162

United States
2000 3,530
1975 1,509

Latin America
2000 1,092
1975 326

Boundary representation is not necessarily authoritative

0    1500 kilometers
0    1500 miles

Figures (in hundred millions of constant 1975 U.S. dollars) are for the medium-growth case.

503702 8-78

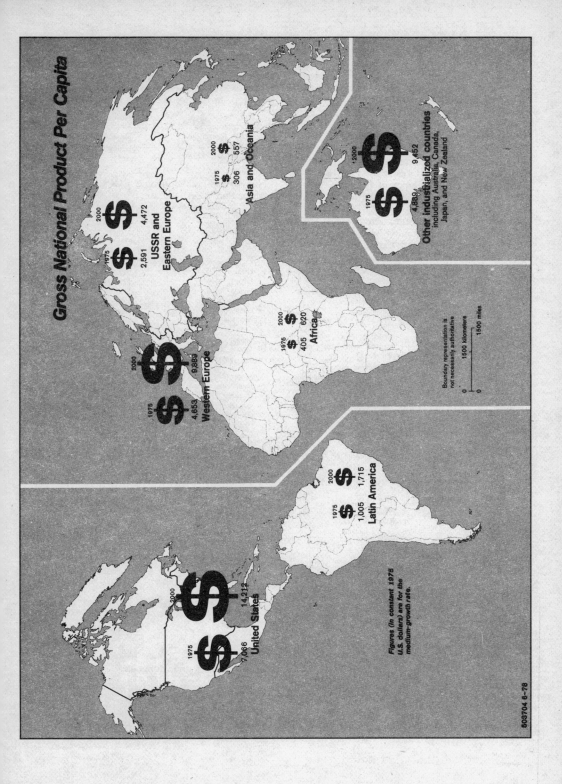

# Gross National Product Per Capita

**USSR and Eastern Europe**
1975 2,591
2000 4,472

**Asia and Oceania**
1975 306
2000 557

**Other industrialized countries** including Australia, Canada, Japan, and New Zealand
1975 4,889
2000 9,452

**Western Europe**
1975 4,653
2000 9,889

**Africa**
1975 405
2000 620

**United States**
1975 7,066
2000 14,212

**Latin America**
1975 1,005
2000 1,715

Boundary representation is not necessarily authoritative

0          1500 kilometers
0          1500 miles

*Figures (in constant 1975 U.S. dollars) are for the medium-growth rate.*

509704 6-78

WAES growth rates be used in the Global 2000
Study and this, in fact, was done.* Projected
growth rates for the Soviet and Chinese bloc countries were obtained from the CIA.

GNP figures for the industrialized nations in the
WAES report have not been derived from SIM-
LINK. Instead, they have been derived by WAES
from analyses of individual countries. In general,
they are lower than unrealistic expectations of
member nations of the Organization for Economic
Cooperation and Development (OECD), making
them more nearly consistent with the WAES
energy projections.†

Seven growth rate assumptions were made on
the basis of the information obtained from the
World Bank, WAES, and the CIA. The growth
rates are presented in Table 3–1. The countries to
which each assumption applies is as follows.

*Assumption A* applies to the OPEC countries:

| | |
|---|---|
| Algeria | Libya |
| Ecuador | Nigeria |
| Gabon | Qatar |
| Indonesia | Saudi Arabia |
| Iran | United Arab Emirates |
| Iraq | Venezuela |
| Kuwait | |

*Assumption B* applies to the non-OPEC lower-
income LDCs (annual per capita income in 1975
under $200, as denominated in 1972 U.S. dollars).
In South Asia these countries are:

| | |
|---|---|
| Afghanistan | Nepal |
| Bangladesh | Pakistan |
| Burma | Sri Lanka |
| India | |

In sub-Saharan Africa the non-OPEC lower-income LDCs are:

| | |
|---|---|
| Burundi | Niger |
| Central African | Rwanda |
| Republic | Sierra Leone |
| Chad | Somalia |
| Dahomey | Sudan |
| Ethiopia | Tanzania |
| Guinea | Togo |
| Kenya | Uganda |
| Madagascar | Upper Volta |
| Malawi | Zaire |
| Mali | |

---

*The World Bank model is officially described in "The
SIMLINK Model of Trade and Growth for the Developing
World," International Bank for Reconstruction and Devel-
opment Working Paper No. 220, Oct. 1975.

†OECD has a large "Interfutures" study in progress, in
which GNP projections are being made. Draft projections
were considered for use in the Global 2000 Study, but the
Interfutures GNP projections seemed high, and documentation at this stage was inadequate to determine how the
projections had been made.

*Assumption C* applies to the non-OPEC middle-
income LDCs (with annual per capita incomes in
1975 of $200 or over, as denominated in 1972 U.S.
dollars). In East Asia these countries are:

| | |
|---|---|
| Fiji | Philippines |
| Hong Kong | Singapore |
| South Korea | Taiwan |
| Malaysia | Thailand |
| Papua New Guinea | |

Non-OPEC middle-income LDCs in sub-Saharan
Africa and West Asia are:

| | |
|---|---|
| Angola | Mauritania |
| Bahrein | Morocco |
| Cameroon | Mozambique |
| Congo P.R. | Oman |
| Cyprus | Rhodesia |
| Egypt | Senegal |
| Ghana | Syria |
| Israel | Tunisia |
| Ivory Coast | Turkey |
| Jordan | Yemen AR,DM |
| Lebanon | Zambia |
| Liberia | |

In the Caribbean and Central and South America
the non-OPEC middle-income LDCs are:

| | |
|---|---|
| Argentina | Haiti |
| Barbados | Honduras |
| Bolivia | Jamaica |
| Brazil | Mexico |
| Chile | Nicaragua |
| Colombia | Panama |
| Costa Rica | Paraguay |
| Dominican Republic | Peru |
| El Salvador | Trinidad and Tobago |
| Guatemala | Uruguay |
| Guyana | |

*Assumption D* applies to the following industrialized nations:

| | |
|---|---|
| Australia | Japan |
| Austria | Luxembourg |
| Belgium | Netherlands |
| Canada | Norway |
| Denmark | Portugal |
| Finland | Spain |
| France | Sweden |
| Federal Republic of Germany | Switzerland |
| Iceland | United Kingdom |
| Ireland | United States |
| Italy | New Zealand |

*Assumption E* applies to most Eastern European countries and Mongolia:

| | |
|---|---|
| Poland | Czechoslovakia |
| Yugoslavia | Hungary |
| Romania | Bulgaria |
| German Democratic | Albania |
| Republic | Mongolia |

*Assumption F* applies to the U.S.S.R. only.

*Assumption G* applies to the centrally planned economies of Asia:

People's Republic of China    North Korea
Socialist Republic of         Lao People's Democratic
  Vietnam                       Republic
Cambodia

The actual GNP projections are given in Tables 3–2 and 3–3 and summarized in the maps on the following two pages. Table 3–2 presents the projections for each country for the years 1985 and 2000. Table 3–3 provides similar data by regional aggregations for (1) more developed regions and less developed regions, (2) major regions of the world, and (3) 17 selected countries and regions. The first map presents total GNP in 1975 and 2000, the second per capita GNP. All the projections are in constant 1975 U.S. dollars.

The per capita GNP projections were developed for the Global 2000 Study by attributing aggregate GNP growth rates to individual countries and regions and dividing these figures by the Study's population projections for the same countries and regions. This procedure clearly does not take into account country-specific charcteristics, which would cause GNP projections for individual countries to vary from aggregate projections. A consistent set of country-specific GNP projections was not available for the study.

The GNP projections were aggregated (Table 3–3) so as to be comparable with the Study's population projections (Table 3–4). The resulting per capita GNP projections are presented in Table 3–5. Because these calculations were not based on country-specific GNP projections, they should be considered as only roughly suggestive of trends applicable to types of countries rather than specific countries.

Some confusion resulted from this process because the base year (1975) figures used by the CIA and the World Bank are derived using different conversion methodologies. The net result is that the low-growth rate of 2.5 percent for China and the 1975 GNP figure for the U.S.S.R. are regarded by the CIA as too low. It should be noted, however, that the World Bank model used to develop the GNP projections for the LDCs assumed a 6 percent growth rate for the socialist bloc for all growth cases, which significantly exceeds current CIA estimates.

## TABLE 3–1

### Annual Growth Rates, Assumptions A to G

*(Percent)*

| Assumption | Applies to | 1960–72 | 1972–76 | 1976–85 High | 1976–85 Low | 1985–2000 High | 1985–2000 Low |
|---|---|---|---|---|---|---|---|
| A | OPEC countries | 7.2 | 12.5 | 7.2 | 5.5 | 6.5 | 4.3 |
| B | Non-OPEC lower-income LDCs | 3.7 | 2.3 | 4.4 | 2.8 | 3.1 | 2.5 |
| C | Non-OPEC middle-income LDCs | 6.2 | 5.9 | 6.6 | 4.4 | 4.9 | 3.9 |
| D | Industrialized countries (OECD) | 4.9 | 2.0 | 4.9 | 3.1 | 3.7 | 2.5 |
| E | Soviet bloc (except U.S.S.R.) | | | 3.5 | 3 | 3 | 2.5 |
| F | U.S.S.R. | | | 3.5 | 3 | 3 | 2.5 |
| G | China, etc.[a] | | | | | 5.0 | 2.5[b] |

[a] Includes the People's Republic of China, the Socialist Republic of Vietnam, the Democratic People's Republic of Korea, Cambodia, and the Lao People's Democratic Republic.
[b] Growth rates for 1975–2000.

## TABLE 3-2

### GNP Estimates (1975) and Projections and Growth Rates (1985, 2000) by Country[a]

*(Millions of constant 1975 dollars)*

| | Growth Rate Assumption | 1975 GNP | 1975–85 Growth Rate (percent) | | | 1985 Projections | | | 1985–2000 Growth Rate (percent) | | | 2000 Projections | | |
|---|---|---|---|---|---|---|---|---|---|---|---|---|---|---|
| | | | High | Med. | Low | High | Med. | Low | High | Med. | Low | High | Med. | Low |
| **ASIA** | | | | | | | | | | | | | | |
| People's Republic of China | G | 285,960 | 5.0 | 3.75 | 2.5 | 465,799 | 413,225 | 366,053 | 5.0 | 3.75 | 2.5 | 968,362 | 717,808 | 530,154 |
| India | B | 91,810 | 4.4 | 3.60 | 2.8 | 141,220 | 130,764 | 121,010 | 3.1 | 2.8 | 2.5 | 223,242 | 197,872 | 175,259 |
| Japan | D | 495,180 | 4.9 | 4.0 | 3.1 | 798,947 | 732,987 | 671,970 | 3.7 | 3.1 | 2.5 | 1,377,842 | 1,158,714 | 973,213 |
| Bangladesh | B | 8,820 | 4.4 | 3.6 | 2.8 | 13,567 | 12,562 | 11,625 | 3.1 | 2.8 | 2.5 | 21,447 | 19,009 | 16,836 |
| Pakistan | B | 9,830 | 4.4 | 3.6 | 2.8 | 15,120 | 14,001 | 12,956 | 3.1 | 2.8 | 2.5 | 23,902 | 21,186 | 18,764 |
| Socialist Republic of Viet Nam | G | 7,100 | 5.0 | 3.75 | 2.5 | 11,565 | 10,260 | 9,089 | 5.0 | 3.75 | 2.5 | 24,043 | 17,823 | 13,164 |
| Philippines | C | 15,730 | 6.6 | 5.55 | 4.5 | 29,806 | 26,997 | 24,428 | 4.9 | 4.4 | 3.9 | 61,085 | 51,502 | 43,363 |
| Thailand | C | 14,540 | 6.6 | 5.55 | 4.5 | 27,551 | 24,954 | 22,580 | 4.9 | 4.4 | 3.9 | 56,464 | 47,604 | 40,083 |
| Republic of Korea | C | 18,650 | 6.6 | 5.55 | 4.5 | 35,339 | 32,008 | 28,963 | 4.9 | 4.4 | 3.9 | 72,425 | 61,061 | 51,413 |
| Iran | A | 48,820 | 7.2 | 6.35 | 5.5 | 97,847 | 90,359 | 83,392 | 6.5 | 5.4 | 4.3 | 251,647 | 198,875 | 156,816 |
| Burma | B | 3,270 | 4.4 | 3.6 | 2.8 | 5,030 | 4,657 | 4,310 | 3.1 | 2.8 | 2.5 | 7,951 | 7,047 | 6,242 |
| Afghanistan | B | 2,160 | 4.4 | 3.6 | 2.8 | 3,322 | 3,076 | 2,847 | 3.1 | 2.8 | 2.5 | 5,251 | 4,655 | 4,123 |
| Republic of China | C | 14,210 | 6.6 | 5.55 | 4.5 | 26,926 | 24,388 | 22,068 | 4.9 | 4.4 | 3.9 | 55,183 | 46,525 | 39,174 |
| Democratic People's Republic of Korea | G | 6,790 | 5.0 | 3.75 | 2.5 | 11,060 | 9,812 | 8,692 | 5.0 | 3.75 | 2.5 | 22,993 | 17,044 | 12,589 |
| Sri Lanka | B | 1,980 | 4.4 | 3.6 | 2.8 | 3,046 | 2,820 | 2,610 | 3.1 | 2.8 | 2.5 | 4,815 | 4,267 | 3,780 |
| Nepal | B | 1,390 | 4.4 | 3.6 | 2.8 | 2,138 | 1,980 | 1,832 | 3.1 | 2.8 | 2.5 | 3,380 | 2,996 | 2,653 |
| Malaysia | C | 8,690 | 6.6 | 5.55 | 4.5 | 16,466 | 14,914 | 13,495 | 4.9 | 4.4 | 3.9 | 33,746 | 28,451 | 23,956 |
| Iraq | A | 14,260 | 7.2 | 6.35 | 5.5 | 28,580 | 26,393 | 24,358 | 6.5 | 5.4 | 4.3 | 73,503 | 58,090 | 45,804 |
| Saudi Arabia | A | 24,960 | 7.2 | 6.35 | 5.5 | 50,026 | 46,198 | 42,635 | 6.5 | 5.4 | 4.3 | 128,659 | 101,679 | 80,174 |
| Cambodia | G | n.a. | 5.0 | 3.75 | 2.5 | — | — | — | 5.0 | 3.75 | 2.5 | — | — | — |
| Syrian Arab Republic | C | 4,870 | 6.6 | 5.55 | 4.5 | 9,228 | 8,358 | 7,563 | 4.9 | 4.4 | 3.9 | 18,912 | 15,944 | 13,425 |
| Yemen Arab Republic | C | 1,380 | 6.6 | 5.55 | 4.5 | 2,615 | 2,368 | 2,143 | 4.9 | 4.4 | 3.9 | 5,359 | 4,517 | 3,804 |
| Hong Kong | C | 7,520 | 6.6 | 5.55 | 4.5 | 14,249 | 12,906 | 11,678 | 4.9 | 4.4 | 3.9 | 29,202 | 24,621 | 20,730 |
| Israel | C | 12,400 | 6.6 | 5.55 | 4.5 | 23,496 | 21,282 | 19,257 | 4.9 | 4.4 | 3.9 | 48,153 | 40,599 | 34,184 |
| Lao People's Democratic Republic | G | n.a. | 5.0 | 3.75 | 2.5 | — | — | — | 5.0 | 3.75 | 2.5 | — | — | — |
| Lebanon | C | n.a. | 6.6 | 5.55 | 4.5 | — | — | — | 4.9 | 4.4 | 3.9 | — | — | — |
| Jordan | C | 1,240 | 6.6 | 5.55 | 4.5 | 2,350 | 2,128 | 1,926 | 4.9 | 4.4 | 3.9 | 4,816 | 4,060 | 3,419 |
| Singapore | C | 5,640 | 6.6 | 5.55 | 4.5 | 10,687 | 9,680 | 8,759 | 4.9 | 4.4 | 3.9 | 21,902 | 18,466 | 15,548 |
| People's Democratic Republic of Yemen | C | 410 | 6.6 | 5.55 | 4.5 | 777 | 704 | 637 | 4.9 | 4.4 | 3.9 | 1,592 | 1,343 | 1,131 |
| Mongolia | E | 1,000 | 3.5 | 3.25 | 3.0 | 1,411 | 1,377 | 1,344 | 3.0 | 2.75 | 2.5 | 2,198 | 2,069 | 1,947 |
| Bhutan | B | 90 | 4.4 | 3.6 | 2.8 | 138 | 128 | 119 | 3.1 | 2.8 | 2.5 | 218 | 194 | 172 |
| Kuwait | A | 11,280 | 7.2 | 6.35 | 5.5 | 22,608 | 20,878 | 19,268 | 6.5 | 5.4 | 4.3 | 58,144 | 45,951 | 36,233 |
| Oman | C | 1,600 | 6.6 | 5.55 | 4.5 | 3,032 | 2,746 | 2,485 | 4.9 | 4.4 | 3.9 | 6,214 | 5,239 | 4,411 |
| United Arab Emirates | A | 6,870 | 7.2 | 6.35 | 5.5 | 13,769 | 12,715 | 11,735 | 6.5 | 5.4 | 4.3 | 35,412 | 27,985 | 22,067 |
| Bahrain | C | 630 | 6.6 | 5.55 | 4.5 | 1,194 | 1,081 | 978 | 4.9 | 4.4 | 3.9 | 2,447 | 2,062 | 1,736 |

| | A[*] | 1,680 | 7.2 | 6.35 | 5.5 | 3,367 | 3,109 | 2,870 | 6.5 | 5.4 | 4.3 | 8,659 | 6,843 | 5,397 |
|---|---|---|---|---|---|---|---|---|---|---|---|---|---|---|
| Qatar | A | 1,680 | 7.2 | 6.35 | 5.5 | 3,367 | 3,109 | 2,870 | 6.5 | 5.4 | 4.3 | 8,659 | 6,843 | 5,397 |
| **AFRICA** | | | | | | | | | | | | | | |
| Nigeria | A | 23,080 | 7.2 | 6.35 | 5.5 | 46,258 | 42,718 | 39,424 | 6.5 | 5.4 | 4.3 | 118,968 | 94,020 | 74,135 |
| Arab Republic of Egypt | C | 11,550 | 6.6 | 5.55 | 4.5 | 21,885 | 19,823 | 17,937 | 4.9 | 4.4 | 3.9 | 44,852 | 37,816 | 31,841 |
| Ethiopia | B | 2,860 | 4.4 | 3.6 | 2.8 | 4,399 | 4,073 | 3,770 | 3.1 | 2.8 | 2.5 | 6,954 | 6,163 | 5,460 |
| South Africa | D | 33,540 | 4.9 | 4.0 | 3.1 | 54,115 | 49,647 | 45,514 | 3.7 | 3.1 | 2.5 | 93,325 | 78,483 | 65,918 |
| Zaire | B | 3,740 | 4.4 | 3.6 | 2.8 | 5,753 | 5,327 | 4,930 | 3.1 | 2.8 | 2.5 | 9,094 | 8,061 | 7,140 |
| Morocco | C | 7,890 | 6.6 | 5.55 | 4.5 | 14,950 | 13,541 | 12,253 | 4.9 | 4.4 | 3.9 | 30,639 | 25,832 | 21,751 |
| Sudan | B | 4,510 | 4.4 | 3.6 | 2.8 | 6,937 | 6,424 | 5,944 | 3.1 | 2.8 | 2.5 | 10,966 | 9,721 | 8,609 |
| Algeria | A | 12,290 | 7.2 | 6.35 | 5.5 | 24,632 | 22,747 | 20,993 | 6.5 | 5.4 | 4.3 | 63,350 | 50,065 | 39,477 |
| Tanzania | B | 2,560 | 4.4 | 3.6 | 2.8 | 3,938 | 3,646 | 3,374 | 3.1 | 2.8 | 2.5 | 6,225 | 5,517 | 4,887 |
| Kenya | B | 2,900 | 4.4 | 3.6 | 2.8 | 4,461 | 4,130 | 3,822 | 3.1 | 2.8 | 2.5 | 7,052 | 6,250 | 5,535 |
| Uganda | B | 2,880 | 4.4 | 3.6 | 2.8 | 4,430 | 4,102 | 3,796 | 3.1 | 2.8 | 2.5 | 7,003 | 6,207 | 5,498 |
| Ghana | C | 4,580 | 6.6 | 5.55 | 4.5 | 8,678 | 7,860 | 7,113 | 4.9 | 4.4 | 3.9 | 17,785 | 14,994 | 12,627 |
| Mozambique | C | 2,850 | 6.6 | 5.55 | 4.5 | 5,400 | 4,891 | 4,426 | 4.9 | 4.4 | 3.9 | 11,067 | 9,331 | 7,857 |
| Madagascar | B | 1,730 | 4.4 | 3.6 | 2.8 | 2,661 | 2,464 | 2,280 | 3.1 | 2.8 | 2.5 | 4,207 | 3,729 | 3,302 |
| Cameroon | C | 1,940 | 6.6 | 5.55 | 4.5 | 3,676 | 3,330 | 3,013 | 4.9 | 4.4 | 3.9 | 7,534 | 6,353 | 5,349 |
| Ivory Coast | C | 3,350 | 6.6 | 5.55 | 4.5 | 6,348 | 5,749 | 5,202 | 4.9 | 4.4 | 3.9 | 13,010 | 10,967 | 9,234 |
| Rhodesia | C | 3,430 | 6.6 | 5.55 | 4.5 | 6,499 | 5,887 | 5,327 | 4.9 | 4.4 | 3.9 | 13,319 | 11,231 | 9,456 |
| Angola | C | 3,710 | 6.6 | 5.55 | 4.5 | 7,030 | 6,367 | 5,762 | 4.9 | 4.4 | 3.9 | 14,407 | 12,146 | 10,228 |
| Upper Volta | B | 560 | 4.4 | 3.6 | 2.8 | 861 | 798 | 738 | 3.1 | 2.8 | 2.5 | 1,361 | 1,208 | 1,070 |
| Mali | B | 540 | 4.4 | 3.6 | 2.8 | 831 | 769 | 712 | 3.1 | 2.8 | 2.5 | 1,314 | 1,164 | 1,031 |
| Tunisia | C | 4,230 | 6.6 | 5.55 | 4.5 | 8,015 | 7,260 | 6,569 | 4.9 | 4.4 | 3.9 | 16,426 | 13,850 | 11,661 |
| Guinea | B | 710 | 4.4 | 3.6 | 2.8 | 1,092 | 1,011 | 936 | 3.1 | 2.8 | 2.5 | 1,726 | 1,530 | 1,356 |
| Malawi | B | 760 | 4.4 | 3.6 | 2.8 | 1,169 | 1,082 | 1,002 | 3.1 | 2.8 | 2.5 | 1,848 | 1,637 | 1,451 |
| Senegal | C | 1,850 | 6.6 | 5.55 | 4.5 | 3,505 | 3,175 | 2,873 | 4.9 | 4.4 | 3.9 | 7,183 | 6,057 | 5,100 |
| Zambia | C | 2,650 | 6.6 | 5.55 | 4.5 | 5,021 | 4,548 | 4,115 | 4.9 | 4.4 | 3.9 | 10,290 | 8,676 | 7,305 |
| Niger | B | 600 | 4.4 | 3.6 | 2.8 | 923 | 855 | 791 | 3.1 | 2.8 | 2.5 | 1,459 | 1,294 | 1,146 |
| Rwanda | B | 360 | 4.4 | 3.6 | 2.8 | 554 | 513 | 475 | 3.1 | 2.8 | 2.5 | 876 | 776 | 688 |
| Chad | B | 490 | 4.4 | 3.6 | 2.8 | 754 | 698 | 646 | 3.1 | 2.8 | 2.5 | 1,192 | 1,056 | 936 |
| Burundi | B | 370 | 4.4 | 3.6 | 2.8 | 569 | 527 | 488 | 3.1 | 2.8 | 2.5 | 899 | 797 | 707 |
| Somalia | B | 320 | 4.4 | 3.6 | 2.8 | 492 | 456 | 422 | 3.1 | 2.8 | 2.5 | 778 | 690 | 611 |
| People's Republic of Benin | B | 420 | 4.4 | 3.6 | 2.8 | 646 | 598 | 554 | 3.1 | 2.8 | 2.5 | 1,021 | 905 | 802 |
| Sierra Leone | B | 590 | 4.4 | 3.6 | 2.8 | 908 | 840 | 778 | 3.1 | 2.8 | 2.5 | 1,435 | 1,271 | 1,127 |
| Libyan Arab Republic | A | 12,000 | 7.2 | 6.35 | 5.5 | 24,852 | 22,951 | 21,181 | 6.5 | 5.4 | 4.3 | 63,915 | 50,514 | 39,830 |
| Togo | B | 590 | 4.4 | 3.6 | 2.8 | 908 | 840 | 778 | 3.1 | 2.8 | 2.5 | 1,435 | 1,271 | 1,127 |
| Central African Empire | B | 410 | 4.4 | 3.6 | 2.8 | 631 | 584 | 540 | 3.1 | 2.8 | 2.5 | 997 | 884 | 782 |
| Liberia | C | 630 | 6.6 | 5.55 | 4.5 | 1,194 | 1,081 | 978 | 4.9 | 4.4 | 3.9 | 2,447 | 2,062 | 1,736 |
| People's Republic of the Congo | C | 660 | 6.6 | 5.55 | 4.5 | 1,251 | 1,133 | 1,025 | 4.9 | 4.4 | 3.9 | 2,564 | 2,161 | 1,820 |
| Mauritania | C | 410 | 6.6 | 5.55 | 4.5 | 777 | 704 | 637 | 4.9 | 4.4 | 3.9 | 1,592 | 1,343 | 1,131 |
| Lesotho | B | 210 | 4.4 | 3.6 | 2.8 | 323 | 299 | 277 | 3.1 | 2.8 | 2.5 | 511 | 452 | 401 |
| Mauritius | C | 510 | 6.6 | 5.55 | 4.5 | 966 | 875 | 792 | 4.9 | 4.4 | 3.9 | 1,980 | 1,669 | 1,406 |
| Botswana | C | 220 | 6.6 | 5.55 | 4.5 | 417 | 378 | 342 | 4.9 | 4.4 | 3.9 | 855 | 721 | 607 |
| Gabon | A | 1,200 | 7.2 | 6.35 | 5.5 | 2,405 | 2,221 | 2,050 | 6.5 | 5.4 | 4.3 | 6,185 | 4,888 | 3,855 |

*In most cases, gross national income growth rates were projected for groups of countries rather than for individual countries. Thus, the rates which are attributed to individual LDCs in this table are the growth rates applicable to the group with which that country was aggregated for making projections and do not take into account country-specific characteristics.

## TABLE 3–2 (cont.)

| | Growth Rate Assumption | 1975 GNP | 1975–85 Growth Rate (percent) High | Med. | Low | 1985 Projections High | Med. | Low | 1985–2000 Growth Rate (percent) High | Med. | Low | 2000 Projections High | Med. | Low |
|---|---|---|---|---|---|---|---|---|---|---|---|---|---|---|
| The Gambia | B | 100 | 4.4 | 3.6 | 2.8 | 154 | 142 | 132 | 3.1 | 2.8 | 2.5 | 243 | 215 | 191 |
| Swaziland | C | 230 | 6.6 | 5.55 | 4.5 | 436 | 395 | 357 | 4.9 | 4.4 | 3.9 | 894 | 754 | 634 |
| Equatorial Guinea | C | 100 | 6.6 | 5.55 | 4.5 | 189 | 172 | 155 | 4.9 | 4.4 | 3.9 | 387 | 328 | 275 |
| Comoros | B | 70 | 4.4 | 3.6 | 2.8 | 108 | 100 | 92 | 3.1 | 2.8 | 2.5 | 171 | 151 | 133 |
| **EUROPE** | | | | | | | | | | | | | | |
| U.S.S.R. | F | 665,910 | 3.5 | 3.25 | 3.0 | 939,332 | 916,888 | 894,927 | 3.0 | 2.75 | 2.5 | 1,463,449 | 1,377,348 | 1,296,121 |
| Federal Republic of Germany | D | 408,750 | 4.9 | 4.0 | 3.1 | 659,497 | 605,050 | 554,682 | 3.0 | 3.1 | 2.5 | 1,137,350 | 956,470 | 803,345 |
| United Kingdom | D | 214,940 | 4.9 | 4.0 | 3.1 | 346,794 | 318,164 | 291,678 | 3.7 | 3.1 | 2.5 | 598,071 | 502,957 | 422,437 |
| Italy | D | 154,110 | 4.9 | 4.0 | 3.1 | 248,648 | 228,120 | 209,131 | 3.7 | 3.1 | 2.5 | 428,811 | 360,615 | 302,884 |
| France | D | 304,600 | 4.9 | 4.0 | 3.1 | 491,456 | 450,882 | 413,349 | 3.7 | 3.1 | 2.5 | 847,551 | 712,759 | 598,653 |
| Turkey | C | 34,590 | 6.6 | 5.55 | 4.5 | 65,542 | 59,365 | 53,717 | 4.9 | 4.4 | 3.9 | 134,324 | 113,250 | 95,355 |
| Spain | D | 95,630 | 4.9 | 4.0 | 3.1 | 154,294 | 141,556 | 129,772 | 3.0 | 3.1 | 2.5 | 266,090 | 223,773 | 187,949 |
| Poland | E | 98,970 | 3.5 | 3.25 | 3.0 | 139,607 | 136,271 | 133,007 | 3.0 | 2.75 | 2.5 | 217,503 | 204,706 | 192,634 |
| Yugoslavia | E | 31,640 | 3.5 | 3.25 | 3.0 | 44,631 | 43,565 | 42,522 | 3.0 | 2.75 | 2.5 | 69,534 | 65,443 | 61,585 |
| Romania | E | 27,650 | 3.5 | 3.25 | 3.0 | 39,003 | 38,071 | 37,159 | 3.0 | 2.75 | 2.5 | 60,765 | 57,190 | 53,817 |
| German Democratic Republic | E | 71,250 | 3.5 | 3.25 | 3.0 | 100,505 | 98,104 | 95,754 | 3.0 | 2.75 | 2.5 | 156,584 | 147,372 | 138,680 |
| Czechoslovakia | E | 55,040 | 3.5 | 3.25 | 3.0 | 77,639 | 75,784 | 73,969 | 3.0 | 2.75 | 2.5 | 120,959 | 113,843 | 107,129 |
| The Netherlands | D | 76,340 | 4.9 | 4.0 | 3.1 | 123,171 | 113,002 | 103,595 | 3.7 | 3.1 | 2.5 | 212,417 | 178,635 | 150,036 |
| Hungary | E | 26,070 | 3.5 | 3.25 | 3.0 | 36,774 | 35,896 | 35,036 | 3.0 | 2.75 | 2.5 | 57,293 | 53,923 | 50,743 |
| Belgium | D | 59,440 | 4.9 | 4.0 | 3.1 | 95,903 | 87,986 | 80,661 | 3.7 | 3.1 | 2.5 | 165,392 | 139,089 | 116,821 |
| Greece | D | 21,500 | 4.9 | 4.0 | 3.1 | 34,689 | 31,825 | 29,176 | 3.7 | 3.1 | 2.5 | 59,824 | 50,309 | 42,256 |
| Portugal | D | 15,040 | 4.9 | 4.0 | 3.1 | 24,266 | 22,263 | 20,410 | 3.7 | 3.1 | 2.5 | 41,848 | 35,194 | 29,560 |
| Bulgaria | E | 17,770 | 3.5 | 3.25 | 3.0 | 25,066 | 24,467 | 23,881 | 3.0 | 2.75 | 2.5 | 39,052 | 36,754 | 34,587 |
| Sweden | D | 64,580 | 4.9 | 4.0 | 3.1 | 104,196 | 95,594 | 87,636 | 3.7 | 3.1 | 2.5 | 179,694 | 151,116 | 126,923 |
| Austria | D | 35,520 | 4.9 | 4.0 | 3.1 | 57,310 | 52,578 | 48,201 | 3.7 | 3.1 | 2.5 | 98,835 | 83,116 | 69,809 |
| Switzerland | D | 51,510 | 4.9 | 4.0 | 3.1 | 83,109 | 76,247 | 69,900 | 3.7 | 3.1 | 2.5 | 143,327 | 120,532 | 101,236 |
| Denmark | D | 35,030 | 4.9 | 4.0 | 3.1 | 56,519 | 51,853 | 47,536 | 3.7 | 3.1 | 2.5 | 97,471 | 81,970 | 68,846 |
| Finland | E | 24,000 | 4.9 | 4.0 | 3.1 | 38,723 | 35,526 | 32,569 | 3.7 | 3.1 | 2.5 | 66,781 | 56,160 | 47,170 |
| Norway | D | 26,240 | 4.9 | 4.0 | 3.1 | 42,337 | 38,842 | 35,608 | 3.7 | 3.1 | 2.5 | 73,013 | 61,402 | 51,571 |
| Ireland | D | 7,560 | 4.9 | 4.0 | 3.1 | 12,198 | 11,191 | 10,259 | 3.7 | 3.1 | 2.5 | 21,036 | 17,691 | 14,858 |
| Albania | E | 1,450 | 3.5 | 3.25 | 3.0 | 2,045 | 1,997 | 1,949 | 3.0 | 2.75 | 2.5 | 3,186 | 3,000 | 2,823 |
| Cyprus | C | 740 | 6.6 | 5.55 | 4.5 | 1,402 | 1,270 | 1,149 | 4.9 | 4.4 | 3.9 | 2,873 | 2,423 | 2,040 |
| Luxembourg | D | 2,200 | 4.9 | 4.0 | 3.1 | 3,550 | 3,257 | 2,985 | 3.7 | 3.1 | 2.5 | 6,122 | 5,149 | 4,323 |
| Iceland | D | 1,250 | 4.9 | 4.0 | 3.1 | 2,017 | 1,850 | 1,696 | 3.7 | 3.1 | 2.5 | 3,478 | 2,925 | 2,456 |
| **NORTH AND CENTRAL AMERICA** | | | | | | | | | | | | | | |
| United States | D | 1,508,680 | 4.9 | 4.0 | 3.1 | 2,434,176 | 2,233,215 | 2,047,311 | 3.7 | 3.1 | 2.5 | 4,197,912 | 3,530,291 | 2,965,117 |
| Mexico | C | 71,170 | 6.6 | 5.55 | 4.5 | 134,856 | 122,146 | 110,525 | 4.9 | 4.4 | 3.9 | 276,377 | 233,017 | 196,198 |
| Canada | D | 151,730 | 4.9 | 4.0 | 3.1 | 244,808 | 224,597 | 205,901 | 3.7 | 3.1 | 2.5 | 422,189 | 355,045 | 298,206 |

| | | | | | | | | | | | | | | |
|---|---|---|---|---|---|---|---|---|---|---|---|---|---|---|
| Cuba | C | 7,430 | 6.6 | 5.55 | 4.5 | 14,079 | 12,752 | 11,539 | 4.9 | 4.4 | 3.9 | 28,854 | 24,327 | 20,483 |
| Guatemala | C | 3,530 | 6.6 | 5.55 | 4.5 | 6,689 | 6,058 | 5,482 | 4.9 | 4.4 | 3.9 | 13,709 | 11,557 | 9,731 |
| Dominican Republic | C | 3,380 | 6.6 | 5.55 | 4.5 | 6,405 | 5,801 | 5,249 | 4.9 | 4.4 | 3.9 | 13,127 | 11,067 | 9,318 |
| Haiti | C | 810 | 6.6 | 5.55 | 4.5 | 1,535 | 1,390 | 1,258 | 4.9 | 4.4 | 3.9 | 3,146 | 2,652 | 2,233 |
| El Salvador | C | 1,820 | 6.6 | 5.55 | 4.5 | 3,449 | 3,124 | 2,826 | 4.9 | 4.4 | 3.9 | 7,068 | 5,960 | 5,017 |
| Puerto Rico | C | 7,100 | 6.6 | 5.55 | 4.5 | 13,453 | 12,185 | 11,026 | 4.9 | 4.4 | 3.9 | 27,571 | 23,245 | 19,573 |
| Honduras | C | 1,010 | 6.6 | 5.55 | 4.5 | 1,914 | 1,733 | 1,569 | 4.9 | 4.4 | 3.9 | 3,923 | 3,306 | 2,785 |
| Nicaragua | C | 1,510 | 6.6 | 5.55 | 4.5 | 2,861 | 2,592 | 2,345 | 4.4 | 4.4 | 3.9 | 5,863 | 4,945 | 4,163 |
| Jamaica | C | 2,630 | 6.6 | 5.55 | 4.5 | 4,983 | 4,514 | 4,084 | 4.4 | 4.4 | 3.9 | 10,212 | 8,611 | 7,250 |
| Costa Rica | C | 1,790 | 6.6 | 5.55 | 4.5 | 3,392 | 3,072 | 2,780 | 4.4 | 4.4 | 3.9 | 6,952 | 5,860 | 4,935 |
| Panama | C | 1,770 | 6.6 | 5.55 | 4.5 | 3,354 | 3,038 | 2,749 | 4.4 | 4.4 | 3.9 | 6,874 | 5,796 | 4,880 |
| Trinidad and Tobago | C | 2,050 | 6.6 | 5.55 | 4.5 | 3,884 | 3,518 | 3,184 | 4.4 | 4.4 | 3.9 | 7,960 | 6,711 | 5,652 |
| Barbados | C | 310 | 6.6 | 5.55 | 4.5 | 587 | 532 | 481 | 4.9 | 4.4 | 3.9 | 1,203 | 1,015 | 854 |
| Bahamas | C | 530 | 6.6 | 5.55 | 4.5 | 1,004 | 910 | 823 | 4.9 | 4.4 | 3.9 | 2,058 | 1,736 | 1,461 |
| Grenada | C | 40 | 6.6 | 5.55 | 4.5 | 76 | 69 | 62 | 4.9 | 4.4 | 3.9 | 156 | 132 | 110 |
| **SOUTH AMERICA** | | | | | | | | | | | | | | |
| Brazil | C | 107,870 | 6.6 | 5.55 | 4.5 | 204,396 | 185,133 | 167,519 | 4.9 | 4.4 | 3.9 | 418,895 | 353,176 | 297,370 |
| Argentina | C | 39,810 | 6.6 | 5.55 | 4.5 | 75,433 | 68,324 | 61,824 | 4.9 | 4.4 | 3.9 | 154,594 | 130,341 | 109,746 |
| Colombia | C | 13,170 | 6.6 | 5.55 | 4.5 | 24,955 | 22,603 | 20,453 | 4.9 | 4.4 | 3.9 | 51,143 | 43,119 | 36,307 |
| Peru | C | 12,520 | 6.6 | 5.55 | 4.5 | 23,723 | 21,488 | 19,443 | 4.9 | 4.4 | 3.9 | 48,619 | 40,992 | 34,514 |
| Venezuela | A | 26,670 | 7.2 | 6.35 | 5.5 | 53,453 | 49,363 | 45,556 | 6.5 | 5.4 | 4.3 | 137,473 | 108,645 | 85,666 |
| Chile | C | 8,050 | 6.6 | 5.55 | 4.5 | 15,253 | 13,816 | 12,501 | 4.9 | 4.4 | 3.9 | 31,260 | 26,357 | 22,191 |
| Ecuador | A | 3,890 | 7.2 | 6.35 | 5.5 | 7,796 | 7,200 | 6,645 | 6.5 | 5.4 | 4.3 | 20,050 | 15,847 | 12,496 |
| Bolivia | C | 1,770 | 6.6 | 5.55 | 4.5 | 3,354 | 3,038 | 2,749 | 4.9 | 4.4 | 3.9 | 6,874 | 5,796 | 4,880 |
| Uruguay | C | 3,670 | 6.6 | 5.55 | 4.5 | 6,954 | 6,299 | 5,699 | 4.9 | 4.4 | 3.9 | 14,252 | 12,017 | 10,117 |
| Paraguay | C | 1,460 | 6.6 | 5.55 | 4.5 | 2,766 | 2,506 | 2,267 | 4.9 | 4.4 | 3.9 | 5,669 | 4,781 | 4,024 |
| Guyana | C | 450 | 6.6 | 5.55 | 4.5 | 853 | 772 | 699 | 4.9 | 4.4 | 3.9 | 1,748 | 1,473 | 1,241 |
| **OCEANIA and INDONESIA** | | | | | | | | | | | | | | |
| Indonesia | A | 24,180 | 7.2 | 6.35 | 5.5 | 48,462 | 44,754 | 41,303 | 6.5 | 5.4 | 4.3 | 124,637 | 98,501 | 77,669 |
| Australia | D | 76,190 | 4.9 | 4.0 | 3.1 | 122,929 | 112,780 | 103,391 | 3.7 | 3.1 | 2.5 | 212,000 | 178,284 | 149,741 |
| New Zealand | D | 14,460 | 4.9 | 4.0 | 3.1 | 23,330 | 21,404 | 19,623 | 3.7 | 3.1 | 2.5 | 40,234 | 33,836 | 28,420 |
| Papua New Guinea | C | 1,220 | 6.6 | 5.55 | 4.5 | 2,312 | 2,094 | 1,895 | 4.9 | 4.4 | 3.9 | 4,738 | 3,995 | 3,364 |
| Fiji | C | 520 | 6.6 | 5.55 | 4.5 | 985 | 892 | 808 | 4.9 | 4.4 | 3.9 | 2,019 | 1,702 | 1,434 |
| Western Samoa | C | 50 | 6.6 | 5.55 | 4.5 | 95 | 86 | 78 | 4.9 | 4.4 | 3.9 | 195 | 164 | 138 |

## TABLE 3-3

### GNP Estimates (1975) and Projections and Growth Rates (1985, 2000) by Major Regions and Selected Countries and Regions

*(Millions of constant 1975 dollars)*

| | 1975 GNP | 1975-85 Growth Rate | | | 1985 Projections [a] | | | 1985-2000 Growth Rate | | | 2000 Projections [a] | | |
|---|---|---|---|---|---|---|---|---|---|---|---|---|---|
| | | High | Med. | Low | High | Med. | Low | High | Med. | Low | High | Med. | Low |
| | | *percent* | | | | | | *percent* | | | | | |
| WORLD | 6,024,900 | 4.91 | 4.08 | 3.26 | 9,733,054 | 8,990,808 | 8,304,551 | 3.93 | 3.32 | 2.73 | 17,353,097 | 14,676,724 | 12,432,918 |
| More developed regions | 4,891,760 | 4.65 | 3.87 | 3.10 | 7,705,109 | 7,150,251 | 6,635,268 | 3.59 | 3.05 | 2.52 | 13,085,720 | 11,224,326 | 9,636,003 |
| Less developed regions | 1,133,140 | 5.99 | 4.97 | 3.95 | 2,027,945 | 1,840,557 | 1,669,283 | 5.08 | 4.28 | 3.50 | 4,267,377 | 3,452,398 | 2,796,915 |
| MAJOR REGIONS | | | | | | | | | | | | | |
| Africa | 161,580 | 6.10 | 5.18 | 4.26 | 292,001 | 267,731 | 245,315 | 5.05 | 4.32 | 3.60 | 611,741 | 505,210 | 417,223 |
| Asia and Oceania | 696,880 | 5.69 | 4.64 | 3.60 | 1,212,127 | 1,097,289 | 992,655 | 5.08 | 4.16 | 3.27 | 2,550,112 | 2,023,422 | 1,608,551 |
| Latin America [b] | 326,210 | 6.66 | 5.63 | 4.60 | 621,457 | 563,976 | 511,337 | 5.07 | 4.51 | 3.94 | 1,305,630 | 1,092,481 | 913,195 |
| U.S.S.R. and Eastern Europe | 995,750 | 3.50 | 3.25 | 3.00 | 1,404,602 | 1,371,043 | 1,338,204 | 3.00 | 2.75 | 2.50 | 2,188,325 | 2,059,579 | 1,938,119 |
| Northern America, Western Europe, Japan, Australia, and New Zealand | 3,844,480 | 4.90 | 4.00 | 3.10 | 6,202,867 | 5,690,769 | 5,217,040 | 3.70 | 3.10 | 2.50 | 10,697,289 | 8,996,032 | 7,555,830 |
| SELECTED COUNTRIES AND REGIONS [c] | | | | | | | | | | | | | |
| People's Republic of China | 285,960 | 5.0 | 3.75 | 2.5 | 465,799 | 413,225 | 366,053 | 5.0 | 3.75 | 2.5 | 968,362 | 717,808 | 530,154 |
| India | 91,810 | 4.4 | 3.6 | 2.8 | 141,220 | 130,764 | 121,010 | 3.1 | 2.8 | 2.5 | 223,242 | 197,872 | 175,259 |
| Indonesia | 24,180 | 7.2 | 6.35 | 5.5 | 48,462 | 44,754 | 41,303 | 6.5 | 5.4 | 4.3 | 124,637 | 98,501 | 77,669 |
| Bangladesh | 8,820 | 4.4 | 3.6 | 2.8 | 13,567 | 12,562 | 11,625 | 3.1 | 2.8 | 2.5 | 21,447 | 19,009 | 16,836 |
| Pakistan | 9,830 | 4.4 | 3.6 | 2.8 | 15,120 | 14,001 | 12,956 | 3.1 | 2.8 | 2.5 | 23,902 | 21,186 | 18,764 |
| Philippines | 15,730 | 6.6 | 5.55 | 4.5 | 29,806 | 26,997 | 24,428 | 4.9 | 4.4 | 3.9 | 61,085 | 51,502 | 43,363 |
| Thailand | 14,540 | 6.6 | 5.55 | 4.5 | 27,551 | 24,954 | 22,580 | 4.9 | 4.4 | 3.9 | 56,464 | 47,604 | 40,083 |
| South Korea | 18,650 | 6.6 | 5.55 | 4.5 | 35,339 | 32,008 | 28,963 | 4.9 | 4.4 | 3.9 | 72,425 | 61,061 | 51,413 |
| Egypt | 11,550 | 6.6 | 5.55 | 4.5 | 21,885 | 19,823 | 17,937 | 4.9 | 4.4 | 3.9 | 44,852 | 37,816 | 31,841 |
| Nigeria | 23,080 | 7.2 | 6.35 | 5.5 | 46,258 | 42,718 | 39,424 | 6.5 | 5.4 | 4.3 | 118,968 | 94,020 | 74,135 |
| Brazil | 107,870 | 6.6 | 5.55 | 4.5 | 204,396 | 185,133 | 167,519 | 4.9 | 4.4 | 3.9 | 418,895 | 353,176 | 297,370 |
| Mexico | 71,170 | 6.6 | 5.55 | 4.5 | 134,856 | 122,146 | 110,525 | 4.9 | 4.4 | 3.9 | 276,377 | 233,017 | 196,198 |
| United States [d] | 1,508,680 | 4.9 | 4.0 | 3.1 | 2,434,176 | 2,233,215 | 2,047,311 | 3.7 | 3.1 | 2.5 | 4,197,912 | 3,530,291 | 2,965,117 |
| U.S.S.R. | 665,910 | 3.5 | 3.25 | 3.0 | 939,332 | 916,888 | 894,927 | 3.0 | 2.75 | 2.5 | 1,463,449 | 1,377,348 | 1,296,121 |
| Japan | 495,180 | 4.9 | 4.0 | 3.1 | 798,947 | 732,987 | 671,970 | 3.7 | 3.1 | 2.5 | 1,377,842 | 1,158,714 | 973,213 |
| Eastern Europe (excluding U.S.S.R.) | 329,840 | 3.50 | 3.25 | 3.0 | 465,270 | 454,155 | 443,277 | 3.0 | 2.75 | 2.5 | 724,876 | 682,231 | 641,998 |
| Western Europe | 1,598,240 | 4.90 | 4.00 | 3.10 | 2,578,677 | 2,365,786 | 2,168,844 | 3.70 | 3.10 | 2.5 | 4,447,112 | 3,739,862 | 3,141,133 |

[a] Projected growth rates of gross national product were developed using complex computer simulation techniques described in Chapter 16. These projections represent the result of applying those projected growth rates to the 1975 GNP data presented in the 1976 World Bank Atlas.

[b] Includes Puerto Rico.

[c] In most cases, gross national income growth rates were projected for groups of countries rather than for individual countries. Thus, the rates which are attributed to individual LDCs in this table are the growth rates applicable to the group with which that country was aggregated for making projections and do not take into account country-specific characteristics.

[d] Does not include Puerto Rico.

# TABLE 3-4

## Population Estimates (1975) and Projections and Growth Rates (1985, 2000) by Major Regions and Selected Countries and Regions

*(In millions)*

| | 1975 | | | Average Annual Growth Rate 1975-85[a] | | | 1985 | | | Average Annual Growth Rate 1985-2000[a] | | | 2000 | | |
|---|---|---|---|---|---|---|---|---|---|---|---|---|---|---|---|
| | High | Med. | Low | High | Med. | Low | High | Med. | Low | High | Med. | Low | High | Med. | Low |
| | | | | *percent* | | | | | | *percent* | | | | | |
| WORLD | 4,134 | 4,090 | 4,043 | 1.95 | 1.79 | 1.63 | 5,013 | 4,885 | 4,753 | 2.05 | 1.77 | 1.48 | 6,797 | 6,351 | 5,921 |
| More developed regions | 1,131 | 1,131 | 1,131 | 0.79 | 0.69 | 0.60 | 1,224 | 1,212 | 1,201 | 0.79 | 0.59 | 0.40 | 1,377 | 1,323 | 1,274 |
| Less developed regions | 3,003 | 2,959 | 2,912 | 2.35 | 2.18 | 2.01 | 3,789 | 3,673 | 3,553 | 2.42 | 2.12 | 1.81 | 5,420 | 5,028 | 4,648 |
| MAJOR REGIONS | | | | | | | | | | | | | | | |
| Africa | 399 | 399 | 399 | 2.96 | 2.90 | 2.80 | 534 | 531 | 525 | 3.13 | 2.90 | 2.48 | 847 | 814 | 759 |
| Asia and Oceania[b] | 2,318 | 2,274 | 2,228 | 2.13 | 1.93 | 1.75 | 2,861 | 2,755 | 2,651 | 2.17 | 1.86 | 1.59 | 3,951 | 3,630 | 3,359 |
| Latin America[b] | 325 | 325 | 324 | 3.04 | 2.91 | 2.65 | 439 | 432 | 421 | 2.94 | 2.61 | 2.17 | 678 | 637 | 581 |
| U.S.S.R. and Eastern Europe | 384 | 384 | 384 | 0.95 | 0.85 | 0.74 | 422 | 418 | 414 | 0.85 | 0.65 | 0.43 | 480 | 460 | 442 |
| Northern America, Western Europe, Japan, Australia and New Zealand | 708 | 708 | 708 | 0.67 | 0.57 | 0.48 | 757 | 749 | 743 | 0.71 | 0.52 | 0.34 | 842 | 809 | 781 |
| SELECTED COUNTRIES AND REGIONS | | | | | | | | | | | | | | | |
| People's Republic of China | 978 | 935 | 889 | 1.64 | 1.42 | 1.10 | 1,151 | 1,076 | 992 | 1.63 | 1.42 | 1.14 | 1,468 | 1,329 | 1,176 |
| India | 618 | 618 | 618 | 2.43 | 2.14 | 2.04 | 786 | 764 | 757 | 2.52 | 1.95 | 1.69 | 1,142 | 1,021 | 974 |
| Indonesia | 135 | 135 | 135 | 2.22 | 2.15 | 2.03 | 168 | 167 | 165 | 2.28 | 2.05 | 1.59 | 263 | 226 | 209 |
| Bangladesh | 79 | 79 | 79 | 3.08 | 3.02 | 2.93 | 108 | 107 | 106 | 2.94 | 2.67 | 2.39 | 166 | 159 | 151 |
| Pakistan | 71 | 71 | 71 | 3.29 | 3.23 | 3.19 | 98 | 98 | 97 | 3.15 | 2.85 | 2.67 | 156 | 149 | 144 |
| Philippines | 43 | 43 | 43 | 2.59 | 2.28 | 2.01 | 56 | 54 | 52 | 2.44 | 2.09 | 1.68 | 80 | 73 | 67 |
| Thailand | 42 | 42 | 42 | 2.65 | 2.50 | 2.34 | 55 | 54 | 53 | 2.58 | 2.20 | 1.77 | 81 | 75 | 69 |
| South Korea | 37 | 37 | 37 | 2.12 | 1.92 | 1.69 | 46 | 45 | 43 | 2.03 | 1.65 | 1.42 | 62 | 57 | 54 |
| Egypt | 37 | 37 | 37 | 2.73 | 2.62 | 2.41 | 48 | 48 | 47 | 2.56 | 2.12 | 1.54 | 71 | 65 | 59 |
| Nigeria | 63 | 63 | 63 | 2.96 | 2.96 | 2.92 | 84 | 84 | 84 | 3.29 | 3.18 | 2.90 | 137 | 134 | 129 |
| Brazil | 109 | 109 | 109 | 3.35 | 3.25 | 3.05 | 151 | 150 | 147 | 3.16 | 2.78 | 2.55 | 241 | 226 | 214 |
| Mexico | 60 | 60 | 60 | 3.69 | 3.44 | 2.80 | 86 | 84 | 78 | 3.36 | 3.02 | 2.32 | 142 | 131 | 111 |
| United States[c] | 214 | 214 | 214 | 0.96 | 0.70 | 0.52 | 235 | 229 | 225 | 0.94 | 0.55 | 0.27 | 270 | 248 | 234 |
| U.S.S.R. | 254 | 254 | 254 | 1.05 | 0.93 | 0.80 | 282 | 279 | 276 | 0.90 | 0.68 | 0.46 | 323 | 309 | 295 |
| Japan | 112 | 112 | 112 | 0.91 | 0.88 | 0.81 | 122 | 122 | 121 | 0.68 | 0.59 | 0.43 | 135 | 133 | 129 |
| Eastern Europe (excluding U.S.S.R.) | 130 | 130 | 130 | 0.74 | 0.68 | 0.63 | 140 | 139 | 138 | 0.76 | 0.57 | 0.39 | 157 | 152 | 147 |
| Western Europe | 344 | 344 | 344 | 0.35 | 0.33 | 0.30 | 356 | 355 | 354 | 0.52 | 0.43 | 0.31 | 384 | 378 | 371 |

[a] Projections for 1985 and 2000 were developed using the complex simulation techniques described in Chapter 15. These growth rates merely summarize the results of those calculations.
[b] Includes Puerto Rico.
[c] Does not include Puerto Rico.

## TABLE 3-5

### Per Capita GNP Estimates (1975) and Projections and Growth Rates (1985, 2000) by Major Regions and Selected Countries and Regions

*(Constant 1975 U.S. dollars)*

| | 1975 | | | Average Annual Growth Rate, 1975–1985 | | | 1985 | | | Average Annual Growth Rate, 1985–2000 | | | 2000 | | |
|---|---|---|---|---|---|---|---|---|---|---|---|---|---|---|---|
| | High | Med. | Low | High | Med. | Low | High | Med. | Low | High | Med. | Low | High | Med. | Low |
| | | | | *percent* | | | | | | *percent* | | | | | |
| **WORLD** | 1,490 | 1,473 | 1,457 | 3.23 | 2.26 | 1.29 | 2,048 | 1,841 | 1,657 | 2.42 | 1.53 | 0.66 | 2,930 | 2,311 | 1,829 |
| More developed countries | 4,325 | 4,325 | 4,325 | 4.02 | 3.16 | 2.28 | 6,416 | 5,901 | 5,420 | 3.19 | 2.45 | 1.72 | 10,270 | 8,485 | 6,996 |
| Less developed countries | 388 | 382 | 377 | 3.94 | 2.75 | 1.58 | 571 | 501 | 441 | 3.22 | 2.13 | 1.05 | 918 | 587 | 516 |
| **MAJOR REGIONS** | | | | | | | | | | | | | | | |
| Africa | 405 | 405 | 405 | 3.22 | 2.23 | 1.28 | 556 | 505 | 460 | 2.51 | 1.38 | 0.46 | 806 | 620 | 493 |
| Asia and Oceania | 313 | 306 | 301 | 3.86 | 2.66 | 1.43 | 457 | 398 | 347 | 3.44 | 2.27 | 1.07 | 759 | 557 | 407 |
| Latin America[b] | 1,007 | 1,005 | 1,003 | 3.90 | 2.64 | 1.51 | 1,476 | 1,304 | 1,165 | 2.84 | 1.84 | 0.97 | 2,247 | 1,715 | 1,347 |
| U.S.S.R. and Eastern Europe | 2,591 | 2,591 | 2,591 | 2.74 | 2.38 | 2.03 | 3,394 | 3,279 | 3,169 | 2.55 | 2.09 | 1.64 | 4,954 | 4,472 | 4,042 |
| North America, Western Europe, Japan, Australia, and New Zealand | 5,431 | 5,431 | 5,431 | 4.40 | 3.41 | 2.41 | 8,352 | 7,597 | 6,894 | 3.35 | 2.57 | 1.77 | 13,693 | 11,117 | 8,974 |
| **SELECTED COUNTRIES AND REGIONS**[c] | | | | | | | | | | | | | | | |
| People's Republic of China | 322 | 306 | 292 | 3.85 | 2.30 | 0.86 | 470 | 384 | 318 | 3.81 | 2.30 | 0.85 | 824 | 540 | 361 |
| India | 148 | 148 | 148 | 2.37 | 1.45 | 0.40 | 187 | 171 | 154 | 1.36 | 0.84 | -0.04 | 229 | 194 | 153 |
| Indonesia | 179 | 179 | 179 | 5.09 | 4.12 | 3.23 | 294 | 268 | 246 | 4.82 | 3.07 | 1.98 | 596 | 422 | 330 |
| Bangladesh | 111 | 111 | 111 | 1.44 | 0.61 | -0.27 | 128 | 118 | 108 | 0.69 | 0.11 | -0.45 | 142 | 120 | 101 |
| Pakistan | 138 | 138 | 138 | 1.23 | 0.43 | -0.44 | 156 | 144 | 132 | 0.42 | -0.09 | -0.63 | 166 | 142 | 120 |
| Philippines | 369 | 368 | 366 | 4.50 | 3.17 | 1.86 | 573 | 503 | 440 | 3.16 | 2.27 | 1.41 | 914 | 704 | 543 |
| Thailand | 343 | 343 | 342 | 4.19 | 2.98 | 1.81 | 517 | 460 | 409 | 3.07 | 2.15 | 1.29 | 814 | 633 | 496 |
| South Korea | 508 | 507 | 505 | 4.83 | 3.54 | 2.35 | 814 | 718 | 637 | 3.44 | 2.70 | 1.83 | 1,351 | 1,071 | 836 |
| Egypt | 313 | 313 | 313 | 4.10 | 2.89 | 1.71 | 468 | 416 | 371 | 3.31 | 2.22 | 1.33 | 763 | 578 | 452 |
| Nigeria | 367 | 367 | 367 | 4.15 | 3.28 | 2.46 | 551 | 507 | 468 | 3.51 | 2.15 | 0.98 | 924 | 698 | 542 |
| Brazil | 994 | 991 | 991 | 3.44 | 2.23 | 1.11 | 1,394 | 1,236 | 1,107 | 2.29 | 1.58 | 0.72 | 1,959 | 1,563 | 1,232 |
| Mexico | 1,196 | 1,188 | 1,182 | 3.70 | 2.04 | 0.78 | 1,720 | 1,454 | 1,278 | 2.52 | 1.34 | 0.52 | 2,499 | 1,775 | 1,382 |
| United States[d] | 7,066 | 7,066 | 7,066 | 4.35 | 3.28 | 2.12 | 10,819 | 9,756 | 8,719 | 3.42 | 2.54 | 1.55 | 17,917 | 14,212 | 10,974 |
| U.S.S.R. | 2,618 | 2,618 | 2,618 | 2.67 | 2.30 | 1.93 | 3,408 | 3,286 | 3,169 | 2.53 | 2.06 | 1.59 | 4,959 | 4,459 | 4,015 |
| Japan | 4,437 | 4,437 | 4,437 | 4.06 | 3.10 | 2.17 | 6,608 | 6,023 | 5,499 | 3.26 | 2.49 | 1.81 | 10,689 | 8,712 | 7,193 |
| Eastern Europe | 2,539 | 2,539 | 2,539 | 2.85 | 2.55 | 2.24 | 3,364 | 3,265 | 3,169 | 2.60 | 2.16 | 1.73 | 4,945 | 4,500 | 4,097 |
| Western Europe | 4,653 | 4,653 | 4,653 | 4.59 | 3.66 | 2.74 | 7,286 | 6,666 | 6,099 | 3.38 | 2.66 | 1.97 | 11,993 | 9,889 | 8,174 |

*The projections of gross national product and population presented in Tables 3-3 and 3-4 were used to calculate the 1975, 1985, and 2000 per capita gross national product figures presented in this table. The high figures are based on dividing the high GNP figures by the low population figures; the low figures are based on dividing the low GNP figures by the high population figures; the medium figures are based on the medium GNP and population figures. The growth rates summarize the results of these calculations.

[b]Includes Puerto Rico.

[c]In most cases, gross national product growth rates were projected for groups of countries rather than for individual countries. Thus, the rates attributed to individual LDCs in this table are the growth rates applicable to the group with which that country was aggregated for making projections and do not take into account country-specific characteristics.

[d]Does not include Puerto Rico.

# 4  Climate Projections

Because climate has a profound effect on our lives and economies and has possible consequences for the future, we cannot ignore it, yet there are unresolved problems which make statements about future climate very uncertain. This is to say, not enough is known about climate to provide us with a reliable predictive capability.

A particular pattern of climate results from very complex interactions between the atmosphere, oceans, land masses, ice pack and glaciers, vegetation, and, to an increasing extent, man. Depending on the specific interaction mechanism, the reaction time from cause to effect—and the duration of the effect—may range from days to millenia. Changes in one part of the system are interlinked with changes in other parts of the system, so that no part, such as the atmosphere, may be considered in isolation from the others.

Before the future climate can be reliably estimated, science must understand it well enough to build realistic quantitative models that relate cause and effect. This understanding would also serve as a basis for evaluating the impact of variations in any of the causes, both in terms of how important they are and the time scales on which they operate. Such models are as yet primitive and incomplete. Until the climatic interactions are understood and quantified, there can be no reliable climatic prediction capability.

As climate research progresses, internal climatic interlinkages are becoming better understood. Many investigators are also studying causal factors external to the climatic system itself. These factors include solar activity, planetary tides, changes in the earth's orbit and rotation, and man-induced (anthropogenic) alterations of our environment. The latter include carbon dioxide, fluorocarbons, particles in the air, changes due to land use, and heat generated by use of energy. A complete understanding has yet to be achieved.

Carbon dioxide increase is thought to produce warming of the earth by the so-called greenhouse effect. There is less agreement as to the effect of increasing atmospheric particles, which may result in either warming or cooling, depending on many details in the situation.

Study of the interactions of the various climatic subsystems has led to the development of some simple models of global-scale climate behavior. Research into the interaction of sea-surface temperature anomalies and the overlying air has produced seasonal forecasts a season in advance that have a small but statistically significant degree of accuracy. Research on the effects of anthropogenic and volcanic inputs on the earth's heat budget has led to provisional assessments of mean temperature and precipitation changes in future decades and centuries. Validation and further refinement of climate models is urgently needed.

There is wide variation in the use of the word "climate." Some reserve the word climate for averages of climate over a 30-year (or longer) period. Others speak of the climate of individual months, seasons, or years. The discussion of climate in this chapter is based on the latter usage. Most users of the word are usually concerned with the assemblage of weather that makes up a month or a season. Annual crops do not respond to 30-year averages or hemispheric mean temperatures. Useful crop yield models must have at least monthly temperature and rainfall inputs. Also, to be useful, climatic information must be specific to geographical regions and preferably to areas as small as crop districts.

At a range of a month to several decades into the future, descriptions of the climate as aggregates of weather need not be detailed as to timing or sequence in order to be useful. However, they do need to include information on variability and probable extremes. Given estimates of monthly means and variances, fairly accurate estimates may be made of grain production. However, in general, statistical studies have not yet sufficed to establish to what extent the variability of weather within a month or season varies with the average "climate" of the month or season. Climate changes may include changes of climatic variability as well as those of averaging climate.

Despite these difficulties, it can still be said that in the remainder of the century there is likely to be less than a 0.5° C change in the mean sea level temperature of the Northern Hemisphere, and that:

51

- Hemispheric warming or cooling will probably be most pronounced in high latitudes, with little temperature change in the tropics.
- Hemispheric temperature changes will be accompanied by changes in the intensity and pattern of atmospheric circulation and probably changes in the variability of climate.
- These atmospheric circulation changes will probably result in important variations in the longitudinal (east-west) direction and affect the distribution of precipitation, including that in the tropics.

## Climate in the Year 2000

An attempt to quantify perceptions of global climate change to the year 2000 has been the initial focus of an interdepartmental study at the National Defense University (NDU) in Washington, D.C. Subjective probabilities for the occurrence of specified climatic events were elicited in a survey of 24 climatologists from seven countries. Individual quantitative responses to 10 major questions were weighted according to expertise and then averaged, a method of aggregation that preserved the climatologists' collective uncertainty about future climate trends. The aggregated subjective probabilities were used to construct five possible climate scenarios for the year 2000, each having a "probability" of occurrence. The aggregated probabilities of contingent events are compared from scenario to scenario, across zones of latitude, and by time periods.

A discussion of the methodology used in the study will be found in Chapter 17 of this volume. The descriptions of the scenarios that follow are from the report of the first phase of the study. "Climate Change to the Year 2000: A Survey of Expert Opinion," issued by the National Defense University in February 1978.

## The Climate Scenarios

In the text and tables of this chapter, the latitudinal zones are defined as: "polar latitudes," 65° to 90° ; "higher midlatitudes," 45° to 65° ; "lower midlatitudes," 30° to 45° ; and "subtropical latitudes," 10° to 30° .

### Large Global Cooling*

The global cooling trend that began in the 1940s accelerated rapidly in the last quarter of the 20th century. The average global temperature reached its lowest value of the past century a few years before the century ended. By the year 2000, the mean Northern Hemisphere temperature was about 0.6° C colder than in the early 1970s, and climatic conditions showed a striking similarity to the period around 1820. Climatologists explained this large global cooling in terms of natural climatic cycles, partly solar induced and partly attributable to several major volcanic eruptions that occurred between 1980 and 2000. Although most climatologists had expected a continued increase in carbon dioxide to be reflected in global warming, this warming influence was overwhelmed by the natural cooling in the period.

While temperature decreased over the entire globe, the largest decreases occurred in the higher latitudes of the Northern Hemisphere. The north polar latitudes, marked by an expansion of arctic sea ice and snow cover (especially in the north Atlantic sector), had cooled by about 2° C since the early 1970s.* The northern higher and lower middle latitudes cooled by slightly more than 1° C. The subtropical latitudes in both hemispheres showed a 0.5° C decrease in average temperature, while the remainder of the southern latitudes showed a 1° C decrease. The large global cooling trend was also reflected in a significant decrease in the length of the growing season in the higher middle latitudes and a substantial increase in the variability in the length of the growing season from year to year.

By the year 2000, it was also raining less in the higher middle and subtropical latitudes, although precipitation amounts in the lower middle latitudes changed little or possibly increased slightly.

Precipitation also became more variable. The westerlies showed a pronounced shift from the higher middle to lower middle latitudes. This shift brought brief, yet severe, "hit-and-run" droughts as well as severe cold spells (including early and late killing frosts) in the lower middle latitudes. The higher middle latitudes, particularly Canada, from which the westerlies and their associated storm tracks were displaced, suffered an increased incidence of long-term drought and winter cold. In the subtropical latitudes, the subtropical highs tended to displace the tropical easterly rainbelt and, hence, increased the incidence of long periods of hot, dry weather. The center and intensity of the Asiatic monsoon changed dramatically

---

*Statements concerning some details of this scenario reflect a higher degree of certainty than was expressed by the climatologists who participated in this study. See Tables 4–1 A and B for the range of uncertainty.

*One climatologist who inclined to this scenario reasoned that the north polar regions would cool only about 0.5° C, considerably less than the cooling in the middle northern latitudes.

between the late 1970s and the turn of the century. The frequency of monsoon failure in northwest India increased to such an extent that the last decade of the 20th century bore a resemblance to the period from 1900 to 1925. Droughts were also more frequent in the Sahel region of Africa.

## Moderate Global Cooling*

The global cooling trend that began in the 1940s continued through the last quarter of the 20th century. By the year 2000, mean Northern Hemisphere temperature had decreased by approximately 0.15° C compared to the early 1970s. Climatologists explained this trend principally in terms of a natural cooling cycle, moderated by the warming effects of increasing amounts of carbon dioxide in the atmosphere. The cooling cycle was partly solar in origin and partly associated with an increase in volcanic activity.

While temperature decreased over the entire globe, the largest temperature decreases occurred in the higher latitudes of the Northern Hemisphere. Specifically, the polar latitudes of the Northern Hemisphere cooled by 1° C; the higher middle latitudes by 0.4° C; the lower middle latitudes by 0.3° C; and the subtropical latitudes by 0.2° C. The Southern Hemisphere, with its more zonal circulation and larger ocean area, cooled more uniformly and slowly; the average cooling in that hemisphere was about 0.15° C. The extent of the cooling in the higher middle latitudes was not sufficiently large to cause a significant change in the mean length or interannual variability of the growing season.

The growing-season precipitation as well as annual precipitation levels remained unchanged in the lower middle latitudes but decreased slightly in the higher middle and subtropical latitudes. Annual and growing-season precipitation variability increased slightly compared to the 1950–75 period, with the strongest tendency toward increased variability in the subtropical latitudes.

Drought conditions again plagued the midlatitude areas of the United States, corroborating the 20- to 22-year drought cycle hypothesis. In the other midlatitude areas of the world, there were intermittent drought conditions comparable to those of the 1970s. Droughts were also more frequent in the Sahel region, as was monsoon failure in Asia.

## Same as the Last 30 Years*

The global cooling trend that began in the 1940s leveled out in the 1970s. Average global temperature in the last quarter of the 20th century increased slightly; thus, temperatures were more consistent with those in the period from 1940 to 1970. By the year 2000, mean Northern Hemisphere temperature had risen approximately 0.1° C compared to the early 1970s. Climatologists explained that the warming effects of the increasing amounts of carbon dioxide in the atmosphere had balanced a natural cooling cycle. Temperature increases were nearly uniform throughout the Northern and Southern Hemispheres, with slightly more warming in the Northern Hemisphere than in the Southern. No significant changes in the mean length or interannual variability of the growing season were noted.

The annual precipitation levels as well as the growing-season precipitation remained unchanged from the 1941–70 period. Also unchanged was the variability of annual precipitation. However, a small shift toward increased variability in the growing season was detected.

Drought conditions again plagued the midlatitude areas of the United States, corroborating the 20- to 22-year drought cycle hypothesis. In other midlatitude areas of the world, drought conditions recurred also, but not to the same extent as in the United States. On the other hand, favorable climatic conditions returned to India and other parts of Asia. Monsoon failures became more infrequent. Also, the Sahel region, which had suffered severe drought from 1965 to 1973, returned to average weather conditions.

## Moderate Global Warming†

The global cooling trend that began in the 1940s was reversed in the last quarter of the 20th century. By the year 2000, mean Northern Hemisphere temperature had risen by approximately 0.4° C, compared to the early 1970s. Climatologists explained that this increase in temperatures was due principally to the warming effects of increasing amounts of carbon dioxide in the atmosphere, which predominated over a slow, natural cooling effect.

*Statements concerning some details of this scenario reflect a higher degree of certainty than was expressed by the climatologists who participated in this study. See Tables 4–2 A and B for the range of uncertainty.

*Statements concerning some details of this scenario reflect a higher degree of certainty than was expressed by the climatologists who participated in this study. See Tables 4–3 A and B for the range of uncertainty.

†Statements concerning some details of this scenario reflect a higher degree of certainty than was expressed by the climatologists who participated in this study. See Tables 4–4 A and B for the range of uncertainty.

## TABLE 4–1A

### LARGE GLOBAL COOLING

PROBABILITY OF SCENARIO: 0.10
MEAN NORTHERN HEMISPHERE TEMPERATURE CHANGE SINCE 1969: between 0.3° and 1.2°C colder

## PROBABILITY OF TEMPERATURE CHANGE BY LATITUDE

(Compared with 1970-75)

| | | 2.0-3.0°C colder | 1.5-2.0°C colder | 1.0-1.5°C colder | 0.5-1.0°C colder | 0.0-0.5°C colder | 0.0-0.5°C warmer | 0.5-1.0°C warmer | 1.0-1.5°C warmer | 1.5-2.0°C warmer |
|---|---|---|---|---|---|---|---|---|---|---|
| Northern hemisphere | Polar | 0.2 | 0.6 | 0.1 | 0.1 | | | | | |
| | Higher mid-latitude* | | 0.1 | 0.5 | 0.3 | 0.1 | | | | |
| | Lower mid-latitude | | | 0.4 | 0.4 | 0.2 | | | | |
| | Subtropical | | | | 0.5 | 0.5 | | | | |
| Southern hemisphere | Subtropical | | | | 0.5 | 0.5 | | | | |
| | Lower mid-latitude | | | 0.5 | 0.4 | 0.1 | | | | |
| | Higher mid-latitude* | | | 0.6 | 0.3 | 0.1 | | | | |
| | Polar | | | 0.6 | 0.3 | 0.1 | | | | |

*Growing season in higher middle latitudes: Probability of an increase (decrease) in the *length* of the growing season exceeding 10 days is 0.0 (0.9); probability of an increase (decrease) in the *variability* of the length of the growing season in excess of 25% is 0.8 (0.0).

## PROBABILITY OF PRECIPITATION CHANGE BY LATITUDE

(Compared with 1941-70)

| | ANNUAL | | | | GROWING SEASON | | |
|---|---|---|---|---|---|---|---|
| | Increase ⩾ 10% | Change < 10% | Decrease ⩾ 10% | | Increase ⩾ 10% | Change < 10% | Decrease ⩾ 10% |
| Higher mid-latitude | 0.2 | 0.5 | 0.3 | | 0.2 | 0.5 | 0.3 |
| Lower mid-latitude | 0.3 | 0.5 | 0.2 | | 0.3 | 0.5 | 0.2 |
| Subtropical | 0.2 | 0.5 | 0.3 | | 0.2 | 0.4 | 0.4 |

## PROBABILITY OF PRECIPITATION VARIABILITY CHANGE BY LATITUDE

(Compared with average for the previous 25-year period)

| | ANNUAL | | | | GROWING SEASON | | |
|---|---|---|---|---|---|---|---|
| | Increase ⩾ 25% | Change < 25% | Decrease ⩾ 25% | | Increase ⩾ 25% | Change < 25% | Decrease ⩾ 25% |
| Higher mid-latitude | 0.3 | 0.5 | 0.2 | | 0.3 | 0.6 | 0.1 |
| Lower mid-latitude | 0.3 | 0.5 | 0.2 | | 0.3 | 0.5 | 0.2 |
| Subtropical | 0.4 | 0.4 | 0.2 | | 0.4 | 0.4 | 0.2 |

## TABLE 4–1B

# LARGE GLOBAL COOLING

| | Carbon dioxide | Fluoro-carbons | Smoke | Volcanic dust | Other particles |
|---|---|---|---|---|---|
| RELATIVE IMPORTANCE OF CARBON DIOXIDE AND TURBIDITY (PERCENT) DURING THE PERIOD 1975-2000 | 15 | 05 | 20 | 50 | 10 |

| | 1977-80 | | | 1981-90 | | | 1991-2000 | | |
|---|---|---|---|---|---|---|---|---|---|
| | Frequent | Average | Infrequent | Frequent | Average | Infrequent | Frequent | Average | Infrequent |
| PROBABILITY OF MID-LATITUDE DROUGHT* | | | | | | | | | |
| United States | 0.6 | 0.3 | 0.1 | 0.4 | 0.5 | 0.1 | 0.7 | 0.2 | 0.1 |
| Other Mid-Latitude | 0.6 | 0.3 | 0.1 | 0.4 | 0.5 | 0.1 | 0.7 | 0.2 | 0.1 |
| PROBABILITY OF SAHEL DROUGHT** | 0.5 | 0.5 | | 0.5 | 0.4 | 0.1 | 0.6 | 0.3 | 0.1 |
| PROBABILITY OF MONSOON FAILURE*** | | | | | | | | | |
| Northwest India | 0.4 | 0.5 | 0.1 | 0.4 | 0.5 | 0.1 | 0.5 | 0.5 | |
| Other India | 0.5 | 0.4 | 0.1 | 0.4 | 0.5 | 0.1 | 0.6 | 0.3 | 0.1 |
| Other Monsoon Asia | 0.5 | 0.4 | 0.1 | 0.4 | 0.5 | 0.1 | 0.5 | 0.4 | 0.1 |

*Frequent—similar to early to mid-1930s and early to mid-1950s; average—similar to the frequency over the longest period of record available; infrequent—similar to 1940s and 1960s.

**Frequent—similar to 1940-50 and 1965-73 periods; average—similar to the frequency over the longest period of record available; infrequent—similar to 1950-65 period.

***Frequent—similar to 1900-25 period; average—similar to the frequency over the longest period of record available; infrequent—similar to 1930-60 period.

## TABLE 4–2A

# MODERATE GLOBAL COOLING

PROBABILITY OF SCENARIO: 0.25
MEAN NORTHERN HEMISPHERE TEMPERATURE CHANGE SINCE 1969: between 0.05° and 0.3°C colder

## PROBABILITY OF TEMPERATURE CHANGE BY LATITUDE

(Compared with 1970-75)

| | | 2.0-3.0°C colder | 1.5-2.0°C colder | 1.0-1.5°C colder | 0.5-1.0°C colder | 0.0-0.5°C colder | 0.0-0.5°C warmer | 0.5-1.0°C warmer | 1.0-1.5°C warmer | 1.5-2.0°C warmer |
|---|---|---|---|---|---|---|---|---|---|---|
| Northern hemisphere | Polar | | 0.1 | 0.6 | 0.1 | 0.1 | 0.1 | | | |
| | Higher mid-latitude * | | | 0.1 | 0.4 | 0.4 | 0.1 | | | |
| | Lower mid-latitude | | | 0.1 | 0.1 | 0.7 | 0.1 | | | |
| | Subtropical | | | | 0.2 | 0.7 | 0.1 | | | |
| Southern hemisphere | Subtropical | | | | 0.2 | 0.6 | 0.1 | 0.1 | | |
| | Lower mid-latitude | | | 0.1 | 0.2 | 0.3 | 0.3 | 0.1 | | |
| | Higher mid-latitude* | | | 0.1 | 0.2 | 0.3 | 0.3 | 0.1 | | |
| | Polar | | | 0.2 | 0.2 | 0.2 | 0.3 | 0.1 | | |

*Growing season in higher middle latitudes: Probability of an increase (decrease) in the *length* of the growing season exceeding 10 days is 0.1 (0.2); probability of an increase (decrease) in the *variability* of the length of the growing season in excess of 25% is 0.2 (0.1).

## PROBABILITY OF PRECIPITATION CHANGE BY LATITUDE

(Compared with 1941-70)

| | ANNUAL | | | | GROWING SEASON | | |
|---|---|---|---|---|---|---|---|
| | Increase ⋀ 10% | Change ⋁ 10% | Decrease ⋀ 10% | | Increase ⋀ 10% | Change ⋁ 10% | Decrease ⋀ 10% |
| Higher mid-latitude | 0.2 | 0.5 | 0.3 | | 0.2 | 0.5 | 0.3 |
| Lower mid-latitude | 0.2 | 0.6 | 0.2 | | 0.2 | 0.6 | 0.2 |
| Subtropical | 0.2 | 0.5 | 0.3 | | 0.2 | 0.5 | 0.3 |

## PROBABILITY OF PRECIPITATION VARIABILITY CHANGE BY LATITUDE

(Compared with average for the previous 25-year period)

| | ANNUAL | | | | GROWING SEASON | | |
|---|---|---|---|---|---|---|---|
| | Increase ⋀ 25% | Change ⋁ 25% | Decrease ⋀ 25% | | Increase ⋀ 25% | Change ⋁ 25% | Decrease ⋀ 25% |
| Higher mid-latitude | 0.2 | 0.6 | 0.2 | | 0.3 | 0.6 | 0.1 |
| Lower mid-latitude | 0.2 | 0.6 | 0.2 | | 0.3 | 0.6 | 0.1 |
| Subtropical | 0.3 | 0.5 | 0.2 | | 0.4 | 0.5 | 0.1 |

**TABLE 4–2B**

# MODERATE  GLOBAL  COOLING

|  | Carbon dioxide | Fluoro- carbons | Smoke | Volcanic dust | Other particles |
|---|---|---|---|---|---|
| RELATIVE IMPORTANCE OF CARBON DIOXIDE AND TURBIDITY (PERCENT) DURING THE PERIOD 1975-2000 | 20 | 10 | 25 | 30 | 15 |

|  | 1977-80 | | | 1981-90 | | | 1991-2000 | | |
|---|---|---|---|---|---|---|---|---|---|
|  | Frequent | Average | Infrequent | Frequent | Average | Infrequent | Frequent | Average | Infrequent |
| PROBABILITY OF MID-LATITUDE DROUGHT* | | | | | | | | | |
| United States | 0.6 | 0.3 | 0.1 | 0.3 | 0.6 | 0.1 | 0.6 | 0.3 | 0.1 |
| Other Mid-Latitude | 0.6 | 0.4 | | 0.5 | 0.4 | 0.1 | 0.5 | 0.4 | 0.1 |
| PROBABILITY OF SAHEL DROUGHT** | 0.4 | 0.5 | 0.1 | 0.4 | 0.4 | 0.2 | 0.5 | 0.4 | 0.1 |
| PROBABILITY OF MONSOON FAILURE*** | | | | | | | | | |
| Northwest India | 0.4 | 0.5 | 0.1 | 0.3 | 0.5 | 0.2 | 0.4 | 0.6 | |
| Other India | 0.5 | 0.4 | 0.1 | 0.3 | 0.5 | 0.2 | 0.5 | 0.4 | 0.1 |
| Other Monsoon Asia | 0.5 | 0.4 | 0.1 | 0.3 | 0.5 | 0.2 | 0.4 | 0.5 | 0.1 |

*Frequent—similar to early to mid-1930s and early to mid-1950s; average—similar to the frequency over the longest period of record available; infrequent—similar to 1940s and 1960s.

**Frequent—similar to 1940-50 and 1965-73 periods; average—similar to the frequency over the longest period of record available; infrequent—similar to 1950-65 period.

***Frequent—similar to 1900-25 period; average—similar to the frequency over the longest period of record available; infrequent—similar to 1930-60 period.

## TABLE 4-3A

# SAME AS THE LAST 30 YEARS

PROBABILITY OF SCENARIO: 0.30      MEAN NORTHERN HEMISPHERE TEMPERATURE CHANGE SINCE 1969: between 0.05° colder and 0.25°C warmer

## PROBABILITY OF TEMPERATURE CHANGE BY LATITUDE

(Compared with 1970-75)

|  |  | 1.0-1.5°C colder | 0.5-1.0°C colder | 0.0-0.5°C colder | 0.0-0.5°C warmer | 0.5-1.0°C warmer | 1.0-1.5°C warmer | 1.5-2.0°C warmer | 2.0-3.0°C warmer | 3.0-5.0°C warmer |
|---|---|---|---|---|---|---|---|---|---|---|
| Northern hemisphere | Polar | 0.1 | 0.1 | 0.1 | 0.3 | 0.2 | 0.2 | | | |
| | Higher mid-latitude* | | 0.1 | 0.2 | 0.4 | 0.2 | 0.1 | | | |
| | Lower mid-latitude | | 0.1 | 0.2 | 0.4 | 0.2 | 0.1 | | | |
| | Subtropical | | 0.1 | 0.2 | 0.5 | 0.1 | 0.1 | | | |
| Southern hemisphere | Subtropical | | 0.1 | 0.3 | 0.4 | 0.1 | 0.1 | | | |
| | Lower mid-latitude | | 0.1 | 0.3 | 0.4 | 0.1 | 0.1 | | | |
| | Higher mid-latitude* | | 0.1 | 0.3 | 0.4 | 0.1 | 0.1 | | | |
| | Polar | 0.1 | 0.1 | 0.3 | 0.3 | 0.1 | 0.1 | | | |

*Growing season in higher middle latitudes: Probability of an increase (decrease) in the *length* of the growing season exceeding 10 days is 0.2 (0.1); probability of an increase (decrease) in the *variability* of the length of the growing season in excess of 25% is 0.1 (0.1).

## PROBABILITY OF PRECIPITATION CHANGE BY LATITUDE

(Compared with 1941-70)

|  | ANNUAL | | | | GROWING SEASON | | |
|---|---|---|---|---|---|---|---|
|  | Increase ⩾ 10% | Change < 10% | Decrease ⩾ 10% | | Increase ⩾ 10% | Change < 10% | Decrease ⩾ 10% |
| Higher mid-latitude | 0.2 | 0.6 | 0.2 | | 0.2 | 0.6 | 0.2 |
| Lower mid-latitude | 0.2 | 0.6 | 0.2 | | 0.2 | 0.6 | 0.2 |
| Subtropical | 0.2 | 0.6 | 0.2 | | 0.2 | 0.6 | 0.2 |

## PROBABILITY OF PRECIPITATION VARIABILITY CHANGE BY LATITUDE

(Compared with average for the previous 25-year period)

|  | ANNUAL | | | | GROWING SEASON | | |
|---|---|---|---|---|---|---|---|
|  | Increase ⩾ 25% | Change < 25% | Decrease ⩾ 25% | | Increase ⩾ 25% | Change < 25% | Decrease ⩾ 25% |
| Higher mid-latitude | 0.2 | 0.6 | 0.2 | | 0.2 | 0.7 | 0.1 |
| Lower mid-latitude | 0.2 | 0.6 | 0.2 | | 0.2 | 0.7 | 0.1 |
| Subtropical | 0.2 | 0.6 | 0.2 | | 0.3 | 0.6 | 0.1 |

## TABLE 4–3B

# SAME AS THE LAST 30 YEARS

| | Carbon dioxide | Fluoro-carbons | Smoke | Volcanic dust | Other particles |
|---|---|---|---|---|---|
| RELATIVE IMPORTANCE OF CARBON DIOXIDE AND TURBIDITY (PERCENT) DURING THE PERIOD 1975-2000 | 50 | 10 | 10 | 15 | 15 |

| | 1977-80 | | | 1981-90 | | | 1991-2000 | | |
|---|---|---|---|---|---|---|---|---|---|
| | Frequent | Average | Infrequent | Frequent | Average | Infrequent | Frequent | Average | Infrequent |
| PROBABILITY OF MID-LATITUDE DROUGHT* | | | | | | | | | |
| United States | 0.5 | 0.4 | 0.1 | 0.2 | 0.6 | 0.2 | 0.5 | 0.4 | 0.1 |
| Other Mid-Latitude | 0.4 | 0.5 | 0.1 | 0.3 | 0.6 | 0.1 | 0.4 | 0.5 | 0.1 |
| PROBABILITY OF SAHEL DROUGHT** | 0.2 | 0.6 | 0.2 | 0.2 | 0.7 | 0.1 | 0.2 | 0.7 | 0.1 |
| PROBABILITY OF MONSOON FAILURE*** | | | | | | | | | |
| Northwest India | 0.3 | 0.6 | 0.1 | 0.2 | 0.6 | 0.2 | 0.2 | 0.5 | 0.3 |
| Other India | 0.3 | 0.6 | 0.1 | 0.2 | 0.6 | 0.2 | 0.2 | 0.5 | 0.3 |
| Other Monsoon Asia | 0.3 | 0.6 | 0.1 | 0.2 | 0.6 | 0.2 | 0.2 | 0.6 | 0.2 |

*Frequent—similar to early to mid-1930s and early to mid-1950s; average—similar to the frequency over the longest period of record available; infrequent—similar to 1940s and 1960s.

**Frequent—similar to 1940-50 and 1965-73 periods; average—similar to the frequency over the longest period of record available; infrequent—similar to 1950-65 period.

***Frequent—similar to 1900-25 period; average—similar to the frequency over the longest period of record available; infrequent—similar to 1930-60 period.

## TABLE 4-4A

# MODERATE GLOBAL WARMING

PROBABILITY OF SCENARIO: 0.25
MEAN NORTHERN HEMISPHERE TEMPERATURE CHANGE SINCE 1969: between 0.25° and 0.6°C warmer

## PROBABILITY OF TEMPERATURE CHANGE BY LATITUDE

(Compared with 1970-75)

| | | 1.0-1.5°C colder | 0.5-1.0°C colder | 0.0-0.5°C colder | 0.0-0.5°C warmer | 0.5-1.0°C warmer | 1.0-1.5°C warmer | 1.5-2.0°C warmer | 2.0-3.0°C warmer | 3.0-5.0°C warmer |
|---|---|---|---|---|---|---|---|---|---|---|
| Northern hemisphere | Polar | | | 0.1 | 0.1 | 0.2 | 0.2 | 0.2 | 0.2 | |
| | Higher mid-latitude* | | | 0.1 | 0.3 | 0.4 | 0.1 | 0.1 | | |
| | Lower mid-latitude | | | 0.1 | 0.5 | 0.3 | 0.1 | | | |
| | Subtropical | | | 0.1 | 0.6 | 0.2 | 0.1 | | | |
| Southern hemisphere | Subtropical | | | 0.1 | 0.6 | 0.2 | 0.1 | | | |
| | Lower mid-latitude | | | 0.1 | 0.5 | 0.3 | 0.1 | | | |
| | Higher mid-latitude* | | | 0.1 | 0.3 | 0.5 | 0.1 | | | |
| | Polar | | | 0.1 | 0.2 | 0.5 | 0.1 | 0.1 | | |

*Growing season in higher middle latitudes: Probability of an increase (decrease) in the *length* of the growing season exceeding 10 days is 0.4 (0.2); probability of an increase (decrease) in the *variability* of the length of the growing season in excess of 25% is 0.1 (0.2).

## PROBABILITY OF PRECIPITATION CHANGE BY LATITUDE

(Compared with 1941-70)

| | ANNUAL | | | | GROWING SEASON | | |
|---|---|---|---|---|---|---|---|
| | Increase ∧ 10% | Change ∨ 10% | Decrease ∧ 10% | | Increase ∧ 10% | Change ∨ 10% | Decrease ∧ 10% |
| Higher mid-latitude | 0.3 | 0.5 | 0.2 | | 0.3 | 0.5 | 0.2 |
| Lower mid-latitude | 0.2 | 0.6 | 0.2 | | 0.2 | 0.6 | 0.2 |
| Subtropical | 0.2 | 0.6 | 0.2 | | 0.3 | 0.5 | 0.2 |

## PROBABILITY OF PRECIPITATION VARIABILITY CHANGE BY LATITUDE

(Compared with average for the previous 25-year period)

| | ANNUAL | | | | GROWING SEASON | | |
|---|---|---|---|---|---|---|---|
| | Increase ∧ 25% | Change ∨ 25% | Decrease ∧ 25% | | Increase ∧ 25% | Change ∨ 25% | Decrease ∧ 25% |
| Higher mid-latitude | 0.2 | 0.6 | 0.2 | | 0.2 | 0.6 | 0.2 |
| Lower mid-latitude | 0.2 | 0.6 | 0.2 | | 0.2 | 0.6 | 0.2 |
| Subtropical | 0.2 | 0.6 | 0.2 | | 0.3 | 0.5 | 0.2 |

## TABLE 4–4B

# MODERATE GLOBAL WARMING

| | Carbon dioxide | Fluoro-carbons | Smoke | Volcanic dust | Other particles |
|---|---|---|---|---|---|
| RELATIVE IMPORTANCE OF CARBON DIOXIDE AND TURBIDITY (PERCENT) DURING THE PERIOD 1975-2000 | 60 | 15 | 5 | 10 | 10 |

| | 1977-80 | | | 1981-90 | | | 1991-2000 | | |
|---|---|---|---|---|---|---|---|---|---|
| | Frequent | Average | Infrequent | Frequent | Average | Infrequent | Frequent | Average | Infrequent |
| PROBABILITY OF MID-LATITUDE DROUGHT* | | | | | | | | | |
| United States | 0.6 | 0.3 | 0.1 | 0.2 | 0.2 | 0.6 | 0.5 | 0.3 | 0.2 |
| Other Mid-Latitude | | | | | | | | | |
| PROBABILITY OF SAHEL DROUGHT** | 0.3 | 0.4 | 0.3 | 0.3 | 0.4 | 0.3 | 0.3 | 0.4 | 0.3 |
| PROBABILITY OF MONSOON FAILURE*** | | | | | | | | | |
| Northwest India | 0.3 | 0.4 | 0.3 | 0.3 | 0.4 | 0.3 | 0.2 | 0.5 | 0.3 |
| Other India | | | | | | | | | |
| Other Monsoon Asia | | | | | | | | | |

*Frequent—similar to early to mid-1930s and early to mid-1950s; average—similar to the frequency over the longest period of record available; infrequent—similar to 1940s and 1960s.

**Frequent—similar to 1940-50 and 1965-73 periods; average—similar to the frequency over the longest period of record available; infrequent—similar to 1950-65 period.

***Frequent—similar to 1900-25 period; average—similar to the frequency over the longest period of record available; infrequent—similar to 1930-60 period.

## TABLE 4–5A

## LARGE GLOBAL WARMING

PROBABILITY OF SCENARIO: 0.10
MEAN NORTHERN HEMISPHERE TEMPERATURE CHANGE SINCE 1969: between 0.6° and 1.8°C warmer

## PROBABILITY OF TEMPERATURE CHANGE BY LATITUDE

(Compared with 1970-75)

| | | 1.0-1.5°C colder | 0.5-1.0°C colder | 0.0-0.5°C colder | 0.0-0.5°C warmer | 0.5-1.0°C warmer | 1.0-1.5°C warmer | 1.5-2.0°C warmer | 2.0-3.0°C warmer | 3.0-5.0°C warmer |
|---|---|---|---|---|---|---|---|---|---|---|
| Northern hemisphere | Polar | | | | | | 0.1 | 0.1 | 0.2 | 0.6 |
| | Higher mid-latitude* | | | | | 0.1 | 0.5 | 0.4 | | |
| | Lower mid-latitude | | | | 0.1 | 0.5 | 0.2 | 0.2 | | |
| | Subtropical | | | | 0.1 | 0.8 | 0.1 | | | |
| Southern hemisphere | Subtropical | | | | 0.1 | 0.8 | 0.1 | | | |
| | Lower mid-latitude | | | | 0.1 | 0.5 | 0.2 | 0.2 | | |
| | Higher mid-latitude* | | | | | 0.1 | 0.5 | 0.4 | | |
| | Polar | | | | | 0.1 | 0.1 | 0.1 | 0.2 | 0.5 |

*Growing season in higher middle latitudes: Probability of an increase (decrease) in the *length* of growing season exceeding 10 days is 0.8 (0.0); probability of an increase (decrease) in the *variability* of the length of the growing season in excess of 25% is 0.0 (0.7).

## PROBABILITY OF PRECIPITATION CHANGE BY LATITUDE

(Compared with 1941-70)

| | ANNUAL | | | | GROWING SEASON | | |
|---|---|---|---|---|---|---|---|
| | Increase ⩾ 10% | Change < 10% | Decrease ⩾ 10% | | Increase ⩾ 10% | Change < 10% | Decrease ⩾ 10% |
| Higher mid-latitude | 0.4 | 0.5 | 0.1 | | 0.3 | 0.5 | 0.2 |
| Lower mid-latitude | 0.3 | 0.5 | 0.2 | | 0.3 | 0.4 | 0.3 |
| Subtropical | 0.3 | 0.5 | 0.2 | | 0.4 | 0.5 | 0.1 |

## PROBABILITY OF PRECIPITATION VARIABILITY CHANGE BY LATITUDE

(Compared with average for the previous 25-year period)

| | ANNUAL | | | | GROWING SEASON | | |
|---|---|---|---|---|---|---|---|
| | Increase ⩾ 25% | Change < 25% | Decrease ⩾ 25% | | Increase ⩾ 25% | Change < 25% | Decrease ⩾ 25% |
| Higher mid-latitude | 0.2 | 0.5 | 0.3 | | 0.2 | 0.5 | 0.3 |
| Lower mid-latitude | 0.2 | 0.5 | 0.3 | | 0.3 | 0.5 | 0.2 |
| Subtropical | 0.2 | 0.5 | 0.3 | | 0.3 | 0.5 | 0.2 |

## TABLE 4–5B

# LARGE GLOBAL WARMING

| | Carbon dioxide | Fluoro-carbons | Smoke | Volcanic dust | Other particles |
|---|---|---|---|---|---|
| RELATIVE IMPORTANCE OF CARBON DIOXIDE AND TURBIDITY (PERCENT) DURING THE PERIOD 1975-2000 | 90 | 10 | 0 | 0 | 0 |

| | 1977-80 | | | 1981-90 | | | 1991-2000 | | |
|---|---|---|---|---|---|---|---|---|---|
| | Frequent | Average | Infrequent | Frequent | Average | Infrequent | Frequent | Average | Infrequent |
| **PROBABILITY OF MID-LATITUDE DROUGHT*** | | | | | | | | | |
| United States | 0.6 | 0.3 | 0.1 | 0.6 | 0.3 | 0.1 | 0.7 | 0.2 | 0.1 |
| Other Mid-Latitude | 0.5 | 0.3 | 0.2 | 0.5 | 0.3 | 0.2 | 0.3 | 0.3 | 0.4 |
| **PROBABILITY OF SAHEL DROUGHT**** | 0.1 | 0.8 | 0.1 | 0.1 | 0.7 | 0.2 | 0.1 | 0.6 | 0.3 |
| **PROBABILITY OF MONSOON FAILURE***** | | | | | | | | | |
| Northwest India | 0.1 | 0.8 | 0.1 | 0.1 | 0.6 | 0.3 | | 0.2 | 0.8 |
| Other India | 0.1 | 0.8 | 0.1 | 0.1 | 0.6 | 0.3 | 0.1 | 0.2 | 0.7 |
| Other Monsoon Asia | 0.1 | 0.8 | 0.1 | 0.1 | 0.6 | 0.3 | 0.1 | 0.2 | 0.7 |

*Frequent—similar to early to mid-1930s and early to mid-1950s; average—similar to the frequency over the longest period of record available; infrequent—similar to 1940s and 1960s.

**Frequent—similar to 1940-50 and 1965-73 periods; average—similar to the frequency over the longest period of record available; infrequent—similar to 1950-65 period.

***Frequent—similar to 1900-25 period; average—similar to the frequency over the longest period of record available; infrequent—similar to 1930-60 period.

While average global temperature increased moderately, the largest temperature increases came in the higher latitudes. The Northern Hemisphere warmed slightly more than the Southern Hemisphere due to its greater land area and the larger thermal inertia of the southern oceans. In the Northern Hemisphere, the polar latitudes warmed by 1.2° C; the higher middle latitudes by 0.5° C, the lower middle latitudes by 0.3° C; and the subtropical latitudes by 0.25° C. In the Southern Hemisphere, average temperatures over the polar latitudes increased by 0.65° C; the higher middle latitudes by 0.4° C; the lower middle latitudes by 0.3° C; and the subtropical latitudes by 0.2° C. The increase in global temperature was reflected in a moderate increase in the length of the growing season in higher middle latitudes, but no significant change in the interannual variability of the growing season was noted.

Annual precipitation levels increased slightly in the higher middle latitudes but showed little change for lower latitudinal bands. Growing-season precipitation also increased slightly in the higher middle latitudes and subtropical regions but remained unchanged in the lower middle latitudes. Both annual and growing-season precipitation variability remained essentially unchanged except for a slight increase in the variability of growing-season precipitation in subtropical latitudes.

Drought conditions again plagued the midlatitude areas of the United States, corroborating the 20- to 22-year drought cycle hypothesis. Climatic conditions were somewhat more favorable in the Asiatic region and in subtropical North Africa. The frequency of monsoon failure, especially in northwest India, resembled more closely the long-term average; so did the frequency of drought in the Sahel region.

### Large Global Warming*

The global cooling trend that began in the 1940s was dramatically reversed in the last quarter of the 20th century. By the year 2000, the mean Northern Hemisphere temperature had increased by about 1° C compared to the early 1970s. Climatologists explained that this trend was due principally to the warming effects of the increasing amounts of carbon dioxide in the atmosphere.

While temperature increased over the entire globe, temperature increases were more pronounced at higher latitudes. The subtropical lati-

tudes warmed, on the average, by 0.8° C; the lower middle latitudes by 1.0° C; the higher middle latitudes by 1.4° C; and the polar latitudes by a remarkable 3.0° C, compared to the early 1970s. Symmetry prevailed as similar temperature changes were observed in both the Northern and Southern Hemispheres. The increase in temperature was accompanied by a significant increase in the length of the growing season in the higher middle latitudes, as well as by a substantial decrease in the variability from year to year in the length of the growing season.

Precipitation levels generally increased, especially in the subtropical and higher middle latitudes. In the lower middle latitudes there was little net change of precipitation. Annual precipitation variability decreased slightly compared to the 1950–75 period; precipitation variability during the growing season similarly decreased in the higher middle latitudes, but increased slightly in the lower middle and subtropical latitudes.

The warming trend also ushered in more favorable climatic conditions in India and other parts of Asia. These conditions were similar to those of the 1930–60 period. Monsoon failure was infrequent, especially in northwest India. But in the midlatitude areas of the United States, extending from the Rockies to the Appalachians, drought conditions similar to the mid–1930s and the early to mid–1950s prevailed. In other midlatitude areas of the world, notably Europe, the probability of drought declined. The increased levels of precipitation also returned the Sahel region to wetter weather conditions.

## Climate Scenarios for the Global 2000 Study

The NDU scenarios provide a richness of detail that could not be used in the Global 2000 Study. At the beginning of the Study it was assumed that the government's long-term global models would require climatological inputs, and three simplified scenarios—informed by the National Defense University study—were developed. More careful investigation established later that *none of the global long-term models used by the agencies for this Study are capable of accepting climatological inputs. The energy, food, water and forestry projections all assume implicitly a continuation of the nearly ideal climate of the 1950s and 1960s.* Although the climate scenarios developed for the Global 2000 Study could not be incorporated into the Study's projections, the scenarios are reported here to indicate the range of climatic change that should be analyzed in a study of this sort.

---

*Statements concerning some details of this scenario reflect a higher degree of certainty than was expressed by the climatologists who participated in this study. See Tables 4–5 A and B for the range of uncertainty.

The Global 2000 Case I scenario described below is similar to the "same as the last 30 years" scenario in the NDU study. The Case II scenario is intermediate between NDU's "moderate warming" and "large warming"; similarly, Case III is intermediate between NDU's two cooling scenarios. *Note that these scenarios span a narrower range of variation than the National Defense University scenarios and that the narrow span excludes climatological developments that would have a pronounced effect on future demands for and supplies of food, wood, water, and energy.*

The three Global 2000 climate scenarios are:

*Case I: No Change.* Yearly rainfall and temperature statistics are similar to those of the 1941–70 period. Drought conditions in the U.S. continue to occur every 20 to 22 years. Monsoon failures in India become less frequent than recently and the Sahel region of Africa no longer experiences severe drought of the type that occurred in the late '60s and early '70s.

*Case II: Warming.* Global temperatures increase by 1° C. Most of the warming is in the polar regions and the higher middle latitudes, with only slight warming in the tropics. Annual precipitation increases by 5–10 percent, and year to year variance decreases slightly. There is an increased likelihood of U.S. drought conditions similar to those of the mid-'30s.

*Case III: Cooling.* Global temperatures decrease by 0.5° C. Cooling of 1° C occurs in the higher and middle latitudes, with a smaller change in the tropics and subtropics. Precipitation amounts decline and variability increases both from month to month and from year to year. Storm tracks—and the precipitation they bring—shift toward the equator, improving conditions in the upper latitudes of the great deserts and worsening them on the equator side. Severe monsoon failures are more frequent in India, severe droughts more frequent in the Sahel.

The three Global 2000 scenarios are compared in Figure 4–1 with the historical record of temperature changes from the 1870s to the 1970s.

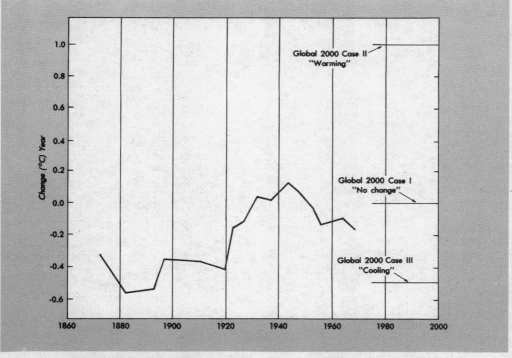

**Figure 4-1.** The three Global 2000 Study scenarios compared with the annual mean temperature changes during the past century for the latitude band 0°–80°N. The period 1941–70 is the zero reference base.

# 5   Technology Projections

Logically, technology is an input to the Global 2000 Study projections much as are population, GNP, and climate. But, because technology is so highly specific to each type of projection, it was impossible to formulate a single set of measures of technological change for all analyses. It was therefore left to the individual experts to make their own assumptions about the effects of technology in their own fields and to develop their projections from those assumptions as well as from the exogenously supplied population, GNP, and climate forecasts. They were requested to make these assumptions as explicit as possible in statements to the Global 2000 Study—often a difficult task, as when trends of technological advance were concealed in time series extrapolations of other input variables, or when it was unclear whether a particular idea was more correctly considered an assumption or a conclusion.

This chapter gathers together the assumptions of technological change made in the individual analyses of the Global 2000 project. For the sake of comprehensiveness, the assumptions behind the development of the input forecasts already considered (population, GNP, climate) are included.

In general, the analyses assume that the adoption and refinement of existing technologies will continue at about the same rate as in the recent past. The verbal analyses often refer to possible technological breakthroughs, and many of the quantitative forecasts extrapolate from historical data taken from the past two or three decades, which were characterized by many such breakthroughs. These forecasts implicitly assume, therefore, that breakthroughs will occur in the future at recent historical rates.

## Population

Technology affects population primarily in the form of birth control, which lowers fertility, and health care, which lowers the death rate. In making the population projections used in the Global 2000 Study, the U.S. Bureau of the Census implicitly assumed continued adoption of both forms of technology at moderate rates by project-

ing generally declining fertilities and mortalities. While the Bureau recognizes the possibility of technological breakthroughs in both fields, some of which are currently under study, it believes that it is uncertain whether any will be perfected and adopted widely enough by the year 2000 to have a significant impact on fertility and mortality levels. Similarly, the Bureau assumed that no regression in either type of technology serious enough to significantly affect their forecasts will occur in the near future-for example, major harmful side effects of existing birth control techniques will not be discovered, and new uncontrollable microbial strains harmful to humans will not develop. While technological advance or regression may occur before 2000 and shift population growth up or down slightly, the Bureau believes that such occurrences will not result in increases or decreases that exceed the limits of its high and low projections.

The discussion of migration in Chapter 2 makes no technological assumptions except that world industrialization will probably continue at about present rates.

## Gross National Product

The GNP forecasts in Chapter 3 were made by analysts in three separate agencies according to somewhat different methods. The forecasts for industrialized noncommunist and communist countries, made by a panel of WAES (Workshop on Alternative Energy Strategies) experts and by the CIA, respectively, are largely the result of subjectively extrapolating historical growth rates. Thus, technology is implicitly assumed to contribute to future economic growth about as it has in the recent past. The WAES panel adjusted its estimates downward to account for the supposed restrictive effect of slowed future population growth. The CIA adjusted its forecasts for parts of Eastern Europe downward on the basis of the availability of energy, thus assuming that technological advance will not completely counteract an increasing scarcity of energy. Initially, however, it based all of its forecasts on direct extrapolation of past trends of GNP and productivity growth, implicitly assuming a continuation of past technological trends.

Forecasts for the less developed countries (LDCs) were made by the World Bank (originally for use by the WAES study) in three stages:

1. Projections were developed by analysts on an independent, country by country basis, relying on a combination of professional judgment and the use of specialized country or regional models. Typically, past rates of increase in the productivity of new capital investment were implicitly projected to continue in the future. These increases were not explicitly attributed to technological change. However, because capital productivity increases in the past resulted partially from technological advance, extensions of the upward trend in productivity presumably imply continued advance.

2. Using a computer-based model, the various country projections were aggregated and adjusted on a globally consistent basis to reflect probable economic growth constraints due to likely limitations in the availability of foreign trade earnings and foreign investment capital. Each LDC group was represented in a way that implicitly assumed that major increases in the productivity of new capital investment will occur in each LDC, in part as a result of technological change (see Chapter 16). For example, in the case of the Other South Asian LDC group, a given investment was implicitly assumed to produce about 60 percent more incremental GDP in 1985 than in 1977 (in constant dollars). However, there is no way to infer the precise extent to which this improved productivity of capital might properly be attributed to technological change.

3. The projections were further adjusted judgmentally by Bank and WAES analysts, but these adjustments were not related to assumptions regarding technological change.

## Climate

The climate forecasts make no assumptions about technology except that industrial processes will continue to release large amounts of carbon dioxide into the atmosphere, with the possible effect of warming the earth's atmosphere. No other foreseeable technological developments before the year 2000 were considered to have a significant effect on the climate of the planet.

## Food

As an econometric projection model, the GOL (grain, oilseed, livestock) model that was used to make the Global 2000 Study's agricultural forecasts assumes that economic variables such as product and input prices will influence food production efficiency as in the recent past. However, provision is also made to incorporate an exogenously estimated trend rate of growth in technology over and above the growth explained by economic variables. This is done by adjusting regional food yield and thus, implicitly, yields per hectare. Yield per hectare is the measure of production efficiency used in the GOL model.

The exogenous adjustments for changes in yield are made in the regional production equations. For each region, GOL has one linear regression equation for each major agricultural product produced locally. In each equation, total production is calculated as a function of endogenously determined crop hectarage, a base crop yield, a time trend variable, and changes in product prices, input prices, and the prices of products competing for inputs. The time trend variable is equal to 1 in the first year of the estimation period, to 2 in the second, and so on. It is intended to capture the effects of factors—other than those included in the total production equation—that influence total yields over time. The most important of these is believed to be technology, which has acted over time to increase yields. The following steps are taken to adjust the estimated coefficient of the trend variable to reflect country analysts' judgments about future productivity trends:

1. GOL supply and demand inputs are used to project roughly the direction of likely future price movements.

2. For each region, a measure of likely pressure on supply calculated from the price projections is used to estimate changes in "innovative technology," which in turn defines the physical or biological limitation on yield per hectare with the best available technology; the estimation thus assumes that technological advance responds directly to economic incentives.

3. The innovative technology level for each region and various data forecasted from the GOL run (see Step 1) are given to the appropriate regional analysts within the Department of Agriculture.

4. On the basis of the data received, each regional analyst re-estimates trend growth in yield to reflect possible constraints or sources of growth not included in the original regression analysis.

5. In each regional production equation of GOL, the coefficient of the time trend variable is recalculated so that the trend increases approximate the values estimated by the regional analyst.

6. The GOL model is run with the judgmentally modified trend coefficients along with the other economic variables cited above. The output of the model is its final forecasts. The yields per hectare that can be calculated from the output are called "adopted technology" because they are the yields per hectare that the regions are projected to actually achieve.

Thus, potential yields per hectare in the future, estimated with data from the GOL model, are used by analysts in adjusting productivity data within the model.

A graph of innovative and adopted technology taken from actual model data is reproduced in Figure 5–1. It is for rice production in Thailand. The first half of each curve is historical data. The right half of the top curve is future innovative technology, calculated as explained in Step 2

above. The right half of the bottom curve is adopted technology calculated as explained in Step 6. GOL was run twice, once for each of two years, to get two points from each kind of technology with which to draw the extrapolations shown. The innovative technology data are what is given to the Thailand regional analyst to consider in setting Thailand's rice output for the adjustment of the GOL model described in Step 3. The adopted technology data points were calculated from the output of the runs as described in Step 6.

Fertilizer consumption per unit of food production, also often considered an important measure of agricultural technology, is estimated subjectively by Department of Agriculture analysts on the basis of the GOL output after the model run is complete. The fertilizer consumption and food

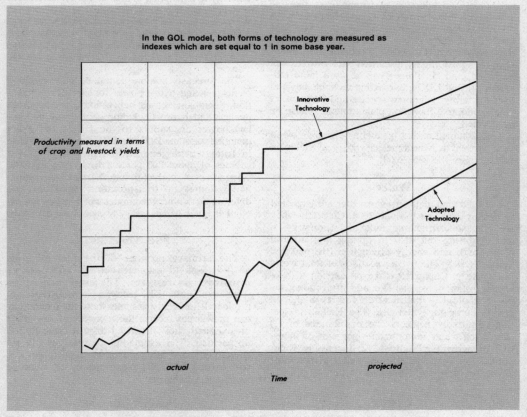

**Figure 5-1.** Innovative and adopted technology levels for rice production in Thailand as projected by the GOL *(grain, oilseed, livestock)* model.

production data in Chapter 6 show an assumption of continued increases in fertilizer use per unit of food output, from about 800 nutrient tons around 1971 to 970 nutrient tons in 1985 and to 1210 nutrient tons in the year 2000.

## Fisheries

The fisheries analysis assumes that the means to harvest and process formerly unfished marine animals, such as Antarctic krill, will be increasingly adopted through the year 2000. Ocean pollution will continue unabated. Technology will soon be ineffective and perhaps counterproductive in increasing catches from natural fisheries because of reduction of fish populations.

## Forestry

The forestry analysis assumes a continued development and adoption of technologies that increase both forest productivity and the percentage of that productivity that can be exploited and used. Particularly in the industrialized countries, the management of forests will become more intensive, uses for formerly discarded parts of trees will be found, and cut timber will be used more efficiently. In the LDCs, harvesting technologies and uses for formerly ignored species and size classes will be adopted; fuelwood plantations may also be established.

Also assumed is that no fuel as cheap as wood is at present will become as widely available in LDCs before the year 2000.

## Water

The following major uses of water are expected to remain the same through 2000. Currently, they are domestic, irrigation, industrial (primarily in manufacturing but also in mining and mineral processing), and energy production (thermal and hydroelectric). The two projections of total world water use in Chapter 9 make no explicit technological assumptions. The Doxiadis projection gives no technological justification for its S-shaped growth curve for water use. The Kalinin projection admittedly neglects the possibilities of (1) decreasing water requirements per unit of industrial or agricultural output, (2) increasing water purification or desalinization, and (3) increasing direct use of unpurified and salt water.

## Energy

The energy forecasts, made with the International Energy Evaluation System (IEES) com-

puter model, assume that only proven techniques for producing final fossil fuels will be widely enough adopted to significantly affect the world energy market by the year 2000. Producers' supply curves, indirectly representing their cost of production, assume no rapid acceleration in yield. The real costs and efficiencies of refining and converting primary fuels and the costs, routes, and modes of transporting intermediate products are also held constant. However, the types of final fuels demanded, the sources of the primary fuels used to make them, the refining and conversion techniques applied in production, and the transportation modes and routes all vary according to relative costs. Large increases in the adoption of existing technologies are also assumed to be possible. The IEES allows world shipping and refining capacities to expand indefinitely to meet world energy demand, and miscellaneous conversions capacity to expand up to high limits. Miscellaneous conversions capacity in 1985 and 1990 is allowed to be as much as two and three times its historical 1975 level, respectively. In general, the expansions in refining and miscellaneous conversions capacities are restricted to the industrialized nations.

The forecasts assume continued new adoption of nuclear and hydro power for electrical generation. Regional electrical generation capacities from nuclear and hydro (including geothermal and solar) power are inputs to the IEES; the exact quantities assumed (Table 5–1) show an increase in total world generation from these power sources of about 200 percent from 1975 to 1990. Capacities of conventional thermal generation, like refining and transportation capacities, are determined within the model but allowed to expand as much as necessary to meet final demands.

## Fuel Minerals

The primary purpose of the fuel minerals analysis was to estimate current world energy resources and reserves. The estimation of resources (all potentially recoverable occurrences of a mineral) implicitly assumes how far technology can or will advance in the recovery of low-grade ores. Exactly how it will advance is typically left unspecified. The estimation of reserves (all resources economically recoverable at current prices with existing technology) assumes by definition no technological change.

## Nonfuel Minerals

The nonfuel minerals demand forecasts were made from combinations of expert judgment and

## TABLE 5-1

### Electrical Generation from Nuclear and Hydro Power Assumed in Energy Forecasts

*(Terawatt-hours per year)*

| | United States | Indus-trialized Coun-tries [a] | Less Devel-oped Coun-tries | OPEC Coun-tries | Centrally Planned Econo-mies |
|---|---|---|---|---|---|
| 1975 | 475 | 1,343 | 240 | 0 | — |
| 1985 | | | | | |
| Low growth | 969 | 2,492 | 585 | 19 | 760 |
| Medium growth | 975 | 2,515 | 585 | 19 | 760 |
| High growth | 976 | 2,516 | 585 | 19 | 760 |
| High prices | 1,045 | 2,584 | 585 | 19 | 760 |
| 1990 | | | | | |
| Low growth | 1,373 | 3,316 | 924 | 64 | 1,350 |
| Medium growth | 1,397 | 3,513 | 924 | 64 | 1,350 |
| High growth | 1,402 | 3,518 | 924 | 64 | 1,350 |
| High prices | 1,555 | 3,670 | 924 | 64 | 1,350 |

[a] Including the U.S.

data analysis. Technology entered the development of the forecasts taken from the 1977 Malenbaum Report (see Chapter 22) in the derivation of intensity-of-use curves. Many of the technological assumptions that influenced the construction of any one curve tended to be highly specific to the mineral and region for which it was drawn. The general technological assumptions implied in the report to underlie all of the curves, with some qualification for individual curves, are:

1. As an economy grows, it first develops or adopts production processes that are relatively mineral-intensive. Then increasingly it refines these processes or shifts away from them, which contributes to a gradual decline in the economy's mineral intensity of use.
2. The advances in mineral production technology necessary to allow continued growth in production will be made. Mineral production will grow through 2000 quickly and reliably enough to make end-use factors, not supply constraints, the dominant determinants of mineral consumption. Economic growth will not be restricted by mineral availability or price; in fact, real mineral prices may decline in the future.

The Bureau of Mines demand forecasts used the judgments of the Bureau's individual commodity analysts, aided by analyses of historical data.

U.S. primary demand for minerals is projected to 1985 and 2000 by use of a regression analysis using the following U.S. economic indicators as explanatory variables: GNP, Federal Reserve Board index of industrial production, gross private domestic investment, new construction, population, and GNP per capita. The historical values of these variables, supplied by the Office of Management and Budget, are taken from the 1954–73 period. Such a regression equation would implicitly assume that the role that technological advance has had in making mineral consumption track the explanatory variables in the past will continue into the future. The forecasts of the regression equations are considered by the individual commodity analysts, who then make the final U.S. forecasts after considering other information relevant to their specific commodity markets, including expected technological advances. The analysts' forecasts for rest-of-the-world demand are made with consideration of various world and regional data, including population, GDP, and GDP per capita, and their own knowledge of world markets and probable technology, but without formal regression forecasts of demand.

## Environment

As Chapter 13 assesses the environmental impact that would result if the other forecasts were valid, it generally accepts their assumptions and conclusions pertaining to technology, in addition to its own technological assumptions. The technological assumptions made specifically for the environmental analysis are listed below. The technological assumptions used to make the other forecasts are not repeated here. The general assumption underlying the entire environmental analysis is that most environmental problems are the result of conflict between population and general economic growth on the one hand and evolved biological systems and physical constants of the globe on the other; technology can aid the management of these problems but not eliminate their cause. The sector-specific assumptions are as follows:

*Population.* The relatively resource-intensive living habits and practices of the industrialized nations will continue to supplant other lifestyles around the world.

*Energy.* There will be a global acceptance of U.S. new source performance standards in the near future. (This is an assumption of the Energy

Systems Network Simulator model used to convert the energy consumption forecasts to emissions forecasts, described in Chapter 19).

*Food*. The productivity increases projected in the food analysis will involve no major breakthroughs in genetic engineering of food crops (such as the development of nitrogen-fixing strains or c–4 grains, which are relatively efficient in photosynthesis) or soil, water, and air management. Plant breeding will continue to reduce the genetic diversity of food crops.

*Minerals*. The means to extract increasingly low-grade mineral ores will continue to be developed and adopted. No breakthroughs in reducing the land disturbance, water use, or waste quantities resulting from mining will occur.

# 6 Food and Agriculture Projections

Recent shifts in world food supplies from surplus toward deficit and back again toward surplus have generated wide concern as to future food balances. This chapter reports on world food projections to 1985 and 2000, emphasizing the problem of food balances in the context of wider resource and environmental balances. The projections are summarized in the maps on the following pages. The analytic framework used to generate the projections and their broad implications are highlighted. Resource balances, estimates of the changing cost and growth in investment required to develop the productive capacity projected to 2000, and the broad environmental implications of the projections are also treated.

## Caveats

Long-range projections, particularly food projections, are subject to several qualifications.

First, estimating changes in population, income, taste, resources, technology, and weather as well as their interrelationships 25 years in the future calls for a number of studies rather than a single paper. The wide range of credible studies analyzing these factors but reaching conflicting conclusions points up the latitude possible in estimating changes in these key variables and their interrelationships. The analyses that follow endogenize as many of these variables and interrelationships as possible but depend to a large extent on output from other models that study individual variables in greater detail.

Second, highly aggregated food projections with so distant a time horizon are not forecasts of what will happen but rather educated guesses of what could happen. Assigning probabilities to projections is consequently difficult; projection studies themselves are designed to test alternatives and to identify potential problems and evaluate possible solutions.

Third, global food projections in particular depend on generally limited and sometimes conflicting data. Any global food analysis must balance the wealth of information available for most of the industrialized countries against the paucity of information available for the less developed and centrally planned countries. The extent to which governments intervene to influence the quantities and prices of food produced and consumed in much of the world also leaves long-range projections subject to wholesale revision as agricultural, food, and trade policies change.

Hence, the food projections presented in this chapter must be seen as broad directional indicators only.

## Model and Methodology

The projections outlined below were generated using a world grain-oilseed-livestock (GOL) model and three smaller sets of aggregate food, arable area, and fertilizer relationships.

GOL is a formal mathematical model made up of roughly 1,000 equations describing the functioning and interaction of the world's grain, oilseed, and livestock sectors. More precisely, GOL is a conglomerate of some 28 regional agricultural sector models made up of grain, oilseed, and livestock supply, demand, and trade equations that sum to a world total. The parameters for the mathematical relationships underlying the models were estimated using data from 1950 through 1975 or were drawn from the literature and the judgment of experts.

The strength of the GOL model lies in its emphasis on cross-regional and cross-commodity quantity and price linkages. The individual grain, oilseed, and livestock sectors within each regional model are linked on the supply side in their competition for resources, and on the demand side as intermediate or finished products in the human diet. Production and consumption across regions are balanced at the world level. Imports and exports sum to zero, and world and regional trade prices are harmonized. Each of the regional models provides for physical factors (such as technical input-output relationships) and economic factors (such as supply, demand, and trade prices). Exogenous inputs include population and income growth rates, agricultural and trade policy assumptions, and weather assumptions.

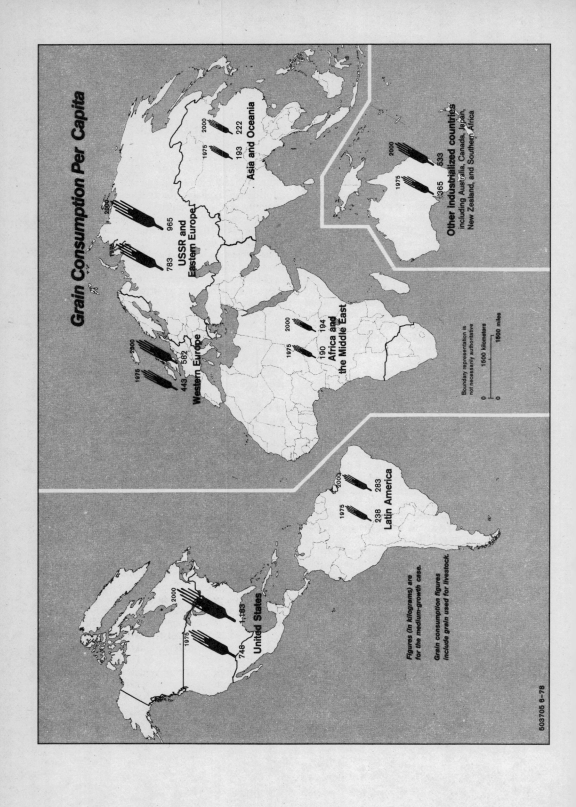

# Grain Consumption Per Capita

**United States**
1975 748
2000 1,163

**Western Europe**
1975 443
2000 582

**USSR and Eastern Europe**
1975 783
2000 965

**Asia and Oceania**
1975 193
2000 222

**Africa and the Middle East**
1975 190
2000 194

**Other industrialized countries**
including Australia, Canada, Japan,
New Zealand, and Southern Africa
1975 365
2000 533

**Latin America**
1975 238
2000 283

Boundary representation is
not necessarily authoritative

0    1500 kilometers
0    1500 miles

Figures (in kilograms) are
for the medium-growth case.

Grain consumption figures
include grain used for livestock.

503705 6-78

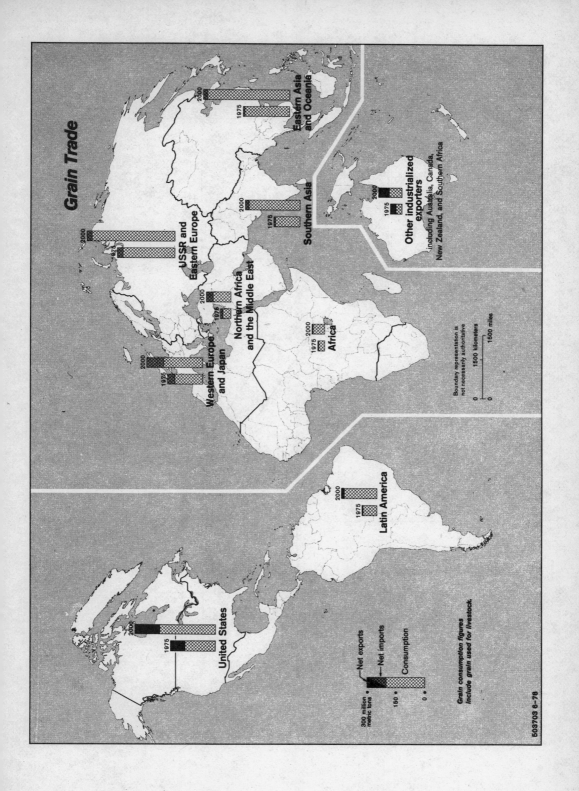

# Grain Trade

**Eastern Asia and Oceania**
2000
1975

**Other industrialized exporters**
including Australia, Canada, New Zealand, and Southern Africa
2000
1975

**USSR and Eastern Europe**
2000

**Southern Asia**
2000
1975

**Northern Africa and the Middle East**
2000
1975

**Western Europe and Japan**
2000
1975

**Africa**
2000
1975

**Latin America**
2000
1975

**United States**
2000
1975

Boundary representation is not necessarily authoritative

0        1500 kilometers
0        1500 miles

Net exports
Net imports
Consumption

300 million metric tons
150
0

*Grain consumption figures include grain used for livestock.*

503703 6–78

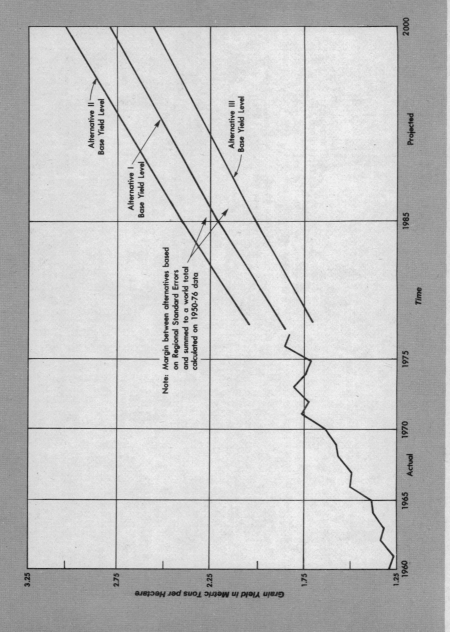

**Figure 6-1.** World grain yields, actual and projected under Alternatives I, II, III.

GOL materials were supplemented with three smaller, informal sets of relationships dealing with aggregate food production and consumption, arable area, and fertilizer use. The first is used to translate GOL output into indices of total food production and consumption; the second and third sets of relationships are used to estimate arable area and fertilizer use. Fertilizer is used as a proxy for a larger collection of inputs, including improved varieties, pesticides, and irrigation. Secondary measures of land-man ratios and use of fertilizer per arable hectare are also generated.

## Scenario Definitions

Three alternative sets of projections were generated for the Global 2000 Study using different income, population, and weather assumptions as well as different assumptions about the rate of petroleum price increases.

Alternative I, a baseline projection, assumes median world population and per capita income growth rates averaging roughly 1.8 percent and 1.5 percent, respectively, through the year 2000 (Tables 6–1 and 6–2). Growth in yields, ultimately raised or lowered by the producer prices generated under a specific alternative, is projected at rates compatible with the technological advances of the past two decades. Weather is held constant—i.e., the impact of weather on yields through 2000 is assumed to be comparable to that of the past 25 years. Agricultural and trade policies are assumed to continue to be largely protectionist in the major importing countries and trade-expansionist in the major exporting countries. Alternative I's median income, population, and weather assumptions are run in combination first with constant energy prices—i.e., assuming petroleum prices do not increase markedly from the real-price highs of 1974–76—and second assuming marked increases more than double the cost of energy inputs by 2000. As will be noted later, the resultant quantity and price ranges quoted under Alternative I reflect not so much uncertainty about petroleum price increases as uncertainty about the ability of the agricultural sector to adjust to changes in input costs.

Alternative II, which defines an optimistic upper bound, assumes lower population growth and higher per capita income growth of about 1.5 percent and 2.4 percent, respectively. Growth in yields is projected assuming favorable weather—i.e., assuming weather through 2000 to be more favorable than weather over the last 25 years. Good weather is assumed to raise yields about the equivalent of one standard error calculated on

1950–75 regional yield series (see Table 6–3 and Fig. 6–1). Alternative II is run assuming petroleum prices remain at their real 1974–76 level through the year 2000.

Alternative III, which defines a lower bound, assumes higher population growth and lower per capita income growth rates of about 2.1 percent and 0.7 percent, respectively. Growth in yields is projected assuming poor weather—i.e., assuming weather through 2000 to be less favorable than over the last 25 years. Yields are projected the equivalent of one standard error below Alternative I levels (see Table 6–3). Alternative III is run assuming that real petroleum prices more than double by 2000.

No provision was made for long-term improvements or deterioration in climate. It is assumed that the world's climate continues largely as reported over the past several decades, or that changes in climate will be small enough to be compensated for by changes in cultural practices and development of new technology. Assuming no significant climate changes, however, does not rule out years of good weather comparable to the late 1960s in the Soviet Union or bad weather years comparable to the mid-1960s in India. The variations in yields between Alternatives II and III provide some measure of the good weather-bad weather range likely without a major change in climate.

## General Results

While the output generated under Alternatives I, II, and III differ with regard to specifics, a number of conclusions hold for all three scenarios. The following general conclusions pertain to Alternative I output.

### Record Growth

*The world has the capacity, both physical and economic, to produce enough food to meet substantial increases in demand through 2000.* The projections are compatible in this regard with a number of other studies suggesting a world food potential several times higher than current production levels. The food growth rates implied in this Study's production and consumption projections are comparable to the record increases reported for the 1950s and the 1960s. Growth in the grain component of total food production and consumption—for which longer historical series are available—is also projected near or above the record rates of the last two decades and more than double the rate of increase for the first half of the century (Table 6–4). *Several significant quali-*

*fications are needed, however, to put this growth into proper perspective.* Driving near-record growth in demand are equally impressive growth in population in the less developed countries (LDCs) and affluence in the industrialized countries. The world's food sector must grow at near-record rates simply to maintain the benchmark per capita consumption levels reported in the late 1960s and

early 1970s (Tables 6–5 and 6–6).

Driving near-record rates of growth on the supply side are marked increases in the resources committed to food production—measured roughly in terms of land under cultivation—and strong gains in productivity—based primarily on wider adoption of technology and increased use of resource-augmenting inputs such as fertilizers and

## TABLE 6–1

### Population Growth Rates, Actual and Projected
(*Percent*)

|  | 1970/1960 | 1985/1975 Alternatives | | | 2000/1975 Alternatives | | |
|---|---|---|---|---|---|---|---|
|  |  | I | II | III | I | II | III |
|  |  |  | *Percent* |  |  |  |  |
| Industrialized countries | 1.09 | .57 | .48 | .67 | .52 | .34 | .71 |
| United States | 1.26 | .70 | .52 | .96 | .55 | .27 | .94 |
| Other developed exporters[a] | 2.28 | 2.05 | 1.99 | 2.15 | 1.80 | 1.60 | 1.94 |
| Western Europe | .80 | .33 | .30 | .35 | .43 | .31 | .52 |
| Japan | 1.04 | .88 | .81 | .91 | .59 | .43 | .68 |
| Centrally planned countries | 1.54 | 1.25 | .99 | 1.45 | 1.21 | .94 | 1.43 |
| Eastern Europe | .70 | .68 | .63 | .74 | .57 | .39 | .76 |
| U.S.S.R. | 1.25 | .93 | .80 | 1.05 | .68 | .46 | .90 |
| People's Republic of China | 1.78 | 1.42 | 1.10 | 1.64 | 1.42 | 1.14 | 1.63 |
| Less developed countries | 2.56 | 2.50 | 2.36 | 2.66 | 2.37 | 2.04 | 2.71 |
| Latin America | 2.82 | 2.91 | 2.65 | 3.04 | 2.61 | 2.17 | 2.94 |
| North Africa/Middle East | 2.74 | 2.75 | 2.61 | 2.86 | 2.75 | 2.44 | 3.05 |
| Other African LDCs | 2.42 | 2.61 | 2.50 | 2.69 | 2.68 | 2.31 | 2.94 |
| South Asia | 2.56 | 2.34 | 2.25 | 2.58 | 2.13 | 1.88 | 2.63 |
| Southeast Asia | 2.68 | 2.50 | 2.34 | 2.65 | 2.20 | 1.77 | 2.58 |
| East Asia | 2.23 | 2.13 | 1.94 | 2.28 | 1.99 | 1.58 | 2.27 |
| World | 1.93 | 1.79 | 1.63 | 1.95 | 1.77 | 1.48 | 2.05 |

[a] Canada, Australia, South Africa.
*Source:* U.S. Bureau of the Census.

## TABLE 6–2

### Per Capita Income Growth Rates, Actual and Projected
(*Percent*)

|  | 1960–1970 | 1985/1975 Alternatives | | | 2000/1985 Alternatives | | |
|---|---|---|---|---|---|---|---|
|  |  | I | II | III | I | II | III |
| Industrialized countries | 3.29 | 3.41 | 4.40 | 2.41 | 2.57 | 3.35 | 1.77 |
| United States | 2.52 | 3.28 | 4.35 | 2.12 | 2.54 | 3.42 | 1.55 |
| Other major exporters[a] | 1.87 | 1.95 | 2.85 | 1.10 | 1.40 | 2.25 | .55 |
| Western Europe | 3.52 | 3.66 | 4.59 | 2.74 | 2.66 | 3.38 | 1.97 |
| Japan | 8.76 | 3.10 | 4.06 | 2.17 | 2.49 | 3.26 | 1.81 |
| Centrally planned countries | 3.65 | 2.35 | 3.22 | 1.50 | 2.20 | 3.15 | 1.25 |
| Eastren Europe | 3.88 | 2.55 | 2.85 | 2.24 | 2.16 | 2.60 | 1.73 |
| U.S.S.R. | 5.17 | 2.30 | 2.67 | 1.93 | 2.06 | 2.53 | 1.59 |
| People's Republic of China | .90 | 2.30 | 3.85 | .86 | 2.30 | 3.81 | .85 |
| Less developed countries | 3.13 | 2.54 | 3.52 | 1.55 | 2.01 | 3.00 | 1.03 |
| Latin America | 2.62 | 2.64 | 3.90 | 1.51 | 1.84 | 2.84 | .97 |
| North Africa/Middle East | 2.79 | 3.95 | 4.70 | 3.35 | 3.20 | 4.15 | 2.26 |
| Other African LDCs | 1.00 | 2.95 | 3.60 | 2.35 | 2.15 | 3.00 | 1.38 |
| South Asia | .73 | 1.12 | 1.91 | .20 | .66 | 1.20 | .15 |
| Southeast Asia | 2.26 | 2.50 | 2.65 | 2.34 | 2.20 | 2.58 | 1.77 |
| East Asia | 2.01 | 3.34 | 4.37 | 2.66 | 2.80 | 3.98 | 1.54 |
| World | 2.80 | 2.26 | 3.23 | 1.29 | 1.53 | 2.42 | .66 |

[a] Canada, Australia, South Africa
*Source:* Global 2000 Study staff.

## TABLE 6–3

### Yield Variations Due to Assumptions Regarding Weather Conditions

| | Variation from Alternative I 1985 and 2000 Yield | Kilogram per Hectare Equivalent | |
|---|---|---|---|
| | | 1985 | 2000 |
| | *Percent* | | |
| Industrialized countries | | | |
| United States | ± 5.75 | 250 | 280 |
| Other developed exporters | ±14.50 | 310 | 400 |
| Western Europe | ± 5.00 | 190 | 220 |
| Japan | ± 4.75 | 190 | 160 |
| Centrally planned countries | | | |
| Eastern Europe | ± 6.25 | 220 | 280 |
| U.S.S.R. | ±11.75 | 240 | 310 |
| People's Republic of China | ± 5.50 | 100 | 130 |
| Less developed countries | | | |
| Latin America | ± 8.00 | 130 | 200 |
| North Africa/Middle East | ± 9.00 | 130 | 200 |
| Other developing Africa | ± 3.50 | 50 | 80 |
| South Asia | ± 4.75 | 60 | 80 |
| Southeast Asia | ± 6.50 | 110 | 160 |
| East Asia | ± 6.00 | 110 | 160 |
| Weighted total above [a] | ± 7.20 | 180 | 220 |
| World aggregated [b] | ± 3.00 | 70 | 90 |

*Note:* Yield variations are calculated on the basis of one standard error of the regression of 1950–75 yield data against time.

[a] Production weighted aggregate of regional variations.

[b] Variation calculated using world yield series.

*Source:* Economics, Statistics, and Cooperatives Service, U.S. Department of Agriculture.

## TABLE 6–4

### Grain Production and Consumption Growth Rates, Actual and Projected (Alternative I)

| | 1973–75/ 1951–55 | 1985/ 1973–75 | 2000/ 1985 |
|---|---|---|---|
| | *Percent* | | |
| Industrialized countries | | | |
| Production | 2.5 | 2.5—1.8 | 1.8—1.7 |
| Consumption | 2.2 | 2.4—2.0 | 1.9—1.8 |
| Exporters | | | |
| Production | 2.6 | 2.9—2.5 | 2.1—2.0 |
| Consumption | 2.1 | 2.7—2.2 | 2.2—2.1 |
| Importers | | | |
| Production | 2.3 | 1.6—0.2 | 1.1—1.1 |
| Consumption | 2.1 | 2.1—1.7 | 1.6—1.5 |
| Centrally planned countries | | | |
| Production | 2.8 | 2.4 | 1.6 |
| Consumption | 3.0 | 2.2 | 1.6 |
| Less developed countries | | | |
| Production | 2.8 | 3.3—3.7 | 3.0—2.8 |
| Consumption | 3.1 | 3.6—3.6 | 2.8—2.6 |
| Exporters | | | |
| Production | 3.2 | 3.1—4.2 | 3.2—2.9 |
| Consumption | 3.5 | 1.7—1.7 | 2.4—2.3 |
| Importers | | | |
| Production | 2.7 | 3.3—3.6 | 3.0—2.8 |
| Consumption | 3.0 | 3.8—3.7 | 2.8—2.7 |
| World | | | |
| Production | 2.7 | 2.7—2.5 | 2.1—2.0 |
| Consumption | 2.7 | 2.7—2.5 | 2.1—2.0 |

pesticides. The rates of growth in production and the relative importance of area and productivity gains shown in Figure 6–2's grain data are representative of the changes projected for the food sector as a whole. Land-man ratios decline throughout the projection period, however, and the productivity gains needed to keep up growth in production come at increasing real cost, particularly if sharp increases in petroleum prices are incorporated into the analysis.

Problems of distribution across and within regions also detract from the high world growth rates shown in Table 6–5. Production and consumption increase at faster rates in the LDCs than in the industrialized countries. LDC growth, however, is from a substantially smaller base. Furthermore, the LDC aggregate and many of the regional totals are somewhat misleading because the difference between individual LDCs—i.e., an Argentina compared with an India, or an Egypt compared with a Bangladesh—are far wider than the differences between the industrialized countries total and the LDC total.

Growth in food production and consumption are not likely to balance at the regional or country levels. Significant increases in trade—exported by a few major surplus producers, including the United States, Canada, Australia, and several emerging exporters such as Thailand and Brazil—

## TABLE 6-5

### Grain and Total Food Production, Consumption, and Trade, Actual and Projected (Alternative I)

| | Grains (million metric tons) | | | | Food (1969–71 = 100) | | |
|---|---|---|---|---|---|---|---|
| | 1969–71 | 1973–75 | 1985 | 2000 | 1969–71 | 1985 | 2000 |
| **Industrialized countries** | | | | | | | |
| Production | 401.7 | 434.7 | 569.5–525.9 | 739.7– 679.1 | 100.0 | 126.6–118.1 | 157.0–143.7 |
| Consumption | 374.3 | 374.6 | 486.2–465.3 | 648.4– 610.8 | 100.0 | 121.0–116.6 | 155.8–147.7 |
| Trade | +32.1 | +61.6 | +83.3–+60.6 | +91.3–+68.3 | | | |
| **United States** | | | | | | | |
| Production | 208.7 | 228.7 | 304.0–297.1 | 416.0– 402.0 | 100.0 | 137.8–134.9 | 184.3–178.5 |
| Consumption | 169.0 | 158.5 | 210.9–199.8 | 290.0– 272.4 | 100.0 | 119.6–114.0 | 160.3–151.3 |
| Trade | +39.9 | +72.9 | +93.1–+97.3 | +126.0–+129.6 | | | |
| **Other developed exporters** | | | | | | | |
| Production | 58.6 | 61.2 | 93.0– 83.1 | 121.9– 106.1 | 100.0 | 139.1–126.7 | 175.4–155.6 |
| Consumption | 33.2 | 34.3 | 47.1– 45.5 | 68.1– 65.2 | 100.0 | 126.8–123.2 | 173.3–166.8 |
| Trade | +28.4 | +27.7 | +45.9–+37.6 | +53.8–+40.9 | | | |
| **Western Europe** | | | | | | | |
| Production | 121.7 | 132.9 | 160.0–133.0 | 182.8– 153.0 | 100.0 | 119.1–105.0 | 133.5–114.6 |
| Consumption | 144.2 | 151.7 | 182.2–175.5 | 225.9– 213.1 | 100.0 | 115.1–111.5 | 138.5–131.6 |
| Trade | –21.8 | –19.7 | –22.2––42.5 | –43.1––60.1 | | | |
| **Japan** | | | | | | | |
| Production | 12.7 | 11.9 | 12.5– 12.7 | 19.0– 18.0 | 100.0 | 102.0–103.6 | 125.0–131.5 |
| Consumption | 27.9 | 30.1 | 46.0– 44.5 | 64.4– 60.1 | 100.0 | 150.7–146.3 | 205.6–192.8 |
| Trade | –14.4 | –19.3 | –33.5––31.8 | –45.4––42.1 | | | |
| **Centrally planned countries** | | | | | | | |
| Production | 401.0 | 439.4 | 567.0 | 722.0 | 100.0 | 138.2 | 174.0 |
| Consumption | 406.6 | 472.4 | 596.0 | 758.5 | 100.0 | 143.3 | 179.9 |
| Trade | –5.2 | –24.0 | –29.0 | –36.5 | | | |
| **Eastern Europe** | | | | | | | |
| Production | 72.1 | 89.4 | 110.0 | 140.0 | 100.0 | 146.2 | 183.2 |
| Consumption | 78.7 | 97.7 | 118.5 | 151.5 | 100.0 | 144.4 | 181.7 |
| Trade | –6.1 | –7.8 | –8.5 | –11.5 | | | |
| **U.S.S.R.** | | | | | | | |
| Production | 165.0 | 179.3 | 230.0 | 290.0 | 100.0 | 137.7 | 172.7 |
| Consumption | 161.0 | 200.7 | 242.5 | 305.0 | 100.0 | 148.5 | 185.9 |
| Trade | +3.9 | –10.6 | –12.5 | –15.0 | | | |
| **People's Republic of China** | | | | | | | |
| Production | 163.9 | 176.9 | 227.0 | 292.0 | 100.0 | 134.0 | 169.0 |
| Consumption | 166.9 | 180.8 | 235.0 | 302.0 | 100.0 | 136.0 | 171.4 |
| Trade | –3.0 | –3.9 | –8.0 | –10.0 | | | |
| **Less developed countries** | | | | | | | |
| Production | 306.5 | 328.7 | 471.7–490.7 | 735.0– 740.6 | 100.0 | 154.4–161.4 | 244.5–247.7 |
| Consumption | 326.6 | 355.0 | 526.0–522.3 | 789.8– 772.4 | 100.0 | 163.4–162.8 | 247.8–242.8 |
| Trade | –18.5 | –29.5 | –54.3––31.6 | –54.8––31.8 | | | |

## TABLE 6-5
### (continued)

| | Grains (million metric tons) | | | | Food (1969–71 = 100) | | |
|---|---|---|---|---|---|---|---|
| | 1969–71 | 1973–75 | 1985 | 2000 | 1969–71 | 1985 | 2000 |
| **Exporters[a]** | | | | | | | |
| Production | 30.1 | 34.5 | 48.5– 54.4 | 78.1– 84.0 | 100.0 | 132.5–142.9 | 209.2–225.0 |
| Consumption | 18.4 | 21.5 | 25.7– 25.5 | 36.7– 36.0 | 100.0 | 122.2–121.7 | 160.8–158.0 |
| Trade | +11.3 | +13.1 | +22.8–+28.9 | +41.4–+48.0 | | | |
| **Importers[b]** | | | | | | | |
| Production | 276.4 | 294.2 | 423.2–436.3 | 656.9– 656.6 | 100.0 | 156.0–158.4 | 247.0–249.3 |
| Consumption | 308.2 | 333.5 | 500.3–496.8 | 753.1– 736.4 | 100.0 | 166.2–164.6 | 254.0–248.9 |
| Trade | –29.8 | –42.6 | –77.1–-60.5 | –96.2–-79.8 | | | |
| **Latin America** | | | | | | | |
| Production | 63.8 | 72.0 | 101.0–111.9 | 182.6–185.9 | 100.0 | 158.7–174.8 | 279.5–284.4 |
| Consumption | 61.2 | 71.2 | 99.5– 98.2 | 168.8–166.0 | 100.0 | 162.7–160.7 | 269.7–265.3 |
| Trade | +3.2 | +0.2 | +1.5–+13.7 | +13.8–+19.9 | | | |
| **North Africa/Middle East** | | | | | | | |
| Production | 38.9 | 42.4 | 56.2– 56.8 | 92.2– 89.0 | 100.0 | 146.3–148.1 | 252.5–257.8 |
| Consumption | 49.5 | 54.1 | 80.6– 79.6 | 127.5–123.7 | 100.0 | 167.4–165.1 | 276.1–267.3 |
| Trade | – 9.1 | –13.8 | –24.4–-22.8 | –35.3–-29.7 | | | |
| **Other African LDCs** | | | | | | | |
| Production | 32.0 | 31.3 | 47.1– 50.0 | 61.3– 63.7 | 100.0 | 150.7–160.2 | 197.1–204.9 |
| Consumption | 33.0 | 33.8 | 51.9– 51.5 | 63.3– 63.0 | 100.0 | 161.2–160.0 | 196.4–196.4 |
| Trade | –1.0 | –2.4 | –4.8– -1.5 | –2.0– +0.7 | | | |
| **South Asia** | | | | | | | |
| Production | 119.1 | 127.7 | 184.2–186.0 | 265.0–259.0 | 100.0 | 154.0–155.5 | 221.8–216.8 |
| Consumption | 125.3 | 135.1 | 199.7–199.0 | 284.3–275.7 | 100.0 | 158.7–158.2 | 226.2–219.4 |
| Trade | –6.2 | –9.3 | –15.5–-13.0 | –19.3–-16.7 | | | |
| **Southeast Asia** | | | | | | | |
| Production | 22.8 | 21.4 | 38.3– 41.4 | 62.0– 65.0 | 100.0 | 179.1–194.3 | 295.3–310.0 |
| Consumption | 19.3 | 17.9 | 30.5– 30.5 | 47.9– 47.0 | 100.0 | 168.0–168.0 | 268.8–263.6 |
| Trade | +3.4 | +3.7 | +7.8–+10.9 | +14.1–+18.0 | | | |
| **East Asia** | | | | | | | |
| Production | 29.9 | 34.0 | 44.9– 44.6 | 71.9– 73.0 | 100.0 | 155.8–154.7 | 251.4–255.3 |
| Consumption | 38.3 | 42.9 | 63.8– 63.5 | 98.0– 97.0 | 100.0 | 173.1–172.3 | 267.7–264.9 |
| Trade | –8.8 | –9.7 | –18.9–-18.9 | –26.1–-24.0 | | | |
| **World** | | | | | | | |
| Production | 1,109.2 | 1,202.8 | 1,608.2–1,583.6 | 2,196.7–2,141.7 | 100.0 | 141.5–140.5 | 194.0–191.0 |
| Consumption | 1,107.5 | 1,202.0 | 1,608.2–1,583.6 | 2,196.7–2,141.7 | 100.0 | 141.5–140.5 | 194.0–191.0 |
| Trade | +1.7 | –0.8 | | | | | |

*Note:* In trade figures + indicates export; minus sign indicates import.
[a]Argentina and Thailand.
[b]All others, including several countries that export in some scenarios (e.g., Brazil, Indonesia, and Colombia).

## TABLE 6-6

### Per Capita Grain and Total Food Production, Consumption, and Trade, Actual and Projected (Alternative I)

| | Grains (kilograms per capita) | | | | Food (1969-71 = 100) | | |
|---|---|---|---|---|---|---|---|
| | 1969-71 | 1973-75 | 1985 | 2000 | 1969-71 | 1985 | 2000 |
| **Industrialized countries** | | | | | | | |
| Production | 573.6 | 592.6 | 718.9– 663.8 | 838.5– 769.8 | 100.0 | 112.9–104.5 | 128.8–118.4 |
| Consumption | 534.4 | 510.7 | 613.7– 587.3 | 735.0– 692.4 | 100.0 | 108.8–104.9 | 127.7–121.2 |
| Trade | +45.8 | +84.0 | +105.1–+76.5 | +103.5–+77.4 | | | |
| **United States** | | | | | | | |
| Production | 1,018.6 | 1,079.3 | 1,331.2–1,301.0 | 1,697.4–1,640.3 | 100.0 | 124.8–122.2 | 156.0–151.1 |
| Consumption | 824.9 | 748.0 | 923.5– 874.9 | 1,183.3–1,111.5 | 100.0 | 108.5–103.4 | 135.9–128.3 |
| Trade | +194.7 | +344.0 | +407.7–+426.1 | +514.1–+528.8 | | | |
| **Other developed exporters** | | | | | | | |
| Production | 1,015.6 | 917.0 | 1,117.4–1,052.1 | 1,052.0– 915.6 | 100.0 | 103.3– 98.6 | 98.6– 88.7 |
| Consumption | 575.4 | 514.0 | 596.3– 576.1 | 587.7– 562.6 | 100.0 | 98.6– 96.0 | 97.5– 94.3 |
| Trade | +492.2 | +415.0 | +581.1–+476.0 | +464.3–+353.0 | | | |
| **Western Europe** | | | | | | | |
| Production | 364.9 | 388.4 | 441.5– 367.0 | 470.7– 394.0 | 100.0 | 111.0– 95.2 | 117.1–101.0 |
| Consumption | 432.4 | 443.3 | 502.8– 484.3 | 581.7– 548.8 | 100.0 | 107.4–104.1 | 121.4–115.5 |
| Trade | -65.4 | -57.6 | -61.3–-117.3 | -111.0–-154.8 | | | |
| **Japan** | | | | | | | |
| Production | 121.7 | 108.5 | 102.1– 103.7 | 142.9– 135.4 | 100.0 | 83.4– 84.5 | 111.3–106.1 |
| Consumption | 267.5 | 274.4 | 375.7– 363.4 | 484.4– 452.3 | 100.0 | 130.4–126.6 | 164.2–154.2 |
| Trade | -138.1 | -175.9 | -273.6–-259.7 | -341.5–-316.7 | | | |
| **Centrally planned countries** | | | | | | | |
| Production | 356.1 | 368.0 | 411.5 | 451.1 | 100.0 | 116.7 | 129.6 |
| Consumption | 361.0 | 395.6 | 432.5 | 473.9 | 100.0 | 122.4 | 135.8 |
| Trade | -4.6 | -20.1 | -21.0 | -22.8 | | | |
| **Eastern Europe** | | | | | | | |
| Production | 574.0 | 693.0 | 788.6 | 921.9 | 100.0 | 132.7 | 153.3 |
| Consumption | 626.6 | 757.4 | 849.5 | 997.6 | 100.0 | 131.1 | 152.1 |
| Trade | -48.6 | -60.5 | -60.9 | -75.8 | | | |
| **U.S.S.R.** | | | | | | | |
| Production | 697.6 | 711.2 | 812.8 | 903.2 | 100.0 | 115.6 | 128.1 |
| Consumption | 663.1 | 796.1 | 856.9 | 949.9 | 100.0 | 127.9 | 141.4 |
| Trade | +16.1 | -42.0 | -44.1 | -46.7 | | | |
| **People's Republic of China** | | | | | | | |
| Production | 216.3 | 217.6 | 237.6 | 259.0 | 100.0 | 108.7 | 117.4 |
| Consumption | 220.2 | 222.4 | 246.0 | 267.8 | 100.0 | 110.3 | 119.1 |
| Trade | -4.0 | -4.8 | -8.4 | -8.8 | | | |
| **Less developed countries** | | | | | | | |
| Production | 176.7 | 168.7 | 182.0– 189.4 | 195.6– 197.1 | 100.0– | 101.7–106.5 | 109.5–110.8 |
| Consumption | 188.3 | 182.2 | 203.0– 201.6 | 210.2– 205.5 | 100.0 | 107.7–106.7 | 111.0–108.6 |
| Trade | -10.7 | -15.1 | -21.0–-12.2 | -14.6–-8.4 | | | |

## TABLE 6-6
### (continued)

| | Grains (kilograms per capita) | | | | Food (1969–71 = 100) | | |
|---|---|---|---|---|---|---|---|
| | 1969–71 | 1973–75 | 1985 | 2000 | 1969–71 | 1985 | 2000 |
| **Exporters[a]** | | | | | | | |
| Production | 491.0 | 521.9 | 541.1– 606.9 | 624.5– 671.7 | 100.0 | 90.6– 97.7 | 102.6–110.4 |
| Consumption | 300.1 | 325.3 | 286.7– 284.5 | 293.5– 287.8 | 100.0 | 83.6– 83.2 | 78.9– 77.4 |
| Trade | +184.3 | +198.2 | +254.4–+322.4 | +331.1–+383.9 | | | |
| **Importers[b]** | | | | | | | |
| Production | 159.4 | 173.8 | 169.2– 174.4 | 180.8– 180.7 | 100.0 | 104.3–106.0 | 110.0–110.8 |
| Consumption | 177.7 | 193.6 | 200.0– 198.6 | 207.3– 202.7 | 100.0 | 111.2–110.1 | 113.3–110.8 |
| Trade | –17.2 | –24.1 | –30.8– 24.2 | –26.5– –21.9 | | | |
| **Latin America** | | | | | | | |
| Production | 236.1 | 241.0 | 247.6– 247.4 | 305.9– 311.4 | 100.0 | 108.2–118.9 | 131.5–133.7 |
| Consumption | 226.5 | 238.3 | 244.0– 240.8 | 282.8– 278.1 | 100.0 | 110.9–109.6 | 127.1–125.1 |
| Trade | +11.8 | +2.7 | +3.7– +33.6 | +23.1– +33.3 | | | |
| **North Africa/Middle East** | | | | | | | |
| Production | 217.1 | 214.6 | 201.8– 203.9 | 218.3– 222.5 | 100.0 | 87.2– 88.3 | 95.9– 98.2 |
| Consumption | 276.2 | 273.8 | 289.4– 285.8 | 301.8– 292.8 | 100.0 | 101.8–100.3 | 105.9–102.2 |
| Trade | –50.8 | –69.8 | –87.6– –81.9 | –83.6– –70.3 | | | |
| **Other African LDCs** | | | | | | | |
| Production | 134.9 | 118.3 | 130.7– 138.7 | 109.0– 113.2 | 100.0 | 98.1–104.3 | 81.2– 84.5 |
| Consumption | 139.1 | 127.7 | 144.0– 142.9 | 112.5– 112.0 | 100.0 | 105.0–104.2 | 81.3– 80.9 |
| Trade | –4.2 | –9.1 | –13.3– –4.2 | –3.6– +1.2 | | | |
| **South Asia** | | | | | | | |
| Production | 161.6 | 162.4 | 170.0– 171.7 | 174.0– 170.0 | 100.0 | 104.6–105.6 | 107.0–104.6 |
| Consumption | 170.0 | 171.8 | 184.3– 183.7 | 186.7– 181.0 | 100.0 | 107.8–107.4 | 109.2–105.8 |
| Trade | –8.4 | –11.8 | –14.3– –12.0 | –12.7– –11.0 | | | |
| **Southeast Asia** | | | | | | | |
| Production | 244.7 | 214.5 | 273.6– 295.8 | 301.9– 316.5 | 100.0 | 116.3–126.4 | 129.2–135.9 |
| Consumption | 207.2 | 182.6 | 217.9– 217.9 | 233.2– 228.5 | 100.0 | 108.9–108.9 | 117.1–114.6 |
| Trade | +37.5 | +31.9 | +55.7– +77.9 | +68.7– +87.5 | | | |
| **East Asia** | | | | | | | |
| Production | 137.3 | 136.0 | 139.9– 138.9 | 161.1– 163.5 | 100.0 | 104.6–104.9 | 121.1–122.8 |
| Consumption | 176.2 | 171.5 | 198.8– 197.8 | 219.5– 217.3 | 100.0 | 116.2–115.6 | 128.7–127.3 |
| Trade | –40.4 | –38.8 | –58.9– –58.9 | –58.5– –53.8 | | | |
| **World** | | | | | | | |
| Production | 311.5 | 313.6 | 337.7– 332.6 | 352.2– 343.2 | 100.0 | 109.5–108.5 | 117.0–114.5 |
| Consumption | 311.0 | 313.4 | 337.7– 332.6 | 352.0– 343.2 | 100.0 | 109.5–108.5 | 117.0–114.5 |
| Trade | +0.5 | +0.2 | | | | | |

Note: In trade figures, + indicates export; minus sign indicates import.
[a]Argentina and Thailand.
[b]All others, including several countries that export in some scenarios (e.g., Brazil, Indonesia, and Colombia).

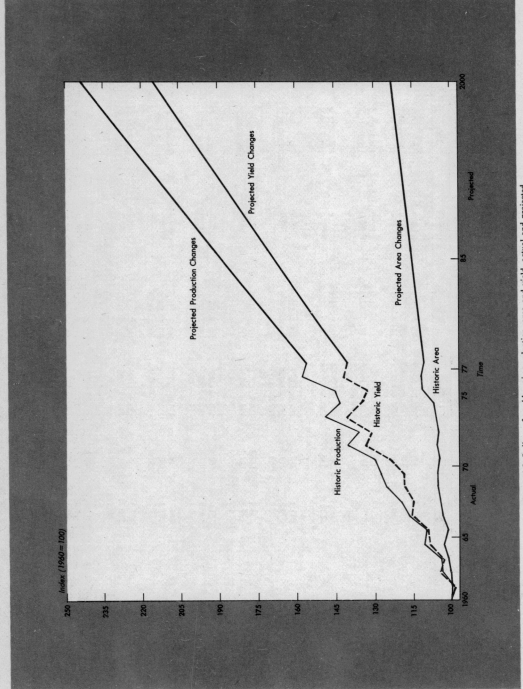

**Figure 6-2.** Indices of world grain production, area and yield, actual and projected.

will be needed to balance excess demand in food-deficit Western Europe, Japan, the centrally planned countries, and parts of developing Africa and Asia. World trade varies from alternative to alternative but exceeds record 1973–75 levels by at least 20 percent by 1985 and 60 percent by 2000.

## Energy Price Impacts

The quantity and price ranges shown in Tables 6–5 and 6–6 reflect model outputs on the impact energy price increases could have on the agricultural sector. The bottom end of the range provides for no marked increase in the price of energy from real 1973–75 levels. The upper end provides for moderately higher real prices by 1985 and substantially higher real prices by 2000. *The range reflects not so much uncertainty about petroleum price increases as uncertainty about the effect changing petroleum prices have on agriculture and the ability of farmers to maintain or expand production while shifting away from energy-intensive inputs.* A variety of cultural practices and management techniques are available in the short and medium terms to minimize the effect of energy price increases. The experience of the past 2–4 years suggests that food and overall agricultural production could well adjust in the long run to substantially higher energy prices, depending on the timing of increases, without the degree of dislocation implied at the upper end of the range.

The model results suggest that, while world production and consumption levels might not be changed measurably by marked but gradual increases in energy prices, major shifts within and across sectors and regions would be likely. The comparative advantage of the resource-endowed LDCs such as Brazil and Thailand, which use relatively few high energy-intensive inputs, would improve. Higher energy prices, however, would likely exacerbate problems of comparative disadvantage in food production common to many of the industrialized and higher-income LDCs.

Adjustments in the food-exporting countries would likely be mixed. In countries such as the United States, higher energy prices could be offset at least partially by increasing the land resources committed to food production and by decreasing on the use of, or increasing returns to, energy-intensive inputs. The comparative advantage of the traditional food-exporting countries would likely deteriorate relative to the resource-endowed LDCs but improve relative to most of the industrialized countries and several of the resource-tight LDCs. The sizes of these changes in comparative advantage are projected to keep the exporters' sales on the world market at or above the levels projected under a constant petroleum price alternative.

Even a rough estimate of the impact of higher energy prices on agricultural production depends on the timing of price increases, long-run rates of technological change, and short-run input flexibility. The real energy price increases projected to 2000 in the energy projections of this study (Chapter 10) are so large as to suggest that the severity of the impact in the long run depends on the rate at which energy-conserving technologies replace existing energy-intensive technologies. Little can be done to project the rate or the impact of such long-run technological change. In the shorter term, however, some estimate of the impact of higher energy prices can be made on the basis of data on energy intensity and judgments as to how much flexibility farmers in a particular country have to change input mixes.

Figure 6–3 can be used to gauge approximate energy intensity and to demonstrate the importance of energy flexibility. Both cross-sectional data for the 30 largest agricultural producers, and time series data for a smaller number of countries suggest the energy-intensity curve is basically S-shaped. Given the position of countries along the curve, there appears to be little question that past increases in productivity have generally depended on marked increases in energy inputs. The impact of any energy price increase, all other things being equal, depends on where a country is on this energy-intensity curve. The efficiency of energy use measured roughly in terms of energy input-product output ratios might well strengthen or weaken the impact of any energy price change, but the general ranking of the countries from right to left would not be likely to change much. The experience of the past 3–4 years of higher energy prices suggests that a country's ability to move back down the curve toward lower energy intensity—i.e., to adjust production techniques without sacrificing the high productivity associated with advanced technology—is particularly crucial.

A review of the adjustments U.S. farmers can and, in many cases, are making suggests that the range of options available even within a basically energy-intensive technology is quite wide. Data from Department of Agriculture and Federal Energy Administration studies estimate that the energy used in the U.S. agricultural sector in 1974 was equivalent to 2,000 trillion Btu (British thermal units) or roughly 5,300 Btu per hectare of total cropped area. As Figures 6–4 and 6–5 indicate, the largest energy expenditures were reported in cultural operations, transportation, irrigation, livestock operations, crop drying, and energy investment in fertilizers and pesticides.

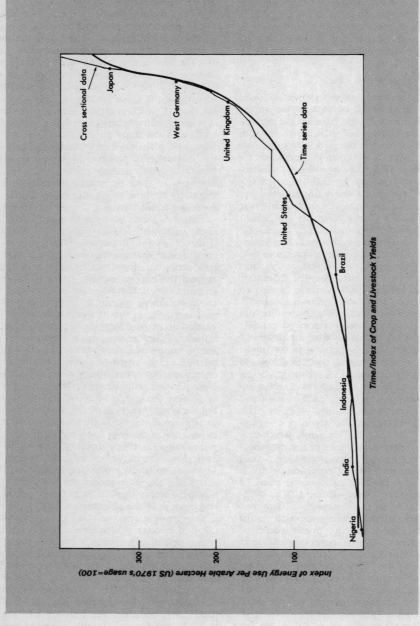

**Figure 6-3.** Energy intensity data. Cross-sectional energy use data plotted against crop and livestock yields for 30 largest food producing countries; 15-year historical series plotted against time for United States and several major European producers.

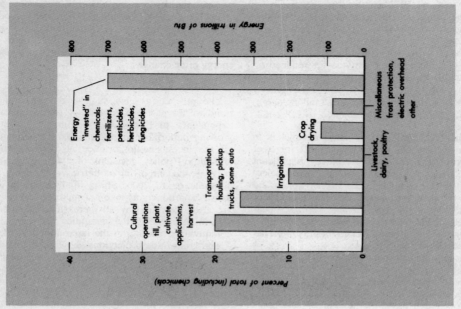

**Figure 6-5.** Energy used in agriculture, plus fertilizer and chemicals, 1974.

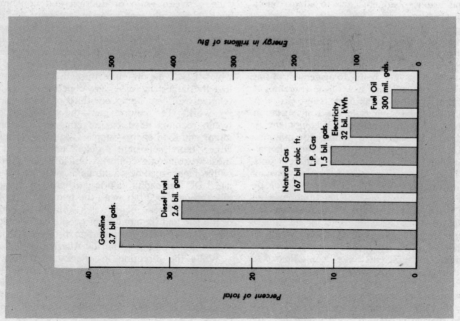

**Figure 6-4.** Energy used in agriculture, 1974.

A review of the literature on energy-saving techniques suggests that considerable reductions in energy use are possible in all of these areas. The energy savings possible from modifying cultural practices, which currently account for 20 percent of energy use, to provide for reduced or minimum tillage are quite large. Net energy savings range up to 50 percent. Moreover, reduced tillage in 1975 amounted to only 35.8 million acres, while conventional tillage amounted to 218.2 million acres.

Another potential area of large savings is in fertilizer use, which currently accounts for over one-third of total energy expenditures. Significant energy savings are possible through proper selection and use of fertilizers. The proper timing and method of application also contribute to fertilizer efficiency. Moreover, considerable savings appear possible by changing mixes of fertilizers to emphasize organic and green fertilizers as well as inorganic chemical fertilizers.

Irrigation engineers also suggest that it is technologically impossible to reduce the 10 percent of total energy use accounted for by irrigation by as much as one half. Reductions in energy consumption of as much as 10–20 percent appear to be possible through minimal efforts to increase irrigation pumping plant efficiency, to upgrade water usage and water scheduling, and to adopt runoff control procedures.

Drying grain for storage—which accounts for 5–10 percent of energy use—is another area of potential saving. There appear to be several ways to reduce grain-drying fuel requirements, including more in-the-field drying, better management of the existing system, and the use of new technical developments such as solar heat. There are also significant potential savings in the transportation sector through more efficient use of equipment.

Keeping these short-term options for minimizing energy inputs in mind, the projection alternatives can be seen in a number of different contexts. Those Alternative I runs assuming constant petroleum prices would be valid either given no increase in petroleum prices or given increases at a fairly even pace—possibly 5–10 percent per year—provided the agricultural sector maximizes short-term energy savings and ultimately substitutes energy-conserving technologies. A number of the model's coefficients have been adjusted to reflect estimates of both short-term flexibility in energy use and the long-term development of energy-conserving technologies as discussed in Chapter 18. The Alternative I projections based on an increasing petroleum price would be valid should agriculture not adjust to gradual energy price increases or should the increases be sudden or much sharper than a graduated 5–10 percent per year. The present capabilities of the GOL model do not permit more precise measurement of the impact of gradually changing petroleum prices or reliable projections of the impact of more extreme energy price changes.

## Continuing Trends

The projections also suggest that the major trends of the past two decades—(1) the increasing dependence of LDCs on food imports; (2) the growing importance of variability in supply; and (3) the increasing importance of the trade and agricultural policy decisions of a few major exporting and importing countries—are likely to continue on to 2000. Shifts in demand toward livestock products as incomes increase, however, are also likely to play an increasingly important role in determining the quantities and prices of commodities moving on the international market.

The grain trade projections shown in Table 6–5 suggest that *the LDCs, excluding food-surplus exporters,\* face sharp increases in the absolute volume of food imports as well as possible increases in the proportion of food imported.* The increased food imports of many of the developing countries, however, are not without positive implications. The grain gap—the difference between grain production and consumption—is generally seen as an indication of the less developed countries' inability to feed themselves. Increases in imports, however, also measure the LDCs ability to supplement limited domestic output with foreign production. A closer look at which LDCs import more through 2000 suggests that the largest increases are concentrated in the relatively affluent upper one-third of the developing world. The calorie gap—the difference between recommended caloric consumption minimums and food energy supplies—suggests a much larger, more persistent problem concentrated in the lowest-income countries but affecting groups within higher-income countries as well. The average LDC per capita calorie gap narrows marginally through 2000 but, with the number of people increasing at near-record rates, the absolute size of the gap and the number of people eating below the recommended minimum is projected to increase under all but optimistic Alternative II.

While the direction, frequency, and size of fluctuations in supply will continue to depend largely on weather, *the importance of variability in supply is likely to increase markedly as world productive capacity is used at significantly higher*

---

\*Primarily Argentina and Thailand, but in some scenarios other LDCs as well, e.g., Brazil, Colombia, and Indonesia.

*levels.* The experience of a number of countries suggests that expansion of cultivation into marginal areas increases susceptibility to weather fluctuations. The resource balances reviewed below indicate that a larger proportion of the world's food supplies will have to be grown on increasingly marginal areas dependent on favorable (rather than normal) rainfall and temperature.

Reserves are likely to increase in importance as a means of ensuring that production windfalls and temporarily low producer prices do not generate production cutbacks in the food-exporting countries. Reserves are also likely to increase in importance as a means of reducing price fluctuations and the market-rationing effect of short-term drops in production in a world of rising real prices.

All three alternatives also suggest that the *agricultural and trade policies of a small number of importers and exporters will play an increasingly dominant role in determining the quantities and prices of food traded on the world market.* The increased importance of policy decisions in the exporting countries would result from their control of scarce excess productive capacity. The experience of the last five years suggests that without marked changes in international trading conventions, the role of major but sporadic importers such as the Soviet Union is also likely to increase. Protectionist agricultural and trade policies currently allow large countries or blocs relatively close to self-sufficiency to avoid the costs of adjusting to world production shortfalls. The current structure of the world market also allows them to pass on part, if not all, of the cost of disruptions in their domestic agricultural economies for absorbtion by the world market. The impact of changes in world supply and demand are consequently likely to be absorbed more and more by countries exporting a large proportion of production and countries importing a large proportion of consumption on a regular basis.

All three alternatives also suggest that, in addition to population and income growth, shifts in consumption patterns are likely to play a major role in shaping demand, particularly beyond 1985. *Growth in demand and shifts in taste away from calorie-efficient diets based on cereals and starches toward less calorie-efficient, livestock-oriented diets will determine to a large extent the demand price of grains, oilseeds, other high-protein feeds, and possibly food prices in general.*

Changes in the proportion of concentrate-fed products in the livestock total will be critical in determining the impact of this shift toward livestock diets and the grain and oilseed balance. Biological limitations on the expansion of the

ruminant herd suggest that a larger proportion of meat supplies will have to come from pork and poultry products heavily dependent on grain and oilseed feeds. Moreover, the world's fish catch is an essentially concentrate-free source of animal protein, and, should the world's fish catch not increase at the 1.5–2.0 percent rate assumed in the model runs, demand for feed to produce a comparable amount of animal protein from pigs and chickens could increase grain and oilseed demand by another 1 percent. The impact on prices and diets worldwide would be relatively small, since less than 6 percent of the world's protein and 1 percent of the world's calories are derived from fish and seafood products. However, in selected countries—such as Japan, where fish accounts for 25 percent of protein supplies and 8 percent of calories—the impact would be very significant.

World grain and overall food balances could tighten further if the lower-income industrialized countries, centrally planned countries, and the higher-income less developed countries were to markedly increase their consumption of livestock products and adopt the grain-intensive feeding techniques of the U.S. World food prices could also be pushed up substancially as price-inelastic food demand in the poorest LDCs competes against more elastic feed demand in the affluent countries.

## Differing Perspectives

All three alternatives also suggest that *the food and environmental concerns of the industrialized and less developed countries are likely to differ widely.* The prime concern in the industrialized countries is likely to be adjustment. The major exporters will continue to face the problem of adjusting their production to higher but widely fluctuating foreign demand. The food-deficit higher-income countries will continue to face the problem of worsening comparative disadvantage and increasingly expensive protectionist agricultural and trade policies. The effect of changing production levels on the environment and the impact of environmental constraints on production costs, however, will be a concern common to all the industrialized countries.

In contrast, the LDCs are likely to face the more pressing problem of expanding production—often regardless of environmental costs—to meet rapidly expanding food needs. Several of the higher-income countries, such as Korea and Taiwan, and several of the resource-constrained countries of North Africa and the Middle East will face the same comparative disadvantage problems as many of the food-deficit industrialized countries, but the bulk of the LDCs will be concerned with environmental quality only after basic human needs are met.

## Alternatives I–III: Results and Conclusions

The projections presented in Tables 6–7 and 6–8 point up a number of alternative-specific conclusions regarding (1) the impacts of population, income, yield, and petroleum price variations in particular regions and over time, (2) the range of possible LDC food consumption improvements through 2000, (3) the variability of world trade and the role of the U.S. as residual supplier, and (4) the range of likely world market price increases.

Before reviewing specific conclusions, however, comments on the range spanned by the alternatives and on short-term versus long-term adjustments are called for.

The range covered by the population and income growth rates for Alternatives II and III is narrow (see Tables 6–1 and 6–2). The range of yield variations is also narrow (see Table 6–3). Given the amount of uncertainty about rates of growth in these variables, the ranges tested here would appear to be too narrow. Moreover, comparisons in terms of absolute production and consumption levels suggest rather minimal differences between alternatives. However, the combination of all the favorable assumptions in Alternative II and all the unfavorable assumptions in Alternative III suggests it is highly probable that the outcome for the world and for major regions would fall within the range bounded by these two alternatives—particularly if analyzed in terms of per capita (rather than absolute) production and consumption levels.

With regard to short-term versus long-term adjustments, the static nature of the GOL model and the long-range specification of its elasticities limit the model to measuring net long-term adjustments. The model can say little about the year to year adjustments within the agricultural sector needed to reach the solutions calculated for 1985 or 2000. Consequently, the fluctuations in endogenous variables generated by the changes in the exogenous variables noted above could well be substantially wider if gauged over a shorter 3- to 5-year rather than a 10- to 20-year period.

### Results

A comparison of the results of the alternatives tested suggests that *the impact of changes in population, income, yield, and petroleum price variables differs widely by regions and over time.* In the food-importing countries of Western Europe and in Japan, with relatively stable yields and low population growth rates, the crucial demand variables both in 1985 and 2000 are likely to be income growth rates and shifts in taste. The crucial determinants of supply are likely to be petroleum prices and domestic agricultural and trade policy decisions. Among the traditional exporters, foreign demand, weather-related fluctuations in yields, and, to a lesser extent, petroleum price increases will be the most relevant considerations. Among the centrally planned countries, yield variations are likely to continue to be the most relevant factors. Among the less developed importing countries, population growth is by far the dominant demand factor, with variability in yields dominating on the supply side.

The importance of each of these exogenous variables changes over time. Petroleum prices become more important as increasingly tight resource supplies narrow the alternatives to energy-intensive food production techniques. Variations in yields are also likely to become more important as agricultural production expands into increasingly marginal areas more susceptible to weather fluctuations. Income growth becomes increasingly important in LDCs as low but sustained growth over the rest of the century pushes per capita levels in the middle-income countries high enough to generate shifts in taste toward grain-fed livestock products.

*With regard to improvements in per capita LDC food consumption, even Alternative II's combination of optimistic supply and demand assumptions suggests gains are likely to be small and poorly distributed.* Annual gains in per capita consumption for the LDCs as a group average less than 0.5 percent but range as high as 1 percent and as low as declining per capita consumption. Given Alternative III's pessimistic assumptions, LDC per capita levels do not grow. While increase in the high-growth regions slows somewhat, per capita consumption levels fall below substandard benchmark 1969–71 levels in low-growth South Asia and Central Africa.

The food problem in many of the LDCs with the slowest growth in consumption appears to be as much a problem of effective market demand as a problem of expanding production. The effect of production constraints—be they limited agricultural resources, inadequate agricultural infrastructure, outdated technology, institutional con-

## TABLE 6-7

### Grain and Total Food Production, Consumption, and Trade (Alternatives I, II, III)

| | 1985 Grain (million metric tons) | | | 1985 Food (1969–71 = 100) | | | 2000 Grain (million metric tons) | | | 2000 Food (1969–71 = 100) | | |
|---|---|---|---|---|---|---|---|---|---|---|---|---|
| | I | II | III | I | II | III | I | II | III | I | II | III |
| **Industrialized countries** | | | | | | | | | | | | |
| Production | 569.5– 525.9 | 568.1 | 536.2 | 126.6–118.1 | 127.3 | 118.2 | 739.7– 679.1 | 730.0 | 683.3 | 157.0–143.7 | 157.1 | 143.5 |
| Consumption | 486.2–465.3 | 515.7 | 455.9 | 121.0–116.6 | 127.1 | 114.6 | 648.4– 610.8 | 687.6 | 590.2 | 155.8–147.7 | 165.7 | 143.6 |
| Trade | +83.3–+60.6 | +52.4 | +80.3 | | | | +91.3–+68.3 | +42.4 | +93.1 | | | |
| **United States** | | | | | | | | | | | | |
| Production | 304.0–297.1 | 297.5 | 309.7 | 137.8–134.9 | 135.1 | 140.2 | 416.0–402.0 | 409.8 | 414.0 | 184.3–178.5 | 181.8 | 183.5 |
| Consumption | 210.9–199.8 | 229.5 | 194.4 | 119.6–114.0 | 129.2 | 111.2 | 290.2–272.4 | 325.0 | 256.8 | 160.3–151.3 | 178.3 | 143.2 |
| Trade | +91.1–+97.3 | +68.0 | +115.3 | | | | +126.0–+129.6 | +84.8 | +157.2 | | | |
| **Other developed exporters** | | | | | | | | | | | | |
| Production | 93.0– 83.1 | 91.5 | 78.7 | 139.1–126.7 | 137.3 | 121.2 | 121.9–106.1 | 126.0 | 107.3 | 175.4–155.6 | 180.6 | 157.1 |
| Consumption | 47.1– 45.5 | 49.9 | 44.2 | 126.8–123.2 | 133.0 | 120.3 | 68.1– 65.2 | 75.9 | 65.9 | 173.3–166.8 | 190.6 | 168.4 |
| Trade | +45.9–+37.6 | +41.6 | +34.5 | | | | +53.8– +40.9 | +50.1 | +41.4 | | | |
| **Western Europe** | | | | | | | | | | | | |
| Production | 160.0–133.0 | 166.0 | 135.5 | 119.1–105.0 | 122.9 | 103.5 | 182.8– 153.0 | 184.3 | 143.0 | 133.5–114.6 | 134.4 | 108.3 |
| Consumption | 182.2–175.5 | 188.8 | 173.3 | 115.1–111.5 | 118.6 | 110.4 | 225.9– 213.1 | 229.9 | 208.5 | 138.5–131.6 | 140.6 | 129.2 |
| Trade | -22.2–42.5 | -22.8 | -37.8 | | | | -43.1–-60.1 | -45.6 | -65.5 | | | |
| **Japan** | | | | | | | | | | | | |
| Production | 12.5– 12.7 | 13.1 | 12.3 | 102.0–103.6 | 104.2 | 96.0 | 19.0– 18.0 | 19.5 | 19.0 | 125.0–131.5 | 139.3 | 138.0 |
| Consumption | 46.0– 44.5 | 47.5 | 44.0 | 150.7–146.3 | 155.2 | 144.8 | 64.4– 60.1 | 66.4 | 59.0 | 205.6–192.8 | 211.5 | 189.5 |
| Trade | -33.5–-31.8 | -34.4 | -31.7 | | | | -45.4–-42.1 | -46.9 | -40.0 | | | |
| **Centrally planned countries** | | | | | | | | | | | | |
| Production | 567.0 | 589.5 | 534.0 | 138.2 | 143.7 | 130.1 | 722.0 | 746.0 | 691.0 | 174.0 | 179.5 | 166.1 |
| Consumption | 596.0 | 597.5 | 578.5 | 143.3 | 143.8 | 139.1 | 758.5 | 755.0 | 730.0 | 179.9 | 179.2 | 173.2 |
| Trade | -29.0 | -8.0 | -44.5 | | | | -36.5 | -9.0 | -39.0 | | | |
| **Eastern Europe** | | | | | | | | | | | | |
| Production | 110.0 | 114.5 | 104.0 | 146.2 | 151.7 | 138.8 | 140.0 | 145.0 | 136.0 | 183.2 | 189.4 | 178.3 |
| Consumption | 118.5 | 119.5 | 116.5 | 144.4 | 145.6 | 142.2 | 151.5 | 151.0 | 148.0 | 181.7 | 181.2 | 177.8 |
| Trade | -8.5 | -5.0 | -12.5 | | | | -11.5 | -6.0 | -12.0 | | | |
| **U.S.S.R.** | | | | | | | | | | | | |
| Production | 230.0 | 245.0 | 210.0 | 137.7 | 146.4 | 126.0 | 290.0 | 305.0 | 270.0 | 172.7 | 181.5 | 161.0 |
| Consumption | 242.5 | 244.5 | 232.0 | 148.5 | 149.7 | 142.2 | 305.0 | 304.0 | 289.0 | 185.9 | 185.3 | 176.3 |
| Trade | -12.5 | +.5 | -22.0 | | | | -15.0 | +1.0 | -19.0 | | | |
| **People's Republic of China** | | | | | | | | | | | | |
| Production | 227.0 | 230.0 | 220.0 | 134.0 | 135.6 | 130.2 | 292.0 | 296.0 | 285.0 | 169.0 | 171.1 | 165.2 |
| Consumption | 235.0 | 233.5 | 230.0 | 136.0 | 135.2 | 133.4 | 302.0 | 300.0 | 293.0 | 171.4 | 170.4 | 166.7 |
| Trade | -8.0 | -3.5 | -10.0 | | | | -10.0 | -4.0 | -8.0 | | | |
| **Less developed countries** | | | | | | | | | | | | |
| Production | 471.7– 490.7 | 485.3 | 470.5 | 154.4–161.4 | 158.9 | 152.9 | 735.0– 740.6 | 757.0 | 745.3 | 244.5–247.7 | 268.2 | 246.4 |
| Consumption | 526.0– 522.3 | 529.7 | 506.3 | 163.4–162.8 | 165.1 | 157.1 | 789.8– 772.4 | 790.4 | 799.4 | 247.8–242.8 | 261.2 | 249.0 |
| Trade | -54.3– -31.6 | -44.4 | -35.8 | | | | -54.8– -31.8 | -33.4 | -54.1 | | | |

## TABLE 6–7(cont.)

### Grain and Total Food Production, Consumption, and Trade (Alternatives I, II, III)

| | 1985 Grain (million metric tons) | | | 1985 Food (1969–71 = 100) | | | 2000 Grain (million metric tons) | | | 2000 Food (1969–71 = 100) | | |
|---|---|---|---|---|---|---|---|---|---|---|---|---|
| | I | II | III | I | II | III | I | II | III | I | II | III |
| **Exporters**[a] | | | | | | | | | | | | |
| Production | 48.5–54.4 | 48.7 | 52.2 | 132.5–142.9 | 133.0 | 139.7 | 78.1–84.0 | 81.0 | 79.3 | 209.2–225.0 | 216.9 | 212.4 |
| Consumption | 25.7–25.5 | 26.1 | 25.6 | 122.2–121.7 | 124.1 | 122.0 | 36.7–36.0 | 37.7 | 39.3 | 160.8–158.0 | 165.2 | 172.2 |
| Trade | +22.8–+28.9 | +22.6 | +26.6 | | | | +41.4–+48.0 | +43.3 | +40.0 | | | |
| **Importers**[b] | | | | | | | | | | | | |
| Production | 423.2–436.3 | 436.6 | 418.3 | 156.0–158.4 | 159.9 | 155.6 | 656.9–656.6 | 676.5 | 666.0 | 247.0–249.3 | 271.9 | 248.8 |
| Consumption | 500.3–496.8 | 503.6 | 480.7 | 166.2–164.6 | 166.3 | 160.9 | 753.1–736.4 | 752.2 | 760.1 | 254.0–248.9 | 268.1 | 254.5 |
| Trade | −77.1–−60.5 | −67.0 | −62.4 | | | | −96.2–−79.8 | −75.7 | −94.1 | | | |
| **Latin America** | | | | | | | | | | | | |
| Production | 101.0–111.9 | 104.3 | 107.6 | 158.7–174.8 | 163.6 | 168.4 | 182.6–185.9 | 195.4 | 188.4 | 279.5–284.4 | 298.4 | 288.1 |
| Consumption | 99.5–98.2 | 103.7 | 97.2 | 162.7–160.7 | 169.2 | 159.2 | 168.8–166.0 | 172.5 | 160.6 | 269.7–265.3 | 275.4 | 257.0 |
| Trade | +1.5–+13.7 | +.6 | +10.4 | | | | +13.8–+19.9 | +22.9 | +27.8 | | | |
| **North Africa/Middle East** | | | | | | | | | | | | |
| Production | 56.2–56.8 | 57.3 | 53.0 | 146.3–148.1 | 149.6 | 136.9 | 92.2–89.0 | 94.5 | 88.1 | 252.5–257.8 | 259.3 | 240.4 |
| Consumption | 80.6–79.6 | 80.9 | 79.9 | 167.4–165.1 | 168.1 | 165.8 | 127.5–123.7 | 125.5 | 132.5 | 276.1–267.3 | 271.4 | 287.7 |
| Trade | −24.4–−22.8 | −23.6 | −26.9 | | | | −35.3–−29.7 | −31.0 | −44.4 | | | |
| **Other African LDCs** | | | | | | | | | | | | |
| Production | 47.1–50.0 | 48.6 | 45.5 | 150.7–160.2 | 155.6 | 145.5 | 61.3–63.7 | 63.1 | 61.5 | 197.1–204.9 | 203.0 | 197.8 |
| Consumption | 51.9–51.5 | 51.5 | 48.5 | 161.2–160.0 | 160.0 | 150.5 | 63.3–63.0 | 60.7 | 62.0 | 196.4–196.4 | 189.1 | 193.2 |
| Trade | −4.8–−1.5 | −2.9 | −3.0 | | | | −2.0–+.7 | +2.4 | −.5 | | | |
| **South Asia** | | | | | | | | | | | | |
| Production | 184.2–186.0 | 190.0 | 178.6 | 154.0–155.5 | 158.9 | 149.3 | 265.0–259.0 | 269.0 | 271.0 | 221.8–216.8 | 225.2 | 226.9 |
| Consumption | 199.7–199.0 | 200.0 | 186.3 | 158.7–158.2 | 159.0 | 148.0 | 284.3–275.7 | 290.7 | 293.9 | 226.2–219.4 | 231.3 | 233.9 |
| Trade | −15.5–−13.0 | −10.0 | −7.7 | | | | −19.3–−16.7 | −21.7 | −22.9 | | | |
| **Southeast Asia** | | | | | | | | | | | | |
| Production | 38.3–41.4 | 38.6 | 39.6 | 179.1–194.3 | 180.6 | 185.5 | 62.0–65.0 | 62.6 | 64.1 | 295.3–310.0 | 298.3 | 305.6 |
| Consumption | 30.5–30.5 | 29.9 | 30.7 | 168.0–168.0 | 164.5 | 169.1 | 47.9–47.0 | 46.0 | 49.9 | 268.8–263.6 | 257.8 | 280.4 |
| Trade | +7.8–+10.9 | +8.7 | +8.9 | | | | +14.1–+18.0 | +16.6 | +14.2 | | | |
| **East Asia** | | | | | | | | | | | | |
| Production | 44.9–44.6 | 46.5 | 43.2 | 155.8–154.7 | 161.4 | 149.7 | 71.9–73.0 | 72.4 | 72.2 | 251.4–255.3 | 253.1 | 252.4 |
| Consumption | 63.8–63.5 | 63.7 | 61.3 | 173.1–172.3 | 172.9 | 166.2 | 98.0–97.0 | 95.0 | 100.5 | 267.7–264.9 | 259.4 | 274.6 |
| Trade | −18.9–−18.9 | −17.2 | −18.1 | | | | −26.1–−24.0 | −22.6 | −28.3 | | | |
| **World** | | | | | | | | | | | | |
| Production | 1,608.2–1,583.6 | 1,642.9 | 1,540.7 | 141.5–140.5 | 144.5 | 137.0 | 2,196.7–2,141.7 | 2,233.0 | 2,119.6 | 194.0–191.0 | 198.0 | 191.5 |
| Consumption | 1,608.2–1,583.6 | 1,642.9 | 1,540.7 | 141.5–140.5 | 144.5 | 137.0 | 2,196.7–2,141.7 | 2,233.0 | 2,119.6 | 194.0–191.0 | 198.0 | 191.5 |
| Trade | | | | | | | | | | | | |

Note: In trade figures, + indicates export; minus sign indicates import.

[a] Argentina and Thailand.

[b] All others, including several countries that export in some scenarios (e.g., Brazil, Indonesia, and Colombia).

## TABLE 6-8

### Per Capita Grain and Total Food Production, Consumption, and Trade (Alternatives I, II, III)

| | 1985 Grain (kilograms) | | | 1985 Food (1969–71 = 100) | | | 2000 Grain (kilograms) | | | 2000 Food (1969–71 = 100) | | |
|---|---|---|---|---|---|---|---|---|---|---|---|---|
| | I | II | III | I | II | III | I | II | III | I | II | III |
| **Industrialized countries** | | | | | | | | | | | | |
| Production | 718.9–663.8 | 719.2 | 669.7 | 112.9–104.5 | 115.2 | 105.0 | 838.5–769.8 | 847.5 | 716.9 | 128.8–118.4 | 131.8 | 108.8 |
| Consumption | 613.7–587.3 | 656.9 | 569.4 | 108.8–104.9 | 115.2 | 102.1 | 735.0–692.4 | 798.3 | 619.2 | 127.7–121.2 | 139.1 | 110.0 |
| Trade | +105.1–+76.5 | +62.3 | +100.3 | | | | +103.5–+77.4 | +49.2 | +97.7 | | | |
| **United States** | | | | | | | | | | | | |
| Production | 1,331.2–1,301.0 | 1,324.6 | 1,322.1 | 124.8–122.2 | 124.2 | 124.0 | 1,697.4–1,640.3 | 1,719.1 | 1,479.5 | 156.0–151.1 | 157.8 | 137.4 |
| Consumption | 923.5–874.9 | 1,021.9 | 829.9 | 108.5–103.4 | 118.9 | 98.7 | 1,183.3–1,111.5 | 1,363.3 | 917.7 | 135.9–128.3 | 154.8 | 107.9 |
| Trade | +407.7–+426.1 | +302.7 | +492.2 | | | | +514.1–+528.8 | +355.8 | +561.8 | | | |
| **Other developed exporters** | | | | | | | | | | | | |
| Production | 1,117.4–1,052.1 | 1,176.1 | 983.1 | 103.3–98.6 | 107.6 | 93.6 | 1,052.0–915.6 | 1,244.5 | 833.8 | 98.6–88.7 | 112.5 | 82.8 |
| Consumption | 596.3–576.1 | 641.6 | 552.2 | 98.6–96.0 | 104.4 | 93.0 | 587.7–562.6 | 749.7 | 512.1 | 97.5–94.3 | 127.4 | 94.1 |
| Trade | +581.1–+476.0 | +534.9 | +431.0 | | | | +464.3–+353.0 | +494.8 | +321.7 | | | |
| **Western Europe** | | | | | | | | | | | | |
| Production | 441.5–367.0 | 459.6 | 372.8 | 111.0–95.2 | 114.8 | 96.5 | 470.7–394.0 | 480.2 | 355.4 | 117.1–101.0 | 119.2 | 92.8 |
| Consumption | 502.8–484.3 | 522.8 | 476.8 | 107.4–104.1 | 110.9 | 102.7 | 581.7–548.8 | 599.0 | 518.2 | 121.4–115.5 | 124.5 | 110.1 |
| Trade | –61.3––117.3 | –63.2 | –104.0 | | | | –111.0––154.8 | –118.8 | –162.8 | | | |
| **Japan** | | | | | | | | | | | | |
| Production | 102.1–103.7 | 107.8 | 100.1 | 83.4–84.5 | 87.3 | 82.0 | 142.9–135.4 | 141.3 | 129.1 | 111.3–106.1 | 110.2 | 101.8 |
| Consumption | 375.7–363.4 | 390.8 | 358.1 | 130.4–126.6 | 135.1 | 124.9 | 484.4–452.3 | 481.2 | 401.1 | 164.2–154.2 | 163.2 | 138.3 |
| Trade | –273.6––259.7 | –283.0 | –258.0 | | | | –341.5––316.7 | –339.9 | –272.0 | | | |
| **Centrally planned countries** | | | | | | | | | | | | |
| Production | 411.5 | 452.5 | 369.6 | 116.7 | 127.6 | 107.2 | 451.1 | 489.2 | 375.3 | 129.6 | 135.6 | 112.8 |
| Consumption | 432.5 | 458.5 | 400.4 | 122.4 | 125.0 | 115.9 | 473.9 | 495.1 | 396.5 | 135.8 | 138.4 | 119.0 |
| Trade | –21.0 | –6.0 | –30.8 | | | | –22.8 | –5.9 | –21.2 | | | |
| **Eastern Europe** | | | | | | | | | | | | |
| Production | 788.6 | 825.5 | 741.3 | 132.7 | 138.4 | 125.4 | 921.9 | 971.9 | 846.2 | 153.3 | 161.1 | 141.6 |
| Consumption | 849.5 | 861.6 | 830.4 | 131.1 | 132.8 | 128.4 | 997.6 | 1,012.1 | 920.8 | 152.1 | 154.2 | 141.2 |
| Trade | –60.9 | –36.1 | –89.1 | | | | –75.8 | –40.2 | –74.6 | | | |
| **U.S.S.R.** | | | | | | | | | | | | |
| Production | 812.8 | 877.5 | 732.2 | 115.6 | 124.6 | 104.5 | 903.2 | 979.7 | 773.9 | 128.1 | 138.7 | 110.3 |
| Consumption | 856.9 | 875.8 | 808.8 | 127.9 | 130.6 | 120.9 | 949.9 | 976.4 | 828.4 | 141.4 | 145.2 | 123.7 |
| Trade | –44.1 | +1.7 | –76.7 | | | | –46.7 | +3.3 | –54.4 | | | |
| **People's Republic of China** | | | | | | | | | | | | |
| Production | 237.6 | 260.0 | 216.2 | 108.7 | 117.8 | 99.9 | 259.0 | 278.0 | 214.0 | 117.4 | 125.2 | 99.0 |
| Consumption | 246.0 | 263.8 | 226.0 | 110.3 | 117.5 | 102.3 | 267.8 | 281.8 | 220.0 | 119.1 | 124.7 | 99.9 |
| Trade | –8.4 | –3.8 | –9.8 | | | | –8.8 | –3.8 | –6.0 | | | |
| **Less developed countries** | | | | | | | | | | | | |
| Production | 182.0–189.4 | 190.4 | 178.3 | 101.7–106.5 | 106.7 | 99.1 | 195.6–197.1 | 210.2 | 176.6 | 109.5–110.8 | 119.5 | 99.1 |
| Consumption | 203.0–201.6 | 207.8 | 191.8 | 107.7–106.7 | 110.8 | 101.8 | 210.2–205.5 | 219.4 | 189.5 | 111.0–108.6 | 116.7 | 99.9 |
| Trade | –21.0––12.2 | –17.4 | –13.5 | | | | –14.6––8.4 | –9.2 | –12.9 | | | |

## TABLE 6-8 (cont.)

### Per Capita Grain and Total Food Production, Consumption, and Trade (Alternatives I, II, III)

| | 1985 Grain (kilograms) | | | 1985 Food (1969–71 = 100) | | | 2000 Grain (kilograms) | | | 2000 Food (1969–71 = 100) | | |
|---|---|---|---|---|---|---|---|---|---|---|---|---|
| | I | II | III | I | II | III | I | II | III | I | II | III |
| **Exporters[a]** | | | | | | | | | | | | |
| Production | 541.1–606.9 | 552.3 | 573.0 | 90.6–97.7 | 92.5 | 94.0 | 624.5–671.7 | 663.7 | 545.6 | 102.6–110.4 | 109.0 | 94.6 |
| Consumption | 286.7–284.5 | 296.0 | 281.0 | 83.6–83.2 | 86.3 | 82.1 | 293.5–287.8 | 308.9 | 270.4 | 78.9–77.4 | 83.0 | 72.7 |
| Trade | +254.4–+322.4 | +256.3 | +291.9 | | | | +331.1–+383.9 | +354.8 | +275.2 | | | |
| **Importers[b]** | | | | | | | | | | | | |
| Production | 169.2–174.4 | 177.4 | 164.1 | 104.3–106.0 | 108.7 | 102.2 | 180.8–180.7 | 194.5 | 163.4 | 110.0–110.8 | 120.3 | 99.4 |
| Consumption | 200.0–198.6 | 204.6 | 188.6 | 111.2–110.1 | 113.1 | 105.6 | 207.3–202.7 | 216.2 | 186.5 | 113.3–110.8 | 119.1 | 101.8 |
| Trade | −30.8–−24.2 | −27.2 | −24.4 | | | | −26.5–−21.9 | −21.7 | −23.1 | | | |
| **Latin America** | | | | | | | | | | | | |
| Production | 247.7–247.4 | 264.3 | 259.6 | 108.2–118.9 | 114.9 | 113.0 | 305.9–311.4 | 346.6 | 286.0 | 131.5–133.7 | 147.8 | 123.6 |
| Consumption | 244.0–240.8 | 262.8 | 234.5 | 110.9–109.6 | 118.7 | 106.9 | 282.8–278.1 | 306.0 | 243.8 | 127.1–125.1 | 136.7 | 110.8 |
| Trade | +3.7–+33.6 | +1.5 | +25.1 | | | | +23.1–+33.3 | +40.6 | +42.2 | | | |
| **North Africa/Middle East** | | | | | | | | | | | | |
| Production | 201.8–203.9 | 209.0 | 188.4 | 87.2–88.3 | 91.0 | 80.1 | 218.3–222.5 | 239.9 | 188.6 | 95.9–98.2 | 107.4 | 80.3 |
| Consumption | 289.4–285.8 | 295.1 | 284.1 | 101.8–100.3 | 104.2 | 99.7 | 301.8–292.8 | 318.6 | 283.7 | 105.9–102.2 | 112.9 | 98.4 |
| Trade | −87.6–−81.9 | −86.1 | −95.6 | | | | −83.6–−70.3 | −78.7 | −95.0 | | | |
| **Other African LDCs** | | | | | | | | | | | | |
| Production | 130.7–138.7 | 136.2 | 125.5 | 98.1–104.3 | 102.3 | 94.0 | 109.0–113.2 | 123.8 | 108.0 | 81.2–84.5 | 92.7 | 80.5 |
| Consumption | 144.0–142.9 | 144.4 | 133.7 | 105.0–104.2 | 105.3 | 97.3 | 112.5–112.0 | 119.1 | 108.8 | 81.3–80.9 | 86.3 | 78.5 |
| Trade | −13.3–−4.2 | −8.1 | −8.3 | | | | −3.6–+1.2 | +4.7 | −0.8 | | | |
| **South Asia** | | | | | | | | | | | | |
| Production | 170.0–171.7 | 177.1 | 160.7 | 104.6–105.6 | 108.9 | 98.8 | 174.0–170.0 | 178.1 | 152.1 | 107.0–104.6 | 109.6 | 93.5 |
| Consumption | 184.3–183.7 | 186.4 | 167.7 | 107.8–107.4 | 109.0 | 98.0 | 186.7–181.0 | 192.4 | 164.9 | 109.2–105.8 | 112.5 | 96.4 |
| Trade | −14.3–−12.0 | +9.3 | −7.0 | | | | −12.7–−11.0 | −14.3 | −12.8 | | | |
| **Southeast Asia** | | | | | | | | | | | | |
| Production | 273.6–295.8 | 282.0 | 278.1 | 116.3–126.4 | 120.1 | 118.4 | 301.9–316.5 | 322.7 | 282.5 | 129.2–135.9 | 138.7 | 120.4 |
| Consumption | 217.9–217.9 | 218.5 | 215.6 | 108.9–108.9 | 109.2 | 107.6 | 233.2–228.5 | 237.1 | 219.9 | 117.1–114.6 | 119.2 | 110.0 |
| Trade | +55.7–+77.9 | +63.6 | +62.5 | | | | +68.7–+87.5 | +85.6 | +62.6 | | | |
| **East Asia** | | | | | | | | | | | | |
| Production | 139.9–138.9 | 148.4 | 131.9 | 104.6–104.9 | 111.2 | 98.5 | 161.1–163.5 | 168.7 | 140.4 | 121.1–122.8 | 126.9 | 105.0 |
| Consumption | 198.8–197.8 | 203.3 | 187.1 | 116.2–115.6 | 118.9 | 109.2 | 219.5–217.3 | 221.3 | 195.5 | 128.7–127.3 | 129.7 | 114.2 |
| Trade | −58.9–−58.9 | −54.9 | −55.2 | | | | −58.5–−53.8 | −52.6 | −55.1 | | | |
| **World** | | | | | | | | | | | | |
| Production | 337.7–332.6 | 354.4 | 315.4 | 109.5–108.5 | 114.0 | 103.0 | 352.2–343.2 | 373.0 | 302.0 | 117.0–114.5 | 126.0 | 104.0 |
| Consumption | 337.7–332.6 | 354.4 | 315.4 | 109.5–108.5 | 114.0 | 103.0 | 352.0–343.2 | 373.0 | 302.0 | 117.0–114.5 | 126.0 | 104.0 |
| Trade | | | | | | | | | | | | |

Note: In trade figures, + indicates export; minus sign indicates import.

[a] Argentina and Thailand.
[b] All others, including several countries that export in some scenarios (e.g., Brazil, Indonesia, and Colombia).

straints, or any combination thereof—are obvious in countries such as Mexico and Egypt. The impact of demand constraints—be they low income, skewed income distribution, foreign exchange shortages, or any combination thereof—are also obvious in countries such as Bolivia and Haiti. The regions showing the smallest improvements through 2000, however, are those with severe supply *and* demand problems. The typical agricultural economy in South Asia and much of Sahelian and Central Africa will be hard pressed to produce an additional 5–10 kilograms of grain per capita over the next 10 years; their consumers, however, are also likely to be hard pressed to demand an added 5–10 kilograms. It should be noted that Alternative II's production increase is relegated largely to reducing imports rather than increasing consumption. The per capita food energy supplies shown in Table 6–9 suggest that *effective* market demand is likely to lag below nutritional demand measured in terms of even the most minimal requirements.

*The results of Alternatives II and III also suggest that world trade is likely to vary far more than world production and consumption.* While world production and consumption vary as much as 10 percent from Alternative II to Alternative III, world trade varies as much as 35 percent. Among the food-deficit countries, variations in the import demand of the centrally planned countries are largest—ranging from 9 to 47 million metric tons in 1985 and 10 to 40 million metric tons in 2000. The import demand of most of the other major importers, including Japan, South Asia, North Africa/Middle East, East Asia, and, to a lesser extent, Western Europe, shows strong but relatively stable growth (Table 6–10).

The surplus productive capacity of the traditional exporters—particularly Canada, South Africa, and Australia—is projected to decrease beyond 1985 as a result of growth in domestic demand. Given the added capacity of several emerging developing exporters, however, excess productive capacity is expected to be more than adequate to balance the highest import demand projected in 2000 but at real prices somewhat above 1973–75 levels. The model implies that the major exporters will continue to play a crucial role in balancing world supply and demand by slowing production in Alternative II-type situations in order to avoid the buildup of price-depressing surpluses, and by increasing export availability under Alternative III-type situations to slow down price increases.

The U.S. is projected to play an increasingly dominant role in this balancing procedure. As the world's residual supplier, the U.S is projected to expand exports faster than the other major traders in a tight world supply situation but to contract exports faster in a loose supply situation. The marked variability of yields in the other major exporters shifts an even larger share of the adjustment on the U.S. in periods of weather fluctuations. As Table 6–10 shows, while the margin between Alternative II and III world export levels is roughly 35 percent in both 1985 and 2000, the margin for exporters excluding the U.S. is 10–20 percent, and the margin for the U.S. is 65–90 percent.

*Alternatives II and III also suggest that the range of possible real-price changes is wide.* Under optimistic Alternative II, an index of real world market prices increases 30 percent from 1969–71 to 2000. Alternative III's tighter supply

## TABLE 6–9

### Daily Caloric Consumption in the Less Developed Countries

| | 1969–71 | 1973–74 | 1985 | | | 2000 | | |
|---|---|---|---|---|---|---|---|---|
| | | | I | II | III | I | II | III |
| | | | *Calories per capita per day* | | | | | |
| Less developed countries | 2165 | 2135 | 2310–2290 | 2350 | 2210 | 2370–2330 | 2390 | 2165 |
| Latin America | 2525 | 2540 | 2690–2670 | 2810 | 2630 | 2935–2905 | 3080 | 2710 |
| North Africa/Middle East | 2421 | 2482 | 2465–2430 | 2525 | 2415 | 2530–2460 | 2655 | 2390 |
| Other African LDCs | 2139 | 2071 | 2245–2230 | 2255 | 2095 | 1840–1830 | 1920 | 1800 |
| South Asia | 2036 | 1954 | 2155–2145 | 2175 | 2005 | 2180–2130 | 2230 | 1985 |
| Southeast Asia | 2174 | 2270 | 2320–2320 | 2325 | 2300 | 2400–2365 | 2425 | 2310 |
| East Asia | 2140 | 2205 | 2310–2340 | 2380 | 2260 | 2505–2480 | 2520 | 2320 |

*Note:* FAO minimum requirements estimated at 2,375 calories per day for Latin America, 2,325 calories in developing Africa, and 2,210 calories in developing Asia. Skewed caloric consumption, however, suggests national caloric consumption averages would have to be 110–125 percent of the minimums to ensure that lowest income classes would be consuming at minimum levels.

*Source:* Tables 6–6 and 6–7.

**TABLE 6–10**

**World Grain Trade Quantities (Alternatives I, II, III)**

| | Historic | | 1985 | | | 2000 | | |
|---|---|---|---|---|---|---|---|---|
| | 1969–71 | 1973–75 | I | II | III | I | II | III |
| | | | *Millions of metric tons* | | | | | |
| **World exports** | | | | | | | | |
| Developed exporters | 68.3 | 100.3 | 139.0–134.9 | 109.8 | 149.8 | 179.8–170.5 | 134.9 | 198.6 |
| United States | 39.9 | 72.9 | 93.1– 97.3 | 68.0 | 115.3 | 126.0–129.6 | 84.8 | 157.2 |
| Other developed exporters | 28.4 | 27.7 | 45.9– 37.6 | 41.8 | 34.5 | 53.8– 40.9 | 50.1 | 41.4 |
| Developing exporters | 11.3 | 13.1 | 22.8– 28.9 | 22.6 | 26.6 | 41.4– 48.0 | 43.3 | 40.0 |
| **World imports** | | | | | | | | |
| Developed importers | 36.2 | 39.0 | 55.7– 74.3 | 61.2 | 69.5 | 88.5–102.2 | 92.5 | 105.5 |
| Centrally planned importers | 5.2 | 24.0 | 29.0 | 8.7 | 46.6 | 36.5 | 9.0 | 39.0 |
| Developing importers | 29.3 | 45.3 | 77.1– 60.5 | 67.0 | 62.4 | 96.2– 79.8 | 75.7 | 94.1 |
| World Total (net export basis) | 79.6 | 113.7 | 161.8–163.8 | 132.4 | 176.4 | 221.2–218.5 | 178.2 | 238.6 |

*Note:* Trade quoted on a net regional basis for total grains and is consequently smaller than trade quoted for individual grains and individual countries.

and doubling of petroleum prices generates more than a 100 percent increase over the same 30-year period. A more detailed analysis of the model's output suggests that the effect of world market price increases varies widely by region and commodity. Countries importing or exporting a large proportion of their total supply on a regular basis, such as Japan and the United States, are strongly affected. In those parts of the world that are near self-sufficiency, the effect of price changes would be substantially smaller. Among the industrialized importing countries near self-sufficiency, higher world prices could strengthen protectionist agricultural and trade policy tendencies. In most of the regions of the world, however, domestic supply and demand pressures and government intervention to minimize the effect of world food price movements on domestic prices would be far more important determinants of actual production and consumption levels. The poorest LDCs accustomed to importing to fill basic food needs, however, could find themselves priced out of the world market to an even greater extent than in 1973–75 should their production shortfalls coincide

with a general Alternative III-type situation (Table 6–11).

## Resources and Inputs

A closer look at the projections suggests that a substantial increase in the share of the world's resources committed to food production will be needed to meet population- and income-generated growth in demand through 2000. A number of recent studies conclude the earth's physical resources and expanding technology can sustain a 4–6 percent rate of growth in food production. Realizing even the 2.1 percent growth to 2000 shown in Table 6–5, however, will entail higher real costs and increased pressure on the world's resource and environmental balances.

### Natural Resources

Table 6–12's arable area data provides one rough measure of food pressure on finite resource supplies. Under all the alternatives tested, growth

**TABLE 6–11**

**International Price Indices (Alternatives I, II, III)**

| | 1969–71 | 1972–74 | 1975–77 | 1985 | | | 2000 | | |
|---|---|---|---|---|---|---|---|---|---|
| | | | | I | II | III | I | II | III |
| | | | | *Real 1969–71 $ = 100* | | | | | |
| World market weighted food prices | 100.0 | 165.0 | 120.0 | 110–130 | 105 | 135 | 145–195 | 130 | 215 |

*Note:* Price index movements indicative of direction of change and order of magnitude only; static nature of the GOL (grain, oilseed, livestock) model and its use of long-run elasticities can understate price adjustments in the short and medium term.

in arable area slows—generally to less than half the rate of increase over the last two and a half decades—despite producer price incentives to accelerate the rate of expansion. Physical constraints, both in the *absolute* sense of running out of cultivatable land and in the *relative* sense of the increasing scarcity of good and reasonably accessible land, affect virtually all of the regions shown in Table 6–5 by 2000 (Fig. 6–6).

Although felt generally throughout the world, pressure on land resources is likely to vary widely and to evoke a number of different responses. The projections suggest that absolute constraints will be most marked in Western Europe, Eastern Europe, Japan, South Asia, China, North Africa and the Middle East, and parts of Central America and East Asia by the early 1990s. Arable area in many of these regions will quite likely begin to contract before 2000 as demand for land for nonagricultural uses increases and as the economic and environmental costs of maintaining cultivated areas near physical maxima becomes prohibitive. Reports on land and water management problems suggest that marginal or submarginal land in Sudano-Sahelian Africa, North Africa and the Middle East, and parts of heavily populated Asia will have to be returned to pasture or

put into an extended fallow rotation if any long-term productivity is to be maintained. Population pressure on arid or semiarid land in these regions in particular has caused soil-fertility losses, deterioration of limited water resources, and declining returns to increasingly costly cultivation. The net return to intensifying use of higher-quality land suggests that economically and environmentally optimum cropped area is far smaller than the potential or maximum area generally measured in physical surveys.

Arable area will undoubtedly continue to expand in other regions of the world, particularly in parts of South America, Central Africa, and East and Southeast Asia. But by 2000, even in these regions where arable area has not reached a maximum, the costs of expansion are likely to be substantially higher as cultivation moves toward forested areas or wasteland, and as water supplies and water management become constraints.

Table 6–13's declining land-man ratios add a population dimension to the problem of absolute and relative constraints on arable area. In general, regions with the tightest absolute constraints report large populations, low incomes, and average caloric consumption levels below recommended minimums.

## TABLE 6–12

### Arable Area, Actual and Projected (Alternative I)

| | 1951–55 | 1961–65 | 1971–75 | Alternative I 1985 | Alternative I 2000 |
|---|---|---|---|---|---|
| | | | *Millions of hectares* | | |
| Industrialized countries | 361.2 | 371.8 | 400.3 | 392.2 | 399.1 |
| United States | 188.5 | 180.5 | 200.5 | 195.0 | 208.0 |
| Other major exporters | 72.5 | 89.0 | 104.0 | 102.0 | 99.0 |
| Western Europe | 95.1 | 96.4 | 90.1 | 89.5 | 87.0 |
| Japan | 5.1 | 5.9 | 5.7 | 5.7 | 5.1 |
| Centrally planned countries | 384.3 | 404.5 | 414.5 | 417.5[a] | 420.0[a] |
| Eastern Europe | 55.0 | 56.0 | 54.4 | — | — |
| U.S.S.R. | 219.8 | 229.5 | 232.5 | — | — |
| People's Republic of China | 109.5 | 119.0 | 127.5 | — | — |
| Less developed countries | 529.2 | 607.1 | 662.0 | 706.0 | 723.5 |
| Latin America | 93.5 | 114.0 | 136.5 | 155.0 | 165.0 |
| North Africa/Middle East | 78.5 | 86.3 | 91.5 | 92.5 | 91.0 |
| Other African LDCs | 116.0 | 146.5 | 160.5 | 175.0 | 182.5 |
| South Asia | 196.0 | 200.5 | 207.5 | 209.0 | 207.0 |
| Southeast Asia | 22.7 | 31.6 | 34.9 | 39.0 | 41.0 |
| East Asia | 22.5 | 28.2 | 31.1 | 35.5 | 37.0 |
| World | 1,274.7 | 1,383.4 | 1,476.8 | 1,513.7 | 1,538.6 |

[a] Arable area in centrally planned countries thought to be at or near maximum. Growth in land used outside the agricultural sector approximately balances arable area increases.

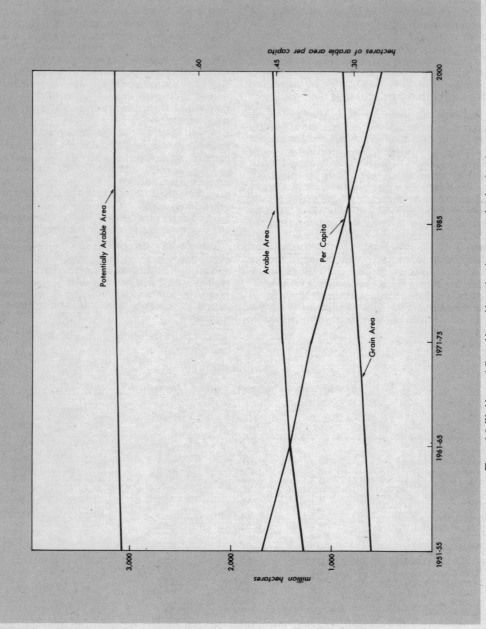

**Figure 6-6.** World potentially arable, arable, and grain area, actual and projected.

## TABLE 6–13

### Arable Area per Capita, Actual and Projected (Alternative I)

| | 1951–55 | 1961–65 | 1971–75 | Alternative I 1985 | Alternative I 2000 |
|---|---|---|---|---|---|
| | | | *Arable hectares per capita* | | |
| Industrialized countries | .61 | .56 | .55 | .50 | .46 |
| United States | 1.17 | .95 | .95 | .86 | .84 |
| Other major exporters | 1.72 | 1.66 | 1.58 | 1.29 | .94 |
| Western Europe | .33 | .30 | .26 | .24 | .22 |
| Japan | .06 | .06 | .05 | .05 | .04 |
| Centrally planned countries | .45 | .39 | .35 | .30 | .26 |
| Eastern Europe | .50 | .47 | .43 | .39 | .36 |
| U.S.S.R. | 1.16 | 1.02 | .93 | .83 | .73 |
| People's Republic of China | .19 | .18 | .16 | .13 | .11 |
| Less developed countries | .45 | .40 | .35 | .27 | .19 |
| Latin America | .56 | .51 | .47 | .38 | .28 |
| North Africa/Middle East | .68 | .58 | .47 | .33 | .22 |
| Other African LDCs | .72 | .73 | .62 | .49 | .32 |
| South Asia | .38 | .32 | .26 | .19 | .13 |
| Southeast Asia | .38 | .41 | .35 | .28 | .20 |
| East Asia | .15 | .15 | .13 | .11 | .08 |
| World | .48 | .44 | .39 | .32 | .25 |

Note: Arable area includes land under temporary crops (double-cropped areas are counted only once), temporary meadows for mowing or pasture, land under market and kitchen gardens (including cultivation under glass), and land temporarily fallow or lying idle.

Source: Economics, Statistics, and Cooperative Service, U.S. Department of Agriculture.

Countries with the broadest latitude for expansion report smaller populations but higher population growth rates and limited agricultural infrastructure and investment monies—factors likely to accelerate growth in their domestic food needs on the one hand while slowing the pace or raising the cost of increases in production on the other.

All three alternatives also suggest substantial pressure to increase not only the quantity of resources committed to agriculture but also the intensity of their use. Increasing use of already cultivated land is possible through multiple cropping, i.e., enlarging harvested area faster than arable area. Even in those countries where resource endowment is such that expansion in arable area is possible, economic returns to intensification are likely to rival returns on developing remaining land and water resources by 1990. In many of the temperate regions unsuited to multiple cropping, similar pressures to intensify are likely to generate changes in land use—shifts out of grasslands into higher-yielding or higher-valued crops, for example, and shortening of fallow periods.

### Resource-Augmenting Inputs

Pressure on the supply side is also likely to generate increases in the use of inputs (such as fertilizer, pesticides, and high-yielding varieties) to augment natural resources. If fertilizer is used as a proxy for a much larger bundle of productivity-expanding inputs, Table 6–14's estimates can be used as rough indications of the growth associated with Table 6–5's projections. The 90–100 percent increase in food production projected through 2000 under Alternative I suggests roughly a 180 percent increase in fertilizer use from 80 million metric tons in 1973–75 to 225 million in 2000. The measures of fertilizer use per arable hectare in Table 6–15 point up the increasingly input-intensive nature of food production through the end of the century.

Expanding food production through increased use of resource-augmenting inputs, however, is subject to diminishing marginal returns. In highly simplistic terms, the 20 million ton increase in fertilizer consumption from the early 1950s to the early 1960s was associated with a 200 million ton increase in grain production suggesting a 10:1 ratio. Growth from the early 1960s through the early 1970s appears to have been at a somewhat lower ratio of 8.5:1. The increases projected under Alternative I imply a further deterioration in this grain:fertilizer ratio to roughly 7.0:1 by 1985 and 5.5:1 by 2000. Ratios within individual regions vary widely, from as low as 3–4:1 in the countries already fertilizing heavily to as high as 10–20:1 in the developing countries at the bottom of what appear to be S-shaped fertilizer response and fertilizer adoption curves. Changes in these world

## TABLE 6–14

### Fertilizer Consumption, Actual and Projected (Alternative I)

| | 1951–55 | 1961–65 | 1971–75 | Alternative I | |
| --- | --- | --- | --- | --- | --- |
| | | | | 1985 | 2000 |
| | | | *Thousands of metric tons* | | |
| Industrialized countries | 13,675 | 25,075 | 39,900 | 57,150 | 84,000 |
| United States | 5,175 | 9,400 | 16,850 | 26,250 | 40,000 |
| Other major exporters | 1,050 | 2,025 | 3,375 | 5,500 | 9,750 |
| Western Europe | 6,525 | 11,850 | 17,650 | 23,000 | 31,000 |
| Japan | 925 | 1,800 | 2,025 | 2,400 | 3,250 |
| Centrally planned countries | 3,525 | 9,100 | 28,125 | 49,250 | 77,500 |
| Eastern Europe | 1,375 | 3,950 | 9,850 | 17,500 | 24,500 |
| U.S.S.R. | 2,000 | 3,700 | 12,850 | 22,000 | 33,500 |
| People's Republic of China | 150 | 1,450 | 5,425 | 9,750 | 19,500 |
| Less developed countries | 1,075 | 3,625 | 11,925 | 28,500 | 58,750 |
| Latin America | 375 | 1,250 | 3,900 | 8,750 | 20,750 |
| North Africa/Middle East | 225 | 650 | 2,000 | 4,250 | 8,750 |
| Other African LDCs | 50 | 175 | 550 | 2,500 | 4,500 |
| South Asia | 150 | 625 | 3,425 | 7,750 | 15,000 |
| Southeast Asia | — | 200 | 450 | 2,000 | 3,500 |
| East Asia | 275 | 725 | 1,600 | 3,250 | 6,250 |
| World | 18,275 | 37,800 | 79,950 | 134,900 | 220,250 |

*Note:* Measures in nutrient tons. Fertilizer total includes nitrogenous fertilizer (N), phosphates ($P_2O_5$), and potash ($K_2O$) used for agricultural production only. Historic usage patterns suggest that the total is made up of approximately 50 percent nitrogenous fertilizers, somewhat over 25 percent phosphates, and somewhat under 25 percent potash.

*Source:* Economics, Statistics, and Cooperatives Service, U.S. Department of Agriculture.

ratios could well be slowed or reversed by either changes in the distribution of scarce fertilizer supplies to increase use in higher-return areas or by technological advances similar to the development of fertilizer-responsive wheat and rice varieties through the late 1950s and early 1960s (Figs. 6–7 and 6–8).

### Water Resources

The key role water plays in developing new resources and intensifying cropping suggests that pressure on water resources is likely to increase even faster than pressure on arable land and inputs. Water management—defined to include conventional irrigation activities as well as flood control, drainage, and soil-erosion control—is already the limiting factor on expanding production in large areas of the world. FAO estimates suggest that over half of the investment in land development of the 1960s and early 1970s was concentrated in water development projects. Future growth in resources committed to agriculture and the successful intensification of resource use are likely to depend to an even greater extent on providing more water and improved water management in the arid and semiarid areas, and on drainage and managing surplus water in the humid and wet areas that together make up well over half of the world's remaining reserves of arable or potentially arable land. As increased pressure on supply generates wider use of high-productivity inputs, water management could become the single most important constraint on increasing yields in the developing world.

### Costs and Investments

All three alternatives indicate that projecting food balances to 2000 is a question not of capacity alone but also of private and public cost. The projection results presented in Tables 6–5 through 6–9 suggest that the world's productive capacity is more than adequate to meet the largest foreseeable increases in demand to the end of the century. However, real food prices are projected to increase even if the price of inputs from outside the agricultural sector are assumed to remain constant. Projected price increases would undoubtedly be even larger if the GOL model's private producer and consumer prices were expanded to reflect the public and social costs associated with developing and maintaining the productive capacity needed in 2000. The margin between public and private costs in the agricultural sector has traditionally been wide. In general, the expense of developing and expanding productive capacity has been funded largely by public investment. Productivity gains have also

## TABLE 6–15

### Fertilizer Consumption per Arable Hectare, Actual and Projected (Alternative I)

| | 1951–55 | 1961–65 | 1971–75 | Alternative I | |
| --- | --- | --- | --- | --- | --- |
| | | | | 1985 | 2000 |
| | | *Kilograms per arable hectare* | | | |
| Industrialized countries | 40 | 65 | 100 | 145 | 210 |
| United States | 30 | 50 | 85 | 135 | 190 |
| Other major exporters | 15 | 25 | 35 | 55 | 100 |
| Western Europe | 70 | 125 | 195 | 255 | 355 |
| Japan | 180 | 305 | 355 | 420 | 635 |
| Centrally planned countries | 10 | 20 | 70 | 120 | 185 |
| Eastern Europe | 25 | 70 | 180 | 315 | 440 |
| U.S.S.R. | 10 | 15 | 55 | 95 | 145 |
| People's Republic of China | 1 | 10 | 45 | 75 | 150 |
| Less developed countries | 2 | 5 | 20 | 40 | 80 |
| Latin America | 5 | 10 | 30 | 55 | 125 |
| North Africa/Middle East | 5 | 10 | 20 | 45 | 95 |
| Other African LDCs | — | 1 | 5 | 15 | 25 |
| South Asia | 1 | 5 | 15 | 35 | 70 |
| Southeast Asia | — | 5 | 15 | 50 | 85 |
| East Asia | 10 | 25 | 50 | 90 | 170 |
| World | 15 | 30 | 55 | 90 | 145 |

*Note:* Measures in nutrient kilograms.
*Source:* Economics, Statistics, and Cooperatives Service, U.S. Department of Agriculture.

depended to a large extent on public investments in education, technology, and extension work.

The relationship between public and private costs have varied widely from country to country due to differing resource endowments and agricultural and trade policies. The most marked differences, however, have been between the industrialized and less developed countries.

Among the industrialized countries—particularly the Western European countries and Japan—governments supplement public investments with farm income and price supports. The projections imply that public costs in many of these countries will have to increase several times faster than private costs—possibly 3 to 4 times faster—if farm production incentives are to be kept high and if new productive capacity is to be developed and old capacity maintained. Public costs will likely increase faster than private costs in several of the LCDs with similar problems of high price supports and limited agricultural resources.

The situation in many LDCs is likely to be in flux beyond 1985. Development policies aimed at taxing the agricultural sector—indirectly by keeping farm prices low, or directly by financing development in other sectors of the economy—have kept public costs much closer to private costs. The projections in Tables 6–5 through 6–8 indicate that a full reversal of conventional public and private cost margins will be necessary by 2000. The public costs associated with the production levels in Table 6–5 are likely to be several times projected private costs. Large public investments in basic infrastructure will be needed; the institutional organization of agriculture in many LDCs leaves the bulk of capital-intensive expansion (as compared to labor-intensive maintenance) of productive capacity to the public sector. Public resources can be injected through market increases in farm returns or directly through development projects. A significant proportion of the capital, goods, and services needed, however, will have to come from foreign sources on a concessional basis if improvements in the agricultural sector are not to slow progress in the rest of the economy.

## Environmental Implications

While the GOL model does not explicitly address environmental issues, the environmental difficulties likely to be associated with the projections outlined above appear to be manageable in theory. Management options within the agricultural sector are wide enough, particularly if supplemented with environmentally sensitive technology, to solve the problems inherent in using a larger proportion of the world's resources in an increasingly intensive manner to produce food.

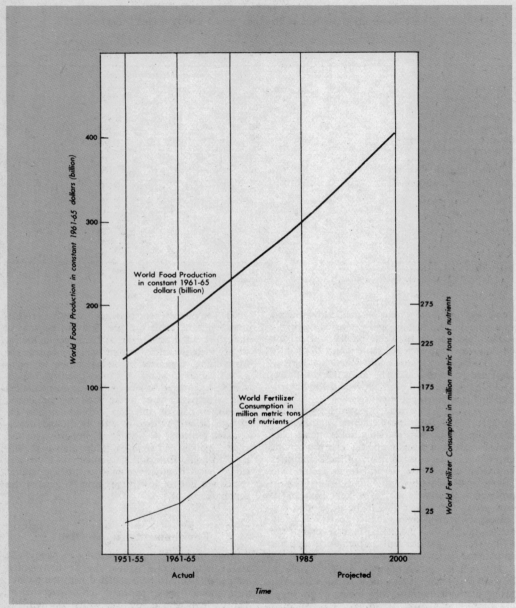

**Figure 6-7.** World food production and fertilizer consumption, actual and projected.

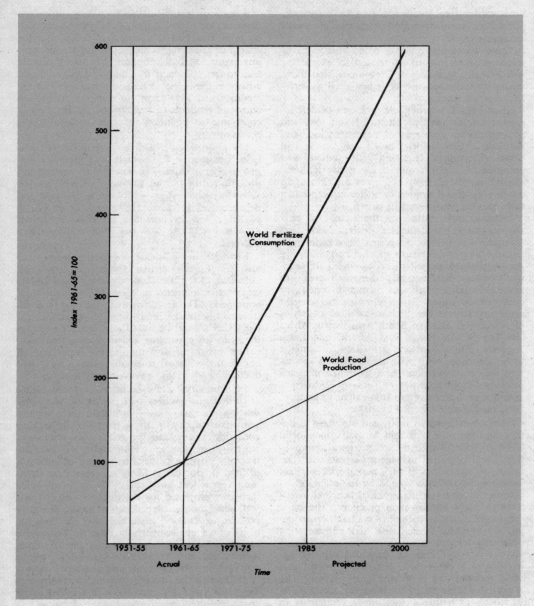

**Figure 6-8.** Indices of world food production and fertilizer consumption, actual and projected.

Environmental problems likely to be associated with future increases in food production are worth cataloging, however.

There appear to be two broad categories of possible problems—those related to expanding and intensifying the use of resources, and those related to increased use of inputs such as fertilizers and pesticides.

Among the first group are problems of deteriorating soil fertility, problems of soil loss and sedimentation, problems of desertification, and problems related to irrigation (such as soil and water salinization, changing water tables, and pollution of water required for nonagricultural uses). If untreated, the problems of this first group cause a gradual deterioration in resource productivity and declining levels of output.

Detailed information on the extent of past fertility losses, erosion losses, desertification, and salinization is limited. Problems have been most marked in countries where man-land pressures are greatest, where agricultural technologies are primitive, where soil conservation measures are limited, and where climate factors do not favor intensive cultivation. Areas reporting the severest problems include the Sudano-Sahelian countries of Africa and areas of South Asia, North Africa and the Middle East, East Africa, and Latin America. Future problems are likely to continue to be associated with pressure to expand agriculture into marginal areas and to utilize marginal resources more intensively. Table 6–12 suggests potential problems even in land-extensive areas of Africa and South America by 2000.

Similar problems in many industrialized countries, including the U.S. and Australia, have been offset to some degree by technological improvements and upgraded management practices. The range of technological and managerial options available, however, is limited by basic land characteristics, tillage techniques, and farmers' incentives to adopt conservation practices. The most successful efforts to date have centered on reducing the intensity of land use and implementing programs for minimum or conservation tillage, contour plowing, terracing, strip cropping, extending dry or green fallow, minimizing runoff and wind erosion, and improving crop rotation. The majority of these programs, however, are likely to be costly in terms of short-range reductions in output or increases in unit production costs.

Among the second group of problems related to increased use of inputs are: fertilizer and pesticide pollution; the increased susceptibility to diseases and pests of high-yield varieties grown in monocultures; the potential toxicity of growth-stimulating additives used in animal husbandry; and the effects of changing techniques in food collection, processing, and distribution. Man-made inputs tend to raise productivity initially; if mismanaged, however, they tend to reduce productivity in the medium and long term, to result in increased output of products of questionable quality, and to contribute to pollution in other sectors of the economy.

The information available on fertilizer and pesticide pollution is fragmentary and generally limited to microstudies. The potential for widespread pollution due to the primary as well as the secondary and tertiary effects of fertilization and pest control is clear. However, the levels of pesticide and fertilizer use projected in Tables 6–14 and 6–15 are well below currently defined maxima.

Fertilizer and pesticide pollution problems can also result from misuse. Even relatively small quantities of ferilizers and pesticides can generate major environmental problems if they are used improperly. The fast growth in the use of fertilizers and pesticides implied by the projections for most LDCs over the next three decades point up the need for expanding and upgrading farm education programs and monitoring input use to ensure the optimum trade-off between food production increases and environmental quality.

In summary, while solutions to foreseeable environmental problems in expanding food production are theoretically available, their application—particularly in those parts of developing countries experiencing the greatest environmental stress—is in question. Ultimately, the environmentally positive or negative nature of increases in food production is likely to depend on short-term versus long-term costs. The real food price increases projected for the decades ahead could well make the short-term costs of environmentally positive agriculture seem high and the long-run costs of an environmentally negative agriculture seem small. In the industrialized countries, internalizing the cost of pollution—translating public costs into private producer and consumer costs—could narrow the margin between short-term and long-term costs and accelerate the move to an environmentally positive agriculture. In most less developed countries, however, questions of grain gaps and calorie gaps are likely to outweigh problems of environment well beyond the year 2000.

# 7 Fisheries Projections

## Marine Fisheries Resources

The total nominal world catch of marine animals in 1975 was 59.7 million metric tons (mmt). The catch from inland areas was 10.4 mmt, which includes some of the diadromous species. Marine fish accounted for 49.3 mmt. The total aquatic catch in 1975 of 69.7 mmt was roughly the same as 1970 (69.6 mmt), the last year of steadily increasing annual catches. Between 1970 and 1975, the average annual total had actually decreased somewhat, primarily, but not entirely, due to the failure of the Peruvian anchovetta fishery (Tables 7–1 and Fig. 7–1).

The trend in marine fish has been downward since the peak year of 1970, demonstrating that the traditional marine fish populations are now

### TABLE 7–1

### Total World Catch and Selected Categories

*(Millions of metric tons)*

|  | Total | Freshwater and Diadromous | Marine Fish | Crustaceans and Mollusks | Mollusks |
|---|---|---|---|---|---|
| 1953 | — | — | 19.1 | 2.6 | — |
| 1954 | — | — | 20.3 | 2.9 | — |
| 1955 | 28.9 | — | 21.3 | 2.8 | — |
| 1956 | 30.8 | — | 22.7 | 2.9 | — |
| 1957 | 31.7 | 5.1 | 22.8 | 3.0 | — |
| 1958 | 33.3 | 5.6 | 24.1 | 3.0 | — |
| 1959 | 36.9 | 6.1 | 26.8 | 3.3 | — |
| 1960 | 40.2 | 6.6 | 29.2 | 3.6 | — |
| 1961 | 43.6 | 7.0 | 32.2 | 3.5 | — |
| 1962 | 44.8 | 6.8 | 35.6 | 3.8 | — |
| 1963 | 46.6 | 7.0 | 36.4 | 4.1 | — |
| 1964 | 51.9 | 7.2 | 40.9 | 4.0 | — |
| 1965 | 53.3 | 7.8 | 39.6 | 4.1 | 2.9 |
| 1966 | 57.3 | 8.1 | 43.0 | 4.3 | 3.0 |
| 1967 | 60.4 | 8.2 | 45.9 | 4.5 | 3.2 |
| 1968 | 63.9 | 9.3 | 48.7 | 5.0 | 3.5 |
| 1969 | 62.6 | 9.8 | 47.2 | 4.7 | 3.2 |
| 1970 | 69.6 | 11.6 | 52.7 | 5.1 | 3.4 |
| 1971 | 70.9 | 12.2 | 52.5 | 5.1 | 3.4 |
| 1972 | 66.2 | 12.4 | 47.2 | 5.3 | 3.6 |
| 1973 | 66.8 | 12.8 | 47.1 | 5.4 | 3.5 |
| 1974 | 70.4 | 12.6 | 50.8 | 5.5 | 3.5 |
| 1975 | 69.7 | 13.4 | 49.3 | 5.8 | 3.8 |

*Source:* Food and Agriculture Organization, *Yearbook of Fishery Statistics: Catches and Landings,* vols. 16, 24, 32, 40.

fully exploited. In fact, many are severely overexploited. The catch of crustaceans has been nearly constant since 1970 at about 2.0 mmt. Mollusks have increased, but in only small amounts. It seems unlikely, therefore, that the generally accepted annual potential of 100 mmt of traditional marine species will be achieved *on a sustained basis.* It is more likely that the potential is nearer the present catch, or about 60 mmt.

Technological and social developments over the next 25 years will not, therefore, cause an increase in sustained yield of the traditional marine fisheries. It is more likely that extended jurisdictions will decrease the actual yield as management under the optimum yield concept brings fishing mortality down to magnitudes more in line with stable, profitable fisheries. Technological advances will likely be needed to just keep the cost of fishing in line with market values. To maintain present yields will also require development of markets for a wider variety of species in order to take advantage of inevitable cyclic changes in species productivity, and implementation of conservational management practices.

To a large extent, the current fisheries yields have been maintained by development of formerly nontraditional species, e.g., capelin and sprat in the northern Atlantic and pollock in the northern Pacific. New fisheries in the next 25 years will continue to develop by seeking species as a replacement for decimated traditional stocks in traditional markets. Species will likely be smaller in size and shorter lived. These fisheries may increase productivity per unit area, but they will also create problems in marketing, particularly for direct consumption. Their development may also restrain rebuilding of traditional stocks because of ecological interactions. The actual theoretical potential of marine protein becomes quite large, 10 to 100 times that of traditional fishery forms, if one is willing to accept that plankton and very small vertebrates can and will be utilized. It is unlikely that a significant stable fishery will develop on these forms with a few possible exceptions.

Utilization of krill in the Antarctic is now developing, and may result in large annual yields

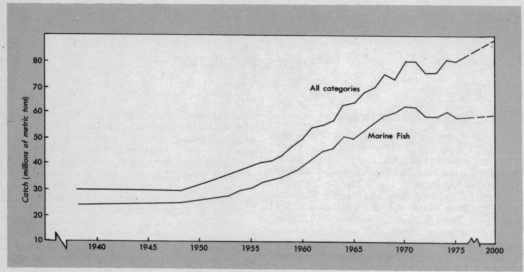

**Figure 7-1.** Annual catch of marine fish and of all marine animals, showing the downward trend in marine fish since 1970.

sometime in the next 10–15 years. There is some potential for developing fisheries on mesopelagic fishes, e.g., lantern fishes, particularly since these are distributed in areas outside of national jurisdictions. Processing and economic considerations will constrain development of both these potentials.

If present trends continue, recreational marine fisheries will increase over the next 25 years to the point where they will have to replace a significant share of the present commercial fishery mortality if the resource is to be managed for sustained, maximal yields. This is now more a development in the U.S. than elsewhere in the world but may become a global problem by the year 2000.

Natural changes in ocean climate will not greatly affect the total potential yield. Species compositions may change and regional productivity may change, but the resource has a basic adaptability which should offset any total changes.

Man-made changes are different. Pollution and physical side effects of other uses such as mineral extraction and powerplants will have an overall negative effect on productivity. If pollution continues unabated as appears to be the prognosis, the effect will be a significant reduction in fishery yields, but there will be a lag in the effects of pollution on the marine resources. Thus, a moderate to low decrease in potential due to this effect would occur during the next 25-year period but would become more severe thereafter.

The 60 mmt marine animal catch in 1975 is roughly equivalent to 12 mmt of protein. It has been calculated that about 36 grams per day per person is an adequate diet of protein (the average daily U.S. protein intake is about 65 grams). Thus, the present fisheries catch would supply about 28 percent of the required protein intake for a population of 4 billion people. This will decrease by 2000 to 25 percent of the requirement for a population of 6 billion people, even if the total aquatic yield increases to 100 mmt.

Culture of marine species probably produces less than 3 mmt currently but has had a real potential for increasing the supply of marine animals. This is particularly true for mollusks (except squid) in estuarine areas. Demand is expected to increase, but primarily in the high-market-price, low-volume species. Production from culture will be slow at first. Over the next 25 years it might double to around 6 mmt.

### Fresh Water Fisheries Resources

The reported harvest of *naturally* produced fresh water fish was about 10 mmt in 1975 and has not increased over the last five years. There appears to be no potential for increased yields from this type of fishery.

The present production from fresh water culture is uncertain. A large share of this is attributed to the People's Republic of China and Asian pond culture. The aquaculture potential in fresh water where nutrition and primary productivity can be artifically enhanced is, perhaps, the greatest of any in terms of realization. The only natural limitation is water supply.

The potential yields of marine and fresh water resources will only be realized if good management, based on a good understanding of the ecosystem, is obtained. The principal ecological research required is on the fundamental processes whereby energy is transformed and distributed in the ecosystem, and on the effects of abiotic factors on productivity and species success.

## Living Marine Resources: Description

The number of different categories (families, genus, species) of marine animals reported in world harvest data is well over a thousand. Because some species are not reported and some not yet exploited, the total numbers of marine species that might enter the harvest would number in tens of thousands. An abbreviated list of species groups used by FAO (the U.N. Food and Agriculture Organization) to report landings is given in Table 7–2. Most of the species are rare or sparsely distributed and do not form a resource significant enough for harvest. Off New England, for example, there are about 200 species of fish, of which only 30 contribute 3,000 or more metric tons each per year and in total amount to 95 percent of the landings. The largest part of the fishery resource is located on or above the continental shelf out to a water depth of 150 fathoms.

Even the species that do provide high yields are not on the average very densely distributed. Adult demersal fish, those associated closely with the bottom, average about one individual per cubic meter. Pelagic fish also average about one per cubic meter. These adult fish range from 0.1 to 100 kg in size. Zooplankton, the small animals that drift in the water column, average about 100 individuals per cubic meter and weigh 0.01 grams or less. Almost all organisms are not uniformly distributed and tend to aggregate in dense concentrations, which provide the basis for today's successful fisheries.

The productivity of some of the richest areas is based on a variable habitat and a multispecies fauna. Sustained yields of from 3.0 metric tons per km$^2$ of surface area (northeast Arctic, New England shelf) to 5.0 (North Sea) have been obtained by intensive fisheries. Most of the shelf area is located well within 200 miles of the coastline.

The largest share of the marine catch (60 percent) in 1975 came from the temperate waters of the northern Pacific and Atlantic oceans. The catch from the central and southern zones followed in order (Table 7–3). The north temperate seas have large areas of very productive shelf,

## TABLE 7–2

### Major Species Groups Reported in World Fishery Landings (FAO)

| | | |
|---|---|---|
| FRESHWATER FISHES:<br>Carps, barbels and other cyprinids<br>Tilapias and other cichlids<br>Miscellaneous freshwater fishes | CRUSTACEANS:<br>Freshwater crustaceans<br>Sea spiders, crabs, etc.<br>Lobsters, spiny-rock lobsters, etc.<br>Squat lobsters, nephrops, etc.<br>Shrimps, prawns, etc.<br>Krill, planktonic crustaceans, etc.<br>Miscellaneous marine crustaceans | MISCELLANEOUS AQUATIC<br>  ANIMALS:<br>Frogs and other amphibians<br>Turtles and other reptiles<br>Sea squirts and other tunicates<br>Horseshoe crabs and other arachnoids<br>Sea urchins, sea cucumbers, and other<br>  echinoderm<br>Miscellaneous aquatic invertebrates |
| DIADROMOUS FISHES:<br>Sturgeons, paddlefishes, etc.<br>River eels<br>Salmons, trouts, smelts, etc.<br>Shads, milkfishes, etc.<br>Miscellaneous diadromous fishes | MOLLUSCS:<br>Freshwater molluscs<br>Abalones, winkles, conchs, etc.<br>Oysters<br>Mussels<br>Scallops, pectens, etc.<br>Clams, cockles, arkshells, etc.<br>Squids, cuttlefishes, octopuses, etc.<br>Miscellaneous marine molluscs | MISCELLANEOUS AQUATIC<br>  ANIMAL PRODUCTS:<br>Pearls, mother-of-pearl, shells, etc.<br>Corals<br>Sponges<br>Aquatic bird guano, eggs, etc. |
| MARINE FISHES:<br>Flounders, halibuts, soles, etc.<br>Cods, hakes, haddocks, etc.<br>Redfishes, basses, congers, etc.<br>Jacks, mullets, sauries, etc.<br>Herrings, sardines, anchovies, etc.<br>Tunas, bonitos, billfishes, etc.<br>Mackerels, snoeks, cutlassfishes, etc.<br>Sharks, rays, chimaeras, etc.<br>Miscellaneous marine fishes | WHALES, SEALS, AND OTHER<br>  AQUATIC MAMMALS:<br>Blue whales, fin whales, sperm<br>  whales, etc.<br>Minke whales, pilot whales, etc.<br>Porpoises, dolphins, etc.<br>Eared seals, hair seals, walruses, etc.<br>Miscellaneous aquatic mammals | AQUATIC PLANTS:<br>Brown seaweeds<br>Red seaweeds<br>Green seaweeds and other algae<br>Miscellaneous aquatic plants |

## TABLE 7–3

### Marine Fisheries Catch by Area, 1975

*(Millions of metric tons)*

|         | Atlantic | Pacific | Total |
|---------|----------|---------|-------|
| North   | 15.9     | 19.3    | 35.2  |
| Central | 6.4      | 9.3     | 15.7  |
| South   | 3.4      | 4.9     | 8.3   |
| Total   | 25.7     | 33.5    | 59.2  |

and the intensity of fishing has been very great as well. These areas border the industrialized countries, which have developed strong coastal fishing fleets. Initial expansion of long-distance fishing fleets took place in the north Atlantic area.

The same countries comprised the 10 leading fishing nations from 1970 to 1975 (Table 7–4). The top two, Japan and the U.S.S.R., have the largest catches from nonhome waters; Cuba has the largest proportion of distant water catches. The 10 leaders take 44 mmt, or about 63 percent of the total. The Republic of South Korea has the largest relative increase in catch since 1970, more than double, followed by Cuba (1.6 times) and Denmark (1.5 times).

## TABLE 7–4

### Catch by Continent and Leading Countries, 1975

*(Millions of metric tons)*

| Rank of 10 Highest |                               | Catch |
|--------------------|-------------------------------|-------|
|                    | Africa                        | 4.5   |
|                    | South Africa                  | 1.3   |
|                    | N. America                    | 4.8   |
|                    | Canada                        | 1.0   |
| 5                  | U.S.                          | 2.8   |
|                    | South America                 | 6.0   |
|                    | Chile                         | 1.1   |
| 4                  | Peru                          | 3.4   |
|                    | Asia                          | 30.7  |
| 8                  | South Korea                   | 2.1   |
|                    | Philippines                   | 1.3   |
|                    | Thailand                      | 1.4   |
|                    | Socialist Republic of Vietnam | 1.0   |
| 3                  | China                         | 6.9   |
| 7                  | India                         | 2.3   |
|                    | Indonesia                     | 1.4   |
| 1                  | Japan                         | 10.5  |
|                    | Europe                        | 12.6  |
| 9                  | Denmark                       | 1.8   |
| 6                  | Norway                        | 2.6   |
| 10                 | Spain                         | 1.5   |
| 2                  | U.S.S.R.                      | 9.9   |

Twenty countries exceeded 1.0 million metric tons. Chile and Peru, notably, depend on one species, the anchovetta, the fishery which failed in 1972 and has not yet recovered. South Africa (pilchard and anchovy) and Norway (capelin) are heavily dependent on one main fishery. The remainder are rather well diversified.

Much of the world catch is taken in or near home waters. The long-distant fleets, however, have been important to many countries, both traditionally (Spain, Portugal) and in the light of recent developments (e.g., Japan, U.S.S.R., Cuba, Poland, Korea).

The leading species group in 1975 catches was the herrings-sardines-anchovies group, which has traditionally been at the top but has dropped from 44 to 30 percent of the 10 leading species groups. The cod-hake-haddock species group is a close second; together the two groups account for about 40 percent of the total catch (Table 7–5). The herrings group is utilized to a large extent for fish meal and oil. The cods are almost totally used for direct human consumption. The redfishes and jacks catches have increased more than the others since 1970.

The total 1975 catch in U.S. continental shelf areas was about 5.8 mmt, the foreign catch in these waters about 3.0 mmt. The U.S. consumes most of its catches in the United States and imports about 70 percent of its total fish consumption. In this respect, it is unique in the world. Almost all of the U.S. catch, except tuna, is taken from the U.S. continental shelf.

## Living Marine Resources: Potential

Several aspects of living marine resources are of prime importance for projecting their use and

## TABLE 7–5

### Leading Species Groups in World Catch, 1970 and 1975

*(Millions of metric tons)*

|                               | 1970 | 1975 |
|-------------------------------|------|------|
| Herrings, sardines, anchovies | 21.6 | 13.7 |
| Cods, hakes, haddocks         | 10.5 | 11.8 |
| Redfishes, basses, congers    | 3.9  | 5.0  |
| Mackerels, cutlassfishes      | 3.1  | 3.6  |
| Jacks, mullets, sauries       | 2.6  | 3.5  |
| Salmons, trouts, smelts       | 2.1  | 2.8  |
| Tunas, bonitos, billfishes    | 2.0  | 1.9  |
| Shrimps, prawns               | 1.0  | 1.2  |
| Squids, octopuses             | 0.9  | 1.1  |
| Flounders, halibuts, soles    | 1.3  | 1.1  |
| Total                         | 49.0 | 45.7 |

productivity. First, they are renewable resources and have the potential for continuing productivity.

The harvest of this productivity is based on the axiom that the net natural rate of growth is changed when population magnitude changes. In particular, when population magnitude decreases from virgin levels, the rate of growth increases and the net increase provides the surplus yield for harvest. The rate of growth is limited, however, being at its maximum in the midrange of density levels, which limits surplus yield.

Between the existing populations of marine plants and animals and their environments an intricate balance has evolved, based on feedback mechanisms that provide the optimal reactions of populations to the natural ecological variations. The populations have co-evolved with a wide range of natural changes and are adapted to them. In terms of our span of time, "What is past is prologue." We do not understand the system well enough to predict the possible changes. Nevertheless, we can be confident the populations will maintain themselves in varying composition but with generally the same productivity. Marine animals have not co-evolved with man, and our interventions cause changes which are potentially very different from those experienced by the natural system and for which the populations do not have the appropriate built-in feedback. Man is not sensitive to the effects of such changes. Our technology has developed to the point where we can drive the ecosystem into a disequilibrium from which recovery is unpredictable. The control we now exert in managing the populations is based entirely on a pervasive and intense fishing mortality that significantly alters population magnitude. The feedback is entirely through our observation of effects and our reactions, both of which are constrained by an economics totally independent of the marine biosphere. The time span of changes in the ecosystem is probably quite out of phase with human desires. Our concepts of optimality are very different from nature's, and our ignorance of the natural system is very great. Thus, man's continuing activities in the marine ecosystem means that maintaining the potential productivity in the long run is problematical, and reduced productivity in the short run is most likely. A significant example of this aspect is the geopolitical treatment of the resources.

Living marine resources are globally considered as a common property to be held and managed in perpetual trust. The scope of commonality is a variable factor and recently has been defined in terms of extended coastal jurisdictions. Division by national boundaries is totally artificial with respect to the resource and, to a lesser extent, the same is true of the offshore limits. Because of differing concepts of optimality and management, national objectives may be quite differently perceived, even for the same population. This tends to further exacerbate the harmony between man and nature that is essential for continued and optimal utilization of the resource. This is critical at present with respect to the effects of fishing but perhaps even more critical in the future with respect to pollution and other man-made changes in the marine environment.

Up to this time, a natural environment has been assumed when studying and estimating the productivity of marine resources. This assumption can no longer be maintained. This creates even greater difficulties in understanding the underlying natural processes than those experienced in the past. The effects of man's changes in the environment are much more subtle, at least initially, than those of the fisheries. They are also probably longer lasting. Hence, detection of their effects (and subsequent correction) will come through a very much delayed and dampened feedback. So much so, that it may be useless to attempt management on the basis of detection and correction. At any rate, the uncertainties create great difficulties in projecting the future course of events.

Productivity of the living marine resources has been estimated using two general methods. One is based on estimating primary productivity, the production of protoplasm or carbon by photosynthesis and then extrapolating the conversion of this energy upwards through the food chain. It can start with estimates of sunlight entering the oceans, with estimates of the standing crop of phytoplankton (chlorophyll), with estimates of the fixation of carbon, or some combination thereof. Beyond this empirical base, the extrapolations into production of other elements in the food chain are based on theoretical assumptions, backed by some experimental work, of the conversion coefficients between trophic layers. The estimates of potential depend to a great extent on definition of the trophic layers or the group of species from which the yield is to be obtained. These decisions or judgments can change estimates by factors of from 10 to 100. It is not always clear what is assumed or what animals are included in the different levels. The other approach utilizes observations of actual fishery yields and field surveys of the resources.

Most of the ocean areas that are productive of fishery resources have been exploited to some degree. Potential can, therefore, be usefully estimated by examining the available statistics and extrapolating therefrom. Lack of accurate reports limits the accuracy of such estimates of cou.se, as does the inference that past performance reflects future potential. Where only surveys of standing stock are available, assumptions about the annual turnover rate must be made, similar to the trophodynamic approach.

In both approaches, the overall world total potential is the most precise, since the sum of regional and species estimates may average out the errors of estimate. The regional estimates will change in accuracy in relation to the amount of data and analyses available. On the other hand, once certain types of areas are defined, and estimates of production per unit area are obtained for some, extrapolation to the total becomes more meaningful. The trophodynamics approach utilizes this feature more successfully than the fishery approach because it does not depend on the vagaries of historical exploitation patterns. The trophodynamic estimates tend to be greater than the fishery-based estimates. The former is estimating a resource potential that includes the total organic biomass in arbitrary categories and is less restained by the implications of practical and feasible fisheries. Thus, the estimates' potential are likely to be biased upward in relation to what may be achieved. They may be biased upward also because the efficiency of transfer of energy may be less than assumed when the populations are being selectively fished, although this is a currently debated issue.

The fishery-based estimates have increased with time. This is characteristic of trend extrapolation methods. The very recent experience of fisheries, however, has led to less optimism about the total extractable amounts of living marine resources. Many of the estimates have been made to promote fishery development by stressing the fact that more is available. But outside of this aspect, some estimates assume that past trends could be simply linearly extrapolated in time and that laws of diminishing returns (limits of biological productivity) would not apply for some time to come. The more specific estimates were often based on the concept and method of maximum sustainable yield. Many of these calculations were based on data from rapidly developing fisheries that were not stabilized to the extent needed for accurate estimates and, because of the opportunistic nature of fisheries, were based on short-term, above-average population magnitudes. Some animal populations do cycle. Fisheries are seldom started at population lows. Improved technology has also masked real declines in populations, but the

possible improvements are limited and the declines have become increasingly apparent in recent years. It has also become apparent that previously observed highs in cycles cannot necessarily be achieved again after intense exploitation. That is, the potential for a population to react to favorable environment is lessened after a high mortality has been exerted upon it, at least within the time spans of 10–20 years, within which the majority of intense fisheries have been developed. This may, in part, be caused by species changes triggered by the selective exploitation.

Relations among species have not explicitly been included in most of the estimates of potential. It is documented that shifts have taken place in some intensely exploited areas (California coast, sardine and anchovy; North Sea, multiple species). It has been observed that the replacement populations tend to be of the smaller sized, shorter-lifespan species. In some cases, yield has been maintained, but often at the expense of heavier fishing. In other cases, yield has decreased, perhaps because the species was less desirable.

In any event, although it has been the case that fishing has been directed at certain desired species, it has also been the case that the gear has not been selective enough. The unselective mortality has, in many cases, been directed at large biomass populations, partly because of the development of long-distant, large-vessel fleets, but it is also due, in coastal fisheries, to the high economic returns. In any mixed species population, which not by accident occurs in most productive areas, the fishing mortality exerted on the smaller biomass species, often inadvertently, is greater than that which will maximize long-run yields. Thus, in general, total area yield has, in many cases, proven to be less than estimates based on individual species assessment. In addition to these factors, many estimates include organisms that have not yet been subjected to exploitation and are in the so-called lower trophic levels.

The potential of these populations is often estimated by multiplying upward from an inverted conversion coefficient the consumption by predator populations. Predator and prey cannot be simply added together. Also, it is not obvious that what was consumed by predators in the system is available to man either from an ecological viewpoint or from a practical technical viewpoint.

Most published studies agree that the north temperate areas of both the Atlantic and Pacific Oceans are now being fished to the full potential. This corresponds to the belt of highly industrialized nations which, with few exceptions, are the world leaders in fishing. The central and southern sectors of fisheries have been developing primarily through long-distance fleet expansion, and the potential is probably greater than present catch—more so for the southern temperate Atlantic and the central Pacific region than the other regions. The total increased yield from lightly exploited areas has been estimated at 30–50 million tons. The species available strongly influence the development of fisheries. Thus, the estimated increase in potential yield over current yield is made up of hakes in the southwest Atlantic and croakers and small pelagics in the central zones. Some increase in cephalopod yield has also been predicted.

Exploration for krill in the Antarctic Ocean (Atlantic sector primarily) is now underway. The potential has been estimated by various authors at 25–100 million metric tons. Doubtless the population is large, but there are many unanswered questions. Do these euphausiids undergo cycles of density, and is a present high what is attracting attention? Will the present turnover rate continue as fishing mortality increases? Will this interfere with recovery of whale populations? The answers are not yet available. The more recent comprehensive fishery-based estimates and the better defined trophodynamic estimates provide a range of potential of 100–150 mmt.

The yields of traditional species in the more heavily exploited areas, which are included in the estimates, have not held up in recent years. In many areas, the so-called nontraditional species are already being harvested (e.g., capelin and squid in the north Atlantic) at maximal levels. Thus much of the hypothesized expansion is in fact a replacement yield and is not additional in terms of potential to the present yields. In addition to the ecological constraints on estimates of potential, the more practical constraints of society (economics, technology, management) will surely reduce the ability to utilize what has been estimated as future potential expansion. For example, the most efficient fishing operation at present will average 50 tons per day in good conditions. The same efficiency applied to zooplankton would average much less than half a ton per day.

These considerations lead to the conclusion that the present world harvest of marine fish of about 60 mmt will not increase on a sustained basis. Furthermore, it will only be maintained with good management of fisheries and protection of the marine environment. The total world harvest of marine renewable resources, based on exploiting natural production, could be increased substantially by the year 2000, perhaps to as much as 100 mmt. To achieve this, however, will require overcoming severe social and economic constraints. Development will have to be carefully planned so that the balance and equilibrium of the marine ecosystem are not radically perturbed. There is not enough information to evaluate the real possibilities of sustained increases in yields, to say nothing of their practicality.

## Marine Pollution

Industrialization, which is heaviest in the Northern Hemisphere, is now introducing pollutants into the oceans in quantities which are beginning to cause significant deleterious effects on resources and the environment. The important coastal zones are being changed at ever increasing rates to the detriment of natural resource productivity.

Worldwide attention to this process is attracted by the more spectacular, acute events that have direct, but short-term, effects on man (large oil spills that affect beaches, heavy metal injections that poison people). The more important effects, however, stem from the largely unnoticed, and undetected, chronic low-level pollution. Because most pollutants fall in the latter category and do not generate public outcry, the general attitude is to consider the oceans as an important resource to be utilized in disposing of the wastes of man. This utilization requires the identification of substances that jeopardize marine resources and human health and the determination of acceptable levels—an extremely slow process because the pathways and effects are extremely complex and long-term. Demonstrable threats to marine resources are seldom available within time spans that could effectively stop the pollution prior to adverse accumulations.

The residence time in the oceans of the pollutants is minimally a matter of decades, but increases to centuries or greater for a host of substances. The process of transport to the ocean and accumulation to detectable, but not necessarily ineffectual, levels is also in many cases a matter of decades or centuries.

How a given material will affect components of the ocean, and how much of a substance or habitat modification jeopardizes a resource requires an ability to predict events in the ocean. This in turn requires a knowledge of the natural processes in the undisturbed system. It is highly problematical that such knowledge will be accumulated rapidly enough to detect and correct adverse effects.

Productivity of marine resources can be reduced by destruction or change of habitat as well as by bio-accumulation of chemicals, most notably in the coastal zones of industrialized countries. Estuarine areas are highly productive, and are an important, and limiting, factor in the life cycles of many species of fish and shellfish. Atmospheric transport of pollutants is also affecting the open ocean environment far from the sites of direct discharge and origin. Man's emissions into the atmosphere are now at least about 10 percent of the naturally occurring flux.

Most of man's activities lead to pollution and physical change of the environment. Most of these changes must be viewed as potentially reducing natural productivity. It is only in physically restricted areas, under controllable and predictable situations, that man can increase productivity. Because such areas are limited, pollution of the oceans at increasing rates will likely have the effect of reducing overall yields of marine resources.

## Marine Aquaculture

Aquaculture, defined as the culture or husbandry of aquatic organisms in fresh or salt water, yielded an estimated 6 mmt of food in 1975—roughly 10 percent of the world production of fishery products. Yields from aquaculture doubled in the period 1970–1975; much of the increase was in high-unit-value species in industrialized countries. Some countries now depend on aquaculture for a significant part of fish and shellfish production. Japanese aquaculture production increased fivefold (to 500,000 metric tons) in the period 1970–1975, while Israel now derives almost half its finfish from aquaculture. United States aquaculture production in 1975 was only 65,000 metric tons, about 3 percent of U.S. fish and shellfish landings, but this limited amount still constituted (in 1975) about a quarter of our salmon production, about two-fifths of our oyster production, and about half of our catfish and crawfish production.

There is cause for reasoned optimism when considering increased food production from aquaculture. Despite institutional, economic, environmental, and technological constraints, global yields are increasing. Intensive culture of high-unit-value species—such as pen-rearing of salmon and raceway culture of shrimp—is approaching the point of economic feasibility, and extensive culture of animals that utilize very short food chains—such as oysters, mussels, and mullet—has the potential for enormous expansion with existing technology. The 1976 FAO World Conference on Aquaculture concluded that even with existing technology a doubling of world food production from aquaculture will occur within the next decade and that a 5–10 fold increase by the year 2000 is feasible if the necessary scientific, financial, and organizational support becomes available.

Development of energy-intensive high-technology culture of species requiring high-protein diets will undoubtedly continue in the next two decades, especially in industrialized countries, but substantial production of herbivorous species in natural waters—designed to yield relatively low-cost animal protein—should expand even more rapidly, particularly in less developed countries, and particularly in tropical and subtropical areas with year-round growing season. An important role of industrialized countries will relate to improvement of the technology required for extensive culture production of inexpensive animal protein in less developed parts of the world by such methods as genetic selection for high food-conversion efficiency and rapid growth, testing of low-cost diets from natural products, and training of technicians. The role of aquaculture in integrated rural development, through provision of better diet, jobs, and cash crops, can be significant in less developed countries. Aquaculture there would be primarily in the form of small-scale, low-technology, labor-intensive operations.

The potential of ocean ranching—not only of anadromous species, but also of coastal-migratory species—will be exploited within the next two decades, and substantial increases in yields (as well as augmentation of fished stocks) can be expected in proportion to public and private investment in this approach to fish production. An important qualifying comment here would be the need for consideration of impacts of introduced populations on natural stocks, and the need to determine and consider the total carrying capacity of the ocean areas involved.

Expansion of food production through aquaculture must be a matter of national policy and national priority—much as the expansion of distant-water fishing fleets was in many countries (particularly the socialist countries with plannned economies) during the 1960s. Included in such policy would be improvement in the technological base, development of legal protection for aquaculture enterprises, control of coastal/estuarine pollution, and encouragement of capital investment. With increasing restrictions on harvests from continental shelf waters of other nations, the aquaculture option should become much more attractive as a protein food source.

## Economic Demand

Projection of past trends in landings into the future assumes that costs of harvesting increasing quantities of fishery products, adjusted for inflation, will not rise more rapidly than in the past. This, in turn, suggests a whole host of other assumptions about fishery technology, species abundance, and patterns of fishery management. World forecasts often ignore geographical differences in population and income growth and the effects of these different rates of growth on world demand for fishery products.

In an effort to overcome some of these difficulties, FAO in 1970 attempted to estimate the income elasticity of demand for world fishery products and to project the demand for food fish to 1975 and 1985 on the basis of 1969 FAO expectations about world population and income trends (Table 7–6). The FAO approach assumed the demand for food fish would grow with world income, but not at the same rate as world income. Thus, for example, U.S. and Canadian demand for food fish would be expected to increase 20

percent for every 100 percent growth in income, Asian demand to increase 109 percent for every 100 percent growth in income, and so on. These estimates depend upon the rather awkward assumption of constant prices for fishery products.

In its world projection to 1985, FAO estimated the demand for industrial fish separately, assuming that the demand for industrial fish was functionally related to the demand for poultry and hogs. Demand of fish meal for poultry and hog production was estimated to grow at a higher rate for the period 1965–1975 than for 1975–1985, so the growth progression was a step function.

Any long-term forecast is bound to present numerous difficulties, but the FAO method poses some special problems. The greatest drawback to the FAO estimation procedures is their lack of adjustment for possible price changes, their use of unchanging country by country income elasticity coefficients for the time of their forecast, their failure to disaggregate by species, and the lack of explanatory information on their derived demand equations for industrial fish.

### TABLE 7–6

### 1970 FAO Projection of Demand for Fish Meal, 1975 and 1985

(*Thousands of metric tons, product weight*)

| | Consumption 1961–63 | 1975 Projected Rate of Increase (*percent per year*) | 1975 Projected Demand | 1985 Projected Rate of Increase (*percent per year*) | 1985 Projected Demand |
|---|---|---|---|---|---|
| Industrialized countries | 2,408 | 4.5 | 4,250 | 3.6 | 5,390 |
| North America | 668 | 2.8 | 960 | 2.4 | 1,140 |
| Europe | | | | | |
| EEC | 734 | 4.4 | 1,280 | 3.5 | 1,620 |
| Northwest Europe | 517 | 4.1 | 870 | 3.1 | 1,040 |
| South Europe | 104 | 8.5 | 300 | 6.7 | 460 |
| Other industrialized countries | | | | | |
| Japan | 340 | 5.8 | 710 | 4.6 | 960 |
| Others | 45 | 8.5 | 130 | 5.9 | 170 |
| Centrally planned countries | 231 | 11.2 | 920 | 8.6 | 1,550 |
| U.S.S.R. | 119 | 11.0 | 460 | 9.2 | 900 |
| Other European countries | 112 | 11.5 | 460 | 7.9 | 650 |
| China | — | — | — | — | — |
| Other Asian countries | — | — | — | — | — |
| Less developed countries | 221 | 8.3 | 620 | 8.9 | 1,560 |
| Latin America | — | — | 310 | — | 710 |
| Africa, South of Sahara | — | — | 30 | — | 130 |
| Near East | — | — | 60 | — | 130 |
| Asia | — | — | 220 | — | 590 |
| World Total | 2,860 | 5.6 | 5,790 | 4.9 | 8,500 |
| Meal from offal | 230 | 6.2 | 500 | 6.6 | 1,000 |
| Demand for meal from fish | 2,630 | 5.5 | 5,290 | 4.7 | 7,500 |
| Demand for fish for meal | 13,150 | 5.5 | 26,450 | 4.7 | 37,500 |

*Note*: To convert the demand for meal from fish to the demand for fish a conversion factor of 5 is used, i.e., it is assumed that 5 tons of fish make 1 ton of meal.

*Source*: Food and Agricultural Organization, *Provisional Indicative World Plan for Agricultural Development*, Rome, 1970.

In 1970 Frederick W. Bell et al. sought to overcome several of the cited disadvantages of the FAO projection methodology. The Bell group undertook to estimate price and income elasticity of demand by species (Table 7–7) and by major consuming country for the years 1975, 1985, and 2000. Incorporated into the Bell analysis was an assumed decline in the income elasticity of demand for food fish for the world starting at 0.68, in 1965, but declining to 0.22 by 1985, and leveling out at about that point. This is in comparison with the FAO estimate which remains at 0.68 throughout their projection. The Bell group assumption of a declining income elasticity is based upon the empirical observation that in general richer countries consume less fish per capita (Fig. 7–2).

The Bell group also incorporated into their model selective assumptions, on a species by species basis, about supply constraints. Their model predicted price increases, sometimes substantial increases. The FAO group did not attempt this, so the two forecasts are somewhat different in their intent. FAO sought to forecast what the world demand would be if prices did not change, while the Bell group attempted to forecast what world prices and quantity demand would be if resource scarcities developed as expected.

Because the Bell Group attempted more than FAO, there were more places where their forecast could go awry. Interestingly enough, both forecasts came out about the same for the 1975 predictions, and both were higher than—but relatively close to—the actual landing of 69.7 mmt (FAO had predicted 74.1 mmt, the Bell Group 74.0). Where the two forecasts diverge is in the later years. For 1985, FAO predicted a demand of 106.5 mmt, the Bell group 78.6. For the year 2000, the Bell group predicted 83.5 mmt; FAO did not make the projection.

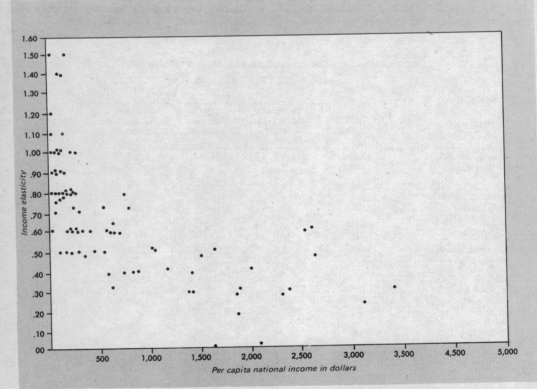

**Figure 7-2.** Per capita national income vs. income elasticity of fisheries demand in 77 countries. (*Frederick W. Bell et al., unpublished manuscript, 1969*)

## TABLE 7–7

### 1970 Bell et al. Projections of World Aggregate Consumption of Fishery Products, 1975–2000

*(Thousands of metric tons, round weight)*

|  | 1965–67[a] | 1975 | 1985 | 2000 | Changes 1965–67 to 2000 (*percent*) |
|---|---|---|---|---|---|
| **Food fish** | | | | | |
| Groundfish | 6,368 | 6,940 | 5,761 | 4,763 | −25.2 |
| Tuna | 1,291 | 1,456 | 1,615 | 1,657 | 28.4 |
| Salmon | 476 | 481 | 485 | 485 | 1.9 |
| Halibut | 58 | 58 | 58 | 58 | 0 |
| Sardines | 871 | 1,464 | 1,848 | 2,370 | 172.1 |
| Shrimp | 634 | 1,066 | 1,347 | 1,479 | 133.3 |
| Lobsters | 137 | 174 | 192 | 145 | 5.8 |
| Crabs | 328 | 481 | 517 | 386 | 17.7 |
| Clams | 478 | 535 | 626 | 694 | 45.2 |
| Scallops | 166 | 236 | 281 | 322 | 94.0 |
| Oysters | 777 | 1,218 | 1,755 | 2,453 | 215.7 |
| Other fish | 25,086 | 32,659 | 41,504 | 53,524 | 113.4 |
| Total food fish | 36,670 | 46.768 | 55,989 | 68,226 | 86.4 |
| Fish meal | 20,440 | 27,170 | 22,634 | 15,196 | −25.7 |
| Total (food and meal) | 57,110 | 78,938 | 78,623 | 83,532 | 46.3 |

[a] Average of actual.

Source: Frederick W. Bell et al., *The Future of the World's Fishery Resources* (National Marine Fisheries Service, File Manuscript No. 65.1) Dec. 1970.

These predictions comprise the best available world demand estimates, although they are both out of date. There is need for a new effort in which price and income elasticities are re-estimated by species and by country, and revised maximum sustainable yield and other supply factor calculations are introduced; projections should then be made on the basis of contemporary estimates of country by country population and income projections.

The FAO projections assumed a world population growth rate to 1985 of 2.1 percent and a per capita income growth of 3.2 percent. The Bell Group assumed a 1.7 percent population growth rate to 2000 and a 3.0 percent growth in per capita income.

World income may rise 3.2–4.1 percent annually from 1975 to 1985, depending upon whether one accepts the low or the high growth rate assumption. From 1975 to 2000 the low projection is 2.9 percent per year and the high 4.2 percent. On the basis of these assumptions, a crude adjustment of the FAO projection suggests a world fish demand for 1985, under the constant price assumption, of 92–98 mmt (as opposed to FAO's projected 106 mmt). A parallel adjustment for the Bell group study suggests 72–76 mmt for 1985 (as opposed to their projected 78.6) and 81–83 mmt for 2000 (as opposed to their projected 83.5).

# 8  Forestry Projections

Twenty-two years ago, forests covered over one fourth of the world's land surface. Now forests cover one fifth. Twenty-two years from now, in the year 2000, forests are expected to have been reduced to one sixth of the land area. The world's forest is likely to stabilize on about one seventh of the land area around the year 2020.*

The economic implications of this transition from a period of global forest wealth to a period of forest poverty are more apparent from the expected change in wood per capita. The world now grows about 80 cu m (cubic meters) per capita of wood in trees large enough to be commercially valuable. In the year 2000, there will be only 40 cu m per capita, even if the deforestation rate stabilizes now. If the deforestation rate continues to increase with population growth, there will be substantially less than 40 cu m per capita.† Yet by the year 2000, GNP is expected to have increased significantly in both the more and less industrialized nations. In the more industrialized nations, consumption of wood products is expected to rise sharply with increasing GNP per capita. Relative prices of industrial wood products, paper, sawn lumber, wood panels, wood-based chemicals, plastics, and many other products, are sure to increase. The effects may be somewhat disruptive, but substitutes will probably be found for the products that become too expensive. No catastrophic changes are foreseen.

In the less developed countries (LDCs), where most of the deforestation will occur, people will forgo the increased use of paper and other industrial wood products that might have been expected to follow increased GNP, and the effect on welfare will be negative but bearable. But industrial wood products are much less important in LDCs than charcoal and fuelwood used for cooking and heating, and poles used for framing structures for shelter. Prices and absolute scarcity will put fuelwood and charcoal out of economic reach of not only the subsistence sector but also much of the market sector of the LDC populations.

---

*The estimates of forest area as a fraction of the world's land area are derived as follows (references are to works in the list of references at the end of this chapter, unless cited in full). The forest area in 1950 was 4.85 billion hectares, according to Whittaker and Likens. That figure excludes woodland, shrubland, and savannah. The forest area in 1973 was about 2.66 billion hectares, according to data from Persson (1974), the Economic Commission for Europe, and J. T. Micklewright ("Forest and Range Resources of the United States and Factors that Affect Their Use," unpublished manuscript prepared for the 8th World Forestry Congress, Oct. 1978). That figure refers to "closed forest". For the United States, closed forest excludes forest land incapable of producing more than 1.4 cubic meters of industrial wood per hectare per year. For Canada, it excludes land incapable of producing stands of trees 4 inches in diameter or larger on 10 percent or more of the area. For the rest of the world, it excludes land where tree crowns cover less than 20 percent of the area and land which has a primary use other than forestry. Interpolating between the 1950 forest area and the 1973 area suggests that 22 years ago the forested area was over 4 billion hectares. The present forest area and the forest area for the year 2000 are calculated by factoring the 1973 area by an annual net deforestation rate of 18 to 20 million hectares. This rate is aggregated data from a variety of sources, including Persson (1974), Sommer, and several series of reports from U.S. embassies in the less industrialized nations. The 1978 forested area is thus calculated to be about 2.57 billion hectares, and the year 2000 area is about 2.1 to 2.2 billion hectares. The assumption that the deforestation rate will not accelerate with population and GNP growth is arbitrary, chosen to be on the conservative side. That the forest area will stabilize at about 1.8 billion hectares follows from the observation that the forests of the more industrialized nations have already stabilized at about 1.45 billion hectares (Micklewright and European Economic Commission) and that about 365 million hectares of forest in the less developed nations is physically or economically inaccessible to logging and land-clearing operations (European Economic Commission and Sommer). At the present deforestation rate, the accessible forests in the less industrialized nations will have been razed before 2020, but the rate will undoubtedly slow down as the forests available for cutting diminish. Thus the inference that the forest area will stabilize around the year 2020. The fractions are derived using 13.003 billion hectares as the world's total land area. That figure is from Persson (1974); it includes 19 percent of arctic regions and excludes the Antarctic, Greenland, and Svalbard.

†The estimates of present and future wood volume per capita were derived by factoring forest areas for each region by the wood volume per hectare for each region as estimated by Persson (1974). The estimates of forest area by region for the year 2000 used in this calculation were derived from the sources cited in previous footnote.

117

To provide some insight into the economic and
environmental transition occurring as a result of
changes in the world's forests, this paper first
discusses the status of forest inventories and the
economic significance of forests from a global
standpoint. Then trends and prospects for forests
and forestry in each of the main geographic
regions are reviewed. The special problems of the
world's most complex ecosystems, the tropical
moist forests, are treated briefly in a separate
section. Finally global linkages that will make the
year 2000 forest situation in the tropics important
to the people of the temperate zone are cited.

## Forest Inventories

Several recent reports have mistakenly indicated that the world contains 4.5 billion hectares
of forests plus over 2.3 billion hectares of open
woodlands.[1] Apparently there is some confusion
over the distinction between "forest land" and
"forest," and it seems to be common practice to
use forest area data from 1950, as though neither
extent of forests nor knowledge about forest areas
were changing. In fact, the world has only about
2.6 billion hectares of closed forest and another
1.2 billion hectares of open woodlands and savan-
nahs, according to the most recent and best global
estimates.[2]

About half of the closed forests are located in
the LDCs of the tropic and subtropic regions,
where exploding populations are rapidly destroying forests for farmland and for fuel. The other
half are in the industrialized nations, mainly the
U.S.S.R., Canada, and the U.S., where their
extent is relatively stable in spite of increasing
demands for forest products. Table 8–1 shows the
distribution of forests by global region.

Information about forest areas is scarce for
many countries. The data that are available are
classified according to widely varying definitions
from year to year and from country to country.
The task of evaluating and synthesizing all these
heterogeneous data was undertaken by the World
Forest Inventory project of the Food and Agriculture Organization (FAO) in the 1950s and 1960s
and, when FAO discontinued the work in the early
1970s, by Reidar Persson at the Royal College of
Forestry in Stockholm. Persson considers the area
data to be "relatively reliable" (accuracy of ± 5–
10 percent) for about half of the world's closed
forest. The data are "poor" (± 40–100 percent)
for about a third of the closed forest area, and
intermediate (± 20 percent) for the rest. The
information on open woodlands is so poor that the

### TABLE 8–1

### World Forested Area by Region, 1973

| | Forest Land | Closed Forest | Open Wood-land | Total Land Area | Closed Forest (% of land area) |
|---|---|---|---|---|---|
| | *Millions of hectares* | | | | *Percent* |
| North America | 630 | 470 | (176) | 1,841 | 25 |
| Central America | 65 | 60 | (2) | 272 | 22 |
| South America | 730 | 530 | (150) | 1,760 | 30 |
| Africa | 800 | 190 | (570) | 2,970 | 6 |
| Europe | 170 | 140 | 29 | 474 | 30 |
| U.S.S.R. | 915 | 785 | 115 | 2,144 | 35 |
| Asia | 530 | 400 | (60) | 2,700 | 15 |
| Pacific area | 190 | 80 | 105 | 842 | 10 |
| World | 4,030 | 2,655 | (1,200) | 13,003 | 20 |

*Notes:* Data on North American forests represent a mid-1970s estimate. Data
on U.S.S.R. forests are a 1973 survey by the Soviet government (see Reference
3). Other data are from Persson (1974); they represent an early-1970s estimate.
Forest land is not always the sum of closed forest plus open woodland, as it
includes scrub and brushland areas which are neither forest nor open woodland,
and because it includes deforested areas where forest regeneration is not taking
place. In computation of total land area, Antarctic, Greenland, and Svalbard are
not included; 19 percent of arctic regions are included.

global figure must be considered an "informed
guess."[3]

The wood resources in the world's forests have
been estimated by extrapolating from detailed
forest inventories carried out in the various regions and biomes.

Most forest inventories are concerned with the
quantity of wood that might be extracted in logs
of commercially useful size. Analysts concerned
with ecological processes, with fuel and other
nonindustrial products, or with biomass conversion and other innovative concepts, need to know
the total forest biomass. It is possible to multiply
the estimates of biomass density for each ecosystem type, as given by Whittaker and Likens[4] by
the present area covered with each major forest
type, as given by Persson. This calculation (Table
8–2) indicates that the total biomass of the world's
forests and woodlands is on the order of 400 to
500 billion tons of carbon.

## Forest Products

Worldwide production of forest products, including fuelwood, as well as wood for construction, for paper and for other industrial products,
totaled at least 2.4 billion cu m (in underbark
roundwood equivalent) in 1975.[5] About half of the
wood harvest is in the industrialized nations where
harvest and production vary with economic
cycles. The other half is in the LDCs where most

## TABLE 8–2

### Biomass of the World's Forests and Woodlands

| Forest Type | 1973 Area (millions ha) | Biomass Density (tons carbon/ha) | Total Biomass (billion tons carbon) |
|---|---|---|---|
| Tropical rain (tropical and subtropical wet evergreen) | 568 | 202.5 | 115 |
| Tropical seasonal (tropical and subtropical moist and dry deciduous) | 1,112 | 157.5 | 175 |
| Temperate evergreen (temperate coniferous) | 448 | 157.5 | 65 |
| Temperature deciduous (temperature broadleaved) | | 135.0 | |
| Boreal (Boreal) | 672 | 90.0 | 60 |
| Woodland, shrubland and savannah (open woodlands) | 1,000 | 22.5 | 22 |
| Total | 3,800 | | 437 |

*Notes:* The data on areas of each forest type are from Persson (1974). The biomass densities for each forest type are from Whittaker and Likens (1975). Persson's forest types are named in parenthesis, indicating how they are assumed to correspond to Whittaker and Likens' ecosystem types for this marriage of the two sets of data. Persson does not disaggregate coniferous and broadleaved temperate forest areas, so it was necessary to use the mean of the biomass density figures for the two types (i.e., 146 tons carbon per hectare); however this manipulation introduces a potential error of less than 5 percent.

of the production is fuelwood for cooking, used by people who are so poor that they are hardly aware of short-term variations in global markets.

Supply factors affecting the production of forest products include not only forest area and standing crop, but also the physical accessibility, species mix and quality of the timber, as well as the availability of capital, labor, and management expertise for road or rail construction and for the other developments necessary to forest exploitation. Factors affecting production from the demand side include size and socioeconomic characteristics of the indigenous population, rates of investment in wood-processing technology, transportation costs to foreign markets, national economic growth rates, and market development achievements. Each nation's annual wood harvest is also strongly affected by institutional and political constraints on forest resource development and exploitation. These constraints vary from political restrictions on international trade to indigenous demand for recreation or other nonconsumptive use of forest resources.

Forest products enter into world trade at all stages—as primary, semiprocessed, processed and manufactured products. As a result, most countries both import and export. With a few exceptions, demand for forest products in industrialized nations is greater than production, so that most industrialized nations are net importers. Many of the less developed nations, on the other hand, produce more nonfuel forest products than they can consume and are net exporters. This complementarity is expected to become even greater during the next 20 years. As it happens, few of the major forest product net exporters are among the more rapidly developing LDCs that are likely to be narrowing the consumption gap by the year 2000. Table 8–3 indicates the rank order of the major net importers and net exporters of forest products.

## The Forest-Man Relationship: Two Systems

Forest resources and the total wood harvest are about evenly divided between the industrialized and the less developed nations. Otherwise, most aspects of the forest-man relationship are profoundly different in the two types of economies. The industrialized nations are three times richer in forest resources per capita. Table 8–4 indicates the distribution of forest area and growing stock per capita in the early 1970s. The gap indicated by these data is widening rapidly. Resources per

## TABLE 8–3

### Major Traders of Forest Products, 1974

| Major Net Exporters | Exports Less Imports (millions $) | Major Net Importers | Imports Less Exports (millions $) |
|---|---|---|---|
| Canada | 4,921 | Japan | 4,365 |
| Sweden | 3,601 | United | |
| Finland | 2,273 | Kingdom | 3,795 |
| U.S.S.R. | 1,552 | Italy | 1,442 |
| Ivory Coast | 706 | German Fed. | 1,439 |
| Indonesia | 666 | France | 1,186 |
| Austria | 540 | Netherlands | 1,085 |
| Malaysia, | | U.S.A. | 746 |
| Sabah | 373 | Belgium-Lux. | 504 |
| Philippines | 237 | Spain | 479 |
| Romania | 218 | Denmark | 472 |
| Malaysia, | | Norway | 416 |
| Peninsula | 200 | Australia | 295 |
| Gabon | 133 | German DR | 284 |
| Chile | 115 | Switzerland | 259 |
| Portgual | 112 | Argentina | 245 |
| New Zealand | 94 | Hungary | 244 |
| | | Hong Kong | 193 |

capita decline in the industrialized countries at the relatively slow rate of population growth (0.6 percent per year), but in the LDCs the rate is the sum of the relatively high population growth rate and the relatively high deforestation rate, which means a decrease of 3–6 percent per year in some nations, and an even faster decrease in others.

The second major difference in man-forest relations in the two types of economies is in the pattern of forest product consumption. The industrialized nations consume over 90 percent of the world's processed forest products, while the LDCs consume nearly 90 percent of the wood used as fuel. The use of wood for fuel in the industrialized nations may increase somewhat, as prices rise for the fuels that have been displacing its use during the past 25 years. The only other factor that seems likely to substantially alter consumption patterns between now and the year 2000 is the impending scarcity of wood for fuel and lumber in the LDCs.

Ecological aspects of the man-forest relations are as disparate as the economic aspects in the developed and developing world. The LDCs have mainly labor-intensive agricultural systems. Increased production to meet the demands of growing populations must come from increasing the labor intensity or from increasing the agricultural land base, which usually implies clearing forests. By contrast, the human ecology of the industrialized nations comprises mainly capital-intensive systems, in which increased agricultural production is generally achieved by investing more capital in already developed land, rather than by

### TABLE 8–4

### Forest Resources per Capita by Geographic Region, mid-1970s

| | Closed Forest Area (ha/cap) | Open Wood-land Area (ha/cap) | Growing Stock (m³/cap) |
|---|---|---|---|
| North America | 2.0 | 0.7 | 179 |
| Central America | 0.5 | 0.02 | 50 |
| South America | 2.4 | 0.7 | 428 |
| Africa | 0.4 | 1.3 | 92 |
| Europe | 0.3 | 0.1 | 27 |
| U.S.S.R. | 3.0 | 0.4 | 310 |
| Asia | 0.2 | 0.3 | 17 |
| Pacific | 3.6 | 4.8 | 390 |
| World | 0.7 | 0.3 | 80 |
| More industrial | 1.3 | 0.4 | 128 |
| Less industrial | 0.4 | 0.3 | 61 |

*Sources:* Population data from Population Reference Bureau (1977); Forest area and volume data from Persson (1974).

clearing forest lands. The natural ecologies are likewise basically different. For the most part, the LDCs are located in the tropics and subtropics, where natural cycles and processes are very rapid and forceful. Most industrialized nations are in the temperate or boreal regions, where energy and materials cycle more slowly through the ecosystems, and where nature is generally less forceful.

Because the man-forest systems of the two types of economies are so dissimilar, they will be treated separately in the remainder of this paper— except for the important links between the two types of systems, including trade, technology transfer, and ecological linkages, which will be considered at the end of the paper.

## Forests and Forestry in the Industrialized Nations

### The U.S.S.R.

The Soviet Union has, by far, the single largest forest resource base in the world, with 785 million hectares of forested land growing 75 billion cu m (overbark) of industrial sized wood. The growing stock is over a third greater than that of the U.S. and Canada combined. The net annual increment in growing stock (growth less natural losses) is on the order of 880 million cu m (overbark), or 1.2 percent of growing stock.[6] This does not mean the resource is unlimited, however.

Fourteen percent of the forested area has such slow growth that it is considered unproductive; another 36 percent is not considered to be commercially exploitable, mainly because it is inaccessible. Thus only 465 million cu m of net annual growth are presently or potentially available with present transportation and harvesting technologies.

Fuelwood production, which takes up about 20 percent of the total cut now, has been declining slowly. Lumber production, which takes the largest share of the wood harvest, about 40 percent, has had hardly any growth during the 1960s and 1970s. Production of pulp, paper, and fiberboard has grown much faster, but the growth rate has been slackening for the past decade. Stagnation of total production of forest products is explained partly by the geographic isolation of the forests, 85 percent of which are in northern and eastern U.S.S.R., far from the population, 85 percent of which is in the southern and western portions of the country. Large areas of European U.S.S.R. are being overcut. For example, the mature stands of Karelia, which account for 5 percent of Soviet total and 20 percent of pulp production, will last only 25 years at the present rate of exploitation.[7]

The future of Soviet forestry is difficult to predict. A large unsatisfied domestic demand for industrial wood products already exists, as indicated by persistant gaps between production targets and actual output of all the major wood products during the past decade. If current trends continue, the Soviet's forest industry will be able to satisfy neither domestic nor foreign demand for its products.

In the longer term, the Soviets need to step up the reforestation programs, which have been neglected in the past. More reliance on Siberian forests will be inevitable, but the distance to western markets is enormous, and exploitation is unlikely to grow rapidly until roads or railways are built for other purposes.

We know little about the reservation of forest environments for aesthetic values, recreation, or other nonconsumptive use in the U.S.S.R. A Tass report claims that forest is being planted at the rate of 2 million hectares per year, much of it as groves around cities for "zones of rest" and on the steppes as shelter belts, which are said to "insure grain yield increases" by up to 25 percent.[8]

**Europe**

Forest is one of the few major natural resources in which Europe can expect to remain reasonably self-sufficient.[9] By the year 2000, total wood consumption is expected to increase by 45 to 80 percent, but European forests should supply 80 percent of the increase.

Europe has about 135 million hectares of commercially exploitable closed forest, with a growing stock of 15 billion cu m (overbark). Another 9 million hectares of closed forest are classed unexploitable, because of very low productivity or inaccessibility, or because they are reserved for various noncommercial uses. The distribution of forest resources among subregions is indicated in Table 8-5. The Nordic countries have the largest share of forest resources and have long been exporters to the rest of Europe. Their great wealth of forests per capita suggests that this relationship will continue indefinitely.[10]

The total wood harvest declined in Europe by 5 percent in 1972 and by 10 percent in 1975. In both years industrial wood production dropped. Whether those declines signal a transition to a period of slowing growth for the forest products industry is uncertain. A 1976 study commissioned by the U.N. Economic Commission for Europe (ECE), *European Timber Trends and Prospects 1950 to 2000,* made predictions for forest products consumption based on alternative assumptions about growth of gross domestic product (GDP). For both high and low GDP growth conditions, the study projects that: (1) fuelwood consumption will continue to decline, though more slowly than in the past; (2) sawnwood consumption will continue to grow, but at a decreasing rate; (3) consumption of paper and wood-based panels will increase at an accelerating rate, and by the year 2000 each will account for a larger portion of total wood use than will sawnwood; (4) supply of wood, including imports, will be less than demand by the year 2000 and will be the main constraint

### TABLE 8-5

### Distribution of European Forest Resources Among Subregions, Early 1970s

| | Exploitable Forest Area (%) | Growing Stock (%) | Net Annual Increment (%) | Fellings (%) | Net Annual Increment per Capita (cu m underbark) | Annual Fellings per Capita (cu m underbark) |
|---|---|---|---|---|---|---|
| Nordic countries | 37 | 29 | 30 | 33 | 6.9 | 7.2 |
| European Economic Community | 21 | 20 | 23 | 23 | 0.3 | 0.4 |
| Central Europe | 3 | 6 | 5 | 5 | 1.5 | 1.3 |
| Southern Europe | 22 | 19 | 19 | 17 | 0.7 | 0.6 |
| Eastern Europe | 18 | 26 | 23 | 22 | 0.9 | 0.8 |
| Total | 100 | 100 | 100 | 100 | 0.8 | 0.7 |
| Measure | 138 million hectares | 13.0 billion cu m underbark | 393 million cu m underbark | 368 million cu m underbark | | |

*Source:* U.N. Economic Commission for Europe, *European Timber Trends and Prospects 1950 to 2000,* pp. 66, 67.

on consumption. Adjusted for the supply constraint, total wood consumption during the 1975
to 2000 period is expected to rise at an annual
compound rate of 1.3 to 2.0 percent, based on
assumed GDP per capita growth of 3.1 to 4.1
percent. The ECE study concludes that if more
countries will begin providing greater incentives
for improved forest management, the projected
growth in consumption to the year 2000 can be
realized without impairing the forests' potential
for sustained production beyond that date.

Environmentally, there will be substantial
changes in European forests during the years to
2000. Few, if any, natural forest areas remain
now; the present structure and composition of the
forest reflects a long history of use and management. As management intensifies, the forests will
become younger and still less diverse. This will
lead to the reduction of some ecological niches
and is likely to cause the extinction of some plant
and animal species and changes in the population
dynamics of others. Meanwhile, pressure is certain to grow for management of forests to enhance
noncommercial values such as ecosystem stability, protection of water quality and flow, air

purification, recreation opportunities, and aesthetic qualities.

No statistics are available on the forest area in
Europe as a whole which has been set aside from
commercial production for use as parks, nature
reserves, protection forests, campsites, and so on.
Most studies lump such areas with the nonprod-
uctive and inaccessible forests, which together
account for about 6 percent of the European
forest.

Forested area is expected to increase in all of
the European subregions, mainly as a result of
afforestation programs. The area of scrub and
open woodlands in southern Europe and especially in Spain should decrease as large areas are
converted to productive closed forest. In the
Nordic countries, natural regeneration has been
more important than planting in the past, but
planting will have to increase during the next
quarter century if the harvests are to be sustained
in spite of the recent tendency to overcutting. In
the rest of Europe, afforestation and reforestation
programs will continue at the pace set during the
past 20 years, about 150 thousand hectares per
year. Table 8–6 indicates the ECE study's fore-

## TABLE 8–6

### Forecasts of the Areas of Forest and Open Woodland in Europe, Year 2000

| | | Forest and Open Woodlands | | | | | |
| | | | | Exploitable Forest | | Other | |
| | Period | Total | Percent of Total Land Area | Area | Percent of Forest and Open Woodlands | Area | Percent of Forest and Open Wood-lands |
|---|---|---|---|---|---|---|---|
| | | *millions of ha* | | *millions of ha* | | *millions of ha* | |
| Nordic countries | 1970 | 58.0 | 52 | 50.5 | 87 | 7.5 | 13 |
| | 2000 | 61.0 | 54 | 51.2 | 84 | 9.8 | 16 |
| European Economic Community | 1970 | 32.6 | 22 | 28.9 | 88 | 3.7 | 12 |
| | 2000 | 34.0 | 23 | 30.6 | 90 | 3.4 | 10 |
| Central Europe | 1970 | 4.8 | 39 | 3.8 | 80 | 1.0 | 20 |
| | 2000 | 5.2 | 43 | 4.5 | 85 | 0.8 | 15 |
| Southern Europe [a] | 1970 | 52.0 | 29 | 29.8 | 57 | 22.1 | 43 |
| | 2000 | 53.2 | 31 | 38.4 | 72 | 15.1 | 28 |
| Eastern Europe | 1970 | 27.7 | 29 | 25.1 | 90 | 2.6 | 10 |
| | 2000 | 29.9 | 31 | 27.4 | 92 | 2.5 | 8 |
| Total | 1970 | 175.0 | 32 | 138.1 | 79 | 36.9 | 21 |
| | 2000 | 183.3 | 34 | 152.0 | 83 | 31.3 | 17 |
| Change 1970–2000 | | | | | | | |
| Area | | +8.3 | | +13.9 | | −5.6 | |
| Percent | | +5% | | +10% | | −15% | |

[a]Including Cyprus and Israel.

*Source*: Economic Commission for Europe, *European Timber Trends and Prospects 1950 to 2000*, p. 80.

casts of the forest areas in the year 2000. For the whole region, the forested area is expected to be 5 percent larger.

## North America

Canada and the United States are about equally endowed with forest resources. Each has over 200 million hectares of productive forest, and each has about 19 billion cu m of growing industrial-sized wood. Most of the U.S. forest is accessible, and it has been used and managed more intensively than the Canadian forest. More use generally means a younger and more rapidly growing forest, and for this reason as well as better growing conditions, annual growth of the U.S. forest is significantly higher than that of the Canadian forest. On a per hectare basis, the U.S. forest grows nearly as rapidly as the European forest. Table 8–7 summarizes the present forest resource situation for North America.

Because of the recent variation from the longer trends in the growth of industrial wood use, the future of North American forestry seems rather uncertain. In the early 1970s, before the recent perturbations in the global industrial economies, the U.S. Forest Service published a study analyzing trends and making projections of demand, supply, and consumption of wood products. That study, *The Outlook for Timber in The United States,* assumed a GNP increase of 4 percent per year during the 1970–2000 period and projected the U.S. demand for wood products would rise by 1.3–2 percent per year, depending on how wood product prices change. Increased harvests of the U.S. forest would depend mainly on changes in relative wood prices and on political decisions regarding intensity of use of the publicly owned forest. Under the various assumptions, the study indicated that the volume of wood supplied from the U.S. forest in the year 2000 would be between 140 and 190 percent of the volume supplied in the year 1970. Most of the volume would come from increased fellings, but part would come from technological advances that

### TABLE 8–7

### North American Forest Resources, Early 1970s

| Resource | Unit | U.S.A. (1970) | Canada (1973) | North America |
|---|---|---|---|---|
| Stocked commercial forest [a] | Million hectares | 194 | 220 | 414 |
| Unaccessible productive forest [b] | Million hectares | 5 | — | 5 |
| Reserved forests (parks, etc) [c] | Million hectares | 8 | 15 | 24 |
| Total productive forest [d] | Million hectares | 207 | 235 | 442 |
| Unstocked commercial forest [e] | Million hectares | 8 | 17 | 26 |
| Open woodlands and other forests of extremely low productivity [f] | Million hectares | 103 | 73 | 176 |
| Growing stock on commercial forest (underbark volume) [g] | Billion cubic meters | 19 | 19 | 38 |
| | Cu meters per hectare | 93 | 75 | 87 |
| Net annual growth on commercial forest land (underbark volume) [h] | Million cubic meters | 527 | 270 | 797 |
| | Cu meters per hectare | 2.6 | 1.1 | 1.8 |
| | Percent growing stock | 2.9 | 1.5 | 2.1 |
| | Cu meters per capita | 2.4 | 11.5 | 3.3 |
| 1974 fellings (underbark volume) [i] | Million cubic meters | 402 | 167 | 545 |
| 1975 fellings (underbark volume) | Million cubic meters | 358 | 147 | 505 |
| 1974 fellings as percent of net annual growth | Percent | 76 | 62 | 68 |

[a] *For the U.S.A.,* commercial forest is defined as forest land producing or capable of producing crops of industrial wood in excess of 1.4 cubic meters per hectare per year in natural stands and not withdrawn from timber use. *For Canada,* commercial forest is defined as forest land suitable for regular harvest, capable of producing stands of trees 4 inches diameter or larger on 10 percent or more of the area, excluding agricultural land currently in use.
[b] This refers to forest *in Alaska* that meets the production criteria but is too inaccessible to be used commercially.
[c] These are forest lands reserved for noncommercial use. Whether all of the 15.5 million hectares reserved in Canada are actually productive forest is not clear from the available sources.
[d] This category excludes some woodland that would meet the tree growth criteria, but is not included in forestry statistics because it has been developed for non-forestry commercial use (e.g., residential land).
[e] *For Canada,* this is probably an underestimate, as it includes only unstocked federal and provincial lands that have been allocated to wood production.
[f] *For the U.S.A.,* this includes stands of pinyon-juniper, woodland-grass, chaparral, subalpine forests, and other woodlands incapable of producing 1.4 cubic meters of industrial wood per hectare per year. *For Canada,* this includes forest land not suitable for regular harvest because of extremely low productivity.
[g] *For the U.S.A.,* this is the volume, suitable for industrial wood use, in trees over 5 inches diameter. *For Canada,* the definition is presumably similar. For both, the unstocked commercial forest area is included in the calculation.
[h] Net annual growth is total growth less volumes of trees dying annually. Apparently it refers to wood in the parts of trees suitable for industrial wood use, and apparently it does not net out the volume lost to forest fires.
[i] Fellings refers to removals plus harvesting losses, apparently only wood of size suitable for industrial wood use is included. This measure is provided to allow comparison of annual fellings to net annual growth. The ratio of fellings to removals was inferred from data provided in U.S. Forest Service (1974), below, and the figures for fellings were calculated by applying that ratio to the removals as reported in FAO (1977).

*Sources:* U.S. Forest Service, *The Outlook for Timber in the United States,* Washington: GPO, 1974; Cliff (1973); Micklewright (1977); FAO (1977); Canadian Forestry Service, "Canada's Forests," Ottawa: 1974.

would make harvesting and processing more efficient. If efficiency of softwood production increases 12 percent by the year 2000, and efficiency
of hardwood production increases 4 percent,[11]
and if hardwood use gains on softwood use to
become a third of the total volume harvested by
2000,[12] then the year 2000 fellings in U.S. forests
could be between 130 and 175 percent of 1970
fellings.

Those projections correspond to a total annual
felling in U.S. forests of from 510 to 690 million
cu m (underbark) of industrial-sized wood. The
lower cut could be accommodated within the
present net annual growth of the forest, which is
estimated at 527 million cu m (underbark). The
higher projection cannot be realized on a sustained
yield basis without a substantial increase in the
net annual growth of the forest, which can only
occur with an increased intensity of management.

Increases in demand for Canadian forest products will depend on the same factors that influence
demand in the U.S., except that rising prices of
wood relative to other products would dampen
demand less for Canada than for the U.S., because Canada would supply a larger proportion of
the U.S. demand under that condition. The Canadian wood harvest is expected to increase by
about 2 percent per year, to reach 215 million cu
m (underbark) in the year 2000.[13] With that
increase, the harvest would still be below the net
annual growth, which is currently about 270
million cu m (underbark). More significantly, it
would be below 240 cu m, which is the Canadian
Forest Service's estimate of the annual cut allowable for sustained yield conditions on the portion
of the Canadian forest that is accessible under
current economic and technological conditions.
Thus there is unlikely to be any strong pressure
for increased intensity of Canadian forest management during the next 25 years.

The condition of the North American forest
environment in the year 2000 will depend to a
considerable extent on economic developments
that will affect management intensity. *The Outlook for Timber in the United States* forecasts
that the U.S. commercial forest area will be 6
million hectares smaller by the year 2000. Similar
estimates are not available for the Canadian
forest; probably the changes will be less as the
smaller population of Canada will be making fewer
demands for alternative uses of forest land.

The fact that the annual harvest is less than the
net annual growth disguises the low rate of
reforestation in North America. The commercial
forest area partially or totally harvested plus the
area burned have averaged about 4 million hec-

tares per year in the U.S. since 1960. During the
same period, the area planted with trees has
averaged about 650,000 hectares per year. The
remainder, except the relatively small portion
dropped from the commercial forest land inventory, is left for natural forest regeneration. If the
trend continues, the U.S. forest will be less
completely stocked than it is now. This will not
significantly affect wood production in the year
2000 but will have a negative effect in the longer
term if reforestation programs are not accelerated.
The situation in Canada, where the area harvested
or burned annually is about 2.5 million hectares,
is similar. The pressure for reforestation in Canada is likely to be lower, and costs of reforestation
there are higher because of the greater problems
of accessibility.

In the year 2000, the North American forest is
likely to be marginally smaller, be less well
stocked, have fewer slow-growing mature trees
and more fast-growing young trees, contain larger
areas reserved for noncommercial use, and have a
lower ecological diversity in the nonreserved
areas. The magnitude of these changes will depend partly on exogenous economic factors and
partly on the attitude of the public towards forest
management.

In recent years, environmental awareness has
increased significantly in both Canada and the
United States. As a result there has been considerable public resistance to forest management
techniques such as clear-cutting, which are economically sound, at least in the short term, but
which are aesthetically disagreeable and environmentally dubious. It is likely the management for
wood production will be constrained on increasing
proportions of the 27 percent of the U.S. commercial forest that is publicly owned and on the 59
percent of the forest that is privately owned by
parties other than forest industry companies. It is
theoretically possible for the managers of the
public forests to increase production of all the
types of benefits provided by the forest, but
without a greatly expanded environmental education effort, it is unlikely that the public will be
well enough informed and motivated by the year
2000 to demand management programs that will
optimize production of all the forest's benefits.

### Pacific Area

Japan is second only to the United States in
volume of wood imported, and is the world's
largest net importer of wood products. Although
Japan has experienced the world's most rapid
increase in industrial wood consumption during

the past 25 years, and although 68 percent of Japan is forested, domestic production has been declining steadily as a result of overcutting during the postwar years and several constraints on use of the existing mature forests.

Japan has a good forestry program, and by the year 2000 the domestic wood production may be rising again. The country will continue to be a major importer for the foreseeable future, however, consuming a substantial proportion of the sawlogs and pulpwood produced in western North America and most of the Philippine mahogany and other high-value logs from Southeast Asia.

The other nations with developed economies and substantial forest areas in the Pacific are Australia and New Zealand. Australia has about 38 million hectares of closed forest, only 20 percent of it coniferous. New Zealand has 6.2 million hectares, 70 percent coniferous. It is a major net exporter of wood products, while Australia is a net importer.

Only vague forecasts of the future of forest environment in the two nations can be given here. Management of the New Zealand forest is relatively intensive and the general trend has been use of monocultures of fast-growing exotic species for reforestation, rather than reliance on natural regeneration of native species. As a result, the New Zealand forest has become less diverse ecologically and more subject to catastrophic losses from pests and diseases. It seems likely that significant proportions of the natural forest will be effectively reserved for noncommercial use.

Tropical rain forest comprises a substantial part of the Australian resources, and it has all the typical rain forest problems of wood heterogeneity, soil instability, climate harshness and poor resiliance after commercial exploitation. Australia's agronomy is capital-intensive, so that production increases can generally be effected better by increasing capital inputs on already cleared land where there are high-quality soils than by clearing forest lands with marginal soils. Until the cost of Australia's wood imports becomes too high, or until technological advances make capital-intensive harvesting and processing of tropical forests more economic, the Australian forest environment is likely to remain relatively stable.

## Summary

Use of land for forests and for agriculture are in approximate equalibrium throughout most of the industrialized nations. Thus the forest area is relatively stable and will be only marginally smaller in the year 2000. The management of

commercial forests will become more intensive, and this will lead to lower ecological diversity. The forest area reserved for noncommercial use will increase in North America, and noncommercial factors will become more prominant in forest management decisions in the other industrialized regions. Except in Europe, Japan, and New Zealand, forests in the year 2000 will be less fully stocked than now, as cutting will continue to outpace tree planting and natural regeneration. For the most part, the cutover land will not be allocated to other uses, however, and will be available for reforestation during the 21st century.

If the industrialized nations recover fully from the economic setbacks of the past few years, then consumption of wood will continue to rise and supplies will begin to be tight within the 1978–2000 period. Production costs for softwood exports will rise as more remote areas must be logged in both the U.S.S.R. and Canada, so prices will rise. The already rising demand for imports from the tropical forests of the less developed countries will increase further.

In the more distant future, rising prices for wood products may lead to improved stocking in the northern forests and to heavier reliance by the wood products industry on plantation forestry in southern Europe, in the southern U.S. and in the tropics.

## Forests and Forestry in the Less Developed Countries

### Demand, Supply, and Deforestation

The LDCs contain nearly half of the world's closed forest area and over half of the growing stock of industrial-sized wood. These forest resources play an important role in economic development by providing subsistance, shelter, employment, resources for development of other sectors, and, for some LDCs, an important export commodity to earn foreign exchange.

The demand for industrial wood products within the LDCs will increase rapidly with economic development, because the elasticity of demand for wood products is high among relatively poor consumers so long as wood supplies are abundant.[14] As income increases further, the demand for paper products rises rapidly. Most of LDCs rely on imports of paper now, but recent technological breakthroughs have made paper production based entirely on mixed hardwoods possible. Where economic development progresses, capital to develop modern wood-processing facilities should become available.

Even where economic progress is not made, demand for forest products has been rising and will continue to rise. Tightening supplies of softwoods in the industrialized nations are causing increased use of hardwoods for sawwood, wood panels, and pulp, and tropical hardwoods have been capturing an increasing portion of this market. Furthermore the demand for fuelwood will rise with the population growth of the LDCs, regardless of progress in industrialization. LDCs now get about one-fourth of their commercial energy from fuelwood; the proportion may decrease where industrialization progresses; but the absolute quantity will probably increase with growth of cottage industries. In any case, most of the fuelwood is used for cooking in residences. Ten years ago it seemed that increased use of bottled gas and kerosene would constrain the rising consumption of wood for residential fuel, but the five-fold petroleum price increases have thrown most of the demand back to wood.

For the near future, the supply side of the forestry picture seems bright for the well-forested LDCs. There is still an abundant supply of virgin tropical timber, and technological advances in processing are resulting in the use of a higher proportion of tree species and size classes. Forest land is generally less expensive in the LDCs than in the industrialized nations, and forest labor is inexpensive and in abundant supply. Finally, the LDCs have a comparative advantage in the development of tree plantations, as the long growing seasons and high insolation available in the tropics result in wood growth rates three to five times higher than in the temperate environments.

Unfortunately, these favorable factors are overshadowed by the specter of deforestation. The forest product supply picture is bright only for the near term. The current forest stock of the LDCs, about 1.1 billion hectares of mature closed forest, is being consumed at the rate of about 20 million hectares per year. About two thirds of the tropical forests are economically accessible, and if the present rate of deforestation were to continue most of the accessible forest would be lost by year 2000. If the rate is assumed to increase with the populations of the LDCs, then virtually all of the accessible tropical forest would be gone by the year 2000.

However, it is more likely that the overall LDC deforestation rate will decline before the year 2000, for the simple reason that the people who are doing most of the cutting will begin to run out of forests to cut. Forests and population are not evenly distributed. Some nations cleared all the forest land accessible to them long ago (e.g., Afghanistan), other densely populated nations that still have substantial forest resources will have lost most of them before the year 2000 (e.g., Indonesia, Thailand), and some sparsely populated nations with vast forests will still have vast forests in the year 2000 (e.g., Gabon, Congo).

The process of deforestation is poorly understood. Apparently most of the forest losses result from clearing and burning for agriculture, with much of the wood being used only to the extent that its ashes constitute fertilizer for one or two season's crops. An estimated 190 million hectares of cleared tropical forests are used for shifting agriculture. After rudimentary clearing, the land is burned and crops are grown for a year or two. Then it is fallowed for about a decade, while a degraded forest develops, and that re-establishes at least some of the soil's fertility for the next round of clearing, burning and planting. The system breaks down as populations increase and the fallow periods are necessarily shortened, and eventually the forest loses its capacity to regenerate and to restore the soil's fertility. The land is abandoned, and often forest is not re-established.

The balance between deforestation caused by shifting agriculture and that caused by farmers clearing land for permanent settlement is unknown, and nothing is known about how the deforestation rate changes as the forest base diminishes. Nor does anyone know how much of the forests now remaining in the LDCs is on arable land, and even the definition of arable may be changing.

The deforestation rate is closely related to the rate of commercial logging. Hardly any of the LDC forests are under intensive management. In most cases, reforestation after logging is left to chance. In densely populated regions, farmers often follow the loggers to complete the process of razing the forest. In less densely populated areas, natural regeneration may result in reforestation, but the forests that result are generally degraded and seldom have commercial value.

How deforestation is related to the fuelwood harvest is another unknown, and the statistics on fuelwood use are only crude guesses. Where the fuelwood comes from is even less well known. Much of the wood, perhaps most of it, is converted to charcoal. This is a cottage industry that supports many farmers clearing forests during their first years in a newly settled area. In other places, rapid deforestation is only for fuel and is independent of the local demand for agricultural land.

Denudation of land, caused by the demand for fuelwood, is thought to be most rapid and to have the most severe environmental consequences in the dry open woodlands of the tropics. In such areas, tree cutting often leads not to a degraded woodland but rather to a desert. [15]

Because so few details are known about the process of deforestation and about the rates at which it occurs under varying economic, demographic, and environmental conditions, it is quite impossible to predict the global condition of forests in the LDCs in the year 2000. It is possible, however, to review current regional conditions, which may give some rough indications of which areas will still have forests 22 years from now.

## Latin America

Closed forests cover about 725 million hectares, over one-third of the total land area of Latin America. Open woodlands cover another 400 million hectares. Nearly all of the softwoods are in Central America. Three-quarters of the tropical moist forest is in the Amazon basin. Open woodlands predominate in parts of Central America, in northeastern and central Brazil, in the Andean valleys of Bolivia, Peru, and Chile, and in the Chaco of Bolivia, Argentina, and Paraguay.

The volume of growing stock of commercial size is higher than in any other region of the world, about 90 billion cubic meters. On a per hectare basis, the volume varies from 92 cu m in Central America, where the forests are similar to those of North America, Europe, and Asia, to over 250 cubic meters in parts of the Amazon Basin. The moist forests are extremely heterogeneous, with up to 100 species per hectare and with plant associations varying greatly over short distances. Only 10 to 30 percent of the standing volume in the Amazon basin is commercially valuable, the rest of the wood is an impediment from the point of view of commercial loggers. For this reason, logging operations have concentrated more on the less dense stands where commercially valuable wood may be more abundant and more accessible.

Deforestation rates vary with population density, as commercial logging operations are not yet well developed in most of Latin America. In the Amazon basin, the deforestation rate is estimated at 4 percent per year. [16] In the past, forests were cut only along the perimeters and along rivers, but new roadway infrastructures are rapidly increasing the accessible area. It seems likely that by the year 2000, the Amazon forest will cover less than half the area it does now. In Central America and northwestern South America, closed forests are diminishing at about 2 percent per year and are likely to be completely removed from arable areas by the year 2000. The deforestation of lowland forests in those areas will depend largely on how the high costs of clearing, drainage, and disease control relate to the demand for increased food production. In Argentina, Paraguay, Bolivia, and Brazil, the rate of clearing of open woodlands will depend on implementation of proposed schemes to make the savannah soil arable. If the new methods work as expected, the savannah woodlands could be significantly reduced by the year 2000, but that will take some pressure off the moist tropical forests, especially in Brazil.

Man-made forests were reported to cover 1.9 million hectares in Brazil and another 1.7 million hectares in the rest of Latin America. It is a small area relative to the deforestation rate, but conservation of the forest environment is not the objective of these plantings. They are industrial wood plantations, about one third conifers and much of the rest eucalyptus, and they do represent a significant beginning for plantation forestry. In Brazil the planting rate is reported to be gaining momentum; in some areas natural forests are razed to provide land for the fast-growing commercial species. Some of the firms involved have had economic setbacks, but it seems likely that in the long run plantations will be providing most of Latin America's wood supply.

Increasing demand for processed wood products in southern Brazil is likely to lead to increased investment in modern facilities that will be able to process a wider variety of species than the present domestic and export markets can use. This will make profitable the exploitation of forest areas where now the commercially valuable species are too widely scattered. The development of a forest products industry and construction of processing facilities is a priority feature in the national planning frameworks of most of the well-forested Latin American nations, though only in Brazil is implementation of such plans likely to have a significant impact on the forest environment by the year 2000.

## Africa

With only about 6 percent of its land area covered with closed forests, Africa is the least forested of the three tropical regions. The continent contains about 180 million hectares of closed forest, 88 percent of which is tropical moist forest in Central and West Africa. The area of open woodlands is estimated to be about three times the area of closed forest.[17]

The 1975 harvest of forest products comprised about 320 million cu m (underbark) of wood, of which 84 percent was fuelwood and charcoal, and 5 percent was unprocessed roundwood used as poles and posts, mainly for construction. Thus only about 11 percent of the harvest, or 35 million cu m, was used for sawn or other industrially processed wood products. About one third of this industrial wood was exported, most of it as logs, most of it to Europe. The rest was consumed within the region, mainly as sawwood for construction. The main exporters, in order of volume exported, are Ivory Coast, Gabon, Cameroon, Ghana, Congo, Nigeria and Zaire. Most of the countries of Africa are net importers of wood. The continent as a whole is a net importer of sawwood, paper, and paperboard, and a net exporter of industrial logs, plywood, veneers, fiberboard, and charcoal.[18]

The demand within Africa for processed industrial wood products is expected to grow by 6 to 9 percent per year between now and the year 2000. However, much of the industrial wood production is likely to continue to be directed to Europe rather than to be traded within Africa, so that the increasing Africa demand is unlikely to be satisfied.

The demand for fuelwood used at the household level is likely to increase at about the rate of population increase, while the demand for fuelwood used for production of commercial energy may increase somewhat faster, as the small-scale industrial sector grows. Supply is already insufficient to meet demand in many countries, and with no economically available substitute for woodfuel, energy consumption per capita has been falling in parts of North Africa.

Changes in the African forest environment have been best researched and described by R. Persson in his 1977 study, *Forest Resources of Africa*.[19] He indicates that agriculture is the main cause of deforestation. The area cleared annually for shifting cultivation in the rainforest zone is 2 to 4 million hectares. There is no estimate of the proportion of this area that is intact natural forest. In the more densely populated humid areas of West Africa, large forest areas are reported to have become denuded and badly eroded wastelands in recent years, because of the pressure to shorten the fallow periods. Persson estimates that 40 million hectares of the rainforest may be under use for shifting cultivation. As rural populations increase and as economic development makes crops more valuable, the shifting agriculturalists are likely to expand into more remote areas of natural forest, and to cause permanent deforestation on larger portions of the areas they are already using.

Permanent agriculture is also likely to take increasing areas of moist forest land in the coming decades. Growing demand for products of tree and bush crops, including coffee, cocoa, and oil palm, will probably result in significant deforestation.

In the seasonally dry areas, shifting cultivation also occurs; often the effects are more deleterious than in the rainforest zone, as the vegetation recovers more slowly. Most of the closed forest in such areas have been insulated from deforestation pressures by tsetse infestations. Gradual progress is being made in tsetse eradication, however, and permanent clearing of most of the woody vegetation is one of the necessary elements in maintaining eradication.

In the open woodlands, gradual denudation results from overgrazing, from burning too frequently for pasture improvement, and from woodgathering for fuel in the more densely populated areas. Since the effect of these factors is too gradual to be easily discernable, there is presently no way to estimate the rate at which the savannah environments are being degraded. Recent attention focused on the desertification process is likely to lead to some study of how open woodlands are changed, and predictions may be possible within a decade.

Persson's and other recent studies have indicated that the moist tropical forests of Africa now cover less than half of the area for which they are designated as the natural vegetation climax. Of course, most of this change is the result of clearing and burning by man and grazing by domestic livestock. The rate at which the change has occured is unknown. It seems likely that the rate has been increasing, and that the next halving of the forested area will occur much more quickly.

Persson and the other sources calculate that the closed forest area of Africa is decreasing by at least 2 million hectares per year and suggest that the rate may be higher. The greatest change is in West Africa, where large populations and large forests both occur. In North Africa, there is probably no net decrease in forested area, as there is limited forest left to cut and as intensive tree planting has begun in several countries. There is an environmental change, however, since the natural vegetation of North Africa continues to be thinned out and the replacement forests are monocultures of single age classes. Catastrophic change does not seem imminent in Central Africa. Gabon, Central African Republic, northern Congo, and southeastern Cameroon all have vast forests and sparse populations. However, if access becomes easier, fast destruction of forests can start, even where populations are relatively low.

By the year 2000, the closed forest area of Africa will have been reduced from 180 to 146 million hectares if deforestation continues at the present rate. It seems likely that the rate will increase, and the forest area may be as small as 130 million hectares by then. Most of the change will have resulted from clearing for agriculture. Timber cutting for industrial wood products is likely to result in changes in botanic composition of the forests, but not in very much deforestation. Woodcutting for fuelwood, charcoal, and poles, on the other hand, will probably cause degradation of open woodlands and complete destruction of many of the mangrove forests. Assuming no changes in current patterns of land use or in priorities of development project funding, substantial areas that are covered now with moist tropical forest will become barren wastelands with soils that have no potential for production, and many areas that are dry open woodlands now will become deserts.

## Asia

The less developed nations of South and Southeast Asia contained about 250 million hectares of closed forest in 1973. China, Mongolia, and the two Koreas contained another 110 million hectares.[20] Since then, South and Southeast Asian forests have probably decreased by about 25 million hectares, while in the more northern countries of Asia, afforestation programs have offset some of the losses, so that the net decline in forest area is probably less. The Asian LDCs have about 135 million hectares of rainforest, 55 million hectares of tropical moist deciduous forest, 95 million hectares of other deciduous forests, and 50 million hectares of coniferous forests.[21]

The Asian subregions are widely variable with regard to the distribution of forest resources. Table 8–8 summarizes data on distribution of resources by subregion.

The 1975 harvest of forest products in Asian LDCs totaled about 650 million cu m (underbark). Fuelwood and charcoal accounted for about 78 percent of the total; unprocessed poles, posts, and pitprops accounted for another 6 percent. Sawn and other processed wood products accounted for 16 percent of the total harvest, or 104 million cu

m. About one-fourth of the wood harvested for processed products was exported, mostly as sawlogs, mostly to Japan. The main exporters, in order of value of forest product exports, were Malaysia, Indonesia, the Philippines, China, Mongolia, Burma, and Thailand.

As in Africa and Latin America, the demand for wood products is expected to rise rapidly in the Asian LDCs, driven by rapid population increases and by substantial gains in GDP per capita. A 1976 study by FAO[22] projected that with GDP increases of 2.5 to 3.5 percent per year, the Asian LDCs would increase consumption of forest products by 2 to 2.5 times during the 1971 to 1991 period, and consumption of fuelwood, as a direct simple function of population growth, was expected to be 1.6 times greater. The projections assumed that relative prices of wood products would remain the same, and that the proportion of wood exported would not increase. The projected consumption rates were then compared to forecasts of sustainable yield from the region's forests to indicate the extent of the wood harvest shortfall that can be expected by 1991.

Supply of wood depends on the volume of growing stock, the net annual growth rate, the rate of cutting and the efficiency of processing. The 1976 FAO study used estimates of growing stock ranging from about 50 cu m per hectare in South Asia and in the communist countries to 75 cu m per hectare in insular Southeast Asia. The net annual growth is estimated at about 2 percent of the growing stock, or 1.5 cu m per hectare per year. Thus the total net annual growth for the region's forest is on the order of 540 million cu m, which is less than the 1975 harvest.

By 1991, more of the annual growth will be occurring in plantations. Most of the plantations to date are in China, where the main objective has been watershed protection. Afforestation to regulate water flow and to counter soil erosion began 30 years ago in China. As many as 100 million hectares may have been planted in the years since, but the survival rate of the seedlings has been low. The Chinese government has not yet released forest statistics on a national level, but the FAO study uses an estimate of about 30 million hectares of plantation trees in China in 1970, plus another 2.3 million hectares in the other Asian LDCs. The plantation area in 1990 is expected to be on the order of 60 million hectares.

Deforestation is occurring most rapidly in the LDCs of tropical Asia. The Green Revolution has caused only about half the food production increases achieved in Asia over the past two decades. The other half has come from expanding

## TABLE 8-8

### Asia—Distribution of Forest Resources by Subregion

Operable Forest Areas
*(millions of hectares)*

| Subregion | Operable Closed Forest | | Inoperable | Total Area of Closed Forest |
| | In use | Total | | |
|---|---|---|---|---|
| Asia Far East region | 279.8 | 378.3 | 158.7 | 537.0 |
| South Asia | 53.2 | 58.5 | 12.0 | 70.5 |
| Continental Southeast Asia | 52.3 | 72.6 | 18.5 | 91.1 |
| Insular Southeast Asia | 36.0 | 71.9 | 32.9 | 124.8 |
| East Asia developing | 4.0 | 5.2 | 1.4 | 6.6 |
| Oceania developing | 2.1 | 16.3 | 23.0 | 39.3 |
| East Asia developed | 24.1 | 24.1 | 1.1 | 25.2 |
| Oceania developed | 29.2 | 29.2 | 20.2 | 49.4 |
| Centrally planned countries | 78.9 | 100.5 | 29.6 | 130.1 |

Growing Stock—Closed Forest

| | Operable Closed Forests | | | Currently Commercial Species | All Closed Forests | | |
| | Total | Coniferous | Broad-leaved | Broad-leaved | Total | Coniferous | Broad-leaved |
|---|---|---|---|---|---|---|---|
| | | | | *million m³* | | | |
| Asia Far East region | 29,000 | 5,600 | 23,400 | 15,000 | 39,000 | 7,000 | 32,000 |
| South Asia | 3,000 | 400 | 2,600 | 1,900 | 3,500 | 600 | 2,900 |
| Continental Southeast Asia | 5,000 | 1 | 5,000 | 3,400 | 6,300 | 50 | 6,200 |
| Insular Southeast Asia | 9,200 | 40 | 9,200 | 5,200 | 13,300 | 50 | 13,200 |
| East Asia developing | 60 | 30 | 30 | 30 | 80 | 40 | 40 |
| Oceania developing | 1,600 | 30 | 1,500 | 700 | 3,000 | 30 | 3,000 |
| East Asia developed | 2,000 | 1,100 | 900 | 800 | 2,100 | 1,100 | 1,000 |
| Oceania developed | 1,500 | 400 | 1,100 | 1,000 | 2,000 | 500 | 1,500 |
| Centrally planned countries | 6,500 | 3,600 | 2,900 | 2,300 | 8,400 | 4,700 | 3,700 |

*Source:* European Economic Commission (1976), pp. 18, 19.

the area harvested, by increasing the crops per year in some places and by clearing new fields in others. The yield increases seem to be reaching a plateau in several of the Asian LDCs, so that an even greater proportion of the needed 3 to 4 percent per year increase in food production may have to come from newly cleared fields.

Forest areas for which conversion to farmland is already planned are substantial in continental and insular Southeast Asia, and shifting agriculture is consuming an increasing portion of both insular and mainland forests. In the Philippines, an estimated 200,000 hectares of forest is destroyed by the shifting farmers each year. In Thailand, they clear an estimated 250,000 hectares per year. In Indonesia, shifting cultivation is said to have devastated about 30 million hectares of forest, which are now degraded grasslands, and the forest currently being used for shifting culti-

vation in that country is estimated at 2 million hectares.

Commercial logging by itself does not necessarily result in destruction of the forest cover, but in most of the Asian LDCs the loggers are responsible for making the forest accessible to farmers. In most cases the settlement of logged-over land is spontaneous, rather than planned.

The FAO study estimates that by 1990, the operable forest area in South Asia and Southeast Asia will be reduced by 34 percent, while the forest area in China and the Koreas will have a 4 percent net increase because of continued afforestation. The study assumes that techniques of harvesting, marketing, and processing will improve so that 90 percent of the logs will be commercially used, as opposed to only 25 percent at present. The study further assumes that the trees outside the closed forests will continue to supply about 250 million cu m of fuelwood per year on a sustained basis.

By the year 2000, the natural closed forests of South and Southeast Asia are likely to be reduced to less than 100 million hectares. The natural forests that remain will be either in inaccessible mountainous or swampy regions, or will be protected by law, or will be so degraded as to be commercially useless. These subregions may have about 5 million hectares of plantation forests by that time. In China, Mongolia, and the Koreas, the forest area may increase slightly, as forest clearing is offset by continued afforestation.

Erosion, siltation, flooding, and other problems associated with deforestation are likely to have become a severe constraint on food production by the year 2000 in South and Southeast Asia. The ecological diversity of the region will be much lower, and populations of the remaining fauna may be expected to fluctuate much more widely, with some species becoming extinct in the low flux and other species becoming hazardous pests in the high flux. It seems likely that some of the region's present potential to support human populations will have been irretrievably lost.

## The Special Problem of Tropical Moist Forests

As already indicated, the most drastic changes in forest resource inventories and in forest environments will occur in the less developed countries. All types of forests in those countries will be affected: evergreen rainforests, moist deciduous forests, dry deciduous forests, and open woodlands. The effects of changes in the first two types will be of greatest importance, for several reasons: first, because the evergreen and deciduous moist forests of the tropics cover larger areas than the other types; second, because the moist forests have less potential for recovery; and third, because the moist forests are genetically and ecologically richer resource systems.

It is useful to distinguish between forest modification and transformation. Modification results from selective logging and from shifting agriculture; transformation results when the original or modified natural forest is totally removed and is replaced by agricultural settlement, man-made forest or wasteland. Modification of moist tropical forests through shifting agriculture is generally believed to result in a permanent degradation of biological productivity. This is because most of the plant nutrients in a tropical moist forest system are held in the standing plant cover, rather than in the soils. As the plants gradually die, fall, and decompose, the enormous mass of vegetation quickly recaptures the nutrients. However, the slash and burn method of the shifting farmers results in sudden release of the plant nutrients at a time when power of the vegetation to recapture the nutrients has been greatly reduced. Because of the quantity and intensity of tropical rains, the soluable nutrients are usually leached too deeply into the earth, and are effectively lost from the ecosystem.

Modification through selective logging seems likely to have a less permanent effect on the forest ecosystems, since at present only a small proportion of the trees are commercially useful, and only the stems of those trees are removed from the forest. Physical destruction that results from selective logging is considerably greater in tropical moist forests than in the temperate zone forests, however. The tropical moist forest is usually multistoried, with commercially valuable trees often limited to those which form the upper-most story. The crowns of such trees are large and vines form strong physical links within and between the several stories. As a result the felling operations are massively destructive. Even more destructive are the extraction operations. In addition to its direct impact on the vegetation, the extraction process disturbs large expanses of the forest floor, often exposing mineral soil to erosion and to other forms of physical and chemical degradation, which occur much more rapidly in hot wet climates than in temperate zone areas.

Most studies of tropical forestry forecast that the number of species and proportion of size classes used will be greatly increased during the next decade. There are several advantages to increased intensity of forest use, the main one being that more wood can be harvested from less land. There are many potential problems however. Nutrient depletion will be increased as greater volumes of wood will be removed. Ecological diversity will be lowered, and consequent population explosions of pest plants and animals are likely to occur. Water yield and quality are likely to suffer if large areas are intensively cut-over, as very little is known about how to forestall water problems in the tropics. The few techniques for water conservation that have been developed are seldom implemented, as the institutional structure is lacking. Effects of intensive forest use on soil structure and soil microorganisms in the tropics are virtually unknown, but are almost certain to be negative. The commercial and environmental quality of the second-growth forest that will follow intensive forest use is another unknown. It will be lower than the quality of second growth that now follows selective logging, unless improved silvicultural techniques are developed and implemented.

Techniques for minimizing the environmental damage that will result from intensified use of tropical moist forests have been proposed, and some research has begun to develop new methods, such as logging in relatively narrow strips, leaving wider strips of natural forest undisturbed. However the capital and institutional constraints on improved management of logged-over areas, and the lack of control that LDC governments have over operations of commercial loggers, are likely to prevent conservation on any substantial portion of the tropical moist forests.

Resource planners for tropical regions have no method with which to determine the balance between the benefits and costs of transforming tropical moist forest land to other uses. The benefits are usually relatively immediate and can be measured in terms of economic gains. This paper has no solution to the problem of weighing benefits against costs. Rather the main environmental costs will be briefly reviewed, to indicate the kinds of changes that may be forecast for the year 2000. These costs include: the risk of creating a useless wasteland; the acceleration of rainwater runoff, with consequent erosion, siltation, and failure to recharge aquifers; the loss of ecological diversity; the more extreme microclimate; and the permanent loss of genetic resources.

The loss of ecological diversity is the most subtle cost. Tropical moist forests are believed to comprise the most complex ecosystems in nature. Their diversity gives them great stability in relation to the kinds of natural changes under which they have evolved. Under conditions of forest destruction by man however, the diversity makes them fragile rather than stable.[23] Where tropical moist forest is removed, that kind of forest and nearly all the species it contains will disappear.[24]

There are other consequences of the loss of the forest's diversity, which may become more immediate costs. Animal communities, like tree communities, are much less diverse after the forest is destroyed. The populations of remnant animals often become very high, and cause massive depredations on newly created croplands.

Water quality, quantity, and timing in tropical streams and aquifers depend to a great extent on the forest cover. Where the cover is maintained, rainwater infiltrates the soil, streams are fed gradually by subsurface flows of relatively clean water, and aquifers are recharged by deep infiltration. Where forest cover is removed from sloping land, more of the rainwater becomes surface runoff and streams are filled suddenly with silt-laden water that may be contaminated with pesticides, fertilizers, or other pollutants. As steeper slopes are deforested, the stream flows become more erratic. Sedimentation in streambeds raises them, further increasing flood frequency and severity. At the same time, groundwater tables fall and wells become seasonal at best. Reservoirs and other irrigation works become choked with silt, and must be dredged at high cost or abandoned and replaced with new, more expensive systems. There is, of course, a limit to the suitable sites for reservoirs.

The effect of tropical moist forest on microclimate is related mainly to the balance between sensible heat and latent heat in the environment. When the forest is razed, the heat that had fueled the evapotranspiration process instead raises the environment's temperature, usually to the detriment of seed germination, plant survival, animal survival, and human comfort. Where soil is poor and natural moist forest is not replaced with year-round agriculture or man-made forest, there may be a positive feedback in the microclimate system that leads to self-generating aridity.

## Global Linkages and the Year 2000 Scenarios

### Global Linkages

Changes in the forest environments of the several regions will impact on global environment and global economic interactions in several ways. The interregional linkages include: availability of genetic resources, trade of forest products, effects of deforestation on climate and on the production and trade of agricultural products, and international transfer of technology for forest management and for wood processing.

During the coming decades, some forest plant and animal species will become extinct as intensified use leads to ecological simplification of the temperate zone forests. More importantly, hundreds of species will become extinct as the moist tropical forests are razed. There will be local effects on ecosystem stability and global effects on agriculture. The genetic reservoir for many tropical crops is in the moist forests. These include bananas, cocoa, oil palm, mango, many other fruits, rubber, lac, and various resins. Improving production from any of these crops may depend, as development of hybrid maize depended, on the availability of wild varieties of the domestic plant. For most such crops, genetic research has hardly begun, and as wild varieties are lost, there is less potential for development of high-yield strains, or of strains resistant to pests, diseases, and drought. Also, opportunities for development of new products, medicines, foods, drinks, resins, specific pesticides, and so forth, are diminished as the tropical moist forests are cleared.

The interregional linkage provided by international trade in forest products will be stronger in some cases and in others will disappear. Japan and Western Europe will be increasingly dependent on Canada and the U.S.S.R. for pulp supplies and for softwood sawlogs. Japan will no longer be able to import sufficient tropical hardwood sawlogs and veneer logs from Asia, and European importers will be paying much higher prices for sawlogs from Africa. Only northern South America is likely to be exporting more sawlogs in the year 2000 than it does now. The United States will probably remain self-sufficient in pulpwood and may become more nearly self-sufficient in sawlogs as the global supply becomes tighter.

Scientists have wondered and speculated about the impact of forests on climate since the time of Plato, but as yet there is no agreement on how deforestation affects regional and global climates. Three mechanisms through which deforestation may be changing climate have been discussed in recent articles. First, the carbon dioxide content of the atmosphere is increased as carbon stored in forest biomass and in forest soils is released. However, the amount of carbon being released to the atmosphere has not been accurately estimated, and the proportion of the $CO_2$ re-stored in wood elsewhere or absorbed by the oceans has not been determined. Measurements of atmospheric $CO_2$ do confirm that the concentration of carbon in the atmosphere has been increasing at the rate of 0.2 percent per year since 1958, and that the rate is accelerating. Most of that increase is due to burning of fossil fuels, however. It seems likely that the $CO_2$ content of the atmosphere will increase by at least 25 percent during the 1978–2000 period, but how this will affect global or regional climates is unknown.[25]

Another mechanism through which deforestation may affect regional or global climate changes is change of the earth's surface albedo, which, along with the increased ratio of sensible to latent heat, may affect the generation and dissipation of tropical easterly waves or may affect the dynamics of general atmospheric circulation.[26] The third mechanism is the increase in dust from deforested areas. At least one climatologist has argued that in the Rajputana region of India, extensive atmospheric dust prevents moist air from rising, and thus inhibits precipitation, causing a man-made desert.[27]

The most significant of the global linkages is probably the impact of deforestation on the welfare of the LDC populations. Energy crises caused by short supplies of oil in the industrial nations will not be more profound than the crises caused by short supplies of fuelwood and charcoal in the LDCs. Fuel consumption per capita is already minimal for both the rural and urban LDC poor. They will have to cut back consumption even more as populations grow and wood becomes scarce. Gradually the urban poor will have to allocate a larger portion of their incomes, and the rural poor a larger portion of their time, to aquisition of the minimum amount of fuel needed for survival. These reallocations of money and time will erode productivity and consequently human welfare.

Deforestation increases food production in the LDCs wherever it leads to an increase in the arable land area. As the limits of arable land are approached, however, continued deforestation suppresses agricultural production. The negative effects include direct environmental processes, such as the siltation of irrigation works, and indirect effects. As wood has become scarce in South Asia, for example, cattle dung and crop residues that once functioned to maintain soil fertility have been used for fuel. In India, Pakistan, Java, Madura, and in parts of Central America and West Africa, the negative effects of deforestation have already begun to constrain food production. It appears likely that by the year 2000, the effects will be severe throughout the tropical regions. Both fuel and food shortages could result in increased LDC demands for aid, and suppression of the LDC economies may reduce markets for the products of the industrialized economies.

**The Year 2000 Scenarios**

The future may be less gloomy than the foregoing implies. To some extent, the negative impacts of deforestation may be offset by reforestation and afforestation programs. Furthermore it may be possible for some countries to slow down the deforestation rates. In Thailand, for example, the government announced in January 1978 that it would begin to use its most extraordinary powers of summary judgment and even execution to punish unauthorized cutting in the national forests. This resolve follows years of failure to enforce the less powerful forest protection laws already in existence. The change was prompted by an increasing frequency of disastrous floods and also by an investigation that indicated the forest resource was being destroyed at the rate of 13 percent per year and would be totally lost within a decade. Whether LDC governments have sufficient control over farmers and loggers remote from the seats of government to keep them from cutting the forests in desperate quest for cropland and wood products remains to be seen.

An optimistic scenario would have governments of the LDCs bringing deforestation under control during the next decade, so that by 1990 forests would be transformed to cropland only where soils were known to be arable. Logging would be accompanied in both the developed and developing world by intensified silvicultural efforts that would assure sustained yields of wood products. Reforestation with mixed species of trees for industrial wood would be greatly accelerated in the LDCs, and a crash program of developing village fuelwood plantations would be implemented. Reforestation and afforestation for watershed protection would be given top priority in the development programs of South and Southeast Asia and Central America, as would the development and diffusion of solar cookers and bio-gas generation plants. Genetic resources would be conserved with programs combining national parks and germ plasm banks. New technologies that increase the efficiencies of forest harvesting and wood processing would be developed and become economic so quickly that the rapidly increasing demands for industrial wood products could be met without overcutting.

While each of the above developments is possible, it seems unlikely that they will all occur in the relatively brief 1978–2000 period.

A more realistic scenario includes some but not all of the above changes in policies and trends. Some changes, such as resolve by a government to spend whatever political capital is necessary to protect its forest resources, are entirely internal matters. Other changes, such as implementation of crash programs for fuelwood plantations, could require aid programs developed by international agencies. Increased investment in silviculture in the industrialized countries and more plantations of fast-growing trees for industrial wood production in the LDCs are most likely developments.

Table 8–9 summarizes forecasts of forest resources by global region for the year 2000. The figures represent a mildly optimistic scenario.

## TABLE 8-9

### Estimates of World Forest Resources, 1978 and 2000

| | Closed Forest (millions of hectares) | | Growing Stock of Commercial Sized Wood in Closed Forests and in Open Woodlands (billions cu m overbark) | |
|---|---|---|---|---|
| | 1978 | 2000 | 1978 | 2000 |
| U.S.S.R. | 785 | 775 | 79 | 77 |
| Europe | 140 | 150 | 15 | 13 |
| North America | 470 | 464 | 58 | 55 |
| Japan, Australia, New Zealand | 69 | 68 | 4 | 4 |
| Subtotal | 1,464 | 1,457 | 156 | 149 |
| Latin America | 550 | 329 | 94 | 54 |
| Africa | 188 | 150 | 39 | 31 |
| Asian and Pacific LDCs | 361 | 181 | 38 | 19 |
| Subtotal (LDCs) | 1,099 | 660 | 171 | 104 |
| | | | | |
| World | 2,563 | 2,117 | 327 | 253 |
| World population (billions) | | | 4.3 | 6.4 |
| Wood per capita (cu m) | | | 76 | 40 |

Source: Based on calculations from preceding tables and deforestation rates cited in the footnote at the beginning of this chapter.

## REFERENCES

1. For example, R. H. Whittaker and G. E. Likens, "The Biosphere and Man," in H. Lieth and R. H. Whittaker, eds., *Primary Productivity of the Biosphere.* New York: Springer, 1975. This is a basic reference for papers on global effects of deforestation, and the data have been used as the current baseline for rather complex models, for example, by R. Revelle, and W. Munk, "The Carbon Dioxide Cycle and the Biosphere," in *Energy and Climate,* Washington: National Academy of Sciences, 1977.

2. R. Persson, *World Forest Resources,* Stockholm: Royal College of Forestry, 1974. This is the most detailed and best documented global forest inventory ever published.

Persson discusses the confidence limits of the data at length and concludes that his global summaries, quoted in this paper, are probably overestimates of the 1973 forest area.

3. Persson, 1974; R. Persson, *Forest Resources of Africa,* Stockholm: Royal College of Forestry, 1977.

4. Whittaker and Likens.

5. Food and Agriculture Organization, *Yearbook of Forest Products,* Rome: FAO, 1977.

6. Data on Russian forest resources are from a 1973 inventory, reported in Economic Commission for Europe, *European Timber Trends and Prospects, 1950 to 2000,* Geneva: FAO, 1976.

7. J. Holowacz, Ontario Ministry of Natural Resources, "The Forests and the Timber Industry of the USSR," unpublished manuscript, 1973; R. N. North and J. J. Solecki, University of British Columbia, "The Soviet Forest Products Industry: Its Present and Potential Exports," unpublished manuscript, 1976.

8. "Planting of Forests in Russia," Tass, May 3, 1973.

9. Food and Agriculture Organization, *Forest Resources in the European Region*, Rome: FAO, 1976.

10. Economic Commission for Europe.

11. E. P. Cliff, *Timber: The Renewable Resource*, Washington: Government Printing Office, 1973.

12. Ibid.

13. Ibid.

14. G. R. Gregory, Forest Resource Economics, New York: Ronald, 1972.

15. E. P. Eckholm, *Losing Ground—Environmental Stress and World Food Prospects*, New York: Norton, 1976.

16. A. Sommer, "Attempt at an Assessment of the World's Tropical Forests," *Unasylva*, 28:112, pp. 5–25.

17. Persson, *Forest Resources of Africa*.

18. Food and Agriculture Organization, *Yearbook of Forest Products*.

19. Persson, *Forest Resources of Africa*.

20. Persson, *World Forest Resources;* Food and Agriculture Organization, *Development and Forest Resources in Asia and the Far East: Trends and Perspectives 1961–1991*, Rome: FAO, 1976.

21. Calculated by factoring the areas in each forest type, as indicated in Persson, *World Forest Resources*, Sommer, and FAO *Development and Forest Resources in Asia*, by the deforestation rates in each subregion.

22. FAO, *Development and Forest Resources in Asia*.

23. Duncan Poore, "The Value of Tropical Moist Forest Ecosystems and the Environmental Consequences of Their Removal," *Unasylva, 28:112, pp. 127–43*.

24. Ibid.

25. Revelle and Munk.

26. R. E. Newall, "The Amazon Forest and Atmospheric Circulation," in W. H. Mathews et al., eds., *Man's Impact on the Climate*, Cambridge, Mass: MIT Press, 1971.

27. R. A. Bryson and T. J. Murray, *Climates of Hunger*, Madison: University of Wisconsin Press, 1977.

# 9 Water Projections

Of all the substances found on the earth, those most fundamental to the existence of man, or to the existence of life itself, are unquestionably water and air. Water comprises some three-quarters of the surface of the earth, including the great oceans, the inland lakes and rivers, and the polar icecaps. Water is the major constituent of living matter, fhether animal or vegetable. The processes of life depend upon a continuous exchange of water between living matter and the environment, and this exchange constitutes an important link in the global hydrologic cycle.

From the time primitive man first organized for the gathering or production of food and clothing, water has been a critical factor in man's economic activities. Lakes, rivers, and oceans have provided sustenance, transportation, and protection. Population centers evolved along the shores of water bodies, and economic development took place along shores and major river valleys.

Increasing development and advancing technology have served to further magnify man's dependence upon water. In modern societies, water is used for human consumption, for transport of wastes, for sanitation in general, for the production of energy, for all types of industrial production, for agricultural production, for transportation, and for recreation.

In order to confine this discussion to the uses of water of most interest to resource planning, only those uses requiring deliberate diversion of water from the hydrologic cycle (by withdrawal from stream, lake, or aquifer) will be considered. This excludes such "in-stream" uses as water transportation, use of water as an energy source, and flood-plain agriculture.

While the identification of water as an important natural resource seems beyond argument, water has not always been viewed as a resource in the same sense as coal, petroleum, mineral ores, timber, and crops. In fact, the management and utilization of water has followed patterns distinctly different from those of other economic resources. The differences may stem from the relative abundance of water in many parts of the world, or from ambiguity concerning the resource nature of water.

In common usage, a resource is something that can be used for supply or support. This definition includes most, if not all, components of the physical environment. Resources that attract the attention of analysts and policymakers, however, are those that display an additional characteristic—scarcity. If all resources were available in unlimited quantity wherever and whenever desired, resource planning and resource management would not be required. Most resources are scarce in some sense, and these scarce (or economic) resources are the legitimate object of national and global concern.

This chapter will examine the resource nature of water, in particular the properties that distinguish it from other scarce resources. Water supply will be discussed, as well as the nature of the demand for water, together with the problems of identifying existing scarcity and of predicting scarcity in the future. Finally, the nature of adjustments to water scarcity, including their implications for other resource stocks, will be reviewed.

## Properties of Water Resources

The concept of water as an economic resource, subject to scarcity and dependent upon rational management, is not universally shared. Water has often been ignored in resource planning efforts or has been presumed to obey economic laws different from those that apply to other resources. The planning and construction of water supply works, the allocation of water among users, the pricing of water—these and other activities have been frequently influenced by the notion that water is virtually "free goods," which should be provided as cheaply as possible in any quantity desired.

Even where water is conspicuously scarce, it may be diverted to low-value uses to the detriment of other users and of future supplies. At the same time, water shortages occur worldwide with increasing frequency, due to drought or other reasons, often leading to serious economic disruption and human suffering.

A number of specific properties of water resources contribute to the tendency to inappropriate water policy and combine to frustrate attempts at rational water resource planning. Six general properties of water resources are listed below.

1. *Water is ubiquitous.* It may be safe to say that no place on earth is wholly without water. In general, vast quantities of water surround most locales of human activity. While the means by which water is moved to the point of use may be of concern, and while the quality of available water may not be all that could be hoped for, the existence of water is a fundamental assumption.

2. *Water is a heterogeneous resource.* While few natural resources are perfectly homogeneous in the environment or in their use, water may be the least homogeneous of all. Although used in the liquid form, water is found as a liquid, a solid, or a gas. As a liquid, it may exist as a lake or a sea, as a flowing stream, or as an underground deposit. Its chemical and biological constituents vary widely. Water uses may range from human consumption to cooling sheets of hot steel, and each use implies constraints on chemical or biological quality. In fact, more than 99 percent of

the water on the globe is unavailable or unsuitable for beneficial use, because of salinity (seawater) or location (polar icecaps). The beneficial use of water requires more than the coincidence of supply and demand; the characteristics of the water supplied must match the requirements of the use for which the water is demanded.

3. *Water is a renewable resource.* The forces of nature constantly renew all water resources. The process is depicted, in broad outline, in Figure 9-1, which divides the hydrologic cycle into three major water locations: the atmosphere, the land, and the oceans. Water falls from the atmosphere as precipitation on both land and oceans. A portion of that falling on land returns to the atmosphere as a consequence of evaporation and of transpiration by living matter. Water that does not return immediately to the atmosphere is stored in lakes and rivers, as icecaps and glaciers, or as underground reserves, or it runs off to the oceans. The water that enters the oceans by precipitation or by runoff from land is essentially returned to the atmosphere by evaporation. The chemical and biological quality of water at various places and

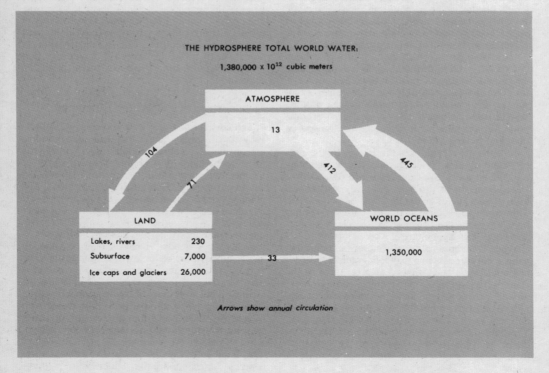

Figure 9-1. Annual circulation of the hydrosphere, in quadrillions of cubic meters.

times is also subject to deterioration and renewal, especially in lakes and streams. An important aspect of the renewability of water is the limited yet significant ability of man to intervene in the renewal process. Modern technology permits the exchange of water between surface sources (lakes, rivers) and ground water sources, the restoration of contaminated water to higher levels of quality, the reclamation of water from the sea, and, in some instances, the alteration of the pattern of precipitation. While such efforts have resource costs in themselves, their possibility modifies the renewability characteristic of water in important ways.

4. *Water may be common property.* Unlike mineral resources, which are relatively well defined in space and subject to private ownership in many societies, water is ubiquitous and nonstationary. Accordingly, property rights in a water resource are typically ill defined or nonexistent (the system of water rights in the Western states constitutes an important partial exception). Since water withdrawals are, in principle, available to all comers without direct charge for withdrawal, any opportunity costs that might be associated with withdrawal are not faced by the withdrawer, and no inherent mechanism for efficient allocation exists. Water is typically treated as a free good by actual users, even during times of scarcity, when many potential users may be excluded. Users recognize the costs of capturing, treating, and transporting water but do not associate cost with the water itself. As a result, past patterns of water use provide only a flawed guide to future, hopefully more efficient, allocations.

5. *Water is used in vast quantities.* Because of the many uses to which water is put and the liberal quantities traditionally associated with many uses, the quantity of water used annually exceeds by far the total quantity used of any other single resource, or of many other resources taken together. In recent years, the total quantity of the world's production of minerals, including coal, petroleum, metal ores, and nonmetals, has been estimated as about $8 \times 10^9$ metric tons per year. Total water use, on the other hand, has been estimated near $3 \times 10^{12}$ metric tons per year, nearly three orders of magnitude larger. This amounts to about 800 metric tons per person per year, *worldwide,* including all water used in (nonhydropower) energy production, in industry, and for irrigated agriculture, as well as water for domestic and municipal uses.

6. *Water is very inexpensive.* For various reasons—including water's common property nature, the nature of water supply technology, and economies of scale—water is very inexpensive. The point-of-use cost of water in the United States is seldom more than $0.30 per metric ton (for municipally supplied water) and may be as little as $0.03 per metric ton (for irrigation water). By contrast, very few minerals can be purchased for as little as $30 per metric ton at the minehead.

In summary, then, water is a substance found almost everywhere on earth, although in many different forms and qualities. Water is renewable, either by natural processes or, to some extent, by human intervention. Most societies have tended to treat water as a common property resource, thus concealing the opportunity costs that may be associated with water use. Water is used in very large quantities and is very inexpensive; aggregate worldwide water use is about three orders of magnitude larger than the total of all mineral products produced, and typical water costs are about three orders of magnitude lower than the costs of the least expensive mineral products.

These properties have important consequences for studies of future water resource trends. Because of the ubiquitousness, the heterogeneity, and the renewability of water, it is difficult to characterize supply, now or in the future. The quantity and quality of the water available at a particular time and at a particular place constitute the relevant supply; aggregate or summary statistics are nearly meaningless.

The common-property characteristic of water, the large quantities used, and the low user costs all act as deterrents to forecasting future water use. While it may be tempting to extrapolate past water-use experience, the possibilities for changes in the structure of use in response to relatively minor adjustments in the way water is managed are so great as to render extrapolation essentially useless. As will be seen in the following section, further problems arise when specific supply forecasts must be compared to specific demand forecasts.

## The Supply of Water

Water available for use in human activities is, for practical purposes, water found in streams, fresh water lakes, and in fresh water aquifers (ground water). While brackish and saline water, including seawater, may be used for some limited purposes and may be rendered useful for other purposes by desalting, total water supply is customarily measured in terms of fresh water available on or under the surface of the land. Since water bodies are constantly replenished, the average rate of replenishment is ordinarily of greater interest than the volume of water available at any specific time. Two major exceptions are: (1) In the case of water withdrawal from streams, some minimum amount of water storage may be required to permit the desired rate of withdrawal in the presence of highly variable streamflow, and (2) certain ground-water deposits, especially in arid or semiarid areas, may be very large by comparison to annual inflows and may be "mined" by setting withdrawals consistently in excess of inflows.

Replenishment of surface and ground-water resources occurs as a consequence of precipitation. A portion of the total quantity of precipitation is returned to the atmosphere by evaporation and transpiration, a portion becomes inflow to the ground-water reserves, and the remainder runs off as surface drainage. In the absence of human withdrawals, inflows to ground-water resources are usually matched by outflows, through springs or seeps, to surface water bodies. A first approximation of the overall rate of replenishment, therefore, may be obtained by measuring the total surface-water discharge from a specific watershed. Unmeasured outflows from ground-water (such as discharges from the ocean floor), net ground-water storage, and/or the existence of ground-water withdrawals may cause this measure to understate the true replenishment rate.

The use of replenishment rate in estimating supply carries further liabilities. As the area under study becomes large (a major river basin, a nation, or a part thereof) the replenishment rate understates the true supply because it fails to reflect reuse possibilities. As each user withdraws and uses water, wastewater flows are generated and returned to the stream or lake. These return flows are then available to other users, water quality permitting. Quality requirements can be met by dilution, by relying on in-stream purification processes, by wastewater treatment before discharge, by water treatment after withdrawal, or by a combination of these. The more effectively the desired water quality can be maintained, the greater the potential for reuse of return flows.

The supply of water available to a given area, therefore, cannot be estimated on the basis of data now available, but a lower bound can be determined by measuring or estimating the total surface water discharge from the area. This annual volume of water is potentially available for withdrawal, although storage facilities might be required to satisfy certain patterns of withdrawal. Additional, unmeasured sources of supply include ground water that leaves the area in some way other than as surface discharge, net additions to

ground-water storage, and return flows from other water users, but data are not available to determine the magnitude or significance of these additions to water supply.

Table 9–1 summarizes estimates of replenishment rates for the populated continents of the earth and for selected nations. The figures represent the excess of precipitation over evapotranspiration. This excess, the net replenishment rate, is expressed in two ways: as cubic kilometers per year and as billion gallons per day. Divided by land area (after converting the second measure to cubic feet per year), these data yield estimates of the average rate of replenishment per unit land area, expressed in millimeters per year and inches per year, respectively. These estimates provide a reasonably comparable index of the relative availability of water at various locations in the world.

Unfortunately, calculations performed on the basis of nations and continents inevitably blur the inherent variation in the data. Many nations, such as the United States, consist of areas which range from very arid to very humid; water may be exceedingly scarce in the Southwest but abundant in the Pacific Northwest. Even so, the average annual runoffs for nations can be seen to range from 4 millimeters for Egypt (not including inflows from other nations via the Nile River) to 1,300 millimeters for the Philippines. The United States is close to the world average at 250 millimeters.

The larger the land area of a nation, the longer the major river systems within the nations, and the more seacoast included, the more seriously these data may understate the true availability of water. On the other hand, environmental considerations may require minimum flows in streams, especially those draining into significant estuaries, which substantially reduce the annual volumes of water that can actually be withdrawn from ground and surface sources. Where surface storage or extensive well fields are required to accomplish a desired withdrawal, economic costs may prevent or delay a potential supply from becoming an actual one.

As a result of the considerations discussed above, it is impossible to make meaningful statements concerning the supply of water available across the world, or throughout any continent or nation. Meaningful statements describing supply can be made only for relatively small areas and then only after detailed on-site investigation of the nature and behavior of the actual water resources available to that area. Therefore, the data presented in this section are included only to illustrate the shortcomings of aggregate calculations and to

## TABLE 9–1

### Estimates of Available Global Water Supply for Continents and Selected Nations[a]

| | Mean Annual Discharge (Water Supply) | | Land Area | | Mean Annual Runoff | |
|---|---|---|---|---|---|---|
| | cubic km/yr | billion gal/day | 1,000 miles[2] | 1,000 km[2] | milli- meters | inches |
| AFRICA | 4,220 | 3,060 | 11,800 | 30,600 | 139 | 5.5 |
| Egypt[b] | 4.0 | 2.9 | 387 | 1,000 | 4.0 | 0.2 |
| Nigeria | 261 | 189 | 357 | 924 | 284 | 11 |
| ASIA | 13,200 | 9,540 | 17,200 | 44,600 | 296 | 12 |
| Bangladesh | 129 | 93.3 | 55.1 | 143 | 915 | 36 |
| China | 2,880 | 2,080 | 3,690 | 9,560 | 300 | 12 |
| India | 1,590 | 1,150 | 1,270 | 3,290 | 485 | 19 |
| Indonesia | 1,510 | 1,090 | 747 | 1,934 | 1,000 | 39 |
| Japan | 396 | 286 | 144 | 372 | 1,070 | 42 |
| Pakistan | 73 | 52.8 | 310 | 804 | 90.2 | 3.6 |
| Philippines | 390 | 282 | 116 | 300 | 1,300 | 51 |
| South Korea | 60 | 43.4 | 38.0 | 98.5 | 609 | 24 |
| Thailand | 171 | 124 | 198 | 514 | 335 | 13 |
| Turkey (both continents) | 172 | 124 | 301 | 781 | 215 | 8.5 |
| U.S.S.R. (in Asia) | 3,320 | 2,400 | 6,760 | 17,500 | 190 | 7.5 |
| AUSTRALIA-OCEANIA (Australia, New Zealand, and Papua New Guinea) | 1,960 | 1,420 | 3,250 | 8,420 | 245 | 9.6 |
| Australia (including Tasmania) | 382 | 276 | 2,970 | 7,690 | 49.8 | 2.0 |
| EUROPE | 3,150 | 2,280 | 3,770 | 9,770 | 323 | 13 |
| U.S.S.R. (entire nation) | 4,350 | 3,150 | 8,650 | 22,400 | 194 | 7.6 |
| U.S.S.R. (in Europe) | 1,030 | 744 | 1,890 | 4,900 | 210 | 8.3 |
| NORTH AMERICA | 5,960 | 4,310 | 8,510 | 22,100 | 286 | 11 |
| Mexico | 330 | 239 | 762 | 1,970 | 165 | 6.5 |
| United States (50 states)[c] | 2,340 | 1,700 | 3,620 | 9,360 | 250 | 9.9 |
| SOUTH AMERICA | 10,400 | 7,510 | 6,880 | 17,800 | 583 | 23 |
| Brazil | 5,670 | 4,100 | 3,290 | 8,510 | 666 | 26 |
| GLOBAL (excluding Antarctica) | 38,900 | 28,100 | 51,600 | 134,000 | 290 | 11 |
| Africa | 3,400 | 2,460 | | 29,800 | 114 | |
| Asia | 12,200 | 8,820 | | 44,100 | 276 | |
| Australia (-Oceania) | 2,400 | 1,740 | | 8,900 | 269 | |
| Europe | 2,800 | 2,030 | | 10,000 | 282 | |
| North America | 5,900 | 4,270 | | 24,100 | 242 | |
| South America | 11,100 | 8,030 | | 17,900 | 618 | |
| Antarctica | 2,000 | 1,450 | | 14,100 | 141 | |
| Global | 39,700 | 28,700 | | 149,000 | 266 | |
| Global (excluding Antarctica) | 37,700 | 27,300 | | 134,000 | 280 | |

[a] Data are rounded to 2 or 3 significant figures.
[b] Egypt is a good example of some nations whose *additional* water supplies come from large rivers entering or passing through the nation but having their upstream source in one or more other nations. The Nile is the major Egyptian water supply, but the Nile is largely fed by precipitation and stream systems located south of Egypt and is therefore not included in the data shown for Egypt.
[c] The figures for the 48 conterminous states are: area, 3,020,000 square miles; mean runoff, 1,800,000 cubic feet per second; water supply, about 1,200 billion gallons per day, or 1,620 cubic kilometers per year.

*Sources:* Runoff data for all but the global areas and continents at end of table were compiled from statistics in M. I. L'vovich, *Global Water Resources and Their Future* (in Russian), 1974, pp. 264–70.
The somewhat comparable data for each continent at the end of the table are from Albert Baumgartner and Eberhard Reichel, *The World Water Balance: Mean Annual Global, Continental and Maritime Precipitation, Evaporation and Run-off,* Amsterdam: Elsevier, 1975.

provide some indication of the gross differences existing among the various regions of the world.

## The Demand for Water

Water is used to perform a wide variety of functions in human society. Among the major uses to which water withdrawn from surface and ground sources may be put are:

- Domestic use
- Industrial use (both in manufacturing and minerals extraction and processing)
- Crop irrigation
- Energy production (not including hydropower)

In each use, some fraction of the amount withdrawn is consumptive use (it is evaporated or incorporated into a product), and the remainder is returned to the environment, where it may be available for later withdrawal by another user.* The distribution of withdrawals among three of these uses (domestic, industrial, agricultural) for 16 selected countries is shown in Figure 9–2.

Data on the above uses have been compiled for the U.S. at 5-year intervals by the U.S. Geological Survey. Scattered data have been compiled for other countries and reprinted and published from

time to time (for example by the Economic Commissions for Europe and for Asia and the Far East). In order to estimate the amount of water use for all regions on a systematic basis in the absence of such first-hand statistics, recourse may be made to comparisons with demographic and related data that are more generally available and which are generally considered in projections of future natural development.

*Domestic use,* for example, can be estimated from data on urban and rural populations, using figures on per capita use where such data are available. Use factors for European countries range from 76 to 270 liters per day per capita, with a general average of 150 liters. Estimates of per capita use for developing countries, published by the World Health Organization, are given in Table 9–2.

*Industrial use* can be estimated from data on the production of various commodities, (e.g., see ECOSOC, 1969). Water-product ratios are highly variable among industrial plants depending, among other things, on the particular plant process, costs

---

* Preferred water use terms used in this chapter are water *withdrawn* (or *withdrawals*), and water *consumed* (consumptive use). Water *withdrawn* is pumped or diverted for use from a stream, lake, or aquifer. After use, part of the water withdrawn returns to a stream, lake, or aquifer, and is available for reuse. The other part has been *consumed* during use—by evaporation, transpiration, drinking by man or beast, or by incorporation into a food or other product. Ther term "consumption" should be avoided because, although usually meaning water withdrawn, the word itself may be confused with "consumed." Water demand, water requirements, and water use also usually refer to water withdrawals rather than water consumed, except when otherwise noted.

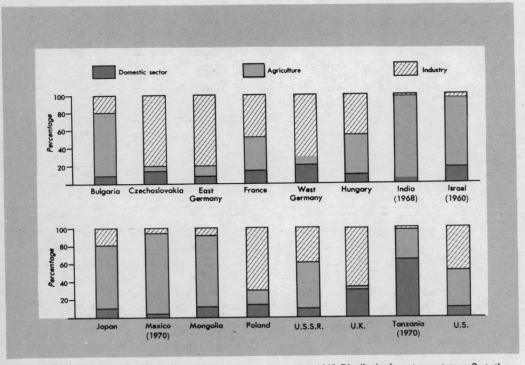

**Figure 9-2.** Distribution of withdrawals among major categories of water use, 1965. Distribution by water-use types reflects the economic characteristics of a nation. *(Adapted from G. R. White et al.,* Resources and Needs: Assessment of the World Water Situation, *U.N. Water Conference, 1977)*

of water, and recycling. For the purposes of this chapter, the ratio of water use to the population engaged in manufacturing is used as a simple measure. For the U.S., the water use/population ratio is 2,500 gallons per day per capita or about 9,500 liters. In several Asian countries, the ratio runs from 2,150 to 8,600 liters per day per capita. The ratio for Japan is about 4,500 liters per day per capita (or 1,640 cubic meters per year per capita). Experience in the U.S. indicates that about 11 percent of industrial withdrawal is consumed.

*Irrigation use* can be estimated from data on irrigated acreage, recognizing that this irrigation use varies climatically, and with the techniques used for irrigation (a maximum under gravity-flow ditch irrigation, a minimum under trickle irrigation schemes).

Irrigation experience in the U.S. indicates that about 3.1 acre-feet per acre (0.95 hectare-meters per hectare) is withdrawn for irrigation. This depth applied to the irrigated area gives the gross amount withdrawn. Of this amount, 17 percent is lost (consumed) in transport to the irrigated lands (largely canal seepage), 59 percent is lost by evaporation for plant growth, leaving 24 percent as return flow from the irrigated lands. In the absence of an adequate return flow, salts build up, destroying soil fertility.

*Cooling water use* in energy production is often expressed in terms of a ratio of water use to kilowatt-hours of generation. This ratio, however, varies with the cooling method used, being large for "once-through" cooling, small for evaporative cooling, and near zero for dry towers.

In the U.S. an average of about 42 gallons (160 liters) per kilowatt-hour is withdrawn for thermal cooling. In recent years the average use has decreased toward 34 gallons (130 liters) as a result of more efficient plants, greater use of cooling ponds and towers, and other changes. About 1.5 percent is consumed through evaporative dissipation.

Data describing water use for various purposes are available from the U.N. *Yearbook* and other sources. Table 9–3 lists such data by nations and continents, as collected from various studies of variable quality, and as estimated by the procedures described above. These readily available statistics have not been compared with alternate sources or checked for internal consistency or accuracy. There are numerous missing data, most notably for the People's Republic of China.

Table 9–4 lists the land areas and average annual water withdrawal for some of the nations and continents listed in Table 9–3. As in the case of water supply data, these large aggregates mask important variations in the data. Within each country, water withdrawals are doubtless concentrated in specific areas, so that certain areas will have withdrawal rates much above that given for the country, and other areas will be much below. Nevertheless, average water withdrawals are seen to vary from a low of just over 1 millimeter for Brazil to a maximum of 301 millimeters for Japan. The latter figure can be traced to very high withdrawals for cooling thermoelectric power plants, as well as relatively high withdrawals for other industrial uses and for crop irrigation.

Forecasts of future water withdrawals require consideration of all the various determinants of water demand. Ideally, each water-using sector would be considered separately, and the factors that influence water use would be identified, quantified, forecast, and combined, using an appropriate demand function, to yield a forecast of future water use. Thus domestic water use would depend upon future lifestyles, family income, family size, water-using appliance technology, and the future price of water for domestic purposes. Future industrial water use would be determined from assumptions regarding technology, industrial output, the price of water, etc. Similarly, agricultural use of water would be expressed in terms of crops, output, irrigation technology, price, and other factors.

Unfortunately, general demand relationships suitable for such estimates on a national and a global basis are not available. The prevailing ambiguity regarding the identity of water as an economic good has tended to discourage the necessary economic modeling. Little examination of the demand for water has occurred, and that has tended to focus on relatively small aggregations.

Further, past management practices have produced historical data of dubious relevance to the future. For example, many countries having substantial irrigated areas have chosen to subsidize the withdrawal of water for irrigation purposes. The result is the displacement of higher-valued uses by agriculture (and the subsequent lack of information about the identity or nature of these uses) and a general lack of experience regarding the applicability of more efficient irrigation technologies, since artificially low prices tend to discourage their use. In other cases, water is allocated administratively without cost, or with negligible cost to the user. Consequently, no direct observations of value, or of the possibilities for reduction of water use during times of shortage, can be obtained.

## TABLE 9–2

### Per Capita Use of Drinking Water in Less Developed Countries, 1970

*(Liters per day)*

| | Present Consumption | | | | | | Future Consumption | | | | | |
| | Urban | | | | Rural | | Urban | | | | Rural | |
| | With House Connections | | With Public Standposts | | | | With House Connections | | With Public Standposts | | | |
| | Min. | Max. | Min. | Max | Min. | Max. | Min. | Max. | Min. | Max. | Min. | Max. |
|---|---|---|---|---|---|---|---|---|---|---|---|---|
| **AFRICA** | | | | | | | | | | | | |
| Botswana | 90 | 1,820 | — | — | 10 | 45 | 90 | 320 | — | 45 | 20 | 45 |
| Burundi | 100 | 350 | 10 | 40 | — | — | 150 | 350 | 40 | 70 | 20 | 40 |
| Cameroon | 100 | 180 | 18 | 34 | 10 | 20 | 120 | 200 | 30 | 50 | 20 | 30 |
| Central African Republic | 50 | 300 | — | 20 | — | — | 75 | 220 | 15 | 20 | — | — |
| Chad | 60 | 400 | 8 | 25 | 5 | 15 | 150 | 400 | 25 | 45 | 20 | 40 |
| Congo | 75 | 100 | 50 | 75 | 10 | 30 | 75 | 100 | 50 | 75 | — | — |
| Dahomey | 10 | 125 | 10 | 30 | 10 | 20 | 80 | 150 | 25 | 50 | 20 | 40 |
| Gambia | 60 | 220 | 50 | 150 | 22 | 50 | 90 | 310 | — | — | — | — |
| Ghana | 36 | 120 | 22 | 36 | 22 | 100 | 115 | 180 | 20 | 55 | 20 | 45 |
| Guinea | 100 | 150 | 40 | 60 | — | — | 100 | 150 | 40 | 60 | — | — |
| Ivory Coast | 20 | 130 | 20 | 40 | 10 | 20 | 40 | 150 | 20 | 40 | 20 | 40 |
| Kenya | 20 | 200 | 5 | 15 | 10 | 20 | 50 | 300 | 20 | 30 | 15 | 75 |
| Lesotho | 55 | 270 | — | — | 27 | 54 | 55 | 270 | 35 | 70 | 35 | 70 |
| Liberia | 95 | 190 | 20 | 40 | 20 | 40 | 115 | 285 | 40 | 80 | 40 | 95 |
| Madagascar | 40 | 250 | 10 | 24 | 4 | 10 | 80 | 250 | — | 25 | 10 | 40 |
| Mali | 10 | 25 | — | — | — | — | 40 | 160 | 30 | 50 | — | — |
| Mauritania | 20 | 200 | 20 | 50 | 10 | 50 | 100 | 300 | 50 | 100 | 30 | 100 |
| Niger | 100 | 300 | 1 | 2 | 3 | 10 | — | — | — | — | — | — |
| Nigeria | 45 | 230 | 45 | 70 | 45 | 45 | 90 | 230 | 45 | 90 | 45 | 70 |
| Senegal | 76 | 96 | 18 | 22 | — | — | 100 | 125 | 20 | 24 | — | — |
| Togo | 60 | 100 | — | — | — | — | — | — | — | — | — | — |
| Uganda | 50 | 500 | 5 | 15 | 5 | 10 | 70 | 700 | 20 | 30 | 10 | 15 |
| Tanzania | 80 | 110 | 40 | 80 | 25 | 50 | 100 | 150 | 55 | 100 | 20 | 40 |
| Upper Volta | 50 | 250 | 5 | 50 | 5 | 20 | 75 | 300 | 10 | 75 | 10 | 50 |
| Zaire | 30 | 250 | 10 | 30 | 20 | 40 | 100 | 300 | 20 | 50 | 5 | 10 |
| Zambia | 200 | 700 | 50 | 90 | 10 | 50 | 130 | 700 | 50 | 90 | 40 | 50 |
| **AMERICAS** | | | | | | | | | | | | |
| Argentina | 300 | 600 | — | — | 100 | 200 | 200 | 350 | — | — | 100 | 200 |
| Barbados | 230 | 1,730 | 23 | 68 | 23 | 910 | 135 | 570 | 23 | 68 | 135 | 570 |
| Bolivia | 60 | 150 | 10 | 25 | 60 | 100 | 150 | 250 | — | — | 80 | 150 |
| Brazil | 80 | 500 | 10 | 50 | 20 | 75 | 100 | 500 | 30 | 50 | 20 | 75 |
| Chile | 180 | 400 | 10 | 20 | 100 | 100 | 250 | 500 | — | — | 100 | 100 |
| Colombia | 113 | 275 | — | — | 40 | 200 | 115 | 300 | — | — | 80 | 150 |
| Costa Rica | 175 | 275 | — | — | 120 | 150 | 200 | 300 | — | — | 150 | 250 |

| | | | | | | | | | | | | |
|---|---|---|---|---|---|---|---|---|---|---|---|---|
| Dominican Republic | 320 | 375 | 55 | 95 | 95 | 130 | 130 | 340 | 55 | 95 | 95 | 130 |
| Ecuador | 140 | 200 | 40 | 40 | 70 | 140 | 100 | — | 40 | — | 60 | 100 |
| El Salvador | 17 | 295 | — | — | 60 | 100 | 60 | 400 | — | — | 60 | 60 |
| Guatemala | 150 | 150 | — | — | 25 | 25 | 100 | 200 | — | — | 25 | 60 |
| Guyana | 270 | 360 | — | — | 135 | 270 | 450 | 550 | — | — | 360 | 550 |
| Haiti | 150 | 200 | 20 | — | — | 175 | — | 225 | 20 | 40 | 20 | 40 |
| Honduras | 20 | 270 | 45 | 70 | 45 | 160 | 140 | 270 | 45 | — | 90 | 135 |
| Jamaica | 320 | 390 | 20 | 50 | 20 | 340 | 320 | 570 | 20 | 50 | 45 | 450 |
| Mexico | 100 | 350 | 40 | 60 | 50 | 100 | 250 | 350 | 40 | 60 | 50 | 250 |
| Nicaragua | 130 | 220 | — | — | 75 | 240 | 150 | 300 | — | 60 | 95 | 150 |
| Panama | 190 | 300 | — | — | 40 | 210 | 80 | 340 | — | — | 60 | 90 |
| Paraguay | 160 | 350 | 10 | 30 | 100 | 160 | 200 | 350 | 10 | 30 | 100 | 200 |
| Peru | 90 | 400 | 25 | 30 | 80 | 150 | 100 | 300 | 30 | 50 | 600 | 100 |
| Uruguay | 120 | 250 | — | — | 100 | 126 | 180 | 262 | — | — | 105 | 190 |
| Venezuela | 200 | 300 | — | — | 150 | 400 | 300 | 600 | — | — | 150 | 200 |
| **EASTERN MEDITERRANEAN** | | | | | | | | | | | | |
| Afghanistan | 60 | 70 | 20 | 30 | 15 | 60 | 20 | 100 | 30 | 50 | 30 | 50 |
| Bahrain | 220 | 420 | 23 | 140 | 110 | 230 | 340 | 360 | 18 | — | 140 | 280 |
| Cyprus | 145 | 275 | 10 | 23 | 90 | 185 | 145 | 320 | — | 36 | 145 | 185 |
| Democratic Yemen | 50 | 180 | 18 | 40 | 10 | 140 | 18 | 230 | 150 | 250 | 50 | 70 |
| Egypt | 100 | 260 | 150 | 40 | 40 | 250 | 40 | 350 | 10 | — | 40 | 60 |
| Ethiopia | 20 | 100 | 10 | 10 | 5 | 40 | 10 | 100 | 20 | 20 | 5 | 15 |
| Iran | 75 | 150 | — | 25 | 40 | 150 | 75 | 190 | — | — | 110 | 150 |
| Iraq | 90 | 200 | — | — | 65 | 160 | 130 | 360 | — | — | 90 | 145 |
| Jordan | 60 | 120 | — | — | 30 | 80 | 60 | 150 | — | — | 40 | 80 |
| Kuwait | 150 | 220 | 70 | 220 | — | 180 | — | 410 | 150 | 220 | — | — |
| Lebanon | 150 | 200 | — | 60 | 80 | 200 | 125 | 250 | — | 70 | 100 | 150 |
| Pakistan | 70 | 180 | 20 | 110 | 20 | 150 | 100 | 220 | 20 | 150 | 50 | 100 |
| Qatar | 150 | 300 | 80 | 50 | 40 | 230 | 80 | 300 | 80 | 50 | 80 | 150 |
| Saudi Arabia | 50 | 400 | 25 | 50 | 25 | 150 | 50 | 250 | 25 | — | 100 | 200 |
| Somalia | —[a] | 250 | 20 | 50 | — | 250 | — | 1,140[b] | 60 | — | — | — |
| Sudan | 45 | 900 | 23 | 32 | 14 | 110 | 42 | 1,140 | — | — | 18 | 45 |
| Syrian Arab Republic | 150 | 200 | — | 10 | 50 | 150 | — | 250 | — | — | — | 75 |
| Tunisia | 100 | 150 | 5 | 10 | 20 | — | — | — | 5 | 10 | 30 | — |
| Yemen | 50 | 80 | 30 | 50 | 20 | — | 40 | — | — | — | 30 | 60 |
| **EUROPEAN REGION** | | | | | | | | | | | | |
| Algeria | 20 | 200 | 10 | 30 | 10 | 80 | 60 | 200 | — | 60 | 50 | 60 |
| Morocco | 60 | 260 | 10 | 20 | 22 | 100 | 70 | 300 | 20 | 30 | 20 | 80 |
| Turkey | 120 | 170 | 60 | 70 | 25 | — | 60 | — | — | — | — | — |
| **SOUTHEAST ASIA** | | | | | | | | | | | | |
| Bangladesh | 45 | 70 | 15 | 25 | 10 | 70 | 20 | 135 | 25 | 45 | 25 | 45 |
| Burma | 100 | 180 | 45 | 100 | 22 | 150 | 60 | 220 | 70 | 120 | 50 | 100 |
| India | 50 | 270 | 5 | — | 25 | 90 | — | 270 | — | — | 45 | 130 |
| Indonesia | 50 | 150 | — | 20 | — | 86 | 100 | 150 | — | 100 | 30 | 60 |
| Mongolia | 24 | 150 | 5 | 60 | — | 187 | — | 420 | 60 | 100 | — | — |
| Nepal | 60 | 100 | 40 | 60 | 40 | 100 | 60 | 200 | 30 | 100 | 60 | 100 |
| Sri Lanka | 170 | 220 | 30 | 50 | 20 | 170 | 70 | 220 | 70 | 50 | 20 | 70 |

## TABLE 9-2 (Continued)

| | Present Consumption | | | | | | Future Consumption | | | | | |
|---|---|---|---|---|---|---|---|---|---|---|---|---|
| | Urban | | | | Rural | | Urban | | | | Rural | |
| | With House Connections | | With Public Standposts | | | | With House Connections | | With Public Standposts | | | |
| | Min. | Max. | Min. | Max | Min. | Max. | Min. | Max. | Min. | Max. | Min. | Max. |
| Thailand | 120 | 180 | — | — | 50 | 100 | 150 | 200 | — | — | 50 | 80 |
| WESTERN PACIFIC | | | | | | | | | | | | |
| Fiji | 140 | 260 | 15 | 140 | — | — | — | 270 | — | — | 9 | 90 |
| Khmer Rep. | 40 | 400 | — | — | — | 15 | 200 | 350 | — | — | 80 | 120 |
| Korea, Rep. of | 150 | 250 | 40 | 80 | 40 | 80 | 100 | 200 | 50 | 150 | 50 | 100 |
| Laos | 50 | 300 | — | — | 20 | 40 | 250 | 250 | — | — | 23 | 110 |
| Malaysia | 18 | 410 | — | — | 14 | 230 | — | — | — | — | — | — |
| Philippines | 110 | 540 | — | — | 40 | 110 | 360 | 1,100 | — | — | 180 | 360 |
| Singapore | — | 220 | — | — | — | — | — | 315 | — | — | — | — |
| Viet-Nam, Rep. of | — | 150 | — | 60 | — | — | — | 300 | — | 60 | — | — |
| Western Samoa | — | 770 | — | — | — | — | — | 220 | — | 50 | — | 100 |
| AVERAGES[c] | | | | | | | | | | | | |
| Africa | 65 | 290 | 20 | 45 | 15 | 35 | 90 | 275 | 30 | 60 | 20 | 50 |
| Americas | 160 | 380 | 25 | 50 | 70 | 190 | 195 | 375 | 30 | 55 | 120 | 195 |
| Eastern Mediterranean | 95 | 245 | 30 | 60 | 40 | 85 | 160 | 310 | 55 | 95 | 70 | 115 |
| European Region | 65 | 210 | 25 | 40 | 20 | 65 | 90 | 250 | 35 | 45 | 35 | 70 |
| Southeast Asia | 75 | 165 | 25 | 50 | 30 | 70 | 125 | 225 | 45 | 85 | 40 | 85 |
| Western Pacific | 85 | 365 | 30 | 95 | 30 | 95 | 230 | 375 | 50 | 85 | 70 | 145 |
| Average | 90 | 280 | 25 | 55 | 35 | 90 | 150 | 300 | 40 | 70 | 60 | 110 |

[a] Magnitude negligible.
[b] Estimation includes garden watering.
[c] Averages rounded to nearest 5 liters.

Source: Frits van der Leeden, *Water Resources of the World: Selected Statistics*, Port Washington, N.Y.: Water Information Center, 1975; original data from World Health Organization, 1973 (data as of Dec. 31, 1970).

## TABLE 9-3
## Water Use for Various Purposes, by Continent and Selected Nations

*(Water use in billions of cubic meters)*

| | Energy Production | | Irrigation | | Industrial (per capita) | | | Domestic (per capita) | | | Water Use Total |
|---|---|---|---|---|---|---|---|---|---|---|---|
| | Genera-tion | Water Use | Area | Water Use | Per-sons in Mfg. | Fac-tor | Water Use | Popu-lation | Fac-tor | Water Use | |
| | $10^9 kw$-$hr$ thermal | $10^9 m^3$ | $10^6 ha$ | $10^9 m^3$ | 1000s | | $m^3$ | Millions | | $m^3$ | $10^9 m^3$ |
| Africa | 86 | 11 | 6.4 | 60.8 | 2,963 | 1,500 | 4.4 | 405 | 30 | 12 | 88 |
| Egypt | 3 | 0.4 | 2.9 | 27.6 | 615 | 1,500 | 0.9 | 38 | 40 | 1.5 | 30 |
| Nigeria | | | | | 172 | 1,500 | .3 | 65 | 40 | 2.6 | |
| Asia | 520 | 68 | 147.4 | 1,400 | 23,600 | 1,300 | 30.7 | 2,290 | | 98 | 1,597 |
| Bangladesh | 1 | 0.1 | | | 260 | 1,000 | .26 | 75 | 40 | 3.0 | |
| China | | | 74.0 | 703 | | | | 853 | 40 | 34 | |
| India | 48 | 0.6 | 37.6 | 357 | 4,800 | 1,000 | 4.8 | 611 | 40 | 24 | 386 |
| Indonesia | 1 | 0.2 | 3.8 | 36 | 925 | 1,000 | .9 | 132 | 40 | 5 | 42 |
| Japan | 378 | 49 | 3.4 | 32 | 11,900 | 1,640 | 19.5 | 112 | 100 | 11 | 112 |
| Pakistan | 4 | 0.5 | 12.0 | 114 | 427 | 1,000 | .4 | 73 | 40 | 3 | 118 |
| Philippines | 10 | 1.3 | 1.0 | 10 | 538 | 1,000 | .5 | 44 | 40 | 2 | 14 |
| South Korea | | | .8 | 7.6 | 1,160 | 1,000 | 1.2 | 35 | 40 | 1 | |
| Thailand | 5 | 0.7 | 1.9 | 18 | 309 | 1,000 | .3 | 42 | 40 | 1 | 20 |
| Turkey | 10 | 1.3 | 1.7 | 18 | 638 | 1,000 | .6 | 41 | 50 | 2 | 22 |
| Australia-Oceania | 61 | 7.9 | 1.4 | 13 | 1,610 | 3,600 | 5.7 | 20 | | 2 | 29 |
| Australia | 56 | 7.3 | 1.3 | 12 | 1,337 | 3,600 | 4.8 | 14 | 90 | 1 | 25 |
| Europe | 1,355 | 176 | 12.2 | 116 | 51,000 | 3,600 | 183.6 | 404 | 100 | 40 | 516 |
| U.S.S.R. | 844 | 110 | 9.9 | 94 | 29,036 | 2,500 | 72.8 | 256 | 70 | 18 | 295 |
| North America | 1,788 | 232 | 21.6 | 205 | 21,270 | 3,600 | 76.5 | 339 | | 38 | 551 |
| Mexico | 24 | 3 | 3.3 | 31 | | | | 60 | 50 | 3 | |
| United States | 1,663 | 216 | 16.9 | 160 | 19,000 | 3,650 | 69.4 | 216 | 150 | 32 | 477 |
| South America | 50 | 6.4 | 3.7 | 35 | 3,653 | 1,200 | 4.4 | 214 | 50 | 11 | 57 |
| Brazil | 4 | 0.5 | 0.14 | 1 | 2,470 | 1,200 | 3.0 | 106 | 50 | 5 | 10 |
| Global | 3,860 | 502 | 192.7 | 1,830 | 104,096 | 2,930 | 305 | 3,670 | 55 | 201 | 2,838 |
| OECD countries | 3,214 | 418 | 33.1 | 314 | 67,400 | | | 755 | 100 | 76 | |

*Source:* United Nations, *Statistical Yearbook, 1977,* New York: 1977; water use computations by U.S. Geological Survey.

Figure 9–3 shows the projected water use to the year 2000 for four Asian countries in percent of the maximum limit of supply as represented by runoff from local precipitation. In these four cases, the maximum developable supply that could be depended upon, without storage, might be between 20 and 70 percent of the maximum limits shown in the figure (100 percent). Storage capacity equivalent to one year's flow can raise this percentage to 80 percent of the maximum limit. "Water consumed" is a more appropriate characteristic than "water withdrawn" for making comparisons with maximum limits of developable water supply, because most water withdrawn is reusable. However, data on "water consumed" are fragmentary or nonexistent in many parts of the world. In the United States, with existing storage capacity of 15 percent of the year's river flow, water withdrawn and water consumed in 1975 was, respectively, 35 and 8 percent of the maximum limit of developable water supply (average runoff).

These problems do not preclude the development of suitable forecasting models; they merely underline the necessity of intensive sector by sector analysis prior to the postulation of such models. They also suggest some of the important deficiencies of forecasting methods that rely on extrapolations of past water-use data. Such methods are likely to produce forecasts seriously in error, especially where water scarcity may increase. Extrapolation alone cannot predict the various economic, technological, and social adjustments known to occur when water becomes, through scarcity, a higher-valued resource. Ex-

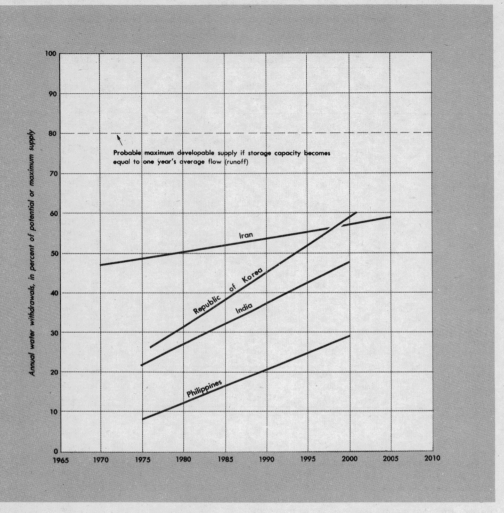

**Figure 9-3.** Projected water use *(withdrawals)* for four Asian countries in percent of maximum limit of supply, as represented by runoff from local precipitation. *(Various country and U.N. reports)*

trapolations have a limited use but should be viewed as highly tentative forecasts.

In spite of the difficulties noted above, several global forecasts of water use have been prepared. Four are discussed here. Three rely on extrapolations of past water use, modified by certain gross adjustments to reflect assumptions regarding changing future conditions of water use. The third forecast attempts, in a relatively crude manner, to identify countries where the availability of water resources could be critical by 2000.

## Doxiadis Projection

In 1967, C. A. Doxiadis published a graph* showing projected increase in the "consumption" (withdrawal) of "water controlled by man." His estimated total for 1975 (2,412 × $10^9$ m³/yr) is in general agreement with the data presented in this

---

*Constantinos A. Doxiadis, "Water and Environment," in *Water for Peace,* International Conference on Water for Peace, Washington, D.C., May 23–31, 1967, pp. 33–60.

## TABLE 9-4

### Average Annual Water Withdrawal per Unit of Land Area, Selected Geographic Units

| | Land Area (millions km²) | Average Annual Water Withdrawals (millimeters per year) |
|---|---|---|
| AFRICA[a] | 30.6 | 2.88 |
| Egypt | 1.00 | 30.0 |
| ASIA[b] | 27.7 | 57.7 |
| India | 3.29 | 9.12 |
| Indonesia | 1.93 | 3.11 |
| Japan | .372 | 301 |
| Pakistan | .804 | 147 |
| Philippines | .300 | 46.7 |
| Thailand | .514 | 38.9 |
| Turkey (Asia and Europe) | .781 | 28.2 |
| AUSTRALIA[c] | 8.42 | 3.56 |
| Australia | 7.69 | 3.25 |
| EUROPE[d] | 27.2 | 19.0 |
| U.S.S.R. (Europe and Asia) | 22.4 | 13.2 |
| NORTH AMERICA[e] | 22.1 | 24.9 |
| United States | 9.36 | 51.0 |
| SOUTH AMERICA | 17.8 | 3.20 |
| Brazil | 8.51 | 1.18 |
| GLOBAL (excluding Antarctica) | 134 | 21.2 |

Note: Data are rounded to three significant figures.
[a] Including Madagascar.
[b] Excluding U.S.S.R. (listed under Europe).
[c] Including New Zealand and Papua New Guinea.
[d] Including entire U.S.S.R. but excluding all of Turkey.
[e] Including Central American countries, Bahamas, Cuba, Dominican Republic, Haiti, and Jamaica.

report for the same set of uses (irrigation, industrial, urban, and rural): $2,336 \times 10^9$ m³/yr.

Doxiadis projected use to increase to $6,500 \times 10^9$ m³/yr by the year 2000, increasing further along a logistic curve to an asymptotic limit of $23,000 \times 10^9$ m³/yr about a century hence. This limit is close to the estimated global supply of fresh water. In the following estimated withdrawals for the year 2000, the largest proportional increase is projected in the industrial and urban uses:

| | 1975 | 2000 |
|---|---|---|
| | Billions of cubic meters per year | |
| Irrigation | 2,000 | 4,600 |
| Industrial | 184 | 950 |
| Urban | 182 | 850 |
| Rural | 46 | 100 |
| Total | 2,412 | 6,500 |

Doxiadis did not provide any explanation of his calculations nor of the regional or continental distribution. Hence, no judgment can be made of their reliability.

## Kalinin Projection

In 1969, the Russian hydrologist G. P. Kalinin published the following estimates of global water requirements by the year 2000.[*]

| | Withdrawn | Consumed |
|---|---|---|
| | Billions of cubic meters per year | |
| Irrigation | 7,000 | 4,800 |
| Domestic | 600 | 100 |
| Industrial | 1,700 | 170 |
| Waste dilution | 9,000 | — |
| Other | 400 | 400 |
| Total | 18,700 | 5,470 |

Kalinin's figures for withdrawals for irrigation and industrial use are greatly in excess of Doxiadis' projections. His domestic-use projections are also higher than those of Dioxiadis. While Kalinin does not explain the derivation of his projections, he does comment:

By the year 2000, half of all the earth's annually renewed water—the 37,000 cubic kilometers [billions of cubic meters] of evaporated ocean water which precipitates on land rather than back into the ocean—will be in use by man. With so high a demand, and the uneven distribution in space and time, work will soon have to be undertaken on an unprecedented scale to regulate run-off and divert the waters of rivers into areas affected by drought. The problem is particularly acute, since demand is growing several times faster than the population. When the world population reaches 20,000 million in the twenty-first century, the demand will be several times greater than in the year 2000.

These water demand forecasts are rough approximations only, because data on growth of population, irrigation, industry and consumption are also only approximate, and estimates of pollution are either too high or too low. Very likely, the future demand for clean, fresh water is exaggerated because: (a) as demand grows, means will be sought to reduce consumption per unit of industrial and agricultural production; (b) some branches of industry could use salt water or brackish water, as is already being done in some cases; (c) desalination of seawater and brackish ground water will increase; and (d) the purifying of polluted water will be improved and accelerated.

Nevertheless, the figures must be regarded as approximately correct for the next thirty-five to fifty years, i.e. until A.D. 2000-15.

In general, population growth, irrigation, or industrial development will exacerbate the con-

*G. P. Kalinin and V. D. Bykov, "The World's Water Resources, Present and Future," Impact of Science in Society (UNESCO), Apr.-June 1969, p. 143.

trasts between have and have-not countries or regions. A percentage increase in water use in a region where the margin is thin would have greater consequences than the same percentage increase in a region where the margin is broad. Moreover, the processes of development in arid areas often lead to changed cultures that are less resilient than the cultural forms they replace. Water development (i.e., storage) decreases the frequency of shortage but may increase the net severity of consequences of droughts that cause excessive demand for stored water.

### The FAO Water Projection

Table 9–5 presents water use projections published by the Food and Agriculture Organization. These projections are of interest because they project separately each of the major sectors of the world water economy.

In commenting on the table and water problems generally, the FAO writes in *The State of Food and Agriculture* (C 77/INF/19, Nov. 1977):

Although irrigated land comprises only 13% of the world's total arable area, irrigation accounts for by far the largest proportion of the total water used by man. . . . Other non-agricultural water uses (for industry, mining and domestic purposes) are now increasing much faster than the use for irrigation. However, a considerable amount of this water is non-consumptive and is recycled, while irrigation continues to be a consumptive use. Irrigated agriculture will therefore continue to be the greatest water consumer in the future.

With a region, country or river basin, the spectrum of uses and withdrawals of water will vary according to climatic and socio-economic conditions, and it is thus necessary to distinguish between consumptive and non-consumptive use. For example, Table [9–6] indicates that, among the countries covered, the highest annual withdrawals per capita occur in the United States and the U.S.S.R., where both irrigated agriculture and industry are highly developed. However, very high withdrawals also take place in non-industrialized countries such as Mexico and India, where there is a large use of water for irrigated agriculture. The figures for Czechoslovakia and the United Kingdom show that per capita demand may be quite low in industrial countries with very low demands for irrigation.

*Water quality*

The need for water resources, however, goes beyond quantity and must also consider quality. The harmful effects of waste disposal on quality are well known, but a major unseen problem is the increasing salinity of water resources with use. This is an inevitable process in nature, but man has greatly accelerated it and, with continued increases in the intensity of use, the problem will become greater.

Guidelines have been drawn up for interpreting the quality of water for irrigation.* Table [9–7] illustrates the application of some of these guide-

---

* R.S. Ayers and D.W. Westcott. *Water Quality for Agriculture*, Irrigation and Drainage Paper No. 29, Rome, FAO, 1976.

### TABLE 9–5

### Estimates of World Water Use in 1976 and Projections to 2000

|  | Total Use in Millions of m³ | | Projected Rate of Growth 1967–2000 in Percent per Year | Fraction of Total Use in Percent | |
|---|---|---|---|---|---|
|  | 1967 | 2000 | | 1967 | 2000 |
| **AGRICULTURE** | | | | | |
| Irrigation | 1,400,000 | 2,800,000 | 2.1 | 70 | 51 |
| Livestock | 58,800 | 102,200 | 1.7 | 3 | 2 |
| Rural Domestic | 19,800 | 38,300 | 2.0 | 1 | 1 |
| **OTHER** | | | | | |
| Urban Domestic | 73,000 | 278,900 | 4.1 | 4 | 5 |
| Industry and Mining | 437,700 | 2,231,000 | 5.0 | 22 | 41 |
| TOTAL | 1,989,300 | 5,450,400 | 3.1 | 100 | 100 |

*Source:* M. Holy, *Water and the Environment*, Irrigation and Drainage Paper No. 8, Food and Agriculture Organization, Rome, 1971.

## TABLE 9–6

### Water Use in Selected Countries, 1965

| | Total Use in m³ per Capita | Percent of Total | | |
| --- | --- | --- | --- | --- |
| | | Municipal and Rural Water Supply | Agriculture | Industry |
| United Kingdom | 200 | 31 | 3 | 66 |
| Czechoslovakia | 285 | 13 | 6 | 81 |
| India | 600 | 3 | 96 | 1 |
| Japan | 710 | 10 | 72 | 18 |
| Mexico | 930 | 4 | 91 | 5 |
| U.S.S.R. | 1.000 | 8 | 53 | 39 |
| United States | 2.300 | 10 | 42 | 48 |

Source: United Nations, *The Demand for Water*, Natural Resources, Water Series No. 3, New York, 1976.

## TABLE 9–7

### Water Quality in Three Selected Irrigation Areas

| | Salinity ECw [a] | Sodium SAR [b] |
| --- | --- | --- |
| GUIDELINE | | |
| No Problem | Below 0.75 | Below 3 |
| Increasing Problem | 0.75–3.0 | 3–9 |
| Severe Problem | Above 3.0 | Above 9 |
| IRRIGATION AREAS | | |
| Mona Project, Pakistan, 1968 | 3.60 | 38.0 |
| Pecos River, United States, 1946 | 3.21 | 8.6 |
| Tigris River, Iraq, 1966–69 | 0.51 | 2.5 |

[a] Electrical conductivity, expressed in mmhos/cm.
[b] Sodium absorption rate, adjusted for calcium and magnesium content.
Source: R. S. Ayers and D. W. Westcott, *Water Quality for Agriculture, op. cit.*

lines to the quality of water in three irrigated areas. The Mona project in Pakistan and the Pecos River in the United States would be classified as having severe or increasing water quality problems for irrigation. The Tigris River would be classified as having no problem, although sodium concentrations would be regarded as borderline.

Increased salinity in water supplies results from the two basic processes of salt loading and salt concentrating. Salt loading is due both to natural causes such as surface run-off and to man-made sources such as industrial waste and return flows from irrigated land. The relative effects of salt loading and salt concentrating on salinity concentrations for the Colorado River in the United States are shown in Table [9–8]. While 59% of the average salinity concentration over the 20 year monitoring period was attributable to natural causes (including evaporation), 41% was due to man's activities (mainly irrigation, which accounted for 37%).

Another major concern in the developing countries is the provision of safe drinking water and the hygienic disposal of wastes. A recent WHO survey, covering 1,600 million people (including those of 88 developing countries), found that 77% of the populations surveyed were not satisfactorily served by community water supplies.*

*Irrigation problems*

Irrigation, or the controlled use of water for agriculture, is playing an increasingly important role in increasing production and in reducing its instability. In the Near East, for example, 70% of the total agricultural production is derived from the 35% of the cultivated area that is irrigated.† The benefits of irrigation go far beyond the mere provision of water, since it creates conditions suitable for the optimum use of other inputs, such as fertilizers and high-yielding varieties.

The total irrigated area of the world was 223 million hectares in 1975, and is expected to rise to 273 million hectares by 1990. Table [9–9] shows estimates of the area equipped for irrigation in the developing market economies in 1975, and targets for new irrigation and the improvement of the existing irrigation in these countries by 1990. Irrigation accounted for 66% of the cropped area in Asia in 1975, 19% in the Near East, 13% in Latin America, and only 3% in Africa. The demand for water for irrigation in the developing

* United Nations, *The Demand for Water*, op. cit.
† M. El Gabaly, *Seminar of Committee on Water Research*, Cairo, 1976.

## TABLE 9–8

**Effect of Various Factors on Salt Concentration of Colorado River[a], United States, 1942–61**

|                                | Cumulative Concentration[b] | Percent of Total |
|--------------------------------|:---:|:---:|
| Natural Sources                | 334 | 47 |
| Evaporation                    | 80  | 12 |
| Irrigation (Salt Contribution) | 178 | 26 |
| Irrigation (Consumptive Use)   | 75  | 11 |
| Municipal and Industrial Sources | 10 | 1 |
| Exports Out of the Basin       | 20  | 3  |

[a] At Hoover Dam.
[b] Expressed in miligrams per liter (mg/l.)
Source: United States Environmental Protection Agency, *Summary Report,* 1971.

market economies would increase between 1975 and 1990 by 438 km³, or more than 30% of the total world use of water for irrigation as estimated in Table [9–5] above.

The major irrigation problems arise from water losses due to ineffective or badly managed systems, and from salinity and waterlogging associated with inadequate drainage. As regards the former, the targets shown in Table [9–9] indicate the need for the improvement of almost half of the existing main and on-farm irrigation systems in the developing market economies. About 40% of these improvements are classified as "major." Even under optimum conditions of efficiency, some 25 to 30% of the water used in irrigation schemes is not utilized by the crop, but is lost in run-off, evaporation and percolation. More often the figure is 50% or even more. More efficient irrigation systems, however, require large investments, which must be returned in higher yields and income. The cost of the improvements included in Table [9–9] has been estimated as U.S. $23,000 million at 1975 prices.

As regards salinity and waterlogging problems, salinization is very often associated with irrigation. The causes include unsuitable soils, irrigation with poor quality water (as discussed above), inadequate soil drainage to remove soluble salts, a high water table, and a high evapotranspiration rate. It is estimated that about half of all the irrigated lands of the world have been damaged by salinization, alkanization and water logging.*

Past neglect of drainage, in conjunction with irrigation, has reduced the productivity of millions of hectares, which must now be reclaimed if at all possible. In some cases, large areas of irrigated

---

* FAO/UNESCO, *Soil Map of the World*, Paris, 1964–74.

land have had to be abandoned as a result of soil salinization. The serious extent of this problem is illustrated in Table [9–9]. Improved drainage should be extended to 52 million hectares of irrigated land in the developing market economies, much of it within the 45 million hectares requiring improvements in the irrigation system. The cost of the drainage improvements shown in Table [9–9] has been estimated as U.S. $13,700 million at 1975 prices.

In Pakistan, out of a total of 15 million hectares of irrigated land, about 11 million [73 percent] suffer from salinity, waterlogging or both, resulting in pronounced reductions in crop yields. In Iraq, more than 50% of the Lower Rafadain Plain suffers from salinity and waterlogging. In Syria, about 50% of the irrigated land in the Euphrates Valley is seriously affected, with crop losses worth about U.S. $30 million annually. In Egypt, some 0.8 million hectares, or 30% of the total, are affected, and in Iran over 15% of the irrigated lands.*

Among other factors to be considered, the most important is disease transmission as a result of irrigation. Schistosomiasis is the most serious of the diseases concerned. Irrigation schemes provide a natural environment for its spread, and in one case 60% of the adults and 80% of the children are affected.† Malaria can also thrive on irrigation projects, when havens for vector breeding become established as a result of defective planning and water management.

The problems of irrigation are immense, but the crop production potential due to irrigation is equally great. The solution lies mainly in the rehabilitation and improvement of existing irrigation schemes and the proper installation and subsequent management of new ones. The installation of new schemes will be particularly important in Africa, where irrigated areas are now expanding rapidly.

### Regional Water Projections

Table 9–10 and the accompanying maps show per capita availability of water‡ in 1971 and projected availability in 2000. These projections were developed by the C.I.A. for the Global 2000 Study and are based on data published in 1971 by the Russian hydrologist M. I. L'vovich in his

---

* M. El Gabaly, *op. cit.*
† M. A. Amin, *Problems and Effects of Schistosomiasis in Irrigation Schemes in the Sudan, Khartoum Bilharzia Project.*
‡ Water availability is defined as annual surface (overland) runoff plus ground-water flows.

## TABLE 9-9

### Irrigation and Drainage in the Developing Market Economies, 1975, and Targets, 1990

|  | Africa | Latin America | Near East | Asia | Total |
|---|---|---|---|---|---|
| IRRIGATION (*thousands of hectares*) |  |  |  |  |  |
| Equipped irrigation area, 1975 | 2,610 | 11,749 | 17,105 | 60,522 | 91,986 |
| *Targets, 1990* |  |  |  |  |  |
| New irrigation | 960 | 3,101 | 4,295 | 13,848 | 22,204 |
| Improvements to existing irrigation | 783 | 4,698 | 9,789 | 29,718 | 44,988 |
| minor | 522 | 2,349 | 6,368 | 17,614 | 26,853 |
| major | 261 | 2,349 | 3,421 | 12,104 | 18,135 |
| Increased water demand (*thousands of cubic meters*) | 20 | 33 | 44 | 341 | 438 |
| DRAINAGE (*thousands of hectares*) |  |  |  |  |  |
| Equipped drainage area, 1975 | 7,044 | 46,585 | 18,212 | 62,501 | 134,342 |
| Improvement targets, 1990 | 5,900 | 19,245 | 9,643 | 43,396 | 78,184 |
| on irrigated land | 1,177 | 2,018 | 7,076 | 42,152 | 52,423 |
| on non-irrigated land | 4,723 | 17,227 | 2,567 | 1,244 | 25,761 |

*Source:* United Nations Water Conference, *Water for Agriculture*, 1977, Annex I.

book *Global Water Resources and Their Future.* The projections from the L'vovich data were obtained simply by calculating the percentage change in population by 2000 and reducing proportionately the per capita water availability.

A simple linear extrapolation based on population growth alone obviously ignores many other important factors that could effect a country's water situation (e.g., the level of agricultural development, degree of urbanization, etc.). Indeed, water availability itself is a relatively crude measure of an overall water situation. Nonetheless, population growth will be the *single* most significant cause of increased future demand, and the projections are useful in giving a general indication of potential future problem areas.

By the year 2000 population growth alone of the world will cause at least a doubling in the demand for water in nearly half of the countries of the world. The greatest pressure will be on those countries with low per capita water availability and high population growth, especially in parts of Africa, South Asia, the Middle East, and Latin America. Much of the increased pressure will occur in developing countries where, if improved standards of living are to be realized, water requirements will expand several times. Unfortunately, it is precisely these countries that are least able, both financially and technically, to deal with the problem.

As pressures on water resources increase, conflicts among nations with shared water resources are likely to intensify. Interstate disputes between upstream and downstream users of multinational river basins are particularly apt to occur over questions of water rights and priorities. Longstanding quarrels over the la Plata (Brazil, Argentina), Jordan (Israel, Jordan), Euphrates (Syria, Iraq), Indus (Pakistan, India), and Ganges (Bangladesh, India) could easily worsen as pressures become critical. And the pressures will become critical: *By 2000 the Ganges basin alone will probably contain more than half a billion people!* The potential for conflict is underscored by the fact that approximately 148 of the 200 first-order river basins* of the world are shared by two countries and 52 by three to ten countries. International cooperation and negotiation will have to be pursued as the primary means of preventing and resolving future disputes.

---

* A first-order river basin is one in which the final destination of the basin water flow is an ocean, closed inland sea, or lake.

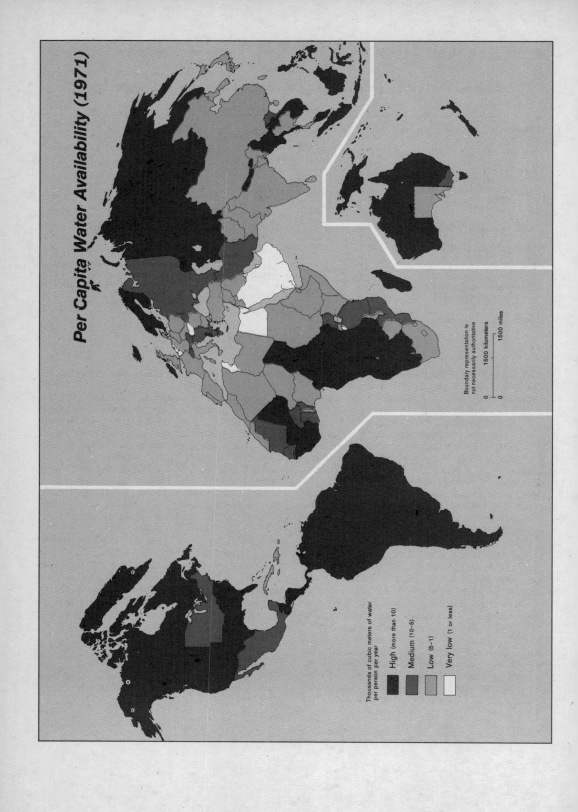

Per Capita Water Availability (1971)

Thousands of cubic meters of water
per person per year

High (more than 10)

Medium (10–5)

Low (5–1)

Very low (1 or less)

Boundary representation is
not necessarily authoritative

0        1500 kilometers

0        1500 miles

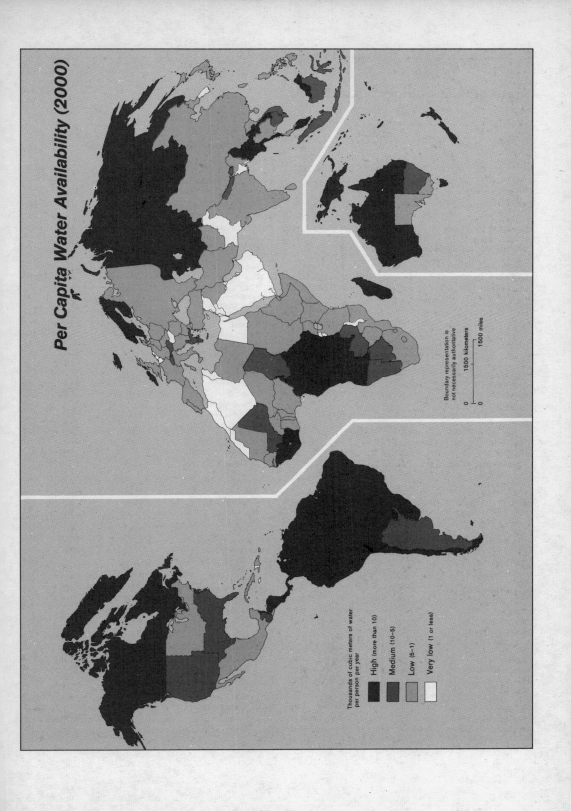

Per Capita Water Availability (2000)

Thousands of cubic meters of water
per person per year

High (more than 10)
Medium (10–5)
Low (5–1)
Very low (1 or less)

Boundary representation is
not necessarily authoritative

0        1500 kilometers
0        1500 miles

## TABLE 9–10

### Per Capita Water Availability, 1971 and 2000

*(Thousands of cubic meters per capita per year)*

| | 1971 [a] | 2000 [b] | Percent Change in Population 1971–2000 |
|---|---|---|---|
| **EUROPE** | | | |
| Finland | 22.5 | 19.9 | 13 |
| Sweden | 24.1 | 21.3 | 13 |
| Norway | 96.9 | 81.4 | 19 |
| Denmark | 3.0 | 2.7 | 13 |
| Iceland | 319.0 | 209.9 | 52 |
| Netherlands | 0.8 | 0.6 | 30 |
| Belgium & Luxembourg | 0.9 | 0.8 | 7 |
| France | 4.6 | 3.8 | 21 |
| Great Britain | 2.7 | 2.0 | 34 |
| Ireland | 13.7 | 11.1 | 23 |
| Switzerland | 7.3 | 6.5 | 13 |
| Austria | 7.7 | 7.6 | 1 |
| Portugal | 2.8 | 2.5 | 13 |
| Spain | 3.9 | 2.8 | 39 |
| Italy | 3.0 | 2.4 | 26 |
| Yugoslavia | 6.0 | 4.6 | 30 |
| Albania | 10.2 | 5.5 | 87 |
| Greece | 7.4 | 6.4 | 16 |
| West Germany | 1.4 | 1.3 | 9 |
| East Germany | 1.2 | 1.2 | 1 |
| Czechoslovakia | 1.9 | 1.5 | 27 |
| Hungary | 0.8 | 0.7 | 20 |
| Romania | 1.8 | 1.3 | 40 |
| Bulgaria | 2.1 | 1.7 | 23 |
| Poland | 1.7 | 1.3 | 35 |
| | | | |
| **ASIA** | | | |
| U.S.S.R. | 17.8 | 13.6 | 31 |
| European Portion | 6.2 | 4.7 | 31 |
| Asian Portion | 39.1 | 29.8 | 31 |
| Mongolia | 36.7 | 14.5 | 153 |
| P.R. China | 3.8 | 2.7 | 42 |
| Japan | 3.8 | 2.7 | 43 |
| North Korea | 5.0 | 2.0 | 153 |
| South Korea | 1.9 | 1.0 | 93 |
| Afghanistan | 4.4 | 2.2 | 96 |
| Iran | 6.0 | 2.5 | 145 |
| Iraq | 3.6 | 1.3 | 173 |
| Turkey | 4.9 | 2.3 | 118 |
| Cyprus | 0.06 | 0.05 | 22 |
| Syria | 3.0 | 1.0 | 165 |
| Countries of the Arabian Peninsula | 0.7 | 0.3 | 106 |
| Pakistan | 1.1 | 0.5 | 125 |
| Bangladesh | 1.8 | 0.9 | 102 |
| India | 2.9 | 1.5 | 92 |
| Sri Lanka | 4.7 | 2.8 | 69 |
| Nepal | 11.0 | 5.6 | 95 |
| Burma | 24.6 | 13.2 | 86 |
| Thailand | 4.8 | 2.0 | 135 |
| Laos | 77.0 | 37.0 | 108 |
| Cambodia | 17.5 | 7.4 | 135 |
| N. Vietnam | 8.2 | 4.9 | 68 |
| S. Vietnam | 11.0 | 5.7 | 92 |
| Philippines | 10.1 | 4.2 | 139 |
| Malaysia, Singapore & Brunei | 33.3 | 14.4 | 132 |

| | 1971 [a] | 2000 [b] | Percent Change in Population 1971–2000 |
|---|---|---|---|
| Indonesia (excluding Western New Guinea & Portuguese Timor | 13.0 | 6.7 | 95 |
| **AFRICA** | | | |
| Tunisia | 0.9 | 0.4 | 126 |
| Algeria | 2.2 | 1.0 | 111 |
| Morocco | 2.1 | 0.9 | 132 |
| Libya | 3.7 | 1.2 | 198 |
| Egypt | 0.1 | 0.05 | 111 |
| Sudan | 4.0 | 1.9 | 107 |
| W. Sahara [b] | 1.8 | 0.9 | 94 |
| Mauritania | 7.0 | 3.6 | 94 |
| Mali | 12.4 | 5.6 | 121 |
| Niger | 3.5 | 1.7 | 101 |
| Benin | 5.7 | 2.7 | 111 |
| Nigeria | 4.7 | 2.4 | 96 |
| Togo | 4.5 | 1.9 | 139 |
| Ghana | 7.8 | 3.1 | 150 |
| Upper Volta | 5.2 | 2.7 | 92 |
| Ivory Coast | 30.8 | 14.3 | 115 |
| Liberia | 198.0 | 89.6 | 121 |
| Sierra Leone | 63.7 | 30.5 | 109 |
| Guinea | 57.6 | 30.8 | 87 |
| Guinea-Bissau | 55.4 | 38.7 | 43 |
| The Gambia | 4.4 | 2.8 | 58 |
| Senegal | 5.9 | 2.9 | 106 |
| Cameroon | 45.9 | 24.4 | 88 |
| Chad | 10.4 | 5.6 | 85 |
| Cen. African Empire | 92.8 | 49.4 | 88 |
| Congo | 192.0 | 108.5 | 77 |
| Zaire | 58.4 | 34.6 | 69 |
| Gabon | 328.0 | 258.3 | 27 |
| Equatorial Guinea | 103.0 | 61.7 | 67 |
| Ethiopia | 4.6 | 2.1 | 115 |
| Somali | 3.9 | 1.8 | 115 |
| Kenya | 3.4 | 1.2 | 191 |
| Uganda | 6.8 | 2.6 | 166 |
| Tanzania | 5.7 | 2.4 | 142 |
| Rwanda | 1.8 | 0.8 | 135 |
| Burundi | 1.0 | 0.6 | 81 |
| Malawi | 2.0 | 1.0 | 108 |
| Zambia | 22.3 | 8.5 | 161 |
| Malagasy Republic | 33.6 | 16.9 | 99 |
| Mozambique | 8.0 | 4.0 | 102 |
| S. Rhodesia | 4.4 | 1.6 | 169 |
| Namibia | 14.3 | 7.4 | 93 |
| Botswana | 13.8 | 7.2 | 92 |
| Rep. S. Africa | 2.9 | 1.3 | 128 |
| Lesotho | 3.9 | 2.1 | 85 |
| Angola | 29.5 | 15.3 | 93 |
| | | | |
| **NORTH AMERICA** | | | |
| Canada | 128.0 | 83.0 | 54 |
| Yukon & N.W. Territories | 5200.0 | 3376.6 | 54 |
| British Columbia | 381.0 | 247.0 | 54 |
| Eastern Provinces | 87.5 | 56.8 | 54 |
| United States (48) | 8.4 | 6.6 | 27 |
| Western States | 12.0 | 9.4 | 27 |
| Northern States | 5.4 | 4.3 | 27 |
| Southern States | 11.6 | 9.1 | 27 |
| Alaska | 2033.0 | 1600.8 | 27 |
| Mexico | 5.5 | 1.9 | 185 |

**TABLE 9–10 (continued)**

| | 1971 [a] | 2000 [b] | Percent Change in Population 1971–2000 |
|---|---|---|---|
| **CENTRAL AMERICA, WEST INDIES** | | | |
| Guatemala | 15.1 | 7.0 | 113 |
| Belize | 123.0 | 63.7 | 93 |
| Salvador | 4.2 | 1.7 | 146 |
| Honduras | 38.0 | 15.3 | 148 |
| Nicaragua | 71.7 | 27.9 | 157 |
| Costa Rica | 41.4 | 22.3 | 86 |
| Panama | 54.8 | 25.1 | 118 |
| Cuba | 3.1 | 1.8 | 74 |
| Jamaica | 1.1 | 0.6 | 93 |
| Haiti | 1.4 | 0.8 | 81 |
| Dominican Rep. | 2.8 | 1.2 | 142 |
| **SOUTH AMERICA** | | | |
| Argentina | 11.9 | 7.7 | 54 |
| Uruguay | 20.4 | 15.9 | 28 |
| Paraguay | 39.3 | 19.0 | 107 |
| Brazil | 59.5 | 26.0 | 128 |
| French Guiana | 2400.0 | 1034.5 | 132 |
| Surinam | 513 | 251.5 | 104 |
| Guyana | 317 | 164.2 | 93 |
| Venezuela | 73.2 | 28.5 | 157 |
| Colombia | 52.7 | 22.5 | 134 |
| Ecuador | 52.2 | 22.7 | 130 |
| Peru | 59.6 | 26.1 | 128 |
| Bolivia | 60.8 | 28.7 | 112 |
| Chile | 47.8 | 28.6 | 67 |
| **AUSTRALIA AND NEW ZEALAND** | | | |
| Australia | 678.0 | 452.0 | 50 |
| W. Australia | 62.6 | 41.7 | 50 |
| N. Territory | 757.0 | 504.7 | 50 |
| S. Australia | 4.5 | 3.0 | 50 |
| Queensland | 76.8 | 51.2 | 50 |
| New South Wales | 12.0 | 8.0 | 50 |
| Victoria | 5.5 | 3.7 | 50 |
| Tasmania | 123.0 | 82.0 | 50 |
| New Guinea Island | 30.4 | 13.9 | 119 |
| New Zealand | 136.0 | 72.0 | 89 |
| N. Island | 56.9 | 30.1 | 89 |
| S. Island | 346.0 | 183.0 | 89 |

[a] These numbers, in thousands of cubic meters per capita per year, have the following approximate meaning: A value of 1.0 or under is a very low availability; 1.0–5.0 is low; 5.0–10.0 is medium; 10.0 or above is high.
[b] The population projections used here are the Bureau of Census medium series developed for this Study. Projections for countries not listed in Chapter 2 were obtained directly from Census personnel. Western Sahara's projection is based on Mauritania's population change figure because available data for Western Sahara was unreliable.
Sources: The 1971 figures were taken from M. I. L'vovich, *Global Water Resources and Their Future* (in Russian), 1974. The 2000 figures were obtained by calculating the percentage change in population and reducing proportionally the per capita water availability.

## Future Water Resources

World water withdrawals for 1975 aggregated less than $3 \times 10^{12}$ cubic meters per year, while the lower-bound supply estimate is more than an order of magnitude greater, nearly $4 \times 10^{13}$ cubic meters per year. Other estimates indicate that nearly 60 percent of all water withdrawn is returned to the environment, so the actual global total of water consumed may be no more than 3 per cent of the aggregate water supply. Barring substantial climatic change, the supply estimate should remain constant throughout the near future, while water withdrawals climb steadily with population and rising agricultural and industrial output. Even if water withdrawals were to increase by a factor of 7 by the year 2000 (the Kalinin forecast), only about 50 per cent of aggregate supply would be withdrawn, and about 15 percent actually consumed.

Comforting as such figures may be, they are misleading. In fact, any significant increase in the rate of water withdrawal, even a doubling by the year 2000, is virtually certain to cause major water supply problems. The use of energy and other resources by the water supply sector will increase dramatically. Water shortages will become more frequent, and their effects will be more widespread and more severe. The availability of water will become an even more binding constraint on the location of economic development. The notion of water as a free good available in essentially limitless quantities will have disappeared throughout much of the world.

These less encouraging predictions stem from recognition of the intensely local nature of a water resource. There exists no world water economy, and it is rarely meaningful to speak of a national water economy. Most water economies exist within smaller hydrologic provinces, in single river basins, adjoining basins connected by water transmission facilities and the like. When the supply in such a limited area falls short of the attempted withdrawals, water shortages occur, regardless of the quantities of water available in neighboring basins. It may also be true that attempted water withdrawals cannot be maintained during a period of low streamflow, even though adequate water is available in the same stream at other times.

This nonuniform distribution of water, both in space and in time, is the fundamental cause of the uniquely local nature of water supply problems. When data are summed or averaged over a number of water supply areas, the nonuniformity is concealed, and water resources may appear to be adequate when, in fact, serious shortages are likely to occur.

When shortages do occur or are considered likely to occur, a number of steps can be taken. First, the supply may be augmented.

One approach to augmentation consists of transferring water in space and/or time so as to meet the requirements of attempted withdrawals. Water is transferred in space by constructing or employing transportation facilities (such as water transmission mains) to move water from an area where it is not required to the area of potential shortage. Water is transferred in time by constructing storage facilities, usually major impoundments on existing streams. Due to the very large quantities of water involved, transmission over large distances is very expensive, requiring large commitments of energy. Major storage projects are also expensive, and may have the added disadvantage of increasing total evaporation, thus reducing the total supply available. Both actions have the potential of permanently altering natural landscapes, and of creating ecological disruptions. However, water shortages that result from a lack of adequate storage capacity may entail high economic and social costs.

Another means of supply augmentation requires increased reuse of return flows from other water users. This may require rearranging the sequence of uses so that those requiring the highest quality come first, followed by users who are increasingly tolerant of lower-quality water. More often, reuse may be increased by the installation of improved treatment facilities, either at the first user's effluent or the second user's intake. Such measures are costly, and they consume significant quantities of energy and, perhaps, various chemicals. Changes in the quality of the environment may occur directly, or as the result of decreased streamflows below the region of more intensive water use.

The second step taken in the case of water shortage involves reducing rates of water use. This may occur through economic incentive, as increasing scarcity drives the price of water higher, encouraging water users to substitute other goods or other inputs for the use of water. It may occur administratively, as users either voluntarily invoke water conservation practices or do so because of regulation or because of reductions in water allocations. Water use may also be reduced by stimulating the introduction of new, less water-intensive technology (cooling towers for power-plants, or drip irrigation).

Finally, when possibilities for supply augmentation and for water-use reduction have been exhausted, and withdrawals still threaten to exceed available supply, water must be allocated among several uses, so that the damages incurred as a result of shortage will be minimized. In the absence of such allocation, the available water is used on a first come, first served basis, until the water supply fails entirely. Supply failure creates a potential for public health problems, industrial shutdowns, and massive crop failures (which also have human health implications).

Some of the measures outlined here can only be implemented after relatively long-term planning and construction (water transmission and storage facilities, for example); others are available on an immediate short-term basis (water-use reduction techniques not involving new technology). The measures requiring construction have the potential of creating adverse environmental effects, and some may imply large increases in the use of energy. It may be advantageous to engage in still longer-term planning, so as to facilitate the location of future water-using activities in areas better able to provide the necessary water. Again, these considerations and findings depend upon specific, area by area analyses of water supply and demand; they cannot be obtained from national aggregate data.

## Conclusions

There will apparently be adequate water available on the earth to satisfy aggregate projected water withdrawals in the year 2000; the same finding holds for each of the continents. Nevertheless, because of the regional and temporal nature of the water resource, water shortages even before 2000 will probably be more frequent and more severe than those experienced today.

By the year 2000 population growth alone of the world will cause at least a doubling in the demand for water in nearly half of the countries of the world. The greatest pressure will be on those countries with low per capita water availability and high population growth, especially in parts of Africa, South Asia, the Middle East, and Latin America. Much of the increased pressure will occur in developing countries where, if improved standards of living are to be realized, water requirements will expand several times. Unfortunately, it is precisely these countries that are least able, both financially and technically, to deal with the problem.

Although irrigated land comprises only 13% of the world's total arable area, irrigation accounts for by far the largest proportion of the total water used by man and will continue to be the greatest water consumer in the future. The total irrigated area of the world was 223 million hectares in 1975, and is expected to rise to 273 million hectares by 1990. As a result the demand for water for irrigation in the developing market economies alone would increase between 1975 and 1990 by 438 cubic kilometers, or more than 30 percent of the current total world use of water for irrigation.

The need for water resources, however, goes beyond quantity and must also consider quality. The harmful effects of waste disposal on quality are well known, but a major unseen problem is the increasing salinity of water resources with use—particularly irrigation use. Increasing salinity is an inevitable process in nature, but man has greatly accelerated it and, with continued increases in the intensity of use, the problem will become greater.

Salinization is very often associated with irrigation. The causes include unsuitable soils, irrigation with poor quality water (as discussed above), inadequate soil drainage to remove soluble salts, a high water table, and a high evapotranspiration rate. It is estimated that about half of all the irrigated lands of the world have been damaged by salinization, alkalinization and waterlogging. In some cases, large areas of irrigated land have had to be abandoned as a result of soil salinization. Past neglect of drainage, in conjunction with irrigation, has reduced the productivity of millions of hectares, which must now be reclaimed if at all possible.

As pressures on water resources increase, conflicts among nations with shared water resources are likely to intensify. Interstate disputes between upstream and downstream users of multinational river basins are particularly apt to occur over questions of water rights and priorities. Long-standing quarrels could easily worsen as pressures become critical.

# 10  Energy Projections

This chapter presents U.S. and world energy forecasts for the midrange (1985–90) and the long range (to the year 2000). The forecasts, made during the spring of 1978, endeavor to reflect a range of uncertainty in future economic and demographic growth by presenting three projections of energy consumption trends. The analysis also examines how these demands would be satisfied by development of energy supply in a market environment. The midrange forecasts were made for the Global 2000 Study. The long-range forecasts, made by other organizations, are compared to the trend in the midrange projections. The regional changes in energy trade and per capita consumption between 1975 and 1990 implied by the forecasts are summarized in the maps on the following two pages.

The conclusions can be summarized as follows. On the consumption side:

- The connection between economic growth and energy demand growth is projected to continue at least through 1990, moderated only by potential price increases.
- Current analysis of the effect of relative and overall levels of energy prices on the structure of energy demand shows that there is a strong potential for fuel substitution in energy consumption.
- However, current medium and high economic growth projections appear to lead to situations in which significantly higher prices for petroleum will be required to equilibrate supply and demand by fuel substitution and other means of petroleum demand reduction.
- In the very long term, there appears to be considerable potential for aggressive, conservation-induced reductions in energy consumption.

On the energy supply side:

- Petroleum production capability is not increasing as fast as demand. Depending upon economic growth and conservation, a supply-constrained market appears to be a strong possibility for the late 1980s.
- In the long term, the rate of petroleum reserve additions appears to be falling. As a result, engineering considerations indicate that world

petroleum production will peak in the 1990–2010 interval at 80–105 million barrels per day, with ultimate resources estimated at 2,100 billion barrels.
- There is a substantial potential for growth in the coal and natural gas supplies beyond the year 2000.

Since there was not sufficient time to evaluate a range of possible global long-term projections, there is a degree of inconsistency in the long-run view that can be resolved only by further careful long-term analysis of the projections or an independent long-run projection exercise.

## Basic Assumptions

The underlying assumptions of the forecasts in this chapter take into account many uncertainties in key variables and thus reflect a range of future outcomes. Projections of energy supply and demand levels require estimates of economic variables as well as estimates of possible technological—and to some extent political—changes. The major variables used to drive the forecasts are: gross domestic product (GDP) and population ranges*; price assumptions; the behavior of the Organization of Petroleum Exporting Countries (OPEC); technological penetration; and conservation.

*GDP/Population Ranges.* Future energy growth is determined primarily by future economic growth, as reflected in GDP and population changes. This analysis assumes that there will be no structural changes. In this analysis, one complete set of projections was developed for each of the Global 2000 medium, low, and high GDP and population growth-rate assumptions. These three economic projections are designed to cover the range of possible outcomes.

*Price Assumptions.* Energy price assumptions affect the levels of consumption and determine the competitiveness of all new technologies. They

---

*Results calculated for the Administrator's Annual Report are not entirely comparable with Global 2000 Study figures because different economic and demographic growth rates were assumed.

# Energy Consumption Per Capita (1975-1990)

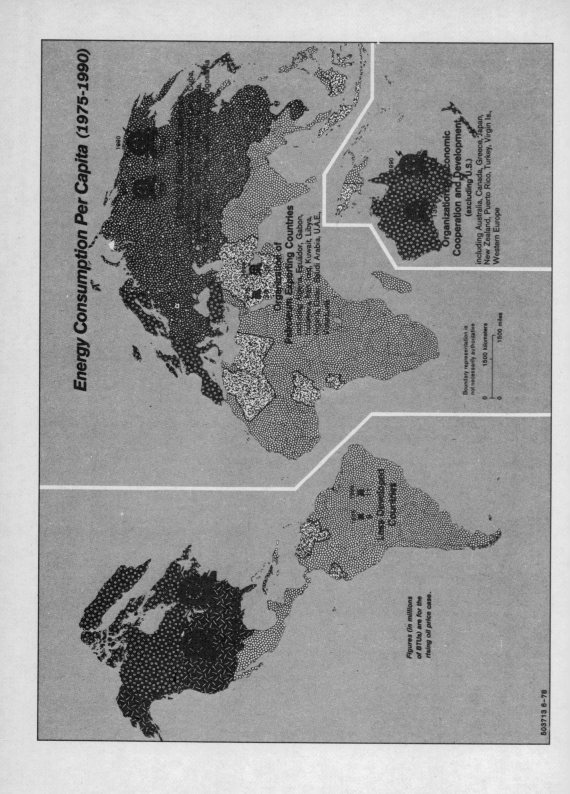

Organization of
Petroleum Exporting Countries
including Algeria, Equador, Gabon,
Indonesia, Iran, Iraq, Kuwait, Libya,
Nigeria, Qatar, Saudi Arabia, U.A.E.,
Venezuela

Organization for Economic
Cooperation and Development
(excluding U.S.)
including Australia, Canada, Greece, Japan,
New Zealand, Puerto Rico, Turkey, Virgin Is.,
Western Europe

Less Developed
Countries

Boundary representation is
not necessarily authoritative

0        1500 kilometers

0        1500 miles

Figures (in millions
of BTUs) are for the
rising oil price case.

503713 6-78

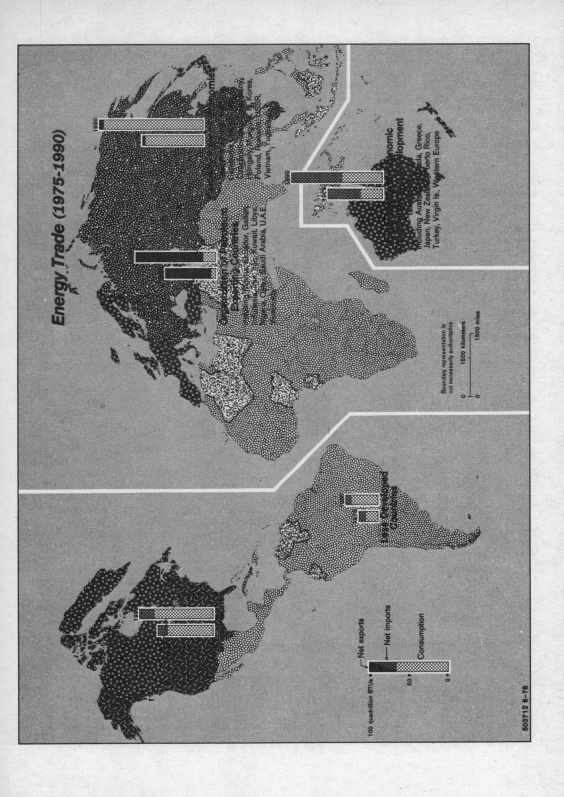

Energy Trade (1975-1990)

Net exports
Net imports
Consumption

100 quadrillion BTUs
50
0

Boundary representation is
not necessarily authoritative

0    1500 kilometers
0    1500 miles

503712 6-78

are dependent not only on traditional supply and demand conditions but also on the actions of the OPEC cartel in adjusting the price of the marginal supply of oil.

The first set of projections in this chapter is based on a constant real oil price of $13 per barrel in 1975 dollars through the year 2000. However, rising oil prices appear to be a strong possibility. Strong upward pressure on world energy prices in the 1980–90 period may result from resource conservation policies of producer countries and rapidly rising world demand. A second projection is then generated, using the assumption that oil prices rise at a real rate of 5 percent per annum between 1980 and 1990.

*OPEC Behavior.* OPEC currently controls the price of international crude oil. More intense competition among oil importing countries for the available OPEC supply is expected in the future, so OPEC pricing policies remain speculative.

It is possible that the demand for oil will exceed maximum world production well before the year 2000. This will ultimately lead to resource depletion, and many OPEC nations face a future where oil is no longer their principal asset. To extend this transition period, some oil producing countries may adopt resource conservation measures and output ceilings, resulting in higher real oil prices.

*Technological Penetration.* The characteristics and economics of technologies can have dramatic effects on the overall projections. Of equal importance are the assumed availability and rate of penetration of competitive technologies. Improved technology can provide for the full utilization of renewable resources in the long run. Most alternative technologies are not now economic, but higher energy prices and limited conventional supply prospects encourage their development. Both hard and soft technologies are considered in the forecasts, with potential impacts being realized in some cases through 1985, in others not until after 2000. The eventual result will probably encompass a blend of different technologies that most efficiently and economically meets the diverse consumption requirements.

*Conservation.* Energy conserving policies may originate from both consumer and producer groups. As energy prices increase demand will decrease. Possible structural changes will further reduce demand. Shifts are introduced by changes in the efficiency of the capital stock either by turning over the stock at a faster than normal rate, by retrofitting the stock, or by introducing new, more efficient capital into the stock. Conservation may also be encouraged through governmental policies aimed at controlling environmental damage.

## Midrange Energy Forecasts, 1985–90

The energy forecasts will be presented in two phases: midrange extrapolations covering 1985–90 and long-range extrapolations extending to the year 2000. This division is made necessary by the differing philosophical approaches used in the forecasts.

This section presents an analysis of three scenarios chosen to illustrate the range of possible variations in world economic and demographic trends, with regional and world energy balances presented for 1985 and 1990. The scenarios are unconstrained in the sense that unlimited world oil supplies are assumed available at constant real oil prices to 1990. A modified energy projection is also developed, assuming annual energy price increases of 5 percent from 1980 through 1990.

The basic assumptions of the model are the analyst's representation of the way the energy system operates. In this analysis this system is understood to be a market in which sellers of natural resources—oil, coal, and gas—are competing to satisfy the demands for energy. In the midrange forecasts demand is based primarily upon past trends, driven by economic activity, energy prices, and the growth of energy-consuming stock. The actual demand for energy products is constrained by technological limits imposed by: our ability to satisfy end-use demands for heat, transportation, mechanical drive, etc., with primary fuels; our ability to generate secondary fuels and energy such as gasoline, distillate, and electricity from primary fuels; and our ability to convey primary fuels to points of conversion and generation.*

The midrange model of the energy market equilibrates supply and demand under these constraints in a competitive market simulation. Forecasts are generated using two equilibrium representations, the Project Independence Evaluation System (PIES) for the U.S. and the International

---

*For example, natural gas remains in Saudi Arabia because there is no practical way to transport it to New York for use as home heat. Likewise, excess natural gas in New York would be useless as a fuel for automobile transportation. These anomalies limit our current ability to satisfy requirements for services. Long-term planning should be directed toward satisfying actual end-use requirements with primary sources. In contrast, midrange planning is predominately concerned with providing secondary fuels, using our existing conversion, transportation, and delivery capability.

Energy Evaluation System (IEES) for the rest of the world. Results of the PIES analysis are used in IEES to represent the United States.

In both PIES and IEES, energy sector demands are determined on the basis of past experience as functions of product prices, economic activity (GNP or GDP), and a lag term to estimate capital stock changes. After determining total sectoral Btu (British thermal unit) demands, individual product demands are estimated as functions of relative prices and stock changes. Given this demand slate, an integrating analysis uses a supply function derived from fuel specific supply and conversion models to produce supply estimates. An iterative approach is then used to adjust prices until an energy market equilibrium is reached between supply and demand. Detailed representations of energy transportation, conversion (by utilities and other processes), and refining are employed to capture the effects of the existing capital stock of coal, oil, and gas consuming equipment and and changes as this equipment is replaced by new building programs. The methodology is described in greater detail in Chapter 20 of this volume.

The two principal uncertainties in forecasting consumption are also the most important variables—economic and population growth. Three alternative projections of each were used as the basis for the low, medium, and high cases (Tables 10–1 and 10–2).

The medium case assumes medium population and GNP growth; the high case assumes low population and high GNP growth; and the low case assumes high population and low GNP growth. For the less developed regions, popula-

## TABLE 10–1

### Real GNP Growth Rate Assumptions

(*Compound annual percent*)

| | 1976–85 | | | 1985–2000 | | |
|---|---|---|---|---|---|---|
| | High | Me-dium | Low | High | Me-dium | Low |
| OPEC | 7.2 | 6.35 | 5.5 | 6.5 | 5.4 | 4.3 |
| Low-income LDCs | 4.4 | 3.6 | 2.8 | 3.1 | 2.8 | 2.5 |
| Medium-income LDCs | 6.6 | 5.55 | 4.5 | 4.9 | 4.4 | 3.9 |
| OECD nations | 4.9 | 4.0 | 3.1 | 3.7 | 3.1 | 2.5 |
| Soviet bloc (excluding U.S.S.R.) | 3.5 | 3.25 | 3.0 | 3.0 | 2.75 | 2.5 |
| U.S.S.R. | 3.5 | 3.25 | 3.0 | 3.0 | 2.75 | 2.5 |
| China | 5.0 | 3.75 | 2.5 | 5.0 | 3.75 | 2.5 |

## TABLE 10–2

### Population Growth Rate Assumptions

(*Compound annual percent*)

| | 1976–85 | | | 1985–2000 | | |
|---|---|---|---|---|---|---|
| | High | Me-dium | Low | High | Me-dium | Low |
| United States | .96 | .70 | .51 | .94 | .55 | .27 |
| Canada | 1.1 | .92 | .70 | 1.20 | .90 | .59 |
| Japan | .91 | .88 | .81 | .58 | .67 | .53 |
| Europe | .35 | .32 | .30 | .48 | .42 | .34 |

*Note:* The energy demands of the less developed countries, OPEC nations, and centrally planned economies are not modeled as being sensitive to population growth rates and therefore are not presented in this table.

tion is not an exogenous variable in the determination of energy demands, so changes in population growth rates influence energy demand only insofar as they are reflected in GNP growth rates. All other exogenous variables are held constant. The common assumptions for this set of projections are:

- A real oil price of $13 per barrel (in 1975 dollars, CIF U.S. East Coast) is maintained through the year 2000.
- OPEC is the world's unconstrained marginal supplier of crude oil.
- The base-case situation for the U.S. includes natural gas regulation and crude oil price control.
- OECD country policies regarding conservation, taxation, import tariffs, and supply development are fixed. (Their relative contributions, shown in the 1978 annual report of the Department of Energy's Energy Information Administration, are discussed below in the uncertainty section.)
- Development policies of the less developed countries (LDCs) continue on their present course (energy demand tied to GDP growth), with no special OPEC oil price arrangement for LDCs.

The result of the calculations is a set of world and regional equilibrium energy balances for 1985 and 1990 for all three growth scenarios (Tables 10–4 and 10–5). Table 10–3 summarizes the forecasts for total oil and total energy.

For 1985 U.S. energy demand ranges from 87 quadrillion Btu (quads) in the low GNP case to 102 quads in the high GNP case, the range for world demand being 329–352 quads. World oil consumption is forecast to be in the range of 71–86 million barrels per day (mb/d) in 1985, with U.S. oil consumption between 19–24 mb/d. Average annual 1975–90 growth rates range from 3.3 to 4.4 percent for total energy and 2.8 to 4.5 percent

## TABLE 10–3

### Total World Oil and Energy Consumption, 1985 and 1990, and Average Annual Growth Rates, 1975–90

|  | Total Oil (thousands bbl/d) | | Total Energy ($10^{15}$ Btu) | | Average Annual Growth Rate 1975–90 (percent) | |
|---|---|---|---|---|---|---|
|  | 1985 | 1990 | 1985 | 1990 | Oil | Total Energy |
| High GNP | 86,318 | 102,266 | 375 | 448 | 4.5 | 4.4 |
| Medium GNP | 78,256 | 90,105 | 352 | 414 | 3.7 | 3.8 |
| Low GNP | 71,235 | 79,581 | 329 | 379 | 2.8 | 3.3 |

for world oil. The corresponding pre-embargo growth rates were 5.1 percent for energy and 7.7 percent for oil for the 1966–73 period. The principal change is the lowering of economic growth rates as higher prices affect consumption and conservation.

In Table 10–5, predicted world energy consumption for 1990 has risen to 379–448 quads and U.S. consumption to 96–111 quads. Both medium and high GNP growth demands for oil exceed estimated OPEC productive capacity and thus are probably infeasible. U.S. oil demand is in the 20–25 mb/d range and world demand between 80 and 103 mb/d. For the same year, U.S. oil imports are predicted at 10–15 mb/d. World coal consumption varies from a high of 5.2 billion short tons per year to 4.6 billion. Natural gas consumption is predicted to be between 59 and 66 trillion cubic feet per year.

### The Role of Uncertainty

The midrange forecasts display a range of possible economic outcomes but do not incorporate uncertainties such as:

- Energy supply from the centrally planned economies. Forecasts of their uncertain role in the international market between 1985 and 1990 range from net exports of 1 mb/d to net imports of 4–5 mb/d.

- Non-OPEC supply. Estimates show an uncertainty of ±3.0 mb/d in 1985 and ±3.5 mb/d in 1990 for the midrange estimate assumed here.

- OECD conservation programs. These were assessed at conservative midrange values in this forecast. A more aggressive upper range assessment places this saving at 2.5 mb/d in 1985 and 3.5 mb/d in 1990.

Figure 10–1 shows the uncertainty bands for projected total demand for OPEC oil. The spread of uncertainty around the base-line economic projections (shown by the shaded bands) illustrates an extreme range of demand levels that consider the highest and lowest possible outcomes. The projected demand for OPEC oil under the high price assumption, discussed below, is also shown in the figure. Rest-of-world demand for OPEC oil becomes lower—approaching the most favorable line—as the non-OPEC supply of oil increases and conservation measures are successful. Higher dependence on OPEC oil results if non-OPEC production is at the bottom of the expected range and energy consumption increases faster than projected. The broad range of possibilities occurs because of the potential difference between non-OPEC supply and demand. Also, the potential error in computing the high and low bands is additive, the extremes being realized only with certain combinations of events. Projections of high, medium, and low made with moderate conservation and supply assumptions can be regarded as the most probable limits.

### OPEC Pricing

Another significant unknown is OPEC pricing policy for Saudi Arabian reference crude. OPEC is a 13-member assembly of countries with a broad range of economic potential, per capita income, oil reserves, and development requirements. Table 10–6 illustrates this range for all less developed, oil exporting countries, including non-OPEC members. Current production levels are compared with capacity and future production potential based upon proved reserves. Note that countries with high per capita incomes such as Kuwait and Saudi Arabia have surplus production capacity and large financial reserves. Because of diversity among OPEC members, the forecast level of oil prices as determined at biannual meetings is based on essentially speculative factors.

From the oil market point of view, OPEC membership is not important because the cartel oil price determines the price of incremental oil production. If the market is viewed as essentially competitive, all oil, regardless of the source, is priced to compete in its own market with oil from this spare capacity.

The low-income countries—Indonesia, Mexico, Nigeria, Algeria—have an incentive to shade their prices relative to the reference price in order to maximize sales and revenues. With their prices slightly lower than the established OPEC price,

## TABLE 10–4
## Regional Energy Balances, 1985

| | United States | Industrial- ized Countries[a] | Less Developed Countries | OPEC Countries | Centrally Planned Economies | World |
|---|---|---|---|---|---|---|
| Oil | | | MEDIUM GNP GROWTH | | | |
| *(thousands bbl/day)* | | | | | | |
| Production | 10,234 | 16,276 | 7,429 | 39,257 | 15,295 | 78,256 |
| Imports | 11,288 | 34,066 | 2,816 | −35,579 | −1,304 | |
| Consumption | 21,522 | 50,342 | 10,245 | 3,678 | 13,992 | 78,256 |
| Natural gas | | | | | | |
| *(billions cu ft/yr)* | | | | | | |
| Production | 16,731 | 29,215 | 3,034 | 5,879 | 18,339 | 56,468 |
| Imports | 1,844 | 3,414 | −600 | −2,164 | −654 | |
| Consumption | 18,575 | 32,629 | 2,433 | 3,720 | 17,684 | 56,468 |
| Coal | | | | | | |
| *(millions short tons/yr)* | | | | | | |
| Production | 1,038 | 1,726 | 426 | 5 | 2,616 | 4,772 |
| Imports | −74 | 97 | −42 | — | −55 | |
| Consumption | 964 | 1,823 | 384 | 5 | 2,561 | 4,772 |
| Nuclear, hydro, solar, geothermal | | | | | | |
| *(terawatt-hr/yr)* | 975 | 2,515 | 585 | 19 | 760 | 3,879 |
| Total energy consumption | | | | | | |
| *(quadrillion Btu)* | 96 | 203 | 39 | 12 | 98 | 352 |
| Oil | | | HIGH GNP GROWTH | | | |
| *(thousands bbl/day)* | | | | | | |
| Production | 10,240 | 16,290 | 7,452 | 47,280 | 15,295 | 86,318 |
| Imports | 13,647 | 40,292 | 3,788 | −43,186 | −894 | |
| Consumption | 23,887 | 56,583 | 11,240 | 4,094 | 14,401 | 86,318 |
| Natural gas | | | | | | |
| *(billions cu ft/yr)* | | | | | | |
| Production | 16,808 | 29,806 | 3,262 | 6,582 | 18,980 | 58,630 |
| Imports | 1,987 | 3,905 | −600 | −2,532 | −773 | |
| Consumption | 18,794 | 33,711 | 2,662 | 4,050 | 18,207 | 58,630 |
| Coal | | | | | | |
| *(millions short tons/yr)* | | | | | | |
| Production | 1,102 | 1,844 | 462 | 6 | 2,394 | 4,706 |
| Imports | −74 | 97 | −42 | — | −55 | |
| Consumption | 1,028 | 1,941 | 420 | 6 | 2,339 | 4,706 |
| Nuclear, hydro, solar, geothermal | | | | | | |
| *(terawatt-hr/yr)* | 976 | 2,516 | 585 | 19 | 760 | 3,880 |
| Total energy consumption | | | | | | |
| *(quadrillion Btu)* | 102 | 220 | 43 | 13 | 99 | 375 |
| Oil | | | LOW GNP GROWTH | | | |
| *(thousands bbl/day)* | | | | | | |
| Production | 10,231 | 16,273 | 7,405 | 32,261 | 15,295 | 71,235 |
| Imports | 9,259 | 28,793 | 1,875 | −28,966 | −1,702 | |
| Consumption | 19,490 | 45,065 | 9,280 | 3,296 | 13,594 | 71,235 |
| Natural gas | | | | | | |
| *(billions cu ft/yr)* | | | | | | |
| Production | 16,677 | 27,847 | 2,807 | 5,307 | 17,831 | 53,791 |
| Imports | 1,724 | 3,160 | −600 | −1,905 | −654 | |
| Consumption | 18,401 | 31,007 | 2,207 | 3,401 | 17,176 | 53,791 |
| Coal | | | | | | |
| *(millions short tons/yr)* | | | | | | |
| Production | 973 | 1,597 | 392 | 5 | 2,305 | 4,299 |
| Imports | −74 | 97 | −42 | — | −55 | |
| Consumption | 899 | 1,694 | 350 | 5 | 2,250 | 4,299 |
| Nuclear, hydro, solar, geothermal | | | | | | |
| *(terawatt-hr/yr)* | 969 | 2,492 | 585 | 19 | 760 | 3,856 |
| Total energy consumption | | | | | | |
| *(quadrillion Btu)* | 90 | 188 | 30 | 11 | 86 | 315 |

[a] All OECD countries, including the U.S.

# TABLE 10–5
## Regional Energy Balances, 1990

| | United States | Industrialized Countries[a] | Less Developed Countries | OPEC Countries | Centrally Planned Economies | World |
|---|---|---|---|---|---|---|
| | MEDIUM GNP GROWTH | | | | | |
| **Oil** | | | | | | |
| *(thousands bbl/day)* | | | | | | |
| Production | 9,756 | 16,281 | 8,006 | 48,823 | 16,995 | 90,105 |
| Imports | 12,085 | 40,635 | 4,546 | −44,091 | −1,090 | |
| Consumption | 21,841 | 56,915 | 12,554 | 4,731 | 15,905 | 90,105 |
| **Natural gas** | | | | | | |
| *(billions cu ft/yr)* | | | | | | |
| Production | 15,920 | 28,635 | 3,759 | 8,759 | 20,793 | 61,880 |
| Imports | 2,424 | 5,105 | −700 | −3,719 | −687 | |
| Consumption | 18,344 | 33,739 | 2,995 | 5,051 | 20,106 | 61,880 |
| **Coal** | | | | | | |
| *(millions short tons/yr)* | | | | | | |
| Production | 1,166 | 1,796 | 502 | 7 | 2,986 | 5,291 |
| Imports | −81 | 115 | −40 | — | −75 | |
| Consumption | 1,085 | 1,911 | 462 | 7 | 2,911 | 5,291 |
| **Nuclear, hydro, solar, geothermal** | | | | | | |
| *(terawatt-hr/yr)* | 1,397 | 3,513 | 924 | 64 | 1,350 | 5,851 |
| **Total energy consumption** | | | | | | |
| *(quadrillion Btu)* | 103 | 231 | 50 | 16 | 117 | 414 |
| | HIGH GNP GROWTH | | | | | |
| **Oil** | | | | | | |
| *(thousands bbl/day)* | | | | | | |
| Production | 9,770 | 16,295 | 8,044 | 60,932 | 16,995 | 102,266 |
| Imports | 14,691 | 49,794 | 6,025 | −55,434 | −385 | |
| Consumption | 24,460 | 66,089 | 14,069 | 5,498 | 16,610 | 102,266 |
| **Natural gas** | | | | | | |
| *(billions cu ft/yr)* | | | | | | |
| Production | 16,122 | 29,411 | 4,048 | 10,580 | 21,832 | 65,871 |
| Imports | 2,512 | 6,290 | −700 | −4,762 | −828 | |
| Consumption | 18,634 | 35,701 | 3,348 | 5,818 | 21,004 | 65,871 |
| **Coal** | | | | | | |
| *(millions short tons/yr)* | | | | | | |
| Production | 1,260 | 1,981 | 558 | 8 | 2,634 | 5,181 |
| Imports | −81 | 98 | −43 | — | −55 | |
| Consumption | 1,179 | 2,079 | 515 | 8 | 2,579 | 5,181 |
| **Nuclear, hydro, solar, geothermal** | | | | | | |
| *(terawatt-hr/yr)* | 1,402 | 3,518 | 924 | 64 | 1,350 | 5,856 |
| **Total energy consumption** | | | | | | |
| *(quadrillion Btu)* | 111 | 256 | 55 | 19 | 118 | 448 |
| | LOW GNP GROWTH | | | | | |
| **Oil** | | | | | | |
| *(thousands bbl/day)* | | | | | | |
| Production | 9,734 | 16,253 | 7,971 | 38,363 | 16,995 | 79,581 |
| Imports | 9,929 | 32,967 | 3,140 | −34,344 | −1,766 | |
| Consumption | 19,663 | 49,219 | 11,111 | 4,019 | 15,229 | 79,851 |
| **Natural gas** | | | | | | |
| *(billions cu ft/yr)* | | | | | | |
| Production | 15,598 | 27,648 | 3,355 | 7,903 | 19,608 | 58,542 |
| Imports | 2,345 | 4,549 | −700 | −3,484 | −364 | |
| Consumption | 17,942 | 32,197 | 2,655 | 4,446 | 19,244 | 58,542 |
| **Coal** | | | | | | |
| *(millions short tons/yr)* | | | | | | |
| Production | 1,075 | 1,631 | 452 | 6 | 2,503 | 4,592 |
| Imports | −81 | 115 | −40 | — | −75 | |
| Consumption | 994 | 1,746 | 412 | 6 | 2,428 | 4,592 |
| **Nuclear, hydro, solar, geothermal** | | | | | | |
| *(terawatt-hr/yr)* | 1,373 | 3,316 | 924 | 64 | 1,350 | 5,758 |
| **Total energy consumption** | | | | | | |
| *(quadrillion Btu)* | 96 | 209 | 45 | 15 | 110 | 379 |

[a] All OECD countries, including the U.S.

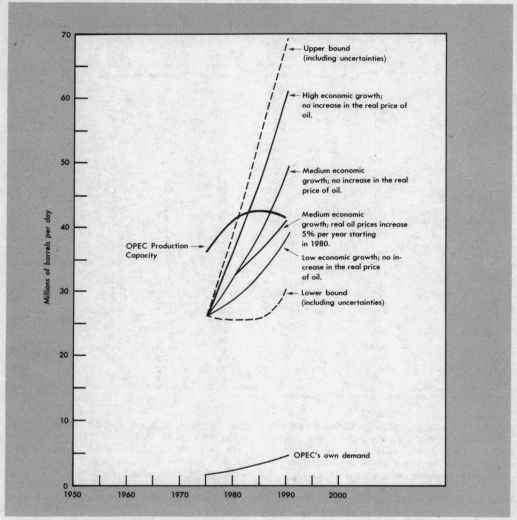

**Figure 10-1.** Projected demand (including OPEC's own demand) for OPEC oil, and OPEC's own demand for OPEC oil.

these countries are able to attract more buyers and thus sell more oil. However, seasonal shifts in demand structure favoring different crude qualities at different times of the year, refining inflexibility, and the institutional arrangements with the major oil companies all tend to make price shading an ineffective revenue-maximizing policy.

OPEC production capacity is projected to exceed demand over the midrange, and this results in some spare capacity. As a result of price shading, this spare capacity is concentrated in

countries with the least desire for income—Kuwait, Iran, Libya, the United Arab Emirates, and Saudi Arabia. These swing countries act as buffers, absorbing seasonal rises and falls in demands.

OPEC pricing policy appears to encompass conflicting objectives. The small, lower-income producers are concerned with maximizing real income, consistent with development plans and future prospects for oil production. In contrast, the large, higher-income producers in the swing group must consider the effects of sudden price

## TABLE 10–6

### Less Developed Oil Exporting Countries: Current Production, Reserves, Population, Income

| | 1977 Production (thousand bbl/day) | 1977 Production Capacity (thousand bbl/day) | Jan. 1, 1978 Reserves (billion bbl) | Future Years of Production | 1975 Production (millions) | 1975 GNP (billion $) | 1975 Per Capital Income ($) | 1977 Account Balances (million $) |
|---|---|---|---|---|---|---|---|---|
| **OPEC Members** | | | | | | | | |
| Algeria | 990 | 1,100 | 6.6 | 16 | 15.7 | 12.3 | 780 | −1,520 |
| Ecuador | 180 | 225 | 1.6 | 20 | 7.1 | 3.9 | 550 | −50 |
| Gabon | 225 | 250 | 2.1 | 23 | 0.5 | 1.2 | 2,239 | −220 |
| Indonesia | 1,690 | 1,800 | 10.0 | 15 | 136.0 | 24.2 | 178 | −580 |
| Iran | 5,650 | 6,700 | 62.0 | 25 | 33.0 | 48.9 | 1,478 | 5,900 |
| Iraq | 2,150 | 3,100 | 34.5 | 31 | 11.1 | 14.3 | 1,282 | 1,950 |
| Kuwait | 1,700 | 3,340 | 67.0 | 55 | 1.0 | 11.3 | 11,280 | 5,750 |
| Libya | 2,050 | 2,500 | 25.0 | 27 | 2.4 | 12.4 | 5,078 | 3,600 |
| Nigeria | 2,150 | 2,400 | 18.7 | 21 | 75.0 | 23.1 | 308 | 290 |
| Qatar | 350 | 650 | 5.6 | 24 | 0.2 | 1.7 | 8,400 | 900 |
| Saudi Arabia | 8,950 | 11,840 | 150.0 | 35 | 8.3 | 25.0 | 3,009 | 20,330 |
| United Arab Emirates | 2,030 | 2,420 | 32.4 | 37 | 0.7 | 6.9 | 10,521 | 5,250 |
| Venezuela | 2,280 | 2,600 | 18.2 | 19 | 12.0 | 26.7 | 2,224 | −150 |
| **Non-OPEC** [a] | | | | | | | | |
| Mexico | 990 | 990 | 14.0 | 39 | 59.9 | 71.2 | 1,188 | |
| Trinidad | 230 | 230 | .7 | 8 | 1.1 | 2.1 | 1,895 | |
| Malaysia | 190 | 190 | 2.5 | 36 | 11.7 | 8.7 | 743 | |
| Bolivia | 35 | 35 | .4 | 27 | 5.6 | 1.8 | 314 | |
| Peru | 90 | 90 | .7 | 22 | 15.4 | 12.5 | 814 | |
| Egypt | 450 | 450 | 2.5 | 15 | 37.2 | 11.6 | 310 | |
| Syria | 200 | 200 | 2.2 | 30 | 7.4 | 4.9 | 657 | |
| Bahrain | 54 | 54 | .3 | 14 | 0.3 | 0.6 | 2,423 | |
| Angola | 195 | 195 | 1.2 | 16 | 6.5 | 3.7 | 573 | |
| Congo | 35 | 35 | .4 | 28 | 1.3 | 0.7 | 497 | |
| Zaire | 24 | 24 | .2 | 17 | 24.7 | 3.7 | 151 | |
| Oman | 350 | 350 | 5.7 | 44 | 0.8 | 1.6 | 2,078 | |
| Brunei | 207 | 207 | 1.6 | 21 | 0.2 | | | |
| Tunisia | 87 | 87 | 2.7 | 84 | 5.6 | 4.2 | 757 | |

[a] For non-OPEC countries, 1977 production is assumed to be production capacity.

movements on the prospects for economic growth in the industrialized countries, the major repository for their investments. As a result, there appears to be a strong incentive for the swing countries to maintain constant real oil prices.

Curtailed oil supplies due to production ceilings could have profound effects on future oil prices, and importing countries must consider the possibility of increasing world oil prices as demand approaches available supply. Figure 10–1 shows potential OPEC oil production, derived from engineering assessments and published production policies, in relation to the projected demand levels. The realization of the estimates depends on both producer country motivation and engineering limitations. Limitations on oil supply from OPEC countries could result from any one outcome or combination of outcomes, including resource conservation by OPEC members with large surplus revenues, technical limitations on field development and infrastructure expansion, and higher

than expected depletion and production declines in the older OPEC countries.

These limits on output would extend the production horizon for some OPEC countries as lesser quantities of oil are produced over a greater number of years. This grace period would give both producing and consuming countries time to prepare for the transition from oil and gas to coal and then to renewable energy sources.

Based on the projections shown in Figure 10–1, the following statements can be made:

- There is a very real possibility that the surplus production capacity in OPEC will disappear as early as 1985 and as late as 1990.

- There is a lower possibility of this occurring either before 1985 or after 1990.

As demand levels approach supply constraints, competitive market demand pressures are expected to result in real price increases. Price changes may also come from OPEC policies, although the timing and magnitude of these changes are difficult to predict. Two broad possibilities to equate world oil demand with OPEC's capacity to produce are (1) OPEC maintaining a passive role, allowing price increases to occur only when demand begins to exceed capacity, or (2) OPEC pursuing an active role by raising prices smoothly each year until some technological backstop becomes competitive. In either case, such a price rise would cause considerable economic impacts. The demand for oil would be reduced, partly because the price had increased and partly because of the depression in economic activity caused by higher prices. In the long run, these higher prices would stimulate a shift to conservation strategies and alternative supply development. Increased conservation efforts would ultimately lower demand.

The effect of a sustained higher OPEC price is projected in Tables 10–7 and 10–8 for 1985 and 1990, showing the balances for world energy in those years, assuming a real price increase of 5 percent per annum for the medium growth case. Demand for OPEC oil imports, as shown in Figure 10–1, relative to the previous medium case, has dropped in response to the higher prices. U.S. oil demand in 1985 is forecast at about 21 mb/d, and world oil demand at 76 mb/d. The respective figures for 1990 oil consumption are 19 and 84. All these forecasts are within the range of the constant price numbers discussed earlier, although U.S. oil consumption in 1990 falls to the lower

limit of the low GNP scenario. Total primary energy consumption in the U.S. is predicted to be 94 quads in 1985 and 100 quads in 1990. Total world energy consumption increases from 335 quads in 1985 to 384 quads in 1990. The resulting average annual growth rate using the higher price assumption is 3.3 percent for total energy.

The possibility of further price increases is still a likely outcome, although the pressure on slack capacity is potentially less in the medium term.

## Long-Range Energy Projections

For the price range assumed in the midrange section, the projections show that the supply situation will tighten rapidly over the 1980–90 period, with a strong possibility of real price increases caused principally by OPEC resource conservation policies that limit production. In the long range, a further tightening in the oil supply situation can be expected due to resource depletion effects. This resource problem is characterized by two phenomena:

1. The world appears to be facing a long-run oil and gas depletion situation, because reserve additions to the production base may not be sufficient to support the growth in demand.

2. The growth rates of energy consumption will have to fall substantially from currently projected levels to be consistent with projected rates of growth in resource production.

**TABLE 10–7**

**Regional Energy Balances with High OPEC Prices, 1985**

| | United States | Industrialized Countries[a] | Less Developed Countries | OPEC Countries | Centrally Planned Economies | World |
|---|---|---|---|---|---|---|
| Oil | | | | | | |
| *(thousands bbl/day)* | | | | | | |
| Production | 10,507 | 16,735 | 7,612 | 36,637 | 15,311 | 76,295 |
| Imports | 10,157 | 31,694 | 2,634 | −33,010 | −1,318 | |
| Consumption | 20,664 | 48,429 | 10,246 | 3,627 | 13,992 | 76,295 |
| Natural gas | | | | | | |
| *(billions cu ft/yr)* | | | | | | |
| Production | 16,934 | 29,750 | 3,034 | 5,651 | 18,462 | 56,897 |
| Imports | 1,833 | 3,345 | −600 | −1,967 | −778 | |
| Consumption | 18,772 | 33,095 | 2,433 | 3,684 | 17,684 | 56,897 |
| Coal | | | | | | |
| *(millions short tons/yr)* | | | | | | |
| Production | 1,055 | 1,764 | 426 | 5 | 2,616 | 4,811 |
| Imports | −74 | 97 | −42 | | −55 | |
| Consumption | 981 | 1,861 | 384 | 5 | 2,561 | 4,811 |
| Nuclear, hydro, solar, geothermal | | | | | | |
| *(terawatt-hr/yr)* | 1,045 | 2,584 | 585 | 19 | 760 | 3,948 |
| Total energy consumption | | | | | | |
| *(quadrillion Btu)* | 94 | 200 | 33 | 12 | 90 | 335 |

[a] All OECD countries, including the U.S.

## TABLE 10–8

### Regional Energy Balances with High OPEC Prices, 1990

|  | United States | Industrial-ized Countries[a] | Less Developed Countries | OPEC Countries | Centrally Planned Economies | World |
|---|---|---|---|---|---|---|
| **Oil** |  |  |  |  |  |  |
| *(thousands bbl/day)* |  |  |  |  |  |  |
| Production | 11,347 | 18,238 | 8,404 | 41,133 | 17,029 | 84,803 |
| Imports | 7,969 | 33,601 | 4,118 | −36,603 | −1,115 |  |
| Consumption | 19,316 | 51,839 | 12,521 | 4,529 | 15,914 | 84,803 |
| **Natural gas** |  |  |  |  |  |  |
| *(billions cu ft/yr)* |  |  |  |  |  |  |
| Production | 16,614 | 29,808 | 3,695 | 9,974 | 20,887 | 64,363 |
| Imports | 2,361 | 6,222 | −700 | −4,741 | −781 |  |
| Consumption | 18,975 | 36,031 | 2,995 | 5,232 | 20,106 | 64,363 |
| **Coal** |  |  |  |  |  |  |
| *(millions short tons/yr)* |  |  |  |  |  |  |
| Production | 1,244 | 1,928 | 502 | 7 | 2,986 | 5,424 |
| Imports | −81 | 115 | −40 |  | −75 |  |
| Consumption | 1,163 | 2,043 | 462 | 7 | 2,911 | 5,424 |
| **Nuclear, hydro, solar, geothermal** |  |  |  |  |  |  |
| *(terawatt-hr/yr)* | 1,555 | 3,670 | 924 | 64 | 1,350 | 6,008 |
| **Total energy consumption** |  |  |  |  |  |  |
| *(quadrillion Btu)* | 100 | 225 | 41 | 15 | 103 | 384 |

[a]All OECD countries, including the U.S.

Together these conditions increase the likelihood of long-run competitive pressure among consumers for oil in the world energy market. This pressure can be partially offset by contributions from both new technologies and conservation measures. Increased supplies of energy can be expected from new energy sources—solar, wind, geothermal, nuclear—as well as from more advanced development of existing sources, including oil shale, coal gasification, and enhanced oil recovery. Utilization of these sources requires demonstration of the necessary technologies on a commercial scale, which involves resolution of uncertainties regarding both the basic cost and availability of the new processes. However, at least to the year 2000, the contribution of technology will not cover the excess of U.S. energy demand over supply. Conservation policies might also be expected to play a role in easing the demand for world energy supplies. Consumers may lower projected demand levels by conserving energy, while producers may choose to conserve resources by establishing production limits.

This section surveys major recent long-run energy projections for the year 2000. The projections have been selected on the basis of being publicly available, either in published or in report form, and represent a range of viewpoints. The projections are not fully consistent or directly comparable, since they were performed at different times and with different assumptions regarding such basic factors as economic growth rates and future oil prices. Despite these difficulties, the projections present a range of possible energy futures. The first part of what follows focuses on two recent global projections, and the second part examines three projections for the U.S. alone.

### Long-Range Global Projections

Possible ranges of world energy demand for the year 2000 were forecast in 1977 by the Workshop on Alternative Energy Strategies (WAES)* and the World Energy Conference (WEC).†

The WAES multicountry study was prepared by independent national experts in each country and integrated to form a single series of consistent international forecasts. Some of the forecasts embodied detailed representation of end-use consumption and conservation possibilities in a multisector input-output representation of the economies of the major countries. Others were based upon much simpler methodologies. The WAES study focused on the key issues of resource depletion in the U.S. by emphasizing either a nuclear or coal technology approach to oil replacement.

The reports to the World Energy Conference at Istanbul included a series of invited papers on

---

*Workshop on Alternative Energy Strategies, *Energy Supply-Demand Integrations to the Year 2000*, Cambridge, Mass.: MIT Press, 1977.
†World Energy Conference, Conservation Commission, *Report on World Energy Demand, 1985–2020*, London: World Energy Conference, 1977.

## TABLE 10–9

### Long-Run World Energy Assumptions

WORKSHOP ON ALTERNATIVE ENERGY
STRATEGIES

| Case:[a] | 1975–85 | | 1985–2000 | | | |
|---|---|---|---|---|---|---|
| | C | D | C1 | C2 | D7 | D8 |
| GDP growth | high | low | high | | low | |
| | 6% | 3.5% | 5% | | 3% | |
| Oil price[b] | $11.50 | $11.50 | $17.25 | | $11.50 | |
| | | | by 2000 | | | |
| Reserve additions | 20 | 10 | 20 | | 10 | |
| (billion bbl/yr) | | | | | | |
| OPEC limit (mb/d) | none | none | 45 | | 40 | |

WORLD ENERGY CONFERENCE

| | 1975–2000 | | | | |
|---|---|---|---|---|---|
| Case: | H–1 | H–4 | H–5 | L–1 | L–4 |
| GDP growth | high | | | low | |
| | 4.2% | | | 3.0% | |
| Price response | none | high | high | none | high |
| Constraints | none | oil | energy | none | oil |

[a] WAES cases C1 and D7 emphasize coal as the replacement fuel; cases C2 and D8 emphasize nuclear energy.
[b] WAES prices per barrel are in 1975 dollars, FOB the Persian Gulf.

world energy resources—coal, oil, and gas—and energy demand for the Conservation Commission. Since these papers were prepared by different groups, the demand study is not wholly consistent with the supply studies. (The authors of the WEC demand analyses were also associated with the WAES group that coordinated the individual country balances.)

The WEC demand cases assume a slightly more pessimistic future than the WAES projections, with 1975–85 world economic growth at 3.0 percent, vs. 3.5–6 percent for WAES. In the 1985–2000 period, WEC and WAES economic growth

rates are roughly comparable (4.2 and 3–5 percent, respectively). Other assumptions are summarized in Table 10–9, and the unconstrained world energy consumption figures are shown in Table 10–10.

The objective of the different forecasts is to define a range of credible futures against which alternative policy options can be tested. The ranges of possible world energy demand by non-centrally planned economies are 338–438 quads (WAES) and 317–507 quads (WEC). These different levels result from varying assumptions about economic growth, energy prices, and policy responses. The WAES scenarios ranged from a "low economic growth/constrained energy price/increasing coal case" to a "high economic growth/rising energy price/increasing nuclear case." Likewise, the World Energy Conference study listed a range of forecasts based on scenarios of high (4.2 percent) and low (3.0 percent) projected economic growth. These cases studied variations in the price response of demand and constraints on energy development.

The WAES analysis predicted gaps in all cases between available Free World oil supplies and desired oil demand (Table 10–11). In the year 2000, the shortages are projected to range from 15–20 mb/d. These "gaps" are the consequence of political limits on oil production that could emerge as early as the 1980s or of limits to the ultimately recoverable oil resources, which seem likely no later than the turn of the century. WAES noted that in reality these gaps will never occur. Rather than forcing a world energy balance, the WAES study indicated that the gaps were measures of the additional effort required to achieve a balance. Prices will rise, economic growth will slow, stronger government policies will be adopted, or other actions will be taken to balance

## TABLE 10–10

### World Energy Demand, Year 2000

(Quadrillion Btu)

| | WAES Cases | | | | WEC Case | Centrally Planned Economies |
|---|---|---|---|---|---|---|
| | C–1 | C–2 | D–7 | D–8 | H–5 | |
| GNP Growth | 5.0% | 5.0% | 3.0% | 3.0% | 4.2% | |
| Renewable resources[a] | 33 | 31 | 24 | 23 | 55 | 27 |
| Nuclear | 60 | 96 | 54 | 82 | 59 | 26 |
| Oil | 196 | 194 | 156 | 155 | 164 | 29 |
| Natural gas | 59 | 55 | 50 | 46 | 22 | 37 |
| Coal | 72 | 62 | 54 | 45 | 64 | 71 |
| Total | 419 | 438 | 338 | 350 | 364 | 190 |
| Total (with centrally planned economies) | 609 | 628 | 528 | 540 | 554 | |

[a] Includes hydro, geothermal, solar, and biomass resources.

## TABLE 10–11

### WAES Oil Balance for Year 2000

*(Millions of barrels per day)*

| | WAES Cases | | | |
|---|---|---|---|---|
| | C–1 | C–2 | D–7 | D–8 |
| **Desired Imports:** | | | | |
| North American | 10.4 | 10.7 | 15.8 | 15.8 |
| Western Europe | 16.5 | 16.4 | 13.2 | 12.5 |
| Japan | 15.2 | 14.4 | 8.2 | 7.9 |
| Rest of Free World outside of OPEC | 11.2 | 9.5 | 9.6 | 9.0 |
| International Bunkers | 5.4 | 5.4 | 4.5 | 4.5 |
| Total | 58.7 | 56.4 | 51.3 | 49.7 |
| OPEC Potential Exports | 38.7 | 37.2 | 35.2 | 34.5 |
| Prospective shortage (gap) | 20.0 | 19.2 | 16.1 | 15.2 |

supply and demand. The size of the gaps merely indicates the magnitude of the adjustment that will be needed in addition to that assumed in the case specification.

Figure 10–2 compares the higher priced growth cases for 1985 and 1990 with the year 2000 forecasts from WAES and WEC (the WAES numbers have been adjusted on the basis of WEC data to include the centrally planned economies).

### Long-Range U.S. Projections

Projections of future energy supply and demand for the United States must be examined in the context of world requirements. Increasing dependence on imported oil in the near term necessitates an international framework. The world price of oil also has a strong influence on the economic competitiveness of alternative energy technologies.

Three long-range U.S. forecasts published during the past year use fundamentally different methodological approaches. These are:

1. The Workshop on Alternative Energy Strategies study, already described.
2. A study by the Stanford Research Institute (SRI),* which utilizes a 50-year representation of supply, conversion, and end-use consumption in a competitive energy market. An unusual and debatable feature of the forecast procedure is that it

---

*Electric Power Research Institute. *Fuel and Energy Price Forecasts*, Report EPRI EA–433, 2 vols., Menlo Park, Calif., 1977.

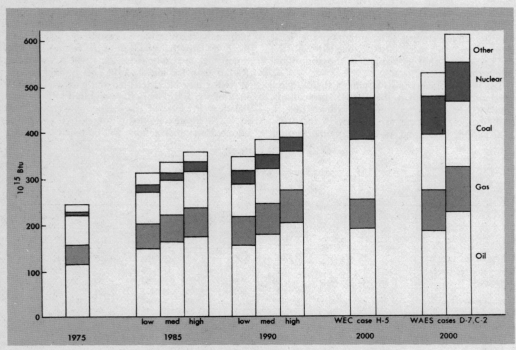

**Figure 10-2.** Comparison of global projections, 1975–2000.

embodies foresight—that is, future shortages influence present decisions in planning representation of the energy market. Decision-makers are assumed to consider the future prices calculated in the model in deciding whether to produce now or later, and whether to expand capacity.

3. A study by Brookhaven National Laboratory and Dale Jorgenson Associates (BNL/DJA),* which uses multiperiod linear programming to represent the technology of supply, conversion, and end-use consumption in conjunction with a long-term, interindustry transaction model of the economy. The solutions emphasize conservation and coal resource development along with significant development of nuclear and renewable resources.

The assumptions of the various cases for the U.S. are shown in Table 10–12 and the outcomes in Table 10–13. The broad range of futures shown in Table 10–13 is in part due to the differences in input assumptions. Total domestic energy consumption is predicted to range between 109 and 143 quads in the year 2000, a narrow band of consumption estimates compared with earlier studies. The most critical supply estimate is future oil availability from domestic sources. WAES domestic oil estimates are lowest at 13–15 quads, SRI the highest at 18–24 quads. The higher estimates result from relatively optimistic assessments of resource availability, the rate of discovery, and the resolution of uncertainties and barriers to resource development. Oil imports vary widely (15–32 quads) depending on world price and the U.S. supply base. Coal consumption is predicted to grow substantially in all scenarios. Estimates of nuclear power range from 22 to 35 quads in 2000. These estimates imply 380–610 gigawatts of generation capacity—a staggering increase from the 163 gigawatts estimated for 1990 for the U.S. in the 1978 annual report of the Department of Energy's Energy Information Administration. Renewable resources including solar and biomass will play a minor but increasingly important role, contributing 1.7–3.9 quads by 2000. Three additional forecasts made by BNL/DRI examining the implications of alternative energy sources and technologies will be discussed later in this chapter.

Basic conclusions that can be drawn from the recent U.S. projections are:

• U.S. oil and gas production from conventional resources will be unlikely to cover the growth in U.S. oil and gas consumption.

*David J. Behling and Edward Hudson, *Policies for Energy Conservation: Potentials, Mechanisms, and Impacts*, Brookhaven National Laboratory, 1978.

## TABLE 10–12

### U.S. Long-Run Energy Assumptions

| Period | Economic Growth (percent) | Oil Prices [a] per barrel) | Technology Emphasized |
|---|---|---|---|
| **WAES case** | | | |
| C | 1975–1985 | 4.4 | $13.00 | |
| C1 | 1985–2000 | 3.5 | 18.75 | Coal |
| C2 | 1985–2000 | 3.5 | 18.75 | Nuclear |
| D | 1975–1985 | 3.2 | 13.00 | |
| D7 | 1985–2000 | 2.5 | 13.00 | Coal |
| D8 | 1985–2000 | 2.5 | 13.00 | Nuclear |
| **SRI** | | | |
| Base | 1975–1985 | 4.6 | 14.09 | |
| | 1985–2000 | 2.9 | 17.86 | Coal |
| Low | 1975–1985 | 2.8 | 12.82 | |
| | 1985–2000 | 1.7 | 15.54 | Coal |
| **BNL/DJA** | | | |
| Base | 1975–1985 | 3.6 | 13.00 | |
| | 1985–2000 | 3.0 | 15.09 | Coal and conservation |

[a] All prices are in 1975 dollars cif. The WAES prices were FOB the Persian Gulf; $1.50 has been added for freight charges.

• However, the rate of growth of U.S. consumption can be cut dramatically in the long run by aggressive conservation policies.

• At least to the year 2000, the contribution of technology—supply enhancement, synthetics production, nuclear generation, and renewable resources—will not make up the excess of U.S. energy demand over supply, and U.S. dependence on world oil resources will continue at least at the current range of 7–10 mb/d.

Figure 10–3 compares the U.S. projections for 1985 and 1990 with the range of year 2000 estimates to provide a perspective for the rising price cases. The comparison shows the divergence of the present base case forecasts, embodying regulatory trends, from the range of free-policy forecasts advocated for the year 2000, none of which is completely consistent with the high, medium, and low growth case specifications.

## Future Oil Potential

The long-range energy forecasts show declining world oil production, concommitant with increasing demand. Future production, of course, is influenced by known reserves, the new discoveries, improved production techniques, level of demand, and OPEC production policies. In the midrange years, governmentally imposed production ceilings could alter the supply position, but

## TABLE 10–13

### Most Recent U.S. Projections for the Year 2000

*(Quadrillion Btu[a])*

|  | BNL/DJA | SRI | | WAES Cases | | | |
|---|---|---|---|---|---|---|---|
|  | Base | Base | Low | C1 | C2 | D7 | D8 |
| Hydroelectric | 3.6 | 3.8 | 3.8 | 4.6 | 4.6 | 3.7 | 3.7 |
| Geothermal | 2.2 | (in hydro) | | 3.0 | 3.0 | 1.2 | 1.2 |
| Solar/biomass | 3.9 | 2.3 | 1.8 | 3.9 | 3.9. | 1.7 | 1.7 |
| Nuclear | 28.5 | 31.6 | 23.0 | 26.0 | 35.2 | 26.0 | 33.1 |
| Domestic oil | 18.8 | 23.5 | 17.9 | 14.9 | 14.9 | 12.7 | 12.7 |
| Imported oil | 26.9 | 14.9 | 14.9 | 19.9 | 20.5 | 32.2 | 32.3 |
| Shale oil | 3.0 | 0.6 | 0.2 | 4.2 | 4.2 | — | — |
| Domestic gas | 17.7 | 20.1 | 15.7 | 14.0 | 14.0 | 11.5 | 11.5 |
| Imported gas | 1.3 | 2.6 | 3.1 | 3.0 | 3.6 | 5.0 | 5.0 |
| Coal (domestic consumption) | 32.6 | 43.8 | 29.0 | 29.8 | 27.1 | 21.1 | 19.1 |
| Other | — | — | — | 1.0 | 1.0 | — | — |
| Total domestic consumption | 138.5 | 143.2 | 109.4 | 124.3 | 132.0 | 115.1 | 120.3 |
| Coal Exports | — | — | — | 18.1 | 7.1 | 14.6 | 8.6 |

[a]One quadrillion Btu = 0.476 million barrels of oil per day (mb/d).

the most important long-range constraint on potential production is the estimated level of recoverable resources. WAES concluded that even without government constraints oil supply in 2000 will meet demand only under the most optimistic assumptions concerning gross additions to reserves.

In 1977 the WEC Conservation Commission prepared a *Report on Oil Resources, 1998–2020*, containing estimates of potential oil production, in parallel with the demand study discussed above. For the oil study, a poll of experts was conducted. The findings, broadly comparable to those of WAES, placed ultimately recoverable worldwide

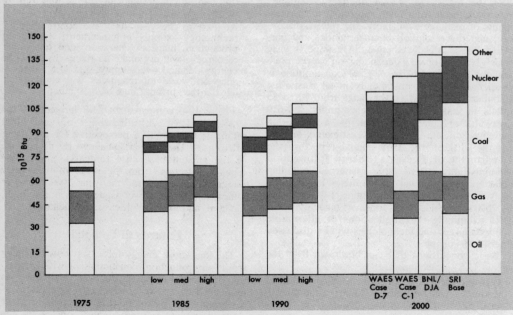

**Figure 10-3.** Comparison of U.S. projections, 1975–2000.

conventional petroleum resources at approximately 2,100 billion barrels (including cumulative production through 1975 of 320 billion barrels). With increased prices and government policies directed at supporting higher production levels, estimated recovery rates could be increased and offshore development continued.

Recovery rate, the ratio of recoverable oil to oil in-place, is an extremely important parameter and susceptible to technological enhancement. If ultimately recoverable world oil resources at a 40 percent recovery rate are 2,000 billion barrels, a 1 percent improvement in recovery rate adds 50 billion barrels of ultimately recoverable oil. To show a relative comparison, current proven reserves for the U.S. are estimated at 31 billion barrels. According to the experts polled, the current world recovery rate, estimated at 25–30 percent, is expected to increase to 40 percent by the year 2000 (in the industrial countries to 45 percent), compared to the present U.S. rate of 32 percent. An increase of that size would compare with a U.S. rate that has risen only 0.3 percent per year over the last two decades.

Based on alternative combinations of ultimately recoverable resources and reserve/production ratios, the WEC examined various levels of maximum technical production capacity. The conclusion of the group was that the most likely production profile would lead to a ceiling of 82–104 million barrels per day, peaking around 1990.

Figures 10–4 and 10–5 illustrate the WEC analysis of the depletion of the world's oil resources. In Figure 10–4, the upper curve shows how cumulative discoveries (reserve additions) would grow if the experts' estimated limit of world resources were approached along a growth curve similar to the pattern shown so far by the United States. The WAES study developed two scenarios using different rates of gross additions to reserves: (1) The 20 billion barrels per year case assumes successful but declining discoveries and an increased contribution from enhanced recovery; (2) the 10 billion barrel per year case assumes rapidly decreasing discoveries and little enhanced recovery.

The model considers high and low economic growth rates, as well as varying oil price levels. A disaggregation of OPEC and non-OPEC production takes into account the possibility of production restrictions. Although these cases result in different levels of peak production and oil production levels in 2000, the underlying conclusion is that potential oil demand in the year 2000 is unlikely to be satisfied by crude oil production from conventional sources. New oil discoveries or

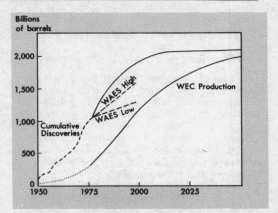

**Figure 10-4.** Cumulative world discovery and production of oil.

higher recovery factors might postpone these peaks a few years but would not reverse the inevitable decline of oil reserves. For comparison, the "WAES high" and "WAES low" curves show the two WAES assumptions of constant reserve additions of 20 and 10 billion barrels per year.

The lower curve in Figure 10–4 was derived from the upper curve by WEC, and shows the cumulative production curve based on depletion of world reserves to an average R/P (reserve/production) ratio of 20. The production is actually calculated by region, with different R/P ratio limits to reflect current national resource conservation strategies. Figure 10–5 displays the same production curve in terms of annual production rates and compares it to a series of world demand growth rates of 2, 3, and 5 percent. Under progressively lower oil demand growth curves, the WEC study implies ultimate failure of world oil production to meet world oil demand in the 1985–2010 time

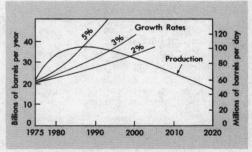

**Figure 10-5.** World maximum oil production at a medium depletion rate and world demand at three growth rates of oil production.

frame. The WAES analysis also indicates this shortfall.

## The Role of Future Technologies

In view of a possible midrange production crisis followed by depletion of the resource base, technological developments will be increasingly necessary to maintain sufficient energy supplies. Alternatives include both new technologies and existing technologies that become economic as energy prices rise. Improvements could occur not only in actual exploration and production techniques but also in electric utility operations, direct fuel consumption, energy conversion, and efficiency levels. Determining the impact of various methods is complicated because each may penetrate the market at a different time, with varying implementation and success rates.

Current predictions of technological implementation are based on research and development status and schedules, projected product costs, anticipated infrastructural requirements, and future governmental regulatory actions.

Among the technologies expected to be competitive before 2000 are heat pumps, enhanced recovery of oil and oil shale, geothermal energy for electricity production in certain regions, solar heating, and light-water fast-breeder reactors. Some marginally competitive sources include solar cooling, synthetic fuels from coal, advanced geothermal techniques, and electric automobiles. Technologies not now economic could become more attractive if prices of conventional energy sources increased, although a 20–30 percent increase in prices would reduce energy demands by 10 percent, so the demands for energy from new technologies still may not exist.

The implications of alternative energy technologies on the total energy system were explored in the Brookhaven National Laboratory study for the following three scenarios:

• Large-scale electrification of demand based upon coal and nuclear fuels.

• Large-scale enhancement of fossil supplies of conventional oil and gas as well as synthetics from coal.

• Large-scale use of renewable resources—solar energy and biomass and process heat from cogeneration.

These scenarios show three plausible mixes of energy technologies for a given economic forecast and level of consumption implementation. Each forecast delivers the same end-use demands for services at the same cost. The means of delivery

of those services are allowed to change across scenarios. Incremental implementation levels for the three cases are shown in Table 10–14. Table 10–15 summarizes resource use in 2000 by fuel and consuming sector. Figure 10–6 illustrates the differences in fuel use under each of the scenarios for 1985 and 2000.

In the large-scale electrification scenario, electricity is substituted for direct use of fossil fuels. Coal and nuclear fuel have the potential to contribute substantially to electricity generation, although there are development impacts that must be considered in both cases. One major area of increased electricity demand is in the use of heat pumps. Fifty percent of new buildings constructed between 1985 and 2000 are projected to have electric heat pumps, the remaining new buildings split evenly between electric resistance heat and fossil fuels. Electric heat pumps also are assumed to have penetrated the industrial market as a source of low-temperature process heat, providing 0.9 quad by the year 2000. This increased industrial use of electricity results from a combination of declining oil and gas supplies for boiler fuel and

## TABLE 10–14

### Incremental Implementation Above Base-Case Levels for Three Alternative Energy Technologies, Year 2000

|  | Thousand megawatts | Quadrillion Btu |
|---|---|---|
| Large-Scale Electrification: |  |  |
| Light-water reactor | 48.7 | 1.02 |
| Enhanced coal recovery | — | — |
| Solar electric | 9.6 | .20 |
| Magnetohydrodynamic | 1.0 | .02 |
| Heat pumps | 16.7 | .35 |
| Advanced coal combustion | 7.2 | .15 |
| Advanced turbines | 1.4 | .03 |
| Geothermal for electricity | 16.2 | .34 |
| Fossil-Based Systems: |  |  |
| Enhanced oil recovery | — | 4.00 |
| Unconventional gas | — | 3.00 |
| Coal recovery | — | .53 |
| Shale oil | — | 2.00 |
| Advanced coal combustion | 1.4 | .03 |
| Coal gasification | — | 2.00 |
| Coal liquefaction | — | 2.00 |
| Decentralized Systems: |  |  |
| Low-head hydropower | 15.3 | .32 |
| Geothermal | — | .53 |
| Biomass gas and liquids | — | .20 |
| Fuels and wastes | — | 1.90 |
| Advanced coal combustion | — | — |
| Solar energy | — | 3.00 |
| Cogeneration | — | 1.67 |

Note: Year 2000 oil imports for the three cases (in equivalent Btu) are: Large-Scale Electrification, 15.52 quads; Fossil-Based Systems, 11.19 quads; Decentralized Systems, 15.16 quads.

## TABLE 10–15

### Resource Use for Three Alternative Technologies, Year 2000

*(Quadrillion Btu)*

| | SRI Base | Alternative Technologies | | |
| --- | --- | --- | --- | --- |
| | | Large-Scale Electrification | Fossil-Based Systems | Decentralized Systems |
| Total primary inputs | 138.5 | 141.3 | 135.7 | 129.7 |
| Oil | | | | |
| Domestic | 18.8 | 18.8 | 22.8 | 18.8 |
| Imported | 26.9 | 26.6 | 22.0 | 28.5 |
| Shale | 3.0 | 3.0 | 5.0 | 3.0 |
| Coal | 32.6 | 32.1 | 33.3 | 26.3 |
| Gas | | | | |
| Domestic[b] | 17.7 | 17.9 | 21.1 | 17.9 |
| Imported | 1.3 | .1 | 2.7 | 3.7 |
| Nuclear[c] | 28.5 | 31.6 | 20.0 | 17.8 |
| Electricity, central (hydro/geo/solar) | 7.7 | 9.2 | 6.8 | 10.2 |
| Electricity, noncentral (other solar/geo) | 2.0 | 2.0 | 2.0 | 3.4 |

[a] Includes wood.
[b] Includes biomass.
[c] Breeder plus light-water reactor.

economics of scale in pollution control technology.

Energy demands in the fossil-based systems scenario are satisfied by heavy reliance on gas and oil in the residential-commercial sector and increased use of coal by industry. The sources of increased gas and oil supplies are higher recovery rates from existing developments and production of oil and gas from unconventional sources, in-

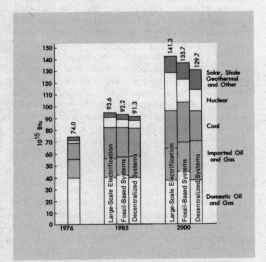

**Figure 10-6.** Primary resources by fuel type for three alternative energy technologies.

cluding shale. Coal gasification and liquefaction also contribute to the total energy supply by 2000. Enhanced crude oil recovery is predicted to supply an additional 1.9 million barrels per day, and unconventional recovery of natural gas contributes an increase of 1.4 million barrels per day (oil equivalent). Coal use by industry is assumed to increase from 4.1 quads in 1976 to 10.7 quads in 1985, reflecting increased direct use of coal as well as cogeneration. Use of liquefied coal as a fuel allows plants to use existing equipment and reduces air pollution levels compared with direct coal use.

The decentralized systems case involves increased use of renewable resources, including biomass and solar energy, and decentralized or small-scale technologies. Electricity from central station powerplants to satisfy final demands is replaced by electricity from decentralized generating facilities using power included as low-head hydropower and cogeneration. One-quarter of the residential housing units are projected to use solar space heating to meet two-thirds of their heating requirements in 2000. As with other new energy sources, higher prices of traditional fuels and technological advances both would encourage the use of solar systems. Congeneration in coal-fired plants is projected to supply 2.3 quads of process heat and 176 billion kilowatt-hours of electricity to industry by 2000.

These three extreme cases have an overall high degree of similarity and indicate that great changes

in the structure of U.S. energy supply by the year
2000 do not appear to be feasible. Despite the
enormous rate of growth of renewable resource
use shown for the decentralized case, the U.S. is
seen to remain fundamentally dependent on fossil
fuels and nuclear power in the year 2000.

On the other hand, the differences in fuel mix
show that we do have options, the choice of
which will have an increasingly significant impact
beyond the turn of the century.

## Energy Impacts

The environmental implications of the energy
projections were assessed quantitatively by the
Biomedical and Environmental Assessment Division of Brookhaven National Laboratory with an
emissions-accounting program called ESNS (for
Energy System Network Simulator). The Brookhaven group was provided with energy projections
for 1985 and 1990 from the International Energy
Evaluation System (IEES) and, as a first approximation, used the ESNS program to assess the
environmental implications of the projections. The
information provided to Brookhaven was insufficient in content to produce a global assessment
for the year 2000 for several reasons:

(1) IEES projections were for 1985 and 1990
only. They did not include base-year estimates or
estimates for years beyond 1990.

(2) IEES projections included no information as
to whether the coal used was to be strip-mined or
deep-mined. Thus, the Brookhaven team could
not estimate land disruption and solid waste
generation caused by mining.

(3) Global projections of future emissions standards by region (i.e., emissions generated per Btu
of fuel, by region) are not available from any
known source.

(4) Although the environmental effects of energy use depends on sector-specific fuel end-use
(e.g., petroleum used in air transportation has a
different impact than that used for automotive
transportation), the IEES output does not provide
such detailed end-use information for the ESNS
model.

The Brookhaven analysts compensated for limitation (4) by using the currently dominant consuming devices for energy end-use. They compensated for (3) by applying U.S. new-source
performance standards on a global basis. No
means were available to compensate for limitations (1) and (2). It should also be noted that
estimates for land disruption and solid waste
generation are incomplete measures, since they

exclude mining, a dominant factor in land disruption and solid waste generation from the energy
sector.

The application of U.S. new-source performance standards on a global basis in the ESNS
calculations is a highly optimistic assumption.
More strict standards may be adopted in some
areas, but, in general, less strict standards can be
expected. Even the U.S. may not be meeting the
current standards by 1985—or even by 1990. In
general, this assumption leads to underestimates
of probable future emissions. The extent of under-
estimation varies by region and by emission type
for regions likely to differ greatly from U.S.
standards, such as many LDCs. The underesti-
mation is large for emissions that are heavily
regulated under U.S. emission standards (sulfur
dioxide and oxides of nitrogen) but small for
regions likely to follow policies similar to those of
the U.S. (such as Western Europe and Japan) and
for environmental impacts (including land use and
solid waste generation) that are not affected by
new-source performance standards.

It should also be pointed out that the emissions
figures do not address some potentially serious
environmental impacts of the energy sector. Estimates of tritium emissions and population exposure refer only to operations occurring in routine
operations in nuclear powerplants; they do not
include estimates for mining and for refining and
reprocessing plant activities. Indirect effects of
energy processes, such as environmental consequences of energy transport (e.g., oil spills, and
impacts of oil pipelines), are also not included.
Since the IEES model outputs were not sufficiently detailed, these issues could not be addressed in depth.

Finally, the Brookhaven estimates are the direct
result of the IEES projections, and therefore
obviously subject to the assumptions implicit in
these projections. For example, the high estimates
of sulfur dioxide and carbon dioxide generation by
the centrally planned economies are a direct result
of the IEES projections of heavy coal use in the
centrally planned economies. To reflect this close
linkage between IEES and ESNS, the following
findings are attributed jointly to IEES-ESNS.

### Findings

The IEES-ESNS findings for the 1985 and 1990
medium-GNP growth scenarios are summarized in
Table 10–16. (The high- and low-GNP growth
findings are in Tables 10–17 and 10–18.) A comparison of 1990 IEES-ESNS emissions projections
with estimates of recent emissions rates from the
technical literature is given in Table 10–19. The

## TABLE 10–16

### Emission Projections, 1985 and 1990, Medium-Growth Case

| | European OECD Countries | U.S. and Canada | Japan | Less Developed Countries | OPEC Countries | Centrally Planned Economies | World |
|---|---|---|---|---|---|---|---|
| **1985** | | | | | | | |
| Carbon dioxide (*billions of short tons*) | 5.2 | 7.54 | 1.68 | 2.81 | 0.89 | 8.99 | 27.1 |
| Carbon monoxide (*millions of short tons*) | 24.7 | 15.2 | 7.25 | 17.2 | 6.22 | 25.4 | 96.0 |
| Sulfur dioxide (*millions of short tons*) | 12.8 | 14.2 | 5.10 | 7.76 | 1.51 | 36.8 | 78.1 |
| Oxides of nitrogen (*millions of short tons*) | 15.1 | 17.1 | 5.27 | 8.99 | 2.68 | 23.4 | 72.5 |
| Particulates (*millions of short tons*) | 6.21 | 9.85 | 2.20 | 7.17 | 0.58 | 38.1 | 64.1 |
| Hydrocarbons (*millions of short tons*) | 2.8 | 2.08 | 0.86 | 1.90 | 0.67 | 3.46 | 11.8 |
| Land use (*millions of acres*) | 13.7 | 18.8 | 3.37 | 11.9 | 0.005 | 15.1 | 62.8 |
| Solid wastes (*millions of short tons*) | 61.9 | 240 | 7.69 | 50.4 | 0.73 | 187 | 547 |
| Tritium (*thousands of curies*) | 103 | 145 | 22.9 | 34.6 | 3.64 | 47.9 | 357 |
| Population exposure (*thousands of man-rems*) | 3.98 | 5.59 | 0.88 | 1.33 | 0.14 | 1.84 | 13.8 |
| Solid high-level wastes (*billions of curies*) | 11.0 | 15.5 | 2.44 | 3.69 | 0.39 | 5.10 | 38.1 |
| **1990** | | | | | | | |
| Carbon dioxide (*billions of short tons*) | 5.90 | 8.29 | 1.88 | 3.42 | 1.15 | 10.2 | 30.9 |
| Carbon monoxide (*millions of short tons*) | 29.4 | 15.6 | 9.20 | 21.1 | 7.97 | 28.9 | 112.0 |
| Sulfur dioxide (*millions of short tons*) | 14.2 | 15.6 | 5.52 | 9.40 | 1.94 | 41.9 | 88.5 |
| Oxides of nitrogen (*millions of short tons*) | 14.9 | 18.2 | 5.84 | 11.0 | 3.46 | 26.7 | 82.0 |
| Particulates (*millions of short tons*) | 6.92 | 11.0 | 2.38 | 8.63 | 0.76 | 43.4 | 73.1 |
| Hydrocarbons (*millions of short tons*) | 1.29 | 2.17 | 1.06 | 2.32 | 0.86 | 3.94 | 13.7 |
| Land use (*millions of acres*) | 15.7 | 21.7 | 4.43 | 15.7 | 0.008 | 21.7 | 79.1 |
| Solid wastes (*millions of short tons*) | 74.2 | 280.0 | 7.75 | 60.4 | 1.02 | 213.0 | 637.0 |
| Tritium (*thousands of curies*) | 178.0 | 225.0 | 42.4 | 74.6 | 12.0 | 118.0 | 650.0 |
| Population exposure (*thousands of man-rems*) | 6.83 | 8.65 | 1.63 | 2.87 | 0.46 | 4.53 | 25.0 |
| Solid high-level wastes (*billions of curies*) | 18.9 | 24.0 | 4.52 | 7.95 | 1.28 | 12.6 | 69.2 |

probable consequences of the projections are discussed below.

*Carbon Dioxide*. As projected, carbon dioxide emissions in 1990 will be about double those of the mid-1970s. The prevailing belief among climatologists is that increases of $CO_2$ emissions on this order of magnitude will not have strong impacts. [1] However, there is growing concern that, if heavy reliance on fossil fuels continues, accumulations of carbon dioxide in the atmosphere will cause seriously disruptive climatic shifts in the early 21st century.

*Particulates*. IEES-ESNS estimates a total of 61–78 million short tons of particulates per year will result from fossil fuel combustions in 1990.

This represents roughly a doubling of energy-related particulate emissions. More than half of these emissions are calculated to come from the centrally planned economies, due to the energy projection of their heavy reliance on coal.

Present global particulate emissions from natural and anthropogenic sources were estimated at 2.6 billion short tons per year—about 50 times the projected 1990 energy-related particulate

emissions.[2] Thus, the energy sector may not have a major impact on the total global particulate levels.

In urban areas the projected doubling of energy-related particulates would degrade the air quality, lowering visibility and contributing to chronic and acute respiratory illnesses. The extent of harm that might be done is difficult to estimate due to (1) lack of knowledge about

## TABLE 10–17

### Emisson Projections, 1985 and 1990, High-Growth Case

| | European OECD Countries | U.S. and Canada | Japan | Less Developed Countries | OPEC Countries | Centrally Planned Economies | World |
|---|---|---|---|---|---|---|---|
| **1985** | | | | | | | |
| Carbon dioxide | | | | | | | |
| (billions of short tons) | 5.81 | 8.31 | 1.88 | 3.02 | .97 | 9.27 | 29.2 |
| Carbon monoxide | | | | | | | |
| (millions of short tons) | 27.4 | 17.4 | 7.89 | 18.2 | 6.69 | 26.2 | 104.0 |
| Sulfur dioxide | | | | | | | |
| (millions of short tons) | 14.3 | 15.5 | 5.73 | 8.35 | 1.63 | 37.9 | 83.3 |
| Oxides of nitrogen | | | | | | | |
| (millions of short tons) | 17.0 | 22.2 | 5.90 | 9.62 | 2.90 | 24.1 | 78.3 |
| Particulates | | | | | | | |
| (millions of short tons) | 6.44 | 10.7 | 2.37 | 7.77 | 0.62 | 39.2 | 67.2 |
| Hydrocarbons | | | | | | | |
| (millions of short tons) | 3.11 | 1.84 | .94 | 2.01 | 0.72 | 3.57 | 12.7 |
| Land use | | | | | | | |
| (millions of acres) | 13.7 | 18.8 | 3.37 | 11.9 | 0.005 | 15.1 | 62.9 |
| Solid wastes | | | | | | | |
| (millions of short tons) | 66.5 | 264.0 | 8.01 | 55.5 | 1.02 | 193.0 | 588.0 |
| Tritium | | | | | | | |
| (thousands of curies) | 103.0 | 149.0 | 22.9 | 34.6 | 3.64 | 47.9 | 361.0 |
| Population exposure | | | | | | | |
| (thousands of man-rems) | 3.98 | 5.71 | .88 | 1.33 | 0.14 | 1.84 | 13.9 |
| Solid high-level wastes | | | | | | | |
| (billions of curies) | 11.0 | 15.9 | 2.44 | 3.69 | 0.39 | 5.10 | 38.4 |
| **1990** | | | | | | | |
| Carbon dioxide | | | | | | | |
| (billions of short tons) | 6.80 | 9.47 | 2.15 | 3.84 | 1.36 | 10.7 | 34.3 |
| Carbon monoxide | | | | | | | |
| (millions of short tons) | 33.6 | 18.6 | 10.5 | 23.6 | 9.36 | 30.2 | 126.0 |
| Sulfur dioxide | | | | | | | |
| (millions of short tons) | 16.4 | 17.8 | 6.38 | 10.5 | 2.28 | 43.7 | 97.0 |
| Oxides of nitrogen | | | | | | | |
| (millions of short tons) | 19.7 | 25.3 | 6.72 | 12.3 | 4.07 | 27.8 | 91.1 |
| Particulates | | | | | | | |
| (millions of short tons) | 7.58 | 12.4 | 2.63 | 9.60 | 0.87 | 45.3 | 78.3 |
| Hydrocarbons | | | | | | | |
| (millions of short tons) | 3.79 | 2.15 | 1.17 | 2.60 | 1.01 | 4.12 | 15.3 |
| Land use | | | | | | | |
| (millions of acres) | 15.7 | 21.7 | 4.43 | 15.7 | 0.009 | 21.7 | 79.2 |
| Solid wastes | | | | | | | |
| (millions of short tons) | 63.7 | 314.0 | 8.32 | 67.9 | 1.46 | 223.0 | 667.0 |
| Tritium | | | | | | | |
| (thousands of curies) | 178.0 | 230.0 | 42.4 | 74.6 | 12.0 | 118.0 | 655.0 |
| Population exposure | | | | | | | |
| (thousands of man-rems) | 6.83 | 8.86 | 1.63 | 2.87 | 0.46 | 4.53 | 25.2 |
| Solid high-level wastes | | | | | | | |
| (billions of curies) | 18.9 | 24.6 | 4.52 | 7.95 | 1.28 | 12.6 | 69.8 |

## TABLE 10–18

### Emission Projections, 1985 and 1990, Low-Growth Case

| | European OECD Countries | U.S. and Canada | Japan | Less Developed Countries | OPEC Countries | Centrally Planned Economies | World |
|---|---|---|---|---|---|---|---|
| **1985** | | | | | | | |
| Carbon dioxide | | | | | | | |
| (billions of short tons) | 4.78 | 6.85 | 1.51 | 2.57 | 0.80 | 7.52 | 24.0 |
| Carbon monoxide | | | | | | | |
| (millions of short tons) | 22.5 | 13.4 | 6.68 | 15.7 | 5.50 | 22.4 | 86.1 |
| Sulfur dioxide | | | | | | | |
| (millions of short tons) | 11.8 | 13.0 | 4.52 | 7.07 | 1.33 | 29.8 | 67.4 |
| Oxides of nitrogen | | | | | | | |
| (millions of short tons) | 13.5 | 15.7 | 4.71 | 8.21 | 2.38 | 19.7 | 64.1 |
| Particulates | | | | | | | |
| (millions of short tons) | 6.3 | 9.02 | 2.03 | 6.56 | 0.54 | 30.6 | 55.0 |
| Hydrocarbons | | | | | | | |
| (millions of short tons) | 2.56 | 1.84 | 0.79 | 1.73 | 0.59 | 2.99 | 10.5 |
| Land use | | | | | | | |
| (millions of acres) | 13.7 | 18.7 | 3.37 | 11.9 | 0.004 | 15.1 | 61.2 |
| Solid wastes | | | | | | | |
| (millions of short tons) | 80.1 | 218 | 7.43 | 45.6 | 0.58 | 149 | 500 |
| Tritium | | | | | | | |
| (thousands of curies) | 103 | 142 | 22.9 | 34.6 | 3.64 | 47.9 | 354 |
| Population exposure | | | | | | | |
| (thousands of man-rems) | 3.98 | 5.44 | 0.88 | 1.33 | 0.14 | 1.84 | 13.6 |
| Solid high-level aastes | | | | | | | |
| (billions of curies) | 11.0 | 15.1 | 2.44 | 3.69 | 0.39 | 5.10 | 37.6 |
| **1990** | | | | | | | |
| Carbon dioxide | | | | | | | |
| (billions of short tons) | 5.20 | 7.31 | 1.62 | 3.05 | 0.97 | 8.42 | 26.6 |
| Carbon monoxide | | | | | | | |
| (millions of short tons) | 26.2 | 13.1 | 8.44 | 19.6 | 6.96 | 25.0 | 99.2 |
| Sulfur dioxide | | | | | | | |
| (millions of short tons) | 12.7 | 13.8 | 4.68 | 8.42 | 1.56 | 33.4 | 74.6 |
| Oxides of nitrogen | | | | | | | |
| (millions of short tons) | 14.8 | 16.2 | 4.44 | 9.74 | 2.88 | 22.0 | 70.7 |
| Particulates | | | | | | | |
| (millions of short tons) | 6.66 | 9.73 | 2.15 | 7.81 | 0.63 | 34.2 | 61.2 |
| Hydrocarbons | | | | | | | |
| (millions of short tons) | 2.94 | 1.85 | 0.38 | 2.14 | 0.73 | 3.35 | 12.0 |
| Land use | | | | | | | |
| (millions of acres) | 15.7 | 21.6 | 4.43 | 15.7 | 0.007 | 21.6 | 79.0 |
| Solid wastes | | | | | | | |
| (millions of short tons) | 75.1 | 243 | 7.49 | 50.2 | 1.02 | 168 | 545 |
| Tritium | | | | | | | |
| (thousands of curies) | 178 | 214 | 42.4 | 74.6 | 12.0 | 118 | 639 |
| Population exposure | | | | | | | |
| (thousands of man-rems) | 6.83 | 8.23 | 1.63 | 2.87 | 0.46 | 4.53 | 24.6 |
| Solid high-level wastes | | | | | | | |
| (billions of curies) | 18.9 | 22.9 | 4.52 | 7.95 | 1.28 | 12.6 | 68.1 |

chemical composition and specific effects of particulates; (2) dependence of the effects on plant siting, air drainage, and other factors; and (3) difficulties establishing clear cause and effect relationships in health problems.

*Sulfur dioxide.* IEES-ESNS projects global emissions of sulfur dioxide to be between 75 and 97 million short tons per year in 1990. Nearly half of this—33 to 44 million short tons—is projected to come from the centrally planned economies and is again attributable to the energy projection that the centrally planned economies will rely heavily on coal as an energy source.

The IEES-ESNS figures for sulfur dioxide emissions are probably substantially lower than will actually be realized. Global emissions of sulfur dioxide are currently about 140 million

## TABLE 10–19

**Recent Estimates of Emissions from Fuel Combustion, Compared with IEES-ESNS Estimates for 1990**

|  | Present Emissions per Year | Calculated Emissions per Year for 1990 |
|---|---|---|
| Carbon dioxide (*billions of short tons*) | 5.4[a] | 27—34 |
| Sulfur dioxide (*millions of short tons*) | 113[b] | 75—97 |
| Oxides of nitrogen (*millions of short tons*) | 52[c] | 71—91 |
| Particulates (*millions of short tons*) | 28[d] | 61—78 |

[a] Council on Environmental Quality, *8th Annual Report*, 1977, p. 190.
[b] Estimated from total global sulfur dioxide generation figures in D. M. Whelpdale and R. E. Munn, in A. C. Stern, ed., *Air Pollution*, vol. 7, 3rd ed., New York: Academic Press, 1977.
[c] E. Robinson and R. C. Robbins, *Emissions Concentrations and Fate of Particulate Atmospheric Pollutants*, Menlo Park, Calif.: Stanford Research Institute, 1971.
[d] Ibid.: calculated using same procedures used for sulfur dioxide estimates.

short tons per year.[3] If U.S. figures are typical throughout the world, then 81 percent of the sulfur oxide emissions (113 million short tons) are from fuel combustion. The IEES-ESNS figures would therefore imply a substantial decrease in sulfur dioxide emissions between now and 2000. These optimistically low projections stem in large part from the assumption that U.S. new-source performance standards will be applied throughout the world. The Environmental Protection Agency's Office of Research and Development estimates that these standards would, in the case of high-sulfur coals, require reductions in emissions from coal combustion to about 20 percent of the unregulated emissions.

Sulfur dioxide and its oxidation products have many adverse effects on biological organisms. These pollutants damage crops and other vegetation. They are respiratory irritants and contribute to acid rain and its damage to fish and vegetation (see the forestry and fresh water projections in this chapter). The extent to which sulfur dioxide emissions from the global energy sector increase or decrease will determine whether the problems associated with sulfur dioxide and sulfates will increase or decrease in the years ahead.

The reduction of atmospheric emissions is not a final solution to the sulfur problem. The chemical-rich sludge that results from desulfurization processes can itself become an environmental hazard. The projected increases in desulfurization imply volumes of sludge large enough to require considerable amounts of land for disposal. Even after the land-use problem is solved, leaching problems can lead to further environmental damage.

*Oxides of Nitrogen*. IEES-ESNS estimates the 1990 emissions of oxides of nitrogen at 71–91 million short tons per year. As a point of comparison, current global emissions from fossil fuel combustion have been estimated at 52 million short tons per year, which is less than 10 percent of the almost 600 million short tons of nitrogen dioxide thought to be released into the atmosphere annually by bacterial action.[2] The Brookhaven 1990 figure, therefore, represents an increase of 30–75 percent over current estimated global emissions from fossil fuel sources. Even though this increase is small compared to natural sources, it may be environmentally significant, since it will occur in urban and industrial areas with high population density, where it will contribute to the formation of photochemical oxidants, the most damaging ingredient in smog.

Human exposure to nitrogen dioxide has been shown to increase susceptibility to respiratory infections and result in increases in chronic respiratory diseases. Ozone, a respiratory irritant formed in the atmosphere through chemical reactions involving nitrogen oxides, is associated with decreased pulmonary functions. It is unclear whether oxides of nitrogen alone have adverse effects on vegetation, but adverse synergistic effects of oxides of nitrogen and sulfur dioxide have been demonstrated. Photochemical smogs containing nitrogen oxides, ozone, and related pollutants are quite damaging to many food crops and to other sensitive vegetation. Nitrogen dioxide and nitrate aerosols contribute to decreased visibility.

*Carbon Monoxide*. IEES-ESNS projects carbon monoxide emissions in 1990 at between 99.2 and 126 million short tons per year. No current estimates of carbon monoxide emissions could be found for comparison. However, the IEES-ESNS figure for 1990 represents a 16 percent increase over the 1985 figure. These increased carbon monoxide emissions are expected to have little environmental effect—except in urban areas—because carbon monoxide released into the atmosphere quickly dilutes to levels believed to be below physiological significance.

*Nuclear Emissions*. Of the radioactive emissions figures produced by IEES-ESNS, the high-level solid wastes, which pose the greatest difficulty (and the greatest potential hazard), are the only ones discussed here.

The problem of high-level radioactive solid waste is not so much in the magnitude of the wastes generated (which is projected to be large) as in the nature of the disposal problem. At present the technical problems of high-level waste disposal are unresolved. The U.S. Department of Energy plans a demonstration project in the next few years, but no commercial facilities are now available in the U.S. With the future of reprocessing plants in question because of their potential to contribute to the proliferation of nuclear weapons, spent fuel rods are rapidly filling existing storage facilities in some countries.

Disposal of nuclear wastes will be a difficult issue even with solution to the technical problems of storage and the political problems of proliferation. Japan and several of the European nuclear countries lack appropriate sites for disposal. Localities with sites more suitable for disposal may resist having nuclear waste facilities developed within their jurisdictions. All but three states in the U.S. have rejected nuclear disposal within their borders.[4]

## Conclusions

Increases in energy use will, *ceterus paribus*, lead to increases of the gaseous emissions generated in the course of energy use. The extent of the increase will depend on what fuels are used and how emissions are regulated. A strategy making heavy use of coal—as in the energy calculation for the centrally planned economies—leads to heavy loadings of particulates, sulfur dioxide, oxides of nitrogen, and carbon dioxide. Worldwide regulation along the lines of the U.S. new-source performance standards would reduce sulfur dioxide emissions to the point where total annual emissions in 1990 could be less than present-day emissions if they were applied on a global basis.

The strongest impacts for the class of energy impacts considered in the Brookhaven analysis are likely to be those on urban air quality. As well as having the aesthetically negative quality of dirtying air and reducing visibility, these air-quality impacts will tend to increase respiratory illnesses and damage to vegetation. In the longer-term, accumulation of atmospheric carbon dioxide may have more impact on the environment than all the other effects of energy use taken together. This probably will not have happened by 2000, though if the world by then has adopted an energy strategy based on coal, oil shale, and other fossil fuels that will still be abundant by 2000, the best scientific evidence presently available indicates that large disruptive climate shifts may occur in the first half of the 21st century.

## REFERENCES

1. Ralph M. Rotty, "Uncertainties Associated with Future Atmospheric $CO_2$ Levels," Oak Ridge Associated Universities, Institute for Energy Analysis, June 1977.
2. E. Robinson and R. C. Robbins, *Emissions Concentrations and Fate of Particulate Atmospheric Pollutants*, Menlo Park, Calif.: Stanford Research Institute, 1971.
3. D. M. Whelpdale and R. E. Munn, in A. C. Stern, ed., *Air Pollution*, vol. 7, 3rd ed., New York: Academic Press, 1977.
4. "Trouble even in New Mexico for Nuclear Waste Disposal," *Science*, Mar. 10, 1978, p. 1050.

# 11 Fuel-Minerals Projections

A consensus is developing that a major shift in the world's patterns of energy utilization is impending. Growing energy demand will deplete conventional energy resources eventually. The problem is more acute for petroleum and natural gas than coal—our most abundant conventional fuel. But there are limits to the role that even coal can play.

Table 11–1 illustrates the estimated energy resources available to the world. It should be clearly understood that a high degree of uncertainty applies to these numbers, as resource estimating is not an exact science. Thus, approximately 161,250 quadrillion Btu (British thermal units) of energy is assumed available for use—if conditions allow. While this seems large, an exercise developed by Vincent E. McKelvey, former Director of the U.S. Geological Survey, shows the impact of exponential growth rates of energy demand.[1] Assuming only the energy availability shown in Table 11–1, and world energy consumption of approximately 250 quadrillion Btu (the 1976 estimate), life of these resources would be:

At 0 percent annual increase in demand rate:
  Resource life = 161,250/250 = 645 years

At 2 percent annual increase in the demand rate:

| Cumulative consumption during | |
|---|---:|
| 1st doubling period (1977–2011) | 12,750 |
| 2nd doubling period (2012–2046) | 25,500 |
| 3rd doubling period (2047–2081) | 51,000 |
| Total 1977–2081 | 89,256 |
| Total 2082–2110 | 71,494 |
| Total | 160,750 |

It would appear that a fourth doubling would be impossible, and that resource life would be less than 133 years.

At 5 percent annual increase in the demand rate:

| Cumulative consumption during | |
|---|---:|
| 1st doubling period (1977–1990) | 5,150 |
| 2nd dubling period (1991–2004) | 10,300 |
| 3rd doubling period (2005–2018) | 20,600 |
| 4th doubling period (2019–2032) | 41,200 |
| 5th doubling period (2033–2046) | 82,400 |
| Total 1977–2046 (70 years) | 159,650 |

## TABLE 11–1

### Recoverable World Nonrenewable Energy Resources

*(Quadrillion Btu)*

| | |
|---|---:|
| Petroleum [a] | 9,634 |
| Natural gas [a] | 8,663 |
| Solid fuels [b] | 120,854 |
| Shale oil [c] | 20,130 |
| Tar sands [d] | |
| Uranium [e] | 1,960 |
| Total | 161,241 |

[a] Based on physical units from Congressional Research Service. *Project Interdependence: U.S. and World Energy Outlook Through 1990.* Washington: GPO, 1977 (based on work done by M. King Hubbert). Conversion factors: 1 barrel oil = 5.8 million Btu; 1 cu ft natural gas = 1,020 Btu.
[b] Based on physical units from World Energy Conference. *Survey of Energy Resources,* 1976. Recoverability of coal assumed to be 50 percent. Conversion factor varies for geographical regions.
[c] Based on physical units from U.S. Geological Survey. Represents identified resources only.
[d] Not estimated, but total energy content of oil in-place is approximately 5,600–9,000 quadrillion Btu, based on physical units in table 11–18.
[e] Based on physical units from World Energy Conference. *Survey of Energy Resources,* 1976. Light-water reactor technology assumed. Conversion factor: 400 billion Btu/short ton of $U_3O_8$.

It would appear that a sixth doubling would be impossible and that resource life would be slightly over 70 years.

The above is a highly artificial example of the effects of continued growth rates on the energy resource base, as the expectation of continued growth is unrealistic. It does point to the problem to be faced as the world shifts from one energy source to another.

Other energy sources have the potentiality for supplying future energy demand. Some, such as solar energy, are renewable while others, such as nuclear fission (using the breeder), thermonuclear fusion (perhaps), and geothermal energy, offer hopes of long-term solution to energy supply. The major problem is bridging the transition from the fossil fuels to the more abundant energy sources.

## Resource Terminology

In discussing resources it is necessary to define two key terms—reserves and resources. For the United States the terminology is based on a U.S.

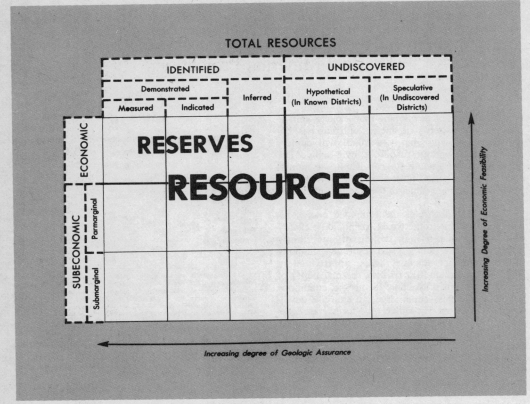

**Figure 11-1.** Classification of mineral resources.

Geological Survey/Bureau of Mines classification system.[2] The system is based on two variables—degree of geologic assurance and degree of Economic feasibility—illustrated in Figure 11-1.

Thus, reserves are identified deposits of minerals known to be recoverable with current technology under present economic conditions. There are three categories of reserves:

*Measured reserves* are identified reserves from which an energy commodity can be economically extracted with existing technology and whose location, quality, and quantity are known from geologic evidence supported by engineering evidence.

*Indicated reserves* are reserves based partly on specific measurements, samples, or production data and partly on projections for a reasonable time period on the basis of geological evidence.

*Inferred reserves* are reserves based upon broad geologic knowledge for which quantitative measurements are not available. Such reserves are estimated to be recoverable in the future as a result of extensions, revisions of estimates, and deeper drilling in known fields.

In most instances these three categories are undifferentiated here. Reserves of coal are sometimes discussed in different terms, as follows:

The *demonstrated coal reserve base* includes measured and indicated in-place quantities of bituminous coal and anthracite located in beds 28 inches or more thick, and subbituminous coal in beds 60 or more inches thick that are located in depths up to 1,000 feet. The demonstrated coal reserve base includes also small quantities of coal located in beds thinner and/or deeper than coal presently mined, for which there is evidence that mining is commercially feasible at this time. The data for lignite include beds 60 inches or more

## TABLE 11–2

### Reserve and Resource Terminology

| Type Resources | Total Reserves | Recoverable Reserves | Other Resources [a] |
|---|---|---|---|
| Solid fuels [b] | Known reserve-in-place | Known recoverable | Additional resources |
| Oil and natural gas | Original reserve-in-place [c] | Proved recoverable reserves | Additional resources |
| Natural gas liquids | | Proved recoverable reserves | Additional resources |
| Oil shale and bituminous sands | | Potential total known recoverable resources | |
| Uranium and thorium | | Known recoverable reserves [d] | Additional resources |

Note: Terminology for hydraulic resources includes installed and installable capacity (power in Mw) and probable annual generation (energy in GWhr/yr). Similar terminology applies, in general, to other renewable resources.
[a] Includes indicated (probable) and inferred (possible) reserves as normally defined.
[b] Total resources are also given for solid fuels.
[c] Includes past cumulative production.
[d] Alternative (Organization for Economic Cooperation and Development) terminology is reasonably assured resources (recoverable at costs up to approximately $26/kg of U or Th). Reasonably assured resources recoverable at costs above $26/kg are regarded as part of additional resources.
Source: Bauer and Carlsmith, p. 47.

thick that can be surface-mined. These are generally located at depths no greater than 120 feet.

*Resources* includes reserves as well as minerals that have been identified but cannot now be extracted because of economic or technological limitations, as well as economic or subeconomic materials that have not as yet been discovered.

*Undiscovered recoverable resources* are quantities of an energy commodity that may be reasonably expected to exist in favorable geologic settings but that have not yet been identified by drilling. Exploration and resulting discovery will permit the reclassification of such resources to the reserves category.

This, of course, is the U.S. system. There are other classification systems. As pointed out by Bauer and Carlsmith,[3] "One of the reasons for a wide disparity in definitions of reserves and resources of energy raw materials among the various regions and nations is that present local usage is based on historical precedents which have evolved under differing social, legal, economic, and technical experiences and commercial practices." For this reason the World Energy Conference (WEC) in its latest reports uses the reserve and resources terminology defined in Table 11–2.

The above classification systems are applicable primarily to stock energy sources, i.e., energy sources having finite quantities. Problems arise in classifying flow and renewable energy forms, for here the concept of time enters. For this reason, renewable energy sources will be shown with their annual output. This is particularly true for hydropower, tidal power, solar energy, etc.

Before turning to the subject of oil resources, some qualifications regarding reserves should be noted. V. E. McKelvey states: We know a good deal about reserves because the deposits compos-

ing them have been identified and their geometry and quality evaluated on the basis of direct evidence. Even so estimates of reserves do not have the exactitudes of inventories of other kinds of stock and they may err by plus or minus 10–25 percent. The assessment of undiscovered resources, however, entails far more hypothesis and much speculation, based on incomplete and sometimes incompatible data, with the hazard, then, that even the most conscientious estimate may be grossly in error.[4]

### Petroleum

Various resource estimators place the quantity of ultimately recoverable petroleum at approximately 2,000 billion barrels. Some of these estimates made since 1970 and cited by M. King Hubbert in the *Project Interdependence* report[5] are presented in Table 11–3.

## TABLE 11–3

### Estimates of World Ultimate Production of Crude Oil Made Since 1970

*(Billions of barrels)*

| Estimators | Organization | Quantity |
|---|---|---|
| J. D. Moody and H. H. Emenik | Mobil Oil Corp. | 1,800–1,900 |
| Richard L. Jody | Sun Oil Co. | 1,952 |
| H. R. Warman | BP, Ltd. | 1,800 |
| William Verneer | Shell | 1,930 |
| H. R. Warman | BP, Ltd. | 1,915 |
| J. D. Moody and R. W. Esser | Mobil Oil Corp. | 2,000 |
| M. King Hubbert | U.S. Geological Survey | 2,000 |

Hubbert's estimates of ultimate production of crude oil are given in Table 11–4. Basically, he estimates that 2,000 billion barrels of oil were available originally, and that approximately 339 billion barrels have already been produced. This leaves 1,661 billion barrels of remaining resources. Of this, 646 billion barrels are reserves,[6] leaving slightly over 1,000 billion barrels to be discovered. Reserves as of January 1, 1978, are shown in Table 11–5 for various regions of the world.

In 1976 the world produced 21.7 billion barrels of oil. Thus, if the production rate remained constant, world reserves of oil would last about 30 years, and total resources about 77 years. This is, of course, not a proper description of the decline pattern of petroleum production. The overall production would decline over time from some peak, and the time involved would be longer than 77 years. A feeling is developing that the peak of petroleum production will occur in the 1990s.

The World Energy Conference recently ran a survey among various resource estimators on their view of ultimately recoverable resources of oil.[7] The average of their low estimates was 1,240 billion barrels; of their median estimates, 1,806 billion barrels; and of their high estimates, 3,110 billion barrels. Most of the incremental oil for the high estimate comes from deep offshore and polar areas (505 billion barrels additional) and the Mid-

dle East (315 billion barrels additional). The degree to which other resource estimators have included deep offshore and polar areas is not readily discernible.

Bernardo F. Grossling of the U.S. Geological Survey has pointed out that many prospective areas of the world have not been extensively drilled. As shown in Table 13–5 the density of drilling per square mile of prospective petroleum area $(mi^2)$ varies from a high of 0.98 wells/mile$^2$ in the United States to a low of 0.0031 wells/mile$^2$ in Africa. As many resource estimates are based on extrapolations from known petroleum areas, some of the least drilled areas may contain resources not showing up in resource estimates.

The 9,634 quadrillion Btu of petroleum resources constitutes 5.4 percent of total recoverable world nonrenewable energy resources.

Two final points on the distribution of petroleum resources and reserves are in order. One is that, in general, reserves and resources are fairly closely correlated, as would be expected. There is one notable exception—and that is the communist countries. These countries have 15 percent of total world petroleum reserves, and are estimated to have 25 percent of total world petroleum resources. Development is at an early to intermediate stage.

A second general point is that, with the excep-

## TABLE 11–4

### World Cumulative Production, Ultimate Production, and Future Resources of Crude Oil as of January 1, 1976

| Region | Cumulative Production | Ultimate Production | Remaining Resources | Energy Content |
|---|---|---|---|---|
| | *Billions of barrels* | | | *Quadrillion Btu* |
| United States and Canada: | | | | |
| United States | 112.118 | 215 | 103 | 597 |
| Canada | 7.217 | 84 | 77 | 446 |
| Total | 119.335 | 299 | 180 | 1,044 |
| Latin America: | | | | |
| Mexico | 5.574 | 30 | 24 | 139 |
| South America | 39.675 | 160 | 120 | 696 |
| Total | 45.249 | 190 | 144 | 835 |
| Europe (excluding communist countries) | 3.220 | 68 | 65 | 377 |
| Africa | 20.598 | 162 | 141 | 818 |
| Middle East | 84.170 | 598 | 514 | 2,981 |
| Asia-Pacific | 9.477 | 96 | 87 | 505 |
| Communist countries | 57.367 | 472 | 415 | 2,407 |
| Additional future discoveries | — | 115 | 115 | 667 |
| World total | 339.416 | 2,000 | 1,661 | 9,634 |

*Note:* Conversion factor: 1 barrel oil = 5.8 million Btu.

*Source:* Library of Congress, Congressional Research Service, *Project Interdependence: U.S. and World Energy Outlook Through 1990.*

## TABLE 11–5

### World Petroleum Reserves, January 1, 1978

| Region | Estimated Proved Reserves | Estimated Production 1977 | Reserves/ Production Ratio |
|---|---|---|---|
| | *Billions of barrels* | | |
| U.S. and Canada | | | |
| United States | 29.50 | 3.01 | 9.8 |
| Canada | 6.00 | .50 | 12.0 |
| Total | 35.50 | 3.51 | 10.1 |
| Latin America | | | |
| Mexico | 14.00 | .36 | 38.9 |
| Central and South America | 26.37 | 1.31 | 20.1 |
| Total | 40.37 | 1.67 | 24.2 |
| Europe (excluding communist countries) | 26.8 | .50 | 53.6 |
| Africa | 59.20 | | |
| Middle East | 366.17 | 7.98 | 45.9 |
| Asia-Pacific (excluding communist countries) | 19.75 | 1.01 | 19.6 |
| Communist countries | | | |
| U.S.S.R. | 75.00 | 4.00 | 18.7 |
| China | 20.00 | .66 | 30.3 |
| Other | 3.00 | .15 | 20.0 |
| Total | 98.00 | 4.81 | 20.4 |
| Total World | 645.85 | 21.73 | 29.7 |

*Source: Oil and Gas Journal. December 26, 1977.*

## TABLE 11–6

### Density of Petroleum Drilling for Selected Areas of the World, as of End of 1975 [a]

| Country or Region | Wells/mile² | Exploratory Wells/mile² |
|---|---|---|
| United States | 0.98 | 0.20 |
| U.S.S.R. | 0.15 | 0.029 |
| Canada | 0.053 | 0.011 |
| Western Europe | 0.019 | 0.0094 |
| Japan | 0.021 | 0.0039 |
| Australia and New Zealand | 0.0016 | 0.0032 |
| South and Southeast Asia [b] | 0.0067 | 0.0031 |
| Latin America [b] | 0.0021 | 0.0029 |
| People's Republic of China [b] | 0.010 | 0.0022 |
| Middle East [b] | 0.0083 | 0.0017 |
| Africa [b] | 0.0031 | 0.0014 |

[a] Density refers to prospective petroleum areas of a country, which are, in general, smaller than the total area of the country.
[b] Development area.

*Source:* Bernardo F. Grossling. "The Petroleum Exploration Challenge with Respect to Developing Nations." in *The Future Supply of Nature-Made Petroleum and Gas: The First UNITAR Conference on Energy and the Future.* Elmsford, N.Y.: Pergamon. 1977.

tion of the U.S.S.R., the industrialized nations with the highest rate of petroleum consumption have the smallest reserves and resources. The implications for future capital transfers are significant.

## Natural Gas

Unlike petroleum, no consensus has developed as to natural gas resources. Some estimates made since 1970 are given in Table 11–7. M. King Hubbert has estimated that the ultimate natural gas production is 10,000 tcf (trillions of cubic feet), of which 1,507 has been produced. This leaves 8,493 tcf available, as illustrated in Table 11–8. Of the available resources, 2,519 tcf consist of reserves, leaving 5,984 tcf still to be found. Reserves are delineated in Table 11–9 for various regions of the world.

In 1976 approximately 50 tcf of natural gas was produced. Assuming continuation of this rate of production, the world would have reserves lasting 44.6 years, and total remaining resources lasting approximately 170 years. As with petroleum, this is not an especially apt description of the production rise and decline of natural gas.

Also, as with petroleum, the sparsity of drilling in certain prospective petroleum areas may indicate understatement of the resources in these regions.

Natural gas resources of 8,663 quadrillion Btu represent 4.8 percent of the total nonrenewable energy resources estimated to be remaining to the world.

## TABLE 11–7

### Estimates Made Since 1970 of Remaining World Resources of Natural Gas

*(Trillions of cubic feet)*

| Estimators | Organization | Quantity [a] |
|---|---|---|
| C. P. Coppack | | 6,660 |
| M. King Hubbert | U.S. Geological Survey | 11,950 |
| | Mobil Oil Corp. | 7,020–7,880 |
| T. D. Adams and M. R. Kirby | | 5,150 |
| | National Academy of Science | 6,900 |
| | Institute of Gas Technology | 9,150–9,550 |
| M. King Hubbert | Congressional Research Service | 8,493 |

[a] Remaining resources converted to ultimate resources by addition of 1.500 tcf previous production to figure. Numbers originally in exajoules and converted on basis of 1 tcf = 1.0885 exajoules.

*Source:* World Energy Conference. *The Future for World Natural Gas Supply. 1985–2020.* Apr. 15, 1977. p. 5.

## TABLE 11-8

### World Cumulative Production, Ultimate Production, and Future Resources of Natural Gas (January 1, 1976)

| Region | Cumulative Production | Ultimate Production | Remaining Resources | Energy Content |
|---|---|---|---|---|
| | | *Trillions of cubic feet* | | *Quadrillion Btu* |
| United States and Canada: | | | | |
| United States | 500 | 1,240 | 740 | 755 |
| Canada | 26 | 663 | 637 | 650 |
| Total | 526 | 1,903 | 1,377 | 1,405 |
| Latin America: | | | | |
| Mexico | 21 | 104 | 83 | 85 |
| South America | 106 | 428 | 322 | 328 |
| Total | 127 | 532 | 405 | 413 |
| Europe (excluding communist countries) | 25 | 517 | 492 | 502 |
| Africa | 81 | 638 | 557 | 568 |
| Middle East | 158 | 1,122 | 964 | 983 |
| Asia-Pacific | 46 | 468 | 422 | 430 |
| Communist countries | 544 | 4,478 | 3,934 | 4,013 |
| Additional future discoveries | — | 342 | 342 | 349 |
| World total | 1,507 | 10,000 | 8,493 | 8,663 |

*Note:* Conversion factor: 1 cubic foot = 1.020 Btu.

*Source:* Library of Congress. Congressional Research Service. *Project Interdependence: U.S. and World Energy Outlook Through 1990.*

## TABLE 11-9

### World Natural Gas Reserves, January 1, 1978

*(Billions of cubic feet)*

| Region | Estimated Proved Reserves |
|---|---|
| United States and Canada: | |
| United States | 210,000 |
| Canada | 58,000 |
| Total | 268,000 |
| Latin America: | |
| Mexico | 30,000 |
| Central and South America | 78,580 |
| Total | 108,580 |
| Europe (excluding communist countries) | 138,190 |
| Africa | 207,504 |
| Middle East | 719,660 |
| Asia-Pacific (excluding communist countries) | 122,725 |
| Communist countries: | |
| U.S.S.R. | 920,000 |
| China | 25,000 |
| Other | 10,000 |
| Total | 955,000 |
| Total World | 2,519,659 |

*Source: Oil & Gas Journal.* Dec. 26, 1977.

As can be seen from Tables 11-8 and 11-9, the communist countries (and the U.S.S.R. in particular) have a significant share of world natural gas reserves and resources. For reserves, the share is 38 percent, and for resources 46 percent. The United States, Canada, and Western Europe have 16 percent of world natural gas reserves and 22 percent of total resources.

## Coal

Coal is a solid, brittle, more or less distinctly stratified, combustible carbonaceous rock, formed by partial to complete decomposition of vegetation. It varies in color from brown to black, and is not fusible without decomposition. It is also very insoluble. Ranks of coal have been established according to the degree of coalification. This is a general indication of carbon content, with anthracite ranking highest followed by bituminous coal, subbituminous coal, and lignite.

World reserves and total resources are shown in Table 11-10. The reserves of 786 billion short tons are recoverable. The total resources of 12,682 billion short tons are in-place coal and must be multiplied by a recoverability factor. For most purposes this is assumed to be 50 percent; thus,

## TABLE 11–10

### Total World Solid Reserves and Fuel Resources

| Continent or Region | Reserves (billion short tons) | Energy Content (quadrillion Btu) | Total Resources[a] (billion short tons) | Energy Content[a] (quadrillion Btu) |
|---|---|---|---|---|
| Africa | 19 | 398 | 106 | 2,209 |
| Asia | 130 | 3,147 | 1,223 | 29,515 |
| Europe | 192 | 3,270 | 770 | 13,128 |
| U.S.S.R. | 151 | 2,328 | 6,294 | 97,294 |
| North America | 229 | 5,478 | 3,978 | 94,993 |
| South America | 7 | 128 | 32 | 594 |
| Oceania | 58 | 822 | 279 | 3,975 |
| Total[b] | 786 | 15,572 | 12,682 | 241,708 |

[a] In-place coal. Recoverability approximately 50 percent.
[b] Data may not add to total due to rounding.
Source: World Energy Conference, Survey of Energy Resources, 1976, Table 1.

the total resource recoverable would be approximately 6,341 billion short tons.

At the 1977 World Energy Conference it was pointed out that the reserves considered technically and economically recoverable constitute only 6 percent of resources, and is probably low. This was attributed to use of extremely strict criteria for assessing and evaluating reserves. In addition, the 50 percent recoverability factor may be too low[8]—a point brought out in greater detail by Paul Averitt.[9] Averitt has also estimated world coal resources. His estimated total resource figure for coal in-place is 16,620 billion short tons—a figure 31 percent higher than the World Energy Conference estimate.[10] Either estimate is far in excess of the amount usable within the time horizon of this study.

At the 1976 rate of coal consumption (3.7 billion short tons per year) coal *reserves* would last for 212 years while recoverable *resources* (total resources at 50 percent recoverability) would last approximately 1,700 years. Growth rates much in excess of zero would sharply decrease these numbers. Still, coal is the world's most abundant fossil fuel.

In contrast to the situation as regards other fossil fuels, the Western nations (the United States, Canada, and Western Europe) have 56 percent of world solid fuel resources based on Btu content. The U.S.S.R. has 15 percent, and the rest of the world has 29 percent. Much the same distribution occurs for resources.

Most resource estimators would say the world possesses abundant coal, fairly evenly distributed over the various continents. Because of the large quantities of coal already located, there has been little effort undertaken in coal deposit research or

exploration. Even more potential may exist beyond the potential already estimated.

Not all resource investigators are in agreement as to the magnitude of the resources of what is commonly called our most plentiful fossil fuel. Gunther Fettweis analyzed worldwide coal resources with more emphasis on technical and economic factors and came up with a world total recoverable resource figure of 1,130 billion short tons.[11] He also pointed out that worldwide distribution of this smaller resource quantity may be rather uneven.

## Nuclear Fuels

Uranium is the fuel used to produce nuclear energy. Unlike other fuels, the technology used will determine the final quantity of energy available. Assuming light-water reactor technology, the uranium requirements for a 1,000 megawatt electrical nuclear powerplant is about 5,400 short tons over its lifetime. (A megawatt is $10^6$ watts.) If the spent fuel is recycled and the unused uranium recovered, this requirement would decline by about 17 percent. Similarly, recycling the plutonium in spent fuel would further reduce uranium requirements by an additional 18 percent.[12] Lifetime requirements for various nuclear powerplant capacities are shown in Table 11–11.

Note that in Table 11–12 total world resources of 4,900 thousand short tons of uranium would thus fuel only 800 gigawatts (800 billion watts) of light-water reactor (or equivalent technology) plants. As a fuel for the present generation of burner reactors, uranium resources now represent a source of limited potential, comparable in magnitude to that of the remaining recoverable re-

194        THE PROJECTIONS

## TABLE 11–11

### Lifetime Uranium Requirements for Nuclear Powerplants

| Installed Nuclear Capacity (Gigawatts) | Lifetime Uranium Requirements (1,000 short tons) |
|---|---|
| 100 | 600 |
| 200 | 1,200 |
| 300 | 1,800 |
| 400 | 2,400 |
| 500 | 3,000 |
| 600 | 3,600 |
| 700 | 4,200 |
| 800 | 4,800 |

Source: Library of Congress, Congressional Research Service. Project Interdependence. p. 285.

sources of oil and gas. The breeder reactor, if deployed, would increase the energy output from this fuel by a factor of from 60–100 times. For this reason stress has been placed by many on building breeder reactors. As a counterpoint, the Nuclear Energy Policy Study Group has stated: "The current assessment of uranium reserves probably substantially understates the supplies that will become available; uranium, at prices making light-water reactors competitive with breeders, will be available for a considerably longer time than previously estimated. New enrichment technologies may also extend these supplies."[13]

Their estimate of 4,876 thousand short tons of uranium at $30 per pound or less is comparable to the 4,900 thousand short tons of the World Energy Conference.

Research continues on not only the breeder reactor but on new types of uranium- and thorium-

cycle burners. Staatz and Olson[14] have come up with a worldwide estimate of 1,435 thousand short tons of thorium oxide recoverable primarily as a by-product, an additional 120,000 short tons of grade higher than 0.1 percent, and 902,000 short tons of lower and 0.1 percent grade. In the United States, the only fuel use of thorium was in high-temperature gas reactors.

## Hydraulic Resources

Conventional hydroelectric developments (ultimately using solar energy) use dams and waterways to harness the energy of falling water in streams to produce electric power. The significant differences between hydropower energy resources and fossil and nuclear fuels[15] are:

- Hydraulic resources are renewable.
- The total potential of hydraulic resources is small compared to fossil fuel resources. Thus their full development could account for only a small part of total energy requirements. Total 1976 world energy consumption was approximately 250 quadrillion Btu. Even if all hydroelectric resources were developed, they could supply only 33.1 quadrillion Btu.
- Hydraulic resources often have other uses—in navigation, flood control, and irrigation—that could interfere with power generation.
- Hydraulic resources convert potential energy to kinetic energy principally for electrical generation purposes, whereas other energy sources first produce heat.

The developed and undeveloped conventional hydroelectric resources of the world are delineated in Table 11–13. Of the total estimated capac-

## TABLE 11–12

### World Uranium Resources

| Continent or Region | Quantity Recoverable at $10–$35/lb (1,000 short tons U308) | Energy Content (quadrillion Btu) | Additional Resources[a] (1,000 short tons U308) | Energy Content (quadrillion Btu) | Total Quantity (1,000 short tons U308) | Total Energy Content (quadrillion Btu) |
|---|---|---|---|---|---|---|
| Africa | 306 | 1,224 | 96 | 383 | 402 | 1,607 |
| Asia | 41 | 164 | 34 | 137 | 75 | 301 |
| Europe | 421 | 1,686 | 91 | 364 | 512 | 2,050 |
| North America | 770 | 3,080 | 2,740 | 10,958 | 3,510 | 14,038 |
| South America | 21 | 85 | 23 | 92 | 44 | 177 |
| Oceania | 268 | 1,074 | 89 | 357 | 357 | 1,431 |
| Total World | 1,827 | 7,313 | 3,073 | 12,291 | 4,900 | 19,604 |

Note: Energy content assumes light-water reactor technology. Conversion factors: 400 billion Btu/short ton for light-water reactors; breeders would be 60–100 times higher.
[a]Includes all indicated and inferred resources in addition to quantity recoverable.
Source: World Energy Conference, 1976.

ity, some 14.2 percent has been developed. This developed capacity is capable of generating 1,348,554 gigawatts or 13.9 percent of the potential hydropower generation capability of the world.

Of the undeveloped capacity left, sparsity of population and remoteness from population centers with large energy requirements leave the economic development of many undeveloped sites in considerable doubt.

Tidal energy is a form of hydraulic resource similar to conventional hydropower. The major differences are:

- Ocean tides are bidirectional, flowing in twice a day and out twice a day.
- Construction materials must be much more corrosion-resistent than those used for fresh water facilities.
- The hydrostatic heads available for tidal energy use are small compared to conventional hydropower installations.

Tidal and topographic factors combine to make energy conversion practicable at nearly 100 sites[16] around the world. The sites considered most viable are listed in Table 11–14.

## Geothermal Energy

Geothermal energy is the natural heat of the earth. The earth's temperature increases toward the core, primarily because of natural nuclear decay and the frictional heat of moving masses of rock. The diffuseness of this energy limits its usefulness to areas where it is concentrated into restricted volumes.

Reserves and resources of geothermal energy must be distinguished from the *resource base*, defined as all of a given material in the earth's crust, whether its existence is known or unknown and without consideration of recovery cost. For geothermal energy, this resource base is all of the heat in the earth's crust (its mean surface temperature is about 15° C). The U.S. Geological Survey (USGS) has estimated that the worldwide heat in the earth's crust to a depth of 10 kilometers is about $10^{24}$ Btu.[17] This is approximately 4 million times the energy consumption for the world in 1975. For the U.S. alone, the USGS estimate of earth heat is $2 \times 10^{22}$ Btu.

Obviously only a small proportion of this large resource base can be considered as a resource. Not only would it be uneconomic and technologically infeasible, but seismic disturbances might result if any substantial fraction of the heat were extracted. The proportion of this resource base that is a resource depends, to a significant degree, on the following factors:

- Depth of extraction
- Assumed temperature distribution
- Effective porosity, specific yield, and permeability of the reservoir rocks
- Physical state of the fluid (water or steam)
- Available technology
- Economics of uses
- Government policy vis-à-vis research and development, leasing, environmental constraints, etc.

Many of the variations in published estimates of geothermal resources are caused by assumptions that differ concerning the above factors.

The U.S. Geological Survey has identified these major categories of the geothermal resource base:

*Hydrothermal convection systems*. These involve circulating hot water and steam that transfer heat from depth to the near surface.

*Hot, young, igneous (volcanic) systems*. These occur where molten magma generated deep within the earth intrudes into the shallow crust. Temperatures are elevated, but there is an absence of natural fluid to carry the heat to the surface.

*Conduction-dominated environments*. These consist of large areas where the heat is transferred from the interior of the earth by conduction through solid rocks.

At present the types of geothermal energy demonstrated to be economic are from the hydrothermal convection systems. They are:

## TABLE 11–13

### Developed and Undeveloped Conventional Hydroelectric Resources of the World

| | |
|---|---|
| Developed: | |
| Capacity (*megawatts*) | 315,137 |
| Average annual generation (*gigawatt hours*) | 1,348,554 |
| Energy content of annual generation (*quadrillion Btu*)[a] | 4.6 |
| Undeveloped: | |
| Capacity (*megawatts*) | 1,911,666 |
| Average annual generation (*gigawatt hours*) | 8,351,720 |
| Energy content of annual generation (*quadrillion Btu*)[a] | 28.5 |
| Total: | |
| Capacity (*megawatts*) | 2,226,803 |
| Average annual generation (*gigawatt hours*) | 9,700,274 |
| Energy content of annual generation (*quadrillion Btu*)[a] | 33.1 |

[a] Based on direct conversion of average annual generation in kilowatt hours to Btu: 1 kWh=3,412 Btu, the actual energy content corresponding to 100 percent efficiency.

*Source:* World Energy Conference, 1976.

## TABLE 11–14

## Major Tidal Power Project Sites, Operational and Potential

| | Approximate Average Tidal Range (*meters*) | Average Annual Energy Output (*gigawatt hours*) | Capacity (*megawatts*) |
|---|---|---|---|
| I. OPERATIONAL PROJECTS | | | |
| Rance, near St. Malo, France | 8¹/₂ | 540[a] | 240[a] |
| Kislaya, Guba, (pilot plant) 40 miles north of Murmansk, Russia | 2¹/₂ | — | 0.4[a] |
| II. POTENTIAL PROJECTS | | | |
| United States: | | | |
| Cook Inlet, Alaska (Turnagain Arm and Knik Arm, A3) | 8 | 10,950[b] | 2,600[b] |
| Passamaquoddy, Maine (M2)[c] | 5¹/₂ | 2,100[d] | 1,000[d] |
| Canada: | | | |
| Minas Basin (B9)[c] | 11¹/₂ | 10,374[d] | 3,200[d] |
| Shepody Bay (A6)[c] | 9¹/₂ | 2,967[d] | 920[d] |
| Cumberland Basin (A8)[c] | 10 | 2,352[d] | 795[d] |
| England: | | | |
| Severn River Estuary, near Bristol[c] | 9 | 20,000[b] | 4,000[b] |
| Solway Firth[c] | 5 | 13,000[b] | 5,000[b] |
| Morecambe Bay | 6 | 10,000[b] | 4,000[b] |
| Carmarthan | 5¹/₂ | 7,000[b] | 2,000[b] |
| France: | | | |
| Minquiers (Cotentin Peninsula) | 8 | 50,000[b] | 15,000[b] |
| Chausey (Cotentin Peninsula) | 8 | 34,000[b] | 6,000 to 12,000[b] |
| Argentina: | | | |
| San Jose, Gulf of San Jose, Chubut Province Valdez Peninsula[c] | 6 | 9,000[b] | 1,000[b] |
| Santa Cruz River | 7¹/₂ | 4,000[b] | — |
| Puerto Gallegos | 7¹/₂ | 2,000[b] | — |
| San Julian | 6 | 400[b] | — |
| Deseado Estuary | 3¹/₂ | 700[b] | — |
| Russia: | | | |
| Gulf of Mezen, White Sea[c] | 6¹/₂ | 2,600[b] | 1,300[b] |
| Okhotsk, northern end of Kamchatka Peninsula | 6 | — | 25,000[b] |
| Kuloi Estuary | 6¹/₂ | 1,300[b] | 500[b] |
| Lumbovskaya[c] | 4¹/₂ | 900[b] | 400[b] |
| Australia: | | | |
| Secure Bay | 7 | 1,700 | 600 |
| Walcott Inlet | 12 | 4,000 | 1,300 |
| George Water | – | 2,500 | 800 |
| St. George Basin | – | 3,500 | 1,000 |
| People's Republic of China: | | | |
| Chientang Kiang[c] | 7 | — | 7,000[b] |
| Gulf of Fuchin Wan | – | — | 1,000[b] |
| Gulf of Shinhwang Wan | – | — | 1,000[b] |
| Gulf of Sanmen Wan | – | — | 1,000[b] |
| Brazil: | | | |
| Itagui[c] | 5 | — | — |
| Sao Luis | 8 | — | — |
| India: Bhaunagar | 7 | — | — |
| Northern Ireland: | | | |
| Strangeford | 3 | 2,000[b] | 200[b] |
| Carlingford | 3¹/₂ | 1,300[b] | 120[b] |
| Guinea Bissau: Porto Gole | 5¹/₂ | — | — |
| North Korea: Yangkakto | 7¹/₂ | — | — |
| South Korea: Inchon | 6 | — | 400 |

[a] Actual output of plant in operation.
[b] Potential output of possible scheme for tidal power.
[c] Known or believed to be under formal study by the government.
[d] Planned output for plant in design or formal planning stage.

*Source:* Stone and Webster Engineering Corp., "Final Report on Tidal Power Study for the United States Energy Research and Development Administration," Boston: Mar. 1977, quoted in Library of Congress, Congressional Research Service, *Project Interdependence.* p. 465.

- Vapor-dominated fields, which produce dry steam at temperatures suitable for power generation.
- High-temperature hot water fields, which produce flash steam suitable for power generation and a large quantity of hot water suitable for low-grade heat applications.
- Moderate-temperature hot water fields, which produce large quantities of water for low-grade heat applications.

There is a high degree of uncertainty in estimating quantitative reserves of any subsurface resource. Geothermal energy development, being a relatively new field, has limited data available for estimating purposes. At present, only the United States has made any effort to estimate its reserves of both low-grade and high-grade geothermal resources (Table 11–15). The regional conductive environments, which include geopressured zones containing exploitable quantities of methane gas, show only trapped heat.

The U.S.S.R. and Hungary are the only other countries that have published data on low-grade geothermal energy resources. Hungary has identified systems containing reserves (represented by water at 100° C) equivalent to 2 billion barrels of oil. It has been estimated that economically exploitable thermal waters underlie 50–60 percent of the territory of the U.S.S.R. The estimate of producible reserves of thermal waters at depths of 1,000–3,500 meters and temperatures of 50–130° C is equivalent to the heat of combustion of 490,000 barrels of oil per day.

As for the rest of the world, the amount of low-grade energy is assumed to be very large. This energy would be suitable for space heating as well as agricultural and industrial application. High-grade geothermal resources suitable for power generation are far more restricted in global distribution and quantity but could furnish significant energy for countries in geologically favorable zones.

## TABLE 11–15

### Estimated Heat Content of Geothermal Resource Base of the United States

| | Heat in the Ground | | | Recoverable with Current Technology |
|---|---|---|---|---|
| | Identified Systems | | Identified (+ Estimate for Undiscovered) | Identified Systems |
| | Number | Heat Content ($10^{15}$ Btu[a]) | Heat Content ($10^{15}$ Btu[a]) | (megawatts for 30 years) |
| Hydrothermal convection systems (to 3 km depth, 10,000 ft, near the maximum depth drilled in geothermal areas) | | | | |
| Vapor-dominated (steam) systems | 3 | 104 | 200 | 1,590 |
| High-temperature hot water systems (over 150°C) | 63 | 1,480 | 6,400 | 10,100 |
| Intermediate-temperature hot water systems (90°–150°C) | 224 | 1,380 | 5,600 | 27,500[b] |
| Total | 290 | 2,964 | 12,200 | |
| Hot igneous systems (0–10 km) | | | | |
| Molten parts of 48 best known systems, including Alaska and Hawaii | | 52,000 | | |
| Crystallized parts and hot margins of same 48 | | 48,000 | | Huge potential |
| Total | | 100,000 | 400,000 | |
| Regional conductive environments (0–10 km; all 50 states subdivided into 19 heat-flow provinces of 3 basic types, Eastern, Basin-and-Range; and Sierra Nevada) | | | | |
| Total, all states | | 32,000,000 | 32,000,000 | 30,800[c] |
| Overall total (as reported) [d] | | 32,103,000 | 32,412,000 | 70,000 |

[a] $10^{15}$ Btu equivalent to heat of combustion of 174 million barrels of petroleum or 39 million short tons of coal.
[b] Nonelectrical use; value is electrical equivalent.
[c] Geopressured resources only (lowest estimate; does not include methane).
[d] Totals may not add due to independent rounding.

Source: D. F. White and D. L. Williams, eds., Geological Survey Circular 726, 1975.

As of 1977, 17 geothermal powerplants, representing 1,472 megawatts capacity, were either "on line" or slated for 1977 or later (Table 11–16). Low-grade geothermal heat applications represent an additional 1,298 megawatts of capacity.

## Oil Shale

The term oil shale, as commonly used, covers a wide variety of laminated, solidified mixtures of inorganic sediments and organic matter that have the common property of yielding oil (shale oil) upon destructive distillation but are only slightly susceptible to the action of solvents. Shales or hard clays partly or completely saturated with oil from an outside source are not considered true oil shales. Shale oils have extremely complex physical and chemical properties that vary with the type of shale from which they are produced and the conditions under which they are distilled from the source rock.[18]

Estimates of identified shale oil resources throughout the world in oil shales richer than 10 gallons per ton are shown in Table 11–17. The quantities shown as recoverable paramarginal resources in the right-hand column of the table represent the more accessible, higher-grade portions of the deposits. Some known oil shale deposits have been only partially appraised, or not appraised at all. Geological studies indicate that large oil shale deposits, as yet unknown, probably exist outside the areas of known shale oil resources. These possible unidentified resources (termed speculative) are thought to be many times as large as the identified world shale oil resources.

Hypothetical oil shale resources (in-place oil) for the world are 450 billion barrels for the 25–100 gallon per ton shale and 8,800 billion barrels for the 10–25 gallons per ton material. Speculative oil shale resources (in-place oil) are estimated at 15,200 billion barrels and 318,000 billion barrels for the two grades, respectively.[19] Exploitation of these resources, if eventually discovered, is expected to be so far in the future as to have no relevance for the year 2000.

Outside the United States, the largest known deposit is the Irati shale deposit in southern Brazil. Although some of the other known deposits in countries other than the United States are richer, they are not nearly as large. Surface mining operations are anticipated for the Irati shale in Brazil. The shale is medium grade, containing about 8 percent kerogen by weight. Shale oil production costs should be reasonable, and prospects for future shale oil production appear good.

In the People's Republic of China, the Manchurian oil shale deposits presently being exploited overlie thick coal deposits. After stripping off the overburden, the oil shale is mined by open pit methods; this is followed by mining of the coalbeds. The grade of shale varies but probably averages about 15 gallons per ton. The mining of both oil shale and coal in this manner, plus fairly efficient processing, results in relatively low costs. Shale oil production is believed to be economical, especially if shale oil is regarded as a by-product of coal production.

In the U.S.S.R. there are a number of oil shale deposits, but the one of primary interest lies in Estonia and the adjacent Leningrad region. This deposit is estimated to contain about 22 billion tons of oil shale, of which about 15 billion tons are considered rich enough and thick enough to mine. For many years underground mining was used almost exclusively. About 10 or 15 years ago, open pit mining was introduced, and its use has been expanding. As a result, mining costs have been reduced. The U.S.S.R. has recently been increasing its oil shale output. A doubling is tentatively indicated as the goal by the early 1980s.[20]

### TABLE 11–16

### Geothermal Powerplants

| Field | Present Plant Capacity (*megawatts*) | Date of Initial Operation |
|---|---|---|
| Larderello, Italy[a] | 380 | 1904 |
| Wairakei, New Zealand | 192 | 1958 |
| Pate, Mexico | 3 | 1958 |
| Geysers, U.S.[a] | 502 | 1960 |
| Matsukawa, Japan[a] | 22 | 1966 |
| Monte Amiata, Italy[a] | 26 | 1967 |
| Otake, Japan | 23 | 1967 |
| Pauzhetsk, U.S.S.R. | 6 | 1967 |
| Namafjall, Iceland | 3 | 1969 |
| Kawerau, New Zealand | 10 | 1969 |
| Tiwi, Philippines | 10 | 1969 |
| Cerro Prieto, Mexico | 70 | 1973 |
| Onikobe, Japan | 25 | 1975 |
| Ahuschapan, El Salvador | 30 | 1975 |
| Hatchoburu, Japan | 50 | 1976 |
| Katsukonda, Japan | 50 | 1977[b] |
| Krafla, Iceland | 70 | 1977[b] |
| Total | 1,472 | |

[a] Fields producing from dry-steam reservoirs. The remainder are hot water reservoirs.
[b] Projected.

Source: Adapted from P. K. Takahashi and B. Chen, "Geothermal Reservoir Engineering," *Geothermal Energy Magazine*, vol. 3, no. 10, 1975, for the Committee on Natural Resources, U.N. Economics and Social Council, *Status of the Use of Geothermal Energy and Future Prospects for Developing Countries* (E/C.7/64, 28), Feb. 1977.

## TABLE 11–17

### Identified Shale Oil Reserves of the World

*(Billions of 42-gallon barrels)*

| | Oil in Place | | Recovera- |
| --- | --- | --- | --- |
| | 25–100 gallons per ton | 10–25 gallons per ton | ble Para-marginal Shale Oil Resources [a] |
| North America | 600 | 1,600 | 80 |
| South America | Small | 800 | 50 |
| Europe | 70 | 6 | 30 |
| Africa | 100 | Small | 10 |
| Asia | 90 | 14 | 20 |
| Australia and New Zealand | Small | 1 | Small |
| World totals | 860 | 2,400 | 190 |

[a] Using present technology and considering only the higher-grade, more accessible portions of deposits; included in the oil-in-place figures.

*Source:* U.S. Geological Survey, *United States Mineral Resources,* USGS Professional Paper 820, 1973.

Approximately one-tenth of an estimated 100 billion barrels of oil in known shale deposits in Zaire is in deposits of relatively high quality, and there appears to be some possibility of eventual development.

In Scotland, once a center of shale oil production, high-grade reserves have been depleted, and there appears to be little prospect for future shale oil production.

## Tar Sands

Tar sands are sedimentary rocks or sands containing a heavy asphaltic substance called bitumen. Characteristics of tar sands vary from one deposit to another with respect to both the host rock and the impregnating material. The sands and rocks have void spaces that are impregnated with bitumen. The impregnating materials vary from semiliquid to semisolid (and in some cases solid) petroleum materials. They range from forms oozing slowly from an outcrop on a warm day to forms difficult to soften in boiling water. Rock types include dolomite, limestone, conglomerate, and shale, as well as consolidated sandstone and unconsolidated sand.

The composition of the rock or sand is mainly quartz, silt, and clay. A typical tar sand consists of approximately 83 percent sand by weight, 13 percent bitumen, and 4 percent water.[21] Bitumen is usually interspersed with collections of water, air, or methane in the tar-sand beds but tends to have a relatively constant chemical composition throughout a given deposit.

Tar sands are known also as oil sands, bituminous sands, and bituminous rocks. Traditionally, they have been treated as a potential petroleum supplement, although in reality the organic material in tar sands is a form of petroleum. The real difference is that tar-sand oil is not producible by the methods commonly used in ordinary oil fields. The bitumen obtained from tar sands is too viscous (5,000–50,000 P at 50° F) to be transportable by pipeline without first being upgraded to a lighter, less viscous oil. Crude tar-sand oil, or bitumen, also is very heavy (usually 6–10° API). However, it can be upgraded by hydrogenation to yield a light syncrude, comparable to a high-API-gravity petroleum.

Tar sands resources are illustrated in Table 11–18. As presently known, the bulk of these resources are concentrated in Canada (731 billion barrels of in-place oil) and Venezuela (200 billion barrels of in-place oil). The Canadian tar sands are concentrated in the Athabasca field.

The Athabasca field in Alberta, Canada, is one of the largest deposits of oil in the world, extending over 21,000 square miles.[22] It is estimated to contain 626 billion barrels of bitumen in-place, with 74 billion barrels lying beneath less than 150 feet of overburden and 552 billion barrels beneath overburden ranging in depths from 150 to 2,000 feet.[23] Estimates of oil in-place in other deposits in the Athabasca region total 105 billion barrels. Thus, the total in-place estimate for the Athabasca region is 731 billion barrels. This does not include the heavy oil in the Canadian Cold Lake area, which is estimated at 164 billion barrels in-place.

One estimate of the oil-generating potential of the Athabasca field is 285 billion barrels, with 85 billion barrels currently possible by open pit mining of near-surface deposits, which are often 200 feet thick.[24] The other 200 billion barrels would have to be recovered by in situ techniques. Another estimate places the total recoverable resource at 250 billion barrels, with 26.5 billion barrels recoverable using established open pit mining and established aboveground recoverable techniques.[25]

Great Canadian Oil Sands, Ltd. has been producing oil from the Athabasca deposit since September 1967. Its plant is the only commercial tar sands facility in operation. Another plant (Syncrude Canada, Ltd.) has been built and is expected to begin operating in the near future. There are no significant extraction plans for any other area of the world.

United States resources of tar sands oil in-place are estimated to be a little over 30 billion barrels. The bulk of these resources is in Utah, whose in-place resources of oil from tar sands are estimated

### TABLE 11–18

### U.S. and World Tar-Sand Oil Resources

(*Billions of barrels*)

| | Total Estimated Oil in-place | Estimated Recoverable Oil | |
| --- | --- | --- | --- |
| | | Using Only Surface Mining and Aboveground Processing | Including Use of in Situ Processing Technology not yet Developed |
| United States [a] | | | |
| Utah | 28 | | |
| California | 0.169–.332 | | |
| Texas | 0.124–.141 | | |
| New Mexico | .037 | | |
| Kentucky | 0.034–.037 | | |
| All other states combined [b] | 1.6 | | |
| Total (rounded) | 30 | 2.5–5.5 [c] | NE [f] |
| Rest of the World | | | |
| Canada [d] | 731 | 26.5–85 | 250–285 |
| Venezuela [e] | 200 | NE | NE |
| Malagasy | 1.750 | NE | NE |
| Albania | 0.371 | NE | NE |
| Trinidad | 0.060 | NE | NE |
| Romania | 0.025 | NE | NE |
| U.S.S.R. | 0.024 | NE | NE |
| Total (rounded) | 934 | NE | NE |
| World Total | 964 | NE | NE |

*Note:* Excludes heavy oil resources, but see footnotes *d* and *e*. Not shown are 600 billion barrels of oil in-place in the Olenek tar sands of the U.S.S.R. (See *Oil and Gas Journal*. Oct. 10, 1977, p. 85).

[a] Heavy oil resources in the U.S. were estimated at 106.8 billion barrels in 1966.
[b] None of the other states has as large an estimated tar-sand oil resource as New Mexico or Kentucky.
[c] Based on information available in 1964.
[d] 626 billion barrels in the Athabasca deposit and 105 billion barrels in other deposits in the Athabasca region. Does not include heavy oil in the Cold Lake Area, which is estimated at 164 billion barrels in-place.
[e] Heavy oil resources in-place in the Orinoco petroliferous belt are estimated at 700 billion barrels.
[f] NE: not estimated.

at about 28 billion barrels.[26] In-place resource estimates for California range from 169 to 322 million barrels—for Texas, 124–141 million barrels—and for New Mexico and Kentucky, about 37 million barrels each. A number of other states have smaller tar-sand resources.

An estimate of resources of bitumen recoverable by known mining methods for near-surface deposits of relatively easy access was made in 1964, based on a compilation of information then available from numerous sources. The estimated resources on this basis were 2.5–5.5 billion barrels.[27] No estimate was made of the oil that might be recovered from U.S. tar sands if satisfactory in situ methods were developed.

### Solar Energy

Solar "insolation," the average rate at which solar energy strikes the earth is about 1,500 Btu/$ft^2$ per day or $42 \times 10^9$ Btu/$mile^2$ per day. This is an enormous flux of energy. In one year an average square mile, such as one located in Asheville, North Carolina, receives about $15 \times 10^{12}$ Btu. By comparison the total net energy consumed in the U.S. in 1976 was about $7.4 \times 10^{16}$ Btu. Thus, 4,900 square miles (less than two hundredths of one percent of the U.S. continental land area) receives on the average the equivalent of the total U.S. energy needs for 1976. At a 10 percent conversion efficiency, only 49,000 square miles (or 1.7 percent of the lower 48 states) would be required to produce the total amount of energy consumed in the U.S. in 1976.[28] The difficulty is, of course, in attaining the proper distribution of this energy in time and location and in matching end-use technologies with this abundant, clean source of energy. Since solar energy is dispersed, it is suitable for a dispersed settlement of people and industry. By contrast, a centralized and concentrated society is needed to minimize distribution losses for efficient use of nuclear technology. There are many ways in which thermodynamic efficiencies can be achieved with solar energy.[29] Many of these possibilities have not yet been adequately investigated, but research in these areas is increasing.

There is currently no systematic collection of data on solar energy resources or consumption in the world. The following discussion will delineate some data on resources, reserves, and consumption, but many of the proposals for use of solar energy overlap, or are contradictory, and estimates based on them are uncertain and open to question.

In discussing solar energy, it is necessary to distinguish between natural collection systems (involving indirect use) and engineered collection systems. The natural collection systems (except for hydropower, which has already been discussed) are considered first.

*Photosynthetic process* (*biomass*). It has been estimated that the world produces $150 \times 10^9$ tons per year of biomass, with an estimated energy content of between 1,500 and 2,400 quadrillion Btu annually.[30] Two ideas under consideration to exploit biomass are:

1. The use of waste products. It is estimated that the U.S. has a resource base of 826 million tons of waste products per year, of which 122 million tons is available for use.[31] This would be burned directly. It is assumed that world resources would be significantly higher.

2. Energy farms. This involves cellulose production, the growth of oil-producing plants, and the production of marine kelp. Under cellulose production, it has been estimated that the U.S. could produce 10 quadrillion Btu of energy per year off 10 percent of forest and range land.[32] If special plants that produce a sap or latex, which is an emulsion, were grown on 10 percent of forest and range land, the resulting energy available would be between 0.5 and 25 quadrillion Btu per year.[33] It has been estimated that the growth of kelp on submerged mesh in the ocean and conversion of the kelp to methane by anaerobic digestion has a resource potential for the world of 1,200 quadrillion Btu per year, and for the United States of 23 quadrillion Btu.[34] It cannot be stressed too strongly, the economic and technical feasibility of these processes has yet to be demonstrated.

*Wind*. Some of the solar energy striking the earth is converted into the kinetic energy of air currents. Although data are sketchy, information on wind velocity patterns indicate certain areas as having strong, fairly constant winds. One method of estimation of total wind energy is based on the natural rate of regeneration as indicated by a summation of surface friction in latitude belts 5° wide. This method indicates that the total energy dissipation rate overland in the Northern Hemisphere in winter would be about $167 \times 10^9$ watts, and $24 \times 10^9$ watts at the same time on land in the Southern Hemisphere. The total wind energy generated overland is therefore about $0.19 \times 10^{12}$ kilowatts, or $1,660 \times 10^{12}$ kWh (kilowatt hours) per year. It is estimated that placement of wind turbines 175 feet in diameter, spaced 16 to the square mile over the entire land area and operating an average of 2,000 hr/yr would yield about $120 \times 10^{12}$ kWh/yr.[35] Scaling this down to cover 2.5 percent of the area of the U.S., or an area about the size of Utah, would provide about $190 \times 10^9$ kWh/yr or about 10 percent of U.S. electrical energy consumed in 1972.

*Ocean thermal energy conversion*. In the tropical regions of the ocean, a temperature difference of 20° C between the surface and deep waters has been observed. In 1929 Georges Claude demonstrated a plant to utilize this heat. The 22 kilowatt plant admitted surface seawater to a low-pressure evaporator, which provided low-pressure steam to a turbine. More recent proposals suggest utilizing an indirect vapor cycle. A secondary working fluid such as ammonia, freon, or propane would expand through a turbine at higher pressures. Cycle efficiency would range between 1.6 percent and 3.2 percent.[36] The estimated power capacity that can be utilized in water adjacent to the United States is 2,000 megawatts.[37]

*Hydropower*. This has already been discussed above.

In addition to natural collection systems, some of the engineered systems are:

*Photovoltaics*. This involves direct conversion of solar energy into electricity. The possible maximum annual contribution to the United States has been estimated at 25 quadrillion Btu/year.

*Thermal collection*. This involves direct use of heat for such purposes as space heating, hot water, industrial heat, etc. Its possible contribution to the United States energy needs is about 7 quadrillion Btu per year. Thermal collection is also used to collect heat for heat engines producing electricity. The possible contribution could run as high as 80 quadrillion Btu per year for the U.S. alone. The possible contributions of both these systems in the world context have not been estimated.[38]

While few present estimates of world energy supply and demand through the year 2000 place much reliance on solar power, some do. (See, for example, A. B. Lovins in "Energy Strategy: The Road Not Taken?"[29].) There is little question that solar already makes an important and often under-valued contribution to the world energy economy. Russell Peterson has noted correctly that without the solar contribution, the entire earth would be more than 400° F cooler than it is now! While the potential of this energy source is large, an assessment of its full potential must await further research and analysis.

## Conclusion

Large quantities of petroleum, natural gas, and solid fuels can still be found and produced. In addition, there exists the strong possibility that exploration in search of as yet undiscovered deposits of fossil fuels will be successful. The probability that technological advance to bring

presently unworkable deposits within economic reach are also high. The major problem is that continued exponential growth in consumption will exhaust these large amounts of resources before the transition to the longer-lived and renewable fuels can be made.

The best summary of the existing energy situation was made by Vincent E. McKelvey when he said:

The era of readily available, cheap fossil fuels is closing and a high order of human ingenuity will be required to extend it and to bring into use another energy resource base. The time necessary to complete these tasks depends not only on the vigor and imagination with which new sources are sought but on the wisdom and restraint exercised in the use of the old.[39]

## REFERENCES

1. Vincent E. McKelvey, Remarks at the International Conference on Energy Use Management, Tucson, Ariz., Oct. 24, 1977.
2. "Principles of the Mineral Resource Classification of the U.S. Bureau of Mines and U.S. Geological Survey," USGS Bulletin 1450–A, Washington: Government Printing Office, 1974.
3. L. Bauer and R. S. Carlsmith, "World Energy Conference Activities in the Field of Surveying World Energy Resources," in M. Grenon, ed., First IIASA Conference on Energy Resources, Laxenburg, Austria: International Institute for Applied Systems Analysis, 1975, p. 47.
4. McKelvey.
5. Library of Congress, Congressional Research Service, Project Interdependence: U.S. and World Energy Outlook Through 1990, Washington: Government Printing Office, 1977, p. 638.
6. Oil and Gas Journal, Dec. 26, 1977, p. 101.
7. World Energy Conference, Conservation Commission Report on Oil Resources, 1985–2020, Executive Summary, London: Aug. 15, 1977, Appendix, p. 18.
8. World Energy Conference, An Appraisal of World Coal Resources and Their Future Availability, Executive Summary, London: Aug. 15, 1977.
9. Paul Averitt, Coal Resources of the United States, January 1, 1974, Geological Survey Bulletin 1412, 1975, pp. 28–31.
10. Ibid., p. 91.
11. Gunther Fettweis, "Contributions to the Assessment of World Coal Resources, or Coal is Not So Abundant," in M. Grenin, ed., First IIASA Conference on Energy Resources, Laxenburg, Austria: International Institute for Applied Systems Analysis, 1975, pp. 476–530.
12. Project Interdependence, p. 285.
13. Nuclear Energy Policy Study Group, Nuclear Power Issues and Choices, Cambridge, Mass.: Ballinger, 1977, p. 32.
14. Mortimer H. Staatz and Jerry C. Olson, "Thorium," in United States Mineral Resources, U.S. Geological Survey Professional Paper 820, 1973, p. 474.
15. The discussion is based on World Energy Conference, Survey of Energy Resources, 1974, New York, Ch. VI.
16. Project Interdependence.
17. Department of the Interior, Panel on Geothermal Energy Resources, "Assessment of Geothermal Energy Resources" (mimeo), June 26, 1972, p. 57ff.
18. U.S. Bureau of Mines Bulletin 415, "Studies of Certain Properties of Oil Shale and Shale Oil," 1938, p. 6.
19. W. C. Culbertson and J. K. Pitman, chapter on oil shale in United States Mineral Resources, U.S. Geological Survey Professional Paper 820, 1973, pp. 500–501.
20. Oil and Gas Journal, Feb. 14, 1977, p. 54.
21. T. J. Peach, "Bitumen Recovery from Tar Sands," Energy Processing (Canada), May-June 1974.
22. Frederick W. Camp, The Tar Sands of Alberta, Canada, 3rd ed., Denver: Cameron Engineers, 1976.
23. L. B. McConville, "The Athabasca Tar Sands," Mining Engineering, Jan. 1975, pp. 19–38.
24. Sam H. Schurr and Paul T. Homan, Middle-Eastern Oil and the Western World, New York: Elsevier, 1971, pp. 59–66.
25. Library of Congress, Congressional Research Service, Energy from U.S. and Canadian Tar Sands: Technical, Environmental, Economic, Legislative, and Policy Aspects, Dec. 1974.
26. H. R. Ritzma, "Oil-Impregnated Rock Deposits of Utah," Utah Geological and Mineral Survey Map 33, Apr. 1973, preprint July 1974, 2 sheets.
27. Ball Associates, Surface and Shallow Oil-Impregnated Rocks and Shallow Oil Fields in the United States, U.S. Bureau of Mines Monograph 12, 1965.
28. William R. Cherry, "Harnessing Solar Energy: The Potential," Astronautics and Aeronautics, Aug. 1973, pp. 30–63 (brought up to date).
29. A. B. Lovins, "Energy Strategy: The Road Not Taken?" Foreign Affairs, Oct. 1976, pp. 65–96: A. B. Lovins, Soft Energy Paths: Toward a Durable Peace, Cambridge, Mass.: Ballinger, 1977; Efficient Use of Energy, American Institute of Physics Conference Proceedings No. 26, New York: 1975 (summarized in Physics Today, Aug. 1975).
30. Jerome Saeman, "U.S. Department of Agriculture Forest Products Laboratory," Chemical Engineering News, Feb. 20, 1977, p. 21.
31. Synfuels Interagency Task Force, "Recommendations for a Synthetic Fuels Commission."

32. Phillips Hahn, "Producing Fuel for Energy Under Intensive Culture," excerpted in *Energy User News*, Dec. 26, 1977, p. 22.

33. "The Petroleum Plant: Perhaps We Can Grow Gasoline," *Science*, Oct. 1, 1976, p. 46.

34. Howard Wilcox, "Ocean Farming," in *Proceedings*, Conference on Capturing the Sun Through Bioconversion, Mar. 10–12, 1976, p. 265.

35. U.S. Congress House Committee on Science and Astronautics, "Solar Energy Research, A Multidisciplinary Approach," Washington: Government Printing Office, 1973.

36. J. H. Anderson and J. H. Anderson, Jr., "Thermal Power from Seawater," *Mechanical Engineering*, Apr. 1966, pp. 41–46.

37. U.S. Energy Research and Development Administration, "Ocean Thermal Energy Conversion Program Summary" (ERDA 76–142), Oct. 1976, p. 1.

38. Richard S. Caputo, "Solar Power Plants: Dark Horse in the Energy Stable," *Bulletin of the Atomic Scientists*, May 1977.

39. McKelvey, op. cit.

# 12   Nonfuel Minerals Projections

There are more than 100 commercial nonfuel mineral commodities—that is, mineral commodities that are not used primarily as fuels—mined, processed, and traded in the world market today. In 1973 the value of all nonfuel minerals produced in the world was $37 billion [1] (excluding processing and transportation costs), or about 1 percent of the gross world product.

This figure does not in itself fully reflect the value of minerals in the world economy. The industrial and agricultural processes that are taken for granted today would be severely disrupted if any one of dozens of critical minerals ceased to be available in dependable, reasonably priced supply. Supply, in turn, has become highly energy-intensive and international in scope. The industrialized countries are dependent on imports—from each other and from the less developed countries (LDCs)—for a portion of their supplies of such basic mineral commodities as bauxite, copper, and iron ore (Table 12–1). Their reliance on imports from the LDCs has increased in recent years as industrial economies have found new uses for formerly unimportant minerals and have partially depleted high-grade domestic deposits of some important minerals. The less developed countries, in turn, rely on exports for foreign exchange and on imports from industrial countries for the sulfur and potash needed for chemical fertilizers. There are therefore many important questions associated with projections of supply, demand, and price of nonfuel minerals.

Unfortunately, economic projections for nonfuel minerals are exceedingly difficult to make. The sheer number of nonfuel mineral commodities present the first difficulty. Matters are complicated further by the fact that significant substitutions in end use occur when one mineral commodity changes price relative to another. Finally, because resources are not uniformly distributed geographically, political considerations become important determinants of price and trade patterns.

To keep the discussion within bounds, this chapter focuses on 19 nonfuel mineral commodities. Six are included because they are basic to modern material life and international trade (alu-

## Table 12–1

### Mineral Imports as a Percentage of Mineral Consumption, 1976

|  | United States | European Economic Community | Japan | U.S.S.R. [a] |
|---|---|---|---|---|
| Bauxite | 88 | 50 | 100 | 44 |
| Chromium | 90 | 95 | 95 | 0 |
| Copper | 16 | 99 | 93 | 4 |
| Iron Ore | 35 | 85 | 99 | 0 |
| Lead | 12 | 85 | 78 | 24 |
| Manganese | 100 | 99 | 90 | 0 |
| Nickel | 61 | 90 | 95 | 0 |
| Tin | 75 | 90 | 90 | 22 |
| Zinc | 60 | 74 | 63 | 13 |

[a] 1975.

Source: U.S. Central Intelligence Agency, *Research Aid: Handbook of Economic Statistics*, Sept. 1977, p. 17. For U.S.S.R. data, V. V. Strishkov, "Mineral Industries of the U.S.S.R.," *Mining Annual Review 1976*, Mining Journal (London); reprinted by the U.S. Bureau of Mines.

minum, copper, iron, phosphate, potash, and sulfur). The remaining 13 (chromium, fluorspar, helium, industrial diamonds, lead, manganese, mercury, nickel, platinum-group metals,* silver, tin, tungsten, and zinc) are included because they illustrate possible future problems.

Projections of demand, supply, and price are taken up sequentially in the following sections. The chapter concludes with a discussion of future issues and questions.

## Demand Projections

Table 12–2 and the map on the page following it present a combination of two sets of mineral demand (or, more precisely, consumption) projections for 1985 and the year 2000.† One set of projections was prepared by Wilfred Malenbaum, Professor of Economics, University of Pennsylvania, in 1977[2]; the other was prepared by the U.S. Bureau of Mines in 1976.[3] Table 12–3 compares these two projections for selected minerals.

---

*Platinum, palladium, iridium, osmium, rhodium, and ruthenium.

†Helium, originally included in this table, has been omitted. The only available datum for helium was average (1971–75) U.S. demand: 570 million cubic feet.

## TABLE 12-2: World Demand for Minerals, 1985 and 2000

| | | Western Europe | Japan | Other Developed Lands[a] | U.S.S.R. | Eastern Europe | Africa | Asia | Latin America | China | United States | Non-U.S. World | World Total |
|---|---|---|---|---|---|---|---|---|---|---|---|---|---|
| **Aluminum[b]** | Aver. 1971–75 | 2862 | 1254 | 528 | 1490 | 827 | 40 | 294 | 333 | 234 | 4388 | 7861 | 12249 |
| (1000 | 1985 | 4637 | 2414 | 890 | 2352 | 1339 | 65 | 453 | 599 | 431 | 7410 | 13180 | 20590 |
| metric tons) | 2000 | 7791 | 4674 | 1565 | 3868 | 2457 | 160 | 884 | 1217 | 827 | 13073 | 23443 | 36516 |
| | Aver. growth (%) | 3.93 | 5.19 | 4.27 | 3.74 | 4.28 | 5.48 | 4.33 | 5.11 | 4.98 | 4.29 | 4.29 | 4.29 |
| **Chromium ore** | Aver. 1971–75 | 1873 | 1127 | 740 | 750 | 744 | 49 | 184 | 109 | 216 | 1149 | 5792 | 6941 |
| (1000 | 1985 | 2951 | 1836 | 1140 | 760 | 1249 | 82 | 302 | 221 | 375 | 1347 | 8916 | 10263 |
| metric tons) | 2000 | 4452 | 3233 | 1877 | 1083 | 2047 | 142 | 526 | 423 | 634 | 1601 | 14417 | 16018 |
| | Aver. growth (%) | 3.39 | 4.14 | 3.64 | 1.42 | 3.97 | 4.18 | 4.12 | 5.35 | 4.23 | 1.28 | 3.57 | 3.27 |
| **Copper, refined** | Aver. 1971–75 | 2422 | 922 | 357 | 1097 | 539 | 21 | 111 | 278 | 290 | 1886 | 6037 | 7923 |
| (1000 | 1985 | 3442 | 1358 | 528 | 1440 | 785 | 38 | 181 | 473 | 486 | 2610 | 8731 | 11341 |
| metric tons) | 2000 | 5231 | 2181 | 715 | 2088 | 1199 | 71 | 311 | 873 | 968 | 3202 | 13637 | 16839 |
| | Aver. growth (%) | 3.01 | 3.37 | 2.71 | 2.51 | 3.12 | 4.80 | 4.04 | 4.50 | 4.75 | 2.06 | 3.18 | 2.94 |
| **Diamond, industrial** | Aver. 1971–75 | | | | The government has no projections. | | | | | | 35 | 50 | 75 |
| (million | 1985 | | | | | | | | | | 37 | 80 | 117 |
| carats) | 2000 | | | | | | | | | | 70 | 150 | 220 |
| | Aver. growth (%) | | | | | | | | | | 4.04 | 4.32 | 4.23 |
| **Fluorspar (F content)** | Aver. 1971–75 | | | | | | | | | | 689 | 1598 | 2287 |
| (1000 | 1985 | | | | | | | | | | 1560 | 3640 | 5200 |
| short tons) | 2000 | | | | | | | | | | 1930 | 5400 | 7330 |
| | Aver. growth (%) | | | | | | | | | | 4.04 | 4.80 | 4.58 |
| **Iron ore** | Aver. 1971–75 | 95 | 53 | 24 | 97 | 27 | 4 | 10 | 15 | 23 | 85 | 346 | 432 |
| (million | 1985 | 133 | 78 | 35 | 144 | 34 | 8 | 18 | 25 | 39 | 101 | 514 | 615 |
| metric tons) | 2000 | 189 | 129 | 49 | 209 | 50 | 14 | 33 | 48 | 65 | 133 | 786 | 919 |
| | Aver. growth (%) | 2.68 | 3.48 | 2.78 | 3.00 | 2.40 | 4.94 | 4.70 | 4.58 | 4.08 | 1.74 | 3.21 | 2.95 |
| **Lead** | Aver. 1971–75 | | | | The government has no projections. | | | | | | 931 | 2461 | 3392 |
| (1000 | 1985 | | | | | | | | | | 1200 | 3960 | 5160 |
| short tons) | 2000 | | | | | | | | | | 1530 | 6040 | 7570 |
| | Aver. growth (%) | | | | | | | | | | 1.43 | 3.51 | 3.14 |
| **Manganese** | Aver. 1971–75 | 4134 | 1667 | 1100 | 6420 | 1157 | 481 | 1384 | 1071 | 998 | 1929 | 18410 | 20339 |
| (1000 | 1985 | 5620 | 2586 | 1168 | 9500 | 1785 | 820 | 2265 | 1890 | 1658 | 2947 | 27292 | 30239 |
| metric tons) | 2000 | 8348 | 4285 | 1743 | 14696 | 2778 | 1513 | 3824 | 3703 | 3168 | 4002 | 44058 | 48060 |
| | Aver. growth (%) | 2.74 | 3.70 | 1.79 | 3.24 | 3.43 | 4.51 | 3.99 | 4.89 | 4.54 | 2.85 | 3.41 | 3.36 |
| **Mercury** | Aver. 1971–75 | | | | The government has no projections. | | | | | | 53 | 183 | 236 |
| (1000 | 1985 | | | | | | | | | | 53 | 190 | 243 |
| flasks) | 2000 | | | | | | | | | | 47 | 222 | 269 |
| | Aver. growth (%) | | | | | | | | | | -0.46 | 0.75 | 0.50 |

| | | | | | | | | | | | |
|---|---|---|---|---|---|---|---|---|---|---|---|
| **Nickel** | | | | | | | | | | | |
| (1000 metric tons) Aver. 1971–75 | 170 | 97 | 17 | 159[b] | 4 | 4 | 7 | | 161 | 458 | 618 |
| 1985 | 246 | 155 | 24 | 242 | 8 | 8 | 13 | | 211 | 694 | 905 |
| 2000 | 345 | 245 | 34 | 360 | 11 | 14 | 24 | | 280 | 1034 | 1314 |
| Aver. growth (%) | 2.76 | 3.63 | 2.70 | 3.19 | 3.97 | 4.94 | 4.85 | | 2.15 | 3.18 | 2.94 |
| **Phosphate rock** | | | | | | | | | | | |
| (million short tons) Aver. 1971–75 | | | | The government has no projections. | | | | | 35 | 88 | 123 |
| 1985 | | | | | | | | | 45 | 162 | 207 |
| 2000 | | | | | | | | | 69 | 387 | 456 |
| Aver. growth (%) | | | | | | | | | 2.64 | 5.86 | 5.17 |
| **Platinum-group** | | | | | | | | | | | |
| (1000 troy ounces) Aver. 1971–75 | 653 | 1765 | 272 | 702[c] | 38 | 141 | 34 | 123 | 1660 | 3728 | 5387 |
| 1985 | 948 | 3146 | 403 | 1218 | 65 | 242 | 79 | 210 | 2442 | 6311 | 8753 |
| 2000 | 1391 | 5765 | 625 | 1806 | 129 | 418 | 158 | 343 | 3335 | 10695 | 14030 |
| Aver. growth (%) | 2.95 | 4.66 | 3.25 | 3.70 | 4.81 | 4.27 | 6.09 | 4.02 | 2.72 | 4.14 | 3.75 |
| **Potash** | | | | | | | | | | | |
| (million short tons) Aver. 1971–75 | | | | | | | | | 6 | 20 | 26 |
| 1985 | | | | | | | | | 9 | 31 | 40 |
| 2000 | | | | | | | | | 12 | 48 | 60 |
| Aver. growth (%) | | | | | | | | | 2.70 | 3.42 | 3.27 |
| **Silver** | | | | | | | | | | | |
| (million troy ounces) Aver. 1971–75 | | | | The government has no projections. | | | | | 124 | 250 | 374 |
| 1985 | | | | | | | | | 160 | 321 | 481 |
| 2000 | | | | | | | | | 230 | 450 | 680 |
| Aver. growth (%) | | | | | | | | | 2.40 | 2.29 | 2.33 |
| **Sulfur** | | | | | | | | | | | |
| (million long tons) Aver. 1971–75 | | | | | | | | | 11 | 38 | 49 |
| 1985 | | | | | | | | | 15 | 50 | 65 |
| 2000 | | | | | | | | | 23 | 87 | 110 |
| Aver. growth (%) | | | | | | | | | 2.88 | 3.24 | 3.16 |
| **Tin** | | | | | | | | | | | |
| (1000 metric tons) Aver. 1971–75 | 69 | 33 | 12 | 18 | 2 | 8 | 7 | 14 | 53 | 180 | 232 |
| 1985 | 84 | 47 | 15 | 24 | 7 | 11 | 11 | 20 | 59 | 242 | 301 |
| 2000 | 111 | 62 | 22 | 31 | 10 | 14 | 16 | 28 | 67 | 326 | 393 |
| Aver. growth (%) | 1.85 | 2.46 | 2.36 | 2.11 | 6.39 | 2.18 | 3.23 | 2.70 | 0.91 | 2.31 | 2.05 |
| **Tungsten** | | | | | | | | | | | |
| (metric tons) Aver. 1971–75 | 11575 | 2758 | 578 | 6645 | 685 | 849 | 1372 | 5386 | 6510 | 33672 | 40182 |
| 1985 | 16860 | 4310 | 834 | 9975 | 1090 | 1510 | 2520 | 8619 | 8420 | 51787 | 60207 |
| 2000 | 24486 | 7011 | 1252 | 14697 | 1807 | 2868 | 4761 | 14080 | 12006 | 80631 | 92637 |
| Aver. growth (%) | 2.92 | 3.65 | 3.02 | 3.10 | 3.80 | 4.79 | 4.90 | 3.77 | 2.38 | 3.42 | 3.26 |
| **Zinc** | | | | | | | | | | | |
| (1000 metric tons) Aver. 1971–75 | 1555 | 673 | 316 | 832 | 24 | 208 | 226 | 190 | 1160 | 4346 | 5506 |
| 1985 | 2178 | 1034 | 459 | 1296 | 38 | 347 | 378 | 298 | 1600 | 6653 | 8253 |
| 2000 | 3116 | 1441 | 704 | 1934 | 71 | 574 | 688 | 528 | 2001 | 10021 | 12022 |
| Aver. growth (%) | 2.71 | 2.97 | 3.13 | 3.30 | 4.26 | 3.98 | 4.37 | 4.01 | 2.12 | 3.27 | 3.05 |

*Note:* Average growth in percent is average growth rate from 1971–75 to 2000. In calculations of average growth rates for the Malenbaum forecasts, in which the base figure is the average annual demand during 1971–75; the base figure is treated as though it were 1974 demand.

[a] Includes Australia, Canada, Israel, New Zealand, South Africa.
[b] Nickel demand figures for the U.S.S.R., Eastern Europe, and China are aggregated under U.S.S.R.
[c] Platinum-group demand figures for the U.S.S.R. and Eastern Europe are aggregated under U.S.S.R.

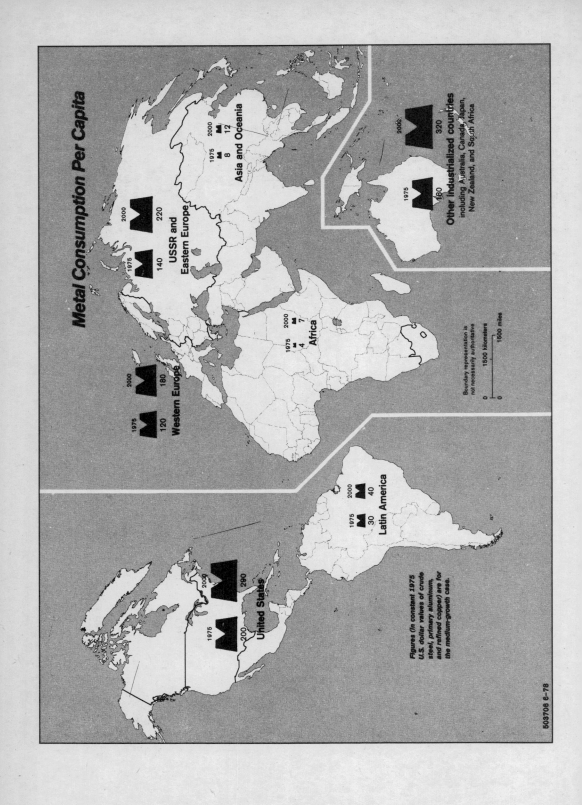

Metal Consumption Per Capita

Western Europe
1975 — 120
2000 — 180

USSR and Eastern Europe
1975 — 140
2000 — 220

Asia and Oceania
1975 — 8
2000 — 12

United States
1975 — 200
2000 — 290

Africa
1975 — 4
2000 — 7

Latin America
1975 — 30
2000 — 40

Other Industrialized countries
including Australia, Canada, Japan,
New Zealand, and South Africa
1975 — 180
2000 — 320

Boundary representation is
not necessarily authoritative

0   1500 kilometers
0   1500 miles

Figures (in constant 1975
U.S. dollar values of crude
steel, primary aluminum,
and refined copper) are for
the medium-growth case.

503706 8-78

## TABLE 12–3

**Comparison of Bureau of Mines and Malenbaum Demand Projections for Selected Metals in 1985 and 2000**

*(Millions of metric tons)*

| | Other Countries | | United States | |
|---|---|---|---|---|
| | Bur. Mines | Malen- baum | Bur. Mines | Malen- baum |
| Aluminum [a] | | | | |
| 1971–75 (avg.) | | 8 | | 4 |
| 1974 | 10 | | 5 | |
| 1985 | 20 | 13 | 10 | 7 |
| 2000 | 41 | 24 | 19 | 13 |
| Iron Ore | | | | |
| 1971–75 (avg.) | | 346 | | 85 |
| 1974 | 431 | | 83 | |
| 1985 | 590 | 514 | 97 | 101 |
| 2000 | 907 | 786 | 117 | 133 |
| Copper [a] | | | | |
| 1971–75 (avg.) | | 6 | | 1.9 |
| 1974 | 4.8 | | 1.8 | |
| 1985 | 9 | 9 | 2.4 | 2.6 |
| 2000 | 16 | 14 | 3.8 | 3.2 |
| Zinc | | | | |
| 1971–75 (avg.) | | 4.3 | | 1.2 |
| 1974 | 4.5 | | 1.3 | |
| 1985 | 6.1 | 6.7 | 1.9 | 1.6 |
| 2000 | 8.4 | 10.0 | 2.8 | 2.0 |

[a] The Bureau of Mines projections and the Malenbaum projections for these minerals are not strictly comparable because of differences in definitions of the commodities. For a more detailed accounting, see table 22–1.

*Source:* Table 12–2.

Neither set of projections meets the needs of the Global 2000 Study. The Bureau of Mines projections are for the United States and "rest of world" only and do not permit the regional disaggregation needed for this study. Neither set of projections could be adjusted to meet the GNP and population assumptions used in the other Global 2000 projections. The inability to match the GNP and population assumptions is particularly important in the case of the Malenbaum projections, which assume that mineral demand is reliably determined as a function of per capita GNP. The Bureau of Mines methodology is not sufficiently defined to allow one to understand precisely the influence of GNP and populations projections. These and other limitations are discussed more fully in Chapter 22.

The demand forecasts of Table 12–2 give a rough idea of what future demand growth could be. Collectively, the 18 mineral commodities (data were unavailable for helium) show a world demand growing at an annual rate of about 3 percent. Three commodities—aluminum, industrial diamonds, and fluorspar—show annual growth rates of over 4 percent, while growth in demand for phosphate rock exceeds 5 percent.

The mineral needs of the world energy industry (and the energy needed to produce these minerals) have not yet received the special attention and analysis that they deserve. The mineral needs of the U.S. energy industry have been analyzed by the U.S. Geological Survey based on the 1974 Project Independence Report. The Survey report concludes, in part:

Expanded energy development and production 1975–90 will necessitate a significant increase in domestic production above that of 1973 for most materials. Averaged over 15 years, the quantities of some materials needed for energy will be a large percentage of 1973 production [Figure 12–1]: for example, aluminum (30 percent), barite (100 percent), bentonite (30 percent), fluorite (58 percent), shipping-grade iron ore (26 percent), and tungsten (78 percent). [Figure 12–2] graphs the data in terms of the percentage of U.S. reserves needed to meet the total energy demand, 1975–90.

A minimum of about 2.5 billion barrels of oil-equivalent (1 bbl = $5.8 \times 10^6$ Btu) may be required to produce 20 selected mineral commodities . . . needed by the energy industries 1975–90, and 18.5 billion barrels of oil-equivalent to produce sufficient supply to meet the overall domestic demand for those minerals during the same period. This amount of energy, equal to more than half of the known U.S. recoverable petroleum reserves, is only a fraction of the energy required to produce the 90 or more mineral commodities used in the total economy. Thus, imports of mineral raw materials . . . and semifabricated or processed material also constitute energy imports. Substitution of domestically produced materials for imports will further stress domestic energy production.

Adequacy of mineral supplies for a sustained economy should be a matter of deep concern, particularly in view of the large quantities of minerals and materials required for energy production and the serious consequences in the event of deficiencies. As was evident in the 1973 oil embargo, political and economic changes and mineral shortages can occur swiftly. Our mineral inventory developed and ready for immediate extraction is nil in the case of some commodities, and in many cases is not equivalent to projected requirements for a decade of U.S. consumption.[4]

Similar analyses are needed for world energy and economic development plans.

The regional subcategories of the demand data in Table 12–2 suggest only a modest increase in the participation of LDCs in world industry. Latin America, Africa, and Asia (including mainland China) used only 7 percent of the world's alumi-

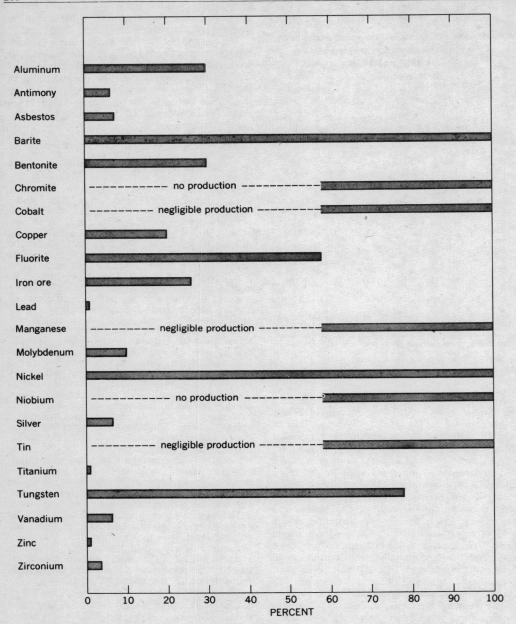

**Figure 12–1.** Average annual demand by energy industries for some commodities, 1975–90, as a percentage of U.S. production in 1973. (*Goudarzi et al., U.S. Geological Survey Professional Paper 1006-B, 1976*)

num production in 1971–75, 9 percent of the copper, and 12 percent of the iron ore. Although the people in these regions will constitute over three-fourths of the world population by year 2000, the projections suggest they will use only 8 percent of the aluminum production, 13 percent of

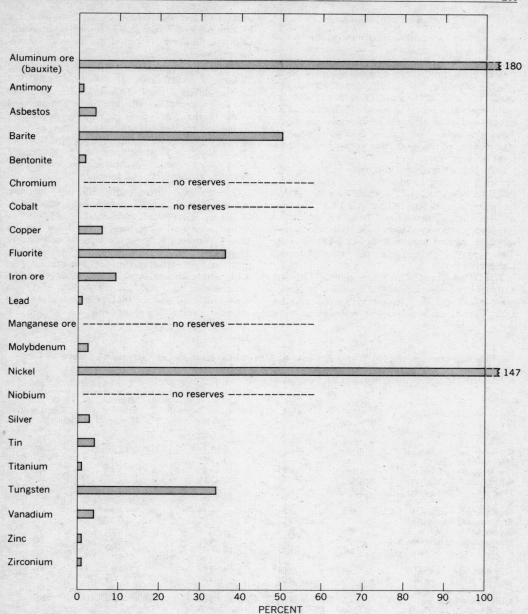

**Figure 12–2.** Percentage of U.S. reserves needed to meet total energy demand for some commodities, 1975–90. (*Goudarzi et al., U.S. Geological Survey Professional Paper 1006-B, 1976*)

the copper, and 17 percent of the iron ore. This is considerably short of the goal (set at the U.N. Industrial Development Organization Conference in Lima in 1975 and endorsed by the Seventh Special Session of the U.N. General Assembly[5]) of expanding the share of Third World countries in world industrial production to 25 percent by the year 2000.

## Supply Projections

Projections of world nonfuel mineral production to 2000 are not available from government or other sources. In the absence of supply estimates, future world production can be assumed to be roughly equal to the quantity demanded as projected in Table 12–2. Since these projections are point estimates, the "demand" figures must be understood to be amounts of minerals consumed. Total production, of course, is always equal to total consumption, neglecting year to year variations in inventories.

Some of the projected increases in supply (i.e., demand) are large, and will require contributions from the two sources of nonfuel minerals—virgin mineral commodities and recycled (or "secondary") mineral commodities. Therefore, the factors influencing the availability of both virgin and recycled mineral commodities need examination. The supply of virgin mineral commodities is considered first.

The stock from which the mining industry extracts ore for processing and refining is termed reserves. The U.S. Geological Survey and the U.S. Bureau of Mines define reserves as "that

portion of the identified resource from which a useable mineral . . . commodity can be economically and legally extracted at the time of determination."[6]

The life expectancies of 1974 world reserves of 18 mineral commodities are shown in Table 12–4 for two different rates of demand. The relatively short life expectancy of some of the commodities listed in the table does not imply impending exhaustion but does indicate clearly that, in order to sustain adequate production in the decades ahead, reserves must be increased for at least a half a dozen minerals—industrial diamonds, silver, mercury, zinc, sulfur, and tungsten.

Over the past few decades, efforts to increase mineral reserves have generally been successful. Of the six minerals just mentioned, world reserves of five nearly or more than tripled from 1950 to 1974.[7] Tungsten is the only mineral commodity whose reserves have declined since 1950. On the other hand, reserves of iron ore, bauxite, copper, lead, and platinum increased by four times or more during the period. A comparison of Tables 12–4 and 12–7 shows that reserves of several mineral commodities, notably chromium, in-

**TABLE 12–4**

**Life Expectancies of 1974 World Reserves of Mineral Commodities of Particular Concern at Two Different Rates of Demand**

| | 1974 Reserves | 1974 Demand | Projected Demand Growth Rate (%) | Demand Static at 1974 Level | Demand Growing at Projected Rates |
|---|---|---|---|---|---|
| Industrial diamonds (million carats) | 680 | 75 | 4.23 | 9 | 8 |
| Silver (million troy ounces) | 6,000 | 374 | 2.33 | 16 | 14 |
| Mercury (thousand flasks) | 4,930 | 236 | 0.50 | 22 | 21 |
| Zinc (million short tons) | 260 | 6.40 | 3.05 | 29 | 21 |
| Sulfur (million long tons) | 2,000 | 49 | 3.16 | 41 | 26 |
| Tungsten (million pounds) | 3,924 | 85 | 3.26 | 45 | 28 |
| Lead (million short tons) | 165 | 3.39 | 3.14 | 47 | 29 |
| Tin (thousand long tons) | 10,120 | 230 | 2.05 | 44 | 31 |
| Copper (million short tons) | 450 | 7.24 | 2.94 | 60 | 35 |
| Fluorine (million short tons) | 38 | 2.29 | 4.58 | 97 | 37 |
| Platinum (million troy ounces) | 297 | 2.70 | 3.75 | 104 | 43 |
| Nickel (million short tons) | 60 | 0.78 | 2.94 | 90 | 44 |
| Iron ore (billion short tons) | 100 | 0.57 | 2.95 | 216 | 68 |
| Chromium (million short tons) | 577 | 2.70 | 3.27 | 249 | 68 |
| Manganese (million short tons) | 2,013 | 10.22 | 3.36 | 268 | 69 |
| Potash (million short tons) | 11,000 | 26 | 3.27 | 430 | 84 |
| Phosphate rock (million short tons) | 17,712 | 123 | 5.17 | 1,659 | 88 |
| Aluminum in bauxite (million short tons) | 3,840 | 17 | 4.29 | 1,199 | 94 |

Note: Corresponding data for helium not available.

Source: Reserves and production data from Bureau of Mines, Mineral Trends and Forecasts, Oct. 1976—except data for industrial diamonds, from Bureau of Mines, Minerals Facts and Problems, Bulletin 667, 1975. Projected demand growth rates from Table 12–2.

creased appreciably even in the few years 1974–77.

Among the pitfalls of interpreting the calculated life of world mineral reserves is the fact that some mines take much longer to exhaust than the average (reserve-lifetime figures are averages that do not take this into account). Furthermore, mine output over time is not typically represented by a straight line to exhaustion and then a vertical drop to zero, but rather by a declining curve.[8]

The demand/supply projections of Table 12–2 assume that part of the future supply of products of mineral origin will be recycled mineral commodities. What portion will come from recycled ("secondary") mineral commodities is not estimated, but rough estimates can be obtained from past experience. In 1974, scrap accounted for 5 percent of U.S. aluminum consumption, 11 percent of chromium, 20 percent of copper, 37 percent of iron, and 39 percent of lead, according to the Bureau of Mines.

The portion of the waste stream that is recycled is influenced by many economic factors. Just as discarded tailings from mining and milling operations are now sometimes reworked in response to changing economic conditions, refuse dumps may someday be "mined" to recover some of the metals and other elements previously discarded. While the potential recoverable amounts have not been estimated, it has been observed by McHale[9] that cumulative world production of iron, manganese, and nickel since 1870 equals one-fourth of their respective present reserves. McHale notes further that the cumulative production of copper and lead equal about half of present reserves, and cumulative production of zinc, tin, and tungsten exceed present reserves. This past production is either still in use or has been discarded. At some point in the future it may be cheaper to recover and recycle some discarded minerals than to mine ores of ever decreasing grade.

## Price Projections

The Global 2000 Study could not obtain nonfuel mineral price projections from the Department of the Interior because the Department does not make such projections. Price projections were made some years ago but were discontinued because they were heavily criticized. The Department normally assumes that the price of refined minerals will remain constant in real terms out to 2000, even if there are significant increases in energy costs.

In fact, the real price of most mineral commodities has been constant or declining for many years. Economists have generally interpreted these trends to mean that no "scarcity" is developing and that no real-price increases are to be expected.[10,11] The trends may be changing,[12] however, and the simple extrapolations behind these projections are being questioned.[13] The techniques for analyzing intercommodity competition that have been developed for energy projections have not yet been applied to nonfuel minerals. Furthermore, developments that can be anticipated in the nonfuel minerals industries—increasing energy costs, gradually declining ore-grades, increased recycling, and requirements for environmental protection—require better methods of analysis than have been used in the past if important nonlinear phenomena are to be considered. Figure 12–3 illustrates the nonlinear increases in energy requirements from mining lower-grade ores.

With diminishing returns in prospect, it is plausible that the price trends in nonfuel minerals will change and real-prices will increase. How much increase might be expected is open to question. Table 12–5 illustrates the prices that

### TABLE 12–5

**Illustration of Nonfuel Mineral Prices Extrapolated to 2000 with a 5 Percent Growth Rate Beginning in 1980**

| | 1976[a] | 1985 | 2000 |
|---|---|---|---|
| | (constant 1970 dollars) | | |
| Aluminum (pound ingot) | 0.32 | 0.41 | 0.86 |
| Chromite (long ton, South Africa) | 30 | 38 | 79 |
| Copper (pound) | 0.45 | 0.58 | 1.21 |
| Diamond, Industrial (carat) | 3 | 4 | 8 |
| Fluorspar (short ton of metspar) | 61 | 78 | 164 |
| Helium (1000 cubic ft) | 15 | 20 | 42 |
| Iron ore (long ton, 51.5 percent Fe) | 14 | 19 | 39 |
| Lead (pound) | 0.14 | 0.18 | 0.38 |
| Manganese (long ton unit of contained Mn) | 1.02 | 1.31 | 2.74 |
| Mercury (76-lb flask) | 67 | 86 | 180 |
| Nickel (pound) | 1.62 | 2.07 | 4.35 |
| Phosphate Rock (short ton) | 14 | 18 | 38 |
| Platinum Group | | | |
| Palladium (troy ounce) | 36 | 46 | 96 |
| Platinum (troy ounce) | 114 | 146 | 306 |
| Potash (short ton unit of $K_2O$) | 0.51 | 0.65 | 1.37 |
| Silver (troy ounce) | 3 | 4 | 8 |
| Sulfur (long ton of elemental S) | 32 | 41 | 66 |
| Tin (pound) | 2.41 | 3.08 | 6.47 |
| Tungsten (pound $WO_3$) | 0.04 | 0.05 | 0.10 |
| Zinc (pound) | 0.23 | 0.29 | 0.62 |

[a] The 1976 price was put into 1970 dollars by dividing its level in 1976 dollars by 1.42, corresponding to an average 6 percent inflation rate.
Source: The 1976 price was obtained from the Bureau of Mines. Future prices were calculated assuming a 5 percent annual increase from 1980 on.

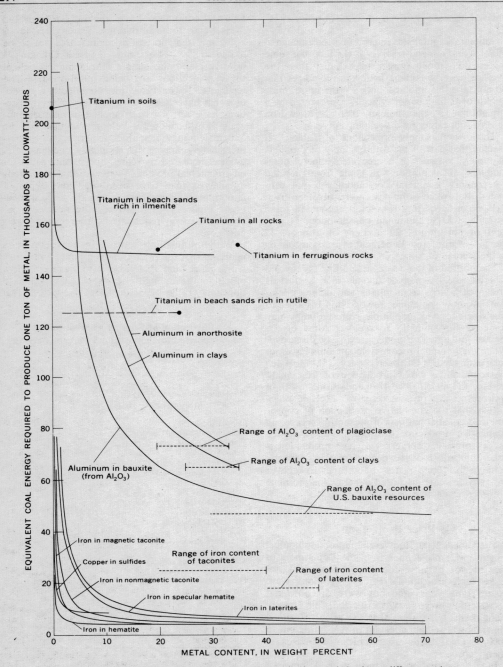

**Figure 12–3.** Energy requirements for recovery of iron, titanium, and aluminum, different grades, various sources. (*Page & Creasey, U.S. Geological Survey* Journal of Research, *Jan.-Feb. 1975*)

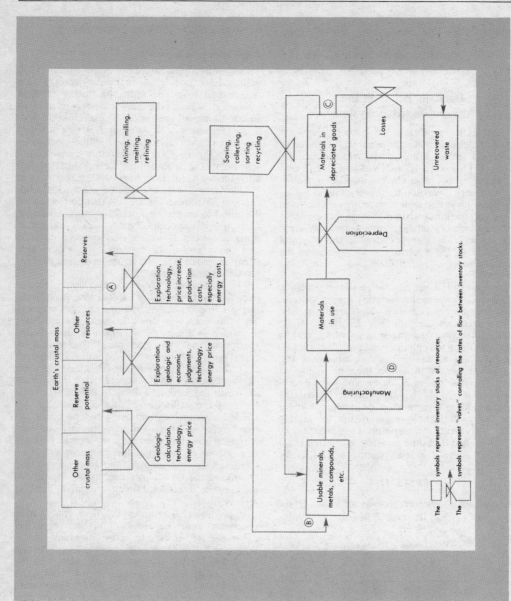

**Figure 12-4.** Mineral product flow and four principal decision points (*A, B, C, D*) in the flow.

would result from a 5 percent per year increase starting in 1980—the same rate as was assumed for energy prices. Table 12–6 compares these prices with projections made for the United Nations.

## Decision Points in the Mineral-Industry System

Meeting the projected 3–5 percent per year growth in demand will require careful attention to the health and stability of the minerals supply system. [14] This system consists of several different types of inventory stocks linked together by flows. The flows are governed by the associated industry, technology, economic conditions, institutions, and government regulations. Stable management of these inventory stocks is an enormously complex matter, not just because of the physical magnitude of the system but also because the stocks themselves are difficult and expensive to measure.

There are four major decision points controlling the primary flows in the minerals supply system. These four principal decision points are designated by the letters A through D in Figure 12–4. At point A, decisions are made as to what can and should be done to replenish reserves. At point B, decisions are made on the mix of virgin and recycled materials to use in their products. At point C, decisions are made on whether a depreciated good should be discarded or saved for recycling. Manufacturers decide at point D where they can reduce their requirements for certain material elements (conservation) and where they should change from one material to another (substitution). Some of the many factors and questions

### TABLE 12–6

### Comparison of Price Projections for Four Metals in the Year 2000

| | From Table 12-5 | Leontief Normalized Prices [a] | |
|---|---|---|---|
| | | Low | High |
| | *(dollars per pound)* | | |
| Copper | 1.21 | .56 | 1.29 |
| Lead | .38 | .15 | .27 |
| Nickel | 4.35 | 1.81 | 3.18 |
| Zinc | .62 | .29 | .29 |

[a] "Normalization" is a process through which the prices projected by the model are adjusted for inflation under the assumption that the average price of all goods consumed will be the same in the future as it was in 1970.

*Source:* Wassily Leontief et al., *The Future of the World Economy*, New York: Oxford University, 1977, p. 45.

involved at each of these four decision points are discussed in the following paragraphs.

**Replenishing Reserves**

Decisions made at point A in Figure 12–4 influence the rate at which mineral reserves are replenished from the stock of "other mineral resources." These other resources consist of three additional major inventories: (1) undiscovered economic resources, (2) undiscovered subeconomic resources, and (3) identified subeconomic resources. Figure 12–5 depicts this classification scheme in the so-called McKelvey box, named after former Geological Survey Director Vincent E. McKelvey, who contributed most to its conception. Since reserves are just that portion of the identified resources from which mineral commodities can be economically and legally extracted, other resources constitute undiscovered deposits and those not quite economically exploitable ("paramarginal") or far from economically exploitable ("submarginal").

The stocks of all resource inventories change over time as the result of exploration, technology, changes in production costs and changes in price. The flows among these inventory stocks are illustrated in Figure 12–6, which is an exploded version of the McKelvey box.* Exploration locates previously undiscovered mineral deposits thus "moving" them into the inventories of identified resources and reserves. This movement augments the identified resource inventories while reducing the undiscovered stocks. Likewise, advances in technology and rising mineral prices can move resources from the paramarginal and submarginal inventories into the economic inventories. However, increased production costs (e.g., increased energy, capital, and labor costs) and environmental constraints can move deposits in the opposite direction. Mining, of course, depletes reserve inventories.

Exploration determines the flow that moves resources from the stock of undiscovered, recoverable resources into reserves. Many factors influence the level of exploratory efforts. Prevailing interest rates and tax policies influence the amount of reserves companies want to hold. High interest rates tend to discourage exploration until the ratio of reserves to annual production becomes

---

*Adapted from John J. Schanz, Jr., "United States Minerals—A Perspective," *Mining Congress Journal*, Feb. 1977, p. 27, and "A Quick-Look Method for Monitoring the Adequacy of Metal Supplies from Canadian Mining for Domestic Needs," Energy, Mines and Resources Canada (Minerals), Mineral Policy Series, Mineral Bulletin MR 165, 1976.

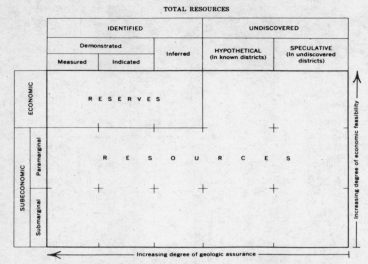

**Figure 12–5.** Classification of mineral resources, the "McKelvey box." (*U.S. Geological Survey Bulletin 1450-A*, 1976)

relatively small. Taxes on reserves also discourage exploration.

Technological advances and increased price of a mineral commodity relative to production costs are the major determinants in the flow of identified paramarginal and submarginal resources into the reserves inventory. Increased real prices offset the high production costs associated with paramarginal (or even submarginal) resources, but at the same time increases in real prices constrain demand and limit the use of mineral commodities in the economy. Over the past decade technology has contributed to a flow of paramarginal and submarginal resources into reserves without increasing relative prices, but continuation of these trends may be more difficult in the future.

Technology is knowledge organized and applied to an objective—in this case the production of nonfuel mineral commodities. This production process involves many factors—labor, water, energy, nonfuel minerals, capital—and the relative mix of the production factors is determined largely by technology.

Much more information (and policy attention) is needed on the influence of technology on the production of mineral commodities. To what extent have past technological developments substituted energy, water, and capital for labor? To what extent has cheap energy contributed to keeping the prices of nonfuel mineral commodities low? What specific technological developments are now expected to influence the future produc-

tion of nonfuel minerals? What will be the energy requirements? The capital requirements? The water requirements? The labor needs? The environmental impacts? Will lower-grade resource stocks become economic? What will be the implications for the price of mineral commodities relative to other goods and services? What indicators should be used to measure technological progress? Has progress been achieved if a technology provides economic access to lower-grade deposits while increasing energy and/or water requirements?

Production costs (relative to nonfuel mineral commodity prices) also need careful examination, because increased production costs relative to market prices can move reserves back to the paramarginal inventory by making production uneconomical. An example from fuel minerals illustrates the point.

At various times during the past decade the per barrel price of oil at which oil shale would become economic has been placed at $5, $7, $10, etc. Yet at an oil price of $14 per barrel, shale is still not economically recoverable, in large part because the increased cost of oil has in turn increased the costs of producing oil from shale. The energy required to produce a unit of energy from shale is large or, to put it another way, the net energy yield is small. In such cases, increases in the price of oil are reflected quickly in increased production costs. As a result, shale may never be more than marginally economic. Similar questions have yet

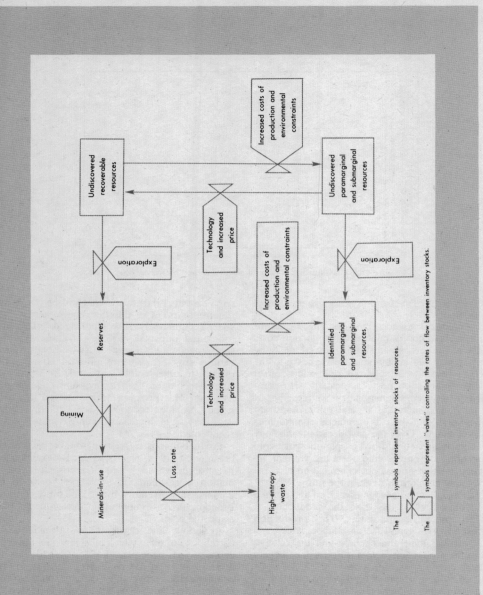

The ☐ symbols represent inventory stocks of resources.

The ⋈ symbols represent "valves" controlling the rates of flow between inventory stocks.

**Figure 12-6.** The exploded McKelvey box, with indicated stocks and flows.

to be carefully answered about paramarginal and submarginal nonfuel mineral resources.

Estimates of resources other than reserves are very uncertain, partly because of conceptual difficulties. How does the investigator decide when a mineral occurrence is too low grade or too difficult to extract or refine to include it as a resource? As a practical matter, investigators do establish cutoff points, selected by professional judgment with limited standard criteria available for guidance.

The question then arises as to what extent mineral resources, as represented by the estimates presented, might be enlarged from other parts of the earth's crust (see Fig. 12–4). McKelvey has suggested that the recoverable resource potential of well-explored chemical elements in the United States is roughly equal to their crustal abundance (percent of the element contained in the earth's crust) times a factor ranging between 1 billion and 10 billion.[15] Ralph Erickson, also of the Geological Survey, elaborated somewhat on the relation-

ship and applied it on a world basis.[16] The recoverable resource potentials implied by this method are included in Table 12–7 for 15 of the elements considered in this chapter. These potentials include undiscovered deposits but exclude all deposits (discovered and undiscovered) not economic at current prices with present technology. Corresponding production and resources data are included in the table for comparison.

The quantity of minerals distributed in the earth's crust down to a depth of 1 kilometer is very large, as indicated in the last column of the table. Most of these minerals, however, generally have such a low concentration that the costs of their extraction and refining are prohibitive.

### The Mix of Virgin and Recycled Materials

The second major decision to be considered (see point B in Fig. 12–4) is the way in which the mix of virgin and recycled materials is determined in the minerals supply system. The factors in-

## TABLE 12–7

### World Production and Reserves in 1977 (Estimated), Other Resources in 1973–77 (as Data Available), Resource Potential, and Resource Base of 17 Elements

*(Millions of metric tons)*

| | Production | Reserves | Other Resources | Resource Potential (Recoverable) | Resource Base (Crustal Mass) |
|---|---|---|---|---|---|
| Aluminum | 17[a] | 5,200[a] | 2,800[a] | 3,519,000 | 1,990,000,000,000 |
| Iron | 495[b] | 93,100 | 143,000[c] | 2,035,000 | 1,392,000,000,000 |
| Potassium | 22 | 9,960 | 103,000 | n.a. | 408,000,000,000 |
| Manganese | 10[d] | 2,200 | 1,100[e] | 42,000 | 31,200,000,000 |
| Phosphorus | 14[f] | 3,400[f] | 12,000[f] | 51,000 | 28,800,000,000 |
| Fluorine | 2[g] | 72 | 270 | 20,000 | 10,800,000,000 |
| Sulfur | 52 | 1,700 | 3,800[h] | | 9,600,000,000 |
| Chromium | 3[i] | 780[i] | 6,000[i] | 3,260 | 2,600,000,000 |
| Zinc | 6 | 159 | 4,000 | 3,400 | 2,250,000,000 |
| Nickel | 0.7 | 54 | 103[e] | 2,590 | 2,130,000,000 |
| Copper | 8 | 456 | 1,770[j] | 2,120 | 1,510,000,000 |
| Lead | 4 | 123 | 1,250 | 550 | 290,000,000 |
| Tin | 0.2 | 10 | 27 | 68 | 40,800,000 |
| Tungsten | 0.04 | 1.8 | 3.4 | 51 | 26,400,000 |
| Mercury | 0.008 | 0.2 | 0.4 | 3.4 | 2,100,000 |
| Silver | 0.010 | 0.2 | 0.5 | 2.8 | 1,800,000 |
| Platinum group[k] | 0.0002 | 0.02 | 0.05[l] | 1.2[m] | 1,100,000 |

[a] In bauxite, dry basis, assumed to average 21 percent recoverable aluminum.
[b] In ore and concentrates assumed to average 58 percent recoverable iron.
[c] In ore and concentrates assumed to average 26 percent recoverable iron.
[d] In ore and concentrates assumed to average 40 percent manganese.
[e] Excludes metal in deep-sea nodules and, in the case of nickel, unidentified resources.
[f] In phosphate rock ore and concentrates assumed to average 13 percent phosphorus.
[g] In fluorspar and phosphate rock ore and concentrates assumed to average 44 percent fluorine.
[h] Excludes unidentified sulfur resources, enormous quantities of sulfur in gypsum and anhydrite, and some 600 billion tons of sulfur in coal, oil shale, and in shale that is rich in organic matter.
[i] In ore and concentrates assumed to average 32 percent chromium.
[j] Includes 690 million tons in deep-sea nodules.
[k] Platinum, palladium, iridium, cesium, rhodium, and ruthenium.
[l] Approximate midpoint of estimated range of 0.03—0.06 million metric tons.
[m] Platinum only.

*Source:* U.S. Bureau of Mines, *Mineral Commodity Summaries 1978; Mineral Commodity Profiles 1977; Mineral Facts and Problems* (Bulletin 667), Washington: Government Printing Office, 1975. Donald A. Brobst and Walden P. Pratt, eds., *United States Mineral Resources* (Geological Survey Professional Paper 820) Washington: Government Printing Office, 1973.

volved are, basically, the quantity and quality of resources available from mining and recycling.

As noted above, the earth's crust contains very large quantities of minerals. It follows, therefore, that the basic long-term issue of mineral-commodity policy for all nations and the world is not the exhaustion of minerals but rather the maintenance of an adequate stock of minerals-in-use in the global economy at manageable economic and environmental costs. Nonetheless, concern over exhaustion persists, stemming in part from confusion over the terms "renewable" and "nonrenewable." Biological resources, are often thought of as "renewable." Nonfuel mineral resources, are usually termed "nonrenewable." Actually in both cases, the reverse is more nearly true.

When passenger pigeons were hunted for savory pigeon-pie filling, they were regarded as a renewable resource. After all, every year the pigeons bred and produced more pigeons. Unfortunately, the take of pigeons exceeded the maximum sustainable yield of this resource and the passenger pigeon population declined. Unlike mineral resources, the remainder of this depleted resource was not scattered across the earth, limiting the take, but concentrated. After each attack, a biologically fatal instinct flocked the birds together again—until the last pigeon was shot. The passenger pigeon resource—the species—is extinct now and will never be replaced. It, like all biological resources, was exhaustible and nonrenewable.

By contrast, mineral resources are (at least in theory) completely renewable. When an atom of copper is used, it is not "consumed" or destroyed but remains an atom of copper potentially available for recovery and reuse. In many cases the cost of recovery and recycling would be exceedingly high. For example, recovery of lead from the waste stream of used tetraethyl lead (in leaded gasoline) would be *very* costly since this lead is scattered along highways across the world as exceedingly fine, diffuse particles. Nonetheless, recovery and reuse of this lead is theoretically possible at some cost of energy, water, labor, and capital. Therefore, in contrast to biological resources, the basic issue of nonfuel mineral resources is not exhaustion or extinction but rather the cost of maintaining an adequate stock of nonfuel mineral commodities within the economy through mining and recycling.

The mix between mining and recycling is determined largely by relative costs. These, in turn, depend to a large extent on the "concentratedness" of the sources of nonfuel minerals.

Entropy is the scientific term that measures how "mixed up" things are. "Concentratedness," as used above, is the opposite of entropy. Concentrated deposits have relatively low entropy and low production costs; low-grade deposits have high entropy and high costs.[17] Combining minerals and materials in alloys and other products and distributing these products throughout the economy increases the entropy of the minerals used; how much entropy is added determines largely the practicality of recycling. The factors that determine the entropy of ores and the wastes from society are therefore highly relevant to maintaining an adequate stock of minerals in use at manageable costs.

Mineral deposits of the lowest entropy (highest grade) are generally used first. It is widely thought that, as low-entropy deposits are depleted, higher-entropy deposits are found in greater abundance. In some types of mineral deposits, there is a graduation from relatively low entropy to relatively high entropy, and the tonnage available increases at a constant geometric rate over some range as the grade decreases.[18] However, there is no geological reason to think that this relationship holds for all ore deposits or that "there must be undiscovered [higher-entropy] deposits of astronomical tonnage to bridge the gap between commercial ore and the millions of cubic miles of crystal rocks that have measurable trace amounts of the various less common metals in them."[19] Much further work is needed to more adequately estimate the ultimate availability of naturally occurring resource deposits and the economic, social, and environmental cost associated with producing them.[20]

## Save It, or Throw It Away?

At point C in Figure 12–4 decisions are made by the final users of products as to whether the depreciated goods are to be "thrown away" or saved for recycling. In part this is a question of personal values: Will a person take the time and go to the inconvenience to see that materials are saved for recycling? In part the question is economic: Are there institutions available for recycling and have the depreciated goods been designed so as to have economic value for recycling?

The most influential decisions affecting the fate of depreciated goods are not made by the final users and recyclers but by the manufacturers who originally designed the depreciated goods. If the original design produces a high-entropy combination of materials, the final user has little choice but to "throw it away." Thus, while decisions on recycling appear to be made at point C in Figure 12–4, most are actually design decisions made at point D.

Some designs facilitate reuse and recycling and thereby increase residence times for minerals-in-use. Other designs make reuse and recycling virtually impossible. "Disposable" products and containers are not designed for easy disposal, in fact disposal of "disposable" products is an increasingly difficult municipal problem. "Disposable" products and containers are designed so that they cannot be reused. Many cannot even be recycled because they are such high-entropy products.

Frozen orange juice containers provide an example of a "disposable" product of a particularly high-entropy design. The metal top is usually a different alloy (or even a different metal) from the bottom. The cylinder itself is composite material—rial heavy paper coated on the outside with ink and plastic and lined on the inside with a metal foil. Minerals and materials combined in such high-entropy designs can be used only once and are thereafter lost to society.

The costs of maintaining an adequate stock of minerals-in-use, therefore, depend not only on adequate reserves and other resources but also on the residence time of the mineral commodities in the economy before they are lost as high-entropy wastes. Product design, the availability of maintenance and spare parts are important considerations, as are the institutional considerations that govern recycling and reuse. Important institutional considerations include the freight rates and tax policies that favor virgin—over recycled—materials and the municipal disposal service (provided at no charge to manufacturers) for the disposal of all products, independent of design. A nation's minerals policy, therefore, extends well beyond reserves, resources, and mining; it includes all factors that lead to high-entropy loss from its stock of minerals-in-use.

High-entropy product designs have an important influence on future material costs and are closely associated with an especially important institutional consideration: Responsibility for the design of most products is separated completely from responsibility for the ultimate disposal of the products designed. The results of this institutional arrangement are often disastrous for those involved in the recycling (secondary-materials) industries. For example, a few years ago beverage producers began using closures that left aluminum rings on the necks of "one-way" bottles with little thought about the implications of this high-entropy design for recycling. Only when recyclers pro-

tested that the aluminum contamination precluded recycling the glass cullet was the product design changed.

Automobiles provide another important example. Automobiles are by nature a high-entropy product containing many materials, but design considerations could greatly facilitate recycling of much of the material. Steel, one of the largest constituent materials in automobiles, is reduced in value significantly by contamination by copper. Were automobile manufacturers responsible for the disposal of depreciated cars, a strong incentive would be established to reduce copper contamination. In fact, if automobiles were leased rather than sold, there might be benefits not only for recycling and solid waste, but also for maintenance and air quality.

The positive effect of institutional responsibility can be seen in the example of scrap wire from telephone installations. Telephone companies are responsible for cleaning up after installations; rather than paying to have scrap wire carted away, attention is given to designs that facilitate recycling of scrap copper wire. Special recycling bags facilitate collection, and insulating materials difficult to separate from the copper are avoided. Similarly, aircraft manufacturers, who are often asked to scrap aircraft, may stamp alloy compositions on parts during manufacture to facilitate recycling. Thus, institutional responsibility for disposal clearly leads to product designs that are very different from those used in the "disposable" products that are ultimately the responsibility of municipal sanitation departments.

## Conservation and Substitution

Point D, the last of the four decision points, in Figure 12–4, is where decisions on conservation and substitution are made. Both conservation and substitution come about as a result of design policies, which respond strongly to technological developments and relative prices.

The demand for nonfuel mineral commodities—like the demand for energy—can be moderated by conservation, but just as with energy, there are costs associated with minerals conservation, costs that may delay major conservation efforts until prices increase significantly.

Substitution also has potential for decreasing the need for the less common metals, provided the substitute material is not highly energy-intensive, like plastics, or is also experiencing supply limitations, like wood and wood products in some regions. Sometimes an alternative process, rather than a different material, reduces or even eliminates the demand for particular uses of a scarce material. There are examples relating to mercury.

Projected demand for mercury, when compared with the resource outlook, suggests that mercury may be one of the first industrial metals to experience significant supply constraints. Furthermore, use of mercury is being restricted in part because of health and environmental hazards. However, acceptable alternatives are now known for most of the major uses of mercury. These alternatives, in effect, substitute for mercury.[21]

Impressive as such developments are, one cannot simply assume that technology will eliminate the need for minerals as they become more scarce. It will probably be very difficult—perhaps impossible—to develop entirely satisfactory substitutes for lead and antimony in storage batteries, manganese for use in desulfurizing steel, nickel and chromium in stainless steel, tin in solder, helium in low-temperature refrigeration, uranium and beryllium in nuclear reactors, tungsten in high-speed tools, mercury in wetted contact relays and arc rectifiers, silver in photography, and palladium as a contact material in telephone electromagnetic relays. Furthermore, it often takes one or two decades for a new technological development to reach the point of widespread use. There can be significant costs and uncomfortable economic dislocations during the transition if stable international supplies are not planned and developed well in advance of anticipated needs.

## Nonfuel Minerals and the North-South Dialogue

Mineral commodities are essential to both developed and developing economies, but in different ways. Developed industrialized economies need access to dependable supplies of inexpensive raw materials. Developing economies need both foreign exchange from mineral commodity exports and refined minerals and materials for development. Mineral policies and prices are therefore a point of potential disagreement between the industrialized nations (predominantly in the northern latitudes) and the less developed nations (primarily to the south). In fact, minerals issues have been a major element in the North-South dialogue.

The demand for nonfuel minerals commodities in the industrialized nations is large. If the fourth of the world's population that inhabits industrial countries were content with a fourth of the world's mineral production, they could furnish their entire needs (except for tin and possibly bauxite) from their domestic deposits and by trade among themselves. At least until the year 2000,

however, industrialized countries are projected to absorb over three-fourths of world nonfuel mineral production.

The per capita demand for nonfuel minerals in the industrialized countries is so high comparatively that these countries use not only their own domestic supplies but import increasingly large quantities from the LDCs. (While some of these resources are re-exported to the less developed countries as manufactured goods, a large portion remains in the developed economies.) As a result, the percentage of world mineral-commodity production traded internationally increased appreciably in the 1950s and 1960s, as shown in Table 12–8. During this same period, real prices of most mineral commodities either decreased or increased only moderately.

Prices are a major concern of those LDCs that export nonfuel mineral commodities. They would, of course, like to receive higher prices for their commodities and argue that the present price of most nonfuel mineral commodities does not reflect the real value of the commodities and is not compatible with the prices charged for the manufactured goods they import. To support the latter point, they note that LDC "terms of trade" with developed areas (unit value index of exports divided by unit value index of imports) for commodities (excluding petroleum) dropped from 109 in 1953 to 84 in 1975 (1970 = 100).[22]

The LDCs' bargaining position is generally not as strong with respect to nonfuel mineral commodities as it is with respect to oil. The OPEC nations have over 70 percent of the proven reserves of petroleum; mineral reserves are not so concentrated. The comparative mineral reserve position of the developed and developing regions is shown in Table 12–9. However, as the industrialized nations continue to deplete their own resources, the LDCs' position will become

### TABLE 12–8

**Percentage of World Production of Selected Minerals Traded Internationally, 1950–70**

|            | 1950 | 1960 | 1970  |
|------------|------|------|-------|
| Aluminum   | 81   | 86   | 103 [a] |
| Copper     | 55   | 66   | 59    |
| Zinc       | 52   | 60   | 60    |
| Fluorspar  | 29   | 42   | 54    |

[a] More than 3 percent of traded aluminum materials derived from drawdowns of mine and smelter stocks.

*Source:* National Commission on Materials Policy, *Toward a National Materials Policy: World Perspective,* Washington: Government Printing Office, Jan. 1973, Appendix.

## TABLE 12–9

### Geographic Distribution of World Resources of Selected Mineral Commodities in 1974

*(Percent of world total)*

| | Northern America, Western Europe, Australia, Japan | | Republic of South Africa, Rhodesia | | U.S.S.R. and Eastern Europe | | Less Developed Countries | |
|---|---|---|---|---|---|---|---|---|
| | Reserves | Total Resources | Reserves | Total Resources | Reserves | Total Resources | Reserves | Total Resources |
| Steel-making commodities | | | | | | | | |
| Iron | 40 | 35 | 1 | 2 | 30 | 27 | 29 | 36 |
| Manganese | 8 | 8 | 45 | 47 | 37 | 38 | 10 | 7 |
| Chromium | 1 | 1 | 96 | 97 | 1 | 1 | 2 | 1 |
| Nickel | 27 | 33 | 3 | 4 | 9 | 8 | 61 [a] | 55 [b] |
| Nonferrous commodities | | | | | | | | |
| Aluminum | 23 | 25 | | | 4 | 3 | 73 | 72 |
| Copper | 31 | 42 | 1 | 2 | 12 | 8 | 56 | 48 |
| Lead | 58 | 65 | | | 21 | 17 | 21 | 18 |
| Zinc | 63 | 63 | | | 15 | 15 | 22 | 22 |
| Tin | 7 | 10 | | | 6 | 7 | 87 | 83 |
| Nonmetallic commodities | | | | | | | | |
| Sulfur | 40 | 57 | | | 18 | 14 | 42 | 29 |
| Phosphate rock | 18 | 12 | 11 | 1 | 3 | 5 | 68 | 82 |
| Potash | 82 | 91 | | | 17 | 8 | 1 | 1 |

[a] Comprises New Caledonia 25 percent and other less developed countries 36 percent.
[b] Comprises New Caledonia 22 percent and other less developed countries 33 percent.

*Source:* Bureau of Mines. *Mineral Facts and Problems*, Washington: Government Printing Office, 1975.

stronger, and continued efforts to establish cartels can be expected.

The future prospects for cartelization efforts is unclear. Some analysts believe that the political, technical, and economic factors responsible for OPEC are unique and that there will never be a comparably effective marketing organization for any other commodity. Others are far less certain. Examples of unity among LDCs have become increasingly evident in recent years, and these countries have much to gain economically by such cooperation. It is clear, however, that the LDCs will be restrained by a desire to maintain employment in their mining and related industries and will therefore be hesitant to encourage industrial countries to turn to alternative sources and substitute materials. Furthermore, all of the non-OPEC LDCs need foreign exchange to pay for essential imports.

Nonfuel minerals play an important role in the balance of payments of the less developed nations. Of the total value of commodity exports (excluding petroleum) by LDCs, eight principal nonfuel minerals constituted 13 percent in 1960 and 11 percent in 1975.[23] Sometimes a single mineral accounts for over half of total exports of a particular country—copper in the case of Chile,

Zambia, and Zaire; iron ore in the case of Liberia and Mauritania; and aluminum in various primary forms in the case of Guinea and Surinam. Tin is nearly as dominant in Bolivian exports, and phosphate rock in Moroccan exports.

Much of the final value of refined minerals is added during processing and refining, and many LDCs want to process their mineral raw materials before export so as to retain as much as possible of the value added by manufacture. Already most bauxite mined in Jamaica is processed to alumina and aluminum metal before export. Collectively, LDCs have set a goal of producing 25 percent of the world industrial production by 2000. Much of the LDC production will be refined mineral commodities.

Mineral deposits beneath the sea are of concern to less developed countries both because these minerals are a possible source of competition and because of a feeling of participation in ownership. Avid Pardo, Maltese Ambassador to the United Nations, succinctly stated the LDC position in his address to the General Assembly on November 1, 1967, when he stressed that the resources in and under the oceans are a "common heritage of mankind." Disputes over who should receive the benefits has delayed the development of seabed resources, the most important of which are the "manganese nodules."

These potato-sized nodules, containing important amounts of nickel, copper, cobalt, and manganese, lie on the ocean floors beneath 1,000 to 20,000 feet of water. The possibility of exploiting these resources has led mining companies in industrial countries to form several consortia to actively develop the necessary dredging and processing technology. Much of the technology has already been developed and tested. Preproduction expenditures are expected to reach $1 billion by 1980. Commercial output may begin in the early 1980s. The prospects for profitable operation are good, but the profits would accrue primarily to industrialized nations since the LDCs have neither the technology necessary to move into deep-seabed mining nor (except for the OPEC nations) the necessary capital.

Annual extraction of manganese nodules from the deep seabed may total 15 million metric tons by 1985, according to estimates by Leipziger and Mudge.[24] These nodules may yield the metal tonnages shown in Table 12–10, plus smaller quantities of some other metals. However, potential environmental impacts have not yet been fully examined, and the LDCs believe that the nodules should be mined by an international authority in which they have significant representation.

At recent United Nations Law of the Sea Conferences, the LDCs have requested the establishment of an International Seabed Resource Authority (ISRA) to control all aspects of deep-seabed mining. It is proposed that the ISRA be an operating institution in competition with (or to the exclusion of) private firms. Whether the operations are public or private, an international tax on resources mined from the deep seabed could yield $200 million to $600 million annually. These funds could then be used to accelerate development in the LDCs, which is the basic objective of a related proposal for the establishment of a New International Economic Order.

Many of the developing countries have come to believe they cannot accomplish their development at a satisfactory rate without basic structural changes in the world economy. Accordingly, a proposal for structural change was presented by the LDCs at the Sixth Special Session of the U.N. General Assembly in 1974. The proposal calls for the establishment of a New International Economic Order, and one of its principal objectives[25] is a more favorable relationship between prices of LDC exports and imports.

Since the Sixth Special Session in 1974, the LDCs have made additional initiatives on commodity prices. An important effort was made at the Fourth U.N. Conference on Trade and Development (UNCTAD) in 1976 to support the prices of 10 commodities, including three nonfuel minerals—bauxite, copper, and tin. Further discussion of the price of these minerals (plus iron ore, manganese ore, and phosphate rock) were held at the 1977 UNCTAD Conference.

One consideration that will become increasingly important in North-South discussions of mineral commodity prices is the fact that high-grade ores in effect have a large "energy content" as a result of their low entropy. It takes less than half as much energy to recover a ton of copper from 4 percent Zambian ore than from 0.3 percent Arizonan ore. Grade and entropy considerations are likely to become more important in the future.

## Conclusions

Projected world demand (when compared with world reserves) of nonfuel resources, shows no immediate prospect of resource exhaustion. On the other hand, significant increases in reserves will be needed to meet projected demand, which does not include a significant increase in LDC demand. As noted in Chapter 22, the projections of LDC demands for nonfuel minerals could be much higher if other assumptions were introduced into the analysis. In any event, the industrialized nations will continue to be heavily dependent on resources imported from LDCs, and both availability and price will depend on developments in the North-South dialogue, especially concerning proposals for a New International Economic Order, for multinational corporation codes, and for Law-of-the-Sea issues.

Such North-South issues, and the prospects for rising energy costs, will deeply affect coming decisions over the exploitability of resources

### TABLE 12–10

### Estimates of Metal Recoveries from Manganese Nodules from the Deep Seabed by 1985

|  | Production (thousands of metric tons) | Percent of 1974 World Production | Percent of Estimated 1985 World Production |
|---|---|---|---|
| Nickel | 225 | 32 | 14 |
| Copper | 180 | 2 | 2 |
| Cobalt | 37 | 125 | 62 |
| Manganese | 3,750 | 40 | 28 |

Source: Danny M. Leipziger and James L. Mudge, *Seabed Mineral Resources and the Economic Interests of Developing Countries*, Cambridge, Mass.: Ballinger, 1976. Data for manganese have been updated.

around the world and the technologies used in the exploitation process. The results could include significant increases in the real price of nonfuel minerals. Recycling could then appear relatively attractive in industrialized nations. The possibilities for recycling, however, depend largely on institutional considerations, especially product-design decisions that determine the entropic state of the resources in depreciated goods. As a result, product-design decisions between now and 2000 may have a significant bearing on resource stocks and prices in the early 21st century.

## REFERENCES

1. F. Callot, "Production et Consommation Mondiales des Minérais en 1973," *Annales des Mines*, Dec. 1975, pp. 13–14; also Charles L. Kimbell and George A. Morgan, "Minerals in the World Economy," in U.S. Bureau of Mines, *Minerals Yearbook 1974*, Washington: Government Printing Office, 1976.

2. Wilfred Malenbaum, *World Demand for Raw Materials in 1985 and 2000*, Philadelphia: University of Pennsylvania, Oct. 1977.

3. U.S. Bureau of Mines, *Mineral Trends and Forecasts*, Washington: Oct. 1976.

4. G. H. Goudarzi, L. F. Rooney, and G. L. Shaffer, "Supply of Nonfuel Minerals and Materials for the United States Energy Industry, 1975–90," in *Demand and Supply of Nonfuel Minerals and Materials for the United States Energy Industry, 1975–1990—A Preliminary Report*, Geological Survey Professional Paper 1006–A,B, Washington: Government Printing Office, 1976.

5. "Report of the 2nd General Conference of the United Nations Industrial Development Organization" (Lima, Mar. 12–26, 1975), UNIDO, May 1975.

6. U.S. Geological Survey, *Principles of the Mineral Resource Classification System of the U.S. Bureau of Mines and U.S. Geological Survey*, Bulletin 1450–A, Washington: Government Printing Office, 1976.

7. John E. Tilton, *The Future of Nonfuel Minerals*, Washington: Brookings, 1977, p. 10.

8. J. Zwartendyk, "The Life Index of Mineral Reserves—A Statistical Mirage," *Canadian Institute of Mining and Metallurgy Bulletin*, Oct. 1974, pp. 67–70.

9. John McHale, "Resource Availability and Growth," *U.S. Economic Growth from 1976 to 1986: Prospects, Problems, and Patterns*, Studies Prepared for Use of the Joint Economic Committee of Congress, Vol. 4, "Resources and Energy," Nov. 16, 1976.

10. Harold J. Barnett and Chandler Morse, *Scarcity and Growth: The Economics of Natural Resource Availability*, Baltimore: Johns Hopkins Press, 1963.

11. Harold J. Barnett, "Scarcity and Growth Revisited," presented at a Resources for the Future conference, Washington, Oct. 19, 1976, in V. Kerry Smith, ed., *Scarcity and Growth Reconsidered*, Washington: Resources for the Future, forthcoming.

12. John J. Schanz, Jr., "United States Minerals—A Perspective," *Mining Congress Journal*, Feb., 1977, p. 27.

13. G. M. Brown, Jr. and B. Field, "The Adequacy of Measures for Signaling the Scarcity of Natural Resources," presented at a Resources for the Future conference, Washington, Oct. 19, 1976, in V. Kerry Smith, ed., *Scarcity and Growth Reconsidered*, Washington: Resources for the Future, forthcoming.

14. Also see: J. F. McDivitt and G. Manners, *Minerals and Men*, Baltimore: Johns Hopkins Press, 1974 (for information on use of materials); Brian J. Skinner, *Earth Resources*, Englewood Cliffs, N.J.: Prentice-Hall, 1969 (for information on geologic occurrence of mineral deposits); Stephen Kesler, *Our Finite Mineral Resources*, New York: McGraw-Hill, 1976, and Charles F. Park, *Earthbound*, San Francisco: Freeman, 1974 (for information on resource scarcity).

15. Vincent E. McKelvey, "Relation of Reserves of Elements to Their Crustal Abundance," *American Journal of Science*, vol. 258–A (Bradley volume), 1960, pp. 234–41.

16. Ralph L. Erickson, "Crustal Abundance of Elements and Mineral Reserves and Resources," in Donald A. Brobst and Walden P. Pratt, eds., *United States Mineral Resources*, Geological Survey Professional Paper 820, Washington: Government Printing Office, 1973, pp. 21–25.

17. For a discussion of entropy as it relates to mineral economics, see Nicholas Georgescu-Roegen, "Matter Matters, Too," in K. D. Wilson, ed., *Prospects for Growth*, New York: Praeger, 1977.

18. S. G. Lasky, "Mineral Resources Appraisal by the U.S. Geological Survey," *Colorado School of Mines Quarterly*, Jan. 1950, pp. 1–27; "How Tonnage-Grade Relations Help Predict Ore Reserves, *Engineering and Mining Journal*, Apr. 1950, pp. 81–85; and "Mineral Industry Futures Can Be Predicted, II," *Engineering and Mining Journal*, Sept. 1955, pp. 94–96.

19. T. S. Lovering, "Mineral Resources from the Land," in National Academy of Sciences, Committee on Resources and Man, *Resources and Man*, San Francisco: Freeman, 1969, p. 114.

20. Donald A. Brobst, "Fundamental Concepts for the Analysis of Resource Availability," presented at a Resources for the Future conference, Washington, Oct. 19, 1976, in V. Kerry Smith, ed., *Scarcity and Growth Reconsidered*, Washington: Resources for the Future, forthcoming; D. A. Singer, "Long-Term Adequacy of Metal Resources," *Resources Policy*, June 1977, pp. 127–33.

21. H. E. Goeller and Alvin M. Weinberg, "The Age of Substitutability," *Science*, Feb. 20, 1976, pp. 683–89.

22. United Nations, *Monthly Bulletin of Statistics*, June 1977, p xxxi.

23. World Bank, *Commodity Trade and Price Trends*, 1977 ed., Washington, Aug. 1977, p. 14.

24. Danny M. Leipziger and James L. Mudge, *Seabed Mineral Resources and the Economic Interests of Developing Countries*, Cambridge, Mass.: Ballinger, 1976.

25. A careful analysis of the need for a New International Economic Order and some of its proposed objectives is contained in Jan Tinbergen (coordinator), *RIO—Reshaping the International Order*, New York: Dutton, 1976.

# 13   Environment Projections

This chapter is the last of the 12 chapters presenting the Global 2000 Study projections. Chapters 2–4 present the driving-force projections (Population, GNP, Climate), which provide basic inputs to the resource projections presented in Chapters 5–12. Attention turns now to the future of the world's environment.

The term "environment" is not easily defined. To some, the word suggests pristine landscapes and wilderness. While these connotations are certainly inherent in most definitions of the term, "environment" is used in this chapter in a much broader sense.

Literally, the environment is the physical and biological surroundings of the organisms under discussion—in this case *Homo sapiens*, the human species. Humankind depends on this life-supporting environment in many complex ways. So intimate is the linkage between humankind and its environment that the distinction between individual and environment blurs. Some of the air we breathe becomes a part of us. The oxygen metabolizes our foods and becomes a part of our flesh and blood; particulates we breath accumulate in our lungs. Some of the liquids we drink become a part of our bodies, as do the toxic substances the liquids sometimes contain. The soils become our food, which in turn becomes our tissues. In fact, the term "environment"—i.e., human *surroundings*—is an inadequate and inaccurate concept because there is not and cannot be a sharp distinction between humankind and its surroundings. In this chapter, for lack of a better alternative, the term "environment" will be used to describe human surroundings, but throughout it should be remembered that in many important ways we and our environment are one.

In analyzing the future of the human environment, it is also important to note the ways in which humankind shapes its environment. Many anthropogenic changes in the environment are beneficial, but some are not. Houses and communities provide many benefits, including shelter from the elements, predators and pathogens. Other anthropogenic changes—such as the contamination of air, water, and soils—have not been wholly beneficial. Some anthropogenic changes are even beginning to threaten goods and services that the environment has heretofore provided free or at minimal cost.

Humankind has habitually taken for granted the goods (e.g., soil fertility, clean plentiful water) and the services (e.g., removal of air pollutants) provided by the environment. The habit persists. The projections reported in the previous chapters are based generally on the assumption that the environment will continue to provide goods and services as abundantly and inexpensively in the future as it has in the past. Many of these general assumptions about future environmental goods and services are brought into question by the analyses in this chapter. In the years ahead, humankind will need to consider more carefully both the environmental implications of its activities and the effects that environmental deterioration generally will have on human activities.

In this chapter, two questions will be asked of all of the Study's other projections: *First,* assuming (1) that the developments projected in the previous chapters actually come about and (2) that present environmental policies remain unchanged, what impacts on the world's environment can be anticipated? *Second,* considering all the projected environmental impacts collectively, how might developments and changes in the world's environment influence the prospects for achieving the projections outlined in the previous chapters?

The analyses are conducted in two steps, as illustrated in Figure 13–1. In the first step, the environmental implications of each of the previous driving-force and resource projections are analyzed. In the second step all of the environmental implications are synthesized and their collective impact back upon the driving-force and resource projections are considered. Were it possible to actually reflect these collective impacts in the earlier projections, the two feedback loops in Figure 13–1 would be closed. In practice, it is possible only to note the kinds of effects that could be expected, but without actually modifying the projections. Thus the feedback loops remain open at two points and the projections continue to be

227

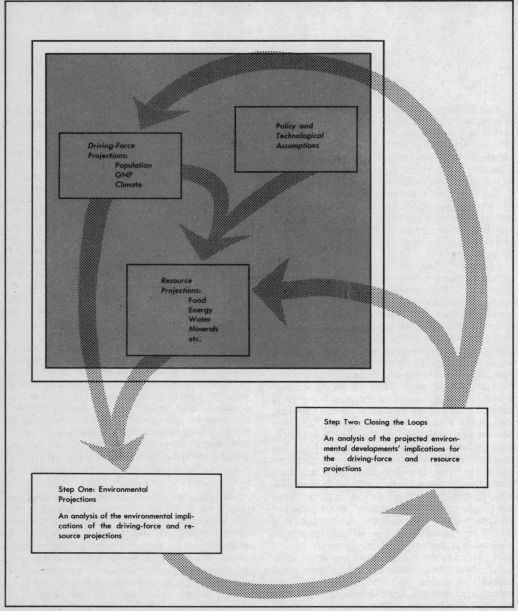

**Figure 13-1.** The two steps in integrating environment into the analysis. The gray box represents the analysis prior to integration with the environmental analysis.

based on rather optimistic environmental assumptions.

The results of the environmental analyses are presented in the following 11 sections of this Chapter. The first step—the analysis of the environmental implications of the previous projections—is presented in the next 10 sections in this order: Population, GNP, Climate, Technology, Food and Agriculture, the Marine Environment, Forestry, Water, Energy, and Nonfuel Minerals. Each of these sections attempts to analyze the environmental developments that might be expected to follow from the corresponding driving-force and resource projections. To assist the reader in recalling the earlier projections, each of the 10 sections begins with a brief summary of the projections being analyzed (under the heading *The Projections,* as on the following page). The second step—the analysis of the effects of environmental developments collectively on the other projections—is presented in the final section: "Closing the Loops: Environmental Feedback to the Other Projections."

Before proceeding to the first of the environmental projections, a few additional points need to be mentioned.

First, an effort has been made to conduct the entire Global 2000 Study with government personnel, government data, and government analytical tools, but unfortunately this objective could not be met in the case of the "Environment Projections" chapter. There is no agency of the government that has the responsibility and capacity to conduct the kind of environmental analysis and synthesis required by the Global 2000 Study. The Environmental Protection Agency (EPA) has a large staff and substantial resources, but EPA is charged with a regulatory mission, not with developing broad, long-term environmental projections. The National Environmental Policy Act (NEPA) assigns a long-term foresight mission (among other responsibilities) to the Council on Environmental Quality (CEQ), but CEQ has never had the staff and resources necessary to carry out all of its assigned functions.

Faced with the fact that no single agency could be expected to prepare the environment projections, the original Global 2000 Study plan called for each agency to prepare an environmental analysis of its projections, using the capabilities it had developed since NEPA initiated the process of environmental impact analysis. This too proved unworkable. As a result of NEPA, most of the agencies now have a substantial capability for environmental analysis. They have assembled the data and analytical tools needed to analyze the environmental impacts of specific project proposals, but with few exceptions they do not have the data and analytical tools needed to perform environmental analyses of long-term plans and global projections. Nor have such analyses been required of them to date.* As a result, most of the environmental analyses that were appended to the agencies projections were quite limited, and the bulk of the environmental analyses and writing for this chapter had to be done by experts outside the government. But although the Study's objective could not be met entirely in the case of the environmental chapter, many government personnel have been involved in reviewing the analyses that follow.

A second point that must be made before the analyses are presented concerns assumptions. An effort was made to avoid abstract environmental projections by relating the analyses as directly as possible to the driving-force and resource projections, but many of the driving-force and resource projections were not explicit enough to permit detailed analyses of their environmental implications, and it was necessary to base some of the environmental analyses on further assumptions. These additional assumptions are described as they occur throughout this chapter.

Third, the environment projections were frequently difficult to develop because much of the data needed on specific topics was not available. In such cases, the analyst was forced either to omit certain topics or to discuss their implications on the basis of fragmentary information. The latter course was chosen whenever the topic seemed important—in which case the discussion was based on the best information available, even if it was only fragmentary.

Fourth, a variety of technologies for environmental protection are considered in the various sections of the chapter. In general, technologies for solving most environmental problems are now available, but there are exceptions. For example, there is no practical means at present for removing oxides of nitrogen from power plant exhaust stacks. The analyses suggest that in most cases economic and policy considerations—rather than the lack of technology—impede environmental protection efforts.

Fifth, the Environment Projections chapter is far longer than any other chapter in the Global

---

*For example hundreds of environmental impact statements have been prepared on individual highways and power plants, but there are no corresponding environmental analyses for the Department of Transportation's year 2000 plan or the Department of Energy's national energy plan.

2000 Study. Its disproportionate length can be justified on two counts: (1) because future trends in the world's environment is a larger than average topic, and (2) because the development of global environmental models is still in its infancy, the environmental analyses—in contrast to the analysis in preceding chapters—are largely discursive, rather than analytical. It should also be mentioned that organizing this long chapter was complicated by the fact that it was necessary to include several topics in more than one section. Every effort has been made to reduce redundancy, however, through footnotes and occasional cross-references to other sections of the chapter.

Finally, the environment projections proceed from the same policy assumption used in the other parts of the Study—namely, that no changes in public policy are anticipated. When applied to the environment, this assumption has many implications. In situations where there is currently no formal environmental management policy, as for example in management of grazing lands in some countries, it is assumed that present lack of management practices will continue. While the resulting prognostications are occasionally grim, they should not be interpreted as statements of what will actually happen, but rather as indications of what is likely to happen if societies do not develop and implement policies that will sustain the health of the environment. Failing this, the analyses suggest strongly that the collective environmental impacts to be anticipated over the next two decades will be sufficiently severe in many areas to alter significantly—and undesirably—the projected population, GNP, and resource trends.

## THE POPULATION PROJECTIONS AND THE ENVIRONMENT

### The Projections

Population levels and their rates of change projected by the U.S. Bureau of the Census are summarized in Table 13–1. The average annual world population growth rate will be 1.8 percent per year throughout most of the 1975–2000 period. By the year 2000, a total of 2.3 billion persons will have been added to the world's population, an increase of 55 percent.

The less developed countries will contribute nine-tenths (2 billions) of the world total increase by 2000. The crude birth rates in the LDCs are projected to decline 21 percent, while life expectancies increase 18 percent (from 54.0 to 63.5 years).* The result is a net annual rate of natural population increase averaging 2.1 percent over the 25-year interval. Asia and Oceania experience the largest numerical increases—60 percent of the total projected world growth. The largest rates of increase occur in Africa (leading to more than a doubling) and in Latin America (a 96 percent increase).

The industrialized countries reduce their population growth rates by about a quarter and experience relatively modest numeric increases: 76 million in the Soviet Union and Eastern Europe (a 20 percent increase) and 101 million in the rest of the industrialized world (a 14 percent increase).

Although the projections do not explicitly address migration and urbanization, there are many indications that the LDCs will experience substantial urban growth by 2000.

### Introduction

The 5 percent increase in world population projected by the Bureau of the Census and summarized in Table 13–1† has many direct and indirect implications for the environment. For example, the direct effects of excrement from an additional 2.2 billion persons can be expected to have a significant impact on the environment in many areas. Still larger indirect effects can be anticipated as

---

*Calculated from Table 8 in U.S. Bureau of the Census, *Illustrative Projections of World Populations to the 21st Century*, Washington: Government Printing Office, 1979.

†Two sets of population projections are presented in Chapter 2. One set was developed by the U.S. Bureau of the Census; the other by the Community and Family Study Center (CFSC)

at the University of Chicago. Both projections were funded by the Population Office of the U.S. Agency for International Development. The Census projections have been used throughout as the Global 2000 Study base case and are summarized in Table 13–1. The CFSC projections were undertaken with a different methodological approach that assumes a rapid

## TABLE 13-1

### Increase in World Population, 1975-2000

| | 1975 | | 2000 | | Increase | |
|---|---|---|---|---|---|---|
| | Popu-lation | Share | Popu-lation | Share | Average Annual | Total |
| | bil lions | per cent | bil-lions | per cent | percent | |
| Industrialized regions | 1.1 | 28 | 1.3 | 21 | 0.6 | 17 |
| Less developed regions | 3.0 | 72 | 5.0 | 79 | 2.1 | 70 |
| World | 4.1 | 100 | 6.4 | 100 | 1.8 | 55 |

*Source:* Bureau of the Census projections. Chapter 2, this volume.

a result of efforts to meet the growing needs of the projected populations for shelter, food, fiber, educational facilities, transportation networks, and employment sites.

The pervasive environmental consequences (both direct and indirect) of the projected population growth make the subject of "Population and the Environment" unmanageably large. Some boundaries must be drawn and limitations established. There are, of course, a number of ways in which this can be done. The choice here has been to discuss in this section those environmental consequences that are directly related to population. The more indirect environmental consequences of population growth—the environmental consequences of increased demands for food, energy, minerals, forestry, etc., to meet the needs of the projected population—are discussed later in this chapter in the sections devoted to those topics. (There are a few exceptions, however; some indirect consequences of population growth—e.g., increased cattle herds for increased populations of nomadic herders—do not fit well in the other sections of this chapter and are therefore discussed here.) While this choice limits the subject

reduction of fertility rates attributed to large expenditures on family planning programs. Both the Census and the CFSC methodologies are discussed in Chapter 15. Since the writing of Chapters 2 and 15, an extensive criticism of the CFSC methodology and projections has been published and rebutted. The criticism appears in Paul Demeny, "On the End of the Population Explosion." *Population and Development Review,* Mar. 1979, pp. 141-62. The response to the criticism is D. J. Bogue and A. O. Tsui, "A Rejoinder to Paul Demeny's Critique, 'On the End of the Population Explosion,' " which is, at this writing, being considered for publication in *Population and Development Review.* Prepublication copies of the Bogue-Tsui rejoinder are available from CFSC, University of Chicago.

matter of this section somewhat, a few further distinctions relevant to the subjects under discussion should be noted.

One distinction involves the different types of pressures that different cultures exert on the environment. In what follows, the world's cultures are categorized as one of two types: either "traditional" or "industrial." This distinction is admittedly a gross simplification, intended only to indicate the relative closeness of a culture to the environment on which it depends. In traditional cultures, the people depend largely on their local environment and are familiar through personal experience with the environmental implications of their numbers and demands. In industrial cultures, the people depend to a much larger degree on environments that are connected with them only by transportation and trade networks, and as a result, such people are often not familiar personally with the full environmental consequences of their population growth and demands.

Although per capita demands on the environment tend to be higher for industrial cultures than for traditional cultures, the distinction is not strictly between the less developed and the developed countries. LDCs contain within them small industrial cultures that make relatively large per capita demands on environments around the world, and the industrialized countries contain traditional cultures that make demands—relatively small per capita demands—primarily on their local environment. (The Amish communities in the U.S. are an excellent example of a traditional culture within a developed country, as is the community and family life-style practiced by some individual environmental advocates.[1]) While the traditional/industrial cultural dichotomy involves major simplifications, it facilitates discussion of some important relationships between population growth and environmental change.

In the following pages, the relatively localized impacts of traditional cultures on their environments are considered first. The discussion of traditional cultures introduces the problem of managing "common" resources, a problem encountered in various forms throughout this chapter. The discussion then turns to the more dispersed pressures that industrial society places on the environment, after which the environmental consequences of changing population distributions are noted, especially the growing concentration of populations in large settlements with minimal public health and other services. Finally, some of the linkages between environment and health are considered.

## Population and the Environment in Traditional Cultures

Traditional cultures, in the sense used here, are cultures that obtain the necessities of life—food, energy, fiber, and shelter—primarily from the local environment with little or no involvement in regional or national trade and commerce. Members of such societies are well aware of their dependence on a healthy environment. Their community values and traditions generally reflect this awareness and encourage a harmonious and sustainable relationship with the environment.[2]

Over the past century industrial cultures have spread and affected, in one way or another, all but a few exceptionally remote traditional cultures. Limited contacts with industrial society have changed some traditional cultures only a little, but in most cases such contacts have set in motion changes significantly affecting the form and function of traditional cultures.

Currently, a majority of the world's rural peoples, who occupy a large fraction of the earth's land, live in modified traditional cultures. There are many such cultures in the less developed countries. Even in the industrialized nations, some native populations still approximate their former traditional cultures—such as the Amish in the U.S., the Eskimos in Canada and Alaska, and the Samis (Lapps) in northern Scandinavia. But trade, medicine, technologies, and other factors have changed practices, values, outlooks, and the relations of such cultures to the environment. The populations of modified traditional cultures often grow at the world's fastest rates and, if unchecked, soon exceed the carrying capacity of the local environments on which they depend. As long as the needs of traditional cultures remain well below the life-support capacity of the local environment, population growth can continue with minimal impacts. As the life-support capacity is approached, however, environmental degradation begins, eroding and reducing the quality of life previously enjoyed. Social tension and conflict over the distribution of increasingly scarce resources often follows. Ultimately, the capability of the environment to support life is undermined and diminished.

Three forms of traditional cultures (and their modified forms) have special significance for the environment: (1) those based on the herding of animals, (2) those based on shifting cultivation, and (3) those who have cut their forests and shifted to settled agriculture. The Global 2000 Study's population projections imply that the populations of all three types will increase signifi-

cantly over the next two decades, with the result that a number of environmental consequences can be anticipated. The effects of expanding populations of herders and shifting cultivators on the environment are discussed below. The environmental effects of population growth among settled agriculturists are discussed later, in the food and agriculture section of this chapter.

### Cultures Based on the Herding of Animals

The world's herding populations, depending upon grasslands or savannas to sustain their livestock, maintain a delicate, often tenuous relationship with their local environments. When herds are managed to sustain the productivity of grassland or savanna ecosystems, grazing can be continued indefinitely without damaging the life-support system. However, when management is neglected, overgrazing often leads to the deterioration or destruction of the rangeland. The extent to which the world's grazing lands are already under pressure is illustrated in the Free Range Grazing Pressure Map in the colored map section of this volume.

Once begun, rangeland deterioration is difficult to control. Most grasslands and savannas are located in semiarid areas, where heavy grazing destroys the ability of plants to resist drought and leads to eventual loss of palatable species in favor of weed species.[3] Range deterioration is almost always accompanied by increased soil erosion. Unfortunately, over much of the world's rangelands today, such overstocking, overgrazing, loss of vegetation, erosion, and associated negative impacts on the hydrologic cycle are accelerating the conversion of productive grazing lands to desertlike wastelands.[4]

The two primary causes of the environmental consequences of overgrazing are (1) expanding human populations accompanied by increasing human demands for larger herds of livestock and (2) efforts to breed and own more livestock as a means of increasing individual and cultural wealth. Together, these two causes lead to accumulating individual pressures on a jointly used, limited resource base.

The protection of such a base in the face of population and economic growth is an exceedingly difficult management problem.[5] Proper management is central to the protection of grazing lands. Unprotected, any jointly used, limited resource suffers a fate often referred to as the tragedy of the commons.*

---

*Protecting a jointly used resource is often an aspect of environmental management. The problems it engenders will be

The tragedy is this: Actions that are in the immediate best interest of each and every individual employing a jointly utilized (common) resource are collectively detrimental to the long-term welfare of the whole society. In his classic essay, "The Tragedy of the Commons," Garrett Hardin describes the tragedy in terms of a grazing commons:

Picture a pasture open to all. It is to be expected that each herdsman will try to keep as many cattle as possible on the commons. Such an arrangement may work reasonably satisfactorily for centuries because tribal wars, poaching, and disease keep the numbers of both man and beast well below the carrying capacity of the land. Finally, however, comes the day of reckoning, that is, the day when the long-desired goal of social stability becomes a reality. At this point, the inherent logic of the commons remorselessly generates tragedy.

As a rational being, each herdsman seeks to maximize his gain. Explicitly or implicitly, more or less consciously, he asks, "What is the utility *to me* of adding one more animal to my herd?" This utility has one negative and positive component.

1. The positive component is a function of the increment of one animal. Since the herdsman receives all the proceeds from the sale of the additional animal, the positive utility is nearly $+1$.
2. The negative component is a function of the additional overgrazing created by one more animal. Since, however, the effects of overgrazing are shared by all the herdsmen, the negative utility for any particular decision-making herdsman is only a fraction of $-1$.

Adding together the component partial utilities, the rational herdsman concludes that the only sensible course for him to pursue is to add another animal to his herd. And another. . . . But this is the conclusion reached by each and every rational herdsman sharing a commons. Therein is the tragedy. Each man is locked into a system that compels him to increase his herd without limit—in a world that is limited. Ruin is the destination toward which all men rush, each pursuing his own best interest in a society that believes in the freedom of the commons. Freedom in a commons brings ruin to all.[6]

Hardin points out in his article that human population growth also unavoidably brings with it increasing demands on the environment. These increasing demands are perhaps most easily observed in traditional herding societies where increased populations lead to a need for increased herds, which in turn lend to degradation of the commons.

Degradation of a commons gives rise to a wide range of environmental and societal stresses. In many cases, social conflicts have their source in the deterioration or destruction of a common resource base. One of the earliest recorded illustrations of social stress caused by growing human and livestock populations utilizing a limited-resource commons is the account of the experiences of Lot and Abram (later Abraham) in the 13th chapter of Genesis. In the biblical case, their cattle and herds became so numerous (as a result of the increases in their population and wealth) that "the land could not support them." Eventually, fighting broke out between the herdsmen of the two families. To resolve the conflict, Abram proposed to Lot that the two families separate and gave Lot his choice of where to go. Lot chose to move toward Sodom and the other towns along the river Jordan; Abram chose the hills of Canaan.

The Genesis solution—separation and movement into new, resource-rich commons—is not a true solution to the tragedy of the commons because it is effective only until all of the entire commons is threatened with overuse and destruction. At this point the basic nature of the tragedy can no longer be ignored, and true solutions must be sought. In his essay, Hardin sets forth his recommended solution—mutual coercion, mutually agreed upon—and explains a number of successful applications of this solution.* (Fishing licenses and catch-limits to protect the sport-fish populations of the commons—lakes and streams—are an example of Hardin's "mutual coercion, mutually agreed upon.")

American Indians, Eskimos, Lapps, and many other traditional cultures evolved solutions to the tragedy that limit their demands on resources held in common.[7] Often these solutions are based on myths, traditions, technologies, and cultural practices that are displaced following contacts with industrial society. The results are generally disruptive and sometimes disastrous.[8] In the case of herding societies, the disruptive influences often

encountered again later in this chapter in connection with the protection of forests, fisheries, oceans, and the atmosphere. The explanation of "the tragedy of the commons" given above applies wherever the tragedy of the commons is mentioned elsewhere in the text.

*In a more recent essay, Hardin discusses his solution in terms of national efforts to protect biotic resources from the tragedy of the commons and concludes that protection of biotic resources is possible under either socialism or free enterprise but not under the system of unregulated commons (Garrett Hardin, "Political Requirements for Preserving Our Common Heritage," Ch. 20 in Council on Environmental Quality, *Wildlife and America*, Washington: Government Printing Office, 1979). Hardin and John Baden propose other solutions in *Managing the Commons* (San Francisco: Freeman, 1977).

## TABLE 13–2

### Number of Cattle and Number of Sheep and Goats, 1955–2000

*(In millions of head)*

| | Cattle | | | | Sheep and Goats | | | |
|---|---|---|---|---|---|---|---|---|
| | 1955 | Annual Growth[a] | 1976 | 2000[a] | 1955 | Annual Growth[a] | 1976 | 2000[a] |
| Developing market economies[b] | 514.3 | 1.7 | 696.3 | 904.3 | 587.8 | 1.3 | 754.3 | 944.6 |
| Africa | 95.0 | 1.7 | 129.9 | 169.8 | 150.3 | 2.1 | 216.8 | 292.8 |
| Far East | 214.8 | 0.9 | 254.0 | 298.8 | 130.5 | 1.7 | 176.6 | 229.3 |
| Latin America | 175.7 | 2.4 | 265.6 | 368.3 | 155.9 | 0.2 | 161.4 | 167.7 |
| Near East | 28.6 | 2.9 | 46.2 | 66.3 | 150.8 | 1.5 | 199.3 | 254.7 |
| Asian centrally planned economies | 57.5 | 1.2 | 71.6 | 87.7 | 101.6 | 2.5 | 154.8 | 215.6 |
| Subtotal | 571.8 | 1.6 | 767.9 | 992.0 | 689.4 | 1.5 | 909.1 | 1160.2 |
| Developed market economies[b] | 225.0 | 1.6 | 302.0 | 390.0 | 364.8 | −0.1 | 359.6 | 353.7 |
| North Africa | 106.4 | 1.6 | 141.7 | 182.0 | 35.3 | −2.7 | 15.0 | 0 |
| Western Europe | 82.0 | 1.1 | 100.6 | 121.9 | 115.7 | −0.5 | 103.0 | 88.5 |
| Oceania | 21.7 | 4.7 | 43.2 | 67.8 | 170.1 | 1.0 | 205.0 | 244.9 |
| Eastern Europe and the U.S.S.R. | 81.2 | 3.7 | 143.9 | 215.6 | 146.7 | 1.1 | 182.0 | 222.3 |
| Subtotal | 306.2 | 2.2 | 445.9 | 605.6 | 511.5 | 0.3 | 541.6 | 576.0 |
| World Total | 878.0 | 1.8 | 1213.8 | 1597.6 | 1200.9 | 1.0 | 1450.7 | 1736.20 |

Source: *The State of Food and Agriculture 1977*, Rome: Food and Agriculture Organization, Nov. 1977, Ch. 3, pp. 3–16 (draft).

[a] Both the annual growth and the projection to 2000 are based on a linear rather than compound (i.e., exponential) growth model. Reviewers of the manuscript felt that, in view of range conditions, an exponential growth model gave unrealistically large animal populations in 2000.
[b] Including countries in regions not specified.

come through modern medical technology, veterinary medicine, and increased access to water.[9] The consequence is often a growth in human and animal populations that cannot be sustained on the available grazing land.[10]

Lands suitable for grazing are limited, and already available rangelands are overpopulated by livestock in many areas (as in the Free Range Grazing Pressure map in the colored map section of this volume). Data on this problem are limited, but its seriousness is illustrated by recent and projected trends in numbers of cattle, sheep, and goats. Table 13–2 summarizes such livestock data for 1955 and 1976 and projects the 1955–76 trends to the year 2000.

The U.N. Food and Agriculture Organization (FAO) estimates that between 1955 and 1976, world cattle populations grew by more than 330 million head. If these trends continue, approximately 380 million additional cattle will be added to the world's herds by 2000. In North America, the Soviet Union, Japan, and Europe, a significant portion of the growth in herds has been on feedlots, but elsewhere much of the growth is on open rangelands.

Much of the global growth of cattle herds is projected to occur in the developing market econ-

omies—from 696.3 million head in 1976 to 904.3 million in 2000, an increase of more than 200 million head. Oceania, Eastern Europe, and the U.S.S.R. have experienced the world's most rapid growth in cattle populations. Oceania's cattle populations, with the world's highest growth rate at 4.7 percent per year, almost doubled in two decades, from 21.7 million in 1955 to 43.2 million in 1976. Eastern Europe and U.S.S.R. cattle populations grew at 3.7 percent per year over the 1955–76 period, from 81.2 million to 143.9 million, and by 2000 are projected to reach 215.6 million, more than three times 1955 levels.

The most rapid recent increases in sheep and goats have been in Africa and the Asian centrally planned economies. Between 1955 and 1976 African sheep and goat populations grew by 66.5 million, and in the Asian centrally planned economies, they rose by 53.2 million. Sheep and goat populations in North America and Western Europe have been declining. If present trends continue, sheep and goats will have largely disappeared from North America by 2000, whereas, worldwide, sheep and goat populations are projected to increase by more than 280 million head between 1976 and 2000.

These recent and projected livestock increases—many of them concentrated in the already heavily utilized, fragile grasslands of Eurasia, the Near East, Africa, the Far East, Oceania, and Latin America—signal accelerating rangeland deterioration, soil erosion, and desertification in these areas. In describing the seriousness of the prospects, the FAO recently reported that global livestock population growth has led to

the serious deterioration of grazing land, particularly in the Sahelian and Sudanian zones of Africa, and in parts of the Near East, the Mediterranean and North Africa. The grazing resources in these areas are to a large extent under arid and semi-arid conditions, and some of them have already been threatened for hundreds and sometimes thousands of years by overuse, leading to complete changes in the vegetation, which have left only shrubs of low palatability. Further increases in grazing pressure and aggravated misuse result in the complete devastation of all vegetation, which finally ends in desertification. The problem has been magnified by the encroachment of cropping onto the grazing area, as a result of faster population growth outside the range area. Similar problems exist in other arid and semi-arid areas, for example, in continental Eurasia, in India and Pakistan, and in Northeast Brazil.[11]

The Global 2000 Study projects further population growth, both within and outside of the world's major grazing lands. Such growth will intensify the pressure on these grazing resources, either for conversion to cropland or for feeding increasing numbers of livestock.[12] In a time when many of the world's free grazing commons have already been overgrazed beyond their ability to recover, the prospect is for even greater devastation of the world's remaining grazing commons by the year 2000.

If the consequences of overgrazing are to be avoided in the areas of the world so threatened, efforts will be needed to relate future herd sizes to the feed resources available. A pioneering global study of livestock feed resources and livestock populations has been completed by the Winrock International Livestock Research and Training Center, Morrilton, Arkansas. The Winrock study starts from an assessment of global livestock feed resources and the potential for their development.[13] This feed potential is then related to herd sizes and composition (to provide projections of possible ruminant populations in 2000) and to the contributions these animals could make toward meeting human needs.

The Winrock projections of feed resources and ruminant populations are summarized in Tables 13–3 and 13–4. Worldwide, the Winrock study foresees the possibility of a 13 percent increase

in forage feed sources, a 75 percent increase in grain feed, a 68 percent increase in feed from by-products of the agricultural industry, a 98 percent increase in feed from oilseeds, and a 21 percent increase in feed from crop residues—an overall increase in ruminant feed resources of 18 percent over the 1970–2000 period. Based on these estimates of feed resources and improved livestock management, Winrock projects that the world's herds could increase over the 1972–2000 period as follows: cattle by 27 percent; buffalo by 29 percent; sheep and goats by 40 percent; total ruminants (cattle, buffalo, sheep, and goats) by 34 percent. The prospects for increases vary markedly from region to region—from a high of 56 percent for sheep and goats in middle America to no increase in a number of other areas.

The Winrock projections differ in important ways from the relatively simple trend projections presented in Table 13–2. The Winrock projections start with the feed resources and attempt an assessment of how these could be developed. Since the projections of Table 13–2 are not as constrained by feed resources, somewhat different results are therefore to be expected. The projected cattle populations, for example, differ in that the Winrock estimates of potential growth are smaller. On the other hand, Winrock believes that the feed resources are potentially available for a larger increase in sheep and goats. However, whatever the animal and whatever the increase, improved range management methods will very much be needed if severe overgrazing of forage resources is to be avoided in the decades ahead. The projected increases in herding populations can only increase the already severe pressure on range and grassland resources in many parts of Asia, the Middle East, north and central Africa, and Central America.

## Cultures Based on Shifting Cultivation

Like the herdsmen just discussed, the cultivators of traditional cultures also place intensifying pressure on the environmental commons as their populations grow. According to one estimate, 25 percent of the world's land surface—primarily in tropical or subtropical regions—is occupied by about 300 million people who practice shifting cultivation.[14] (See the Land Use Patterns map in the colored map section of this volume.) In some areas, traditional agriculturists practicing shifting cultivation on lands that cannot sustain continual intensive agricultural use are beginning to damage permanently the productivity of the area and to reduce its carrying capacity.

## TABLE 13–3

### Winrock Projections of World Feed Resources for Ruminants, by Region

*In billions of Mcal ($10^{15}$ calories)*

#### Forage Sources and Grain

| | Forage Sources | | | | | | Grain | |
| | Permanent Pasture and Meadows | | Arable Lands | | Nonagricultural Lands | | | |
| | 1970 | 2000 | 1970 | 2000 | 1970 | 2000 | 1970 | 2000 |
|---|---|---|---|---|---|---|---|---|
| North America | 470 | 515 | 615 | 700 | 175 | 125 | 205 | 335 |
| Middle America | 215 | 350 | 60 | 70 | 30 | 15 | 3 | 5 |
| South America | 1,130 | 1,170 | 230 | 295 | 230 | 110 | 15 | 15 |
| Western Europe | 310 | 310 | 220 | 220 | 40 | 30 | 95 | 170 |
| Eastern Europe | 115 | 145 | 85 | 85 | 10 | 10 | 35 | 65 |
| U.S.S.R. | 300 | 310 | 575 | 670 | 15 | 15 | 50 | 100 |
| China | 250 | 360 | 75 | 85 | 20 | 15 | 2 | 5 |
| North Africa, Middle East | 180 | 200 | 150 | 230 | 15 | 10 | 5 | 15 |
| Central Africa | 850 | 900 | 240 | 300 | 310 | 300 | 1 | 1 |
| Southern Africa | 190 | 205 | 25 | 30 | 15 | 15 | 3 | 5 |
| India | 15 | 55 | 415 | 450 | 15 | 10 | 3 | 15 |
| South and Southeast Asia | 70 | 445 | 220 | 245 | 130 | 50 | 1 | 5 |
| Japan | 5 | 10 | 25 | 25 | 1 | 1 | 5 | 15 |
| Oceania | 580 | 495 | 175 | 360 | 10 | 10 | 15 | 15 |
| Rest of world | 140 | 140 | 5 | 10 | 3 | 3 | 1 | 1 |
| World total | 4,820 | 5,610 | 3,115 | 3,775 | 1,019 | 719 | 439 | 767 |

#### Other Sources

| | Agri-Industry By-products | | Oilseeds | | Crop Residues | | World Total | | Percent of World | |
| | 1970 | 2000 | 1970 | 2000 | 1970 | 2000 | 1970 | 2000 | 1970 | 2000 |
|---|---|---|---|---|---|---|---|---|---|---|
| North America | 15 | 20 | 25 | 55 | 440 | 500 | 1,945 | 2,250 | 16 | 15 |
| Middle America | 1 | 1 | 1 | 1 | 65 | 80 | 375 | 522 | 3 | 4 |
| South America | 5 | 10 | 2 | 5 | 195 | 325 | 1,807 | 1,930 | 14 | 13 |
| Western Europe | 10 | 15 | 25 | 55 | 275 | 280 | 975 | 1,080 | 8 | 7 |
| Eastern Europe | 5 | 10 | 5 | 10 | 175 | 180 | 430 | 505 | 3 | 3 |
| U.S.S.R. | 25 | 30 | 10 | 15 | 370 | 430 | 1,345 | 1,570 | 11 | 11 |
| China | 5 | 5 | 1 | 1 | 540 | 595 | 893 | 1,066 | 7 | 7 |
| North Africa, Middle East | 5 | 20 | 2 | 2 | 110 | 135 | 467 | 612 | 4 | 4 |
| Central Africa | 10 | 10 | 1 | 1 | 130 | 160 | 1,542 | 1,672 | 12 | 11 |
| Southern Africa | 1 | 1 | 1 | 1 | 25 | 35 | 260 | 292 | 2 | 2 |
| India | 30 | 65 | 5 | 5 | 270 | 350 | 753 | 950 | 6 | 7 |
| South and Southeast Asia | 10 | 20 | 1 | 1 | 235 | 300 | 667 | 1,066 | 5 | 7 |
| Japan | 2 | 2 | 2 | 10 | 45 | 45 | 85 | 108 | 1 | 1 |
| Oceania | 3 | 5 | 1 | 1 | 35 | 105 | 819 | 991 | 6 | 7 |
| Rest of world | 1 | 1 | 1 | 1 | 35 | 40 | 186 | 196 | 2 | 1 |
| World total | 128 | 215 | 83 | 164 | 2,945 | 3,560 | 12,549 | 14,810 | 100 | 100 |

Source: H. A. Fitzhuhg, H. J. Hodgson, O. J. Scoville, T. D. Nguyen, and T. C. Byerly, *The Role of Ruminants in Support of Man*, Morrilton, Ark.; Winrock Livestock Research and Training Center, Apr. 1978.

When conducted in moderation on suitable slopes and at human population levels within the carrying capacity of the environment, shifting cultivation is a sound and appropriate practice. Under moderate demands, shifting agriculture is usually sustainable for long periods of time and with low requirements for energy subsidies or external capital. A recent U.N. report noted that shifting agriculture "achieves high productivity per man-day with small capital investment. . . .

## TABLE 13-4

### Winrock Projections of World Ruminant Populations, by Region

| | Cattle | | | Buffalo | | | Sheep and Goats | | | Camels[a] |
|---|---|---|---|---|---|---|---|---|---|---|
| | 1972 | 2000 | Percent Increase | 1972 | 2000 | Percent Increase | 1972 | 2000 | Percent Increase | 2000 |
| | *millions* | | | *millions* | | | *millions* | | | *millions* |
| North America | 130 | 156 | 20 | – | – | – | 21 | 25 | 19 | – |
| Middle America | 39 | 59 | 51 | – | – | – | 16 | 25 | 56 | – |
| South America | 190 | 286 | 51 | 0.1 | – | – | 142 | 214 | 51 | 6,154 |
| Western Europe | 89 | 107 | 20 | 0.1 | 0.1 | 0 | 94 | 113 | 20 | – |
| Eastern Europe | 35 | 42 | 20 | 0.3 | 0.5 | 67 | 43 | 52 | 21 | – |
| U.S.S.R. | 102 | 123 | 21 | 0.4 | – | – | 145 | 218 | 50 | 307 |
| China | 63 | 82 | 30 | 29.7 | 38.6 | 30 | 129 | 194 | 50 | 17 |
| North Africa, Middle East | 44 | 57 | 30 | 4.8 | 6.2 | 29 | 216 | 323 | 50 | 6,165 |
| Central Africa | 116 | 150 | 30 | – | – | – | 157 | 235 | 50 | 7,656 |
| Southern Africa | 16 | 19 | 19 | – | – | – | 45 | 67 | 49 | – |
| India | 179 | 179 | 0 | 57.9 | 75.3 | 30 | 108 | 130 | 20 | 1,464 |
| South and Southeast Asia | 75 | 112 | 49 | 33.2 | 43.1 | 30 | 75 | 113 | 51 | 1,489 |
| Japan | 4 | 4 | 0 | – | – | – | – | – | – | – |
| Oceania | 37 | 33 | 19 | – | – | – | 224 | 269 | 20 | – |
| Rest of world | 11 | 13 | 18 | – | – | – | 19 | 27 | 42 | 1,059 |
| World total | 1,130 | 1,435 | 27 | 126.6 | 168.8 | 29 | 1,435 | 2,005 | 40 | 24,311 |

*Source:* H. A. Fitzhugh, H. J. Hodgson, O. J. Scoville, T. D. Nguyen, and T. C. Byerly, *The Role of Ruminants in Support of Man,* Morrilton, Ark.: Winrock International Livestock Research and Training Center, Apr. 1978.

[a] Camel populations were not available for 1972.

If cultivation is not prolonged, rapid regeneration of secondary forest vegetation occurs when the land is abandoned."[15]

The importance of the phrase "if cultivation is not prolonged" must be emphasized. Sustainable shifting agricultural requires periodic fallow periods for the cultivated lands to rebuild soil fertility.[16]

The possibilities for maintaining an adequate fallow cycle are closely related to size of the shifting cultivator population, and to the land area available. The Global 2000 Study's projections suggest that the size of these populations will increase by 50–70 percent by 2000. The amount of land burned* and cultivated each year by shifting cultivators will also increase. Where will this land come from?

Virgin forest lands are not likely to be available to meet all of the increased land needs of shifting cultivators. In the forestry projections in Chapter 8, approximately one fifth of the world's remaining forests are projected to be removed by 2000. By far the largest portion of the forest losses will occur in developing countries with large populations of shifting cultivators. As a result of reduced forested areas and the spread of settled agriculture, shifting cultivators will be forced to return with increasing frequency to lands previously cleared and cultivated. Fallow periods will unavoidably shorten, leading to nutrient losses, adverse shifts in the species composition in the naturally occurring flora and fauna (a reduction of overall species diversity and an increasing preponderance of weed species), and deleterious alterations of the soil structure.[17] Although crops may be grown temporarily in some areas following a short fallow period, the ultimate result of shortening the fallow cycle is increased nutrient leaching from soils, accelerating competition from weeds, and declining yields.[18]

The projected growth of shifting cultivator populations will also lead to increased use of marginal and submarginal lands. Such lands have generally been avoided in the past because of the known agricultural risks and low yields typical of such areas. However, as good land becomes scarcer, the erosion-prone soils of steep slopes and the lateritic soils of humid tropics are likely to be cultivated. Steep slopes erode rapidly when cleared,

*Little has been written about the local and global effects on air quality and climate of burning for agricultural clearing and weed control, but accidental forest fires have somewhat similar effects (see "Air Quality and Smoke from Urban and Forest Fires: An International Symposium," Washington: National Academy of Sciences, 1976). One of the primary atmospheric effects is thought to be a large contribution of particulates. It is now also thought that this burning contributes to the accumulating concentrations of carbon dioxide in the earth's atmosphere (George M. Woodwell et al., "The Carbon Dioxide Problem: Implications for Policy in the Management of Energy and Other Resources," report to the Council on Environmental Quality, July 1979.)

increasing flooding, drought, and siltation down-stream. Similarly, lateritic tropical soils can quickly become unproductive when misused. If intensive shifting cultivation is continued in such areas, even the forest's ability to regenerate can be threatened. [19]

The populations of traditional cultures—both herdsmen and shifting cultivators—already exert large, population-related environmental effects on approximately a quarter of the world's land area. The Land Use Patterns map and Free Range Grazing Pressure map (in the colored map section) show large expanses of the globe now peo-pled by herdsmen, pastoralists, and peoples practicing shifting crop culture. Although data on these populations and their effects on the envi-ronment are quite limited, most experts agree that large and growing numbers are involved. [20] Al-ready major reductions in the productivity of parts of Eurasia, the Near East, Africa, Oceania, and Latin America have been observed. [21] Some of the productivity losses are very severe. [22] Reductions in land productivity by as much as 90 percent were reported for several areas during the 1977 U.N. Conference on Desertification. [23]

The Global 2000 Study's population projections indicate that by 2000 the populations of traditional cultures will have increased significantly, nearly doubling in some areas. If present trends con-tinue, these populations can be expected to con-tinue growing well into the 21st century,* but in some areas, the trends may change. Evidence is accumulating that agricultural and grazing lands in parts of Africa, Asia, the Near East, and Latin America are already under such heavy stress that they simply cannot be expected to retain their present productivity through another two decades of intensifying human and animal population pres-sure. [24] In such areas, further population growth makes major losses of biological life-support ca-pacity virtually inevitable.

## Population and the Environment in Industrialized Cultures

Like traditional cultures, modern industrial cul-

---

*Erik Eckholm points out that many of the cultivators re-sponsible for deforestation, soil erosion, etc., are not "tradi-tional" shifting cultivators but rather landless castoffs of modern development processes. They are not ecologically skilled like tribal people, but are trying to farm wherever they can. Driven by population growth, unequal land tenure, and unemployment, these people are moving onto hillsides and desert margins. Poverty itself is a cause of some forms of environmental deterioration. (Erik Eckholm, *The Dispos-sessed of the Earth: Land Reform and Sustainable Develop-ment*, Washington: Worldwatch Institute, June 1979.)

tures,* place population-related pressures on the environment. They face the same basic problem of the tragedy of the commons, but there are at least three important differences between indus-trial and traditional cultures. First, an additional person in an industrial society makes larger de-mands on the world's resources than does an ad-ditional person in a traditional society. Second, the environmental pressures produced by an ad-ditional person in an industrial society are trans-mitted by transportation and commerce over a much wider geographic area than are those of an additional person in a traditional society. Third, the economies of industrial cultures are much more complex than those of traditional cultures, complicating the analysis—and even the percep-tion—of population-related environmental im-pacts of industrial cultures.

It is often asserted that some small percentage (e.g., 6 percent) of the world's population living in industrial cultures consumes some dispropor-tionately large share (e.g., 60 percent) of the world's resources. While this assertion is true in some generalized sense, the percentages often quoted are not as easily developed as the asser-tions might suggest. One of the major difficulties in comparing the resource consumption (e.g. com-mercial energy) of an "average" person in an in-dustrial society with that of an "average" person in a traditional society is that the industrial person uses a significant portion of the resources to pro-duce products that are ultimately exported and "consumed" in other countries. Food is probably the resource that is easiest to compare directly because relatively little human energy (the end product of food consumption) is exported as com-pared to the human energy exported in industrial products,† Tables 13–5 and 13–6 present data on

---

*The populations of most industrial cultures and nations are increasing both as a result of natural increase and as a result of immigration. The effects of immigration are discussed briefly in Chapter 2. One of the problems associated with demographics in industrial cultures is that those immigrants who enter a country illegally avoid contact with the govern-ment and are often not counted in official census figures. As immigration continues, the demographic importance of un-counted persons will increase. A demographic analysis by Robert Cook (available from the Environment Fund, Wash-ington) suggests that as of mid-1979, the official population figures for the United States are about 3 percent low, in part because of uncounted immigrants residing illegally in the U.S. Concern has already been expressed about the accuracy that will be achievable in the 1980 Census (T. R. R. Reid, "Billion-Dollar Nosecount of '80 Fated to be Wrong," *Washington Post*, June 10, 1979, p. A2).

†Even here, the comparison is not clear-cut because there is a significantly higher human energy content in the goods ex-ported by traditional cultures (such as oriental rugs) than in most industrial goods.

## TABLE 13–5
### Annual Grain Consumption per Capita in the 20 Most Populous Countries, 1975[a]

| | Kilograms |
|---|---|
| United States | 708 |
| U.S.S.R. | 645 |
| Spain | 508 |
| France | 446 |
| Federal Republic of Germany | 441 |
| Turkey | 415 |
| Italy | 413 |
| United Kingdom | 394 |
| Mexico | 304 |
| Egypt | 286 |
| Japan | 274 |
| Brazil | 239 |
| Thailand | 225 |
| People's Republic of China | 218 |
| Bangladesh | 203 |
| Pakistan | 171 |
| Philippines | 157 |
| Indonesia | 152 |
| India | 150 |
| Nigeria | 92 |

Source: Lester R. Brown, *The Twenty-Ninth Day*, New York: Norton, 1978, p. 200.

[a] Includes grain consumed both directly and indirectly (in the form of meat, milk, and eggs).

## TABLE 13–6
### Energy Consumption per Capita in the 20 Most Populous Countries, 1974[a]

| | Kilograms of Coal Equivalent |
|---|---|
| United States | 11,485 |
| Federal Republic of Germany | 5,689 |
| United Kingdom | 5,464 |
| U.S.S.R. | 5,252 |
| France | 4,330 |
| Japan | 3,839 |
| Italy | 3,227 |
| Spain | 2,063 |
| Mexico | 1,269 |
| Brazil | 646 |
| People's Republic of China | 632 |
| Turkey | 628 |
| Egypt | 322 |
| Philippines | 309 |
| Thailand | 300 |
| India | 201 |
| Pakistan | 188 |
| Indonesia | 158 |
| Nigeria | 94 |
| Bangladesh | 31 |

Source: Lester R. Brown, *The Twenty-Ninth Day*, New York: Norton, 1978, p. 202.

[a] Excludes firewood and dung.

the food and commercial energy consumption per capita in the 20 most populous countries. The relatively "industrial" nations clearly tend to have substantially higher per capita consumption of both food and energy than the relatively "traditional" nations.

Another approach to comparing the resource and environmental impacts of industrial and traditional societies is to compare the discarded waste from each. In traditional societies very few resources are lost as waste. Even human excrement is returned to the soil where it adds nutrients. In industrial societies, wastes of every kind are extensive and environmentally damaging.

In the United States, for example, industrial solid wastes generated in 1977 totaled about 344 million metric tons, and the amount of these wastes is growing at about 3 percent per year.[25] The Council on Environmental Quality (CEQ) reports that solid wastes from residential and commercial sources were estimated at 130 million metric tons in 1976. Based on present trends and policies, the projection for 1985 is 180 million metric tons. These rising waste generation rates reflect increasing use of raw materials and energy.[26] Currently, the average person in the United States produces about 1,300 lbs. of municipal solid waste annually.[27]

The cost of disposing of this waste is high—$9 billion in 1977—and the rate of resource recovery is low—about 7 percent.[28] CEQ reports* that the recovery rate could be tripled by individuals setting aside recyclable materials such as newspapers, glass, and metal for separate collection or delivery to recycling centers.[29] The composition of municipal refuse generated in the United States in 1977 is illustrated in Table 13–7. In addition to reducing per capita mineral resource demands,[30] recycling has energy-saving and environmental advantages. CEQ reports, for example, that making steel reinforcing bars from scrap instead of from virgin ore takes 74 percent less energy and 51 percent less water, creates 86 percent less air pollution emissions, and generates 97 percent less mining wastes.[31]

Per capita wastes and demands on environmental and other resources in the United States are not typical of all industrial societies, but in general an "industrial person" seems likely to have a larger impact on the world's resources and

*Since this text was written, CEQ has reported further on resource recovery. (See Council on Environmental Quality, "Municipal Solid Wastes," in *Environmental Quality: the Tenth Annual Report of the Council on Environmental Quality*, Washington: U.S. Government Printing Office, 1979.)

## TABLE 13–7

**Post-Consumer Residential and Commercial Solid Waste Generated and Amounts Recovered, by Type of Material, 1977**

*(As-generated wet weight, in millions of tons)*

| | Gross Discards | Material Recovery | | Net waste disposed of | | |
|---|---|---|---|---|---|---|
| | | Quantity | Percent | Quantity | Percent of Total Waste | Percent of Nonfood Product Waste |
| Paper | 49.2 | 10.2 | 20.7 | 39.0 | 28.6 | 46.9 |
| Glass | 14.7 | 0.5 | 3.4 | 14.2 | 10.4 | 17.1 |
| Metals | 13.7 | 0.4 | 2.9 | 13.3 | 9.8 | 16.0 |
| Ferrous | 11.9 | 0.3 | 2.5 | 11.6 | 8.5 | 13.9 |
| Aluminum | 1.4 | 0.1 | 7.1 | 1.3 | 1.0 | 1.6 |
| Other nonferrous | 0.4 | 0.0 | 0.0 | 0.4 | 0.3 | 0.5 |
| Plastics | 5.3 | 0.0 | 0.0 | 5.3 | 3.9 | 6.4 |
| Rubber | 3.3 | 0.2 | 6.1 | 3.1 | 2.3 | 3.7 |
| Leather | 0.6 | 0.0 | 0.0 | 0.6 | 0.4 | 0.7 |
| Textiles | 3.0 | 0.0 | 0.0 | 3.0 | 2.2 | 3.6 |
| Wood | 4.7 | 0.0 | 0.0 | 4.7 | 3.4 | 5.6 |
| Total nonfood product waste | 94.5 | 11.3 | 12.0 | 83.2 | 61.0 | 100.0 |
| Food waste | 23.8 | 0.0 | 0.0 | 23.8 | 17.4 | 28.6 |
| Yard waste | 27.3 | 0.0 | 0.0 | 27.3 | 20.0 | 32.8 |
| Miscellaneous inorganic wastes | 2.2 | 0.0 | 0.0 | 2.2 | 1.6 | 2.6 |
| Subtotal | 147.8 | 11.3 | 7.6 | 136.5 | 100.0 | 164.0 |
| Energy recovery | | +0.7 | 0.5 | −0.7 | | |
| Total recovery | | 12.0 | 8.1 | | | |
| Total net disposal | | | | 135.8 | | |

*Source:* Franklin Associates (Prairie Village. Kan.). *Post-Consumer Solid Waste and Resource Recovery Baseline: Working Papers,* draft prepared for the Resource Conservation Committee. U.S. Environmental Protection Agency. May 16. 1979. p. 22.

environment than a "traditional person." Furthermore, the industrial person has less direct experience of the impacts being made on the environment than the traditional person because the industrial person is separated by distance from many of the more severe forms of environmental degradation caused by modern industrial cultures.[32] To many urban members of industrial societies, energy comes from an electrical outlet and food comes from grocery stores. Relatively few have had anything to do with the strip mines, power plants, and nuclear waste facilities involved in producing "clean" electricity or with the air and water pollution associated with steel manufacturing and with the chemicals used in "industrial" agriculture. The complex economic web of trade and commerce extends the environmental impacts of each additional industrial person across oceans and continents (see the map Extent of Commercial Activity in the colored map section of this volume).

The complexities of trade and industrial commerce do not alter the fact that increases in industrial populations and their wealth—like increases in herdsmen and cattle—threaten the resources of the environmental commons. The fundamental population-related problem presented by the tragedy of the commons[33] faces both traditional and industrial societies. As Garrett Hardin has shown, common environmental resources can be protected by "mutual coercion, mutually agreed upon" both under socialist and under market economic systems.[34] The socialist approach is illustrated by the examples of the Soviet Union[35] and China[36]. The market (or mixed) economy approach is illustrated by U.S. efforts, among others.[37] It should be noted, however, that both socialist and market economic systems face two incompletely resolved difficulties in protecting the resources of the environmental commons: They place a monetary value on environmental resources and weigh present and future costs and benefits of resources and protective measures.

Under the theory of market economies, the

price of a good (or service) has a major influence on demand, and to the extent that environmental costs are included in market prices, the market can help control the demand for and use of the environmental commons. A valuation problem arises because many environmental costs (e.g., degraded water and air quality or loss of species and wilderness) are borne by a large portion—or all—of society. Called "externalities" by economists, these costs are generally not included in the price of a particular good or service. Unless environmental costs are included in the market price, the market cannot act to protect the environment.* Similar environmental valuation problems arise under socialist economic systems, because government-set prices often fail to reflect external costs any more adequately than market prices.

The second problem involved in using either socialist or market economic systems to protect the environmental commons is that of intergenerational equity.[38] In most societies, a present-value approach is used in economic decision-making. Under the present value approach, future benefits and costs are valued less (i.e., are discounted) relative to current benefits and costs. The higher the discount rate the more difficult conservation and environmental protection become.[39]

Whatever economic system is involved, increased numbers of people lead to increased environmental pressures. The magnitude and character of these pressures depends significantly on the type of culture. The Global 2000 Study's projections suggest that the populations of traditional cultures will be growing rapidly (at more than 2 percent per year in some cases) in the decades ahead. Increased overgrazing and shortened fallow cycles will aggravate erosion, forest losses, and desertification. In parts of Eurasia, the Near East, Africa, Oceania, and Latin America, the land cannot be expected to retain even its present productivity under another two decades of intensifying stress, as discussed in later sections of this chapter. The Global 2000 Study's projections show the population growth rates of industrial societies falling by about a quarter by 2000. The

*Energy provides an example of the externalities problem. There are many external environmental costs of energy production that are not now included in the market price of energy. Although this problem is not resolved, much thought is being given to alternative methods of including external costs into the market price of goods. William Ramsey's *Unpaid Costs of Electrical Energy: Health and Environmental Impacts from Coal and Nuclear Power* (Baltimore: Johns Hopkins, 1979) provides a useful introduction to this problem.

population increase in the Soviet Union, Europe, and North America (about 200 million) is small compared to the rest of the world (about 2 billion), but the per capita resource and environmental impacts of industrial societies are relatively large. However analyzed, population increase throughout the world must be regarded as a major source of stress on the common environmental resources of the earth.

## Population Distribution and the Environment

The nature of the demands and impacts a population makes on its environment depends in part on how its people are distributed over the land. For both developing and industrialized nations, this distribution has been changing. The trend has been toward a decreasing proportion of the world's population living in rural areas and an increasing proportion living in urban areas.

Over the past two centuries the growth of relatively dense human settlements has been rapid, even more rapid than the growth of the world's population. Between 1800 and 1950, the world's population increased by a factor of 2.6. Over this same period the number of persons living in human settlements of 20,000 or more increased from 22 million to more than 500 million, a factor of 23. The populations of large industrial cities (100,000 or more inhabitants) in America, Europe, Oceania, and the Soviet Union grew still faster, increasing by a factor of 35. Recently, however, urban expansion in developed countries (especially in Europe) has slowed. Large cities in the LDCs grew less rapidly than large cities in the industrialized nations during this period, but since 1900, LDC urban growth has accelerated.[40]

United Nations reports suggest that trends toward urbanization may continue.[41] In 1950, 29 percent of the world's population lived in urban settlements. The urban population share grew to 39 percent in 1975 and is projected to approach 50 percent by 2000.[42] Using the Global 2000 Study's medium world population figure, 50 percent urbanization would mean more than 3 billion urban residents in 2000. Such a population distribution would have significant environmental implications in both less developed and industrialized nations.[43]

### Urbanization and the Environment in the LDCs

How much urban growth can be expected in the LDCs by the year 2000? The Global 2000 Study's projections do not include detail regarding

## TABLE 13-8

### Urban Population in All Cities of 100,000 or More

|  | 1950 | 1975 | 2000 |
|---|---|---|---|
|  | *millions* | | |
| World | 392 | 903 | 2,167 |
| Industrialized countries | 262 | 503 | 756 |
| Less developed countries | 130 | 480 | 1,411 |

Source: *Trends and Prospects in the Populations of Urban Agglomerations 1950–2000, as Assessed in 1973–1975.* New York: United Nations 1975

## TABLE 13-9

### Estimates and Rough Projections of Selected Urban Agglomerations in Developing Countries

|  | 1960 | 1970 | 1975 | 2000 |
|---|---|---|---|---|
|  | *Millions of persons* | | | |
| Calcutta | 5.5 | 6.9 | 8.1 | 19.7 |
| Mexico City | 4.9 | 8.6 | 10.9 | 31.6 |
| Greater Bombay | 4.1 | 5.8 | 7.1 | 19.1 |
| Greater Cairo | 3.7 | 5.7 | 6.9 | 16.4 |
| Jakarta | 2.7 | 4.3 | 5.6 | 16.9 |
| Seoul | 2.4 | 5.4 | 7.3 | 18.7 |
| Delhi | 2.3 | 3.5 | 4.5 | 13.2 |
| Manila | 2.2 | 3.5 | 4.4 | 12.7 |
| Tehran | 1.9 | 3.4 | 4.4 | 13.8 |
| Karachi | 1.8 | 3.3 | 4.5 | 15.9 |
| Bogota | 1.7 | 2.6 | 3.4 | 9.5 |
| Lagos | 0.8 | 1.4 | 2.1 | 9.4 |

Source: U.N. estimates and medium variant projections, as published in *Department of State Bulletin*, Fall 1978, p. 17.

rural or urban populations, but an estimate of the LDCs' urban growth can be obtained from United Nations information.

Projections reported by the U.N. Secretariat indicate that urban areas will absorb 59 percent of the increase in LDC population between 1975 and 2000.[44] The Global 2000 Study projects a net population growth of 2.0 billion persons in the developing nations. Applying the U.N. urban percentage to this figure, the urban populations of the LDCs would increase by about 1.2 billion by 2000. As illustrated in Table 13-8, U.N. projections are similar, but somewhat higher.

Most of the projected increase would occur in existing cities, and as a result many LDC urban populations would become almost inconceivably large. For example, by 2000 Mexico City would house nearly 32 million persons—about 4 times New York City's present population.[45] São Paulo would surpass 26 million.[46] Altogether, more than 400 cities would be expected to pass the million mark, most of them in developing countries.[47] The projected growth of selected LDC cities is illustrated in Table 13-9.

The most rapid urban growth of less developed countries occurs in the "uncontrolled settlements"—urban slums and shantytowns, where sanitation and other public services are nonexistent or, at best, minimal. Already more than half of the populations of many larger cities—for example, Buenaventura in Colombia, Ismir and Ankara in Turkey, and Maracaibo in Venezuela—live in uncontrolled settlements,[48] as do more than a quarter of the populations of Baghdad, Seoul, Calcutta, Taipei, Mexico City, and Rio de Janeiro.[49] Recent estimates indicate that the populations of many uncontrolled settlements are doubling in size every 5–7 years, while the urban populations as a whole double every 10–15 years.[50] The more rapid growth of the uncontrolled settlements means that as time goes on, a larger fraction of the LDC urban population will be living in these settlements. In Bombay, where uncontrolled settlements are among the largest in the world, 45 percent of the 6 million urban popula-

tion in 1971 was living in squatter villages and slums, and the squatter-slum population was growing at 17.4 per cent per year.[51]

The rapid growth of LDC urban populations will create unprecedented pressure on sanitation and other public services by 2000. Waste disposal, water, health care, shelter, education, food, and employment will be needed for approximately 1.2 billion additional urban residents. Simply to provide in 2000 the same per capita services that now exist, the LDCs will need to increase all of the services, infrastructures, and capital of their cities by roughly two-thirds—and this massive increase would provide no net improvement in services. The degree to which public services are provided will, in large measure, determine future environmental conditions in LDC cities.

Safe drinking water and sewage disposal are two of the most basic indicators of LDC urban environmental conditions. While conditions improved over the 1970–75 period, large numbers of LDC urban residents still do not have access to safe drinking water. A 1975 World Health Organization (WHO) survey[52] indicated that at that time 24 percent of the urban populations in LDCs did not have house water connections, or even access to standpipes, and 25 percent were without even household systems for excreta disposal.*

Progress in providing basic LDC urban services also appears to have varied significantly according to income group. The WHO survey found the

---

*For comparison, 78 percent of the LDC rural population did not have access to an adequate water supply, and 86 percent were without even household systems for excreta disposal.

installation of piped indoor water connections were running well in excess of anticipated rates; thus, it was proposed that the 1980 target for installation of connections from piped public water supplies be moved upward from 60 to 68 percent. On the other hand, service from public standpipes increased slower than anticipated, and the proposed target for this form of service has been moved downward from 40 to 23 percent.[53] These trends suggest that service is being provided more rapidly to the relatively affluent middle-class neighborhoods than to the very poor in the rapidly growing uncontrolled settlements.

Provision of potable drinking water in LDC cities is a service closely related to the problems of sewage treatment and disposal. A 1976 report found that only 3.3 percent of the world's LDC urban population lived in dwellings connected to sewer systems that were in turn connected to some form of conventional treatment facility or oxidation pond. The dwellings of another 23.7 percent were connected to sewer systems without any form of sewage treatment capability. Household systems—pit privys, septic tanks, and buckets— were used by 42.1 percent. The remaining 30.9 percent did not even have a pit privy.[54]

While WHO reports that over the 1970–75 period an increasing percent of LDC residents are served by sewers, the projected growth of slums and uncontrolled settlements projected in the years ahead present an unprecedented challenge. In São Paulo, the number of homes served by sewers increased over the 1940–75 period, but the proportion of urban dwellers served by sewers dropped from 38 percent to 29 percent over the same period.[55] The high capital costs of Western-style sewage systems lead many development specialists to advocate less costly composting toilets as an alternative.[56]

Without basic hygienic facilities, LDC urban populations face the constant threat of epidemics and the daily reality of rampant infectious disease. The health impacts of sewage pollution of water are already serious in LDCs. Growing populations—and the resultant sewage burdens in streams, rivers, and lakes and along coastlines—are spreading several waterborne diseases in many urban communities. Recent figures on the impact of waterborne diseases in developing countries show that such diseases are responsible for 40 percent of the affected countries' mortality and 60 percent of their morbidity. In areas occupied by more than 67 percent of the world's population, dysentery, typhoid, cholera, and hepatitis, the major causes of death, can be linked to inadequate sewage treatment.[57]

Environmental problems in LDC urban areas are by no means attributable to growth only in the poorest classes; growth in the more affluent classes also creates environmental problems. One indicator of the environmental stress produced by growth of the affluent classes is the increasing numbers of automobiles and the associated air pollution. Although statistics on LDC urban air quality are very limited, a few examples will serve to indicate some of the general trends:

- In Caracas, Venezuela, the motor vehicle population grew at an annual rate of around 10 percent prior to 1974. With the increase in incomes brought about by 1973 oil price increases, the figure rose roughly 20 percent during 1974 and 1975. Vehicles now produce 90 percent of the air contaminants in Caracas. At peak traffic hours, the carbon monoxide concentrations reach 40–45 parts per million (ppm); the average urban concentration is 25–30 ppm.[58] An 8-hour exposure to even 20 ppm is described by the U.S. Environmental Protection Agency as "very unhealthful."[59]

- Air pollution problems in most LDC cities are made worse by the fact that many automobiles used are old and in poor state of repair, and their engines release relatively high amounts of carbon monoxide, particulates, and smog-producing hydrocarbons. In addition, other motorized vehicles causing relatively high releases of air pollutants (motorbikes, scooters, motorcycles) are common in LDC cities. LDC urban air pollution problems are further intensified by the lack of vehicular air pollution control laws and associated emission-control devices for internal combustion engines.

- Ecologist Carlos Bustamante of Peru's National University of Engineering noted recently that Lima's serious air pollution problems are not just due to its low diffusion of contaminated air (Lima is surrounded on three sides by Andean foothills). He claimed much of the problem was due to the city's numerous old and poorly maintained vehicles and estimated that such vehicles emit five times more pollution than new cars.[60]

- In the capital city of Ankara, the Turkish Health Ministry recently reported that the air was laden with 2.5 times more sulfur dioxide and four times more smoke than the maximum levels set by WHO. Because of this condition, the Ministry reports that cases of bronchitis, asthma, pneumonia, heart attacks, and other diseases caused by the air pollution have sharply increased.[61]

- Bombay, India, is another city suffering from serious air pollution. A recent government survey found that, largely because of industrial growth, pollutants enter the area's air at the rate of 1,000 tons every four hours.[62] The air pollutants include 38.4 percent carbon monoxide, 33.4 percent sulfur dioxide, and 9.8 percent oxides of nitrogen. In one residential area of Bombay, the residents were found to be inhaling very large amounts of sulfur dioxide every day, and most were suffering from cough, constant sneezing, asthma, bronchitis, chest pain, and fatigue.[63] Bombay's nearly 300,000 automobiles have added to the air pollution caused by local industry, magnifying the respiratory disease impacts.[64]

Migration to cities will continue to be a major component of urban growth in LDC nations as long as rural populations, especially the rural poor, believe that urban areas offer greater economic opportunities than rural areas. As urban populations continue to expand, however, economic and environmental conditions may change. Existing trends indicate that the problems of air and water pollution can be expected to worsen, and the spread of waster-borne diseases—and even the disposal of the dead*—will present increasing threats to human health. Urban economies will be hard pressed to keep pace. Housing and employment are in short supply, and energy will present increasing difficulties, especially for the LDC's urban poor. Many can no longer afford kerosene or gas and depend on firewood and charcoal. In some areas the price of firewood has increased at rates exceeding international oil price increases[65] (see also the forestry section of this chapter). The FAO reports that in some areas of

Asia and Africa, firewood now absorbs 15–25 percent of household income.[66]

Will the trends continue? Some observers are beginning to have doubts. Harold Lubell, project leader for an International Labor Organization study of six major Third World cities, concludes that "there appears to be a saturation point, and when this is reached migration falls off in response to declines in the urban economy."[67] Lester R. Brown, President of the Worldwatch Institute, questions whether sufficient food will be available to LDC cities, either from other countries or from domestic sources in large enough quantities and at low enough prices to allow the urbanization trends to continue for many more years.[68] In effect, negative feedback may slow the growth of already overcrowded cities.

If present trends do continue to 2000, urban populations would approach a majority of the world's population,[69] and the largest urban areas would be in the LDCs. The economic and environmental challenges implied by these trends are enormous. Whether these challenges can be met to the degree necessary if the trends are to continue is an open question.

## Urbanization and the Environment in Industrial Nations

Over the past several decades population patterns in most industrial nations have changed significantly. Rural to urban migration has created large national majorities of urban dwellers, declining populations in most small towns and villages, the consolidation and mechanization of farms, and a concurrent decline in the number of small, family-owned farms. Rapid growth of various transport systems (particularly highway and air) has lead to high personal mobility and rapid growth of single-family houses and "townhouse complexes" in suburban areas. Urban and suburban installation of potable-water, sewer, and electric and fossil fuel energy systems for households is nearly complete. Although some of these changes have also been occurring to a degree in some developing nations, such changes are relatively well advanced in industrial nations.

The environmental consequences of these patterns of population distribution and human settlement, many of which have already been touched upon, are numerous. One factor needing emphasis concerns the importance of the low (even the falling) real price of energy and other raw materials during the period of urbanization in the industrialized nations.

During the 1950s and 60s, the low real cost of

---

*Disposal of the dead presents fewer physical and health problems in countries where religion and custom encourage cremation. In cultures where burial is preferred and space is scarce, public health issues become more important. The difficulties are most severe in LDC cities following an earthquake or some other temporary cause of high mortality but can occur in industrialized countries as well. A particularly striking example of the cumulative problems that burial can present occurred in France during the late 1700s. The principal cemetery in Paris had accumulated some 2 million bodies in a space of only 131 by 65 yards. The *Smithsonian* magazine reports: "This human compost heap was 30 feet deep and extended seven feet above ground. In 1780, in a catastrophic landslide, the walls of an entire apartment block adjoining the cemetery gave way and 2,000 corpses slid into the cellars, giving off a stench that well-nigh asphyxiated the residents above. It was clear that new arrangements were urgently needed. But the turmoil of the French Revolution and the establishment of the Napoleonic Empire precluded the opening of [the new] Père-Lachaise [cemetery] until 1804." (Robert Wallace, "The Elegies and Enigmas of Romantic Père-Lachaise," *Smithsonian*, Nov. 1973, pp. 108–15.

energy encouraged a variety of wasteful and inefficient designs. Homes, offices, and factories were built with minimal insulation and energy-conserving features. Labor-saving, but energy-intensive, appliances and machinery spread throughout the culture. Agriculture and industry became increasingly energy-intensive and less labor-intensive. Production of vehicles expanded rapidly, and their weight and horsepower grew substantially. Simultaneous massive investments in highway and road construction led to rapid growth of energy-inefficient single-family homes in suburban communities, often around decaying inner cities. Oil-based chemicals, plastics, and fabrics replaced many natural materials, such as wood, wool, and cotton. All this was made possible by cheap, abundant energy, especially fluid fuels, and all of this has now changed.

Some of the environmental, resource, and economic costs of the past decades of urbanization have been analyzed for the United States in "The Costs of Sprawl," a study prepared by the Real Estate Research Corporation for the Council on Environmental Quality and other federal agencies in 1975.[70] This study documents how, in contrast to urban sprawl, higher-density, better-planned communities require less energy for cooling and heating, stimulate less automobile use, and conserve water. They produce about 45 percent less air pollution than sprawling communities, reduce storm water runoff, and allow more land, wildlife, and vegetation to be protected in parks and open spaces.

Now that the era of inexpensive, widely available energy has come to an end, the implications for both population distribution and environmental quality are likely to be profound. Although the future shape of cities in industrial nations is not yet clear, it is certain that such communities will be confronting radical transformation from energy-wasteful to energy-conserving societies. Smaller, well-insulated homes, and increasing shifts to townhouses and condominiums are trends already underway in housing. Slower driving speeds, smaller and more efficient automobile engines and greater use of public transport are energy-conserving transportation measures already beginning to take effect. Recycling of materials and increased reliance once again on renewable sources of materials (especially wood) may also reduce societal energy requirements[71] but might also increase the competition for land.

The fundamental nature of the long-term change was indicated briefly in the 1977 U.S. National Energy Plan (NEP).[72] The NEP noted that a basic aspect of the energy problem in the U.S. is that abundant cheap energy has led to the development of a stock of capital goods, such as homes, cars, and factory equipment, that uses energy inefficiently.[73] The NEP went on to note that a transition to an era of substantially more expensive and less abundant energy is in progress and that as a part of this transition, changes in capital stocks will be needed.[74] These changes, if started soon, can be accomplished incrementally.

In reviewing the NEP, the Office of Technology Assessment (OTA) noted that energy efficiency in the use of capital stocks depends in significant part on how the stocks are distributed over the nation and that changes in patterns of capital distribution and transportation are long-range and fundamental and will take more than one generation to complete.[75] The OTA report recommends guidelines, leadership and incentives to initiate the process now. Its point might be summed up as follows:

The United States and other industrial nations will face an exceedingly difficult energy problem in 2000 if its patterns of capital distribution are still based on the sprawl that is so characteristic of many industrial cities; yet because of the long depreciation times associated with transportation, communication, sewage, and other systems associated with sprawling types of land-use patterns, the major capital systems of most industrial cities in 2000 will look much like those that existed in 1977 unless the "guidelines, leadership, and incentives" called for by OTA are established immediately. The distribution patterns of major capital systems can be changed only over a period of decades, not within a few years.

At least in the U.S., the dependence on and the passion for the private automobile is not likely to change easily. The U.S. Bureau of the Census recently completed a study of some of the ties between Americans and their automobiles. The study found, among other things, that while the use of car pools and mass transportation probably increased after the 1973–74 Arab oil embargo, the increase was apparently only temporary. By 1975:

• Of 80.1 million Americans going to work each day, 52.3 million (65 percent) were driving alone.

• Another 15.6 million (19.4 percent) were driving, but with other passengers in the car or truck.

• Only 4.8 million (6 percent) used public transportation, and 3.8 million (4.7 percent) walked.

• The remaining 3.6 million (4.5 percent) used bicycles or motorcycles or worked at home.

- The average commuter trip was 9 miles each way and was 20 minutes in duration.[75a]
- The proportion of mass-transit users among those employing vehicles actually *decreased* from 10 percent to just over 6 percent in 1975.

Despite the abiding passion and dependence, the future of the private automobile is in doubt not only in the U.S. but throughout the world. Virtually every other use of dwindling petroleum resources has been found to have a higher priority than that of the private automobile.[75b] However, it will be difficult to eliminate dependence on the private automobile without fundamental changes in population and land-use patterns. As discussed briefly in the energy section of this chapter, the choice of future energy systems and technologies—large-scale centralized systems or small-scale decentralized systems—will have a major influence on the population and land-use patterns than can be expected in the future.

Whether or not in direct response to energy developments, the trend toward urbanization in some industrial nations has begun to change. In the U.S., for example, signs began to appear after 1970 that many of the nation's larger cities—New York, Los Angeles, Detroit, Seattle, Chicago, and St. Louis—were declining in population.[76] At the same time, much of the nation's fastest population growth has shifted to rural areas. From 1970 to 1975, 7 million people emigrated from U.S. central cities to suburbs and other nonmetropolitan areas.[77]

However these trends continue, the industrial nations of the world face a period of perhaps 50 to 100 years of transition. Over the next decades, choices will have to be made, not only in energy development but in many other sectors of industrial society (such as food production and water and minerals supply) that will encounter problems of scarcities and resource degradation. How these choices are made will profoundly affect patterns of future development and human settlement in industrial nations.

### Urbanization and the Environment—Summary

Urban growth, due largely to the migration of poor people from rural areas, may have created cities in the developing countries of unprecedented sizes by the year 2000. On the other hand, it is possible that rural development plus a decline in economic and public health conditions in LDC cities will slow the migration somewhat. In any event, it is anticipated that the most rapidly growing parts of these cities will be the uncontrolled settlements where large numbers of the poor exist

without access to even basic public services such as potable water and sewage disposal. At anticipated growth rates, it is doubtful that the services of many LDC cities can be increased rapidly enough to provide services at even the present per capita level.[78] Raw sewage, air pollution, lack of housing, poor and crowded transport, inadequate fire protection, and disease will present increasing difficulties within these cities. Immediately outside the cities, firewood gatherers, animal grazers, and charcoal-makers will strip the surrounding areas of accessible trees, shrubs, and grasses. As the area of degradation widens, there are likely to be losses of indigenous plants and animals, aggravated soil erosion, and increased risk of serious flooding.[79]

In the industrial nations, future trends in urbanization are not clear, but designs that conserve resources, especially energy, will become increasingly attractive. The era of rapid growth in industrialized nations fueled by high consumption of resources, particularly relatively clean, inexpensive, and abundant petroleum fuels, has ended. In the future, consumption patterns of both rural and urban settlements of industrialized nations will be altered by inevitable shifts from a high-consumption to a conservation approach.[80] Before the year 2000, industrialized nations will be forced to make major choices relating to their future energy and resource industries and their production technologies—choices that will have profound implications for population distribution and environmental quality throughout the 21st century.

## The Population Projections and Human Health

The life expectancy of a population is perhaps the most all-inclusive and widely measured indicator of a nation's environmental health. In the absence of safe drinking water, sewage systems, adequate food and shelter, medical services, and controls over toxic pollutants and disease vectors and hosts, the release of environmental pathogens and pollutants, life expectancies are low. With these basic environmental conditions met, life expectancies are high.[81]

It is generally believed that as economic development proceeds, one of its major benefits is a combination of beneficial environmental conditions that increase the average period of productive life. The increased life expectancy is brought about in three stages according to a theory that has been expressed succinctly by Dr. N.

R. E. Fendall, former director of medical services for Kenya:

1. In the earliest stages of development, the epidemiological picture is determined largely by an endemic infectious disease situation with a high prevalence of parasitosis, gastroenteritis, respiratory diseases, malnutrition, and vector-borne diseases.

2. As living standards rise and environmental conditions improve, the endemic infectious disease problems are brought under control, and measles, whooping cough, poliomyelitis and other bacterial and virus diseases dominate the epidemiological picture.

3. In the final stage of economic development, the degenerative diseases of a cerebrosclerotic nature, hypertension, heart failure, diabetes, psychosomatic diseases, and cancer comprise the major portions of ill health. Undernutrition gives way to overnutrition and the severity of the disease pattern shifts from the child to the aged. [82]

This theory, in effect, underlies the projections of life expectancy made by the Bureau of the Census for the Global 2000 Study. These projections (see Chapter 2) assume that future economic progress and development will lead to environmental conditions that will in turn result in increased life expectancy. For the world as a whole, life expectancy is projected to increase 6.7 years (11 percent) by the year 2000 (from 58.8 years in 1975 to 65.5 years in 2000). For the LDCs, the projected increase is 18 percent (form 54.0 to 63.5 years), and for the industrialized countries, 3 percent (from 71.1 to 73.3 years). In no country is life expectancy projected to decline.

Since the advent of preventive immunization against communicable diseases, life expectancies have improved steadily. The continuing trend of life expectancy is illustrated and compared in Table 13–10 with the Bureau of Census projections developed for the Global 2000 Study. For the world as a whole, a 15 percent increase was achieved over the 1950–70 period. Life expectancies increased everywhere, but the most dramatic increases were in the less developed countries—a 21 percent increase overall. Asia achieved a striking 24 percent increase.

On closer examination, the life expectancy data show another important development: The rate of increase of life expectancy has slowed. For the world as a whole, the average annual increment in life expectancy declined from 0.64 to 0.34 years over the 1950–70 period. Further increases in life

expectancy have been particularly difficult to achieve in the industrialized nations, where child mortality is relatively low. Degenerative diseases (e.g., cancer, heart disease, cerebrovascular disease) have proven very difficult to prevent or control. In the LDCs, decreases in infant and child mortality have been difficult to achieve, and progress in increasing life expectancies has slowed there too.

The Bureau of the Census life expectancy projections are based on an examination of past trends, not on an examination of the causes of mortality and the prospects for changes in these causes. The causes are largely associated with environmental problems, and the prospects for change need to be examined. The problems and prospects for improvements are quite different in the industrialized countries than in the less developed countries.

### Environment and Health in the LDCs.

Mortality statistics show that in most LDCs high mortality rates among infants and children are the primary statistical contributors to low life expectancies. A 1975 World Bank Policy Paper containing vital statistics for 67 countries lists 19 countries with per capita incomes of less than $200 per year. [83] Of these, only 2 had infant mortality rates below 10 percent, while 10 had rates 15 percent or higher. By contrast, only 4 of the 16 countries with per capita incomes of over $700 had child mortality rates greater than 5 percent; 8 had rates of less than 3 percent. [84]

The World Bank also notes that the rate at which life expectancies have improved in less developed countries has declined since 1955—from 2.7 years in the periods 1950–55 and 1955–60 to 2.6 years in 1960–65 and to only 2.0 years in 1965–70. [85] A particularly significant factor in the slowdown of the decline of LDC mortality appears to be that mortality in childhood has shown a somewhat greater resistance to decline than mortality at some later ages. [86]

The persistence of infectious diseases (above all diarrhea) that cannot be conquered with modern medicine is, in large part, responsible for slowing the decline in infant mortality. Malaria control, antibiotics, and immunization programs have brought some quick, dramatic gains, but further progress depends on improvements in nutrition and sanitation, which are coming along slowly, if at all. According to Dr. John Bryant (formerly with the Rockefeller Foundation, now with the office of International Health, U.S. Department of Health, Education and Welfare):

## TABLE 13–10

## Levels and Trends of Life Expectancy at Birth, 1950–2000

### Life Expectancy at Birth, in Years

|  | 1950/55 | 1955/60 | 1960/65 | 1965/70 | 1975[a] | 2000[a] |
|---|---|---|---|---|---|---|
| World | 46.7 | 49.9 | 52.2 | 53.9 | 58.8 | 65.5 |
| Industrialized countries | 65.0 | 68.2 | 69.5 | 70.3 | 71.1 | 73.3 |
| Less developed countries | 41.6 | 45.0 | 48.0 | 50.4 | 54.0 | 63.5 |
| Africa | 36.1 | 38.5 | 40.8 | 43.0 | 46.2 | 57.4 |
| Latin America | 52.3 | 55.3 | 57.7 | 59.5 | 63.1 | 70.3 |
| Asia | 42.5 | 46.3 | 49.8 | 52.5 | 54.3[b] | 63.7[b] |

### Average Annual Increment in Life Expectancy at Birth, in Years

|  | 1950/55–1955/60 | 1955/60–1960/65 | 1960/65–1965/70 | 1975–2000[a] |
|---|---|---|---|---|
| World | 0.64 | 0.46 | 0.34 | 0.27 |
| Industrialized countries | 0.64 | 0.26 | 0.16 | 0.09 |
| Less developed countries | 0.68 | 0.60 | 0.48 | 0.38 |
| Africa | 0.48 | 0.46 | 0.44 | 0.45 |
| Latin America | 0.60 | 0.48 | 0.36 | 0.29 |
| Asia | 0.76 | 0.70 | 0.54 | 0.38 |

Source: World Population Prospects as Assessed in 1973, New York: U.N. Department of Economic and Social Affairs. 1977, pp. 138 ff.

[a] Calculated from Bureau of the Census, Illustrative Projections of World Populations to the 21st Century, Washington: Government Printing Office, 1979, p. 91 Table 8. Weighting is 105 for males; 100 for females.
[b] Asia and Oceania

The great weapons of modern medicine are aimed at the patho-physiology of disease and its susceptibility to pharmaceutical, immunological, or surgical attack. Health services are designed to deliver these weapons mainly through the hands of doctors. The dismal fact is that these great killers of children—diarrhea, pneumonia, malnutrition—are beyond the reach of these weapons.

If children sick with these diseases reach the physician, there are sharp limits to what he can do. Diarrhea and pneumonia are often not affected by antibiotics, and the frequent presence of malnutrition makes even supportive therapy difficult or futile. And even these interventions by the physician, whether or not they are therapeutically effective, are only sporadic ripples in a running tide of disease. We are speaking of societies in which, at any given time, a third of the children may have diarrhea and more than that may be malnourished. Their lives are saturated with the causes—poverty, crowding, ignorance, poor ventilation, filth, flies. [87]

The causes of high infant-mortality rates are well known and closely linked to environmental conditions. As shown in Table 13–11, the diseases most often fatal during early childhood in a developing area (in this case, Latin America) are fecally related and airborne contagious diseases. Although diseases such as cholera, typhoid, and polio all contribute to the mortality statistics, in-testinal parasites and various infectious diarrheal diseases are probably the most devastating of the fecally related types. Surveys of parasite-infected populations frequently show from 70 to 90 percent infestations. [88] In Egypt, Iran, and Venezuela, the monthly incidence of diarrhea among preschool children has been estimated to be 40–50 percent. [89]

The effects of diarrhea, pneumonia, and intestinal parasites are greatly aggravated by undernutrition, which is the major underlying cause of death among children. Deaths from infection nearly always result from a combination of undernutrition and infection. When women are undernourished, too frequent pregnancies result in malnutrition for the mother and baby, low average birth weights, and poor resistance to disease.

The prospects for reducing malnutrition are mixed. The Global 2000 Study food projections, in the medium case, show only limited improvement in per capita food availability and, in some instances, declines. Furthermore, when food distribution among income classes is taken into consideration, the number of malnourished, disease-vulnerable children is likely to increase by 2000. Increased death rates in parts of Asia have already been observed during poor crop years. [90]

To further complicate the situation, many of the diseases most threatening health in developing countries are becoming increasingly resistant to drugs now being used in their treatment. [91] Already drug-resistant pathogen strains* have contributed to severe epidemics in several LDCs:

- In Central America between 1968 and 1971, a dysentery pandemic occurred in which the drugs normally used to treat the disease proved ineffective. [92] The strain—*Shigella dysenteriae 1*—had high mortality rates in both Guatemala and El Salvador. In Guatemala alone, an estimated 12,500 people died from the disease in 1968 (200 out of every 100,000 inhabitants). [93]
- In Mexico in 1972, an epidemic of typhoid fever appeared on a scale unprecedented in modern times. [94] The strain—*Salmonella typhi*—has resistance to a wide range of drugs. [95] The outbreak lasted for months and involved four Mexican states. Large numbers of persons of all ages and varying socioeconomic groups were affected. [96]
- In recent years resistance to commonly used therapeutic agents against malaria has increased substantially in South America and Southeast Asia. There is every reason to believe that these resistant strains will spread, thus hampering treatment and eradication. [97]

In short, there is growing evidence that numerous pathogens and vectors† are evolving strains that are resistant to many of the common and least expensive drugs. [98] While new drugs will continue to be developed, the new drugs are often more expensive and effective against a smaller group of pathogens than those that they replace. [99] Excessive use of commom antibiotics both by humans [100] and in animal feed [101] may increase the rate at which resistant strains evolve. The most

---

*Pathogen resistance to drugs is not limited to developing countries; it causes increased mortality in industrialized societies as well ("Rise of Antibiotic-Resistant Bacteria," *Science News*, Aug. 24/31, 1974, p. 119). Certain staphylococcus infections (especially in hospitals) and gonorrhea in particular are growing problems. There are many indications that drug resistance in pathogens will continue to increase throughout the world (Marietta Whittlesey, "The Runaway Use of Antibiotics," *New York Times Magazine*, May 6, 1979, p. 122). Coastal waters off New York have been contaminated with both sewage and mercury. Tests show that bacteria in these waters have developed varying degrees of resistance to ampicillin, tetracycline, kanamycin, and streptomycin, and research with both the genus *Vibro* and the genus *Bacillus* led to the conclusion that ampicillin resistance and mercury resistance are genetically linked (Marine Ecosystems Analysis Program, *New York Bight Project Annual Report for FY 1976–76T*, Boulder, National Oceanic and Atmospheric Administration, 1977, p. 28).

† See the food and agriculture section of this chapter for a discussion of the increasing problems of insecticide resistance and immunities developing in strains of insect vectors.

inexpensive, common antibiotics are widely available without prescription even in remote rural LDCs. [102] And the appearance of resistant bacterial strains may not be due only to low probability mutations; it is now thought that epidemic diseases may suddenly acquire resistant traits through higher-probablility contacts with more common, harmless intestinal species that have already evolved their own resistance. [103]

If the reduced LDC mortality figures projected in the population chapter are to be achieved, progress must be made in controlling the fecally related diseases, the airborne diseases, and the increased mortality associated with these diseases as a result of nutritional deficiency. These diseases are largely of environmental origin and can be controlled only through improved environmental and sanitation conditions and through improved nutrition and education, all of which require capital investment, as well as through changes of habits and cultural traditions. As discussed above under urbanization in the LDCs, there is reason to question whether the needed improvements in sanitary and environmental conditions will occur. By the year 2000, sanitary conditions in some areas may even deteriorate. This situation, worsened by increasing scarcities of food and energy in poorer regions, could lead to an increase, rather than a decrease, in mortality rates among some populations. [104]

## Environment and Health in the Industrialized Nations

Two important developments in health conditions are occurring in the industrialized nations. First, life expectancies are continuing their trend of many years, increasing slowly. In the U.S., for example, the rate of increase of life expectancy averaged 0.53 years per year over the 1940–50 period but fell to 0.15 years per year for the 1950–60 decade and to 0.12 years per year for the 1960s. Over the first five years of the 1970s, the annual rate has increased to an average 0.32 years, bringing the U.S. life expectancy at birth to 72.5 years. [105]

The second development relates to causes of death. Although there is much dispute over particulars, medical experts generally agree that the causes of the diseases and accidents responsible for most fatalities and prolonged periods of ill health in affluent societies (heart disease, lung disease, cancer, stroke, highway accidents) are now related largely to life-styles and environmental circumstances. Frequently mentioned as con-

## TABLE 13–11

**Percentages of Deaths of Children Under the Age of Five Due to Fecally Related and Airborne Diseases or Malnutrition, Latin America, Selected Areas**

| | Fecally Related Disease | Airborne Disease | Nutritional Deficiency | Total |
|---|---|---|---|---|
| Chaco, Argentina (rural) | 40 | 36 | 2 | 79 |
| San Juan, Argentina (central urban) | 38 | 32 | 3 | 72 |
| San Juan, Argentina (suburban) | 34 | 38 | 8 | 80 |
| San Juan, Argentina (rural) | 35 | 42 | 8 | 84 |
| Chaco Resistencia, Bolivia (rural) | 52 | 27 | 6 | 84 |
| La Paz, Bolivia (urban) | 29 | 55 | 3 | 87 |
| Viacha, Bolivia (rural) | 25 | 65 | 0 | 91 |
| Recife, Brazil (urban) | 42 | 41 | 5 | 88 |
| Ribeirao Preto, Brazil (urban) | 49 | 36 | 2 | 87 |
| Ribeirao Preto, Brazil (rural) | 50 | 29 | 3 | 81 |
| Ribeirao, Preto Franca, Brazil (rural) | 55 | 20 | 7 | 82 |
| Sao Paulo, Brazil (urban) | 40 | 33 | 5 | 78 |
| Santiago, Chile (central urban) | 31 | 37 | 6 | 73 |
| Santiago, Chile (suburban) | 33 | 38 | 3 | 74 |
| Cali, Colombia (urban) | 44 | 25 | 15 | 84 |
| Cartagena, Colombia (urban) | 38 | 23 | 17 | 78 |
| Medellin, Colombia (urban) | 49 | 22 | 11 | 82 |
| San Salvador, El Salvador (urban) | 52 | 28 | 6 | 86 |
| San Salvador, El Salvador (rural) | 51 | 22 | 13 | 86 |
| Kingston, Jamaica (urban) | 37 | 21 | 5 | 63 |
| St. Andrew, Jamaica (rural) | 23 | 23 | 23 | 69 |
| Monterrey, Mexico (urban) | 43 | 35 | 4 | 83 |

*Source:* Ruth R. Puffer, and Carlos V. Serrano, *Inter-American Investigation of Mortality in Childhood, Provisional Report,* Washington: Pan American Health Organization, Sept. 1971. pp. 133–54.

tributing factors are limited exercise, cigarette smoking, alcohol consumption, exposure to toxic chemicals, chronic psychological stress, and diets high in fats, salt, and refined carbohydrates.[106] Changes in these contributing factors must occur if the increased life expectancy projected in the Global 2000 population projections is to be achieved in the industrialized countries. What are the prospects?

The prospects for change are mixed, at least in the U.S. The adverse effects of smoking have received much attention since the Surgeon General's report of a decade ago, but smoking habits have changed relatively little. Over the 11-year period from 1965 to 1976 smoking among males declined about 10 percentage points (from 52.4 to 41.9 percent of the male population) and about 2 percentage points for women (from 34.1 to 32.0 percent of the female population).[107] Efforts are being made to control toxic substances, but there will be long lags in identifying and removing toxic substances from the environment.[108] Cancer is the only major cause of death that has continued to rise from 1970 to 1976, and environmental (i.e., exogenous nongenetic) factors contribute 80–90 percent of the present cancer cases.[109] Little change seems in prospect for the life-styles and institutional demands that are the root cause of much stress. However, many persons are making efforts to improve their physical fitness. Some persons are changing their dietary habits, but the Global 2000 food projections (see Table 13–17) show the industrialized nations increasing their already high per capita food consumption still further to 130–35 percent of the standards recommended by the Food and Agriculture Organization. Efforts to reduce energy consumption have increased life expectancies in at least one way: Accidental deaths associated with motor vehicle accidents have declined by 25 percent between 1972 and 1975, due primarily to reduced speeds.[110] However, due to lax enforcement of the new speed limits, speed and accidents are both increasing again.

## Conclusions

The discussion in this and other sections of this chapter make clear that the projected levels of human population will exert significant pressures on the environment, both directly and indirectly. Environmental impacts will occur in both traditional and industrial cultures.

A number of traditional cultures have existed for centuries in relative equilibrium with their environments. Today, population growth, changing technologies, and altered life-styles have rendered the balancing mechanisms ineffective. Highly evolved social-ecological systems are breaking down with disastrous results for both humans and their life-supporting environment.

The threat to most ecosystems in less developed regions is illustrated in the last four maps in the colored map section at the end of this volume. These maps show the extensive overlap between the areas of high population density, limited agricultural potential, and intense land use. In parts of Asia, Africa, and Latin America, the productivity of the life-supporting ecosystems can be expected to decline as a result of another two decades of intensifying pressure.

The Global 2000 population projections show no significant slowing in growth through the year 2000, and increases can be anticipated well into the 21st century. A large portion of the 6.4 billion persons projected for 2000 will be desperately poor. Biological resources and the environment generally as well as economies will be stressed just to meet basic human needs. Income disparities and limited educational opportunities will compound the difficulties.

Population-related pressures on the environment are also expected to increase in the industrialized countries. Although population growth in these countries is much less than in the LDCs, the resource requirements and waste production of an "industrial person" is large. Trade and commerce spread the environmental impacts of increased industrial populations over very wide areas.

Environmental factors will complicate preventive health measures in both less developed and industrialized countries. Poor sanitary conditions will hamper efforts to eradicate the diseases that have the largest influence on mortality rates in the LDCs. In the industrial nations, environmental factors and life-styles may lead to the continued prevalence of premature deaths.[111] Curative health measures will be complicated in both developing and developed countries as a result of increased pathogen resistance to many common and inexpensive drugs.

## THE GNP PROJECTIONS AND THE ENVIRONMENT

### The Projections

The medium-growth* Gross National Product (GNP) projections, developed from World Bank, CIA, and nongovernmental data, are summarized in Table 13–12. GNP is projected to grow exponentially at 3.6 percent per year, increasing 145 percent by 2000. The industrialized countries' GNP grows more slowly than the world average, increasing by 129 percent. The less developed countries more than triple their GNP, but the magnitude of the LDC increase ($2.4 trillion) is much less than the magnitude of the increase in the industrialized countries ($6.3 trillion). Nonetheless, the LDC share of the world's total GNP is projected to rise from 18 to 24 percent.

On the average these trends, when combined with the trends inherent in the population projections, imply that real per capita incomes increase by about a third—more in countries with rapid economic and slow population growth, less in countries with slow economic growth and rapid population growth. In some cases (Pakistan, India, Bangladesh), little or no growth in real per capita income is projected. The GNP projections do not address the distribution of GNP (or income) among socioeconomic classes within countries and give no indication of any changes that might occur in the composition of GNP.

---

* The GNP projections in Chapter 3 are based on rates for low, medium, and high growth. Only the medium-growth case is considered here.

### Introduction

Although economic activity certainly has many environmental effects, GNP estimates are not an adequate basis from which to deduce detailed environmental impacts. At best, GNP figures provide an indication of the volume of economic activity, but with virtually no hint of the content. The content of GNP is particularly important in connection with the environment; as the U.S. Commission on Population Growth and the American Future observed, "An irony of [present] economic measurement is that the value of goods and services represented by the GNP includes the cost of producing the pollutants as well as expenditures for cleaning up afterward."[112] Without knowledge of the specific goods and bads and the services and disservices to be produced, only a very general discussion of the environmental implications of GNP projections is possible.

Nonetheless, GNP projections do provide some clue to future environmental problems, particularly with respect to pollution and waste generation and resource consumption. By the year 2000, even the slowest growing economy is projected to have nearly doubled its GNP, while more vigorous economies will have more than tripled theirs. Barring major changes in the kinds of goods (and bads) and services (and disservices) produced—and barring major changes in the technologies employed and in the share of GNP devoted to environmental protection—certain rough proportional increases in waste and pollution generation and in resource consumption can be anticipated.*

In the paragraphs that follow, the implications of GNP growth for pollution and waste generation and for resource consumption are considered very briefly. (The specific implications of the projected resource developments are discussed in later sections of this chapter.) Then, toxic substances—a topic that relates more to GNP growth than any of the other projections—are discussed briefly.

## Pollution and Waste Generation

Unless there are very significant structural changes in the world's economies, increased eco-

* This observation depends to a degree on where sectorally the GNP growth occurs. In industrialized countries, economic growth has become increasingly concentrated in the relatively clean service sector, rather than in the more polluting extractive and manufacturing sectors. GNP growth in the LDCs, which will occur largely in primary and secondary sectors, will probably have relatively larger impacts on the environment over the next two decades. Furthermore, as discussed in Chapter 14, the GNP model assumes that the proportion of GNP allocated to environmental pollution will not increase markedly in the LDCs, and the energy model assumes that the real cost of environmental protection will not significantly increase the cost of building or operating future energy facilities in the industrialized countries.

### TABLE 13–12

**GNP Trends, 1975–2000, Medium-Growth Rate**

*(In trillions [$10^{12}$] of constant 1975 U.S. dollars)*

|  | 1975 | | 2000 | | Increase | |
|---|---|---|---|---|---|---|
|  | GNP | Share | GNP | Share | Average | Total |
|  |  | *percent* |  | *percent* | *percent* | |
| Industrialized countries | 4.9 | 82 | 11.2 | 76 | 3.4 | 129 |
| Less developed countries | 1.1 | 18 | 3.5 | 24 | 4.7 | 218 |
| World | 6.0 | 100 | 14.7 | 100 | 3.6 | 145 |

*Source:* Chapter 2, this volume.

nomic activity can be expected to produce larger quantities of waste materials and more residual wastes. Whether these residual wastes actually enter the environment as pollutants depends on policies for, and expenditures on, environmental protection. The projected economic growth will have one of two effects (or a combination of both): increased release of wastes and pollutants into the environment or increased costs of keeping the waste and pollution out of the environment.

Increased environmental pollution can occur in at least two ways: first, as a result of relaxed or unmet ambient (or source-emission) standards; second, as a consequence of increased numbers of emission sources, all of which meet unchanged source-emission standards. As the number of sources (or the volumes discharged from existing sources) increases, source-emission standards (per unit of effluent discharged) must be tightened just to maintain present environmental conditions.

Tightening standards to compensate for increased economic activity may become quite expensive. For example, if the number of sources meeting a 94 percent emission standard doubles, the standard must be tightened to 97 percent, just to break even. If the discharges triple, increased pollution occurs unless the standards are tightened to 98 percent. As the standard approaches 100 percent, the costs of meeting the standard generally increase very rapidly. Thus, the projected doubling or tripling of economic activity can be expected to lead to either an increasing proportion of GNP being devoted to pollution control, to more pollution, or to both—unless there are innovations in production processes, by which "wastes" are recycled and used (as in the pulp and paper industry, which now uses "waste" as an energy source).

## Resource Consumption

The projected increases in GNP imply increased demand for both renewable and nonrenewable resources. Meeting these resource demands will have many environmental implications.

The Global 2000 Study's nonrenewable resource projections (i.e., the energy and minerals projections of Chapters 10–12) are based on various assumed linkages to GNP. For example, as discussed in Chapter 14, the LDC minerals projections assume that LDC economies will become more mineral-intensive as growth continues; the LDC energy projections suggest that LDC economies will not increase in energy intensiveness as industrialization proceeds. In the industrialized economies, the models assume that GNP growth will lead to little change in energy intensiveness and to decreasing minerals intensiveness. Whatever the actual relationship is between GNP and nonrenewable resources, increased environmental impacts can be anticipated in the mining, refining, and energy sectors as a result of increased economic activity. The environmental impacts of the projected increase in demand for nonrenewable resources are considered in other sections of this chapter.

Renewable resources are also of critical importance to the health of the world's economies. As Lester R. Brown, President of Worldwatch Institute, has observed:

Four biological systems—fisheries, forests, grasslands, and croplands—form the foundation of the global economic system. In addition to supplying all our food, these four systems provide virtually all the raw materials for industry except minerals and petroleum-derived synthetics. The condition of the economy and of these biological systems cannot be separated. As the global economy expands . . . pressures on earth's biological systems are mounting. In large areas of the world, human claims on these systems are reaching an unsustainable level, a point where their productivity is being impaired. When this happens, fisheries collapse, forests disappear, grasslands are converted into barren wastelands, and croplands deteriorate.[113]

The environmental impacts of projected increases in demand for renewable resources are considered in other sections of this chapter.

## The Use of Chemicals in the Development of Societies*

Reports can be found documenting the use of chemicals dating back to antiquity. The utilization of chemicals to enhance living conditions can be traced to the simple use of metals in the development of glazing materials for ceramic utensils. Other uses of metals are found, for example, in the development of bronze, initially for weaponry, then for the creative arts. Accounts are also found of the use of metals in the development of medical practice, such as the use of mercury for medicinal purposes by the Romans. The reliance by civilizations on chemicals in order to improve their living conditions has had a long history in Western civilization.

By the same token, however, the use of chemicals in an adverse sense also has had a long history, beginning with the use of extracts from the fruit of the hemlock by the Greeks. This was followed by the Romans, who used other forms of poisons, and later still by those who participated in the Italian court intrigues of the Renaissance era. This, of course, continued into the end of the 19th century with the development of trinitrotoluene (TNT) and the use of chemicals in modern warfare in World War I.

It was not until the end of the 19th century that the use of chemicals in society began to become widespread. It was at this point that reliance on natural sources for chemicals became so strong that the sources of supplies began to lag significantly behind the demands society placed upon them. This led to the development of experimental chemistry in Europe for the express purposes of synthesizing new chemicals to replace those originally obtained from natural sources. This development coincided with the discovery that crude oil, which was initially used as a replacement for whale oil, could also be used as a new source of supply for chemicals. A new scientific discipline emerged, to expand the utility of crude oil: organic chemistry.

With the advent of organic chemistry, the synthesis of every imaginable organic compound originating from crude oil feedstock began. In part, this activity was the domain of the scientist in order to further understand the mechanisms of organic chemical reaction rates. Uses for the increasing number of organic compounds synthesized by the organic chemists was left to others,

---

* This section was added at the suggestion of the U.S. Department of State, while Chapter 13 was in press. It is the work of Mr. Jack Blanchard in the Office of the Assistant Secretary for Oceans and International Environmental and Scientific Affairs, Department of State. Since toxic chemicals are a major source of pollutants in the coastal waters of the world's oceans, they are also discussed below, in the section on the marine environment.

however, to develop. An example of such a process was DDT. It was considered a novel compound by organic chemists in the early 1940s. It was not until the latter stages of World War II, however, that it was found to have pesticide activity and was used extensively as a disinfectant. Subsequently, its use as an overall general pesticide expanded enourmously after the war. It was used widely and it was inexpensive. Only recently have we realized its adverse effects: pesticide resistance, thinning of eggshells, and its appearance in foodstuffs worldwide. Indeed, the field of organic chemistry spawned an impressive expansion of new pharmaceuticals which led to striking advancements in medical health practices. In time, the advent of novel synthetic organic chemicals quickly found commercial uses, such as plastics and even artificial diamonds. Just before the World War II, U.S. production of synthetic organic materials was less than 1 billion pounds per year. By 1978, U.S. production had risen to approximately 172 billion pounds annually.[114]

The use of chemicals in the 20th century has become so widespread that it can be said that their presence is ubiquitous. Along with this expanded reliance of chemicals, however, has been an increasing awareness in recent years of the unintended adverse impact to the environment and public health due to the widespread use of chemicals. Society has come to rely extensively on chemicals and is now beginning to realize the problems that have been created with the manufacture, use, transportation, and disposal of chemicals. For the advantages that chemicals have given societies, which have been overwhelming, there have also been disadvantages which have proven striking. We are now beginning to realize how extensive these disadvantages are, and in industrialized societies remedial measures are being developed to respond to the more serious problems chemicals pose to the environment and public health.

At the Governing Council meeting of the United Nations Environment Programme in 1978, it was estimated that 4 million identifiable chemicals are in common use, with the worldwide value of chemical sales in excess of $300 million annually and with over 30,000 chemicals in commercial use. There are some 1,000 new chemicals brought on to the market annually.[115] With regard to international trade in chemicals among OECD-member countries, this amounted to approximately $50 billion in 1976.[116]

Along with this expanded use of chemicals, however, has been an increasing awareness in recent years of the unintended adverse impact to the environment and public health following long-term low level exposures to chemicals. Society has come to rely extensively on chemicals in order to improve its living conditions. This heavy reliance on chemicals, however, has begun to elicit concerns about the benefits when evaluated with the unintended risks associated with their use. These risks have been associated with every facet in the utilization of chemicals, from their manufacture and use to their transportation and disposal.

Examples of such risks to chemicals abound, not only in the technical press, but the lay press as well. There can be no dispute that radium, originally used on watch faces for luminescent figures, causes cancer. Similarly that dibromochloropropane (DBCP) developed as a herbicide causes sterility in males following occupational exposures.[117] Also that vinyl chloride monomer, the precursor to polyvinyl chloride, causes angiosarcoma of the liver.[118] Transportation of bulk chemicals has periodically resulted in major accidents requiring the evacuation of whole communities in order to protect them from clouds of poisonous gas, explosives, or other hazards.[119] Similarly, disposal of chemicals until recently has never been regulated. Environmental contamination of the Hudson and James Rivers by PCBs[120] and Kepone,[121] respectively, of the Love canal in New York State,[122] and of Hardeman County, Tennessee,[123] and Seveso, Italy, are examples of large-scale industrial disposals of chemicals, which in time have proven injurious to communities.

Where does the control of chemicals begin in order to provide society with some protection? How will the uses of chemicals be tempered in order to provide a rational basis for their continued use? The projected outcome may not be difficult to develop if current practices are taken into consideration. The major question remains as to whether controls on chemicals will be adequate to allow for their continued use by society while maintaining an acceptable measure of protection from exposures associated with their manufacture, use, transportation, and disposal.

Chemicals will continue to play an integral role in the development of societies of both industrialized nations and less developed countries. The roles played by these societies with regard to the control of toxic substances may not be changed materially by the year 2000.

Industrialized countries have begun to institute regulatory controls on chemicals. As national programs have been developed in the last few years, continued examples of adverse environmental and public health damage coupled with society's increasing concerns, have led to this development. As governments move to implement their respective national programs, two major goals are being addressed: (1) protection of public health and environment and (2) recognition that economic impacts associated with these controls should not impede unduly (or create unnecessary economic barriers to) technological innovation. These issues have international ramifications. Considerable movement has been made in attempting to reach consensus among industrialized countries regarding the control of chemicals. It seems prudent to project that some form of international cooperation will take place in the future, hopefully well before the year 2000.

A different set of problems exist, however, for less developed countries. In these instances, examples already exist with regard to governments who perceive themselves at some disadvantage relative to industrialized countries in protecting themselves from adverse exposures to chemicals. Developing countries, and in some cases less developed countries, have indicated that insufficient data are available to them in order to develop adequate control programs. Few developing countries have the capacity to cope with the sophisticated analyses required to assess the risks of imported or locally manufactured chemicals, and multinational chemical manufacturers are locating plants in the LDCs to avoid the regulations that already exist in many industrialized nations. In view of these problems, the LDCs have asked the United Nations Environment Programme (UNEP) for assistance in developing and strengthening their capabilities for evaluating chemicals, food, drugs, and cosmetics. [124]

The projections for less developed countries for the year 2000 in dealing with chemicals are less amenable to generalizations. It can be said that they will, of course, rely on UNEP as well as other multilateral organizations to provide the basic technical skills for controlling the manufacture, use, transportation, and disposal of chemicals. Some countries may incorporate directly part or all of the control programs implemented by industrialized countries. As such the work of developed countries in harmonizing regulatory controls in chemicals becomes quite important to both the chemical-exporting countries and the chemical-importing countries.

The level of control of chemicals by the year 2000 may be somewhat anticipated on the basis of developments already under way. Within industrialized societies, the environmental movement has established a substantial body of legislative mandates designed to protect public health and the environment from pollutants from industrial sources. This activity has been concerned with toxic chemicals. Many of these programs have been adopted by the World Bank in establishing environmental guidelines for developing countries desirous of undertaking rapid growth in their economies. [125] While environmental controls are being imposed in industrial countries, less developed countries will be able to benefit from these efforts.

With regard to direct controls in chemicals themselves, the picture is a bit less clear. Industrialized countries have identified the characteristics of those chemicals which could be regarded as having unacceptable effects on humans and their environment. These generally are persistence, wide distribution, and bioaccumulation leading to biological effects, and they form the basis of their respective chemical control programs. [126] Since pollution readily crosses political boundaries, there is a definite correlation that can be expected to occur between control programs in industrialized and those in less developed countries, the only mitigating aspects being economics, technical expertise, and societal factors. In time, one would expect that regulatory controls of toxic substances, once initiated by industrialized countries, will also be adopted by nonindustrialized countries.

As less developed countries improve their economies, a transfer of information on the control of chemicals will be expected to occur. In time, the differences will be one of a degree of enforcement from country to country. Society cannot live without chemicals. It is clear, on the other hand, that society cannot live without controls on chemicals. Somewhere in between will be found the position of the broad range of societies, their disparities measured by their willingness to coexist with chemicals in their environment.

## Conclusions

The Global 2000 Study projects the GNP of the world to increase from $6 trillion in 1975 to $14.7 trillion in 2000. Because GNP figures include the cost of producing pollution as well as cleaning up afterward, they are an inadequate basis for anticipating environmental impacts. However, the GNP projections imply increasing demand for both renewable and nonrenewable resources. Short of major changes in the structure of the world's economies, meeting the projected resource demands will lead to increases in environmental pollution or increases in the proportion of

GNP devoted to environmental protection, or both. The environmental implications of meeting the projected demands are analyzed in other sections of this chapter.

## CLIMATE CHANGES AND THE ENVIRONMENT

### The Projections

Because of the difficulty of climatological modeling, it is not possible currently to produce generally agreed-upon quantitative climate projections. Instead, the CIA developed for the Global 2000 Study three climatological scenarios,* each of approximately equal probability, and described the principal characteristics and probable broad-scale effects of each. The three scenarios, discussed in detail in Chapter 4, are, in brief:

CASE I: NO CHANGE. Climate conditions approximate those of the 1941–70 period.

CASE II: WARMING. A general warming, mainly in the polar and higher middle latitudes, is associated with smaller year to year variation in precipitation and with slight increases in global precipitation but, at the same time, with a greater likelihood of continental drought in the U.S.

CASE III: COOLING. Cooling in the higher and middle latitudes is associated with a decrease in precipitation amounts and an increase in month to month and year to year variation in precipitation, a general equatorward shift of storm tracks, more frequent failures of the monsoon over India, and recurrent severe droughts in the Sahel (as during the 1972–74 period).

Aspects of the energy, forestry, food, and GNP projections, which also have the potential to influence (and be influenced by) climate, are listed here in summary form.

*The Energy Projecions* through 1990 show annual increases in the demand for oil of 3.0 percent; oil will supply 47 percent of the 1990 energy demand. (See Chapters 10 and 20 for an explanation of the 1990 limit to the energy projections.) It is projected that coal will furnish one-fifth of the total energy for 1990. Nuclear and hydroelectricity production will treble and will furnish 16 percent of the 1990 energy demand. Natural gas usage will have increased 43 percent by 1990 to satisfy 17 percent of the demand.

*The Forestry Projections* anticipate deforestation at rates that will reduce total forested areas on the earth by 16–20 percent by 2000.

*The Food and Agriculture Projections* foresee a 90–100 percent increase in total world production. This increase is based on a small (5 percent) increase in arable land and a 70–100 percent increase in productivity of land under cultivation. Much of the increased productivity is a result of more than a doubling of fertilizer† use per hectare for the world as a whole, and a quadrupling of fertilizer use per hectare in the LDCs.

*The Gross National Product Projections* show trends toward increases in real per capita incomes by about one-third, with greater increases in countries with rapid economic growth but slow population growth, and smaller increases in countries with slow economic—but rapid population—growth.

---

* The three climatological scenarios developed by the CIA were based in part on five scenarios developed jointly by the National Oceanic and Atmospheric Administration, the Department of Agriculture, the National Defense University and the Central Intelligence Agency.
† In the USDA projections, the term "fertilizer" is used to denote fertilizers and other yield-enhancing inputs, including pesticides and herbicides.

## Introduction

Present comprehension of long-range climatic phenomena is so limited that scientists have no generally accepted bases for predicting with assurance the magnitudes—or even the directions—of possible changes in the earth's climate over the next several decades. Yet it is known that the climate of the 1950s and 1960s was exceptionally favorable and that, on the basis of past experience, the earth can expect both more variable and less favorable climate in the future. Some human activities, especially those resulting in releases of carbon dioxide into the atmosphere, are known to have the potential to affect the world's climate. Whether future climate changes will be predominantly of natural or human origin is not known, and the pace at which they will occur and the severity of their consequences are unknown quantities. Many experts nevertheless feel that changes on a scale likely to affect the environment and the economy of large regions of the world are not only possible but probable in the next 25–50 years.

The Global 2000 Study group, faced with the need to estimate the effects of climate change on the environment over the next quarter century, decided to use the recent survey of expert opinion[127] conducted by the National Defense University as a basis for the three scenarios described briefly above. Environmental implications of each of the Global 2000 Study climate scenarios will be examined here,*together with aspects of some of the other projections that have implications for world climate.

## The Climate Scenarios

An analysis of the environmental impacts of the three Global 2000 climate scenarios must begin with a brief glance at the National Defense University (NDU) study on which they are based.[128]

The five climate scenarios of the NDU study were developed by a panel of experts in climatology. All had the same basic information; each had his own ideas and opinions as to the nature, dimensions, and consequences of the climate changes that could be expected over the next 25 years. Both human-caused (anthropogenic) and natural influences were considered. Increased fossil fuel combustion and clearing of forests for food production are examples of possible anthropo-

genic influences. Natural influences are exemplified by changes in solar radiation, volcanic activity, and shifting ocean currents, all of which can have significant effects on climate.

All members of the panel had available detailed evidence of climate variation, both during human history and during the geological history of the planet, indicating that significant natural variations could occur between the present and the year 2000.

The benign climate of the 1950s and the 1960s was by no means typical of the integlacial (or postglacial) period the earth has been experiencing for approximately the last 10,000 years.[129] This 20-year period was most favorable for agriculture and food production over much of the cultivated areas of the industrialized high-technology nations; a climate a few degrees warmer or cooler could have been considerably less favorable.[130]

Consideration of current trends in temperatures and of the history of climate over the past 10,000 years led the NDU panel of experts to five alternative climate scenarios for the next 25 years; (1) Large Warming, (2) Moderate Warming, (3) No Change, (4) Moderate Cooling, and (5) Large Cooling. The three Global 2000 Study scenarios are related to these five as follows: Case I (*No Change*) is essentially identical to the NDU No Change scenario; Case II (*Warming*) falls between the NDU Moderate Warming and Large Warming scenarios; Case III (*Cooling*) falls between the NDU Moderate Cooling and Large Cooling scenarios.

The climatological considerations[131] behind the Global 2000 Study scenarios are, briefly:

*Case I: No Change* might occur if warming and cooling effects should happen to balance one another between now and 2000.

*Case II: Warming* might occur if the warming effect of atmospheric carbon dioxide were to predominate over all other effects.

*Case III: Cooling* might occur if the global cooling trend that began in the 1940s were to continue, possible as the result of an increase in volcanic activity (and related dust) or a (sunspot-cycle-related) decrease in the solar energy reaching the earth.

## Environmental Consequences of the Climate Scenarios

Details of the Global 2000 Study's Case I (No Change) scenario are given in Chapter 4 under the heading "Same as the Last 30 Years." The major premise is that the warming effects of increasing $CO_2$ in the atmosphere will compensate

---

* The probability of occurrence of the Case I scenario (No Change), is 0.30; of Case II (Warming), approximately 0.25; of Case III (Cooling), also 0.25. Estimated from the probability figures for the five National Defense University scenarios given in Tables 4–1A through 4–5A in Chapter 4.

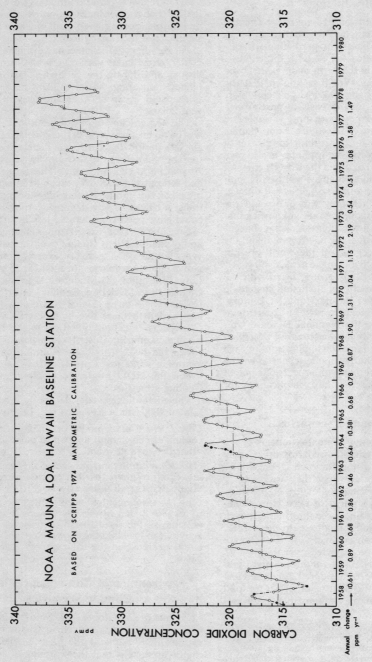

**Figure 13–2.** Trend since 1958 in the concentration of carbon dioxide in the atmosphere (parts per million by volume), as monitored at the National Oceanic and Atmospheric Administration's Mauna Loa Observatory, Hawaii, 19.5° N latitude, 3,401 meters altitude. (*L. Machta, NOAA Air Resources Laboratories, 1979*)

for the cooling effects of a natural cycle of falling temperatures. The environmental consequences of this scenario on changes in energy usage, agriculture and food production, and forestation are minimal. Furthermore, since none of the government's present long-term global models can utilize climate inputs, *all of the Global 2000 Study environmental impact projections are based on the assumption that the Case I (No Change) scenario will actually occur.* Thus, the environmental impacts of the Case I scenario are incorporated in those projections.

The Case II (Warming) scenario has, of course, somewhat different environmental implications. This scenario leads to an increase of 1° C in global temperatures, with most of the warming in the polar regions and the higher middle latitudes. Precipitation increases are predicted for the higher middle latitudes with little change elsewhere. Fewer extremely cold winters might be expected, but the chance that the interior of the U.S. would experience hot summers and widespread drought conditions resembling those of the mid-1930s is likely to increase. The warming would be substantially beneficial to Canadian and Soviet wheat production; it would be moderately detrimental to wheat in Argentina, Australia, and India and marginally unfavorable to corn (maize) in Argentina and the U.S.[132] The effects on energy usage, while not calculated, are probably negligible. Deforestation would probably increase in the higher middle latitudes as more of the land became arable. Pressures on forests elsewhere would depend on population growth and concomitant needs for food, fuelwood, building materials, and other forest products.

The Case III (Cooling) scenario leads to a global temperature decrease of 0.5° C, with 1° C cooling in the higher and middle latitudes and smaller changes near the equator. Precipitation amounts decrease, and month to month and year to year variability increases. Storm tracks shift equatorward, bringing precipitation to the higher latitudes of deserts, but causing equatorward expansion of these deserts. Monsoon failures would become more frequent and severe in India, and the Sahel would experience more frequent severe droughts. Wheat yields in Canada and the Soviet Union would be reduced, but other key crops would not be severely affected.[133] The demand for energy would increase, particularly in the middle and higher latitudes, where increasing amounts of energy would be needed for heating. Also, greater variability of climate might call for higher levels of heating-fuel reserves. Additional demands for energy might also result from attempts to relieve drought effects in densely populated areas by producing water in massive desalinization programs. Forested areas at higher latitudes of the Northern hemisphere would become less accessible, and grow more slowly.

## Impact of the Other Projections On Climate

Climatologists have identified two general types of factors that influence climate: human activity (anthropogenic influences) and natural factors (geological, oceanic, and ice feedback effects and astronomical effects). The following paragraphs focus primarily on the anthropogenic influences implied by the other Global 2000 Study projections, especially the GNP, food and agriculture, forestry, and energy projections. These projections are considered in terms of their potential effects on the factors thought most likely to alter the world's climate.

Most experts agree that the most potentially harmful changes in climate on a global scale would result from increases of atmospheric carbon dioxide and other "greenhouse gases" (such as fluorocarbons and nitrous oxide), from changes in the quantity and character of particulate matter in the atmosphere, or from a partial destruction of the ozone layer. Changes in the earth's surface albedo (a measure of reflectivity), and increases in residual heat released as a consequence of energy use are also known to be factors in local, regional, or—in extreme cases—global changes in climate.

### Carbon Dioxide

Carbon dioxide ($CO_2$) is a colorless, tasteless, nontoxic gas. It is exhaled by all animals as a product of metabolism and is absorbed by plants as part of the process of photosynthesis. $CO_2$ is a basic product of the combustion of all hydrocarbons, including fossil fuels and wood. It is not subject to economically practical control by any pollution-control technology. The amounts produced annually are so large that the only possible means of disposal is discharge to the atmosphere.

The carbon dioxide content of the atmosphere has been increasing since routine observations began. Preindustrial (ca. 1860–90) atmospheric $CO_2$ content is estimated by most experts at approximately 290 ppm (parts per million by volume)[134]; measurements show the 1976 content to be 332 ppm.[135] The upward trend is easily seen in Figure 13–2, which shows rather large seasonal variations superimposed on the long-term trend. The average concentration increased by about 5 percent in the 20-year period 1958–78.

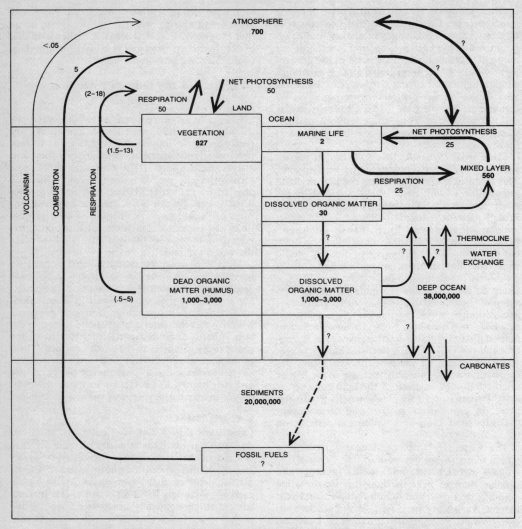

**Figure 13–3.**   Global pools and flows of carbon. Pools are expressed in billions of metric tons of carbon, flows in billions of metric tons of carbon per year. (*From "The Carbon Dioxide Question," by George M. Woodwell, copyright 1978 by Scientific American, Inc., all rights reserved*)

The increasing atmospheric concentration of $CO_2$ is of concern because of the so-called greenhouse effect. In a greenhouse (or solar collector), shortwave solar radiation (light) from the sun passes through the glass and is re-radiated as infrared longwave, heat radiation from the soil and other surfaces inside the greenhouse. The heat energy radiated upward is trapped inside of the greenhouse by the glass, which cannot transmit longwave radiation to the colder outside environ-ment. The $CO_2$ in the atmosphere acts in much the same way as glass, permitting solar radiation to pass through to the earth's surface but intercepting some of the heat radiated upward from the surface toward space and reradiating it back toward the surface. With steadily increasing atmospheric $CO_2$, the balance between incoming and outgoing radiation can be maintained only if surface and lower-atmospheric temperatures increase.

There is still some uncertainty on exactly where all of the additional $CO_2$ is coming from, where it goes, and whether the rate of increase will remain constant or change. The general picture, however, is reasonably well established, at least out to the year 2000.[136] Since the total amount of carbon in the earth-atmosphere system is constant, the carbon being added to the atmosphere pool must come from a nonatmospheric carbon pool somewhere within the system. Figure 13–3 shows the various pools of carbon in the earth-atmosphere system and the flows of carbon between pools. Most experts consider that carbon from the combustion of fossil fuels is the main cause of increasing $CO_2$ in the atmosphere, but recently others have suggested that deforestation (and the associated oxidation of the fixed carbon in plants and humus) may contribute approximately as much to the increase of atmospheric $CO_2$ as the combustion of fossil fuels.[137]

Global 2000 Study projections are not sufficiently precise to permit accurate calculations of how much $CO_2$ will accumulate in the atmosphere in the coming decades. However, significant increases in atmospheric $CO_2$ levels can be anticipated on the basis of the forestry and energy projections: Deforestation and fossil fuel combustion are both projected to increase significantly. On the basis of the Study's projections of fossil fuel combustion alone, the Brookhaven National Laboratory estimates that annual emissions of $CO_2$ will increase by 35–90 percent by the year 1990.*

Not all the $CO_2$ released into the atmosphere by these and other processes accumulates in the atmosphere. Past records and computations show that atmospheric carbon dioxide has been increasing by only about 46 percent of the $CO_2$ released into the atmosphere annually.[138] An amount equivalent to the remaining 54 percent is removed by plants through the process of photosynthesis and by the surface waters of the ocean, which take up the $CO_2$ in solution.[139] The amount removed from the atmosphere by these processes is dependent on the atmospheric concentration of $CO_2$. From biology and chemistry it is known that, in general, the greater the concentration of $CO_2$ in the atmosphere, the more is removed by vegetation and the oceans. However, the increasing concentration of $CO_2$ in the oceans (which may reduce the ability of ocean surfaces to dissolve $CO_2$) and the projected deforestation could conceivably reduce the rate of absorption and cause

an acceleration in the current annual rate of increase in atmospheric $CO_2$. No one knows for sure how these and other[140] circumstances will combine in the years ahead, but after a careful study of the matter, the National Academy of Sciences anticipates that, if present trends continue, a four- to eightfold increase of atmospheric $CO_2$ concentration is entirely possible by the latter part of the 22nd Century.[141] A four- to eightfold increase in atmospheric $CO_2$ concentration would have exceedingly serious consequences. Even a doubling would have very serious consequences, and several scientists feel that, if present trends continue, a doubling is likely to occur during the first half of the 21st Century.

The major contribution to an increased concentration of atmospheric $CO_2$ is the combustion of fossil fuels. Over the past 30 years fossil fuel combustion has increased at about 4.3 percent per year. About half of the $CO_2$ released by fossil fuel combustion remains in the atmosphere while the other half is taken up by plants and ocean waters, or is otherwise removed from the atmosphere. If these trends continue, the atmospheric content of the atmosphere could reach twice that of preindustrial times by 2025–2050.[142] The rates of increase are dependent on energy strategies yet to be chosen, but an illustrative range of cases is shown in Figure 13–4. The rapid increases shown in the figure are due in part to an assumed continuation in the growth of fossil fuel combustion and in part to a shift toward coal and synthetic fuels produced from coal, both of which produce somewhat more $CO_2$ per unit of heat produced than do oil and gas.

The increased $CO_2$ concentrations implied by a continuation of present trends have momentous implications. The Geophysics Study Committee of the National Academy of Sciences has studied the prospects with one of the most complete climate models yet developed for examining such problems. The Committee has observed:

For even a doubling of carbon dioxide in the atmosphere, the model predicts about a 2° –3° C rise in the average temperature of the lower atmosphere at middle latitudes and a 7 percent increase in [global] average precipitation. The temperature rise is greater by a factor of 3 or 4 in polar regions. For each further doubling of carbon dioxide, an additional 2° –3° C increase in air temperature is inferred. *The increase in carbon dioxide anticipated for A.D. 2150 to A.D. 2200 might lead to an increase in global mean air temperature of more than 6° C*—comparable with the difference in temperature between the present and the warm Mesozoic climate of 70 million to 100 million years ago. [Emphasis in the original.][143]

---

* See the Energy System Network Simulator (ESNS) estimates in Chapter 10.

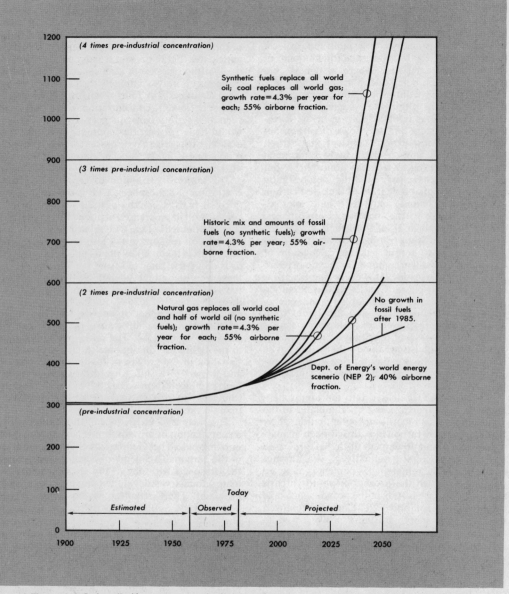

**Figure 13-4.** Carbon dioxide concentrations implied by various energy scenerios. Synthetic fuels derived from coal are assumed to release 3.4 x 10$^{15}$ grams of carbon in $CO_2$ per 100 quads of energy. Airborne fraction is the percent of emitted $CO_2$ that remains in the atmosphere. *(U.S. Department of Energy)*

## TABLE 13–13

### Global Summary of Sources and Annual Emissions of Atmospheric Particulate Matter

| | Natural Sources | Anthropogenic Sources |
|---|---|---|
| | *Millions of metric tons per year* | |
| Primary particle production | | |
| Fly ash from coal | – | 36 |
| Iron and steel industry emissions | – | 9 |
| Nonfossil fuels (wood, mill wastes) | – | 8 |
| Petroleum combustion | – | 10–90 |
| Incineration | – | 4 |
| Agricultural emission | – | 10 |
| Cement manufacture | – | 7 |
| Miscellaneous | – | 16 |
| Sea salt | 1,000 | – |
| Soil dust | 428–1,100 | ? |
| Volcanic particles | 4 | – |
| Forest fires | 3–150 | ? |
| Subtotal | 1,500–2,300ª | 100–180 |
| Gas-to-particle conversion | | |
| Sulfate from H₂S | 130–200 | – |
| Sulfate from SO₂ | | 130–200 |
| Nitrate from NOₓ | 60–430 | 30–35 |
| Ammonium from NH₃ | 80–270 | – |
| Organic aerosol from terpenes, hydrocarbons, etc. | 75–200 | 15–90 |
| Subtotal | 350–1,100ª | 175–325 |
| Total | 2,000–3,400ª | 275–500ª |

Source: Adapted from George D. Robinson, "Effluents of Energy Production: Particulates," in Geophysics Study Committee, *Energy and Climate,* Washington: National Academy of Sciences, 1977, p. 62.

ª Subtotals and totals do not sum exactly due to rounding.

## Particulates

At any given time the earth's atmosphere, at various levels above the ground, carries billions of tons of many different kinds of particles in various concentrations. These particulate accumulations are of both natural and anthropogenic origin.[144]

Table 13–13 lists the kinds, amounts, and sources of particulate matter in the atmosphere. The figures in this table are estimates only; for the most part they were extrapolated from data that are limited both in accuracy and length of record, and assumptions used in the extrapolations were sometimes arbitrary in nature.

The effects of atmospheric particulates on climate are varied. Their size, shape, color, electromagnetic properties, and distribution in the atmosphere determine how they affect the balance of solar and terrestrial radiation, the formation of clouds and rainfall, the surface temperature of the earth, and the quality of air for both plant and animal life.[145]

Naturally produced particulates tend to have more widespread and more chronic effects than those produced by human activity. For example, volcanic activity injects particulates high into the atmosphere, where they tend to reflect much more of the incoming solar radiation than do particles generated by human activity, which tend to remain at lower altitudes.[146] Volcanic particles are known to have been carried completely around the world and to have remained in the atmosphere from one to three years.* Clouds of dust particles from desert areas are sometimes carried thousands of miles by the prevailing winds.[147] These heavy clouds of dust may suppress cloud formation and the occurrence of precipitation, and could be implicated as a cause of drought.[148]

A general atmospheric effect of particulates involves the scattering and reflection of solar radiation back into space, thus reducing the amount of solar energy reaching the earth's surface.† With this effect in mind, it has occasionally been speculated that the cooling effect of anthropogenic particulates might just balance the warming effect of $CO_2$ accumulations. All the Global 2000 Study's projections of fossil fuel combustion, deforestation, agricultural production, and GNP generally imply increases in particulate emissions. The ESNS (Energy System Network Simulator) findings reported in Chapter 10 indicate that over the next two decades there will be significantly more emissions from energy conversion. If desertification, conversion of forests to agriculture, and general removal of vegetative cover continue, the amount of particulates contributed by windblown dust will increase—perhaps significantly.

Can the effects of increased particulates and $CO_2$ emissions be expected to be mutually balancing? The definitive study of this question has yet to be done, but on the basis of present information, the answer seems virtually certain to be no. Anthropogenic particulates do not have enough effect. The National Academy of Sciences reports:

---

* The National Defense University global climate scenario for Large Cooling is based in part on the cooling effect of particulates released by several major volcanic eruptions assumed to occur between 1980 and 2000 (see Chapter 4).

† The scattering and reflective properties of particulates vary considerably with the size and other properties of the particles. While the most common effect is as described above, some particles absorb enough solar radiation to produce a warming effect.

We can greatly increase emission of the kind of particle now produced by combustion in industrial communities without greatly changing the integrated radiative properties of our planet's disk as seen from space, unless, as may be the case, the increased particle loading changes the albedo of cloud. . . . [However,] there is little doubt that an increase in particles and sulfurous emissions to a magnitude that might have global climatic consequences would be intolerable from the point of view of community health.[149]

The Academy's passing reference to cloud albedo is significant. Particulates and aerosols are known to provide condensation nuclei important in the formation of clouds, but it is not known how the types of particles and aerosols that are likely to be added to the atmosphere in the years ahead would affect cloud formation. The effect is likely to be quite nonlinear, at least in some respects—i.e., relatively modest changes in particulate loadings may lead to significant changes in cloud cover. The linkage between condensation nuclei and cloud formation has been termed one of the most frequently overlooked, yet potentially most serious consequences of industrial pollution.[150] More research in this area will definitely be needed.

## Ozone

The atmosphere consists of two major layers; the troposphere extending upward to 8 to 16 kilometers and, above that, the stratosphere extending up to about 50 kilometers. Temperature decreases with increasing altitude throughout the troposphere, but a permanent temperature inversion exists at the tropopause, with temperatures *increasing* with altitude in the stratosphere. Temperatures rise by roughly 65° C over a height interval of 35 kilometers. The temperature rise is caused by the stratospheric layer of ozone ($O_3$).[151]

The ozone layer has two important and interrelated effects. First, it absorbs ultraviolet (UV) light in the UV–B band (optical wavelengths ranging from 290–320 nanometers) and so protects all life on the earth from the harmful effects of this radiation. Second, by absorbing the UV radiation, the ozone layer heats the stratosphere, causing the temperature inversion.[152] The effects of temperature inversions in limiting vertical mixing in the atmosphere are well known as a result of the pollution problems of inversion-prone areas such as Los Angeles. This same effect is at work in the stratosphere.* Various waste products produced

in, or migrating slowly into, the stratosphere may remain there for years until they are converted to other substances in the stratosphere or are transported downward into the troposphere, where they can be removed by various processes, including rain. The difficulty is that the effluents of several human activities are being trapped by the temperature inversion in the stratosphere, where they react in ways that deplete the ozone.[153] The human activities now thought to have varying degrees of adverse impact on the ozone layer include the release of chlorofluorocarbons from pressurized cans and other sources,[154] jet aircraft flight† in the stratosphere,[155] and the use of nitrogen fertilizers in agriculture.[156] The Global 2000 Study's projections all suggest that, unless regulatory policies change, these activities and emissions will continue to increase.

The effect of effluents (hydrocarbons and oxides of nitrogen) from jet flights in the stratosphere has been studied in reports by the U.S. Department of Transportation and the National Academy of Sciences.[157] The effect depends greatly on the number of flights and the performance of the jet engines. Concern has centered primarily on supersonic transport (SST), since these aircraft fly higher in the stratosphere than subsonic jets. The Department of Transportation report estimates the size and properties of future SST fleets that would be required to pay off development costs and return a fair profit. On the basis of these estimated fleet sizes, updated for improvements in technology, the National Academy of Sciences estimates that the impact of such a fleet might ultimately be a reduction of ozone by about 6.5 percent, with an uncertainty range of 1–10 percent, whereas current stratospheric flights reduce ozone by less than 0.1 percent.[158]

The effect of chlorofluorocarbon release has been studied by the National Academy of Sciences and others.[159] Using recently updated informa-

---

* While the wastes mix only very slowly vertically, they spread horizontally relatively rapidly, reaching all longitudes of the world in about a week and all latitudes within months. There is therefore little that any one nation or region can do to protect the ozone layer above it. Like carbon dioxide, the ozone problem is global in scope.

† Based on a 1975 report by the National Academy of Sciences. A very recent opinion by the Academy's Committee on Impacts of Stratospheric Change—as yet unpublished—suggests that jet aircraft may not be as much of a problem as suggested in previously published reports and may actually increase ozone (personal communication, Apr. 3, 1979, from J. Murray Mitchell, Jr., senior research climatologist, National Oceanic and Atmospheric Administration). Opinions, however, are still in a state of flux (see, for example, Anthony J. Broderick, "Stratospheric Effects from Aviation," *Proceedings*, 13th Propulsion Congress, Orlando, Fla., July 1977, and his "Stratospheric Effects from Aviation," *Journal of Aircraft*, Oct. 1978, pp. 643–55). The discussion presented here is based on National Academy of Sciences published reports.

tion,[160] the Academy reports that continued use of chlorofluorocarbons at the 1974 rate would reduce the global ozone by 14 percent over the next 50 years, with a 4–40 percent range of uncertainty. If the rate of production were to increase in proportion to the Global 2000 Study's GNP projections, the impact would be much larger.

The Academy has also studied the impact of anthropogenic nitrogen fixation on stratospheric ozone.[161] The linkage between fertilizer and ozone comes through the release of nitrous oxide ($N_2O$) during the denitrification of fixed nitrogen. The processes involved are much more complex than for either SST emissions or chlorofluorocarbon emissions, and yet they have been studied far less.[162] Assuming a 2–3 times increase in manufactured and legume-produced nitrogen fertilizer,* the Academy estimates that the global ozone would be reduced by 3.5 percent, with a range of uncertainty of 0.4–13 percent.[163]

It now appears, therefore, that definite and adverse effects on the ozone layer do exist in varying magnitudes as a result of (1) aircraft exhaust in the stratosphere, (2) chlorofluorocarbon and other halocarbon emissions, and (3) nitrogen fertilizer use. The Global 2000 Study's projections suggest that all three activities can be expected to increase by the year 2000. At present, there is tremendous uncertainty associated with the relative magnitude of the impacts of these three human activities, but all three now appear to be within an order of magnitude of each other,[164] with chlorofluorocarbons apparently having the greatest impact. While scientific assessment is still in flux and might shift significantly, the most recent work on the subject continues to support these general conclusions.[165]

How serious are depletions of global ozone? The consequences are related both to climate modification and to the amount of ultraviolet radiation reaching living organisms on the earth. The temperature inversion in the stratosphere is caused by the solar energy absorbed by ozone. A change in the ozone would lead to a significant change in the temperature distribution of the stratosphere, and probably to a small (but as yet uncertain) change in the pattern of temperature and rainfall over the earth's surface as well. These climatic changes are currently thought likely to be small compared to the potential changes that could occur as a result of carbon dioxide accu-

mulations in the atmosphere.[166] The effects of increased amounts of ultraviolet (UV) radiation may be more serious.

Ozone-induced changes in UV radiation would change one of the conditions that has almost certainly influenced the evolution of life on earth so far, and a significant UV increase can be expected to precipitate a disturbance in the existing balance of life virtually everywhere on the planet.[167] The National Academy of Sciences reports:

All unshielded cells are highly vulnerable to sunlight and may be killed by relatively short exposure to full sunlight. While such cells and organisms are generally protected to varying degrees in nature so that they experience sublethal doses of radiation, any increase in UV radiation could be considered to increase the pressure against survival. Because of the relationships between species in ecosystems, damage to one species might jeopardize an entire ecosystem. Hence, the potential effects of any elevation of the present UV–B levels of sunlight reaching the earth's surface should be taken most seriously.[168]

Cancer is the best-established direct threat to the human species. There is compelling evidence that UV radiation is a cause of skin cancer.[169] A 10 percent decrease in stratospheric ozone appears likely to lead to a 20–30 percent increase in this type of cancer,[170] but the increase may vary significantly from area to area (e.g., in the Andean or Tibetan highlands it could be higher than the world average).

The indirect threat of UV radiation to human welfare may be even larger than its direct effect.[171] It is known that, for small changes, UV radiation reaching the ground increases about 2 percent for each 1 percent decrease in stratospheric ozone.[172] It is also known that increased exposure to UV radiation adversely affects plants. Plants that have been exposed to supplemental UV in growth chambers or greenhouses have shown a 20–50 percent inhibition of growth, a 10–30 percent decline in chlorophyll content (and a similar decline in capacity for photosynthesis), and up to a 20-fold increase in the frequency of harmful mutations.[173] Seedlings are even more sensitive to UV radiation than mature plants, and single-celled algae are extremely sensitive. Algae can withstand only a few hours' exposure to even natural sunlight, and enhanced UV is expected to cut the survivable exposure time by as much as a factor of 2.[174] Enhanced UV radiation also appears to be extremely lethal to fish and crustacean larvae, and has been shown to produce burns and induce tumors on those organisms surviving exposure.[175] At the present time, the accumulating research

---

* The Global 2000 Study's agricultural projections are based on a doubling of fertilizer application worldwide and a quadrupling in the LDCs. Over and above these increases, large amounts of fertilizer may be applied in the intensive silvicultural methods projected to occur in forestry.

data seem to indicate that ecosystems may be significantly disrupted by increased levels of ultraviolet radiation.

There are a number of steps that can be taken to limit the reduction of the earth's ozone layer. The emissions of chlorofluorocarbons can be limited by legislation. The U.S. has enacted such legislation[176] and hopes to persuade all industrialized nations to establish similar limitations. Supersonic flying can also be regulated if further research indicates the need.* But the world cannot easily dispense with nitrogen fertilizers even if future research should indicate that they contribute more to ozone depletion than recent findings suggest. The National Academy of Sciences has published an economic analysis† of the costs and benefits of chemical fertilizers and reports that the present discounted value of damages is small because of the distant nature of the projected impacts.[177] On the basis of this analysis, the Academy states that "in our opinion, the current value to society of those activities that contribute to global nitrogen fixation far exceed the potential cost of any moderate (e.g., up to a decade) postponement of action to reduce the threat of future ozone depletion by $N_2O$ [from nitrogen fertilizer use]."[178]

### Albedo and Heat

The Global 2000 Study's forestry, energy, minerals, agriculture, and GNP projections all point to significant changes in land use§ and significant releases of waste heat. These changes will certainly influence local climates, and may even affect regional or global climate.

Perhaps the most significant land-use change anticipated is the 16–20 percent reduction in the world's forests over the next two decades, as pro-

jected in Chapter 8. This reduction of 420 million hectares involves roughly 3 percent of the earth's continental land surface and about 1 percent of the earth's total area.

The most direct linkage between change of land use and climate is through change of surface albedo.* Evergreen forests have an albedo of 7–15 percent. Dry, plowed fields have an albedo of 10–15 percent; deserts, 25–30 percent; fresh snow, 85–90 percent; and asphalt, 8 percent.[179]

The global changes in land use over the next two decades are by themselves probably not so extensive as to cause a significant change in global climate, but they are certainly sufficient to cause local changes in many areas. In some cases beneficial changes will occur as, for example, when restored park and forest lands improve local climate, but adverse change—including desert conditions—can also be anticipated.[180]

Urbanization is another land-use trend known to affect local weather and climate. Typical changes resulting from urbanization are shown in Table 13–14.

The energy projections in Chapter 10 anticipate an almost 50 percent increase in energy demand by 1990. All human energy use ultimately ends up as residual heat and much of it—especially in thermal generation of electricity—is converted to heat immediately on use.† Already, residual heat releases are comparable or larger than the solar input in some reasonably large local areas.[181] The anthropogenic energy releases over the 60 square kilometers of Manhattan are almost 4 times the solar energy falling on the area; even over sprawling Los Angeles (3,500 square kilometers) the anthropogenic heat released now totals 13 percent of the solar flux.[182]

Although it has long been known that releases of residual heat influence local climates, it has generally been thought that thermal pollution would probably not affect global climate because anthropogenic heat is now, and is expected to remain, a small percentage of the solar influence on global weather.[183] As shown in Table 13–15, fossil fuel combustion increased by a factor of 8

* During the 1976 U.N. Environment Programme's Governing Council Meeting, the U.S. sponsored a resolution calling for an international meeting on the regulation of supersonic flying. The meeting, held in Washington in March 1977, prepared a world plan of action on the ozone layer, which is reported in *Ozone-Layer Bulletin* (U.N. Environment Programme, Nairobi), no. 1, Jan. 1978.
† The Academy's report notes that this economic analysis has limitations and is not a broad-scale assessment of the full costs and benefits of current or projected patterns of global food production and energy use. The analysis addresses a 3.5 percent decrease in stratospheric ozone, using discount rates ranging from 3 to 8 percent. Changes in temperature and in ultraviolet radiation are considered. Incre se  UV radiation is assumed to have negligible effects on plants.
§ Surface changes are thought to affect climate through (1) changes in albedo, (2) changes in surface "roughness" (by affecting drag on winds), (3) changes in water storage capacity (affecting wetness), and (4) changes in heat storage capacity. Only albedo effects are discussed here.

* Albedo (as defined in the National Science Board/National Science Foundation *Patterns and Perspectives in Environmental Science,* 1972, p. 66) is the percentage of the amount of the incident solar radiation reflected by a land or water surface. For example, if the sun radiates 100 units of energy per minute to the outer limits of the atmosphere, and the earth's surface receives 80 units per minute (the atmosphere absorbs 20 units) and then reflects 40 units upward, the albedo is 50 percent.
† Roughly two-thirds of the primary energy needed in the thermal generation of electricity (primarily by coal and nuclear plants) is lost immediately as waste heat.

## TABLE 13–14

### Typical Climate Changes Caused by Urbanization

| Type of Change | Comparison with Rural Environs |
|---|---|
| **Temperature** | |
| Annual mean | 0.5–1.0° C higher |
| Winter minima | 1.0–3.0° C higher |
| **Relative Humidity** | |
| Annual mean | 6% lower |
| Winter | 2% lower |
| Summer | 8% lower |
| **Dust Particles** | 10 times more |
| **Cloudiness** | |
| Cloud cover | 5–10% more |
| Fog, winter | 100% more frequent |
| Fog, summer | 30% more frequent |
| **Radiation** | |
| Total on horizontal surface | 15–20% less |
| Ultraviolet, winter | 30% less |
| Ultraviolet, summer | 5% less |
| **Wind Speed** | |
| Annual mean | 20–30% lower |
| Extreme gusts | 10–20% lower |
| Calms | 5–20% more |
| **Precipitation**[a] | |
| Amounts | 5–10% more |
| Days with 0.2 inch | 10% more |

*Source:* After H. E. Landsberg, in W. H. Matthews et al., eds., *Man's Impact on the Climate,* Cambridge, Mass.: MIT Press, 1971, p. 168.

[a] Precipitation effects are relatively uncertain.

## TABLE 13–15

### Selected Annual Energy Supply Rates for the Earth[a]
*(Billions of watts)*

| | |
|---|---|
| ¼ Solar constant (extra-atmospheric irradiance) | 178,000,000 |
| Insolation absorbed at ground level | 90,000,000 |
| Dissipated by friction in atmospheric circulations | 1,500,000 |
| Photosynthesis (production by living vegetation) | 40,000 |
| Geothermal heat (by conduction in crust) | 32,000 |
| 1970 Rate of fossil fuel burning | 8,000 |
| Infrared radiation from full moon | 5,000 |
| Dissipated by friction in ocean currents and tides | 3,000 |
| Solar radiation received via reflection from full moon | 2,000 |
| Dissipated by friction in solar tides of the atmosphere | 1,000 |
| 1910 Rate of fossil fuel burning | 1,000 |
| Human body heat | 600 |
| Released by volcanoes and hot springs (geoconvection) | 300 |
| 1960 Rate of hydroelectric power production | 240 |
| Dissipated as heat in lightening discharges | 100 |
| Radiation from bright aurora | 25 |
| Received from space by cosmic radiation | 15 |
| Dissipated mechanical energy of meteorites | 10 |
| Total radiation from all stars | 8 |
| Dissipated by friction in lunar tides of the atmosphere | 5 |
| Solar radiation received as zodiacal light | 2 |

*Source:* After Office of Research and Development. U.S. Environmental Protection Agency, *Changes in Global Energy Balance,* Washington, Oct. 1974.

[a] These whole globe averages represent annual gigawatts ($10^9$W) of power totaled over the earth's surface.

between 1910 and 1970, but solar energy is still far and away the most important energy source in human affairs. However, it has been noted that although anthropogenic heat inputs will be localized, they may be strong enough to alter local or regional components of the world climate system.[184] In turn, changes triggered in individual components of the system may have effects throughout the world. Examples of local effects are given in Table 13–16.

The energy research group at the International Institute of Applied Systems Analysis (IIASA)* near Vienna has studied this problem with the general circulation model of the United Kingdom Meteorological Office.[185] The IIASA group found that large heat releases (such as one might expect from "power parks") could trigger changes in re-

* An international effort to accomplish East-West cooperation through joint work with the use of systems analysis tools. The Institute is well supported by both the U.S and the U.S.S.R.; Canada, Czechoslovakia, France, and German Democratic Republic, Japan, the Federal Republic of Germany, Bulgaria, Italy, Poland, the United Kingdom, Austria, Hungary, Sweden, Finland, and the Netherlands also participate.

gional elements of the global system, and that these in turn produced global effects in the model runs. The kinds of global changes produced depended on where the heat source was located. The IIASA group concluded that the results of these model experiments indicate a possible global atmospheric response to large heat discharges, which must be borne in mind for planning purposes and also investigated further.[186]

## Conclusions

Both the National Defense University survey of expert opinion and the analysis of the possible climatic implications of the Global 2000 Study's other projections lead to the same general conclusions: (1) Climate will continue to vary in the future, just as it always has in the past, in a largely unpredictable manner. (2) Apart from this characteristic variability, no substantial net trend of

## TABLE 13–16

### Effects of Large Heat Additions to the Atmosphere

| Phenomenon | Energy Rate (Mw) | Area (km²) | Energy-Flux-Density (W/m²) |
|---|---|---|---|
| Large brush fire[a] | 100,000 | 50 | 200 |

Consequences: (Relatively small energy-flux rate, very large area.) Cumulus cloud reaching to a height of 6 km formed over 0.1 area of fire. Convergence of winds into the fire area.

| | | | |
|---|---|---|---|
| Forest fire whirlwind[b] | | | |

Consequences: Typical whirlwind: Central tube visible by whirling smoke and debris. Diameters few feet to several hundred feet. Heights few feet to 4,000 ft Debris picked up—logs up to 30 in. in diameter and 30 ft long.

| | | | |
|---|---|---|---|
| World War II fire storm[c] | | 12 | |

Consequences: Turbulent column of heated air 2.5 mi in diameter. Fed at base by inrush of surface air; 1.5 mi from fire, wind speeds increased from 11 to 33 mph. Trees 3 ft in diameter were uprooted.

| | | | |
|---|---|---|---|
| Fire at Hiroshima[d] | | | |

Consequences: (10–12 hr after atomic bomb.) "The wind grew stronger, and suddenly—probably because of the tremendous convection set up by the blazing city—a whirlwind ripped through the park. Huge trees crashed down; small ones were uprooted and flew into the air. Higher, a wild array of flat things revolved in the twisting funnel." The vortex moved out onto the river, where it sucked up a waterspout and eventually spent itself.

| | | | |
|---|---|---|---|
| Surtsey volcano[e] | 100,000 | < 1 | 100,000 |

Consequences: Permanent cloud extending to heights of 5–9 km. Continuous sharp thunder and lightning, visible 115 km away. (Phenomenon probably peculiar to volcano cloud with many small ash particles.) Waterspouts resulting from indraft at cloud base, caused by rising buoyant cloud.

| | | | |
|---|---|---|---|
| Surtsey volcano[f] | 200,000 | 1 | 200,000 |

Consequences: Whirlwinds (waterspouts and tornadoes) are the rule rather than the exception. More often than not there is at least one vortex downwind. Short inverted cones or long, sinuous horizontal vortices that curve back up into the cloud, and intense vortices that extend to the ocean surface.

| | | | |
|---|---|---|---|
| French Meteotron[g] | 700 | 0.0032 | 219,000 |

Consequences: ". . . artificial thunderstorms, even tornadoes, many cumulus clouds . . . substantial downpour." Dust devils.

| | | | |
|---|---|---|---|
| Meteotron[h] | 350 | 0.016 | 22,400 |

Consequences: 15 min after starting the burners, observers saw a whirl 40 m in diameter . . . whirlwind so strong burner flames were inclined to 45°

| | | | |
|---|---|---|---|
| Single large cooling tower | 2,250 | 0.0046 | 484,000 |

Consequences: Plume of varying lengths and configurations.

| | | | |
|---|---|---|---|
| Array of large cooling towers [48,000 Mw(e) NEC; area 48,000 acres] | 96,000 | 194 | 495 |

Consequences: Unknown.

Source: Ralph M. Rotty, "Energy and the Climate." Institute for Energy Analysis, Oak Ridge Associated Universities, Sept. 1976, pp. 15–16.
[a] From R. J. Taylor et al., "Convective Activity Above a Large-Scale Brush Fire." Journal of Applied Meteorology, vol. 12, 1973, p. 1144.
[b] From H. E. Graham, "Fire Whirlwinds." Bulletin of American Meteorological Society, vol. 36, no. 3, 1955, p. 99.
[c] From H. Landsberg, "Fire Storms Resulting from Bombing Conflagrations." Bulletin of American Meteorological Society, vol. 28, no. 2, 1947, p. 72.
[d] From J. R. Hersey, Hiroshima, New York: Bantam, 1946, pp. 50–51.
[e] From A. G. Borne, "Birth of an Island," Discovery, vol. 25, no. 4, 1964, p. 16.
[f] From S. Thorarinsson and B. Vonnegut, "Whirlwinds Produced by the Eruption of Surtsey Volcano." Bulletin of American Meteorological Society, vol. 45, no. 8, 1964, p. 440.
[g] From J. Dessens, "Man-made Thunderstorms," Discovery, vol. 25, no. 3, 1964, p. 40.
[h] From J. Dessens, "Man-made Tornadoes," Nature, vol. 193, no. 4810, 1962, p. 13.

climate in the direction of either warming or cooling is anticipated between now and 2000.

These conclusions, however, are not the end of the climate story. Human societies around the world have become (and are becoming increasingly) dependent on favorable climate. Less favorable climates are known to have occurred in the past, and the less favorable climate of the 1971–73 period demonstrated just how vulnerable world societies have become to weather and climate change. The Global 2000 Study's projections (all based on the assumption of no significant climatic change) point to a world in 2000 that is even more vulnerable to weather and climate change than the world of today. Furthermore, scientists now know that several human activities have reached a scale that, over periods of several to many decades, has the potential to alter the world's climate significantly. These anthropogenic influences on global climate include carbon dioxide emissions and release of chemicals affecting the ozone layer as well as potential land-use changes, aerosol and particulate generation, and heat releases.

The import of anthropogenic influences on climate lies no† in any imminent threat of massive climatic change, but rather in the inadequacy of present knowledge and the inability of institutions to make society respond effectively if evidence of serious consequences develops. Probably the most serious anthropogenic threats to the stability of climate are $CO_2$ emissions and releases of chemicals that deplete stratospheric ozone. In both cases it is impossible for an individual nation to protect itself against the consequences of other nations' actions. These problems are truly global in scope, and there is no human institution now established that can adequately address them.

In commenting on its carbon dioxide findings, the National Academy of Sciences concluded: "If the preliminary estimates of climate change in the latter part of the twenty-second century are validated, a reassessment of global energy policy must be started promptly because, long before that destined date, there will have been major climatic impacts all over the world." [187] Other studies now underscore the Academy's concern, and point to significant changes in $CO_2$ concentrations by 2000 or shortly thereafter: [188]

The key word in the Academy's admonition is "promptly." Unfortunately, given the limitations cited above, it is difficult to imagine how a reassessment of *global* energy policy could be undertaken promptly. Considering the uncertainties in the magnitude of $CO_2$ sources and sinks and the limited research that has been done in these areas, it could easily be more than a decade before a definitive conclusion is reached just on how to project $CO_2$ concentrations accurately. Even given definitive projections, several decades of intensive research will be required to reach agreement on the climatological implications of increasing $CO_2$ concentrations. Lacking a world institution with an energy mission, how long would a global reassessment of a world energy policy require? And given a change in policy, how long would be

needed to implement any basic change in the world's energy capital, infrastructure, and economy? By the time the world is prepared to address seriously the climatological implications of world energy policy, commitments (e.g., to intensified use of coal and to deforestation) may have become so well established that a basic change in the global energy economy might be as economically catastrophic as the climatic change itself. Thus, to delay a careful and prompt international assessment of the carbon dioxide problem could lead to capital commitments and forest policies that make irreversible accumulations of $CO_2$ in the atmosphere essentially unavoidable. Similar difficulties could develop in connection with the stratospheric ozone layer as the world's growing population becomes increasingly dependent on biologically and synthetically produced nitrogen fertilizers.

In the decades ahead, the finite capacity of the atmosphere to absorb various anthropogenic chemical emissions without catastrophic climate change must be recognized as an extremely important resource, a resource vital to and held in common by all nations. Protecting this resource will raise perplexing and troublesome questions: Which nations should be allowed to burn how much coal or to replace how much forest with food crops? How are global $CO_2$ discharges to be monitored and controlled?

The capacity of the atmosphere to absorb $CO_2$ may be a resource that is even more limited than either forests or fossil fuels, and questions concerning the allocation of "$CO_2$ disposal rights" could conceivably overshadow all other energy issues. [189] Similarly, if protecting the ozone layer requires limitations on the emissions from spray cans, air conditioners, supersonic aircraft, and nitrogen fertilizers, the right to deplete the atmosphere's limited ozone resource can be expected to go first to agriculture.

Even within individual nations, the making of major decisions in these regards can be expected to place a strain on existing institutions and to require long periods of time for debate. On a global scale, there is no adequate institution and no precedent for such decisions or the cooperation they would require.

While no major worldwide climatic changes are expected by 2000, anthropogenic forces affecting the world's climates will be accelerating, and unless these forces and their effects are soon studied, monitored, and analyzed much more carefully, human institutions will be ill prepared to make some of the difficult choices that may be required in the 1980s or at the latest in the 1990s.

## THE TECHNOLOGY PROJECTIONS AND THE ENVIRONMENT

### *The Projections*

Each of the agencies making projections for the Global 2000 Study made its own projections (and/or assumptions) of technological developments in its particular area of concern. In general, the technological projections and assumptions are implicitly, rather than explicitly, incorporated in each agency's overall contribution to the Study. As a result it is not always possible to state precisely what technological developments are projected or assumed. Nonetheless, a general pattern is discernible. On the whole, the technological projections and assumptions imply that production- and yield-enhancing technologies will continue to be developed and disseminated as fast as they have been over the past few decades—or faster. Further, the agencies generally assume that new technologies will be deployed as fast as (or faster than) they have in the past, and that the technologies will not produce adverse side effects (of an economic, environmental, social, or resource nature) that would limit their application.

The more specific technological assumptions associated with the projections are as follows:

*Population Projections.* Birth control (family planning) and health care, technologies will be disseminated and used to a greater extent than in the past two decades. The technological developments of industrialization, as they impinge on natality and mortality, will continue at or above historically observed rates.

*Gross National Product Projections.* In the industrialized world, technology is assumed to contribute to future economic growth as it has in the recent past. The productivity of new investment capital will increase, in part a result of technological change, at about the historically observed rate of 0.5–1.5 percent per year.

*Fisheries Projections.* The projections assume that technologies for harvesting and processing nontraditional living marine resources will be adopted increasingly through the year 2000.

*Food and Agriculture Projections.* The projections assume that yields per hectare will continue to increase at rates comparable to those of the past two decades.

*Forestry Projections.* Continued progress is assumed in increasing forest yields per hectare, and in decreasing losses incurred during processing or from previously underutilized species and from disease.

*Energy Projections.* Due to technological developments, the real costs of production, refining, and marketing of energy products will remain essentially constant. Large increases in the adoption of existing technologies are assumed to be possible. It is assumed that, collectively, nuclear and hydroelectrical generation (which are lumped together in the Department of Energy projections) will approximately triple between 1975 and 1990. The technologies for fossil fuel production and use are assumed to respond to variations in relative costs, resulting in shifts from oil and natural gas to coal.

*Nonfuel Minerals Projections.* Technological advances in production technology necessary for continued growth in production will be made. As high-grade ores are depleted, technological developments will hold the real cost of minerals and materials constant. Mineral use per dollar of GNP will tend to decrease as economies enlarge and mature.

None of the projections assumes specific major technological breakthroughs, (such as harnessing of the fusion process for energy production), and none assumes failures of existing technologies (such as the evolution of antibiotic-resistant diseases, or the termination of nuclear power development due to inadequate reactor safety or waste disposal methods).

For three reasons, no attempt will be made to analyze the environmental implications of the technological projections and assumptions made by the contributing agencies. First, the technological projections and assumptions are, for the most part, too inexplicit to permit an adequate assessment of their environmental implications. Second, technology is knowledge—especially scientific knowledge—applied to practical or productive ends, and since the principal environmental implications of a particular technology occur in the economic sector in which it is applied, its environmental implications are analyzed individually in the other sections of this chapter. Third, the interesting and important environmental questions about technologies emerge not from an analysis of a particular technology but from an analysis of alternative technological options. The last point deserves elaboration.

Both developed and less developed nations have had considerable experience with the unforeseen social and environmental impacts of technology and development. Neither Henry Ford nor the purchasers of his Model Ts foresaw that automobile exhaust would become an environmental health problem. Similarly, university agricultural facilities involved in the development of modern agricultural equipment failed to anticipate adverse social impacts—such as unemployment among farmworkers and urban migration—and were taken by surprise recently when 19 farmworkers and a California Rural Legal Assistance group sued the University of California over the development of sophisticated harvesting machines, which the farmworkers alleged were a threat to their livelihood. The suit contends that harvesting machines in the California tomato industry alone have displaced 32,000 workers and that thousands more have been displaced by university-developed machinery in vegetable fields and fruit orchards.[190] One certainly cannot infer from this development that all harvesting machinery is bad, but the farmworkers' suit does illustrate the extent to which questions are being raised about the impact of technology—questions that in even the relatively recent past might have been thought external to decisions concerning technological priorities.

New institutions are developing in response to the growing awareness of the social and environmental impacts that follow in the wake of new technologies. In the United States, the Office of Technology Assessment was instituted to assist Congress in assessing the social, economic, and environmental consequences of new and emerging technologies. Internationally, the United Nations Conference on Science and Technology for Development (UNCSTD) was designed to consider both technological choice and the transfer of technologies among nations.

The international transfer of technologies has important environmental implications. In fact, some of the most serious environmental problems have come from the direct transfer of technologies from temperate-zone industrial societies to tropical environments in less developed societies.[191] Many of these environmental problems are due to lack of understanding of how tropical- and arid-zone ecosystems differ from temperate-zone systems. For example, many tropical river basin development projects have stabilized irrigation systems to provide increased agricultural production, only to discover such stabilized-irrigation agriculture provided ideal environments for the spread (via snail vectors) of such serious waterborne diseases as schistosomiasis.[192]

Economist E. F. Schumacher and his colleagues of the Intermediate Technology Group in London have pioneered efforts over the past two decades to develop "appropriate" technologies, i.e., technologies that are ecologically gentle and adaptable to the economic, resource, and social structures of a particular society. Schumacher presented his thoughts on technology in *Small is Beautiful: Economics as if People Mattered*. In this well-known book, Schumacher goes beyond environmental compatability to identify four basic propositions for choosing technologies for developing societies:

- First, that workplaces have to be created in the areas where the people are living now, and not primarily in metropolitan areas into which they tend to migrate.
- Second, that these workplaces must be, on average, cheap enough so that they can be created in large numbers without this calling for an unattainable level of capital formation and imports.
- Third, that the production methods employed must be relatively simple, so that the demands

for high skills are minimized, not only in the production process itself but also in matters of organization, raw material supply, financing, marketing, and so forth.

• Fourth, that production should be mainly from local materials and mainly for local use. [193]

The industrialized nations face corresponding choices in defining and developing appropriate "postindustrial" technology. The environmental problems that are passed on to the next generation will be greatly influenced by whether industrialized countries—as well as less developed countries—encourage technologies that conserve energy and other natural resources, increase employment, and minimize pollution and other impacts on the environment, or whether these countries continue to develop technological innovation primarily for increasing per capita consumption of goods and services. [194]

## Conclusions

Many of the environmental impacts discussed in other sections of this chapter are the consequences of past technological choices. The health of the environment during the 21st century will be shaped significantly in both developing and industrialized countries by the choices of technologies made over the next two decades. Fortunately, a wide range of technologies are available that appear to be environmentally, socially, and economically sound, but it is by no means clear that these technologies will be chosen. [195] How political and social controls affect the choice and diffusion of technologies in the early stages of their development will have monumental implications for the environmental conditions passed on to the next generation. Indeed, the choice of technologies may be the area in which society will have the greatest latitude and leverage in shaping the future of the global environment.

## THE FOOD AND AGRICULTURE PROJECTIONS AND THE ENVIRONMENT

### The Projections

The food and agriculture projections developed by the U.S. Department of Agriculture* foresee a 90–100 percent increase in total world production over the 1970–2000 period. This increase, however, is the equivalent of only a 10–15 percent increase in per capita production. The real price of food is projected to increase from 30 to 115 percent over 1969–71 prices.

The projections increases are based in part on a projected 4 percent increase in arable area. Although this expansion of arable area involves a substantial increase in the world's harvested area over the record high levels reported for the first half of the 1970s, the rate of increase in arable area is significantly slower than in the postwar period. The slowed expansion is due in large part to the growing capital costs of adding increasingly remote and marginal lands to the production base. The slowed rate of increase leads to an increased number of people supported per hectare. Globally during the first half of the 1970s, 2.6 persons were supported per arable hectare; by 2000 the figure is projected to rise to 4.0. In the LDCs the ratio is projected to rise from 2.9 in the early 1970s to 5.3 in 2000, excluding China.

---

* Half of the Study's food projections reported in Chapter 6 assume that energy prices remain constant in real terms (at 1974–76 prices) to the year 2000. The figures presented under Alternative II (see Chapter 6) assume that energy prices remain constant. The double set of figures presented under Alternative I reflect possibilities ranging from constant to increasing energy prices. (The first of the two Alternative I entries is for constant energy prices; the second entry is for rising energy prices.) Alternative III explicitly presents results based on real energy prices rising as projected in the Study's energy projections in Chapter 10. Alternative III also assumes high population growth rates, lower income growth rates, and weather less favorable than that of the past 25 years. The food projections under this alternative show the real price of food increasing by 115 percent over the 1970–2000 period. For

LDCs overall, average per capita daily calorie consumption remains constant at the 2,165 calorie per capita levels of 1969–71. Per capita calorie consumption declines for the North Africa/Middle East region, other African LDCs, and South Asian areas and increases for Latin America and the Southeast Asia and East Asia areas. The percentages of decline in per capita consumption (relative to 1969–71 levels) are as follows: 1 percent for the North Africa/Middle East area, 16 percent for the other African LDCs, 3 percent for the South Asian area. Fertilizer consumption and increase in arable area are not projected for the specific case of rising energy prices. World grain trade increases 200 percent, from 79.6 million metric tons in 1969–71 to 238 million in 2000. Grain imports increase as follows: 190 percent for developed importers, 650 for centrally planned country importers and 220 for LDC importers.

The remainder of the increase in production comes from a projected 70–100 percent increase in productivity, (i.e., substantially higher crop yields per hectare). Implicit in the projected productivity growth is a more than doubling of fertilizer* use per hectare for the world as a whole and a quadrupling of fertilizer use per hectare for LDCs. The food projections also note a continued diminishing of marginal return to increases in fertilizer use. In simplified terms, a 1-kilogram increase in fertilizer use at the world level appears to have generated about an 8-kilogram increase in grain production in the early 1970s; a 1-kilogram increase in fertilizer use in 2000 is projected to generate less than a 6-kilogram increase in production. Water, which is already a limiting factor in agricultural production in large parts of the world, will become even more of a limiting factor by 2000. As noted in the food and agriculture projections (Chapter 6), the projected increases in food production imply large public-sector investments in irrigation, agricultural extension, and land reclamation.

The projected increases in demand will be generated by the projected increases in population and, to a lesser extent, by increases in per capita income. Increases in both production and demand are likely to be unevenly distributed and are therefore expected to generate both a marked increase in international trade and a widening of the differences between per capita consumption in the different regions of the world. Net declines in caloric consumption per capita are projected for most areas of developing Africa south of the Sahara; negligible gains in caloric consumption are expected for South Asia and parts of the rest of the developing world.

As noted in Chapter 4 ("Climate"), the Study's food projections implicitly assume that no significant change in the climate will occur relative to that experienced over the last several decades. However, the projections do explicitly consider variations in weather by providing for fluctuations in yields similar to weather-related variations experienced during the 1950–77 period. The projections take into account ecological stresses, such as deterioration in soil fertility, and hydrologic irregularity induced by deforestation, but only to the extent that these problems have occurred in the past and—given past experiences—are likely to occur in the future. Ecological stresses are linked to the projections by assuming that steps will be taken to alleviate the impact of these stresses on production. The costs of taking the preventive steps are expensive and contribute significantly to the increased real cost of producing and consuming food. The required capital is assumed to be available.

## Introduction

The food projections present a complex picture of interacting factors that will affect the environment. The growing populations and incomes projected increase the demand for food at a time when increasing the stock of arable land will have become more difficult and expensive. A reduced rate of expansion of arable land will place further importance on increasing yields, but yield-enhancing techniques are themselves showing signs

* In the Department of Agriculture's projections for this Study, the term "fertilizer" is used as a proxy for a group of productivity-expanding inputs, including pesticides, herbicides, and high-yield grain varieties, as well as chemical fertilizers in the usual meaning of the term. The projections are not detailed enough to specify any change in the relative proportions of these various inputs.

of limitations. Further, the *nonrenewable* resources on which agriculture is based—fossil fuels, genetic strains, and soils—are being diminished rapidly in some areas. All of these developments will have environmental implications, some of which will directly influence the prospects for future food production.

This point has already been forcefully made by the Council on Environmental Quality. The Council's 1977 report "The Food-People Problem" discusses the situation in the following terms:

In the race to provide food for the expanding world population, improper farming practices—including overly intensive cultivation, too heavy a reliance on marginally productive semi-arid lands, and inadequate conservation measures—

are increasing the erosion and depleting the nutrients of topsoils. The result . . . is reduced fertility of the land, lowering its capacity for food
production.

In many parts of the world, hillsides are being
deforested to make way for more farms and to
provide fuel for cooking food. The rains no longer
soak into the ground but run off in the form of
uncontrollable torrents which tear away the soil
under cultivation, flood the low lying cropland,
and clog reservoirs and irrigation canals with silt.
Left behind are barren slopes that later become
abandoned.

Environmental degradation has been barely
noticeable amid increased farm production resulting from the technological improvements of
the "Green Revolution," made particularly effective by fertilizers and pesticides. However, rapidly growing population and growing affluence
continue to increase the demand for food, while
at the same time losses in soil fertility which reduce land's capacity to produce are occurring
across the world.

According to a U.S. survey of 69 countries with
1.8 billion people:

- Overgrazing and overcropping, which result in
  heavy loss of soil by erosion, are serious problems in 43 countries with 1.4 billion people.
- Serious irrigation problems were recorded in
  eight arid countries attempting to increase food
  production.
- Heavy loss of forests has occurred in at least 24
  developing countries. Principal reason for converting forest to cropland and grazing fields is
  to meet the demand for food.
- Water problems resulting from deforestation
  have appeared in 16 countries in the form of
  critical water shortages, and in 10 countries in
  the form of increased flooding. Some countries
  shared both drought and flooding. [196]

The implications of the Global 2000 Study's
food projections for the environment are discussed in the following five sections. First, the
food projections are analyzed in terms of their
implications for human nutrition—an important
aspect of environmental quality—and in terms of
the kinds of pressures that agricultural activities
will exert on other parts of the environment.
Other subjects of environmental concern include
soil deterioration, the ecological effects of fertilizers and pesticides, crop vulnerability (the genetic instability induced by simplification of
ecosystems and reduction of genetic resources),
and the implications of the food projections for
nonrenewable fossil fuels.*

*In addition to the discussions that follow, several direct es-
timates and broad directional indicators of environmental
change are presented in the food and agriculture projections
themselves (Chapter 6).

## Food and the Human Environment

Food is an essential element in environmental
quality for the human population. Without an
adequate diet, vulnerability to disease is increased, capacity to perform physical work is limited, and (in children) mental and physical
development is impaired. Nutritional requirements vary with age, sex, occupation, height, and
weight. As a rough guide to human nutritional
needs, the U.N. Food and Agriculture Organization (FAO) [197] has estimated minimum caloric
requirements for various regions.* The degree to
which the FAO standards are met provides an
important indication of the nutritional dimension
of human environment and, indirectly, an indication of the pressures on local agriculture.

Table 13–17 compares recent and projected per
capita calorie consumption with the FAO minimum standards for various regions of the world.
As noted in Chapter 6, real-price increases will
be needed to pay for more costly land development and yield-enhancing technologies implicit in
the projected figures. Some regions will be better
able than others to pay the increasing real prices,
and consequently the prospects reflected in the
table vary widely from region to region. The prospects are good in the industrialized countries and
the centrally planned economies. In the affluent
developed countries, diets can be expected to become more diversified while calorie consumption
rises to perhaps 135 percent of FAO standards.
The increased consumption in these regions brings
to mind the problem of malnutrition due to over-
consumption (i.e., overeating) cited in several recent studies. [198]

The consumption statistics for the industrialized
countries and centrally planned economies do not
fully indicate the magnitude of the pressures for
increased agricultural production in these regions.
Many are critically dependent on imports. In one
case, the food projections in Chapter 6 show a
food-importing centrally planned economy increasing its grain purchases by 650 percent by the
year 2000. Pressure will also be high in those exporting countries experiencing balance of payment problems. Agricultural sales provide a
significant amount of foreign exchange for some
countries. In 1975–77 in the U.S., for example,

* Of course, adequate nutrition also requires protein and other
nutrients, many of which will also be increasing in price. The
discussion here is limited to caloric requirements. See Joint
FAO/WHO ad hoc Expert Committee, "Energy and Protein
Requirements," Rome: Food and Agriculture Organization,
1973; and World Food Study and Nutrition, vol. 1, Washington:
National Academy of Sciences, 1975.

## TABLE 13–17

### Daily per Capita Calorie Consumption, Historic and Projected, by Region, with Percent of FAO Minimum Standards

| | Historic | | Projected for 2000 | |
|---|---|---|---|---|
| | 1969–71 | 1973–74 | Alternative II[a] | Alternative III[b] |
| | *Figures in parentheses are percents of FAO minimum standards[c]* | | | |
| Industrialized countries | 3,180 (122) | 3,340 (128) | 3,500 (135) | 3,400 (130) |
| Centrally planned economies | 2,600 (107) | 2,665 (110) | 2,940 (121) | 2,860 (118) |
| Less developed countries | 2,165 (94) | 2,135 (93) | 2,390 (104) | 2,165 (94) |
| Latin America | 2,525 (106) | 2,540 (107) | 3,080 (130) | 2,710 (114) |
| North Africa/Middle East | 2,421 (104) | 2,482 (107) | 2,655 (114) | 2,390 (103) |
| Other African LDCs | 2,139 (92) | 2,071 (90) | 1,920 (83) | 1,800 (77) |
| South Asia | 2,036 (92) | 1,954 (88) | 2,230 (101) | 1,985 (105) |
| Southeast Asia | 2,174 (98) | 2,270 (103) | 2,425 (110) | 2,310 (105) |
| East Asia | 2,140 (97) | 2,205 (100) | 2,520 (114) | 2,320 (105) |

*Source:* Data for industrialized countries and centrally planned economies are from Table 6–8, Chapter 6, this study; data for LDCs are from Table 6–9. Conversion from the food indexes was performed by the Department of Agriculture.

*Note:* Caloric requirements and per capita caloric consumption figures are calculated from measures of total food supply (adjusted for nonfood use, and processing losses and waste) divided by midyear population. Intake below 80–90 percent or above 120–130 percent of the FAO minimum requirement is unlikely, given basic body metabolism. Therefore projected per capita caloric levels outside a range of 80–130 percent of caloric minimums reflect an unusually small or large waste or processing margin rather than a sustained daily per capita intake in the 1,700–1,800 calorie range or in the 3,300–3,400 calorie range.

[a] Real price of energy remains constant, with low population growth, high income growth, and less favorable weather.
[b] Real price of energy increases as projected in Chapter 10, with high population growth, low income growth, and less favorable weather.
[c] FAO's minimum, country-specific caloric requirements imply regional requirements of 2,375 calories per capita per day for Latin America, 2,325 for developing Africa, 2,210 for developing Asia (2,300 for the LDCs as an aggregate), 2,600 for the industrialized countries, and 2,420 for the centrally planned economies.

grain sales provided over 10 percent of all U.S. foreign sales.[199]

Prospects in the LDCs are mixed. Diet improvements for the poorest two-thirds of the world's population are likely to be small or not forthcoming at all. As shown in Table 13–17, diets are projected to improve in Latin America and in Southeast and East Asia. Diets also improve in South Asia under the optimistic assumptions (including constant energy prices) of Alternative II. But with the assumptions of increasing energy prices, high population growth, low income growth, and less favorable weather (Alternative III), average per capita calorie consumption declines in South Asia and in the LDCs south of the Sahara.*

The full implications of these calorie consumption levels depend on an additional measure—the statistical distribution of diets above and below calorie consumption averages. Studies by the U.S. Department of Agriculture and the World Bank[200] suggest that calorie distribution in the LDCs is sufficiently skewed that national average calorie consumption levels would have to be at least 110–120 percent of the FAO minimum before consumption in lower-income groups could be ex-

pected to approach the recommended minimum.* Keeping this added distribution factor in mind, the projected increase in per capita calorie consumption would probably be adequate to improve Latin American diets (under all three alternatives) and Southeast Asian and East Asian diets (under selected alternatives) to the extent that low-income groups would have access to minimum food supplies. Consumption in the rest of the developing regions—and in the LDCs as a whole—would fail to increase fast enough to meet the minimum needs of the lowest-income groups, which possibly make up one-third to one-half of the total world population. The World Bank, taking these inequities into account, estimates that malnourished persons in the LDCs could increase from the current figure (400–600 million) to as many as 1,300 million by the year 2000.[201]

There has been hunger and malnutrition somewhere in the world for virtually all of recorded history, but as National Academy of Sciences President Philip Handler has observed,

The character of malnutrition has changed markedly in the last 40–50 years. The classical defi-

---

* Alternative I (see Chapter 6) presents a range for the medium case. The first number presented in the Alternative I entries reflects conditions with constant energy prices; the second entry is for rising energy prices. The Nutritional implications of Alternative I are presented in Chapter 6.

* Policies leading to a more equitable income distribution could reduce this skewness and result in a far larger improvement in diets than reflected in the regional consumption averages. However, the analysis throughout this Study is limited to one policy option, namely the continuation of present policies.

ciency diseases—beriberi, scurvy, pellagra, rickets, sprue—have almost disappeared. Only xerophthalmia due to Vitamin A deficiency continues as a serious problem, causing blindness in large numbers of children. Instead, there is marasmus, and kwashiorkor—both forms of general protein-calorie insufficiency and iron deficiency anemia. Thus, nutritional status is now rarely the consequence of ignorance; malnutrition now reflects lack of food, not lack of scientific understanding. [202]

In short, nations throughout the world will be pressured to substantially increase agricultural output to respond to growth in demand. Demand will be driven by both population and income growth, but in different proportions in different areas. In the LDCs, approximately a third to a half of the world's population will experience a calorie shortfall. Most food-importing nations will produce as much as possible to alleviate negative trade balances. Exporters, especially the U.S., will encourage grain production to help offset the balance of payment pressure created by continued heavy oil imports. While the demand for food will be high everywhere, the strains on the agricultural sector are likely to be highest in South Asia and in LDCs south of the Sahara. These pressures will affect the environment adversely through soil deterioration, through use of pesticides and abuse of fertilizers, and through the consequences of monocultures of inbred crop varieties.

## Deterioration of Soils

The amount of land available for cultivation changes when new lands are brought into production, when existing croplands deteriorate and are abandoned, and when croplands are converted to other uses. The projections suggest that, even with substantially higher food prices, only relatively modest amounts of additional land can be expected to be brought into production by 2000. This prospect accentuates the importance of increasing yields and, in turn, of maintaining and improving soil fertility. Yields can be enhanced with fertilizers but only at an increasing cost and only as long as an adequate soil structure remains. The condition of soils is of central importance now, and its importance is likely to increase in the years ahead. The trend, unfortunately, is one of deteriorating soil conditions.

To what extent does soil deterioration on existing croplands affect the world's agricultural potential? The limited data available can only suggest the outlines of an answer to this question, [203] showing scattered but alarming examples

of soil deterioration.* The primary problems include: (1) loss of topsoil to erosion, (2) loss of organic matter, (3) loss of porous soil structure, (4) build-up of toxic salts and chemicals.

Given the limited data, there are several approaches that might be used in assessing the influence of soil deterioration on agricultural production to the year 2000. First, as has been done in the Global 2000 Study's food projections, one can assume that farmers throughout the world will be aware of the potential problems, will successfully charge more for their produce, and will use the additional income to counteract potential ecological problems. The technologies and management techniques now available are assumed to be brought to bear on ecological problems as they emerge, so as to limit their adverse impact on expanding production. This approach does not assume that adverse effects do not occur but rather that the capital, knowledge, and incentives necessary to employ presently known solutions will be available. Under this assumption, the impacts of ecological problems on agricultural production do not increase markedly beyond the current level. This approach is subject to criticism because it is based on assumed developments—specifically, the adoption of environmentally sensitive technologies and management policies—that may or may not occur.

Another approach is to extrapolate on the basis of the present limited knowledge of world soil deterioration. For example, the 1977 U.N. Conference on Desertification projected that if present trends continue, the world will have lost one-third† of its arable lands due to desertification and

---

* Changes in soil quality cannot be directly and accurately measured over large geographic areas, and too few sample measurements have been made to obtain a detailed statistical picture at the global (or even, with few exceptions, at the national) level. Presently, rates of soil deterioration for large geographic areas can be estimated only on the basis of fragmentary evidence: data from experimental plots, studies of stream-water siltation, archeological and historical studies of once verdant lands now turning to desert, and remote sensing satellite images used to assess vegetative and other characteristics. The limited number of cases where site-specific data are available include examples of disastrous soil deterioration, and evidence of deterioration can be found in scattered observations from around the world. [204] The study of world soil conditions is further complicated in many regions by the use of synthetic fertilizers and high-yielding varieties, which may maintain or even increase production for a time, temporarily masking losses of soil and deteriorating soil structure.

† Erik Eckholm has noted in a private communication an inability to find anyone who will take responsibility for this U.N. projection. Eckholm himself sees the problem as serious, but not quite this serious. He has described his own perceptions of the problem in Erik Eckholm and Lester R. Brown, *Spread-*

other causes by 2000.[205] This approach is open to criticism because of the limited knowledge on which it is based. The approach used in the following paragraphs is simply to catalog and describe the principal elements of what is now known of world land degradations.

The five major agents of soil loss are: (1) desertification (the process of land deterioration associated with desert encroachment, usually caused by overly intense grazing, shortened fallow periods, and consumption of woody plants as fuel); (2) waterlogging, salinization, and alkalinization, which commonly occur when irrigation systems, particularly in arid lands, apply water in ways that are incompatible with soil drainage and other soil and water characteristics; (3) soil degradation that follows deforestation on steep slopes and in many humid tropical areas; (4) general erosion and humus loss occurring in major agricultural regions as a consequence of routine agricultural practices; and (5) loss of lands to urbanization, road building, village expansion, and other land-consuming developments associated with economic and population growth.

### Desertification.

Desertification* will probably be a major modifier of landscapes between now and 2000. If all the lands identified by the U.N. as having a high or very high probability of desertification were to become desert by 2000, deserts would occupy more than three times the 7,992,000 square kilometers they occupied in 1977.[206] Most of the land lost would be pastureland, but losses in cropland could also be significant. As shown in the accompanying map, most of the losses would probably take place in Africa and Asia. Desertification is

---

*ing Deserts—The Hand of Man,* Washington: Worldwatch Institute, Aug. 1977. Present losses to desertification are apparently on the order of 6 million hectares per year (60,000 square kilometers): 3.2 million hectares of rangeland, 2.5 million hectares of rainfed cropland, and 125,000 hectares of irrigated farmland (Margaret R. Biswas, "United Nations Conference on Desertification in Retrospect," Laxenburg, Austria: International Institute for Applied Systems Analysis, Sept. 1978, p. 31). According to "Desertification: An Overview," U.N. Desertification Conference Aug. 1977, areas undergoing severe desertification now cover about 30 million square kilometers, or 23 percent of the earth's ice free land area.

*Desertification is a broad, loosely defined term encompassing a variety of, ecological changes that render land useless for agriculture or for human habitation. Deserts rarely spread along well-articulated frontiers; rather, they pop up in patches where abuse, however unintended, destroys the thin cover of vegetation and fertile soil and leaves only sand or inert earth. (Erik Eckholm and Lester R. Brown, *Spreading Deserts—The Hand of Man,* Washington: Worldwatch Institute, Aug. 1977, pp. 7–8).

an active ongoing phenomenon, and its implications are not a matter of speculation. The economic bases of several West African countries, including Mauretania, Senegal, Upper Volta, Mali, Niger, and Chad have recently been undermined through the extensive desert expansion that occurred during the 1968–73 drought. These countries will find recovery difficult, as the damage done to soils was long-term. Sudan, Somalia, Ethiopia, Kenya, and Tanzania have also suffered degradation of soils associated with the recent drought.[207]

As already stated, one of the leading causes of desertification is overgrazing. As shown in the Free Range Grazing Pressure map in the colored map section, a large amount of land surface is used for free range grazing. Livestock populations have grown rapidly over the last few decades, and in the LDCs much of the increase has been in free-ranging animals. Globally the population of cattle rose by 38 percent over the 1955–76 period—including a 62 percent increase in the Near East and a 51 percent increase in Latin America. Over the same period, global sheep and goat populations increased by 21 percent, with a 52 percent increase in the Asian centrally planned economies and a 44 percent increase in Africa.[208] A portion of this increase has been in countries with rapidly expanding feedlot operations, but in many areas the increases in free-ranging livestock populations have pushed above the levels that can be indefinitely sustained by the land—given current pasture management policies and the limited application of available (but expensive) technologies for the protection of rangelands. In some regions, such as Rajasthan in India, increases in the land under cultivation have reduced available pastureland and intensified pressure on remaining pastures. The result has been severe declines in soil productivity and in some areas the actual creation of deserts of blowing sands.[209]

It is easy to underestimate the statistical probability of a drought. The 1968–73 drought in the African Sahel was so long and so severe that many experts suspected that a climatic shift had occurred. However, several statistical analyses of climatological data prepared for the 1977 U.N. Conference on Desertification suggest that the 5-year Sahelian drought was within the range of statistical expectation and therefore should not be thought of as a climatic shift or a fluke. Moreover, the analyses suggested a statistically significant tendency for dry years to occur in succession. Thus the Sahel can expect a recurrence of such a drought.[210] In most arid areas the oldest people can, on average, remember having experienced

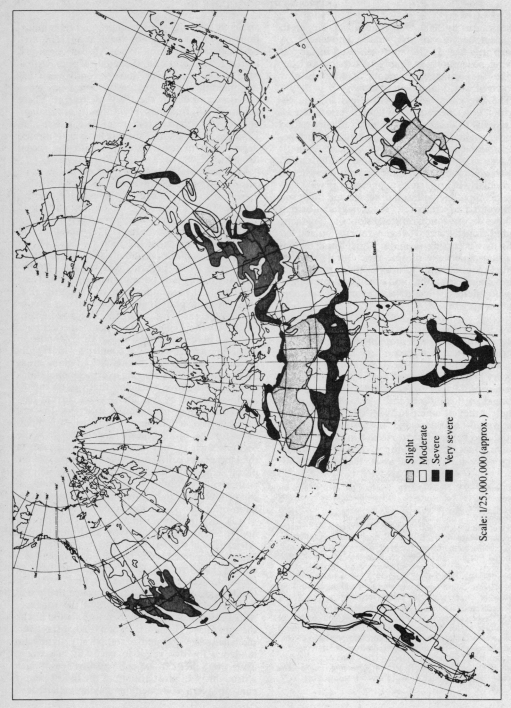

Slight
Moderate
Severe
Very severe

Scale: 1/25,000,000 (approx.)

Desertifification Map (U.N. Desertification Conference, 1977)

about four major droughts, some of which extended over several years. While most areas do not experience droughts as frequent or as severe as those in the Sahel, the probability of adverse weather is often underestimated, especially during periods of good weather.

The example of the Sahel also raises questions relating to populations, carrying capacity, and assistance. Drought always means hardship, but in cases like the recent Sahelian drought, where conditions exceed mere hardship and include severe famine and ecological decline, the role of human and animal population levels must be examined as potentially major contributors to suffering.[211] Where drought occurs periodically, the livelihood systems of the peoples there become adapted to coping with the consequences of drought. In these situations, the U.N. notes, great care must be exercised in external efforts to assist so that the adapted livelihood systems are not disrupted.[212]

## Waterlogging, Salinization, Alkalinization

Many irrigation projects also take their toll. The causes vary, as discussed below, but worldwide an estimated 125,000 hectares of irrigated land are lost from production each year due to waterlogging, salinization, and alkalinization.[213] This loss rate amounts to only about .06 percent per year of the world's total irrigated land.[214] If it remains constant through the year 2000, about 2.75 million hectares (approximately 1.4 percent of the world's total irrigated land) will be out of production. These losses have more impact than averaged figures suggest because irrigated land is almost always the most productive land in a given region. But even assuming average productivity, 2.75 million hectares represents the food supply (with average yields) for more than 9 million people.*

Problems of waterlogging, salinization, and alkalinization occur in arid regions where irrigation systems supply water to the soil faster than drainage can remove it. The excess water raises the water table to a level near the ground surface. Evaporation brings dissolved soil salts to the surface where they inhibit plant growth and form a mineral crust. The water that returns to local streams and rivers is often so laden with salts that

---

*A Department of Agriculture representative has pointed out that with higher yields (2,000 kilograms) 2.75 million hectares could feed more than 15 million people. Furthermore, even when lands are not abandoned, waterlogging, salinization, and alkalinization are reducing the yields on ever larger amounts of land—annually and cumulatively.

irrigation downstream is impaired (see the water section of this chapter for further information on this point).

Seepage from unlined canals is often even more of a problem than the water intended for irrigation. Canal seepage may cause the water table to rise, waterlogging the soil and transporting salts from lower soil horizons to the surface.

Such problems reach extreme proportions in Pakistan even as early as the 1960s. At that time in the Sind, one of Pakistan's two major provinces, 49 percent of all agricultural land was moderately or severely waterlogged, 50 percent was highly saline, and 27 percent was moderately saline, according to U.N. data. In the Punjab, the other major agricultural province, over 30 percent of all agricultural land was reported suffering from salinization. Massive soil reclamation projects in Pakistan have had some success, particularly in reducing waterlogging, but reclamation of saline soils has been slow.[215]

The situation in Pakistan is far from unique. In Afghanistan, waterlogging, salinization, and alkalinization are evident in most agricultural areas.[216] In Argentina, 2 million hectares of irrigated land are adversely affected by waterlogging, salinization, or alkalinization.[217] And in Peru, 300,000 out of 800,000 hectares of coastal irrigated land are affected by salinization or waterlogging.[218] In fact, virtually every nation with a sizable irrigated area is now adversely affected by these problems.

In the U.S., for example, some of the nation's richest farmlands are threatened. The San Joaquin Valley provides a recent, well-studied example. About 400,000 acres (160,000 hectares) of irrigated farmland in the San Joaquin Valley currently are affected by high, brackish water tables that pose an increasingly serious threat to productivity. Approximately 1.1 million acres (450,000 hectares)—about 13 percent of the total valley—ultimately will become unproductive unless subsurface drainage systems are installed. The salting problems of the valley have been compared to those that resulted in the collapse of civilization in Mesopotania and Egypt's upper Nile when early signs of agricultural overproduction were not heeded. Loss of the productive capacity of the San Joaquin Valley lands would be a serious loss to the people who work them, to the economic community of the valley, to the State of California, and to the country as a whole. The agricultural output of the valley is now estimated at $4 billion annually. To prevent this loss, a comprehensive system for management and disposal of the saline effluent of on-farm subsurface drainage systems has been proposed.[219] Similar problems are also being observed in California's Imperial Valley.

Reclamation of degraded irrigated lands is a slow and costly process, often requiring construction of major public works, drainage, and corrective soil chemistry and structure. Lands that are waterlogged but have no problems with accumulated salts can generally be restored by reducing the water seepage rate and improving drainage, which can be costly but at least shows immediate results. Salinized and alkalinized soils, on the other hand, generally can't be restored without washing the accumulated salts out of the soil. In arid lands where such problems occur, passing enough water through the soil to carry away excess soil salts is difficult, costly, and time-consuming. In most instances, drainage problems make it impossible to simply pour huge quantities of water over the soil, and major hydraulic engineering is required. Furthermore, once washed out, the salts may reach ground-water supplies or become deposited in downstream regions, thus moving the problem rather than solving it. In many cases it is only possible to move the salts down in the soil profile.

In conclusion, history shows that when the desert is made to bloom, it sometimes does so only as a day flower, soon to wither under the stressful interaction of soil and sun. Poorly managed irrigation is often a major cause. The U.N. Conference on Desertification has focused attention on these problems, and the ecological and technological aspects of reclamation and prevention are beginning to be understood.[220] However, many drylands scattered across the world are showing early signs of salinization. By 2000 these areas may have experienced major declines in fertility unless major educaional efforts are made and capital is provided. The technology is available, but high costs and poor management (often including no water charge, thus encouraging overwatering and inadequately designed drainage) may significantly limit its appliction.

### Deforestation

In their natural state, most regions of the globe receiving moderate-to-high rainfall would be forested. When forests are cut, particularly in tropical and semitropical lands (where rainfalls are violent and biochemical reactions are relatively rapid) and on steep slopes (where soils are usually thin and easily eroded), accelerated soil erosion occurs, accompanied by increased seasonal flooding, low flows, and siltation.

Haiti is an example of what advanced deforestation can do to an agricultural system. With a tight 5.3 persons per arable hectare, Haiti has effectively lost the forests on its watersheds. Farmers looking for a small patch of land, hungry cows and goats, and firewood gatherers have reduced the country's forests to 9 percent of their original extent. Droughts and floods are unmoderated by forest buffers; erosion is rampant; irrigation and hydroelectric systems are silting in; and the quality of the soils is declining.[221]

Information on watershed deforestation from U.S. Embassy officials (see Appendix C) and from the U.S. Agency for International Development,[222] suggests that Thailand, Brazil, Costa Rica, the Philippines, Burundi, the Ivory Coast, Burma, India, Indonesia, and many other nations may be facing similar problems, at least locally, if not on a nationwide scale. For example, the U.S. Embassy in Thailand reports that under the combined influences of firewood gathering, slash-and-burn agriculture, and large-scale illegal poaching of protected forests, the country's entire forest area cover could be effectively cleared by 1987, and even the most optimistic estimates of the rate of destruction offer no hope of significant forest stands in Thailand beyond 1993. As a result of its deforestation, Thailand suffers increasingly from both flood and drought, and while Thailand's arable area is still expanding, the general impression left by the U.S. Embassy reports is that erosion is already serious and likely to become more so.

As will be discussed more fully in the forestry section of this chapter, deforestation, particularly of mountain slopes forming the watersheds to heavily populated agricultural regions, appears likely to create serious obstacles to achieving the food projections summarized above, and hence also to the fulfillment of basic food needs for tens of millions of the world's people.

### General Erosion

Given the scenarios developed in the agricultural forecasts in this volume, it can be anticipated that hydrologic destabilization will increase rates of erosion and loss of soil organic matter through the year 2000. By that time many croplands that are now producing well will be facing serious soil problems if current cultivation practices continue.

Because corn (maize) is relatively poor at holding soil, the corn-growing lands—about 7.5 percent of all lands in cultivation, producing roughly one-fifth of the world's grain—will fare the worst. The United States, as the world's largest corn producer, is in particular danger.

The U.S. Soil Conservation Service considers soil losses of 1 ton per acre for shallow soils and 5 tons per acre for deep soils to be the maximum that can be sustained annually without harming productivity. Although difficult to estimate, the extent to which soil losses exceed this figure appears to be great. For example, a survey of 283 U.S. farms in the Midwest, Great Plains, and Pacific Northwest recently conducted by the General Accounting Office (GAO) found that 84 percent had annual soil losses in excess of 5 tons* per acre.[223] In Iowa and Illinois, the two corn-dominated states covered by the GAO study, half the farms surveyed lost betwen 10 and 20 short tons per acre per year. These findings are consistent with those of other studies.[224]

Gently sloping lands planted to corn, millet, or cotton often lose as much as 20 tons of soil per acre per year, at which rate they will have lost approximately 3 inches of soil by the year 2000.[225] Steeper slopes might double or even quadruple these figures and conceivably experience soil losses of 6 inches to a foot or more by the year 2000 wherever the main crop does not provide good soil cover. The significance of these losses depends on local soil depths, but to date the seriousness of such losses have been masked largely by energy subsidies in terms of fertilizers—subsidies that will be increasingly expensive and difficult to maintain in the decades ahead.

Wheat is relatively good at holding soil. Five to 10 tons of soil loss per acre per year are commonly reported losses for wheat, at which rate approximately 1.5 inches of soil could be lost by the year 2000.[226] Terraced rice cultivation appears to be the most soil-conserving of all. It has been calculated that Chinese, Japanese, and Korean practices may add more to the soil, through addition of canal dredging to the fields, than is washed away.[227] Very low rates of erosion can also be attained by crop rotations, such as alternative plantings of corn, wheat, and clover, which restore organic matter and keep the earth well covered at most times.

Loss of organic matter follows trends similar to those observed for erosion. It is particularly severe with crops such as corn and soybeans, which do not provide a dense soil cover or sodlike root structure. Organic matter is also lost if crop residues are burned to protect crops against disease, as they often are in the U.S., or if crop residues and manure are used as fuel, as they are increasingly in developing regions faced with firewood shortages. Rotation schemes, fallow periods, and green manuring can reduce losses or permit buildup. However, until 1973 relatively inexpensive chemical fertilizers and high crop prices discouraged fallowing and encouraged continuous cropping. Since 1973 fertilizer prices have risen, but although the Global 2000 Study's energy projections suggest that the price of energy-intensive fertilizers will increase significantly in the years ahead, the high effectiveness of chemical fertilizers may continue to make the use of organic fertilizers less attractive.

Loss of organic matter is critical for two reasons: (1) organic matter serves to retain soil structure and moisture, and (2) breakdown of soil organic matter adds carbon dioxide to the atmosphere, potentially leading to climatic change. As shown in Figure 13–3, the pool of carbon in soil systems is thought to be larger than that in forests and living organisms. The effects of converting fixed carbon in both forests and soil systems to carbon dioxide are discussed above in the climate section of this chapter.

### Losses to Development

When land is subjected to the intense uses characteristic of urban and industrial development, it is in effect permanently lost for food production. Furthermore, urban and industrial developments are often located on some of a nation's, or the world's, *best* agricultural land—rich, irrigated, alluvial soils in gently sloping river valleys. Such lands lost to urban and industrial growth often involve taking lands out of production and therefore represent an *actual* loss of production as opposed to a *potential* loss.

The loss of both producing and potentially producing land has serious implications for food-importing nations. For example, the total irrigated land in Egypt has remained virtually unchanged over the past two decades. Old producing lands are lost to development almost as fast as additional hectares are irrigated with water from the Aswan Dam.[228]

The worldwide losses of agricultural land to development are difficult to estimate on the basis of the limited data now available. A recent report by Lester Brown, President of Worldwatch Institute, brings together most of what is now known.[229] Brown projects that, if present trends in urban development and growth continue, development between 1975 and 2000 will claim 25 million hectares of cropland. While this is only about 2 percent of the world crop base, it is enough land (assuming even average productivity) to feed some 84 million people.

Increases both in urbanization (growth of the urban population) and suburbanization (the geographical spread of urban settlements) have ac-

## TABLE 13–18

### Loss of Agricultural Lands, 1960–2000, Selected Industrialized Countries

|  | Average Annual Rate of Loss 1960–70 | Projected Cumulative Loss 1978–2000 |
|---|---|---|
|  | Percent | |
| Austria | 0.18 | 5 |
| Belgium | 1.23[a] | 24 |
| Denmark | 0.30 | 6 |
| Finland | 0.28[b] | 6 |
| France | 0.18 | 4 |
| West Germany | 0.25 | 5 |
| Japan | 0.73[c] | 15 |
| Netherlands | 0.48[d] | 10 |
| New Zealand | 0.05 | 1 |
| Norway | 0.15 | 3 |
| Sweden | 0.33 | 7 |
| Turkey | 0.04 | 1 |
| United Kingdom | 0.18 | 4 |
| United States (excluding Alaska) | 0.08 | 2 |
| Weighted total |  | 2.5 |

Source: 1960–70 data from Organization for Economic Cooperation and Development, Interfutures. Ch. 13."Physical Environment." Paris, May 16, 1977 (draft), p. 22.

[a] 1959–70.    [b] 1959–69.    [c] 1965–75.    [d] 1966–72.

celerated the rate at which agricultural land is lost to development. A recent study by the Organization for Economic Cooperation and Development (OECD) indicates that in the OECD (industrialized) countries urban land area has been growing about twice as fast as the population.[230] This trend is due in part to sprawling residential patterns. In 1972 each additional U.S. suburbanite required 0.15 hectares of land (0.09 hectares of which was taken out of cultivation) for development purposes. This loss is nearly half the *average* agricultural land per capita (0.19 hectares) projected for the LDCs by the year 2000.[231] On a percentage basis, even higher loss rates are being experienced in some industrialized nations (see Table 13–18). Surveys in developing countries show lower per capita land losses to development, but the high rates of population growth and the limited amounts of prime farmlands are likely to make such losses equally important in the LDCs.

In the face of rising energy costs, it is unclear whether the trend toward urban, suburban, and industrial sprawl will continue or reverse. Energy concerns will gradually encourage both greater compactness (for the efficiency needed by large centralized energy facilities) and more decentralization (for the more diffused, land-intensive, and

self-sufficient settlement patterns that efficiently use solar and other small-scale renewable sources of energy, such as windmills, biogas plants and biomass). However these forces eventually balance out, it seems likely that significant amounts of land will be removed from cultivation or potential cultivation between now and 2000. The OECD countries again provide an example. Should 1960–70 rates of land loss continue, the OECD countries will have lost an average of 2.5 percent of their agricultural lands by 2000, as shown in the table. A substantial portion of the higher cost of food production projected for 2000 in Chapter 6 is a direct result of the costs of expanding arable area to compensate for development losses.

Over and above losses to urbanization and suburbanization, agricultural lands are being lost to expanding rural populations and villages around the world. The data available on these losses are limited. Lester Brown, who finds evidence that villages frequently expand onto cropland, reports that India, a nation of 600,000 villages, projects nonagricultural land use to expand by 9.8 million hectares (or 60 percent) between 1970 and 2000.[232] Overall, world losses of agricultural land to village expansion have not been estimated.

The food projections in Chapter 6 include explicit consideration of land lost to development.* The above discussion is presented as support for the estimates used and cited in the Study's food projections, although it provides only an indication of the gross changes known to be occurring.

### By the Year 2000

This discussion of global deterioration of soils has considered (1) desertification, (2) waterlogging, salinization and alkalinization, (3) the effects of deforestation, (4) general erosion and humus loss, and (5) loss of land to urbanization and village expansion. These problems are widely recognized by national and world leaders and efforts are being made to reduce rates of deterioration and to restore soils. The 1977 U.N. Conference on Desertification is an example of these efforts.

---

*In the GOL (grain, oilseed, and livestock) model used by the Department of Agriculture for the food projections, development-related land losses are specified as a negative function of population growth. Specifically, the assumed losses range from 0.03 hectares per capita in LDCs to 0.1 hectares per capita in the developed countries. The Department notes that to date losses of arable area to development have been offset substantially by larger gains through settlement of new lands or by reclamation of old lands. With the supply of potentially arable area finite and the cost of reclamation increasing, losses due to development are likely to become increasingly important.

Most instances of soil deterioration are reversible, at least in theory. Given sufficiently large commitments of time, capital, energy, technical knowledge, and political will, most land deterioration can be slowed, stopped, or even restored. The problem is that in practice the time and knowledge required and the economic, resource, and political costs involved make many cases of soil deterioration virtually irreversible.

The difficulty in controlling the five types of land deterioration can be seen in examples in the United States. Luther Carter has described the economic problem in part, noting that despite the billions spent on it, the problem of soil erosion persists.[233] The General Accounting Office has recently pointed to the need to give soil conservation top priority in order to meet future food needs.[234] Salinization continues to be a threat to important U.S. croplands.[235] Prime agricultural lands continue to be lost to urban sprawl, resource development, roads, and shopping centers.[236] The Department of Agriculture's Soil Conservation Service (SCS) reported that in 1975 soil losses on U.S. cropland amounted to almost 3 billion tons, an average of about 9 tons per acre. Although this was excessive, it was less than the estimated 4 billion tons of topsoil that would have been lost in 1975 if farmers had followed no conservation practices at all.[237] The SCS report concluded that to sustain U.S. crop production indefinitely at even present levels, soil losses must be cut in half. The SCS has developed a plan for reducing soil losses, but the plan has not been implemented, probably in part because it would lead to a 5–8 percent increase in production costs. It might also reduce food output somewhat in the short run.[238]

Not just in the U.S. but throughout the world, the fate of soil systems depends on societies' willingness to pay the short-run resource and economic costs to preserve soils for long-run benefits. Whether the soils of the world will deteriorate further or be reclaimed will depend in large part on the ability and willingness of governments to make politically difficult policy changes. Soil protection requires a stable society and well-developed institutions. A society stressed by warfare, hunger, internal turmoil, and corruption, or obsessed with modernization to the point that it ignores the fate of its agricultural lands, will be fortunate if the productivity of its land does not diminish significantly in the decades ahead.

The political difficulties cannot be overemphasized. Often solutions to soil problems will require resettlement, reduction of herd sizes, restrictions on plantings, reforms in land tenure, and public works projects that will fail without widespread cooperation from the agrarian population. The costs will be immediately apparent; the benefits will seldom be seen in less than half a decade and in some cases may not be apparent for a generation or more. Unless a government is trusted by its people or can afford to offer long-term financial incentives, it will have difficulty implementing soil conservation programs.

The soil conditions that can be expected by the year 2000 are critically dependent on policy changes during the intervening years. Assuming no policy change—the standard assumption underlying all of the Global 2000 Study projections—*significant deteriorations in soils can be anticipated virtually everywhere, including in the U.S.* Assuming that energy, water, and capital are available, it will be possible for a time to compensate for some of the deterioration by increasing the use of yield-enhancing inputs (fertilizer, irrigation, pesticides, herbicides, etc.), but the projected increases in energy (and chemical fertilizer) costs will make this approach to offsetting soil losses ever more expensive. Without major policy changes, soil deterioration could significantly interfere with achieving the production levels projected in this Study.

## Ecological Effects of Fertilizers and Pesticides

Historically, fertilizer use is correlated with the use of a number of yield-enhancing agricultural inputs including pesticides and herbicides. The projections in Chapter 6 are based on the assumption that growth in fertilizer use is representative of the growth in all yield-enhancing inputs. Therefore the "fertilizer" projections are intended to apply to a full package of yield-enhancing inputs.

However, from an ecological perspective, fertilizers and pesticides have very different effects. It is therefore important in the environmental analysis to examine factors that might alter the historic correlation. Thus, the discussions that follow begin with a brief consideration of some of the factors that will influence the relative growth of fertilizers and pesticides and herbicides. Fertilizers are considered first.

### Fertilizers

Chapter 6 projects that by 2000 global use per hectare of "fertilizer" (as defined in that chapter) will be 2.6 times that of the record levels reported in the early 1970s. Usage in LDCs is projected to quadruple, and usage in the centrally planned and market economies is projected to increase by factors of 2.3 and 2.1 respectively. Since the area under cultivation is projected to increase only slightly, the *per hectare* usage of fertilizers in all regions can be expected to increase at essentially the same rates as the total applications. In the discussion that follows, it is assumed that actual fertilizer use will follow closely these indicative "fertilizer" projections.

In assessing the environmental implications of the projected fertilizer usage, it is important to obtain some sense of the magnitude of projected fertilizer use relative to natural flows of basic nutrients. The Scientific Committee on Problems of the Environment (SCOPE) of the International Council of Scientific Unions estimated in 1976 that if current rates of increase in nitrogen fertilizer production were to continue, synthetic nitrogen fixation—which then amounted to about 26 percent of natural, terrestrial fixation— would be equal to natural fixation by 1983.[239] The ecological ramifications of an alteration of this magnitude in a basic nutrient cycle are unclear, as are the ramifications of the parallel and equally significant changes in the phosphate nutrient cycle.

While U.S. Department of Agriculture officials regard the global levels of fertilizer use projected for 2000 to be safe when applied carefully by trained personnel, they are aware that improper use leads to increased dangers. Improper use can aggravate rather than alleviate problems of soil deterioration and declining fertility. Furthermore, even with careful application adverse effects of fertilizer usage have been observed, or are suspected, in aquatic and marine systems, in the atmosphere, and in terrestrial ecosystems.

Scientific understanding of atmospheric influences is not yet well developed, but it is reported by the National Academy of Sciences that nitrous oxide from fertilizer usage, when it makes its way into the stratosphere, reacts in a fashion that depletes the ozone layer. If this phenomenon turns out to be serious, the world could find itself in the tragic situation of having to support the human population at the cost of subjecting the world's biota to damaging dosages of cosmic and ultraviolet radiation, at least one effect of which would be increased incidence of skin cancer in human beings.*

From the perspective of ecology, the known terrestrial effects of increased fertilizer usage are surprisingly benign. The addition of large amounts of three critical nutrients (phosphorus, potassium,

and fixed nitrogen) might be expected to produce many changes in soils. The most apparent effect is simply the intended increase in plant growth. One potentially adverse effect concerns the accelerated decomposition of organic matter in soils. As nitrogen is often the limiting nutrient for decomposition of soil organic matter, increased nitrogen usage contributes to reduction of soil organic matter, thus degrading soils and contributing carbon dioxide to the atmosphere.[239a]

As soon as virgin soil is plowed, the decomposition of its organic matter accelerates, and soil quality (especially tilth, porosity, and water-absorbing capacity) begins to deteriorate. It was once thought that the application of nitrogen fertilizer would rebuild the organic matter in croplands by stimulating more plant growth, the residue of which would be added to the soil.[239b] However, it was demonstrated early[239c]—and confirmed again more recently[239d]—that under modern farming methods the organic matter in soils cannot be maintained at anything approaching its virgin state. Generally, soil organic matter declines to an equilibrium value of 40–60 percent of the orginal content. Soil quality deteriorates as well. While in most cases crop yields can be maintained through the continual application of chemical fertilizers, through plowing with large heavy tractors, and through irrigation, the modern methods of farming tend to lock agriculture into a particular mode of cultivation and resource allocation if high yields in degraded soils are to be maintained.[239e]

Consequences of increased fertilizer use for aquatic systems are more serious than terrestrial effects and include eutrophication[240] and nitrate contamination of drinking water supplies.[241] The phosphorus component of fertilizers is thought to contribute most to eutrophication in affected lakes, but nitrogen is also important. Nitrogen contributes most to eutrophication in coastal waters. More than 70 percent of the nitrogen entering surface waters is from nonpoint agricultural sources. Even the input of nitrogen from rainwater is a sufficient nutrient loading in some lakes to support a moderate increase in biotic activity. An important part of the fixed nitrogen in precipitation enters the atmosphere as a result of ammonia volatilization, chiefly from animal wastes.[242]

The levels of nitrogen that pose hazards to human health—about 10 milligrams of nitrate per liter of water—are roughly an order of magnitude higher than the levels that produce eutrophication and are relatively rare at the rates at which fertilizers are now used. The primary population at risk is that of infants under the age of three. In-

---

*See the climate section of this chapter for further information on nitrous oxide and other chemicals that deplete the ozone layer.

fants consuming synthetic milk formula mixed with nitrate-contaminated water may experience the toxic effect known as methemoglobinemia. This disease is readily diagnosed, and is rapidly reversible with clinical treatment. After the age of 3 months, vulnerability to methemoglobinemia decreases rapidly. In the U.S., concentration of nitrates above 10 milligrams per liter are rare. The primary risk is from wellwater on or near farms, especially in areas where soil and hydrologic conditions favor the accumulation of nitrate in groundwater.

While mortality from methemoglobinemia is now extremely rare, the presence of high levels of nitrate in drinking water supplies poses a health hazard that is already a valid concern in at least some regions of the United States, and the projected doubling to quadrupling of fertilizer applications by 2000 could make this disease more serious and more widespread.[243]

## Pesticides and Herbicides

The first step in examining the future environmental implications of pesticides is to assess whether their usage globally is likely to continue to be correlated with the "fertilizer" package projected in Chapter 6. This assessment is difficult because data on pesticide use are not published for most countries, and thus it is not possible to quantify past trends in any detail or to project future developments. It is known that a large fraction—probably more than half—of all pesticides are applied to a few high-value, commercial crops (especially cotton, vegetables, and tobacco) and that demands for these crops are expected to continue growing steadily. The applications of pesticides to food grains are relatively small.

The Food and Agriculture Organization succeeded in gathering some data for the LDCs in 1975 and found that pesticide use in the LDCs had increased by about 50 percent over the two year period 1971–73 and that consumption for 1974–77 was expected to increase more slowly, at about 9 percent per year.[244] These figures are significantly influenced by the heavy use of pesticides in India, Mexico, and Argentina. If this slowed rate of increase (9 percent per year) continues, LDC pesticide use by 2000 would still be more than 10 times the 1971–73 rate. The FAO growth estimates are therefore considerably higher than the "fertilizer" projection of Chapter 6.

The FAO survey revealed further that half the pesticides used in the LDCs were generally persistent organochlorines (DDT, aldrin, and other chlorinated hydrocarbons). This is to be expected.

Though more environmentally damaging, organochlorines are markedly less expensive in most applications than the less persistent, more specific alternatives, and are also far safer for farmers to apply because of less short-term toxicity to humans. If the conclusion to the food projections in Chapter 6 is correct—namely, that in most LDCs food demands "are likely to outweigh problems of the environment well beyond 2000"—the use of DDT and other persistent pesticides can be expected to continue in proportions much like those found at present.[245]

The future use of pesticides in the industrialized nations is equally difficult to project both because of data limitations and because of growing interest in changing practices. The "fertilizer" indicator in Chapter 6 implies moderate increases (by a factor of 2.1) over 1971–75 average consumption by 2000. The banning of DDT and other persistent insecticides by much of the industrialized world during the last decade suggests that increases in insecticide usage there will be discriminating, emphasizing compounds with less persistent ecological effects than the compounds likely to be used in the LDCs. Furthermore, there is growing interest in several industrialized nations in the techniques of integrated pest management* (IPM).[246] Although there is not at this time a prevailing policy to encourage IPM, increasing pest resistance and simple economics may encourage a shift. If widely applied, IPM would reduce the use of pesticides.

The rapid increase in the use of herbicides in the developed regions in the last two decades can be expected to continue. If no-till planting, which involves heavy use of herbicides, is widely adopted in the next few decades—and there is reason to expect that it will be—very rapid increases in herbicide usage can be expected.

No-till planting is the practice of eliminating field preparation entirely and planting on top of the residue of the previous crops. Minimum tillage refers to the practice of minimizing field preparation—principally plowing, but also tillage with disc harrows, drags, and cultivators—for planting. There are both advantages and disadvantages in no-till and minimum-till practices. Crop residues

---

*The Council on Environmental Quality defines integrated pest management as follows: IPM employs a combination of techniques to control crop-threatening pests. Maximum reliance is placed on natural pest population controls and a combination of suppression techniques—cultural methods, pest-specific diseases, resistant crop varieties, sterile insects, attractants, augmentation of parasites or predators, or chemical pesticides as needed.

are often breeding places for pests, which increases the need for pesticides or other pest control measures. Fertilizer placement options are reduced and, as a result, fertilizers may be inefficiently utilized and fertilizer runoff increased. Also, extensive use of herbicides is involved. Nonetheless, no-till and minimum-till techniques appear to have potential for reducing energy inputs and for conserving soil resources. The use of these techniques has grown roughly 300 percent in the U.S. since the start of the decade. They account today for roughly a quarter of farmland preparation, and some experts expect them to be used very extensively in the future.

What, then, are the prospects for future utilization of pesticides and herbicides? In the following discussion, it is assumed that world pesticide (and herbicide) use will increase at approximately the same rates as the "fertilizer" indicator in the Department of Agriculture projections in Chapter 6, that is, they will more than double over the 1975–2000 period. In the LDCs the increase is likely to be fourfold, and possibly as much as sixfold if the FAO estimated increase of 9 percent per year is sustained.

The environmental problems anticipated from increases in pesticide use are suggested by problems that have already occurred and can be expected to continue.[247] They include: (1) biological amplification and concentration of persistent pesticides in the tissues of higher-order predators, including humans; (2) development of increased resistance to pesticides by numerous insect pests, and hence possible declines in yields through increased vulnerability to pests; (3) destruction of natural pest controls such as insect-eating birds and predatory insects, and hence further increases in the cost of—and decreases in the effectiveness of—preventing crop losses caused by pests; (4) emergence of new pests previously not troublesome; and (5) increased poisonings of farm workers and families from nonpersistent pesticides.

The first of these problems, biological amplification (or concentration), is familiar because of the extensive attention it received (due initially to the pioneering work of Rachel Carson) in the years preceding the bans in several developed countries on the use of DDT.* Here it is appropriate to note only that biological concentration is a continuing problem. Although monitored concentrations of DDT in the environment have been shown to be declining in those industrialized countries that have banned DDT,[248] concentrations are

virtually certain to continue to increase in those LDCs where DDT is still being used extensively. Unfortunately, very little information is available on DDT concentrations in LDC environments because almost no monitoring is being done.

The second problem, biological resistance, has received less popular attention than the first, but is equally important. Biological resistance to pesticides develops in pest species because repeated pesticide usage places species under an evolutionary pressure such that those individuals in a pest population that possess some immunity to pesticides are the most likely to survive and reproduce. Malaria-transmitting mosquitoes, plant-eating mites,[249] and other insects that have been regularly exposed to pesticides are showing great genetic flexibility in developing tolerance or resistance to insecticides. The three examples that follow were selected from the many available and illustrate the seriousness of this problem.

1. In California, a state that makes heavy use of pesticides, a large number of pest species attacks crops. Of this large number, 25 species have been found to cause major damage (i.e., losses of $1 million or more per species in 1970). The genetic flexibility of these species is indicated by the fact that, at some location in the world, 21 of those 25 species have been found to be resistant to one or more pesticides: 16 to DDT, 16 to organophosphates, and 10 to cyclodines. In California alone, 17 of the 25 species were found to be resistant to one or more types of insecticide.[250]

2. Disease vectors that have been heavily controlled by use of insecticides have shown great ability to tolerate their intended poisons. The National Academy of Sciences (using World Health Organization data) documents the growing number of vector-insect species (e.g., body lice) showing tolerance to important pesticides over an extended period, as shown in the following table.[251]

| | DDT | Dieldrin | Organo-phosphate Compounds | Total |
|---|---|---|---|---|
| 1956 | 27 | 25 | 1 | 33 |
| 1962 | 47 | 65 | 8 | 81 |
| 1969 | 55 | 84 | 17 | 102 |
| 1974 | 61 | 92 | 27 | 109 |

Of the anopheline (malarial) mosquitoes, 41 have been found resistant to dieldrin and 24 to DDT. One species, *Anopheles albimanus Wiederman*, has become resistant not only to dieldrin and DDT but to malathion and certain other or-

*For some uses, that is. The bans do not prevent the use of DDT for controlling health-threatening insect vectors.

ganophosphate and carbonate insecticides, *thus showing itself resistant to all the major chemical groups that are used to combat malaria vectors.*[252] If pesticide resistance becomes widespread in other species of malarial mosquitoes, control of malaria would be badly hampered, and its incidence could be expected to rise sharply.

3. Cotton, which receives about 50 percent of all the pesticides applied in the U.S.,[253] now attracts several pests that have developed immunity to all currently available and registered pesticides. In cotton-growing districts across Central America, the U.S. Southwest, Southern California, and Australia, the situation has become so severe that growers in many places have been forced either to give up cotton growing or to shift to integrated pest management techniques. Some districts have endured the cost of as many as 30–50 pesticide applications a year to a single crop.[254]

As long as pesticides are used, pest resistances can be expected to continue to develop. By the year 2000 there will almost certainly be more pesticide-resistant pests and more crops for which there are no effective pesticides. There will also be more registered pesticides. How the continuing struggle with insect pests will stand in 2000 will depend on pest control policies, chemical technologies, and biological technologies. Newer pesticides are generally more selective, but also more expensive than those they replace. The techniques of integrated pest management offer new hope,[255] but the transmittal of these techniques requires a significant amount of field and laboratory research on insect ecology, and therefore commitments of both time and money. Also IPM methods depend heavily on the very species most seriously threatened by pesticides—the beneficial insect species that prey upon agricultural pests.

The third problem of increased pesticide use is simply that pesticides destroy natural pest controls. The discussion here focuses on predatory insects, but insect-eating birds are also affected.

Insecticides are usually more damaging to predator insect species than they are to pests, because (1) predators may be poisoned through ingesting poisoned pest species as well as directly through the effects of the pesticide*; (2) since predator populations are always less numerous and generally less fecund than their prey, predator populations have less genetic material from which to develop immunities to pesticides, take longer to regain their numbers after insecticide application,

and face a higher probability of being reduced to such a low level that they cannot recover; (3) the predator species are eliminated both directly through the effects of insecticides and indirectly through the loss of their normal food when the insects on which they feed are eliminated.

Often predatory insects are made locally extinct through pesticide applications. When predatory insects are eliminated, herbivorous pest species multiply rapidly leading to severe pest outbreaks. Farmers often respond to such outbreaks with still heavier application of pesticides, reducing further the chances that predator species might be reestablished.

Also, in such predator-free environments, species that have previously been benign become major pests. Mites, which are now major pests in fruit culture, became pests only after the start of heavy use of pesticides in fruit cultivation. Similar histories can be found for many insect species, including Hessian flies, and several major pest species of the cotton plant. Insecticides are probably largely responsible for new insect pests in agriculture.[256]

Successive developments of biological resistance and releases of new pest species will decrease the effectiveness of the projected increases in pesticide use. Diminishing returns on pesticide investments can go on only so long before crop losses will force a major change in strategies of pest control. The techniques of integrated pest management[257] and biological controls appear now to offer good alternatives. Although there are as yet few policy commitments to IPM or biological controls, interest is growing.

## By the Year 2000

The pressure to increase agricultural yields is projected to more than double the application rates of nitrogen and phosphorous fertilizers and pesticides. This growth in fertilizer use implies that before 2000 the annual industrial rate of fixing of nitrogen for agricultural purposes will exceed the total global rate of nitrogen fixation by natural systems. The full implications of a modification of this magnitude in a basic nutrient cycle are not clear and have not yet been studied carefully, but potentially adverse effects are known or suspected. Nitrate contamination of fresh water supplies and eutrophication of fresh and estuarine waters are among the adverse effects known to be possible, and potentially serious reductions in the atmospheric ozone layer are suspected by some knowledgeable scientists. The increased use of pesticides can be expected to continue to reduce

*In general, predators are more susceptible to pesticides than the pest species they hunt.

pest populations, but with diminishing returns since insect resistances to pesticides will continue to develop and predator populations will continue to be depleted. By 2000 the techniques of integrated pest management and biological controls may be in much wider use than today.

The overall environmental impacts are difficult to estimate because so many uncertain variables are involved. Rising food prices (where people can afford to pay them) may allow producers to endure the higher costs of increased pesticide use at diminished returns; increased resistance to pesticides may increase losses, thereby increasing food prices still more; or increased pesticide prices may make IPM more competitive. The rate at which pest resistance will diminish returns on investments in chemical controls will depend both on the way the chemicals are used and on the progress of chemical technology in finding new insecticides. New chemical pesticides will be developed but will require time and money for registration, adoption, and application.

There are similar uncertainties for the variables relating to fertilizers. Will the LDCs—where the marginal returns on fertilizer investments are greatest—be able to afford fertilizers? How serious a threat do fertilizers pose for the upper atmosphere? How far and how rapidly will the biologically based technologies for nitrogen fixation develop and be applied?

With all this uncertainty, it is not possible to project precisely how these variables will develop over the next two decades. It is only possible to note that the foreseeable trend is one of heavy and increasing dependence—often with diminishing returns—on both synthetic fertilizers and chemical pesticides. The potentially adverse atmospheric effects associated with continued heavy dependence on synthetic fertilizers is one of the most understudied and potentially serious global environmental questions. Pest control strategies also need much further study. Many experts feel that strategies based on biological controls and integrated pest management offer much greater possibilities for improvement than do chemical technologies alone, and a gradual shift toward integrated and biological control techniques seems probable in both the industrialized countries and the LDCs.

## Crop Vulnerability: Genetic Considerations

With only modest increases in arable land expected, the food projections imply strong pres-

sures to continue increasing yields through genetic technologies. Following two decades of developments in agricultural genetics, two trends can be expected in response to the continuing strong pressures. The first is for further genetic improvements in key plant and animal species to raise yields.* Developments in this area will entail greater dependence on inbred strains manifesting a high degree of genetic uniformity. The second trend is the shift toward monoculture cultivation of a few relatively high-yielding, low-cost, staple food crops. Together, these two trends will lead to further genetic hybriding and further replacement of lower-yielding, diversified cropping patterns with extensive, often contiguous, patterns. The short-term effect will be increased yields, but in the long run, questions of crop vulnerability must be considered.

These two factors—dependence on inbred strains and the shift toward monoculture cultivation—have become more closely interrelated over the past two decades as pressure to expand food production has grown. It has been estimated that by the early 1970s over four-fifths of the world's food supplies were derived from less than two dozen plant and animal species.[258] One expert estimates that as much as four-fifths of the world's population depends for sustenance on wheat or rice.[259] The exact figures are not important. The point is that the already narrow genetic base of the world's major food crops may become even more narrow. Plant diseases are constantly evolving ways to overcome plant resistances, requiring plant breeders to develop new resistant strains. The tens of thousands of genotypes of the major crop species are the raw materials from which plant breeders work, and these stocks of genetic raw materials are being reduced as natural habitats are lost. Increased reliance on a narrowing gene pool and more extensive monoculture of food staples could lead to sudden unanticipated widespread losses in world food production. How likely and how serious is such a disaster? There is no easy or precise answer to the question. Past history suggests that the probability of a major genetic failure is low but increasing.

The following paragraphs discuss three aspects of increasing genetic vulnerability. The first is historic in nature. Past examples demonstrate both the difficulty of controlling pest or disease infections in areas of extensive monoculture, and

---

*Questions are being raised as to how much further yields can be increased by genetics and technology. See for example N. F. Jensen, "Limits to Growth in World Food Production," *Science*, July 28, 1978, pp. 317–20.

the severe implications of failures. The second and third aspects relate to concerns voiced by plant geneticists themselves: that present trends toward uniform strains and loss of genetic reserves could raise the frequency and severity of pest-related and disease-related crop failures significantly by 2000, and that the costs of even relatively minor genetic failures (genetic in the sense that a crop population is genetically unable to protect itself from pathogens and pests) may ultimately outweigh gains from genetically increased yields, even if major catastrophes do not occur. Such a development would be a catastrophe by itself, eventually.

## Historical Examples

One of the best known examples of a genetic/monoculture crop failure is the massive failure of potato crops of the 1840s in Ireland and Europe. An estimated 2 million people starved to death in the wake of the blight, and a similar number were forced to emigrate.[260] The potato famine was not a unique phenomena; there are many other examples. Wheat rust epidemics have caused localized famines since the Middle Ages. The European wine industry was nearly destroyed three times in the last century by three different plant diseases. Between 1870 and 1890 coffee rust transformed Ceylon from the world's largest coffee-growing nation into a country unfit for coffee-growing. Shortly after the turn of the century, two separate, highly destructive epidemics struck the widely cultivated Gros Michael banana.[261] A fungus devastated the Bengali rice crop in 1942, leading to the deaths of tens of thousands.[262] In 1946 a large fraction of the U.S. oat crop, which was comprised almost entirely of a strain called Victoria, was lost to a fungus epidemic.[263] While these genetically related crop failures have all had very serious impacts on the human populations involved, some genetic failures have been even more damaging ecologically. For example, the American chestnut is virtually extinct due to the chestnut blight, and elms are becoming ever scarcer due to Dutch elm disease.

Serious outbreaks of genetically related crop diseases continue. For example, after existing as a minor disease for 14 years, race 15B of the wheat stem rust erupted in the early 1950s into a full-blown epidemic. It destroyed 75 percent of the Durham variety in the 1953 U.S. spring wheat crop as well as 35 percent of the bread wheat crop in that season.[264]

Another example occurred in 1970. A corn fungus disease, *Helminthosporium maydis*, reached epidemic proportions in large areas of the corn belt. An estimated 80 percent of U.S. corn acreage was highly susceptible because of both the genetic composition of the corn and the contiguous monoculture used across large areas of the states involved. The disease did not spread to all susceptible areas, but it did manage to reduce U.S. corn production by 15 percent (710 million bushels). It is no exaggeration to call the response of the seed corn industry heroic. There is a fascinating story of efforts to locate stocks of normal cytoplasm, which were then in short supply.[265] If the U.S. seed industry had not been sufficiently adaptable in developing a technical fix—it replaced approximately 80 percent of its sales with an alternative (and much harder to produce) product*—losses in 1971 and 1972 might have been much greater than in 1970.[266] Nonetheless, the effect on the price of seed was significant. The price of seed corn in 1970–71 was $18–$25 per bushel; the mean price was $20. The price has risen steadily ever since to a mean of $48 per bushel during the 1976–77 season.[267] This 140 percent increase is due in large part to the increased difficulty of producing blight-resistant seed.

## The Danger of Present Trends Toward Monoculture and Genetic Uniformity

It is almost always the case that a hard fight on one front means fewer defenses elsewhere. So it is generally with breeding plants for high yields. Modern plant breeding is based largely on the use of inbred, uniform strains,[268] and the most inbred strains appear to have weakened in their natural resistance to pathogens and pests. The inbred products manifest a high degree of genetic uniformity. The increasing cultivation of strains of high-yield varieties will result in great increases in the degree of genetic uniformity of major crops throughout the world. As a result the fraction of the crop at risk in the event of a trait-specific epidemic will also increase, as will the ease with which disease or insect pests can spread across large areas of contiguous monoculture. As a result, the probable geographic extent of the epidemic may expand in the years ahead. Furthermore, since water enhances the transmission of many plant diseases, the projected in-

---

*The vulnerable strain in this case was a male-sterile cytoplasm, which allowed the breeder to cross strains in the field, using natural pollination rather than employing an expensive manual process to avoid self-fertilization of the two strains. The fungus forced the seed industry to go back to hand detasseling. (C. E. Yarwood, "Man-Made Plant Diseases," *Science*, Apr. 10, 1970, pp. 218–20.)

creases in the amount of irrigated cropland may further increase the vulnerability of crops to disease throughout the world.[269] Furrow or flood irrigation, for example, creates conditions that favor the growth of pathogens requiring high soil moisture (e.g., *Pythium*), and sprinkling irrigation favors diseases spread by splashing water and rain (e.g., bacterial blight and anthracnose of bean).[270]

Simultaneously, the genetic resources available for combatting diseases are dwindling. In the event of a major new crop epidemic, plant breeders sort through thousands of varieties of the afflicted plant species, hoping to identify a resistant strain that can be interbred with other varieties to impart disease resistance without reducing productivity or imparting undesirable characteristics. Finding a resistant strain depends on the quality of the available seed bank. In general, the more tough wild varieties available, the better the chance of finding an appropriate resistant strain.[271]

However, the varietal stock is diminishing. The wild strains (from which modern high-yielding varieties were originally bred) are not usually cultivated and are being obliterated by widespread and increasing destruction of habitat. High-yield varieties are being adopted everywhere, replacing the myriad native strains that local farmers have developed over centuries. These strains, often uniquely suited to local conditions, are rarely preserved when farmers shift to high-yield varieties. The increases in the use of high-yield varieties implicit in the food projections of Chapter 6 will worsen this situation.[272]

A recently discovered plant related to corn (maize) dramatically illustrates the potentially catastrophic losses that can occur when plant species are lost. Corn, an annual plant, must be planted every year at the expense of labor, erosion, and fossil fuel subsidies. A plant known as teosinte, an ancestor of corn, was thought to have had several varieties, some annual and some perennial. If a perennial variety of teosinte could be found, modern plant breeding techniques might permit the development of a perennial corn. For many years, only annual varieties of teosinte were discovered. Unfortunately, teosinte grew in only limited areas of Mexico where they were regarded locally as weeds, and it was feared that the perennial varieties—if they ever existed—had been eradicated.

In 1910 a perennial variety of teosinte was discovered.[273] The variety discovered (*Zea perennis*) has the long-sought perennial properties, but unfortunately it has 40 chromosomes and can not be crossed with modern corn, which has 20 chromosomes. The discovery of *Zea perennis* established the fact that a perennial variety of teosinte had in fact existed, but it seemed increasingly likely that the 20-chromosome variety had been lost.

In late 1977 Raphael Guzman, a botany student at the University of Guadalajara, found a new variety of teosinte growing in a remote, mountainous region of Mexico in the state of Jalisco. Guzman's variety (*Zea diploperennis*) has now been examined by Dr. Hugh H. Iltis, Director of the Herbarium at the University of Wisconsin, who reports that *Zea diploperennis* is a perennial variety with the 20 chromosomes necessary for cross-breeding with corn.

The discovery of *Zea diploperennis* opens the possibilities of not only perennial corn, but of corn that can be grown over wide ranges of climate and soil. Furthermore, since *Zea diploperennis* grows successfully in cool, damp places where fungus diseases (such as the 1971 corn blight) abound, crossbreeding may produce varieties that are more resistant to the diseases that now plague corn farming.

Cross-breeding has begun, and fertile offspring have been produced. Dr. Iltis now feels certain that the perennialness of *Zea diploperennis* can be crossed into corn, but cautions that perhaps 10–20 years will be required.

The sobering fact, however, is that the benefits from *zea diploperennis* could easily have been lost, just as the potential benefits from many other plant species are being lost now, especially in the tropics. Dr. Iltis writes of *Zea diploperennis*:

This species could easily have become extinct [before its discovery], and may yet become [extinct] in the wild in the near future. . . . Just this winter I spent 10 weeks exploring for primitive corn in southern Jalisco, Mexico. There is wholesale mass destruction of vegetation [in progress there] on a gigantic scale (e.g., virgin tropical deciduous forest near Puerto Vallarta, 30,000 hectares at a time) by pushing of vegetation into piles with bulldozers, then burning the piles and planting sorghum. . . . The destruction is enormous, terrible and devastating. . . . None of this vegetation has . . . been studied or . . . represented in preserves. Much of such destruction was originally U.S. instigated to "help . . . raise more food." . . . One could not think of a more effective policy . . . to help destroy a livable world![274]

Dr. Iltis has recommended that the mountain range where *Zea diploperennis* was discovered be established as a national park. Instead, he reports, the area is being deforested to provide jobs and to supply wood for making broom handles.[275]

Plant breeders around the world are aware of the rapid rate at which species are being lost, and efforts are being made to protect genetic resources. An International Board for Plant Genetic Resources has been established in Rome with U.N. and national government funding. The Board is encouraging a variety of seed collection, storage, and documentation schemes.[276] The U.S. Department of Agriculture maintains an extensive collection of crop plant specimens which includes more then 60,000 small-grain specimens, but concern is increasing over corporate control of genetic resources. Seed companies owned by multinational conglomerates have large private seed reserves and are lobbying the U.S. Congress to extend patent protection to plant varieties.[276a] The institutes responsible for breeding Green Revolution varieties are developing and expanding their collections, and the Soviet collections are as extensive as our own, if not more so. But as plant geneticist Jack Harlan has pointed out, many of these collections leave much to be desired:

I know these collections too well. Some are better than others; some are better maintained than others. All are incomplete and shockingly deficient in some kinds of materials. They tend to be enormously redundant in certain races showing seemingly endless repetition of combinations and permutations of common items and are cluttered with accessions that float from experiment station to experiment station. On the other hand, some races are hardly represented at all and the wild and weedy gene pools are conspicuously missing. In no collection is there an adequate sampling of the spontaneous races that are the most likely sources of disease and pest resistance. On the whole, the collections we have are grossly inadequate for the burden they will have to bear.[277]

This narrowing of the gene pool may hinder plant breeding in coming years: Traits possessed by local plants (such as tolerance to adverse and eroding soil conditions or insect and bird predation), which may be required by the high-yielding varieties to adapt them to local environmental conditions, may be lost.

Animal genetic resources are facing problems like those affecting the pool of plant genes. Local breeds of livestock are disappearing almost as rapidly as are local crop strains. Due to artificial insemination, changes in livestock populations that might formerly have taken centuries now take place in a few decades. About 80 percent of the cattle strains indigenous to Europe and the Mediterranean are threatened with extinction. Elsewhere, many of the tropical cattle strains are low in numbers, and programs for their genetic improvement are often weak. Native poultry and pig strains are also threatened in some developing regions. Very little is known about genetic resources for goats, water buffalo, camels, alpacas, llamas, cultivated fish species, and other domesticated animal varieties.[278] Therefore it is not possible to evaluate the loss of genetic diversity among these types of livestock as readily as among crop plants and their progenitors.

## Minor Genetic Failure

Regardless of whether major disasters occur, it is clear that further development (or even maintenance) of genetically specialized, high-yield crop strains that are also defensible against pests and diseases will be increasingly difficult. There will be occasional pest and pathogen outbreaks from genetic failures, i.e., when the natural or inbred resistance of a plant (or animal) strain is overcome by pests or pathogens. Many plant breeders now expect a new variety of wheat to last only about a decade before pests and pathogens evolve a way around the variety's defenses.[279] The high-yield Mexican wheats that touched off much of the Green Revolution were carefully bred for resistance to stem rust, leaf rust, and stripe rust. Recently, however, this resistance appears to have begun to break down, and 10 years appears to be the longest that a wheat variety can withstand the constantly evolving attack of the three rusts.[280] As a result, peasant and commercial farmers using high-yield seeds will have to learn to shift varieties when the ones they are using become vulnerable. Furthermore, the production and distribution of seed will have to be developed to the point that one major variety can be substituted for another over large areas on very short notice.*

The trends point to problems for plant breeders. When favored strains cease to be effective, good monitoring and management may be capable of limiting losses, but difficulties will mount. As the probability of plant epidemics increases (due to inbreeding, decreased species disease re-

---

*A far better approach might be to simply avoid monocultures altogether. Plant pathologist J. Artie Browning has described the advantages of diverse cultures modeled on natural ecosystems. He notes: "When used as part of a *diverse* [plant] population, a frequency of only about 30% [resistant plant strain] can be considered adequate protection against the most virulent and prevalent group of strains of the pathogen!" ("Relevance of Knowledge About Natural Ecosystems to Development of Pest Management Programs for Agro-Ecosystems," *Proceedings of the American Phytopathological Society,* 1974, pp. 191–99.)

sistance, and monoculture) and as the number of genetic resources available declines (due to loss of wild habitat and the replacement of local strains with high-yield varieties), major food losses will be increasingly difficult and costly to avoid.

The less developed countries in the tropics may be particularly susceptible to genetic crop failures in the years ahead. The traditional staple foods and export crops of the tropics are often more vulnerable than the global staples, either because they are propagated asexually (with the consequence that all plants in a large area are genetically identical) or because the present collections of their genetic material are very limited—or both. [281] Notable among such vulnerable crops are: plantation crops, such as rubber, oil palm, coffee, and cocoa (whose seeds resist normal methods of storage with the result that the collections of germ plasm are extremely limited); and tropical roots and tubers, such as yams, taro, sweet potato, and cassavas (which are both extremely difficult to store and are commonly propagated by dividing roots, a form of propagation that leads to genetically identical plantings). [282] For crops such as these, the stage is set for disasters on the scale of the coffee blight that ruined Ceylon's coffee industry and the potato blight that struck Ireland.

Genetic engineering may, at some point, reduce dependence on naturally evolved sources of disease-resistant genetic material, but to date there has been little success in the use of induced mutations for generating agriculturally useful plant varieties. [283] Plant cell culturing might eventually improve photosynthetic efficiency and the amino acid balance in plants (from the human point of view) and lead to asexual propagation of crop plants. [284] Should this happen, the world may face even greater genetic uniformity in crops.

Areas in which science and technology could definitely help in combatting genetic vulnerability include increased systematization of existing collections, computerized reference systems, better international exchange of plant disease information, improved warning systems, genetic heterogeneity in agro-ecosystems, and live collections in protected, representative ecosystems.

### By the Year 2000

If present trends continue, increasing numbers of people will be dependent on the genetic strains of perhaps only two dozen plant and animal species. These strains will be highly inbred, and the plant strains may have reduced pest and disease resistance and may be planted in large, contiguous monocultures. Plant and animal epidemics will occur as they have in the past, except that in the future the number of human lives at risk may not be in the millions (as was the case in the Irish potato famine) but in the tens or even hundreds of millions. While the magnitude of the risks involved cannot be measured precisely, the world's history of crop failures due to pests and diseases (including the recent U.S. corn blight) demonstrates that the probabilities of a major failure are not negligible. Furthermore, the costs of even a minor failure would be so high they might offset the gains in yields expected from extensive monocultures of high-yield varieties.

### Food and Nonrenewable Fossil Fuels

Modern high-yield agriculture is heavily dependent on fossil fuel inputs.[*] As Philip Handler, President of the National Academy of Sciences, has observed,

The great gains in cereal production have occurred where modern energy-intensive agriculture—as developed in the United States, largely with federal research support—has combined applied genetics, irrigation, pesticides and herbicides, fertilizer and mechanization to the increase of yields. In effect, modern agriculture utilizes sunlight to transmute fossil fuels into edible crops. [285]

The gains and developments noted by Dr. Handler are illustrated in the U.S. corn (maize) data presented in Table 13–19 (inputs and outputs expressed in common measures) and Table 13–20 (inputs and output expressed in energy equivalents). Perhaps most notable are the declining labor input and the increasing energy inputs through machinery, gasoline, fertilizers, pesticides, herbicides, drying, irrigation, electricity, and transportation. Yields also increase—by 138 percent from 1945 to 1970—but on a list of the 20 major world food crops and nations that regularly achieve the highest yields per hectare of each, the United States, as of 1974, does not appear even once. [286] Furthermore, the energy input table shows that the number of calories returned in food energy per calorie of input energy declines by almost 25 percent over the 1945–70 period. Overall, the U.S. now uses the equivalent of approximately 80 gallons of gasoline to grow an acre of corn.

Increases in energy inputs have been observed throughout the entire U.S. food system. Processing, packaging, and distribution in all ultramodern food systems require about three times as much energy as the production itself. [287] The overall en-

---

[*]The implications of higher energy prices for the Global 2000 Study's food projections are discussed in Chapter 6.

## TABLE 13–19
### Average Energy Inputs per Acre in U.S. Corn Production, 1940–70

| Input | 1945 | 1950 | 1954 | 1959 | 1964 | 1970 |
|---|---|---|---|---|---|---|
| Labor (*hours per acre*) | 23 | 18 | 17 | 14 | 11 | 9 |
| Machinery (*thousands of kilocalories*) | 180 | 250 | 300 | 350 | 420 | 420 |
| Gasoline (*gallons*) | 15 | 17 | 19 | 20 | 21 | 22 |
| Nitrogen (*pounds*) | 7 | 15 | 27 | 41 | 58 | 112 |
| Phosphorus (*pounds*) | 7 | 10 | 12 | 16 | 18 | 31 |
| Potassium (*pounds*) | 5 | 10 | 18 | 30 | 29 | 60 |
| Seeds for planting (*bushels*) | 0.17 | 0.20 | 0.25 | 0.30 | 0.33 | 0.33 |
| Irrigation (*thousands of kilocalories*) | 19 | 23 | 27 | 31 | 34 | 34 |
| Insecticides (*pounds*) | 0 | 0.10 | 0.30 | 0.70 | 1.00 | 1.00 |
| Herbicides (*pounds*) | 0 | 0.05 | 0.10 | 0.25 | 0.38 | 1.00 |
| Drying (*thousands of kilocalories*) | 10 | 30 | 60 | 100 | 120 | 120 |
| Electricity (*thousands of kilocalories*) | 32 | 54 | 100 | 140 | 203 | 310 |
| Transportation (*thousands of kilocalories*) | 20 | 30 | 45 | 60 | 70 | 70 |
| Corn yields (*bushel*) | 34 | 38 | 41 | 54 | 68 | 81 |

*Source:* D. Pimentel et al., "Food Production and the Energy Crisis," *Science,* Nov. 2, 1973, pp. 443–48.

## TABLE 13–20
### Energy Inputs in U.S. Corn Production (in kilocalories)

| Input | 1945 | 1950 | 1954 | 1959 | 1964 | 1970 |
|---|---|---|---|---|---|---|
| Labor[a] | 12,500 | 9,800 | 9,300 | 7,600 | 6,000 | 4,900 |
| Machinery[b] | 180,000 | 250,000 | 300,000 | 350,000 | 420,000 | 420,000 |
| Gasoline[c] | 543,400 | 615,800 | 688,300 | 724,500 | 760,700 | 797,000 |
| Nitrogen[d] | 58,800 | 126,000 | 226,800 | 344,400 | 487,200 | 940,800 |
| Phosphorus[e] | 10,600 | 15,200 | 18,200 | 24,300 | 27,400 | 47,100 |
| Potassium[f] | 5,200 | 10,500 | 50,400 | 60,400 | 68,000 | 68,000 |
| Seeds for planting[g] | 34,000 | 40,400 | 18,900 | 36,500 | 30,400 | 63,000 |
| Irrigation[h] | 19,000 | 23,000 | 27,000 | 31,000 | 34,000 | 34,000 |
| Insecticides[i] | 0 | 1,100 | 3,300 | 7,700 | 11,000 | 11,000 |
| Herbicides[j] | 0 | 600 | 1,100 | 2,800 | 4,200 | 11,000 |
| Drying[k] | 10,000 | 30,000 | 60,000 | 100,000 | 120,000 | 120,000 |
| Electricity[l] | 32,000 | 54,000 | 100,000 | 140,000 | 203,000 | 310,000 |
| Transportation[m] | 20,000 | 30,000 | 45,000 | 60,000 | 70,000 | 70,000 |
| Total inputs | 925,500 | 1,206,400 | 1,548,300 | 1,889,200 | 2,241,900 | 2,896,800 |
| Corn yield (output)[n] | 3,427,200 | 3,830,400 | 4,132,800 | 5,443,200 | 6,854,400 | 8,164,800 |
| Kcal return/input kcal | 3.70 | 3.18 | 2.67 | 2.88 | 3.06 | 2.82 |

*Source:* David Pimental et al., "Food Production and the Energy Crisis," *Science,* Nov. 2, 1973, p. 445.

[a] It is assumed that a farm laborer consumes 21,777 kcal per week and works a 40-hour week. For 1970, from Table 13–17: (9 hours/40 hours per week) × 21,770 kcal per week = 4,900 kcal.
[b] The machinery needed to farm 62 acres of corn was estimated to have required 244,555,000 kcal. This machinery was assumed to function for 10 years. Repairs were assumed to be 6 percent of total machinery production. Hence, a conservative estimate for the production and repair of farm machinery per acre of corn for 1970 was 420,000 kcal. A high for the number of tractors and other types of machinery on farms was reached in 1964 and continues. The number of tractors and other types of machinery in 1945 were about half what they are now.
[c] Gasoline: 1 gallon = 36,225 kcal.
[d] Nitrogen: 1 pound = 8,400 kcal, including production and processing.
[e] Phosphorus: 1 pound = 1,520 kcal, including mining and processing.
[f] Potassium: 1 pound = 1,050 kcal, including mining and processing.
[g] Corn seed: 1 pound = 1,800 kcal. This energy input was doubled because of the effort employed in producing hybrid seed corn.
[h] Only about 3.8 percent of the corn grain acres in the United States were irrigated in 1964, and this is not expected to change much in the near future. An estimated 905,600 kcal is required to irrigate an acre of corn with an acre-foot of water for one season. Since only 3.8 percent of the corn acres are irrigated (1964–70), it was estimated that only 34,000 kcal were used per acre for corn irrigation. The percentage of acres irrigated in 1945 was based on trends in irrigated acres in agriculture.
[i] Insecticides: 1 pound = 11,000 kcal, including production and processing.
[j] Herbicides: 1 pound = 11,000 kcal, including production and processing.
[k] When corn is dried for storage to reduce the moisture from about 26.5 percent to 13 percent, 408,204 kcal are needeed to dry 91 bushels (*Corn Grower's Guide,* Aurora, Ill.: Grace and Co., 1968, p. 113). About 30 percent of the corn produced in 1970 was estimated to have been dried, as compared to an estimated 10 percent in 1945.
[l] In 1970, agriculture consumed about 310,000 kcal per acre for fuel used to produce electricity.
[m] The number of calories burned to transport machinery and supplies to corn acres and to transport corn to the site of use was estimated to be about 70,000 kcal per acre in 1964 and 1970 and about 20,000 kcal per acre in 1945.
[n] A bushel of corn was considered to weight 56 pounds, and each pound was assumed to contain 1,800 kcal.

ergy requirements of the U.S. food system are illustrated in Figure 13–5. On a per capita basis, David Pimental estimates that U.S. crop production alone requires about 112 gallons of gasoline per person per year. [288]

The commercial energy requirements for modern and traditional production of rice and corn (maize) are compared in Table 13–21. The only commercial energy input in traditional agriculture is the energy used in making simple tools and implements. But when the commercial energy inputs are low, the yields are also low. In transitional agriculture, more commercial energy is used especially for machinery, fuel, fertilizer, pesticides, improved seeds, and transportation. In transitional agriculture commercial energy inputs may increase by a factor of 10 or more over the commercial energy used in traditional agriculture. Yields may more than double. Modern agriculture involves commercial energy inputs that are more than 100 times those of traditional agriculture. Yields achieved are double to triple those achieved with traditional agriculture. [289]

The energy intensiveness of high-yield agriculture has been studied extensively[290] and is discussed briefly in the food projections in Chapter 6. While the concerns that have emerged cannot be discussed in any detail here, a few need to be mentioned.

The basic concern is that in becoming highly dependent on fossil fuels, modern high-yield agriculture is also becoming vulnerable—both in the short and the long run. In the short run (the next two decades), energy-intensive agriculture will become increasingly vulnerable to the vicissitudes of the energy sector. Even now a sudden price increase or a sudden interruption of petroleum or natural gas supplies could severely affect world agricultural production, raise food prices, and increase the numbers of people who cannot afford adequate food.* If the energy intensiveness of agriculture continues to increase over the next two decades as implied by the projections, the potential disruptiveness (measured in terms of the numbers of persons unable to obtain adequate

nourishment) of an energy supply interruption might well become twice what it is today.

In the long run, agriculture becomes vulnerable through reliance on a depleting resource. David Pimentel estimates that if the world's petroleum reserves were used *exclusively* to provide the world's population with the average U.S. diet as now produced with modern, energy-intensive agricultural methods, the entire 415 billion barrel reserve would last a mere 29 years—or 107 years if all potential reserves (about 2,000 billion barrels) became available. If the world population were to subsist on corn grain only, the same potential petroleum reserves would provide enough energy to supply food for a population of 10 billion for 448 years![291]

The prospect of increasing energy dependence and vulnerability in agriculture has led to some preliminary examinations of alternative approaches. [292] Most of the options so far examined involve relatively small farm units, less substitution of fossil energy for human energy and skill, and the use of "intermediate" or "appropriate" technologies. [293]

The prospect of relatively small farm units raises questions of economic efficiency, and it is encouraging to note that the U.S. Department of Agriculture, in its publication "The One-Man Farm," considers that food production on a small scale can be as efficient as production on a larger scale:

The fully mechanized one-man farm, producing the maximum acreage of crops of which the man and his machines are capable, is generally a technically efficient farm. From the standpoint of costs per unit of production, this size farm captures most of the economies associated with size. The chief incentive for farm enlargement beyond the optimum one-man size is not to reduce unit costs of production, but to achieve a larger business, more output, and more total income. [294]

Encouraging as some of the preliminary investigations are, two points must be kept in mind. First, present trends are overwhelmingly in the direction of further energy intensiveness of agriculture; *major* technological and policy changes would be required to reverse this trend. Second,

---

*In this connection it should be noted that energy-intensive food is "inexpensive" in the United States only because per capita income is high by world standards. U.S. costs of production in the U.S. are high compared to those of many other countries. For example, the cost of producing 1,000 kcal of plant product is estimated to be about $38 in the U.S. and about $10 in India (Pimental et al., "Food Production and the Energy Crisis," *Science*, Nov. 2, 1973, p. 448). Because many LDCs can produce food less expensively than the U.S., some observers expected LDCs to export significant amounts of food

(and cotton and rubber) to earn foreign exchange, even though their own populations are malnourished. Land tenure is a contributing factor. Much good farmland in the LDCs (and increasingly in the industrialized nations) is held by landlords or corporations and is farmed for export, not local consumption. Such exports, if they develop significantly, would also affect the U.S. balance of payments (CIA National Foreign Assessment Center, "The Role of the LDCs in the U.S. Balance of Payments," Washington, Sept. 1978).

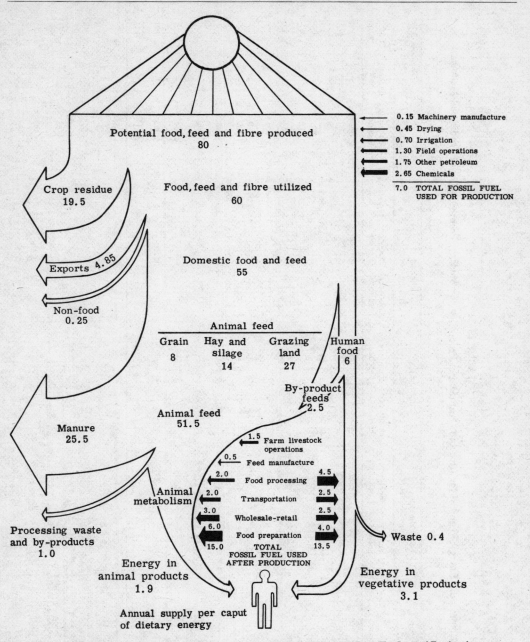

**Figure 13–5.** Energy flow in the U.S. food chain, in billions of joules. (*From* The State of Food and Agriculture 1976, *FAO, 1977; adapted from F. C. Stickler et al.*, Energy from Sun to Plant, to Man, *Deere & Co., 1975*)

## TABLE 13–21

### Commercial Energy Required for Rice and Corn (Maize) Production, by Modern, Transitional, and Traditional Methods

| | Rice | | | | | | Maize | | | |
| | Modern (United States) | | Transitional (Philippines) | | Traditional (Philippines) | | Modern (United States) | | Traditional (Mexico) | |
| Input | Quantity per hectare | Energy per hectare | Quantity per hectare | Energy per hectare | Quantity per hectare | Energy per hectare | Quantity per hectare | Energy per hectare | Quantity per ha. | Energy per ha. |
|---|---|---|---|---|---|---|---|---|---|---|
| | | $10^6$ joules | | $10^6$ joules | | $10^6$ joules | | $10^6$ joules | | $10^6$ joules |
| Machinery and implements[a] | $4.2 \times 10^9$ joules | 4,200 | $335 \times 10^6$ joules | 335 | $173 \times 10^6$ joules | 173 | $4.2 \times 10^9$ joules | 4,200 | $173 \times 10^6$ joules | 173 |
| Fuel[b] | 224.7 liters | 8,988 | 40 liters | 1,600 | – | – | 206 liters | 8,240 | – | – |
| Nitrogen fertilizer[c] | 134.4 kg | 10,752 | 31.5 kg | 2,520 | – | – | 125 kg | 10,000 | – | – |
| Phosphate fertilizer[d] | – | 605 | – | – | – | – | 34.7 kg | 586 | – | – |
| Potassium fertilizer[e] | 67.2 kg | – | – | – | – | – | 67.2 kg | 605 | – | – |
| Seeds[f] | 112.0 kg | 3,360 | 110 kg | 1,650 | 107.5 kg | – | 20.7 kg | 621 | 10.4 kg | – |
| Irrigation[b] | 683.4 liters | 27,336 | – | – | – | – | $351 \times 10^6$ joules | 351 | – | – |
| Insecticides[g] | 5.6 kg | 560 | 1.5 kg | 150 | – | – | 1.1 kg | 110 | – | – |
| Herbicides[g] | 5.6 kg | 560 | 1.0 kg | 100 | – | – | 1.1 kg | 110 | – | – |
| Drying | $4.6 \times 10^9$ joules | 4,600[h] | – | – | – | – | $1,239 \times 10^6$ joules | 1,239 | – | – |
| Electricity | $3.2 \times 10^9$ joules | 3,200[h] | – | – | – | – | $3,248 \times 10^6$ joules | 3,248 | – | – |
| Transport | $724 \times 10^6$ joules | 724[h] | $31 \times 10^6$ joules | 31 | – | – | $724 \times 10^6$ joules | 724 | – | – |
| Total | | 64,885 | | 6,386 | | 173 | | 30,034 | | 173 |
| Yield (kg/ha) | | 5,800 | | 2,700 | | 1,250 | | 5,083 | | 950 |
| Energy input yield per unit ($10^6$ joules/kg) | | 11.19 | | 2.37 | | 0.14 | | 5.91 | | 0.18 |

Source: Food and Agriculture Organization. The State of Food and Agriculture 1976. Rome. 1977. p. 93

[a] Energy input to produce 1 kg of equipment assumed to be $68.7 \times 10^6$ joules
[b] One liter of fuel assumed to contain $40 \times 10^6$ joules.
[c] Production of 1 kg of nitrogen fertilizer assumed to require $80 \times 10^6$ joules.
[d] Production of 1 kg of phosphate fertilizer assumed to require $14 \times 10^6$ joules.
[e] Production of 1 kg of potassium fertilizer assumed to require $9 \times 10^6$ joules.
[f] Production of 1 kg of high-quality seed assumed to require $30 \times 10^6$ joules in the United States and $15 \times 10^6$ joules in the Philippines and Mexico.
[g] Production of 1 kg of pesticide assumed to require $100 \times 10^6$.
[h] Assumed to be similar to figures given for maize by David Pimental et al., "Food Production and the Energy Crisis," Science, Nov. 2, 1973, p. 444.

population growth may make energy-intensive agriculture inevitable. The People's Republic of China has probably been more successful than any other country in developing its agriculture with minimum energy requirements. The Chinese experience and other experiments[295] demonstrate clearly that there are alternatives to the most energy-intensive agricultural methods. Yet even China has been forced by the food needs of an expanding population to import energy-rich chemical fertilizers and has contracted for the construction of 13 large nitrogen fertilizer plants.[296]

## Conclusions

It has often been observed that agricultural resources are renewable: A hectare of farmland can grow as many as three crops annually; soil fertility can be maintained and often improved; biomass can be consumed and yet grow again another year. While these points are all true, they do not provide an adequate perspective for consideration of agricultural prospects in the decades ahead, particularly beyond the year 2000.

There are three critically important facts to be kept in mind when considering agricultural prospects for the future. First, agriculture is now and will continue to be based largely on depletable resources. Second, at present these depletable resources—crucial to the maintenance and renewal of land, water, and other renewable agricultural resources—are being consumed, extinguished, and eroded at rates that cannot be sustained indefinitely. Third, for the foreseeable future, there is no end in sight to increasing population levels and to escalating needs for agricultural production.

The depletable nature of a number of basic agricultural resources has been given inadequate attention in the past. There has even been occasional confusion as to what the basic resources of agriculture are. Biomass is not a basic agricultural resource, but genetic stocks of crop plants and of domestic animals and beneficial insects are. These agricultural resources are being depleted or rendered extinct at an accelerating rate that alarms many scientists. Soil is a basic agricultural resource, but it is a depleting, salifying, and eroding resource. Lost soil fertility often can be restored, but only after long periods of time and at great cost. Furthermore, in some instances soil fertility simply cannot be renewed: Soils lost by erosion, by urban and industrial expansion, and by hydroelectric development are permanent losses for agriculture. Solar energy is a basic agricultural resource, but fossil fuels are too. Fossil fuels are

a depletable, nonrenewable resource, required for production of chemical fertilizers, pesticides, and fertilizers, and for mechanization and irrigation. Water, too, is a basic agricultural resource, but an exhaustible resource of finite extent, threatened by competing uses, dissolved salts, and acid rain.

The knowledge, technologies, and management techniques needed to protect the basic, depletable resources of agriculture are generally established, but often not known or available where they are most needed. Careful cultivation practices and well-known techniques of terracing, for example, can reduce soil losses. The preservation of habitat for the maintenance of genetic stocks requires no elaborate technologies. But the technological knowledge and capital necessary to successfully use marginal soils is not available to many of the farmers who will be forced to use these soils in the years ahead. Similarly the skills needed for safe and effective use of fertilizers or for alternative methods of pest control are not widely available in many less developed countries.

Although further research is certainly called for (e.g., the atmospheric effects of nitrous oxide from fertilizer applications is not known with certainty), the skills and technologies needed to limit virtually all of the environmental pressures implicit in the Global 2000 Study's food projections are already available. The big question is: Will these skills and technologies be used?

There is no clear answer to this question. Conflicts are involved. The need to increase agricultural production will certainly continue since a large fraction of the world's population is inadequately nourished even now and since throughout the foreseeable future the world's population is projected to continue growing. Historically, increases in agricultural production have come both from increasing the lands under cultivation and from increasing yields per hectare. Options for increasing the lands under cultivation are now limited and expensive, and becoming more so. Therefore efforts to increase yields on lands already under cultivation can be expected to intensify. Unless marginal lands are introduced with skill and moderation, and unless efforts to increase yields are carefully managed, environmental stresses will follow—erosion, laterization, alkalinization, salinization, waterlogging, urban encroachment, and loss of plant, animal, and predator-insect species. If unabated, these stresses could lead initially to a significant reduction in the expansion of food production and in time to a serious reduction in the world's capacity to maintain food production. As noted in the beginning of this section, the Global 2000 food projections are based on the assumption that steps will be taken to keep the impact of these stresses in line with past experience. If these stresses are not controlled, they could bring into serious question even the modest increases in per capita food availability projected in Chapter 6.

To what extent will farmers, governments, and international organizations act to protect the world's depletable agricultural resources? Several nations have already faced the kinds of agriculturally related environmental pressures that are expected to occur worldwide. Some of these nations have successfully maintained or expanded their agricultural capacities. The People's Republic of China and Israel are examples. Several other nations, of which Haiti and Ethiopia are examples, have so far been unable to respond successfully. Most nations have yet to experience the pressures and face the policy decisions.

Success in efforts to protect depletable agricultural resources will require a concerted public effort to set priorities for both food production and

environmental protection and to finance ecologically positive technologies and management techniques. Issues relating to land tenure will also be important.[297] Unfortunately, efforts to maintain and expand the productivity of agricultural resources often increase unit costs and reduce production, at least in the short run. In the face of increasing costs of food, it is uncertain that the public support required to accomplish these objectives will be made even in the affluent industrialized nations—and far less certain in the LDCs, which face the greatest pressures to increase food production in years ahead.

The agricultural and population policies that nations develop over the next two decades will have lasting significance. The possibility of a serious erosion and depletion of the world's depletable agricultural resources cannot be ignored. Unless the pressures on these resources are addressed and resolved, at least in part before the year 2000, it appears virtually certain that the world's per capita food production will slow, stagnate, or even decline during the first half of the 21st century.

## THE PROJECTIONS AND THE MARINE ENVIRONMENT

### The Projections

Many of the Global 2000 projections and their implicit consequences have implications for the future of the marine environment. The projections that are most relevant are as follows:

*Population.* A 45–65 percent increase in human population will lead to substantial increases in the amount of coastal development.

*Gross National Product.* Coupled with projected population growth, doubling and tripling of GNPs will lead to global increases in water and airborne pollutants and to increases in economic activities—such as dredging and the construction of port facilities—that alter the coastal marine environment.

*Agriculture.* An increase by a factor of 2.5 in global use of fertilizer, pesticides, and other yield-enhancing inputs will lead to a marked growth in the quantities of nutrients and toxic chemicals entering the marine environment.

*Fisheries.* The intense demand projected for fishery resources (83.5 million metric tons by 2000) will result in severe pressure on preferred stocks and increased exploitation of nontraditional, smaller, and shorter-lived species. Pollution and physical destruction of marine habitats will impede the growth of aquaculture in estuarine and coastal areas, effectively reducing the overall potential yields of living marine resources.

*Forestry.* A 15–20 percent decrease in the area under forest cover, with most of the reduction taking place in LDCs, will lead to a sizable increase in the silt loads of tropical river systems and thus to increased silt deposition in estuaries, deltas, and on adjacent coastal shelves.

*Water.* Hydraulic engineering of freshwater systems will alter salinity concentrations and cyclic flows in estuaries, and will interfere with the life cycles of organisms that spend part of their lives in the ocean and part in freshwater. Because nutrients will be trapped behind new dams, the quantity and quality of estuarine and coastal productivity will be adversely affected.

*Energy.* More offshore drilling, more marine transport of oil, and more portside storage and processing facilities will be needed to sustain the projected 3.3–4.4 percent annual increase in demand for oil. More petroleum pollutants will enter the oceans. Proliferation of onshore and offshore power plants will result in extensive use of oxidants and other biocides (especially chlorine) to prevent biological fouling in cooling towers, entrainment, and thermal pollution, altering the habitat of marine organisms. The increased use of nuclear energy may lead to accidental release or to deliberate disposal of radioactive materials into the oceans.*

*Nonfuel Minerals.* More mining wastes will be produced and more mineral products will be in circulation, due in part to increased production of various minerals from lower grade ores. As a result, more of these wastes will enter the earth's air and freshwater systems and, eventually, the oceans. Of particular concern are toxic wastes resulting from increased production of several heavy metals. Chromium production is projected to increase annually by 3.3 percent, copper by 2.9 percent, lead by 3.1 percent, mercury by 0.5 percent, and zinc by 3.1 percent. Increased industrial dredging for gravel and coral sands will also have significant local impacts. If initiated, deep-sea mining operations will produce locally disruptive effects on open-ocean ecosystems.

In summary, while the projections are usually not sufficiently detailed to provide specific quantitative estimates, they do imply a variety of impacts on the marine environment. Worldwide population growth will contribute to increased economic development of the earth's coastlines and their estuaries. Industrial, agricultural, and domestic pollution, coupled with hydraulic engineering of freshwater systems, will adversely affect biological productivity in coastal waters and interfere with aquaculture. Growing demand for commercially preferred fish will increase pressures on these stocks. Overfishing may increase, and a growing proportion of the global catch will be composed of nontraditional species. Continued deforestation will lead to destructive silt deposition in river estuaries, deltas, and on adjacent coastal shelves. More energy-related pollutants—petroleum hydrocarbons, radioactive materials, and waste heat—will enter the oceans, and the increased production of various minerals will add to the amount of toxic wastes entering coastal waters. Dredging and deep-sea mining will disrupt coastal and oceanic ecosystems.

## Introduction

The earth is truly a water planet. The waters of the oceans cover 71 percent of the earth's surface and amount to 97 percent of the earth's total water supply. So vast is this volume that more than 200,000 years would be needed by a river the size of the Amazon to drain the world's oceans.

For an understanding of the future of the

---

*There are two emerging energy technologies that deserve note here — Ocean Thermal Energy Conversion (OTEC) and deep water hydrocarbon exploration. Neither of these technologies are projected to be making a major contribution to the world's energy supplies by 1990 (where the DOE projections stop), but both may be in early growth stages by 2000. Both may have very significant impacts on the marine environment.

The OTEC technology utilizes the temperature difference between the warm surface water and the cold deep water to generate electricity. OTEC plants are likely to be anchored in deep waters close to subtropical and tropical islands. Each plant may take in and discharge as much water as the flow of a large river. Environmental effects could include death of vast numbers of plankton, and larvae of coastal and oceanic fishes and benthic organisms by entrainment through heat exchang-

ers, chemical anti-fouling treatments using chorine or other biocides, and thermal shock.

Hydrocarbon exploration and production will occur in progressively deeper waters, introducing into vulnerable oceanic ecosystems unprecedented quantities of drilling muds and cuttings, well treatment fluids, oily brines, natural gas flared underwater, and oil spills. Oil spills are a special concern because production in oceanic waters will probably be by seabed systems rather than above-water platforms, making blowout repairs and spill cleanup operations particularly difficult. (*Ocean Thermal Energy Conversion 1977: Environmental Development Plan (EDP)*, Washington: U.S. Department of Energy 1978; James J. Geraghty et al., *World Atlas of the United States*, Port Washington, N.Y.: Water Information Center, 1973.)

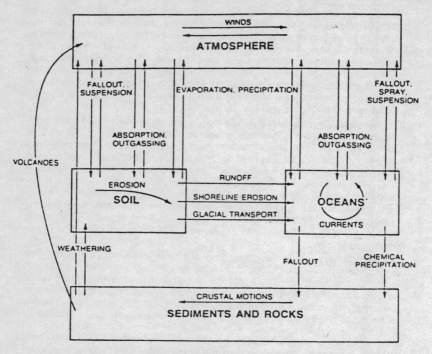

**Figure 13–6.** Transport mechanisms linking the oceans with the other principal parts of the physical world. (From *Ecoscience: Population, Resources, Environment* by Paul R. Ehrlich, Anne H. Ehrlich, and John P. Holdren. *W. H. Freeman and Company, Copyright © 1977, p. 69*)

world's environment, the immensity of the oceans is important for two reasons. First, because of their size and other properties, the oceans have a major role in determining the energy flows and the macroenvironment of the entire planet. Thus the condition of the oceans is of planetary significance. Second, the oceans' enormous size provides a large amount of dilution and stability. As a result, change comes slowly to the oceans, and changes are often difficult to detect and even more difficult to control.

The major flows involved in the oceans' influence on the world's macroenvironment are illustrated in Figure 13–6. Through evaporation, precipitation, and runoff, the oceans are linked with the atmosphere and soil in determining the primary flows of solar energy and thus the planet's temperature distribution and climate. The massive heat storage capacity of the oceans is one of the strongest stabilizing influences on the planet's climate.

The absorption and outgassing flows noted in Figure 13–6 are simplified representations of the

highly complex carbon and oxygen cycles, which, through photosynthesis in plants and respiration in most organisms, further link oceans, soil, and atmosphere. In the oceans, minute phytoplankton annually fix 40 billion tons of carbon from carbon dioxide and release billions of tons of oxygen.[298] Both oxygen and carbon dioxide gases are exchanged with the atmosphere. Settling and decomposition provide nutrients and energy to life in the lower ocean-water strata.

Although there are still uncertainties, the major stabilizing functions of the oceans—the water, oxygen and carbon cycles—are not likely to be seriously disrupted over the next two decades. The major impacts on the oceans are more likely to occur as a result of yet another function of the oceans, namely, as the ultimate receptacle for much of the world's unwanted waste materials—toxic substances, sediments, agricultural chemicals, oil, sewage, and solid litter.

The flows toward the oceanic "sink" are also illustrated in Figure 13–6. Most of the waste flows start on land and move through runoff, dumping, evaporation, precipitation, fallout, and absorption into the ocean waters. Marine transportation, seabed oil development, and seabed mining also contribute to the flow of damaging wastes.

A major impact on living marine resources is implied by the Global 2000 Study's projections. These resources now make an important contribution to the economics, health, and welfare of many nations. Fisheries contribute about 2 percent of the food calories consumed globally by humans, and directly supply approximately 14 percent of the world's animal protein consumed by humans. In a number of LDCs and industrialized nations, such as Iceland, Japan, the Philippines, and Vietnam, animal protein from ocean organisms is a major component of the national diet, in some cases making up over one-half of animal protein consumption.[299] Any reduction in calories and protein from the oceans will have serious implications for the populations of such areas.

Major changes in the composition of living marine resources are anticipated, especially in the coastal waters. These changes will come about as a result of habitat destruction and waste deposition and concentration, and particularly from pollutants such as synthetic organic chemicals and heavy metals. In some areas habitat destruction is proceeding rapidly and is a major threat. Contamination of the marine environment occurs at different rates in different areas. Its seriousness depends on a number of considerations.

Because of their enormous volume, ocean waters are potentially capable of much dilution of polluting wastes. However, the ocean waters themselves are not the ultimate resting place for many wastes entering the oceans. Some materials are biologically degraded; others are transported by particulate fallout and chemical precipitation to the sediments of the ocean floor, as indicated in Figure 13–6. The rate at which wastes reach various parts of the ocean is therefore important in determining their concentration and ultimate fate. There is extreme variation in the times required.

There are two basic kinds of marine ecosystems: coastal and oceanic. Table 13–22 briefly describes these two ecosystems and indicates (1) the type of pollution affecting each kind, (2) the effects of the pollution, and (3) the duration of the effects. One fact that stands out strikingly in the table is that the highly productive coastal waters—including the world's estuaries, coastal wetlands, reefs, and the many marginal seas over the continental shelves and slopes[300]—account for only 10 percent of the total area of the global marine environment, whereas the relatively less productive (biologically speaking) open oceans constitute 90 percent.

An important distinction between coastal and oceanic waters is the large difference in the duration of effects from various pollutants, many of which have only relatively short-term effects in coastal waters. Although these effects are ex-

## TABLE 13–22

### Categories of Ocean Areas and Types of Pollution, with Effects on Uses and Their Duration

| Types of Pollution | Effects on Uses and Pollution Trends | Duration of Effects |
|---|---|---|
| COASTAL WATERS *(10 percent of total area; 99 percent of total fish production[a])* | | |
| Sewage; industrial wastes; litter; petroleum hydrocarbons | Living resources destroyed or rendered unusable; industrial uses of seawater adversely influenced; amenities reduced; recreational values diminished | Short-term; mainly during period of discharge |
| Synthetic organic chemicals; metals; radioactivity | Living resources decreased or rendered unusable | Long-term; metals and synthetic organic chemicals deposited in sediments may be released for a long time through normal leaching and/or dredging disturbance |
| OPEN OCEAN *(90 percent of total area; 1 percent of total fish production[b])* | | |
| Synthetic organic chemicals; metals; petroleum hydrocarbons; radioactivity | Increasing concentrations in water and organisms may indicate dangerous trends | Long-term; duration depends on the residence time of pollutant |

Source: Michael Waldichuk, *Global Marine Pollution: An Overview*, Paris: UNESCO, 1977. p. 12.
[a] Including fish production from upwelling area.   [b] Excluding fish production from upwelling area.

tremely serious in some instances, their intensity may be reduced rapidly after the discharge is terminated. Other pollutants can have longer-term effects due to bioaccumulation and accumulated sedimentary deposits. In the open ocean, pollutants have the potential to produce delayed effects. In addition to bioaccumulation and interactions with coastal zone sediments, pollutant effects on the open ocean are prolonged, since most ocean waters below a depth of 100 meters exchange with surface and coastal waters relatively slowly—usually over time periods on the order of hundreds or thousands of years.[301]

Because deep open-ocean waters are so different from coastal waters in the rate at which they receive and experience the effects of pollutants, these two major ocean areas will be considered separately. The implications of the Global 2000 Study projections for coastal waters are considered first under the following topics: coastal development; coastal pollution; and overexploitation of living marine resources.

The implications of the projections for the deep open-ocean waters must be examined separately. Not enough time will have elapsed by the year 2000 for projected developments to greatly affect these waters. The discussion of the open ocean, therefore, will be primarily in terms of the trends established over the next two decades that will ultimately have implications for oceanic ecosystems.

## Effects of Coastal Development

The earth's coastal waters and ecosystems are important for human society because they are highly productive biologically and because they support a wide range of economic activities. These ecosystems are strongly influenced by changes in the physical and biological conditions of the coastal seabed and adjacent land.[302] Many of the Global 2000 Study's projections suggest a variety of coastal developments that can be expected to cause extensive and adverse changes in the biological productivity of the world's coastal zones.

In the next two decades, a significant consequence of many of the Global 2000 projections will be a dramatic growth in coastal development. Population pressures will lead to rapid rates of coastal settlement and urbanization, especially in LDCs. Rivers emptying into estuaries will be dammed to ensure adequate supplies of water for burgeoning metropolitan areas and agriculture. Rising GNPs and energy demand will encourage the expansion of coastal industrial facilities, and the consequent development will have serious impacts upon the marine environment.

Coastal dredging is likely to be extensive. The Global 2000 Study's minerals, technology, energy, population, and GNP projections indicate that offshore dredging for landfill, improved port and waterway facilities, and construction material can be expected to continue. Coastal dredging of anchorages and channels destroys the immediate benthic area and, through sedimentation, can affect more distant zones. Commercial dredging of gravel, coral, and coral sands is already conducted in many areas in waters as much as 100 meters in depth.

Marine transportation is still the cheapest, most energy-efficient mode of transporting materials in bulk, and the Study's food, minerals, and energy projections suggest that it will accelerate at least as much over the next few decades as in the last few. Gross registered tonnages of ocean vessels have grown by 9 percent annually during recent years, while the volumes transported have increased by 6–9 percent.[303] If present growth rates continue, marine transport will have increased three to sevenfold by the year 2000. To accommodate the increased marine traffic, existing port facilities will have to be expanded significantly, and corresponding increases in secondary economic activities and human settlement in coastal areas can be anticipated. Dredging, filling, paving, and construction of terminals, factories, settlements, and service roads will increase noise, air and water pollution, and will greatly reduce productivity, diversity, and stability of coastal and adjacent ecosystems. Increasing marine traffic may bring proportional increases in catastrophic spills and chronic pollution from discharges of ballast and tank washings. However, international agreements requiring the use of navigation aids, segregated ballast tanks, and other features to reduce oil pollution should diminish adverse effects of increased marine traffic.[303a]

A less widely recognized problem is "biological pollution," the introduction of nonnative species into coastal ecosystems. Newly introduced species freed of their natural predators, parasites, and competitors can severely disrupt food webs, diversity, and stability and may effectively eliminate valuable native living marine resources. Besides marine transportation-related sources of biological introduction such as ballast waters, bio-fouling on vessels and mobile drilling rigs, and sea level canals, nonnative species may be introduced deliberately or accidentally, as in clumps of transplanted oysters.[303b]

Once established, settlements, factories, refineries, power plants, and port facilities along the coastal zones are not easily—nor are they likely to be—relocated. Furthermore there is a limit to the modification feasible should their presence or their delayed, indirect environmental impact prove severely damaging to coastal ecosystems. The expected result of the next two decades of development along coastlines is damaging physical alteration or total destruction of habitat—particularly in estuaries and wetlands and on coral reefs—that will adversely affect marine organisms and natural nutrient and waste cycling processes.

## Impacts on Estuaries and Coastal Wetlands

Estuaries,* and the salt marshes and mangrove communities that make up coastal wetlands, are globally widespread. One third of the population of the United States lives and works in regions surrounding estuaries, and of the 10 largest metropolitan areas in the world, seven border existing or former estuarine regions (New York, Tokyo, London, Shanghai, Buenos Aires, Osaka, and Los Angeles). Estuaries and coastal wetlands accumulate natural riverborne sediments as well as wastes from nearby urban areas. Nutrients are cycled in estuaries and wetlands. Large phytoplankton and zooplankton populations responsible for the high productivity of global coastal fisheries, as well as benthic plant production, algae, salt marsh grasses, seagrasses and mangrove communities result from this rich nutrient supply. It is estimated that 60–80 percent of the commercial marine fisheries species are dependent upon estuarine ecosystems during part or all of their life cycles.[304]

Salt marshes and mangrove communities are distributed all over the world and are either associated with estuaries or coastal barrier islands.[305] Intertidal salt marshes are an exceptionally fertile part of coastal zone estuarine ecosystems. Salt marsh grasses recycle mineral and organic nutrients entering the marsh environment, creating an area of biological productivity that can yield 10 tons of organic material per acre per year.[306] Cyclic tidal flooding circulates detritus and dissolved nutrients to other marsh areas and to offshore organisms. Much of the decomposing plant matter goes to the floor of the marsh, producing rich deposits of organic peat. Ultimately, low tidal marshes can actually build themselves up and out of the tidal range,[307] contributing to

coastline stabilization. Lush salt marshes also provide a habitat for a wide variety of fish, shellfish, wildfowl and mammals. Many ducks, geese and other waterfowl use coastal wetlands as resting stations and feeding grounds during migratory movements. Fish such as flounder and bluefish may make transient use of marshes for feeding, overwintering or as nurseries.[308]

Like salt marshes and estuaries, tropical mangrove communities are highly productive. The net primary production from mangrove ecosystems is utilized by a variety of organisms in a complex, detritus-based food web. As a transitional ecological belt, mangroves serve to protect the shoreline, are a source of raw materials for human populations, act as a shelter for bird and mammal species, and are nursery and breeding grounds for freshwater and marine organisms. A large number of commercially important fish and shellfish of the tropical coastal waters depend directly or indirectly on mangrove communities for food and shelter during their lives.[309]

The water, food, climate, and population projections imply that future water-supply and conservation efforts may include construction of freshwater dams and irrigation works. However useful these projects may be, they may reduce the diversity, productivity, and stability of the marine environment. Already, the damming of rivers flowing into estuaries reduces the size of wetlands and diminishes the flow and alters periodicity of freshwater entering the coastal zone. As yet, little definitive information is available with which to anticipate the ultimate effect of such human manipulation of the hydrology of salt marshes and mangrove communities,[310] but it can be reasonably expected that global damming or diversion of estuarine river systems will disturb or destroy many estuarine habitats for fish and wildlife, and will disrupt the normal processes of nutrient supply and cycling. As a consequence, estuarine ecosystems and their distribution and abundance of plants and animals can be expected to be significantly altered.[311]

Salt marshes have historically been filled or dredged to accommodate the needs of human settlements, agriculture, and industry the world over.[312] The alteration of salt marsh wetlands continues today for the establishment of new residences, for recreation, and industry. In the United States, commercial "finger-fill" lagoons have been dredged out of salt marsh to provide docking space for marinas and land for housing sites.[313] Salt marshes have been dredged for boat and ship harbors in the course of commercial development of coastal barrier islands as well.[314] These practices

---

*"Estuary" has been used to describe the lower reaches of a river in which seawater mixes with freshwater. The definition can be expanded to include bays, inlets, gulfs, and sounds into which several rivers empty and in which the mixing of fresh- and saltwater occurs. (Charles B. Officer, "Physical Oceanography of Estuaries," *Oceanus*, Fall 1976, p. 4).

are environmentally detrimental. Instead of the healthy flushing of salt marsh organic matter into adjacent waters, the organic matter collects on the stagnant canal bottoms, depleting the oxygen from the canal waters, thus killing or driving away valuable fish and shellfish.[314a] Leftover dredge spoils from channel and boat basin construction—and from their subsequent maintenance dredging—often have been dumped on nearby undisturbed wetlands, where they smothered established plant life and bottom-dwelling animals, polluted soil and water, and drastically altered the overall topography of the marsh.[315] Dredge spoils are often dumped in offshore coastal waters, and the resulting spoil deposits smother and intoxicate benthic organisms. Sediments mobilized and resuspended by bottom currents and upwellings can also move the spoil material inshore, or pollute more removed areas.[315a]

Salt marsh lands have been regarded globally as prime areas for industrial siting. Marshes also bear the brunt of the often environmentally destructive aftermath of economic development. For example, new refineries, power stations, and dikes are being planned for construction on marshy European coastlines.[316] Rivers carrying industrial pollutants contaminate their own estuarine marshes as well as those adjoining or connected by coastal currents; chemicals, metals, and petroleum pollutants carried to the sea in the Rhine River have tended to move northward to pollute the Wadden Zee tidal flats in the Netherlands.[317]

Mangrove ecosystems are also facing destruction through development. In many countries with large and rapidly expanding populations, mangrove areas are seen as areas for human settlement and zones of more intensive exploitation—as in southern Florida, U.S.A., where extensive areas of mangrove have been bulldozed and then filled with dredged sediments to create land for housing developments.[318]

Mangrove communities have been destroyed to make way for other forms of land use such as fish ponds, urban development, and industrial sites. Coastal mining, logging without replanting, and military defoliation have destroyed mangroves as well.[319] Destructive influences on mangrove communities also include the diversion or regulation of freshwater streams and rivers. The resulting reduction of freshwater flows cause estuarine soils to become excessively salinized, a condition in which mangroves cannot survive. As a result of these varied development practices during the 1960s and 1970s, there has been widespread and rapid degradation or destruction of extensive mangrove areas along the coasts of the Americas, Africa, east and west Malaysia, the Philippines, Indonesia, Vietnam, Singapore, east and west India, east and south Australia, and south Thailand.[320]

## Impacts on Coral Reefs

The loss to the marine environment of coral reef ecosystems is great. Coral reefs are among the most extensive and productive shallow marine communities.[321] Reef habitats, comparable in complexity and diversity to tropical rain forests,[322] provide food and shelter for approximately one-third of all fish species and for seemingly countless invertebrates, some of which contain or produce a wide range of pharmacologically active compounds. In addition, reefs function as buffers against ocean forces. As self-repairing, energy-dissipating breakwaters, they protect thousands of miles of continental and island coastlines from erosion in Southeast Asia, the Middle East, the Central and South Pacific and the Caribbean.[323]

Coral reefs in the U.S. Virgin Islands, Micronesia, the Seychelles, Puerto Rico, the Bahamas, Hawaii, and Florida have been damaged or destroyed entirely as a result of poorly planned and managed dredging.[324] Continued destruction of coral reef habitats through dredging activities will ultimately affect the marine environment and its coastal productivity and protection capabilities.

In short, anticipated coastal development will lead to large-scale destruction of estuaries, coastal wetlands (salt marshes and mangroves), and coral reefs. Notwithstanding the vital role of these areas in maintaining coastal productivity and protection, coastal development during the present century has already reduced the total world acreage significantly.[325]

If present trends continue throughout the next two decades, the increases in human population density and industrial and commercial activity will have yet more substantial effects on the biological productivity of the oceans' coastal waters. The habitats provided by estuaries, salt marshes, mangrove communities, and reefs will suffer the stresses of coastline development, and their loss will contribute significantly to changes in size and species composition of the global fisheries catch.

## Coastal Pollution

Coastal waters the world over constantly receive direct injections of polluting materials through river discharge, coastal outfalls, dumping, and atmospheric transport.[326] The agriculture, population, minerals, forestry, and energy projections suggest that the amount of pollutants entering the coastal zones will increase between now and the year 2000. Toxic chemical contamination, as yet largely uncontrolled, is likely to have the most damaging impact. While only a small number of all toxic chemicals are of agricultural origin, even the projected increases in pesticide and herbicide use have serious implications for the coastal environment. Pollution from expanding use of fossil fuel energy sources will continue to afflict coastal waters and their living resources. The impact of sewage, silt, and fertilizer nutrients will grow and have critical local and regional consequences. As GNPs rise globally, the volume of solid wastes discarded or deposited in the oceans will increase as well.

Collectively, the anticipated amount of coastal pollution is seen to be a major problem for the marine environment in the future. Pollutant stress on ocean life forms can cause chemical-physical damage to cell membranes or tissues, modification of biochemical reactions, buildup of microbial pathogens, low environmental oxygen levels, viral infections, skeletal anomalies, and genetic abnormalities. Several indicators point to rising levels of pollution in coastal waters. In fish, a degenerative disease syndrome aptly named "fin erosion" is associated with degraded estuarine or coastal environments and has been observed in U.S. coastal waters, in Tokyo Bay, and in the Irish Sea. A similar condition affects crabs, lobsters, and smaller crustaceans.[327] In the New York Bight, heavy municipal and industrial pollution and long-term dumping of dredge, sewage, and industrial wastes has caused fouling of shellfish gills by parasites and detritus.[328] The collection of contaminated shellfish is prohibited in certain areas because of hazards to human health.*

## Toxic Waste Pollution

Toxic waste pollution (also discussed above in the section entitled, "The GNP Projections and the Environment.") will be discussed here because many toxic substances eventually find their way into the sea via the atmosphere or continental runoff. By either route, toxic waste pollution is one of the most serious threats to the health of the coastal oceans.

---

*Trends in shellfish contamination and the closure of shellfish beds in the U.S., as well as a description of the innovative Mussel Watch—a monitoring program that uses mollusk tissue pollutant levels as an indicator of estuarine environmental quality—are discussed in "Ecology and Living Resources," Council on Environmental Quality, *Environmental Quality 1979*, Washington: Government Printing Office, forthcoming.

Toxic substances include those that are carcinogenic (causing cancer), mutagenic (producing mutations), and teratogenic (causing birth defects). Many toxic substances possess two—or even all three—of these specific properties.

Over 4 million chemical compounds have been reported to the American Chemical Society for listing in the Society's registry. Of the chemicals listed, about 70,000 are now in production in the United States, 50 in quantities greater than 1.3 billion pounds per year.[329] Unfortunately, not all 70,000 will be adequately tested for toxicity or environmental hazards. Studies to determine environmental persistence, transport, and long-term biological effects are expensive both in time and money, and the substances to be measured are often not only low in concentration but accompanied by other substances that produce synergistic effects and complicate analysis of the data. Relatively few contaminants have been monitored to the point where trends can be detected, and links between human health and the contaminants at the levels at which they occur are only tenuously understood.[330]

One of the gravest perils to human and marine life is that relatively persistent toxic chemicals and metals might build to dangerous levels before being detected, as occurred in the mercury-poisoning incident at Minamata Bay, Japan (see Table 13–28, below). The Minamata Bay tragedy is by no means the only instance in which long-lived toxic chemicals have been released in a way that will ultimately lead to their entry into the oceans. The Kepone contamination of the James River in Virginia provides another example.

Until it was ordered to stop in 1975, a Hopewell, Virginia chemical company under contract to Allied Chemicals had been dumping quantities of chemical waste into the James River in the course of manufacturing the insecticide Kepone. About 1.5 million gallons of highly toxic material were created and dumped. In 1976, the strange symptoms that had been exhibited by workers at the plant manufacturing this white-powder chemical compound were attributed to Kepone poisoning. The acute physical symptoms of this poisoning are evident, but its long-term effects on humans and animals are still unknown. Since Kepone is bioaccumulative and environmentally persistent, aquatic life downriver from Hopewell and in the James River estuary will be affected for many years, even though the source of pollution has been eliminated.[331]

Polychlorinated biphenyls (PCBs) have been in use for half a century. More recently they have been discovered to cause cancer in laboratory animals, and skin diseases, jaundice, and liver damage in humans. In the Baltic Sea, only a few thousand gray seals remain of a population estimated to be 20,000 in 1940, due to the seal's diet of PCB-contaminated fish.[332] In the United States, the Toxic Substances Control Act of 1976 prohibits the sale of PCBs after July 1, 1979, but this persistent chemical will remain in commercial products, municipal dumps, soils, and the sediments of streams, lakes, and ocean coastal zones for years to come.

The Hudson River, already contaminated with a complex mixture of toxic substances, was further contaminated in the early 1970s by approximately 440,000 pounds of PCBs, discharged there by two General Electric capacitor plants. Now, much of the PCB contamination, lodged in the river sediments over a 40-mile stretch between Troy Dam and Hudson Falls, poses a health threat to the 150,000 upstate New Yorkers who drink the river water, as well as a threat to commercial fisheries in the Hudson's estuary. Approximately 6,000 pounds of the accumulated contaminant spills over Troy Dam each year.

In 1976, General Electric agreed to pay the State of New York $4 million for the removal of the polluted sediment. Two years later, the New York State Department of Environmental Conservation was requesting $25 million in federal funds to remove 75 percent of the contaminant from 30–40 of the most contaminated spots in the riverbed. Estimates for dredging the entire 40 miles of polluted sediments are in the hundreds of millions, and would take about 10 years and cause destruction of local sediment life for at least a year or two in each section of the river dredged.[333] In the absence of decontamination, most of the PCBs will ultimately be deposited in the Atlantic Ocean.

Pollution of the James and Hudson Rivers are dramatic illustrations of toxic substance contamination that ultimately is transported to the oceans. While these instances are massive and serious in and of themselves, hundreds of thousands of smaller daily losses of chemicals around the world have even greater implications for the oceans. In the next few pages, marine environmental problems arising from toxic wastes will be discussed by type of pollutant: synthetic organic chemicals, heavy metals, and radioactive materials.

### Synthetic Organic Chemicals

Large numbers of different synthetic chemicals enter the oceans through rivers, the atmosphere and offshore coastal dumping of chemical wastes and are now ubiquitous in the oceans.[334] The effects of most of these chemicals has not been carefully studied, and even if the knowledge were available, the numbers of chemicals and their even more numerous effects could not be fully addressed here. The discussion is therefore limited to a few examples from a group of chemicals—halogenated hydrocarbons—about which there is both concern and understanding (albeit limited) of their effects on marine ecosystems. Three heavy halogenated hydrocarbons are considered first, followed by examples of lighter halogenated hydrocarbons.

DDT, polychlorinated biphenyls (PCBs), and hexochlorobenzene are heavy halogenated hydrocarbons over which there continues to be concern. DDT is still widely used in both agricultural and vector control programs in many nations. As discussed in the food and agriculture section of this chapter, the Global 2000 food projections anticipate a large increase—on the order of 2 to 4 times the present amount—in the use of pesticides over the next 20 years. Persistant pesticides such as DDT will almost certainly continue to be used in large and increasing quantities in many areas, especially in the LDCs.

Atmospheric transport is the principal pathway by which DDT and its metabolites reach the oceans.[335] Regional DDT contamination has been shown to have caused reproductive failure in birds and fish. In some cases DDT has proved to be toxic to fish,[336] and has interfered with their chemoreception and natural behavior patterns.[337]

PCBs—stable, relatively insoluble and nonflammable compounds—are now widespread pollutants of the marine environment as a result of inadvertent spills and leakage, breakage of containers, and evaporation. Besides being dangerous to human health, they are toxic to some marine organisms.[338] PCBs (and other heavy halogenated hydrocarbons including DDT and its metabolites, and dieldrin) are known to adversely affect vital estuarine phytoplankton communities. Field and laboratory experiments have shown that a variety of normal functions—including growth, photosynthesis, and cellular development—are inhibited in phytoplankton when they are exposed to chlorinated pesticide concentrations ranging from 1 to 10 parts per billion. Sustained high concentrations were observed to cause cell rupture and ultimate death. As a result, these chemicals in the marine environment may adversely affect natural food chains by altering the quantities and sizes of phytoplankton available for zooplankton grazing. Such changes could in turn disrupt trophic interactions within an estuarine community and could bring about changes in the species composition of many marine ecosystems. [339]

Hexachlorobenzene (HCB) is a stable, unreactive compound used as a grain fungicide and a component in some pesticides. It is produced as a by-product in the manufacture of many chlorinated hydrocarbons. HCB is widely used as a fungicide in the Near East, Australia, the United States, and Eastern and Western Europe. [340] The National Academy of Sciences has identified HCB as a danger to human health and to the environment. Once transferred to the oceans via atmospheric fallout, waste-dumping, or coastal outfalls containing pesticide residues, HCB is resistant to chemical, biological, or physical degradation. [341] It is now present in terrestrial and aquatic food webs, and has been observed to be concentrated in some marine organisms at levels similar to those of DDT and the PCBs. [342]

Halogenated hydrocarbons of low molecular weight are also of concern, but their effects in the environment are different from those of heavier molecules. Compared to the heavy halogenated hydrocarbons, such as DDT, the PCBs, and dieldrin, compounds of lower molecular weight are more water-soluble. They are found in aerosol propellants, fumigants, fire extinguishers, solvents, dielectric insulators, and are used as intermediates of organic synthesis. It is estimated that 6,000 tons of one of these compounds (trichlorofluoromethane) enter the world's oceans annually. [343] These compounds readily evaporate and remain in the atmosphere long enough to make transfer to the oceans highly likely. While low molecular weight compounds are now ubiquitous in the atmosphere and in surface waters, [344] concentrations observed so far in the oceans are six orders of magnitude below the concentrations that cause toxic effects in mammals and aquatic organisms. [345] The long-term impact of these chemicals at low concentrations is unknown, and a continuing buildup of these chemicals could significantly increase both their concentrations and their potential biological consequences.

One aspect of the long-term buildup of synthetic organic chemicals applies to both heavy and light molecules. Unless monitoring increases significantly, pollutant concentrations may grow to unmanageable proportions before they are recognized. By that time, they may have become ecologically dangerous and, even if inputs were to cease, the effects of the materials continuing to circulate in the ecosphere would be manifested for years afterward. DDT use offers an example of this phenomenon. [346] It has been observed that the effects of DDT pollution on a localized or

regional scale begin to subside in individual species 3–5 years after input to the ecosystem has halted. [347] On a global scale, however, simulation models suggest that if world application were phased out, a downturn in bioaccumulation and physiological effects might not occur for decades because of the DDT residue remaining in atmospheric, soil, and oceanic reservoirs (Fig. 13–7).

## Heavy Metals

All naturally occurring heavy metal elements are found in the oceans at some concentration. Those metals introduced by human society enter via rivers, industrial outfalls and domestic sewers, and through atmospheric transport and offshore dumping of waste materials. As a result, pollution of the marine environment by metals is most evident in the coastal zones, especially where mixing processes between coastal and oceanic waters are slow, facilitating accumulation. [348] Due to their oceanic omnipresence, most heavy metals are now bioaccumulated to some degree in one or more

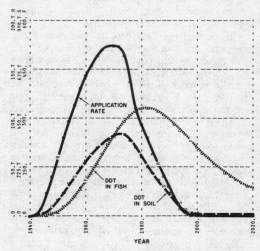

**Figure 13–7.** The effect of a gradual reduction, starting in 1971, in the use of DDT from a simulation model. The usage rate is assumed to reach zero by the year 2000. The usage rates are historically correct through 1971, when it is assumed that a world decision to phase out the use of DDT is reached. Shortly thereafter, the concentration of DDT in soil begins to decline, but the concentration of DDT in fish continues to increase for 11 years and does not return to the 1971 level until 1995. The response of DDT concentrations in animals further up the food chain—birds and humans, for example—are subject to even longer delays. (*Jørgen Randers, in D. L. and D. H. Meadows, eds., Toward Global Equilibrium, Cambridge, Mass.: Wright-Allen Press, 1973; reprinted by permission of the distributors, MIT Press*)

components of the marine food web.[349] Trace metal concentrations have been measured in fish and shellfish in coastal waters of the United States and New Zealand, the North Atlantic, the North Sea, and other European coastal areas.[350] According to the Global 2000 Study projections, the annual production and circulation of most metals is expected to increase between now and the year 2000. In many cases the rate of accumulation in the oceans of metals injected by human activity is expected to exceed the natural rate (Table 13–23).

The effect of heavy metal concentrations on the development of marine organisms is only beginning to be understood. However, the characteristics of heavy metals are significant. They are among the most environmentally persistent substances. They cannot be transmuted or destroyed and, in concert with certain bacteria, have the insidious attribute of combining with organic substances to form highly toxic metallo-organic compounds. Sometimes these compounds are discharged directly into ocean waters. For example, the "mercury poisoning" at Minamata, Japan, involved spent chemical catalysts containing metallo-organic methyl mercury.[351]

The highest mercury concentrations in ocean organisms are found in the top predators of the food chain. In the past decade there has been concern that the concentration of mercury may increase as more of the metal is released into the environment. However, recent studies suggest that the present mercury levels in these pelagic life forms should not be expected to increase with society's continued use of the metal. The estimated total mercury content of the world ocean mixed layer is currently two orders of magnitude greater than the annual production by human society; therefore, measurable man-made alteration of mercury levels in the open ocean is not probable in the short term. It does appear likely that regional pockets of high-level coastal mercury pollution will continue to exist, due primarily to industrial processes.[352]

Besides input from rivers, urban outfalls, and dumping, concentrations of iron and copper metals in the ocean are atmospherically transported from specific industrial sources, particularly the smelting industry processes for copper and the processes of the iron, steel, and titanium dioxide industries for iron. The National Academy of Sciences has estimated that coal combustion is also one of the most significant human sources of iron and copper introduction to the sea.[353] These metals are partially released during combustion and carried to the oceans in fly-ash particulate matter.

## TABLE 13–23

### Estimates from Annual River Discharges of Amounts of Metals Injected into the Oceans Annually by Geological Processes and by Man

|  | By Geological Processes (in rivers) | By Man (in mining) |
|---|---|---|
|  | *(in thousands of metric tons)* | |
| Iron | 25,000 | 319,000 |
| Manganese | 440 | 1,600 |
| Copper | 375 | 4,460 |
| Zinc | 370 | 3,930 |
| Nickel | 300 | 358 |
| Lead | 180 | 2,330 |
| Molybdenum | 13 | 57 |
| Silver | 5 | 7 |
| Mercury | 3 | 7 |
| Tin | 1.5 | 166 |
| Antimony | 1.3 | 40 |

Source: Michael Waldichuk, *Global Marine Pollution: An Overview*, Paris: UNESCO, 1977, p. 20.

Current levels of oceanic introduction of iron and copper will not result in major overall concentration changes but will probably increase. Global industrial development will provide a growing source of metallic emissions that will easily enter the world oceans.[354]

Cadmium poisoning in Japan has stimulated an interest in the possible effects of this metal on the marine ecosystem. As with most other metals, cadmium enters the oceans through continental outfalls and the atmosphere. Its bioaccumulation in organisms consumed by humans could potentially be a threat to health. Any significant cadmium pollution would be expected to occur in the coastal zones, and localized high concentrations of cadmium could contaminate marine organisms in coastal waters. However, open-ocean surface water pollution by cadmium metal does not seem probable, at least in the near future.[355]

It appears that, up to this point, lead is the only stable metal element that has exhibited widespread increased concentrations in the ocean. It has been nearly 20 years since concentrations in the oceans were demonstrated to be attaining significant levels through anthropogenic sources.[356] These concentrations have been altered in coastal waters, mainly as a result of the use of lead alkyls as antiknock additives in fuels of internal combustion engines. Lead aerosols have been responsible for the increase of this metal in the coastal surface waters of the Pacific, Atlantic, and Mediterranean Oceans. Once introduced into the sea via coastal runoff and the atmosphere, lead quickly interacts with the marine biota. Concern exists over how human health may be affected by the consumption of lead-contaminated marine resources. [357]

Following a course similar to that of lead in the marine environment, other trace metals still incompletely investigated may have increased their concentration in the surface layers of the global ocean. This is especially possible in northern hemispheric waters surrounding regions of high fossil fuel combustion, cement production, and other industrial activities. [358]

Ultimately, most reactive heavy metals are deposited relatively rapidly in the sediments of the coastal zones, seemingly out of the water layers where they may play a determinate role in biological processes. [359] However, metal accumulation in sediments poses potential problems. Measurement of the extent of metal concentrations have only begun, as have studies of the mechanisms for redistribution of metals back into bottom water and their uptake by benthic organisms. [360] One study has examined the amounts and distribution of six trace metals—cadmium, chromium, copper, nickel, lead, and zinc—in the water and sediments of Raritan Bay, a polluted estuary of the New York Bight. Large amounts of metal-laden municipal and industrial wastes have accumulated in the bay, forcing the termination of shellfish harvesting, decreasing benthic diversity and reducing the yield of commercial fishery species. Metal concentrations in Raritan Bay bottom sediments have been found to be similar to other estuarine areas in the United States and in the United Kingdom. [361] Anoxic coastal sediments containing precipitated mercury sulfide also may release their deposited mercury upon contact with aerated waters. [362]

## Artificial Radioactive Materials

The Global 2000 energy projections foresee significant growth in the worldwide development and use of nuclear energy, and this increased nuclear activity may result in increased flows of radioactive materials into the marine environment.

The history of radioactive contamination of the oceans provides a useful context for considering possible future contamination. The largest source of radioactive materials entering the oceans has been nuclear explosions detonated by the United States, the U.S.S.R., the United Kingdom, France, the People's Republic of China and India. Up to 1968 the world's oceans had received much of the radioactive debris from 470 nuclear explosions. Two biologically active fission products—cesium–137 and strontium–90—have been produced at levels of 21 and 34 megacuries, respectively, and much of this material has now entered the oceans. [363]

Although the nuclear test ban has substantially reduced the rate at which radioactive materials enter the oceans, nuclear energy production and the use of radioactive materials has continued the flow of radioactive isotopes into the terrestrial environment and ultimately into the oceans.

The three broad types of radioactive species have been introduced to the marine environment: (1) transuranic elements used as nuclear fuels, such as uranium, neptunium, curium and plutonium; (2) the radionuclides produced as fission products or as induced radioactive species, such as strontium-90 and cesium-137; and (3) the activation products resulting from the interaction of nuclear particles with the components of nuclear reactors and weapons, such as zinc-65 and iron-55. As early as 1972, scientists had detected 52 artificially produced radionuclides in the marine environment. [364]

In the decades ahead, the largest source* of radioactive materials entering the oceans will probably be the nuclear fuel cycle, i.e., the production, use, reprocessing and disposal of nuclear fuels. The Department of Energy projects more than a 200 percent increase in nuclear energy by 2000. How extensive this source will be depends critically on how carefully the fuel cycle is managed.

Table 13–24 presents a projection of the inventory of radionuclides in the world's oceans that has been reported by UNESCO. The total artificial radioactivity in the oceans in 2000 is projected to be of the same order of magnitude as it was in 1970, i.e., about $10^9$ curies. Tritium from nuclear reactors increases by three orders of magnitude over the 30-year period, reaching something on the order of $10^8$ curies. The largest artificial contribution continues to be tritium from nuclear explosions. The total artificial radioactivity introduced remains two orders of magnitude less than the total natural background of potassium-40 at $5 \times 10^{11}$ curies, but some of the artificially introduced radionuclides have effects quite different from those of natural potassium-40. [365]

It is not known to what further levels the various radioactive elements could safely be accommodated in the marine environment, especially in crucial coastal zones. So far, only modest efforts have been made to study the environmental impact these substances have upon individual marine organisms or their communities. Transuranics,

---

*Assuming that atmospheric testing of nuclear devices is not resumed.

## TABLE 13–24

### Total Inventory of Artificial Radionuclides Introduced into the World Oceans, 1970 and 2000

|  | 1970 | 2000 |
|---|---|---|
|  | *Curies* | |
| Nuclear explosions (worldwide distribution) | | |
| Fission products (exclusive of tritium) | $2–6 \times 10^8$ | $? \times 10^8$ [a] |
| Tritium | $10^9$ | $? \times 10^9$ [a] |
| Reactors and reprocessing of fuel (restricted local distribution) | | |
| Fission and activation products (exclusive of tritium) | $3 \times 10^5$ | $3 \times 10^7$ |
| Tritium | $3 \times 10^5$ | $? \times 10^8$ |
| Total artificial radioactivity | $10^9$ | $10^9$ |
| Total natural potassium-40 | $5 \times 10^{11}$ | $5 \times 10^{11}$ |

*Source:* A. Preston et al., as reported in Edward E. Goldberg, *The Health of the Oceans,* Paris: UNESCO, 1976, p. 81.

[a] Assuming that atmospheric nuclear testing will continue at about the 1968–70 rate.

fission products, and induced radioactive species are now found in seawater and in the ocean biota almost universally. The biological or environmental significance of this contamination is virtually unknown.[366]

### Fossil Fuels

The Study's energy projections anticipate a global growth in commercial energy demand, and a resulting rise in the production and use of fossil fuel energy resources. Driven by expanding GNPs, population needs, and technological advances, this increased energy usage will certainly aggravate the already serious problems of coastal zone degradation by fossil fuel pollutants. The proportions of fuel oil and gas supplies extracted from the seabed are significant and increasing. While large oil spills caused by blowouts and tanker collisions can have disastrous local effects on coastal zone ecosystems, the discharges from the routine transportation, production, and use of oil and gas are greater in volume and may present a long-term threat to the marine environment. Estimates of the quantities of petroleum hydrocarbons entering the oceans annually are presented in Table 13–25.

As oil exploration continues worldwide, increasing numbers of extraction facilities will be established in coastal zone areas. Sublethal and long-term damage to marine organisms and eco-

systems may result from chronic discharges and accidental low-volume spills during normal offshore and dockside operations, from disposal of drilling muds and cuttings, and from disturbance of the seabed and coastal wetlands by platform and pipeline construction. Losses incurred during transportation and processing also contribute to low-level petroleum contamination, as do inputs from the atmosphere, coastal municipal and industrial waste outfalls, and urban and river runoff.[367] Increased coal combustion and conversion can also be expected to contribute to oceanic pollution. Mining wastes, secondary pollutants associated with trade and transport, and the byproducts of processing and primary combustion of coal will enter coastal waters via the land and the atmosphere.

The manner and severity with which fossil fuel pollutants affect the marine environment varies. Different factors—such as oil dosage and type, weather and water conditions, and the seasonal behavior patterns of marine organisms—influence the biological impact of petroleum hydrocarbons on ocean life and habitats.[368] Nearshore petroleum discharges cause more extensive and permanent damage to organisms and life cycles in estuaries and coastal wetlands than those further offshore. Biological recovery of oil-inundated

## TABLE 13–25

### Best Estimates of Petroleum Hydrocarbons Introduced into the Oceans Annually

| Source | Best Estimate | Probable Range |
|---|---|---|
|  | *(millions of metric tons)* | |
| Natural seeps | 0.6 | 0.2–1.0 |
| Offshore production | 0.08 | 0.08–0.15 |
| Transportation | | |
|   LOT tankers | 0.31 | 0.15–0.4 |
|   Non-LOT tankers | 0.77 | 0.65–1.0 |
|   Dry docking | 0.25 | 0.2–0.3 |
|   Terminal operations | 0.003 | 0.0015–0.005 |
|   Bilges bunkering | 0.5 | 0.4–0.7 |
|   Tanker accidents | 0.2 | 0.12–0.25 |
|   Nontanker accidents | 0.1 | 0.02–0.15 |
| Coastal refineries | 0.2 | 0.2–0.3 |
| Atmosphere | 0.6 | 0.4–0.8 |
| Coastal municipal wastes | 0.3 | – |
| Coastal nonrefining industrial wastes | 0.3 | – |
| Urban runoff | 0.3 | 0.1–0.5 |
| River runoff | 1.6 | – |
| Total | 6.113 | |

*Source:* National Academy of Sciences, *Petroleum in the Marine Environment,* Washington, 1975, p. 6.

wetlands is a complex process, and the time required for recovery varies widely.[369]

The coastal effects of oil pollution may be of longer duration than previously thought. Components of oil are now known to remain in estuarine wetland sediments for as long as eight years after an initial spill,[370] continuing to affect benthic organisms and altering biological productivity. A marsh grass community has been observed to have been unable to reestablish itself even three years after an oil spill. Over the three years of observation, erosion rates in the salt marsh were found to be 24 times greater than those in nearby unaffected areas.[371]

If subjected to large enough amounts of oil and petroleum hydrocarbon products, either through accidental spills or extended low level inputs, a sea-surface hydrocarbon microlayer can form to cover the adjacent coastal ocean areas. This hydrocarbon film can act as a differential accumulation layer for trace materials such as toxic heavy metal ions, vitamins, amino acids, and lipophilic chlorinated hydrocarbon pollutants, including DDT residues and PCBs. The combination of these materials near or at the ocean surface could significantly affect coastal ocean ecosystems. Such "microslicks" have been observed to interfere with the normal development of fish eggs during spawning seasons, and some scientists suspect microslicks of inducing changes within phytoplankton communities.[372]

Although the long-term implications of low-level oil contamination are just beginning to be understood, it is now well established that petroleum hydrocarbons adversely affect a wide variety of marine organisms physiologically and behaviorally.[373] Significant petroleum contamination of wetland sediments resulting from repeated small spills and/or effluent discharges have already occurred along West German, British, French, and Italian coastlines, as well as those of the U.S.[374] Such polluting input can be expected to increase globally as fossil fuel production, transportation, and use grow during the next two decades.

As the search for oil and gas intensifies, exploration and extraction will take place in areas previously untouched. The marine environment in parts of the Arctic is now vulnerable to conditions accompanying the exploitation of fossil fuel resources. The construction of artificial drilling islands, dredged up from bay bottoms, will have locally adverse effects on Arctic sea life, as will low level losses of oil incurred during routine production and transportation. Accidental large volume spills or well blowouts would pose serious problems, for the very nature of the far northern

environment would make cleanup efforts and ultimate ecosystem recovery especially difficult.[375] Exploitation of fossil fuel resources in the Antarctic region could create similar difficulties. There would certainly be localized environmental effects of oil processing and transport activities; repeated accidental spills could have serious cumulative effects on Southern Ocean ecosystems.

## Sewage, Fertilizer Nutrients, and Sedimentation

The Global 2000 Study projections for water, population, forestry, and food and agriculture imply that there will be a growth in coastal pollution from sewage, fertilizers, and land runoff sedimentation. These problems are seen to be particularly acute in the coastal zones of less developed countries. Unprecedented urban growth will give rise to an increase in the volume of untreated sewage entering estuarine rivers and coastal waters. Intensified agricultural activity and the concomitant twofold to threefold increase in global fertilizer use will add to already large amounts of chemical nutrients carried into estuaries, wetlands, and coral reefs. Projected deforestation will destroy watersheds, exacerbate erosion, and create large nutrient-laden silt loads in rivers running to the sea. Upon entering estuaries and coastal areas, river waters will release their suspended sediment and organic matter, creating conditions of coastal water overproductivity and contributing to problems of sedimentation that are especially destructive of coral reefs. While the dangers of both nutrient and sediment pollution are known, there has been little study of what the ultimate consequences of this pollutant combination may be. In the short term, however, it appears that nutrients and sediments, together with physical alteration of estuaries and reefs, will produce localized cases of estuarine and coastal eutrophication.

Coastal wetlands are naturally able to absorb contaminants from polluted tidal water. Since most salt marshes are either located in estuaries or have freshwater flowing into them, their ability to retain contaminants running off the land help to prevent further transport of pollutants to the sea. Marshes of *Spartina* grasses can biologically fix inorganic nitrogen, creating high levels of plant productivity equal to that of intensively managed agricultural areas.[376] Mangrove soils are effective nutrient reservoirs too and are exceptional environments for the removal of nitrogen in sewage. In salt marshes, extreme enrichment of inorganic nitrogen is counteracted by its bacterial conversion to nitrogen gas. However, as capable as wetlands are in utilizing large volumes of nutrients, the presence of excessive amounts of nitrogen, like those contained in sewage and fertilizer runoff, could eventually result in an overproductivity of coastal waters that takes the form of coastal algal blooms[377] and could cause eutrophication of localized estuarine and wetland areas.

In tropical waters, sewage pollution can also result in the growth of coral-smothering algae, causing reef degradation and sometimes leading to the sedimentary production of toxic levels of hydrogen sulfide. Pollution-intolerant reef species then decrease. The more tolerant species take over the community, and the reef ecosystem is altered, sometimes permanently.

The exposure of reefs to land runoff sedimentation has, so far, been the greatest single cause of reef destruction.[378] Ongoing activities such as deforestation, intensive agricultural practices, livestock grazing, and dredging and filling operations are currently leading to extensive sedimentation of reef waters in tropical coastal waters. Natural growth of reef-forming polyps requires favorable conditions of salinity and relatively warm, turbulent or upwelling water to bring nutrients and cleanse away waste materials.[379] When functioning naturally, a coral reef ecosystem sustains the life cycles of all of its individual components, but when the reef-growth system is disturbed, imbalances develop as certain reef organisms either leave or die. Most corals cannot live if heavily coated or buried by sediment particles, and reduced light intensity caused by turbid waters significantly affect growth rates and species diversity.[380]

Other causes of reef destruction include heavy freshwater runoff due to deforestation, excessive salinity (produced by desalinization plants), and thermal pollution.[381] The resuspension of sediment in dredging operations effectively blocks any regeneration of already damaged coral colonies.[382] Once destroyed, a coral reef has little hope for regeneration. If healing reef growth does occur in the absence of pollutants, the time for restoration to any semblance of its natural state can easily be a matter of decades.[383]

### Solid Wastes.

Solid waste disposal in the coastal zones is—for the short term—one of the least serious of marine pollution problems. While foreign material can adversely affect coastal ecosystems, its current impact is generally as a localized nuisance and human health hazard. However, considering the population, GNP, and forestry projections, greater quantities of solid wastes should be expected to enter the oceans between now and the year 2000.

The sea floor, surface waters, and beaches of the earth's marine environment are littered with man-made materials originating from deliberate, incidental, or accidental waste disposal.* Solid waste, often referred to as "litter," is of two types: (1) refuse originating on land, consisting of packaging materials (plastic, metal, cloth, glass, or wood), and (2) refuse from ships released during fishing, recreation, or cargo-carrying operations.[384] The amount of solid wastes entering the world's oceans each year—a large part of which is released in harbors, ports, or other coastal water areas— is estimated to be in the millions of tons (Table 13–26).

Floating litter is mainly a coastal zone problem and affects both commercial and biological activity. Nylon ropes and plastic sheets floating just beneath the sea surface easily foul ship propellors. Wood debris and submerged logs can present sudden and serious navigational problems. The effect of litter on ocean organisms is apparent also. Plastic sheets can also smother benthic organisms. Sheer plastics, mistaken for jellyfish, have been eaten by sea turtles, small plastic objects been injested by fish, and plastic bags caught on the heads of sea mammals are known to have caused suffocation. In coastal waters adjacent to logging and pulp mill activities, solid and liquid wood wastes have been found to be destructive of ocean organisms and habitats.[385]

On the whole, given current practices and the projections of the Global 2000 Study, a growth in marine pollution can be expected in the next 20 years. Outfalls and the atmosphere will inject industrial, municipal, and agricultural chemical and metal wastes into coastal waters. Pollutants from fossil fuel extraction, transportation, and energy production will contribute significantly to spoilation of the marine environment. Population growth, deforestation, and intensive agriculture will all contribute to the volume of sewage, nutrient chemicals, and sediments entering coastal

---

*Disposal of solid wastes in the oceans can be carried to extremes, as it has in the New York Bight, resulting in unpleasant localized impacts on the marine environment. The Marine Ecosystems Analysis Program of the National Oceanic and Atmospheric Administration (NOAA) has described one incident as the infamous "summer 1976 floatables event," during which "beaches along the south shore of Long Island were inundated by a variety of floating litter. Included among the materials washed ashore were tar and grease balls, charred wood, garbage and trash (e.g., watermelon rinds, chicken heads, styrofoam beads, paper, and plastic wrappers), and sewage-related items (e.g., condom rings, diaper liners, and tampon applicators)." (*New York Bight Project: Annual Report for FY 1976*, NOAA Environmental Research Laboratories, Boulder, Dec. 1977, p. 29.)

## TABLE 13–26

### Annual Ocean Litter Estimates

| Source | Litter (millions of metric tons) |
|---|---|
| Passenger vessels | 0.028 |
| Merchant shipping | |
| Crew | 0.110 |
| Cargo | 5.600 |
| Recreational boating | 0.103 |
| Commercial fishing | |
| Crew | 0.340 |
| Gear | 0.001 |
| Military | 0.074 |
| Oil drilling and platforms | 0.004 |
| Catastrophe | 0.100 |
| Total | 6.360 |

*Source:* National Academy of Sciences, *Assessing Potential Ocean Pollutants,* Washington, 1975, p. 422.

waters. Unsightly and unhealthy solid waste pollution will develop into problems of greater magnitude and areal extent. The most serious impact of pollutants will be on the organisms and ecosystems of the coastal zones. Living marine resources will be affected by disease and by the reduction and spoilation of viable habitat resulting from pollutant increases. The greatest uncertainty over coastal pollution concerns the specific level of the pollution and the future of international efforts to control it.

## Overexploitation of Living Marine Resources

The Global 2000 food and population projections point to a growth in global demand for living marine resources. However, the fisheries projections themselves suggest that the trend in ever increasing annual yields may have peaked and that future catch tonnages may not be able to readily meet this demand. Increasing pressure by commercial fisheries will place great stresses on living resource populations and lead to an overexploitation of traditional species. Catch compositions will shift to greater amounts of nontraditional species. A significant proportion of these smaller, shorter-lived species will continue to be utilized in ways other than direct human consumption. The policies and practices applied to marine mammals are in flux. In the face of extinction, the survival of many species depends on rational scientific and societal management decisions.

### Fisheries

The Global 2000 Study population and food projections suggest that the demand for seafood will increase, encouraging still more fishing activity. The degradation of coastal zone habitats—either through physical destruction for development or through constant injection of various pollutants—will contribute to changes in species composition and the quantity of the global catch. Future gross catch statistics therefore may show a constant or increasing yield, but the catch will become composed of progressively less traditional products. Advances in fishing and processing technologies, by helping the gross catch figures to remain high, will effectively conceal the degree to which overfishing is undermining the utility and value of the world catch.

The coastal oceans are the crucially important sites of the world's fisheries: At least half of the marine life forms directly utilized by humans come from coastal waters; nearly all of the remainder come from coastal and oceanic upwellings.* Although these upwellings occur in approximately 0.1 percent of all oceanic areas, they are among the world's most productive fisheries.[386]

Over the last three to four decades, intensive fishing activity has produced a shift in the species composition of the global catch away from the traditionally preferred species toward species at lower trophic levels and of less economic value. A growing proportion is being converted to fertilizer and fishmeal for animal feed. Before 1940, a negligible portion of the catch was used in meal production; by the mid-1970s, 35 percent was being used for making meal and oil.[387] Thus the fish catch directly used for human consumption in 1975 was closer to 45 million metric tons than the 70 million often cited. Use of the ocean fisheries for animal feed is somewhat analogous to fattening livestock on high quality grain. The fish catch—like the grain—would be more efficiently utilized if it were consumed directly by humans and if animals were raised primarily on plant species and other foods of no value as human food. Whether the shift to fertilizer and fishmeal can be attributed partially to the need to find a market for the less preferred species or to the fact that fishmeal has been made into a more marketable product, the shift itself is clear.

---

*Upwelling areas occur where winds and prevailing boundary currents allow cold, nutrient-laden water to rise from below. Upwellings create areas of high primary productivity, which consequently allow the production of large stocks of fish.

Intensive fishing activity appears to have helped reduce the absolute yield of the global fisheries catch. Improved fishery technologies have greatly aided the overexploitation of most traditional stocks. Until 1971, global total fisheries production had increased annually at a rapid rate. However, in 1972 a combination of natural ocean current inversions and the prolonged strain of overfishing on fish populations drastically reduced the population size and thus the yield from the Peruvian anchovy fishery.[388] This reduction in yield appears to have contributed significantly to the 1972 world decline in catch tonnage and to the subsequent fluctuations in total annual yields.[389]

### Marine Mammals and the Marine Environment

Constant global demand, shortsighted management of living resources, and overexploitation have caused the severe depletion, and in some cases the extinction, of a number of marine mammal species. Marine mammals—which include whales, porpoises, dolphins, seals, sea lions, sirenians, sea otters, and polar bears—have historically been hunted to the brink of extinction. Some animals, such as whales, have been attacked one species at a time and with increasing technological expertise (see Table 13–27). As marine biologist Kenneth Norris has written, "The contest has now become so grossly unequal that no evasion on the part of the animals has any effect. Their only defense is scarcity."[390]

Abusive overutilization of a living marine resource results in the loss of a full range of benefits—tangible, intangible, realized, or potential—to both present and future generations. Such benefits include economic and nutritive values, aesthetic contributions, and important roles in maintenance of the health and stability of the marine ecosystem.[391]

Ecosystem effects may be a crucially important factor; no species exists alone, and exploitation of one species has some impact on other components of the habitat. Yet present harvesting procedures consider only the effects on individual species, or groups of species in isolation, and do not recognize the need for predicting the impact on the cycle of reciprocal relationships within the ecosystem. The impact of overexploitation may include changes (1) in the population of competing or symbiotic species within the functional group of the exploited species, (2) in the vegetation structure and carnivore populations where the exploited species is a herbivore, and (3) in numbers of prey where the exploited species is a carnivore. These are only first-order responses,

### TABLE 13–27

### Effect of Whaling on Stocks of Ten Species of Whales

| Species | Virgin Stock | 1974 Stock | 1974 Stock as a Percentage of the Virgin Stock |
|---|---|---|---|
| | *(thousands)* | | |
| Sperm | | | |
| both sexes | 922 | 641 | 69 |
| male | 461 | 212 | 45 |
| female | 461 | 429 | 93 |
| Fin | 448 | 101 | 22 |
| Minke | 361 | 325 | 90 |
| Blue | 215 | 13 | 6 |
| Sei | 200 | 76 | 38 |
| Bryde | 100 | (40)? | ? |
| Right[a] | (50)? | (2)? | ? |
| Bowhead[a] | (10)? | (2)? | ? |
| Humpback | 50 | 7 | 14 |
| Gray[a] | 11 | 11 | 100 |
| Total | 2,367 | 1,218 | 51.4 |

*Source:* Victor B. Scheffer, "The Status of Whales," *Pacific Discovery,* vol. 29, no. 1, 1976, p. 3.

[a] Not currently being hunted.

and consequent changes in more remote parts of the system are probable.[392]

International efforts to regulate whaling have been protracted.[393] The somewhat more responsible management techniques now established by the International Whaling Commission are seriously hindered by the lack of accurate whale-population data needed to determine harvest quotas. In the United States, the Marine Mammal Protection Act of 1972 is the first national legislation that makes the healthy maintenance of the ecosystem the primary objective of marine mammal management.[394]

Major uncertainties arise when evaluating the consequences of the Global 2000 Study's projections on the environmental quality of marine fisheries. A good knowledge of the ecological effects of marine resource overexploitation has yet to be gained, and agreement has yet to be reached over whether current reduced catch yields are a trend or only a temporary fluctuation in fisheries population cycles. The productivity of future fisheries depends on the development of cooperative marine management practices. Inherent in this course will be the problem of how to regulate internationally commonly utilized living resources. Unilaterally declared 200-mile economic zones may both aggravate and alleviate the evolution of fisheries overexploitation. Only time, and a clear perception of current and potential environmental conditions, will tell how successful these management efforts will have been.

In conclusion, the Study's projections indicate that loss of habitat, pollution, and overexploitative living-resource management policies will significantly affect the integrity and ultimate productivity of the world's coastal waters. Economic development along the coastal zone will destroy or alter ecosystems crucial to the life cycles of many fisheries species. Chemicals, fossil fuels, solid and sewage wastes, agricultural nutrients, and eroded sediments will pollute ecosystems and degrade marine communities. Growing demand for food to feed rapidly multiplying populations will lead to great stresses on global fisheries and cause a further shift in total yields and species composition. Population pressures, concerted economic development, and an increased need for food will have cyclic effects and eventually impact upon those very areas, the coastal zones, from which basic sustenance and livelihood is derived.

## Open Oceans

The open oceans differ from coastal waters, both in the time scales of the processes taking place within them and in their capacity to absorb, dilute, and disperse waste materials. The environmental conditions of the deep sea are quite unique. It is an immense area that is relatively stable over long time periods, has little topographic complexity, and receives low inputs of energy. Most benthic animals are small mud-dwelling and mud-feeding creatures of great variety and long evolutionary history. Natural deep-sea disturbances consist of events such as mud slumps, fish and invertebrate activity, and large objects settling from the surface.[395]

As a result of their vast size and the nature of their ecosystems, environmental change in the open oceans necessarily occurs very slowly. It can be expected that the Global 2000 Study projections will cause no major impact on the earth's open oceans by the year 2000. However, the projections do indicate that over the next 20 years world society will establish certain trends that, sustained over the long term, will eventually cause measurable change in the oceanic environment. Most importantly, long-lived toxic substances will continue to accumulate in open ocean waters and inevitably affect oceanic ecosystems for many years into the future. Deep-sea mining, if initiated without adequate knowledge and precautions will also have the potential to disrupt the ecosystems of extensive benthic and pelagic areas.

## Pollution of the Open Oceans

The Global 2000 energy, GNP, nonfuel minerals, and agriculture projections imply that increasing amounts of toxic pollutants will continue to be produced in the decades ahead. Toxic chemicals enter oceanic waters three ways. Major quantities are deposited in coastal waters and subsequently carried into oceanic waters by currents and living organisms. Significant amounts are also deposited directly from the atmosphere. Large and probably increasing amounts will be deposited directly into surface and deeper oceanic waters by accidental spills, operational discharges and intentional dumping.

Oceanic ecosystems differ from coastal ecosystems by assimilating pollutants from land-based, coastal, and oceanic sources over a longer time period. Most pollutants enter marine waters as fine particles, as liquids, or in dissolved form. The pollutants are then adsorbed onto fine sediment and detrital particles that are consumed by zooplankton in the water column. The zooplankton incorporate the pollutants into their bodies and eject them as packaged fecal pellets. Dead organisms and feces settle quickly, leading to a rapid accumulation of chemicals in oceanic depths.[395a]

In the cold oceanic bottom waters, metabolism and natural sedimentation are very slow,[395b] and as a result, pollutants are biologically degraded or immobilized in sediments at a much slower rate than in coastal waters. A related consequence of the slow degradation and immobilization of pollutants is that deep sea communities are exposed to pollutants for long periods of time. Lengthy exposure to even low concentrations of pollutants is likely to be especially damaging to the organisms of the deep oceanic waters because they have evolved in one of the most stable, least varying ecosystems in the biosphere, and have had little need to develop adaptations to deal with environmental change.[395c]

Given their enormous volume, oceanic waters can accept a certain amount of waste material. Yet the oceans' capacity to dilute is ultimately finite. Marine scientist Edward Goldberg has expressed concern that over an extended period of time the introduction of pollutants into the oceans could lead to a long-term buildup of toxic material, causing "widespread mortalities and morbidities" in ocean organisms.[396] Once this condition is reached, Goldberg writes, there would be "no turning back. The great volume of the open ocean makes the removal of a toxic substance, identified by a catastrophic event, an endeavor beyond mankind's capabilities with the technologies of today or of the foreseeable future."[397]

## Deep-Sea Mining

The potential environmental implications of mining the deep seabed are not yet fully understood but are being studied by the U.S. National Oceanic and Atmospheric Administration, the International Union for the Conservation of Nature and Natural Resources, and the American Society for International Law.

In a preliminary effort to assess what the ecological impact of deep-sea mining might be, the National Oceanic and Atmospheric Administration (NOAA) has monitored test-mining activities in the Pacific Ocean. [398] The short-term, near-field effects of seabed mining have been evaluated to some extent; they include the action of the ore collector itself, pelagic and benthic plumes generated by deep seabed collection, and damage to benthic and pelagic organisms.

NOAA stated in its preliminary estimates [399] that deep-ocean mining will have very marked impacts on the sea floor and in the 20 to 50 meters of water above the point of discharge of the bottom effluent. The NOAA-monitored mining test has found this to be true in varying degrees. The ore collector contact zone—the portion of the seafloor actually mined and an area of several meters on either side of the collector track—is the site of severe, long-term environmental destruction. [400] Under present techniques, ore collection on the seabed also creates a benthic plume of suspended sediment as thick as a few tens of meters. The resedimentation from a benthic plume is easily measurable near the collector track, yet diminishes rapidly as the distance from the track increases. NOAA concluded that initial test monitoring has shown the resedimentation to not measurably affect benthic organisms at sites removed from the collector track. [401] However, the available study methods constrained the ability of the monitoring team to track the benthic plume and observe its effects on the deep sea benthic organisms.

The surface plume is a cloud of turbid waste water that extends with decreasing intensity and detectability downcurrent from the mining ship after its discharge. After monitoring the mining activity and conducting initial laboratory tests, NOAA concluded that the surface plume has no observable deleterious effects on the rate of primary productivity. The effects of the plume sediments on penetration of light into the euphotic zone are as yet undetermined. Preliminary investigations show no detectable "in-plume" mortality of zooplankton; experiments are being conducted to assess the possible uptake of plume-related particulates by zooplankton. [402]

The International Union for the Conservation of Nature and Natural Resources [403], Morges, Switzerland, feels that the eventual environmental consequences of deep seabed mining may be more serious than anticipated or observed, for the following reasons:

1. Deep sea organisms may have very long generation times—a benthic clam was recently described as taking 200 years to reach sexual maturity—and may be extremely vulnerable to alteration of their environment.*

2. In the process of bringing dredged materials to the surface, sediments and bottom water will be released. Settling times for sediment may be very slow—on the order of 20 meters per year—and intensive dredging operations may create extensive surface plumes. One estimate states that several hundred thousand square miles of the Pacific may be layered with sediment in the 100 meters below the surface by 1990. Clouding of waters may have adverse effects on many organisms, and species composition of the phytoplankton community may be altered due to transport of dormant spores from the bottom to surface waters.

3. An estimated 70–96 percent of the nodules, by volume, will end up as processing waste, and processing them will require large quantities of chemical reagents and energy. The wastes, which will include heavy metals, may be quite toxic to marine life, and regardless of whether the operations take place on the coast or offshore, it is likely that they will produce both chemical and thermal pollution.

On the other hand, a report prepared for the American Society of International Law states that if strict controls and regulations are established soon by the United States and other countries involved, adverse impact could be minimized and deep-sea mining could be made environmentally acceptable. [404]

## Conclusions

Overall, what implications do the Global 2000 projections have for the marine environment? In large part, the answer is uncertain. The limited

---

*The deep ocean floor exhibits very low rates of recovery from damage. Even after a period of two years, densities of life in an altered area can be an order of magnitude lower than those of surrounding sediments. Benthic species composition remain different from the undamaged encircling environment for a similiar period of time (J. Frederick Grassle, "Diversity and Population Dynamics of Benthic Organisms," *Oceanus*, Winter 1978, pp. 42, 43, 45.

detail in the projections, combined with inadequacies in present knowledge of the oceans, leave many questions unanswered. However, a few general conclusions can be drawn.

First, there is no evidence to suggest that the major regulatory functions of the world's oceans will be substantially disrupted during the next two decades. The oceans' heat and energy storage capacity and its influence on global climate are not expected to undergo major modifications. The oceanic role in the global oxygen, carbon, and water cycles will not be drastically affected by the year 2000.

Second, the most significant impacts of the events foretold in the projections will probably occur in the coastal zones. These impacts will stem from the projected pressures of overfishing, the projected increase in the installation of new transportation and industrial facilities, and the projected discharge of toxic wastes and petroleum hydrocarbon products. As a result of these projected developments, the future pollution, alteration and destruction of estuaries, coastal wetlands and coral reefs may be anticipated.

Spoilation of coastal waters and disruption of estuarine and wetland ecosystems may have grave implications for the continued productivity of global fisheries—including aquaculture—and for the general viability of many ocean organisms. It is known that a large fraction of marine fishes depend, during some period in their lives, on estuarine ecosystems, coastal wetlands (including salt marshes and mangroves), and coral reefs. The extent to which the world's potential fish catch has already been affected by losses of coastal wetlands, estuaries and coral reefs is unknown, but certainly large, continuing losses may be expected to produce adverse effects. Furthermore, overfishing will continue to stress coastal fish communities; fisheries catches will be composed of species at lower trophic levels; and the proportion of these species used for animal feed and fertilizer rather than for human consumption will increase.

Coastal zones everywhere will be affected in one way or another. The use of DDT and other persistent pesticides in African, Latin American, and Asian countries for vector control and agricultural pest control is expected to increase in the next few decades, and the quantities of these persistent chemicals entering the coastal waters and the open ocean will increase accordingly.[405] The global input of herbicides and other agricultural chemicals will also increase, as will urban and industrial pollution and the destruction of estuarine and coastal wetland habitats.

In many respects the degradation of the marine environment in the next few decades parallels the terrestrial "tragedy of the commons," with the same complex problem of how to protect a jointly used, limited resource in the face of population and economic growth. No assured source of funds, no unified strategy, and no authority adequately protects the global marine environment from overuse or misuse. Unilaterally declared two hundred mile limits encourage coastal states to protect their ocean resources, but the oceans themselves do not recognize such arbitrary boundaries; they will transport pollutants throughout their environment regardless of political delimitations.[406] International agreements on the control of marine pollution have addressed contamination by petroleum and radioactive materials. Dumping of wastes at sea has also been considered in international conventions, but the largest sources of marine pollution—land-based outfalls, runoff, and atmospheric emissions of synthetic organic chemicals and heavy metals—are largely exempt from regulation by international agreement. The exploration and exploitation of the deep seabed are also still unregulated.[407] The United Nations Environment Programme (UNEP) is helping nations to protect and manage shared oceanic zones through its Regional Seas Programme. Of eight regional seas programs now designated by UNEP, that for the Mediterranean is the most developed. Assessment of coastal and open-ocean pollution is being conducted by most of the states surrounding the Mediterranean; they are also involved in marine environmental planning and management, the development of legislation, and institutional and financial arrangements. Although difficulties remain concerning both individual and collective responsibilities and capabilities, UNEP's Regional Seas Programme is advancing the cause for international cooperation in the prevention of ocean pollution.[408]

To further complicate the management of the marine commons, there are societal delays in responding to even catastrophic environmental problems. The Minamata Bay incident in Japan, involving mercury poisoning through consumption of contaminated fish, is a case in point. As shown in Table 13-28, 17 years elapsed between the time the mercury-laden catalysts were first discharged into the bay and the observation of neurological disorders in the fishermen and their families. Three more years elapsed before the agent causing the disease was identified, and another 14 years passed before the chemical factory was held legally responsible for its actions and ordered to compensate the victims or their fam-

## TABLE 13–28

### Timetable of Societal Responses to Mercury Pollution of the Ocean, Minamata Bay, Japan, 1939–73

| Year | | Years Elapsed Since Pollution Began |
|------|--|------|
| 1939 | Chemical production begins on the shores of Minamata Bay; the factory discharges spent catalysts containing mercury into the bay. | 0 |
| 1953 | Birds and cats in the bay area act oddly; the behavior disorder becomes known as "disease of the dancing cats." | 14 |
| 1956 | Neurological disorders observed among Minamata Bay fishermen and their families. | 17 |
| 1959 | High concentrations of mercury ascertained in bay fish and in dead patients; an independent study shows disease was methyl mercury poisoning and factory effluent the likely source. | 20 |
| 1960 | Chemical company denies relationship of mercury to the disease but finds new discharge sites for waste; several new cases break out at new site. | 21 |
| 1961–64 | Very small compensations paid by the chemical company to disease victims and to fishermen for loss of livelihood. | 22–25 |
| 1965 | A second outbreak occurs at Niigata, Japan, where an acetyldehyde factory discharges spent mercury catalysts into the river. | 26 |
| 1967 | Niigata patients initiate a civil action, presumed to be the first large civil suit brought against a polluter in Japan. | 28 |
| 1971 | Niigata District Court pronounces judgment against the Niigata factory; compensation awarded the 77 Niigata victims or their families. | 32 |
| 1973 | Kumamoto District Court finds Minamata Bay factory culpable and orders company to pay reasonable compensation to victims or their families. | 34 |

Source: Edward D. Goldberg, *The Health of the Oceans*, Paris: UNESCO, 1976, pp. 21–23; Paul R. Ehrlich, et al., *Ecoscience: Population, Resources, Environment*, San Francisco: Freeman, 1977, p. 574.

ilies.* And many more years will pass, if ever, before all of the consequences will have run their course. If societal delays on the order of decades are involved in the responses of a single nation, how long a time might be required for all of the nations of the world to respond if the oceans were observed to be evolving into a "toxic broth?"[409]

Global society is currently in a reactionary mode in its dealings with the marine environment:

Problems develop, and society reacts—after a time. Considering the magnitude of the short- and long-term problems to be faced, a determined shift to a more anticipatory mode is now appropriate. Although dead or dying global oceans will not be in evidence by the year 2000, what happens over the next two decades will be a major determinant of the health and productivity of the marine environment in the 21st century.

## THE FORESTRY PROJECTIONS AND THE ENVIRONMENT

### The Projections

The CIA forestry projections anticipate that the present net global deforestation rate of 18–20 million hectares per year will continue through the end of the century.† About one-fifth of the world's land surface is now covered by closed forests. By the year 2000, the projected deforestation will shrink

---

*Two years later, in 1975, a survey disclosed that there had been 3,500 victims of the disease and that an additional 10,000 persons might develop symptoms of the disease in the future (Paul R. Ehrlich et al., *Ecoscience*, San Francisco: Freeman, 1977, p. 574).

†Estimates of the annual rate of global deforestation vary widely. Data from the governments of tropical countries indicate a net annual deforestation of 6.4 million hectares during the 1975–80 period, and an optimistic projection of those countries' plans indicates the rate will decline to 4 million hectares per year by the 1995–2000 period (J. P. Lanly and J. Clement, *Present and Future Forest and Plantation Areas in the Tropics*,

Rome: Food and Agriculture Organization, Jan. 1979). A more widely used estimate of tropic deforestation is 10–12 million hectares per year (used, for example, by Edouard Saouma in "Statement by the Director-General of the Food and Agriculture Organization," 8th World Forestry Congress, Jakarta, Oct. 16–28, 1978). The substantially higher estimate used in this study takes into account the common disparity between the official designation of areas as forests and the actual use of the land by farmers, as well as the disparity between official intentions and actual accomplishments in the tropical nations.

forest cover to one-sixth of the land surface. As illustrated in Table 13–29, most of the deforestation will occur in the LDCs, whose humid tropical forests and open woodlands are steadily being felled and converted to farmland and pasture. This trend is impelled by several forces: the expansion of agricultural frontiers into forested areas in order to supply food as populations increase; the demand for fuelwood and charcoal; the demand for tropical forest products by industrialized nations; and the demand within the LDCs for paper and other forest-derived products as incomes rise. In North America and the U.S.S.R., on the other hand, only small reductions in forested areas are expected, while in Europe some increase in forests is anticipated.

The combination of increasing population growth and decreasing forest area will result in a decline in stocks of commercial-sized timber per person. In the industrialized countries, such stock will fall from the present 142 cubic meters per capita to 114 cubic meters per capita in the year 2000, with consequent rises in the real price of wood and some increases in the use of substitutes for wood products. In the LDCs over the same period, stocks will plummet from the present 57 cubic meters per capita to 21 cubic meters per capita, resulting in serious shortages of firewood, building materials, and other forest-derived benefits.

Forest management practices will also change. In the industrial nations, forest management will become increasingly intensive as efforts are made to boost commercial wood yields. In the less developed countries, the planting of plantation forests may increase toward the end of the century, but over the next two decades denuded areas and degraded forests resulting from planned agricultural settlement and from unplanned cutting will become far more extensive.

## Introduction

Of all the environmental impacts implied by the Global 2000 Study's projections, the forest changes, summarized in Table 13–29, pose one of the most serious problems, particularly for the less developed regions of the world.[410] When forests are removed, water and nutrient cycles are destabilized, and soil is left unprotected from rainfall and from the sun's heat, often leading to a sharp decline in soil fertility and to harsh extremes of temperature and moisture that reduce agricultural potentials.[411] Where catchments are deforested, the result is destabilization of steep slopes and increased flooding, both of which jeopardize downstream land and water use. Where humid tropical lowlands are deforested and recovery does not occur, sterile soils—capable of supporting little more than tenacious inedible grasses—may be exposed. When followed by burning, overcultivation, and overgrazing, deforestation is merely the first step in the process of converting forest lands into barren wastelands. This transformation occurred centuries ago in much of the Mediterranean basin and the Middle East and has already occurred during this century in wide areas

**TABLE 13–29**

**Estimates of World Forest Resources, 1978 and 2000**

| | Closed Forest (millions of hectares) | | Growing Stock (billions cu m overbark) | |
|---|---|---|---|---|
| | 1978 | 2000 | 1978 | 2000 |
| U.S.S.R. | 785 | 775 | 79 | 77 |
| Europe | 140 | 150 | 15 | 13 |
| North America | 470 | 464 | 58 | 55 |
| Japan, Australia, New Zealand | 69 | 68 | 4 | 4 |
| Subtotal | 1,464 | 1,457 | 156 | 149 |
| Latin America | 550 | 329 | 94 | 54 |
| Africa | 188 | 150 | 39 | 31 |
| Asia and Pacific LDCs | 361 | 181 | 38 | 19 |
| Subtotal (LDCs) | 1,099 | 660 | 171 | 104 |
| Total (world) | 2,563 | 2,117 | 327 | 253 |

| | Growing Stock per Capita (cu m biomass) | |
|---|---|---|
| Industrial countries | 142 | 114 |
| LDCs | 57 | 21 |
| Global | 76 | 40 |

Source: Table 8–9 and forestry projections, Chapter 8, this volume.

of Africa and South Asia.[412] By the end of the century it may well have occurred throughout large areas of Africa, Asia, and Latin America.

Drastic reductions in global forest area, coupled with a simultaneous growth in demand for wood products, are sure to lead to efforts to intensify the management of the remaining forests to raise yields and to increased areas of timber plantations. These trends will have both positive and negative environmental impacts. Well-managed plantations and production forests (especially in temperate areas) can ease the cutting pressure on natural forests, but production forests are biologically less diverse, are poorer habitats for native animals,[413] and, in some instances, may be inferior to natural forests in soil and water conservation values.[414] Energy-intensive fertilizers, pesticides, and herbicides may be required, creating runoff and associated problems. Still, given the projected demands for forest products, intensified wood and fiber production will be absolutely necessary in many areas, especially in the tropics, if other large areas are to be preserved as natural forests.

In the discussion that follows, the environmental consequences of deforestation in the LDCs are examined first, then the effects of more intensive management in the remaining forests of both the LDCs and the industrialized nations, followed by a brief consideration of possible global effects of the expected changes in forest environments.

## Deforestation in the LDCs

The world's forests are quite diverse, ranging from dense tropical rain forests to sparsely wooded savannas, from dwarf krummholz forests along alpine timberlines to thickets on semiarid chaparral land.[415] To simplify the discussion, however, all forests will be classified here into one of two broad categories: (1) closed forests, where dense tree canopies preclude the growth of grasses, or (2) open woodlands, where canopies are more open and ground cover includes grasses and forbs.

### Closed Forests

Closed forests in the LDCs present difficult management challenges. Commercial timber cutters usually operate on a "cut-and-get-out" basis, making no effort to manage for perpetuity. The forest is "high-graded" of commercially valuable species, while much of the remaining vegetation is destroyed by the logging operations. Land for crops is often cleared (frequently by burning) with little or no use made of the wood,* and valuable

---
*Wood ashes do yield crop nutrients—until they are leached out, which is often quite quickly.

timber, such as teak, is sometimes used only for firewood. Although management regulations of some kind have now been established in almost every nation for public forests (and in some nations even for private forests), the ability to enforce such regulations is commonly limited, since the responsible agencies have insufficient personnel and inadequate budgets.[416] The need for land-use planning based on soil capabilities and site features is widely recognized, but the pace of planning is glacial, and land-use changes—forced by population growth and economic development—are proceeding rapidly.[417]

The disruption of water systems is the most certain environmental consequence of forest elimination. Deforestation is most rapid in the very region where water systems are most vulnerable: the equatorial (tropical) belt, lying between 15 degrees north and 15 degrees south latitude in Africa and America, and bulging up to 30 degrees north in Asia. The equatorial belt receives almost half the globe's total terrestrial rainfall. Many areas within this band receive over 3 meters of rainfall a year, and the rain is substantially more erosive than elsewhere in the world.[418] Until they are removed, the multistoried tropical forests buffer the force of torrential rains, absorb water, and slow runoff. Deforestation of this belt will have serious effects on the flows in the major river systems such as the Mekong, the Ganges, the Amazon, the Congo, and their tributaries; the shorter rivers of the equatorial island systems will also be affected. The effects will be felt in all zones of the equatorial-belt watersheds. Effects range from landslides in the mountains and siltation of reservoirs and irrigation areas to the smothering of marine life with silt in coastal areas.[419]

The extent to which populations in the Asian equitorial belt are dependent on indirect agricultural benefits from forests differs considerably from that of populations in the non-Asian areas of the belt. The Asian populations will be considered first.

*The Asian Equatorial Belt.* Most Asian forests lie above rich alluvial valleys and basins, the majority of which are intensively farmed and irrigated, and several of which support the largest, densest agricultural populations on earth. Almost one-fourth of humanity lives in these valleys and basins and depends for subsistence on critical irrigation water derived from forested watersheds. In India, Pakistan, and Bangladesh alone, about 500 million people depend on water running off the Himalayan watershed, and a similar number in East and Southeast Asia depend on water from the Himalayan and adjacent mountain systems.

Most of the humid Asian equatorial belt is subject to heavy rains during the monsoon and to relative drought during the rest of the year. Consequently, the intensive river basin farming depends on flood control and drainage for wet-season crops and on irrigation for any double-cropping. The loss of water control thus spells disaster.

Waterflows in the Asian river basins depend on what happens to the forests on the slopes of the Himalayan and other Asian mountain systems. How the millions of people living in these watersheds manage the land and forests will determine the stability of the streamflows available to the billion or so people living downstream. Unfortunately present land-use trends offer little hope that the forests will be conserved. The mountain people's populations are increasing by over two percent per year according to the projections in Chapter 2, and they perceive no alternative to clearing the forests to meet their needs. Many practice a combination of cropping and animal herding, and livestock populations are growing apace with the human populations.[420] Overgrazing is widespread and getting worse. Fire, routinely used to clear new croplands and to temporarily improve pastures, often gets out of control.[421] Commercial cutting has reduced the forest cover of the Himalayan watershed by as much as 40 percent in the past 30 years, and only an estimated 10 percent of the total area now under management by man in the East and West Himalayas of India (30,000 square kilometers) is still tree-covered.[422] Transformation of montane ecosystems into alpine deserts has become an immediate problem for large mountain populations; landslides and catastrophic floods are becoming annual disasters.[423]

The most severe consequences in the coming decades will occur downstream, across national boundaries in some cases. The potential for international disputes resulting from Himalayan deforestation was highlighted in several U.S. Embassy cables sent in response to Global 2000 Study queries (see appendix C). For example, the U.S. Embassy in Dacca cabled:

Should population pressures lead to large-scale removal of forest cover in Nepal and Assam, Bangladesh as a whole would be adversely affected by the increased runoff. Under present conditions the country is subject to periodic severe flooding, and the prospect of more frequent and damaging floods would threaten both the productivity of the land and large portions of the population. This may be the most significant environmental problem facing Bangladesh by the year 2000.

From the U.S. Embassy in New Delhi:

The combination of both overgrazing and stripping of trees for fuel is making a serious impact on the Himalayan watershed. Effects are seen in landslides, flooding on the Gangetic Plain, lowering of the ground-water table, and reservoir siltation. . . . Resolving the sociological problems of forestry management would appear to be as problematical as finding the resources for reforestation. Supplying an alternative means for the economic survival of the people currently using the forests for their livelihood must proceed simultaneously with good forestry practices.

And from the American Embassy in Islamabad, Pakistan:

The scale of the problem overwhelms scattered attempts to reverse the negative trends. Good forestry practices are not implemented, and no one really knows how much, if any, effective reforestation is taking place. Disruption of watershed cover is responsible for declining soil fertility, accelerated soil erosion, and increasingly severe flooding. . . . The forestry institutes, which direct the few programs, have proven to be inadequately financed and unable to meet either the immediate or the long-term needs of forest preservation.

Similar situations, where deforestation is undermining agriculture downstream, are reported (in the communications reproduced in Appendix C) from Thailand, Indonesia, and the Philippines, and are undoubtedly also occurring in Vietnam, Burma, Laos, and Malaysia.

*The Non-Asian Equatorial Belt.* Outside Asia, the dependency of the downstream populations on upstream forestry practices is less intense. The non-Asian portions of the equatorial belt are not so heavily populated and do not support a major portion of the earth's settled agriculture. However, even outside of Asia deforestation of watersheds will affect not only natural systems but also the downstream reservoirs, ports, cities, and transportation facilities, all of which will suffer from flooding, sedimentation, and decreased dry-season water levels.[424]

Events in Panama provide a microcosmic picture of what will occur on a much wider scale throughout tropical Africa and Latin America. All the water for operation of the Panama Canal comes from the watershed of Lake Gatun. Farmers have cleared forest from about half the watershed, and operation of the canal is already threatened by destabilization of water flows and by sedimentation of the lake and its reservoirs.

In May 1977, the surface of Lake Gatun dropped 3 feet below the level needed for full canal operation. Ships had to send part of their cargo across the isthmus by land, and some large carriers had to detour around the Horn. Such interruptions in the Canal's performance can be expected to become increasingly frequent if the trends in deforestation cannot be reversed.[425]

The highlands of Ethiopia and of the Peruvian, Equadorian and Bolivian Andes have long suffered from the effects of deforestation and are especially vulnerable to the consequent ecological deterioration. While their salubrious climates often attract more human settlements than the surrounding lowlands, the mountain terrain makes most soils prone to erosion whenever farming becomes intensive.[426] The hilly rainforest areas of West Africa are likewise subject to severe erosion, as population pressure forces shifting cultivators to shorten or eliminate fallow periods.[427] Consequently, some areas have already become useless badlands.

The elimination of tropical forests has several other damaging effects that are less dramatic than catastrophic floods. As regions are deforested, they lose much of the cooling effect of shade evapotranspiration and develop harsh microclimates.[428] Soil, fauna and flora are exposed to the full force of the sun, rain and wind. Plants that can survive are often vigorous weeds. Vain attempts are made to control the tough, inedible grasses that choke out other vegetation by more frequent burning, and the fires eat further into the remnant stands of trees, accelerating the decrease in life-support capacity.

## Open Woodlands

Knowledge of open woodlands is fragmentary, as they are included in few resource inventories. They are thought to cover about 30 percent of the earth's total forest area, or about 1.2 billion hectares, but they contain less than 10 percent of the total global stock of wood. About half of the earth's total extent of this type of ecosystem is located in Africa, about 15 percent is in North America, and 12 percent in South America.[429]

Open woodlands in the tropics are found in semiarid zones, where rainfall is insufficient to support a dense closed forest. In these dry areas, fire is an effective tool for weed control and land-clearing. Being sparse, open woodland can supply only relatively small quantities of fuel for expanding populations and, in many countries (such as Sudan, Chad, Niger, Yemen, Iran, Afghanistan, Pakistan, India, and Nepal), have been nearly eliminated by wood gatherers.[430] Open

woodlands are most often used as rangeland, and their regeneration is inhibited by burning and overgrazing. Although most open forest species are fire-resistant, the trees in many regions have been decimated by too frequent or too severe burning in attempts to make short-term improvements.[431]

The transformation of open woodland to desert is well documented and has in many instances taken place within living memory. Where firewood gathering, overgrazing and uncontrolled burning occur, soil nutrients are leached beyond the reach of remnant plants, soil organic matter is depleted, erosion by wind and water becomes severe, and the ultimate consequence is often desertification. A large scale shift of vegetational belts is underway with desert encroaching into dry prairie, dry prairie into savanna, and savanna into forest.[432] By 2000 this succession will have sharply reduced the rangeland possibilities of the overused open woodlands.

## Prospects for Amelioration

The demand for forest products, grazing land, and cropland will be high in the decades ahead, and the trends for both open woodlands and closed forests imply much tropical deforestation in the equatorial belt. Can these trends, and the associated environmental impacts, be reversed? The prospects are mixed. Many complex interacting factors are involved. No amelioration can be anticipated until there is awareness and, given awareness, explicit program ideas, then testing and demonstration. But forests are long-term resources, and economic considerations—especially during times of high discount rates—encourage short-term thinking. Finally, technologies are being developed which will make forest clearing quicker and less expensive. These factors all require examination.

There is a need for increased awareness both locally and within institutions. The Chipko Andolan "tree hugger" movement in northern India is an interesting example of growing awareness at the local level. The following passage is paraphrased from S.K. Chauhan's 1978 article[433] describing that movement:

Literally linking arms against indiscriminate deforestation by the lumber industry, these Himalayan villagers protectively hug the trees when lumberjacks approach to fell them! The Chipko movement's primary objective is to force the state government of Uttar Pradesh to change its antiquated forest policy. Most of the deforestation that takes place in this area is not because of wood collecting to meet basic energy needs but the result of the insatiable demand of the lumber industry.

After a serious flood and landslide five years ago, people of this region came to realize that their lives were intricately interwoven with the surrounding forest, and that official policy since colonial times had been tearing that web apart. As the thick, broad-leaf forests on the mountain tops were slowly sold away, the humus sponge that held the monsoon water back disappeared. Perennial streams now dry up soon after the monsoon season, and the collection of firewood has become a major preoccupation of the hill women. This deforestation has increased soil erosion and decreased local agricultural productivity.

The ecological usefulness of the government's afforestation programs in the region can be disputed. Under these programs, most of the felled oaks, rhododendron, and other broad-leaf trees are replaced with pine, because they grow faster and their wood is wanted in the market. But pine forests do not produce any humus to absorb water or increase soil fertility. Without urgent, proper management of these forests, the agricultural economy of a vast region of plains as well as hills will be threatened.

The Chipko leaders have organized large voluntary afforestation programs, planting broad-leaf trees in mountain areas and along riverbanks to halt erosion and provide a source of fuelwood. Yet the fact that the villagers themselves practice such conservation techniques, and feel impelled to bodily prevent the razing of trees, illustrates the failure of the country's development strategy. Instead of trying to link the life and economy of the local people, and thereby their development, with the rational exploitation of the only resource surrounding them (in this case, the forests) the government continues to support policies that regard these resources as things to be sold to the highest bidder.

Much more than local awareness is called for; institutional awareness and concern is imperative. In recent years there have been some encouraging signs of institutional awareness, at least at the international level. These developments include the establishment of the United Nations Environmental Program and the development of the World Bank policy for environmental as well as industrial forestry. [434] The U.S. Department of State and its Agency for International Development recently sponsored a strategy conference on tropical deforestation. [435] The papers presented at the Seventh World Forestry Congress, held in Buenos Aires in 1972, are probably the most comprehensive set of papers on silviculture as it is practiced today around the world. [436] Numerous LDC governments (including Malaysia, the Philippines, Thailand, India, China, and South Korea) are now showing serious concern over deforestation, [437] and these institutional developments may foreshadow increased financial support for forest management in the LDCs. However, forest conservation and reforestation projects will continue to face stiff competition for funds and institutional support. Industrial and agricultural projects that show a quick profit and give a more immediate response to the LDC's urgent need for economic growth are likely to continue to receive higher priority. Forestry projects that do receive priority and funding will still face formidable ecological, bureaucratic, and (perhaps even more formidable) sociological obstacles.

Several types of programs have been proposed to offset the adverse effects of deforestation in the LDCs. These proposals include:

- Better management of existing forest resources;
- Reforestation;
- Tree Plantations;
- Rangeland management with grazing controls and pasture improvement;
- Restriction of new land clearing, based on soil capability studies;
- Development of agro-forestry techniques for people who now have no alternative to planting annual crops on steep slopes;
- Dissemination of more efficient wood cooking stoves;
- Development of bio-gas and solar stoves to replace wood and charcoal burners; and
- Intensification of agriculture and other employment-creating forms of rural development in order to reduce the agricultural pressures on the remaining forest lands.

The *technical* feasibility of implementing some of these proposals in some less developed countries (especially those in the more temperate zones) has been tested in recent years. Agro-forestry projects (especially for palm oil) have been developed over the past decade in Malaysia, [438] and significant reforestation has been accomplished over the past two decades in the People's Republic of China. [439] Industrial wood plantations have been established in parts of Angola, Argentina, Brazil, Chile, India, Indonesia, Kenya, the Republic of Korea, Malawi, Morocco, Tanzania, and Zambia. [440] A village fuelwood plantation program is underway in the Republic of Korea. [441] Experiments with agroforestry are being carried out in the Philippines [442] and in Nigeria. [443] However, outside of the countries just named, few of these programs have gone beyond the demonstration stage.

Tropical deforestation is caused by a combination of (1) need for additional agricultural land, (2) need for additional fuelwood, and (3) a sustained world demand for tropical woods operating in the absence of effective and enforced programs for forest conservation and management. Synergisms are often involved. For example, although a growing population of subsistence farmers is clearing land to grow food, access to such land is possible in many cases only because commercial logging operations have opened the forests in response to growing domestic and foreign demand for wood products.[444] Access and transportation are also factors in the economics of clearing steep slopes. Even if the soil washes away after only one or two crops, farmers can support themselves over several seasons of clearing by selling firewood or charcoal on the regional market if transportation is available.[445] One of the causes of the growing world demand for forest products is, of course, population growth, but income is also a major factor, and the U.N. Food and Agriculture Organization (FAO) is well aware of both. Edouard Saouma, FAO Director General, stated recently that, based on projections of past trends:

Over the next 16 years it is expected that consumption of forestry products will rise by 75 percent to an annual roundwood equivalent of 4,000 million m³. If international development strategies were to increase the buying power of the masses of people in the developing world, even by a small fraction, projected consumption figures would be far higher.[446]

In addition, possibilities for earning foreign exchange, needed by many LDCs to reduce large foreign debts, will continue to be a motivating factor in establishing tropical forest policy[447] and will therefore also influence the possibilities for ameliorating the tropical deforestation trends.

While techniques and technologies are being developed that will assist in protecting and expanding forests, other technical developments may affect the future of tropical forests adversely. A variety of faster, less costly technologies are being developed to replace cutting and burning, the traditional methods of clearing. For example, Agent Orange, the chemical defoliant used widely by U.S. armed forces in Vietnam, is reportedly available in farm supply stores in the Amazon basin, where it is used to clear land for cultivation.[448] The chemical 2,4,5-T, one of two herbicides contained in Agent Orange and invariably contaminated with the toxic compound dioxin, is now banned in the United States[449] because it has been linked with birth defects and miscarriages.*

Another innovative technique for efficient clearing of tropical forests in Brazil is the *correntao*.[450] This involves the use of very large anchor chains, roughly 100 meters in length and weighing up to 10 tons. Enormous tractors attached to each end drag them through the forest, uprooting trees and everything else in the path.† Still another technological development likely to significantly affect at least the Brazilian tropical forests is the "floating papermill." In 1978, industrialist Daniel Ludwig's floating papermill (longer than two football fields in size) was towed from its construction site in Japan through the Indian and Atlantic Oceans to its final destination along the Jari River, a tributary of the Amazon. *Time* magazine, reporting on the $250 million plant, commented that by 1981 the factory "will turn out 750 metric tons of bleached kraft pulp a day, enough to make a single strand of toilet paper stretching more than 6-½ times around the world. . . . To feed the mill's appetite, Ludwig's crews have cleared nearly 250,000 acres of jungle so far and planted 81 million fast-growing trees.[451] Eventually, Ludwig plans to "tame" an area of rain forest almost the size of Connecticut.

What then are the prospects for amelioration of the tropical deforestation trends in the LDC? While there are a number of important and encouraging demonstration projects, environmentally significant conservation and reforestation practices cannot be expected unless and until technically competent institutions are provided with more resources and authority.[452] Sociological research on community cooperation and institutions will also be necessary if village-level woodlots to meet woodlot and environmental needs are to be widely established.[453]

## By the Year 2000

Assuming no change in policy (the standard policy assumption of the Global 2000 Study's projections), deforestation can be expected to continue as projected in Chapter 8. Deforestation will affect the rural segments of the LDC populations most severely. Small farmers in South and Southeast Asia, already among the world's poorest, will

---

*The Comptroller General of the United States has recommended that the Department of Defense conduct a survey of any long-term medical effects on military personnel who were

likely to have been exposed to herbicides in South Vietnam (*Health Effects of Exposure to Herbicide Orange in Vietnam Should Be Resolved*, Washington: U.S. General Accounting Office, Apr. 6, 1979.)

†This technique was used earlier (and may have been developed initially) in the United States, where it was used in arid-zone range management. Undesirable woody vegetation was scraped from the land with heavy chains, after which preferred range grasses were sown. (John Valentine, *Range Development and Improvement*, Provo: Brigham Young Univ. Press, 1974, p. 516.)

face yet harder times as waterflows from the mountain watersheds become more erratic and as reservoirs essential for irrigation are filled with silt eroded from the deforested slopes. In Africa, herdsmen will find that rangeland will recover more slowly (where it does recover) from periodic droughts. Throughout the LDCs millions of farmers using shifting agriculture will experience sharply declining harvests as yields fall and the short fallow periods fail to restore soil fertility.

A consequence of deforestation and simultaneous population growth is that wood for fuel will be in short supply and more people will be forced to use grass, crop residues, and animal dung for cooking fuel, further endangering land productivity, since these organic materials are essential for the maintenance of soil quality. As prices for commercial fuel increase and gathered fuels become scarcer, the costs (both monetary and temporal) of boiling water and cooking food may become prohibitive for the poorest populations, especially in areas where fuelwood plantations have not been established.

## Increased Intensity of Forest Management

As explained in Chapter 8, the real price of forest products is expected to rise in the coming two decades. The rising prices will enhance the profitability of investments in forest management, and forests can be expected to become increasingly subject to human control and manipulation through intensive silviculture and tree farming.

While it is not possible to know precisely how fast intensive silviculture will develop, the trend is clear. It is also clear that there will be both positive and negative environmental consequences. On the positive side, the higher yields resulting from faster growth of wood in the intensively managed stands and from more complete exploitation of accessible natural stands should take some pressure off the less accessible forest areas and thus allow the preservation of some forests in their natural state. Wood from intensively managed stands could certainly enhance the human environment for those who depend on firewood and charcoal for domestic fuel. On the negative side, a number of adverse environmental effects are anticipated, some of which raise questions about the basic viability of intensive silviculture, especially in the tropics.

The technological problems involved, are similar in many ways to those of intensive agriculture. Both intensive silviculture and intensive agriculture involve high-yield strains and monocultures. Plant geneticists have been at work not only on grains but also on trees, and there are hopes that fast-growing supertree plantations[454] will be to forestry what Green Revolution methods have been to agriculture.* However, monocultures of genetically identical trees face essentially the same problems as monocultures of genetically identical grains. These basic problems were discussed at some length for the case of the Green Revolution in the food and agriculture section of this chapter; a few points particularly relevant to intensive silviculture and tree farming will be considered here.

A major, perhaps underestimated problem faced by both intensive silviculture and intensive agriculture is the increasing energy subsidies they require. The fossil fuel subsidies inherent in intensive agriculture have received much attention and have been discussed extensively in the literature (and earlier in this chapter), but the energy requirements of intensive silviculture have been examined relatively little. A 1970 study[455] found that fertilization and shorter rotation resulted in a 38 percent increase in Douglas fir production, while costs (excluding any costs of environmental protection) increased 64 percent. Still higher cost increases could be anticipated if the energy subsidies had been priced at the post-1973 level. Nonetheless it is certainly true that trees grow rapidly in the tropics, producing rotation times as short as 10 years. Attention is now being focused on nitrogen-fixing species that may not require fertilizer. More attention to and testing of indigenous species are needed, rather than further attempts to grow a few exotic species. But no matter what species are ultimately chosen, the energy subsidies inherent in intensive silviculture deserve closer examination before major commitments are made.

Another difficulty in applying the intensive Green Revolution methods to forests is that the time between harvests is so much longer for trees than for grains. A combination of genetics and management practices is expected to reduce temperate-zone growth cycles from 150 to 40 years for Douglas fir and from 60 to 35–40 years for southern pine.[456] Nonetheless, the exposure period for genetically identical monocultures of trees

---

*In 1975, the journal of the American Forest Institute looked forward to an increase of 100 percent in the productivity of land in the production of wood and an increase of 300 percent in fiber yields ("More Wood, Faster," *Green America*, Fall 1975).

(even in the tropics) will always be long compared with the corresponding exposure period for grains. As with grains, pests and pathogens may evolve ways to overcome the genetic defenses of single strains, producing plant epidemics comparable to the southern corn blight or the Dutch elm disease.[457]

As with the deforestation problem, the negative environmental impacts of intensive silviculture will probably be more severe in the tropics than in the temperate zones. Foresters and biologists have suspected for some time that the great ecological diversity of tropical forests, which makes them exceptionally stable under natural conditions, also makes them exceptionally vulnerable to permanent damage from logging operations and that natural forest stands degrade severely when subjected to intense use.[458]

Most silvicultural methods have been developed by foresters in the temperate zones and are of doubtful suitability or utility for forests of the humid tropics. A substantial research investment must be made to develop appropriate silvicultural methods for tropical environments. However, the time lag inherent in forestry research (a growth cycle measured in decades, as opposed to months for grains) delays the economic return from tropical forest research investments, making it difficult to obtain support for forestry research in the LDCs. In the absence of extensive tropical forestry research, technological breakthroughs are not likely, and the application of doubtful forest management methods can be expected to continue for at least several decades.

There are other reasons for environmental concern about increased silvicultural intensity: (1) In both the industrialized nations and the LDCs, the ability of many forest soils to sustain short-rotation tree cropping is doubtful. Recent U.S. research indicates that even in quickly recovering temperate-zone forests, the loss of soil nutrients following a clear-cutting operation is significant.[459] (2) There is some evidence that plantations of uniformly aged trees do not stabilize watersheds as well as the natural forests that preceded them. (3) Applications of pesticides and fertilizers are likely to affect ecosystem elements other than the trees they are intended for, reducing the diversity of both flora and fauna and threatening the health of forest lakes and streams. (4) In some places intensively managed forests may even become sources of pollution (from fertilizers and other applied chemicals), where they once functioned as filters of air and water.[460]

Given all these problems, how rapidly can the methods of intensive silviculture be applied? Even

with the higher prices anticipated for forest products, there are serious difficulties in the way of rapid, global developments in intensive silviculture, and the pace of application promises to be slower than was the case for intensive agricultural methods.

To date, experience with intensive silviculture is limited to a very small number of complete planting-to-harvest cycles. Furthermore, as shown in Chapter 8, intensive silviculture is being practiced at present on a regional scale only in Europe, although significant local developments are taking place in Japan, North America, the People's Republic of China, Brazil, South Korea, and New Zealand. Less intensive techniques, such as regulation of livestock, pest control and reforestation are practiced on parts of the forests in most industrialized countries and on scattered sites in many LDCs. In most forests outside Europe and North America, however, the only management inputs are fire control and occasional cutting.

As a result of all of these present and potential problems, and because of limited planting-to-harvest experience, most businessmen and investors consider plantation forestry outside of the temperate zone an unproven technology.[461] Many decades will pass before the questions created by these problems have been answered. Investors will be slow to move into intensive silviculture, particularly in the tropics. Because of technical problems, most multinational forest product companies do not expect that the incentives* will warrant large-scale commercial planting before the 1990s.[462] It is even less certain when and if publicly sponsored and local commercial enterprises will undertake plantation forestry projects on a scale that would alleviate local and global firewood scarcities.

For all these reasons, major industrial wood harvests from manmade tropical forests are not likely to begin by the year 2000. Nonetheless, locally important harvests of wood for fuel and for village-level construction could be realized by 2000, and important watershed protection could be achieved in some areas where policies and attitudes are now changing and where fast-growing tree species are available.

*Several years ago, Brazil established strong tax incentives for reforestation, and a substantial amount of planting was done hastily by corporations and large landowners in the country's subtropical areas. Under these incentives, the area devoted annually to commercial planting was about three times the goal set by the Food and Agriculture Organization for all of Latin America. Brazil, however, has now reduced the tax incentives. (Gordon Fox, "Commercial Forestry," Proceedings, U.S. Strategy Conference on Tropical Deforestation, Washington: Department of State, Oct. 1978.)

## Global-Scale Environmental Impacts

There are two global-scale environmental impacts to be anticipated from the forestry projections. First is a potential impact on the world's climate. Second is a significant reduction in the number of plant and animal species on the planet.

### Changes in Climate

The anticipated change in global forest inventory may affect global climate patterns by increasing the amount of carbon dioxide in the atmosphere. Climatologists have been aware of a steady increase in atmospheric carbon dioxide ($CO_2$) for many years, and some, as already stated in Chapter 4, have expressed concern that a global warming trend may result. Until recently, it was assumed by most experts* that nearly all of the increase was coming from the burning of fossil fuels and that the earth's plants were absorbing some of the excess. However, recent calculations that take deforestation into account indicate that carbon stored in the biomass has been decreasing rather than increasing. One rough estimate indicates that as much as half the carbon in the earth's biomass may be stored in the forests, much of it in the tropics, and that current rates of forest clearing may be releasing amounts of carbon dioxide approximately equivalent to the amounts coming from fossil fuel consumption.[463] Others feel that these amounts and rates are probably lower. It is well known that not all of the $CO_2$ released to the atmosphere remains there, but there is still debate over the sinks. Some of the released $CO_2$ is stored in new forest growth, but the net decrease in wood volume projected in this study implies an acceleration of the $CO_2$ buildup that may have significance for climate as early as 2050.

### Changes in Biological Diversity

The second global change implied by the forestry projections is a significant reduction in biotic diversity. The extent to which the diversity of the flora and fauna is maintained provides a basic index to the ecological health of the planet. Presently the world's biota contains an estimated 3–10 million species.[464] Until the present century, the number of species extinguished as a result of human activities was small, and the species so affected were regarded as curiosities. Between now and 2000, however, the number of extinctions caused by human activities will increase rapidly. Loss of wild habitat may be the single most important factor. The projected growth in human population and economic activity can be expected to create enormous economic and political pressure to convert the planet's remaining wild lands to other uses. As a consequence, the extinction rate will accelerate considerably.

The death of an individual is very different from the death of a species. A species is a natural biotic unit—a population or a series of populations of sufficient genetic similarity that successful reproduction between individuals can take place. The death of an individual of a particular species represents the loss of one of a series of similar individuals all capable of reproducing the basic form, while the death of a species represents both the loss of the basic form and its reproductive potential.

Extinction, then, is an irreversible process through which the potential contributions of biological resources are lost forever. In fact, plant and animal species are the only truly nonrenewable resources.[465] Most resources traditionally termed "nonrenewable"—minerals and fossil fuels—received that label because they lack the reproductive capability. Yet most nonbiological compounds and elements are, at least in theory, fully renewable. Given sufficient energy, nonbiological resources can be separated, transformed, and restored to any desired form. By contrast, biotic resources—species (not individuals) and ecosystems—are completely nonrenewable.* Once extinguished, species cannot be recreated. When extinct, biotic resources and their contributions are lost forever.

How many extinctions are implied by the Global 2000 Study's forestry projections? An estimate was prepared for the Global 2000 Study by Thomas E. Lovejoy of the World Wildlife Fund. Dr. Lovejoy's analysis, together with a tabular summary of the results, is presented on the next four pages. His figures, while admittedly rough, are frightening in magnitude. *If present trends continue—as they certainly will in many areas—hundreds of thousands of species can be expected to be lost by the year 2000.*

Extinction, of course, is the normal fate of virtually all species. The gradual processes of natural extinction will continue in the years ahead, but the *extinctions projected for the coming decades will be largely human-generated and on a scale that renders natural extinction trivial by comparison.*

---

*G. E. Hutchinson is an exception. In 1954 he estimated that the increase in atmospheric $CO_2$ from forest destruction was about equal to that from the burning of fossil fuels ("The Biochemistry of the Terrestrial Atmosphere," in G. P. Kuiper, ed., *The Solar System,* Chicago: Univ. of Chicago Press, 1954, vol. II, pp. 371–433).

*Also see the discussion of this point in Chapter 12.

# A PROJECTION OF SPECIES EXTINCTIONS*

Virtually all of the Global 2000 Study's projections—especially the forestry, fisheries, population, and GNP projections—have implications for the extinction of species. Accepting these projections as correct, how many extinctions can be anticipated by 2000?

Probably the largest contribution to extinctions over the next two decades will come as a result of deforestation and forest disruption (e.g. cutting "high-grade" species), especially in the tropics. The forestry projections in Chapter 8 provide an estimate of the amount of tropical deforestation to be expected. The question then is: What fraction of the species now present will be extinguished as a result of that deforestation?

Possible answers are provided by the curves in Figure 13–8. The curves in this figure do not represent alternative scenarios but rather reflect the uncertainty in the percent of species lost as a result of a given amount of deforestation. The endpoints are known with more accuracy than other points on the curves. Clearly, at zero deforestation the resulting loss of species is zero—and for 100 percent deforestation, the loss approaches 100 percent. The reasons for the high losses at 100 percent deforestation are as follows.

The lush appearance of tropical rain forests masks the fact that these ecosystems are among the most diverse and fragile in the entire world. The diversity† of tropical forests stems in part from the tremendous variety of life zones created by altitude, temperature, and rainfall variations.[467] The fragility of tropical forests stems from the fact that, in general, tropical soils contain only a very limited stock of nutrients. Typically, the nutrients in tropical soils are only a small part of the total inventory of nutrients in the tropical ecosystem. Most of the nutrients are in the diverse flora and fauna of the forests

themselves. Tropical forests sustain themselves through a rapid and highly efficient recycling of nutrients. Little nutrient is lost when an organism dies, but when extensive areas of forest are cleared, the nutrients are quickly leached out and lost.[468]

Studies have shown that there are a wide variety of tropical soils. Some (such as those in lowland swamps) are rich, but most are either thin, infertile, and highly acidic, or thick and highly leached of nutrients. Recent aerial surveys of the Amazon basin, for example, indicate that only 2 percent of the soils are suitable for sustained agriculture.[469] Once cleared, the recycling of nutrients is interrupted, often permanently. In the absence of the forest cover, the remaining vegetation and exposed soil cannot hold the rainfall and release the water slowly. The critical nutrients are quickly leached from the soils, and erosion sets in—first, sheet erosion, then gully erosion. In some areas only a few years are required for once dense forest lands to turn to virtual pavements of laterite, exposed rock, base soil, or coarse "weed" grasses. The Maryland-sized area of Bragantina in the Amazon basin is probably the largest and best-known area to have already undergone this process, becoming what has been called a "ghost landscape."[470]

With formerly recycled nutrients lost through deforestation and its aftereffects, the capacity of a tropical rain forest to regenerate itself is highly limited and much less than that of a temperate forest. The possibilities for regeneration are limited further by the fact that the reproductive biology of many of the tree species found in mature tropical forests is adapted to recolonizing small patches of disturbed forest rather than the large areas now being cleared.[471] As a result and in spite of rapid succession rates, the disruption and simplification from deforestation of tropical rain forests is, for the most part, irreversible, given the time scale necessary to preserve the present mature and diverse biota. While a few attempts at reforestation to natural tropical forest are being made, only limited success has yet been

---

*This projection was developed for the Global 2000 Study by Dr. Thomas E. Lovejoy of the World Wildlife Fund.
†Diversity here is used simply in the sense of numbers of species. Ecologists sometimes use more complex indices of ecological diversity.

*Efforts to meet basic human needs and rising expectations are likely to lead to the extinction of between one-fifth and one-seventh of all species over the next two decades.* A substantial fraction of the extinctions are expected to occur in the tropics.

The lost potential of the earth's biological resources is often neglected in considering the con-

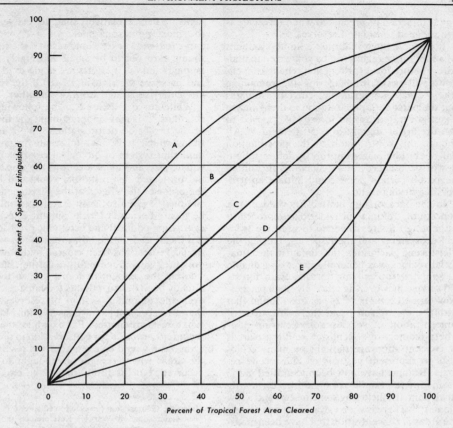

**Figure 13-8.** Loss of species through clearing of tropical forest areas—five projections.

achieved (e.g., in Puerto Rico). More typically, tropical forests are either cleared and abandoned, or (if the soil and economics permit) converted to plantation forests of high-growth species such as *Eucalyptus, Pinus,* and *Gmelina,* which are not suitable for the diverse local fauna found in mature tropical forests.

As a consequence (and for purposes of the rough calculations here) the rain forest areas modified by deforestation can be expected, with few exceptions, to include a negligible number of the species that were present in the virgin forests. The estimate used for the end-

point of the curves in the figure for 100 percent deforestation is therefore a 95 percent loss of species. So much for the endpoints of the curves.

The general shape of the curves (convex, linear, or concave) depends in large part on the size of the areas needed to preserve the ecosystems on which the species depend. Unfortunately, little is known about the size of these areas.[472] Most tropical species occur at exceedingly low densities. Dispersal (to compensate for local extinctions) is probably an important part of their biology,[473] and this survival strat-

sequences of deforestation in the tropics. Tropical forests contain both the richest variety and the least well known flora and fauna in the world. It would be difficult to overstate the potential value

of this huge stock of biological capital, which, if carefully managed, could be a rich, sustainable source of building materials and fuel, as well as medicinal plants, specialty woods, nuts, and fruits.

egy is impeded or precluded when forest areas are reduced to isolated reserves.

It is also known that only a limited amount of a rain forest region can be converted to non-forest before local (or regional) changes in climate will occur, endangering the remaining forest areas. For example, current estimates put the percent of precipitation in the Amazon basin generated by the forest (as opposed to the ocean) at slightly over 50 percent. [474] Although this contribution to the precipitation will not be eliminated entirely by deforestation, it will be reduced, and reductions in rainfall beyond a certain point could initiate an irreversible drying trend.

In the face of our limited knowledge, the concept of "refugia" provides one approach to estimating the areas needed to preserve tropical ecosystems and their species. During the Pleistocene glaciations, the climate in the equatorial regions was generally dryer and unable to support tropical rain forests. Rain forests did survive, however, in relatively small patches, now termed refugia. [475] It has been found that within the Amazon basin there are areas of concentration of species not occurring elsewhere (centers of endemism), and these areas of concentration are thought by many ecologists to represent vestiges of Pleistocene refugia. Refugia have now been identified in the basin for a few families of organisms (primarily small animals, including some insects and a few plants). [476] There is wide variation in size among the areas of concentration that have been measured, the smallest areas being for the class with the most species (i.e., insects). And, of course, the smaller the area of concentration, the more vulnerable the species are to extinction by reason of deforestation and loss of habitat.

How then should the curves in Figure 13–8 be drawn? Assuming that the refugia concept applies generally to all tropical forests, a convex curve (curve A or B) would result if the refugia turn out to be relatively small and if the refugia should happen to be cleared first. A linear curve (curve C) would result from random cutting if the refugia were not adjacent but overlapping, or were relatively small. (The limited data now available suggest that the re-

fugia are in fact relatively small for classes with the most numerous species. [477]) A concave curve (curve D or E) would result if the refugia should turn out to be small and highly overlapping, and (a) if efforts are made to identify and preserve the refugia, or (b) if the refugia are widely separated from one another.

While curve D is used in the following calculations, [478] it may underestimate the impacts of the projected deforestation.* Were it possible—which it is not—to create instantly a minimum system of biological reserves of adequate size and ideal location, the impacts of the projected deforestation would still be on the order of the effects of the Pleistocene glaciations. [479] Even so, such a system would not be secure because of local climatic effects and ever rising political and economic pressures. It is difficult to estimate how much of the world's tropical forest has been cleared and how such pressures will influence future cutting, but considering the amount of forest known to have already been destroyed, it is too late to achieve even the minimum system of reserves. Furthermore, present global conservation plans for rain forests are limited. For example, the *most ambitious proposal* for conservation in the Amazon basin would be site parks and reserves in the areas where refugia are thought to have occurred, but the total area of the parks and

---

*Even the deforestation projected in Chapter 8 may have been underestimated. Warwick Kerr predicts the loss of all Amazon forests (B. Dickson, "Brazil Learns Its Ecological Lessons the Hard Way," *Nature*, vol. 275, 1978, pp. 684–85), and P. W. Richards (op. cit.) predicts the loss of all untouched rain forests by the century's end. Very recently, however, some new information has become available for the tropical forests of the Amazon basin. According to Larry Rohter (op. cit.), Brazil's National Space Research Institute analyzed 32 photographs taken from a Landsat satellite and estimated in late 1978 that as much as one-tenth of the Brazilian Amazon forest has been razed. This is an area larger than the state of Texas and probably does not include areas that are now forested but are no longer diverse, virgin forest. On the matter of future cutting, the Brazilian Government is reported to be studying the use of "risk contracts" for the large-scale logging in the Amazon basin. The Superintendency for the Development of the Amazon (SUDAM) has identified approximately 100 million additional acres (between 5 and 10 percent of the total area of the Amazon basin) for timber exploitation.

---

However, if present trends continue, sustained benefits from this capital will never be realized. Unique local plants and animals will be unknowingly and carelessly destroyed. Particularly well-

adapted or fast-growing local trees will be cut before their fruits or seeds are collected. Predatory insects and plants with herbicidal or insecticidal properties will be lost for lack of observation and

## TABLE 13–30

### Extinctions of Species Implied by the Global 2000 Study's Projections

| | Present Species[a] (in thousands) | Projected Deforestation[b] | Loss of Species[c] | Extinctions[d] (in thousands) |
|---|---|---|---|---|
| **LOW DEFORESTATION CASE[b]** | | | | |
| Tropical forests | | | | |
| Latin America | 300–1,000 | 50 | 33 | 100–333 |
| Africa | 150–500 | 20 | 13 | 20–65 |
| S. and SE. Asia | 300–1,000 | 60 | 43 | 129–430 |
| Subtotal | 759–2,500 | | | 249–828 |
| All other habitats | | | | |
| Oceans, fresh water, nontropical forests, islands, etc. | 2,250–7,500 | – | 8[e] | 188–625 |
| Total | 3,000–10,000 | | | 437–1,453 |
| **HIGH DEFORESTATION CASE[b]** | | | | |
| Tropical Forests | | | | |
| Latin America | 300–1,000 | 67 | 50 | 150–500 |
| Africa | 150–500 | 67 | 50 | 75–250 |
| S. and SE. Asia | 300–1,000 | 67 | 50 | 150–500 |
| Subtotal | 750–2,500 | | | 375–1,250 |
| All other habitats | | | | |
| Oceans, fresh water, nontropical forests, islands, etc. | 2,250–7,500 | – | 8[e] | 188–625 |
| Total | 3,000–10,000 | | | 563–1,875 |

[a] The total of 3–10 million species (see reference 85) are assumed to be distributed roughly as follows: 10 percent in the virgin forests of the Amazon (P. H. Raven, personal communication to T. E. Lovejoy, 1974), 5 percent in African tropical forests, 10 percent in south and southeast Asian tropical forests, and 75 percent elsewhere (oceans, fresh water, nontropical forests, islands, etc.). It should be noted that the figures for the percentage of the world's biota in tropical rain forests are comservative. Many estimates (see Norman Myers, *The Sinking Ark,* London: Pergamon, forthcoming, 1979) place 30–40 percent of the total in the moist tropics and 70–80 percent in the tropics as a whole.
[b] See the forestry projections in Chapter 8.
[c] Derived from curve C in Figure 13–8.
[d] Calculated as the percent loss of species times the present number of species.
[e] The combined effects of loss of habitat, presence of toxic substances, eutrophication, desertification, simplification of forests in the temperate zones, acid rain, etc.—spread over five continents and the two-thirds of the planet's surface covered by the seas—are assumed to lead to a loss of one-twelfth of the planet's biota.

reserves would comprise only 5 percent of the total land area of the Amazon.[480] Such a system would mimic the distribution of forests at the height of the Pleistocene glaciations.[481]

What then is a reasonable estimate of global extinctions by 2000? Given the amount of tropical forest already lost (which is important but often ignored), the extinctions can be estimated as shown in Table 13–30. In the low deforestation case, approximately 15 percent of the planet's species can be expected to be lost. In the high deforestation case, perhaps as much as 20 percent will be lost. This means that of the 3–10 million species[482] now present on the earth, at least 500,000–600,000 will be extinguished during the next two decades. The largest number of extinctions can be expected in the insect order—many of them beneficial species—simply because there are so very many species of insects. The next highest number of extinctions will be among plants. While the projected extinctions refer to all biota, they are *much* larger than the 1,000 bird and mammal species now recognized as endangered.[483] Clearly the extinctions caused by human activities will rise to unprecedented rates by 2000.

study. Diverse assemblies of gigantic trees, their understories, and their resident communities of mammals, birds, and insects—natural wonders every bit as unique and beautiful as the Grand Canyon—will be irreparably lost. In short, the projected loss of tropical forests represents a massive expenditure of biological capital, an expenditure so sudden and so large that it will surely limit the future benefits that even careful management and husbanding can sustain from the remaining biotic resources of the earth.[466]

## Conclusions

The Global 2000 Study's forestry projections have serious implications for the environment. In the Asian LDC's, deforestation will cause extensive erosion and will destabilize waterflows, adversely affecting the agriculture on which a quarter of the world's total human population depends. In the tropical zones of Africa and Latin America, deforestation will lead, in many cases, to the loss of the nutrients and to reduction of the soil quality essential for the recovery of the forests. Desert encroachment can be anticipated in parts of nearly every continent. Extinctions of species caused by human activities will explode to rates never before observed, perhaps on the same order as during the Pleistocene glaciations.[484]

The deforestation will be caused by a combination of population increase and economic growth. Currently the primary cause is agricultural expansion. By 2000, agriculture will have expanded about as far as it can, and fuelwood and forest product demands will become the primary causes. Populations needing firewood, charcoal, plots for agriculture, lands for grazing, and materials for village construction are projected to continue their rapid growth over the next two decades. In the industrialized nations, slower population growth coupled with economic growth and high per capita consumption of forest products will also have a large impact on world forests through increased demands for wood and paper products. The demand for commercial timber and paper in the less developed countries, while starting at a low base, is rising considerably faster than that in the industrialized countries, and as a result a rising number of LDCs are becoming dependent on forest-product imports.[485]

Prospects for amelioration of these trends are mixed, at best. On the one hand, there are a large number of difficulties. Silvicultural methods developed primarily in the temperate zones are of doubtful utility in the tropics, where most of the deforestation will occur. Intensive silviculture (tree plantations), patterned after Green Revolution agriculture, is a much-discussed hope but its methods face the same problems (including energy-intensiveness and genetic vulnerability of single-strain monocultures) as Green Revolution agriculture and over much longer planting-to-harvest periods. Experience with these methods (especially in the tropics) is limited to a few growth cycles at most. Investors are cautious, and major world plantings are not expected before the 1990s at the earliest because the economic incentives do not match the risks involved. On the other hand, the need for small-scale village woodlots is now recognized by international aid agencies and by many national governments, and many programs of this sort are now planned or underway.[486]

The tragedy of forests is that, like the commons,[487] they are another example of a common resource subject to misuse—but on a global scale. While forest lands are owned by individuals (or governments), forests provide community, national, and international benefits that go well beyond the benefits usually considered in forest management decisions. Moderation of temperatures, stabilization of waterflows, protection of soils, and provision of habitats for a wealth of unexamined biotic resources are some of the benefits of forests that accrue to society as a whole and do not enter into the normal calculus of forestry economics.

The difficulty—some would say, the impossibility—of managing common resources is well known. Garrett Hardin has written about the specific problem of managing and protecting commons-type biological resources.[488] He concludes that biotic resources cannot be preserved under commons management, and that socialism or private enterprise are the only workable alternatives, both of which have limitations. The socialism approach suffers from the problem of *quis custodiet ipsos custodes?* (who will watch the watchman himself?). The private enterprise approach, Hardin argues, has a serious weakness in the way it deals with time, the question being: Can conservation be accomplished over time solely as a result of economic self-interest?

Aldo Leopold, a wise and insightful observer of biotic resources and economic systems, considered this question and concluded:

A system of conservation based solely on economic self-interest is hopelessly lopsided. It tends to ignore, and thus eventually to eliminate, many elements in the land community that lack commercial value, but that are (as far as we know) essential to its healthy functioning. It assumes, falsely, I think, that the economic parts of the biotic clock will function without the uneconomic parts.[489]

More recently, economic analysis has provided further support for Leopold's conclusion.[490] A common approach to management decisions under private enterprise is to calculate the present value of the future stream of benefits to be obtained from alternative management strategies. Other things being equal, management strategies that maximize the present value of discounted future benefits are generally preferred.

What benefits are to be considered, and at what discount rate? Forest benefits to the entire watershed (e.g., water stabilization, erosion control, temperature moderation, species protection, recreation) are often not included in the calculations because they are "external" benefits, i.e., benefits not accruing to the self-interest of the forest landowner. Discount rates are also important because conservation by its very nature concerns itself with future values. As Hardin explains, "The higher the interest rate on money, the more difficult it is to conserve for the future. Or as economists put it: the higher the interest rate, the more heavily the purely rational man must discount the future. . . . Compound discounting, which increases as interest rates increase, diminishes and in the long pull virtually destroys [future values]."[491] And the Global 2000 Study's projections suggest that interest rates will remain high. Virtually every one of the projections is based on the assumption that large amounts of capital investment will be made in the sector; these investments of scarce capital can be expected to keep interest rates quite high.

Scott Overton and Larry Hunt of the University of Oregon have examined the implications of the present-value approach to forest management. Their particular concern was whether this approach to management and conservation would keep the forest system in equilibrium at an optimal, sustainable yield. They concluded that the conventional economic analysis (ignoring the external costs and benefits of forests to the wider society) "must lead to a pattern of high cuts now and lower cuts later . . . to shorter and shorter rotations to the point of depletion of the resource, and to the conversion of forest lands to other uses until the relative price of forest products rises sufficiently high that the *economic* system is in equilibrium.[492]

It seems likely, therefore, that without basic changes in forest policy throughout much of the world, the environmental consequences of the Global 2000 Study's forestry projections are virtually inevitable. Even the bases for such policy changes are unclear. It is not at all obvious what should be done in each geographic area, and technology is certainly not the whole answer.[493] In general, localized approaches and solutions will probably be needed, but until all of the societal benefits of forests are taken into consideration in making forest policy and management decisions, societies around the world can expect that the forest-related environmental benefits that are taken for granted today will continue to slip away and will be sadly reduced in number and quality by the end of the century.

## THE WATER PROJECTIONS AND THE ENVIRONMENT

### *The Projections*

The Study's water resource projections, developed by the Department of the Interior and the Central Intelligence Agency, assume that water supply is constant and that demand increases with growth in population, expansion of irrigated agriculture, and increased industrial activity. The projections stress the severe limitations associated with supply-demand balance. But since regional or local quantitative data are lacking, global aggregates are presented (see Table 13–31).

The present global supply of fresh water (i.e., total runoff) is large relative to demand, at least in theory. Supply is now about 10 times demand but by the year 2000 is projected to be 3.5 times demand. This projection dramatizes the rapidity with which human demand is catching up with the world's theoretical availability of fresh water. However, even these figures are misleading because of the extreme seasonal and geographic unevenness in the distribution of water resources. Even now local and regional deficits occur on a seasonal and, increasingly, perennial basis.

Given present data limitations, the prospects for water in 2000 can be assessed only qualitatively. Based on examples from many areas, the projections anticipate serious water shortages in many nations or regions. Water development projects will be pursued, but severe shortfalls are expected in deficit areas. Areas noted as being particularly susceptible to water shortage include parts of Africa, North America, the Middle East, Latin America, and South Asia. Conflicts among competing water-demanding economic sectors and among nations drawing water from the same river systems are anticipated.

As a further complication, water supplies from streams and rivers may become less reliable in regions where deforestation is stripping watersheds bare. The projected decrease in the world's forests from 20 percent to 16 percent of the land surface by 2000 will take place largely in the LDCs, where needs for water already exceed supplies in some regions.

The water projections assume no climatic change. However, in the event of a cooling trend supplies would be adversely affected as a result of a more erratic pattern of rainfall. A warming trend, on the other hand, might reduce variability and increase supplies slightly, but in the central United States droughts might become more common.

## Introduction

It is not possible to analyze the environmental implications of the water projections with precision because environmental impacts tend to apply to specific river basins or other hydrological units, and the water projections summarized in Table 13–31 could not achieve that level of detail. Nonetheless, five environmental topics related to the projections of water supply and to the consequences of water development and use are explored:

- Environmental developments affecting water supply (deteriorating catchments in river basins, acid rain, climatic change);
- Impacts of hydraulic works;
- Water pollution (of urban and industrial origin and of agricultural origin);
- Water-related diseases; and
- Extinction of freshwater species.

This range of topics reflects the multiplicity of characteristics, uses, and values of the water resource: Water is essential to human health and well-being; water is habitat for a diversity of aquatic life; water is a major component (and determinant) of the environment. In short, water is unique among resources in the diversity of its characteristics, uses, and values.

## Environmental Developments Affecting Water Supply

Worldwide, two environmental developments are likely to have an impact on water supply by 2000: catchment and river basin deterioration and regional or global changes in climate. The trends in catchment and river basin deterioration are clearly discernible and accelerating. Climatic trends are less clear but just as important. Deteriorating

catchment and river basin conditions will adversely affect water supplies by increasing variability. Climatic change could further increase variability.

### Deterioration of Catchments and River Basins

From the standpoint of both water supply and water quality, the condition of a catchment or river basin is determined largely by the flora on the upper portions of the basin. The high, often steep portions of the basin usually receive a large proportion of the rainfall, and the flora on these slopes are critically important in determining the quality and flows of water throughout the basin.

A continuous mantle of vegetation in the upper portions of a basin has many benefits. The vegetation breaks the fall of the raindrops, absorbing the kinetic energy before it can dislodge soil particles. The vegetation also slows the runoff and enhances the absorptive properties of the soils. Where vegetation is present over the upper por-

### TABLE 13–31

### Projected Global Supply and Demand for Water by the Year 2000

*Cubic kilometers per year*

| | Projected Demand | | |
| | With-drawn | Con-sumed[a] | Supply[b] |
|---|---|---|---|
| Irrigation | 7,000 | 4,800 | |
| Domestic | 600 | 100 | |
| Industrial | 1,700 | 170 | |
| Waste dilution | 9,000 | | |
| Other | 400 | 400 | |
| Total | 18,700 | 5,470 | 37,700 |

*Source:* The work of G. P. Kalinin, as presented in Chapter 9.
[a] Not returned to streams or rivers.
[b] Taken to be the mean annual discharge of all rivers.

tions of a river basin, the basin's water is generally relatively well regulated and clean.

In the absence of vegetative cover, rain flows off a basin's steep upper slopes as it would off a tin roof. The full kinetic energy of the raindrops is available to dislodge soil particles. A relatively unobstructed surface accelerates the runoff, producing greater flood peaks downstream.* The kinetic energy of the enhanced floods tears away riverbanks, broadens channels, and damages or destroys canals, bridges, and other hydrological developments. Canals and dams are rapidly filled with sediments eroded from upstream, and topsoils are carried far downstream to be deposited ultimately in estuaries and oceans, often adversely affecting biological productivity. Aquifers are not recharged, and in the dry season flows are low. As a result, the removal of vegetation—especially forests—from the upper portions of river basins and catchments increases erosion, reduces water quality, damages hydrologic developments, and reduces the water available during the dryer season.[494] On very steep (therefore unstable) slopes, removal of vegetation can trigger landslides and flows of debris. In the Cape Verde Islands, narrow, irrigated valleys have been buried meters deep by soil and debris swept down from denuded side slopes by intense rains.[495]

Deforestation, burning, overgrazing, and some cultivation practices all have potential for adversely affecting river basins and catchments. The Global 2000 forestry and agriculture projections both suggest that by 2000 such practices will have extended much further into the upper portions of river basins and catchments (see Chapters 6 and 8 and Appendix C).

Deforestation is one of the most serious causes of deterioration of catchments. In steep, high-rainfall zones such as the midslopes of the Andean and Himalayan mountains, forests are indispensable for protecting catchments and controlling runoff. Removal of trees, however, does not invariably jeopardize water supplies. In regions with moderate relief and low rainfall, removal of

forests and the substitution of other soil-binding vegetation that consumes less water (such as grasses) can improve lower-basin water supplies by increasing runoff—at the cost of tree growth. Scientifically controlled cutting of catchment vegetation has been employed in the United States and some other countries to increase runoff, or water yield, in dry regions.[496] To be successful this practice requires strong, enlightened institutional programs for careful land and water management over much of the affected basin. In most of the world there is as yet no such institutional capability, and as a result, the projected deforestation will in virtually all cases lead to adverse water impacts.

Burning, overgrazing, and cultivation practices that expose the soil for long periods can be expected to increase in many areas over the next two decades, contributing further to catchment deterioration. These practices intensify the extremes of flooding and aridity by reducing soil porosity and water storage capacity, by reducing organic matter, and by increasing compaction. In soils that are overgrazed, frequently burned, or continuously cultivated, organic matter (largely mulch from vegetative debris) can become sufficiently depleted to cause soil drought. Without the absorbent properties of these organic materials, soils are less able to retain moisture, and shifts in vegetation occur. The vegetation able to survive in such soils is typical of climates that are more arid than actual rainfall indicates. The intensification of soil drought is already in evidence in the African Sahel and other semiarid regions,[497] and much further deterioration of the water retaining properties of soils can be anticipated on the basis of the population and food projections.

## Acid Rain

Acid rain is an environmental problem closely related to energy development. It deserves special note here because of its effects not only on water bodies over much of the world but also on many other parts of the biosphere.

While the Global 2000 energy projections are not specific enough to permit a detailed analysis of the future prospects for the acid rain problem, a few points can be made. First, increases in coal combustion in the magnitudes projected (13 percent by 1990) will significantly increase the production of the two primary causes of acid rain—sulfur oxides ($SO_x$) and oxides of nitrogen ($NO_x$). The 58 percent increase in oil combustion projected to occur by 1990 will also increase both $SO_x$ and $NO_x$ emissions; the 43 percent increase pro-

---

*The development of large urban areas can produce similar effects. Roofs, streets, and other impervious surfaces both increase the volume and shorten the duration of runoff, leading to flash floods and serious erosion downstream. In Arlington, Virginia, for example, the county's Environmental Improvement Commission has estimated that 50 percent of the land area in this suburban community as of 1972 had been covered over or in some way made impervious, and as a result damaging flash floods now occur in what were formerly small streams (*Arlington's Environmental Quality—1972*, County Planning Office, Arlington, Va., 1972). Since 1972 much more of the county has been made impervious, and an additional large highway is now under construction.

jected in natural gas combustion will also increase $NO_x$ emissions. Technologies are available to remove sulfur oxides, but their removal is expensive and probably will not be required uniformly throughout the world. There is no practical technology for the removal of oxides of nitrogen from stack gases; the only control now available involves reduced combustion temperatures, which limit efficiencies. The water-quality consequences of increased emissions, especially increases of $NO_x$ emissions, need to be considered carefully.

The immediate consequence of both $SO_x$ and $NO_x$ emissions is the acidification of precipitation. These gaseous compounds react in the atmosphere to form sulfuric acid and nitric acid, which, in turn, precipitate out of the atmosphere in both rain and snow. The acidified precipitation falls anywhere from a few hundred to a few thousand miles away from the source, depending on the strength of the prevailing winds.[498] As a result, the pH of rainfall is known to have fallen from a normal value of 5.7 to 4.5–4.2 (high acidic values) over large areas of southern Sweden, southern Norway, and the eastern U.S.[499] In the most extreme case yet recorded, a storm in Scotland in 1974, the rain was the acidic equivalent of vinegar (pH 2.4).[499a] Equivalent changes have almost certainly occurred elsewhere, for example, downwind of the German, Eastern European, and Soviet industrial regions. Effects of acid rain are only beginning to be understood but have now been observed in lakes, rivers, and forests, in agricultural crops, in nitrogen-fixing bacteria, and in soils.

The clearest ill effects of acid rainfall observed to date are on lake fisheries. A survey of over 1,500 lakes in southwestern Norway, which has acid rainfall problems similar to those of southern Sweden, showed that over 70 percent of the lakes with a pH below 4.3 contained no fish. This was true for less than 10 percent of the lakes in the normal pH range of 5.5–6.0.[500] Similar effects have been found in lakes in the Adirondack mountains of New York[501] and in some areas of Canada.[502] Acid rain appears to be the cause of both the low pH and the extinction of the fish (see also the discussion of fresh water extinctions in the fisheries section of this chapter). Within the last 20 years salmon disappeared from many Norwegian rivers, and trout soon followed. Measurement in such rivers almost always shows a decline in pH, usually attributable to acid rain. Similar occurrences have been observed in Sweden.[503]

Effects of acid rain on forest growth are only beginning to be understood. The effects on tree-seed germination are mixed.[504] Reductions in natural forest growth have been observed in both New England and Sweden.[505] One study tentatively attributed a 4 percent decline in annual forest growth in southern Sweden to acid rain.[506] Other observers feel that a decline in Scandinavian forest growth has not been conclusively demonstrated but suspect that the even more acidic rainfall expected in the future will cause slower growth.[507]

The effects of acid precipitation on leafy vegetation have been studied in the United States in the states of Maryland and West Virginia. While no major damage has yet occurred, one study concludes that current levels of acidity in rainfall present little margin of safety for foliar injury to susceptible plant species, but with the increasing emissions of pollutants that contribute to the formation of acid rain, there is substantial risk of surpassing the threshhold for foliar effects in the future.[508]

Little research has been undertaken on the effects of acid rain on large natural ecosystems, but one interesting study has now been done for the boundary-waters canoe area and the Voyageurs National Park (BWAS-VNP) wilderness areas in the north central United States. The findings are as follows:

Acid precipitation, by causing increased acidity in lakes, streams, pools and puddles, can cause slight to severe alteration in communities of aquatic organisms. . . . Bacterial decomposition is reduced and fungi dominate saprotrophic communities. Organic debris accumulates rapidly. Nutrient salts are taken up by plants tolerant of low pH (mosses, filamentous algae) and by fungi. Thick mats of these organisms and organic debris may develop which inhibit sediment-to-water nutrient and mineral exchange, and choke out other aquatic plants. Phytoplankton species diversity, biomass and production are reduced. Zooplankton and benthic invertebrate species diversity and biomass are reduced. Ultimately the remaining benthic fauna consists of tubificids and Chironomus (midge) larvae in the sediments. Some tolerant species of stoneflies and mayflies persist, as does the alderfly. Air breathing insects (water boatman, backswimmer, water strider) may become abundant. Fish populations are reduced or eliminated, with some of the most sought after species (brook trout, walleye, smallmouth bass) being the most sensitive and therefore among the first to be affected. Toxicity or elevated tissue concentrations of metals may result either from direct deposition or increased mobilization or both. Amphibian species may be eliminated. And finally, populations or activities of higher terrestrial vertebrates that utilize aquatic organisms for food or recreation are likely to be altered.[509]

The study concludes that "as more lakes are eventually impacted, the whole philosophy behind the wilderness experience that forms the basis of the establishment of the BWCA-VNP will be violated and the part of the BWCA which provides recreation will be reduced. Few people who utilize the BWCA-VNP could be expected to enjoy the areas made fishless by pollution from human activity."

The effects of acid rain on nonforest agricultural crops are under study and are beginning to be reported. Shoot and root growth of kidney bean and soybean plants have been found to be markedly reduced as a result of simulated acid rain of pH 3.2.[510] Similarly, nodulation by nitrogen-fixing bacteria on legumes is significantly reduced by simulated acid rain.[511] The growth of radish roots has been observed to decline by about 50 percent as the pH of rain falls from 5.7 to 3.0.[512]

The sensitivity of soils to acidification by acid rain varies widely from area to area, depending largely on the amount of calcium in the soil.[513] Calcium buffers the soil against acidification, but is leached out by acid rain; this leaching of calcium and soil nutrients has been found to increase with decreasing pH, and the pH of soils has been observed to decline more rapidly with more acidic rains.[514] The acidic soils that can result from acid rain could be expected to significantly reduce crop production in the affected areas unless large amounts of lime were applied.

In addition to damaging biota and soils, acid rain damages materials extensively over wide areas.[515] Even stone is being severely damaged. A dramatic example of the effects of acid rain and air pollution on stone is provided by the Egyptian obelisk moved from Egypt to New York in the 1890s (Fig. 13–9). While the inscription on the east face of the monument is still legible, the inscription on the west face has been destroyed by chemicals in the city's air, driven by New York's prevailing westerly winds.

The 13 percent increase in coal combustion by 1990 implies that large areas in and near industrial areas will continue to receive highly acidic rainfall. The rainfall in these areas is likely to become increasingly acidic as $SO_x$ and $NO_x$ emissions increase. The areas affected are likely to extend hundreds to thousands of miles downwind from the sources, a total geographic area large enough to include many lakes, watersheds and farmlands. The combined adverse effects in these areas on water quality (and indirectly on soil quality and plant growth) are likely to become increasingly severe.

## Climatic Change

Water supplies and agriculture can be severely affected by climatic changes that are well within the range of historic experience. Changes in global temperatures could lead to either an increase or decrease in both the amount and variability of rainfall. The climate projections therefore have definite significance for water availability in the future.

The Global 2000 Study's climate projections provide little guidance, however, because of disagreement among climatologists on future trends. As discussed in Chapter 4 and in the Climate section of this chapter, the experts are more or less evenly divided over the prospects for warming or cooling, and most felt that the highest probability is for no change.[516] Faced with this uncertainty, the Global 2000 Study devised three climatic scenarios of roughly equal probability. There is considerable uncertainty as to the pattern of rainfall to be associated with these climate scenarios, but it is thought by many climatologists that global warming would lead to slight increases in precipitation in many areas and less year to year variation. (The central U.S., however, might experience more frequent drought.) A cooling trend is thought by many to be associated with less precipitation and increased year-to-year variation.

In short, there is much uncertainty about future global climate because of the present lack of agreement on causes, effects, and trends. Uncertainty over climate—and therefore also over water supplies and agricultural harvests—can be expected to lead to projects for the storage and regulation of water and to the development of food reserves in anticipation of unfavorable years.

Even if it were absolutely certain that the variability and amount of water supply would not deteriorate in the years ahead, there would still be reason to anticipate further projects to increase the storage and regulation of water and to develop food reserves. Population growth, urbanization, and the extension of both agriculture and forestry into more arid and variable regions has made the social and economic impacts of variability of water supplies greater than in the past. In the years ahead the impacts of even present variability can only become greater. As nations attempt to bring more marginal lands into production, fluctuations in water supply will quickly translate into social and economic vulnerability. Therefore, even in the absence of any climatic deterioration, incentives will be present to maintain food-grain reserves, accelerate water conservation efforts,

**Figure 13-9.** A monument to acid rain and air pollution—"Cleopatra's Needle," sent from Egypt to New York City in the 1890s. The inscription on the east face (*left*) is still legible; the inscription on the west face (*right*) has been erased by chemicals in the city's air, driven by the prevailing westerly winds. Ninety years in New York has done more damage to the stone than 3,500 years in Egypt. (*U.N. photo*)

modify macro- and microclimates, and develop hydraulic works to reduce the risk and uncertainty in water availability. What will be the environmental consequences of these efforts?

## Impacts of Hydraulic Works

Both the prospect of destablizing deforestation in the upper portions of river basins and the certainty of continued (possibly even increased) climatic variability will encourage the development of hydraulic works for flow regulation, electrical generation, irrigation, and flood control. The Global 2000 Study's water projections assume increased withdrawals of water for all uses, but make no projections as to how additional water supplies will be developed or where supplies might fall short of future need. To meet the projected withdrawals a considerable expansion of engineering works for water regulation and distribution will be required, especially in regions with highly variable rainfall. By one estimate, 12,000 cubic kilometers of runoff will be controlled in the year 2000 by dams and reservoirs—30 percent of the total world runoff and three times the estimated 4,000 cubic kilometers now stored in the world's reservoirs.[517]

In the LDCs, where most of the world's untapped hydropower potential is located, river basin development schemes that integrate flood control, power production, and irrigation will be implemented for a number of reasons:

• The indispensable role of irrigation in increasing food production;

• The limited amounts of naturally fertile, well-drained, well-watered soils remaining to be brought into production;

• The need to control the floods of large rivers (e.g. Yellow River, Lower Mekong River) where floods have been more or less tolerated in the past; and

• The need for electricity in economic development.

The environmental impacts of large river basin development schemes can be great. In the case of large dams, the impacts include:

• The inundation of farmland, settlements, roads, railroads, forests, historic and archeological sites, and mineral deposits;
• The creation of artificial lakes, which often become habitats for disease vectors such as the mosquitoes that transmit malaria and the snails which transmit schistosomiasis;
• The alteration of river regimes downstream of dams, ending the biologically significant annual flood cycle, increasing water temperature, and sometimes triggering riverbank erosion as a result of an increased sediment-carrying capacity of the water;
• The interruption of upstream spawning migrations of fish; and
• Water quality deterioration.

Irrigation systems have their own environmental problems:

• Danger of soil salinization and waterlogging in perennially irrigated areas;
• Water weeds, mosquitos, and snail infestation of drainage canals, with the danger of malarial and schistosomiasistic infections spreading in areas where these diseases exist, especially in parts of Africa and Latin America; and
• Pollution of irrigation return water by a variety of agricultural chemicals, with negative consequences for aquatic life and for the human use of downstream waters.

While the benefits of dams and irrigation development may outweigh the costs, environmental impacts have a definite bearing on the benefit/cost ratios of river basin development schemes. Plans for the development of the Lower Mekong River Basin illustrate this point.

A series of engineering, economic, social, and environmental studies of the Lower Mekong Basin has been carried out under the aegis of the United Nations Committee for Coordination of Investigations. The development plan that has emerged from these studies calls for the construction over a 20-year period of a series of multipurpose dams and associated irrigation works for the basin, which is shared by Thailand, Laos, Cambodia and Vietnam.[518] In 1974 the portion of the basin downstream from the People's Republic

of China supported about 33 million persons. Assuming the adoption of birth control methods at rates based on other South Asian experience, the U.N. studies project this population to grow ultimately to or beyond the Lower Mekong Basin's present food-production capacity, which is estimated to be potentially adequate for 123 million persons. To feed the expanded population by the end of the century, it will be necessary to expand paddy rice production from 1970s 12.7 million tons to 37 million tons. The studies suggest that this increase of nearly 200 percent cannot be achieved without flood control and new irrigation. It is estimated that multiple dams in the Lower Mekong River system could add up to 5 million hectares of land for double-cropping of rice and might provide enough food to support an additional 50 million persons in the basin.[519] The dams would generate badly needed power, and the reservoirs could, with proper management, become productive fisheries.

The proposed dams in the Lower Mekong Basin will involve significant social costs. For example, the reservoir behind the Pa Mong—the largest dam proposed for the Mekong River—would force the resettlement of 460,000 persons, mostly in Thailand. Land for resettlement en masse in large communities is not available, and Thailand is faced with the prospect of paying these people an estimated $626 million (approximately $1,400 each) to leave without a planned alternative, a situation euphemistically referred to as "self-settlement."[520]

The situation in the Mekong River Basin happens to be relatively well understood because 20 years of internationally coordinated studies have examined the entire river basin as a single planning unit. Other densely populated river basins in Asia, Africa, and Latin America are the focus of similarly ambitious schemes, but in most cases there are no coordinated studies or even adequate data. Consequently the full social and economic costs of these proposed projects can scarcely be estimated.

The environmental costs are just as hard to estimate. It is known that large dams produce very considerable ecological impacts on rivers and estuaries in temperate and subtropical areas. The Aswan Dam in Egypt is a case in point.

A considerable list of costly impacts are associated with the High Aswan Dam and the irrigation development that has subsequently taken place in the Nile Delta. They have been recently documented by Julian Rzoska[521] in a ten-years-later assessment, as well as by earlier researchers such as Kassas, George, and van der Schalie.[522] Here are some of their findings:

- 100,000 people had to be relocated from the reservoir site, which extends into Sudan. The people were mostly flood plain farmers of Nubian origin.
- The ancient Nubian temples were inundated (a considerable portion of them were salvaged intact in a UNESCO-organized emergency operation).
- The dam traps sediments that formerly enriched the flood plain as well as the Mediterranean Sea, with a loss in natural soil productivity and the collapse of the sardine fishery that once provided half of Egypt's fish.
- Waves and tides are now eroding the delta, which formerly was extending into the Mediterranean, and a reduction in the agriculturally important delta is slowly occurring.
- Year around irrigation in the delta, which represents 60 percent of Egypt's farmland, has elevated the water table and caused salinization, now being remedied through expensive drainage works financed by the World Bank.
- Schistosomiasis is rapidly spreading throughout the rural population as a consequence of the spread of the snail intermediate hosts in the irrigation canals, the lack of sanitary facilities and the continual exposure of the dense rural population.
- The water hyacinth spread almost uncontrollably throughout the canal systems, where it harbors snails and interferes with water flows.

This controversial project's benefits include an 8,000 megawatt electricity generating potential, and a doubling of agricultural potential on perennially irrigated soils.

While the extensive consequences of the Aswan Dam are reasonably well known and established, relatively little is known about the ecological effects of dams in tropical areas, where most of the need and potential is located. The animal species native to tropical rivers, estuaries, and oceans have frequently evolved life cycles that are linked to annual floods and the patterns of salinity and nutrient fluxes that accompany the floods. Regulation of river flows can therefore be expected to significantly affect large numbers of estuarine and oceanic organisms. Similar impacts can be anticipated in freshwater species. Their decline is not likely to be compensated by the development of aquaculture, especially if pollution seriously impairs water quality.

## Water Pollution

The Global 2000 Study projections point to worldwide increases in urbanization and industrial growth and in the intensification of agriculture—trends that, in turn, imply large increases in water pollution in many areas.

### Water Pollution of Urban and Industrial Origin

By the year 2000, worldwide urban and industrial water withdrawals are projected to increase by a factor of about 5, reaching 1.8–2.3 trillion cubic meters (see Chapter 9). The higher figure is almost equal to the total annual runoff of 2.34 trillion cubic meters from the 50 United States. Most of the water withdrawn for urban and industrial use is returned (treated or untreated) to streams and rivers. If 90 percent is returned, the total combined discharge of water flowing through sewers and industrial outfalls by the year 2000 will be on the order of 1.6–2.1 trillion cubic meters.

Urban and industrial effluent will be concentrated in the rivers, bays, and coastal zones near the world's largest urban-industrial agglomerations. In the developing world—where 2 billion additional persons are projected to be living by 2000 and where rapid rates of urbanization continue—urban and industrial water pollution will become ever more serious because many developing economies will be unable or unwilling to afford the additional cost of water treatment.

Few LDCs have invested heavily in urban and industrial waste treatment facilities. As a result the waters below many LDC cities are often thick with sewage sludge and wastes from pulp and paper factories, tanneries, slaughterhouses, oil refineries, chemical plants, and other industries. One consequence of this pollution is declining fishing yields downstream from LDC cities. For example, the inland catch in the eastern province of Thailand, 696 tons in 1963, fell to 68 tons by 1968, and it is thought that water pollution, particularly from Bangkok, was the main cause of the decline.[523] Similar, though less extreme, declines have occurred around the world in freshwater systems, and in bays, lagoons, and estuaries. Frequently the changes are not measured but become apparent with the appearance of eutrophication, poisonous red tides, and the decline of inland fishing occupations.[524]

Efforts to control the effects of pollution from LDC cities can lead to international disputes. An example is the dispute that occurred in 1976 over India's withdrawal of water from the Ganges to flush out the port of Calcutta during the dry season when the water was needed in Bangladesh for irrigation.[525]

The reuse of urban and industrial waste water is likely to increase as urban populations expand rapidly in the water-short regions of West Asia and in arid portions of Mexico, Africa, and the U.S. Southwest. The use of waste water for irrigation will serve to recycle nutrients that would otherwise overload the absorptive capacity of rivers; however, a careful management and monitoring will be required to avoid pollution of ground-water and human exposure to disease pathogens, heavy metals, and other toxic substances.[526]

The use of water as the transport media for sewage is being questioned because of its high capital requirements, its potential for pollution, and its energy intensiveness. Composting toilets that avoid the water medium entirely have been developed and are being used more widely.[527]

Some water pollution problems are linked directly to air pollutants from urban and industrial areas, particularly from emissions of sulfur and nitrogen oxides from electric power plants burning fossil fuels (see "Acid Rain," above). The increased use of coal (a rich source of both sulfur and nitrogen oxides) promises a growing contribution of acid to rain water and to lakes. There is no known, economically practical method for controlling $NO_x$ emissions. Control of $SO_x$ emissions from coal is now technologically possible but is estimated to increase electricity costs by 6–15 percent. It seems that the price of "live" lakes will be high.[528]

Urbanization and industrial growth, in addition to increasing various forms of water pollution, will also increase the consumptive uses of water. Evaporative cooling for thermal-electric generating facilities is one of the fastest-growing consumptive uses of water.

Large amounts of water are used to remove waste heat from thermal-electric (primarily coal and nuclear) power plants, but until recently relatively little of this water has been consumed (i.e., evaporated). Until the early 1970s in the U.S. most of the waste heat from electricity generation—which amounts to approximately two-thirds of the total primary energy input to electrical generation*—was dissipated by means of once-through

---

* Nuclear plants typically convert roughly one-third of their primary energy input to electricity; the remaining two-thirds is usually lost as waste heat. Fossil-fuel-fired plants are only slightly more efficient. Over and above these losses, transmission-line losses are significant (A.L. Velikanov, *Hydrologic Problems Stemming from Energy Development*, U.N. Water Conference, Jan. 27, 1977, p. 6). The large amount of energy lost as waste heat is at the heart of some of the most intense criticism of energy policies that increase electrical generation for end uses that do not necessarily require electricity. See, for example, Amory B. Lovins, *Soft Energy Paths*, Cambridge, Mass.: Ballinger, 1977, and *Efficient Use of Energy*, American Institute of Physics Conference Proceedings no. 25, summarized in *Physics Today*, Aug. 1975.

cooling. With once-through cooling, large quantities of river, lake, or ocean water are pumped through condensers and returned to the natural water body approximately 10° C warmer. Between 1950 and 1972 annual water withdrawals in the U.S. for thermal-electric power plant cooling jumped from 50 billion to 275 billion cubic meters—2.5 times the average flow (110 billion cubic meters) of the lower Mississippi River—surpassing irrigation withdrawals in volume.[529]

Concern for biological and ecological damage caused by water intakes and by thermal pollution in the U.S. resulted in the promulgation in 1974 of standards for levels of thermal discharge to water bodies by power plants, but in 1976 the standards were remanded by court order. At present, thermal pollution has a low priority at the Environmental Protection Agency.[530] Thermal pollution impacts are numerous and generally deleterious in mid to low latitudes. In high latitudes waters are naturally so cold that aquatic life processes are slowed, and in these areas heated discharges from power plants can stimulate production of fish and other organisms. In the tropics, on the other hand, where waters are naturally warm and many species live near their upper temperature tolerance, thermal discharges are often lethal. At all latitudes increased temperature reduces the dissolved oxygen in the water, stressing aquatic fauna by speeding metabolic rates while at the same time depleting oxygen supplies.[531] Other impacts include:

- Destruction of small organisms such as fish larvae and plankton entrained in the cooling water intake and poisoned by antifouling biocides.
- Reduction of fish abundance, biomass, and species diversity in downstream thermal "plumes."
- Synergistic exacerbation of the stresses caused most organisms by other factors such as increased salinity, biological oxygen demand, and toxic substances.
- Shifting of the balance among algae species to favor blue-green algae, which create taste and odor problems in municipal water supplies.
- Sudden changes of temperature during startups and shutdowns, causing death of many sensitive species.[532]

The remanding of the 1974 Environmental Protection Agency regulations on thermal pollution left U.S. problems of thermal pollution unresolved. New plants tend to utilize evaporative cooling towers rather than once-through cooling because of insufficient volumes of water available rather than because of ecological considerations.[533] As a result, thermal water pollution in the U.S. may remain at about 1976 levels, while local atmospheric heat and humidity loadings in areas around new power plants increase. The U.S. Water Resources Council estimates that the consumptive use of water by the country's electrical generating facilities will increase rapidly (650 percent between 1975 and 2000).[534]

The net consumption (i.e., evaporation) of water can also be expected to continue increasing elsewhere in the world during the years ahead as thermal-electric generation grows and supply constraints and environmental considerations encourage shifts away from once-through cooling to evaporative cooling towers. A. L. Velikanov has estimated for the United Nations that waste heat discharged from thermal-electric plants throughout the world in 1973 was sufficient to evaporate 7–8 cubic kilometers ($km^3$) of water if cooling towers had been in use everywhere.[535] This estimate may be low. European energy specialist Wolf Häfele calculates that if Europe had been using cooling towers exclusively in 1974, Europe alone would have been evaporating water at an annual rate of 16 $km^3$. [536] Häfele expects this consumption to reach 30 $km^3$ per year by 2000. Although this represents only about 1 percent of Europe's yearly runoff of 2800 $km^3$, the additional consumptive demand on Europe's water resources would be significant.

## Water Pollution of Agricultural Origin

Extensive pollution from fertilizer runoff can be expected, especially in developed, densely populated regions, if worldwide fertilizer usage increases from 55 kilograms per hectare (kg/ha)—the average 1971–75 rate—to around 145 kg/ha as projected. The U.S. Department of Agriculture projects fertilizer application rates in Japan, Western Europe, and Eastern Europe to reach 635, 355, and 440 kg/ha, respectively, by 2000 (see Table 6–15).* At these application rates it will be difficult to avoid at least some increase in the nitrogen pollution of water supplies and eutrophication of bodies of water.

The LDCs are likely to experience increasing water pollution by pesticides, especially chlorinated hydrocarbon insecticides used in irrigated rice culture and export crop production. The Food and Agriculture Organization expects that pesticide usage in the LDCs will grow at 10 percent per year for at least the near future. Should this

trend continue until 2000, the volume of pesticides used in the LDCs will have increased more than sevenfold.[537] Presently, about half the pesticides used in the LDCs are organochlorines, a trend that may continue because organochlorines are substantially less expensive than the more specific, less destructive and less persistent alternatives.

A sevenfold increase in the use of persistent pesticides in Asia would virtually eliminate the culturing of fish in irrigation canals, rice paddies, and ponds fed by irrigation water.[538] Organochlorine insecticides continue to collect in aquatic systems years after they have been applied and affect waters many miles downstream. At moderately high concentrations, they kill fish.[539] Already, many Asian farmers are reluctant to buy fry for their paddies or ponds for fear that pesticide pollution will kill the stock.[540] The amount of protein forfeited could be substantial. Per hectare yields of fish from well-tended ponds can be as high as the per hectare yields of rice, i.e., 2,500 kg/ha animal protein vs. 2,500 kg/ha carbohydrate.[541] Cage culture yields are extraordinarily high and show great commercial promise in several developing countries, as long as waters are not poisoned by pesticides. Projected pesticide increase seriously threatens both freshwater and brackish water aquaculture in much of Asia. If pesticide trends continue, aquaculture in Latin America and Africa will eventually face the same threat.

The protein that fish culture could provide is badly needed, especially in the humid tropics where aquaculture can thrive. Moreover, while alternative forms of producing animal protein tend to increase the pressures on already stressed soil systems, fish culture places no strain on terrestrial systems and is complementary to the careful water management schemes required for sustained agricultural production in many parts of the humid tropics. The FAO estimates that culture of fresh water and marine organisms could reach 20–30 million metric tons by 2000—between one-third and one-half of the present marine catch.[542] Further pesticide pollution will sharply diminish this promising prospect.

Increased pesticide use will also create water contamination problems in industrialized nations. To cite but one example: California health officials report that they have found dangerous levels of a pesticide—dibromochloropropane (DBCP) in half of the irrigation and drinking water wells they have tested in one of the state's major agricultural areas, the San Joaquin valley. The U.S. Environmental Protection Agency banned the use of DBCP in 1977 on 19 fruit and vegetable crops

---

* The projection assumes that real energy prices remain constant to 2000; fertilizer projections were not reported for the Global 2000 standard case of rising energy prices.

after tests showed that the pesticide caused sterility in the workers who manufactured it and caused cancers in laboratory animals. Two years after the ban, California health officials found residues averaging 5 parts per billion (ppb) in the wells tested. The State has recommended that all wells showing more than 1 ppb of DBCP be closed to human consumption. At that level, one case of cancer is expected for every 2,500 persons who use the wells. Arizona health officials have tested 18 wells near Yuma and found 6 wells with concentrations of 4.6–18.6 ppb. of DBCP. The Environmental Protection Agency has allowed continued use of an estimated 10 million pounds of DBCP annually in the U.S. on crops such as soybeans, citrus fruits, grapes and nuts but is now considering restricting this amount.[543]

Other pesticides may not cause as many problems with water. California officials report that DBCP is the only pesticide they tested that shows a tendency to be absorbed into ground-water. Nonetheless, the projected increases in pesticide usage will create a variety of water contamination problems in the industrialized nations as well as in the less developed countries.

Irrigation will also add large amounts of salt contamination to the waters of many areas.[544] The water-use projections reveal that by the year 2000 between 4,600 and 7,000 billion cubic meters of water will be withdrawn for irrrigation. Approximately 25–30 percent will be returned to streams carrying dissolved salts. In very arid areas return water is heavily contaminated with salts, concentrated by high rates of evaporation.

Salt pollution of arid-zone rivers draining away from irrigated lands will ultimately make the rivers unfit for further irrigation use in their lower reaches, as has already happened to the Shatt-al-Arab River, in Iraq and the Lower Colorado River in the U.S.[545] The Shatt-al-Arab was formed by the Tigris and Euphrates Rivers, whose delta soils were once covered with extensive date-palm and citrus orchards.

One remedy—a very costly and energy-intensive remedy—for the salt pollution of rivers is to desalinate the water. A 104 million gallon per day desalting facility will soon be in operation on the Lower Colorado River. Now under construction at Yuma, Arizona, this plant will be the largest desalting plant in the world, costing over $300 million. It is needed to fulfill a U.S. agreement with Mexico to deliver water in the Colorado River with a total dissolved solids content (including salts) of no more than 115 milligrams per liter (mg/1). Because of the leaching of salts from fields upstream, the dissolved-solids content had increased to 850 mg/1 and was expected to reach 1,300 mg/1 by 2000. Most plant species cannot tolerate water with more than 500 mg/1 of dissolved solids.[546]

## Water-Related Diseases

Water related diseases have been an unfortunate accessory to irrigation systems and dams as well as to pollution by human wastes and are virtually certain to become more prevalent during the rest of the century as more of the water environment becomes affected by human activities and wastes.

A wide variety of water developments can increase the incidence of water-related diseases. The creation of ponds, reservoirs, and irrigation and drainage canals in the course of water resource development, and the widespread inadequacy of waste water disposal systems in LDC cities, all favor the persistence or spread of a number of such diseases. In recent years new irrigation systems and reservoirs in Middle and North Africa and West Asia have provided ideal habitats for the intermediate snail host of schistosomiasis, which has spread dramatically among rural populations.[547] This debilitating disease of the intestinal and urinary tract now affects an estimated 250 million people throughout the world, approximately 7 percent of the entire human population. In some irrigation-project and reservoir areas, up to 80 percent of the population is affected.[548]

In addition to schistosomasis there are numbers of other serious water-related diseases. These include malaria, filariasis (elephantiasis), and yellow fever, all of which are transmitted by mosquitoes. Onchocerciasis, "river blindness" disease, is transmitted by flies. Paragonimiasis is a disease transmitted by a snail. Poorly managed water resource development projects, as well as the impact of urbanization on aquatic habitats and water quality, contribute to the spread of all of these diseases. Diseases typical of waste water contaminated by human feces—cholera, typhoid fever, amoebic infections, and bacillary dysentery— can become problems anywhere in the world. In LDCs today almost 1.5 billion persons are exposed to these diseases for lack of safe water supplies and human waste disposal facilities. Largely for this reason infant deaths resulting from diarrhea continue at a high rate. Every day 35,000 infants and children under five years of age die throughout the world; most of these deaths occur in LDCs.[549] Schistosomiasis afflicts 200 million people in 70 countries and elephantiasis is estimated to cripple 250 million more.[550] In parts of

Asia where night soil is extensively used as fertilizer, roundworm (*Ascaris*) infections will continue to be a threat because the roundworm's eggs are not easily killed.

Water-related diseases are not limited to countries that cannot afford sewage treatment. In industrialized countries the treatment of city waste waters with chlorine presents a different kind of water-related health problem—the possibility of cancer. When chlorine reacts with organic compounds in waste water, one of the resulting by-products is chloroform, a carcinogen. Elevated rates of fatal gastrointestinal and urinary cancer are reported by some scientists in communities that utilize water supplies contaminated with chloroform.[551] The U.S. National Academy of Sciences has recommended that strict criteria be applied in setting limits for chloroform in drinking water.[552]

## Extinction of Freshwater Species

The International Union for Conservation of Nature and Natural Resources notes in the draft of its *World Conservation Strategy* that 274 fresh water vertebrate taxa are threatened by extinction as a result of habitat destruction. This number is larger than the number of similarly threatened vertebrate taxa in any other ecosystem group.[553]

It is not surprising that a large number of freshwater species are threatened with extinction through loss of habitat in view of the major changes that are occurring in freshwater systems. Damming, pollution, channelization, and siltation are causing massive alterations in freshwater ecosystems throughout the world. Fresh water species endemic to specific lakes, rivers, or upper reaches of river branches are particularly vulnerable because they are often easily extinguished by changes in water chemistry (the effects of acid rain for example), modification of streambed contours, alteration of water temperature, or the imposition of dams that prevent species from reaching their spawning grounds. Because of the anticipated increase in pollution and in manipulation of freshwater systems, many of the species now threatened may be extinct by 2000, and many now relatively common species may be on the way to extinction.

The trends in freshwater extinctions will be difficult if not impossible to reverse. In many areas political and social realities will stand in the way of installing expensive pollution control systems, of changing dam sites, or of reducing pesticide usage or coal combustion in order to save a fish or amphibian whose existence may be known to only a few people and whose value and impor-tance may be perceived by fewer still. As a result, high rates of extinction among freshwater species are expected to continue.

## Conclusion

Freshwater, once an abundant resource in most parts of the world, will become increasingly scarce in coming decades for two reasons. First, there will be greater net consumption, by cooling towers and, especially, by irrigation so that the total supply will decline. Second, pollution and the impacts of hydraulic works will effectively limit the uses of freshwater—and therefore, in effect, the supply. The deterioration of river basin catchments, especially as a result of deforestation, will increase the variability of supply, accelerate erosion, damage water development projects, and degrade water quality. It seems inevitable that the function of streams and rivers as habitat for aquatic life will steadily be sacrificed to the diversion of water for irrigation, for human consumption, and for power production, particularly in the LDCs.

The 1977 U.N. Water Conference served to focus global attention on the critical problems of managing the world's water resources in the coming decades. In the LDCs the development of water resources for irrigation and power is a key to providing for the economic needs of expanding populations. At the same time the ecological impacts of hydraulic works and of pollution from agricultural fields and urban industrial concentrations is greatly diminishing the capacity of water systems to support fish that are sorely needed to supplement meager diets. The lack of safe water supplies and of methods for sanitary disposal of human waste and waste water means that as many as 1.5 billion persons are exposed to fecally related disease pathogens in drinking water. These problems of water supply and quality in LDCs are so severe as to be matters of survival for millions of persons.

In industrial nations, water supply and quality will pose more subtle and therefore more complex questions of trade-offs and conflicts among users (or values) of freshwater. Water resources management in such nations is concerned not with human survival but with balancing demands for water resources against considerations of quality-of-life. But scarcities and conflicts are becoming more acute, and by the year 2000 economic, if not human, survival in many industrial regions may hinge upon water quality, or water supply, or both.

Perhaps the most underrated aspect of freshwater systems throughout the world is their function as aquatic habitat. At some point, high social and economic costs will follow the continued neglect of the water quality needed to maintain ecosystem health. This point may be marked by the failure of fish farms, or by a decline of the capacity of streams to accommodate wastes, or by the decline or disappearance of species that may possibly be of great future value. Given the criticality of the other uses of freshwater resources, the future integrity of aquatic habitats is by no means assured. In fact, since aquatic habitats are much more difficult to know and monitor than terrestrial ones, it is in serious doubt.

## THE ENERGY PROJECTIONS AND THE ENVIRONMENT

### The Projections

Assuming a 5 percent annual increase (starting in 1980) in the real price of oil, the Department of Energy, projects a growth in demand for commercial energy (i.e., energy from fossil fuels and from nuclear and hydro sources) of 3.0 percent per year for the 1975–90 period.* Total world commercial energy use (energy conversion) is projected to increase about 56 percent in 15 years—from 246 quadrillion ($10^{15}$) Btu to 384 quadrillion Btu in 1990.

The projected distribution of this increase among energy sources is illustrated in Table 13–32. The world's dependence on oil increases from 46 to 47 percent of total energy use. Annual oil consumption is projected to increase 66 quadrillion Btu ($11.4 \times 10^9$ barrels), a 58 percent increase in oil use over 15 years. Coal's share is projected to increase 13 percent; by 1990, 20 percent of all the energy used is projected to come from coal. Natural gas usage is projected to grow by 43 percent, providing 17 percent of the world's commercial energy in 1990. Nuclear and hydroelectricity production† are projected to increase by 226 percent (more than tripling); by 1990 they account for about 16 percent of the world's *primary* energy uses, but (after subtracting losses of waste heat) provide only about 6 percent of the world's usable energy. Solar energy, other than conservation and hydroelectric, is not projected to be making a significant contribution to the world's energy production by 1990.

The distribution of the increased use of commercial energy forms among regions of the world is illustrated in Table 13–33. Energy consumption in the United States increases by 41 percent, less rapidly than the 87 percent increase in other industrialized countries. The LDCs increase their use of commercial energy forms by 64 percent, but because these countries use such a small amount of commercial energy now, the 15-year growth adds only one percentage point to their fraction of the world total. The OPEC countries use a relatively small, but rapidly growing (more than 6 percent per year), fraction of the world's primary energy. The centrally planned economies increase their annual energy use by 34 percent, but their share of the world total declines from 31 to 27 percent. Overall, the global use of primary energy increases by 56 percent.

Projected changes in per capita use of primary energy are illustrated in Table 13–34. U.S. per capita energy use increases by 27 percent over 15 years, from 553 percent of the world average to 586 percent. The other industrialized countries increase their per capita energy use more rapidly (72 percent) to reach 325 percent of the world average by 1990. The LDCs (including OPEC countries) increase their per capita consumption by 27

---

*Because of the complexities of the world energy situation, the Department of Energy did not feel its projections could be extended beyond 1990. See chapters 10 and 20 for further details.

†The Department of Energy projections lump together nuclear and hydroelectric generation; most of the increase must be in nuclear generation because most of the large undeveloped hydroelectric sites are in the LDCs, and few of these will be developed over the next 15 years.

percent, to reach 19 percent of the world average. (The OPEC countries, even though their populations are relatively small, account for 36 percent of the combined LDC-OPEC increase in energy use.) The centrally planned economies increase their per capita energy use by 12 percent but decline relative to the world average from 97 percent to 90 percent. For the world as a whole, per capita annual energy use increases 20 percent from 60 million to 72 million Btu. The world average oil consumption in 1990 will be the equivalent of approximately 12 barrels of oil per person per year. The global variation ranges from about 73 barrels per person per year in the U.S. to about 2.4 barrels per person in the LDCs (including the OPEC countries).*

## Introduction

The DOE energy projections are based largely on an industrialized country perspective. The projections in Tables 13–32, 13–33, and 13–34 focus exclusively on what might be termed the commercial energy sources—oil, coal, natural gas, and nuclear and hydro sources—used primarily in industrialized economies. Important as these commercial energy sources and their environmental impacts are, they provide an incomplete picture of energy development and use and of environmental impacts over the next two decades.

In the less developed countries, noncommercial, organic fuels—wood, crop wastes, charcoal, and dung—are collected and burned daily by an estimated 1.5 billion persons, approximately 40 percent of the total human population. These energy sources are used extensively throughout rural

regions and even in cities, but because of their low energy content both per unit weight and per unit volume, they are not commonly traded in international commerce. Nevertheless, these organic fuels are traded locally and are vitally important to the economies in which they are used. Furthermore, their use has environmental implications of a significance comparable to that of commercial energy sources.

Two other categories of energy need to be mentioned briefly. One might be termed traditional sources; the other high-technology sources. The traditional sources involve well-established techniques and technologies for converting solar, wind, and water power into useful work. Examples include sailing ships, windmills, water mills and wheels, hydraulic rams, solar drying and distilling, charcoal-fired smelters and forges, and human and draft animal power. Not much importance has been assigned to these traditional sources of energy over the last several decades in the industrialized nations until recently, when "intermediate" and "appropriate" technologies[554]

---

* These projections were made by DOE in 1978, and DOE has revised its estimates since. See, for example, *National Energy Plan II,* Washington: Department of Energy, May 1979.

---

**TABLE 13–32**

**Global Primary[a] Energy Use, 1975 and 1990, by Energy Type**

| | 1975 | | 1990 | | Percent Increase (1975–90) | Average Annual Percent Increase |
|---|---|---|---|---|---|---|
| | $10^{15}$ Btu | Percent of Total | $10^{15}$ Btu[b] | Percent of Total | | |
| Oil | 113 | 46 | 179 | 47 | 58 | 3.1 |
| Coal | 68 | 28 | 77 | 20 | 13 | 0.8 |
| Natural gas | 46 | 19 | 66 | 17 | 43 | 2.4 |
| Nuclear and hydro | 19 | 8[c] | 62 | 16[c] | 226 | 7.9 |
| Solar (other than conservation and hydro)[d] | – | – | – | – | – | – |
| Total | 246 | 100 | 384 | 100 | 56 | 3.0 |

*Source:* The 1990 figures are from the Department of Energy's projections in Chapter 10 and note b, below. The 1975 figures for the centrally planned economies were taken by DOE from K. A. D. Inglis, *BP Statistical Review of World Oil Industry, 1976,* London: British Petroleum Company, Ltd., 1976; the other 1975 figures are from DOE's own sources.

[a] All of the nuclear and much of the coal primary (i.e., input) energy is used thermally to generate electricity. In the process, approximately two-thirds of the primary energy is lost as waste heat. The figures given here are primary energy.
[b] The conversions from the DOE projections in Table 10–8 were made as follows: *Oil:* 84.8 × 10⁶ bbl/day × 365 days × 5.8 × 10⁶ Btu/bbl = 179 × 10⁶ Btu. *Coal:* 5,424 × 10⁶ short tons/yr × 14.1 × 10⁶ Btu/short ton [DOE figure for world

average grade coal] = 77 × 10¹⁵ Btu. *Natural gas:* 64.4 × 10¹² ft³/yr × 1,032 Btu/ft³ = 66 × 10¹⁵ Btu. *Nuclear and Hydro:* 6,009 × 10¹² Wh [output]/yr × 3.412 Btu/Wh × 3 input Btu/output Btu = 62 × 10¹² Btu.
[c] After deductions for lost (waste) heat (see note a), the corresponding figures for output energy are 2.7 percent in 1975 and 6.0 in 1990.
[d] The IIES projection model is able to include solar only as conservation or hydro.

## TABLE 13–33

### Regional Distribution of Global Primary Energy Use, 1975 and 1990

| | 1975 Annual Use | | 1990 Annual Use | | Percent Increase (1975–90) | Average Annual Percent Increase |
|---|---|---|---|---|---|---|
| | $10^{15}$ Btu | Percent of Total | $10^{15}$ Btu | Percent of Total | | |
| United States | 71 | 29 | 100 | 26 | 41 | 2.3 |
| Other industrialized countries | 67 | 27 | 125 | 33 | 87 | 4.2 |
| Less developed countries | 25 | 10 | 41 | 11 | 64 | 3.3 |
| OPEC countries | 6 | 2 | 15 | 4 | 150 | 6.1 |
| Centrally planned economies | 77 | 31 | 103 | 27 | 34 | 1.9 |
| World | 246 | 100 | 384 | 100 | 56 | 3.0 |

Source: The 1990 figures are from Department of Energy's projections in Chapter 10. The 1975 figures for the centrally Planned Economies were taken by DOE from K. A. D. Ingles, *BP Statistical Review of World Oil Industry, 1976*, London: British Petroleum Company, Ltd., 1976; the other 1975 figures are from DOS's own sources.

## TABLE 13–34

### Per Capita Global Primary Energy Use, Annually 1975 and 1990

| | 1975 | | 1990 | | Percent Increase (1975–90) | Average Annual Percent Increase |
|---|---|---|---|---|---|---|
| | $10^6$ Btu | Percent of World Average | $10^6$ Btu | Percent of World Average | | |
| United States | 332 | 553 | 422 | 586 | 27 | 1.6 |
| Other industrialized countries | 136 | 227 | 234 | 325 | 72 | 3.6 |
| Less developed countries[a] | 11 | 18 | 14 | 19 | 27 | 1.6 |
| Centrally planned economies | 58 | 97 | 65 | 90 | 12 | 0.8 |
| World | 60 | 100 | 72 | 100 | 20 | 1.2 |

Source: The energy figures are from the Department of Energy (see Chapter 10 and Table 13–33). The population figures were obtained from the Bureau of the Census (see Chapter 2).

[a] Since population projections were not made separately fot the OPEC countries, those countries have been included here in the LDC category.

began to attract attention. Now these and related technologies are being reexamined by many groups, including the National Academy of Sciences, and it is generally agreed that many traditional technologies and techniques and their modern elaborations (e.g., methane generation) show great promise for rural development applications.[555] A major advantage of the modernized traditional sources is their small-scale, decentralized nature, which allows a wide range of applications especially in poor rural areas.

The high-technology category of energy sources includes a number of technologies now being researched or undergoing development. There are many examples: large-scale synthetic fuel production from coal, nuclear fusion, nuclear fission breeder reactors, hydrogen fuel, solar photovoltaic cells for direct electrical generation, large wind turbines for electrical generation, and large scale geothermal and ocean thermal energy conversion. Most of these high technologies are very large-scale approaches to energy supply and are beyond the reach of the poorest regions of the world.

In the discussion that follows, the environmental impacts of the Department of Energy (DOE) projections for commercial energy in industrialized society are considered first. The Brookhaven National Laboratory (BNL), under contract with DOE, analyzed the environmental implications of the DOE projections, but the analysis, as will be explained more fully below, does not provide an adequate basis for assessing the environmental consequences of future energy developments, largely because of technological uncertainties. Technology is then discussed in terms of the spectrum of alternatives and the various environmental consequences implied by these alternatives. The environmental implications of possible future high technologies are not discussed because these technologies are not projected by DOE as making significant contributions to the world's energy economy by 1990.

The environmental impacts of noncommercial organic fuels used in the LDCs is considered next, together with two "intermediate" or "appropriate" technologies that are becoming commercialized to a degree in some LDCs: methane gas and charcoal. Since the DOE projections did not include noncommercial energy sources, the discussion of organic fuels, charcoal, and methane is based largely on projections and estimates developed by the United Nations.

## Commercial Energy in Industrial Societies

The environmental implications of the DOE energy projections cannot be analyzed in detail for two reasons. First, the analytical tools needed for the assessment of the environmental consequences of even national (let alone global) energy projections are still being developed. Second, the DOE energy projections for the Global 2000 Study are not sufficiently detailed to permit the full application of even the presently available tools for environmental analysis. Consider first the limitations in available tools for environmental analysis.

Much has been written, and continues to be written, about the environmental aspects of energy development. Probably the largest portion of this work in the U.S. is being conducted or sponsored by one agency or another of the federal government.* Most of the analyses and reports are highly detailed and lack both the breadth and synthesis required for policy analysis and for the Global 2000 Study.

In spite of the large numbers of energy-environment studies, the information and analytical framework needed to systematically, comprehensively, and objectively compare the impacts of

alternative energy strategies do not exist. Recently, however John P. Holdren has proposed a framework for such analysis.[556] The framework, in its barest outline, involves the following sequence:

1. Identification of the *sources* of effects on the environment, in the form of specific technological systems and activities;
2. Identification and characterization of the *inputs* to the immediate environment that are produced by these sources, where "input" is taken to encompass what is put into, taken out of, or done to the surroundings;
3. Analysis of the *pathways* by which the inputs lead to stresses on the components of the environment at risk;
4. Characterization and quantification of these *stresses*;
5. Analysis of the *responses* of the components at risk to the stresses imposed;
6. Identification and quantification of the *costs* to human well-being associated with these responses.[557]

At present, the six steps of this sequence cannot be completed systematically for any nation, let alone for the world. *Sources* can now be identified in terms of specific technological systems and activities, but most national (and all global) energy projections and scenarios do not provide the basic source information in the detail needed for a comprehensive environmental analysis. Large volumes of data of mixed quality on pollution and residual *inputs* into the environment are being gathered in "data bases." However, the assembling and synthesizing of this data into a coherent, readily usable form is proceeding only relatively slowly. (Basic environmental input data are now being summarized in a large data book[558] by the office of the Assistant Secretary for the Environment, DOE. When complete, this volume will provide an important and useful source of data on the amounts of pollutants various energy

---

*The volume of energy-environment research and analysis sponsored by the government is staggering. The Environmental Protection Agency has developed a directory just to assist government personnel and other interested persons in locating the principal government officials involved in the program ("Who's Who in the Interagency Energy/Environment R&D Program," June 1978). In April 1977, the Energy Research and Development Administration published a 4-volume *Inventory of Federal Energy-Related Environment and Safety Research for FY 76*, totaling approximately 1,500 pages.

Debate surrounds the energy-environment research agenda. The Department of Energy has obtained research recommendations from consultants (e.g., METREK Division of the MITRE Corporation *International Aspects of Energy and the Environment: Status and Recommendations*, Apr. 1978).

Congressional committees and the Council on Environmental Quality have developed their own views (see Congressional Research Service, "Research and Development Needs to Merge Environmental and Energy Objectives," prepared for the House Subcommittee on Environment and the Atmosphere, Mar. 1978; and the Council's "Environment and Conservation and Energy Research and Development: Assessing the Adequacy of Federal Programs," Government Printing Office, Sept. 1976). The following two books by INFORM, a nonprofit environmental research group in New York City, provide an excellent overview of industrial research on new energy technologies: Stewart W. Herman and James S. Cannon, *Energy Futures: Industry and the New Technologies*, 1976; Walter C. Patterson and Richard Griffin, *Fluidized-Bed Energy Technology: Coming to a Boil*, 1978.

## TABLE 13–35

### U.S. Source Documents on the Effects of Pollutants

| Subject | Title | Source[a] | Year |
|---|---|---|---|
| Air pollution | *Air Quality Criteria for Nitrogen Oxides* | EPA | 1971 |
| | *Nitrogen Oxides* | NAS | 1977 |
| | *Air Quality Criteria for Hydrocarbons* | HEW | 1970 |
| | *Air Quality Criteria for Sulphur Oxides* | HEW | no date |
| | *Sulfur Oxides* | NAS | 1978 |
| | *Air Quality Criteria for Photo Chemical Oxidants* | HEW | 1970 |
| | *Ozone and Other Photo Chemical Oxidants* | NAS | 1977 |
| | *Air Quality for Particulate Matter* | HEW | 1969 |
| | *Particulate Polycyclic Organic Matter* | NAS | 1972 |
| | *Air Quality Criteria for Carbon Monoxide* | HEW | 1970 |
| | *Carbon Monoxide* | NAS | 1977 |
| Water pollution | *Quality Criteria for Water* | EPA | 1976 |
| | *Drinking Water and Health* | NAS | 1977 |
| Climate | *Energy and Climate* | NAS | 1977 |
| Land disruption | *Permanent Regulatory Program Implementing Section (501)(b) of the Surface Mining Control and Reclamation Act of 1977* | DOI | 1979 |
| | *Rehabilitation Potential of Western Coal Fields* | NAS | 1974 |
| Thermal pollution | *The Environmental Effects of Thermal Discharges* | EPA | 1974 |
| | *Biological Effects of Once-Through Cooling* | UWAG | 1978 |
| Low-probability, high-risk events | *Reactor Safety: Assessment of Accident Risks in U.S. Commercial Nuclear Power Plants* | NRC | 1975 |
| | *The Risks of Nuclear Power Reactors: A Review of the NRC Reactor Safety Study* | UCS | 1977 |
| | *Risk Assessment Review Group Report to the U.S. Nuclear Regulatory Commission* | NRC | 1978 |
| | *Liquefied Energy Gases Safety* | GAO | 1978 |
| Radioactive pollution | *The Effects on Population of Exposure to Low Levels of Ionizing Radiation* | NAS | 1972 |
| | *Radiological Quality of the Environment in the U.S., 1977* | EPA | 1977 |
| | *Report of the Interagency Task Force on Ionizing Radiation* | HEW | 1978 |
| | *The Effects on Populations of Exposure to Low Levels of Ionizing radiation* | NAS | 1979 |
| Synthesis of U.S. energy-related environmental impacts | *The Strategic Environmental Assessment System*[b] | DOE | 1978 |

[a] In the order in which the abbreviations appear in the table: U.S. Environmental Protection Agency; National Academy of Sciences; U.S. Department of Health, Education, and Welfare; U.S. Department of the Interior; Utility Water Act Group, Richmond, Va.; U.S. Nuclear Regulatory Commission; Union of Concerned Scientists, Cambridge, Mass.; U.S. General Accounting Office; U.S. Department of Energy.
[b] The U.S. Government does not have a model capable of a synthesis of all energy-related environmental impacts along the lines of Holdren's 6-step sequence discussed in the text, but the Strategic Environmental Assessment System (SEAS) is used by DOE for its environmental analysis (see, for example, DOE's Office of the Assistant Secretary for Environment, *National Energy Plan II, Appendix: Environmental Trends and Impacts,* May 1979, p. 2). Also, there is no single source of documentation for the SEAS model, but Richard J. Kalagher et al. indicate in a recent DOE-sponsored report that "documentation on the SEAS methodology, data bases, and other detailed information on the system" may be found in the 31 references listed on page 95 of the report (*National Environmental Impact Projection No. 1,* McLean, Va.: MITRE Corp., Dec. 1978).

sources put into the environment.) Information on *pathways, stresses, responses,* and *costs* is still incomplete and fragmented (see Table 13–35). Given the fragmentary information available for many of the six steps in the sequence, it is not surprising that at present adequate analytical models do not exist for translating environmental inputs from even a national energy projection or scenario through the pathways, stresses, and responses to the costs to human well-being,* and

* The model now being used by the Department of Energy—the Strategic Environmental Assessment System (SEAS)

considering the complexities involved, time will be needed to improve the models.

In view of the present limitations in capabilities for the analysis of environmental consequences of energy projections, the most that could be hoped for in the Global 2000 Study's analysis was a clear indication of inputs only—the environmental inputs from world energy developments out to the year 2000. However, even this relatively

model—is more integrated than many national energy models. Some results from the SEAS model are discussed later in this section.

modest goal proved impossible for several reasons. First, the DOE projections do not extend to 2000. Because of technical, political, economic, and policy uncertainties (see Chapters 10 and 20 for further details), the DOE was unable to extend its projections beyond 1990. Second, the DOE energy projections are not sufficiently detailed to permit anything but the broadest of environmental assessments. The fraction of coal to be strip-mined is not projected; the percent sulfur in the coal to be burned is not specified; nuclear and hydroelectric generation—technologies with quite different environmental effects—are lumped together.

Given the incomplete and tentative nature of the energy projections, a detailed and systematic environmental analysis could not be expected. However, DOE was asked to provide at least a general analysis of the environmental implications of its projections, and the Department contracted this work to the Brookhaven National Laboratory (BNL).

## Environmental Analysis—The Brookhaven National Laboratory Projections

The DOE–BNL environmental projections include energy-related air pollutant emissions (carbon dioxide, carbon monoxide, sulfur dioxide, oxides of nitrogen, particulates, and hydrocarbons), radioactive emissions (tritium, population exposure to radiation, and solid high-level waste), land-use requirements, and solid-waste generation. Unfortunately, the simplifying assumptions underlying the DOE–BNL environmental projections severely limit the usefulness of the results. These assumptions are: (1) that by 1985 all energy facilities throughout the world will be retrofitted to meet U.S. new-source performance standards* for sulfur dioxide, oxides of nitrogen, particulates, and hydrocarbons; and (2) that for other environmental emissions and effects, emissions per fuel unit produced and consumed will remain at presently estimated values. The DOE–BNL land-use and solid-waste estimates pertained only to those aspects of the energy system for which DOE was able to supply Brookhaven with projections (unfortunately this excluded strip-mining). The estimates thus give only a partial picture of en-

___

* See *Clean Air Act*, 42 U.S.C. 1857 et seq. In its *Eighth Annual Report—1977* (p. 26), the Council on Environmental Quality writes—concerning the 1977 amendments to the Act— that "sections of the Amendments provide a more vigorous definition of new-source performance standards requiring performance at least as good as that which could be obtained by using the 'best technological system of continuous emission reduction.' "

ergy-related effects. No base-year (1975) residual emission figures could be provided because the DOE energy projections did not include base-year figures.* Given these assumptions and limitations, the DOE–BNL figures must be regarded at best as lower bounds on the expected environmental impacts.

The DOE–BNL environmental projections are presented in Tables 10–16, 10–17, and 10–18 of Chapter 10 for three cases in which oil prices are assumed to remain constant out to 1990. The Global 2000 Study's base case—oil prices increasing at 5 percent per year starting in 1980—was not analyzed. However, the low-growth case leads to a total world energy consumption similar to that in the Global 2000 Study's base case, but the mix of technologies is of course different. The DOE–BNL residuals projections for the low-growth case are shown in Table 13–36. The DOE–BNL environmental projections are discussed in detail in Chapter 10 and will not be discussed here. Because of fundamental limitations in the DOE–BNL approach, remedial efforts would be insufficient. Another approach is needed.

## Environmental Analysis—Another Approach

The energy problem has several dimensions— political, economic, resource, technological, environmental, social—and difficult decisions will be required of each nation in each of these areas. The basic difficulty in developing projections of the environmental consequences of energy development* is that few nations have yet made these difficult decisions. As a result, there is much uncertainty as to the approaches and technologies that will be used.

In the discussion that follows, the resource and economic aspects of the energy problem are examined briefly to establish a framework for the spectrum of technological alternatives various nations are now considering. The environmental consequences of the technological options at the ends of the spectrum are then discussed and compared. This comparison, based on U.S. national studies, provides a range of possible environmental consequences. Finally, the comparison is extended globally, with particular attention to environmental impacts of energy development that could have significant implications for some of the other Global 2000 Study projections.

*The Resource Problem.* Essentially, the resource aspects of the commercial energy problem

___

* Late in the study, DOE did provide a limited amount of base-year data, which have been used in Tables 13–32, 13–33, and 13–34.

## TABLE 13–36

### Projected Annual Emissions: 1985 and 1990, Low-Growth Case[a]

| | European OECD Countries | U.S. and Canada | Japan | Less Developed Countries | OPEC Countries | Centrally Planned Economies | World |
|---|---|---|---|---|---|---|---|
| **1985** | | | | | | | |
| Carbon dioxide | | | | | | | |
| (billions of short tons) | 4.78 | 6.85 | 1.51 | 2.57 | 0.80 | 7.52 | 24.0 |
| Carbon monoxide | | | | | | | |
| (millions of short tons) | 22.5 | 13.4 | 6.68 | 15.7 | 5.50 | 22.4 | 86.1 |
| Sulfur dioxide | | | | | | | |
| (millions of short tons) | 11.8 | 13.0 | 4.52 | 7.07 | 1.33 | 29.8 | 67.4 |
| Oxides of nitrogen | | | | | | | |
| (milliions of short tons) | 13.5 | 15.7 | 4.71 | 8.21 | 2.38 | 19.7 | 64.1 |
| Particulates | | | | | | | |
| (millions of short tons) | 6.3 | 9.02 | 2.03 | 6.56 | 0.54 | 30.6 | 55.0 |
| Hydrocarbons | | | | | | | |
| (millions of short tons) | 2.56 | 1.84 | 0.79 | 1.73 | 0.59 | 2.99 | 10.5 |
| Land use | | | | | | | |
| (millions of acres) | 13.7 | 18.7 | 3.37 | 11.9 | 0.004 | 15.1 | 61.2 |
| Solid wastes | | | | | | | |
| (millions of short tons) | 80.1 | 218 | 7.43 | 45.6 | 0.58 | 149 | 500 |
| Tritium | | | | | | | |
| (thousands of curies) | 103 | 142 | 22.9 | 34.6 | 3.64 | 47.9 | 354 |
| Population exposure | | | | | | | |
| (thousands of man-rems) | 3.98 | 5.44 | 0.88 | 1.33 | 0.14 | 1.84 | 13.6 |
| Solid high-level wastes | | | | | | | |
| (billions of curies) | 11.0 | 15.1 | 2.44 | 3.69 | 0.39 | 5.10 | 37.6 |
| **1990** | | | | | | | |
| Carbon dioxide | | | | | | | |
| (billions of short tons) | 5.20 | 7.31 | 1.62 | 3.05 | 0.97 | 8.42 | 26.6 |
| Carbon monoxide | | | | | | | |
| (millions of short tons) | 26.2 | 13.1 | 8.44 | 19.6 | 6.96 | 25.0 | 99.2 |
| Sulfur dioxide | | | | | | | |
| (millions of short tons) | 12.7 | 13.8 | 4.68 | 8.42 | 1.56 | 33.4 | 74.6 |
| Oxides of nitrogen | | | | | | | |
| (millions of short tons) | 14.8 | 16.2 | 4.44 | 9.74 | 2.88 | 22.0 | 70.7 |
| Particulates | | | | | | | |
| (millions of short tons) | 6.66 | 9.73 | 2.15 | 7.81 | 0.63 | 34.2 | 61.2 |
| Hydrocarbons | | | | | | | |
| (millions of short tons) | 2.94 | 1.85 | 0.38 | 2.14 | 0.73 | 3.35 | 12.0 |
| Land use | | | | | | | |
| (millions of acres) | 15.7 | 21.6 | 4.43 | 15.7 | 0.007 | 21.6 | 79.0 |
| Solid waste | | | | | | | |
| (millions of short tons) | 75.1 | 243 | 7.49 | 50.2 | 1.02 | 168 | 545 |
| Tritium | | | | | | | |
| (thousands of curies) | 178 | 214 | 42.4 | 74.6 | 12.0 | 118 | 639 |
| Population exposure | | | | | | | |
| (thousands of man-rems) | 6.83 | 8.23 | 1.63 | 2.87 | 0.46 | 4.53 | 24.6 |
| Solid high-level wastes | | | | | | | |
| (billions of curies) | 18.9 | 22.9 | 4.52 | 7.95 | 1.28 | 12.6 | 68.1 |

Source: Department of Energy–Brookhaven National Laboratory projections.

[a] The important assumptions behind the figures in this table are discussed briefly in the text of this chapter and, more fully, in Chapter 10.

facing the world is that convenient, easily transported, relatively clean-burning petroleum and natural gas resources are being depleted. As these resources become increasingly scarce, a transition to other forms of energy must be made. How quickly the transition must be made depends upon how much oil will ultimately be recovered and how rapidly the oil is used.

While there is still uncertainty and debate over how much oil will ultimately be recovered, estimates are becoming more refined. The lack of consensus on estimates of ultimately recoverable conventional world oil resources stems (1) from several economic, technical, and geologic uncertainties that are not likely to be resolved soon, and (2) from a failure to fully utilize existing public

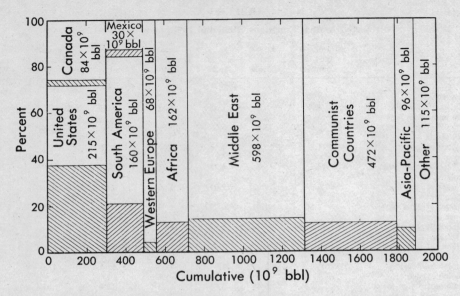

**Figure 13–10.** Distribution and present production of ultimately recoverable conventional crude oil resources of the world. Shaded areas represent cumulative production to date. (*M. King Hubbert, in Congressional Research Service,* Project Interdependence: U.S. and World Energy Outlook Through 1990, *Washington, 1977, p. 644*)

information about world oil resources. A recent report prepared for the Central Intelligence Agency by Richard Nehring of the Rand Corporation provides a detailed, publicly available description of the known recoverable crude oil resources of the world and an explicitly reasoned estimated range of ultimately recoverable conventional crude oil resources.[559]

The Nehring report focuses on the relatively small number of giant oil fields, defined as fields having an ultimate recovery of 500 million barrels or more. These giant oil fields contain more than 75 percent of the known recoverable oil resources of the world. Their comprehensive examination provides an efficient means of assessing world oil resources.

After a lengthy and detailed analysis, Nehring concludes[560] that the ultimate recoverable conventional crude oil resources of the world are somewhere between 1,700 and 2,300 billion barrels.* Nehrings "best estimate" of the ultimately

recoverable conventional crude oil resources of the world (i.e., the middle of his range) is 2,000 billion barrels. The global distribution of this resource is illustrated in Figure 13–10, in which the shaded areas indicate the fractions of the ultimately recoverable crude oil resources that have already been produced. The United States has produced the largest fraction of its crude oil resources (approximately 50 percent); Canada, Mexico, and Western Europe have produced relatively small fractions of theirs.

How fast will the world's crude oil resources be consumed? This question cannot be answered with precision. As Nehring notes, the future depletion rate will depend on (1) the production policies of OPEC, (2) the development of technology for offshore Arctic and deepwater exploration and production, and (3) the existence of the necessary economic incentives to producers and refiners. However, it is possible to estimate roughly how long the world's crude oil resources will last.

---

* These figures were estimated prior to the recent reports of a major oil province in Mexico. The Mexican find, therefore, may be considered to be one of "the two to four major oil provinces" that Nehring expects to be discovered and developed. The Mexican find is large, probably on the order of 50–60 billion barrels of petroleum (as opposed to "oil equiva-

lent"). This amount is roughly equal to 10 percent of the petroleum ultimately recoverable in the Middle East or 50 percent of the oil yet to be produced in the United States—or about 3 percent of the ultimately recoverable crude oil resources of the world.

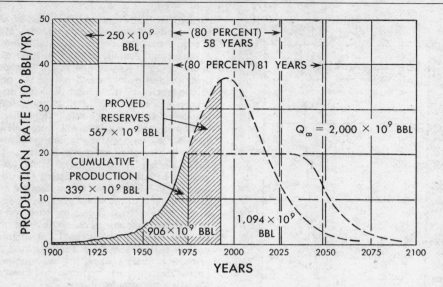

**Figure 13–11.** Possible production rate curves for the world's ultimately recoverable crude oil resources. (*M. King Hubbert in Congressional Research Service*, Project Interdependence: U.S. and World Energy Outlook Through 1990, *Washington, 1977, p. 642*)

The production rate curve for any finite resource—including crude oil—has a bell shape. The production rate starts at zero when the resource was first tapped. The curve then rises as the production rate increases. Ultimately, the curve must peak and return to zero as the oil resource is exhausted. On such a curve, a steep rise in the real costs of discovery and production can be anticipated. The total area under the curve must equal the total oil ultimately economically recoverable.[561]

Using 2,000 billion barrels (Nehring's best estimate) for the ultimately recoverable resource, Figure 13–11 illustrates two possible shapes of the future crude oil production rate curve for the world. In both cases, the total area under the curves is equal to the total ultimately recoverable conventional crude oil resource of the world (2,000 billion barrels), and the initial portion of the curves corresponds to historic experience. The symmetric curve rises to a peak about 1990, declining thereafter. The second curve shows that if petroleum production were held at about 1975 rates, the decline in production could be postponed for about two decades. The symmetric curve assumes that 80 percent of the world's total ultimately recoverable conventional resources are consumed over a 58-year period; with production

limited to the 1975 rate, 80 percent of the resources are consumed over an 81-year period.

The resource aspect of the world's commercial energy problem is, in essence, that crude oil (and natural gas) cannot continue to grow at historical rates. Figure 13–12 illustrates the problem for crude oil. The rapidly rising curve continues the growth trend experienced in the 1950s, 60s, and early 70s. The lower curve is the symmetric production curve (from Fig. 13–11) for the world's ultimately recoverable conventional crude oil resources. The rapidly growing gap is an indication of the resource aspect of the world's commercial energy problem.

*The Economic Problem.* The economic aspect of the world's commercial energy problem stems largely from the observation[562] that GNP and energy growth have been correlated in the past, as illustrated in Figure 13–13 for the U.S. The concern is that (1) if GNP measures social welfare and (2) if growth in GNP is both correlated with and caused by energy growth, reduced energy growth would necessarily affect social welfare adversely. However, there are many reasons to doubt these two suppositions. It is well known that GNP is not an adequate or satisfactory measure of social welfare. Furthermore, there is wide variation among nations and regions in the amount

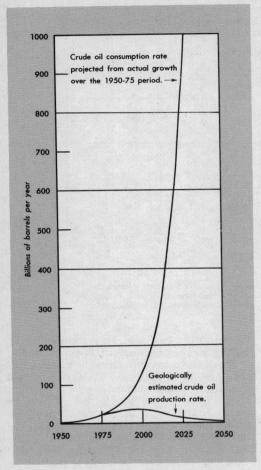

**Figure 13-12.** Geologically estimated global crude oil production rates compared with consumption rates projected from actual growth over the 1950–75 period. The production curve is from Figure 13–11; the consumption curve is projected from historic consumption rates over the 1900–75 period.

of GNP (and welfare) produced per unit of energy used,* and the hypothesized causal linkages between energy use and GNP (and welfare) are clearly subject to varying degrees of efficiency.[563]

---

* A study prepared by the MITRE Corporation for the Department of Energy (Richard J. Kalagher et al., "National Environmental Projection No. 1," Dec. 1978, p. 83) forecasts that by 1990 the U.S. economy will generate $19 billion of GNP per quad ($10^{15}$ Btu) of energy supply, up about 19 percent from the 1975 performance of $16 billion GNP per quad of energy supply.

Since GNP figures include the value of services performed in cleaning up the environment as well as economic activities that create pollution, social welfare could actually increase as a result of reduced GNP, at least to the extent that more efficient use of energy could reduce the polluting component of GNP without reducing the beneficial component.* While all of the future consequences are still not entirely clear, the social, economic, and environmental consequences of alternative energy paths are important considerations in projecting an energy future.

*The Technological Options.* There are many ideas as to how the United States and other nations might best respond to the resource and economic aspects of the world energy problem. The most widely discussed ideas are based on the use of increased amounts of energy derived from five primary energy sources: coal, oil, natural gas, nuclear fission, and solar. Increased use of each of these primary sources has environmental impacts. These impacts are described briefly in the following paragraphs.

• Coal production and use involve serious environmental problems, most of which can be limited through control measures.

Worker health and safety is a special concern with coal. Coal mining is a hazardous occupation, even when careful attention is given to maintaining a safe and healthy workplace. Without such attention, frequent accidents and a high incidence of black-lung disease would be the norm.

Adverse land and water impacts are also a prime concern. Without proper controls, surface mines can lead to large-scale land disruptions. Natural habitats can be largely destroyed, and farmlands can be rendered unproductive. The physiological and ecological character of the affected regions can be markedly changed. Land subsidence is a common occurrence with deep mines. Water pollution, especially acid mine drainage, is associated with both surface and underground mines.

Without adequate controls, coal combustion can release considerable amounts of air pollutants, including sulfur dioxide, nitrogen oxides, particulates, and trace metals. These pollutants

---

* Further support for this point is provided by the forthcoming report of the Demand and Conservation Panel of the National Academy of Sciences' Committee on Nuclear and Alternative Energy Systems (discussed in part in "U.S. Energy Demand: Some Low Energy Futures," *Science*, Apr. 14, 1978, pp. 142–52), and in the report of the Energy Project at the Harvard Business School (Robert Stogaugh and David Yergin, eds., *Energy Future*, New York: Random House, 1979).

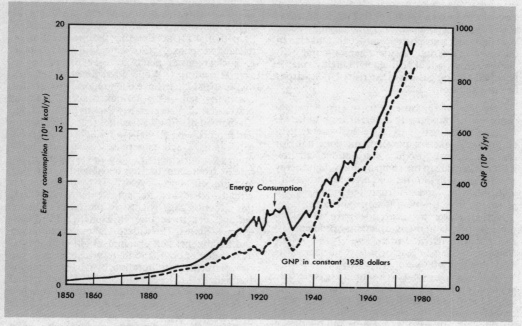

**Figure 13-13.** Historical growth of GNP and commercial energy use in the United States, 1850-1976. (*U.S. Statistical Abstracts*)

can produce health or ecological concerns on a local, regional, national, and sometimes even international scale.

The ecological effects associated with acid rains have only recently become of widespread concern. The combustion of coal and other fossil fuels produces oxides of sulfur and nitrogen that acidify rain over wide areas. (The acid rain problem is discussed extensively in the water section of this chapter.)

The combustion of coal and other fossil fuels releases carbon dioxide, contributing to the problem of its accumulation in the atmosphere. Global atmosphere $CO_2$ levels have already increased by about 10 percent above pre-industrial concentrations. The global consequences of continued $CO_2$ buildup are not well understood, but there is concern that a gradual, irreversible, and potentially dangerous change in the world's climate could occur over the next century as a result of the "greenhouse effect." (The $CO_2$ problem is discussed extensively in the climate section of this chapter.)

• Oil produces environmental impacts that are both similar to and different from those produced

by coal. The environmental impacts associated with the combustion of oil and coal are generally similar, but on a per unit energy basis tend to be less severe with oil. The comparison, however, is not completely straightforward because some of the impacts are not fully commensurable. (The problem of comparability becomes more acute with energy sources that are even more dissimilar—e.g., coal versus nuclear energy.)

The most prominent generic environmental difference between coal and oil concern production and transportation. The problems of production and transportation of oil include the likely disruption of some pristine areas (such as the arctic and antarctic regions), the possibility of blowouts during the exploration and drilling phases, and the likelihood of major spills due to transportation accidents. Ocean transportation by supertanker is of particular concern. Over the last decade, large oil spills from supertankers have become a global problem. Chronic oil pollution from many sources, land- and marine-based, also remains a serious concern.

• Natural gas produces substantially less air pollution per unit of energy than either oil or coal.

Being gaseous under normal conditions, it poses less risks to land and water during overland transport. Natural gas, however, is increasingly being liquefied and transported via ocean tankers. In the event of a serious accident near a major population center, a tanker filled with highly volatile liquefied natural gas poses the risk of a disastrous fire or explosion.

• Nuclear energy raises a set of environmental concerns that are largely different from those associated with fossil fuels. Electrical energy generation at a nuclear power plant does not, for example, directly produce conventional air pollution. Also, due to the comparatively high energy content of uranium ores that are presently available, much less land is disrupted to produce a unit of energy from uranium than from coal.

Nuclear power, however, does have several important societal and environmental problems associated with its widespread use. These include concerns related to reactor safety, nuclear waste disposal, and international security.

Nuclear reactor safety is a continuing issue. The possibility of a truly catastrophic accident, involving a reactor meltdown that releases considerable amounts of radiation and could lead potentially to thousands of deaths and billions of dollars of property damage, has been a concern since the beginning of the technology. Elaborate safety measures with several levels of redundancy have been developed to prevent such an event. Even though the likelihood of a major accident at a carefully designed, maintained, and managed reactor is small, its precise value is uncertain and nonzero. The actual degree of risks under various conditions of design, maintenance, and management continues to be the subject of intensive analysis. Needless to say, if nuclear power plants are not subject to careful design, maintenance, and management, these facilities pose far greater risks to public health and welfare.

The total global amounts of nuclear waste generated by reactor operations have grown steadily. Nuclear waste products are toxic, highly radioactive, and long-lived. Some of the radioactive isotopes in nuclear wastes remain dangerously radioactive for hundreds of thousands of years, a period many times longer than recorded history. Safe disposal will require extended containment in sites that are stable over geological periods of time. Many disposal techniques have been proposed but none has yet been established as fully satisfactory. Research aimed at resolving this problem must receive greater attention than in the past.

Nuclear power may also increase the risk to world security, both through the possibility of added vulnerability to terrorist actions and through its potential for accelerating the proliferation of nuclear weapons. Acts of vandalism and sabotage to nuclear power plants have been reported in several countries. While no radioactive releases due to such attacks have been reported so far, this possibility remains a serious concern. Nuclear power may also accelerate weapons proliferation. The spread of sensitive facilities (e.g., enrichment and reprocessing plants) can result in direct access to weapons-usable materials. To date, the technology for enriching uranium and separating plutonium from spent fuel has been tightly controlled and limited almost exclusively to those nations already possessing nuclear weapons. However, this situation may change in the future if more nations seek to acquire enrichment and reprocessing facilities. The widespread use of plutonium and highly enriched uranium would increase the availability of both, and thereby also increase the risk of further proliferation of nuclear weapons throughout the world while offering no substantial advantage over the continued use of low-enriched uranium in the nuclear energy facilities of those nations that do not now have nuclear weapons. Furthermore, a substantial disadvantage could occur in that a proliferation of nuclear weapons capability would diminish world security and in turn threaten the energy security of all nations.

• Solar energy is available in several forms, including hydropower, wind power, organic material (biomass), ocean thermal energy conversion, and direct sunlight. Its environmental problems vary markedly both in kind and in degree from one technology to another. Even for a given technology, the environmental implications depend on the scale of the facility and on site-specific factors.

Hydro facilities that generate electricity usually generate from a few kilowatts to thousands of megawatts. Environmental concerns associated with hydropower include the disruption of river flows and aquatic life, flooding of land and wetland habitats, potential public health problems related to ecosystem changes, and possible long-term effects on agricultural production at those locations where the reservoir is used for irrigation.

Energy production via large and small wind systems also raises a number of minor but consequential environmental concerns. These include safety problems associated with blade or tower failure, worker and neighborhood exposure to noise, electromagnetic interference, and windmill aesthetics.

The potential environmental problems associated with increased reliance on biomass could be severe. As noted elsewhere in this Study, LDCs have been particularly subject to the overuse of biomass for basic energy needs. The problems in some LDCs include widespread deforestation and the loss of essential nutrients due to the use of animal wastes to meet domestic energy requirements. These problems are already very critical in some countries and may become even more critical in the future.

By comparison, the use of bioenergy in industrialized countries appears to pose problems of considerably smaller magnitude. These include the possibility of small- to moderate-scale ecological effects due to the development of intensive biomass "farms," air pollution associated with the increased use of fuelwood, and air and water pollution associated with the production of liquid or gaseous fuels from biomass.

Ocean thermal energy conversion (OTEC) systems pose several environmental problems (see "The Projections and the Marine Environment" above), whose nature, magnitude, and effects are still somewhat uncertain. Three unexplored areas provide the source of this uncertainty. First, the technology is evolving rapidly and is subject to substantial modifications. Second, the specific nature of the impact of OTEC facilities in an ocean environment is not well understood. Third, the aggregate environmental impact of an OTEC "farm" is unknown. The most important concerns identified so far include: the need to avoid ecology sensitive areas by proper site selection; displacement of sufficient oceanic water to alter the temperature and chemical characteristics of the marine environment; entrainment and possible destruction of marine organisms; and corrosion of metallic surfaces, which could lead to the buildup of toxic substances in the marine food chain.

The potential methods of harnessing direct solar radiation range from large-scale electrical generating installations to small-scale applications for home space heating, hot water, and electricity. The vast majority of the applications appear to be relatively benign environmentally. Most of the environmental impacts are typically associated with the production of equipment rather than operation. Large-scale solar "power towers" and solar cells in space to generate microwave power beamed to earth are possible exceptions. Ongoing research is aimed at the better identification of the environmental effects associated with these and other systems.

Given these primary sources of energy—coal, oil, natural gas, nuclear fission and solar—there are a wide spectrum of mixes under consideration by nations around the world as possible solutions to their energy problems. The spectrum ranges from heavy dependence on nuclear energy and nonrenewable fossil fuels (especially coal) with minimal attention to the productivity and efficiency of energy use on the one hand, to heavy emphasis of renewable resources (especially the various forms of solar energy), increased productivity (i.e., end-use conservation), and increased efficiency in the energy sector (i.e., thermodynamic matching of energy source to end-use requirements*) on the other. These two extremes of the solution spectrum are now widely referenced to as the "hard" and the "soft" paths. [564]

The hard path/soft path dichotomy is a convenient means of capsulizing the *range* of environmental impacts that may be expected from energy development in the decade ahead. While both the hard path and the soft path have environmental impacts, their relative difference in emphasis on conservation, productivity, efficiency and renewable/nonrenewable sources leads to very different environmental impacts. For a time, the most complete comparisons of hard and soft path scenarios were provided by the writings of Amory Lovins [565] and his critics, [566] but a number of additional studies are now available. Most of the new studies are not strictly hard path or soft path studies, but are definitely closer to one end of the spectrum or the other. The discussion that follows relates these studies to the hard and soft path concepts and compares environmental consequences. Finally, the range of energy-related environmental impacts that might be experienced globally in 2000 is considered briefly in light of the comparison.

## The Hard Path

Studies of hard path options abound. The discussion here is limited to two. The first is the work of the World Energy Conference (WEC), which

---

* The degree to which the energy industry requires primary energy to deliver end-use energy for the needs of society is illustrated by the example of converting coal to another form of energy, namely electricity. If three lumps of coal are burned in a thermal power plant to generate electricity, *the energy sector of the economy loses the energy from two lumps of coal as waste heat.* Similar losses occur in the conversion of coal to synthetic fuels. Such inefficiencies in the energy sector can be minimized by matching thermodynamically the quality of the energy delivered to the quality of the energy needed for the performance of particular end uses.

provides what is probably the most complete global hard path scenario yet developed, but has only a very limited environmental analysis.* The second is U.S. national energy scenario developed by the U.S. Department of Energy. The environmental implications of the DOE scenario have been analyzed much more fully than the WEC scenario.

*The World Energy Conference Study.* The relatively hard path scenarios developed by the WEC anticipate significant growth in both coal and nuclear. The WEC analysis,† noting that ultimately production regulates demand, projects potential world primary energy production in 2000 at 690 exajoules (EJ).§ The potential production mix is as follows: coal, 170 EJ; oil, 195 EJ; gas, 143 EJ; nuclear, 88 EJ; hydraulic, 34 EJ; unconventional oil and gas, 4 EJ; renewable solar, geothermal, and biomass, 56 EJ.[567]

The WEC presents a range of energy demand projections for 2000. All of the projections are based on assumed rates of economic growth and assumed elasticities of energy use relative to income and price. High growth ("H") cases and low growth ("L") cases were developed using the following assumed annual economic growth rates:

|  | OECD Nations | Centrally Planned Economies | Less Developed Countries | World |
|---|---|---|---|---|
| High growth | 3.7 | 4.5 | 5.3 | 4.1 |
| Low growth | 2.8 | 3.2 | 3.8 | 3.0 |

The income and price elasticities vary from case to case. The high-growth case H3 includes only the impact of a significant price response and results in a demand of about 680 EJ (646 quad) in 2000—an increase of a factor of two over energy use in 1972 (the study's base year). The H5 scenario includes not only the high price response, but also oil utilization constraints and vigorous conservation measures, which exceed the normally expected consumer response to higher energy prices. The H5 assumptions result in a demand of about 560 EJ (532 quad) in 2000—an increase of about a factor of 1.7 over 1972 use. The low-growth case L4 assumes a high price response, further oil constraints, further conservation measures, and the use of oil primarily for premium uses. The L4 assumptions result in a demand of about 520 EJ (494 quad)—an increase of about 1.5 times over 1972 use.[568]

The World Energy Conference's consideration of environmental constraints is confined to one page in its current work.[569] This brief discussion recalls for the reader the assumption in the WEC analysis that current environmental and antipollution standards will remain unchanged. The discussion continues by noting that of course standards will change; and because "in the case of an emergency an ample supply of energy is given a higher priority than at least the more marginal concern for the environment, . . . we believe that proper measures to prevent energy shortages should form a part of a comprehensive and responsible environmental policy."[570]

The WEC environmental assessment continues, "It is often said that the least-polluting joule is the one never produced. This is not necessarily true. In fact many antipollution measures, adopted, or proposed, require the use of more energy rather than less.[571]

The WEC concludes its environmental discussion with a call for more environmental analysis. It should be noted that environmental considerations are one of the three major topics on the program of the next WEC conference.[572]

*The DOE hard path scenario.* The Department of Energy recently contracted with the MITRE Corporation to analyze the environmental implications of a DOE scenario that lies close to the hard end of the spectrum of energy paths. The scenario, known as Projection Series C, is one of a set developed by DOE's Energy Information Administration and reported in the Administration's annual report.[573] In Table 13–37, Projection Series C* is compared with the original definition of the hard path. While there is a close correspondence between the scenario and the definition, this is not the "hardest" of the scenarios being considered by DOE. The DOE-sponsored MITRE analysis[574] describes this scenario as a "business-as-usual" scenario, characterizing "a middle range of energy futures likely to result if

---

* The scenarios developed by Workshop on Alternative Energy Strategies (WAES) might also have been considered here, but they exclude nations having centrally planned economies and have no more environmental analysis than the WEC work.
† The WEC projections extend to 2020, but to facilitate comparison with other figures in this report, the WEC figures presented here are the ones for 2000.
§ 1 EJ = $10^{18}$ joules = $0.95 \times 10^{15}$ Btu = 0.95 quad.

*Since the above was written, DOE has published a similar environmental analysis of National Energy Plan II (NEP-II). The NEP-II scenario for low-priced oil ($21/bbl in 2000) is based on the identical average annual growth rate in primary energy conversion—2.82 percent per year. The NEP-II scenario for high-priced oil ($38/bbl in 2000) has a slightly slower average annual growth rate in primary energy conversion—2.60 percent per year.

policies in existence prior to the passage of the National Energy Act* are continued.

The DOE-MITRE analysis of Projection Series C is based on present and anticipated environmental regulations, many of which are under attack or in question. Among these regulations, the air and water quality regulations are particularly important.†

Based on these and other assumptions, the DOE-MITRE report presents a mixed and incomplete picture through 1990 of the U.S. environmental future implied by the Projection Series C

*Deregulation provided for in the National Energy Act will gradually raise the cost of domestic oil and gas to world price levels, but will not significantly alter the basic strategy characteristic of Projection Series C.
†The MITRE analysis (pp. 19, 59–60) describes its assumptions about these regulations as follows:
"The 1970 Clean Air Act Amendments to the Air Quality Act of 1967 ('Clean Air Act') provide the legislative basis for most environmental regulations and assumptions used in this section of the report. The Clean Air Act stipulated that the federal government set National Ambient Air Quality Standards (NAAQS) for five pollutants: total suspended particulates, sulfur dioxide, nitrogen dioxide, hydrocarbons, and carbon monoxide. Each state was then required to develop and submit a State Implementation Plan (SIP) to the Environmental Protection Agency (EPA) Administrator. The SIP specifies strategies to achieve the level of air quality established by the NAAQS for individual polluting categories in all regions of the state. EPA also set New Source Performance Standards (NSPS) for selected industrial categories. Compliance with both the SIP and NSPS is assumed in the environmental forecasts of this report, although full compliance with SIP standards is not assumed until 1985. It is assumed that new sources coming on line after 1975 meet EPA's original NSPS standards until the revised NSPS regulations of the Clean Air Act Amendments of 1977 become effective.
". . .The revised NSPS regulations require the use of the 'Best Available Control Technology' (BACT) for new major emitting facilities. This BACT requirement has been simulated for new coal-fired electric utilities (projected to be operational in 1984 or later) and new industrial boilers (initiated in 1981 or later). . . .
"Title II of the Clean Air Act (as amended in August 1977) specifies emission limits (in grams of pollutant per vehicle mile traveled over the lifetime of a vehicle) for mobile pollution sources. These emission limits have been translated by EPA into emission factors (also expressed in grams per mile) which account for increasing pollutant emissions as the vehicle ages. In several cases, the emission factors for new vehicles are lower than the emission limits set because increasing emissions due to vehicle deterioration are accounted for by increasing emission factors over time. . . . The Federal Water Pollution Control Act stipulated that the Environmental Protection Agency (EPA) develop industry-specific guidelines limiting releases of major pollutants. . . . The effluent limitations developed by EPA set two levels of guidelines: 'Best Practicable Technology' (BPT) currently available, to be met by July 1, 1977; and 'Best Available Technology' (BAT) economically achievable, to be met by July 1, 1983. This DOE-MITRE study assumes that 100 percent industrial compliance with BPT standards will be achieved in 1979, and with BAT standards by 1985."

hard path scenario. The treatment of air pollution covers most of major energy related pollutants: sulfur oxides, hydrocarbons, carbon monoxide, nitrogen oxides, hydrocarbons and particulates, but omits carbon dioxide.* The discussion of water pollution covers total dissolved solids and nitrogen discharges. Water consumption is projected, but no indications of land disruption and loss by mining (especially coal strip-mining and uranium mining) are provided. Solid wastes (especially scrubber sludge and ash) are projected, but nuclear wastes and radiation associated with the nuclear fuel cycle are not. Despite its limitations, this is one of the broadest and most complete environmental assessments yet provided by DOE in its energy scenarios and strategies.† The principal findings are exerpted briefly below.

According to the DOE-MITRE report, the en-

* The major importance of carbon dioxide to the formulation of energy policy is discussed in a recent report sent by four scientists to the Council on Environmental Quality (George M. Woodwell, Gordon J. MacDonald, Roger Revelle, and C. David Keeling, "The Carbon Dioxide Problem: Implications for Policy in the Management of Energy and Other Resources," Washington: Council on Environmental Quality, July 1979).
† There is wide variation in the extent to which environmental considerations have been included in major domestic and world energy studies. In the U.S., for example, the Federal Energy Administration's 1974 *Project Independence Report* included a brief 15-page environment assessment (Chapter 4), addressing a wide range of environmental impacts associated with six scenarios for $7 and $11 oil, but without much integration and synthesis. The 1974 report of the Ford Foundation's Energy Policy Project (*A Time to Choose*, by S. David Freeman et al., Ballinger, 1974) anticipated higher oil prices and included a reasonably thorough environmental assessment in its analysis of alternative energy policies (p. 179). The 1977 Congressional Research Service report *Project Interdependence* discussed briefly the environmental constraints associated with various possible energy sources. The National Academy of Science's *Implications of Environmental Regulations for Energy Production and Consumption* (1977) is very detailed on those environmental impacts now being regulated in the U.S.
*The National Energy Plan* (Executive Office of the President, 1977) integrates general environmental considerations at many points, but specifics are limited. The Department of Energy did not prepare an environmental impact statement for the plan, but an "environmental assessment statement" is expected to be released in 1979 (John Pearson, Energy Information Administration, personal communication, 1979). In May 1979, DOE submitted a revised National Energy Plan (NEP II) to Congress, containing an appendix, *Environmental Trends and Impacts,* that addresses the environmental consequences of the revised plan and its energy-pricing proposals, similar in scope to the DOE-MITRE report discussed in the text above.
Outside the U.S., there is also wide variation in the ways in which energy and environment are considered. The Secretariat for Future Studies in Sweden has produced two reports on energy that contain extensive and integrated consideration

## TABLE 13–37

## Comparison of the Hard Path Definition and the Energy Information Administration's Projection Series C

| Hard Path Definition | Projection Series |
|---|---|
| Twin goals: sustaining growth in energy consumption (assumed to be closely and causally linked to GNP and to social welfare) and | The Projection Series C scenario projects the following trends in macroeconomic and energy consumption: |
| minimizing oil imports | Increased petroleum imports. The costs of production and distribution for all energy sources except oil and gas were held constant by the Energy Information Administration. Changes in oil and gas costs, however, are induced through alternative assumptions regarding their physical availability. The Projection Series C case postulates a constant real price of imported oil of $15.32 per barrel in 1978 dollars. |
| Rapid expansion of the coal sector (mainly coal strip-mined and converted into electricity or synthetic fuels). | Coal production, particularly in the West, will increase dramatically, reflecting increased demand brought about by higher (post-1973) prices of oil and gas, particularly for electricity generation. Electricity sales will grow at 4.8 percent per year, rather than the historic 7 percent, reflecting saturation of air conditioning and major appliances that included high rates of penetration during the 1960s. This is consistent with the 5 percent growth from 1970 to 1976 and 4.2 percent from 1976 to 1977. |
| Rapid expansion of the oil and gas sectors (increasingly from arctic and offshore wells). | Increased oil imports. Domestic oil production will increase slightly over current levels because of the development of Alaskan oil fields and the outer continental shelf. Lower 48 production of natural gas will continue to decline, although less rapidly, after Alaskan North Slope gas distribution systems are completed. Fuel shares in the industrial economic sector indicate a shift from gas to oil and, to a lesser extent, to electricity, reflecting declining gas supplies. |
| Rapid expansion of the nuclear fission sector (especially in fast breeder reactors). | Large increases in nuclear power. |
| Limited or no use of solar and conservation technologies. | Solar technologies are not expected to contribute significantly to total energy supply through 1990. The key elements in supply-demand patterns through 1990 are assumptions about the degree of energy conservation in general and of oil and gas in particular, as a result of economic presssures and mandatory conservation measures introduced 1973. One example of such measures is the imposition of fuel efficiency standards for automobiles. |

|  | 1975 | 1985 | 1990 |
|---|---|---|---|
| GNP (*billions of 1972 dollars*) | 1,202 | 1,803 | 2,017 |
| Energy consumption (*quadrillion Btus*) | 70.6 | 94.6 | 108.5[a] |

Source: Hard path definition—Amory B. Lovins, *Soft Energy Paths: Toward a Durable Peace*, Cambridge. Mass.: Ballinger, 1977. p. 26. Projection Series C—Richard J. Kalagher et al., "National Environmental Impact Projection No. 1," McLean. Va.: MITRE Corp., Dec. 1978. pp. 1, 150.

[a] Compare the Department of Energy's projection for the Global 2000 Study, which has the U.S. consuming 100 quadrillion Btus in 1990 (Table 13–33).

of environmental impacts ("Energy and Society: Conceptual Outline Introducing a Futures Study," Dec. 1975; and Måans Lönnroth et al., *Energy in Transition: A Report on Energy Policy and Future Options*, Mar. 1977). The 1977 *World Energy Outlook: A Reassessment of Long-Term Energy Developments and Related Policies*, prepared for the Organization for Economic Cooperation and Development, does not explicitly consider the environmental dimension of energy prospects. The lengthy report of the Workshop on Energy Strategies (*Energy: Global Prospects 1985–2000*, McGraw-Hill, 1977) concludes its consideration of environment in less than two pages (p. 41). The global energy analysis work of the International Institute of Applied Systems Analysis is oriented primarily toward economic and resource considerations but does contain a limited environmental dimension (see, for example, W. Häfele, "Energy Options Open to Mankind Beyond the Turn of the Century," International Conference on Nuclear Power and Its Fuel Cycle, Schlossburg, Austria, May 1977; and Häfele and W. Sassin, "The Global Energy System," *Annual Review of Energy*, vol. 2, 1977).

The international environmental group Friends of the Earth has published books on world energy strategies (Amory B. Lovins, *World Energy Strategies: Facts, Issues and Options*, Ballinger, 1975) non-nuclear energy options (Lovins and John H. Price, *Non-Nuclear Futures: The Case for an Ethical Energy Strategy*, Ballinger, 1975), and soft energy paths (Lovins, *Soft Energy Paths: Toward a Durable Peace*, Ballinger 1977), all of which contain general but not highly detailed considerations of social, political, and physical environments. The Rockefeller Foundation sponsored *World Energy Survey* by Ruth Leger Sivard (World Priorities, Leesburg, Va., 1979) contains a brief environmental discussion. The various reports of the World Energy Conference (WEC) contain nothing on the environmental aspects of energy issues (Robert J. Raudebaugh, Executive Director of WEC's U.S. National Committee, personal communication, Feb. 15, 1979). The WEC, however, plans to include environmental considerations in two of the four major program divisions at its 1980 meeting (11th World Energy Conference, 1980, "Energy for Our World," Technical Program with Instructions for Authors, 1979).

vironmental implications of the Projection Series C hard path scenario are as follows:

- Little or no improvement is shown for sulfur oxide ($SO_x$) emissions. All improvements occur by 1985 when it is assumed that standards for existing sources will have been met. If $SO_x$ emissions are to be reduced by 1990, the retirement of old plants must be accelerated or the standards tightened.
- Large increases in nitrogen oxide ($NO_x$) emissions are anticipated. Throughout the forecast period, combustion activity (primarily by electric utilities) is responsible for the majority of $SO_x$ and $NO_x$ releases.
- Significant national reductions are expected by 1990 in the emissions of particulates, hydrocarbons, and carbon monoxide.
- Large increases in dissolved solids (especially sulfates, creating acid problems) are anticipated.
- Little or no improvement is shown for point-source nitrogen releases to water.
- Significant national reductions are expected by 1990 in point-source discharges of major water pollutants such as biochemical oxygen demand, suspended solids, total phosphorus, and numerous metals.
- Large increases in ash and scrubber sludge are anticipated.
- High-Btu gasification of coal is expected to produce major increases in cyanide releases in regions with gasification plants unless zero discharge regulations are imposed.
- Thermal discharges are not calculated, but large increases in water consumption for evaporative cooling are anticipated. Both utilities and other manufacturing industries contribute substantially to increased water consumption by 1990. The increasing role of nuclear-powered generation is a factor in this increase. Development of both energy and manufacturing activity may be seriously limited by existing or anticipated water shortages in several regions of the country.

The DOE-MITRE report does not address the following energy-related environmental considerations:

- Land losses to facilities development, uranium mining, and strip-mining are not calculated or discussed.
- Nuclear wastes and radiation from the nuclear fuel cycles are not calculated or discussed.
- Occupational safety and health issues are not addressed.

When the environmental trends are viewed at the regional and local levels, the picture reveals impacts that are otherwise masked by the national trends. Figure 13–14 summarizes the most significant energy-related regional impacts.

The DOE-MITRE report describes the environmental trends from the Projection Series C hard path scenario as "a middle ground of likely environmental futures" for the U.S. How typical might such impacts be for other industrial economies?

Serious as many of the DOE-MITRE environmental trends are, they may underestimate the impacts that would follow in many nations from a hard path energy policy. This is because the degree of environmental protection assumed in the DOE-MITRE report requires significant national commitments of capital, resources, and labor. The report notes that

Total pollution control costs (capital plus operating and maintenance expenditures) will increase at an annual rate of 3.1 percent between 1975 and 1990, but will decline relative to GNP.

Direct and indirect energy requirements for pollution control are projected to increase by 50 percent between 1975 and 1990, but will account for no more than 3.7 percent of total U.S. energy use in any one year. . . . The number of persons in 1990 that will be employed directly or indirectly in pollution control-related activities is estimated to be 1.8 million, or 1.6 percent of total U.S. employment.

It is not clear that all industrial nations (perhaps even including the U.S.) will be able or willing to commit as much of their capital, resources, and labor to environmental protection as is assumed in the DOE-MITRE report.

There are a number of variations of the hard path. The most significant differences among these variations concern the major sources of additional primary energy. Some variations involve a large growth in nuclear energy; others involve large increases in coal combustion. The environmental implications of these two variations are significantly different, and their economic advantages and disadvantages differ from region to region.

The primary argument for nuclear power in the U.S., for example, has been that it would produce cheaper electricity than alternative energy sources. Early advocates suggested that fission would produce electricity "too cheap to meter." Nuclear power has certainly no prospect of becoming too cheap to meter. As a result, the basic argument of its cost advantage over alternative sources has been questioned frequently with the charge that if all costs were properly accounted for, and sub-

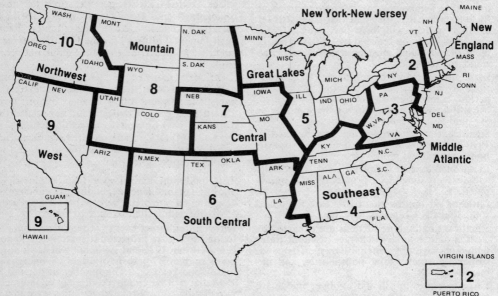

### Region 1

TDS discharges double due primarily to electric utilities. Slight increase in particulate emissions. Moderate increase in $SO_x$ emission due to conversion to coal.

### Region 2

Arsenic discharges double due to pharmaceuticals industry. Moderate increase in $SO_x$ emission due to conversion to coal. High amounts of sludge generated by 1990.

### Region 3

Sulfate discharges increase by 1/5 due to coal mining activities. Substantial decline in $SO_x$ and particulate emissions by 1990. High sludge and NCSW volumes from electric utilities and industrial boilers burning coal by 1990.

### Region 4

TDS releases triple due to electric utilities and chemical industry. Several non-ferrous metals and chlorides discharges double by 1990. High particulate emissions in 1975 with substantial decline by 1990. High sludge and NCSW volumes by 1990.

### Region 5

TDS discharges increase by 1/2 due to electric utilities and chemical industry. High sludge and NCSW volumes by 1990 due primarily to electric utilities and industrial boilers burning coal.

### Region 6

Projected increases in energy related water consumption by 1990 may face strong competition from other sources. TDS and chloride discharges more than double by 1990 due to organic chemicals industry. Cyanide releases increase by 1/2 due to high BTU coal gasification. Largest projected increase in $SO_x$ emissions. Regional increases in $SO_x$ from new coal burning electric utilities and industrial boilers.

### Region 7

Large portion of national cyanide discharges in 1990 due to high BTU coal gasification. Regional increases in $SO_x$ due to new coal combustion. Increases in sludge and NCSW generation due to new coal burning facilities.

### Region 8

Projected increases in energy related water consumption may face strong competition from other uses. Cyanide releases more than double due to high BTU coal gasification. Substantial sulfate releases from coal mining and electric utilities activities. Large increases in NCSW generation by 1990 due to oil shale activities.

### Region 9

Large increases in NCSW volumes by 1990 primarily in California. $SO_x$ emissions decline.

### Region 10

TDS discharges double due to electric utilities. Potassium releases doubles due to smelting.

**Figure 13–14.** Major regional trends associated with the DOE-MITRE Projection Series C (Hard Path) Energy Development Scenario. In the regional analyses, TDS stands for total dissolved solids; NCSW stands for noncombustible solid wastes. (*National Environmental Impact Project No. 1, MITRE Corp., Dec. 1978*)

sidies stripped away, nuclear power would not be competitive with alternative energy sources.[575] The Ford Foundation's nuclear energy policy study group addressed this question and concluded in 1977, before the Three Mile Island nuclear reactor accident in Pennsylvania, that in the United States nuclear energy based on uranium, but not plutonium, is somewhat less costly than coal, but that in much of the country "the choice is so close and the uncertainties sufficiently large that the balance could easily shift either to increase or eliminate the small average advantage that nuclear power presently enjoys."[576]

For Japan and Western Europe, the Ford study concludes that

a shift to heavy reliance on coal would require increasing dependence on imports from the United States and Eastern Europe. The political acceptability of such dependence is not clear. There is also a question as to how large a foreign market [for coal the United States] could supply and still meet its own growing domestic demand. For these reasons, a greater preference for nuclear power should be expected in these countries than in the United States.[577]

For the LDCs, the Ford study concludes that the demand for nuclear power is "very uncertain":

Nuclear power may be competitive in some twenty developing countries by the year 2000, and others may install it for noneconomic reasons. As a practical matter, the large, 1,000 MWe nuclear power plants now being built [by commercial manufacturers] to achieve economies of scale are not matched to the small power grids of most developing countries. More suitable, smaller plants (less than 600 MWe) would have significantly higher capital cost per kilowatt and, in the absence of demand, are no longer being built. For these reasons, nuclear power may be ruled out as an economic energy option for many developing nations.[578]

In the U.S. and many other countries, decisions on major electric power facilities are made by utility executives based on costs to the utilities (after government subsidy) rather than on costs to the nation as a whole. The costs of decommissioning old plants and disposing of nuclear wastes are minimized because of the uncertainty of those costs. Recent accidents—such as occurred at Three Mile Island in Pennsylvania[579] have raised interest rates, and underwriters point to the possible need for further costly regulations, designs, and plant shutdowns.[580] As a result, the costs of nuclear power—including those costs perceived

by utilities and banks—may become increasingly comparable with coal.*

While there are many factors beyond purely economic ones involved in the choice of national energy policy beyond the purely economy factors. Nonetheless, a number of recent decisions seem to support the conclusions of the Ford study. In the U.S., the states of California and Montana have limited the construction of new nuclear facilities until the federal government will have demonstrated a capacity to safely dispose of the nuclear wastes.[581] Sites for nuclear plants and disposal areas continue to present a problem; only the states of Washington, New Mexico, and Nevada are still sympathetic to locating new waste disposal sites within their boundaries.[582] The governors of the only three states now willing to accept even low-level nuclear wastes recently wrote to the Nuclear Regulatory Commission and the Department of Transportation demanding tightened enforcement of safety rules on the shipment of nuclear wastes if their states are to continue receiving radioactive materials. The Governor of South Carolina cut off shipments from the damaged reactor at Three Mile Island.[583] In Europe, antinuclear sentiments significantly contributed to a change of government in Sweden,[584] and voters elected to terminate work on a nearly complete nuclear plant in Austria in 1978.[585] In the Federal Republic of Germany, the construction of a nuclear reprocessing plant considered essential to Germany's energy program for the next two decades was recently "postponed indefinitely."[586] European expectations for nuclear energy can be seen in the history of OECD projections for 1985 nuclear-generating capacities shown in Figure 13–15. It seems likely, therefore, that at least until 2000, the hard path option will include some nuclear power (primarily existing plants) but will emphasize coal.

### The Soft Path

There are many ideas about the technologies most appropriate to a soft path future. These technologies were originally defined in terms of five characteristics:

---

*The costs of the Three Mile Island accident are now thought to be higher than the first estimates. Repairing the damaged reactor (unit 2) will cost not $140 million, but $240–320 million; in addition, the cost of replacing the reactor core is estimated at $60–85 million; the utility will not be permitted to restart the undamaged reactor (unit 1) for 18 months to 2 years, leading to costs—over and above those directly attributable to the accident—of $14 million per month. ("Costs Still Climbing at Three Mile Island," *Science,* Aug. 3, 1979, p. 475)

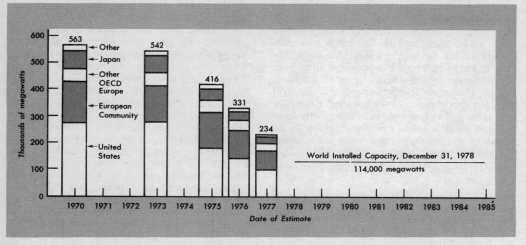

**Figure 13-15.** OECD countries' projections of 1985 nuclear generating capacity for the world, by dates of estimates. (*From "Nuclear Energy," Central Intelligence Agency, Aug. 1977, p. 39; world installed capacity data from U.S. Department of Energy, Energy Information Administration.*)

1. They rely on renewable energy flows that are always there whether we use them or not, such as sun and wind and vegetation: on energy income, not on depletable energy capital.
2. They are diverse, so that as a national treasury .runs on many small tax contributions, so national energy supply is an aggregate of very many individually modest contributions, each designed for maximum effectiveness in particular circumstances.
3. They are flexible and relatively low technology—which does not mean unsophisticated, but rather, easy to understand and use without esoteric skills, accessible rather than arcane.
4. They are matched in scale and in geographic distribution to end-use needs, taking advantage of the free distribution of most natural energy flows.
5. They are matched in *energy quality* to end-use needs [thus increasing the productivity of the primary energy used].[587]

The number of national soft path and low-energy studies from around the world has increased rapidly in the last few years. Several of these studies for some of the nations having energy-intensive economies are discussed in the following pages.*

*The Solar Sweden Study.* One of the most thorough national soft path studies now available is

*Readers interested in a more complete inventory and continuing reporting of national soft-path studies are referred to the journal *Soft Energy Notes* (San Francisco, Friends of the Earth).

the *Solar Sweden* report produced by the Secretariat for Future Studies in Stockholm.[588] This report addresses the feasibility of basing the Swedish energy supply *completely* on solar energy (solar radiation, hydro power, wind power, and wave power) in the not too distant future. (Complete dependence on solar energy would be difficult for Sweden since it is quite far north and receives only about 40 percent of the solar energy per unit area that is received by countries in North Africa.) While the report does not advocate that Sweden turn solely to solar energy, the report concludes that *by 2015 Sweden could shift entirely to solar energy without prohibitive costs and without major changes in life styles.*

The *Solar Sweden* analysis is based on a number of assumptions. The goods and services produced are assumed to double relative to 1975. The efficiency with which energy is used to produce the goods and services is assumed to increase as illustrated in Table 13–38. Care is taken to match the quality of an energy source with the quality required for particular end uses, as described in Table 13–39. The quality of the energy delivered remains essentially unchanged. The resulting energy system is illustrated in Figure 13–16. The final value for energy use in 2015 is not quite 500 $\times$ $10^{12}$ watt hours (WH), compared with 390 $\times$ $10^{12}$ WH in 1975. (The corresponding figures in quads are 1.7 and 1.3, respectively.)

The *Solar Sweden* energy system is very diversified. Production and use of biomass dominates and includes energy plantations on land and in

## TABLE 13–38

*Solar Sweden* Assumed Production of Goods and Services and Specific Energy Use, 1975 and 2015

| | Energy | | Goods and Services Produced in 2015 Relative to 1975 | |
|---|---|---|---|---|
| | 1975 | 2015 | Production | Specific Energy Need[a] |
| | *TWH*[b] | | *Percent* | |
| Production of goods | 165 | 264 | +100 | −20 |
| Production of services | | | | |
|   Transport | 75 | 75 | +100 | −50 |
|   Other | 70[c] | 70[d] | +100 | −50 |
| Housing, including domestic electricity | 80 | 80 | +40 | −30 |
| Total end use | 390 | 489 | | |
| Conversion losses | 25[e] | 79[f] | | |
| Total supply | 415 | 568 | | |

Source: Thomas B. Johansson and Peter Steen. *Solar Sweden*, Stockholm: Secretariat for Futures Studies, 1978. p. 26.

[a] Energy required to produce a unit of goods or services.
[b] 1 TWH = $10^{12}$ watt hours = $3.41 \times 10^{-3}$ quads.
[c] Of which space heating is approximately 40 TWH.
[d] Of which space heating is approximately 31 TWH.
[e] Losses in electricity distribution and refineries.
[f] Losses occur mainly in domestic methanol production.

the sea and the use of straw, reeds, and logging waste. Solar heating is used for space heating together with district heating based on plants fueled with biomass for combined generation of electricity and heat. The electricity sector becomes relatively large and the proportion of electricity larger than today. Electricity is produced from hydro power, wind power, and solar cells and in fuel cells and plants for combined generation. By making the latter into relatively small units, they can be located to minimize energy waste, e.g., by using the waste heat for space heating. Methanol, from biomass, is introduced into the transport sector.

In making its economic calculations, the *Solar Sweden* report assumes that the costs for the renewable energy system are and remain those that can be foreseen for the 1980s. The calculations show that building up such a system is compatible with the assumed doubling of the production of goods and services, implying an increase of approximately 2 percent annually. Of this annual increase approximately one-eighth goes to the new energy system, and the remaining seven-eighths are necessary to increase the production of goods and services. Thus, the report concludes, a renewable energy system does not demand a lower standard of living, but merely requires that part of the increase in goods and services is utilized to create such a system.

In discussing the advantage of a solar Sweden, the report notes that the energy system it sketches is domestic, and that as a result, uncertainties concerning the possibilities of importing various energy raw materials do not exist. Balance of payment is not to any large extent influenced. The use of many different dispersed energy sources makes the system relatively invulnerable. The system is preferable from the environmental point of view because it limits emissions and does not increase the risk of catastrophic occurrences.

But the environmental implications of the solar Sweden energy system are not completely beneficial. The report notes that the demand on land

## TABLE 13–39

*Solar Sweden* Percent Distribution of Energy, by Energy-Quality Categories A–I, 1971 and 2015[a]

| | 1971 | | | 2015 | | |
|---|---|---|---|---|---|---|
| | Industry | Transport | Other | Industry | Transport | Other |
| A Lighting, small motors | 2 | | 15 | 5 | | 40 |
| B Electricity for chemical processes | 3 | | | 3 | | |
| C Stationary motors | 15 | | | 17 | | |
| D Transports | 3 | 100 | | 2 | 100 | |
| E Process heat (> 1000°C) | 22 | | | 23 | | |
| F Process heat (500–1000°C) | 9 | | | 9 | | |
| G Process heat (100–500°C) | 26 | | | 26 | | |
| H Process heat (< 100°C) | 9 | | | 9 | | |
| I Low temperature heat (space heating) | 11 | | 85 | 6 | | 60 |
| Total | 100 | 100 | 100 | 100 | 100 | 100 |
| Percent of total energy use | 41 | 17 | 42 | 54 | 15 | 31 |

Source: Thomas B. Johansson and Peter Steen. *Solar Sweden*, Stockholm: Secretariat for Futures Studies, 1978. p. 26.

[a] The quality classification A–I are not strictly thermodynamic but are user oriented.

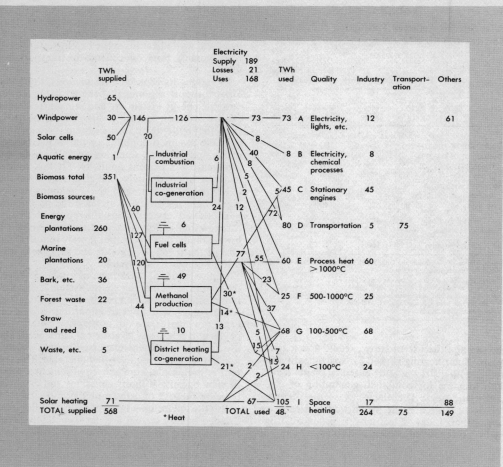

**Figure 13-16.** The Solar Sweden energy system for the year 2015. The supply from renewable sources and the amounts from each are given on the left. The end use of energy is divided into energy quality categories A through I on the right. The linkage between supply and use is shown in the center of the figure. Numbers indicate the energy (in TWh=10¹² watt-hours) represented by each line. (From "Solar Sweden," Stockholm, 1978, p. 32)

is great because of the low intensity of solar radiation in Sweden. It is estimated that approximately 3 million hectares would be needed, mainly for energy plantations. As now conceived, the plantations would need to be heavily fertilized, particularly with nitrogen. Methods of controlling damage from game animals, rodents, fungi, and insects would also be needed. The environmental problems of managing large-scale energy plantations—and ecologically acceptable management techniques—are discussed in two related Swedish reports.[589]

Finally, the *Solar Sweden* report acknowledges conflicts of interest concerning the 3 million hectares that would be needed for energy plantations. The other sectors most interested in utilizing the same areas would probably be the forest industry and recreation. The forest industry in Sweden currently uses approximately 23 million hectares. Wind power, etc., might meet with resistance from those who own recreational houses near the plants. Therefore, an important question is how Swedish society should balance the interests of forest industry, recreation, and energy production in the future. The report concludes that these interests can be balanced and conflicts resolved with farsighted planning.[590]

*Soft Energy Studies in Canada.* Canada has also given thought to soft energy scenarios for its future[591] and has examined the possibilities for energy plantations. The Canadian Ministry of Energy, Mines, and Resources, in its *Tree Power* report,[592] assessed the energy potential of forest biomass in Canada for three technologies: (1) direct electricity generation or cogeneration, (2) conversion to methanol, and (3) low Btu gasification. Costs were established, where possible. The Canadian forest resources are large, and the report notes that data on the extent of Canadian forest resources are "severely lacking." Using various estimates of the resource, the report estimates that the total annual productivity of the forest is about $400 \times 10^6$ ODt (oven-dried metric tons), equivalent in energy to $8 \times 10^{18}$ joules. The present Canadian wood harvest of $51 \times 10^6$ ODt for all purposes has an energy content of about $1 \times 10^{18}$ joules. The report concludes:

The medium term to 1990 will realize more forest energy but will require changes in harvesting technology and forest management practice as well as development of conversion and end use technologies.

Over the longer term to 2025, the extensive forest and energy plantations could provide a large fraction of the carbon based fuel requirements. However a development program including extensive environmental assessment of the impacts of such large scale use will be needed. For example, the effect of collecting forest residue in the medium term and of plantations in the longer term could be to strip the soil of nutrients.[593]

*U.S. Studies.* In the U.S., the Department of Energy has indicated its interest* in consideration

---

*The DOE interest in what it terms "small-scale, appropriately distributed technology" was expressed most clearly at a public briefing on January 26, 1978, in Washington. The official transcript of this briefing (published as *DOE Role in Support of Small-Scale Appropriately Distributed Technology*, DOE Office of Consumer Affairs, Aug. 1978) is available from the National Technical Information Service. The specific programmatic efforts reported in the briefing are summarized in Table 13–4.

†As of August 1978, it was established that the Standing Committee would be chaired by the Assistant Secretary for Conservation and Solar Applications, and that the Committee would have representatives from the DOE Offices of Energy Technology, Energy Research, Environment, and Policy and Evaluation (p. 144 of the briefing cited in the previous note). As of this writing (March 1979), no Committee members had been appointed, and the Committee's purpose had not been resolved.

of soft path options by establishing a Standing Committee on Soft Technology under the R&D Coordinating Council† and by initiating a small-grants program for several studies. These studies are listed and described briefly in Table 13–40.

The DOE-sponsored California Distributed Energy Study[594] is probably the most detailed and thorough soft path analysis now available. The study analyzes hypothetical future energy systems for the State of California in the year 2025. Assuming a doubling of population, a tripling of total economic activity, and a quadrupling of energy prices by 2025, the study reaches four important conclusions for the State:

1. It is possible to achieve a balance between energy demand and energy supply only through strict attention to conservation for buildings, improved efficiencies of end-use appliances, and improved efficiencies in industry.[595]
2. It is possible, in purely technical terms, to come quite close to operating the postulated advanced, post-industrial society in California using indigenous, sustainable resources.[596]
3. The environmental impacts of certain "soft" technologies—notably increased end-use efficiency, active and passive solar heating and cooling with individual building or neighborhood units, fuel production from biomass in the form of wastes, and dispersed on-site wind generators—will prove markedly smaller than those of virtually all of the traditional "hard" technologies, as well as smaller than those of the more centralized technologies for harvesting renewables.[597]
4. To achieve a distributed [soft] energy outcome which is approximately that described [in the California study] by a time close to 2025 requires that implementation begin almost at once.[598]

While the California Distributed Energy Study is the only detailed soft path study now available, a number of studies have examined aspects of a soft path for the whole of the U.S. The findings and conclusions of approximately 40 related studies have been drawn together by the Council on Environmental Quality (CEQ) in a recent report that compares the hard and soft paths for the United States.[599] Some of the major findings reported by CEQ are as follows:

- There is now clear evidence that the United States can maintain a healthy economy without the massive increases in primary energy called for under the hard path.
- Recent macroeconomic analyses indicate that there is a more loose and flexible linkage be-

## TABLE 13-40

## U.S. Department of Energy Studies Underway as of August 1978 to Examine "Soft Path" Options

| Subject or Title | Responsible DOE Office | Budget | Description |
|---|---|---|---|
| Small-Grants Program | Conservation and Solar | $3 million (FY 78) $8 million (FY 79) | This program provides small grants (up to $50,000) for conservation and solar efforts. The $3 million pilot program started in Region 9 and was heavily over subscribed. Approximately 1,100 grant requests were received; approximately 100 were funded. The budget has now been increased to $8 million for all 10 federal regions. A preliminary report on the effectiveness of the grants has been prepared.[a] |
| Appropriate Technology Characterization | Policy and Evaluation | $250,000 | Contract to Arthur D. Little, Inc., Cambridge, Mass., for an engineering notebook describing the technical and economic aspects of "appropriate," "soft," and "transitional" technologies. A draft has been circulated for review at DOE, but as of March 1979, the report was not publicly available.[b] |
| "California Case Study: Decentralized Energy Systems" | Policy and Evaluation | $700,000 | This study, conducted jointly by the Lawrence Berkeley Laboratory and the Lawrence Livermore Laboratory, is probably the most thorough and detailed examination of a "soft path" option for a specfic region—California. The DOE preface to the study indicates that it was undertaken largely as a response to "Energy Strategy: The Road Not Taken," by Amory B. Lovins (Foreign Affairs, Oct. 1976). Two reports and many supporting documents have been produced.[c] Further work on this topic has been proposed by the two laboratories involved, but DOE, as of March 1979, was not willing to fund additional work. |
| "Any Town USA" | Policy and Evaluation | $240,000 | SRI International was to provide a study on how a "typical" American town might look under a soft path solar future. The study was completed in 1977 but was never published or publicly released by DOE. A limited number of copies of the report are available directly from SRI International.[d] |
| Energy Futures: Solar and Nuclear Alternatives | Policy and Evaluation | $500,000 | This study at the Institute for Energy Analysis, Oak Ridge Associated Universities, has two objectives: (1) to project the contribution that solar energy might make by the year 2020; (2) to investigate how far nuclear development could continue if all additional reactors were located on sites where nuclear reactors are already located or under construction. DOE representatives report that the contractor was unable to develop the solar portion of the study to any extent; the contractor reports that DOE lost interest in the solar portion of the study. In any event, as of March 1979, a nuclear report was available, but the solar report was incomplete.[e] |
| Overview of Soft Energy Paths and Decentralized Energy Systems in the United States | Environment | Not applicable | This subject was ultimately subsumed under "Alternative Energy Futures" below. |
| Development of Community Level Technology Assessments | Energy Technology | $500,000 (FY 78) $250,000 (FY 79) | As a part of a longer study, contractors were to work with local communities to develop "self-assessments of solar futures." As of March 1979, one contractor had started work, and Requests for Proposals (RFPs) are pending. No report was publicly available at that time, but one report prepared under the program may be obtained from another source.[f] |
| Alternatives Energy Futures | Environment | $179,000 | This work was contracted to the Argone National Laboratories and in turn subcontracted to the Center for Energy Studies in the Department of Industrial Engineering. The work was done by faculty and students as a part of Industrial Engineering Course 235 at Stanford University. As of March 1979, no report was publicly available from DOE, but a report was expected to be available from Stanford.[g] |

## TABLE 13–40 (cont.)

| Subject or Title | Responsible DOE Office | Budget | Description |
|---|---|---|---|
| Less Developed Countries | International Affairs | $1,600,000 | This joint DOE/State Department program of cooperative assistance to selected developing countries is intended to provide a complete and objective energy assessment, including all the basic data and information needed for the development of an energy plan for the country being analyzed. A wide range of energy options—both nuclear and nonnuclear—are considered with emphasis given to employing indigenous resources. An assessment of Egyptian energy options is now complete and has been very well received by Egypt and international development and lending institutions.[h] A report on Peru is in progress, and five other reports are being considered. |

*Source:* U.S. Department of Energy, Office of Consumer Affairs, *DOE Role in Support of Small-Scale Appropriately Distributed Technology,* Official Transcript of Public Briefing and Addendum on Jan. 26, 1978. CONF–780132, Washington: National Technical Information Service. Aug. 1978. p. 144. Budgets and descriptions of studies are based on information provided by the responsible DOE offices and DOE contractors.

[a] DOE San Francisco Operations Office, Appropriate Energy Technology Program, *Summary of Projects: Appropriate Energy Technology, Pilot Regional Program,* 1978 (available from Appropriate Energy Technology, DOE, 1333 Broadway, Oakland, Calif. 94612); DOE Div. of Buildings and Community Systems, Assistant Secretary for Conservation and Solar Applications, "Appropriate Technology: A Fact Sheet," Washington, 1977; "Report to Congress on Appropriate Technology Pilot Regional Program," undated, unpublished (available from, Jerry D. Duane, DOE, Office of the Assistant Secretary for Conservation and Solar Applications).
[b] Edward Blum, DOE, Office of the Assistant Secretary for Policy and Evaluation, personal communication, Mar. 1979.
[c] Paul P. Craig and M. D. Levine, "Distributed Energy Systems in California's Future: Issues in Transition," Lawrence Berkeley Laboratory, Jan. 16, 1979 (draft).
[d] John Reuyl et al., *Solar Energy in America's Future: A Preliminary Assessment,* Menlo Park, Calif.: SRI International, Mar. 1977.

[e] The nuclear report is M. J. Ohanian et al., *Feasibility of a Nuclear Citing Policy Based on Existing Cites,* Oak Ridge: Institute for Energy Analysis, Nov. 1979. As of May 1979, the Institute was still planning seven topical reports on solar energy: two were final, three were being revised following review, one was under a new review, one was still being written. The final reports are as follows: R. W. Gilmer and R. E. Meunier, "Electric Utilities and Solar Energy: The Service Contract in a New Social Context," Oak Ridge Associated Universities, Apr. 1979; final reports being revised at Oak Ridge Associated Universities are (with dates of draft): R. W. Gilmer "The Social Control of Energy: A Case for the Promise of Decentralized Solar Technologies," Apr. 2, 1979; W. D. Devine, Jr., "Energy Accounting for Solar and Alternative Energy Sources," Jan. 1979; D. B. Reister and W. D. Devine, Jr., "Total Costs of Energy Services," Mar. 1979. The following draft is being reviewed: D. A. Boyd, "The Stochastic Sun: Identifying the Recoverable Resource," Mar. 1979.
[f] C. T. Donovan et al., *Energy Self-Sufficiency in Northampton, Massachusetts,* Jan. 3, 1979 (available from A. S. Krass, School of Natural Science, Hampshire College, Amherst, Mass. 01002).
[g] Grant Ireson et al., *Alternative Energy Futures: An Assessment of Options for U.S. Society to 2025,* Institute for Energy Studies, Stanford University, forthcoming, 1979.
[h] DOE Developing Countries Energy Program, *Egypt-United States Cooperative Energy Assessment,* Washington, 1978. 5 vols.

tween energy use and the economy than previously thought.

- These studies generally conclude that low energy growth is not only consistent with continued economic expansion and a high standard of living but can also have a positive effect on employment and can provide an important weapon in the fight against inflation.
- Much of the energy saved by a departure from the hard path would be realized in the form of reduced imports of oil and natural gas for which Americans pay a high price both economically and in terms of national security. Improvements in U.S. balance of payments can be anticipated principally due to reduced dollar outflows for direct purchases of foreign fuels.

The CEQ conclusion, in short, is that the United States can do well, indeed prosper, on much less energy than has been commonly supposed.

But what about the environmental impacts of a departure from the hard path? The CEQ report also provides one of the more complete national comparison now available of scenarios related to

the hard and soft path environmental impacts. This comparison is made on the basis of two energy supply futures[600] (see Table 13–41).* Future I, with a total demand of 85 quads (1 quad = $10^{15}$ Btu) reflects a strong, sustained commitment to conservation (higher energy productivity) and the use of renewable energy sources. In Future II, energy demand grows by 1.9 percent per year reaching 120 quads by 2000.

The CEQ report compares the environmental impact of these two energy futures as follows:

The most important difference in energy supply between the two futures described above arise from the need to place great emphasis on coal and nuclear in Future II. In the high-growth future these two sources collectively supply 2.1 times as much energy (an additional 34 quads) in the year 2000 as they would in the low-energy future. Although it is not feasible to describe completely

*The CEQ report is not a true comparison of hard and soft paths for the U.S. because both of the energy supply futures contains the same solar component (19 quads). For a true hard/soft comparison for the U.S., it would be necessary to replace the 19 quads of solar in Future II with an additional 19 quads of coal or nuclear.

## TABLE 13–41

**Energy Supply in 1977 and Two Supply Scenarios for the Year 2000**

*Quads (10¹⁵ Btu) of Primary Fuels*

|              | 1975 | 2000 Future I | 2000 Future II |
|--------------|------|---------------|----------------|
| Oil and gas  | 56.5 | 40            | 46             |
| Solar*       | 4.2  | 19            | 19             |
| Nuclear      | 2.7  | 8             | 18             |
| Coal         | 14.1 | 18            | 37             |
| Total        | 77.5 | 85            | 120            |

*Source*: Council on Environmental Quality. *The Good News About Energy*. Washington: Government Printing Office. 1979. p. 20.

ª The solar category includes all renewable energy sources. The 4.2 quads includes 1.8 quads from biomass, which is usually not included in national energy statistics.

the details of these two futures, specific, important environmental impacts related to the additional use of coal and nuclear energy in Future II have been estimated and presented in Table [13–42]. . . . Although the total impacts of all these trends is highly uncertain, it is nonetheless clear that a national—indeed, global—policy emphasizing energy conservation [(i.e., increased productivity in the energy sector) and benign sources] will allow the world more flexibility and time to maneuver in the event of incipient, adverse developments.[602]

*Low Energy Study for Denmark.* Domestic nonrenewable energy sources are limited in Denmark. In the face of rapidly rising energy costs, the country has been considering a variety of options for reducing its needs for foreign oil. Much of the energy analysis in Denmark has assumed that little departure from traditional energy growth rates could be accomplished without serious economic implications. A 1976 study, sponsored jointly by the Niels Bohr Institute and the International Federation of Institutes for Advanced Study,[603] found much more flexibility in the GNP-energy relationship than had been assumed in the past.

The Danish study examines the economic consequences of two scenarios out to 2005. One scenario assumes a continuation of the traditional growth in energy use (3–5 per cent per year); the other assumes a reduced growth (under 1.5 per cent per year). In the traditional-growth scenario, energy is used more or less traditionally. In the reduced-growth scenario, major efforts are made to increase the thermodynamic efficiency with which the energy is used.

The study found that over a 15-year period Denmark could make major reductions in its en-

ergy requirements without harm to general economic development. The energy savings for the two cases are illustrated in Figures 13–17 and 13–18. Overall, the study concluded that the reduced energy growth, while requiring somewhat larger investments over the next 15 years, produced a

## TABLE 13–42

**Relative Environmental Impacts of Low- and High-Energy Growth Futures**

|  | 1977 | 2000 Future I | 2000 Future II |
|--|------|---------------|----------------|
| Coal production (*millions of tons/year*)ª | 613 | 782 | 1,609 |
| Cumulative coal mined, 1977–2000 (*millions of tons*)ᵇ | — | 16,000 | 25,500 |
| Cumulative area strip-mined, 1977–2000 (*square miles*)ᶜ | — | 1,200ˡ | 2,000ᵐ |
| Cumulative area affected by subsidence (*square miles*)ᵈ | — | 1,400–3,300ⁿ | 2,300–5,300º |
| Number of coal power plants (*nominal 1,100 MW*)ᵉ | 200 | 243 | 500 |
| Number of nuclear power plants (*nominal, 1,100 MW*)ᶠ | 43 | 135 | 304 |
| Area required for transmission lines for new coal and nuclear plants (*square miles*)ᵍ | — | 3,900 | 16,500 |
| Radioactive tailings to supply uranium for 1977–2000 (*million tons*)ʰ | — | 400 | 800 |
| Volume of low-level radioactive wastes generated, 1977–2000 (*millions of cubic feet*)ⁱ | — | 34 | 66 |
| Spent fuel generated, 1977–2000 (*thousands of tons*)ʲ | — | 61 | 120 |
| Total spent fuel generated over lifetimes of plants constructed through the year 2000 (*thousands of tons*)ᵏ | — | 121 | 274 |

*Source:* Council on Environmental Quality. *The Good News About Energy*. Washington: Government Printing Office. 1979. pp. 23–24.

ª Nominal tons at 23 million Btu each.

ᵇ Assuming linear growth in production.

ᶜ Assuming (1) one-fialf of coal is mined in the West, one-half in the Midwest and East; and (2) all of Western coal and one-half of rest is strip-mined. Area disturbed: 50 acres per million tons in the West and 100 acres elsewhere. See *Energy/Environment Fact Book*, DOE/EPA, Dec. 1977, p. 60.

ᵈ Assuming 230 to 529 acres affected per ton of coal mined, depending on mining techniques. See *Energy Alternatives: A Comparative Analysis*, University of Oklahoma, Science and Public Policy Program, May 1975, pp. 1–56.

ᵉ Assumes 70 percent of coal will continue to be used by electric utilities, capacity factors will average 55 percent and individual plant efficiencies 35 percent.

ᶠ Assumes capacity factors of 60 percent and average efficiencies of 33 percent.

ᵍ Based on an average value of 17,188 acres per gigawatt of capacity. See *Energy and the Environment: Electric Power*, CEQ, Aug. 1973, p. 42, note 8.

ʰ Assuming 0.1 percent uranium ore, 0.25 percent tailings assay, and annual loading of 30 tons of fuel per reactor per year.

ⁱ *Based on an annual volume of 16,500 cubic feet per plant-year. See "Report to the President by the Interagency Review Group on Nuclear Waste Management," Oct. 1978, p. D–6 (draft).*

ʲ *Assuming 30 tons discharged per reactor per year.*

ᵏ *Assuming 30 tons discharged per reactor per year and 30-year plant lifetimes.*

ˡ *3,108 sq km.*

ᵐ *5,180 sq km.*

ⁿ *3,626–8,547 sq km.*

º *5,957–13,727 sq km.*

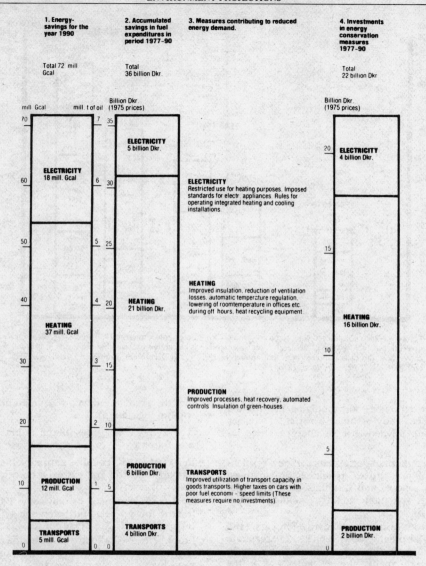

1. Energy-savings for the year 1990

Total 72 mill Gcal

mill Gcal    mill. t of oil

| | |
|---|---|
| 70 | 7 |
| | |
| ELECTRICITY 18 mill. Gcal | |
| 60 | 6 |
| | |
| 50 | 5 |
| | |
| HEATING 37 mill. Gcal | 4 |
| 40 | |
| | |
| 30 | 3 |
| | |
| 20 | 2 |
| | |
| PRODUCTION 12 mill. Gcal | 1 |
| 10 | |
| TRANSPORTS 5 mill. Gcal | |
| 0 | 0 |

2. Accumulated savings in fuel expenditures in period 1977–90

Total 36 billion Dkr.

Billion Dkr. (1975 prices)

| |
|---|
| 35 |
| ELECTRICITY 5 billion Dkr. |
| 30 |
| 25 |
| HEATING 21 billion Dkr. |
| 20 |
| 15 |
| 10 |
| PRODUCTION 6 billion Dkr. |
| 5 |
| TRANSPORTS 4 billion Dkr. |
| 0 |

3. Measures contributing to reduced energy demand.

**ELECTRICITY**
Restricted use for heating purposes. Imposed standards for electr. appliances. Rules for operating integrated heating and cooling installations.

**HEATING**
Improved insulation, reduction of ventilation losses. automatic temperature regulation. lowering of roomtemperature in offices etc. during off hours, heat recycling equipment.

**PRODUCTION**
Improved processes, heat recovery, automated controls Insulation of green-houses.

**TRANSPORTS**
Improved utilization of transport capacity in goods transports. Higher taxes on cars with poor fuel economi - speed limits (These measures require no investments).

4. Investments in energy conservation measures 1977–90

Total 22 billion Dkr

Billion Dkr. (1975 prices)

| |
|---|
| 20  ELECTRICITY 4 billion Dkr. |
| 15 |
| HEATING 16 billion Dkr. |
| 10 |
| 5 |
| PRODUCTION 2 billion Dkr. |
| 0 |

**Figure 13–17.**  Survey of energy savings in Denmark, 1977–90; "mill Gcal" = millions of gigacalories = $10^{15}$ calories; Dkr = Danish kroner. (*Sven Bjørnholm,* Energy in Denmark, 1990 and 2005, *Neils Bohr Institute, 1976, p. 34*)

considerable overall advantage to the economy— also to the reliability of Danish energy supplies and to the environment.

*Low-Energy Study for the United Kingdom.* In London, the International Institute for Environment and Development has studied the potential for energy conservation in the U.K. [604] The Institute's study uses the official U.K. Department of Energy estimates of GNP growth* and examines

* For the next 10–15 years GNP is assumed to grow as fast as, or faster than during the 1960s. By 2025 GNP roughly doubles in one case; it trebles in another.

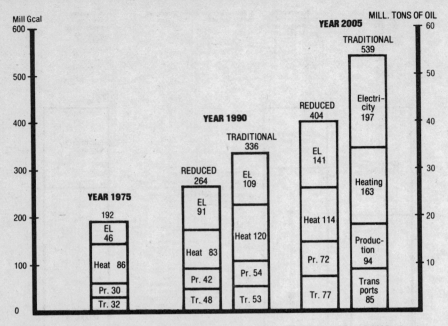

**Figure 13–18.**   Traditional and reduced demand for energy in Denmark, 1990 and 2005, showing quantities of fuel by type of demand. Fuel consumption is calculated by assuming the losses in the fuel conversion and distribution system that applied in 1975. (*Sven Björnholm*, Energy in Denmark, 1990 and 2005, *Neils Bohr Institute, 1976, p. 35*)

alternative strategies for supplying the needed energy. The study assumes a series of policies encouraging efficient use of energy. These include:

- Improved thermal performance of new residential dwellings, offices, public-sector buildings, such as schools and hospitals, and industrial buildings (by tightening the building regulations);
- Energy performance standards for cars (and possibly also light-goods vehicles) to accelerate and ensure the timely implementation of technical developments already under way in the motor industry;
- Energy performance standards for major household electrical goods and cooking stoves to ensure the introduction of relatively simple, low cost improvements (such as better insulation) and similar standards for lighting;
- Possible legislation to reduce the use of oil in heating homes, offices, and public-sector buildings, as well as in industrialized boilers ("possible legislation," because the authors believe

that the gradual reduction assumed may occur without legislation).

The study's conclusions (in the authors' words) are as follows:

- In 2000 the U.K. could be entirely self-sufficient on North Sea oil and gas even on central estimates of reserves.
- Coal production need be only some 120 million [metric tons] a year, far below the 170 million target in the [U.K.] "Plan for Coal."
- From 1976–2000 we have assumed the construction of only 4.5–6.5 GW [gigawatts] of nuclear capacity, or three to five average-sized stations, compared to 30 GW in the current Department of Energy reference forecast. If more were built there would be such a surplus of generating capacity that a choice would have to be made between leaving nuclear stations idle and reducing coal production to uncomfortable low levels.
- Over the same period, only 26–30 GW of generating capacity of all kinds need be built (most of it replacing existing plant) compared to 83 GW in the Energy Department's reference fore-

cast. The saving in capital investment would be around £26–30,000 million for the plant alone, or well over £1,000 million a year. We would be most surprised if this did not greatly exceed the costs of all the energy conservation measures we have assumed for all sectors and fuels.

- After 2000 the only significant fuel shortfalls are in North Sea oil, taking the central estimate of reserves. This "gap" reaches an annual 36–47 million [metric tons] of oil by 2025 in the Low and High cases respectively, or roughly half recent levels of oil imports. It could be filled from several sources, either from the large quantities of crude oil that should even then be flowing in world trade or by the import of liquid fuels made from crops grown in the tropical belts. . . .

- Coal production need be only 128–148 million [metric tons] in 2025, or well below the present target for 2000.

- Electricity output can be met by building only 6 GW of nuclear capacity in the first quarter of the next century. Nuclear power in our projections thus becomes a peripheral issue and could be abandoned as an option if—for whatever reason—it became prudent to do so. We have, however, assumed a continuing nuclear programme at a "tick over" level sufficient to keep the industry alive as an insurance measure.

- The fast breeder reactor and the plutonium fuel cycle, with all their risks of nuclear weapon proliferation and public opposition, could be shelved indefinitely.[605]

## Commercial Energy in Industrial Societies— Environmental Prospects

The DOE projections and the hard and soft path studies reviewed here all suggest that major—perhaps even massive—changes in the world's commercial energy economy will inevitably be in progress well before 2000 and that these changes in the energy economy could well bring with them major environmental consequences throughout the world. The type and magnitude of the environmental impacts depends largely on the choice of technologies to be employed in the energy sector of the economy to provide energy for end-use needs, i.e., the production of goals and services.

As already noted, there is a spectrum of technological options open for the future of the energy sector. The spectrum ranges from the soft path (emphasizing both efficient use of energy in the energy sector itself and renewable forms of energy, especially solar, for primary sources) to the hard path (emphasizing large increases in primary energy production, especially coal and nuclear generation of electricity and the production of synthetic fuels). Options at the soft path end of the spectrum lead to a relatively efficient energy sector, capable of meeting end-use needs with less primary energy imputs than possible with options near the hard end of the spectrum. Every option along the hard-soft spectrum produces social and environmental side effects. While most studies suggest that options toward the soft end of the spectrum produce impacts less serious than options toward the hard end, the soft options too have their effects. The *Solar Sweden* report discussed above candidly acknowledges concern over intensive energy plantations, and the brief mention in the report of the International Institute for Environment and Development of "the import of liquid fuels made from crops grown in the tropical belts" might involve some significant environmental implications outside the U.K.

It is now widely recognized and accepted that the largely undesirable side effects of energy-sector development must be taken into account in the selection and development of energy futures, but it is not yet widely understood that these side effects—rather than resource or narrow economic considerations—define the energy dilemma in the long term. As noted in the DOE-sponsored California Distributed Energy Study:

The energy problem resides fundamentally in the fact that the relation between energy and well-being is two-sided. The application of energy as a productive input to the economy, yielding desired goods and services, contributes to well being; the environmental and social costs of getting and using energy subtract from it. At some level of energy use, and for a given mix of technologies of energy supply, further increases in energy supply will produce incremental social and environmental costs greater than the incremental economic benefits—that is growth [in energy consumption] begins to do more harm than good. This level can be said to define a rational "limit to growth," as distinct from a strictly physical one.

That such a level, beyond which energy growth no longer pays, exists in principle for any mix of technologies of supply and end-use is easily shown from basic economics and physical science; predicting its magnitude exactly is much harder, the more so because social costs even less quantifiable than environmental ones may dominate. Lovins[606] evidently believes that the United States is already near or beyond the point, given the "hard" energy technologies on which it relies, where further growth hurts more than it helps. Whether he is right or wrong about exactly where we are now, however, or in specific judgments about the merits of "hard" versus "soft" technologies, it is clear that energy policy for the long term should be shaped by awareness that social-environmental costs, not exhaustion of resources, will limit the amount of human well-being derivable from energy. Maximizing this quantity will require striving for technologies of energy supply with low social and environmental costs per unit of energy delivered, and fostering patterns and technologies of energy end-use that squeeze from each such unit the maximum contribution to human well-being.

This perspective, then, elevates environmental and social characteristics to the top of the list of criteria used to select supply technologies from the menu of genuinely long-term options—fission breeder reactors, fusion, direct and indirect harnessing of solar flows, and possibly some forms of geothermal energy. It rationalizes the possibility that society will choose to pay more (in economic terms) for a more benign energy source than for a less benign one. And it argues for using, as a criterion for selecting short-term and transition energy sources, the extent to which these promote and facilitate the transition to a longer term energy future built on more benign sources and efficient end-use.

Given a perspective that places environmental and social impacts at the heart of the energy predicament rather than on the periphery, it becomes essential to compare the impacts produced by alternative energy options systematically, comprehensively, and objectively.[607]

The environmental and social impacts of alternative energy options for the next two decades have not been compared "systematically, comprehensively, and objectively" for the U.S., let alone the world. While these ideas will never be fully achieved, progress is being made and should continue. For the U.S., the DOE-MITRE study,* DOE-sponsored California Distributed Energy Study, and the CEQ comparison of alternative energy futures—all three summarized above—are the most current (but still highly inadequate) efforts. On the world level, the primary analyses now available that address energy-related environmental and social impacts are a few very brief reports by the U.N. Environment Programme[608] and the works by Lovins already cited.† On the

basis of the analyses now available, only two things can be said. The first is that the more efficient energy sector produced by soft path options leads to a need for less primary energy. The second is that, to the extent that primary energy production leads to undesirable social and environmental impacts and to the extent that soft path technologies are less damaging to the environment, a shift toward the soft path options can be expected to reduce these impacts.*

Systematic, comprehensive and objective analyses of alternative energy options are urgently needed. These studies will not be done easily or quickly, but in their absence it may be difficult to obtain public support of any choice of energy policy. As time goes on, the situation (as Fig. 13–12 suggests) will only become more urgent, and options may become more restricted. Lovins, for example, argues that some options will be effectively foreclosed by delay.[609] (There have been sharp exchanges between Lovins and his critics on this point.[610]) It is clear, however, that the world's remaining petroleum resources need to be invested wisely in infrastructure, and capital needs to be well matched to genuinely long-term energy options. The choice of both the long-term options and the transitional approaches can be facilitated by further attention to, and analysis of, the associated social and environmental impacts.

## Noncommercial Fuels

The preeminent noncommercial fuel throughout the world is wood. (Charcoal, also important,

*Since this text was drafted, DOE released its second National Energy Plan (NEP-II), which includes an appendix on environmental impacts (DOE Office of the Assistant Secretary for Environment, *National Energy Plan II, Appendix: Environmental Trends and Impacts,* Washington, May 1979). The appendix contains information quite similar to the DOE-MITRE study, plus an analysis of the environmental implications of specific NEP-II initiatives.

†Several persons reviewing the manuscript of this Study suggested adding to these the report of the Workshop on Alternative Energy Strategies (*Energy: Global Prospects 1985–2000,*

New York: McGraw-Hill, 1977) and the works of the World Energy Conference (see especially World Energy Commission of the World Energy Conference, *World Energy: Looking Ahead to 2000,* New York: IPC Science and Technology Press, 1978). Neither is appropriate. The WAES report deals with only a part of the world and concludes its treatment of the environment in less than two pages. The WEC, as noted earlier, is only now beginning to consider the environmental implications of energy sector development (Robert J. Raudebaugh, Executive Director of the WEC's U.S. National Committee, personal communication, Feb. 15, 1979).

*Additional analyses on these points are becoming available. These include the report of the Energy Project at the Harvard Business School (Robert Stobaugh and David Yergin, eds., *Energy Future,* New York: Random House, 1979) and the forthcoming report of the Demand and Conservation Panel of the National Academy of Sciences' Committee on Nuclear and Alternative Energy Systems (discussed in part in "U.S. Energy Demand: Some Low Energy Futures," *Science,* Apr. 14, 1978, pp. 142–52). Both reports point to the advantages of an efficient energy sector of the economy and to the economies of conservation. This last point is made effectively in *Energy: The Case for Conservation* by Denis Hayes (Worldwatch Paper 4, Washington: Worldwatch Institute, Jan. 1976). All three reports support the general points made in the text above.

is derived from wood.) Only in the developing countries, however, does firewood continue to be a major fuel; 90 percent of the worlds fuelwood consumption is in the LDCs.[611] Worldwide, the energy derived from wood amounted to $13.3 \times 10^{15}$ Btu in 1974, roughly the same amount as the total from hydroelectric sources.[612] Dried dung (providing an estimated $1.7 \times 10^{15}$ Btu in 1974) and crop residues (providing an estimated $1 \times 10^{15}$ Btu in 1974) are the other major noncommercial fuels.[613] They are important in densely populated regions, such as northern India's Gangetic Plain, and in the treeless Andean mountains in South America. Thus the noncommercial fuels— wood, charcoal, dried dung, and crop residues— are all organic fuels.

Statistics concerning noncommercial, organic fuels are incomplete, due to the inherent difficulties in collecting such data, and to the relative lack of attention given these forms of energy by governments and world organizations. The United Nations Food and Agriculture Organization (FAO) has attempted over the past decade to survey these fuels even partially.

It is not possible to make a precise distinction between commercial and noncommercial fuels. Large quantities of firewood are marketed commercially, and the statistics now available on wood consumption include wood converted to commercial charcoal (estimated at 5 percent of the total fuelwood consumption) along with noncommercial firewood. Dung is also sold to some extent, so that its noncommercial designation is not entirely accurate. Furthermore, crop residues are increasingly being used along with animal manure in the production of methane gas on a commercial basis, so that the noncommercial category is not precise in this case either. Although the discussion that follows focuses on the noncommercial uses of these organic fuels, there is a discernible trend toward commercialization.

Wood, dung, and crop wastes are used throughout the LDCs as a source of energy for the preparation of meals and for heating. An estimated 1.0–1.5 billion persons[614] (more than a quarter of the total world population) use fuelwood as their primary energy source for cooking. Most of these persons are located in rural areas where firewood has traditionally been a free good. An additional 100 million or more persons use dried dung and crop wastes for the same purpose.[615]

Global estimates of the share of noncommercial energy in the total energy picture in developing countries vary widely from a high of 70 percent to a low of 30 percent.[616] It is known that these fuels (wood, dung, and crop wastes) account for approximately 56 percent of the total energy consumption in India and 58 percent of the total in Africa. Commercial energy—coal, gas, oil, electricity, and charcoal—is used almost exclusively by the wealthiest 20 percent of the people in poor countries.[617]

It was once hoped that fossil fuels (especially kerosene) would reduce fuelwood and charcoal use, thereby decreasing deforestation pressures. The rapid increases in fossil fuel prices since 1973, however, have largely eliminated this hope. The rate of growth in LDC kerosene consumption has been slowed significantly, and the demand for fuelwood and charcoal is thought to be rising rapidly, in spite of percentage increases in the prices of these fuels that are as large or larger than the percentage increases in the price of fossil fuels. Switching from kerosene to fuelwood has been reported in parts of Africa[618] and is probably occurring in many other poor LDC areas where fuelwood is still relatively plentiful. As a result, the demand for fuelwood and charcoal in the years ahead may grow as fast as—or even faster than— LDC populations.

The primary environmental consequences of fuelwood consumption are those associated with deforestation, described earlier in this chapter. In the paragraphs that follow, a few additional energy-specific impacts associated with fuelwood are presented. The discussion then turns to the impacts of the use of dung and organic residues for fuel impacts which are serious for soil productivity. The discussion concludes with a consideration of the prospects for controlling the environmental impacts of noncommercial fuels.

### Fuelwood

Today there is an inverse relationship between the level of economic development and the use of fuelwood. The poorest countries or regions use the most fuelwood; it is the principal source of fuel for the poorest families in these regions. Domestic energy requirements in developing countries range from a low of 0.2 m³ (cubic meters) of wood per person per year burned in open cookfires in tree-short South Asia,[619] to a medium of 0.5 m³ in the warm tropics and to a high of over 2 m³ per person per year in the colder uplands, where wood is burned for both cooking and warmth.[620] The average annual per capita consumption where wood is abundant is about 1 m³ (approximately 450 kg of wood),* but it drops to

---

*For comparison, a cord of wood (a common measure in the U.S.) is a pile measuring 4 × 4 × 8 feet (128 ft³ or 3.6 m³). Therefore, 1 m³ of wood is less than 0.3 cord.

less than 0.5 m³ in wood-poor areas such as China, India, the Near East, and North Africa. [621]

The demand for fuelwood in developing countries is estimated (largely on the basis of data collected before the major oil price increases started in 1973) to have been growing 1–2 percent per year. Based on this growth rate, the FAO projected in 1976 that consumption would reach 2 billion cubic meters annually by the year 2000. [622] In contrast, fuelwood consumption in developed nations was falling at the rate of 6 percent per year in 1975 and represented less than 1 percent of the total energy consumed by these countries. [623] (This downward trend, however, may now have been reversed as a result of the recent rapid increases in the cost of fossil fuels.) In 1977 the FAO revised its estimate upwards to a 2.2 percent annual increase in demand in LDCs and predicted that by 1994, there would be a fuelwood shortage of 650 million cubic meters annually in wood-poor countries. [624] For comparison, this figure is roughly one quarter of the year 2000 fuelwood consumption projected by the FAO.

Wood is the only household fuel for most of the rural families in the developing world, and even urban families meet as much as 25 percent of their fuel needs with fuelwood. [625] However, because of its high weight per unit fuel value, wood is seldom collected from farther away than 10 kilometers and ordinarily is not transported by road from beyond 50 kilometers. Therefore scarcities tend to be local. Still, as scattered rural populations deplete local wood resources, entire regions become treeless, and an increasing effort must be exerted to find and carry wood to the home. In the arid Sahel of Africa, the gathering of fuelwood has become a full-time job, requiring in places 360 person-days per year per household. [626] Urban families, too far from collectible wood, spend 20–30 percent of their income on wood in some West African cities. Large industries involving trucks or animal carts exist to bring fuelwood into cities. [627] When demand is concentrated in large towns or cities, the surrounding areas become barren to a distance of as much as 50–100 kilometers. [628]

FAO's annual shortfall of 650 million cubic meters of fuelwood by 1994 is an alarming projection. It implies the reduction of essential fuel consumption, expanded deforestation, increased wood prices and growing amounts of dung shifted from field to fireplace. [629] The fuelwood problem is every bit as great for the poor LDC rural dweller as is the problem of increased petroleum costs for the more affluent citizen of the developed world.

There are no panaceas or quick fixes for the fuelwood problem. Tree plantations established today will require at least 10 years of growth prior to harvest, and growth rates are slow in the semi-arid regions where scarcities are already critical. In the Sahel, annual production of wood in native scrub forests, on a continuous basis, ranges from less than 0.5 m³ per hectare at the desert's edge—or enough for only one person's fuel needs—to up to 5 m³ per hectare in the less arid belt adjacent to the wooded savanna. [630] Near the wooden savanna, a hectare of well-tended forest could satisfy the fuel needs of a family of six or more. [631] Since the region's remaining forest stock has not yet been measured, the extent of the present fuelwood supply is not known, but local scarcities are evidenced by the treeless landscapes around towns. The Club du Sahel* notes that where populations exceed 25 persons per square kilometer, total deforestation is inevitable, and many areas of the Sahel have already surpassed this population density. [632] By the year 2000, the Club estimates that total firewood consumption will increase from the 1975 figure of 16 million to 33.5 million cubic meters, including 9.8 million burned in cities. [633] To meet this demand it is calculated that 150,000 hectares per year of forest plantations would have to be established—50 times the present rate of 3,000 hectares per year. [634]

The picture is not all bleak, however. Wood can be conserved through the use of more efficient stoves. In many areas the potential for conservation exists for ample village woodlots. The constraints in most areas are more sociological than technical, though the difficulty of sociological constraints is not to be underestimated. [635]

## Charcoal

The manufacture and commercial use of charcoal appears to be increasing in the LDCs, where it is used primarily for cooking and heating in rural and urban areas. Much of the increase is in urban areas. The increasing use of charcoal in cities is explained by a combination of factors: increases in prices of kerosene, liquid gas, and electricity; lack of fuelwood as deforestation extends beyond distances from which it can be economically transported; and increasing urbanization of LDC populations. [636]

Information on the production and use of charcoal is not routinely collected by many nations, and as a result the data now available are not sufficient for making detailed projections. However, the information that is available from sev-

---

* An international voluntary association of nations, organized to mobilize assistance to drought stricken Sahelian states.

eral countries indicates increases in both the rate of consumption and the price of charcoal in LDCs.[637] In Ghana, which has desert scrub, savanna woodlands, and humid evergreen forests, charcoal consumption in 1975 was estimated at over 280,000 tons, and use was growing at an estimated 2.7 percent per year.[638] Kenya's consumption in 1972 was 310,000 tons, half of it in cities, and demand was growing at 7 percent per year.[639] For the poor communities that ring cities in Kenya, charcoal is now the major fuel. In Mozambique, 6,000 families earn their livelihood by supplying charcoal to the capital city Maputo.[640] Even in rural areas of East Africa, up to 50 percent of the people buy their charcoal.[641] In Sudan and Thailand, charcoal represents over 40 percent of the wood consumed for fuel; in India, however, its use is relatively small.[642] In general, the pattern appears to be one of an increasing trade in charcoal in urban markets, particularly in low-income quarters, and an increasing amount of charcoal manufacture.

While most charcoal is used for domestic cooking and heating, Brazil, the world's largest charcoal producer, uses most of its production for smelting pig iron, 45 percent of which is smelted with charcoal. Brazil burned 3.6 million tons of charcoal in smelters during 1978 and this figure is expected to increase at 10 percent per year, doubling every 7 years.[643] In the State of Minas Gerais, where 56 smelters supply 85 percent of Brazil's pig iron, virtually all of the original 55 million hectares of forest have been removed, largely for charcoal production. At present rates of cutting, there will be no more savanna forest in Minas Gerais by 1982.[644] To ensure a continuing supply of wood and charcoal, the Brazilian government enacted a law in 1967 requiring wood-using industries to be self-sufficient in wood by 1982. A successful program of fiscal incentives (now reduced) resulted in the establishment of over 1.5 million hectares of eucalyptus by late 1978.[645]

The actual combustion of charcoal fuel has minimal direct environmental impact. It is cleaner-burning than wood or coal. Its sulfur content is roughly one tenth that of even coking coal, making it an ideal smelting fuel.[646] It has twice the caloric value of most air-dried wood, at less than half the weight, and as a result it can be transported from much greater distances than wood. The carbonization process used to make charcoal consumes some energy to drive off water and other volatile substances, but if wood is used as the energy source, it is energy that otherwise probably would not be used or sold because of local surpluses or the cost of transporting the wood.

The indirect environmental effects of charcoal use are more significant. Because charcoal is such an attractive alternative fuel for urban uses, and because its manufacture is a simple and universally known technology, future conversion of forests and other vegetation to charcoal will continue to be an important and probably increasing activity in LDCs. Uncontrolled deforestation and its consequences (described earlier in this chapter) will therefore be a parallel and increasing result of intensified charcoal trade and manufacture. A related social consequence will be a decline in self-sufficiency among rural dwellers who will lose the natural vegetation they now exploit for multiple purposes—medicine, construction materials, tool woods, food, livestock forage, vegetable gums, etc.[647] The establishment of fast-growing fuelwood plantations of such species as eucalyptus will ensure a continuing supply of fuelwood, but will not replace the numerous other uses of native vegetation. These environmental and related socioeconomic consequences will be particularly noticeable in the areas around large cities, out to a distance of perhaps as much as 200 kilometers, depending upon the cost of transport. If the land is available and plantings can be encouraged and protected, large blocks of eucalyptus (or other fast-growing species such as pines or the acacia *Leucaena*) can be expected to replace the diverse, slower-growing native forests in the vicinity of large cities. Otherwise, the native forests near cities may simply be removed and not replanted.

### Dung and Crop Residues as Fuel

Once fuelwood demands exceed forest production, a variety of stresses and changes begin. Arid regions have virtually no alternatives to fuelwood, and after it is gone desertification is speeded. In more humid agricultural regions that have become deforested, the alternative open to poor people is to turn to burning dung and crop residues (stalks, hulls, etc.) for cooking and warmth.

The shift to dung and crop residues is already well advanced in the treeless Gangetic Plain of India, Nepal, other parts of Asia, and the Andes of South America.[648] The FAO reports that in 1970 India burned 68 million tons of cow dung and 39 million tons of vegetable waste, representing 35 percent of her total noncommercial energy consumption.[649] Worldwide, an estimated 150–400 million tons of dung are burned for fuel, the lower estimate being equivalent to 13 percent of the amount of energy provided by firewood.

Dry dung has about the same caloric value as wood per unit weight. [650]

The burning of dung and crop residues is a disastrous loss. For the world's poor, these organic materials are the only sources of the nutrients needed to maintain the productivity of farmlands. It is the poorest people—the ones least able to afford chemical fertilizers—who are now being forced to burn their organic fertilizers. The combustion of dung and crop residues is equivalent to burning food. One ton of cow dung contains enough nutrients to produce 50 kilograms of food grain, which in turn can feed one person for four months. [651] The burning of almost 70 million tons of cow dung in India wastes nutrients equal to more than one-third of India's chemical fertilizer use. [652]

In the LDCs the potential contribution of organic materials (including human wastes) to soil fertility is enormous. The Food and Agriculture Organization reports that in a study done by J. C. C. van Voorhoeve for the World Bank the amount of nitrogen, potassium, and phosphorus potentially available to the LDCs from organic sources in 1971 was 7.8 times the amount actually applied that year as chemical fertilizer, worth $16 billion at 1973 prices. For 1980, the van Voorhoeve study found that at least 80 million metric tons of organic nutrients—worth $21 billion— could be supplied from organic sources. [653] If the amount of dung burned increases in proportion to population growth (the same assumption made for fuelwood consumption), 250–670 million tons per year would be burned annually by 2000, representing a loss of approximately 5–13 million metric tons of nitrogen (assuming 2 percent nitrogen dry weight). In monetary terms, these lost nutrients would be worth roughly $2 billion annually.

It is essential to understand that while inorganic substitutes exist for organic sources of nitrogen, potassium, and phosphorus, there is no substitute for organic matter itself. The proteins, cellulose, and lignins that comprise plant residues increase the porosity and water-holding capacity of soils, thereby serving to prevent erosion and provide the conditions needed for good root development. [654] Organic matter is also the food for the soil's microbiological life, which slowly converts and releases nutrients (and trace elements) in forms and at rates that plants can assimilate. [655]

## Bio-Gas

Methane gas, also known as marsh gas, can be obtained from organic wastes by means of a relatively straightforward technology. [656] Manure and plant wastes are fed into enclosed chambers of brick, concrete, or steel construction. Anaerobic bacterial digestion of the organic matter produces methane $(CH_4)$ and carbon dioxide $(CO_2)$, the products of bacterial respiration. The environmental consequences of this growing form of energy production are generally quite positive. The resulting sludge retains all of the mineral salts and nitrogen (although little of the cellulose or carbohydrates) in the original material. Thus, the fertilizing benefits of the organic wastes are retained in the sludge* while the energy value of the manure and crop residues is captured in the form of methane gas. The energy value of the gas produced ranges from 18,630 to 26,080 kilojoules (500–700 Btu/ft$^3$) per cubic meter. In small farm applications the gas is piped directly to the kitchen for cooking.

Small-scale bio-gas plants have been the subject of intensive research and development in recent years, especially in India and the People's Republic of China. A major focus of this research has been on family-size plants (2–3 m$^3$ of gas per day). The offal from at least five cows (or an equivalent amount from other animals or humans) is needed to produce this amount of methane. Since many rural poor do not have so many animals, this source of energy is not accessible individually to the poorest rural people. India and China are developing larger bio-gas plants (10 m$^3$ of gas per day) that show considerable promise for community use. [657]

Both China and India have begun developing bio-gas production facilities. China has already built 7 million bio-gas plants and a total of 70 million are targetted for 1985. [658] India plans to build 100,000 bio-gas plants per year for the next decade. This rather modest number would affect only 1–2 percent of India's people; it would process the manure of only 2–4 percent of India's cows and recover only 100,000 metric tons per year of nitrogen fertilizer. [659] Presently, India has only 7,000 bio-gas plants. [660] Taiwan, South Korea, and Thailand are also promoting this form of energy development.

Problems of operation and maintenance, initial cost, and social equity have impeded rapid diffusion of this promising technology, [661] but the many benefits of bio-gas technology assure it an important role in the decades ahead.

---

* There is another advantage. The digestion process kills many pathogens affecting both plants and humans, thus improving human health and reducing the transfer of crop diseases from year to year. This advantage is particularly important in those areas where night soil is used as fertilizer.

## Noncommercial Fuels—Environmental Prospects

Growing populations and increasing prices of commercial fuels (especially fossil fuels) can be expected to lead to rapidly increasing demands for organic noncommercial fuels. This increasing demand will lead to many environmental impacts.

The environmental impacts of deforestation have been discussed earlier in this chapter ("The Forestry Projections and the Environment") and will not be repeated here. One general outcome of deforestation is, of course, a shift to other sources of fuel, such as organic matter. A single and disastrous consequence can readily be predicted: decline in soil productivity and the decline, therefore, in the production of food for humans and animals. More specifically, a number of physical and environmental effects of diminished levels, or disappearance of, organic matter in soils can be determined:

- Diminished capacity of soils to hold water, therefore greater susceptibility to drought during dry periods, exacerbated by loss of lignin by-products.
- Decreased porosity, therefore poorer aeration and absorption of water and more difficult tilling plus a tendency to become compacted and, during rains, waterlogged, leading to erosion and fast runoff.
- Less adhesion between soil particles and greater susceptibility to erosion by wind or water.
- Reduced reservoir of plant nutrients (and therefore reduced fertility) and greater loss of nutrients to leaching action of soil water.
- Overall loss in productivity of the land.

These effects have long been known [662]; avoiding them through husbandry of soil organic matter has been a hallmark of wise farming for thousands of years.

In regions with scarce fuel supplies, it is not likely that cattle populations will grow and compensate for the increased burning of dried dung. As noted in Tables 13–2 and 13–4, cattle populations will increase in many areas but on overgrazed lands; the animals will eat less and produce less dung as land productivity declines. The situation may lead to a self-accelerating downward trend in soil productivity, driven by efforts of increasing populations to survive on decreasing quantities of plant production.

In regions with steep slopes erosion may be the *coup de grace* for lands which have been deprived of organic matter, reducing them in extreme cases to bare rock and in wide areas to infertile soils, which will require decades or more of careful management and conservation if they are to be returned to productivity. Such severe hillside erosion has already been documented in Central America, the Andean region of Latin America, the East African Highlands, and the Himalayan hills. [663] In less steep landscapes, the land will simply produce less food and plant matter, and both animals and people will go hungry or starve—or migrate if the alternative exists. Adverse climatic developments aggravate declining productivity, as experience in the Sahel has shown.

A reversal of these alarming trends is being sought by the World Bank, the Food and Agricultural Organization of the United Nations, and U.S. Agency for International Development, [664] and other organizations that have studied the problem. [665] Reduction in the use of wood, dung, and plant residues for fuel could be achieved by several means:

- *Use of kerosene.* This is judged to be too expensive for the poorest people.*
- *Improved efficiencies in the technologies used in the production of charcoal.*
- *Improved efficienty of fuel use.* This is the most promising option. Open fires waste over 90 percent of the heat generated. Improved stoves, of which a number of designs exist suited to different cultures, can reduce wood consumption by 70 percent. [666]
- *Utilization of methane digesters.* This process holds much promise, but requires an initial capital outlay of several hundred dollars, and the possession of livestock. Thus, it holds little promise for the dilemma of the poorest people (no free fuel and no ability to purchase an alternative), but the process does save the value of organic matter while also exploiting its energy. [667]
- *Development of fuelwood plantations.* This is a promising solution after a few years to a decade for growth, but is beset by lack of institutional capabilities for large scale plantation programs, as well as social and economic problems at the local level (see Chapter 8).
- *Solar and wind energy.* There is increasing interest in the use of solar energy for cooking and for irrigation pumping and of wind for pumping and other energy needs.

---

* The World Bank is concerned about the effects of increasing world oil prices on non-OPEC developing economies and has initiated a new program to accelerate petroleum exploration and production in the non-OPEC developing countries. (See *A Program to Accelerate Petroleum Production in the Developing Countries*, Washington: World Bank, January 1979.)

What then are the prospects for noncommercial, organic fuels by the year 2000? The answer—to the extent that it can be given—depends largely on which geographic region is being considered. Potentials for organic matter production vary among regions by a factor of 10 or more, as do population densities. Awareness of the importance of organic fuels is growing rapidly in some areas, less rapidly in others. The role of cattle husbandry and traditional methods of cooking and disposing of organic wastes also show cultural variations, which not only influence the practice of using organic fuels but also the potentials for socially and economically feasible alternatives. However, further increases in population and further increases in the costs of fossil fuels imply substantially increased pressures on organic fuel resources virtually everywhere by the year 2000.

## Conclusion

How the many nations of the world will respond to the rapidly changing energy situation is uncertain, and as a result it has not been possible for the Department of Energy to develop energy projections that extend to the year 2000. While DOE did prepare projections that extend to 1990, the information required to analyze the environmental implications of these projections is not available. As a result, it has been necessary to limit the discussion of environmental impacts to a qualitative consideration of a range of energy development options bounded by the hard and soft paths. From this qualitative consideration it is clear that all energy sources have environmental impacts associated with their development and use. The energy challenge to each nation over the next two decades is to develop an energy economy that balances the advantages of more energy with the disadvantage of the environmental and social impacts. While the situation is still very uncertain, trends are emerging for both the commercial and the noncommercial energy economies.

At present, the world's commercial energy sector (fossil fuels, nuclear energy, and hydropower) is developing a structure that is much nearer the hard path end of the spectrum of options than the soft path end. If the overall, primary-energy growth rate projected by the Department of Energy out to 1990 were to continue to 2000, the result would be a commerical energy economy consuming 517 quads (517 × 10$^{15}$ Btu) annually, more than double the 1975 figure. If, in addition, this commerical energy were to be supplied by a global energy sector similar in composition of that described in Table 13–41 for the United States,

the consequences might be expected to include the following proportionate increases in the environmental impacts described in Table 13–42:

- Several thousand million tons of coal production per year by 2000.
- Approximately one hundred thousand million tons of coal mined cumulatively, 1975–2000.
- Many thousands of square kilometers of land strip-mined cumulatively.
- Many thousands of square kilometers of land affected by subsidence cumulatively.
- Approximately one thousand (nominally 1,100 Mw) coal power plants.
- Several hundred (nominally 1,100 Mw) nuclear power plants.
- Several tens of thousands square kilometers required for transmission lines for electricity generated by new coal and nuclear plants.
- Approximately 1,000 million tons of radioactive tailings from supplying uranium, 1977–2000.
- Approximately ten million cubic meters of low-level radioactive wastes.
- A few 100,000 tons of spent nuclear fuel, 1977–2000.
- Several 100,000 tons of spent nuclear fuel generated over the lifetimes of the plants constructed through the year 2000.

While these estimates are highly uncertain, they are the best estimates that can be made with the projections and data currently available, and they do indicate the order of magnitude of the cumulative impacts of a global hard path over the decades ahead.

In addition to its environmental impacts, the global hard path option will maintain and increase thermodynamic inefficiencies in the energy sector itself. Large amounts of energy will be used in converting one form of energy to another, and the resulting energy forms will not in many cases be efficiently matched thermodynamically to end-use requirements.

As the soft path studies illustrate, requirements for nonrenewable primary energy (and the associated environmental impacts) could be reduced by increasing the thermodynamic efficiency in the energy sector, by increasing the contribution of renewable sources of primary energy, and by increasing end-use conservation. However, the DOE energy projections show only relatively small shifts in these directions through 1990.

Trends in the world's noncommercial energy economy lead to environmental consequences that are quite different from those implied by the commercial economy. The FAO projection of a 650 million cubic meter annual shortage of firewood in the LDCs means that approximately a quarter of the needed fuelwood in the LDCs may not be available. The shortfall implies increased deforestation and shifts to alternative fuels (dung and crop residues). Both the deforestation and the shift to alternative fuels will have adverse affects. The deforestation will enhance erosion and destabilize stream flows. The combustion of dung and crop residues will deprive the soil of needed nutrients and organic matter.

The most serious environmental impacts implied by the noncommercial energy trends could be reduced significantly by extensive development of village woodlots and the use of methane generators. Encouraging initiatives in both areas have been noted above. Nevertheless, if present trends continue, the organic fuel needs of increased LDC populations can be expected to seriously affect forestry and agriculture in large parts of Africa, Asia, and Latin America by the year 2000.

By then, the commercial and noncommercial energy sectors may be having increasing effects on each other. Higher costs of kerosene can be expected to expand the use of organic fuels in LDCs, increasing further the pressures on LDC forests. The resulting deforestation and wood combustion will contribute potentially significant amounts of carbon dioxide to the atmosphere and will reduce the amount of vegetation available globally to absorb $CO_2$—developments that, in turn, will increase concerns in the world's commercial energy economy over the climatological consequences of continued and expanded fossil fuel combustion.

## THE NONFUEL MINERALS PROJECTIONS AND THE ENVIRONMENT

### The Projections

Collectively, the demand for the 18 nonfuel minerals considered in the projections prepared by the Department of the Interior, was expected to grow at around 3 percent per year, slightly more than doubling between 1975 and 2000. In most cases it appears possible to accommodate the projected growth of mineral demand, but there are a number of unanswered questions concerning the price at which demand will be met, especially if energy prices increase significantly above their present levels. As higher-grade resources in accessible locations are exhausted, new mining ventures will tend to exploit lower-grade deposits and deposits in less accessible parts of the world with more fragile environments. Some of the projected increases in supply are large and will require contributions of both virgin and recycled materials. The industrialized nations will continue to depend heavily on resources imported from LDCs and are projected to absorb over three-fourths of the world's nonfuel mineral production until at least the year 2000.

### Introduction

The Global 2000 Study projections indicate that in the decades ahead there will be increasing needs both for mineral resources and for environmental conditions beneficial to biological resources. These two resource needs, at least in the context of present policy and practice, are to a degree in conflict. Thus tensions between materials demand and environmental quality can be expected to continue. In the past—and even to a greater degree now—mineral resource policy has been based on the assumption that mining is the most appropriate use for mineral-bearing land. Not long ago in the United States, however, the Study Team on Environmental Problems Associated with Metallic and Nonmetallic Mineral Resources, working under the sponsorship of the National Academy of Sciences, advised against making the assumption that mining is necessarily the most appropriate use of mineral-bearing land.[668] The goal recommended by the U.S. Secretary of Interior is a proper balance between mineral extraction and environmental protection.[669] Achieving that balance in the U.S. and elsewhere will require significant changes of policy and practice, as well as significant expenditures. According to a United Nations estimate, the cost of abating all world pollution due to mining by the year 2000 would be about $200 billion, or 1–2 percent of the product value.[670]

Richard A. Carpenter, Executive Director of the National Academy of Sciences' Commission on Natural Resources, has summarized the situation as follows:

The tensions between availability of materials and quality of the environment will increase with economic growth and the appreciation of environmental values. These tensions can be relieved to an extent by internalizing the costs of environmental protection so that they are reflected in the price of materials. . . .

Environmental protection regulations will result in (i) increased costs for many materials; (ii) disruptive changes in uses of materials, due to environmental characteristics and revised cost of effectiveness calculations; (iii) restrictions on the siting of processing and manufacturing installations; (iv) preemption of access and surface rights to some mineral bearing lands, particularly those that are federally controlled; (v) diversion of capital from new production facilities; and (vi) frustrating delays in decisions, such as those affecting leasing and plant siting.

In return for these generally undesirable disruptions in the continued development and supply of materials, society will obtain: (i) improved quality of air and water; (ii) long-term protection of the natural ecosystems of which man is a part; (iii) more efficient allocation of natural resources on the basis of more accurate and complete accounting of costs; (iv) improved human health through decreased contamination of the environment with toxic substances; and (v) conservation of materials through a closing of the production, use, and disposal cycle.

Ingenuity and a more complete understanding of the parts and interactions of the energy, materials, and environmental system can do much to reduce the tensions in these conflicts and bring about equitable trade-offs among societal goals.[671]

Significant environmental damage can be anticipated from the projected increases in mineral production and utilization. These impacts will be felt as a continuation of both the direct and the indirect consequences of mining on land. Mining the seabed will present new and unique environmental impacts. The three types of impacts are discussed below.

# Direct Environmental Effects of Mining on Land

As shown in Table 13–43, mines, quarries, and wells yielded about 21 billion short tons of refined mineral materials worldwide in 1976 (25 billion if oil and gas are included). Of the quantity produced, roughly 16 billion tons were nonmetallic minerals, mainly stone, sand, and gravel; 8 billion tons were fuels; and nearly 1 billion tons were metals.

Most mineral resource production now occurs in the industrialized countries. About 14 billion tons of refined mineral materials were produced in Japan, Canada, Australia, South Africa, and the industrialized countries of Europe in 1976; 4 billion tons were produced in the United States, and 7 billion tons in the less developed countries. This marketed mineral output amounted to 2 tons per person annually in the LDCs, 20 tons per person in the United States, and 16 tons per person in the other industrialized countries (Fig. 13–19).

Direct effects of mining on the landscape, such as surface disturbance, deposition of overburden and tailings, and generation and disposal of pollutants, tend to be roughly proportional to the quantity of minerals extracted. Such effects, in the absence of measured data, can therefore be roughly estimated by applying conversion coefficients to estimates of future production. Estimates of utilized land areas and generated mining wastes derived in this manner are presented below, after which their implications for air and water resources are discussed briefly.

## Land Use in Mineral Production

The extent of the earth's surface disturbed by worldwide mining operations has never been measured accurately. It is estimated in Table 13–43 at roughly 1.5 million acres per year in 1976, growing to 3 million acres per year by 2000 (excluding surface disturbed by oil and gas operations). The land area that will be directly disturbed during the 1976–2000 period is approximately 60 million acres, or 94,000 square miles—an area roughly equal to West Germany, or 0.2 percent of the earth's total land surface. By comparison, the southern border of the Sahara Desert, by moving steadily southward during the last 50 years, is believed to have encompassed some 250,000 square miles of land once suitable for agriculture or grazing,[672] and it is expected that the closed forests of the world will be reduced by 1.72 million square miles between 1978 and 2000.[673]

However, the projected figure (94,000 square miles of land expected to be directly disturbed by mining over the next quarter century) is misleadingly small. The mines themselves are not the only areas disturbed by mining operations. It has been said that the least of the problems is "the hole in the ground." Mining operations are responsible for water and air pollution, for destruction of fish and wildlife habitats, for erosion, and for the impairment of natural beauty many miles from the mine sites. The extensive areas indirectly affected by mining are not included in the 94,000 square mile figure, and virtually no data are available

## TABLE 13–43

### Estimated Land Area Utilized for World Mineral Production Compared with Annual Production, 1976–2000

| Mineral Commodity | Ratio of Mineral Production (in millions of short tons) to Acres of Land Utilized in the U.S. in 1971[a] | 1976 Production (billions of short tons) | 1976 Land Utilized (thousands of acres) | 1985 Production (billions of short tons) | 1985 Land Utilized (thousands of acres) | 2000 Production (billions of short tons) | 2000 Land Utilized (thousands of acres) |
|---|---|---|---|---|---|---|---|
| Stone | 30 | 7.7 | 231 | 8.2 | 246 | 14.8 | 444 |
| Sand and gravel | 50 | 6.9 | 345 | 10.5 | 525 | 17.3 | 865 |
| Commodities not elsewhere specified[b] | 60[c] | 1.5 | 90 | 2.2[c] | 132 | 3.5[c] | 210 |
| Clays | 120 | 0.6 | 72 | 0.8 | 96 | 1.1 | 132 |
| Bituminous coal[d] | 130 | 3.5 | 455 | 4.0 | 520 | 4.8 | 624 |
| Iron (in ore) | 170 | 0.5 | 85 | 0.8 | 136 | 1.1 | 187 |
| Phosphate rock | 260 | 0.1 | 26 | 0.2 | 52 | 0.5 | 130 |
| Copper | 12,670 | 0.008 | 101 | 0.013 | 165 | 0.022 | 279 |
| Uranium[e] | 200,000 | 0.000025 | 5 | 0.000107 | 21 | 0.000193 | 39 |
| World total (excluding petroleum and natural gas) | | 20.8 | 1,410 | 26.7 | 1,893 | 43.1 | 2,910 |

Note: Production figures assume U.S. 1971 ratio of marketable production to land utilized (column 1). Production figures for 1985 and 2000 are U.S. Bureau of Mines projections for demand, which is assumed to be matched by production.

[a] Millions of short tons produced : acres of land utilized.
[b] Mainly cement, anthracite coal, salt, and other nonmetallic minerals, but excluding petroleum and natural gas.
[c] Estimated figure, based on the relative contributions of cement, anthracite coal, salt, and other nonmetallic minerals.
[d] This fuel mineral is included for purposes of comparison.
[e] Figures do not include centrally planned economies; data was not available.

Sources: Ratios calculated from U.S. Bureau of Mines, Land Utilization and Reclamation in the Mining Industry, 1930–71, 1974. Production data for 1976 from U.S. Bureau of Mines, Mineral Commodity Summaries, 1978. Production estimates for 1985 and 2000 from U.S. Bureau Mines, Mineral Trends and Forecasts, 1976.

on the overall amounts of land disturbed by mining.

Mining directly disturbs land in a number of ways. According to United States experience over the 1930–71 period, 59 percent of such land was utilized for excavation and 38 percent for disposal of mine and mill waste; the remaining 3 percent either subsided or was otherwise disturbed by underground workings. [674]

Large areas have been directly disturbed by surface mining for certain metals—in Malaysia for tin, in New Caledonia for nickel, in Australia for titanium, and on various Pacific islands for phosphate. [675] Work has begun near Hambach, West Germany, on an open-pit lignite mine that will cover 30 square miles of what are (or were) farms, forests, and villages. [676] A proposed bauxite mine in Western Australia will destroy the only forest in a million square mile area. The mining company answers critics that it believes most of the trees have an incurable root disease. The company has also offered to attempt reforestation. [677]

By 1977, land directly disturbed by surface mining in the United States totaled 5.7 million acres. [678] The strip mining of bituminous coal accounted for the largest part of this. The thinner the coal seam, the greater the area disturbed for a certain quantity of coal. In the western United States, for example, the mining of 30-foot seams of Wyoming coal disturbs 25 acres of land for every million tons produced, whereas mining 10-foot seams of Washington, Arizona, Colorado, or Utah coal disrupts 72–80 acres per million tons of coal recovered. [679] There is 12 times as much coal available by deep mining in the United States as by stripping, [680] but although deep mining appears to cause less land degradation than surface mining, it entails greater occupational hazard and discomfort and greater cost.

The nonfuel minerals commodities principally responsible for direct land disturbance during mining are sand and gravel, stone, copper, iron, clays, and phosphate rock ore. Table 13–43 provides estimates and projections of the areas disturbed worldwide during the mining of these commodities in the years 1976, 1985, and 2000.

# ABOUT 40,000 POUNDS OF NEW MINERAL MATERIALS ARE REQUIRED ANNUALLY FOR EACH U.S. CITIZEN

8000 LBS.
STONE

8000 LBS.
SAND AND GRAVEL

660 LBS.
CEMENT

450 LBS.
CLAYS

430 LBS.
SALT

1400 LBS.
OTHER
NONMETALS

1000 LBS.
IRON AND STEEL

46 LBS.
ALUMINUM

16 LBS.
COPPER

14 LBS.
ZINC

11 LBS.
LEAD

31 LBS. OTHER
METALS

## PLUS

7650 LBS.
PETROLEUM

5200 LBS. COAL

4200 LBS.
NATURAL GAS

1/7 LB. URANIUM

## TO GENERATE:

ENERGY EQUIVALENT TO 300 PERSONS WORKING AROUND-THE-CLOCK FOR EACH U.S. CITIZEN

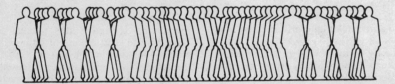

# U.S. TOTAL USE OF NEW MINERAL SUPPLIES IN 1975 WAS ABOUT 4 BILLION TONS !

**Figure 13–19.** Consumption of new mineral materials per person in the United States in 1975. (*U.S. Bureau of Mines,* Status of the Mineral Industries 1976)

The figures, admittedly approximate, were derived for each commodity by observing the ratio of production tonnages to land acreages disturbed and utilized in the United States in 1971 (as reported in a Bureau of Mines study[681]) and applying these ratios to the Bureau's projections of world mineral demand (which were equated with production).

There are several factors influencing the accuracy of the area estimates in the table. The mix of mining methods used in the United States, especially the ratio of surface to underground mining, differs from that of the world as a whole. The United States is also atypical in that it exploits much low-grade ore deep beneath the surface. It should also be remembered that as miners everywhere deplete the world's high-grade, accessible ores, they will be turning to deposits requiring even more surface disturbance. Some new production processes (such as leaching ores in place) show promise for reducing the land requirements of mining, but it is doubtful that these processes will be in widespread use before 2000. Lastly, it should be noted that the projected production figures have a wide range of uncertainty, which carries over into the land utilization figures.

In addition to land disrupted by "the hole in the ground," other land is affected by mining wastes. Furthermore, dust and toxic materials from the wastes generated in mining and refining often spreads to surrounding areas, reducing their ability to support life.

The wastes from mining and the early stages of refining are usually bulky, and sometimes toxic. For many deposits, the tons of earth that must be moved to expose the ore body exceed the tonnage of ore ultimately recovered from the site. This surface material removed (the "overburden") and the residue left after processing (the "tailings") are usually discarded in open piles.

Accurate data on the worldwide magnitude of mining waste generated annually are not available, but it is known that in industrialized countries the mining and cleaning of coal produces more waste than the extraction of any nonfuel mineral. According to the Organization for Economic Cooperation and Development, annual accumulations of coal mining waste are 90 million metric tons in the United States, 60 million tons in West Germany, and 56 million tons in the United Kingdom.[682] Uranium is also responsible for large amounts of mining waste. Nonfuel mineral commodities whose extraction is accompanied by considerable waste include (in descending order of apparent magnitude of waste) copper, iron ore, phosphate rock, stone, and clays.

Table 13-44 gives estimates of the amount of waste generated by the world output of six mineral commodities.* The estimates are rough approximations, derived by multiplying world production or projected demand by the ratio of marketable product to waste experienced in the United States in 1975.[683] While these estimates suffer from the same kinds of limitations as the estimates in Table 13-43, they do suggest that world production of the six commodities (totaling 9 billion tons) generated approximately 14 billion tons of waste in 1976. The projection for 2000 is 18 billion tons of commodities produced and 34 billion tons of waste. Future mining and milling wastes are expected to increase faster than the output of mineral commodities, partly because the demand for minerals with high ratios of waste to marketable product (phosphate rock, copper, and uranium)

is projected to increase faster than the demand for minerals with low waste to product ratios (stone and clays). The actual increase of waste will probably be greater than the increase in Table 13-44, which does not take into account the fact that, as time goes on, the average grade of ores worked will generally be lower.

Several countries are now seeking ways to protect agricultural land, forests, and waterways from pollution from mine wastes. In the Philippines, where mines discharge 140,000 tons of waste daily, the country's Bureau of Mines is investigating potential uses of some of the mine waste as material for cement, ceramics, and construction.[684] There is plenty of waste to work with. For example, nonfuel mining operations in the United States in 1975 moved 4.2 billion tons of material, of which 2.6 billion tons represented crude ore and 1.6 billion tons mining waste; 94 percent of the crude ore and 99 percent of the mining waste was from surface mines.[685]

What happens to mined-out land after operations move on or cease? When nothing is done, the abandoned and useless sites usually remain an ugly, hazardous area and a major source of water pollution, air pollution, and soil erosion. Vegetation is slow to regenerate naturally because of displaced soil, steep slopes, and drainage, which usually is acid, alkaline, or saline. These problems are particularly acute in areas where coal has been strip mined.[686]

According to the Environmental Protection Agency,[687] representative annual rates of erosion from various land uses are as follows:

| Land Use | Metric Tons per Square Kilometer | Short Tons per Square Mile | Relative Rate (Forest=1) |
|---|---|---|---|
| Forest | 8.5 | 24 | 1 |
| Grassland | 85 | 240 | 10 |
| Abandoned surface mine | 850 | 2,400 | 100 |
| Cropland | 1,700 | 4,800 | 200 |
| Active surface mine | 17,000 | 48,000 | 2,000 |
| Construction | 17,000 | 48,000 | 2,000 |

Reclamation efforts can reduce the environmental damage caused by mining wastes. Mining companies—at least in some nations—are increasing the incidence and degree of reclamation of mined lands. These efforts are largely in response to conservation movements and more stringent legislation.

Although world data on the extent of reclamation of mined-out lands are not available, some information for the United States is available. Of U.S. land used for mining in the 1930–71 period, 40 percent has been designated "reclaimed."[688]

---

* As indicated above, coal generates an enormous quantity of mining waste, but data corresponding to that presented in Table 13-44 could not be obtained for coal.

## TABLE 13-44

### Estimates of Solid Wastes Generated Annually by World Production of Selected Mineral Products, 1976–2000

| Mineral Product | Ratio of Tons of Waste to Tons of Marketable Product (U.S. 1975) | | 1976 | | | 1985 | | | 2000 | | |
|---|---|---|---|---|---|---|---|---|---|---|---|
| | Mining Waste | Milling Waste | Marketed Production | Mining Wastes | Milling Wastes | Marketed Production | Mining Wastes | Milling Wastes | Marketed Production | Mining Wastes | Milling Wastes |
| | | | | | | | | Millions of short tons | | | |
| Stone | 0.073 | 0.008 | 7,700 | 600 | 100 | 8,192 | 600 | 100 | 14,849 | 1,100 | 100 |
| Clays | 0.85 | Negligible | 580 | 500 | -* | 761 | 600 | -* | 1,061 | 900 | -* |
| Iron ore | 3.46 | 2.13 | 987 | 3,400 | 2,100 | 1,293 | 4,500 | 2,800 | 1,947 | 6,700 | 4,100 |
| Phosphate rock | 4.45 | 2.84 | 118 | 500 | 300 | 207 | 900 | 600 | 456 | 2,000 | 1,300 |
| Copper | 501 | 188 | 8 | 4,000 | 1,500 | 13 | 6,500 | 2,400 | 22 | 1,100 | 4,100 |
| Uranium | 14,235 | 673 | 0.04 | 600 | 30 | 0.1 | 1,400 | 100 | 0.2 | 2,800 | 140 |
| Total (all six commodities) | | | 9,393 | 9,600 | 4,000 | 10,466 | 14,500 | 6000 | 18,335 | 24,500 | 9,800 |

*Note:* Figures for mining and milling wastes assume U.S. 1975 ratios of marketable production to waste (columns 1 and 2), usually rounded to the nearest 100 million tons. Production figures for 1985 and 2000 are U.S. Bureau of Mines projections for demand, which is assumed to be matched by production.

* Less than 500,000 tons.

*Source:* U.S. Bureau of Mines, "Mining and Quarrying Trends in the Metal and Nonmetal Industries," in *Minerals Yearbook 1975; Mineral Commodity Summaries 1978;* and *Mineral Trends and Forecasts,* 1976.

However, the quality of the reclamation varies considerably. In some cases the effort has been minimal; in others serious difficulties are presented by hilly terrain and limited rainfall.

Land reclamation success stories are heard from many other nations. For example, in Ostrava, Czechoslovakia, red oak has started to grow on coal dumps characterized by steep slopes and very limited soil.[689] American Metal Climax, Inc. of New York conducts a project to farm its acquired coal lands (at Sullivan, Indiana) before strip mining and plans to develop the land's most productive resources after mining.[690] A cement plant at Bamburi, on Kenya's Indian Ocean coast, has rehabilitated hundreds of acres of land from which it quarried coral limestone; the area now has a forest of 30,000 trees, a productive farm, and fish ponds.[691]

As of mid-1977, 70 percent of the land disturbed by surface mining and needing reclamation in the United States was not under any legal requirement to be reclaimed.[692] This situation led to the Surface Mining Control and Reclamation Act of 1977. The law, which applies only to coal lands, stipulates that mined-over areas be returned approximately to their original contours. A tax on currently produced surface coal will be used to finance the reclamation of "orphaned" lands left from earlier operations. Slopes of more than 20 degrees on waste dumps are prohibited.[693]

Compliance with the new reclamation law is estimated to add from 50 cents to $4.00 to the cost of producing a ton of surface-mined coal in the United States.[694] Rehabilitating coal fields in the western United States, parts of which have a dry climate, would cost an estimated $925 to $2,750 per acre.[695] According to an Argonne National Laboratory study, reclamation of mined land in some localities (such as certain phosphate rock sites in Florida) may be a profitable endeavor if proper land use planning and marketing strategies are employed.[696]

Under present policy in most nations, the mining of a particular piece of land is usually permitted even when mining operations conflict with other uses of the land. However, stipulations and conditions are increasingly being made that take other potential land uses into consideration. In a few cases, mining has even been prohibited for environmental reasons. For example, the Rio Tinto Zinc Corporation was prohibited from mining in the Snowdonia National Park, Wales.[697] The Swedish Government has assured environmental groups and local authorities it will refuse to issue requested permits for strip mining mineral-bearing slate deposits in the Naerke area of southern Sweden.[698] In a region of Western Australia recently experiencing a diamond rush, the government set aside as off limits to mining a 440 square mile park near Cape Londonderry.[699] Ecological (as well as economic) factors figured significantly in the decision of the Puerto Rican Department of Natural Resources to not allow Kennecott Copper Corporation and American Metal Climax to mine an estimated 243 million tons of copper reserves on the island.[700] The United States has largely closed its national parks to mining; it has also prohibited surface mining of coal on prime farmlands unless they can later be restored to their original productivity and has prohibited mining that damages water supply.[701] Trends such as these may reduce to a degree the land disruption caused by mining, but they will also increase somewhat the cost of mineral products.

## Impact of Mineral Production on Air Quality

Air pollution generated from mining and processing activities (particularly high-temperature metallurgical operations) produces serious environmental and health problems. Air pollutants of particular concern are sulfur oxides, particulates, asbestos, radionuclides (radium and radon), coke oven emissions, arsenic, lead, and fluorides.[702]

Most sulfur oxide contamination of the atmosphere is caused by the combustion of fossil fuels, especially coal, but in addition, sulfur oxides go up the stacks of smelters treating sulfide ores of metals such as copper, nickel, lead, and zinc.

In 1974 U.S. copper smelters emitted 8,214 tons of sulfur oxides daily, 10 percent of the nation's total. However, smelter emissions are being reduced. The 1974 emissions were 33 percent below previous highs and the 1986 emissions are expected to be 90 percent below the earlier peak.[703] Unfortunately, such reductions are not the trend everywhere. The Cuajone copper mining and smelting project in Peru will soon double emissions and effluents from the site; it is expected that 60,000 tons of sulfur oxides will be released into the air and 30 million tons of tailings discharged into the sea annually. The World Bank, one of the project's lenders, has persuaded the borrower to accept, in principle, the incorporation of a number of environmental safeguards in project design.[704] The copper-nickel smelters of the Sudbury district of Ontario, Canada, emit 2.7 million tons of surfur oxides annually, causing losses of timber with a value of $117,000 per year in a 720 square mile zone of severe damage.[705] Such sulfur oxides contribute more widely, of course, to the problems of acid rain discussed in

this chapter in the section entitled "Water Projections and the Environment." They are also known to increase the incidence of asthma, chronic bronchitis, and emphysema.[706]

Uranium-mill tailings present a radioactive air pollution problem. The radium in the tailings decays to the radioactive gas radon, whose decay products are responsible for the high incidence of lung cancer among uranium miners in Europe and the United States.[707] Piles of uranium tailings in the United States total 140 million tons and could reach a billion tons by the year 2000.[708] Lyman J. Olsen, director of the Utah State Division of Health, reports that thousands of people work and live in close proximity to the tailings pile of an inactive uranium-mill site in Salt Lake City and are exposed to radioactive dust, radon gas and its decay products, and gamma radiation.[709] An active uranium mill near Grants, New Mexico, has dumped 23 million tons of tailings on 265 acres; the pile rises to a height of 100 feet. Covering such dumps with 8–12 feet of clay would reduce the radon eminations to twice background levels.[710] The cost of safe disposal of all uranium tailings in the United States is conservatively estimated at $140 million.[711]

Although radiation at phosphate rock mines is apparently a somewhat lesser problem,[712] the Global 2000 Study projections of a doubling to quadrupling of fertilizer use by the year 2000 imply an increase in the amount of radioactive phosphate waste. In Florida radiation from phosphate wastes is already an issue. According to a preliminary report by the U.S. Bureau of Mines, there could be a twofold increase in the incidence of lung cancer among persons living in structures built on reclaimed phosphate lands in Florida.[713]

## Impact of Mineral Production on Water Quality

Surface and underground water is frequently polluted by effluents of mining and milling operations and by rainfall or stream action on solid mine and mill wastes. Thirty-four percent of waste water discharged by all major U.S. industrial groups in 1973 was from production of primary metals, 8 percent from petroleum and coal products, and 1 percent from stone, glass, and clay products.[714]

One example of water pollution from mining is acid mine drainage, which is caused by the reaction of water and air with sulfur-bearing minerals in coal or metal mines and dumps. The sulfuric acid produced in this reaction enters streams, lakes, and rivers where it lowers the pH, killing many forms of life.

Another notable example of water pollution by

mining wastes is the dumping of salt wastes by East German potash mining companies into the Werra River. The Werra, which weaves across the border between East and West Germany, flows into the Weser River, which is now so salty that the city of Bremen can draw on it for only 20 percent of its water supply.[715] In addition, wastes from potash mines in France have long been implicated as one of the primary sources of contamination of the Rhine River.

In 1978, a series of earthquakes affecting Japan's Izu Peninsula caused the collapse of earthen dams holding mine wastes containing poisonous sodium cyanide. Fish were killed not only in the Mochikoshi and Kano Rivers but as far away as Suruga Bay.[716]

The Philippine Inter-Agency Committee on Environmental Protection has reported the discharge of about 100,000 tons of mine tailings per day in eight major river systems in the country, affecting an estimated 130,000 hectares of agricultural land.[717] The Japan International Cooperation Agency is expected to study the feasibility of a project for collecting tailings from at least four of the six major copper mines in the Baguio district of the Philippines and transporting them by pipeline for discharge into the Lingayen Gulf.[718]

In Peru, tailings from copper mines are polluting the San Juan, Mantaro, Locumba, and Moche rivers with iron, acid, magnesium, and other metals. The World Bank recommends a Mantaro cleanup project to be completed by 1980 to bring the iron content of the waste outflow down to 0.1 gram per liter and to reduce the acidity by 99.9 percent.[719]

As part of the opening of a molybdenum mine at Urad, Colorado, American Metal Climax constructed diversion structures and two miles of underground pipeline so that streams will flow around and under the mill and tailings areas and emerge from the property uncontaminated. The streams involved are part of the water supply for Golden, Colorado. A reservoir, holding water for mining and milling the ore, will be open to the public for camping, fishing, and the enjoyment of the surroundings.[720]

The Reserve Mining Company, a subsidiary of Armco Steel and Republic Steel Corporations has dumped approximately 67,000 tons of iron ore waste (taconite tailings) daily into Lake Superior for the past 23 years. The wastes contain microscopic asbestos fibers from a mine at Babbitt, Minnesota, and an ore-processing plant at Silver Bay, Minnesota.[721] Asbestos fibers are now present in the drinking water of Duluth and other communities that draw water from the lake. Air-borne asbestos fibers are known to cause serious lung diseases, including a particularly dangerous form of cancer. Whether similar problems arise from the drinking of water containing asbestos has not been established. Nevertheless, state and federal courts have determined that a potential health hazard exists[722] and have ruled that Reserve must change to on-land disposal. It is estimated that the required pollution control facilities will cost $370 million.

The increased mining that follows from the Global 2000 Study's projected demand for fuel and nonfuel minerals could easily increase the amount of water pollution from mining activities. Present policies may limit the effects somewhat, but the quality of water used for drinking, irrigation, and fish culture can be expected to be adversely affected in at least some areas.

## Indirect Effects of Mining on Land

The direct effects of most mining operations on land, while not negligible, are localized and relatively small compared to many other forms of human economic activity such as farming, forestry, and urbanization. By contrast, the indirect effects of mining can be quite large, especially since the infrastructure developed for mining operations often permits a large number of other activities that would be very difficult or impossible to carry on without it. Among the many indirect effects of mining on land are the boom-and-bust cycle, access roads, demand for renewable resources, and energy requirements. Each will be briefly considered here.

The boom-and-bust cycle of communities near mining and refining centers is a virtually inevitable consequence of the nonrenewable nature of mineral resources. Demographic and economic instabilities usually result.* In the short run, small communities may be unable to supply the community services needed by the overwhelmingly large numbers of new citizens drawn to a new

_____
* The U.S. Department of Housing and Urban Development has prepared a report suggesting how to manage growth when an area is suddenly affected by the rapid growth accompanying resource exploitation. The report focuses primarily on growth associated with energy development but applies equally to growth associated with the exploitation of nonfuel minerals. It includes brief case studies of the impacts of growth associated with the Jim Bridger Power Plant in Sweetwater County, Wyoming, the nuclear power plant in Calvert County, Maryland, and oil production and coal mining in Campbell County, Wyoming; the effects of North Sea oil and gas production on Scotland are also examined. (*Rapid Growth from Energy Projects—Ideas for State and Local Action—A Program Guide*, Washington: Department of Housing and Urban Development, 1976.)

mining operation. In the long run (of a decade or two), these services may not be needed at all.

D. B. Brooks and P. W. Andrews, in reviewing the problem of boom-and-bust cycles on a global basis for a 1973 United Nations Symposium on Population, Resources and Environment, noted that:

Even if mining communities are more carefully planned today, their inherent tendency to deplete their reason for existence cannot be ignored, because the result is often a depressed region with high unemployment and few services. Such problems are intensified by the cyclical nature of investment in minerals, so that there tend to be cycles, every 20 to 40 years, during which a nation is faced with waves of mine closures. [723]

This type of local economic instability is exacerbated by the relative isolation of mining from the rest of the economy. Mining generally does not spawn significant amounts of associated industrial or manufacturing activities, especially if carried out in remote areas.

Mining activities, especially in remote areas, require improved access roads. The access roads built to mines often lead to other forms of natural resource exploitation that are undesirable if uncontrolled. As happened in coal mining regions of Southern Appalachia and in the copper and silver mining regions of Chile, forests are often removed from a wide area around the mine, either to provide timber for mining operations, housing construction, railroad ties, and fuel, or simply because improved transportation makes previously inaccessible forests exploitable.

The excessive production, use, and marketing of charcoal is a case in point. A few countries still use charcoal to smelt and refine ores, among them Brazil, Argentina, Malaysia, Australia, and India. [724] The consequences of this practice are illustrated by what is happening in Brazil. The once extensive, mixed-hardwood open woodlands of the Brazilian plateau are being rapidly consumed. In the state of Minas Gerais, it is estimated that by 1982, 45 million hectares of forest will have been cut down, largely for conversion to charcoal to smelt pig iron. [725] The destabilizing impact of this deforestation on soils and the hydrological cycle is discussed in more detail in the energy section of this chapter.

Not all energy for mining and processing comes from renewable sources. Most energy for the mining and metals industries comes from nonrenewable sources, and these energy requirements lead to yet another indirect consequence of the projected increases in mining activities.

Like the technologies of the Green Revolution in agriculture and the intensive silviculture discussed elsewhere in this chapter, the technologies of mining and processing are energy-intensive and are becoming more so. The worldwide energy dependence of mining and processing has not been studied carefully, but the linkages between energy and minerals in the U.S. has been examined to some extent. The reason for concern over the energy-intensiveness of mining and processing is that lower-grade ores generally require more energy for extraction, processing, and refining at a time when energy costs are projected to increase significantly in the years ahead. As Earl Hayes notes,

Each material has a fixed lower bound of ore grade, below which energy costs make processing uneconomic. . . . Energy costs [in general] rise rapidly as ore grade decreases. At some lower limit, say 0.25%, the energy expenditures dominate the whole recovery picture. Technological improvements in rock disintegration, transportation and concentration will have to be made if such low-grade ores are to be considered reserves—that is, resources that can be processed economically. [726]

Hayes also notes that in 1971 the energy inputs for processing metallic and nonmetallic minerals totaled $69 \times 10^{15}$ Btu. The net energy output was $57 \times 10^{15}$ Btu. The U.S. materials industry uses over 20 percent of the nation's energy to process materials: 8 percent for metals, 7.8 percent for chemicals and allied products, 4 percent for petroleum refining, and 2 percent for nonmetallics. Steel, aluminum, plastics, cement, and gasoline account for half of the 20 percent. [727]

As these figures make clear, the projected worldwide increases in minerals production can be expected to have a number of indirect environmental consequences through the associated demands for energy.

## Effects of Mining the Seabed

As mentioned in Chapter 12, if the politics of the ocean floor are adequately resolved and if manganese nodules prove economically competitive with the ores for which they would substitute, large-scale mining of the ocean floor may commence before the year 2000. The environmental implications of mining the seabed have already been discussed in detail in this chapter in the section on "The Projections and the Marine Environment."

## Conclusions

The environmental consequences of an approximate doubling of the global mining of nonfuel

## TABLE 13-45

### Apparent Opportunities for Further Mineral Development

| Country | Mineral | Value of World Output, 1968 (in millions of 1968 dollars) | Percent of World Reserves | Percent of World Output |
|---|---|---|---|---|
| Zambia | copper | 7,740 | 10 | Quite small |
| Chile | copper | 7,740 | 19 | 12 |
| Thailand | tin | 750 | 32 | 9 |
| Indonesia | tin | 750 | 12 | Quite small |
| U.S. | zinc | 1,450 | 27 | 12 |
| U.S. | lead | 775 | 37 | 14 |
| Cuba | nickel | 1,100 | 24 | Quite small |
| Morocco | phosphorus | 835 | 42 | 13 |
| Guinea | bauxite | 340 | 34 | Quite small |
| Australia | bauxite | 340 | 34 | 15 |

Source: Rex Bosson and Bension Varon. *The Mining Industry and the Developing Countries.* New York: Oxford. 1977. App. G.

minerals between now and 2000 are difficult to assess. Possibilities for considerably expanded production seem to exist in countries having large portions of the world's reserves of critical, high-value minerals (Table 13-45). Major new resource discoveries have been reported in ecologically fragile areas such as the seabed, the Amazon basin, Oceania, Siberia, and south central Africa. A disproportionate fraction of resource development is expected to take place in the LDCs, where environmental protection measures may be limited.

Smelting, refining, and milling usually occur in major industrial centers rather than at the mine site, but mineral exploitation and processing can have devastating impacts on extraction and concentration sites and their adjoining communities. Although the mining and concentration operations may continue for only a decade or two, they leave permanent scars on the landscape, especially in the case of open pit mines, which can be very deep.[728] Superficial mining of ores such as bauxite that are the result of weathering or are found in sedimentary formations may be less destructive of the land, which can be restored to productive forests, to pasture, or even to farmland if precautions and ecological conditions are adequate. The recovery of such sites will take many

more years in arid or cold (tundra) regions than in hot humid regions, however. How long it will take for mining scars to heal in the oceans is still highly uncertain.

The indirect effects of boomtowns, new transportation systems, and other infrastructures associated with mining operations may be more lasting and significant than the direct effects. Land and water for mining and refining will in many cases be in direct competition with agriculture, forestry, urban water supplies and other uses. Conflicts with local populations over the use of land and water resources can be expected to increase. In West Germany opposition was encountered when an entire village was relocated recently to make room for a coal mine.[729] In central Florida, opposition has been raised to phosphate mining because of competition for the water used in beneficiating the ore.

These and other environmentally related conflicts will increase in the years ahead as the minerals industry is forced to turn to poorer, less accessible, more energy-demanding ores than those presently being exploited. As a result, the environmental damage done by mining is likely to increase markedly unless policies change and production technologies and practices improve significantly.

## CLOSING THE LOOPS

### Introduction

The previous 10 sections of this chapter have

considered the Global 2000 Study's projections for population, GNP, climate, technology, food and agriculture, forestry, marine and coastal resources, water, energy, and nonfuel minerals for the purpose of determining what impact those projections will have *on the environment* between now and the year 2000. In the final sections of this chapter, however, the perspective will be reversed. The focus will shift to the impact that the environmental developments presented in the preceding 10 sections would have *on the population, economic, and resource projections* of Chapters 2–12.

Figure 13–1 at the beginning of this chapter illustrates a reversed—ecological—perspective, showing first how population, economic, and resource factors affect environment (as presented in the preceding 10 sections of this chapter) and how, in turn, the environment feeds back upon (affects) population, economy, and resources. While Figure 13–1 illustrates, at least conceptually, how the feedback loops are closed in nature, it must be emphasized that in the discussion that follows the feedback loops are not actually closed analytically, and that they cannot be closed with the government's current models.

The problem is that the government's present analytical tools for making population, GNP, and resource projections are not designed to accept explicit environmental feedback. Most of these models simply assume implicitly that the environment will do what it has done in the past, only more so; and this assumption leads to discrepancies between the environmental assumptions of the population, GNP, and resource projections and the environmental conditions implied by these projections. Put simply, the environment cannot do what some of the projections assume it will do.

Although there is no way in which revised, more realistic environmental assumptions can be entered into the projection models, it is possible to (1) compare each model's environmental assumptions with the environmental conditions implied by the population, GNP, and resource projections, (2) note the discrepancies (which would not exist if the environmental feedback effects were actually present in the models), and (3) consider how the discrepancies might affect the population, GNP, and resource projections *if* it were possible to alter the environmental assumptions to eliminate the discrepancies. Since it is not possible to alter the environmental assumptions in the population, GNP, and resource projections, the discrepancies remain, and the projections retain their basically open-loop, linear

character.* Nonetheless, the examination of the discrepancies and their implications provides a step toward a more ecological perspective.

As a preparation for shifting to this more ecological perspective on the future world environment, it is helpful to review the impacts upon the environment already presented in this chapter. Because, from the environmental point of view, economic and political boundaries are of very limited relevance, it is necessary to organize the information around major environmental classifications—terrestrial, atmospheric, aquatic—rather than around the economic and political jurisdictions considered heretofore. This is essential as a first step in closing the feedback loops because, for instance, many of the projections imply changes in the aquatic environment, and all of these changes need to be considered in comparing the future aquatic environment with the water assumptions in the various projections. Similarly, several of the projections imply changes in soil conditions, and it is the overall soil conditions that result from all the changes that need to be compared with the projections' implicit assumptions about soils. In such cases, how is the whole ecological perspective to be determined on the basis of fragmented projections—and then again how is the whole environmental future to be made relevant to fragmented projection models?

The approach used here is to gather the implications of the fragmented projections into one extensive table—Table 13–46. This table is organized *primarily* by the earth's major environments: terrestrial, atmospheric, aquatic. This primary organization establishes the holistic perspective characteristic of the environment. The *secondary* organization of the table is by major geographic groupings: global, regional (i.e., continental or more than one nation state), and local (i.e., subcontinental, individual nation states, or smaller economic or political units). The "local" category is further subdivided into "rural" and "urban." This organization of the table demonstrates the relationship of economic and geopolitical areas.

In the text that follows Table 13–46, the future world environment is discussed first in terms of the three major environments (still in the original perspective of projections impacting on the environment) so that the overall ecological description of the future world environment can finally

---

*These missing feedback loops and many other deficiencies in the government's current analytical capabilities are discussed in Chapter 14 and succeeding chapters of Parts II and III.

## TABLE 13-46

## Summary of Impacts on the Environment Implied by the Global 2000 Study's Population, GNP, and Resource Projections, by Major Environments

### A. TERRESTRIAL ENVIRONMENTS

| | Global | Regional (continental or more than one nation state) | Local (subcontinental, individual nation states, or smaller) | |
|---|---|---|---|---|
| | | | Urban | Rural |
| **Population** | No impact projected. | No impact projected. | Arable land lost to new or expanding human settlements by the year 2000 is projected to be 25 million hectares. | Increased numbers of subsistence farmers in LDCs will result in deterioration in land productivity, overgrazing, and deforestation. |
| **GNP** | No impact projected. | Slow economic growth rates in densely populated LDCs will increase the pressures of people and domestic animals on land. | Continued terrestrial disposal of toxic industrial and urban wastes will create potential health hazards in both industrialized countries and LDCs. | No impact projected. |
| **Climate** | No impact projected. | No impact projected. | No impact projected. | No impact projected. |
| **Technology** | No impact projected. | No impact projected. | No impact projected. | No impact projected. |
| **Agriculture and food** | Land productivity is declining in many industrialized countries as well as LDCs. Losses of range and farmland to desertification by 2000 could total 2,800 million hectares, primarily in Africa and Asia. One half the total irrigated land is already damaged by waterlogging, salinization, and alkalinization. By 2000, an additional 2.75 million hectares could be lost or damaged. | Regional germ plasm in traditional crops is being lost as increasingly marginal lands are being brought under cultivation and local varieties are replaced by high-yield varieties. | No impact projected. | Soil erosion and compaction will be a continuing—perhaps intensifying—problem for intensively-cropped, clean-tilled land in both industrialized countries and LDCs. Heavy dependence on pesticides will further deplete insect predator populations, reducing the crop protection offered through insect ecology, but the trend toward integrated pest management may compensate or even rehabilitate some areas. |
| **Fisheries and marine developments** | No impact projected. | No impact projected. | No impact projected. | No impact projected. |
| **Forest exploitation** | Hundreds of thousands of species of plants and animals will be extinct by 2000—a major reduction of a global genetic resource. | Between 1975 and 2000, 446 million hectares of forests will be removed to meet global demands for forest products, fuelwood, and agricultural land. | No impact projected. | Critical catchment areas and inherently unstable land will become destabilized by deforestation leading to erosion and land slippage. |

|  |  |  |  |
|---|---|---|---|
|  | No impact projected. | ricultural land. The deforestation will occur primarily in the LDCs and will: (1) cause irreparable or long term damage to the land by exposing the soil to sun and rain; (2) render up to 600,000 species of plants and animals globally extinct; (3) destabilize slopes of catchments, especially in the Himalayan range and other mountains of Asia and in Latin American ranges.<br><br>Deforestation rates are relatively slow in industrialized countries, balanced by plantations. | Habitats for wildlife (including predators of agricultural pests) will be destroyed in large amounts. |
| Water resource development and regulation | No impact projected. | No impact projected. | Large impoundments will inundate agricultural lands, forests, mineral deposits, human settlements, roads, etc., especially in densely populated LDC areas. |
| Energy | In industrialized regions (North America, Eastern and Western Europe, Japan, U.S.S.R., South Africa, and Australia) energy development by 2000 will result in:<br>• Thousands of millions of tons of coal mined annually.<br>• Approximately one hundred thousand million tons of coal mined cumulatively over the 1975–2000 period.<br>• Many thousands of square kilometers of land strip-mined cumulatively.<br>• Many thousands of square kilometers (collectively) of land adversely affected by subsidence.<br>• Land for approximately 1,000 coal power plants (nominal 1,100 Mw).<br>• Land for several hundred nuclear power plants (nominal 1,100 Mw). | Where LDC urban poor rely on charcoal or firewood, urban demand will result in total denudement of surrounding countryside to as great a distance as 100 kilometers. | Strip mining of coal and uranium will cause land disturbance, and mine tailings will pose radiation danger. |

## A. Terrestrial Environments (cont.)

| Global | Regional (continental or more than one nation state) | Local (subcontinental, individual nation states, or smaller) | |
|---|---|---|---|
| | | Urban | Rural |
| | • Several tens of thousands of square kilometers of land for transmission lines for new coal and nuclear plants. | | |
| | • Approximately 1,000 million tons of radioactive tailings from supplying uranium for the 1975–2000 period. | | |
| | • Approximately 10 million cubic meters of low-level radioactive wastes. | | |
| | • A few 100,000 tons of spent nuclear fuel. | | |
| | • Several 100,000 tons of spent nuclear fuel over the lifetimes of the plants constructed through the year 2000. | | |
| | Coal development can be expected to be most intense in those areas with large coal deposits (U.S. and Eastern Europe); nuclear development most intense in those areas with limited coal resources (Western Europe, Japan). | | |
| | In the less developed regions (North and Middle Africa, parts of the Middle East, much of Asia, parts of Latin America), the energy impacts will be primarily in organic fuels leading to: | | |
| | • A 650 million cubic meter annual shortfall in fuelwood before 2000, causing (1) combustion of even small bushes and aggravated erosion and desertification, and (2) increased use of dung and crop residues for fuel. | | |

| | | | | |
|---|---|---|---|---|
| Nonfuel minerals | • Annual combustion of 250–670 million tons of dung by 2000, depriving the soils of the equivalent of $2 billion in chemical fertilizer. | No impact projected. | No impact projected. | The mining of quarries of bauxite, sand, gravel, and limestone, as well as the mining of metallic minerals from hard rock, will result in long-term—sometimes permanent—local land disturbance and loss. |

### B. ATMOSPHERIC ENVIRONMENTS

| | | | | |
|---|---|---|---|---|
| Population | No impact projected. | No impact projected. | No impact projected. | No impact projected. |
| GNP | Some spray-can propellants and some high-altitude aircraft flights may contribute to the depletion of the ozone layer. | No impact projected. | LDC air pollution—especially by toxic substances—will increase if polluting industries move from areas with strong environmental standards to areas with limited or no standards. | |
| Climate | No impact projected. | No impact projected. | No impact projected. | No impact projected. |
| Technology | No impact projected. | No impact projected. | No impact projected. | No impact projected. |
| Agriculture and food | Nitrous oxide release to air from bacterial conversion and nitrogen fertilizer may contribute to depletion of the ozone layer. DDT and other organochlorines enter the atmosphere where they accumulate and are precipitated out in rain, which ultimately will contaminate the oceans. | No impact projected. | No impact projected. | Pesticides sprayed from aircraft may create local air quality problems and poison people and animals. Smoke and dust will create local air quality problems. Land clearing will cause greater weather and microclimate extremes. |
| Fisheries and marine developments | No impact projected. | No impact projected. | No impact projected. | No impact projected. |

## A. Atmospheric Environments (cont.)

| | Global | Regional (continental or more than one nation state) | Local (subcontinental, individual nation states, or smaller) Urban | Local (subcontinental, individual nation states, or smaller) Rural |
|---|---|---|---|---|
| Forest exploitation | 446 million hectares of forest will be lost as an absorber of atmospheric carbon dioxide ($CO_2$). CO₂ will be added to the atmosphere as a result of burning a portion of the trees that were on the 446 million hectares cleared. | No impact projected. | No impact projected. | Noticeable increase in humidity will occur near reservoirs and irrigation systems. |
| Water resource development and regulation | No impact projected. | No impact projected. | No impact projected. | Slight increase in humidity near reservoirs and irrigation systems. |
| Energy | $CO_2$ emissions will increase to 26–34 billion short tons per year, roughly double the CO₂ emissions of the mid-1970s.<br><br>446 million hectares of CO₂-absorbing forests will be lost.<br><br>Burning of much of the wood on 446 million hectares will produce more CO₂.<br><br>Decomposition of much soil humus will release more CO₂.<br><br>Establishment of trends in fossil fuel combustion and deforestation, which will lead inevitably to significantly larger concentrations of CO₂ in the earth's atmosphere during the 21st century.<br><br>A doubling of the CO₂ concentration by 2050 could increase the average temperature of the earth by about 3°C, melting much of the polar ice over an estimated period of 200 years and flooding large | In industrialized regions of the world (North America, Eastern and Western Europe, Japan, U.S.S.R., South Africa, and Australia) the annual production and combustion of several thousand million tons of coal will produce regionally significant emissions of particulates, carbon monoxide, nitrogen oxides, sulfur oxides, and toxic heavy metals.<br><br>In some areas, emission control standards will limit or reduce some emissions. In the U.S. for example, the Department of Energy estimates that under present standards, national emissions of sulfur oxides will decline until 1985 and increase thereafter.<br><br>In the less developed regions, increased combustion of wood, dung, and coal is not expected to result in multinational or continental air quality problems. | Coal combustion will result in 5 to 20 times more air pollutants (CO, NO$_x$, SO$_2$, hydrocarbons, smoke, smog) than at present and higher temperatures than surrounding countryside.<br><br>LDC cities will probably not demand emission controls on coal power and heating plants, and as a result will experience large increases in many air pollutants, especially sulfur oxides and particulates. | Hotter local weather will occur where forests have been removed for fuelwood or charcoal. |

|  |  |  |  |  |
|---|---|---|---|---|
|  | amounts of coastal land. | Increased emissions of sulfur and nitrogen oxides will acidify the rain over wide areas. |  | No impact projected. |

## C. Aquatic Environments

|  |  |  |  |  |
|---|---|---|---|---|
| Nonfuel minerals | No impact projected. | No impact projected. | No impact projected. | No impact projected. |
| Population | No impact projected. | No impact projected. | Human wastes create increasingly severe water pollution problems in many LDC urban areas. | No impact projected. |
| GNP | No impact projected. | Pollution by toxic wastes from petrochemical, metallurgical, and other industries will accumulate in regional seas and gulfs with slow or restricted water circulation (e.g., Red Sea, Caspian Sea, Persian Gulf, Mediterranean). | In or near large cities—especially in the middle-income LDCs—serious water pollution by organic and inorganic wastes, some highly toxic, can be expected from areas of industrial concentration and ports. Construction on coastal and wetland habitats will reduce spawning and breeding habitats and damage reefs. |  |
| Climate | Climate change of sufficient magnitude to influence global water supplies are thought possible by 2000, but there is no consensus on either the climate change or the associated change in water supply. | Climate change of sufficient magnitude to influence regional water supplies is thought possible by 2000, but there is no consensus on either the climate or the associated change in water supply. | Climate change of sufficient magnitude to influence local water supplies are thought possible by 2000, but there is no consensus on either the climate change or the associated change in water supply. |  |
| Technology | No impact projected. | No impact projected. | No impact projected. | No impact projected. |
| Food and agriculture | No impact projected. | Consumptive (evaporative) use of water for irrigation will increase. Surface waters will contain increased amounts of salts, fertilizers, and pesticides. Persistent pesticides and their degradation products, especially the organochlorine group, will accumulate in marine sediments and bioaccumulate in marine food chains. | Pesticide, fertilizer and other chemical manufacturing plants may pollute local waters with effluents. | Streams receiving runoff from farmlands, especially irrigated lands, will receive increased quantities of pesticides, herbicides, sediments, nitrites, and nitrates. Persistent pesticides in runoff will contaminate sediments and nearshore waters and damage spawning and breeding waters. Feedlots and food-processing plants will pollute local waters with organic wastes, depressing dissolved oxygen levels and killing fish. |

## C. AQUATIC ENVIRONMENTS (cont.)

| | Global | Regional (continental or more than one nation state) | Local (subcontinental, individual nation states, or smaller) Urban / Rural |
|---|---|---|---|
| Fisheries and marine development | Intensive commercial fishing will continue to deplete oceanic stocks of tuna and other traditionally preferred species. | Populations of preferred fish species may decline in some regional seas (e.g., the Mediterranean) as a result of intensive fishing and pollution. The 200-mile economic zone, on the other hand, may lead to improved management of some regional and national fisheries. | Fishing in heavily polluted rivers, coastal waters, and estuaries will decline or become restricted due to health hazards of toxic chemicals and pathogens. |
| Forest exploitation | No impact projected. | Extensive deforestation and land-clearing will alter the hydrology of major rivers, exaggerating extreme high and low flows. | Local streamflow and seasonal floods will increase in basins with deforested watersheds. Aquifer recharge will diminish following deforestation, reducing ground-water supplies and increasing vulnerability to drought. Intensive tree-farming will add fertilizers and pesticides to local waters. |
| Water resource development and regulation | No impact projected. | Large-scale dams, impoundments, and modifications of river flows will significantly alter salinity, temperature, and flows of nutrients in estuaries, disrupting the life cycles of many organisms and adversely affecting biological productivity in the affected waters. | Hazards of schistosomiasis, malaria, and other water-borne diseases will be increased significantly through irrigation projects that create and expand habitats for the vectors and hosts of these diseases. Increasing consumptive use of water will diminish the capacity of streams and rivers to carry and degrade wastes, including soil salts. Impoundments on smaller rivers to store water, control floods, and generate electricity will alter hydrologic regimes to the detriment of aquatic productivity, only partially compensated for by still-water fisheries in reservoirs. |
| Energy | Open oceans will be polluted by oil from tankers and by atmospheric fallout from the combustion of fossil fuels. | In the industrialized regions of the world (North America, Eastern and Western Europe, Japan, U.S.S.R., South Africa, and Australia), there will be several aquatic | Oil pollution of ports, coastal waters, and estuaries from accidental losses occuring during transfers, or from groundings or collisions. Local waters will experience thermal and other kinds of pollution as a result of coal and nuclear generating plants with once-through cooling, |

impacts of energy development: Acidic drainage from approximately one thousand million tons of coal mined annually will affect water quality and aquatic life over large areas.

Lakes in southern Scandinavia and eastern Noth America will become acidified as a result of acid rain and snow.

Oil from offshore wells and tankers (operational discharges and accidental spills), and terrestrial runoff will pollute coastal and open ocean areas.

Large increases in the number of coal and nuclear power plants will create a large impact on the aquatic environment through once-through cooling or consumptive, evaporative cooling.

In the less developed regions, two aquatic impacts of energy development can be expected: Stream and river flows will be destabilized as a result of deforestation for fuelwood; oil development and export in petroleum exporting countries will adversely affect water quality and aquatic resources.

which alters aquatic ecology, lowers dissolved oxygen, kills fish eggs, and may cause fish kills.

Consumptive use of water for evaporative cooling in generating plants may be large enough to affect stream flows in some areas, potentially reducing the ability of streams to absorb wastes and degrading water quality locally.

Local streams and rivers will be polluted by acidic drainage from mines.

Nonfuel minerals

No impact projected.

Deep-sea mining is not expected to produce seriously adverse effects in the short run (years) but the long-term, ultimate effects of bottom disruption, turbidity in the deep ocean waters, and the processing of wastes are still very uncertain.

Deep-sea mining will produce silt and processing wastes that may be locally damaging to marine ecosystems.

## TABLE 13–46 (cont.)

### D. Low Probability, High-Risk Events Affecting All Environments

| | Global | Regional (continental or more than one nation state) | Local (subcontinental, individual nation states, or smaller) — Urban | Rural |
|---|---|---|---|---|
| Climate | As populations grow, forcing the use of more marginal and arid lands, world food production will become more vulnerable even to (relatively) high-probability variations in climate. | Regional manifestations of the global problem will be significant, especially for South Asia, the United States, the U.S.S.R., and the Sahel region of Africa. | Vulnerability, large increases in prices, and supply interruptions will be especially high in urban areas. | Vulnerability is less in rural areas but, locally, will be severe, as in the African Sahel. |
| Food and agriculture | Habitat for the wild progenitors of major food crops will continue to be lost while single-variety monocultures expand. As a result, there would be an increased probability of plant epidemics (e.g., the U.S. problem with corn blight in the early 1970s), which could significantly affect world food supplies and markets. Increased dependence of agriculture on fossil fuel intensive inputs increases the vulnerability of crop production to disruptions of energy supplies. | Regional manifestations of the global problem will be experienced. | Urban areas will be more vulnerable to increased prices and supply interruptions. | Rural areas will be less vulnerable than urban areas to supply interruptions and increased prices. |
| Energy | The increased use of nuclear energy increases the probability of further nuclear proliferation and of nuclear terrorism. | A 226 percent increase in nuclear and hydroelectric (mostly nuclear) generation by 1990 (several hundreds of plants by 2000), will increase the probability of a serious accident in a nuclear reactor or in some other portion of the nuclear cycle. | Local manifestations of the global and regional impacts will be experienced. Increased marine transport of liquefied energy gases will increase the risks of fires or explosions in ports. | No impact projected. |

*Note:* Throughout Table 13–46 the word "will" is used in the sense that an impact will follow if the population, GNP, and resource projections are fulfilled and if there is no change in current environmental projection policies.

be related back to the environmental assumptions in projection models for the discussion of discrepancies and their implications in the section entitled, "Assumptions, Discrepancies, and Feedback."

It should be emphasized here once again that the entries in Table 13–46 and in the following section ("The Global Environment in 2000") summarize impacts *on the environment* implied by the Global 2000 Study's population, GNP, and resource projections. Where an entry in the table indicates "No impact projected," it means simply that the Global 2000 Study's projections for population, GNP, and resources do not imply an impact in this particular area. For example, although there are many indirect implications of the projected increase in human population, the projected increase is not expected to have a direct, global effect on the world's soils. As a result, the first entry in Table 13–46 under Terrestrial Environment is "No impact projected."

## The Global Environment in 2000

Most· aspects of environmental deterioration are not global in scale, but those that are are serious and troubling indeed. They are serious not only because they develop slowly on a massive scale but also because they are usually not subject to any quick technological fixes. They are troubling not only because data and knowledge on their development and causes are often only sketchy, but also because the institutions studying and addressing these problems are underfunded and understaffed. Furthermore, solutions to many global environmental problems are related directly or indirectly to economic development and population stabilization efforts, and therefore programs to address global environmental problems must inevitably become involved in some of the world's most difficult and complex social, political, and economic problems.

Serious environmental developments on a global scale are clearly in evidence—on the land, in the atmosphere, and in the water. The global problems of the terrestrial environment are considered first.

*The World's Terrestrial Environment in 2000.* The world has only recently begun to take measure of the universal and momentous nature of trends in the condition of the terrestrial environment. The data now available are largely a result of a series of specialized international conferences and studies sponsored by the United Nations. The general picture is that of a decline in soil quality and productive capacity over much of the planet,

but especially in the difficult or marginal environments, such as mountains, arid lands, and very humid regions. The most massive losses or damages to the world's lands, forests, and genetic wealth have been taking place and will continue to take place in the less developed regions of Africa, Latin America and Asia, but the industrialized countries are also being affected.

Some reference figures are helpful in adding perspective to the discussion of the future of the terrestrial environment. The most basic of these figures is the earth's total area: 51,000 million hectares (510 million square kilometers) or 197 million square miles. Of the earth's total surface, more than 70 percent is ocean (361 million sq km). About 25 percent (132 million sq km) is ice-free land. About 5 percent (26 million sq km) is closed forest and 2 percent (12 million sq km) is open forest and range land. Deserts now cover about 2 percent of the surface area (7.9 million sq km). About 3 percent (15 million sq km) is arable land. Irrigated land amounts to less than 1 percent of the arable total, as does the total urban area.

Table 13–47 presents the major trends in the world's terrestrial environment. In geographic terms, desertification is the most sweeping change. If unchecked, the process of desertification that is claiming range land and some crop land, especially in Africa and Asia, will more than triple the present 7,922 thousand square kilometers of desert in the world, possibly by 2000. Twenty one

## TABLE 13–47

### Projected Changes in Global Vegetation and Land Resources, 1975–2000

| | 1975 | 2000 | Change | Percent Change |
|---|---|---|---|---|
| | *millions of hectares* | | | |
| Deserts | 792 | 1,284 | +492 | +62 |
| Closed forests | 2,563 | 2,117 | −446 | −17 |
| Irrigated area | 223 | 273 | +50 | +22 |
| Irrigated area damaged by salinization and related problems* | 111.5 | 114.6 | +3.1 | +3 |
| Arable land | 1,477 | 1,539 | +62 | +4 |

*Source:* Global 2000 Study projections.

a. Estimated as follows. In Chapter 9 it is estimated that half of the world's total irrigated area is already damaged; thus the 1975 figure is approximately 111.5 million ha. The U.N. estimates (*Desertification: An Overview,* U.N. Conference on Desertification, 1977, p. 12.) that approximately 125,000 ha are degraded annually due to waterlogging, salinization, and alkalinization. Assuming that this annual figure remains constant to the year 2000, a total of 3.1 million ha. would be added to the damaged area, bringing the total to 114.6 million ha.

percent of the earth's ice-free surface would then be desert.

At the other climatic extreme—the humid tropics—deforestation is projected to remove 446 million hectares of closed forest by 2000, thus reducing the amount of the earth's surface covered with closed forests from one-fifth to one-sixth of the total. Because of the low fertility of many soils in the humid tropics, the removal of tropical forests may represent a onetime exploitation with high long-term costs, especially for the survival of local flora and fauna.

At no time in recorded history has the specter of species extinction loomed so ominously. Largely a consequence of deforestation and the "taming" of wild areas, the projected loss over two decades of approximately one-fifth of all species on the planet (at a minimum, roughly 500,000 species of plants and animals) is a prospective loss to the world that is literally beyond evaluation. The genetic and ecological values of wild or newly identified species continue to be discovered. They represent an irreplaceable evolutionary legacy whose value, particularly the value of the many expected to be lost in the tropics, will certainly increase especially if the earth's climate becomes warmer. The fact that humankind derives most of its food from no more than 15 species of plants masks to some extent the importance of genetic extinction, but not for the plant breeders who rely on the traits of wild progenitors of domestic plants in their continuing battle against pests and disease and in efforts to increase yields.

Arable land for agriculture is projected to increase by about 4 percent over the next two decades to a total of 15.4 million square kilometers. This global projection, however, hides a number of important considerations. In some areas the amount of arable land is actually projected to decline. Where arable land is projected to increase, the projection is based on the assumption that capital will be available to bring the land into cultivation at two to three times the present cost per hectare. Furthermore, overall basic land productivity is declining in many areas.

Irrigated lands, a part of the productivity problem, are projected to increase by about 28 percent, again assuming that large amounts of capital will be available for water regulation and irrigation projects. However, one-half of the world's irrigated soils are presently suffering the effects of salinization and alkalinization resulting from inadequate drainage and poor water management. The amount affected will increase during the rest of the century. Barring unprecedented improvements in water and soils management, the historic and present intractability of this problem does not bode well for irrigation in arid zones. While the areas affected are relatively small, irrigated lands generally have exceptionally high yields, and their loss, or even their reduced productivity, is therefore very important. In the U.S., for example, the extremely productive San Joaquin Valley in California is experiencing increasing problems of salinization.

Worldwide, the productivity of arable, unirrigated land is declining in many areas due to overintensive use. While in the industrialized countries, a loss in natural productivity is partially obscured by heavy use of increasingly expensive, petroleum-based chemical fertilizers, that is not the case in the LDCs. While lack of comprehensive data limits appreciation of the phenomenon, observations in Africa and in India and elsewhere in Asia point to continuing erosion, loss of organic matter, shortened fallow periods, and declining soil quality in the decades ahead.

The prospect of declining soil quality can be seen to be very serious when viewed against a backdrop of increasing population densities on arable lands. The trends in arable hectares per capita throughout the world are illustrated in Figure 13–20. With less than 2000 square meters (one-fifth of a hectare, or one-half acre) of arable land per capita projected for the year 2000 in the LDCs, continuation of the deterioration in soil quality and natural productivity would be disastrous. Nonetheless, since birth rates are not projected to decline to replacement levels anytime soon and since little additional land will be brought into cultivation, very intensive use—and abuse—of land can be expected to continue well into the 21st century.

While there are definite global trends toward soil loss, soil deterioration, and species extinctions, these terrestrial trends are generally subject to remedial action on a national or even local scale. By contrast, the atmosphere and the oceans are examples of global resources held in common, and all nations must inevitably participate in the resolution of problems in these areas. *Institutionally,* therefore, the problems of the atmospheric and aquatic environments are even more difficult of solution than those of the terrestrial environment.*

---

*It can be reasonably argued that terrestrial resources are also, in effect, a global commons problem. Foreign economic assistance and international trade in oil, grain, and forest products involve many nations directly or indirectly in the fate of other nations' terrestrial environments. Nonetheless, each nation does have significantly more control over its soils, forests, and fresh water resources that it does over its share of the world's atmosphere and oceans.

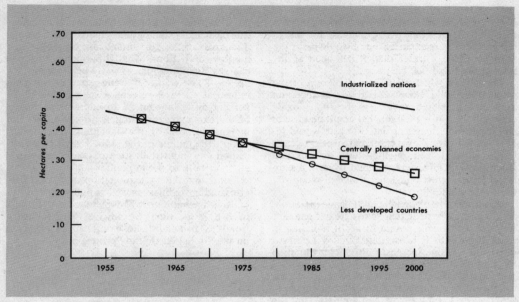

**Figure 13-20.** Arable land per capita, 1955, 1975, and 2000. (*From Chapter 6, Table 6-13*)

*The World's Atmospheric Environment in 2000.* Two global atmospheric changes resulting from anthropogenic pollutants are of great consequence over the long term: the increase in concentrations of carbon dioxide ($CO_2$) and the depletion of the ozone layer in the stratosphere.

Most climatologists expect a general, global warming as a consequence of increased atmospheric concentrations of $CO_2$, but the timetable for significant global warming is not agreed upon. The National Academy of Sciences projected a 6° C warming by the latter half of the 22nd century, but it appears very likely that significant global climatic warming could occur long before that time. A panel of scientists assembled by the Department of Energy anticipates that a doubling of atmospheric $CO_2$ would result in a 2–3° C warming as early as the year 2050. [730]

U.S. analyses of early warming trends are supported by World Meteorological Organization (WMO) reports on atmospheric carbon dioxide. The WMO also suggests that with a doubling of $CO_2$ the global average temperature would increase by almost 3° C above its present level [731] and that gradual warming of the lower atmosphere, expecially at high altitudes, would create global and regional climatic effects detectable before the end of this century and significant before

the end of the next. [732] The Declaration of the 1979 World Climate Conference of the WMO states that the burning of fossil fuels, deforestation, and changes of land use have increased the $CO_2$ content in the atmosphere by about 15 per cent during the last century and are continuing to increase $CO_2$ concentrations by about 0.4 per cent per year. [733]

Most recently, four scientists reported to the Council on Environmental Quality on the $CO_2$ problem, noting—among other things—that the time is at hand when industrialized nations must begin careful consideration of the implications of their energy policies for the $CO_2$ balance of the atmosphere. The scientists concluded: "If we wait to prove that the climate is warming before we take steps to alleviate the $CO_2$ build-up, the effects will be well underway and still more difficult to control. The earth will be committed to appreciable changes in climate with unpredictable consequences. The potential disruptions are sufficiently great to warrant the incorporation of the $CO_2$ problem into all considerations of policy in the development of energy. [734]

A global warming would mean more rain and a melting of polar ice, with a consequent rise in sea level. Temperature increases in polar regions would be 3 or 4 times greater than global averages. If the West Antarctic ice sheets were to melt,* it could raise sea levels worldwide by 5 meters.[735] Even if only a 1° C increase in average temperature were experienced, it would make the earth's climate warmer than it has been at any time in the last 1,000 years.[736]

The date at which significant depletion of the ozone layer could take place is at least as uncertain as the date for significant effects of carbon dioxide accumulation. It is thought that continued use of chlorofluoromethanes at the 1974 rate would reduce global ozone by 14 percent over 50 years. Gases emitted from high-altitude aircraft and from nitrogen fertilizers, thought to have a similar, if lesser, effect on ozone, would also contribute to the depletion.

Ozone absorbs ultraviolet and cosmic radiation, and as a result its depletion allows greater amounts of these biologically potent forms of radiation to reach the earth. It is estimated that a 1 percent decrease in ozone increases ultraviolet radiation by 2 percent. The known consequences of increased ultraviolet radiation include a greater incidence of skin cancer in humans and damage to other species (both plants and animals), but the biological impacts of increased ultraviolet radiation have not been studied extensively.

*The World's Aquatic Environment in 2000.* Over the next two decades, changes in the world's aquatic environment are expected to occur primarily on or near land. Freshwater will be affected most, followed by changes in coastal marine waters and habitats. The deep open-ocean waters interact only very slowly with surface and coastal waters and are not expected to change significantly by 2000.

The precise nature of freshwater pollution is highly localized, but the general problem of water quality deterioration is global in scope. In the less developed regions, pollution of water supplies by disease pathogens or parasites is perhaps the major problem. In industrialized and urbanized regions, pollution of waterways and ground water by municipal sewage and industrial wastes (toxic chemicals and heavy metals) are principal concerns. In rural areas, nonpoint pollutants—fertilizers, pesticides, salt-laden irrigation drainage, and other contaminants emitted from sources that are difficult or impossible to pinpoint—are of universal concern.

Ultimately, rivers carry many freshwater pollutants to the oceans, and over the next two dec-

*Scientists believe that with a 6° C increase in the earth's average temperature, the melting would require about 200 years.

ades coastal waters will be steadily polluted by oil, persistent chemicals (including organochlorine pesticides), and by heavy metals, even though discharges of these pollutants are controlled in a number of nations. The U.S. alone now discharges 50 million tons of waste per year into the ocean—80 percent of it dredge spoils, 10 percent industrial waste, 9 percent sewage sludge, and 1 percent miscellaneous.[737] In addition, increased offshore oil and gas drilling, a projected 7 percent increase in ocean traffic (including the transport of oil), the mining of the seabed, and the urbanization and industrialization of coastal areas will all contribute to ocean pollution.

Continuing heavy exploitation of coastal fisheries and upwellings, as well as pollution and loss of estuarine habitats, will deplete preferred stocks of fish (e.g., tuna) worldwide. The following trends for fish and shellfish populations are based on the Global 2000 Study projections:

|  | Annual Harvest (in millions of metric tons) | Trend |
|---|---|---|
| Marine species | 60 | Peak, 1970 |
| Freshwater species | 10 | Peak, 1975 |
| Marine aquaculture | 3 | Increasing, 1979 |
| Freshwater aquaculture | 3 | Increasing, 1979 |
| Total | 76 | |
| Demand in year 2000 | 83.5 | |

The 200-mile economic zone may lead to improved management of marine fisheries, but the pressures on these resources are expected to continue to increase.

*Low-Probability, High-Risk Events Affecting All Environments.* By 2000 the world will be more vulnerable to several low-probability high-risk events. Food production will be more vulnerable to fluctuations in climate and to disruptions in energy supplies for fertilizer production, farm machinery fuel, and irrigation. Loss of wild progenitors of major food crops could lead to increased difficulty in maintaining pest and pathogen resistance in high-yield hybrids. A major shift to nuclear power could make the energy sector vulnerable, should a major nuclear accident occur. And a *major* shift to coal could make the energy sector vulnerable, should a serious problem develop with $CO_2$. While it may be that none of these difficulties will occur, the disruptive potential of such events will increase significantly by 2000.

## Special Regional Problems

In addition to the worldwide environmental developments just described, Table 13–46 includes a large number of regional developments involving continents or more than one nation state. Six regional developments are discussed here: (1) the increasing use of coal combustion by industrial regions; (2) their increasing use of nuclear power; (3) fuelwood shortages in rural LDC areas; and developments in (4) regional seas, (5) transnational river basins, and (6) wet tropical regions.

*Industrial Regions Turning to Coal.* Two large industrial regions are rich in coal resources—the United States and Eastern Europe. It is likely that the coal resources of these regions will be developed much more extensively over the next two decades. While it is not possible to anticipate the environmental consequences in detail, there are broad implications for the land, air, and water of these regions.

The land impacts are primarily associated with coal mining, power plant facilities, and transmission lines. Worldwide, over the 1977–2000 period, approximately 100,000 million tons of coal can be expected to be mined, reaching the rate of several thousand million tons per year by 2000. Strip-mined land would total tens of thousands of square kilometers, and subsidence would affect an additional tens of thousands of square kilometers. Land for more than 1,000 coal-fired power plants would be needed. Additional transmission lines would require many tens of thousands of square kilometers. Much of the affected land would be in the United States and Eastern Europe.

The atmospheric impacts would include significant increases in combustion residuals—particulates, heavy metals, carbon monoxide, nitrogen oxides, and sulfur oxides. Emissions of most of these residuals would depend on the control measures applied, but no economically practical technology is available to control the release of oxides of nitrogen.

The aquatic impacts of increased coal combustion include thermal discharges, increased consumptive uses, and acid drainage. Once-through cooling kills many small organisms and young fish, causes damaging variations in water temperatures and reduces dissolved oxygen concentrations. Evaporative cooling towers are projected to cause the second largest increase in consumptive use of water, and in parts of water-scarce Europe, water for cooling towers may be subject to limiting constraints until other needs have been met. In the

U.S., water for coal processing and the production of synthetic fuels may pose constraints in the arid West. Increased deep- and surface-mining could easily lead to much water pollution in the U.S. and Europe, especially with silt and acid. The U.S. has recently passed strip-mining legislation, but it remains to be seen how effectively the legislation can be enforced.

Increased emissions of oxides of nitrogen and sulfur will aggravate another aquatic effect of increased coal combustion—the acidification of rain. Acid rain is already a problem not only for northeastern Europe and the U.S. but also for neighboring states. Weather patterns carry the emissions and contaminated water vapor north of the industrial centers in northern Europe and the northeastern U.S. Thousands of lakes and streams in southern Sweden and Norway, in the U.S. Adirondacks, and in adjacent areas in Canada have been damaged—perhaps irreparably—by acid rain. These waters normally yield abundant arctic char, salmon, and trout, but are losing much of their aquatic life as the acidity increases. Lower forms of aquatic life and juvenile life forms are extinguished by the excessive acidity caused by the rain. Evidence has now been presented suggesting that the emissions that cause acid rain may travel more than 10,000 kilometers to contribute to atmospheric haze in the Arctic.[738] The shift to more coal use will aggravate future acid rain problems.

*Industrialized Regions Turning to Nuclear Power.* Neither Western Europe nor Japan have large coal resources and may, as a result, turn increasingly to nuclear power in the decades ahead. A shift toward nuclear power would bring its own environmental impacts, starting with the mining of uranium. In addition to the land disturbed, thousands of millions of tons of radioactive tailings will result from supplying uranium for the world over the 1977–2000 period.

The nuclear plants and transmission lines themselves require large amounts of land. The projected 226 percent increase in nuclear and hydroelectric generation by 1990 (most of it nuclear) will require hundreds of additional nuclear power plants. By the year 2000, the spent nuclear fuel will accumulate in amounts measured in hundreds of thousands of tons. There will also be more than 10 million cubic meters of low-level wastes that will have to be stored somewhere. In view of local opposition to locating such plants in many areas and of even more widespread opposition to storing radioactive wastes in most localities, it is not at all clear where these plants will be located or where the radioactive materials will eventually be stored.

The reactor accident and its aftermath at Three Mile Island, Pennsylvania, in March and April 1979, dramatized the hazards of nuclear power. Subsequent reviews and investigations are sharpening the basis for assessing and reducing the risks of nuclear power, but it is now virtually certain—at least in the United States—that the development of nuclear power will be delayed. It will be more closely regulated and, as a result, will become more expensive.

*Fuelwood Shortages in the LDCs.* By 1994, there will be a 650 million cubic meter shortfall in fuelwood in the LDCs, according to the Food and Agriculture Organization. This shortfall is about one-half the present fuelwood consumption in LDCs and would furnish the cooking and heating needs of approximately 650 million persons. Today, by comparison, an estimated 1.5 billion persons warm themselves and cook with wood. The numbers will surely increase as long as the price of alternative fuels continues to increase more rapidly than income.

The fuelwood shortage will be felt throughout the world, especially in the semiarid regions. These same semiarid regions are threatened by desertification, and of course fuelwood exploitation of the slow-growing trees in open woodlands and "bush" of Africa and Asia is one of the primary causes of desertification. Fuelwood shortages will also affect the populations of high mountains in LDCs where tree growth is slow and human numbers are high—the Himalayas, the Hindu Kush range, the Andes of South America, and other, lesser massifs.

Statistical data on the open woodlands of the world and the woody vegetation of semiarid regions are limited, but it is known that approximately 50 percent of the world's total open woodlands are in Africa and 12 percent in South America. The fuelwood crisis has already afflicted Africa seriously and shows no sign of easing soon. Firewood and charcoal production account for 90 percent of the total forest exploitation on that continent. In the Sahel, the present rate of reforestation, an inconsequential 3,000 hectares per year, is far, far below the 150,000 hectares that needs to be planted there each year if future demands are to be met.

To reverse the fuelwood shortage trend, truly dramatic increases in the establishment of fuelwood plantations will have to be made worldwide. If the trend is not reversed, all other vegetation (and dung as well) will be used for fuel in the affected areas, as is already the case in parts of India, Nepal, Sahelian Africa, and South America. Most of the people living in semiarid zones threatened by desertification are pastoralists and herdsmen, and the resulting disappearance of soil organic matter will have disastrous effects on their ability to feed themselves and their animals. The carrying capacity of the land will decline as soils lose the fertility and water-holding capacity provided by organic matter. Outmigration or starvation (or both) will accompany this scenario of land degradation. As many as 600 million people now living in the zones threatened by desertification would cause (and would ultimately be victimized by) this process.

*Pollution of Regional Seas.* Many regional seas, or gulfs with relatively poor circulation, are suffering from land-based pollution introduced by rivers or directly by sewage pipes from cities and industrial sites. The Mediterranean Sea, the Persian Gulf, and the Caspian Sea exemplify this problem.

The threat to the Persian Gulf is growing rapidly. Sixty percent of all the oil carried by ships throughout the world moves through the shallow Persian Gulf. There are 20 existing or planned major industrial centers along the coast. Heavy pollution of the Persian Gulf as well as the Mediterranean has resulted in international, antipollution agreements and action plans, sponsored by the United Nations Environment Program. These plans, a first step toward cleanup, are also intended to prevent further deterioration and to improve documentation concerning pollution levels and the resources affected. [739]

*Transnational River Basin Development.* Of the world's 200 large rivers, 148 are shared by two states and 52 by 3–10 countries each. Examples include the Nile, shared by Ethiopia, Uganda, Sudan, and Egypt; the lower Mekong River, shared by Laos, Thailand, Vietnam, and Cambodia; the Plata, shared by Brazil, Bolivia, Uruguay, Paraguay, and Argentina; and the Ganges shared by Nepal, India, and Bangladesh.

Large-scale development in transnational river basins often have environmental impacts that extend across national borders. Difficult political problems of international equity result from the ecological and socioeconomic impacts that follow from urgently needed dams and by flood-control, drainage, and irrigation projects. Downstream states may experience costs while upstream states enjoy the benefits. Reduced flows, sudden changes in flows (related to generation of peak power), dislocation of populations from reservoir sites, water-related diseases (such as malaria and schistosomiasis) associated with man-made lakes and irrigation projects, and water quality problems resulting from agricultural runoff—all are problems of river development with the potential to stir up international conflicts. Rivers, such as the Euphrates and the Jordan, running through water-short regions will be especially susceptible to development conflicts.

The LDCs in particular will have to grapple with these difficult problems, since their hydroelectric power generating potential is relatively undeveloped. Increased petroleum prices have greatly enhanced the economics of hydroelectric power in the LDCs, and the needs for flood control and increased irrigation (assumed in the food projections) are similarly compelling.

*Wet Tropical Regions.* Forty percent of the remaining 1,680 million hectares of "closed" tropical forest will have been destroyed by 2000, according to the forestry projections in Chapter 8. Much or most of this destruction will occur in the Amazon Basin, in the Indonesian territories of Sumatra, Kalimantan, and West Irian, and in Papua New Guniea. Equatorial Africa's small amount of closed tropical forest (approximately 40 million hectares) will be all but gone by 2000. Increases in firewood gathering, shifting agriculture, permanent agriculture, and industrial forestry will all contribute to this destruction of the world's tropical forests.

The fate of these deforested areas remains in doubt. The intensification of shifting agriculture through shortened fallow periods will degrade large areas or force their conversion to grazing land. Relatively little of the forested land is projected to have been converted to permanent agriculture. Portions may succumb to laterization while other areas will be invaded by cogon grass (*Imperata cylindrica*) or other vigorous weed species that will be virtually impossible to exclude as soil fertility declines. Regions with almost sterile soils will become useless, covered with grass too coarse for cattle. This case is exemplified by the quartzite sands of the Gran Sabana regions of Venezuela, once forested by broadleafed trees, now covered only by short grass. There has been no natural regeneration of the trees. Large areas will be degraded forest—devoid of commercially valuable species—but will still be heavily vegetated.

In addition to the loss of productivity, deforestation of these humid regions will render extinct as much as one-half of their genetic heritage, representing anywhere from 375,000 species to well over a million. The loss is incalcuable since most of the tropical gene pool has not been identified and studied, but if the wet tropics contain one-third of the world's species, as scientists have estimated, the projected losses will be truly momentous.

## Deterioration of Urban Environments

A general worsening of urban environments in the less developed countries is a virtual certainty, with population growth and poverty as the most important factors. As illustrated in Table 13–48, the population of LDC cities is projected to grow at the extraordinary rate of 4.3 percent per year, almost tripling over the 1975–2000 period. Of the 2.2 billion total world increase in population between 1975 and 2000, almost half—930 million additional persons—will live in LDC cities. The *increase* in LDC urban populations is projected to be larger than the entire 1975 urban population of the world. Although LDC economic growth is expected to be concentrated in urban areas, it is doubtful that LDC cities will have the resources necessary to keep pace with the increasing needs for public services and facilities.

To keep pace with the projected increases in needs during the next two decades, LDC cities would have to essentially triple all of the facilities and services that have been built up over the past centuries. The chances of this happening are unlikely at best. Water supplies and sanitation services in most LDC cities and surrounding slums are already being rendered obsolete by rapid population influxes. Almost 1.5 billion persons in LDCs—more than one-third of the world's total population—presently lack safe water and waste disposal facilities. LDC cities will also be hard pressed to provide food and the sanitary conditions for safe food distribution. Most LDC cities have only very limited sewage systems, or none at all. Noise, congestion, and air pollution are as bad—or worse—in many LDC cities as they are in industrialized nation cities. Infant mortality

### TABLE 13–48

### Urban Population in All Cities of 100,000 or More

|  | 1950 | 1975 | 2000 |
|---|---|---|---|
|  |  | *millions* |  |
| World | 392 | 983 | 2,167 |
| Industrialized countries | 262 | 503 | 756 |
| Less developed countries | 130 | 480 | 1,411 |

*Source: Trends and Prospects in the Populations of Urban Agglomerations 1950–2000, as Assessed in 1973–1975, New York: United Nations, 1975.*

continues to be high in LDC urban slums and uncontrolled settlements partly because of diseases (such as diarrhea) related to poor sanitation and contaminated water and because of inadequate diets, which increase susceptibility to diseases. Already most of the 35,000 infants and children under the age of 5 who die throughout the world each day were born and died in the LDCs, and the proportion is likely to increase in the years ahead.

Urban populations in industrialized countries are also projected to increase over the next two decades, but at a relatively manageable 1.6 percent per year. However, even this growth rate leads to a 50 percent increase over the 1975–2000 period.

Urban areas in industrialized countries are likely to be most adversely affected by deteriorating air quality resulting from a large increase in coal combustion and from the possibility that some nations will relax emission standards so as to reduce the economic costs of emission control. While national energy plans are by no means firm, and while the energy projections anticipate only a modest 13 percent increase in coal combustion by 1990, many observers anticipate large increases. The health and environmental consequences of an increased use of coal will be determined by the stringency of environmental controls. If there is no change of policy (the Global 2000 Study's standard assumption) emissions can be expected to begin increasing in at least some parts of the world. In the U.S., for example, a middle-range energy scenario developed by the Department of Energy shows sulfur oxide emissions decreasing through 1985 but increasing thereafter as a result of increased coal combustion and the slow retirement of old power plants. Similar trends can be expected elsewhere. In fact, in some areas there may even be efforts to relax present emission standards because of the economic costs entailed.

However, the human health consequences of exposure to air pollutants may be more serious in LDC cities than in the cities of industrialized nations. Emissions from increased coal combustion in LDC cities are not likely to be tightly regulated, and some highly polluting industries (including some emitting toxic substances) are avoiding regulations in industrialized nations by locating plants in LDCs, where there are far fewer regulations.[740] Furthermore, the health impacts of air pollutants in LDC cities are likely to be complicated—especially in the poorer sections— by poverty, disease, and poor nutrition.

## Assumptions, Discrepancies, and Feedback

With completion of the description of the future world environment as it is implied by the population, GNP, and resource projections of Global 2000, the shift can now be made to an examination of the effect the environment will have *on* these population, GNP, and resource projections. As illustrated in Figure 13–1 earlier in this chapter, this is the point at which the closing of the feedback loops can begin. As already noted, the loops cannot actually be closed analytically here, but the implications of the lack of closure can be analyzed to a degree. The basic process to be used is (1) to identify the environmental assumptions, both implicit and explicit, that were made in developing the population, GNP, and resource projections, (2) to compare these assumptions wth the future world environment (terrestrial, atmospheric, and aquatic), as treated in the preceding section and in Table 13–46, (3) to note the differences (discrepancies) between the assumptions and the environmental perspective, and (4) to consider how these discrepancies would feed back to and alter the population, GNP, and resource projections.

The actual tracing through of the assumptions, discrepancies, and effects becomes quite complicated because of the number of feedback loops involved. The two loops shown in Figure 13–1 linking back to the two driving-force projections (population, and GNP) and the resource projections are highly simplified representations of the myriad ways the environment influences the prospects for future developments in populations, GNP, and resources. Analysis of these influences on the population and GNP projections is particularly complex because many of the environmental influences from these projections come indirectly through the resource projections.

As an aid to systematic discussion of these many influences, Figure 13–21 presents a conceptual model of the major feedbacks linking the environmental projections back to the other projections. This conceptual model underlies the discussion that follows. The Global 2000 population, GNP, and resource projections imply a future world environment (summarized in Table 13–46). When this world environment is compared with the assumptions that are inherent in the population, GNP, and resource projections, a number of significant discrepancies appear. The discrepancies generally result from unrealistic assumptions in the population, GNP, and resource projections about the ability of the environment

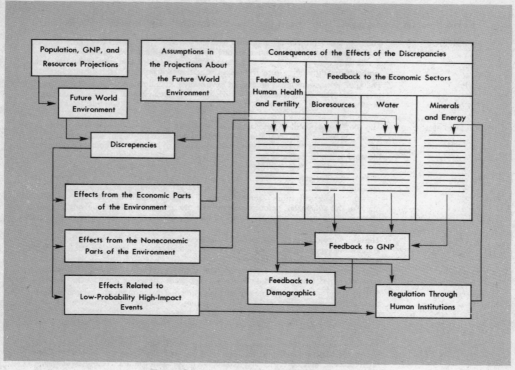

**Figure 13-21.** Conceptual model for closing the loops.

to supply increased goods and services. The effects of the discrepancies are traced through the environment to consequences which feed back to human health and the economic sectors. The collective consequences are subsequently traced on through the human health and the economic sectors for their secondary consequences and their feedback to the GNP and demographic projections. The discussion of the feedback to the economic sectors includes illustrative economic impacts that are referred to later in the discussion of feedbacks to GNP.

Developments in the environment have virtually no *direct* effect on the mineral and energy sectors of industrialized economies. (Fuel and nonfuel deposits and mining operations are not affected directly by, for example, water pollution, air pollution, and species extinctions.) However, there are significant indirect effects. These indirect effects arise largely through human health effects and low-probability high-impact events that lead (through human institutions) to tighter

environmental (and safety and health) regulation of the mineral and energy sectors.

The effects of the discrepancies that feed back onto human health and the economic sectors are disaggregated into two categories in Figure 13-21: effects from the "economic" and effects from the "noneconomic" parts of the environment. The distinction is between those aspects of the environment on which markets place economic value (e.g., land, water, forests, fish stocks) and those aspects of the environment on which markets place relatively little—or no—economic value (e.g., population of insect predators, pollinating insects, decomposer organisms, and nitrogen-fixing bacteria; spawning habits; and a variety of biological and ecological *processes*, such as the annual flooding or drying cycles that trigger reproductive behavior in fish and other species). This distinction is made to emphasize a point made years ago by Aldo Leopold, namely, that one cannot expect the "economic" parts of the

## TABLE 13–49

### Environmental Assumptions Inherent in the Population, GNP, and Resource Projections

| | |
|---|---|
| Population | The population projections anticipate declines in fertility and mortality, partly because of an assumption that environmental conditions affecting human populations will improve significantly over the next two decades. The lack of consideration of migration assumes implicitly that differences in environmental conditions will not lead to significant migration. |
| GNP | The GNP projections make no explicit environmental assumptions. Implicitly, however, they assume that over the next two decades the environment will supply goods and services free (or at no increase in cost), in vastly increased amounts and without breakdown or interruption. |
| Food and agriculture | The food and agriculture projections take into account losses of arable land due to urbanization and assume (1) that other losses and deterioration of soil will occur at about the same rate as in the past, (2) that losses of soil and soil fertility can be made up through the application of increased amounts of fertilizers, pesticides, and irrigation water, and (3) that losses to insects and plant diseases will not increase significantly. |
| Forestry | The forestry projections assume that the adverse effects of deforestation and forest simplification will not reduce the rapid rate of large amounts of deforestation, especially in the tropics. The projections assume, further, that serious deterioration of soils will follow much of the anticipated deforestation but that there is potential for applying intensive methods of silviculture through the use of rapidly growing species and, possibly, the use of fertilizers. |
| Water | The water projections do not specfically address environmental developments that may affect water supplies and quality; they assume implicitly that environmental developments will not significantly alter future water supplies. |
| Marine | The marine projections note that pollution of the ocean will ultimately, if continued, adversely affect fish stocks and catches but significant effects are not expected by 2000. |
| Energy | The energy projections make no explicit environmental assumptions and assume implicitly that environmental considerations and regulations will not interfere with achieving the 56 percent increase in the use of fossil fuel and nuclear energy projected for 1990. The projections also assume that there will be no significant increase in the cost of pollution control. |
| Minerals | The minerals projections include no explicit environmental assumptions and assume implicitly that the environmental implications of mining and refining will not lead to further regulation and increased costs, and that lands now containing mineral resources or reserves will not be protected in any way that would make the mineral resources unavailable for exploitation. |

environment to function without the "noneconomic" parts.

The environmental assumptions inherent in the population, GNP and resource projections are summarized in Table 13–49. With few exceptions, the models do not have provisions for explicit environmental assumptions, and as a result, the environmental assumptions tend to be implicit and, in some cases, quite vague.

Before discussing the assumptions of the individual projections, a point concerning time lags must be stressed. The population, GNP, and resource projections imply a number of environmental impacts that will not nearly have run their courses by 2000. The continued flow of long-lived, toxic organochlorines (e.g., PCBs and DDT) into the world's oceans is but one example. In these cases, time lags occur between the causal action (the developments implied by the population, GNP, and resource projections) and the ultimate feedback, through the environment, back to the projection.

In many cases (such as soil deterioration, species extinctions, and $CO_2$ accumulations) the projections lead to environmental feedbacks that will not have produced their total effect until well beyond 2000.

### Feedback to the Forestry Projections

Of all the resource projections, the forestry projections may have the most significance for the future world environment. Feedback to these projections is therefore taken up first.

The forestry projections are based on only a few environmental assumptions: (1) that the adverse effects of deforestation will not lead to regulation and control of deforestation, especially in the tropics; (2) that serious deterioration of soils will follow much of the anticipated deforestation in the tropics; and (3) that in most of the areas to be deforested there is potential for intensive methods of silviculture using fast-growing species and, possibly, fertilizers. The projections themselves, being extrapolations of historic trends, assume that the 18–20 million hectare annual net deforestation rate will remain constant despite growth in population and economic activity.

There are relatively few discrepancies between the environmental assumptions underlying the forestry projections and the future world environment implied by all of the projections. Serious soil deterioration is expected. In some tropical areas there may be potential for intensive silvicultural methods with pesticides, fertilizers, and fast-growing species. However, this potential certainly does not extend to all of the areas expected to be deforested, and where the potential does exist, it will be reduced by the extinction of both locally adapted, fast-growing tree species and insect predators, especially birds and predatory insects.

The environment projections summarized in Table 13–46 imply a significant increase in the acidity and extent of acid rain. This development may reduce forest growth in some areas, especially in northern Europe, the northeastern U.S., southern Canada, and parts of the U.S.S.R. Acidification of soil may also occur over a period of years. The acid rain phenomena will probably reduce rates of growth and increase the difficulty of reforestation efforts.

The environment projections also imply that significant forest areas will be inundated by water development projects. For the most part the affected areas will be deforested before flooding; so the primary effect on the forestry projections would be to reduce the area available for reforestation.

The most significant environmental assumption in the forestry projections is that the adverse effects of deforestation will not lead to regulation and control. The adverse effects of deforestation—deterioration of soils (permanent in some cases), the extinction of hundreds of thousands of species, the destabilization of hydrologic flows, the increase in atmospheric carbon dioxide ($CO_2$), the loss of large amounts of $CO_2$-absorbing vegetation—are all of such significance as to raise the possibility of a major change in forest policy throughout the world, especially in the LDCs. Although there are some small encouraging signs in individual countries (as noted in Chapter 8 and in the forestry section of this chapter), large, rapidly growing populations of the rural poor in many LDCs make careful management of forests for timber production and other uses increasingly difficult. The forests of mountain regions, so essential to soil protection and runoff control, are particularly endangered by encroaching populations of land-hungry rural poor. The slow-growing trees of the open forests of the world's arid lands are similarly vulnerable to expanding rural populations and their needs for wood for fuel and construction. And finally, it must be remembered that the forestry projections assume that the net rate of deforestation will *not* increase with increasing populations.

All things considered, the environmental assumptions underlying the forestry projections are generally consistent with the environment projections, and environmental feedback is not likely to alter the forestry projections significantly. If anything (as the forestry projections also conclude), the anticipated loss of only one-fifth of the world's remaining forests over the next two decades "represents a mildly optimistic scenario."

## Feedback to the Water Projections

As noted in the water projections, meaningful statements describing water supply can be made only for relatively small areas, and then only after detailed on-site investigations of the water resources available. Unfortunately, data are not forthcoming for assessing global water resources and their future on an area by area basis, and as a result the water projections are presented on the basis of national and world averages.

The averaging process vastly overstates available water resources. Virtually every area as large as a nation has areas with substantial surpluses of water as well as areas of water shortage. The U.S. is an example. The Pacific Northwest as a region has ample—even surplus—water, whereas the Southwest has severe water limitations. The aggregation of the water resources of these two regions into average figures for the U.S. implicitly assumes that water from surplus areas can be made available to water-limited areas. In reality, however, surplus water throughout the world goes unused. Some of it will continue to go unused unless large numbers of very large, very expensive hydraulic works are constructed. Some of it will remain unused because of the energy and economic costs of lifting water considerable heights.

The projections focus on rates of replenishment of water resources. The rates of replenishment are assumed to be measured approximately by the total surface drainage from an area. This assumption overestimates water resource replenishment in some areas and underestimates it in others. The assumption overestimates replenishment in areas drawing on fossil waters because here the replenishment is essentially zero. In other areas the assumption underestimates replenishment (or at least the availability of water of altered quality) because it neglects reuse possibilities.

The projections address both withdrawals of water (water that is potentially available for reuse) and consumptive use of water (largely evaporative uses that preclude reuse) but do not consider in-stream uses. Issues relating to transportation, aquatic habitats, water as an energy resource, flood-plain agriculture, and water quality are not considered.

In addition to the assumptions and emphases mentioned above, the water resource projections are based on several other important assumptions.

The projections assume that an approximate 50 percent increase in world population and a 146 percent increase in economic activities will roughly double the demand for water in nearly half of the countries of the world by the year 2000. They recognize that arid regions will experience water shortages long before 2000 but do not address the shortages that will be entailed by the need to preserve river flows for carrying away wastes. Existing water quality problems for irrigation (i.e, salt) and potable water supplies (pathogens and toxic substances) are noted but are not related quantitatively to the water shortages already occurring in many localities. The projections set forth various ways to deal with water shortages: augmentation of supplies (storage and reuse), reduction of water use (pricing policy, regulation, technological innovation), and allocation. The influence of possible climate changes and of anticipated land-use changes on supplies are not considered. Interrelationships between water quality and flow on the one hand and the living resources of streams, lakes, and the oceans on the other are not taken into account.

A comparison of the assumptions underlying the water projections with the environmental projections brings out a number of discrepancies. These discrepancies relate to the effects of (1) land-use changes, (2) possible climate changes, (3) changes in consumptive uses, (4) changes in water quality, and (5) habitat changes.

*Effects of Land-Use Changes.* Perhaps the most significant land-use change projected for 2000 is extensive deforestation, which has dramatic implications for water availability. Lacking the regulating effect of forests in the upper elevations of river basins, water flows will become more extreme during both the high and low flow periods. Water supplies will be reduced in both quantity and quality. The reduction in quantity will be a result of rapid runoff, which cannot be retained for later use. The reduction in quality will be a result of the increased silt loads that accompany increased erosion.

The LDC forests will be most affected. The tropical rivers of Africa and Latin America carry enormous quantities of water and will become highly destructive if their peak flows are augmented. Similar problems can be anticipated in parts of Africa and in Asia. The remaining forests of the Himalayan range are particularly important since the waters of the range feed a number of large rivers that supply the needs of millions of persons. It is estimated that by the year 2000 the Ganges Basin alone will contain 500 million persons, who will be dependent on that river for agricultural, industrial, and drinking water.

The steep and rugged terrain of the Himalayas and the Andean ranges prohibit the construction of the large dams that might tame their rivers and regulate their flows. Consequently only vegetative cover and special land management can be employed to control runoff. The denuding of catchments will exaggerate high flows and high sediment loads, and will reduce dry-season flows. These changes will in turn lead to extreme problems in the management of irrigation systems and impoundments throughout the affected regions.

A world survey has yet to be made of the economic impact on water projects of the sedimentation, greater fluctuations in flow, and more frequent flood peaks that result from vegetative changes in steep catchments. It was expected that large impoundments such as Volta Lake in Ghana or Lake Nasser behind the Aswan Dam would have useful "lives" of 100 years or more, but these and other lakes and dams will have much shorter lives if sedimentation increases. Wherever major denuding occurs upstream of a large reservoir, accelerated filling by sediments is likely to become evident by the year 2000, and in small rivers with high sediment loads, impoundments may become economically infeasible because of the short time it would take them to fill with sediment.

Deforestation would also affect ground-water recharge and, ultimately, flows from springs. This effect is well established, but the extent of its impact across the world is undocumented and difficult to assess because subsurface water movements can only be determined by carefully executed surveys using radioactive isotopes or dyes.

*Effects of Possible Changes in Climate.* In addition to the effects of deforestation, potential changes in climate would certainly affect water supplies. There is not full agreement among climatologists either as to the climate changes anticipated or as to their consequences for water supplies, but many climatologists associate increased variability and reduced rainfall with a cooling trend, and increased rainfall (except perhaps in the south central area—dustbowl of the 1930s—of the U.S.) with an increase in temperature.

*Effects of Changes in Consumptive Uses.* Over and above the effects of deforestation and possible climatic change, water availability will be influenced by increased consumptive uses of water for irrigation and for the discharge of waste heat through evaporative cooling towers. Thermal electric (coal and nuclear) power plants discharge approximately two-thirds of their input energy as waste heat; increasingly these discharges are through evaporative cooling towers. By 2000 the consumptive use of water for waste heat discharges is expected to be regionally significant in the U.S., Europe and Japan.

The biggest increase in consumptive (evaporative) use of water will come about as a result of the growth in irrigated agriculture.

Irrigation is already the largest consumptive use of water, and although the agricultural projections are not specific as to the amount of additional irrigation implied, it is clearly large. The projections suggest that the pressure on water resources due to irrigation of arid lands is likely to increase even more rapidly than pressures on arable land resources, which will increase by only about 4 percent in area by the year 2000 over the 1971–75 average figure. The increased consumptive use of water in agriculture will decrease the supply of water available for other uses, especially for energy applications.

*Effects of Changes in Water Quality.* Irrigation will decrease water availability in yet another way. Salts washed out of the soils will enter streams and rivers, contributing to a general decrease in water quality and in some areas effectively reducing water supplies by rendering water unfit for reuse.

There is an important linkage between the environmental implications of the agricultural and water projections. The agricultural projections anticipate both increases in irrigated land and a net increase in arable land over and above land losses. To achieve the increase in arable and irrigated land anticipated, marginal arid lands will be brought into cultivation, in some areas through irrigation and the removal of soil salts. However, the problems of salinization in irrigated soils are resolved only by flushing salts out of the soil with water. The rivers and streams that receive the salt-laden drain water become increasingly salty. As the water projections note, the buildup of concentrations of salts in rivers flowing through irrigated lands in arid regions is inevitable. The result downstream is water unfit for irrigation. This phenomenon has no solution other than the removal of salts.

Desalting rivers is expensive. A 104-million gallon per day desalting plant under construction at Yuma, Arizona, will cost an estimated $315 million. It will reduce the salinity of the Colorado River as it passes from the U.S. into Mexico from 850 milligrams per liter (mg/l) to 115 mg/l in accordance with a 1973 agreement. Without the plant, the Bureau of Reclamation projected that salinity levels would climb to 1,300 mg/l milligrams per liter by 2000, and that every additional milligram per liter of salt would cause an equivalent of $230,000 in damages annually to water users in the lower reaches of the river.[741]

Desalting rivers also requires energy. The Yuma plant will require 4.3 megawatts of hydroelectric energy to run the pumps that supply pressure for reversed osmotic desalinization. The electric generative use of the water, therefore, also competes with irrigation use. Of the plant's input waters, 70 percent emerge at 250 parts per million (ppm) salt concentration and flow back into the river; 30 percent emerge at 9,000 ppm and flow into a briny lagoon. Wind and solar generation methods are being considered to reduce the hydroelectric demands of the plant.

If the assumption in the food and agriculture projections is correct—namely that there will be significant increases in the agricultural use of arid lands through irrigation—large water losses (through evaporation) from the supplying streams and rivers are inevitable. At the same time, salts will be flushed out of the soils. More salt and less water means higher salt concentrations downstream. Accordingly, one of two results will follow: Irrigated farming costs will either increase significantly so as to include the cost of salt removal, or the salts from the fields of farmers upstream will be added to those in the fields of farmers downstream.

Salts are not the only way in which the environmental implications of the food projections impact on water quality. The use of fertilizers, pesticides, and herbicides is projected to double on a global average but to quadruple in the LDCs. The fertilizer runoff will lead to the eutrophication of many lakes and streams especially in the LDCs. Contamination with pesticides will reduce the possibilities for aquaculture, reducing the availability of badly needed fish protein. Probably the net effect in the LDCs will be to reduce the amount of water that is safely available for fish culture and for human consumption.

Other decreases in water quality will also occur. In addition to salts and pesticides, increasing amounts of fertilizers, toxic substances, oil, disease pathogens, acids (from mine drainage and acid rain), and sediments can be expected to enter the world's waters, especially in the LDCs. The net effect will again be either a reduction in the safety of the water available for various uses or increased costs of protecting water supplies.

The economic costs of water protection are significant. In the U.S., for example, a predecessor of EPA—the Federal Water Pollution Control Administration (FWPCA)—attempted to estimate the ultimate costs of water protection in 1970 as this nation was beginning seriously to clean up its waters. The FWPCA concluded that it would cost $4.4 billion to bring municipal water treatment systems up to desired standards, and that additional needs related to urban and suburban growth would bring the total to $10 billion for the 1970–75 period.[742] The total public expenditures in the U.S. on water-pollution control for the 1977–86 period is now estimated to be on the order of $200 billion,[743] and the portion of these costs associated with potable water may go still higher.

*Habitat Changes.* Both the water and the food projections explicitly or implicitly assume the development of many more water-regulation projects—dams, dikes, canals, etc. The severe ecological consequences of many of these projects are beginning to be examined more carefully during the planning process. As a result, some planned projects can be expected to be delayed, redesigned, or dropped in the years ahead.

The LDCs can anticipate the largest ecological impacts as a result of future water development for two reasons. First, the industrialized nations have already developed most of their water resources, and while some further development will occur, it will probably proceed with caution informed by the ecological results of earlier, less cautious developments. Water resources in the LDCs are less developed and more likely to proceed with relatively less careful consideration of the ecological consequences.

The second reason is that water development leads to a number of severe ecological changes in the LDCs that do not occur (or occur to a much lesser degree) in the industrialized nations. Probably the most significant of these ecological changes is the spread of habitat for disease vectors and hosts. The implications of large dams and irrigation projects for the spread of malaria, schistosomiasis, and river blindness will be of increasing concern to water planners throughout the world, and it is likely that a number of large water developments now planned in LDCs will be delayed or abandoned in the years ahead when their ecological implications are better understood. In this way ecological and habitat considerations will feed back to influence the water projections.

The preceding comparisons of the assumptions underlying the water projections with the environmental projections bring out a number of discrepancies relating to changes in land use, climate (possibly), consumptive uses, water quality, ecology, and habitat. These discrepancies cannot be related quantitatively to the water projections, but they all support the general conclusion of the water projections, namely that throughout the world, even before the year 2000, shortages of water of usable quality can be expected to become more frequent, more extensive, and more severe than those being experienced today.

### Feedback to the Food and Agriculture Projections

The environmental assumptions in the food and agriculture projections take into account some, but not all, of the influences that follow from the environmental projections. The major environmental assumptions underlying the food and agriculture projections are as follows:

• Weather variability (but not global climate change) is analyzed as the principal variable in the three alternative projections of food production, and as a result climate overall is assumed to remain favorable over the next two decades.

• Some land is assumed to be lost to urbanization (and perhaps other causes), but the amounts assumed lost to specific causes are not indicated. Trends in *net* arable area provide some clues and are given in Chapter 6 in Table 6–12. By 2000, the amounts of arable land in North Africa, the Middle East, and South Asia are projected to *decline* (relative to areas under cultivation in 1985) as the "economic and environmental costs of maintaining cultivated areas near physical maxima become prohibitive."

• The projections assume that increasing inputs of fertilizer and irrigation and other energy-intensive inputs will compensate for erosion and the other forms of land deterioration now being experienced throughout the world.

• Deterioration of range lands is not specifically addressed in the projections and is assumed implicitly not to be a constraining factor on the projected livestock production.

• The projections assume that substantially increased amounts of water will be available for irrigation, but the specific water assumptions are unclear. The text of Chapter 6 indicates that water management for irrigation could become the single most important constraint to increasing yields in the LDCs, but the quantitative implications of water constraints are not analyzed. Also, the extent to which irrigation is leading to the salinization of soils is not discussed.

• The continuing losses of diverse local (and wild) crop strains is implicitly assumed not to adversely affect the success of plant breeders in developing still higher-yielding varieties and protecting food crops against pests and pathogens. Yields are assumed to continue increasing at essentially the same rates as in the past two decades.

• Pollution by pesticides and fertilizers is assumed not to constrain the use of pesticides and fertilizers. Pollution is mentioned in Chapter 6 as a potential problem particularly in the LDCs, but it is also implied that these countries will have neither the capacity nor the motivation to control fertilizer and pesticide pollution, especially if controls would reduce yields.

It is notable that the projections foresee only a small increase (about 4 percent) in arable land over the last quarter of this century, and after 1985 decreases are projected in some regions. Land limitations and production constraints, especially water shortages, lead to a decline in per capita food production relative to 1970 levels in North Africa, the Middle East, and the Central African LDCs, and only slight increases in South Asia. In other words, over the period of the projections there will be no major improvement in the food supply for the world's poorest populations, and what improvements do occur will require an increase of 95 percent in the real price of food.

Against this sobering outlook, a comparison of the environmental assumptions in the food projections with the environmental projections gives little reason for optimism. Discrepancies are apparent in connection with land deterioration, losses of genetic resources, pest and disease management problems, water problems, and the effects of air pollution.

*Effects of Land Deterioration.* Erosion, salinization, alkalinization, waterlogging, compaction, and loss of organic matter are all aspects of the soil deterioration processes at work throughout the world. While soil deterioration is a less easily quantified phenomenon than land lost to urban sprawl, its effects are being felt in both LDCs and industrialized nations.

In the industrialized nations, the primary forms of land deterioration are erosion, compaction, and salinization. The projections assume that continued and increasing quantities of energy-intensive inputs (especially chemical fertilizers, but also irrigation water, herbicides, and pesticides) will compensate for basic declines in soil conditions and productivity. This assumption is supported by past experience. In the U.S., for example, almost two-thirds of the crop land needs treatment for erosion and compaction, but as a result of increasing energy-intensive inputs, yields continue to increase and many large farms continue to make a profit.[744]

The discrepancy between the assumptions of the food projections for industrialized countries and the environmental projection involves the feasibility of continued increases in energy-intensive inputs over the next two decades. Diminishing returns are experienced; input costs are increasing rapidly with energy prices; adverse externalities (such as the effects of toxic pesticides on human and animal health* and ground-water pollution) are becoming matters of concern.

Although there are admittedly some significant exceptions, the issue in most industrialized nations is not irreparable soil damage but the increasing vulnerability of the agricultural sector of the economy to disruption. Present practices lead to three forms of vulnerability. First, present farming practices with energy-intensive inputs and cost-cutting methods lead to soils that are less able to absorb and retain water; rain and irrigation are both of less help to crops, and the soils are more vulnerable to wind erosion during a drought or a shift to a period of dryer climate. Second, diminishing returns on increasingly expensive energy-intensive inputs can be sustained only to a

---

*Many workers in LDC countries use pesticides without adequate training or protection. In Central America, for example, there were 19,300 medically certified pesticide poisonings over the 5-year period 1971–76. Most of the poisonings (17,-000) occurred in El Salvador and Guatemala where there are about 360 cases per year for each 100,000 persons. By comparison, in the U.S. there are only about 0.17 cases per 100,000 persons. In Central America pesticides have also contaminated animals. In 1976 about 500,000 pounds of beef imported to the U.S. from El Salvador were rejected for levels of up to 95 parts per million of DDT; the U.S. threshold level is 5 ("Toxic chemicals: How More than 50 Nations on Five Continents Handle Their Most Deadly Pollutants," *World Environment Report*, June 18, 1979, p. 2).

point, and along the way further soil damage (especially erosion and compaction leading to hardpan soils) will accumulate. When damage is far enough advanced, productivity drops regardless of added fertilizers. Some U.S. soils have reached and passed that point. [745] Third, the food needs of an increasing world population combined with rapid increases in energy prices could lead either to a very rapid increase in the cost of food (effectively pricing a much larger portion of the world's population out of the market) or to a relatively sudden and disruptive shift away from energy-intensive methods of agriculture. Restoration of mildly damaged soils could be accomplished over a decade with fallowing and green manuring with leguminous cover crops, but restoration of severely damaged land would require much longer, and a disruptive effect on production could be expected during the restorative period. The food projections in Chapter 6 note that there are a variety of cultural practices and management techniques available to reduce agricultural dependence on energy-intensive inputs, but the projections question the ability of farmers to maintain or expand production levels while shifting away from energy-intensive inputs.

There is little question, however, that rising input costs and further diminishing returns are in prospect and that a careful and objective analysis of scientific and public policy options for reorientating trends in agriculture is needed. Evidence is accumulating that present research and policy priorities are in need of reorientation, [746] but short-term and institutional interests are also involved. In this connection, David Vail of Bowdoin College asks a very relevant question about agriculture in the industrialized nations: "In view of the power, objectives, and past behavior of the industries (and government agencies) that have shaped and promoted [energy-]intensive technology, is it reasonable to expect a transformation of priorities just because it would be in society's long-run interest?"[747]

For the LDCs, the food projections assume that land deterioration will not be more serious than in past decades because farmers will be aware of the problems, will institute practices preventing more extensive deterioration, and will charge more for their crops to cover increased costs. There is a significant discrepancy between these assumptions and the environmental projections.

Basically, the environmental projections anticipate significant increases in the intensity of use of agriculture lands in the LDCs and very few preventive or remedial measures. The primary LDC remedial measures implied by the food projections are a fourfold increase in the use of fertilizers, herbicides, and pesticides and a large increase in irrigation. With the projected increase in energy costs, and with the environmental (and political) implications of the implied water development, it seems unlikely that remedial or preventive measures will be able to counter the pressures for overuse. Furthermore, the environmental projections suggest that deforestation will increase the degradation of the LDC agricultural lands, both through more erratic streamflows and increased erosion and through a fuelwood shortage, which will result in an increase in the burning of dung that would otherwise have been returned to the soil as nutrients.

The economic consequences of land deterioration are more immediate in the LDCs than in the industrialized countries. Overgrazing, desertification, and salinization are major problems. Harold E. Dregne, chief of the U.N. Environment Programme's working groups on desertification, finds the total annual production losses due to desertification and salinization (an estimated $15.6 billion [748]) to be distributed as follows: $3.3 billion due to waterlogging and salinization of irrigated land; $6.7 billion due to range deterioration; $5.6 billion due to deterioration of rainfed crop land. Most of these losses would be borne by the LDCs. Dregne computed the production loss potential at 40 percent of production on irrigated lands (due to salinization), 60 percent on range land, and 25 percent on rainfed crop land. Average gross incomes per hectare from lands not affected by desertification or salinization were estimated at $400 for irrigated land, $90 for rainfed crop land and $3.50 for range land.

Another measure of the economic impact of land deterioration is the estimated cost of remedial measures. According to the Committee on Problems of the Environment of the International Council of Scientific Unions (SCOPE), it would cost $25 billion to rehabilitate 50 million hectares with the heaviest salt damage. [749] The U.N. Environment Program estimates that it will cost $400 million a year to combat desertification. [750] So far no global price tag has been placed on halting erosion or overgrazing.

*Effects of Genetic Resource Losses.* The food and agriculture projections assume that yields will continue to increase at essentially the same rate as over the past two decades. The yield increases come in part from distribution of technologies already demonstrated in field experiments and in part from further experimental improvements, especially in seed. Improvements in seed involve both increased plant productivity and increased (or at least maintained) resistance to plant pests and pathogens. To achieve these ends, local strains of crop species are needed, and these are being lost rapidly.

The projected extinction of one-fifth of all species—plants and animals—on the planet is an indication of the overall pressure on genetic resources. Most of these extinctions will occur as a result of tropical deforestation. The genetic losses of most concern to agriculture are not so much located in tropical forests as in dry and marginal lands where local strains of important food grains have evolved high-yield or disease-resistant traits. These local strains are being lost in two ways. First, local strains are lost as more and more farm lands are put into production with commercial rather than local seed. Second, land-clearing is destroying habitat for many local wild varieties.[751]

Concerned plant scientists are increasing their efforts to collect varieties of crops from all over the world before they are lost. The International Rice Research Institute has a collection of 45,000 rice strains in Los Banos, Philippines but considers that its collection is only a fraction of the world's known rice germ plasm.[752] There is little doubt that large numbers of local strains will be lost in the decades ahead. Without new genetic materials to work with, there are very real limits to what plant breeders can accomplish.

Although the genetic losses most significant to present-day agriculture are far more likely to occur in the fields of subsistence cultivators than in tropical forests, the extinctions in tropical forests also have implications for future agriculture. Tropical forests contain wild progenitors of many important crops—cocoa, rubber, oil palm, pineapple, and many nuts and fruits, as well as medicinal plant species and many plants of unexplored food and medical potential. Should the world's climate become warmer and wetter, as many climatologists believe likely, these and other tropical species could become exceedingly important.

Finally, it should be mentioned that, livestock genetic resources are also being lost at a rapid rate and without extensive efforts at preservation. Livestock, especially ruminants, are important in the world's food future because of their capacity to convert cellulose plant materials (indigestible to humans) into high-quality protein.

*Effects of Pest and Disease Management Problems.* The food projections assume that agricultural pests and diseases will not present more difficult problems in the future than they have in the past. The projections anticipate that these problems will be managed through a global doubling in the use of pesticides. A still larger increase in pesticides is anticipated for the LDCs.

By contrast, the environmental projections suggest that pest and disease problems will increase, especially if reliance continues to be placed primarily on pesticides. The methods of integrated pest management* may offer a more effective alternative, but continued dependence on pesticides will enhance resistance in pests and decimate predator populations. Extensive monocultures of genetically identical plants will further increase vulnerability.

The economic impact of pest management problems will be felt particularly in cash and export crops. The problems caused by heavy applications of pesticides have been well demonstrated in cotton fields of the world[753] as well as on plantations of tea, oil palm, vegetables, and fruits.[754] In Northeastern Mexico 250,000 hectares of cotton were totally destroyed by the bollworm *Heliothis* when it became resistant to all of the pesticides used against it.[755] Similar problems of resistance were experienced in Texas where the costs of protecting cotton in the Rio Grande Valley were higher than anywhere else—11 percent of the total production costs. In 1966 cotton farmers in the U.S. were using 47 percent of all pesticides used by U.S. farmers,[756] and pest control costs had become inordinately high.

Although many cotton farmers, especially in the U.S., Mexico, and Peru, are shifting to integrated pest management techniques for cotton, pesticides applied to cotton elsewhere in the world continue to represent a large share of the total pesticide chemical usage. In fact, in LDCs export corps (including cotton) receive most of the pesticides now used.[757]

The projected 100 percent increase in food production by 2000 is weakened to the extent that it assumes that a doubling of the world average application rate of pesticides to food crops (and a quadrupling of the application rate in the LDCs) will enhance production. Modest applications of pesticides in conjunction with the ecological and cultural techniques of integrated pest management generally contribute to increased yields in the short run, but massive increases in the use of pesticides alone will definitely increase the chances of major increases in pest resistance over the next two decades, as has happened already in cotton.

---

*"Integrated pest management" applies to a wide array of pest management techniques that greatly reduce the use of pesticides and rely more on biological controls and cultural techniques.

The assumption in the food projection that further adoption of existing high-yield technology will occur is in essence an assumption that larger monocultures of genetically identical strains will increase. This assumption implies increased vulnerability of food staples. The establishment of still larger monocultures of rice, wheat, and corn propagated from an excessively narrow genetic base enhances the probability of crop epidemics on a scale even larger than the 1972 corn blight epidemic in the U.S. The potential economic impact of such an epidemic is enormous. While a useful quantification of this potential is not possible, the possibility is real and is increased by the trends assumed in the food projections.

*Effects of Air Pollution.* The food projections assume that the adverse effects of air pollutants on agricultural production will not increase over the next two decades, but the environmental projections point to a number of potential increases in air pollution, some of which can be expected to affect agriculture adversely.

The increased combustion of coal will produce at least three combustion products of potential significance to agriculture, namely, sulfur oxides ($SO_x$), nitrogen oxides ($NO_x$) and carbon dioxide ($CO_2$). Increased $CO_2$ in the air could increase plant growth, but $SO_x$ and $NO_x$ emissions are known to have adverse effects on plants. $SO_x$ emissions can be controlled with the technology now available, so the extent of emissions depends on national pollution control standards. In the U.S., for example, present standards would reduce $SO_x$ emissions until about 1985, when emissions would start increasing again. $NO_x$ emissions cannot be controlled with existing pollution control technologies. The energy projections are not sufficiently detailed or precise to permit an estimate of the areas that will be exposed to increased concentrations of $SO_x$ and $NO_x$.

Air pollution already causes significant damage to agricultural crops. In the U.S., air pollution damage to crops in Southern California alone cost farmers $14.8 million per year during the 1972–76 period. The losses amounted to 2 percent of the crop categories affected. Celery, potatoes, and tomatoes were especially hard hit.

Over the next two decades the impact of air pollutants on agriculture can be expected to increase, especially for farmers downwind of industrial centers. The effects may be particularly severe near industrial centers in LDCs. [758]

*Effects of Aquatic Changes.* The food projections assume that water resources will be available to effectively utilize a doubling in the application of fertilizers. (The twofold increase is a world average; a quadrupling of fertilizer use is anticipated in the LDCs.) The projections note that water management could become the single most important constraint on increasing yields in the developing world.

The environmental projections lend strong support to the concern over water constraints not only in the developing world, but also in industrialized nations. Competition with energy development will be intense in parts of many industrialized nations (e.g., the Western U.S.). While neither the water assumptions in the food projections nor the water projections themselves are sufficiently detailed to permit a close comparison, much examination of regional water supplies would be needed to determine if the water assumptions of the food projections are fully justified.

In addition to water supply, the environmental projections point to two other aquatic developments that will affect the food projections. One concerns the acidity of rain water, the other, variations in supply.

The increased emissions of sulfur oxides and nitrogen oxides from coal combustion are causing rainfall over wide areas to become more acidic. Much of the eastern half of the United States and parts of southern Canada, northern Europe, and southern Scandinavia have all been affected. The effects of acid rain on crops and soils are only beginning to be investigated, but it is already known that simulated acid rain adversely affects the growth of some food crops, including soybeans and kidney beans. It is also known that over a period of 3–5 years simulated acid rain begins to acidify soils. Most food crops do not grow well in acid soils. The extent to which acid rain will adversely affect food production is still unknown, but over the next 20 years it will probably have much more effect than is assumed in the food and agriculture projections in Chapter 6.

The implications of the anticipated deforestation for streamflows also apply to agriculture in large portions of the developing world. The absence of forest cover in the upper reaches of river basins tends to exaggerate both peak and minimum flows. As a result, flooding and erosion will be increased during rainy periods, and irrigation potentials will be reduced during dry periods. This effect is not considered in the development of the food projections.

As the preceding paragraphs have indicated, there are apparently many discrepancies between the environmental assumptions underlying the food projections and the environmental projections made in the food and agriculture section of this chapter. Land deterioration is likely to be more extensive than assumed. The assumed primary reliance on chemical fertilizers to maintain soil fertility will lead to further soil deterioration as well as to increased costs and economic vulnerability. Lost genetic resources will reduce the prospects for additional decades of yield increases. The assumed primary reliance on pesticides as a pest management strategy implies further pesticide resistance in pest populations and decreased populations of pest predators. Air pollution will have adverse effects, as will acid rain. Although the water assumptions are not explicit, the adverse effects of deforestation on water supplies will further complicate an already difficult situation.

If these apparent discrepancies could be taken into account, the feedback from the environmental projection would alter the food projection in several ways. Most basically, per capita food consumption might well be less than that projected in Alternative III in Chapter 6, namely, a 4 percent increase worldwide, a decline of 20 percent in Africa and the Middle East, and increases only in the U.S., the U.S.S.R., and in Eastern and Western Europe. The real cost of food might increase more than the 100 percent projected, and even before 2000 those LDC economies that are largely agrarian may experience a decline in the growth of their GNP.

## Feedback to the Fisheries Projections

The fisheries projections make several environmentally related assumptions concerning marine fisheries, freshwater fisheries, and aquaculture.

For marine fisheries, the projections assume that:

- Increasing demand for marine fish will not lead to overfishing so severe that it depletes fish stocks.
- Continuing pollution of coastal waters with oil, pesticides, heavy metals, and other toxic substances will have an overall negative effect on the quality or quantity of marine fish catches. However, the projections implicitly assume that such pollution will not be severe by the year 2000.
- Continuing losses of estuaries and coastal wetlands will not significantly reduce natural marine productivity by 2000.
- Improved fishing technologies will not be used in ways that threaten fisheries.
- The present world harvest of marine fish of about 60 million metric tons (mmt) will not in-

crease on a sustained basis; careful planning and management could, in theory, raise the harvest of natural marine production to 100 mmt by 2000; and economic model projections based on continued population and GNP growth lead to a fish demand in 2000 of 81–83 mmt.

For freshwater fisheries, the projections assume that:

- Natural freshwater fisheries are fully exploited at the present 10 mmt catch.
- Environmental deterioration will not adversely affect this natural freshwater catch.

For aquaculture (fresh- and saltwater), the projections assume that:

- There is a significant potential for expanding the present 6 mmt harvest of largely high-unit-value species.
- This potential will not be seriously affected by environmental developments over the next two decades.

The environmental projections show developments that will adversely affect natural production of fish, both marine and freshwater, and that will reduce the potential for both freshwater and marine aquaculture. The only question is how soon will the adverse effects be felt.

Feedback from both continued pollution of coastal waters and the loss of coastal habitat could significantly affect the marine fisheries projections. Discharges of oil, pesticides, heavy metals, and other toxic substances are expected to continue to increase, especially in LDC coastal waters. By 2000, the impact on fisheries may not be universal, but many areas will experience continuing or increasing contamination by long-lived pollutants that may decrease production regionally or severely contaminate marine resources.

The continuing losses of coastal habitats—estuaries, salt marshes, mangrove communities, etc.—may not lead to a significant global decline in marine fisheries by 2000. Nonetheless, it is known that most important marine species are dependent at some point in their life cycles on such habitats, and continued loss of these habitats must ultimately have significant impacts on marine fisheries—impacts that could begin to be felt before 2000.

An example illustrates the economic significance of coastal marine habitats in the U.S.: Estimates made in the northeastern United States and the Gulf of Mexico demonstrate that fish production alone on an acre of submerged coastal wetlands has an annual value (in 1970 dollars) of $380, which over even a relatively short 20-year life period represents $7,980 at a 5 percent discount rate. However, for every acre of coastal wetlands dredged or filled, the production of two additional acres is lost because of the resulting disruption by siltation and other impacts. As a result, a single acre of coastal wetlands lost to dredge and fill operations represents $23,940 in lost seafood production potential alone,* and coastal wetlands provide many other ecological benefits that have not been included in this estimate. [759]

Marine fish production will also be affected by hydrologic developments on the land. The productivity of coastal waters is enhanced by the normal flows of rivers and the sediments and organic matter they bring to the ocean food chain. This function of rivers is being increasingly impaired by large dams which control floods, regulate flows, and trap sediments and organic matter. The food and the water projections implicitly assume that a large number of dams and reservoirs will be constructed by 2000. The importance, magnitude, and timing of the resulting impact on ocean fisheries can be deduced from examples but cannot be projected in any detail. (In some cases the impact on marine fish production may be offset to some degree by new fish production in the reservoirs.) The effect of the Aswan Dam on the Mediterranean's sardine fishery is a well-known example of this phenomenon.

The effects of irrigation development, increased sewage discharge from LDC cities, and increased use of pesticides and fertilizers could seriously affect both the projected freshwater catch and aquaculture. Irrigation development often adversely affects habitats for freshwater fish by increasing temperatures, reducing the oxygen content of the water and increasing salinity. The projected increase in the use of fertilizers will enhance algal blooms, eutrophication, and depletion of dissolved oxygen in reservoirs and lakes. Acid rain from increased coal combustion will acidify lakes in many industrialized nations, eliminating the use of the lakes for aquaculture or the natural production of fish. Pesticide residues from a doubling to a quadrupling of pesticide applications will pollute streams, rivers, reservoirs, and lakes, killing small fish.

---

*These figures are not intended to establish a precise value for coastal wetlands. Estimated values vary widely and are hard to estimate (See "The Value of Wetlands" in Elinor Lander Horwitz, *Our Nation's Wetlands: An Interagency Task Force Report*, GPO stock no. 041–011–00045–9, Washington: U.S. Government Printing Office, 1978, pp. 28–29). The figures are used here only as an indication of real, non-zero value for coastal wetlands.

Coastal and estuarine breeding and spawning waters for many oceanic fish will also be affected, especially in regional seas. In the Mediterranean, for example, coastal aquaculture, which now yields 165,000 tons of fish each year, is seriously threatened by land-based pollution, as are the 700,000 tons caught annually in the open Mediterranean. The $5.0 billion price tag on the cleanup of the Mediterranean Sea is well justified by the benefits of conserving these fisheries resources as well as the 100 million visitor per year tourist industry and the 100 wetland sanctuaries for birds and marine life. [760]

Brackish-water fish ponds line the coasts of many Asian countries and yield highly prized Chinese milkfish and shrimp. They too are seriously threatened by pollution, particularly pesticides in runoff but also by toxic substances in municipal and industrial effluents. [761] Paddy rice *cum* fish culture operations are also jeopardized by pesticides in water and an important nutritional impact results, since snails, crabs, and small fish which normally inhabit flooded rice paddies are a major source of protein for farm families throughout Asia. [762]

As the preceding paragraphs have indicated, there are a number of potential and apparent discrepancies between the assumptions of the fisheries projections and the environmental projections. If the apparent discrepancies could be eliminated in the analysis, the accumulative effects of the environmental trends, in conjunction with increasing demands for fishery products, could lead to a decrease in the world's total fishery resources. The anticipated environmental developments will certainly have a negative effect on these resources because the trends are largely disruptive and poisoning. When these effects would be felt is open to speculation, but there is a distinct possibility that the adverse effects of continued environmental deterioration will have noticeably affected many fishery resources before 2000.

### Feedback to the Minerals Projections

The environmental projections are not likely to have significant direct feedbacks to the nonfuel minerals/projections because mineral production is not particularly sensitive to environmental conditions. A change in air quality, for example, has little direct effect on mining.

There are indirect feedbacks, however, that may be significant. As land disruption, water pollution, and air pollution affect human health and the nonmining sectors of the economy, human institutions (e.g., governments, insurance companies, etc.) may impose further regulations that will reduce the environmental impacts of mining and increase mining costs.

The nonfuel mineral projections are not based on any explicit environmental assumptions. Implicitly, they assume that environmental regulations will not significantly constrain world mining activities over the next two decades. They assume further than the nonfuel minerals sector will receive all of the water and energy needed for the projected growth. All of these assumptions are somewhat questionable.

Water, for example, is needed in the mining and processing of both fuel-mineral and nonfuel-mineral ores, and water availability could be an important constraint. While the amounts needed for mining are relatively small (in the U.S. they amount to only about 2 percent of total withdrawals), and while the water-quality requirements are relatively low, water resources will become increasingly constrained everywhere. Competition for water between agriculture, minerals development, and energy production will become much more intense in the years ahead.

The use of energy in mining and refining may be more troubling. The energy requirements of declining ore grades has not yet been examined carefully, and the economics of mining will certainly be affected by further increases in energy costs. The economic recoverability of some resources now classed as (economically recoverable) reserves may even be affected if energy prices continue to rise sharply.

Finally, laws and regulations to preserve environmental quality may be tightened in the future as the projected increases in mining and refining activities impact on land, air, and water resources. However, the assumptions underlying the projections—no tightening of the laws and regulations controlling the environmental impacts of mining—are consistent with the Global 2000 Study's overall assumption of no policy changes between the present and the year 2000.

### Feedback to the Energy Projections

Like the nonfuel minerals projection, little or no direct environmental feedback is expected to commercial energy production (coal, oil, gas, plus nuclear and hydro generation) in the industrialized nations, but significant feedback may be involved in the LDCs' use of organic fuels.

The energy and fuel mineral projections do not make explicit assumptions about the future environment but implicitly assume that environmental laws and regulations will not limit development or significantly increase costs over

the next two decades. The energy projections assume further that there will be no constraints on the water or energy needed for energy development.

Large amounts of water are needed for coal mining, synthetic fuel production, and oil-shale production, and at least in the arid west, these water needs will conflict with mining and agricultural needs. In 1978, the U.S. Water Resource Council anticipated increasing pressures on water resources in the Missouri and Upper Colorado River basins, where coal and oil-shale mining are developing, but beyond those areas, the Council foresaw no other major conflicts between the water needs of the coal industry and of other water users.[763] The water picture in the U.S. may change, however, if there is a significant increase in the production of synthetic fuels, which require large amounts of water.

Water for evaporative cooling at nuclear and coal-powered electric generating plants may also present problems in some areas. In Western Europe, for example, withdrawals for evaporative cooling may present a constraint when added to all other water demands. In the U.S., consumptive cooling water withdrawals are expected to be the fastest-growing component of water use over the 1975–2000 period, increasing from 1.3 to 7.8 percent of total water consumption. Overall, water can be expected to become more of a constraint than is assumed in the energy, agriculture, and nonfuel minerals projections.

Like water, energy itself is a critical input in energy development. The energy projections implicitly assume that adequate energy will be available for energy development, conversion, and delivery. In fact, the energy efficiency of the energy sector (end-use energy supplied per unit of primary energy used) may decrease as a result of the projected increases in primary energy conversion to secondary energy forms, especially electricity and (perhaps) synthetic fuels. This means that the energy sector itself will require increasing amounts of primary energy in order to supply a given amount of end-use energy need in the economy. Net energy analysis and energy efficiency are not a part of the current energy projections, and its seems likely that the energy efficiency of the energy sector will be examined more extensively in the years ahead. Ultimately, some of the assumptions underlying the energy projections may be brought into question.

Energy development in the industrialized nations will produce significant environmental impacts over the next two decades, and the laws and regulations relating to its development may change significantly. The energy projections, however, assume no change in environmental regulations and no significant increases in the cost of environmental protection. This assumption is consistent with the Global 2000 Study's overall assumption of no policy change.

In the LDCs, there will be feedback from the environmental projections to the energy projections in two ways. First, deforestation from all causes will contribute to the growing shortages of fuelwood. Second, deteriorating range conditions may reduce the amount of dung available for fuel.

### Feedback to the GNP Projections

The feedback of the evironmental projections to the GNP projections (and also to the population projections, which are considered next) is more complex than the feedbacks considered so far. The complexities arise both from the several linkages through which environmental feedback influences GNP and from the indirect nature of the feedbacks.

Environmental developments influence GNP in at least three different ways. One way is through the influence that environmental developments have on individual economic sectors, which in turn influence the total GNP. Another is through the influence that human health has on GNP. Finally, the economic activity associated with environmental protection efforts also influences GNP.

These three linkages from the environment to GNP are not easily discerned in the assumptions that underly the GNP projections. While there are no explicit environmental assumptions in those projections, they seem to assume implicitly that the environment will continue to provide each economic sector with the same goods and services as in the past, but in substantially increased amounts, without interruption and without increase in cost (generally taken to be zero). The discrepancies that follow from this assumption are, of course, somewhat different for the industrialized countries than for the LDCs.

*Feedback to the Industrialized Economies.* Feedback from the environment through the various sectors of the economy have been discussed in the preceding sections on forestry, water, food, fisheries, nonfuel minerals, and energy. These feedbacks involve parts of the environment that are economically valued (e.g., land and forests), as well as parts that are not valued economically (e.g., populations of predator insects). An attempt has been made to include in these discussions a few indications of the costs of lost environmental goods and services. (The estimated

loss of seafood production totaling—by one estimate—nearly $24,000 for each acre of dredged coastal wetlands is but one example.*) Unfortunately, available data on such losses are so incomplete that the cost figures cannot even be termed spotty, but they make a basic point: The goods and services provided by the environment—from the decomposition of wastes to the absorption of carbon dioxide—contribute substantially but subtly to the GNP in each economic sector. Projected losses in environmental goods and services will significantly affect every economic sector, but especially—but not exclusively—those involving renewable resources.

There will also be feedback from the nonrenewable resource sectors. For example, different energy strategies allow for comparable degrees of environmental protection with very different capital (and GNP) implications. All of the projections are based on the assumption of no capital constraints. In actual fact, capital is scarce and expensive, and intense competition among the sectors can be expected over the next two decades as efforts are made to develop a new energy economy, raise food production, increase water availability, increase mineral production, *and* protect the environment. Increasing costs of obtaining many resources can be expected to contribute to inflation and capital scarcity, thus indirectly affecting GNP.

Feedback from environmental protection efforts to GNP is also subtle and complex. No studies have yet been done of this feedback for industrialized economies as a group, but the issue has been examined for the U.S. economy.

The U.S. study, recently done by Data Resources, Inc. (DRI) for the Environmental Protection Agency (EPA), analyzes the economic effects of federal air and water pollution control programs over the 1970–86 period. The DRI study arrived at the following conclusions:

• The extra investment required for the federal air and water pollution control programs has a positive economic effect until 1981, after which it turns slightly negative due to inflation and reduced productivity. As a result the real GNP would be 1.0 percent lower at the end of the period than if there has been no incremental pollution control expenditures.

---

*The figures used here are only illustrative. Estimates vary widely. (See "The Value of Wetlands," in Elinor Lander Horwitz, *Our Nation's Wetlands: An Interagency Task Forced Report,* GPO Stock No. 041–011–00045–9, Washington: U.S. Government Printing Office, 1978, pp. 28–29.

- The federal air and water pollution control programs are slightly inflationary, adding 0.3 percent to the overall rate of inflation each year through 1986.
- Employment benefits remain constant, even after construction ends, due to the labor needed in operation and maintenance of pollution control equipment and installations.[764]

At the time of the DRI study's release, EPA's administrator pointed out that the DRI study did not measure many of the benefits of cleaner air and water, and as a result depicted the worst possible economic impact. Had the study been more complete, the negative impacts might have been largely counterbalanced or outweighed by consideration of benefits such as enhanced agricultural production, greater fish harvests, lower maintenance and depreciation costs for materials and processes affected by air and water pollution, and improved health.[765]

The EPA administrator's comments on the DRI study refer to the third type of feedback from the environment to GNP, namely the linkage through human health. While again no studies for the industralized nations as a group have been done, the impacts of air pollution on human health in the U.S. have been studied in a report, also prepared for EPA, by a group of resource economists at the University of Wyoming. Completed in 1979, the study documents a very significant linkage between environment, health, and GNP. It concludes that the health benefits from a 60 percent reduction in air pollution would amount to a total annual savings of $40 billion ($185 per person)—$36 billion representing a decrease in illnesses and $4 billion, a decrease in mortality rates.[766] The major health benefits associated with the reduction in air pollution particulates were more on-the-job time for everyone and increased productivity of those people suffering from chronic illnesses associated with air pollution. The Environmental Protection Agency estimated on the basis of the figures above that the 12 percent decrease *in particulates alone* that has been achieved between 1970 and 1977 provides $8 billion in health benefits each year compared to the total 1977 expenditures on *all air pollutants* from stationary sources (the primary sources of particulates) of $6.7 billion.[767]

The linkages between the environment and GNP involve a number of subtleties; the linkages through human health and soil conditions provide two interesting examples. In the case of human health, improvements in air quality increase productivity and time on the job, both of which contribute to increased GNP. But these are not the only effects. An improvement in health *reduces* the goods and services delivered by the medical sector of the economy, thus *diminishing* GNP. Similar subtleties occur in the case of soil health. Declines in soil quality due to compaction and erosion are known to be occuring widely in the U.S., but by replacing lost fertility with energy-intensive inputs, declining soil productivity may actually increase GNP—but at the cost of (among other things) increased dependence on foreign sources of energy. These two examples suggest that in industrialized countries the linkages between environmental developments and GNP may be quite different from the linkages between environmental developments and national welfare.

*Feedback to the LDC Economies.* The model used to develop GNP projections for the LDCs makes environmental assumptions that are similar to those contained in the GNP models of industrial economies. Neither of the GNP models makes explicit assumptions about goods and services provided by the environment; both assume implicitly that environmental goods and services will be available without interruption in much larger quantities and at no increase in cost. Furthermore, in the case of the model of the LDC economies, it is assumed that environmental considerations are relatively unimportant compared with trade with developed nations. This last assumption is inherent in the model's structure, under which the LDC economies are assumed to expand only through trade with industrialized countries, and as a consequence, can grow only when industrial economies are growing. This last assumption has been questioned both as to its necessity and its desirability for the LDCs.

Actually, the same three types of linkages relate environmental developments to GNP in the industrialized countries as in the LDCs. The three linkages—through the economic sectors, through human health and productivity, and through expenditures on environmental protection—are probably even more important in determining GNP (and welfare) in the LDCs than in the industrialized nations.

Linkages through the economic sectors illustrate this last point. In the LDCs, the industrial sectors (such as oil, chemicals, steel, and manufacturing) are by definition less developed (i.e., industrialized), and the economic sectors based on renewable resources (forestry, fisheries, agriculture) are the economic mainstays of the domestic economy. Environmental deterioration strongly affects the renewable resource sectors. Deforestation is, simply put, a matter of living from biological capital, not from its dividends, and the LDCs' tropical forest capital will largely be spent by 2000. Fuelwood shortages will increase the use of dung for fuel, reducing the recycling of nutrients to the soil, and so will adversely affect the agricultural sector. Deforestation will exaggerate peak and minimum streamflows, which will increase erosion, degrade water quality, and reduce productivity in the agricultural and fisheries sectors. Overgrazing will deplete grass and range land resources, which will speed up desertification and adversely affect the agricultural sector. Efforts to increase agricultural production with pesticides, fertilizers, and irrigation will require increasingly expensive energy-intensive inputs, which may in turn intensify balance of payment problems to a greater extent than they increase domestic GNP. The projected quadrupling of agricultural chemical usage would also adversely affect the fisheries sector. In short, projected environmental developments in the LDCs can be expected to have pervasive adverse effects on GNP through the vitally important agricultural, forestry, and fisheries sectors of the economies.

The effects of environmental developments on GNP via human health and productivity are equally strong. The projected increases in urbanization in the absence of adequate sewage and potable water facilities can only lead to significant increases in the incidence of fecally related contagious disease and morbidity generally. The quadrupled use of pesticides will (and already has) lead to major increases in worker illness and poisoning. The water development projects implied by the food projections will expand habitats for disease vectors, increasing the incidence of schistosomiasis, river blindness, and malaria. Widespread malnutrition will complicate the increased morbidity. The combined effects of the projected environmental developments can be expected to significantly reduce human productivity and GNP in the LDCs.

To date many of the LDCs have not made major investments in industrial pollution control technologies, and the GNP projections assume that laws and regulations affecting industrial pollution control expenditures in the LDCs will not be increased significantly over the next two decades. This assumption is consistent with the Global 2000 Study's overall assumption of no policy change.

In the absence of stringent pollution control laws and regulations, multinational corporations engaged in highly polluting industrial processes may find the LDCs increasingly attractive sites for their plants. Industries involved in the production of toxic substances may become especially interested in LDC locations.[767a] Increased industrial activity, even of the highly polluting sort, may increase the GNP of LDC economies—and perhaps even national welfare—but before this possibility is accepted as valid, the adverse effects of the pollution on other economic sectors and on human productivity need to be examined carefully.*

In both LDCs and industrialized countries, environmental developments influence GNP directly through economic sectors, indirectly through human health and productivity, and, subtly, through expenditures on environmental protection. The Global 2000 Study's projections of GNP make no explicit assumptions about the environment but implicitly assume that environmental developments will not reduce GNP growth in either developed or developing countries. A comparison of this assumption with the preceding paragraphs reveals many discrepancies. While it is not possible to modify the GNP projections to eliminate these discrepancies, a more adequate consideration of environmental developments in the GNP projections would probably lead to lower estimates of GNP growth, especially in the LDCs. In any case, environmental deterioration will impair the quality of life in both industrialized and developing countries, and "additions" to GNP required to offset pollution or health damages might more properly be substituted since they do not involve a net increase in *desired* goods and services.

## Feedback to the Population Projections

Feedback from the environmental projections to future population levels occurs through the effects of environmental changes on health, mortality, fertility, and migration. The feedback through health, mortality, and fertility will be most significant for the LDC population projec-

---

*M. Greg Bloche, a Yale medical student, has recently interviewed the minister of health in the People's Republic of China on the subject of the environmental and health impacts of industrialization. He reports that China is having the same difficulties as industrialized nations in coping with rapid increases (a doubling over two decades) in the illnesses of industrialization—cancer, hypertension, and heart diseases. He also reports familiar tensions in carefully and objectively examining the merits of environmental standards and quotes the minister of health as remarking tersely: "Of course the Ministry of Health wants high standards and the Ministry of Industry wants low standards. You can spend less money on low standards." (M. Greg Bloche, "China Discovers Health Perils Accompany Modernization," *Washington Post*, Aug. 19, 1979, p. A21.)

tions. The feedback through migration will also affect LDC demographics to a small extent and will have a relatively long-lasting effect on populations in some industrialized nations.

*Feedback to the Population Projections for the LDCs.* The environmental assumptions underlying the LDC population projections are largely subassumptions of the fertility and mortality rate assumptions. Fertility rates and mortality rates are not projected by the population model, but rather are fed into the model as a large number of time-series assumptions/projections. The environmental assumptions underlying the externally developed fertility and mortality projections are the assumptions that need examining here.

To understand how environmental assumptions enter into the fertility and mortality assumptions/projections, the methods by which these projections were developed must first be reviewed briefly (a more detailed explanation will be found in Chapters 2 and 15). The process is basically this: The fertility rate (or mortality rate) for the base year is estimated on the basis of available data and is then projected forward in time, using one or two methods—either a general continuation of past trends or the establishment of a "target" figure for the final year of the projection. Under both approaches, the projected fertility rate (or mortality rate) is adjusted upward or downward to take into account assumed influences of the environment and other factors, such as the availability of family planning services.* There are two environmentally related assumptions used in developing and adjusting the projections of the LDC fertility rates: (1) continued moderate social and economic progress in all LDCs throughout the projection period and (2) a more or less continuous decline in fertility rates throughout LDC societies caused in part by the assumed continuation of social and economic progress. The environmentally related assumption underlying the mortality rate assumption/projection is basically that, to the extent that improved sanitation, nutrition and environmental conditions have led to decreased mortality rates in the past, continued improvements will lead to similar decreases in mortality rates in the future.

There appear to be a number of discrepancies between the Global 2000 Study's low-fertility, low-mortality population assumptions/projections and the Study's environmental projections. The population projections assume continued improvements in human welfare throughout LDC societies. Discrepancies between this assumption and the environmental projections can be seen for large aggregate areas of the LDC nations, for large rural LDC areas, and increasingly for LDC urban areas.

The assumed continued moderate social and economic progress throughout the LDCs appear to be contradicted by trends in GNP, food, and energy. The per capita GNP projections—even without correction for decreased goods and services from the environment—do not show moderate increases throughout the LDCs. In the medium case, growth in per capita GNP slows to 0.1 percent per year for parts of South Asia for the 1985–2000 period. Per capita GNP growth for the entire African continent slows to less than 1.4 percent per year for the same period, and although figures for the poorest countries in Africa are not available separately, they are certain to be much lower than the continental average. Food consumption per capita does not show moderate increases throughout the LDCs. For the LDCs overall, per capita daily caloric consumption—again, with no reductions for anticipated environmental problems—increases only slightly, from 93 percent of FAO minimum standards for the 1973–74 period to 94 percent in 2000. This single percentage point increase masks declines for the poorest LDC nations and for the poorest classes in all LDC societies. Per capita daily calorie consumption in the Central African LDCs falls from 90 percent of FAO minimum standards for the 1973–74 period to 77 percent in 2000.* The energy sector will also affect health. The projected doubling of world energy prices will force the LDCs, chronically short of foreign exchange, to depend increasingly on domestic organic fuels. But the Food and Agriculture Organization projects that by 1994 there will be a fuelwood shortfall of 650 million cubic meters annually, approximately one quarter of the fuelwood consumption projected by FAO for the year 2000. The health hazards associated with undercooked foods and inadequate heat are well known. In short, the aggregate

---

*At the request of the U.S. Agency for International Development, two sets of demographic projections were developed for the Global 2000 Study. One set was developed by the U.S. Bureau of the Census, the other by the Community and Family Study Center (CFSC) of the University of Chicago. The two projections use basically the same environmental assumptions but differ significantly in their assumptions concerning the effectiveness of family planning progams. Further details on the differences between the two sets of projections is provided in Chapters 2 and 15 and in Paul Demeny, "On the End of the Population Explosion," *Population and Development Review*, Mar. 1979, pp. 141–62, and in Donald J. Bogue and Amy Ong Tsui, "A Rejoinder to Paul Demeny's Critique," May 1979 (draft submitted to *Population and Development Review*).

*The figures for per capita daily calorie consumption are from Alternative III of the food and agriculture projections in Chapter 6—the only alternative that includes increasing energy costs.

projections of GNP, food, and energy—even without any correction for environmental deterioration—do not suggest continued moderate progress for all segments of the populations throughout the LDCs.

Beyond the broad, aggregate trends, rural LDC areas will experience problems uniquely their own. The pressure on all agricultural lands will increase enormously. The number of persons that will have to be supported per arable hectare will increase from 2.9 in the 1970–75 period to 5.3 by 2000. The expansion of irrigation facilities implicitly assumed in the food projections will substantially increase habitats for disease vectors. Malaria-carrying mosquitos are developing progressively greater resistance to the major pesticides used to control them. The quadrupled use of pesticides assumed in the food and agriculture projections will lead to increased pesticide pollution and poisonings.

The largest impacts on LDC health, however, may occur in the urban areas. Over the last quarter of this century the urban population of the world is projected to increase from 39 percent to almost 50 percent. The largest increases will occur in LDC cities. Mexico City is projected to increase from 10.9 million in 1975 to 31.6 million in 2000, roughly three times the present population of metropolitan New York City. Calcutta is projected to reach nearly twice New York's present population by 2000. Jakarta's population more than triples to reach 16.9 million. Altogether, it is projected that 1.2 billion additional persons—roughly a quarter of the present total world population—will be added to LDC cities, and the most rapid growth will be in uncontrolled settlements, where populations are now doubling every 5–7 years. Financial resources are not likely to be available to the poor in uncontrolled settlements or to their city governments, even for providing safe water. Sewage facilities will be limited at best. Fecally related diseases can be expected to increase. The forestry and energy projections suggest that warm, dry, uncrowded housing will be even less available than now—a condition that will foster the transmission of contagious diseases. Pathogen resistance to the least expensive antibiotics and other drugs is becoming more common in the treating of many diseases, including malaria, typhoid, dysentery, and the venereal diseases. This increased resistance, along with continued malnutrition, will make epidemics more frequent and harder to control.

Overall, there appear to be significant discrepancies between the environmental projections and the assumptions underlying the population projections for the LDCs. If it were possible to correct these discrepancies by incorporating feedback from environmental projections into the demographic projections for the LDCs, some significant numerical changes would probably occur. The projections for Pakistan are a case in point.

The environmental and other projections for Pakistan do not support the general assumption underlying the population projections, namely, continued moderate increases in social and economic welfare. Even before any environmental considerations are taken into account, growth in Pakistan's per capita GNP is projected essentially to come to a halt during the 1985–2000 period, and there are many environmental considerations to be taken into account in Pakistan. Virtually every environmental feedback discussed in the past few paragraphs applies to Pakistan. Therefore, to the extent that the fertility and mortality rates for Pakistan were assumed to be lowered by continued moderate increases in social and economic welfare, the rates are too low. If environmental feedbacks had been explicitly taken into account, life expectancies might have been projected to remain about the same or to increase only slightly rather than to rise by an average of nine years.* Similarly, something less than a 28 percent decline in the crude birth rate (from 44.54 to 32.12) might have been anticipated, even with a fairly strong family planning program.

If environmental feedback were to be explicitly considered throughout the population projections, analogous adjustments would be necessary in the projections for many other LDC countries, including Haiti, Thailand, Mexico, India, Indonesia, Bolivia, Bangladesh, and the countries of sub-Saharan Africa.

*Feedback to the Population Projections for the Industrialized Countries.* The feedbacks to the population projections for the industrialized nations are relatively few compared to those for the LDC population. The linkages are primarily through the health implications of energy development and through migration.

The energy projections show clearly that by 2000 a transition away from petroleum must be well in progress for most industrialized nations. The choices lie along a spectrum that ranges from the soft path (a highly efficient energy sector using a minimal amount of primary energy drawn as much as possible from solar and other renewable sources) to the hard path (a relatively inefficient energy sector using relatively large amounts of primary energy drawn from coal and nuclear

---

*For females, the projected increase over the 1975–2000 period is from 53.63 to 63.95 years (19 percent) in the medium series of the Bureau of Census projections; for males the increase is from 54.50 to 62.30 years (14 percent).

sources). Most nations have yet to choose among their options, but when the choice is made, it will have significant health implications. The hard path coal option implies increasing problems with particulates, oxides of sulfur, and oxides of nitrogen, all of which have health adverse effects. The hard path nuclear option implies increasing problems of disposal of radioactive wastes from uranium mining, from low-level nuclear wastes, and from spent nuclear fuel, and radiation problems as well. The soft-path renewable-resource options also present a number of health problems. The energy projections do not extend to 2000, and it is not possible to predict how nations will make their energy choices. Whatever the choices are, however, they can be expected to have significant and varied health implications, but are unlikely to significantly affect population growth.

The other major feedback from the environmental projections to the population projections for the industrialized nations involves migration. International migration is a difficult subject from many perspectives, including that of the demographer. The demographer's problem is that migrants are often in violation of immigration laws, and as a result avoid being counted in a census.

Difficult as the problem is for demographers, the projected LDC population growth coupled with the projected LDC environmental trends suggests that there will be increasing pressures from international migration. Although the flows cannot be quantified and projected precisely, increased migration can be anticipated from North Africa to Europe, from South Asia to the oil-rich nations of the Middle East, and from Central to North America (Mexico City, for example, is only about 500 miles from the Mexican-U.S. border).

Even the limited statistics available for the United States illustrate the demographic significance of migration. The so-called natural increase (excess of births over deaths) for the U.S. is now roughly 1.3 million per year. Approximately 400,000 foreign visitors per year remain in the country illegally, and in addition approximately 800,000 successfully enter the country illegally each year, adding about 1.2 million persons to the U.S. population annually, an amount almost identical with the natural increase of about 0.6 percent per year.* As a result, the population growth rate for the U.S. is probably closer to 1.2 percent per year than the 0.6 percent per year estimate given in Table 2–12 in Chapter 2. Similar (and probably

increasing) immigration can also be expected for parts of Europe and the Middle East.

It is thus clear that feedback from the environmental projections to the population projections has implications for the population estimates for both LDC and industrialized nations. For the industrialized nations, migration may increase growth rates in some cases by one half of a percentage point or so. For the LDCs, the effects are more complex and dependent on the situation in individual countries. If environmental factors could have been taken into account explicitly throughout the Global 2000 Study population projections, the total world estimates for 2000 might well have been about the same as the present projection—a 46–64 percent increase to a total world population of 5.9–6.8 billion in 2000—but for somewhat different reasons: Birth rates would have generally been somewhat higher and life expectancies lower .

## Summing Up

The foregoing analysis of the environmental feedbacks to the Global 2000 projections reveals numerous and serious differences (discrepancies) between the projected future world environment and the assumptions that were used in the population, GNP, and resource projections of Chapters 2–12. Many of the study projections assume implicitly that terrestrial, aquatic, and atmospheric resources will continue to provide goods and services in ever increasing amounts without maintenance, moderation, or protection.† Such

---

*These estimates were obtained in 1976 by Justin Blackwelder, president of the Environmental Fund, Washington, from the U.S. Immigration and Naturalization Service (INS) and were published by the Environmental Fund in 1976 in "U.S. Population Larger Than Official Census Figures." The INS has since stopped making such estimates, and will not now confirm or deny the estimates (E. Collison, INS Staff Investigator,

personal communication, 1979). Anne Ehrlich suggests that the figures are too high (personal communication, 1979). *The Golden Door,* a recent book on migration between Mexico and the United States attempts to trace the history of the 800,000 estimate (Paul R. Ehrlich, Loy Bilderback, and Anne Ehrlich, New York: Ballantine, 1979, p. 180). INS Staff Investigator E. Collison suggests the recent work of Clarice Lancaster of the U.S. Department of HEW and Frederick Scheuern of the U.S. Social Security Administration as a widely accepted estimate. Clarice Lancaster and Frederick Scheuern estimate that in 1970 there were between 2.9 and 5.7 million illegal aliens in the U.S. ("Counting the Uncountable: Some Initial Statistical Speculations Employing Capture-Recapture Technique," paper presented at the American Statistical Association Annual Meeting, 1977).

†In the U.S., this and related assumptions have been questioned with increasing frequency by many groups. The relationship between the environment and human economic institutions is highly complex, and many environmental leaders believe that some basic value changes will be needed before a sustainable relationship can develop. Several feminist writers have drawn interesting parallels between the values underlying the relationship between humankind and Mother Nature on the one hand and values underlying relationships between men and women. See, for example: Susan Griffin, *Woman and Nature: The Roaring Inside Her,* New York: Harper, 1978; Mary Daly, *GYN/ECOLOGY: The Metaphysics of Radical Feminism,* Boston: Beacon, 1978; and Dorothy Dinnerstein, *The Mermaid and the Minotaur: Sexual Arrangements and Human Malaise,* New York: Harper, 1978.

assumptions are unrealistic. The Global 2000 Study's environmental analyses point to many areas where the capacity of the environment to provide goods and services can no longer be taken for granted. There are two reasons. First, the demand for environmental goods and services is outstripping the capacity of the environment to provide, as both population and per capita consumption expand. Second, in many areas the ecological systems that provide the goods and services are being undermined, extinguished, and poisoned. While informed and careful management of the environment might still increase the goods and services it provides in some areas, in other areas the demands placed on the environment are approaching, and in some areas have exceeded, its sustainable carrying capacity.

Added insight into the meaning of the Global 2000 Study's projections can be obtained by comparing them with a National Academy of Sciences estimate of the ultimate carrying capacity of the global environment. The Academy's 1969 report, *Resources and Man,* concluded that the world population must be stabilized at levels considerably lower than 10 billion, if human life is to be comfortably sustained within the resource limits of the earth.[768] The Academy also concluded that, even by sacrificing individual comfort and choice, the human population is unlikely ever to exceed 30 billion persons.

Information that has become available since 1969 tends not only to confirm the Academy's findings but to point to even more severe limits. For example, the Academy based its conclusion as to the earth's carrying capacity on the assumed availability of 61 million hectares more arable land than was projected by the U.S. Department of Agriculture for the Global 2000 Study. The Academy's report assumed a sustainable fish catch 40 million tons per year higher than the National Oceanic and Atmospheric Administration has estimated for the Global 2000 Study.* In its estimates, the Academy had assumed that one-half of the world's potentially arable land was under cultivation so that a twofold increase in production could be expected by developing the other half, and two additional twofold increases could be obtained by increased productivity and innovation respectively, leading to an eightfold potential increase in food production. Its study made no mention of the productivity losses re-

sulting from salinization (which now affects half of the world's irrigated soils), or of the soil losses and hydraulic destabilization that will accompany the projected deforestation. Nor did the Academy anticipate the rapid rise in the cost of energy-intensive fertilizers and pesticides. In short, the vast majority of the information that has become available over the past decade suggests that the Academy's estimate is reasonable, perhaps even optimistic: The earth's carrying capacity, under intensive management is about 10 billion persons "with some degree of comfort and individual choice," and about 30 billion otherwise.

The world's population picture has, of course, changed since the Academy's report in 1969, when there were about 3.6 billion persons and the total was increasing at about 2 percent per year. In 1979, there are approximately 4.3 billion persons, and the number is increasing at about 1.8 percent per year. The Global 2000 Study's projections suggest that by 2000 there will be about 6.35 billion persons, and that the number will increase at about 1.7 percent per year. Clearly, if present demographic trends continue, population growth will not stop—i.e., the annual percentage increase will not fall to zero—until well into the 21st century. If a net reproductive rate of 1.0 (replacement fertility) could somehow be achieved in 2000, the world's population would peak at approximately 8.4 billion by about the year 2100.[769] If it were to continue growing at the rate projected for 2000 (1.7 per unit per year), the world population would reach 10 billion in 2027, and 30 billion in 2091.

As of 1980, the year 2027 is 47 years away. To put it another way, a child born in 1980 will be 47 years old in 2027. Persons now under the age of 24 years can expect to live to 2027 (assuming a 70-year life expectancy). They may be living in a world whose population is approaching the maximum number that an intensively managed earth can sustain with, as the National Academy puts it, "some degree of comfort and individual choice." What are the major environmental developments that these persons may observe?

The Global 2000 Study's environmental projections, based on the assumption of no changes in policy, point to major changes in all three of the earth's major environments—terrestrial, aquatic, and atmospheric. The projections also point to a group of emerging environmental problems, some of which are global in scope, some of which involve vicious circles of causality, and some, increased societal vulnerability. By and large, these environmental problems will be difficult to resolve, even with major policy changes.

---

*It is perhaps notable that the historically steep upward trend in marine fish catch peaked at 60 million tons just as the National Academy of Sciences made its estimate of a 100 million ton potential.

In the terrestrial environment, the basic change to be anticipated is a general deterioration of soil quality over most of the earth. The immediate causes vary from one area to another, but generally involve demands on local ecosystems and soils and population growth that will be impossible to sustain. Desertification will claim large areas in the LDCs of Africa, Asia, and Latin America, as will erosion following shortened fallow cycles and tropical deforestation. Erosion, compaction, and hardpanning will affect increasingly large areas in the industrialized nations, as will salinization, alkalinization, and waterlogging of irrigated lands everywhere. Farm land will continue to be lost to urban and village expansion.

The global aquatic environment will also deteriorate generally, both in its saltwater and freshwater portions. Freshwater will be slowed by dams and irrigation works, warmed by waste heat from energy facilities (thus reducing the oxygen content), reduced in flow by more consumptive (i.e., evaporative) uses such as irrigation and evaporative cooling for energy facilities, salted by irrigation drainage, eutrophied by fertilizer runoff and sewage, acidified by acid mine drainage and acid rain, destablized by deforestation, and polluted by silt, pesticides, and other toxic substances. Freshwater habitats for disease vectors will increase. Habitats for species that require swift, clean, cool water (like salmon in the U.S.) will decline. Coastal marine waters will suffer from loss of important habitats—estuaries, salt marshes, mangroves, reefs—as well as from heavy pressure on fish and mammal populations, continued pollution by crude oil from offshore extraction, marine transport, and terrestrial runoff, and an influx of toxic materials, the effects of which will continue to be experienced for decades, at a minimum.

The atmosphere will—again, under the assumption of no change in present policies—receive increasing amounts of effluents from coal combustion. Oxides of nitrogen and sulfur will cause increased health problems and will produce acid rain. Particulates will increase health problems. Carbon dioxide emissions resulting from deforestation and from all forms of fossil fuel combustion (especially increased use of coal and synthetic fuels) will continue to increase the global concentration of $CO_2$ in the atmosphere, creating conditions that many scientists believe could raise the average temperature of the earth, melt polar ice, raise sea levels, and flood coastal areas during the 21st or 22nd century. Some spray-can propellants and refrigerants, some high-altitude aircraft flights, and nitrogen fertilizers will release

chemicals in varying amounts that tend to reduce concentrations of ozone in the upper atmosphere, potentially increasing the amount of ultraviolet radiation, which is damaging to plants, animals, and humans.

Several developments are anticipated that will affect all three major environments (air, water, land). The release of toxic substances, including pesticides, is being controlled increasingly in industrialized nations, but under present policies growing amounts of these substances can be expected to enter the air, land, and water in LDCs. Materials emitting low-level radiation will be released in increased amounts into all three environments. Oxides of nitrogen and sulfur from fossil fuel combustion will increase atmospheric concentrations, acidify rain, and ultimately alter chemical balances in surface waters and soils over wide areas. The rate of extinctions of species in all three environments will increase dramatically, leading to the loss of perhaps one-fifth of all plant and animal species by 2000.

Some new classes of environmental problems will become more evident and more important—among them: problems that require global cooperation; problems that are very long-lived; problems that lead to increasing social vulnerability; and problems that originate in vicious-circle types of causations.

Problems of the global commons—the earth's atmosphere and oceans—can be expected to become more important and urgent in the years ahead. Management of global $CO_2$ and ozone concentrations are probably the most important and difficult issues of the global commons, but the protection of marine mammal populations (a global-commons problem on which some progress has already been achieved) will continue to be a concern. Institutional mechanisms for dealing with these issues are limited. The International Maritime Consultative Organization (IMCO) has made significant progress in dealing with oil pollution from tankers, but has made little progress in reducing the flow of toxic substances into the oceans. The U.N.-sponsored Law of the Sea Conference constitutes one of the broadest efforts made so far to deal with such problems, but the slowness of the progress made by this conference and related follow-up activities illustrates the extreme difficulties involved in achieving the necessary cooperation on issues related to the global commons. Efforts to manage $CO_2$ and ozone concentrations on a global scale are just beginning, and considering the issues involved—fossil fuel combustion, deforestation, high-altitude flight, perhaps even the rate of use of nitrogen fertilizers—agreements can be expected to be at least as difficult to reach as in the case of the Law of the Sea.

Multilateral cooperation on only a somewhat smaller scale will be required to deal with a number of terrestrial, coastal, and freshwater environmental issues. Desertification problems often cross national boundaries, as do some of the herding populations involved. Deforestation is being driven not only by domestic needs, but also by multinational markets and corporations. Protection of regional seas will be impossible without multilateral cooperation, and the protection and management of many river basins will require cooperation among two or more nations as well. Since the needs of upstream and downstream users often conflict, river development and management may become an increasing source of conflict among nations as water resources become still more heavily committed.

Long-lived toxic pollutants also present a new class of environmental problems. Many toxic substances—heavy metals, radioactive materials, and some toxic chemicals—have very long lives, and their release or mobilization into the environment creates changes for which there is no apparent remedial action. Mercury, lead, high-level radioactive wastes, dioxin, and PCBs are examples. Many metals, some of which bioaccumulate, are highly toxic, and once mobilized by mining, refining, dredging, or industrial processes, are expected to produce adverse effects for decades—or centuries—to come, especially in the oceans. The consequences are many and varied. It is well known, for example, that the utility of biological resources (e.g., fish and shellfish) has been degraded or destroyed by heavy metals, but it is less well known that some bacteria have developed resistance to mercury poisoning and as a consequence also to several antibiotics. (Research with the genus *Vibrio* and the genus *Bacillus* have led to the conclusion that the antibiotic and mercury resistances are genetically linked and caused by the mercury exposure.[770]) High-level radioactive wastes are extremely toxic and must be kept safely separated from the environment for tens of thousands of years, a period that exceeds the stable life of any civilization in history, and even exceeds the period of recorded history. Long-lived toxic chemicals present similar problems. While several industrial nations are now tightening regulations for the use and disposal of toxic chemicals, the controls are far from adequate. Even determining which individual chemicals are toxic will be difficult, and the problem of the synergistic toxicity of two or more chemicals presently lacks a feasible solution.[771] Furthermore, old chemical dumps (such as the Love Canal dumpsite in New York State),[772] contaminated river bottoms (such as those of the Hudson River in New York[773] and the James in Virginia),[774] and contaminated lands (such as the environs of Seveso, Italy)[775] will continue to pose threats to animals—and human life—for many years to come.

Another class of environmental pressures is leading to increased vulnerability, especially in the world's food production and energy systems. Food production around the world is leading to various forms of soil deterioration. Fertility is being maintained, pests controlled, and yields enhanced through energy-intensive (or more specifically, fossil fuel-intensive) inputs of fertilizers, chemicals, and fuels for tractors and irrigation motors. The food needed to feed the population projected for 2000 can be produced only through the continued and increased dependence of agriculture on fossil fuels. The increased vulnerability that this trend implies is illustrated by the disruption in energy supplies caused recently by the change of government in a single nation—Iran, by no means the largest of the world's energy suppliers. The vulnerability of energy-intensive agriculture is increased further by expanded areas of genetically similar (or identical) monocultures, by expansion of agriculture into increasingly arid and marginal lands, and by the projected deforestation (which exaggerates seasonal variations in water availability and thus increases vulnerability to drought).

In the energy area, increased reliance on nuclear energy will create another environmentally related vulnerability. The accident at Three Mile Island in Pennsylvania demonstrated dramatically that nuclear accidents, whatever their probability, can and do happen. In the Three Mile Island accident, relatively little damage was done to the environment, but radioactive gases were released, and the governor of Pennsylvania felt it necessary to partially evacuate an area within five miles of the stricken plant. As a result of the accident, and of concern over the safety of a second reactor at the same site built by the same manufacturer, a significant fraction of the electric energy supply for Pennsylvania has been lost for a period of years. Public concern is now such that another serious accident or a terrorist attack* could lead to a significant curtailment in nuclear generation in many countries. The projected 226 percent increase in nuclear generation by 1990 will increase this vulnerability.

---

*There have been a significant number of attacks on nuclear installations. See Michael Flood, "Nuclear Sabotage," *Bulletin of the Atomic Scientists*, Oct. 1976, pp. 29–36.

Finally, there is a growing class of environmental problems that will be extremely difficult to resolve because of a vicious circle of causes and effects. This class of problems is particularly acute in the land-deterioration/population-growth phenomenon in some of the poorest rural areas in the LDCs: Environmental deterioration is accelerated by further population growth; human reproduction rates are kept up by poor living conditions (and other social welfare problems);[76] and living conditions decline further as the environmental resources deteriorate.

The important linkages between the population, welfare, and resource demands have long been recognized and included in development plans and projection models, but the linkages from the environment back to population, welfare, and resources have often been neglected. So it is with the Global 2000 Sudy's projections. As illustrated in Figure 13–1, the linkages from the population and GNP projections to resource demands are well established. This chapter has analyzed the environmental implications of the population, GNP, and resource projections and has attempted to close the feedback loops linking the projected future world environment back to the other projections. While the feedback loops could not actually be closed, the environmental assumptions underlying the population, GNP, and resource projections were identified and compared with the environmental future these projections imply. The environmental assumptions implicit in the population, GNP, and resource projections amount in many cases to an assumption that the environment will provide its goods and services in much larger amounts, without interruption, and without increase in cost. The environmental analysis suggests that this assumption is, in many cases, unrealistically optimistic. The analysis also shows that the goods and services provided by the environment can no longer be taken for granted.

## REFERENCES

### Population Section

1. Wendell Berry, *Unsettling of America,* San Francisco: Sierra Club, 1977, pp. 210–17.
2. See, for example, Colin M. Turnbull, *The Forest People: A Study of the Pygmies of the Congo,* New York: Simon and Schuster, 1962.
3. Raymond F. Dasmann et al., *Ecological Principles for Economic Development,* New York: Wiley, 1973, p. 82.
4. *Conservation and Rational Use of the Environment,* UNESCO and FAO report to the U.N. Economic and Social Council, Mar. 12, 1968.
5. Garrett Hardin and John Baden, eds., *Managing the Commons,* San Francisco: Freeman, 1977.
6. Garrett Hardin, "The Tragedy of the Commons," *Science,* Dec. 13, 1968, pp. 1243–48.
7. For two particularly interesting examples, see the story of the Tasaday in John Nance, *The Gentle Tasaday: A Stone Age People in the Philippine Rain Forest,* New York: Harcourt, 1975; and the story of the decline of the Mayan civilization as told in Harold M. Schmecht, Jr., "Study Depicts Mayan Decline," *New York Times,* Oct. 23, 1979, p. C1, and in E. S. Deevey et al., Mayan Urbanism: Impact on a Tropical Karst Environment," *Science,* Oct. 19, 1979, pp. 298–306.
8. See, for example, Colin M. Turnbull, *The Mountain People,* New York, Simon and Schuster, 1972. This phenomenon extends beyond herding societies. See, for example: D. A. Schanche, "King, Cripple-Makers Rule Cairo's Army of Beggars," *Washington Post,* Sept. 2, 1978, p. A–11; Abdell Atti Hamed, *Adventures of a Journalist at the Bottom of Egyptian Society,* Cairo: Akbar al Yom Publishing House, 1974.
9. *Arid Lands in Transition,* Harold E. Dregne, ed., Washington: American Association for the Advancement of Science, 1970.
10. Ibid.
11. *The State of Food and Agriculture.* Rome: Food and Agriculture Organization, Nov. 1977 (draft), ch. 3, pp. 3–16.
12. Ibid.
13. T. C. Byerly et al., *The Role of Ruminants in Support of Man,* Morrilton, Ark.: Winrock International Livestock Research and Training Center, Apr. 1978; T. D. Nguyen and H. A. Fitzhugh, *WINROCK MODEL for Simulating Ruminant Production Systems,* Morrilton: Winrock, Dec. 1977.
14. Robert B. Batchelder and Howard F. Hirt, "Fire in Tropical Forests and Grasslands," U.S. Army Natick Laboratories, June 1966, pp. 136, 168 (this excellent report is available from the National Technical Information Service).
15. *Tropical Forest Ecosystems: A State of Knowledge Report,* Natural Resources Research XIV, Paris: UNESCO/UNEP/FAO, 1978, pp. 467–81.
16. Ibid., p. 475.
17. Dasmann et al., op. cit.
18. P. H. Nye and D. J. Greenland, *The Soil Under Shifting Cultivation,* Technical Communication No. 51, Bucks, England: Commonwealth Agricultural Bureaux, 1960.
19. *Tropical Forest Ecosystems,* op. cit., pp. 470–76.
20. R. F. Watters, *Shifting Agriculture in Latin America,* Rome: Food and Agriculture Organization, 1971.
21. Lester R. Brown, *The Worldwide Loss of Cropland,* Washington: Worldwatch Institute, Oct. 1978; "Desertification: An Overview," U.N. Conference on Desertification, 1977; Erik P. Eckholm, *Losing Ground: Environmental Stress and World Food Prospects,* New York: Norton, 1976.
22. For further details, see the forestry section of this chapter, also Chapter 8 and App. C, and "Proceedings of the U.S. Strategy Conference on Tropical Deforestation," Washington: U.S. Agency for International Development, 1978.
23. U.N. Conference on Desertification, Earthscan Press Briefing Document No. 6, Aug. 1977.
24. Eckholm, *Losing Ground,* op. cit.; App. C of this volume; "Desertification: An Overview," op. cit.
25. *Environmental Quality 1978,* annual report of the Council on Environmental Quality, Washington: Government Printing Office, 1979, ch. 3.

26. Ibid.
27. Ibid.
28. Ibid.
29. Ibid.
30. Denis Hayes, *Repairs, Reuse, Recycling–First Steps Toward a Sustainable Society,* Washington: Worldwatch Institute, Sept. 1978.
31. *Environmental Quality 1973,* annual report of the Council on Environmental Quality, Washington: Government Printing Office, 1974, p. 204.
32. The obscuring of environmental impacts that results from trade and commerce is brought out in Edward Goldsmith and John P. Milton, eds., "The Future of America," *The Ecologist,* Aug./Sept. 1977, pp. 245–340.
33. Hardin, "Tragedy of the Commons," op. cit.
34. Garrett Hardin, "Political Requirements for Preserving Our Common Heritage," Ch. 20 in Council on Environmental Quality, *Wildlife and America,* Washington: Government Printing Office, 1979.
35. Thane Gustafson, "The New Soviet Environmental Program: Do The Soviets Really Mean Business?" *Public Policy,* Summer 1978, pp. 455–76; Marshall I. Goldman, *The Spoils of Progress: Environmental Pollution in the Soviet Union,* Cambridge, Mass., MIT, 1972.; Donald R. Kelly et al., *Economic Superpowers and the Environment: United States, Soviet Union and Japan,* San Francisco; Freeman, 1976.
36. Susan Swannack-Nunn et al., *State-of-the-Environment Profile for the People's Republic of China,* Washington: National Council for U.S.–China Trade, Apr. 1979. Also see B. J. Culliton, "China Adopts New Law for Environmental Protection," *Science,* Oct. 26, 1979, p. 429.
37. An excellent history of U.S. efforts to protect its environment will be found in J. Clarence Davies III and Barbara Davies, *The Politics of Pollution,* 2d ed., Indianapolis: Bobbs-Merrill, 1975; also see P. R. Portney, ed., *Current Issues in U.S. Environmental Policy,* Baltimore: Johns Hopkins, 1978.
38. Talbot Page, *Conservation and Economic Efficiency: An Approach to Materials Policy,* Baltimore: Johns Hopkins, 1977, ch. 7; Kenneth J. Arrow, "The Rate of Discount for Long-Term Public Investment," in Holt Ashley et al., *Energy and the Environment: A Risk Benefit Approach,* New York: Pergamon, 1976, pp. 113–41.
39. Ibid.
40. *The Determinants and Consequences of Population Trends,* vol. 1, New York: U.N. Dept. of Economic and Social Affairs, 1973.
41. "Trends and Prospects in Urban and Rural Population, 1950–2000, as Assessed in 1973–74," New York: Population Div., U.N. Dept. of Economic and Social Affairs, Apr. 25, 1975, p. 10.
42. Ibid.
43. An excellent introduction to this topic, prepared for the U.N. Conference on Human Settlements, is Barbara Ward, *The Home of Man,* New York: Norton, 1976.
44. "Trends and Prospects in Urban and Rural Population, 1950–2000," op. cit., p. 11.
45. "Third World Urban Sprawl," *ILO Information* (U.S. ed.), vol. 6, no. 4, 1978, pp. 1, 9.
46. Ibid.
47. "Trends and Prospects in the Populations of Urban Agglomerations, 1950–2000, as Assessed in 1973–1975," ESA/P/WP.58, New York: Population Div., U.N. Dept. of Economic and Social Affairs, Nov. 21, 1975.
48. Peter H. Freeman, "The Environmental Impact of Rapid Urbanization: Guidelines for Policy and Planning," Washington: Office of International and Environmental Programs, Smithsonion Institution, 1974, table 12, p. 42.
49. Peter H. Freeman, ed., *The Urban Environment of Seoul, Korea: A Case Study of Rapid Urbanization,* Washington: U.S. Agency for International Development, Nov., 1974.
50. "World Population: The Silent Explosion," *Department of State Bulletin,* Fall 1978, pp. 17–18.
51. Ward, op. cit., p. 193.
52. World Health Organization, "Community Water Supply and Wastewater Disposal," May 6, 1976, p.4.
53. Ibid., p. 5.
54. J. R. Simpson and R. M. Bradley, "The Environmental Impact of Water Reclamation in Overseas Countries," *Water Pollution Control,* vol. 77, no. 2, 1978, p. 223.
55. Ibid.
56. Bruce McCallum, *Environmentally Appropriate Technology,* Dept. of Fisheries and Environment, Canada, Apr. 1977, pp. 109–11; Lane deMoll, ed., *Rainbook: Resources for Appropriate Technology,* New York: Schocken, 1977, pp. 191–94.
57. World Health Organization, "Disposal of Community Wastewater," Technical Report Service no. 541, 1974.
58. Elaine de Steinheil and Hilary Branch, "Enforcing Environmental Law in Venezuela," *World Environment Report,* Feb. 27, 1978, p. 3.
59. William F. Hunt et al., *Guideline for Public Reporting of Daily Air Quality: Pollutant Standards Index,* U.S. Environmental Protection Agency, Aug. 1976.
60. Loretta McLaughlan, "Peruvian Ecologist Urges Lima to Enact Air Pollution Law," *World Environment Report,* Aug. 14, 1978, p. 5.
61. Sam Cohen, "Sulphur Dioxide in Ankara's Air Found Twice that of WHO Standard," *World Environment Report,* Dec. 19, 1977, p. 5.
62. R. Murali Manohar, "Massive Air Pollution in Bombay Cause of Respiratory Ailments," *World Environment Report,* May 8, 1978, p. 5.
63. Ibid.
64. Ibid.
65. Erick Eckholm, *The Other Energy Crisis: Firewood,* Washington: Worldwatch Institute, 1975.
66. *State of Food and Agriculture,* op. cit., p. 25.
67. "Third World Urban Sprawl," op. cit.
68. Lester R. Brown, *The Twenty-Ninth Day,* New York: Norton 1978.
69. "Trends and Prospects in Urban and Rural Population, 1950–2000," op. cit.
70. Council on Environmental Quality, U.S. Dept. of Housing and Urban Development, and U.S. Environmental Protection Agency, "The Costs of Sprawl: Environmental and Economic Costs of Alternative Residential Development Patterns at the Urban Fringe," Washington: Government Printing Office, Apr. 1974; also see the Council's "The Quiet Revolution in Land Use Control" and "The Growth Shapers," Washington: Government Printing Office, 1971, 1976.
71. Hayes, op. cit.
72. Executive Office of the President, "The National Energy Plan," Washington: Government Printing Office, Apr. 1977.
73. Ibid., p. VII.
74. Ibid., pp. VIII, X.
75. Office of Technology Assessment, "Analysis of the Proposed National Energy Plan," Washington: Government Printing Office, Aug. 1977, pp. 197–80.
75a. *The Journey to Work in the United States: 1975,* Washington: Government Printing Office, July 1977; Spencer

Rich, "Auto Data Reflect an Abiding Passion," *Washington Post*, July 22, 1979, p. A20.

75b. L. R. Brown, C. Flavin, and C. Norman, *Running on Empty: The Future of the Automobile in an Oil Short World*, New York: Norton, 1979.

76. *Environmental Quality 1978*, op. cit. p. 220; also see U.S. Bureau of the Census, *Geographic Mobility: March 1975 to March 1978* and *Social and Economic Characteristics of the Metropolitan and Nonmetropolitan Population: 1977 and 1970*. Washington: Government Printing Office, Nov. 1978.

77. *Environmental Quality 1978*, op. cit., p. 227.

78. George J. Beier, "Can Third World Cities Cope?" Washington: Population Reference Bureau, Dec. 1976.

79. Eckholm, *Losing Ground*, op. cit.; Dasmann et al., op. cit.; *Tropical Forest Ecosystems*, op. cit.

80. *Canada as a Conserver Society: Resource Uncertainties and the Need for New Technologies*, Ottawa: Science Council of Canada, Sept. 1977.

81. U.N. Dept. of Economic and Social Affairs, *The Determinants and Consequences of Population Trends: New Summary of Findings on Interaction of Demographic, Economic and Social Factors*, vol. 1, New York, 1973.

82. N. R. E. Fendall, "Medical Care in the Developing Nations," in John Fry and W. A. J. Farndale, eds., *International Medical Care*, Wallingford, Pa.: Washington Square East, 1972, p. 220.

83. World Bank, "Health," Sector Policy Paper, Washington, Mar. 1975, annex 2, pp. 72–73; also see M. C. McHale et al., *Children in the World*, Washington: Population Reference Bureau, 1979, pp. 30–34.

84. World Bank, op. cit.

85. Ibid., p. 7.

86. Tim Dyson, "Levels, Trends, Differential and Causes of Child Mortality—A survey," *World Health Statistics Report*, vol. 30, no. 4, 1977, pp. 289–90.

87. John Bryant, *Health and the Developing World*, Ithaca, N.Y.: Cornell, 1969, p. 39.

88. W. J. van Zijl, "Studies on Diarrhoeal Diseases in Seven Countries by the WHO Diarrhoeal Diseases Advisory Team," *Bulletin of the World Health Organization*, vol. 35, no. 2, 1966, pp. 249–61.

89. Ibid.

90. Lester R. Brown, *World Population Trends: Signs of Hope, Signs of Stress*, Washington: Worldwatch Institute, Oct. 1976, pp. 15–25.

91. Sheldon M. Wolff and John V. Bennetts, "Gram-Negative Rod Bacteremia," *New England Journal of Medicine*, Oct. 3, 1974, pp. 733–34; Henry E. Simmons and Paul D. Stolley, "This is Medical Progress? Trends and Consequences of Antibiotic Use in the United States," *Journal of the American Medical Association*, Mar. 4, 1974, pp. 1023–28; LaVerne C. Harold, "Transferable Drug Resistance and the Ecologic Effects of Antibiotics," in M. Taghi Farvar and John P. Milton, eds., *The Careless Technology, Ecology and International Development*, Garden City: Natural History Press/Doubleday, 1972, pp. 35–46.

92. Wolff and Bennett, op. cit.

93. Eugene J. Gangarosa et. al., "An Epidemic-Associated Episome?," *Journal of Infectious Diseases*, Aug. 1972, pp. 215–18.

94. Ibid.

95. J. Olarte and E. Galindo, "Factores de resistencia a los antibióticos encontrados en bacterias enteropatógenas aisladas en la Ciudad de México," *Reviews of Latin American Microbiology*, vol. 12, 1970, pp. 173–79.

96. Pan American Sanitary Bureau, Regional Office of the World Health Organization, *Weekly Epidemiological Report*, no. 22, 1972, pp. 129–30.

97. World Health Organization, *Weekly Epidemiological Record*, Oct. 14–Nov. 11, 1977. pp. 325–70; June 23–30, 1978, pp. 181–96.

98. Marietta Whittlesey, "The Runaway Use of Antibiotics," *New York Times Magazine*, May 6, 1979, p. 122.

99. Ibid.

100. Ibid; Janice Crossland, "Power to Resist," *Environment*, Mar. 1975, pp. 6–11.

101. Office of Technology Assessment, *Drugs in Livestock Feed*, vol. I, *Technical Report*, Washington: Government Printing Office, 1979.

102. Whittlesey, op. cit.

103. Ibid.

104. Davidson R. Gwatkin, "The Sad News About the Death Rate," *Washington Post*, Dec. 2, 1978, op ed page; and his "The End of an Era: A Review of the Literature and Data Concerning Third World Mortality Trends," Washington: Overseas Development Council, forthcoming.

105. U.S. Public Health Service, National Center for Health Statistics, *Vital Statistics of the United States*, vol. 2, sec. 5, *Life Tables*, Hyattsville, Md., 1977, pp. 5–15.

106. There is a very extensive literature on this topic. For a small sample, see Michael J. Hill, "Metabolic Epidemiology of Dietary Factors in Large Bowel Cancer," *Cancer Research*, Nov. 1975, pp. 3398–3402; F. R. Lemon and T. T. Walden, "Death from Respiratory System Disease Among SDA Men," *Journal of the American Medical Association*, vol. 198, 1966, p. 117; Roland L. Phillips, "Role of Life-Style and Dietary Habits in Risk of Cancer Among Seventh-Day Adventists," *Cancer Research*, Nov. 1975, pp. 3513–22; Denis P. Burkitt, "Epidemiology of Cancer of the Colon and Rectum," *Cancer*, July 1971, pp. 3–13; "Statement of Dr. D. M. Hegsted," in U.S. Senate Select Committee on Nutrition and Human Needs, *Dietary Goals for the United States*, Washington: Government Printing Office, Feb. 1975, p. 3; Jacqueline Verrett and Jean Carper, *Eating May Be Hazardous to Your Health: How Your Government Fails to Protect You from the Dangers in Your Food*, New York: Simon and Schuster, 1974; Erik P. Eckholm, *The Picture of Health: Environmental Sources of Disease*, New York: Norton, 1977.

107. U.S. Public Health Service, *Health, United States 1978*, Washington: Dept. of Health, Education, and Welfare, 1978, pp. 220–21.

108. "Report to the President by the Toxic Substances Strategy Committee," Washington: Council on Environmental Quality, Aug. 1979 (public review draft).

109. Richard Doll, "Introduction," and J. W. Berg, "Worldwide Variations in Cancer Incidence as Clues to Cancer Origins," in H. H. Hiatt et al., eds, *Origins of Human Cancer*, Cold Spring Harbor, New York: Cold Spring Harbor Laboratory, 1977. Also see Thomas H. Maugh II, "Cancer and Environment: Higginson Speaks Out," *Science*, vol. 205, 1979, pp. 1363–66.

110. U.S. Public Health Service, *Annual Summary for the United States, 1977: Births, Deaths, Marriages, and Divorces*, pp. 28–29, and *Monthly Statistics Report—Provisional Statistics*, Washington: Dept. of Health, Education, and Welfare, 1977, 1979.

111. Ibid.

### GNP Section

112. Commission on Population Growth and the American Future, *Population and the American Future*, Washington: Government Printing Office, Mar. 27, 1972, p. 48.

113. Lester R. Brown, *The Global Economic Prospect: New Sources of Economic Stress*, Washington: Worldwatch Institute, May 1978, p. 6.
114. J. Krieger et al., "Facts and Figures for the U.S. Chemical Industry," *Chemical and Engineering News*, vol. 57, 1979, pp. 32–68.
115. U.N. Environment Programme, *State of the Environment 1978*, United Nations, Nairobi, 1978.
116. Organization for Economic Cooperation and Development, Chemicals Committee, *Chemicals in the Environment*, Paris, 1977.
117. U.S. Dept. of Labor, Occupational Safety and Health Administration, "Occupational Exposure to 1,2-Dibromo-3-chloropropane (DBCP) Occupational Safety and Health Standards," *Federal Register*, Mar. 17, 1978, pp. 11514–33.
118. Thomas H. Milby, ed. *Vinyl Chloride: An Information Resource*, Washington: National Institutes of Health, Mar. 1978.
119. U.S. Senate Committee on Commerce, Science, and Transportation, *Hazardous Materials Transportation: A Review and Analysis of the Department of Transportation's Regulatory Program*, Washington: Government Printing Office, 1979, pp. 13–14.
120. Environmental Defense Fund and the New York Public Interest Research Group, *Troubled Waters: Toxic Chemicals in the Hudson River*, New York, 1977.
121. *Environmental Quality 1977*, annual report of the Council on Environmental Quality, Washington: Government Printing Office, 1977, pp. 15–16.
122. US Environmental Protection Agency, *EPA Activities Under the Resource Conservation and Recovery Act—Fiscal Year 1978*, Washington: Government Printing Office, 1979, pp. 1–3.
123. Dick Kirschten, "The New War on Pollution is Over the Land," *National Journal*, 1979, pp. 603–6; John Walsh, "Seveso: The Questions Persist Where Dioxin Created a Wasteland," *Science*, Sept. 9, 1977, pp. 1064–67; John C. Fuller, *The Poison that Fell From the Sky*, New York: Random House, 1977, p. 94; Thomas Whiteside, "A Reporter at Large: Contaminated," *New Yorker*, Sept. 4, 1978, pp. 34–81 (published also as *The Pendulum and the Toxic Cloud*, New Haven: Yale, 1979).
124. Report of the Governing Council of the United Nations Environment Programme on the Work of its Fifth Session, Governing Council Decision 85(v), Nairobi, May, 1977.
125. World Bank, *Sociological Planning and Political Aspects*, Aug. 1978, ch. 7.
126. Study Group on Unintended Occurrence of Pesticides, *The Problems of Persistent Chemicals: Implications of Pesticides and Other Chemicals in the Environment*, Paris: Organization for Economic Cooperation and Development, 1971.

### Climate Section

127. "Climate Change to the Year 2000: A Survey of Expert Opinion," Washington: National Defense University, 1978.
128. Ibid.
129. P. R. Crow, *Concepts in Climatology*, New York: St. Martin's, 1971, p. 480 ff.; C. E. P. Brooks, *Climate through the Ages*, New York: Dover, 1949.
130. *Climate and Food: Climatic Fluctuation and U.S. Agricultural Production*, Washington: National Academy of Sciences, 1976.
131. Well-developed introductions to the issues of climatic change are provided in Paul R. Ehrlich et al., *Ecoscience: Population, Resources, Environment*, San Francisco: Freeman, 1977, pp. 672–94; Ralph M. Rotty, "Energy and the Climate," Oak Ridge: Institute for Energy Analysis, Sept. 1976; Bert Bolin, "Energy and Climate," Stockholm: Secretariat for Future Studies, Nov. 1975. More detailed information is provided in U.S. Committee for the Global Atmospheric Research Program, *Understanding Climatic Change: A Program for Action*, Washington: National Academy of Sciences, 1975; Study of Man's Impact on Climate, *Inadvertent Climate Modification*, Cambridge, Mass.: MIT, 1971; Study of Critical Environmental Problems (SCEP) *Man's Impact on the Global Environment*, Cambridge, Mass.: MIT, 1970; Geophysics Study Committee, *Energy and Climate*, Washington: National Academy of Sciences, 1977.
132. "Crop Yields and Climate Change: The Year 2000," Washington: National Defense University, Dec. 1978, (draft abstract of Task II final report).
133. Ibid.
134. Rotty, op. cit.
135. U. Siegenthaler and H. Oeschger, "Predicting Future Atmospheric Carbon Dioxide Levels," *Science*, vol. 199, 1978, pp. 388–95.
136. Geophysics Study Committee, op. cit.
137. For a relatively simple discussion of the phenomena, see G. M. Woodwell, "The Carbon Dioxide Question," *Scientific American*, Jan. 1978, pp. 34–43. Also see G. M. Woodwell et al., "The Biota and the World Carbon Budget," *Science*, Jan. 13, 1978, pp. 141–46; G. E. Hutchinson, "The Biochemistry of the Terrestrial Atmosphere," in G. P. Kuiper, ed., *The Solar System*, Chicago: University of Chicago, 1954, vol. 2, pp. 371–433. For a recent counteropinion, see W. S. Broecker et al., "Fate of Fossil Fuel Carbon Dioxide and the Global Carbon Budget," *Science*, vol. 206, 1979, pp. 409–18.
138. Siegenthaler and Oeschger, op. cit.
139. Ibid.
140. Peter G. Brewer, "Carbon Dioxide and Climate," *Oceanus*, Fall 1978, pp. 13–17.
141. Siegenthaler and Oeschger, op. cit.
142. For an especially clear introduction, see the short report by Gordon J. F. MacDonald: *An Overview of the Impact of Carbon Dioxide on Climate*, McLean Va.: MITRE Corp., Dec. 1978; also see U.S. Office of Technology Assessment, *The Direct Use of Coal*, Washington: Government Printing Office, Apr. 1979, pp. 226–30; *Carbon Dioxide Emissions from Synthetic Fuels Energy Sources*, Washington: Dept. of Energy, August 8, 1979.
143. Geophysics Study Committee, op. cit., p. 4.
144. George D. Robinson, "Effluents of Energy Production: Particulates," in Geophysics Study Committee, op. cit.
145. Ibid.
146. A Miller and J. C. Thompson, *Elements of Meteorology*, Columbus, Ohio: Merrill, 1970; A. G. Borne, "Birth of An Island," *Discovery*, vol. 25, no. 4, 1964, p. 16.
147. J. Ernst, "African Dust Layer Sweeps into SW North Atlantic Area," *Bulletin of the American Meteorological Society*, vol. 55, no. 11, 1974, pp. 1352–53; J. B. Lushine, "A Dust Layer in the Eastern Caribbean," *Monthly Weather Review*, vol. 103, no. 5, 1975, pp. 454–55.
148. R. A. Bryson and T. J. Murray, *Climates of Hunger: Mankind and the World's Changing Weather*, Madison: University of Wisconsin, 1977.
149. Robinson, op. cit., p. 70.
150. Rotty, op. cit., p. 19.
151. A. Kh. Khrgian, *The Physics of Atmospheric Ozone*, Leningrad: Hydrometeorological Institute, 1973 (English translation, 1975), pp. 31–32.

152. *Environmental Impact of Stratospheric Flight: Biological and Climatic Effects of Aircraft Emissions in the Stratosphere,* Washington: National Academy of Sciences, 1975, pp. 5–7, 9–10.
153. "Response to the Ozone Protection Sections of the Clean Air Act Amendments of 1977: An Interim Report," Washington: National Academy of Sciences, 1977.
154. *Halocarbons: Environmental Effects of Chlorofluoromethane Release,* Washington: National Academy of Sciences, 1976.
155. *Environmental Impact of Stratospheric Flight,* op. cit.
156. *Nitrates: An Environmental Assessment,* Washington: National Academy of Sciences, 1978; W. C. Wang et al., "Greenhouse Effects due to Man-Made Perturbations of Trace Gases," *Science,* Nov. 12, 1976, pp. 685–90. Also see G. L. Hutchinson, A. R. Mosier, "Nitrous Oxide Emissions from an Irrigated Cornfield," *Science,* Sept. 14, 1979, pp. 1125–27.
157. A. J. Grobecker et al., "The Effects of Stratospheric Pollution by Aircraft," report of the Climatic Impact Assessment Program, Washington: Department of Transportation, 1975; *Environmental Impact of Stratospheric Flight,* op. cit.
158. *Nitrates,* op. cit. pp. 362–63.
159. *Halocarbons,* op. cit.; Council on Environmental Quality and Federal Council for Science and Technology, "Fluorocarbons and the Environment," Washington: Government Printing Office, 1975.
160. *Nitrates,* op. cit., p. 364.
161. Ibid., especially ch. 7.
162. Ibid., p. 362.
163. Ibid. p. 361.
164. Ibid., p. 363.
165. R. P. Turco et al., "SSTs, Nitrogen Fertilizer and Stratospheric Ozone," *Nature,* Dec. 28, 1978, pp. 805–7; Paul J. Crutzen and Carleton J. Howard, "The Effect of the $HO_2$ + NO Reaction Rate Constant on One-Dimensional Model Calculations of Stratospheric Ozone Perturbations," *Pure and Applied Geophysics* (Milan), vol. 116, 1978, pp. 497–510.
166. *Environmental Impact of Stratospheric Flight,* op. cit., p. 7; Geophysics Study Committee, op. cit., p. 4.
167. *Environmental Impact of Stratospheric Flight,* op. cit., p. 45.
168. Ibid., p. 49.
169. Ibid., pp. 177–221.
170. Ibid., p. 13.
171. Ibid., pp. 222–31.
172. Ibid., p. 11.
173. Ibid., p. 47; *Results of Research Related to Stratospheric Ozone Protection,* U.S. Environmental Protection Agency, Jan. 1978.
174. *Environmental Impact of Stratospheric Flight,* op. cit., p. 47.
175. *Results of Research Related to Stratospheric Ozone Protection,* op. cit.
176. Section 153 of the Clean Air Act, as amended.
177. *Nitrates,* op. cit., ch. 11.
178. Ibid., p. 18.
179. Geophysics Study Committee, op. cit., p. 97.
180. Weather Modification Board, "A U.S. Policy to Enhance the Atmospheric Environment," Washington: Department of Commerce, Oct. 21, 1977; "Desertification: An Overview," op. cit.
181. Rotty, op. cit., p. 15.
182. Ibid.
183. SCEP, *Man's Impact on the Global Environment,* op. cit.
184. S. F. Singer, "The Environmental Effects of Energy Production," in S. F. Singer, ed., *The Changing Global Environment,* Dordrecht; Netherlands: Reidel, 1975, pp. 25–44.
185. A. H. Murphy et al., "The Impact of Waste Heat Release on Simulated Global Climate," Laxenburg, Austria: International Institute of Applied Systems Analysis, Dec. 1976, p. 23.
186. Geophysics Study Committee, op. cit., p. 4.
187. Ibid.
188. See especially George M. Woodwell et al., *The Carbon Dioxide Problem: Implications for Policy in the Management of Energy and Other Resources,* Washington: Council on Environmental Quality, July 1979; also see references cited in Reference 142.
189. Woodwell et al., *The Carbon Dioxide Problem,* op. cit.

**Technology Section**

190. Cynthia Gorney, "University Is Sued Over Development of Sophisticated Harvesting Machines," *Washington Post,* Jan. 18, 1979, p. A11.
191. See, for example, the case histories in M. Taghi Farvar and John P. Milton, eds., *The Careless Technology: Ecology and International Development,* New York: Doubleday, 1972.
192. Raymond F. Dasmann et al., *Ecological Principles for Economic Development,* New York: Wiley, 1973, pp. 182–235.
193. E. F. Schumacher, *Small is Beautiful: Economics as if People Mattered,* New York: Harper, 1973, p. 165.
194. A thoughtful discussion of some of the options for a postindustrial technological society is provided in Willis W. Harman, *An Incomplete Guide to the Future,* Stanford, Calif.: Stanford Alumni Association, 1976.
195. Colin Norman, "Soft Technologies, Hard Choices," Washington: Worldwatch Institute, June 1978.

**Food and Agriculture Section**

196. "Demand for Food Production Reduces Land's Capacity to Produce," Council on Environmental Quality news release, Mar. 13, 1977, announcing publication by the Council on Mar. 14, 1977, of Paul F. Bente, Jr., "The Food People Problem: Can the Land's Capacity to Produce Food Be Sustained?"
197. Joint FAO/WHO ad hoc Expert Committee, "Energy and Protein Requirements," Rome: Food and Agriculture Organization, 1973.
198. See, for example, Erik Eckholm and Frank Record, *The Two Faces of Malnutrition,* Washington: Worldwatch Institute, 1976; *World Food and Nutrition Study,* interim report, Washington: National Academy of Sciences, 1975.
199. U.S. Department of Agriculture, Economics, Statistics, and Cooperative Service, "Report Assessing Global Food Production and Needs as of March 31, 1978," Washington, Mar. 1978.
200. S. Reutlinger and M. Selowsky, *Malnutrition and Poverty,* World Bank Occasional Paper 23, Washington, 1976.
201. Robert McNamara, "Address to the 1978 Annual Meeting of the World Bank–International Monetary Fund Board of Governors," Washington, Sept. 1978.
202. Philip Handler, "On the State of Man," address to the annual convocation of Markle Scholars, National Academy of Sciences, Sept. 29, 1974.
203. An excellent listing of the literature available in this area will be found in Lester R. Brown, *The Worldwide Loss of Cropland,* Washington: Worldwatch Institute, Oct.

1978; for U.S. data, see U.S. Department of Agriculture, Economic Research Service, "American Agriculture: Its Capacity to Produce," Washington, Feb. 1974.

204. Erik P. Eckholm, *Losing Ground: Environmental Stress and World Food Prospects* New York: Norton, 1976.

205. "Desertification: An Overview," U.N. Conference on Desertification, Aug. 1977, p. 11.

206. *The State of Food and Agriculture 1977,* Rome: Food and Agriculture Organization (draft), calculated from table 3–28.

207. "Desertification: An Overview," op. cit., pp. 5–6; *Desertification: Environmental Degradation in and Around Arid Lands,* Boulder: Westview Press, 1977.

208. Erik Eckholm and Lester R. Brown, *Spreading Deserts—The Hand of Man,* Washington: Worldwatch Institute, Aug. 1977; *State of Food and Agriculture 1977,* op. cit., table 3–14.

209. Ibid., p. 13; "Case Study on Desertification—Luni Development Block, India," U.N. Conference on Desertification, Aug. 1977, especially pp. 39ff.

210. F. Kenneth Hare, "Climate and Desertification: Background Document," U.N. Conference on Desertification, Aug. 1977, p. 36.

211. "Population, Society and Desertification," U.N. Conference on Desertification, Aug. 1977.

212. "Desertification: An Overview," op. cit., pp. 7–8; "Synthesis of Case Studies of Desertification," U.N. Conference on Desertification, Aug. 1977.

213. "Desertification: An Overview," op. cit., p. 12.

214. Calculated from data in ibid. and *Production Yearbook 1975,* Rome: Food and Agriculture Organization, 1976.

215. "Case Study on Desertification: Mona Reclamation Experimental Project, Pakistan," U.N. Conference on Desertification, Aug. 1977.

216. "Transnational Project to Monitor Desertification Processes and Related Natural Resources in Arid and Semi-Arid Areas of Southwest Asia," U.N. Conference on Desertification, Aug. 1977.

217. "Transnational Project to Monitor Desertification Processes and Related Natural Resources in Arid and Semi-Arid Areas of South America," U.N. Conference on Desertification, Aug. 1977, p. 8.

218. Ibid., p. 12.

219. U.S. Bureau of Reclamation, California Dept. of Water Resources, and California State Water Resources Control Board, *Agricultural Drainage and Salt Management in the San Joaquin Valley,* Fresno, Jan. 1979.

220. "Ecological Change and Desertification" and "Technology and Desertification," U.N. Conference on Desertification, Aug. 1977.

221. "Haiti: A Study in Environmental Destruction," *Conservation Foundation Letter,* Nov. 1977, pp. 1–7.

222. Walter Parham, "LDC Deforestation Problem: A Preliminary Data Base," U.S. Agency for International Development, Technical Assistance Bureau, Mar. 8, 1978 (manuscript).

223. U.S. General Accounting Office, "To Protect Tomorrow's Food Supply, Soil Conservation Needs *Priority* Attention," report to the Congress by the U.S. Comptroller General, Feb. 14, 1977.

224. See, for example, Luther J. Carter, "Soil Erosion: The Problem Persists Despite the Billions Spent on It," *Science,* Apr. 22, 1977, pp. 409–411; D. Pimentel et al., "Land Degradation: Effects on Food and Energy Resources," *Science,* Oct. 8, 1976, pp. 149–155; R. Blobaum, "Loss of Agricultural Land," Washington: Council on Environmental Quality, 1974; R. A. Brink, "Soil Deterioration and the Growing World Demand for

Food," *Science,* Aug. 12, 1977, pp. 625–30; Brown, *Worldwide Loss of Cropland,* op. cit.

225. Approximated from table 9.7 in Harry O. Buchman and Nyle C. Brady, *The Nature and Properties of Soils,* 6th ed., New York: Macmillan, 1960.

226. Calculated from data in ibid. and Pimentel et al., "Land Degradation," op. cit., table 1.

227. F. H. King, *Farmers of Forty Centuries: Permanent Agriculture in China, Korea, and Japan,* Emmaus, Pa.: Rodale, 1973, and New York: Gordon Press, 1977 (reprints of the original 1911 ed.).

228. "Physical Environment," ch. 13 in Organization for Economic Cooperation and Development, *Interfutures,* Paris, May 16, 1977 (draft).

229. Brown, *Worldwide Loss of Cropland,* op. cit.

230. Organization for Economic Cooperation and Development, op. cit.

231. Ibid.

232. Brown, *Worldwide Loss of Cropland,* op. cit.

233. Luther J. Carter, "Soil Erosion: The Problem Persists Despite the Billions Spent on It," *Science,* Apr. 22, 1977, pp. 409–11.

234. U.S. General Accounting Office, op. cit.

235. See, for example, *Environmental Quality 1970,* p. 41, and *1971,* pp. 107–8, annual reports of the Council on Environmental Quality, Washington: Government Printing Office, 1970, 1971; U.N. Environment Programme, "Overviews in the Priority Subject Area—Land, Water and Desertification," Feb. 1975; "Technology and Desertification," op. cit.

236. An excellent introduction with extensive additional references is provided in the short Council on Environmental Quality (CEQ) report by R. Blobaum, already cited, especially pp. 7–11. Also see CEQ's *Environmental Quality 1970,* op. cit., pp. 173–75; *1971,* p. 63; *1973,* pp. 215, 306; *1974,* p. 343; *1975,* pp. 163, 179–80, 451; *1977,* pp. 90–91; and CEQ, *The Costs of Sprawl,* Washington: Government Printing Office, Apr. 1974.

237. U.S. Department of Agriculture, Soil Conservation Service, "Cropland Erosion," Washington, June 1977.

238. Brown, "Worldwide Loss of Cropland," op. cit.

239. R. Soderlund and B. H. Svensson, "The Global Nitrogen Cycle," in Svensson and Soderlund, eds., *Nitrogen, Phosphorus, and Sulphur—Global Cycles,* Stockholm: Ecological Bulletin, 1976, p. 66.

239a. Martin Alexander, *Soil Microbiology,* New York: Wiley, 1961, pp. 263–66.

239b. F. E. Allison, *Soil Organic Matter and its Role in Crop Production,* New York: Elsevier, 1973.

239c. Frank J. Stevenson, Chapter 1 in W.V. Bartholomew and Francis E. Clark, eds., *Soil Nitrogen,* Madison, Wis.: American Society of Agronomy, 1965, p. 33.

239d. V. W. Meints et al, "Long Term Trends in Total Soil N as Influenced by Certain Management Practices," *Soil Science,* vol. 124, 1977, pp. 110–16.

239e. Daniel Kohl, Washington University, St. Louis, Mo, personal communication, 1979.

240. *Eutrophication: Causes, Consequences, Correctives,* Washington: National Academy of Sciences, 1969; Programme on Man and the Biosphere, "Consultative Group on Project 9: Ecological Assessment of Pest Management and Fertilizer Use on Terrestrial and Aquatic Ecosystems (Part on Fertilizers)," Rome: UNESCO, Jan. 1974.

241. *Drinking Water and Health,* Washington: National Academy of Sciences, 1977, pp. 411–25.

242. *Nitrates: An Environmental Assessment,* Washington: National Academy of Sciences, 1978, pp. 5–15.

243. Ibid.

244. "Pesticide Requirements in Developing Countries: Summary of Replies to FAO Questionnaire," Food and Agriculture Organization, 1975.

245. For but one small example, see P. Lernoux, "Crop Spraying in Northern Colombia Causing Ecological Disaster," World Environment Report, New York: Center for International Environment Information, Sept. 1978.

246. There is a growing literature on integrated pest management. See for example: Council on Environmental Quality, Integrated Pest Management, Washington, Nov. 1972 and Integrated Pest Management: Status and Prospects in the United States (forthcoming, 1979); "Integrated Pest Management," California Agriculture (special issue), Feb. 1978; Pest Control: Strategies for the Future, Washington: National Academy of Sciences, 1972; Committee on Scholarly Communication with the People's Republic of China, Insect Control in the People's Republic of China, Washington: National Academy of Sciences, 1972; D. Pimental, ed., World Food, Pest Losses, and the Environment, Boulder: Westview Press, 1978, pp. 17–38, 163–84.

247. See H. L. Harrison et. al., "Systems Study of DDT Transport," Science, Oct. 30, 1970, pp. 503–8; G. M. Woodwell et. al., "DDT in the Biosphere: Where Does It Go?," Science, Dec. 10, 1971, pp. 1101–7; Programme on Man and the Biosphere, "Expert Consultations on Project 9: Ecological Assessment of Pest Management and Fertilizer Use on Terrestrial and Aquatic Ecosystems (Part on Pesticides)," UNESCO, 1974.

248. Environmental Quality 1975, op. cit., pp. 368–76.

249. A detailed discussion of the role of pesticides and predators in the control of plant-eating mites is provided in C. B. Huffaker et. al., "The Ecology of Tetranychid Mites and Their Natural Control," Annual Review of Entomology, 1969, pp. 125–74; J. A. McMurty et al., "Ecology of Tetranychid Mites and their Natural Enemies: A Review, Pt. 1, Tetranychid Enemies: Their Biological Characters and the Impact of Spray Practices," Hilgardia, 1970, pp. 331–90.

250. Robert F. Luck et al., "Chemical Insect Control—A Troubled Pest Management Strategy," BioScience, Sept. 1977, p. 608.

251. "Pest Control and Public Health, in Pest Control: An Assessment of Present and Alternative Technologies, Washington: National Academy of Sciences, 1976, vol. 5, p. 219.

252. Ibid.

253. Council on Environmental Quality, Integrated Pest Management 1972, op. cit., p. 4.

254. Ray F. Smith and Harold T. Reynolds, "Some Economic Implications of Pesticide Overuse in Cotton," in California Dept. of Food and Agriculture, New Frontiers in Pest Management: Conference Proceedings, Sacramento, Dec. 1977, pp. 25–34.

255. See reference 246, above.

256. See Paul R. Ehrlich et al., Ecoscience: Population, Resources, and Environment, San Francisco: Freeman, 1977, ch. 11; Luck et al., op. cit., pp. 606–11.

257. See, for example, F. W. Plapp and D. L. Bull, "Toxicity and Selectivity of Some Insectides to Chrysopa carnea, a Predator of the Tobacco and Bud Worm," Environmental Entomology, June 1978, pp. 431–34; F. W. Plapp and S. B. Vinson, "Comparative Toxicities of Some Insecticides to the Tobacco Bud Worm and Its Ichneumonid Parasite, Compoletis sonorensis," Experimental Entomology, June 1977, pp. 381–84.

258. Normal Myers, The Sinking Ark, New York: Pergamon, 1979.

259. Jack R. Harland, "Genetics of Disaster," Journal of Environmental Quality, 1972, pp. 212–15.

260. Judith Miller, "Genetic Erosion: Crop Plants Threatened by Government Neglect," Science, Dec. 21, 1973, p. 1232; G. L. Carefoot and E. R. Sprott, Famine on the Wind: Man's Battle Against Plant Disease, Chicago: Rand McNally, 1967, p. 81.

261. Carefoot and Sprott, op. cit., pp. 53, 54, 98, 117, 119, 130–32, 138, 139.

262. Miller, "Genetic Erosion," op. cit., p. 1232.

263. Genetic Vulnerability of Major Crops, Washington: National Academy of Sciences, 1972, pp. 13, 14.

264. Carefoot and Sprott, op. cit., pp. 194–201.

265. A. J. Ullstrop, "The Impacts of the Southern Corn Leaf Blight Epidemic of 1970 and 1971, Annual Review of Phytopathology, 1972, pp. 37–50; L. A. Tatum, "The Southern Corn Leaf Blight Epidemic," Science, Mar. 19, 1971, pp. 1113–16; A. L. Hooker, "Southern Leaf Blight of Corn—Present Status and Future Prospects," Journal of Environmental Quality, 1972, pp. 244–49.

266. Tatum, op. cit.

267. U.S. Department of Agriculture, Agricultural Marketing Service, unpublished data.

268. M. W. Adams et al., "Biological Uniformity and Disease Epidemics," BioScience, Nov. 1, 1971, pp. 1067–70.

269. C. E. Yarwood, "Man-Made Plant Diseases," Science, Apr. 10, 1970, pp. 218–20.

270. W. C. Snyder et al., California Agriculture, vol. 19, no. 5, 1963, p. 11.

271. A good overview of these problems is provided in Genetic Vulnerability of Major Crops, Washington: National Academy of Sciences, 1972.

272. A readable introduction to the problems of preserving genetic resources is provided in Erik Eckholm, Disappearing Species: The Social Challenge, Washington: Worldwatch Institute, July 1978; also see Marc Reisner, "Garden of Eden to Weed Patch," Natural Resources Defense Council Newsletter, Jan.-Feb. 1977; Conservation of Germplasm Resources: An Imperative, Washington: National Academy of Sciences, 1978; Genetic Improvement of Seed Proteins, Washington: National Academy of Sciences, 1976; Programme on Man and the Biosphere, "Expert Panel on Project 8: Conservation of Natural Areas and of the Genetic Material They Contain," Morges, Switzerland: UNESCO, Sept. 1973; Myers, op. cit.; Commission on International Relations, Underexploited Tropical Plants with Promising Economic Value, Washington: National Academy of Sciences, 1975; Grenville Lucas and A. H. M. Synge, "The IUCN Threatened Plants Committee and Its Work Throughout the World," Environmental Conservation, Autumn 1977; International Union for Conservation of Nature and Natural Resources Threatened Plants Committee, List of Rare, Threatened and Endemic Plants in Europe, Strasbourg, 1977.

273. Hugh H. Iltis et al., "Zea diploperennis (Gramineae): A New Teosinte from Mexico," Science, Jan. 12, 1979, pp. 186–88; also see Walter Sullivan, "Hope of Creating Perennial Corn Raised by a New Plant Discovery," New York Times, Feb. 5, 1979; Richard Orr, " 'Mexico Connection' May Improve Corn," Chicago Tribune, Feb. 18, 1979; "Maize Seeds Plant Hope," Milwaukee Sentinel, Jan. 30, 1979.

274. Hugh H. Iltis, personal communication, Mar. 5, 1979.

275. "Maize Seeds Plant Hope," op. cit.

276. Erik Eckholm, "Disappearing Species," op. cit.

276a "Seeds of Trouble," editorial, *Washington Post,* Nov. 10, 1979, p. A22.

277. Harlan, op. cit., p. 214.

278. *The State of Food and Agriculture 1977,* op. cit., pp. 3-40-3-43.

279. *CIMMYT Review 1974,* Centro Internacional de Mejoramiento de Maiz y Trigo (International Maize and Wheat Improvement Center), Mexico, 1974, p. 7.

280. Ibid.

281. O. H. Frankel and J. G. Hawkes, eds., *Crop Genetic Resources for Today and Tomorrow,* New York: Cambridge Univ. Press, 1975.

282. Ibid.

283. *Genetic Vulnerability of Major Crops,* Washington: National Academy of Sciences, 1972, ch. 5.

284. P. S. Carlson and J. C. Polacco, "Plant Cell Cultures: Genetic Aspects of Crop Improvement," *Science,* May 9, 1975, pp. 622-25.

285. Handler, op. cit.

286. *Production Yearbook 1974,* Rome: Food and Agriculture Organization, 1974.

287. Lester R. Brown, *The Twenty-Ninth Day,* New York: Norton, 1978, p. 145.

288. D. Pimentel et al., "Food Production and the Energy Crisis," *Science,* Nov. 2, 1973, pp. 447-48.

289. *The State of Food and Agriculture 1976,* Rome: Food and Agriculture Organization, 1977, p. 93.

290. See, for example, ibid., ch. 3; Pimentel et al., "Food Production," op. cit.; Arjun Makhijani and Alan Poole, *Energy and Third World Agriculture,* Cambridge, Mass.: Ballinger, 1975; G. Leach, "Energy and Food Production," *Food Policy,* Nov. 1975, pp. 62-73.

291. Pimentel et al., "Food Production," op. cit., p. 448.

292. See, for example: U.S. Department of Agriculture, Economic Research Service, "The One-Man Farm," Washington, Aug. 1973; Makhijani and Poole, op. cit.; William Lockeretz et al., "A Comparison of Production, Economic Returns, and Energy Intensiveness of Corn Belt Farms that Do and Do Not Use Inorganic Fertilizers and Pesticides," St. Louis: Center for the Biology of Natural Systems, Washington Univ., July 1975; *The Journal of the New Alchemists,* vols. 1-4, 1973-77; W. Berry, *The Unsettling of America: Culture and Agriculture,* San Francisco: Sierra Club, 1977.

293. E. F. Schumacher, *Small is Beautiful: Economics as if People Mattered,* New York: Harper, 1973. For an introduction to the technical issues associated with technology transfer for agricultural development, see: D. Goulet, *The Uncertain Promise: Value Conflicts in Technology Transfer,* New York: IDOC/North America, 1977.

294. U.S. Department of Agriculture, Economic Research Service, "The One-Man Farm," op. cit., p. V.

295. See reference 292, above.

296. Henry J. Groen and James A. Kilpatrick, "China's Agricultural Production," in U.S. Congress, *Chinese Economy Post-Mao: A Compendium of Papers Submitted to the Joint Economic Committee,* vol. 1 *Policy and Performance,* Washington, Nov. 9, 1978, pp. 632-34.

297. Erik Eckholm, *The Dispossessed of the Earth: Land Reform and Sustainable Development,* Washington: Worldwatch Institute, June 1979.

### Marine Environment Section

298. Bert Bolin, "The Carbon Cycle," *Scientific American,* Sept. 1970, pp. 126, 131.

299. Paul R. Ehrlich et al., *Ecoscience: Population, Resources, Environment,* San Francisco: Freeman, 1977, pp. 352, 354.

300. Edward D. Goldberg, *The Health of the Oceans,* Paris: UNESCO, 1976, p. 17.

301. Ibid., p. 19.

302. Goldberg, op. cit., p. 17.

303. "Marine Overview," op. cit., pp. 8, 9.

303a *The International Conference on Tanker Safety and Pollution Prevention,* London: Inter-Governmental Maritime Consultative Organization, 1978.

303b Walter R. Courtenay, Jr. and C. R. Robins, "Exotic Organisms: An Unsolved, Complex Problem," *Bio-Science,* vol. 25, June 23, 1975, pp. 306-13.

304. Ivan Valiela and Susan Vince, "Green Borders of the Sea," *Oceanus,* Fall 1976, p. 10; Charles B. Officer, "Physical Oceanography of Estuaries," *Oceanus,* Fall 1976, pp. 3, 4; SCEP Work Group on Ecological Effects, "Phosphorus and Eutrophication," in William H. Matthews et al., eds., *Man's Impact on Terrestrial and Oceanic Ecosystems,* Cambridge, Mass.: MIT, 1971, p. 321; R. Eugene Turner, "Intertidal Vegetation and Commercial Yields of Penaeid Shrimp," *Transactions of the American Fisheries Society,* vol. 106, no. 5, 1977, pp. 411-16.

305. Valiela and Vince, op, cit., p. 100.

306. Eugene P. Odum and Armando de la Cruz, "Particulate Organic Detritus in a Georgia Salt Marsh-Estuarine System", in *Estuaries,* George Lauff, ed., Washington: American Association for the Advancement of Science, 1957.

307. Paul J. Godfrey, "Barrier Beaches of the East Coast," *Oceanus,* vol. 19, no. 5, Fall 1976, p. 31.

308. Valiela and Vince, op. cit., p. 14.

309. UNESCO, Div of Marine Sciences, "Human Uses and Management of the Mangrove Environment in South and Southeast Asia, September—October 1977," Paris, Oct. 12, 1978, pp. 1, 2; Scientific Committee on Oceanic Research (SCOR), "Minutes—SCOR Working Group 60 on Mangrove Ecology, May 16-18, 1978, San José, Costa Rica," p. 2; Lawrence E. Jerome, "Mangroves," *Oceans,* Sept.-Oct. 1977, p. 42.

310. Ibid.

311. "Marine Overview," op. cit., p. 31; B. J. Copeland et al., "Water Quantity for Preservation of Estuarine Ecology," in Ernest F. Gloyna and William S. Butcher, eds., *Conflicts in Water Resources Planning,* Center for Research in Water Resources, Univ. of Texas at Austin, 1972, pp. 107-26.

312. Valiela and Vince, op. cit., p. 11.

313. Elinor Lander Horwitz, *Out Nation's Wetlands: An Interagency Task Force Report,* Washington: Government Printing Office, 1978, p. 44.

314. Godfrey, op. cit., p. 37.

314a W. N. Lindall, Jr. et al., "Fishes, Macroinvertebrates, and Hydrological Conditions of Upland Canals in Tampa Bay, Florida," *Fishery Bulletin,* (National Oceanic and Atmospheric Administration), vol. 71, no. 1, 1973, pp. 155-63.

315. Horwitz, op, cit., p. 46.

315a M. Grant Gross, "Waste-Solid Disposal in Coastal Waters of North America," in William H. Matthews, Frederick E. Smith and Edward D. Goldberg, eds., *Man's Impact on Terrestrial and Oceanic Ecosystems,* Cambridge, MA: The MIT Press, 1971, p. 258.

316. Valiela and Vince, op. cit., p. 13.

317. Ibid., p. 12.

318. UNESCO, Div. of Marine Sciences, op. cit., p. 1; Jerome, op. cit., p. 44.

319. UNESCO, Div. of Marine Sciences, op. cit., p. 2.

320. Ibid.; Scientific Committee on Ocean Research, op. cit., pp. 8, 9; Dr. Samuel Snedacker, University of Miami Rosensteil School of Marine and Atmospheric Sciences, personal communication to Dr. Elliott A. Norse, Council on Environmental Quality, 1979.

321. R. E. Johannes, "Pollution and Degradation of Coral Reef Communities," in E. J. Ferguson Wood and R. E. Johannes, eds., Tropical Marine Pollution, Amsterdam: Elsevier, 1975.

322. P.R. Ehrlich, "Population Biology of Coral Reef Fishes," Annual Review of Ecology and Systematics, Sept. 1975, pp. 211–47.

323. Robert E. Johannes, "Life and Death of the Reef," Audubon, Sept. 1976, pp. 45, 46; Johannes, "Pollution and Degradation," op. cit., p. 13.

324. "Life and Death of the Reef," op. cit., p. 50.

325. V. J. Chapman, ed., Ecosystems of the World, vol. 1, Wet Coastal Ecosystems, Amsterdam: Elsevier, 1977, p. 1.

326. Michael Waldichuk, Global Marine Pollution: An Overview, Paris: UNESCO, 1977, p. 32; E. D. Goldberg, "Atmospheric Transport" in Donald W. Hood, ed., Impingement of Man on the Oceans, New York: Wiley, Interscience, 1971, pp. 75–88.

327. Carl J. Sindermann, "Environmentally Related Diseases of Marine Fish and Shellfish," Marine Fisheries Review, Oct. 1978, p. 43; New York Bight Project: Annual Report for FY 1976, Marine Ecosystems Analysis Program, Boulder: NOAA Environmental Research Laboratories, Dec. 1977.

328. New York Bight Project, op. cit., p. 25.

329. Environmental Quality, 1978, annual report of the Council on Environmental Quality, Washington: Government Printing Office, 1978, p. 178.

330. American Chemical Society, Cleaning Our Environment: A Chemical Perspective, Washington, Oct. 1978, pp. 2, 4.

331. Environmental Quality 1978, op. cit., p. 183; John C. Fuller, The Poison that Fell from the Sky, New York: Random House, 1977.

332. Robert H. Boyle, "Getting Rid of PCBs," Audubon, Nov. 1978, p. 150.

333. Ibid.; "N.Y. Plan to Remove PCBs," Science News, July 15, 1978, p. 39.

334. Waldichuk, op. cit., p. 22.

335. Goldberg, op. cit., p. 47.

336. Waldichuk, op. cit., p. 22.

337. John Todd, personal communication, 1979, concerning research done at San Diego State University in 1969 in 18 ecosystems with 9 species of fish.

338. Waldichuk, op. cit., pp. 22.

339. New York Bight Project, op. cit., pp. 25, 26; Goldberg, op, cit., p. 61.

340. Goldberg, op. cit., p. 66.

341. Assessing Potential Ocean Pollutants, Washington: National Academy of Sciences, 1975, pp. 190, 202.

342. Ibid. pp. 191–202; Goldberg, op. cit., p. 66.

343. Waldichuk, op. cit., p. 22.

344. Goldberg, op. cit., p. 48.

345. Assessing Potential Ocean Pollutants, op. cit., p. 122.

346. George M. Woodwell et al., "DDT in the Biosphere: Where Does It Go?" Science, Dec. 10, 1971, pp. 1101–7.

347. Paul R. Spitzer et al., "Productivity of Ospreys in Connecticut—Long Island Increases as DDT Residues Decline," Science, Oct. 20, 1978, pp. 333–34; Daniel W. Anderson et al., "Brown Pelicans: Improved Reproduction off the Southern California Coast," Science, Nov. 21, 1975, pp. 806–8.

348. Waldichuk, op. cit., p. 17; Goldberg, op. cit., p. 114.

349. Waldichuk, op. cit., p. 17.

350. Richard A. Greig and Douglas R. Wenzloff, "Trace Metals in Finfish from the New York Bight and Long Island Sound," Marine Pollution Bulletin, Sept. 1977, pp. 198–200; R. A. Greig et al., "Trace Metals in Sea Scallops Placopecten magellanicus, from Eastern United States," Bulletin of Environmental Contamination and Toxicology, New York: Springer, 1978, pp. 326–34.

351. Goldberg, op. cit., p. 99.

352. Ibid., p.112.

353. Assessing Potential Ocean Pollutants, op. cit., p. 333.

354. Ibid., p. 301.

355. Goldberg, op. cit., pp. 113, 114.

356. Waldichuk, op. cit., p. 20; T. Chow and C. Patterson, "The Occurrence and Significance of Lead Isotopes in Pelagic Sediments", Geochemica et Cosmochemica, vol. 26, 1962, pp. 263–306; M. Rama and E. Goldberg, "Lead-210 in Natural Waters", Science, vol.13, 1961, pp. 98–99.

357. Goldberg, op. cit., p. 109.

358. Ibid., p. 114.

359. Ibid.

360. E. Goldberg et al., "A Pollution History of Chesapeake Bay," Geochemica et Cosmochemica, vol. 42, 1978 pp. 413–25.

361. Richard A. Greig and Richard A. McGrath, "Trace Metals in Sediments of Raritan Bay," Marine Pollution Bulletin, Aug. 1977, pp. 188–192; Ruth Waldhauer et al., "Lead and Cooper in the Waters of Raritan and Lower New York Bays," Marine Pollution Bulletin, Feb. 1978, pp. 38–42.

362. Goldberg, Health of the Oceans, op. cit., p. 112.

363. Ibid., pp. 79–97.

364. Ibid.

365. Ibid.

366. Ibid.

367. Council on Environmental Quality, OCS Oil and Gas: An Environmental Assessment, vol. 1, Washington, Apr. 1974, p. 112.

368. Petroleum in the Marine Environment, Washington: National Academy of Sciences, 1975, pp. 83–84.

369. John H. Vandermeulen, "The Chedabucto Bay Spill—Arrow, 1970," Oceanus, Fall 1977, pp. 31–39.

370. Howard L. Sanders, "The West Falmouth Spill—Florida, 1969," Oceanus, Fall 1977, pp. 15–24.

371. George R. Hampson and Edwin T. Moul, "Salt Marsh Grasses and #2 Fuel Oil," Oceanus, Fall 1977, pp. 25–30.

372. Petroleum in the Marine Environment, op. cit., pp. 52–53; A Crosby Longwell, "A Genetic Look at Fish Eggs and Oil," Oceanus, Fall 1977, pp. 46–58.

373. Council on Environmental Quality, OCS Oil and Gas, op. cit., pp. 106–111; Goldberg, Health of the Oceans, op. cit., p. 134; Donald F. Boesch et al., Oil Spills and the Marine Environment, Cambridge, Mass.: Ballinger, 1974, pp. 8–9; Frederick P. Thurberg, et al., "Some Physiological Effects of the Argo Merchant Oil Spill on Several Marine Teleosts and Bivalve Molluscs," from In the Wake of the Argo Merchant, Center for Ocean Management Studies, University of Rhode Island, Kingston, 1978; George R. Gardner, "A Review of Histopathological Effects of Selected Contaminants on Some Marine Organisms," Marine Fisheries Review, Oct. 1978, pp. 51–52; John J. Stegeman, "Fate and Effects of Oil in Marine Animals," and Jelle Atema, "The Effects of Oil on Lobsters," Oceanus, Fall 1977, pp. 59–73.

374. John W. Farrington, "The Biogeochemistry of Oil in the Ocean," *Oceanus*, Fall 1977, p. 9.
375. Douglas Pimlott et al., *Oil Under the Ice: Offshore Drilling in the Canadian Arctic*, Canadian Arctic Resources Committee, Ottawa, 1976.
376. Valiela and Vince, op. cit., pp. 14, 16.
377. William E. Odum and R. E. Johannes, "The Response of Mangroves to Man-Induced Environmental Stress," in *Tropical Marine Pollution*, op.. cit.; Valiela and Vince, op. cit., pp. 14, 16.
378. Johannes, "Pollution and Degradation," op. cit., pp. 14–17; Johannes, "Life and Death of the Reef," op. cit., pp. 48–50.
379. Burrell, op. cit.
380. Johannes, "Pollution and Degradation," op. cit., pp. 14–15; Johannes, "Life and Death of the Reef," op. cit., pp. 48–50.
381. Ibid.
382. Johannes, "Pollution and Degradation," op. cit., pp. 19, 20; Johannes, "Life and Death of the Reef," op. cit., p. 50; "Marine Overview," op. cit., pp. 8, 40.
383. Johannes, "Pollution and Degradation," op. cit., pp. 21–22.
384. Goldberg, *Health of the Oceans*, op. cit., p. 19; J. B. Coltron, Jr., "Plastics in the Ocean," *Oceanus*, vol. 18, no. 1, 1974, pp. 61–64; Edwin Carpenter et al., "Polystyrene Spherules in Coastal Waters," *Science*, vol. 178, 1972 p. 749.
385. Waldichuk, op. cit., pp. 31, 32; Carpenter et al., op. cit.; Gardner, op. cit., pp. 51, 52.
386. Goldberg, *Health of the Oceans*, op. cit., p. 17.
387. "Marine Overview," op. cit., p. 11.
388. John Gulland, "The Harvest of the Sea," in W. W. Murdoch, ed., *Environment: Resources, Pollution, and Society*, Sunderland, Maine: Sinauer Press, 1975, pp. 167–89; C. P. Idyll, "The Anchovy Crisis," *Scientific American*, June 1973, pp. 22–29.
389. Ehrlich et al., *Ecoscience*, op. cit., pp. 354–55.
390. Kenneth S. Norris, "Marine Mammals and Man," in Howard P. Brokaw, ed., *Wildlife and America*, Washington: Government Printing Office, 1978, pp. 320–21.
391. Sidney J., Hold and Lee M Talbot, ed., "The Conservation of Wild Living Resources," final report, Airlie House (Va.) Workshops, Feb., Apr. 1975, p. 4; Lee M. Talbot, "History, Status and Conservation Problems of the Great Whale Populations," Symposium on Endangered Species, American Association for the Advancement of Science annual meeting, Feb. 28, 1974, p. 24.
392. Holt and Talbot, op. cit., p. 11.
393. Ehrlich et al., op. cit., pp. 360–61.
394. Public Law 92–522, 92nd Congress, H.R. 10420, Oct. 21, 1972, 86 Stat. 1027.
395. J. Frederick Grassle, "Diversity and Population Dynamics of Benthic Organisms," *Oceanus*, Winter 1978, pp. 42, 43, 45.
395a Susumu Honjo and Michael R. Roman, "Marine Copepod Fecal Pellets: Production, Preservation and Sedimentation," *Journal of Marine Research*, vol. 36, 1978, pp. 45–57.
395b K. L. Smith, Jr., "Benthic Community Respiration in the NW Atlantic Ocean: *In Situ* Measurements from 40 to 5200 m," *Marine Biology*, vol. 47, 1978, pp. 337–47.
395c Howard L. Sanders, "Evolutionary Ecology and the Deep Sea Benthos," in *The Changing Scenes in Natural Sciences 1776–1976*, Academy of Natural Sciences, 1977, pp. 223–43.
396. Goldberg, *Health of the Oceans*, op. cit., pp. 19.
397. Ibid.
398. Robert E. Burns, "Effect of a Deep Ocean Mining Test,"

NOAA Pacific Marine Environmental Laboratory, Seattle, Aug. 1978.
399. "Deep Ocean Mining Environmental Study—Phase I," progress report, *National Oceanic and Atmospheric Administration*, Boulder, Aug. 1976, pp. xii–xiv, 152–54.
400. Burns, op. cit.
401. Ibid.
402. Ibid.
403. "Marine Overview," op. cit., p. 41.
404. Richard A. Frank, *Deepsea Mining and the Environment*, Report to the Working Group on Environmental Regulation of Deepsea Mining, American Society of International Law, St. Paul: West, 1976, p. 2.
405. Goldberg, *Health of the Oceans*, op. cit., pp. 50, 51.
406. Waldichuk, op. cit., p. 38.
407. Ibid.
408. U.N. Environment Programme, "Report of the Executive Director," Feb. 20, 1978, pp. 139–66; Baruch Boxer, "Mediterranean Action Plan: An Interim Evaluation", *Science*, Nov. 10, 1978, pp. 585–90.
409. Goldberg, *Health of the Oceans*, op. cit., p. 19.

## Forestry Section

410. For a recent insightful analysis of the implications of tropical forest losses, see Norman Myers, *The Sinking Ark*, Elmsford, N.Y.: Pergamon, 1979.
411. Peter Sartorius, "Sociological and Environmental Consequences of the Reduction or Elimination of Primary Tropical Forests," in *Technical Conference on the Tropical Moist Forests*, Rome: Food and Agriculture Organization, 1977; Eneas Salati et al., "Origem e Distribucão das Chuvas na Amazônia," *Interciencia*, July-Aug. 1978, pp. 200–05.
412. George P. Marsh, *The Earth as Modified by Human Action*, New York: Scribner, 1885; Erik Eckholm, *Losing Ground: Environmental Stress and World Food Prospects*, New York: Norton, 1976.
413. See, for example, the discussion of the poor habitat value of eucalyptus plantations, which are replacing millions of hectares of native forest in Minas Gerais, Brazil in *Planoroeste II*, 3 vols. Belo Horizonte: Secretaria de Estado de Planejamento e Coordenação Geral, Secretaria de Agricultura, Secretaria de Estado de Ciência e Tecnologia, 1978.
414. Samuel H. Kunkle, "Forestry Support for Agriculture Through Watershed Management, Windbreaks, and Other Conservation Measures," Washington: U.S. Forest Service, Oct. 1978.
415. Betty J. Meggers et al., eds., *Tropical Forest Ecosystems in Africa and South America: A Comparative Review*, Washington: Smithsonian Institution Press, 1973, pp. 313, 324. For more detailed studies of shifting agriculture/forest systems, see: P. H. Nye and D. J. Greenland, *The Soil Under Shifting Cultivation*, Burks, England: Commonwealth Agricultural Bureaux, 1960, 156 pp.; R. F. Watters, *Shifting Cultivation in Latin Ameria*, Forestry Development Paper No. 17, Rome: Food and Agriculture Organization, 1971.
416. Douglas R. Shane, "A Latin American Dilemma: Current Efforts to Develop the Tropical Forest Areas of Thirteen Latin American Nations," U.S. Strategy Conference on Tropical Deforestation, Washington, June 12–14, 1978 (manuscript).
417. *Tropical Forest Ecosystems: A State-of-Knowledge Report*, Natural Resources Research XIV, Paris: UNESCO, 1978, pp. 317–553; also *Conservation and Rational Use of the Environment*, U.N. ECOSOC, 44th Session, Agenda Item 5(d), 1968; Raymond F. Dasmann et al.,

*Ecological Principles for Economic Development*, New York: Wiley, 1973, pp. 51–75.

418. M. L'voich, *Global Water Resources and their Future*, Moscow, 1974; and *Tropical Forest Ecosystems*, op. cit., pp 35–56; Joseph A. Tosi, Jr., and Robert F. Voertman, "Some Environmental Factors in the Economic Development of the Tropics," *Economic Geography*, vol. 40, no. 3, 1964; Norman Hudson, *Soil Conservation*, Ithaca: Cornell University Press, 1971, pp. 179–95.

419. Raymond F. Dasmann et al., op cit., pp. 208–12; Robert N. Allen, "The Anchicaya Hydroelectric Project in Colombia: Design and Sedimentation Problems," in M. Toghi Farrar and John P. Milton, eds., *The Careless Technology: Ecology and International Development*, New York: Doubleday, 1962, pp. 318–42. For coastal sedimentation from interior erosion, see Carleton Ray, *Marine Parks for Tanzania*, Washington: Conservation Foundation, Oct. 1968, pp. 11, 17.

420. *The State of Food and Agriculture 1977*, Rome: Food and Agriculture Organization, Nov. 1977 (draft), pp. 3-4-3-19, Lester R. Brown, *The Global Economic Prospect: New Sources of Economic Stress*, Washington: Worldwatch Institute, May 1978, p. 9; also see the "Population" section of this chapter.

421. Robert B. Batchelder, "Spatial and Temporal Patterns of Fire in the Tropical World", in *Proceedings, Tall Timbers Fire Ecology Conference, No. 6*, Tallahasse, 1967, pp. 171–90.

422. "Mountains," in *A World Conservation Strategy*, Morges, Switzerland: International Union for Conservation of Nature and Natural Resources, Jan. 1978 (draft), p. 8.

423. Ibid., pp. 8–9; also see Appendix C, especially the cables from Dacca and New Delhi.

424. Dasmann et al., op. cit.

425. Frank Wadsworth, "Deforestation—Death to the Panama Canal," in U.S. Agency for International Development, *Proceedings of the U.S. Strategy Conference on Tropical Deforestation*, Washington, Oct. 1978.

426. Edward G. Farnworth and Frank B. Golley, eds., *Fragile Ecosystems: Evaluation of Research and Applications in the Neotropics*, New York: Springer, 1974.

427. "Shifting Cultivation and Soil Conservation in Africa," Soils Bulletin 24, Rome: Food and Agriculture Organization, 1974; R. Persson, *Forest Resources of Africa*, Stockholm: Royal College of Forestry, 1977.

428. Duncan Poore, "The Value of Tropical Moist Forest Ecosystems and Environmental Consequences of their Removal," *Unasylva*, vol. 28, nos. 112–13, 1976 pp. 127–43.

429. Calculated from Reidar Persson, "The Need for a Continuous Assessment of the Forest Resources of the World," Eighth World Forestry Congress, Jakarta, Oct. 16–28, 1978.

430. For a general introduction to these problems, see Erik Eckholm, "The Other Energy Crisis: Firewood," Washington: Worldwatch Institute, 1975; Eckholm, *Losing Ground*, op. cit.; Erik Eckholm and Lester R. Brown, "Spreading Deserts—The Hand of Man," Washington: Worldwatch Institute, July 1978. Also see "Arvores por Ferro, " *Veja* (Brazil), Nov. 8, 1978, pp. 77–78.

431. Water Deshler, "An Examination of the Extent of Fire in the Grassland and Savanna of Africa Along the Southern Side of the Sahara," in *Proceedings of the Ninth International Symposium on Remote Sensing of Environment*, Environmental Research Institute of Michigan, Ann Arbor, 1974, pp. 23–29. Also see Batchelder, op. cit.; Robert B. Batchelder and Howard F. Hirt, *Fire in Tropical Forests and Grasslands*, U.S. Army Natick Lab-

oratories, 1966; R. Rose Innes, "Fire in West African Vegetation," in *Proceedings, Tall Timbers Fire Ecology Conference, No. 11*, Tallahassee: 1972, pp. 147–73; O. C. Stewart, "Fire as the First Great Force Employed by Man," in W. L. Thomas, Jr., *Man's Role in Changing the Face of the Earth*, Chicago: Univ. of Chicago, 1956, pp. 115–33.

432. M. Kassas, "Desertification versus Potential for Recovery in Circum-Sahara Territories," in Harold E. Dregne, ed., *Arid Lands in Transition*, Washington: American Association for the Advancement of Science, 1970, p. 124.

433. S. K. Chauhan, "Tree Huggers Save Forests", *Development Forum*, Sept. 1978, p. 6.

434. "Forestry: A Sector Policy Paper," Washington: World Bank, Feb. 1978.

435. U.S. Department of State and U.S. Agency for International Development, *Proceedings of the U.S. Strategy Conference on Tropical Deforestation*, Washington, Oct. 1978.

436. A summary of the Seventh World Forestry Congress and a list of the 142 papers is in "Commission I: The Silviculturists," *Unasylva*, Special Issue, no. 104, 1972, pp. 15–30; individual papers are available from the authors or on microfiche from the Food and Agriculture Organization, Rome. The proceedings of the Eighth Congress (Jakarta, 1978) should provide a comprehensive updated overview when available.

437. Erik Eckholm, *Planting for the Future: Forestry for Human Needs*, Washington: Worldwatch Institute, February 1979.

438. Chapter 8, this volume.

439. Jack Westoby, "Forestry in China," *Unasylva*, no. 108, 1975, pp. 20–28; Jack Westoby, "Making Trees Serve People," *Commonwealth Forestry Review*, vol. 54, no. 3–4, 1975; S. D. Richardson, *Forestry in Communist China*, Baltimore: Johns Hopkins University Press, 1966; William K. Kapp, *Environmental Policies and Development Planning in Contemporary China and Other Essays*, Paris: Mouton, 1974; For an illuminating discussion of the extent to which China has extinguished species to provide more land for "useful" plants, see Anita Thorhaug, ed., *Botany in China*, Stanford: Stanford Univ., forthcoming, 1980; and *Plant Species in the Peoples' Republic of China*, Washington: National Academy of Sciences, 1978.

440. Eckholm, *Planting for the Future*, op. cit.; pp. 11, 37; *Forestry: A Sector Policy Paper*, op. cit., p. 28.

441. Hans Gregersen, "Appraisal of Village Fuelwood Plantations in Korea," U.N./FAO, SIDA Project Case Study No. 2, St. Paul, Minn., 1977 (draft).

442. N. Vietmeyer and B. Cottom, "Leucaena: Promising Forage and Tree Crop for the Tropics," Washington: National Academy of Sciences, 1977; Michael D. Benge, "Banyani: A Source of Fertilizer, Feed and Energy for the Philippines," USAID Agricultural Development Series, Manila, 1977.

443. R. M. Lawton, "The Management and Regeneration of Some Nigerian High Forest Ecosystems," in: *Tropical Forest Ecosystems*, op. cit., pp. 580–88; and H. Ray Grinnell, "A Study of Agri-Silviculture Potential in West Africa," Ottawa: International Development Research Centre, Oct. 1977.

444. Willem Meijer, *Indonesian Forest and Land Use Planning*, Lexington: Univ. of Kentucky, Botany Department, 1975.

445. Ibid.; T. E. Lovejoy, "The Transamazonica: Highway to Extinction," *Frontiers*, Spring 1973.

446. Edouard Saouma, "Statement by the Director-General of FAO," Eighth World Forestry Congress, Jakarta, Oct. 16–28, 1978.

447. Larry Rohter, "Amazon Basin's Forests Going Up in Smoke," *Washington Post*, Jan. 5, 1978, p. A14.

448. Ibid.

449. Clive Cookson, "Emergency Ban on 2,4,5-T Herbicide in U.S.", and Alistair Hay, "Dioxin: The 10 Year Battle that Began with Agent Orange," *Nature*, Mar. 8, 1979, pp. 108–09.

450. Rohter, op. cit.

451. "Daniel Ludwig's Floating Factory: A Giant Pulp Mill for the Amazon Wilderness," *Time*, June 19, 1978, p. 75.

452. J. G. Bene et al., "Trees, Food and People," Ottawa: International Development Research Centre, 1977; Robert O. Blake, "Response to Date—Institutions," in *Proceedings of the U.S. Strategy Conference on Tropical Deforestation*, U.S. Dept. of State, Oct. 1978, pp.25–30; "Forestry: A Sector Policy Paper," op. cit.; Jack C. Westoby, "Forest Industries for Socio-Economic Development," Eighth World Forestry Congress, Jakarta, Oct. 1978.

453. Eckholm, "Planting for the Future," op. cit.

454. Norman E. Johnson, "Biological Opportunities and Risks Associated with Fast Growing Plantations in the Tropics," *Journal of Forestry*, Apr. 1976.

455. A. E. Lugo, "Ecological Role of Fertilizers in Relation to Forest Productivity and Dollar Subsidy by Man," in *Proceedings of the Florida Section*, Society of American Foresters, Gainesville, Fla., 1970, pp. 21–33.

456. "Watching the Trees Grow—From Space," *Nation's Business*, Jan. 1979, p. 57.

457. J. L. Keas, and J. V. Hatton, "The Implication of Full-Forest Utilization on Worldwide Supplies of Wood by Year 2000," *Pulp and Paper International*, vol. 17, no. 6, 1975, pp. 49–52.

458. A. Gomez-Pompa et al., "The Tropical Rain Forest: A Nonrenewable Resource," *Science* vol. 177, 1972, pp. 762–65; Duncan Poore, "The Value of Tropical Moist Forest Ecosystems and the Environmental Consequences of Their Removal," *Unasylva*, vol 28, no. 112, 1976, pp. 127–43; J. Ewel and C. Conde, "Potential Ecological Impact of Increased Intensity of Tropical Forest Utilization," Madison, Wis.: U.S. Department of Agriculture, Forest Service Forest Products Research Laboratory, 1976 (manuscript).

459. G. E. Likens et al., "Recovery of a Deforested Ecosystem," *Science*, vol. 199, 1978, pp. 492–96.

460. Carl Olof Tamm et al., "Leaching of Plant Nutrients from Soil as a Consequence of Forestry operations," *Ambio*, vol. 3, no. 6, 1974, pp. 211–21.

461. William Gladstone, Manager, Tropical Forestry Research, Weyerhaeuser Company, personal communication, June 1978.

462. Ibid.

463. G. M. Woodwell et al., "The Biota and the World Carbon Budget," *Science*, Jan. 13, 1978, pp. 141–146.

464. P. H. Raven et al., "The Origins of Taxonomy," *Science*, vol. 174, 1971, pp. 1210–13; "Trends, Priorities and Needs in Systematic and Evolutionary Biology," *Systematic Zoology*, vol. 23, 1974, pp. 416–39.

465. *Environmental Quality 1978*, annual report of the Council on Environmental Quality, Washington: Government Printing Office, Dec. 1978, pp. 328–30.

466. For discussions of these points, see *Underexploited Tropical Plants with Promising Economic Value* and *Conservation of Germplasm Resources: An Imperative,* Washington: National Academy of Sciences, 1975 and 1978; Erik Eckholm, *Disappearing Species: The Social Challenge,* Washington: Worldwatch Institute, July 1978.

467. Joseph A. Tosi, Jr., "Climatic Control of Terrestrial Ecosystems: A Report on the Holdridge Model," *Economic Geography*, Apr. 1964, pp. 173–81, especially p. 178.

468. National Research Council. *Soils of the Humid Tropics,* Washington: National Academy of Sciences, 1972; Tamm et al., op. cit; P. W. Richards, "The Tropical Rain Forest," *Scientific American*, vol. 169, no. 6, 1973, pp. 58–67.

469. Rohter, op. cit.

470. Ibid.

471. Tamm et al., op. cit.; Richards, op. cit.; Gomez-Pompa et al., op. cit.

472. See D. S. Simberloff and L. B. Abele, "Island Biogeography Theory and Conservation Practice," *Science*, vol. 171, 1976, pp. 285–86; J. Terborgh, "Island Biogeography and Conservation: Strategy and Limitations" (response to Simberloff and Abele), *Science*, vol. 193, 1976, pp. 1028–29; T. E. Lovejoy and D. C. Oren, "Minimum Critical Size of Ecosystems," in R. L. Burgess and D. M. Sharpe, eds., *Forest Island Dynamics in Man-Dominated Landscapes,* New York: Springer, 1979; J. M. Diamond and R. M. May, "Island Biogeography and the Design of Natural Reserves," in R. M. May, ed., *Theoretical Ecology: Principles and Applications,* Oxford: Blackwell, 1976, pp. 163–86; E. O. Wilson and E. O. Willis, "Applied Biogeography," in M. L. Cody and J. M. Diamond, eds., *Ecology and Evolution of Communities,* Cambridge, Mass: Harvard University Press, 1975, pp. 522–34.

473. T. E. Lovejoy, "Bird Diversity and Abundance in Amazon Forest Communities," *Living Bird*, vol. 13, 1975, pp. 127–91; C. S. Elton, "Conservation and the Low Population Density of Invertebrates Inside Neotropical Rain Forest," *Biological Conservation*, vol. 7, 1975, pp. 3–15; G. E. Hutchinson, *Principles of Population Ecology,* New Haven: Yale Univ. 1978.

474. E. Salati et al., "Origem e Distribuiçâ das Chuvas na Amazônia," *Interciencia*, vol. 3, 1978, pp. 200–5; and N. A. Villa Nova et al., "Estimativa da Evapotranspiração na Bacia Amazônica," *Acta Amazônica*, vol. 6, 1976, pp. 215–28.

475. J. Haffer, "Speciation in Amazonian Forest Birds," *Science*, vol. 165, 1969, pp. 131–37.

476. Ibid.; J. Haffer, *Avian Speciation in Tropical South America, with a systematic Survey of the Toucans* (Ramphastidae) *and Jacamars* (Galbulidae)," Cambridge, Mass.: Nuttall Ornithological Club, 1974; P. E. Vanzolini, "Paleoclimates, Relief, and Species Multiplication in Equatorial Forests," in Meggers et al., op. cit., pp. 255–58; G. T. Prance, "Phytogeographic Support for the Theory of Pleistocene Forest Refuges in the Amazon Basin, Based on Evidence From Distribution Patterns in Caryocaraceae, Chrysobalanaceae, Dichapetalaceae, and Lecythidaceae," *Acta Amazônica*, vol. 3, 1973, pp. 5–28; K. S. Brown, Jr., "Centros de Evolução, Refúgios Quaternários e Conservação de Patrimônios Genéticos na Regiâo Neotropical: Padrões de Diferenciação na Ithomiinae (*Lipidoptera: Nymphalidae*)", *Acta Amazônica*, vol. 7, 1977, pp. 75–137.

477. Brown, op. cit.

478. Support for a curve of this sort is suggested in A. Sommer, "Attempt at an Assessment of the World's Tropical Forests," *Unasylva*, vol. 28, 1976, pp. 5–25.

479. T. E. Lovejoy, "Refugia, Refuges and Minimum Critical

Size: Problems in the Conservation of the Neotropical Herpetofauna", in W. E. Duellman, ed., *South American Herpetofauna: Its Origin, Evolution and Dispersal,* Lawrence, Kan.: Museum of Natural History, Univ. of Kansas, 1979.

480. G. B. Wetterberg, et al., "Umma Anális de Prioridades em Conservação da Natureza na Amazônia," Seria Tecnica No. 8, Brasilia: Ministerio da Agricultura, 1977.

481. Lovejoy, "Refugia," op. cit. The concept of Pleistocene refugia in present tropical forest areas and the applicability of this concept to conservation will be explored during meetings to be held in Caracas, Venezuela, Feb. 8–13, 1979, under the auspices of the Association for Tropical Biology.

482. Raven et al., op. cit.; "Trends, Priorities and Needs," op. cit.

483. *Red Data Book,* Morges, Switzerland: International Union for Conservation of Nature, vol. 1, *Mammalia,* in press; vol. 2, *Aves,* by W. B. King, 1978

484. Lovejoy, "Refugia," op. cit.

485. Eckholm, "Planting for the Future," op. cit.

486. Ibid.

487. Garrett Hardin, "The Tragedy of the Commons," *Science,* vol. 162, 1968, pp. 13–18.

488. Garrett Hardin, "Political Requirements for Preserving Our Common Heritage," in Council on Environmental Quality, *Wildlife and America,* forthcoming, 1979, pp. 310–16.

489. Aldo Leopold, *A Sand County Almanac,* New York: Ballantine, p. 251 (originally published by Oxford University Press, 1949).

490. See especially Scott Overton and Larry Hunt, "A View of Current Forest Policy, with Questions Regarding the Future State of Forests and Criteria of Management," in *Transactions of the Thirty-Ninth North American Wildlife and Natural Resources Conference,* Washington; Wildlife Management Institute,1974, pp. 334–53, Also see John Maynard Keynes, *Essays in Biography,* New York: Meridian, 1956; Daniel Fife, "Killing the Goose," *Environment,* vol. 13, no. 3, 1971, pp. 20–27.

491. Hardin, "Political Requirements," op. cit., p. 315.

492. Overton and Hunt, op. cit.

493. Hardin, "Political Requirements," op. cit., p. 316.

## Water Section

494. Food and Agriculture Organization, *Soil Conservation and Management in Developing Countries,* FAO Soils Bulletin 33. Rome, 1977; *Guidelines for Watershed Management,* FAO Conservation Guide 1, Rome, 1977; E. Eckholm, *Losing Ground,* New York: Norton, 1976.

495. P. H. Freeman, et al., *Cape Verde: Assessment of the Agricultural Sector,* report submitted to the Agency for International Development, McLean, Va.: General Research Corporation, 1978.

496. H. W. Anderson et al., *Forests and Water: Effects of Forest Management on Floods, Sedimentation and Water Supply,* Pacific Southwest Forest and Range Experiment Station report, Washington: U.S. Forest Service, 1976.

497. M. Kassas, "Desertification versus Potential for Recovery in Circum-Saharan Territories," in H. E. Dregne, ed., *Arid Lands in Transition,* Washington: American Association for the Advancement of Science, pp. 123–142; "Status of Desertification in the Hot Arid Regions; Climate Aridity Index Map; Experimental World Scheme of Aridity and Drought Probability," U.N. Conference on Desertification, 1977.

498. A. P. Altschuller, "Transport and Fate of Sulfur and Nitrogen Containing Pollutants Related to Acid Precipitation," unpublished report to the Environmental Protection Agency; George M. Hidy et al., "International Aspects of the Long Range Transport of Air Pollutants," report prepared for the U.S. Department of State, Westlake Village, Calif.: Environmental Research and Technology, Inc., Sept. 1978.

499. Commission on Natural Resources, National Research Council, *Implications of Environmental Regulations for Energy Production and Consumption: A Report to the U.S. Environmental Protection Agency from the Committee on Energy and the Environment,* Washington: National Academy of Science, 1977, vol. 6, p. 68; Northrop Services, Inc., "Interim Report: Acid Precipitation in the United States—History, Extent, Sources, Prognosis," a report to the Environmental Protection Agency, Corvallis, Ore.: Environmental Research Laboratory, Dec. 18, 1978; J. N. Galloway et al., "Acid Precipitation in the Northeastern United States," *Science,* vol. 194, 1976, pp. 722–24; G. E. Likens, "Acid Precipitation" *Chemical Engineering News,* vol. 54, 1976, pp. 29–44.

499a G. E. Likens, et al., "Acid Rain," *Scientific American,* Oct. 1977, pp. 43–51.

500. George R. Hendrey et al., "Acid Precipitation: Some Hydrobiological Changes," *Ambio,* vol. 5, no. 5–6, 1976, pp. 224–27. For a good general overview of the impact of acid precipitation in Norway, see Finn H. Braekke, *Impact of Acid Precipitation on Forest and Freshwater Ecosystems in Norway,* SNSF-Project, NISK, 1432 Aas-NHL, Norway, Mar. 1976.

501. C. L. Schofield, "Acid Precipitation: Our Understanding of the Ecological Effects," in *Proceedings of the Conference on Emerging Environmental Problems: Acid Precipitation,* U.S. Environmental Protection Agency Region II, New York, 1975.

502. D. M. Whepldale, "Large Scale Atmospheric Sulphur Studies in Canada", *Atmospheric Environment,* vol. 12, 1978, pp. 661–670; Roderick W. Shaw, "Acid Precipitation in Atlantic Canada", *Environmental Science and Technology,* vol. 13, no. 4, Apr. 1979, pp. 406–11; Ross Howard, "48,000 Lakes Dying As Ontario Stalls", *Toronto Star,* Mar. 10, 1979, p. C4.

503. Arild Holt-Jensen, "Acid Rains in Scandinavia," *Ecologist,* Oct. 1973, pp. 380–81.

504. Jeffrey J. Lee and David E. Webber, "The Effect of Simulated Acid Rain on Seedling Emergence and Growth of Eleven Woody Species," unpublished report, Corvallis Environmental Research Laboratory, U.S. Environmental Protection Agency, Corvallis, Ore.; Braekke, op. cit., pp. 53–59.

505. National Academy of Sciences, *Implications of Environmental Regulations for Energy Production and Consumption,* Washington, 1977, p. 66.

506. Leon S. Dochinger and Thomas A. Seliga, "Acid Precipitation and the Forest Ecosystem," *Journal of the Air Pollution Control Association,* Nov. 1975, p. 1105.

507. Holt-Jensen, "Acid Rains in Scandinavia," op. cit., pp. 381–82; Carl Olof Tamm, "Acid Precipitation: Biological Effects in Soil and on Forest Vegetation," *Ambio,* vol. V. no. 5–6, 1976, pp. 235–38; Braekke, op. cit., pp. 53–59.

508. J. S. Jacobson and P. Van Leuken, "Effects of Acidic Precipitation on Vegetation" in S. Kasuga et al., eds., *Proceedings of the Fourth International Clean Air Congress,* Tokyo: Japanese Union of Air Pollution Prevention Associations, 1977, pp. 124–27.

509. Gary E. Glass, "Impacts of Air Pollutants on Wilderness Areas of Northern Minnesota," Environmental Research

Laboratory–Duluth, U.S. Environmental Protection Agency, Mar. 5, 1979, pp. 129–30 (draft).

510. Stephan Gage, assistant administrator, research and development, U.S. Environmental Protection Agency, personal communication, 1979.

511. D. S. Shriner, "Effects of Simulated Rain Acidified with Sufuric Acid on Host-Parasite Interactions," *Journal of Water and Soil Pollution,* vol. 8, no. 1, 1976, pp. 9–14.

512. Norman Glass, U.S. Environmental Protection Agency, Corvallis, Ore., Environmental Research Laboratory, personal communication, 1979.

513. W. H. Allaway, "pH, Soil Acidity, and Plant Growth," and N. T. Coleman and A. Mehlich, "The Chemistry of Soil, pH," in *Soil: The 1957 Yearbook of Agriculture,* Washington: Government Printing office, pp. 67–71 and 72–79.

514. John O. Reuss, "Chemical/Biological Relationships Relevant to Ecological Effects of Acid Rainfall," Corvallis, Ore.: National Environment Research Center, U.S. Environmental Protection Agency, June 1975; Dale W. Johnson and Dale W. Cole, "Anion Mobility and Soils: Relevance to Nutrient Transport from Terrestrial to Aquatic Ecosystems," U.S. Environmental Protection Agency, June 1977.

515. Environmental Protection Agency, Air Pollution Control Office, *Air Quality Criteria for Nitrogen Oxides,* Washington: Government Printing Office, Jan. 1971; National Research Council, Committee on Medical and Biologic Effects of Environmental Pollutance, *Nitrogen Oxides,* Washington: National Academy of Sciences, 1977; U.S. Department of Health, Education, and Welfare, National Air Pollution Control Administration, *Air Quality Criteria for Hydrocarbons,* Mar. 1970, and *Air Quality Criteria for Sulphur Oxides,* undated. Washington: Government Printing Office.

516. "Climate Change to the Year 2000," Washington: National Defense University, 1978.

517. K. Szesztay, "Summary: Hydrology and Man-Made Lakes," in William C. Ackermann et al., eds., *Man-Made Lakes: Their Problems and Environmental Effects,* Washington: American Geophysical Union, 1973.

518. Committee for Coordination of Investigations of the Lower Mekong Basin, *Pa Mong Optimization and Downstream Effects Study: Environmental Effects of Pa Mong,* Bangkok: Mekong Secretariat, 1976.

519. Ibid.

520. Ibid.

521. Julian Rzoska, "A Controversy Reviewed," *Nature,* June 10, 1976, pp. 444–45.

522. Mohammed Abdul-Fatah Kassas et al., "Impact of River Control Schemes on the Shoreline of the Nile Delta"; Carl George, "The Role of the Aswan High Dam in Changing the Fisheries in the Southeastern Mediterranean"; Henry van der Schalie, "World Health Organization Project Egypt 10: A Case History of a Schistosomiasis Control Project," all in T. Farvar and J. P. Milton, eds., *The Careless Technology: Ecology and International Development,* New York: Doubleday, 1972.

523. *The State of Food and Agriculture 1971,* Rome: Food and Agriculture Organization, 1971, p. 152.

524. Ibid., pp. 152–53.

525. A. T. Abbas, "Problems of Water Resource Development in Bangladesh," U.N. Water Conference, 1976.

526. Office of Water Program Operations, "Application of Sewage Sludge to Cropland: Appraisal of Potential Hazards of Heavy Metals to Plants and Animals," Washington: U.S. Environmental Protection Agency, No. 15, 1976; Bernard P. Sagik and Charles A. Sorber, eds., *Risk*

*Assessment and Health Effects of Land Application of Municipal Wastewater and Sludges,* conference proceedings, San Antonio: Center for Applied Research and Technology, University of Texas, Dec. 1977; G. W. Leeper, *Managing the Heavy Metals on the Land,* New York: Marcel Dekker, 1978.

527. Bruce McCallum, *Environmentally Appropriate Technology,* Ottawa: Ministry of Fisheries and Environment, Mar. 1975, p. 115; Lane de Moll, ed., *Rainbook: Resources for Appropriate Technology,* New York: Schocken, 1977, pp. 191–94.

528. J. T. Dunham et al., "High Sulfur Coal for Generating Electricity," in P. H. Abelson, ed., *Energy: Use, Conservation and Supply,* Washington: American Association for the Advancement of Science, 1974, pp. 83–88.

529. G. H. Davis and L. A. Wood, "Water Demands for Expanding Energy Development," USGS Circular 703, Washington: U.S. Geological Survey, 1974.

530. John Lun, U.S. Environmental Protection Agency, personal communication, 1979.

531. P. R. Ehrlich et al., *Ecoscience: Population, Resources, Environment,* San Francisco: Freeman, 1977, p. 670.

532. Ibid.; and C.C. Coutant and S.S. Talmadge, "Thermal Effects," *Journal of Water Pollution Control Federation,* June 1977, pp. 1369–1425.

533. John Lun, op. cit.

534. U.S. Water Resources Council, *The Nation's Water Resources: 1975–2000,* Washington: Government Printing Office, Dec. 1978.

535. Velikanov, op. cit.

536. Wolf Häfele, "Energy Choices that Europe Faces: A European View of Energy," in Abelson, op. cit. pp. 97–104.

537. U.S. Agency for International Development, *Environmental Impact Statement on the AID Pest Management Program,* vols. 1 and 2, Washington, May 13, 1979; also its *Environmental and Natural Resource Management in Developing Countries: A Report to Congress,* vols. 1 and 2, Washington, Feb. 1979.

538. R. Pantulu, *Role of Aquaculture in Water Resource Development: A Case Study of the Mekong Project,* Bangkok Secretariat, 1974 (manuscript).

539. Environmental Protection Agency, *Quality Criteria for Water,* Washington, 1976

540. Pantulu, op. cit.

541. Ibid. Also see Barbara J. Culliton, "Aquaculture: Appropriate Technology in China," *Science,* Nov. 2, 1979, p. 539; and R. Zweig and W. O. McLarney, "Aquaculture," *Journal of the New Alchemists,* (Woods Hole, The New Alchemy Institute), 1977, pp. 63–82.

542. Food and Agriculture Organization, "The Potential of Fisheries to Developing Countries and the Requirements for Investment," FAO Fisheries Circular 343, Rome, 1977.

543. Bill Richards, "Toxic Chemical Found in California Wells," *Washington Post,* June 15, 1979, p. A2.

544. "Desertification: An Overview," U.N. Conference on Desertification, 1977.

545. Farvar and Milton, op. cit.

546. U.S. Bureau of Land Reclamation, "Increasing Available Water Supplies Through Weather Modification and Desalination," U.N. Water Conference, New York, 1976.

547. Farvar and Milton, op. cit.

548. Jane Stein, *Water: Life or Death,* Washington: International Institute for Environment and Development, June 1977; *Environmental Aspects of a Large Tropical Reservoir: A Case Study of the Volta Lake, Ghana,* Wash-

ington: Office of International and Environmental Programs, Smithsonian Institution, 1974.

549. Erik Eckholm, *The Picture of Health,* New York: Norton, 1977.

550. Letitia Obeng, "Water and Health," in International Institute for Environment and Development, *Clean Water for All,* Washington, 1976, pp. 13–18.

551. Talbot Page et al., "Drinking Water and Cancer Mortality in Louisiana," *Science,* July 2, 1976, pp. 55–57.

552. *Drinking Water and Health,* Washington: National Academy of Sciences, 1977.

553. *World Conservation Strategy,* Morges, Switzerland: International Union for Conservation of Nature and Natural Resources, Jan. 1978 (draft), p. WCS/Strategy/4.

## Energy Section

554. E. F. Schumaker, in *Small Is Beautiful: Economics as if People Mattered* (New York: Harper, 1973), is one of those who drew attention to the importance of intermediate or appropriate technology.

555. National Research Council, *Energy for Rural Development* and *Methane Generation from Human, Animal and Agricultural Wastes,* Washington: National Academy of Sciences, 1976, 1977.

556. John P. Holdren, "Environmental Impacts of Alternative Energy Technologies for California," in *Distributed Energy Systems in California's Future,* vol. 2, Washington: Government Printing Office, May 1978.

557. Ibid., p. 4.

558. Richard J. Kalagher et al., *Environmental Data for Energy Technology Policy Analysis,* Office of the Assistant Secretary for Environment, Department of Energy, Mar. 10, 1978 (draft).

559. Richard Nehring, "Giant Oil Fields and World Oil Resources," Santa Monica, Calif.: Rand Corp., June 1978.

560. Ibid., p. 85.

561. M. King Hubbert, "World Oil and Natural Gas Reserves and Resources," in Congressional Research Service, *Project Interdependence: U.S. and World Energy Outlook Through 1990.* Washington: Government Printing Office, Nov. 1977, pp. 632–44.

562. See, for example, Edison Electric Institute, *Economic Growth in the Future: The Growth Debate in National and Global Perspective,* New York: McGraw-Hill, 1976; Workshop on Alternative Energy Strategies, *Energy: Global Prospectives 1985–2000,* New York: McGraw-Hill, 1977.

563. Amory B. Lovins, "Energy Strategy: The Road Not Taken,"*Foreign Affairs,* Oct. 1976; Amory B. Lovins, *Soft Energy Paths: Toward a Durable Peace,* Cambridge, Mass.: Ballinger, 1977; Hugh Nash, ed., *Progress as if Survival Mattered,* San Francisco: Friends of the Earth, 1977. For further details on the relationship between energy and GNP, see Sam H. Schurr and Joel Darmstader, "Some Observations on Energy and Economic Growth," in *Future Strategies for Energy Development: A Question of Scale,* proceedings of a conference at Oak Ridge, Tenn., Oak Ridge Association Universities, 1977, pp. 280–97.

564. Lovins, "Energy Strategy" and *Soft Energy Paths,* op. cit. Also see P. R. Ehrlich et al., *Ecoscience: Population, Resources, Environment,* San Francisco: Freeman, 1977, Ch. 8, 14, and 15.

565. Lovins, "Energy Strategy" and *Soft Energy Paths,* op. cit.

566. All major criticisms of Lovins' work have been collected by the Senate Select Committee on Small Business and Committee on Interior and Insular Affairs and published in a report of more than 2,000 pages: *Alternative Long-Range Energy Strategies: Additional Appendixes—1977,* Washington: Government Printing Office, Dec. 9, 1976.

567. World Energy Commission of the World Energy Conference, *World Energies: Looking Ahead to 2020,* New York: IPC Science and Technology Press, 1978.

568. Ibid.

569. Ibid., p. 228.

570. Ibid.

571. Ibid.

572. Robert J. Raudebaugh, executive director of WEC's U.S. National Committee, personal communication, Feb. 15, 1979.

573. DOE Energy Information Administration, "Projections of Energy Supply and Demand and Their Impacts," in *Administrator's Annual Report to Congress, 1977,* Washington, Apr. 1978, vol. 2.

574. Richard J. Kalagher et al., *National Environmental Impact Projection No. 1,* McLean, Va.: MITRE Corp., Dec. 1978.

575. Ford Foundation Nuclear Energy Policy Study Group, *Nuclear Power Issues and Choices,* Cambridge, Mass.: Ballinger, 1977, p. 7.

576. Ibid., p. 8.

577. Ibid., p. 11.

578. Ibid.

579. Eliot Marshall, "H$_2$ Bubble Is Unexpected Source of Trouble," and "A Preliminary Report on Three Mile Island," *Science,* Apr. 13 and 20, 1979, pp. 152–53 and 280–281.

580. Tim Metz, "Financial Fallout: Post Accident Costs May Be Biggest Hurdle for Nuclear Expansion," *Wall Street Journal,* Apr. 24, 1979, p. 1; "Assessing the Damage at Three Mile Island," *Science,* May 11, 1979, pp. 594–96.

581. "Montana Passes a Nuclear Initiative," *Science,* Nov. 24, 1978, p. 850.

582. Luther J. Carter, "Nuclear Wastes: Popular Antipathy Narrows Search for Disposal Sites," *Science,* Sept. 23, 1977, p. 1265–66.

583. David S. Broder, "U.S. Gets Ultimatum on Nuclear Waste," *Washington Post,* July 11, 1979, p. A2.

584. "European Doubts About Nuclear Power", *Science,* Oct. 8, 1976, p. 164; Robert Skole, "Sweden's Nuclear Election," *The Nation,* Oct. 9, 1976, pp. 334–37.

585. "Austria Declines to Start a Nuclear Power Program," *Science,* Nov. 24, 1978, p. 850; "Austrians Turn Down Nuclear Power Plant in Close Referendum," *Washington Post,* Nov. 6, 1978, p. A24.

586. John Vinocer, "West Germany Postpones Building a Key Atom Plant," *New York Times,* May 17, 1979, A7.

587. Lovins, *Soft Energy Paths,* op. cit. pp. 38–39.

588. Thomas B. Johansson and Peter Steen, *Solar Sweden: An Outline to a Renewable Energy System,* Stockholm: Secretariat for Futures Studies, 1978.

589. Lars Emmelin and Bo Wiman, *The Environmental Problems of Energy Production,* Stockholm: Secretariat for Future Studies, 1978 (Swedish); Lars Emmelin and Bo Wiman, "Environmental Report," in *Preliminary Report from the Energy Commission, Group A, Safety and Environment,* Stockholm: Ministry of Industry, Oct. 1977 (Swedish).

590. Johansson and Steen, op. cit.

591. W. R. Derrick Sewell and Harold D. Foster, *Images of Canadian Futures: The role of Conservation and Renewable Resources,* Ottawa: Environment Canada, 1976.

592. Peter Love and Ralph Overend, *Tree Power: An Assessment of the Energy Potential of Forest Biomass in*

*Canada,* Ottawa: Ministry of Energy, Mines and Resources, 1978.

593. Ibid., p. ix.
594. *Distrbuted Energy Systems in California's Future,* Interim Report, Washington: Government Printing Office, May 1978. 2 vol.
595. Ibid., vol. 1, p. vi.
596. Ibid.
597. Ibid., vol. 2, p. 60
598. Ibid., vol. 1, p. ix.
599. Council on Environmental Quality, *The Good News About Energy,* Washington: Government Printing Office, 1979.
600. Ibid, p. 23.
601. Department of Energy Impacts Panel, *Domestic Policy Review of Solar Energy,* Washington, Oct. 1978.
602. Council on Environmental Quality, op. cit.
603. Sven Bjórnholm, *Energy in Denmark, 1990 and 2005: A Case Study,* Copenhagen: The Niels Bohr Institute, Sept. 1976.
604. Gerald Leach et al., *A Low Energy Strategy for the United Kingdom,* Cambridge, England: J. W. Larman, 1979.
605. Ibid., pp. 18, 19.
606. Lovins, *Soft Energy Paths,* op. cit., p. 26.
607. Holdren, op. cit., pp. 1–3.
608. "Regional Information on Industry and Environment," in *Industry and Environment,* Nairobi: U.N. Environment Programme (UNEP), 1979; *National Energy Policies: An Overview,* Nairobi: UNEP, 1979; *Solar 2000,* Nairobi: UNEP, 1979.
609. Lovins, *Soft Energy Paths,* op. cit., pp. 59–60.
610. *Alternative Long-Range Energy Strategies,* op. cit.
611. Food and Agriculture Organization, *The State of Food and Agriculture, 1976,* Rome, 1976, Ch. 3.
612. Ibid.
613. Ibid.
614. Ibid.
615. Ibid.
616. Food and Agriculture Organization, *The State of Food and Agriculture,* op. cit. p. 89; also see Arjun Makhijani and Allan Poole, *Energy and Agriculture in the Third World: A Report to the Energy Policy Project of the Ford Foundation,* Cambidge, Mass.: Ballinger, 1975, p. 19.
617. Arjun Makhijani, *Energy Policy for the Rural Third World,* London: International Institute for Environment and Development, 1976.
618. D. Brokensha and B. Riley, "Forest, Foraging, Fences and Fuel in a Marginal Area of Kenya," Univ. of Calif., Santa Barbara, prepared for the Firewood Workshop, sponsored by USAID's Africa Bureau, June 1978; "The Double Problem of Charcoal," *"The Center Report* (Nairobi, Environmental Liaison Center) vol. 3, no. 3, Aug. 1978.
619. Erik Eckholm, Personal communication, 1979.
620. J. E. M. Arnold and J. Jongma, "Fuelwood and Charcoal in Developing Countries," *Unasylva,* vol. 29, no. 118, 1978, pp. 2–9.
621. Ibid.
622. Food and Agriculture Organization, *The State of Food and Agriculture, 1976,* op. cit.
623. World Bank, *Forestry Sector Policy Paper,* Washington, 1978.
624. FAO Committee on Forestry, "A Forecast of Wood Consumption," *Unasylva,* vol. 29, no. 118, 1978, pp. 33–34.
625. Arnold and Jongma, op. cit.
626. Food and Agriculture Organization, *The State of Food and Agriculture,* op. cit.

627. Erik Eckholm, personal communication, 1979.
628. Arnold and Jongma, op. cit.
629. Erik Eckholm, *Planting for the Future: Forestry for Human Needs,* Washington: Worldwatch Institute, Feb. 1979, p. 30.
630. F. R. Weber, "Economic and Ecologic Criteria of Forestry and Conservation Projects in the Sahel," prepared for the USAID Sahel Development Program, Boise, Idaho: International Resource Development and Conservation Services, 1977.
631. Ibid.
632. Club du Sahel, and Comité Permanent Inter-Etats de Lutte contre la Sécheresse dans le Sahel, *Energy in the Development Strategy of the Sahel: Situation, Perspectives, Recommendations,* Paris: Club du Sahel, 1978.
633. Ibid.
634. Ibid.
635. Erik Eckholm, *Planting for the Future,* op. cit.
636. Weber, op. cit. Brokensha and Riley, op cit.; "The Double Problem of Charcoal," op. cit.
637. Brokensha and Riley, op. cit.; W. M. Floor, "Energy Options in Rural Areas of the Third World," 8th World Forestry Conference, Jarkarta, Oct. 1978.
638. Tze I. Chiang, et al., *Pyrolytic Conversion of Agricultural and Forestry Wastes in Ghana: A Feasibility Study,* prepared for USAID, Atlanta: Georgia Institute of Technology, 1976.
639. "The Double Problem of Charcoal," op. cit.
640. Clark University Program for International Development, *Fuelwood and Energy in Eastern Africa,* Worcester, Mass.: Clark Univ., 1978.
641. Ibid.
642. J. E. M. Arnold, "Wood Energy and Rural Communities," 8th World Forestry Congress, Jakarta, Oct. 1978.
643. "Arvores por Ferro," *Veja* (Brazil), Nov. 8, 1978, pp. 77–78.
644. Ibid.
645. Peter H. Freeman, "Environmental Aspects of Development in the Paracatu River Basin, Brazil," submitted to the Organization of American States, Washington: Threshold Inc., 1978.
646. D. E. Earl, *A Report on Charcoal,* Rome: Food and Agriculture Organization, 1974.
647. Brokensha and Riley, op. cit.
648. Makhijani, *Energy Policy, op. cit.;* Food and Agriculture Organization, op. cit.; Erik Eckholm, *The Other Energy Crisis: Firewood,* Washington: Worldwatch Institute, 1975.
649. Food and Agriculture Organization, op. cit.
650. Ibid.; Arnold and Jongma, op. cit.
651. Lester Brown, Personal communication, 1979.
652. Arnold and Jongma, op. cit.; Eckholm, *The Other Energy Crisis,* op. cit.; Erik Eckholm, personal communication, 1979.
653. Food and Agriculture Organization, *Organic Materials in Soil Productivity,* FAO Soils Bulletin 35, Rome, 1977, pp. 94–95; see also J. J. C. van Voorhoeve, *Organic Fertilizer Problems and Potential for Developing Countries,* Washington: World Bank Fertilizer Study, Background Paper 4, 1974.
654. U.S. Department of Agriculture, *Soil: The 1957 Yearbook of Agriculture,* Washington: Government Printing Office, 1957.
655. Food and Agriculture Organization, *Organic Materials,* op. cit.
656. National Research Council, *Methane Generation,* op. cit.
657. Food and Agriculture Organization, *Organic Materials,* op. cit.

# Methodology and Environmental Maps

## Methodology Maps

The first five maps which follow depict the various ways in which the regions of the world are represented in five key methodologies used to develop the Global 2000 Study projections. These maps and methodologies are as follows:

- GNP Projections (SIMLINK methodology)
- Population Projections (Cohort-component methodology)
- Food Projections (GOL methodology)
- Energy Projections (IEES methodology)
- Nonfuel Minerals Projections (IOU methodology)

Each methodology has its own way of dividing and aggregating the world into regions. These regional patterns differ. Moreover, some methodologies make many regional discriminations; others, only a few. In order to clarify these patterns and levels of regional detail, on each map a distinctive color is assigned to each region separately distinguished by the relevant methodology.

Some methodologies develop projections for each region separately, with no simulated interactions between regions. The maps depicting these methodologies make use of very thick boundaries between regions: ▬▬▬

Other methodologies develop projections for each region on an interactive basis. The maps depicting these methodologies make use of thinner boundaries between regions: ────

Though some methodologies simulate all endogenous regions in equal detail, others simulate different groups of regions at different levels of detail. Within maps depicting these latter methodologies, similar colors have been assigned to regions within groups simulated at the same level of detail:

More intense colors have been assigned to those regions modeled in greater detail:

Less intense colors have been assigned to those regions modeled in lesser detail:

## Environmental Maps

The last five maps illustrate various themes developed in the environmental projections.

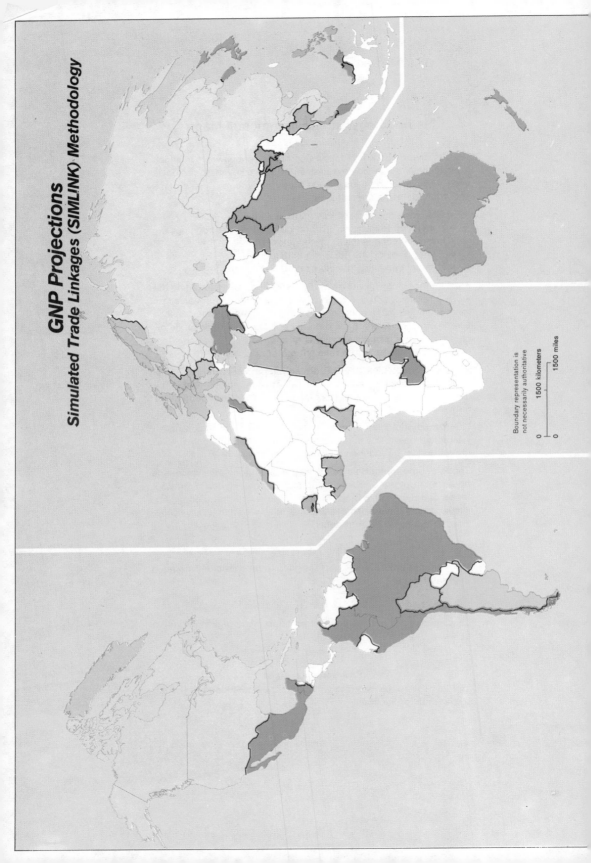

# GNP Projections
## Simulated Trade Linkages (SIMLINK) Methodology

Boundary representation is
not necessarily authoritative

0        1500 kilometers
0        1500 miles

# Partially Interactive Endogenous Regions Modeled in Equal Detail

## LDC regions endogenously represented

India

Low-income Africa

Lower-middle income

Middle income

Upper-middle income

Other South Asia

## Regions exogenously represented as markets for LDC exports of primary commodities, manufactured goods, and services

Japan and Oceania

North America

Western Europe

## Regions exogenously represented as markets for LDC exports of manufactured goods and services

Socialist countries

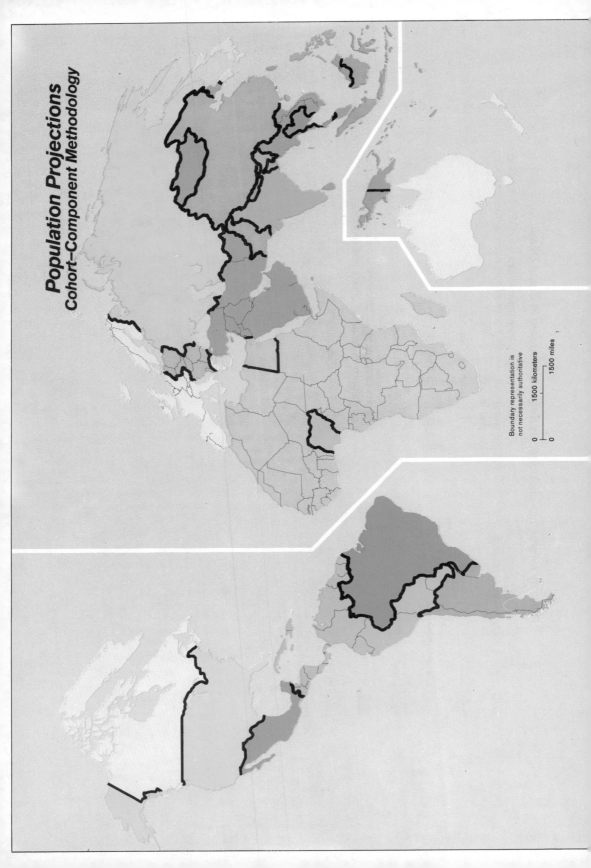

**Population Projections**
*Cohort–Component Methodology*

Boundary representation is
not necessarily authoritative

0          1500 kilometers

0          1500 miles

## Independent Regions Modeled in Equal Detail

Bangladesh

Brazil

Eastern Europe

Egypt

India

Indonesia

Japan

Mexico

Nigeria

Pakistan

People's Republic of China

Philippines

South Korea

Temperate South America

Thailand

Union of Soviet Socialist Republics

United States

Other Africa

Other Asia and Oceania

Other industrialized market countries

Other Latin America

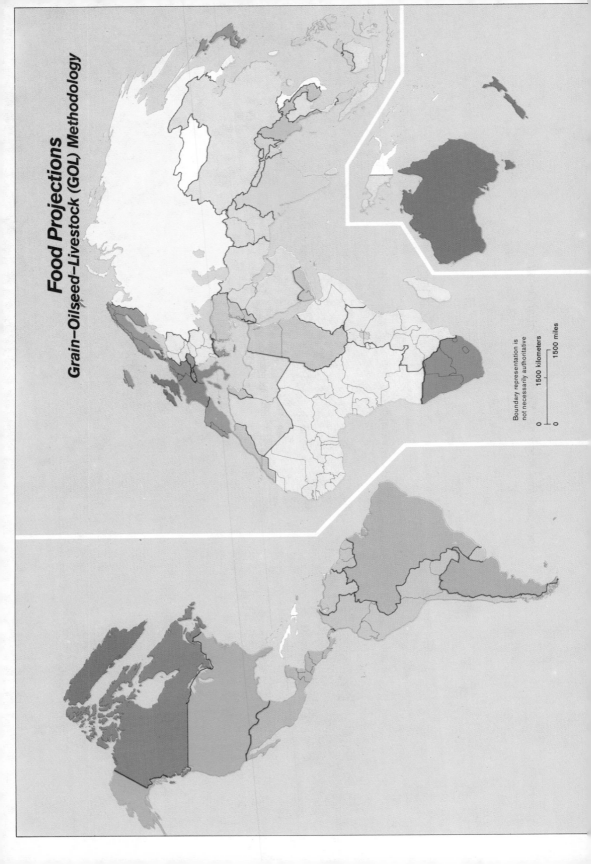

## Food Projections
### Grain–Oilseed–Livestock (GOL) Methodology

Boundary representation is
not necessarily authoritative

0        1500 kilometers

0        1500 miles

# Interactive Regions Modeled at Different Levels of Detail

**Regions which include detailed equations for grain, livestock, and dairy products**

- Canada
- Japan
- Oceania
- Southern Africa
- United States
- Benelux, France, Italy, West Germany
- Denmark, Ireland, United Kingdom
- Other Western Europe

**Regions which include detailed equations for grain and livestock**

- Argentina
- Brazil
- Central America

**Regions which include detailed equation for grain**

- Central Africa
- East Africa
- East Asia, high income
- East Asia, low income
- India
- Indonesia
- North Africa and Middle East, high income
- North Africa and Middle East, low income
- Thailand
- Venezuela
- Other South America
- Other South Asia
- Other Southeast Asia

**Regions which include only trade equation for grain and livestock**

- China
- Eastern Europe
- Union of Soviet Socialist Republics

**Regions which include only trade equations for livestock and dairy products**

- Rest of world

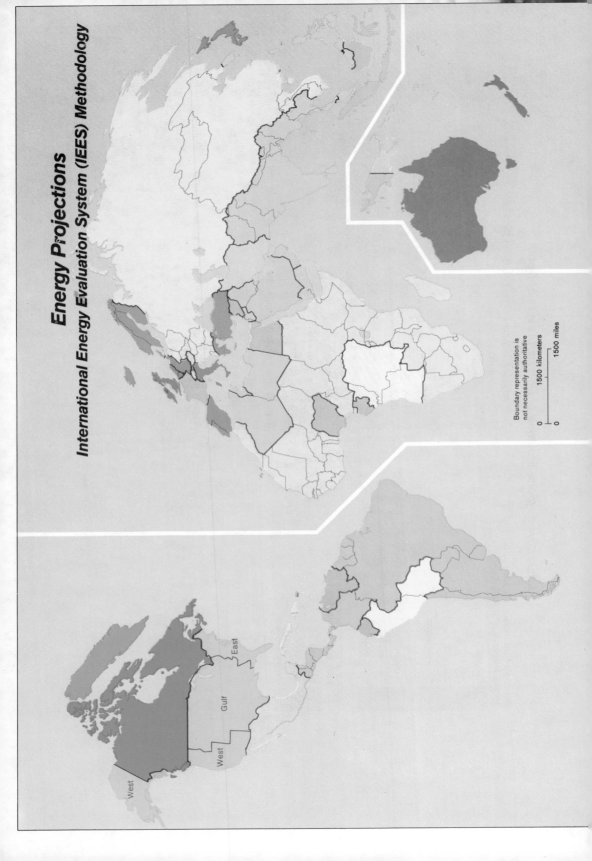

# Energy Projections
## International Energy Evaluation System (IEES) Methodology

West

Gulf

East

West

Boundary representation is
not necessarily authoritative

0          1500 kilometers
0          1500 miles

# Interactive Regions Modeled at Different Levels of Detail

### Regions which include detailed equations for energy demand, petroleum refining, and electricity generation

- Australia, New Zealand
- Austria, Switzerland
- Benelux
- Canada
- France
- Greece, Turkey
- Italy
- Japan
- Puerto Rico, Virgin Is.
- Scandinavia
- Spain, Portugal
- United Kingdom, Ireland
- West Germany

### Regions which include detailed equations for petroleum refining and electricity generation

- East  U.S. East Coast
- Gulf  U.S. Gulf Coast
- West  U.S. West Coast

### Regions which include detailed exogenous estimations of crude oil production

- Indonesia
- Iran
- Libya, Algeria
- Nigeria, Gabon
- Persian Gulf (Arab)
- Venezuela, Ecuador

### Regions which include only simplified demand relationships

- Angola, Congo, Zaire
- Asian exporters
- Bolivia, Peru
- Egypt, Syria, Bahrain
- Mexico
- Other Africa
- Other Asia
- Other Caribbean
- Other Latin America

### Regions for which supply and demand calculations are largely exogenous

- Centrally planned economies

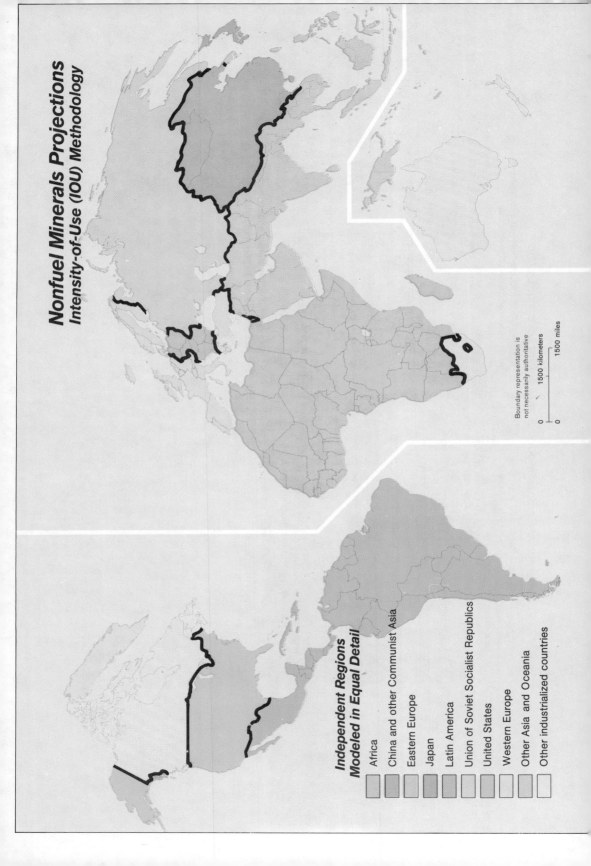

## Nonfuel Minerals Projections
### Intensity-of-Use (IOU) Methodology

### Independent Regions
### Modeled in Equal Detail

Africa
China and other Communist Asia
Eastern Europe
Japan
Latin America
Union of Soviet Socialist Republics
United States
Western Europe
Other Asia and Oceania
Other industrialized countries

Boundary representation is
not necessarily authoritative

0        1500 kilometers
0        1500 miles

# Extent of Commercial Activity

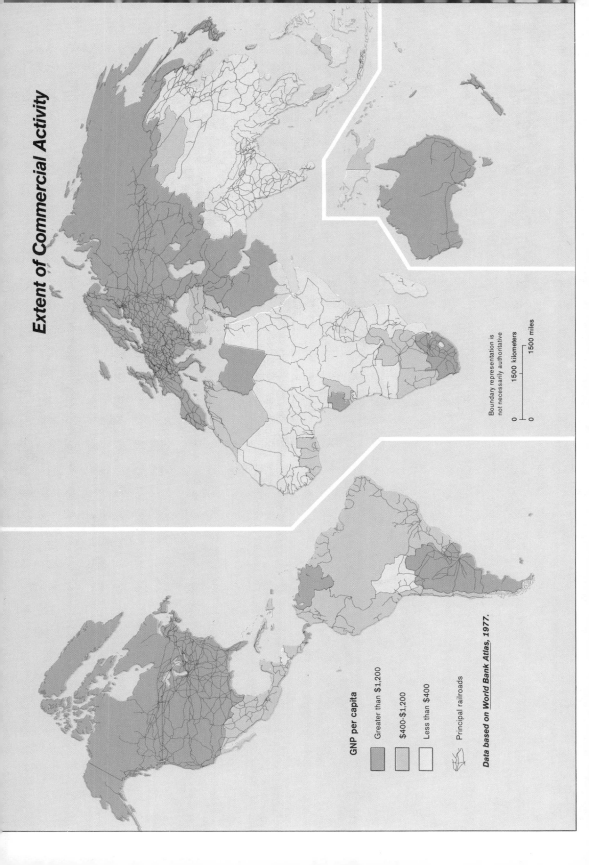

**GNP per capita**

Greater than $1,200

$400–$1,200

Less than $400

Principal railroads

*Data based on World Bank Atlas, 1977.*

Boundary representation is
not necessarily authoritative

0        1500 kilometers

0        1500 miles

# Population Density (1975)

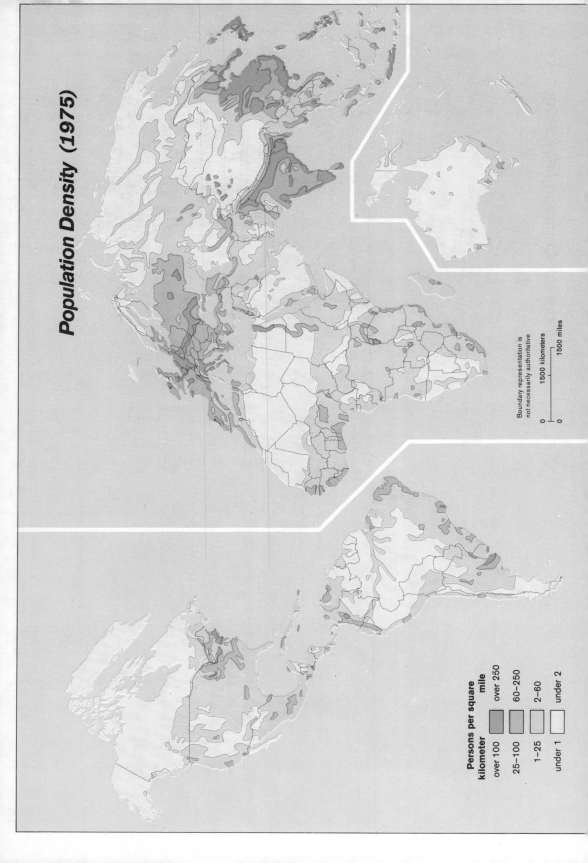

**Persons per square**

| kilometer | mile |
|---|---|
| over 100 | over 250 |
| 25–100 | 60–250 |
| 1–25 | 2–60 |
| under 1 | under 2 |

Boundary representation is
not necessarily authoritative

0        1500 kilometers

0        1500 miles

# Agricultural Production Potential

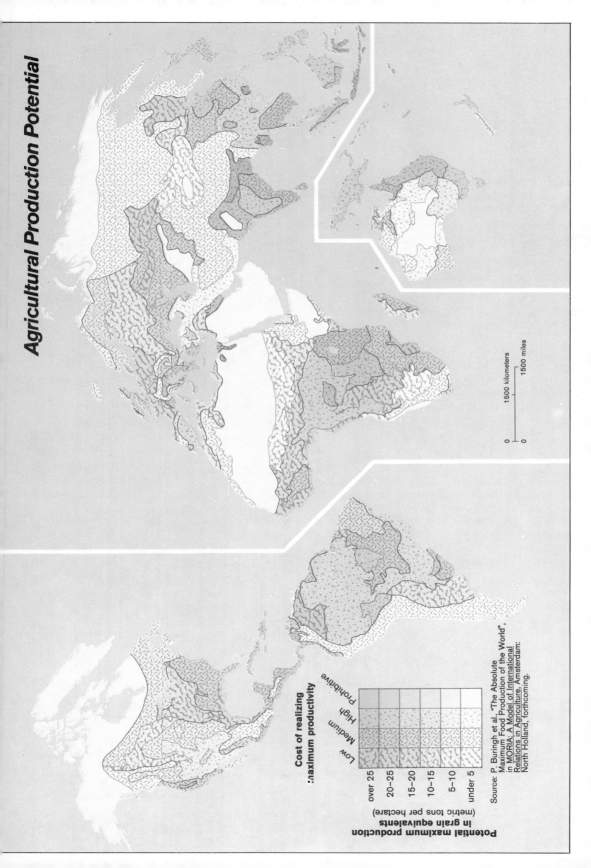

**Cost of realizing maximum productivity:**

Low  Medium  High  Prohibitive

**Potential maximum production in grain equivalents**
(metric tons per hectare)

over 25
20–25
15–20
10–15
5–10
under 5

0    1500 kilometers
0    1500 miles

Source: P. Buringh et al. "The Absolute
Maximum Food Production of the World",
in MOIRA: A Model of International
Relations in Agriculture, Amsterdam:
North Holland, forthcoming.

# Land Use Patterns (1975)

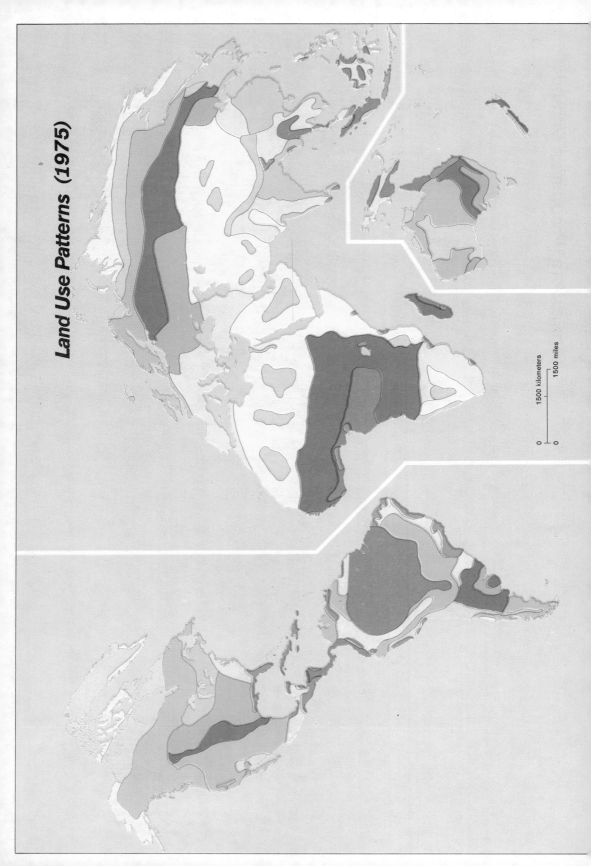

1500 kilometers

1500 miles

Large farms, temperate crops, plains agriculture

Rice (paddy), usually interspersed with mountains and forests

Small farms; various systems including mixed and shifting cultivation, excluding rice, often interspersed with forests

Tropical forest, hunting, fishing, gathering, shifting cultivation

Temperate forests, forestry, hunting, fishing, gathering

Dairy farming

Tropical plantation crops

Rich grazing lands supporting wild or domestic species interspersed with sedentary agriculture

Poor grazing lands

Nomadic and semi-nomadic herding interspersed with primitive cultivation, non-forested

Unproductive land

# Free Range Grazing Pressure

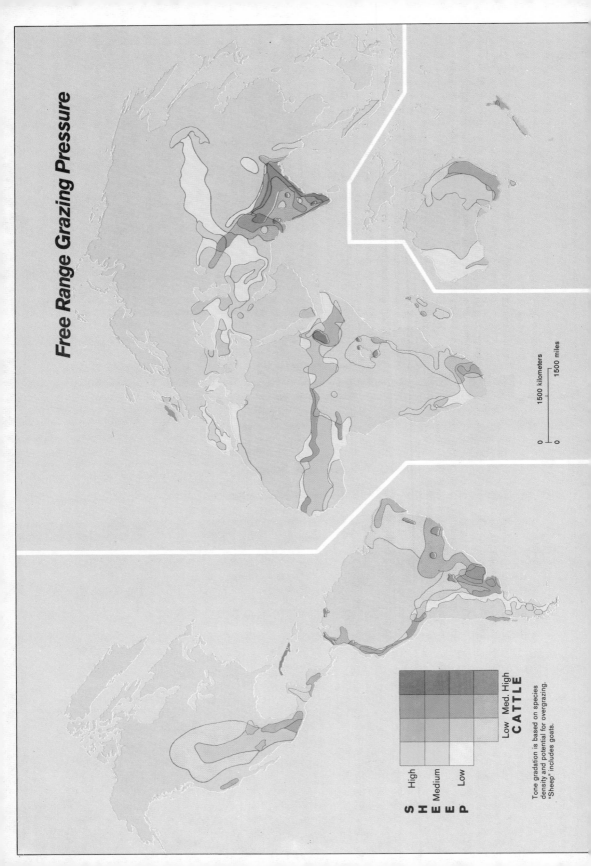

1500 kilometers

1500 miles

0

0

**S** High
**H** 
**E** Medium
**E** 
**P** Low

Low Med. High
**CATTLE**

Tone gradation is based on species
density and potential for overgrazing.
"Sheep" includes goats.

658. D. Thery and Van Giap Dang, "The Chinese Biogas Phenomenon" *Ecodevelopment News*, Dec. 1978, pp. 15–16.
659. Makhijani and Poole, op. cit.
660. W. M. Floor, "Energy Options in Rural Areas of the Third World," 8th World Forestry Conference, Jarkarta, Oct. 1978.
661. Ibid.; National Research Council, *Energy for Rural Development*, op. cit., and *Methane Generation*, op. cit.
662. U.S. Department of Agriculture, *Soil*, op. cit.; Food and Agriculture Organization, *Organic Materials*, op. cit.
663. Erik Eckholm, *Losing Ground*, New York: Norton, 1976; also see the observations on environmental deterioration woven into Peter Matthiessen, *The Snow Leopard*, New York: Viking, 1978.
664. D. French, "Firewood in Africa," Firewood Workshop, USAID Africa Bureau, Washington, June 1978.
665. Makhijani, *Energy Policy*, op. cit.
666. Arnold and Jongma, op. cit.
667. Makhijani, *Energy Policy*, op. cit.; National Research Council, *Methane Generation*, op. cit.; Food and Agriculture Organization, *China: Recycling of Organic Wastes in Agriculture*, FAO Soils Bulletin No. 40, Rome, 1977; Thery and Dang, op. cit.

**Nonfuel Minerals Section**

668. National Academy of Sciences and National Academy of Engineering, *Man, Materials and Environment*, Cambridge, Mass.: MIT, 1973, p. 88.
669. U.S. Department of the Interior, "Environmental Issues and the Mineral Industry," in *Mining and Minerals Policy*, Washington: Government Printing Office, July 1976, Ch. 7, pp. 95–105.
670. United Nations, *Environmental Impacts on the Growth and Structure of the World Economy*, E/AC.54/L.76, 1975.
671. Richard A. Carpenter, "Tensions Between Materials and Environmental Quality," *Science*, Feb. 20, 1976, pp. 665–68.
672. U.S. Agency for International Development, *Desert Encroachment on Arable Lands: Significance, Causes and Control*, Washington, Aug. 1972.
673. See the forestry projections in Chapter 8.
674. James Paone et al., *Land Utilization and Reclamation in the Mining Industry, 1930–71*, Bureau of Mines Information Circular 8642, Washington: Government Printing Office, 1974.
675. Raymond F. Dasmann, *Environmental Conservation*, New York: Wiley, 1976, p. 356.
676. J. M. Bradley, "W. Germany to Develop World's Largest Open Pit Lignite Mine," *World Environment Report*, July 4, 1977, p. 5.
677. Don Lipscombe, "Australian Conservationists Lose to Giant Alumina and Gas Projects," *World Environment Report*, Sept. 11, 1978, p. 3.
678. U.S. Soil Conservation Service, *Status of Land Disturbed by Surface Mining in the United States as of July 1, 1977, by States*, Advisory CONS–5, Washington, Feb. 9, 1978.
679. *Rehabilitation Potential of Western Coal Fields*, Washington: National Academy of Sciences, 1974.
680. Energy Policy Project of the Ford Foundation, *Exploring Energy Choices: A Preliminary Report*, New York: Ford Foundation, 1974.
681. Paone et al., op. cit.
682. Peter Dewhirst, "OECD Reports on Waste Material Use in Road Construction," *World Environment Report*, July 3, 1978, p. 5.
683. John L. Morning, "Mining and Quarrying Trends in the Metal and Nonmental Industries," in Bureau of Mines, *Minerals Yearbook 1975*, Washington: Government Printing Office, 1977.
684. Arthur Miller, "Philippines Seeking to Recycle, Reduce Waste in Mining Operations," *World Environment Report*, Oct. 24, 1977, p. 5.
685. Morning, op. cit.
686. Argonne National Laboratory, *Land Reclamation Program Annual Report July 1976-October 1977*, ANL/LRP–2, Argonne, Ill., 1978, p. 7.
687. *Methods for Identifying and Evaluating the Nature and Extent of Non-Point Sources of Pollutants*, EPA–430/9–73–014, Washington: Environmental Protection Agency, Oct. 1973, p. 6.
688. Paone et al., op. cit.
689. "Czechs Reclaim Coal Strip Mines by Planting Acorns," *World Environment Report*, Aug. 15, 1977, p. 8.
690. Human Resources Network, *The Handbook of Corporate Social Responsibility-Profiles of Involvement*, Radnor, Pa.: Chilton; 1975, p. 179.
691. Charles Harrison, "UNEP Hails Rehabilitation Of Limestone Quarry in Kenya," *World Environment Report*, Feb. 27, 1978, p. 1.
692. U.S. Soil Conservation Service, op. cit.
693. *Environmental Quality 1977*, annual report of the Council on Environmental Quality, Washington: Government Printing Office, 1977, pp. 87–89.
694. Ibid., p. 331.
695. David Sheridan, "A Second Coal Age Promises to Slow Our Dependence on Imported Oil," *Smithsonian*, Aug. 1977, p. 35.
696. J. R. LaFevers, et al., "A Case Study of Surface Mining and Reclamation Planning, International Minerals, and Chemical Corp. Phosphate Operations, Polk County, Fla.", *Integrated Mined-Area Reclamation and Land Use Planning*, vol. 3B, Argonne, Ill.: Argonne National Laboratory, 1977.
697. Dasmann, op. cit.
698. "Sweden Refuses Permits For Strip Mining of Slate," *World Environment Report*, Feb. 14, 1977, p. 6.
699. "Create Land Reserve at Scene of Diamond Boom," *World Environment Report*, Aug. 28, 1978, p. 8.
700. Ariel Lugo, Council on Environmental Quality, personal communication, 1979.
701. *Environmental Quality 1977*, op. cit., pp. 87; 89, 90.
702. *Asbestos: The Need for and Feasibility of Air Pollution Controls*, Washington: National Academy of Sciences, 1971; *Relationship Between Environmental Quality, Health, and Safety and the Availability and Price of Minerals*, Washington: Environmental Protection Agency, Nov. 17, 1978.
703. Ibid.
704. *Environment and Development*, Washington: World Bank, June 1975, pp. 17–18.
705. S. N. Linzon, "Effects of Sulfur Oxides on Vegetation," *Canadian Forestry Chronicle*, vol. 48, no. 4, 1972, pp. 1–5.
706. Carl M. Shy, "Health Hazards of Sulfur Oxides," *American Lung Association Bulletin*, Mar. 1977, pp. 2–7.
707. Luther J. Carter, "Uranium Mill Tailings: Congress Addresses a Long-Neglected Problem," *Science*, Oct. 13, 1978, pp. 191–95.
708. Ibid.
709. Ibid.
710. Ibid.
711. Ibid.
712. *Preliminary Findings, Radon Daughter Levels in Structures Constructed on Reclaimed Florida Phosphate Land,*

Washington: Environmental Protection Agency, Oct. 1975.

713. *Phosphate—1977,* Mineral Commodity Profiles MCP-2, Washington: Bureau of Mines, May 1977, p. 14.

714. *Relationship Between Environmental Quality, Health, and Safety,* op. cit.

715. J. M. Bradley, "East and West Germany Squabble Over Polluted Werra River," *World Environment Report,* Oct. 24. 1977, p. 2.

716. A. E. Cullinson, "Collapse of Slag Yard Dams in Japan Pollutes Two Rivers," *World Environment Report,* June 5, 1978, p. 5.

717. "Environmental Protection Unit Established in Philippines," *World Environment Report,* June 20, 1977, p. 8.

718. "Japanese Agency Studies Filippino Mine Wastes," *World Environment Report,* May 22, 1978, p. 8.

719. Loretta McLaughlan, "Chemical Congress in Peru Indicts Copper Mine Pollution of Rivers," *World Environment Report,* Dec. 5, 1977, p. 6; "New Peruvian Method Recovers Copper From Water," *World Environment Report,* July 4, 1977, p. 6.

720. Human Resources Network, op. cit., p. 180.

721. "Reserve Mining Company to Remain in Minnesota," *New York Times,* July 8, 1978, p. 35; M. Howard Gelfan, "Mining Firm Wins a Round in Dumping Fight With State," *Washington Post,* Feb. 1, 1977, p. 43.

722. Irving J. Selikoff, "Asbestos in Water," in *Water—Its Effect on Life Quality,* Seventh International Water Quality Symposium Proceedings, Lombard, Ill.: Water Quality Research Council, 1974.

723. D. B. Brooks and P. W. Andrews, "Mineral Resources, Economic Growth and World Population," in P. H. Abelson and A. L. Hammond, eds., *Materials: Renewable and Nonrenewable Resources,* Washington: American Association for the Advancement of Science, 1976, pp. 41–47.

724. D. E. Earl, "A Report on Charcoal," Rome: Food and Agriculture Organization, 1974.

725. "Arvores por Ferro," *Veja* (Brazil), Nov. 8, 1978, pp. 77–78.

726. Earl T. Hayes, "Energy Implications of Materials Processing," in Abelson and Hammond, op. cit., pp. 33–37.

727. Ibid.

728. Harry M. Caudill, *Night Comes to the Cumberlands: Biography of a Depressed Area,* Boston: Little, Brown, 1963.

729. Bradley op. cit.

**Closing the Loops**

730. William P. Elliot and Lester Machta, eds., *Workshop on the Global Effects of Carbon Dioxide from Fossil Fuels, 1977,* Washington: U.S. Department of Energy, May 1979, p. 24.

731. *Report of the Scientific Workshop on Atmospheric Carbon Dioxide, 1976* Geneva: World Meteorological Organization, 1977, p. 13.

732. *World Climate Conference: Declaration and Supporting Documents,* Geneva: World Meteorological Organization, Feb. 1979, p. 4.

733. Ibid., p. 4.

734. George M. Woodwell, et al., "The Carbon Dioxide Problem: Implications for Policy in the Management of Energy and Other Resources," Washington: Council on Environmental Quality, July 1979.

735. "Making the Most of the $CO_2$ Problem" *Science News,* Apr. 14, 1979, p. 244. Op. cit.

736. William W. Kellog, "Facing Up to Climatic Change," *Ceres,* vol. 11, 1978, pp. 13–17. Kellog, op. cit.

737. Committee on Environmental Improvement, *Cleaning Our Environment: A Chemical Perspective,* Washington: American Chemical Society, 1978, p. 209.

738. Richard A. Kerr, "Global Pollution: Is the Arctic Haze Actually Industrial Smog?," *Science,* July 20, 1979, pp. 290–93.

739. "Gulf States to Attend Kuwait Conference," U.N. Environment Program, press release, Nairobi, Apr. 14, 1978.

740. Barry Castleman, "The Export of Hazardous Factories to Developing Nations," *International Journal of Health Services,* forthcoming, 1979; "Trouble for Export," *Washington Post,* Aug. 27, 1979, p. A26. In addition, the Health Hazard Export Study Group of the University of Connecticut Health Center will sponsor a conference on the Exportation of Hazardous Industries to Developing Countries on Nov. 2 and 3, 1979 at Hunter College, New York City. The conference will be held in conjunction with the annual meeting of the American Public Health Association. Conference proceedings will be available in Jan. 1980 from ABT Associates, Cambridge, Mass.

741. "Increasing Available Water Supplies Through Weather Modification and Desalination," New York: U.N. Water Resources Branch, 1976.

742. Clyde LaMotte, "The U.S. Plan to Control Water Pollutions," *Ocean Industry,* June 1970. pp. 39–45.

743. *Environmental Quality 1978,* annual report of the Council on Environmental Quality, Washington: Government Printing Office, 1978, p. 446.

744. David Pimentel et al., "Land Degradation: Effects on Food and Energy Resources," *Science,* vol. 194. 1976, pp. 149–55.

745. See *Conservation Foundation Newsletter,* Dec 1978.

746. Robert C. Oelhaf, *Organic Agriculture,* New York: Wiley, 1979; also see William Tucker, "The Next American Dust Bowl," *Atlantic Monthly,* July 1979, pp. 38–49.

747. David Vail, "The Case for Organic Farming." *Science,* July 13, 1979, pp. 180–81.

748. Harold E. Dregne, cited in "Desertification: What is it? Where is it? Who has it? Is it expensive? How does it happen?" *IUCN Bulletin,* (International Union for the Conservation of Nature and Natural Resources), Aug./Sept., 1977, p. 45.

749. Scientific Committee on Problems of the Environment, "Arid Lands in Developing Countries: Environmental Effects," Paris: International Council of Scientific Unions, 1976.

750. United Nations Environment Program press release, Nairobi, Sept. 14, 1977.

751. "Perennial Corn Hope," *Development Forum,* Mar. 1979, p. 5.

752. "Riceless World?" *Development Forum,* Mar. 1979, p. 5.

753. O. Beingolea Guerrero, "Integrated Pest Control, Latin America," Conference on Environmental Sciences in Developing Countries, Nairobi, Feb. 1974.

754. Lim Guan Soon, "Integrated Pest Control, Asia," Conference on Environmental Sciences in Developing Countries, Nairobi, Feb. 1975.

755. Guerrero, op. cit.

756. Ray Smith, "Economic Aspects of Pest Control," Univ. of Calif., Berkeley, 1970 (unpublished paper).

757. *The State of Food and Agriculture, 1976,* Rome: Food and Agriculture Organization, 1976.

758. Richard M. Adams et al., *Methods Development for Assessing Air Pollution Control Benefits,* vol. 3, *A Preliminary Assessment of Air Pollution Damages for Se-*

*lected Crops Within Southern California,* Washington: Environmental Protection Agency, Feb. 1979.

759. Anne K. Robas, *South Florida's Mangrove-Bordered Estuaries: Their Role in Sport and Commercial Fish Production,* Sea Grant Information Bulletin no. 4, Univ. of Miami, 1970.

760. United Nations Environment Programme, *The Mediterranean Action Plan,* Nairobi, 1977; also see the program's 1977 press releases nos. 85, 147, and 162.

761. *Coastal Zone Pollution in Indonesia with Emphasis on Oil: A Reconnaissance Survey,* Washington: Smithsonian Institution, 1974.

762. Asia Bureau, U.S. Agency for International Development, "Environmental Assessment of the Small Farm Systems in the Phillipines," Washington, 1978.

763. U.S. Water Resource Council, *The Nation's Water Resource, 1975–2000,* vol. 1, *Summary,* Washington: Government Printing Office, 1978.

764. "The Macroeconomic Impact of Federal Pollution Control Programs: 1978 Assessment," report submitted to the Environmental Protection Agency and the Council on Environmental Quality by Data Resources, Inc., Cambridge, Mass; Jan. 11, 1979.

765. D. M. Costle, "The Benefits of a Cleaner Environmental," *EPA Journal,* Jan. 1979, pp. 2–3.

766. Thomas D. Crocker et al., *Methods Development for Assessing Air Pollution Control Benefits,* vol. 1., *Experiments in the Economics of Air Pollution Epidemiology,* Washington: Environmental Protection Agency, Feb. 1979.

767. "Health Benefits from Stationary Air Pollution Control Appear Substantially More than Costs," Environmental Protection Agency, press release, Mar. 29, 1979.

767a Castleman, op. cit.

768. National Academy of Sciences, Committee on Resources and Man, *Resources and Man,* San Francisco: Freeman, 1969, p. 5.

769. There is an extensive literature on this general subject. For a short introduction, see Lester R. Brown et al., *Twenty-Two Dimensions of the Population Problem,* Washington: Worldwatch Institute, Mar. 1976. For a well articulated Marxist perspective on this subject, see Mahmood Mamdani, *The Myth of Population Control,* New York: Monthly Review Press, 1972.

770. National Oceanic and Atmospheric Administration, *New York Bight Project Annual Report for FY 1976–76T,* Boulder: Marine Ecosystems Analysis Program, Dec. 1977, p. 28.

771. Council on Environmental Quality, *Report to the President by the Toxic Substances Strategy Committee: Public Review Draft,* Washington, Aug. 1979.

772. Dennis Hanson, "Earthlog," *Audubon,* Nov. 1978, pp. 14, 16–17; "A Nightmare in Niagara," *Time,* Aug. 14, 1978, p. 46.

773. Robert H. Boyle, "Getting Rid of the PCBs," *Audubon,* Nov. 1978, p. 150; "N.Y. Plan to Remove PCBs" *Science News,* July 15, 1978, p. 39.

774. *Environmental Quality 1978,* op. cit., p. 183; John C. Fuller, *The Poison that Fell from the Sky,* New York: Random House, 1977, p. 94.

775. John Walsh, "Seveso: The Questions Persist Where Dioxin Created a Wasteland," *Science,* Sept. 9, 1977, pp. 1064–67; Fuller, op. cit.; Thomas Whiteside, "A Reporter at Large: Contaminated," *New Yorker,* Sept. 4, 1978, pp. 34–81 (published also as *The Pendulum and the Toxic Cloud,* New Haven: Yale, 1979).

776. See references 769.

Part II

# Analysis of Projection Tools:
# The Government's Global Model

# 14 The Government's Global Model: The Present Foundation

This chapter introduces Part II of the Global 2000 Study's *Technical Supplement*. Part I (Chapters 1–13) responded to the first aspect of the President's directive establishing the Study: to make a "study of the probable changes in the world's population, natural resources, and environment to the end of the century." Part II (Chapters 14–23) responds to the second aspect of the President's directive: that "this study will serve as the foundation of our longer-term planning."*

Specifically, Part II describes and analyzes the set of formal computer-based models and less formal computational procedures used to develop the projections presented in Part I. It is these models and procedures, rather than the projections themselves, that constitute the real "present foundation" for the government's longer-term planning. This is because:

- These models and procedures embody—in an outward and visible form—many of the assumptions present in the minds of those responsible for the government's longer-term planning.
- These models and procedures are actually used by Government planners to help delineate the implications of those assumptions, to test and revise those assumptions where appropriate, and more generally to provide analytic support for long-term policy decisions.

A presentation of the government's present foundation for longer-term planning requires both a holistic overview of the entire set of models and procedures underlying the projections and a detailed examination of each model and procedure. This first chapter of Part II provides the holistic overview, while Chapters 15–23, which follow,

describe and analyze each element of the set individually. This chapter can be thought of as primarily examining the external relationships among a set of "black boxes," whereas Chapters 15–23 explore the internal contents of each black box in detail. For the reader's convenience, a summary description of each "element" (or black box) is provided at the end of this chapter.

## The "Government's Global Model"

Throughout Part II of this volume, the set of formal models and the less formal computational procedures used to develop the Study's projections are referred to, collectively, as the "government's global model" (for projecting probable changes in the world's population, natural resources, and environment to the end of the century).* Of course, the U.S. Government does not presently have an integrated computer model of the world. In fact, it may at first seem inappro-

---

*Additional specialized terms and phrases used in Part II:

*Computer-based model*—For the purposes of the Global 2000 Study, a computer program which simulates the behavior of some real-world phenomenon (for example, population growth or the patterns of world food trade) by using mathematical equations to make projections.

*Input*—Data (including assumptions) required before use can be made of a computer-based model or other computational procedure.

*Output*—Data created as a result of making use of a computer-based model or other computational procedure.

*Endogenous calculations*—Calculations performed by a computer-based model or other computational procedure.

*Exogenous calculations*—Calculations performed either in preparing input before making use of a computer-based model or other computational procedure, or in preparing output after making use of a computer-based model or other computational procedure.

*Dynamically calculated projections*—For the purposes of the Global 2000 Study, projections made endogenously for a future year that are dependent in part on projections (also made endogenously) for a preceding year or years.

*Statically calculated projections*—For the purposes of the Global 2000 Study, projections made endogenously for a future year that are independent of projections made endogenously for a preceding year or years. Exogenous changes in the input determine the year for which the projections are being calculated.

---

*Part III of this volume (Ch. 24–31) also responds to the second aspect of the President's directive by describing, analyzing, and comparing several highly integrated, long-term, global models not currently in extensive use by the U.S. government. These models and their projections provide important additional insights for use in analyzing the Global 2000 Study's projections and otherwise strengthening the present foundation for the government's longer-term planning.

priate for this report to make reference to this collection of analytic procedures as though it were a fully integrated entity—with a food sector maintained by the Department of Agriculture, an energy sector maintained by the Department of Energy, an environmental sector scattered through many agencies, and so forth.

Instead, each agency has its own idiosyncratic way of projecting the future, based on its own responsibilities and interests. These different approaches were never designed to be used as part of an integrated, self-consistent system like the "government's global model." They were designed by different people, at different times, using different perspectives and methodologies, to meet different needs. While many are widely recognized as making outstanding use of state-of-the-art analytic procedures appropriate to their respective sectors, they produce projections that are mutually inconsistent in important ways.

Nevertheless, there are at least three compelling reasons for describing and evaluating these different approaches as a collective whole:

1. The various sectoral models and calculation procedures (arbitrarily aggregated in this discussion into a set of 11 "elements") have, to a limited degree, actually been developed and maintained in ways that involve mutual interactions via an informal, almost glacial process.
2. Projections developed using these elements have generally been used by the government and others as though they had been calculated on a mutually consistent basis.
3. These elements should be capable of being used on a mutually consistent basis—regardless of how they have actually been developed and maintained, and regardless of how their projections have generally been used. In fact, the President implicitly directed that the elements be used and evaluated in this way when he commissioned the Global 2000 Study.

The U.S. Government has a large collection of analytic procedures for anticipating future trends in a wide range of areas. The Global 2000 Study asked the federal agencies to develop projections using the methodologies that they routinely use for this purpose.

These methodologies—or tools—can be considered collectively as elements of the government's overall global model. Normally these elements are not employed in ways that ensure that the assumptions they use are mutually consistent. For the purposes of this study, ensuring consistency became a high priority, and every effort was made to enhance interactions and consistency among elements.

But in spite of the discipline established by the Study to ensure consistency, a number of internal contradictions were inherent in the analysis and, unavoidably, they remain. To put it more simply, the analysis shows that the executive agencies of the U.S. Government are not now capable of presenting the President with internally consistent projections of world trends in population, resources, and the environment for the next two decades.

These contradictions do not completely invalidate the overall results of the Study—in fact, the Study's projections are the most consistent such set the government has ever produced—but they do suggest that the results of the projections understate the severity of potential future problems. The analysis also points to ways in which the quality of the government's long-term analytic tools can be improved.

One of the most important findings of the Study is that the sectoral trends projected in Part I interact with each other in the real world in ways that are not represented in the government's global model—essentially because of the institutional context in which the elements of the model were developed and are being used. This context emphasizes sectoral concerns at the expense of interactions among sectors and leads to distorted and mutually inconsistent projections. Important decisions—involving billion-dollar federal programs and even the national security—are partially based on these projections.

In the discussion that follows, the "present foundation" (the government's global model) is first described in terms of its scope and in terms of the linkages between its elements. With this overall description to work from, the operation of the elements as a collective whole is analyzed. The implications of this analysis are then examined with regard to (1) interpreting the projections and (2) strengthening the present foundation. Finally, the 11 elements of the government's global model are summarized, using a fixed format to facilitate comparisons.

The remainder of this chapter is divided into five sections and several subsections, as follows:

## Description of the Present Foundation

The government's present foundation for longer-term planning—the government's global model, as previously defined—is more than the sum of its parts. It is the sum both of its 11 elements and of the linkages among them. For the reader's convenience, the projections and detailed discussions in this volume related to each of the 11 elements are cross-referenced in Table 14–1.

The discussion that follows first reviews the decisions made in defining the scope of the Global 2000 Study, then describes the linkages that existed prior to the President's directive establishing the Study, and, finally, describes the linkages established under the limited discipline imposed by the Study.

### Scope of the Global 2000 Study

Within the scope of the President's directive, several decisions were made that played a major role in determining the ultimate shape of the Global 2000 Study by alternately selecting and excluding factors and considerations related to long-term global analysis:

1. The mandate of the Global 2000 Study was to focus on trends and changes rather than on goals. The Study was to look ahead, primarily to the year 2000 but not much beyond. It was concerned with biophysical matters, as opposed to social, political, and economic developments. While economic considerations were introduced in a limited way to help tie the projections together, economic, political, and social, considerations were essentially outside the scope of the Study.

2. Analytic methods were used wherever possible, to the exclusion of more normative or qualitatively descriptive approaches that might have been used to gather ideas and opinions from country and sectoral experts.* Naturally, the government makes use of many computational procedures for policy analysis other than those used by the Global 2000 Study, and many organizational units make use of sources other than those relied on by the Study. But, in general, those other procedures produce projections that are either not global and long-term, (i.e., to the end of the century, as defined by the President's directive) or not generally used by the governmental unit with primary responsibility for developing the type of projections required for this Study. Hence, such procedures were not included among the 11 elements comprising the government's global model appropriate for meeting the objectives of this Study.†

3. Wherever possible, use was made of the tools, data, and capabilities available within the federal government. This choice was made to fa-

**TABLE 14–1**

**Index to Projections and Detailed Discussions Related to Each of the 11 Elements of the Government's Global Model**

| Element | Projections Developed Using the Element Part I, Chapter | Detailed Description of the Element Part II, Chapter |
|---|---|---|
| *In the order presented in the last section of this chapter* | | |
| 1. Population | 2 | 15 |
| 2. GNP | 3 | 16 |
| 3. Climate | 4 | 17 |
| 4. Technology* | 5 | 23 |
| 5. Food | 6 | 18 |
| 6. Fisheries, Forestry, Water | 7,8,9 | 19 |
| 7. Energy | 10 | 20 |
| 8. Energy residuals | 10 | 20 |
| 9. Fuel minerals | 11 | 21 |
| 10. Nonfuel minerals | 12 | 22 |
| 11. Environment | 13 | 19 |

* A composite element, bringing together under a single heading the various assumptions and approaches related to the technological innovations used by the different elements, together with their deployments and impacts.

*For example, the field anomaly relaxation method for projecting whole-body future patterns, developed by the Stanford Research Institute.
† Broad surveys of other models used by the U.S. Government are provided in *A Guide to Models in Governmental Planning and Operations,* Washington: Environmental Protection Agency, Aug. 1974, and in G. Fromm et al., *Federally Supported Mathematical Models: Survey and Analysis,* Washington: National Science Foundation, June 1975. A discussion of the evolving role of models in governmental processes is provided in M. Greenberger et al., *Models in the Policy Process,* New York: Russell Sage Foundation, 1976.

cilitate an evaluation of the present foundation for longer-range planning—but as a result of this decision, the contributions of many tools available in universities, the private sector, and other institutions were omitted. A further consequence of this choice is that individual agency views were not cross-evaluated with other perspectives from the private sector, except to the extent that these may have been incorporated in the views and criticisms of the Study's advisers.

4. Among the tools available in the federal government, it was necessary to pick and choose specific topical areas within the broader categories of population, natural resources, and the environment. Some of these choices were voluntary, others were not. For example, grasslands are a resource that could not be evaluated in the time available. While mineral consumption is projected, mineral demand, supply, and price are not projected because the government has no capability to project these on a global basis. The long-term global environmental analysis was assembled from a large number of sources, most of them outside the government, since the government has no capacity for such analysis that could be brought to bear on the Study.

5. Among the many variables selected for projection, some basic disaggregations were made, but disaggregation was not possible in every case or, necessarily, in even the most significant cases. For example, the number, age, and sex of the world's human populations were considered, but other factors (for example, educational, rural-urban, racial, religious, income, and other socioeconomic distributions) were not. Total energy consumption was considered, but not in terms of the end-use requirements for low-grade versus high-grade forms of energy; no net energy considerations were included. Out of nearly 100 resources traded internationally, only 12 were considered. Competition among crops for arable land was not specifically considered. Also, the environmental projections could not be geographically disaggregated in many cases because of the limitations of available data.

## Linkages Prior to the Global 2000 Study

Each of the various agencies and departments of the executive branch of the federal government has always had some capacity to make long-term assessments of global trends related to population, natural resources, and the environment—such as the assessments discussed in Appendix A. Recent examples include *World Population: 1977* by the Bureau of the Census, *World Food Situation and Prospects to 1985* by the Department of Agriculture, *Mineral Facts and Problems* by the Bureau of Mines, and *World Energy Prospects* by the Department of Energy's predecessor, the Federal Energy Administration.

Prior to the Global 2000 Study, such reports were generally prepared largely independently of each other.* Little formal attempt was made to ensure that the assumptions used by one agency were consistent with those used by another. Little consideration was given to mutual interactions and feedback over time. Little heed was paid to intersectoral problem areas and concerns that were not the immediate responsibility or a special interest of that particular agency. Instead, it was implicitly assumed that long-term issues relating to population, natural resources, and the environment could be studied and analyzed on a largely independent basis.

Interaction among various elements of the government's global model still tends to occur very infrequently. Even the activities of the interagency task forces cited in Chapter 1 and discussed at greater length in Appendix A have done little to improve coordination among the government's numerous computational procedures. This is due largely to the relatively narrow focus and brief life span of most of those procedures. They tend to focus on a single set of narrowly conceived factors directly relevant to specialized sectoral concerns and to give priority to more pressing and parochial short-term tasks.

While it is true that the individual reports discussed in Appendix A have been independently prepared, there has always been some interaction between the agencies as they proceeded to formulate their projections. But most interactions occur as part of a relatively slow process. In general, one agency completes and publishes a study report, which, when read by other agencies, informs the future study efforts of those agencies.

Those individual studies have not all been undertaken at the same time, of course, nor have they necessarily made use of mutually consistent assumptions. Thus, while some feedback (and some interaction) does occur, as manifested in the process just described (and occasionally in formal and informal task force collaborations), such feedback tends to be extremely limited. Nevertheless, when viewed from this perspective, a quasi-integrated governmental global model can be seen

---

*The extent to which formal collaborative joint task force efforts were undertaken is discussed in Appendix A. The trend has been increasing, but the Global 2000 Study is the first official study to use all 11 elements concurrently.

that is more than the sum of a set of independent elements and their respective projections.

A signal indication of the relative lack of direct interaction among the elements and associated experts (prior to the Global 2000 Study) was provided when the Global 2000 staff met with the agency experts responsible for the maintenance and operation of the 11 elements of the government's global model. With one or two exceptions at the most, none of the agency experts had met each other previously, and none knew anything about the assumptions, structures, requirements, and uses of the others' calculation procedures—although on occasion they were required to make use of projections developed by the other elements.

## Linkages Under the Limited Discipline of the Global 2000 Study

The various agencies' miscellaneous published projections could have been used as the Global 2000 Study's projections, but while this would have addressed the first aspect of the President's directive establishing the Study, it would not have addressed the second. The foundation thus established would have been of unknown reliability, making interpretation of the projections uncertain. Moreover, no basis would have been established for strengthening the present foundation.

Therefore, a special limited discipline was established for the Global 2000 Study—that is, a conscious choice was made (1) to employ, wherever possible, the very tools and data used within the federal government, and (2) to employ those tools and data on the most coordinated basis feasible within the constraints of the Study. In keeping with this decision, the Global 2000 Study's central staff established three criteria to be followed in developing the Study's projections, namely, that the projections be developed using analytical procedures, wherever possible, which were essentially (1) long-term, (2) global, and (3) in general use by the agencies primarily responsible for the type of projections required by the Study.

It was also clear that the normal linkages and mode of operation of the government's global model were not adequate for the Global 2000 Study, and so a special effort was made to increase linkages between the elements and to improve the consistency of these assumptions by:

• Using the output from one element as the input to another whenever this was readily feasible within the time and resource constraints of the Study.

• Providing special opportunities for relevant agency experts to exchange views with each other in order to encourage them to make their elements (and derived projections) more mutually consistent.

• Providing special opportunities for the various agency experts to exchange views with and receive comments from various experts not directly affiliated with the participating agencies. This also was done to encourage the agency experts to make the elements (and their derived projections) more mutually consistent.

The initial assignments of responsibility to the appropriate agencies have already been presented in Chapter 1. The agencies identified experts, both inside and outside the agencies, whom the agencies considered most appropriate for discharging the responsibility of preparing the projections requested by the Study's central staff. These "agency experts" (identified in the Acknowledgment section of the Preface) then became responsible for selecting and utilizing analytical procedures that they felt best met the Study's criteria.

The agency experts were asked to produce a first draft of their projection in just six weeks, at which time they, the Study staff, and a small group of outside experts* met for a weekend synthesis meeting. The purpose of the meeting was to improve the consistency of the projections and to begin—at least subjectively—to consider the implications of the natural resource and environmental projections for the independently derived projections of gross national product (GNP) and population. A certain amount of difficulty was anticipated in this preliminary meeting, and, in fact, many inconsistencies were revealed. The experts then decided collectively how best to adjust and modify the projections to improve the internal consistency of the whole set. The final projections were prepared during the following two months.

The projections had to be undertaken as part of a sequential process, since the structures of the elements themselves precluded their being used simultaneously. This process is illustrated in Figure 14–1.

While this sequential process permitted some interaction among the various elements of the government's global model, many important linkages could not be included at all. In particular, the population and GNP projections that were

---

*These experts are also identified in the Acknowledgments section of the Preface to this volume. A discussion of their activities, together with a summary of their views, is presented in Appendix B.

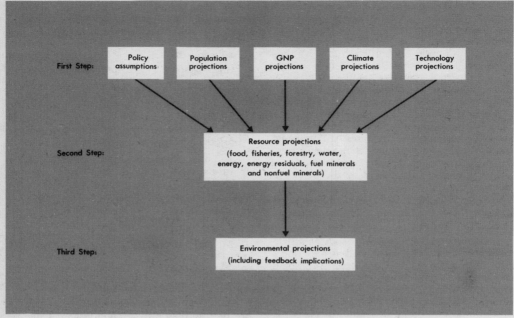

**Figure 14-1.** Sequential steps followed in linking elements of the government's global model.

prepared during the first step were based largely on extrapolations of past trends and were uninformed by interactive feedback from the resource and environmental projections or from each other. The resource and environmental analyses also projected developments that could significantly feed back to and influence each other, but these feedbacks were also not represented by explicit linkages.

Although an attempt was made to develop projections of resource consumption and environmental impacts using a single source for population projections and GNP projections, this effort was only partially successful.* While projections provided by these single sources were used in preparing the Study's food and energy projections,

they were not used in preparing the climate, technology, fisheries, forestry, water, fuel minerals, and nonfuel minerals projections. Nor were they used explicitly in preparing the environmental projections derived from the other projections.†

The limited extent to which both vertical and horizontal linkages were actually established for the Study is indicated in Figure 14–2. Additional steps were taken by the Study in order to obtain some indication of the extent to which the environmental impacts projected by the Study would have influenced the Study's other projections—had they been available and taken into account when those projections were made. These steps were discussed previously in the "Closing the Loops" section of Chapter 13 and are therefore

---

*Another initial objective was to examine the implications of the projections as they applied to a specific geographic region. This examination would have provided another test of the consistency of the projections and would also have given the global (sometimes nebulous) projections a more specific geographic reference for policy analysis. Unfortunately this examination could not be completed within the time and resource constraints of the Study because of the major differences in the ways that the various models represent geographic regions. Nonetheless, an effort was made in the preparation of Chapters

15–23 to provide the reader with as much detailed numeric information as possible on one arbitrarily selected region—North Africa. The interested reader may wish to examine further the additional problems and inconsistencies exposed by drawing this information together for purposes of comparison.

† Similarly, it was not possible to ensure that the assumption of no significant policy change was followed in developing the various projections (as shown later, in Table 14–2 and summarized in the element descriptions at the end of this chapter).

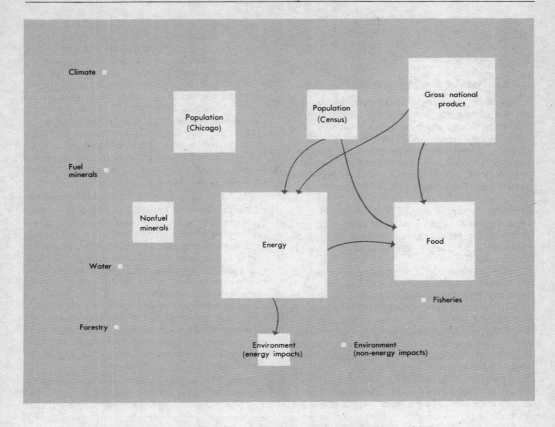

**Figure 14-2.** Linkages achieved between elements of the government's global model. Areas are proportional to the complexity of explicit quantitative relationships. The small squares represent negligible complexity.

not discussed further in this chapter, nor included in Figure 14-2.

Attempts by the Study to link together the elements of the government's global model focused entirely on linking the outputs of one element with the inputs of another. Because of the severe difficulties encountered in meeting even this limited objective, no attempt was made to evaluate deeper linkage opportunities or the challenges related to melding the various structures and paradigms.

A crude measure of uncertainty surrounding the projections was obtained as part of the limited discipline of the Global 2000 Study by requesting all participants to provide high, medium, and low variations of their projections wherever feasible. In practice, the high, medium, and low variations

that were prepared in making the resource and environmental projections were largely obtained by varying the population and GNP assumptions on which they were based. Most of the participating agency experts were reluctant to assign either statistical or subjective estimates of relative probability to these variations.

Even under the limited discipline of the Global 2000 Study, multiple sources for population and GNP projections were used in developing many of the Study's other projections. For this reason, inconsistencies unavoidably abound in the Study's collected set of projections—as well as for other reasons which will be discussed later in this chapter. Nevertheless, under the discipline of the Study, more consistency was achieved regarding linkages as basic as the use of consistent population and GNP projections than in any previous official governmental projections related to long-term, global trends in population, natural resources, and the environment.*

## Analysis of the Present Foundation

The tacit assumption underlying the development and use of each separate element of the government's global model has been that long-term global trends in population, natural resources, and the environment can be projected separately in an essentially consistent and accurate manner. This assumption is false. As will be seen in the following analysis, projections from the government's global model fail to meet the most fundamental test of consistency—that the basic conclusions of an analysis shall not contradict its basic premises. And because the conclusions are not mutually consistent, they cannot be accurate.†

While consistency is a necessary prerequisite for accuracy, consistency alone does not ensure accuracy. Projections which should be and are consistent can nevertheless be wrong. Moreover, certain real-world phenomena in a state of dynamic disequilibrium (for example, markets where supply and demand are not in balance) would be inaccurately represented by projections in which supply and demand were statically balanced in accordance with a foolish consistency.

Nor does accuracy ensure usefulness. The ultimate usefulness of a projection (and, in a sense, its accuracy) can only be judged relative to its intended purpose. And it is likely that different criteria should be used to evaluate different projections, depending on the purposes for which the projections were developed. For example, some

projections are best evaluated in terms of how well the underlying equations are fitted to past data. Others are best evaluated in terms of how well the equations can be defended as logically representing relationships existing in the real world. Some projections are best evaluated in terms of how accurately and precisely they predict (1) the timing of events in the real world or (2) the particular values pertaining to certain variables at particular times. Others are best evaluated in terms of how well they illuminate possible future patterns of behavior, even if the timings and magnitudes of the patterns they project are not precisely accurate.

The various elements of the government's global model were not designed to be used on a fully mutually consistent basis, even though projections developed using them are often treated as though they were. Therefore, it is in a sense unfair to the designers of these elements to analyze them on a holistic basis—even though a holistic perspective is, as discussed in the previous section, a basic requirement of the President's directive creating the Study. Moreover, it would have been more unfair to the designers of the elements to note that the elements are capable of performing a number of agency-specific functions not required under the mandate of the Global 2000 Study.

Despite the numerous inconsistencies which are about to be analyzed, the projections developed for this Study using the government's global model are the most complete and internally consistent ever developed by the executive agencies of the government. The central staff of the Global 2000 Study concluded, as have many of the Study's advisers, that the overall findings are

---

*The projections reported in this Study are based on the collective judgment of the agency experts who participated in the effort. In an effort to ensure internal consistency, several adjustments were required in individual agency projections. As a result, the projections may not agree completely with projections previously published by the participating agencies. Since the manuscript has not been subjected to formal interagency clearance procedures, the agencies are not responsible for any errors in fact or judgment that may have occurred in making these adjustments.

† One of the problems in analyzing models (and one of the strengths of models) is that models change over time. The models analyzed here are the models used to develop the Global 2000 Study projections. Since the projections were developed, several of these models have been modified, improved, or expanded, in some cases in response to problems and issues identified in the course of this study. The Department of Agriculture has established links to the International Institute for Applied Systems Analysis in Vienna and with the Mesarovic-Pestel World Integrated Model. The Department

of Energy is exploring feedback relationships to GNP. The Central Intelligence Agency is developing an expanded capability for nonfuel minerals analysis and projections. The World Bank has developed a new economic model which, Bank analysts report, eliminates many of the problems identified in this report. New projections also differ from those prepared for the Global 2000 study. The World Bank is projecting lower growth rates. The Department of Energy now expects oil price increases to occur sooner than projected and to have more impact on economic growth. The Department of Agriculture anticipates increases in the real price of food to occur sooner. The Bureau of the Census now expects life expectancies to increase more slowly than projected in some countries. While there have been changes in both individual models and projections, nothing has changed fundamentally concerning the problems of inconsistency and internal contradiction that occur when an effort is made to integrate the projections from the various elements of the government's global model. The basic problem addressed by this chapter has not changed and is not soon likely to change significantly.

valid, for reasons that will be discussed later in this chapter in the section entitled "Interpreting the Projections."

The essential problem with the current elements of the government's global model (and the projections derived from them) is, of course, the fact that they were designed to simulate sectoral aspects of long-term global trends largely to the exclusion of interactions between and among sectors. This design is no institutional accident but is in conformity with the bureaucratic division of responsibility within the executive agencies.* But real-world phenomena interact—especially in the longer term—in ways that do not conform to the bureaucratic division of responsibility or to narrowly focused sectoral models. Hence, the government's global model in its present form can only imperfectly project the consequences of these interactions. Furthermore, in the absence of ongoing institutional incentives to address cross-sectional interactions, the present form of the government's global model is not likely to change significantly in the foreseeable future.

The following analysis of the government's global model addresses six subjects: (1) the ubiquitous and important inconsistencies in the government's global model; (2) the extent to which the inconsistencies result from the use of diverse sources of information; (3) the extent to which the inconsistencies are due to the absence of important feedback relationships; (4) the various structural differences between the elements that make calibration difficult; (5) some of the institutional factors that underlie the discrepancies—including the use of the elements to develop projections intended primarily for advocacy purposes.

## Inconsistent Variable Values

The 11 elements of the government's global model make use of many of the same variables—for example, population growth rates. Some assumed values are assigned to these variables prior to making use of an element, while other values are calculated as an intermediate or final step in developing an element's projections.

In many cases, the values assigned to the same variables by different elements are inconsistent

*This fragmented approach is not unique to the executive branch. The U.S. Congress, through its committee structure, faces similar (but somewhat different) difficulties in systematically analyzing interrelated issues.

with each other.* For example, one set of projections assumed that population growth rates in the less developed countries (LDCs) would decline significantly, while another calculated that they would not. One set of projections assumed that per capita gross national product (GNP) in the LDCs would increase significantly, while another calculated it would not.

In order to help the reader understand the collective implications of these numerous inconsistencies, the following discussion is divided into four subsections, each of which addresses an important set of inconsistent variable values (the overwhelming number of environmental projection findings—discussed at length in Chapter 13—which explicitly contradict major variable values involving virtually all the other elements, are not included). The first subsection concerns population and GNP growth rates; the second and third, commodity trade prices and volumes; the fourth, capital and resource utilization. Each subsection consists of a paragraph providing a brief perspective on a set of inconsistencies, a diagram visually summarizing the set, and an itemization of specific inconsistencies.† The inconsistencies presented are representative but not exhaustive; nor are the four aggregates into which they have been grouped exhaustive. Other aggregates could have been assembled to make other points, but these four seemed sufficient to establish the ubiquity and seriousness of the inconsistencies.

### Inconsistent Population and GNP Growth Rates

The Global 2000 Study population and GNP projections were developed independently of each other and appear to be mutually inconsistent. Because these projections were used to calibrate several of the Study's other projections, the distortions created by their inconsistencies have skewed those other projections. Additional dis-

*The variables described here as inconsistent are not always precisely or even approximately commensurable. Therefore, the "inconsistencies" cited in this discussion should be understood as apparent only and subject to further verification. It was not possible to reconcile them more closely with each other within the time and budget constraints of the Global 2000 Study.

† In these somewhat technical itemizations, many methodologies and reports are referred to by short names or abbreviations—for example, the "cohort-component methodology" or the "WAES study." Providing even a brief explanation of these terms in this context would have distracted the reader's attention from the inconsistencies that are the focus of the immediate discussion. The reader is referred to the final section of this chapter for a brief explanation of these terms and to Chapters 15–23, where each is described at greater length.

crepancies were created when still other projections in the preceding chapters utilized population and GNP projections developed independently of the Study.

Figure 14–3 illustrates some of the inconsistencies regarding population and GNP growth rates. Four of the 11 numbered "elements"* considered in this chapter are involved: population (1), GNP (2), food (5), and nonfuel minerals (10). Four apparent inconsistencies are discussed below: (A) LDC social and economic development, (B) LDC population growth, (C) world population growth, and (D) GNP growth in LDCs. The arrows represent linkages that should or did occur. The broad end of the arrow is attached to the source of a particular type of information; the arrowhead indicates where the information is required as an input. The plus and minus symbols locate points of apparent inconsistency in the linkages.

A. *LDC Social and Economic Development.* The food element (5), the GNP element (2), and the population element (1), of the government's global model appear to have posited different rates of LDC social and economic development. Specifically, the Department of Agriculture's GOL (Grain, Oilseed, Livestock) model projected (in the medium-growth case, over the 1970–2000 period) that global per capita food consumption will increase only slightly and that this increase will not be evenly distributed, so that declines will be experienced in some LDCs. Similarly, the WAES (Workshop on Alternative Energy Sources) study, which is an integral part of the GNP element (2), projected (in the medium-growth case, which averages the two WAES cases, over the 1985–2000 period) that in some countries (e.g., Brazil, Mexico, Bangladesh) real per capita GNP (calculated using the Global 2000 Study's population projections) is likely to increase only marginally and that in others (e.g., Pakistan) real per capital GNP is likely to decline. In contrast, the Census Bureau's cohort-component methodology assumed (in all three cases, over the 1975–2000 period) that all LDCs will continue to make moderate progress in social and economic development.

B. *LDC Population Growth.* The population element (1) and the GNP element (2) appear to have posited different population growth rates in the LDCs. Specifically, the Census Bureau's co-hort-component methodology projected (in the medium-growth case, over the 1975–2000 period) that the LDCs will not experience significantly lower total population growth rates over the 1985–2000 period relative to the 1975–85 period—that is, the average annual growth rate over the 1985–2000 period (2.09 percent) was projected to be only 0.07 percentage points lower than the average annual growth rate over the 1975–85 period (2.16 percent).* In contrast, the WAES study arbitrarily reduced all GNP growth rates (including those of the LDCs) by roughly 10–30 percent (in both WAES cases, over the 1985–2000 period) to reflect the projected impact of assumed declining population growth rates on GNP growth.

C. *World Population Growth.* The population element (1) and the nonfuel minerals element (10) appear to have posited different population growth rates for the industrialized nations relative to world population growth rates. Specifically, the Census Bureau's cohort-component methodology projected (in the medium-growth case, over the 1975–2000 period) that average annual U.S. and U.S.S.R. population growth (0.6 and 0.8 percent, respectively) will be significantly lower than average annual world population growth (1.8 percent)—despite, for example, a projected 20 percent increase in U.S. fertility rates over the same period. In contrast, the 1977 Malenbaum Report relied upon by the Department of the Interior assumed (in the one case presented, over the 1973–2000 period) that average annual U.S. and U.S.S.R. population growth (1.0 and 1.3 percent, respectively) will be less dramatically lower than average annual world population growth (1.9 percent).

D. *GNP Growth in LDCs.* The GNP element (2) and the nonfuel minerals element (10) appear to have posited different GNP growth rates in the LDCs. Specifically, the WAES study projected (in the medium-growth case, which averages the two WAES cases, over the 1975–2000 period) that collectively African, Asian, and Latin American GNP will increase roughly 5 percent per year. In contrast, the IOU (Intensity of Use) methodology relied upon by the Department of the Interior assumed (in the one case presented, over the 1973–2000 period) that collectively African, Asian and Latin American GNP will increase roughly 3.5 percent per year.

---

*The number following each element is the sequence number arbitrarily assigned to that element in the last section of this chapter.

*In the Bureau of the Census high-growth series, the average annual population growth rate in the LDCs actually increases from 2.32 percent per year over the 1975–85 period to 2.39 percent per year over the 1985–2000 period.

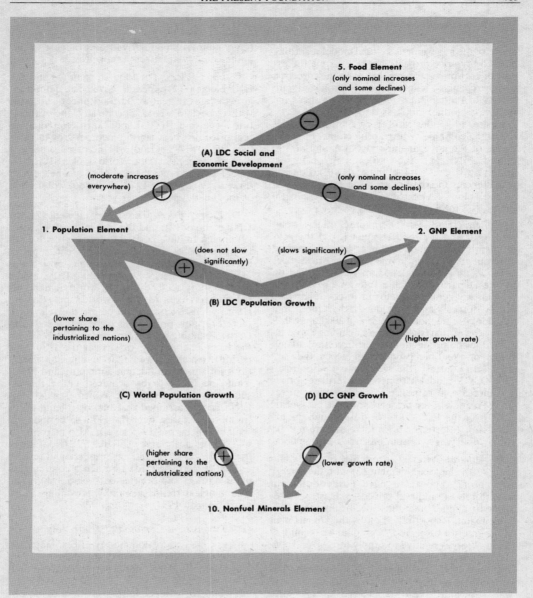

**Figure 14-3.** Inconsistent population and GNP growth rates.

## Inconsistent Commodity Trade Prices

Major disparities exist among many of the elements of the government's global model regarding commodity price projections. Not merely the extent of real-price changes, but even the direction of such changes, is inconsistently projected with regard to fundamental price variables involving fertilizer, nonfuel minerals, food, and energy.

Figure 14–4 illustrates major inconsistencies regarding commodity price projections. Five elements of the government's global model are involved: GNP (2), food (5), energy (7), fuel minerals (8), and nonfuel minerals (10). Four inconsistencies in commodity trade prices are discussed below: (A) fertilizer prices, (B) mineral prices, (C) food prices and (D) energy prices.

A. *Fertilizer Prices.* The nonfuel minerals element (10) and the food element (5) of the government's global model appear to have posited different growth rates in real fertilizer prices. Specifically, the 1977 Malenbaum Report relied on by the Department of the Interior projected "a gradual weakening of demand forces relative to supply forces" and concluded, therefore, that "the long-term tendency, 1985 and 2000, may thus be for lower materials prices [including those involved in the production of fertilizers] relative to prices of the final products in which they are used." In contrast, the Department of Agriculture's GOL model assumed that fertilizer prices will increase in response to rising energy prices (in the rising-energy-price case and the pessimistic case, over the 1970–2000 period), though the exact assumed fertilizer price increases are not explicitly disaggregated from other cost assumptions.

B. *Mineral Prices.* The nonfuel minerals element (10), the GNP element (2), and the energy element (7) appear to have posited different growth rates in mineral prices—at least, with respect to copper and tin. Specifically, the 1977 Malenbaum Report relied on by the Department of the Interior projected "a gradual weakening of demand forces relative to supply forces" and concluded, therefore, that "the long-term tendency, 1985 and 2000, may thus be for lower materials prices relative to prices of the final products in which they are used." In contrast, the World Bank's SIMLINK (SIMulated trade LINKages) model assumed growth in average real prices for copper and tin (in all three cases, over the 1975–85 period) to be roughly 5.2 and 2.5 percent per year, respectively. Also in contrast, the Energy Department's IEES (International Energy Evaluation System) model assumed (in all four cases, over the 1975–90 period) that the various resources indirectly required to produce energy (e.g., nonfuel minerals) will be available in unlimited supply at current real prices.

C. *Food Prices.* The food element (5) and the GNP element (2) appear to have posited different growth rates in real-world food prices—at least, with respect to wheat. Specifically, the Agriculture Department's GOL model projected that the real price of wheat (in the medium-growth case, over the 1970–85 period) will increase 2.1 percent per year. In contrast, the World Bank's SIMLINK model assumed that the real world price of wheat (in all three cases, over the 1975–85 period) will decline at roughly 0.6 percent per year.

D. *Energy Prices.* The energy element (7), the GNP element (2), and the fuel minerals element (9) appear to have posited different growth rates in energy prices—at least, with respect to petroleum prices. Specifically, preliminary projections made by the Energy Department's IEES model for the Study showed that the world demand for petroleum is likely to exceed world supply (at constant real 1978 prices) well before the year 2000; therefore, new projections were developed arbitrarily assuming a 5 percent per year increase (in the rising-energy-price case, over the 1980–1990 period), which showed that equilibrium conditions for supply-and-demand quantity and prices would be likely to be achieved under this assumption. In contrast, the World Bank's SIMLINK model assumed that real petroleum prices (in all three cases, over the 1975–85 period) will remain constant at 1975 levels. Also in contrast, U.S. Geological Survey Circular 725 (from which the Study's U.S. oil and gas resource and reserve estimates were derived) assumed a continuation of 1974 prices and of price-cost relationships and technological trends generally prevailing a few years prior to 1974.

## Inconsistent Commodity Trade Volumes

As in the case of commodity prices, major disparities exist among many of the elements of the government's global model regarding commodity trade volume projections. The GNP projections, for example, assumed lower growth rates in world food trade than projected by the food element and higher growth rates in world minerals trade than projected by the nonfuel minerals element.

Figure 14–5 illustrates some of the major inconsistencies regarding commodity trade volumes. Four elements of the government's global model are involved: GNP (2), food (5), fisheries

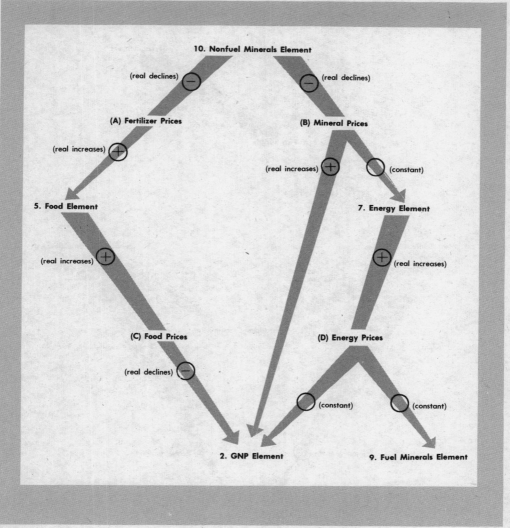

**Figure 14-4.** Inconsistent commodity trade prices.

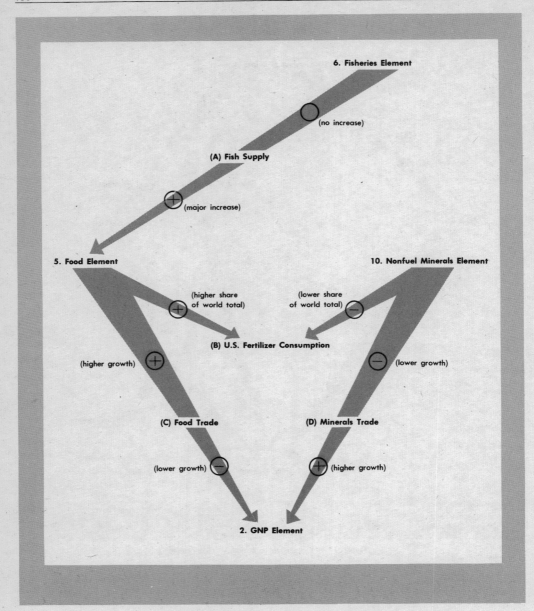

**Figure 14-5.** Inconsistent commodity trade volumes.

(6), and nonfuel minerals (10). Four inconsistencies are discussed below: (A) fish supply, (B) U.S. fertilizer consumption, (C) food trade, and (D) minerals trade.

A. *Fish Supply.* The fisheries element (6) and the food element (5) of the government's global model appear to have posited different growth rates in world fish catches. Specifically, the Commerce Department's judgmental forecasting procedures projected (in the medium case, the only case projected, over the 1975–2000 period) that while catches of some species may increase, others are likely to decrease, keeping the total annual fish catch essentially constant. In contrast, the Agriculture Department's total food submodel assumed in essence that the size of each country's fish catch (except in the case of Japan) will provide a constant percentage of the food needs of each country (in all four cases, over the 1975–2000 period), implicitly requiring that the annual fish catch for each country (except Japan) increase at essentially the same rate as population.

B. *U.S. Fertilizer Consumption.* The food element (5) and the nonfuel minerals element (10) appear to have projected different growth rates in U.S. fertilizer consumption relative to growth rates in the rest of the world—at least, with respect to phosphate rock (which is used primarily for fertilizer). Specifically, the Agriculture Department's fertilizer submodel projected growth in U.S. fertilizer consumption (in the medium, constant-energy-price case, the only case projected, over the 1973–2000 period) to be somewhat lower (3.2 percent per year) than in the rest of the world (4.0 percent per year). In contrast, the Interior Department's calculations (loosely based on the 1972 Malenbaum Report) projected growth in U.S. consumption of phosphate rock (in the most probable case, over the 1973–2000 period) to be significantly lower (2.6 percent per year) than in the rest of the world (5.9 percent per year).

C. *Food Trade.* The food element (5) and the GNP element (2) appear to have posited different growth rates in world food trade—at least, with respect to wheat. Specifically, the Agriculture Department's GOL model projected growth in trade in wheat between all countries (in the medium-growth case, over the 1970–85 period) to be 4.1 percent per year. In contrast, the World Bank's SIMLINK model assumed growth in trade in wheat between the industrailized nations and the LDCs (in all three cases, over the 1975–85 period) to be 2.5 percent per year.

D. *Minerals Trade.* The nonfuel minerals element (10) and the GNP element (2) appear to have posited different growth rates in quantities of minerals traded in world markets—at least with respect to aluminum and zinc. Specifically, the IOU methodology relied upon by the Department of the Interior projected growth in world consumption of primary aluminum and zinc (in the one case presented, over the 1973–85 period) to be 4.2 and 3.3 percent per year, respectively. In contrast, the World Bank's SIMLINK model assumed growth in trade in a collective category of certain key minerals (namely, bauxite, lead, phosphate rock, silver, and zinc) between the industrialized nations and the LDCs (in all three cases, over the 1975–85 period) to be 6.3 percent per year.

## Inconsistent Capital and Resource Utilization

No consistent accounting was made of capital and resource allocations among the eleven elements of the government's global model. Thus, significant omissions or double-counting may have been implied in projected levels of water availability and some forms of capital investment. Significant omissions or double-counting may also be involved in assumptions regarding the future allocation of land and labor. But it is impossible to compare these assumptions in this discussion, since they were completely inexplicit in almost all elements and could not be inferred without extensive analysis beyond the scope and resources of the Global 2000 Study.

Figure 14–6 illustrates some of the significant omissions or double-counting that may have occurred regarding capital and resource utilization. Six elements of the government's global model are involved: GNP (2), food (5), water (6), energy (7), energy residuals (8), and nonfuel minerals (10). Four inconsistencies are discussed below: (A) water availability, (B) investment in agricultural inprovement, (C) investment in pollution control, and (D) LDC resource consumption.

A. *Water Availability.* The water element (6), the food element (5), the GNP element (2), the energy element (7), and the nonfuel minerals element (10) appear to have posited different levels of water availability. Specifically, the judgmental forecasting procedures used by the Study's water consultants projected (in the medium case, the only case presented, over the 1975–2000 period) that problems of water shortage will be more widespread and severe by 2000 than they are now—in part as a result of extensive deforesta-

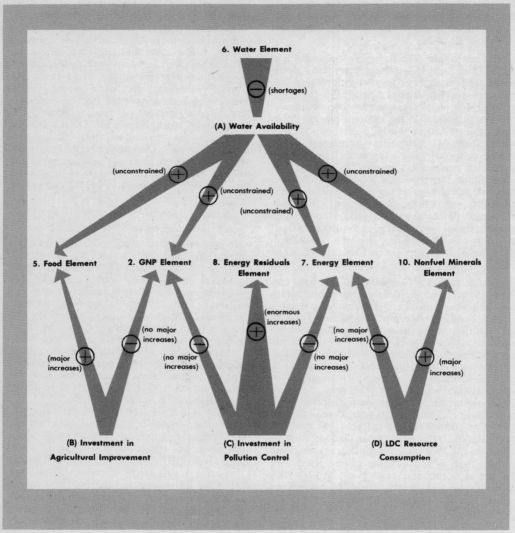

**Figure 14-6.** Inconsistent capital and resource utilization.

tion. In contrast, the Agriculture Department's GOL model assumed (in all four cases, over the 1970–2000 period) no explicit limitations on water availability (at current real prices), although limitations on arable land were explicitly considered. Also in contrast, the World Bank's SIMLINK model assumed (in all three cases, over the 1975–85 period) that foreign exhcange earnings rather than savings, capital, or labor will constrain GNP growth in the LDCs; resource availability (e.g., water) was not assumed to be a binding constraint. Also in contrast, the Energy Department's IEES model assumed (in all four cases, over the 1975–90 period) that the various resources indirectly required to produce energy (e.g., water) will be available in unlimited supply at current real prices. Also in contrast, the IOU methodology relied upon by the Department of the Interior assumed (in the one case presented, over the 1973–2000 period) that long-term growth in minerals and materials consumption will not be governed by supply limitations (e.g., water).

B. *Investment in Agricultural Improvement.* The food element (5) and the GNP element (2) appear to have assumed different growth rates in investment for agricultural improvement. Specifically, the Agriculture Department's GOL model assumed (in all four cases, over the 1970–2000 period) that major increases in public and private investment will be made throughout the world to increase cropped areas. In contrast, the World Bank's SIMLINK model assumed (in all three cases, over the 1975–85 period) that the proportion of an LDC's GNP allocated for agricultural improvement will not vary markedly from recent historic experience.

C. *Investment in Pollution Control.* The energy residuals element (8), the GNP element (2), and the energy element (7) appear to have assumed different growth rates in investment for pollution control. Specifically, the Energy Department's IEES–ESNS (International Energy Evaluation System–Energy System Network Simulator) model assumed (in all three cases, 1975–90) that an extremely large investment in pollution control technologies will be made by all countries by 1985 so that by that time all energy conversion facilities throughout the world will meet or will have been retrofitted to meet 1978 U.S. new source performance standards for carbon monoxide, sulfur dioxide, nitrous oxides, and particulates. In contrast, the World Bank's SIMLINK model assumed (in all three cases, over the 1975–85 period) that the proportion of an LDC's GNP allocated for environmental protection will not vary markedly

from recent historic experience. Also in contrast, the Energy Department's IEES model assumed (in all four cases, over the 1975–90 period) that the real cost of applying technology to protect the environment will not significantly increase the real cost of building or operating energy facilities in the future.

D. *LDC Resource Consumption.* The energy element (7) and the nonfuel minerals element (10) appear to have assumed different growth rates in LDC resource consumption, although comparisons are not easily made. Specifically, the Energy Department's IEES model implicitly assumed (in all four cases, over the 1975–90 period) that industrialization within the LDCs will not cause LDC resource consumption (energy, in this case) to increase faster than the LDCs growth in GNP. In contrast, the IOU methodology relied upon by the Interior Department assumed (in one case presented, over the 1973–2000 period) that industrialization within the LDCs will require them to consume increasing amounts of resources (in this case, minerals and materials) per unit of per capita GNP as industrialization proceeds.

## Use of Diverse Sources of Information

There are a number of inconsistencies among the elements of the government's global model due to the different elements making use of different sources of information for the same sets of assumptions.

For example, many federal agencies, including the Departments of Agriculture, Energy, and the Interior have customarily made use of international population estimates and projections developed by organizations other than the Bureau of the Census. These estimates vary widely, as may be seen in the following recent estimates of the average annual rate of LDC population growth in 1975:

|  | *Percent* |
|---|---|
| U.S. Agency for International Development | 1.88 |
| U.S. Bureau of the Census | 2.25 |
| U.N. Secretariat, Population Division | 2.34 |
| Environmental Fund (privately sponsored) | 2.55 |

Projections of future population growth rates are usually even more divergent than these estimates of past population growth rates.

Many federal agencies have also often made use of divergent international GNP projections developed by organizations other than the World Bank's Economic Analysis and Projections Department. The State Department's Agency for International Development, for example, has cus-

## TABLE 14–2

### Selected Contrasting Assumptions of the 11 Elements of the Government's Global Model

| The 11 Elements of the Government's Global Model | Cases Presented | Selected Policy Assumptions | Selected Population Assumptions | Selected GNP Assumptions | Selected Climate Assumptions | Selected Technology Assumptions |
|---|---|---|---|---|---|---|
| 1. Population | a. High-growth case<br>b. Medium-growth case.<br>c. Low-growth case | Major extension of family planning throughout the world | Zero net migration between regions | Moderate social and economic progress throughout the world over the 1975–2000 period | Not considered | No major technology breakthroughs or setbacks affecting fertility or mortality rates |
| 2. GNP | a. High-growth case<br>b. Medium-growth case<br>c. Low-growth case | Continuation or implementation of prudent policies to maximize export earnings | Major reduction in population growth rates in all countries over the 1985–2000 period | GNP growth in LDCs largely dependent on industrial nation GNP growth | Not considered | Major increasing returns on most LDC gross capital investment |
| 3. Climate | a. Warming case<br>b. Constant temperature case<br>c. Cooling case | Deliberate human efforts to modify climate excluded | Not explicitly considered | Not explicitly considered | Extreme climatic change not considered | Deliberate human efforts to modify climate excluded |
| 4. Technology | The same technology assumptions usually applied to all cases pertaining to a given element; no coordination of assumptions among different elements | Extensive deployment of family planning, nuclear-power and air pollution-abatement technologies (some of which may require significant policy changes in some countries) | No major technical breakthroughs or setbacks affecting fertility or mortality rates | Major increasing returns on most LDC capital investment | Deliberate human efforts to modify climate excluded | Major technological progress in almost all projections; no technological setbacks or adverse side effects anticipated |
| 5. Food | a. Optimistic case<br>b. Middle case<br>c. Pessimistic case<br>d. Rising-energy-price case | Major public and private investment in agricultural land development continued; worldwide shift toward more fossil-fuel-intensive agricultural techniques | a. Global 2000 low-growth case<br>b. Global 2000 medium-growth case<br>c. Global 2000 high-growth case<br>d. Global 2000 medium-growth case | a. Global 2000 high-growth case<br>b. Global 2000 medium-growth case<br>c. Global 2000 low-growth case<br>d. Global 2000 medium-growth case | Explicit assumption of no climatic change | Widespread deployment of fertilizer and other yield-enhancing inputs, producing steadily increasing yields—comparable to the increases experienced over the past two decades. |

| Selected Food Assumptions | Selected Fisheries, Forestry, and Water Assumptions | Selected Energy Assumptions | Selected Energy Residuals Assumptions | Selected Fuel Minerals Assumptions | Selected Nonfuel Minerals Assumptions | Selected Environmental Assumptions |
|---|---|---|---|---|---|---|
| Not explicitly considered (except as noted under "Selected GNP Assumptions") | Not explicitly considered (except as noted under "Selected GNP Assumptions") | Not explicitly considered (except as noted under "Selected GNP Assumptions") | Not explicitly considered (except as noted under "Selected GNP Assumptions") | Not explicitly considered (except as noted under "Selected GNP Assumptions") | Not explicitly considered (except as noted under "Selected GNP Assumptions") | Not explicitly considered (except as noted under "Selected GNP Assumptions") |
| Lower trade volumes at lower prices than Global 2000 food projections | Not explicitly considered | Unlimited energy at constant real prices | Not considered | Unlimited energy at constant real prices | Higher trade volumes at higher prices than Global 2000 nonfuel minerals projections | Not explicitly considered |
| Not explicitly considered | Not explicitly considered | Not explicitly considered | Not explicitly considered | Not explicitly considered | Not explicitly considered | Not explicitly considered |
| Widespread deployment of fertilizer and other yield-enhancing inputs, producing steadily increasing yields comparable to the increases experienced over the past two decades. | Development of less wasteful methods for harvesting nontraditional fish species; development of less wasteful methods and of methods for exploiting nontraditional forestry species; water assumptions unknown | Widespread deployment of light-water nuclear electric power plants | By 1985, all countries' energy facilities retrofitted to meet U.S. new source performance standards for CO, $SO_x$, $NO_x$, and particulates | Continuation of the price-cost relationships and technical trends generally prevailing in years prior to 1974 assumed in all U.S. oil and gas resource and reserve estimates | Increasingly less intensive mineral use in highly industrialized countries; increasingly more intensive mineral use in LDCs. | Side effects of technology, coupled with institutional and social problems, appear to be the root cause of many of the world's most serious environmental problems; but technology can also solve many problems |
| No major increase in meat share of LDC diets | Major increases in fish catches implicitly assumed; adverse impacts of deforestation not considered; explicit assumption of unlimited water at constant real prices | a. Constant energy price<br>b. Constant energy price<br>c. Global 2000 rising-energy-price case<br>d. Global 2000 rising-energy-price case (In all cases, unlimited energy supply assumed at cited costs) | Not considered | No fuel resource constraints (other than price) | No nonfuel minerals resource constraints (except energy price effects) | No large scale land degradation due to environmental or human factors (other than urbanization) and no increased pest resistance. |

**Table 14–2** (cont.)

| The 11 Elements of the Government's Global Model | Cases Presented | Selected Policy Assumptions | Selected Population Assumptions | Selected GNP Assumptions | Selected Climate Assumptions | Selected Technology Assumptions |
|---|---|---|---|---|---|---|
| 6. Fisheries | A single medium case. | Improved management of fisheries and protection of the marine environment on a worldwide basis | Assumptions not explicit | Assumptions not explicit | Not considered | Development of methods for harvesting nontraditional fish species |
| Forestry | A single medium case | Some policy changes throughout the world regarding current deforestation practices | Assumptions not explicit | Assumptions not explicit | Not considered | Development of less wasteful production techniques and of methods for exploiting nontraditional forestry species |
| Water | a. Higher case<br>b. Lower case | Unknown | Unknown | Unknown | Unknown | Unknown |
| 7. Energy | a. Optimistic case<br>b. Middle case<br>c. Pessimistic case<br>d. Rising-energy-price case | Implementation of more effective energy conservation programs within the OECD countries; OPEC countries to supply oil to meet residual demand up to their maximum production capacity | a. Global 2000 low-growth case<br>b. Global 2000 medium-growth case<br>c. Global 2000 high-growth case<br>d. Global 2000 medium-growth case | a. Global 2000 high-growth case<br>b. Global 2000 medium-growth case<br>c. Global 2000 low-growth case<br>d. Global 2000 medium-growth case | Not considered | Widespread deployment of light-water nuclear electric power plants |
| 8. Energy residuals | a. Optimistic case<br>b. Middle case<br>c. Pessimistic case | Major public and private investment in air pollution abatement technologies by all countries | Not explicitly considered (except as derived from preceding energy projections) | Not explicitly considered (except as derived from preceding energy projections) | Not considered | By 1985, all countries' energy facilities retrofitted to meet U.S. new source performance standards for $CO$, $SO_x$, $NO_x$, and particulates |
| 9. Fuel minerals | A single medium case | Continuation of 1974 prices assumed in all U.S. oil and gas resource and reserve estimates | Not considered | Not considered | Not considered | Continuation of the price-cost relationships and technical trends generally prevailing in years prior to 1974 assumed in all U.S. oil and gas resource and reserve estimates |

| Selected Food Assumptions | Selected Fisheries, Forestry, and Water Assumptions | Selected Energy Assumptions | Selected Energy Residuals Assumptions | Selected Fuel Minerals Assumptions | Selected Nonfuel Minerals Assumptions | Selected Environmental Assumptions |
|---|---|---|---|---|---|---|
| Not considered | Water projections not considered | Not considered | Not considered | Not considered | Not considered | No significant pollution affecting growth of fishery stocks; no significant losses of estuarian areas |
| Not considered | Water projections not considered | Not considered | Not considered | Not considered | Not considered | No significant impacts affecting forest growth (e.g., acid rain, increased UV radiation, or increased pest resistance) |
| Unknown | Unknown | Unknown | Unknown | Unknown | Unknown | Unknown |
| Not considered | No nonfuel resource constraints in the industrialized countries (except as limited by GNP); bio-energy resource constraints in the LDCs | Net energy not explicitly considered | Not considered | Not directly related to the Study's fuel minerals projections | No nonfuel resource constraints (except as limited by GNP) | Not explicitly considered |
| Not considered | No resource constraints | a. Global 2000 optimistic case b. Global 2000 middle case c. Global 2000 pessimistic case | No capital investment constraints | Not considered | Not considered | By 1985, all countries' energy facilities retrofitted to meet U.S. new source performance standards for CO, SO$_x$, NO$_x$, and particulates |
| Not considered | Not explicitly considered | Not directly related to Study's energy projections | Not considered | Net energy not explicitly considered | Not explicitly considered | Not explicitly considered |

**Table 14–2** (cont.)

| The 11 Elements of the Government's Global Model | Cases Presented | Selected Policy Assumptions | Selected Population Assumptions | Selected GNP Assumptions | Selected Climate Assumptions Selected | Selected Technology Assumptions |
|---|---|---|---|---|---|---|
| 10. Nonfuel minerals | A single medium case | No changes | Single set of projections derived from U.N. projections | Single set of projections based on Malenbaum's personal judgment | Not considered | Increasingly less intensive mineral use in highly industrialized countries; increasingly more intensive mineral use in LDCs |
| 11. Environment | Same cases as provided for each element, but generally only medium cases analyzed | No policy changes (except as derived from preceding projections) | Global 2000 medium case | Global 2000 medium case | Several environmental developments assumed potentially capable of influencing global climate | Technologies are generally available to address the world's most serious environmental problems (e.g., soil erosion and deterioration); social and institutional problems (not technological problems) are often the primary impediment to environmental protection |

tomarily relied on the World Bank's generally more optimistic individual country analyses. The Department of Agriculture's Economics, Statistics, and Cooperatives Service has customarily used projections developed by the U.N. Food and Agriculture Organization (FAO). The Department of Energy's Energy Information Administration has used projections made by the intergovernmental Organization for Economic Cooperation and Development (OECD). The Interior Department's Bureau of Mines has relied on international economic projections developed by Professor Wilfred Malenbaum of the University of Pennslyvania.*

Under the limited discipline achieved by the Global 2000 Study, much more consistent use than heretofore was made of the projections developed using the population and GNP elements by other elements of the government's global model. Nevertheless, inconsistent assumptions abound, as shown in Table 14–2, which provides a cross-index of selected, diverse assumptions used by the elements. Many of these inconsistent assumptions are described in greater detail in the summaries of the various elements presented in the last section of this chapter and in Chapters 15–23.

Even a single set of assumptions may contain internal inconsistencies as a result of being compiled from diverse sources. For example, the U.S. government does not maintain its own single, consistent source of GNP projections. The GNP projections most frequently used pertaining to the

---

*The FAO and OECD projections have tended to be significantly higher than those of the World Bank and Professor Malenbaum. Moreover, these projection differences have tended to be significantly greater on a regional or country by country basis than on a global basis.

| Selected Food Assumptions | Selected Fisheries, Forestry, and Water Assumptions | Selected Energy Assumptions | Selected Energy Residuals Assumptions | Selected Fuel Minerals Assumptions | Selected Nonfuel Minerals Assumptions | Selected Environmental Assumptions |
|---|---|---|---|---|---|---|
| Not considered | Explicit assumption of no resource constraints | Explicit assumption of no resource constraints | Explicit assumption of no environmental constraints | Explicit assumption of no resource constraints | Explicit assumption of no resource constraints | Explicit assumption of no environmental constraints |
| Global 2000 rising-energy-price case | Global 2000 medium case | Global 2000 rising-energy-price case | Global 2000 medium case | Global 2000 medium case | Global 2000 medium case | Considered extensively on a comprehensive, interrelated basis |

OECD countries* are those assembled by the headquarters staff of the OECD. The most frequently used GNP projections for the LDCs are those developed by the World Bank. The most frequently used GNP projections for the centrally planned economies are those developed by the U.S. Central Intelligence Agency.

Each of these sources prepares its projections using different statistical conventions and independently developed assumptions regarding the future. Such GNP projections are therefore not internally consistent, as noted in Chapter 3. Because they are not collectively maintained by the

*The Organization for Economic Cooperation and Development includes the following countries: Australia, Austria, Belgium, Canada, Denmark, Finland, France, the Federal Republic of Germany, Greece, Iceland, Ireland, Italy, Japan, Luxembourg, the Netherlands, New Zealand, Norway, Portugal, Spain, Sweden, Switzerland, Turkey, the United Kingdom, and the United States.

U.S. government, it was not possible within the mandate and constraints of the Global 2000 Study to examine in any detail the assumptions underlying the GNP projections routinely used by the government.* What information is available suggests that population, resources, and the environment are not taken into account through any explicit functional relationships and are included only judgmentally, if at all.

Three further problems related to the use of diverse sources for GNP projections are noted below. They are representative of the types of problems encountered when diverse sources are also used for population, food, energy, and other projections:

*However, one important computer model used to develop GNP projections (the World Bank's SIMLINK model) is discussed in some detail in Chapter 16.

1. The GNP projections published by the OECD for its member nations are widely regarded as "pious hopes." To obtain a measure of realism, the World Bank has routinely adjusted the OECD projections substantially downward before using them. Further downward adjustments were made by the WAES study* (and recommended for Global 2000 Study use by World Bank analysts) to account for the fact that those GNP projections have in the past been based on the assumption made by individual OECD nations that they will be able in the future to import unrealistically large amounts of OPEC oil.

2. The World Bank's projections of LDC growth rates assume that the primary force driving LDC economic progress is growth in the economies of the industrialized countries. As yet, neither the theory nor the specific numbers involved in this assumption have been adequately validated. The theoretical and numeric basis underlying the GNP projections for the centrally planned economies are subject to even less general agreement.

3. The Global 2000 Study's per capita GNP figures come directly from combining the population and GNP projections, which were developed independently of each other and have been shown previously in this chapter to be mutually inconsistent. Moreover, in projecting beyond about 10 years, all the Study's GNP projections have been based on a simple exponential growth model involving an assumed percentage of annual compound growth. This exponential growth assumption produces absurd results in the long run† and assumes implicitly that no resources or environmental constraints will be encountered that cannot be overcome by unspecified technological developments (which themselves are further assumed to create no constraining resource or environmental problems). To the extent that the GNP projections include any consideration of population, natural resources, or the environment, that consideration is exogenous, judgmental, and not open to examination or verification.

---

*The World Alternative Energy Strategies study sponsored by the Massachusetts Institute of Technology, which is discussed in Chapter 16. The GNP projections for LDCs developed for that study are presented as part of the Global 2000 Study's GNP projections in Chapter 3.

† World Bank analysts note that their official GNP projections rarely extend more than 10 years into the future. The exponential growth rates mentioned above were developed as a special accommodation to the needs of the WAES study and were never intended to be applicable beyond the year 2000.

## Absence of Feedback

A second critical factor accounting for the inconsistencies previously presented is the general lack of feedback between elements of the government's global model. Under the limited discipline (described earlier in this chapter) established by the Global 2000 Study, only a few basic linkages were made between the elements, as shown schematically in Figure 14–2. But even if a much more strict and comprehensive discipline had been possible (for example, the use of single sources of information for related input assumptions required by the elements), two fundamental structural problems related to feedback would have been encountered in attempting to link the elements together on a consistent basis:

- The elements have been designed to accommodate only the sequential unidirectional linkages previously shown in Figure 14–1—that is, the population and resource projections must precede the resource projections, which must precede the environmental projections.

- The sets of assumptions which are made prior to using many of the elements are "frozen" in the sense of not being responsive to changed conditions in the course of projection computations.

These two problems are actually two dimensions of the same feedback issue. The first problem, regarding sequential unidirectional linkages, focuses on intersectoral distortions—the fact that certain sectors are represented in the government's global model as influencing others, but as not themselves being influenced by others. The second problem, regarding "frozen" sets of assumptions, focuses on temporal distortions—the fact that the general absence of feedback produces increasingly severe inconsistencies the further into the future the projections are extended.

*Sequential Unidirectional Linkages.* In most of the elements of the government's global model, population and GNP are conceived as "driving forces." Given assumed levels of population and GNP, the various elements calculate the consumption of food, energy, minerals, and other resources. But no calculations are made regarding the influence of the scarcity or abundance of food, energy, minerals, and other resources—as projected by their respective elements—on population or GNP. Similarly, no calculations are made regarding the influence of environmental factors—as projected by the environmental element—on population, GNP, or the various natural resources.*

In the case of the population projections, for example, certain extremely general assumptions are made regarding social and economic development, and in many cases these are inconsistent with the projections developed by other elements. But there is little or no provision in the population element itself that would allow precise, explicit, quantitative adjustments in the element's calculations to be made in response to the precise, explicit, quantitative calculations made by the other elements.

In short, the issue is not merely that the reverse linkages have not been made (for example, from per capita food consumption to population) but that the current structural design of the elements generally precludes their being made. The population and GNP elements are essentially incapable of taking precise account of the results of the natural resource projections. And the population, GNP, and natural resource elements are incapable of taking precise account of the results of the environmental projections. In actuality, of course, they take little or no account of them at all—precise or imprecise. While the environmental element is not capable of taking the results of the population, GNP, and resource elements precisely into account, it does at least consider them qualitatively.

It should also be noted here that even if the models were structured so as to facilitate the establishment of the needed reverse linkages, many of the linkages would have to be established conjecturally because the empirical evidence presently available is limited. However, even a conjectural linkage would, in most cases, be far preferable to the assumption of no linkage when such an assumption is known to be significantly in error. Furthermore, if sensitivity tests show the linkage to be a critical and sensitive linkage, priority can thus be established for the collection of needed empirical data.

*"Frozen" Sets of Assumptions.* Each element of the government's global model makes use of sets of assumptions (i.e., time-series inputs) which may be thought of as "frozen." They are frozen in the sense that they are determined prior to

using the element and are not altered in response to changed conditions implied by calculations made by the element and by the other elements. In other words, there is no feedback from the element's computations to the original set of frozen assumptions.

For example, as already shown in Figure 14-2:

- The population projections were developed with fixed assumptions regarding social and economic progress.
- The gross national product projections were developed with fixed assumptions regarding population growth.
- The energy projections were developed with fixed assumptions regarding population and GNP growth.
- The food projections were developed with fixed assumptions regarding increases in population, GNP, and energy prices.
- The population, GNP, and resource projections were developed with fixed assumptions concerning the environment.
- The environmental projections were developed with fixed assumptions concerning the population, GNP, and resource projections.

In some cases, the set of fixed or frozen assumptions used by one element may summarize the projections developed through the complex calculations of another element. Often these complex calculations are summarized in the form of simple time-series data or fitted equations. In other cases, the set of frozen assumptions may come from a source entirely outside the government's global model and may explicitly contradict calculations made by another element of that model. Often these frozen assumptions are not explicitly stated in quantitative terms, but may nevertheless be inferred—for example, in terms of some commodity being available in unlimited supply or at constant real prices, or both.

The government's long-term global projections implicitly assume either (1) that the use of frozen sets of assumptions would produce logically consistent projections or (2) that any inconsistencies would be relatively inconsequential in view of simplifications made in the overall representation of the global system and data uncertainty. These assumptions tend to be valid for short-term (i.e., 1–2 year) projections—where, in the absence of major dislocations, major trends generally tend to perpetrate themselves forward smoothly—but are increasingly dubious when the projections extend for 5, 10, 20, or more years. As projections are extended further into the future, feedback in-

---

*The very significant effects that the environmental projections could be expected to have on the population, GNP, and resource projections are discussed under "Closing the Loops" in Chapter 13. However, as pointed out in that chapter, all of the projections retain their basically open-loop character because none of the missing feedback linkages could actually be established through direct dynamic effects on the elements' calculations.

teractions become increasingly important as major trends collide with one another and are deflected from their original paths in complex ways. The elements of the government's global model are generally not structured and linked together in a way that allows such deflections to occur. As a result, the trends override one another and produce increasingly serious inconsistencies as the projections move further into the future.

## Structural Incompatibilities

Any model of reality necessarily selects and excludes relationships and data in order to clarify the issues it is intended to simulate. Thus, the 11 elements of the government's global model naturally embody simplifications, limitations, and omissions that may well have been entirely appropriate for the purposes for which the elements were originally designed, but which make effective coordination between elements extremely difficult. The inability or failure to transfer information represented in one element according to one set of structural conventions to a different element utilizing a different set of structural conventions provides a third explanation for the inconsistencies previously presented.

Most elements, for example, make use of different conventions for representing the world geographically, which makes coordination difficult. Some elements provide great detail on the Western industrialized nations and little detail on the LDCs, or vice versa, while most provide almost no detail on the centrally planned economies. Some elements are fundamentally incapable of simulating interactions among separate geographic regions except through changes in exogenous assumptions (so that interregional adjustments cannot be taken into account by them). Other elements are fundamentally interregional, that is, their basic purpose is to project future interregional trade balances, based on the assumption that static economic equilibrium conditions will obtain in the future in a way that maximizes total world economic efficiency for the sector for which the projection is developed.

A perspective on the geographic differences among those elements with the most complex explicit quantitative relationships is presented in the first five maps in the colored map section. These maps illustrate the extent to which each element (1) aggregates (or disaggregates) the various regions of the world and (2) makes independent (or interdependent) projections for those regions. The maps also show the level of detail represented in each aggregate.

Most elements make use of different conven-

tions for representing temporal change, which also adds to the difficulties of coordination. Some elements are theoretically capable of projecting well beyond the year 2000, others were not designed to project beyond 1985 or 1990. Some elements were designed to calculate equilibrium balances between supply and demand at equilibrating prices and are fundamentally incapable of simulating change over time, except through changes in exogenous assumptions. This means that they cannot take into account dynamic disequilibria. Other elements are fundamentally dynamic—that is, their basic purpose is to display trends and modes of behavior over time.

Other major structural differences and limitations include:

- Many elements are based on analytic methods that require crucial interdependent variables to be projected independently in advance.
- Many require these variables not to exceed historial ranges or rates of growth.
- Most are incapable of simulating fundamental structural change.
- Many have limited capacity to integrate inconsistent inputs developed using other analytical methods.

Many of these differences are summarized on an element by element basis in Table 14–3. A more complex account of them is provided in the last section of this chapter and in Chapters 15–23.

## Institutional Factors Underlying the Discrepancies

Many institutional factors underlie the inconsistencies. As Table 14–3 shows, each of the 11 elements of the government's global model was developed in a different bureaucratic context. It would be surprising indeed if the elements did not significantly differ from each other since each was developed

- by different people (even experts differ among themselves),
- at different times (the real world changes over time),
- using different perspectives and methodologies (which use different simplifying assumptions and different computational techniques),
- to meet different needs (affecting the selection of assumptions and the validation of calculations).

Moreover, it would be naive not to recognize that projections and the procedures used to pro-

## TABLE 14-3

**Selected Institutional and Structural Differences Among the Elements of the Government's Global Model**

| Element | Primary Source of Projections | Primary Computational Procedures | First Major Use | Major Geographic Representation | Temporal Representation | Number of Cases Examined |
|---|---|---|---|---|---|---|
| 1. Population | Census Bureau; University of Chicago | Cohort-component methodology | Early 1930s | The world in 23 independent regions | 1975–2000 (dynamically calculated) | 3 |
| 2. GNP | WAES Study (MIT) and World Bank | SIMLINK model; judgmental extrapolation | 1974 | Primarily 6 LDC aggregates, with limited interaction | 1975–85 (dynamically calculated) 1985–2000 (informally extrapolated) | 3 |
| 3. Climate | National Defense University study (CIA) | Weighted expert opinion | 1977 | The world in 8 regions | 1977–80, 1981–90, 1991–2000, (discontinuously calculated) | 3 |
| 4. Technology | Diverse independent sources | Diverse unrelated methodologies | Diverse | Usually global only | No consistent representation | 1 per element |
| 5. Food | Department of Agriculture | GOL model | 1974 | The world in 28 interrelated regions | 1985 2000 (discontinuously calculated) | 4 |
| 6. Fisheries, forestry, and water | NOAA; CIA; Department of the Interior | No explicit quantitative model | Diverse | Typically by interrelated ecosystem | 2000 (informally extrapolated) | 1,1,2 |
| 7. Energy | Department of Energy | IEES model | 1977 | The world in 5 interrelated regions | 1985 1990 (essentially discontinuously calculated) | 4 |
| 8. Energy residuals | Department of Energy | IEES-ESNS model | 1978 | The world in 5 independent regions | 1985 1990 (discontinuously calculated) | 3 |
| 9. Fuel minerals | Independent expert (affiliated with the Departments of Energy and the Interior) | Eclectic (based on many previous studies) | Diverse | No consistent representation | No temporal dimension | In general, 1 |
| 10. Nonfuel minerals | Professor Malenbaum (University of Pennsylvania) | IOU methodology | 1972 | The world in 10 independent regions | 1985 2000 (discontinuously calculated) | 1 |
| 11. Environment | Multiple sources coordinated by Study staff | No explicit quantitative model | Diverse | The industrial and developing economies and selected ecosystems, on an interrelated basis. | Generally 2000 (informally extrapolated) | No consistent selection of cases |

duce them have frequently been criticized by Congressional committees and others as subject to influences not purely analytical in origin. Each agency has its own responsibilities and interests, its own constituencies, and its own pet projects. Often, an agency finds it helpful to use advanced analytic techniques (and associated projections) as weapons in the adversary process of initiating, justifying, and defending its programs. As a result, there have been many occasions in which the elements (and associated projections) of the government's global model have been used in support of (or in opposition to) highly controversial programs, and the credibility of the projections has become a subject for debate. This has been especially true in recent times, as both the issues and the advanced analytic procedures used for examining the issues have become increasingly complex and, in a sense, incomprehensible to many nonexperts.

Under these conditions, government agencies have occasionally been accused of falsifying the data on which their projections are based or of adding "fudge factors" to equations to produce desired results. While these accusations are relatively infrequent, agencies have often been accused of carefully tailoring the assumptions underlying their analyses so as to ensure that desired results are attained in a way that is analytically defensible. To the extent that these circumstances occur, they contribute to the inconsistencies previously presented.

## Interpreting the Projections

The preceding analysis has identified inconsistencies, incompatibilities, and other problems, which must inevitably raise questions regarding the validity of the projections presented in Part I, Chapters 2–13. Some of these problematic issues are discussed below.

### Validity of the Basic Findings

Before discussing the implications of the problems identified in the preceding section of this chapter, it is important to point out that the projections presented in Part I nevertheless represent the most consistent set of projections ever developed making use of the set of elements that constitute the government's global model. No alternative governmental projections currently available provide a more logically coherent foundation for the government's longer-term planning. This is, of course, because the Global 2000 Study represents the first occasion in which even an effort (regardless of its deficiencies) has been made to apply—collectively and consistently—the global, longer-term methodologies routinely used by the government to project trends regarding population, natural resources, and the environment.

With this in mind, it may be helpful for the reader to review some of the most basic findings of Part I. Only the most fundamental adjustments to the elements of the government's global model would change the basic thrust of the following findings.

*Population.* Total world population growth rates will not decline significantly by the year 2000. Instead, roughly twice as many additional new people will be added to the world's population over the 1975–2000 period (on a net basis) as were added over the 1950–1975 period. A very large proportion of this population growth will occur in the LDCs, particularly in South Asia, Africa, and Latin America.

*GNP.* Per capita GNP Increases about 55 percent worldwide, but increases only marginally in several LDCs. The problems leading to the decline in the growth of per capita GNP will become more intense over the 1985–2000 period.

*Climate.* Should any climate change occur, its most adverse effects (largely involving changes in average temperature, precipitation patterns, and weather variability) are likely to be felt in the temperate regions, where most of the world's major food-exporting nations are located.

*Food.* Global per capita food consumption will not increase significantly, despite major increases in real food prices and in agricultural investment. Declines in per capita food consumption will occur in many of the poorest LDCs, with the most rapid declines occurring over the 1985–2000 period.

*Resource Prices.* The real prices of food, fish, lumber, water, and energy will increase significantly, with the steepest increases occurring over the 1985–2000 period.*

*The Environment.* Major strains will be placed on ecological systems throughout the world and, as a result, the goods and services that have heretofore been provided by the environment can no longer be simply taken for granted. The significant deterioration in terrestrial, aquatic, and atmospheric environments projected to occur around the world will inevitably impact adversely on agricultural productivity, human morbidity and mortality, overall economic development, and perhaps even on climate—among other factors. These strains are likely to be felt most strongly in the LDCs toward the end of the century, though there is much current evidence of their existence.

---

* This particular finding raises several important economic questions. If the real prices of these commodities increase as projected, for what corresponding commodities will real prices decrease? If no compensating real-price decreases are projected, what do these "real" price increases mean theoretically—or even semantically? Unfortunately, even attempting to develop answers to these difficult questions would have exceeded the time and resource constraints of the study.

In short, increasingly severe stresses will be felt on a global basis toward the end of the century. These stresses will be most severe in the world's poorest nations, but the industrialized countries will also feel their effects.

It is the conclusion of the staff of the Global 2000 Study and many of the Study's advisers that these basic findings are qualitatively correct, even taking into account the many current deficiencies of the government's global model. There are three major reasons for holding this view:

1. They represent no radical departures, for the most part, from projections published over many years by their respective sources.
2. They are supported collaterally, for the most part, by alternative projections developed by numerous organizations with similar sets of sectoral concerns.
3. They are supported (in terms of many of their most basic thrusts) by projections developed using a set of less complex but more highly integrated global models.*

If anything, the severity of the effects of these basic trends may be understated, due to the very limited feedback between the elements of the government's global model. This view is largely corroborated by projections developed using more highly integrated models.

It is also the conclusion of the staff of the Global 2000 Study and many of the Study's advisers—in view of the preceding analysis in the government's global model—that it is impossible to assign a high probability to any of the specific numeric projections presented in the preceding chapters.

**Biases Due to Inconsistent Variable Values**

The complex patterns of bias caused by the inconsistent variable values used by different elements of the government's global model make adjustment extremely difficult. In particular, a chicken-and-egg problem is encountered in attempting to make simple quantitative adjustments to any single set of projections developed by a single element of the model.

For example, the assumptions about GNP that were made in order to develop the population projections are contradicted by the GNP projections. Specifically, the population projections were based on the assumption that significant reductions in fertility will occur because of improved social and economic conditions throughout the world. But the projections of per capita GNP do not show significant improvements in economic

* These nongovernmental projections are described, analyzed, and compared in considerable detail in Part III of this volume.

conditions in many parts of the world, especially those with the most rapidly growing populations.*

Similarly, the assumptions about population that were made in order to develop the GNP projections are contradicted by the population projections. Specifically, the GNP projections were adjusted downward for the 1985–2000 period because of an assumption that population growth rates will have declined by that time. But the population projections show the world population growth rate continuing at an essentially constant 1.8 percent per year.

If one begins by adjusting the GNP projections (to resolve the obvious inconsistency regarding population), then they are adjusted upward (to take into account the lack of decline in population rates). Potentially, this makes the GNP projections consistent with the population projections (leaving the population projections unchanged).

If, on the other hand, one begins by adjusting the population projections (to resolve the obvious inconsistency regarding GNP), then they are adjusted upward (to take into account the lack of improvement in social and economic conditions). If the per capita GNP figures are then recalculated, social and economic conditions are seen to be even worse than before and another upward adjustment to the population figures is required, and so on until a limit perhaps is reached (greatly increasing the population projections). Conversely, if the second step is to readjust the GNP projections, a balance may then be struck making the population projections consistent with the GNP projections (by significantly increasing both the population and GNP projections).

Does one begin, then, by assuming the GNP projections to be correct and adjusting the population projections, or vice versa (or something in between)? Where is the lever and where is the fulcrum?

These problems are compounded as more elements and relationships are taken into consideration—such as the following:

• For example, the food projections show that in certain regions of the world (notably North Africa and the Middle East) there will be some declines in food per capita (even using the apparently too low population projections). This finding reinforces the finding of the per capita

* It should be noted, however, that these per capita GNP projections do not take into account possible shifts in patterns of distribution that could either increase or decrease the per capita incomes of different economic groups within a given population, even assuming a fixed level of overall per capita GNP.

GNP projections that social and economic conditions will not improve throughout the world.

- The food projections also assume that there will be no constraints on water development for agriculture. But this is contradicted by the water, forestry, and environmental projections, implying that a downward adjustment should be made to the food projections. This in turn would lead to a downward adjustment to the per capita food projections.

- The food projections also assume that land deterioration from intensive use will not occur. But this is contradicted by the environmental projections,* implying the need for further downward adjustments to the food projections and per capita food projections.

- Downward adjustments to the per capita food projections would necessitate increases in the population projections, lowering further the per capita food projections and requiring yet another round of adjustments.

- Higher population projections would in turn probably increase the severity of water problems (due to more pressures from fuelwood demand and increased deforestation) and the rate of land deterioration (due to more intensive farming practices), further lowering the food projections and the per capita food projections. Thus, the adjustment process would have to continue until a limit was reached (if ever).

Again, if one wanted to adjust the food, GNP, or population projections for consistency (as opposed to attempting to actually adjust and rerun the elements themselves on some more integrated basis), where is one to begin—or end? Where is the lever and where is the fulcrum?

---

* Because the environmental projections show that the combined environmental impacts of all other projections have the potential to alter almost all the other projections in generally adverse ways, there is some justification for concluding that the Global 2000 Study's projections are by and large "optimistically" biased and in need of a "pessimistic" correction. But before projections can be meaningfully described as optimistic or pessimistic, the values by which they are being judged must be made clear. For whom, where, and at what time are projections optimistic or pessimistic? Are projections of extensive firewood combustion optimistic or pessimistic for those who need heat now? Are the same projections optimistic or pessimistic for their children, or for plant breeders needing genetic resources? Projections and models are not value free, and hence relative optimism or pessimism is very much in the eye of the beholder. The perspectives and values of an American farmer and an improverished citizen from an LDC in evaluating the prospect of future food price increases by the year 2000 might be very different, so that it is not necessarily helpful to attempt to characterize the projections as biased favorably or unfavorably without careful qualifications.

## Strengthening the Present Foundation

While few concrete, quantitative steps can be taken to adjust the projections presented in Chapters 2–13 in order to improve their reliability (for reasons just discussed), several options exist for improving the current form of the government's global model itself, so that subsequent projections will become significantly more reliable. In view of the fact that billions of dollars in federal funds are currently expended based on decisions using projections developed by the various agencies, it should not be difficult to develop cost justifications for appropriate improvements. Several minor improvements to the government's global model have already been made in the course of executing the present Study, and further minor improvements are possible in the near future if a moderate commitment of the necessary resources is made. But it should also be recognized that major improvements will require (1) a new institutional commitment to the development of long-term, global analytic procedures throughout the government, and (2) a much greater investment in time and resources than was available to the Global 2000 Study.

### Need for an Ongoing Institutional Mechanism

The numerous problems currently associated with the government's global model are primarily symptoms of a deeper, more fundamental problem. The dubious assumptions, omissions, inconsistencies, and incompatibilities are only technical manifestations of a severe institutional problem: The executive branch of the government currently has no ongoing institutional entity with the explicit responsibility and authority necessary for resolving such technical and philosophical problems. In the absence of such an entity, it is difficult to imagine how the government's capabilities for longer-term analysis and planning can improve significantly.

The Study's agency experts are generally aware of the limitations in the present elements of the government's global model. With few exceptions, the agencies are planning to develop new computational procedures that will eventually replace those used now. But unless some coordination is provided, there is little reason to think that the new procedures will be any more compatible, consistent, or interactive than the present ones. A priority task, therefore, is to survey the development plans related to long-term, global analysis of all of the relevant agencies—with the objective of coordinating the modification of existing sectoral elements (or, where appropriate, the development of new sectoral elements) and of coordinating the specific needs of the agencies.

Discussions with the Study's agency experts already indicate that several additional analyses are needed if the completed Global 2000 Study is to be of maximum benefit to the agencies. Finding answers to the following questions deserves the highest priority:

1. What are the strategic and economic implications of the trends now foreseen?
2. What policy changes might be pursued to alter the trends in a desirable manner?
3. What technologies might contribute most significantly to the evolution of a more desirable future?

Fortunately, the Study has already provided a basis for initiating an increased level of interagency cooperation and coordination on data exchange and model formulation.

### Potential Technical Improvements

The extent to which relatively modest incremental modifications of the government's existing models could permit more synergistic interaction and feedback than was achieved in the Global 2000 Study is clearly an important area for early investigation. Simple modifications (e.g., developing projections in which all elements use the Study's population and GNP projections) would be relatively inexpensive and could be made relatively rapidly. Similarly, somewhat more consistent projections could be achieved simply through the imposition of a somewhat more extensive amount of coordination and arbitration. In many instances the agencies choices of different data sources and different simplifying assumptions may be inadvertent. The pressure of short-term tasks often requires the agencies' modeling experts to make expeditious simplifications, which are rarely reviewed in depth and which are difficult to revise once made. Other discrepancies may reflect real differences of opinion among the agencies responsible. But whether inadvertent or substantive, these discrepancies should be amenable to resolution through interagency negotiation and arbitration—if a suitable institutional mechanism could be held responsible for identifying the discrepancies and encouraging the negotiation and arbitration.

Iterative adjustments might further improve the projections. For example, the results of all the Global 2000 Study's projections could be used as the basis for a new set of assumptions in the existing models for the development of new GNP and population projections. These new GNP and population projections could then be used to develop new resource and environmental projections. If this cycle were repeated one or more times, it might provide a stronger degree of temporal and intersectoral interaction and consistency. But such cycles could only be executed on a block-recursive basis—that is, a full set of projections would have to be obtained from one element before making projections for another element that required the former element's projections. At best, the procedure is likely to be clumsy, time-consuming, and expensive, and there is no assurance that closure (or even moderate convergence) would be possible. Even if a major attempt had been made to resolve many of the more obvious inconsistencies and incompatibilities among the elements, major structural inconsistencies would remain, making convergences and the verification of convergences problematic.

As Chapters 15–23 demonstrate, the present elements of the government's global model are sufficiently dissimilar that incremental improvements of the kinds discussed above would be of only limited utility. Put simply, there is no possibility that the present sectoral elements of the government's global model could be used on a fully integrated, simultaneous, and interactive basis. Severe structural and computational differences among the elements preclude their being operated in this manner. Furthermore, to achieve even a modest degree of consistent, simultaneous interlinkage would require such extensive modifications of the present elements that the creation of an entirely new family of elements might well be more cost-effective.

It is doubtful, however, that the government will find it convenient anytime soon to work with a single large computer model of the world. In fact, attempting to develop and maintain a single all-purpose model might not be well advised, even in the long run. On the one hand, the departments and agencies have individual and unique projection needs that could not be satisfied easily with a single large global model. On the other hand, one model is not likely to ever be capable of providing the diverse perspectives on issues essential to the sound formulation of policy. A more pluralistic approach would therefore appear to be both desirable and necessary.

Such a pluralistic approach could incorporate several of the following principles:

• All major development and use of analytic procedures related to long-term global projecting in a government agency would continue to be undertaken by the agency or under its sponsorship—using funds and personnel allocated specifically for this purpose.

- A major effort would be made to encourage much more extensive development and use of existing and new long-term global models.
- A major effort would also be made to ensure that governmentwide protocols were established and enforced regarding documentation standards, access, reproducibility, and comparisons with standard series projections, together with other steps to facilitate public understanding of the elements of the government's global model and derived projections.

## Incorporating Broader Perspectives

Several important steps could be taken to ensure that a broader range of perspectives is drawn upon than is currently the case in developing and making use of the government's global model. For example:

1. *A coordinating body to improve understanding of models.* At present, information related to the Study projections and their underlying methodologies is not easily examined by even the policymakers and members of Congress, let alone the private sector and general public. The basic documentation on the elements of the government's global model is incomplete and of mixed quality and is only now being made available to the public as the third volume of the Global 2000 Study. If the government's computer-based tools and models are to achieve their potential for benefiting policy analysis, ways must be found to facilitate understanding of the assumptions on which they are based. One or more coordinating bodies might give attention to this problem, representing both the perspectives of analytic expertise and social, political, and economic experience.

2. *Increased interaction with the private sector, educational institutions, other national efforts, and international agencies.* Since all models are simplifications of reality, one basic purpose of a model is to provide a basis for its own improvement. An important part of any process for improving the sectors of the government's global model is increased interaction with individuals and organizations that could help to improve the government models. The private sector has much data and much familiarity with particular economic sectors. Therefore, an organized private sector review of the assumptions and structures of the government's longer-term models could both improve the models and reduce the number of unanticipated changes in government policy.

Modeling in educational institutions needs to be encouraged to provide both new techniques and diversity of perspectives in the available models. Since other nations and international agencies face similar analytical problems, more extensive and penetrating interaction among professionals would be helpful in extending techniques and information around the world.

3. *A more useful and internally consistent capability for longer-range analysis and planning.* This must start with an improved exchange of information. At present, even the agency experts responsible for the development, use, and maintenance of the individual sectoral elements of the government's global model have little knowledge of the assumptions, methodologies, and requirements of the other sectoral elements. The third volume of the Global 2000 Study will provide a reference manual on the various sectoral models, but much more is needed. Opportunity should be provided not only for the agencies' modeling experts, but also for experts from congressional staffs, the private sector, educational institutions, and the general public to learn about these models and to gain experience in their use. Increased understanding and ideas for improvements are sure to result from such information exchanges.

4. *Improved documentation of the elements of the government's global model.* Better documentation is badly needed. The third volume of the Global 2000 Study provides an initial attempt to draw the pieces together, but the basic reference documents should be available from a single source. Furthermore, the quality of the documentation—especially regarding descriptions of assumptions underlying the projections—needs to be improved. Impartial validation should also occur.

## Summary Descriptions of the 11 Elements

Each of the 11 elements of the government's global model is described here in terms of nine topics of particular relevance to the analysis presented earlier in this chapter.

Source of the designated projections
Explicit linkages to other elements of the government's global model
Critical policy and technology assumptions
Analytic methodology used to develop the projections
Brief description of the methodology
First major use of the methodology

Geographic representation within the methodology

Temporal representation within the methodology

Cases analyzed for the Global 2000 Study using the methodology

The 11 elements are described in the order in which they appear in Table 14–1. Much of the material presented below is encapsulated in Tables 14–2 and 14–3.

## 1. Population Element

*Source.* At the suggestion of the Agency for International Development (AID) of the U.S. Department of State, two independently developed sets of population projections were prepared for the Study. The Bureau of the Census of the U.S. Department of Commerce developed the projections that were subsequently used in preparing the Study's energy and food projections and its per capita GNP projections. The Community and Family Study Center at the University of Chicago developed alternative projections, which highlight the potential impact of family planning programs on population size and structure.

*Explicit Linkages to Other Elements of the Government's Global Model.* The Census and Chicago population projections were not developed taking into explicit account any of the Study's other projections. However, the Census projections were subsequently used in developing the Study's food and energy projections (and the derived energy-residual and environmental-impact projections).

*Critical Policy and Technology Assumptions.* With regard to policy, all population cases assumed that almost all countries that do not already do so will make family planning services available to an appreciable portion of the population during the 1975–2000 period, and that countries with family planning programs now in operation will extend coverage, particularly in rural areas. This meant, for example, that in the Census projections for Bangladesh (in the medium-growth case; over the 1975–2000 period) fertility rates were exogenously projected to decline 40 percent, as discussed in Chapter 15.

With regard to technology, no major breakthroughs or setbacks affecting fertility or mortality rates (e.g., regarding birth control devices or medical discoveries) were assumed.

*Analytic Methodology.* Both the Census and Chicago projections make use of the cohort-component methodology. The name of this methodology refers to the fact that each "cohort" of a given population (each group of males or females born in the same year) is treated separately and explicitly with respect to each major demographic "component" (mortality, fertility, and net migration). Each set of projections was prepared using somewhat different versions of a FORTRAN computer program of about 1,000 lines (including extensive comments).

Chicago's exogenous fertility projections also make use of an additional, explicit quantitative methodology. Given a population's 1975 fertility rate and the "strength" in 1975 of its family planning programs, Chicago's computer-based methodology projects future fertility rates, relying entirely on explicitly defined assumptions regarding the future development and efficacy of family planning programs; no other factors are considered in making these projections.

*Brief Description.* The cohort-component methodology projects population size and structure based on exogenous projections of mortality, fertility, and net migration rates.

Only demographic variables are considered in developing the population projections. No explicit mathematical relationships are used at any point that involve nondemographic factors—such as the size and distribution of per capita income; requirements for food, housing, schools, jobs, or medical facilities; likely welfare expenditures; educational opportunities; work roles and opportunities for women or men; or the influence of environmental factors on health. Internal migration (for example, between rural and urban areas or between social classes) is not represented, nor are differential growth rates for separate ethnic, racial, or religious groups.

*First Major Use.* Although the cohort-component methodology, developed in the 1930s, has been used extensively by demographers for decades, it was not until the late 1960s that the Bureau of the Census began making major use of it to develop international population projections, at the request of AID. At that time, AID asked Census to develop a model that would avoid what appeared to be biases contained in U.N. population estimates and projections, and subsequently to perform various policy analyses.

Several years later, in August 1977, AID asked the University of Chicago to develop a new projection methodology and undertake projections which would take more explicit account of the likely future impact of family planning programs (which AID was encouraging) on population size and structure. The Chicago population projections presented in the Study, developed in response to this request, emphasize the potential efficacy of AID's programs. Thus, the Chicago high, medium, and low world population projections for the year 2000 are 3 to 12 percent lower than the Census projections.

*Geographic Representation.* The cohort-component methodology can be used to develop projections for any appropriately defined population. Separate projections were prepared for 23 countries and subregions for the Global 2000 Study, at the request of the Study's central staff. These 23 areas include collectively all the world's population; moreover, the 12 less developed countries for which individual projections were made represent 75 percent of the current total population of the LDCs.

In the case of the Global 2000 Study, projections for each of the 23 countries or subregions were made independently of each other, and summed as appropriate. Migration between countries or subregions was assumed to be zero, for analytic reasons explained in Chapter 15.

*Temporal Representation.* Projections of a given population's size and structure were made dynamically—on a year by year, sequential basis. These projections were based on exogenous projections of mortality and fertility. For the Global 2000 Study, projections were presented in Chapter 2 for each 5-year interval of the 1975–2000 period.

*Cases Analyzed.* Three sets of projections were developed by both Census and Chicago: a high-growth, a medium-growth, and a low-growth case. In general, Census and Chicago used different estimates of current population sizes and structures and different mortality and fertility projections. Within both the Census and Chicago projections, variations among the high-growth, medium-growth, and low-growth cases were based entirely on different fertility rate projections (and in the Census projections, in the case of China, on different estimates of actual population size in 1975). Mortality assumptions and the zero net migration assumption did not vary within either the Census set of projections or within the Chicago set of projections.

## 2. Gross National Product Element

*Source.* No U.S. agency is responsible for developing a consistent set of long-term GNP projections for all the world's nations. Therefore, on the recommendation of the U.S. Agency for International Development of the U.S. Department of State, the Global 2000 Study turned to the office within the World Bank Group responsible for estimating consistent GNP projections for the Western industrialized nations and less developed

countries through 1985.* On the recommendation of Bank staff members, the Global 2000 Study supplemented the Bank's projections with GNP growth rates to the year 2000 developed for the 1977 Workshop on Alternative Energy Strategies (WAES), sponsored by the Massachusetts Institute of Technology.

The WAES group had first developed its own projections for the Western industrialized nations, and then—with the assistance of World Bank staff members—developed a consistent set of LDC projections using World Bank analytic tools. The World Bank and WAES projections were subsequently supplemented for the Global 2000 Study with projections for the centrally planned economies (CPEs), developed by the U.S. Central Intelligence Agency. Unfortunately, the GNP projections for the CPEs presented in this volume are considered unrealistically low by the CIA, when viewed together with the Study's other GNP projections (due to statistical differences discussed briefly in Chapter 3). However, it should be noted that the CPE growth rates used by the World Bank in developing the LDC growth rates for the WAES Study are much higher than those reported in this volume.

*Explicit Linkages to Other Elements of the Government's Global Model.* The GNP projections were not developed taking into explicit account any of the Study's other projections, except that the per capita GNP projections were subsequently calculated using the Study's population projections (developed by the Bureau of the Census). However, the GNP projections were subsequently used in developing the Study's food and energy projections and the derived energy-residual and environmental-impact projections.

*Critical Policy and Technology Assumptions.* No major policy changes were assumed. With regard to technology, however, all the GNP projections for the LDCs assumed that the productivity of capital in almost all of the LDCs will increase significantly over the 1975–85 period. This meant, for example, that in the other-South-Asia LDC group, a given investment could be thought of as producing 60 percent more incremental GNP in 1985 than in 1977 (in constant dollars), as discussed in Chapter 16.

*Analytic Methodology.* Most of the GNP projections (those for the LDCs) were developed making use of a dynamic, block-recursive computer model known as SIMLINK (SIMulated trade LINKages). The model contains over 200

---

*The World Bank Group is an international organization affiliated with the United Nations.

econometric structural equations and is written in approximately 1,500 lines of FORTRAN.

*Brief Description.* SIMLINK simulates world trade between the industrialized nations and the LDCs. Its purpose is to aggregate and adjust, as appropriate, the economic growth projections developed for individual LDC nations by World Bank analysts, so as to take account explicitly and consistently of likely limitations in the worldwide availability of foreign trade earnings and foreign investment capital. If these adjustments were not made, projections made by both the individual LDCs and World Bank analysts would sum to implausible levels of world trade and foreign investment.

Trade between industrialized nations or between LDCs is not explicitly represented in SIMLINK, nor is primary commodity trade between the LDCs and the CPEs. Current debt levels and growth trends in these levels are also not explicitly accounted for.

No explicit account is taken by SIMLINK of future population sizes and structures or of potential environmental impacts. Resources are represented primarily on the basis of historic cost-price relationships and past trends in growth of production.

*First Major Use.* An early version of SIMLINK began to be applied in 1974. One of the first applications examined the potential direct effect of recent and potential changes in the international price of oil on LDC economic growth rates (which are of crucial financial importance to the World Bank). The model supported the Bank's view that the direct impact of changes in the price of oil on LDC economic growth would be minor. However, the model also showed that changes in the growth rates of the industrialized nations, which might also be affected by changes in the price of oil, would have major direct impact on LDC economic growth.

*Geographic Representation.* SIMLINK treats the Western industrialized and socialist nations exogenously as four aggregates, each with its own GNP growth rate and elasticity of demand for LDC exports of manufactured goods. The LDCs are selectively represented by six aggregates: India, other-South-Asia countries, low-income Africa, lower-middle-income countries, middle-income-countries, and upper-middle-income countries. Each aggregate is treated at the same level of detail. SIMLINK simulates trade between each of the six LDC aggregates and (1) the Western industrialized nations and (2) the CPEs. Trade among the six LDC aggregates is not simulated,

nor is trade between the industrialized nations and the CPEs.

Several simplifying assumptions were made in developing the SIMLINK model. Within each of the six LDC aggregates, geographically and socioeconomically diverse LDCs—such as (1) Argentina, Jamaica, and Yugoslavia, or (2) Bolivia, Thailand, and Morocco—are treated as if they were single entities because they have roughly the same levels of per capita income. Many LDCs are not included in the model. For example, the OPEC income-surplus nations were not explicitly represented in the version of SIMLINK used for the WAES Study. However, those LDCs that are specifically included are said by Bank analysts to represent most of the population and national income of the LDCs.

*Temporal Representation.* Projections of world trade directly affecting the LDCs are based on exogenous projections of (1) Western industrial and CPE growth rates, trade volumes, and prices for many major commodities and (2) inflation rates for all years to be covered by the projection. After these exogenous projections are completed, SIMLINK projects LDC economic growth rates sequentially, year by year.

Bank analysts note that SIMLINK was not constructed to make projections beyond 1985, that they have little confidence in using it to develop longer-term projections, and that they have recently replaced it with a more comprehensive system of models. For the WAES Study, SIMLINK projections were developed for the 1975–90 period and extrapolated judgmentally to 2000.

*Cases Analyzed.* High, medium, and low GNP projections were used in the Global 2000 Study. The high and medium projections derive largely from figures developed for the WAES Study. The high-growth case generally projects a continuation of 1960–72 growth patterns, whereas the low-growth case projects a continuation of the patterns characteristic of the 1973–75 period—just sufficiently above that period's population growth to allow an advance in real global GNP per capita. The third (medium-growth) set of projections was developed by averaging the growth rates used in the high and low projections.

## 3. Climate Element

*Source.* The Global 2000 Study's climate projections were developed by the Central Intelligence Agency (CIA), based on an interagency research project on climate conducted by the National Defense University (NDU), with participation by the U.S. Department of Defense, the

U.S. Department of Agriculture, and the National Oceanic and Atmospheric Administration of the U.S. Department of Commerce. The first of the NDU project's four tasks—to define and estimate the likelihood of changes in climate during the next 25 years and to construct climate scenarios for the year 2000—was completed in February 1978, and the results were published in the National Defense University report entitled *Climate Change to the Year 2000.*\* The remaining three tasks of the NDU project included (1) estimating the likely effects of possible climatic changes on selected crops in specific countries, (2) evaluating the domestic and international implications of these specific climate-crop cases, and (3) transmitting the research results to individuals and organizations concerned with the consequences of climatic changes in fields other than agriculture.

*Explicit Linkages to Other Elements of the Government's Global Model.* The climate cases were not developed taking into direct account any of the Study's other projections, nor were they used in developing any of those projections, since, as it turned out, none of the other elements used to develop the Study's other projections was capable of directly taking into account any climatic variation from patterns established over the past 2–3 decades.

*Critical Policy and Technology Assumptions.* With regard to both policy and technology, deliberate human efforts to modify climate were excluded from the analysis.

*Analytic Methodology.* A special survey methodology devised by the Institute for the Future (hereafter referred to as the NDU methodology) was used to gather, weigh, and consolidate the views of numerous experts on climate. The purpose of the NDU project was not to forecast climate change or reach a consensus on how climate will change, but rather to synthesize reasonable, coherent, and consistent possibilities for world climate to the end of the century, and to put plausible bounds on the likelihood of each of these possibilities occurring.

*Brief Description.* The CIA developed three simplified cases for the Global 2000 Study, based primarily on the more complex and highly qualified findings of the NDU report. The approach

used in developing the NDU report was to seek and weigh a wide range of expert opinion. This synthesized survey approach seemed likely to yield the most meaningful results obtainable, in view of the fact that there is currently no single well-accepted quantitative model of the causal forces thought to determine climate.

In the first of the NDU project's four tasks, a questionnaire defining five future climate possibilities was prepared and completed by a diverse group of climatological experts. The emphasis of the project was placed primarily on assessing probabilities related to (1) average global temperature, (2) average latitudinal temperature, (3) carbon dioxide and turbidity (including particulates), (4) precipitation change, (5) precipitation variability, (6) midlatitude drought, (7) Asian monsoons, (8) Sahel drought, and (9) the length of the growing season.

Individual responses were weighted by each participant's expertise, as evaluated by self and peers, and responses to this questionnaire were then used to calculate complex topographical probability functions associated with each specified case.

*First Major Use.* The NDU methodology was first developed and used in connection with this particular NDU study in the mid-1970s, although it is related to Delphi-survey techniques developed over the past two decades.

*Geographic Representation.* The NDU study developed separate probability functions primarily with regard to each of eight regions (polar, higher midlatitude, lower midlatitude, and subtropical regions in both Northern and Southern Hemispheres). Geographic causal linkages between the phenomena occurring in these regions were informally assessed on an individual, undocumented basis by each of the participants in the study.

*Temporal Representation.* Probability functions were assessed for three time periods: 1977–80, 1981–90, and 1991–2000. Temporal causal linkages between the phenomena occurring in these time periods were informally assessed on an individual, undocumented basis by each of the participants.

*Cases Analyzed.* The three climate cases developed for the Global 2000 Study represent simplifications of three of the five NDU cases, namely, they approximate the three more moderate cases projected by the report as most probable. However, it should be kept in mind that in excluding the more extreme, large-scale changes, the Global 2000 Study has omitted consideration of climatological developments that could have an

---

\* These climate "projections" are actually scenarios (in the sense of being internally consistent statements of possible future developments), rather than "projections" (in the sense of being foreseeable consequences of present trends). In order to facilitate comparisons with the other element descriptions in this chapter, they will henceforth be referred to as "cases" in this discussion.

extremely pronounced effect on the Study's other projections.

The following three world-climate cases were developed for the 1975–2000 period. They differ primarily with regard to assumed future global temperature and precipitation patterns.

| Case | Temperature | Precipitation |
|------|-------------|---------------|
| No change | Similar to 1941–70 period (i.e., less variability than over the past 100–200 years). | Similar to 1941–70 period (i.e., less severe drought in the Sahel and less monsoon failure in India than recently experienced). |
| Warming | Global temperatures increase by 1° C, with only slight warming in the tropics. | Annual precipitation increases 5–10 percent and becomes less variable; probability of U.S. drought increases. |
| Cooling | Global temperatures decrease by 0.5° C, with only slight cooling in the tropics. | Precipitation amounts decline and variability increases; probability of U.S. drought increases. |

## 4. Technology Element

*Source.* This section brings together under one heading (as a major element of the government's global model) the disparate methods used by the other elements of the government's global model to project rates of technological innovation, deployment, and impact. The fact is that no government agency has unique responsibility for projecting future rates of technological change for use in other official projections and forecasts. As a result, each agency develops its own technological projections and forecasts on a virtually independent basis.

This practice was also followed in developing the Global 2000 Study's projections. The Study's assumptions concerning future rates of technological change were determined independently by the various agencies for their individual contributions to the Study.

*Explicit Linkages to Other Elements of the Government's Global Model.* No explicit linkages were made between any of the other 10 elements of the government's global model with respect to technology. Those elements from which projections were developed using projections developed by other elements, however, could be thought of as incorporating implicitly the technology assumptions of those other elements (often inconsistently).

*Critical Policy and Technology Assumptions.* No explicit, consistent policy assumptions were made with regard to technological innovation, deployment, or impact. However, some representative critical technological assumptions are cited below, under "Cases Analyzed." In general, technological progress is assumed, potential setbacks are not considered, and adverse side effects are not considered.

*Analytic Methodology.* Over the years, government agencies have developed a wide variety of diverse methodologies for projecting (often implicitly) technological assumptions. These technological projections are then incorporated in projections and forecasts of other variables of interest. In some cases, these technological projections are made in advance of making use of the methodologies which comprise the other elements of the government's global model; in other cases, they are calculated concurrently with other calculations made using the methodology. The actual techniques used by the various elements to project technological innovation, deployment, and impact are so idiosyncratic that a more explicit overall description (such as that provided in Chapter 23) is not feasible here.

*Brief Description.* Most technologies were projected to yield increasing benefits over time at exponential rates corresponding to recent historical experience. In some cases, the deployment of existing technology was projected to occur at rates faster than recent historical experience (e.g., in the population projections and energy-residual projections). The potential adverse and dysfunctional consequences of technological innovation and deployment were almost never explicitly considered, except in the environmental projections.

*First Major Use.* The agencies' overall projection methodologies generally have unique ways of incorporating the underlying technology assumptions. Therefore, the first major use of the diverse methodologies for technological projections tended to coincide with the first major use of the overall projection methodologies of which they are a part. Little or no consistency was imposed regarding the rate at which technological advance is projected in various fields (e.g., in response to allocations of federal research budgets), and the Global 2000 Study represents the first time the government's various approaches to longer-term, global technological projection have even been cursorily examined on a collective basis in an official executive branch report.

*Geographic Representation.* Most projections assumed that all regions of the world will be culturally and physically capable of accepting technological change to approximately the same extent and at approximately the same rates.

*Temporal Representation.* No systematic attempt was made by the Study to assure the use of consistent assumptions regarding likely future rates of technological innovation, deployment, and impact collectively in the Study's projections. Therefore, it is unlikely that the temporal representation of technological change among the various elements is to any degree consistent, although the inexplicit character of the way technology is represented in many elements of the government's global model makes this virtually impossible to assess.

*Cases Analyzed.* No consistent, systematic projections of technology per se were made for the Study, but diverse technological assumptions were incorporated in all of the other projections developed for the Study. Some key examples are provided below:

- All the population projections assumed that almost all countries that do not already do so will make family planning technologies and services available to an appreciable portion of the population during the 1975–2000 period, and countries with family planning programs now in operation will extend coverage, particularly in rural areas. This meant, for example, that in the Census projections for Bangladesh (in the medium-growth case), fertility rates were exogenously projected to decline 40 percent over the 1975–2000 period, as discussed in Chapter 15.

- Almost all the GNP projections for the LDCs assumed that the productivity of capital in the LDCs will increase significantly over the 1975–85 period. This meant, for example, that in the other-South-Asia LDC group, a given investment could be thought of as producing 60 percent more incremental GNP in 1985 than in 1977 (in constant dollars), as discussed in Chapter 16.

- All the food projections assumed that the widespread deployment of fertilizer and other yield-augmenting inputs (together with other factors) will lead to further increased yields comparable to the increases experienced over the past two decades (the period of the Green Revolution). This meant, for example, that annual LDC grain production was projected to increase 125 percent over the 1975–2000 period (in the medium case), as discussed in Chapter 5.

- All the energy projections assumed the widespread deployment of light-water nuclear electric power plants. This meant, for example, that electrical generation from nuclear and hydropower sources was projected to increase about 200 percent over the 1975–90 period (in the medium case), as discussed in Chapter 5.

- All the energy-residual projections (i.e., projections of residuals such as pollutants or waste heat from energy conversion processes) assumed implicitly that major public and private investment will be made in pollution abatement technologies so that by 1985 all energy facilities in all countries will have met or have been retrofitted to meet 1978 U.S. new source performance standards for various emissions, as discussed in Chapter 10.

## 5. Food Element

*Source.* The Study's food projections were developed by the U.S. Department of Agriculture's Economics, Statistics, and Cooperatives Service.

*Explicit Linkages to Other Elements of the Government's Global Model.* The projections are based on the Study's population projections (developed by the Bureau of the Census) and GNP projections. In addition, the Study's rising-energy-price projections were used in developing the two food cases (which assume increasing petroleum prices) and the Study's associated environmental projections. However, no Study projections (other than population, GNP, and energy) were directly used in developing the Study's food projections (i.e., no use was made of the Study's projections involving climate, fisheries, forestry, water, energy residuals, fuel minerals, nonfuel minerals, or the environment).

*Critical Policy and Technology Assumptions.* With regard to policy, the projections all assumed that major public and private investment in agricultural land development will be made. With regard to technology, they assumed that widespread deployment and use of fertilizer and other yield-augmenting inputs (together with other factors) will lead to further increased yields comparable to the increases experienced over the past two decades (the period of the Green Revolution). This meant, for example, that annual LDC grain production (in the medium case, over the 1975–2000 period) was projected to increase 125 percent.

*Analytic Methodology.* A computer-based static-equilibrium model known as the GOL (Grain, Oilseed, Livestock) model was the primary tool used in developing the food projections. The

GOL model consists of approximately 930 econometric equations, which are solved simultaneously.

Three additional procedures were used to make projections of arable area, total food production and consumption, and fertilizer use. They were developed since the fall of 1977 specifically for the Study, and were based on the application of comparatively simple computational procedures to some of the results of the GOL calculations. These additional calculations were made without the use of a computer-based model.

*Brief Description.* The GOL model projects world production, consumption, and trade quantities and prices in grains, oilseeds, and livestock products based on exogenous projections of population, GNP, growth in crop yields due to the deployment of more efficient yield-enhancing technology, and other variables. The model's structure is most detailed for grain; other food products are represented in less detail. Collectively, the relationships incorporated in the model are said to represent approximately 70–80 percent of total world food production, consumption, and trade. No environmental considerations (other than land scarcity and weather) are explicitly represented in the model. Similarly the public and social costs associated with developing and maintaining the productive capacity required by 2000 are not explicitly represented in the model.

*First Major Use.* Along with other analyses, the model was initially used in 1974 to generate projections supporting the U.S. position paper for the Rome Food Conference sponsored by the Food and Agriculture Organization. The model's initial projections showed that over the next decade the world could produce enough grain (at real prices above the relatively low prices of the late 1960s) to meet the demands of (1) a largely cereal diet in the developing world and (2) a moderately rising grain-feed meat diet (based in part on grain-fed livestock) in the industrial nations. The U.S. position paper prepared for the conference made use of these projections to support policy views favoring, in general, the limiting of government intervention in domestic and world food markets, and questioning, in particular, the need for an extensive international system of government-owned food reserves.

*Geographic Representation.* A total of 28 closely interrelated regions are represented at varying levels of detail. The 28 regions consist of 8 regions of Western industrial nations, 3 regions of centrally planned economies, and 17 regions of less developed countries (LDCs). All regions have crop equations, but not all regions have full livestock sectors. The centrally planned regions are represented solely by collapsed international trade equations (that is, area yield and production projections are generated by "satellite" models, while consumption is calculated as production plus or minus trade).

*Temporal Representation.* The GOL model is a static equilibrium model. It is described as static in that it does not dynamically develop projections on a year by year basis. Instead, its projections are derived from estimated values for an initial base period, directly adjusted to correspond to anticipated equilibrium conditions in a final year, without calculating successive values for the intervening years. This process of one-step projecting is based on the assumption that the world's grain-oilseed-livestock production and trade system was in rough equilibrium (supply equaled demand at the reported market price) in the base period and that the solution calculated for any single future year will also be in rough equilibrium. The GOL model is thus extremely limited in its capacity to simulate the many important aspects of agricultural market behavior that are in a state of dynamic disequilibrium over periods exceeding one year.

GOL projections for 1985 and 2000 were developed for the Global 2000 Study starting with 1969–71 (average) base-line conditions (adjusted somewhat using data through 1976) and projecting to 1985 and 2000.

*Cases Analyzed.* Four projections of world food production, consumption, and trade were developed for the Study, based on different assumptions for population growth, GNP growth, weather, and the real price of petroleum. The four food cases* are summarized below:

| Cases | Population Growth | GNP Growth | Weather | Real-Price of Petroleum |
|---|---|---|---|---|
| Medium | Medium | Medium | Same as last three decades | Constant ($13/bbl., 1978 dollars) |
| Optimistic | Low | High | More favorable than last three decades. | Constant ($13/bbl., 1978 dollars) |
| Pessimistic | High | Low | Less favorable than last three decades | Increasing (5 percent per year in real terms, 1980–2000) |
| Rising energy price | Medium | Medium | Same as last three decades | Increasing (5 percent per year in real terms, 1980–2000) |

*The "cases" are referred to as "alternatives" and "scenarios" in Chapters 6 and 18. Alternative I of Chapter 6 embodies both the medium and the rising-energy-price cases; Alternative II is the optimistic case; Alternative III is the pessimistic case. In these cases, the changes in assumptions regarding weather (a term used to refer to relatively short-term variations within historic norms) are not considered equivalent to changes in assumptions regarding climate (a term used to refer to fundamental long-term change).

## 6. Fisheries, Forestry, Water Element

*Source.* Because of their methodological similarities, the fisheries, forestry, and water projections are described together here as if they were one element in the government's global model. The fisheries projections were developed by the National Oceanic and Atmospheric Administration of the U.S. Department of Commerce and by outside consultants. The forestry projections were developed by the Central Intelligence Agency, with assistance from the Department of Agriculture and the Department of State (and its Agency for International Development). The water projections were developed by the Department of the Interior, with assistance from the CIA and outside consultants.

*Explicit Linkages to Other Elements of the Government's Global Model.* The fisheries, forestry, and water projections were not developed taking into direct account any of the Study's other projections or each other, nor were they used in developing any of the Study's other projections, except the environmental impact projections.

*Critical Policy and Technology Assumptions.* With regard to policy, the fisheries projections assume, on a worldwide basis, good management of fisheries and protection of the marine environment; the forestry projections assume some policy changes throughout the world regarding current deforestation practices; the water projections' policy assumptions are unknown. With regard to technology, the fisheries projections assume the invention of methods for harvesting nontraditional species; the forestry projections assume the invention of both less wasteful production techniques and methods for exploiting nontraditional species; the water projections' technology assumptions are unknown.

*Analytic Methodology.* Descriptive and judgmental analyses (rather than elaborate mathematical models) were used in developing the fisheries, forestry, and water projections.

*Brief Description.* The fisheries production (supply) projections were based on empirical evidence and ecological theory. The fisheries consumption (demand) projections were based on broadly generalized assumptions about the relationships between population, income growth, and income elasticities of demand for marine products. Together, these projections suggest that future fish consumption will be constrained by production and price.

The forestry projections were based on a review of the literature of forest economics and ecology, combined with informed judgment. In cases where sources were in conflict (for example, when ecological and anthropological projections came to different conclusions regarding the sustainability of slash-and-burn agriculture), the source with the stronger empirical evidence was preferred.

Two sets of projections of water availability were presented by the Department of the Interior and the CIA: (1) the lower projection of increases in the "consumption" (withdrawal) of "water controlled by man" over the 1975–2000 period was developed by C. A. Doxiadis; (2) the higher projection of global water requirements by the year 2000 was developed by Russian hydrologist G. P. Kalinin. The projections were apparently not chosen by the Department of the Interior for their excellence, but because other global water projections could not be found or developed.

*First Major Use.* The fisheries and forestry projections were developed specifically for the Global 2000 Study. In the case of the water projections, the Doxiadis projections were originally published in the report, "Water for Peace," prepared for the International Conference on Water for Peace held in Washington, D.C., in 1967. The Kalinin projections were originally published in UNESCO's *Impact of Science in Society,* April-June 1969.

*Geographic Representation.* Projections involving fisheries, forestry, and water resources are severely complicated by the fact that the boundaries of the political jurisdictions responsible for gathering information on them and for managing them do not coincide with the natural boundaries of the ecological systems involved. These complications are greatest in the case of the fisheries projections, which had to be made largely on the basis of species rather than geographic region. In the case of the forestry projections, the supply, demand, and price of forest products were considered separately for each of the major forest regions of the world. A separate section was devoted to the problems of the humid tropics.

In the Study's water projections, the point is made that there is no such thing as a global water economy in the same sense as, for example, a global economy for minerals and fuels. Since the cost of transporting water tends to be high when large distances are involved, water problems tend to be local or regional, rather than global.

*Temporal Representation.* The fisheries, forestry, and water projections are either based on straight-line (linear) or exponential (nonlinear) extrapolations of past trends.

*Cases Analyzed.* Only a single medium case was evaluated for the fisheries and forestry projections; both a lower and a higher set of water projections were presented. The specific assumptions behind these cases (to the extent they are known) are reported in Chapters 7, 8, and 9.

### 7.  Energy Element

*Source.* The Study's energy projections were developed by the Energy Information Administration of the U.S. Department of Energy.

*Explicit Linkages to Other Elements of the Government's Global Model.* The Study's population projections (developed by the Bureau of the Census) and GNP projections were used in developing the energy projections. None of the Study's other projections were used, but the energy projections were used in developing the Study's food, energy residuals, and environmental projections (but not in developing the climate, fisheries, forestry, water, fuel minerals, or nonfuel minerals projections).

*Critical Policy and Technology Assumptions.* With regard to policy, all the energy projections assumed the implementation of more effective energy conservation policies within the member countries of the Organization for Economic Cooperation and Development (OECD). With regard to technology, all the energy projections assumed the widespread deployment of light-water nuclear electric power plants. This meant that electrical generation from nuclear and hydropower sources was projected (in the medium case, over the 1975–2000 period) to increase more than 200 percent, as discussed in Chapter 5.

*Analytic Methodology.* The energy projections were made with a computer-based static-equilibrium model known as the International Energy Evaluation System (IEES). IEES is a family of complex supply, demand, and production models, integrated by means of a large linear-programming-matrix representation of approximately 2,000 rows and 6,000 columns. The data quantifying world energy supply and demand, and production and transportation costs necessary for these integrating calculations, are supplied by six IEES submodels. These submodels have been assembled independently of one another, and are executed sequentially, drawing on their own outside data sources.

*Brief Description.* The IEES model projects world energy production, consumption, and trade, based on exogenous projections of population, GNP, trends in the international price of petroleum, and other variables. The model emphasizes the fossil fuel sector by providing elaborate detail for petroleum (and related fuels) and coal while incorporating significantly less detail for nuclear energy, solar energy, energy conservation programs, firewood, and emerging technologies. For example, solar energy is not explicitly represented and can be included in the projections only by an exogenous assumption of a given solar contribution to electrical generation or to conservation. Supply of nuclear facilities is determined largely outside of the model by exogenous projections and assumptions.

The IEES system of models is structured around a single large integrating linear-programming matrix representation. According to the model's theory, the world energy market operates as a free market whose equilibrium minimizes the total cost of meeting the world's energy demands at a specific, assumed price of oil.* Demand and supply are balanced through a price mechanism that adjusts marginal costs of supply and demand to equal values through iterative adjustments. The Organization of Petroleum Exporting Countries (OPEC) is assumed to provide as much oil as might be wanted (up to its maximum production capacity), independent of the price of oil assumed for the model run.

There are several important assumptions implicit in the operation of the IEES price mechanism. In each year projected, energy production outside of OPEC is assumed to respond within limits to prevailing energy prices, with little or no time lag. Oil production outside of OPEC generally does not meet demand, and IEES achieves supply-demand balance by assuming OPEC meets the residual demand (which in some runs exceeds the OPEC maximum production capacity) at whatever oil price prevails in the year in question. The energy production alternatives are assumed to be selected solely on the basis of meeting projected demand at the lowest possible global cost. In general, only gross energy production figures are presented; net energy production figures (i.e., gross energy production less the energy consumed in obtaining the gross energy production) are not calculated. Forms of energy supply which are not generally traded internationally (except hydropower and geothermal energy) are not represented in the model.

---

* In the analyses performed for the Global 2000 Study, the OPEC oil price scenario (constant at $13 per barrel in 1975 dollars until 1980, then increasing at 5 percent per year) was assumed. However, the Department of Energy does have an Oil Market Simulator (OMS) model with which the Department makes medium term forecasts of OPEC oil prices. OMS is calibrated to ILES and in forecasting runs annually equilibrated oil supply with the oil demand projected by ILES.

Since OPEC currently provides such a significant share of the oil used by the U.S. and other nations, the IEES model's assumptions about OPEC are of critical importance. IEES assumes (in all cases analyzed for this Study) that OPEC will provide as much oil as can be consumed independent of the exogenously projected price. However, if projected OPEC production exceeds OPEC capacity, an oil price increase is implied.

Generally, IEES is used to study the world balance of energy supply and consumption for specifically assumed oil prices—given essentially exogenous supply estimates for all energy sources. Interfuel trade-offs in consumption and conservation are the key results calculated.

The social or environmental effects of the energy sector are not evaluated by IEES, nor is resource depletion explicitly represented in the model. While gross national product is included as one of the major determinants of energy demand, IEES implicitly assumes that GNP growth is independent of energy availability and price.

*First Major Use.* IEES is based on the same analytic structure as the Project Independence Evaluation System (PIES), the initial computer-based model developed to analyze U.S. energy-policy options following the 1973–74 oil embargo.* IEES makes international projections that are consistent with the PIES domestic projections. Thus, IEES is essentially a copy of the PIES structure (a few deviations were necessary) using international data. The first major public analysis performed by IEES was released for distribution in 1978 (and previously circulated in 1977 in a form intended for limited distribution). It supports the view that petroleum demand is likely to exceed the production capacity of the OPEC nations in the mid-1980s, assuming real petroleum prices do not increase significantly above 1975 (real) prices in the near future.

*Geographic Representation.* IEES simulates a modern competitive energy market that deals primarily in fossil fuels. Four groups of countries are represented in the model at varying levels of detail: member countries of OECD, the OPEC countries, the CPEs, and the less developed countries. The OECD countries, which consume 80 percent of the world's oil production and are generally the world's most industrialized nations, are treated most extensively in the demand submodel

---

* PIES was originally used to analyze ways of achieving President Nixon's goal of energy independence for the United States by 1980. While the results showed that such a goal was unachievable by 1980, the model suggested that the goal could be attained by 1985, if the Administration's proposed energy policies were adopted.

analyses, although all of the submodels produce data for every part of the world. In contrast, the energy economies of the LDCs are not treated in detail and in fact contain significant omissions. For example, the large proportion of LDC energy economies based on firewood and other biofuels is not represented.

*Temporal Representation.* Although some of its submodels exhibit dynamic behavior, IEES is essentially a static-equilibrium model. Like the GOL model used to develop the Study's food projections, IEES is "static" in that it does not dynamically develop its projections year by year with developments in one year influencing opportunities and difficulties in succeeding years. The IEES projections are made in a one-step process that starts in a base year (e.g., 1975) and progresses directly to the final year (e.g., 1990) under the assumption that the international energy system is in equilibrium and optimally efficient during the intervening years.

The time-dependent characteristics of the IEES projections derive entirely from exogenous projections used as driving inputs to the IEES model. In the main part of the IEES system, variables change over time only in direct response to changes in exogenously projected variables.

The model's static equilibrium projections for a given year are internally independent of its projections for all other years and may well be inconsistent with projections for other years. However, the demand submodel (which serves as the basis for the initial demand estimates) is an annual dynamic model which imposes some intertemporal consistency. The model develops its projections for a given year based on exogenously projected economic and resource conditions for that one year only, without explicitly considering developments that might be anticipated beyond the year in question. The model therefore operates as if the planners' goals were to optimize for just that year, without any further planning for successive years. One exception is that demand data can be (and are) exogenously adjusted to reflect energy conservation measures expected to be implemented by the OECD countries.

Projections for the Study were made for 1985 and 1990, but not for 2000. IEES was not constructed to project beyond 1990, and at this time Department of Energy analysts have little confidence in using it to develop longer-term projections or in extrapolating such projections judgmentally.

*Cases Analyzed.* Four projections of world energy production, consumption, and trade were developed for the Study. These projections were primarily based on different assumptions regarding population growth, GNP growth, and the real price of petroleum, as summarized below*:

| Case | Population Growth | GNP Growth | Real Price of Petroleum |
|------|------|------|------|
| Medium | Medium | Medium | Constant ($13/bbl., 1978 dollars) |
| High | High | Low | Constant ($13/bbl., 1978 dollars) |
| Low | Low | High | Constant ($13/bbl., 1978 dollars) |
| Rising energy price | Medium | Medium | Increasing (5% per year in real terms, 1980–90) |

## 3. Energy Residuals Element

*Source.* The projections of energy residuals were developed by the Brookhaven National Laboratory, under contract to the Department of Energy's Office of Technology Impacts.

*Explicit Linkages to Other Elements of the Government's Global Model.* Like the Study's energy projections, the study's energy residuals projections are derived (via the energy projections) from the Study's population and GNP projections. However, they neither influenced any of the Study's other projections (other than the environmental projections) nor were they influenced by any of the Study's other projections (i.e., climate, food, fisheries, forestry, water, fuel minerals, or nonfuel minerals projections).

*Critical Policy and Technology Assumptions.* With regard to policy and technology, all the energy residuals projections (i.e., projections of residuals such as pollutants or waste heat from energy conversion processes) assumed implicitly that major public and private investment will be made in pollution abatement technologies so that by 1985 all energy conversion facilities throughout the world will have been retrofitted to meet the 1978 U.S. new source emission standards for carbon monoxide, sulfur dioxide, oxides of nitrogen and particulates.

*Analytic Methodology.* The energy residuals projections were developed using a highly simplified version of a computer-based network model or accounting tool known as the Energy Systems Network Simulator (ESNS). ESNS is currently capable of calculating the emissions of 435 energy-conversion processes, using 69 exogenously derived coefficients to transform energy consumption figures into estimates of residuals.

* The "cases" are referred to as "scenarios" in Chapters 10 and 20.

*Brief Description.* The simplified version of ESNS used in the Study makes repeated use of the following equation, summed across end-use (sectoral) categories and across fuel-type categories:

Total regional residuals generated (by emissions type)
= Total regional energy conversion (by fuel type)
× residuals generated (by emission type) per unit of energy conversion.

The national (i.e., U.S.) ESNS model was modified for use in this Study by adapting it to accept (as input) the results of the International Energy Evaluation System (IEES)—the model used to develop the Study's energy projections. The adaptation was difficult since (1) the international version could not be developed without making assumptions about emissions control standards on a worldwide basis, (2) the output from the IEES model (particularly the estimates of fuel consumption by end uses for the LDCs, the OPEC regions, and the centrally planned economies) were too aggregated for use in the ESNS model, and (3) the IEES projections for the Global 2000 Study do not include a base case—such as 1975—to which residuals in later years can be compared.

The adapted ESNS model is therefore severely limited by the capability of IEES, and the resulting model is best thought of as the IEES-ESNS model. An especially critical limitation to the value of the IEES-ESNS analysis is the assumption that by 1985 all countries will have met the U.S. new source performance standards discussed above.

*First Major Use.* ESNS itself was first developed in 1975 to assist the U.S. Energy Research and Development Agency (a predecessor agency of the U.S. Department of Energy) in analyzing the residuals implicit in the energy developmental programs it was advocating. The present Study marks the first time the ESNS model has been used to make long-term global projections.

*Geographic Representation.* The geographic representation in ESNS is necessarily the same as in the IEES energy projections—that is, the world is represented as four major regions or groups of nations: OECD Countries (also represented separately), the OPEC countries, the centrally planned economies, and the LDCs.

*Temporal Representation.* The temporal representation is necessarily the same as in the case of the energy projections—i.e., projections were developed for 1985 and 1990 and not for previous or subsequent years.

*Cases Analyzed.* The three cases analyzed are

necessarily the same as those analyzed in the energy projections—the low, medium, and high cases—except that the fourth (rising-energy-price) case was not analyzed.

## 9. Fuel Minerals Element

*Source.* The Study's estimates of fuel minerals reserves and resources were developed from a variety of sources since no one federal agency has exclusive responsibility for producing such estimates. These sources included the U.S. Geological Survey (USGS) of the Department of the Interior, the Department of Energy (DOE), and some private organizations, most notably the World Energy Conference (WEC). A consistent set of estimates was compiled, compared, and interpreted for the Study by a government expert who had worked with both DOE and Department of the Interior's Bureau of Mines.

*Explicit Linkages to Other Elements of the Government's Global Model.* The fuel minerals projections were not derived from any of the Study's other projections—including the Study's energy projections—nor were they used in developing any of the Study's additional projections other than the environmental projections.

*Critical Policy and Technology Assumptions.* With regard to policy, the U.S. oil and gas resource and reserve estimates assume a continuation of 1974 energy prices. With regard to technology, the U.S. oil and gas resource and reserve estimates assume a continuation of price-cost relationships and technological trends generally prevailing in years prior to 1974.

*Analytic Methodology.* The methods used to derive fuel resource and reserve estimates vary, to some extent, with the organization that gathered the estimates. In general, the organizations cited above made use of secondary rather than primary sources of information—that is, they queried corporations and other organizations and totaled these various estimates, or they adapted estimates that other organizations had derived previously from similar sources.

*Brief Description.* While field surveys and explorations are the best primary source of information, it has been necessary in this Study to rely primarily on secondary or tertiary sources. For example, the resource figures for solid fuels used in this Study are based on WEC estimates. The WEC sends questionnaires to the participating countries, requesting information on reserves, resources, maximum depth of deposit, minimum seam thickness, and other critical factors. In many cases, methods of estimating reserves and re-

sources differ significantly from country to country. As a result, it has not been possible to describe a consistent systematic methodological approach, even for individual fuel minerals.

*First Major Use.* The USGS, in addition to reviewing other sources of information, has been doing its own field geological research for decades to support its U.S. resource and reserve estimates. However, in 1974, the USGS reported new oil and gas estimates based on new techniques, which are discussed briefly in Chapter 21. The new oil and gas estimates are significantly lower than previous estimates, so the present USGS estimates may be thought of as dating from 1974. WEC started using its survey techniques to estimate reserves and resources prior to World War II and has published estimates periodically ever since. DOE develops its own estimates of U.S. coal reserves using techniques developed by its various predecessor agencies. For oil and natural gas reserve figures, DOE relies largely on estimates made by the U.S. Geological Survey, updated by DOE's own survey's and augmented for the most current months by data published by the American Petroleum Institute and the American Gas Association, trade associations of the oil and gas industries.

*Geographic Representation.* No consistent pattern of geographic representation has been followed in developing the fuel minerals projections.

*Temporal Representation.* Both resource and reserve estimates are dynamic concepts. Exploration shifts resources from the undiscovered category to the identified category. Economic and technological developments move resources between the economic and subeconomic categories. Reserves are those resources that are identified as economic and have not yet been depleted.

The Global 2000 Study's resource and reserve estimates do not have a dynamic perspective. The estimates presented are based on a static concept; they are applicable to a particular year but have no other time dimension. In general, they are based on the assumption that there will be a continuation of current price-cost relationships and technological trends, although the U.S. oil and gas resource and reserve estimates (derived from USGS Circular 725) assume a continuation of 1974 prices and of generally prevailing pre-1974 price-cost relationships and technological trends.

*Cases Analyzed.* Only one set of estimates was developed for the Study, but in many instances the probabilities associated with different measures of statistical variance have also been indicated.

## 10. Nonfuel Minerals Element

*Source.* The Study's nonfuel mineral-consumption projections were assembled by the Study's central staff, with assistance from the U.S. Department of the Interior's Bureau of Mines and outside consultants. Since the Bureau does not have and could not produce the disaggregated international projections needed for this Study, the Study's projections were based in large part (at the suggestion of the Bureau) on projections developed in 1972 by Wilfred Malenbaum for the National Commission on Materials Policy and were supplemented by projections prepared in 1977 by Malenbaum for the National Science Foundation. Malenbaum's projections cover 12 minerals and materials, said to account for 80–90 percent of the value of the total world mineral production. Consumption projections for an additional 75 minerals and materials have also been developed by the Bureau of Mines, making use of Malenbaum's analysis.

To facilitate review and comparison with the other trends presented in this Study, only a representative subset of these consumption projections is presented in Chapter 12. This subset consists of 10 minerals and materials projected by Malenbaum and 9 additional minerals projected by the Bureau of Mines.

Explicit price projections are not available from either the Department of the Interior or from Malenbaum's published analyses.

*Explicit Linkages to Other Elements of the Government's Global Model.* The nonfuel minerals projections were not derived from any of the Study's other projections, nor were they used in developing any of the Study's additional projections (other than the environmental impact projections).

*Critical Policy and Technology Assumptions.* With regard to policy, no significant changes are assumed. With regard to technology, the projections assume increasingly less intensive mineral use in highly industrialized countries and increasingly more intensive mineral use in the LDCs.

*Analytic Methodology.* Both the 1972 and 1977 Malenbaum projections were developed using a methodology known as the Intensity of Use (IOU) analysis. This methodology utilizes simple arithmetic procedures based on the relative intensity with which a given commodity is projected to be consumed per unit of per capita gross domestic product (GDP). This relative intensity of use is referred to as the material's IOU statistic. A relatively high IOU statistic indicates that a relatively large quantity of a given commodity is projected to be consumed per unit of per capita GDP.

*Brief Description.* In the 1977 Malenbaum Report (which was the report relied upon primarily by the Study) consumption projections for 12 minerals and materials were developed independently of each other, using the IOU methodology. They were based on exogenous projections of GDP and population, in combination with an extrapolation of historic relationships between mineral consumption and per capita GDP (developed according to IOU theory).

IOU theory assumes that as less developed countries industrialize, they use increasing quantities of minerals per unit of per capita GDP; conversely, it assumes that as industrial countries move toward postindustrial status, they use decreasing quantities of minerals per unit of per capita GDP. Malenbaum's use of IOU methodology also assumes explicitly that long-term growth in minerals and materials consumption will not be governed by supply limitations—whether due to depletion, environmental constraints, price increases, or other factors. In particular, it assumes explicitly that future consumption of minerals and materials will be largely independent of price, though Malenbaum notes that—to the vague and imprecise degree that prices are considered—they are projected to decline.

*First Major Use.* The IOU methodology is said to have been developed by the International Iron and Steel Institute in 1972 and tends to produce lower consumption projections than other methodologies (since it assumes that increasing economic growth in the industrial countries requires increasingly less consumption of minerals and materials per unit of per capita economic growth). Malenbaum's studies based on this particular methodology were used by the National Commission on Materials Policy to demonstrate the feasibility of striking a balance between the national need to produce goods on the one hand and to protect the environment on the other.

*Geographic Representation.* In the Malenbaum mineral-consumption projections the world is divided into 10 countries or groups of countries, treated independently and at the same level of detail. The Bureau of Mine's projections are disaggregated geographically into only two parts: the United States and the rest of the world.

*Temporal Representation.* The IOU methodology involves no endogenous dynamic calculations. Projections for any given year are based entirely on exogenous population and GDP projections and IOU assumptions. The exogenous population and GDP assumptions must be aggregated in the same way as the data used to project future trends in the IOU statistics and must be consistent with the historical data used to develop the IOU relationships. The 1977 Malenbaum Report presented historical estimates for the 1971–75 period and earlier, and projections for 1985 and 2000.

*Cases Analyzed.* For a variety of reasons it was not possible to obtain nonfuel minerals projections specifically for the Global 2000 Study. As a result it was necessary to rely entirely on previously published projections—namely, the 1977 Malenbaum Report—which presents only one set of consumption projections: the medium one. This set of projections is based on Malenbaum's population and GDP projections, which differ in complex ways from those of this Study (see Chapter 22).

The Bureau of Mines' projections for an additional 75 minerals and materials are made for three cases: a probable, high, and low case. However, the Bureau's assumptions are not sufficiently explicit or documented to determine exactly how these assumptions relate to those of the Study, and so only the Bureau's probable case projections have been presented in Chapter 12.

## 11. Environment Element

*Source.* The environmental projections were prepared by the Study's central staff, with assistance from the Environmental Protection Agency, the Agency for International Development of the U.S. Department of State, the Council on Environmental Quality, and outside consultants. In particular, the Council on Environmental Quality and the Environmental Protection Agency conducted extensive reviews of the drafts of Chapter 13. On the basis of the first of these reviews, the Study's central staff rewrote the environmental chapter over a period of about six months. The primary contributions to the final draft came from several persons: Gerald O. Barney, Study Director; Jennifer Robinson, a member of the Study's central staff; Peter Freeman, a free-lance environmental and development consultant; Jeffrey Maclure, a member of the Study's central staff; Allan Matthews, a retired foreign service officer; Bruce Ross, an ecologist on the staff of the Central Intelligence Agency; Thomas Lovejoy of the World Wildlife Fund, Washington, D.C.; Paul Lehr, a Washington-area writer specializing in climatological issues; and Richard Hennemuth, Assistant Director of the Northeast Marine Fisheries Laboratory, National Oceanic and Atmospheric Administration, Woods Hole, Massachusetts.

*Explicit Linkages to Other Elements of the Government's Global Model.* The Study's environmental projections were based primarily on the medium cases of all of the Study's other projections. Although they were directly used by none of the Study's other projections, a serious attempt was made to assess how feedback from the combined influence of all of the environmental impacts would feed back to influence the population, GNP, and resource projections. The basic conclusion of this analysis was that feedback from the environmental projections would have significantly altered the population, GNP, and resource projections if it had been possible to include this feedback explicitly.

*Critical Policy and Technology Assumptions.* With regard to policy and technology, no major changes were assumed other than those implicitly carried forward from the other study projections from which the environmental impact projections were derived.

*Brief Description.* The original plan of the Study called for each participating agency to analyze the environmental implications of its own projections. It was assumed that in responding to the requirements of the National Environmental Policy Act, each of the agencies would have developed a capacity to analyze the environmental implications of its trend projections. As it turned out, most do now have some capacity for environmental analysis, but only rarely is the capability available for examining the environmental implications of long-range global projections. As a result, the environmental analyses that came appended to the agencies' projections, with some exceptions, were minimal or nonexistent. Confronted with this situation, the Study's central staff was forced to strengthen the contributions that had been made and to prepare environmental analyses in those cases where none had been contributed. A number of consultants assisted to accelerate the work, but the extended environmental analysis unavoidably delayed the Study. Along the way it became clear that the government presently has only a very limited analytical capacity for integrated, long-term projections of global environmental trends.

*Analytic Methodology.* The environmental projections were made using the descriptive, deductive, and inductive methods of scholarly and scientific research. Whenever possible, the environmental analyses emphasized the qualititative and quantitative aspects of the ability of the environment to support human life and to provide goods and services. Particular attention was given to situations in which the goods and services provided by healthy environmental systems are threatened for large portions of the world's population or over large geographical areas. Special attention was given to situations where widespread or irreversible damage to the environmental systems now threatens to occur. Uncertainties were unavoidable in the environmental analysis because there are still many gaps in scientific knowledge and data in this field.

The environmental projections or analyses were made from two different perspectives. One perspective started with each of the other (nonenvironmental) projections reported in the Study and analyzed the implications of that projection for the environment. This perspective is analogous to that involved in the preparation of the environmental impact statements required by the National Environmental Policy Act. The other perspective started with the overall environmental impacts of all the projected trends and analyzed the feedback implications of all these environmental impacts collectively on each of the other (nonenvironmental) projections. The government does not routinely perform analysis from this second (feedback) perspective, but parts of the annual *Environmental Quality* reports of the Council on Environmental Quality are analogous in intent.

*First Major Use.* The environmental analyses were necessarily developed specifically for this Study; however, they are based on techniques that have been in widespread use for decades.

*Geographic Representation.* Like the fisheries, forestry, and water projections, the environmental projections are complicated by the fact that the boundaries of the political jurisdictions responsible for management and data collection do not coincide with the natural boundaries of ecological systems. Whenever possible, the environmental analysis is presented in terms of geographical subdivisions that correspond to the areas of particular ecological systems (e.g., a river basin or watershed). In many cases, data limitations made it necessary to use national subdivisions in discussing specific examples of problems, when ecological boundaries would have been more appropriate.

*Temporal Representation.* In most cases environmental impacts are projected to the year 2000. They are developed generally from straight-line (linear) and from exponential (nonlinear) extrapolations of past trends, and from inference from ecological theory.

*Cases Analyzed.* As previously noted, the environmental projections were based primarily on the medium cases of the Study's other projections. Although they themselves were not used in developing any of the Study's other projections, a special analysis was subsequently prepared discussing many of the implications of the environmental projections with regard to the other (nonenvironmental) projections of the Study. This special analysis is presented as part of Chapter 13.

# 15 Population

## Census Projections

The Bureau of the Census (in the U.S. Department of Commerce) collects and publishes estimates and projections of worldwide population growth trends and demographic parameters, in addition to its major task of gathering material on the people and economy of the United States. Responsibility for developing these estimates and projections rests with the International Demographic Data Center in the Bureau's Population Division and with the Bureau's Foreign Demographic Analysis Division.

The Bureau of the Census's international demographic program was initiated in 1954 but did not receive any major impetus until the late 1960s, when improved statistical support was required by the State Department's Agency for International Development (AID). Previously, AID relied on official U.N. projections, published every five years, which were sometimes influenced by the interests of member states and were not considered sufficiently timely or flexible to meet the policy analysis needs of the Agency. Thus, in response to the requirements of AID and other federal agencies, the Bureau of the Census established and maintains a comprehensive set of population and related social and economic statistics for all nations of the world, with particular emphasis on the less developed countries (LDCs).

Fully reliable mortality and fertility statistics for most of these nations are not available from conventional sources, such as the official birth and death registers maintained by most LDCs. Therefore, in developing population projections (which require these statistics), the Bureau must estimate past mortality and fertility rates and assess other demographic conditions from incomplete data, making adjustments where appropriate after evaluating all data for possible errors. Only after such adjustments are made are the data suitable as a base for making projections. As a result, past demographic estimates (as well as future projections) are based on the professional judgment of the Bureau and may differ significantly from estimates made by other professional organizations.

Estimates of past population growth rates (derived from estimates of past mortality and fertility rates and past population structures) illustrate those differences. For example, the Census Bureau estimates that the population of the less developed world was increasing at an annual rate of 2.25 percent in 1975, compared to the U.N. estimate of 2.34 percent, a figure 4 percent greater. Since estimates of underlying mortality and fertility rates are nearly the same for the two agencies for 1975, this difference in the growth rates is presumably due to the different estimates of the population age structure.* Other organizations show much wider differences in their estimates of past growth rates in the less developed world. For example, AID estimates a 1975 growth rate of 1.88 percent and the Environmental Fund, 2.55 percent.[1]

Projections of the future are even more divergent than estimates of the past. Some experts at the 1978 annual meeting of the American Association for the Advancement of Science, for example, suggested that by the year 2000, the world may contain a billion fewer people than shown in projections by the U.N. agencies and other organizations. Other experts disagree, pointing to recent increasing birth rates in countries as diverse as Taiwan and the United States.

Many federal agencies, including the Departments of Agriculture, Energy, and the Interior, often rely on international population estimates and projections developed by organizations other than the Bureau of the Census—for example, the U.N. Population Division or the World Bank—apparently because the U.N. and World Bank estimates and projections are more widely known. Rarely, if ever, have these federal agencies critically compared the Census projections with those developed by other institutions. Other federal agencies, particularly AID, make more extensive use of the Census estimates and projections, in conjunction with those developed by other organizations.

---

* Conversely, the U.N. projects that the LDC population growth rate over the 1995–2000 period will be 4 percent lower than in the medium growth Census Bureau projections.

## Chicago Projections

At the suggestion of AID's Office of Population, for comparative purposes, an alternate set of population projections was provided to the Global 2000 Study by the University of Chicago's Community and Family Study Center. These projections (hereafter referred to as the Chicago projections) utilize a methodology that emphasizes the potential impact on population size of national efforts to provide family planning services. The projections are currently being used by AID to develop projections of the following critical social statistics related to population for selected countries: (1) size of the school-age population, labor force, and elderly population; (2) requirements for food, housing, schools, jobs, and medical facilities; and (3) trends in urbanization.

Both the Census and Chicago projections have been presented in Chapter 2. The high-, medium-, and low-growth Chicago projections of total population in the year 2000 are, respectively, 12, 7, and 3 percent lower than the Census projections. These differences reflect Chicago's lower baseyear estimates of population size and fertility and Chicago's assumption that means of regulating fertility will be available throughout the world on an organized basis by the year 2000.

Because of the need to focus the Global 2000 Study on a limited number of scenarios and because the Census projections were made by a federal agency, only the Census projections have been used in developing the food and energy projections of the Study, which required exogenous population projections. Other projection methodologies used by the Study (which in many cases also required exogenous population projections) made use of various other, independently developed, projections.

## Key Analytic Methodology

Both the Census and Chicago projections are based on the cohort-component method of population projection developed by the Scripps Foundation in the early 1930s. This method, now the standard procedure for projecting population throughout the world, uses exogenous estimates of initial population size, disaggregated by age and sex, and exogenous age- and sex-specific projections of mortality, fertility, and net migration trends in order to produce age- and sex-specific projections of population size on a year by year basis. The name "cohort-component" refers to the fact that each "cohort" of total population (i.e., each group of males or females born in the same year) is treated separately and explicitly

with respect to each major demographic "component" (mortality, fertility, and net migration).

Standard statistical procedures were applied to develop both the Census and Chicago exogenous estimates of initial population and future mortality rates. Similar procedures were followed in developing the Census exogenous estimates of future fertility rates. But the Chicago exogenous estimates of future fertility rates were based on the application of a more complex quantitative methodology, which relied on different basic assumptions regarding the principal factors that influence fertility rates. Both the Census and Chicago projections assume that no migration will occur between any countries of the world during the period 1975–2000.

The Chicago methodology for projecting fertility trends was first developed at the University's Community and Family Study Center in August 1977, and is still being refined. The preliminary estimates dealt with the speed with which family planning programs are likely to be adopted by the various nations of the world and probable efficacy of these programs. These estimates were reviewed by a panel of demographic experts in September 1977. The panel members were critical of many aspects of the study and, in general, felt that the efficacy of family planning programs was greatly overstated. This criticism was supported by additional quantitative analyses already in progress at Chicago.

Adjustments reducing the estimated effects of family planning programs on crude birth rates by approximately 50 percent were therefore made by the Chicago group, and an extensive set of population projections for various countries and regions of the world was prepared for the Global 2000 Study in October 1977, which were roughly 10–20 percent lower than the Census projections. A final set of projections for all countries of the world was provided to the Global 2000 project in February 1978. They included a revision of regional projections, for which only rough estimations were available earlier. These are the projections, roughly 5–10 percent higher than Chicago's previous projections, which are presented in Chapter 2.

Both sets of projections were developed with the aid of computer programs written in FORTRAN and run on IBM 370/168 computers. The Census cohort-component program consists of approximately 1,100 lines of programming instructions, including extensive comments and supported by a program for estimating projected life tables of approximately 200 lines and a program for estimating projected age-specific fertility rates of approximately 15 lines.* The Chicago cohort-component program consists of approximately 800 lines of programming instructions, including comments. In addition, the Chicago fertility methodology utilizes a separate 30-line FORTRAN program to calculate total fertility rates and a 15-line FORTRAN program to transform the total fertility rates into age-specific fertility.

## Basic Principles

The cohort-component methodology is focused almost entirely on the following basic demographic equation:

Net population change = births − deaths ± net migration.

In order for this relationship to hold, it must refer to a fixed territory, and there must be no measurement error in any of the components. Regional and total world population projections are obtained by simply summing the relevant country and subregion projections, assumed independent of each other. Additions to a population within a given area are made when a birth occurs or a migrant arrives; conversely, population numbers are decreased through death or emigration.

Factors that determine the rates at which these events occur are peripheral to the methodology and their influence is almost always exogenously estimated. Explicit projections of mortality, fertility, and net migration are required by the cohort-component methodology. However, the factors that underlie these projections are usually not explicitly specified. Not only are they not precisely quantified, but often they are not even precisely identified. The Chicago fertility projections constitute a rare exception to this rule. Moreover, with regard to net migration, any balancing of projected flows of immigrants and emigrants between different populations must be performed exogenously if country and subregion projections are to be consistent with each other. Consistency was obtained in the case of the Global 2000 Study by assuming zero net migration.

Under the cohort-component methodology, population projections are developed exclusively on the basis of (1) an initial estimated population structure for a given base year, in terms of the various population cohorts by sex, and (2) a set of exogenous projections of mortality, fertility, and net migration rates for each year covered by the projection, specified for each of the various population cohorts. A cohort of population (or, more properly, a birth cohort) is the total number of males or females within a population born in the same year and therefore of the same age, though cohorts can also be specified for periods other than a year. For example, a 5-year cohort would refer to the group of males or females within a population born during the same 5-year period.

Projections are developed sequentially on a year by year basis, starting with a base-year estimate of the population structure of the region or country. Each cohort is projected to age a year according to its exogenously estimated mortality rate (expressed in terms of a survival ratio) and any exogenously estimated net migration (which may be expressed either in terms of a rate or an absolute number). Births are calculated by multiplying each female cohort in the fertile ages by its exogenously estimated fertility rate for that year (expressed in terms of annual births per thousand women of a given age group). These calculations produce a new population structure, which differs from the original base-year structure and is used as the new base year for calculating the subsequent year's population structure.

Because mortality, fertility, and net migration rates are exogenously estimated for all years covered by the projection in advance of any calculations to project overall population structure for those years, the cohort-component methodology implicitly assumes that age-specific mortality, fertility, and net migration rates are not directly related to overall population structure. For example, although the total number of births projected for a given year is dependent on the number and age composition of fertile women just projected for the preceding year, the fertility rates themselves are independent of other population statistics. This means, in effect, that the probability of a woman having a child in a given year is assumed to be independent of the ratio of men to women or the ratio of dependents to persons of working age.

The cohort-component methodology also implicitly assumes that exogenously estimated mortality, fertility, and net migration rates are not directly related to the impact of future population size and structure on the allocation of economic resources or the development of social policy. For example, although exogenous projections of mortality rates are implicitly based on projected trends in economic growth and the modernization of social programs, they are not explicitly based on precise, quantitative relationships involving any of

---

* Estimation of base-year demographic parameters by the Bureau of the Census is also accomplished making use of the computer programs presented in the Bureau's *Computer Programs for Demographic Analysis*, by E. Arriaga, P. Anderson, and L. Heligman, (Washington, GPO, 1976).

the following variables: per capita income; requirements for food, housing, schools, jobs, or medical facilities; likely welfare expenditures (explicitly taking into account a country's projected investment and foreign exchange requirements); the influence of environmental factors; and potential fundamental economic, social, or political change.

Most demographers making use of the cohort-component methodology agree that many of these relationships are important determinants of population structure. However, they also point out that there is no general agreement among demographers as to what kind of influence each of these factors has on mortality, fertility, and net migration. Agreement is also lacking on how such influences should best be represented quantitatively in terms of equation structures and on the values that should be given to coefficients and exponents within particular equations.

Some demographers emphasize the importance of a country's cultural context, social norms, and general economic situation in determining fertility levels and trends. Many of these argue that high fertility rates can be projected to decline only if other major social changes are concurrently projected. These might include the achievement of a large per capita increase in national income, a more equitable distribution of national income, a widely available good health care system, increases in the number and scope of opportunities for women, improved opportunities for educating children, and the attainment of means—other than large families—of guaranteeing security in old age.

Other demographers emphasize the importance of facilitating the direct regulation of fertility itself through the practice of contraception, sterilization, or abortion. Many assert that changing socioeconomic contexts can have little influence in reducing high fertility rates if information and technologies related to fertility regulation are not widely available. They also point out that projecting the implementation of effective national programs to make them available implicitly assumes that the other improvements in socioeconomic conditions will be occurring at the same time.

Still other demographers question whether making available information and technologies related to regulating fertility is likely to have much influence in producing significant fertility rate reductions in many countries with strong pro-natalist traditions. Some point out that higher per capita incomes appear to be associated with higher fertility rates in many LDC populations.

Demographers also point out that there is little general agreement among economists and social scientists as to the influence of population size and structure on the economic and sociologic variables that might, in turn, influence population size and structure. Some economists assert that high population growth creates pressures on limited natural resources, reduces private and public capital formation, and results in additions to capital resources being used to maintain, rather than increase, the stock of capital per worker. Others point to positive effects, such as economies of scale and specialization, the possible spur to favorable motivation caused by increased dependency, and the more favorable attitudes, capacities, and motivations of younger—compared with older—populations.

Thus, rather than pick a set of explicit relationships that might not be readily defensible on an individual basis, Census Bureau demographers prefer to state that levels and trends in mortality, for example, are related to many factors, including the quantity and quality of food and housing, the degree of various economic pressures, the availability of medical knowledge, personnel, and supplies, and the extent of public health programs. They project levels and trends in mortality exogenously as summary statistics with no specific accounting for the individual influence of each of these factors and indicate that it may often be inappropriate to revise these exogenous projections to take into account different assumptions regarding any one variable (for example, food availability). According to the Census demographers, given the large number of factors that determine mortality, different reasonable assumptions regarding food availability could all be consistent with previously projected mortality assumptions.

For similar reasons, both the Census and Chicago projections for the Global 2000 Study assume that net migration between countries after 1975 will be zero. This assumption in part reflects a decision to simplify the projections and meet the deadlines set by the project. The cohort-component methodology requires that the careful balancing of flows of immigrants and emigrants between separate populations be performed exogenously— a laborious process that the methodology does not facilitate. Moreover, statistical material related to past international migration is largely incomplete and unreliable so that simple trend extrapolation is difficult and of limited usefulness.

However, the zero net migration assumption also reflects the fact that there is only limited agreement among economists or social scientists as to what causal factors (in what equations with what coefficient or variable values) are, or are likely to be, the main determinants of international migration trends under various circumstances. As it happens, the zero net-migration assumption has been approximately valid for most nations of the world in the past but has been clearly invalid for several—of which the United States is one of the most conspicuous. The assumption of zero net migration for the period 1975–2000 is thus based more on lack of time, resources, data, and theory than on a belief that this component will actually remain zero. Projecting major international migrations, of course, could have had a significant impact on many of the other projections developed for the Global 2000 Study. But projecting the magnitude and direction of such migrations, as in the case of projecting the dimensions and direction of climatological change, would have been somewhat arbitrary and extremely uncertain.

Many demographers feel that highly uncertain relationships should not be specified explicitly in developing population projections. The methodology, they feel, should either treat such relationships implicitly in developing exogenous mortality, fertility, and net migration projections, or it should disregard them altogether. *The Chicago fertility projection methodology represents an exception to this rule.* It makes comparatively daring assumptions regarding the widespread adoption and efficacy of family planning programs, expressing these assumptions in explicit, quantitative terms, and it uses the fertility projections thus obtained as exogenous inputs for making population projections.

The Chicago fertility projection methodology is based on five major assumptions:

1. Two major factors in determining the future course of a nation's fertility are the date at which it sponsors a national program to distribute fertility regulation ervices and the level of effort at which it implements that program.

2. Countries with no family planning programs now may be expected to begin at least weak (partial) programs within the very near future, and nations with weak or moderate family planning programs may be expected to strengthen them substantially. By the end of the century, every nation on earth is expected to have at least some kind of a substantial public or private planning effort.

3. Steady but not necessarily spectacular progress may also be expected in other areas of economic and social development (i.e., efforts to reduce infant mortality, promote adult literacy, raise the standard of living, and promote community development will continue at about present

rates). In other words, rapid fertility decline does not result solely from economic development or family planning progress but from both at once.

4. The projected rate of fertility decline will be directly proportional to the amount of family planning effort and the quality of those efforts, which, in turn, encompasses some variation to be found across continents, cultures, religious groups, and levels of economic activity.

5. The pace of decline of fertility will be that of a reverse S curve. When birth rates are high and family planning programs are still gaining social acceptance, the pace will be slow. As birth rates fall to lower levels, the rate of decline will accelerate to a maximum when the crude birth rate is between 20 and 38 births per thousand members of the total population. In this interval, the pace may be very rapid. When the crude birth rate reaches the lower 20s, complete saturation of contraception will have been approached. Non-adopters at this point will likely be young people starting families and a few reactionary late adopters. Fertility decline will continue, but at a decelerating rate until it reaches a replacement or near-replacement level.

These assumptions are explicitly quantified in a set of tables that present projected declines in total fertility rates over the 1975–2000 period as a function of the 1975 estimated values for (1) the total fertility rate and (2) the level of effectiveness of family planning programs within a given country or region. Only one set of tables is used to project fertility declines for all regions and countries for a given scenario; each of the three Global 2000 Study scenarios has its own set of tables. Only declines can be projected; no events or trends projected to occur after 1975 affect the fertility projections, which are solely a function of the two 1975 statistics noted above. The different sets of tables used to create the different scenarios embody different assumptions regarding the pace at which family planning programs might be adopted or strengthened and the projected efficiencies of the program. The tables were developed by the Chicago staff on the basis of statistical analyses of selected countries and critical review by other demographers.

Many demographers have suggested that the Chicago fertility projection methodology overemphasizes the influence of family planning programs on fertility rates, but few have proposed alternative methodologies to account for the influence of these programs in combination with other factors. In fact, most demographers, though they argue that the causality is more complex, agree with assumptions 1 and 2 above regarding the widespread adoption of family planning programs by the year 2000 and the subsequent decline in fertility, though they argue that the causality is more complex. For example, the Census fertility projections were based on the following set of assumptions, which resembles the fertility assumptions used in preparing the U.N. population projections:

1. The less developed countries will continue to make moderate progress in social and economic development during the 1975–2000 period.

2. Fertility rates will decline as LDCs undergo social and economic development. In the long run, fertility rates will decline more or less continuously, though some temporary plateaus may be encountered.

3. Almost all countries that do not already do so will make family planning services available to an appreciable portion of the population during the 1975–2000 period, and countries with family planning programs now in operation will extend coverage, particularly in rural areas.

4. Knowledge and methods of limiting family size will become better known and will be better used among populations that wish to reduce fertility, and expansion of these practices will expedite the process of fertility decline. In countries where rapid social and economic progress and strong desires for smaller families coincide, fertility decline will be very rapid.

Both the Census and Chicago assumptions (regarding projected fertility declines) may suggest to some that these fertility declines will be accompanied by equally rapid, concomitant declines in population growth rates in most countries. While declining growth rates are projected for some countries, it should be noted that although fertility rates declined in most regions of the world over the 1960–75 period, total world population grew at almost exactly the same rate during 1970–74 as during 1960–70 (1.9 percent per year), as shown in Figure 15–1. It is not surprising, then, that although the Study assumes declining fertility rates for most countries over the 1975–2000 period, world population growth is projected to continue at a constant rate (1.8 percent per year) over most of this period (1975–95) in the Census medium-growth projections. This assumes that in Bangladesh, for example, fertility rates will decline roughly 40 percent over the 1975–2000 period; it also assumes, in contrast, that fertility rates will increase 20 percent in the United States and 10 percent in Western Europe over the same period.

Both the Census and Chicago projections premised their exogenous projections of declining worldwide fertility rates on a continuation of recent trends of improvement in economic and social welfare. Yet the GNP projections for the Global 2000 Study show rates generally below recent historic experience. For some very poor countries, per capita GNP and per capita food consumption growth rates are in fact projected to be negative for the latter period.

Moreover, the fertility and mortality projections also assume that, although moderate progress will be made in improving means of both death and birth control, no major technical breakthroughs will occur. This is not considered unreasonable in view of the fact that breakthroughs, the major determinant of the decline in fertility and mortality will be the extent of diffusion of existing technologies throughout the population, especially in rural areas. A further assumption implicit in both sets of population projections is that the extent and rate of diffusion of existing technologies will be greatly influenced by the abilities of governments to diffuse such technologies through family planning and public health programs.

As a result, although improvements in birth control technology—for example, an oral contraceptive with fewer side effects, a pill that could be taken less frequently, a male pill, or reversible sterilization—may occur, as well as improvements in mortality-reduction technology, such as simple, easily applied, effective means for controlling gastroenteritis or eliminating schistosomiasis—it is unclear whether these technological advances will have an important effect on fertility and mortality levels by the year 2000. Accordingly, they are not represented in the projections.

It has also been implicitly assumed that there will be no technological regression (for example, no further accumulation of evidence of harmful side effects of birth control pills or of sterilization or no major loss of effective means of controlling smallpox). Technological breakthroughs or regressions would only move the projections slightly closer to the low or high series considered likely to form the upper and lower population limits, according to the demographers who prepared the projections for the year 2000.

## Basic Components

In terms of the requirements of the Global 2000 Study, the cohort-component methodology produces explicit estimates of future population growth based on exogenous estimates of mortality, fertility, and net migration (although the pro-

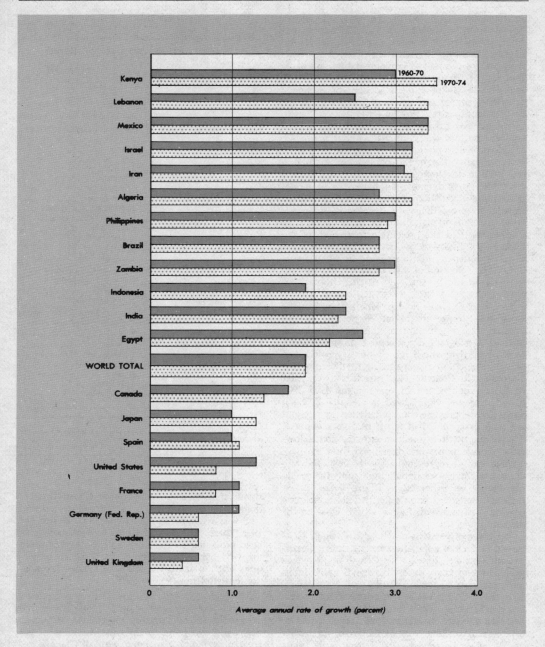

**Figure 15-1.** Population growth, selected countries, 1960–70 and 1970–74. *(Social Indicators 1976, Bureau of the Census, 1977)*

jections developed for the Global 2000 project assume zero net migration). The Chicago projections are based on a more explicit fertility forecasting methodology, devised from exogenous estimates of the rate of implementation and likely efficacy of family planning programs. Neither methodology takes explicit account of economic growth, resource requirements and availabilities, or environmental impacts. However, both methodologies assume that recent trends related to these factors will continue without major adjustment or disruption.

Specifically, the cohort-component methodology used in developing both sets of projections is executed by a dynamic computer-based model performing calculations on a year by year basis. Population projections are developed independently for individual countries or regions. The Census and Chicago projections prepared for the Global 2000 Study were developed separately for the 23 countries and subregions listed in Table 15–1. The selection of the countries and subregions was made by the staff of the Global 2000 Study.

The 12 LDCs for which separate projections were made represent about 75 percent of the current total population of the less developed regions. A geographic perspective on the methodology underlying these projections is provided in one of the colored maps used to illustrate the discussion in Chapter 14. Projections were prepared for each of the 25 years in the 1975–2000 period, and are summarized in Chapter 2. Each projection reports the total population by age and sex. Age is specified in terms of 5-year cohorts.

A high-growth, a medium-growth, and a low-growth projection were developed for each geographic entity, representing the highest, the medium, and the lowest population counts that could reasonably be expected in future years, given present trends and knowledge. Actual population growth is expected to follow a path close to the medium projection.

The three projections originate from single base-year estimates of population age structure, mortality, and fertility, although the Census and Chicago projections in many cases use significantly different estimates as well as different base years. Generally, 1975 was used in both sets of projections, when reasonably firm estimates of population size and fertility and mortality levels could be established for that year. Otherwise, an earlier base year was selected. The Census projection's treatment of the People's Republic of China is the most prominent example of a case where the selection of an earlier base year was of major

## TABLE 15–1

### Regions, Subregions, and Countries for Which Population Projections Were Developed

| Region | Subregions and Countries [a] |
|---|---|
| Africa | Egypt |
| | Nigeria |
| | Remainder of Africa |
| Asia and Oceania | People's Republic of China |
| | India |
| | Indonesia |
| | Bangladesh |
| | Pakistan |
| | Philippines |
| | Thailand |
| | South Korea |
| | Remainder of Asia and Oceania (excluding *Australia* and *New Zealand*) |
| Latin America | Brazil |
| | Mexico |
| | *Temperate South America* |
| | Remainder of Latin America |
| U.S.S.R. and Eastern Europe | *U.S.S.R.* |
| | *Eastern Europe* [b] including *Albania* and *Yugoslavia* |
| Northern America, Western Europe, Japan, Australia and New Zealand | *U.S.* and *Canada*, including *Greenland, Bermuda, St. Pierre*, and *Miquelon* |
| | *Western Europe* [c] |
| | *Japan* |
| | *Australia* |
| | *New Zealand* |

[a] Countries in italics are "more developed." All others are "less developed."
[b] Eastern Europe includes *Bulgaria, Czechoslovakia, German Democratic Republic, Hungary, Poland,* and *Romania.*
[c] Western Europe includes *Channel Islands, Denmark, Faeroe Islands, Finland, Iceland, Ireland, Isle of Man, Norway, Sweden, United Kingdom, Andorra, Gilbraltar, Greece, Italy, Malta, Portugal, San Marino, Spain, Austria, Belgium, France, Federal Republic of Germany, Liechtenstein, Luxembourg, Monaco, Netherlands,* and *Switzerland.*

significance in shaping the three Census projections. The most recent year for which reliable data was available for China was 1953. Hence, for 1975, three estimates of China's population have been projected by the Bureau of the Census from the 1953 base year, whereas the Chicago projections use the same projection of Chinese population growth from 1953 to 1975.

The high, medium, and low Census projections for each country and subregion use the same exogenous set of mortality projections. (China is the single exception to this rule, because of the great uncertainty associated with all Chinese demographic data.) Each Census projection also uses the same exogenous set of migration projections—namely, that net migration after 1975 between all countries will be zero.* Only the exogenous fertility projections are varied to produce the three population projections for each region and country.

The Chicago projections were developed in much the same way. They also assume zero net migration, but generally use different base-year estimates and different mortality and fertility projections. For the purposes of the Chicago fertility projections, each country covered was further identified as having a strong, moderate, weak, or no family planning effort, based on World Bank assessments.

As previously noted, much of the data underlying both projections is neither of good quality nor very timely. Theoretically, annual data on population growth or natural increase can be obtained from national vital registration systems or ongoing continuous surveys, but in practice neither of these two data collection systems is prevalent in the LDCs. Of 52 LDCs in a recent Census Bureau Study,[2] only eight currently have vital registration systems for birth and death data that are at least 90 percent complete. With the exception of Sri Lanka, all of these countries are in Latin America (Chile, Costa Rica, Guatemala, Guyana, Jamaica, Panama, and Uruguay). An additional five countries (Egypt, Tunisia, El Salvador, Nicaragua, and the East Bank of Jordan) have registration of births (but not deaths) with an estimated completeness of at least 90 percent. Six countries have ongoing continuous surveys, of which three (Lesotho, India, and Brazil) are currently collecting data that may be used to estimate growth rates or rates of natural increase on an annual basis.

In the absence of reliable data from vital registration systems and continuous surveys, countries must rely on censuses and ad hoc surveys for estimating levels and trends in population growth. By using the censuses conducted during the 1956–76 period, intercensal growth rates can be derived for 35 of the 52 countries reviewed. Egypt, Tunisia, the Republic of South Korea, and the Philippines each conducted more than two censuses during this period; therefore at least two intercensal growth rates can be computed for each of these countries.

Most of the countries reviewed have conducted at least one census or survey that collected data on both births and deaths; therefore they have estimates of population growth for at least one

point in time. Only four countries have conducted two or more such censuses, and 10 have conducted two or more surveys that collected such data. Thus, it is possible to obtain estimates of the trend in population growth for only a few of the 52 countries. Trends in the fertility component can be estimated for an additional 18 countries that collected data on births from two censuses, and for 15 countries that collected data on births from two or more surveys. None of these data collections, however, provides annual estimates of the level or trend in population growth or the components of change.

Existing vital registration systems afford the greatest potential for supplying regular and timely estimates of change; however, the time lag between collection and availability of data is often several years (for census data it is sometimes as great as six years, for survey data, generally only one to two years). While censuses and surveys may be taken at regular intervals, they cannot provide annual estimates of population growth. With the exception of those few countries which have reliable vital registration data, demographers are only now receiving enough information to measure population changes that occurred in the late 1960s and early 1970s.

## Basic Procedures

### Endogenous Population Size Projections

The following steps are followed by the Census Bureau's cohort-component program in developing population projections for a given country or region:

1. Begin by reading in the exogenous base-year estimates of the number of males and females in each 5-year cohort of the population (for example, the number of males aged 20–24).

2. Disaggregate these base-year estimates so that they are specified in terms of each single-year cohort of the population (for example, the number of males aged 20). This disaggregation is accomplished using an interpolation function that generates a smooth convex curve relating decreasing cohort size to increasing cohort age.

3. Then read in the exogenous mortality, fertility, and net migration, and fertility statistics estimated to be applicable to the base-year population during the base year. Mortality and net migration statistics are specified for each 5-year cohort of males and females, while fertility statistics are specified for each 5-year cohort of fertile females (for example, births per thousand females aged 15–19).

---

*For three countries in the Census projections (Mexico, the Philippines, and South Korea), migration through 1975 was projected in developing 1975 base year estimates utilizing earlier demographic data.

4. Disaggregate these mortality and net migration statistics so that they are specified in terms of each single-year cohort of the population. The mortality statistics are disaggregated using an interpolation function that generates a smooth convex curve relating decreasing survival ratios to increasing cohort age. The net migration statistics are disaggregated using an interpolation function that generates a skewed normal pattern with increasing cohort age, reflecting the assumption that most migration occurs in the working-age cohorts. The fertility statistics do not need to be disaggregated as annual births can be estimated by simply applying the annual average fertility rate for a 5-year cohort to the number in the cohort.

5. Read in the mortality, fertility, and net migration statistics projected as applicable to a somewhat changed population during a future year. As before, mortality and net migration statistics are specified for each 5-year cohort of males and females, while fertility statistics are specified for each 5-year cohort of females in the fertile ages.

6. Disaggregate the new mortality, fertility, and net migration statistics so that they are specified in terms of each single-year cohort of the population using the same disaggregation procedures described in step 4.

7. Calculate mortality statistics for the intervening years, using simple linear extrapolation.

8. Calculate net migration statistics for the intervening years, using simple linear extrapolation.

9. Calculate fertility statistics for the intervening years, using simple linear extrapolation.

10. Calculate successively, for each year for which mortality, fertility, and net migration statistics have been projected, the number of males and females in each single-year cohort of the population, according to the following sequence:

(a) add in half the year's net migration, which may be positive or negative; (b) survive the population forward a year according to projected survival ratios; (c) add in the other half of the year's net migration; (d) determine the number of new births by taking the projected number of females in each fertile cohort during the year, averaging the number before and after the migration and survival calculations are made, and multiplying by the appropriate fertility rate; (e) determine the number of surviving newborn infants at the end of the year, using the relevant projected survival ratio.

11. Use as the new base-year estimate the number of males and females in each single-year cohort of the population, as most recently projected, and repeat steps 5 through 11 until population figures have been calculated for all the years for which a projection is desired.

A similar sequence of steps is followed by the Chicago cohort-component program.

## Population Size: Egyptian Example

*In much of the rest of this chapter, Egypt has been used as an example to delineate similarities and differencs between the Census and Chicago uses of the cohort-component methodology. Differences in these examples point up, among other things, the extent to which projecting population statistics is an art rather than an exact science.*

Growth in the size of the Egyptian population as projected by the Census use of the cohort-component methodology is presented in Figure 15–2. As can be seen, Egyptian population grew at an average annual rate of 2.4 percent during the 1950–75 period and is projected to grow at almost the same rate (2.3 ± 0.4 percent), during the 1975–2000 period.

The same example from the Chicago projections (Fig. 15–3) shows a significantly lower annual growth rate for Egypt during the 1975–2000 period (1.8 ± 0.1 percent) than either past experience or the Census projections indicate. Both the Census and Chicago projections estimate that in the year 2000, Egyptian population will constitute 1.0 percent of world population.

The projections differ because they are derived from different base-year estimates of Egyptian population size in 1975 and make use of different exogenous projections of mortality and fertility rates. The Census 1975 population size estimate is lower than the Chicago estimate and the Census mortality rate projections are lower, but the Census fertility rate projections are higher, producing generally higher population size projections for Egypt in the year 2000. Both projections assume that no net migration will occur, no new technologies related to fertility or mortality rates will be developed, and recent trends in economic growth and modernization will continue.

The difference between the two estimates of Egyptian population size on July 1, 1975, arises because the Chicago projections are based on World Bank estimates of the 1975 population. In contrast, the Census projections are based on the preliminary count of the November 1976 Egyptian census (adjusted backward to July 1, 1975, based

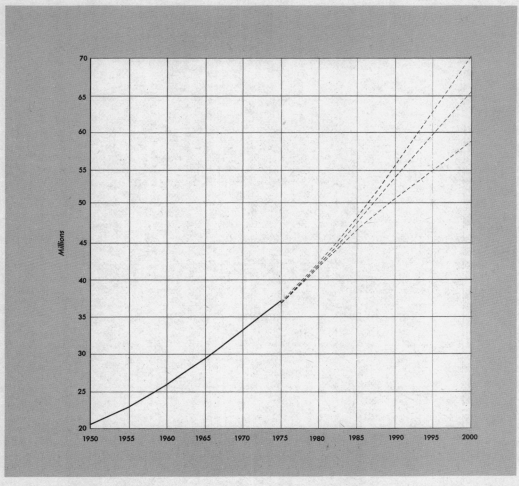

**Figure 15-2.** Egyptian population growth, 1950–2000, Census projections. Figures for 1950–75 are from *World Population 1975: Recent Demographic Estimates for the Countries and Regions of the World*, Bureau of the Census, 1976. Estimates were updated for the Global 2000 Study, resulting in a discontinuity at 1975 in the 1950–75 population time series. A revised, consistent 1950–75 time series is being prepared in conjunction with the Bureau's *World Population: 1977*, to be published in 1978.

on registered births and deaths, with births adjusted for 2 percent underregistration and deaths adjusted for 4 percent underregistration). Since only a preliminary census total was available, the census was not adjusted for coverage error. Because no age distribution from the 1975 census was available, the age distribution for 1975 from the U.N. medium variant projections was also accepted as the base-year age distribution for the Bureau of Census projections as well as for the Chicago projections.

**Exogenous Mortality Rates**

Both the Census and Chicago projections make use of the same two-step procedure in developing exogenous projections of mortality. First, target life expectancies at birth are projected at 5-year intervals over the period for which the forecast is to be made. Then, these figures are translated into survival ratios over the 5-year period for each 5-year cohort of the population (for example, males aged 20–24).

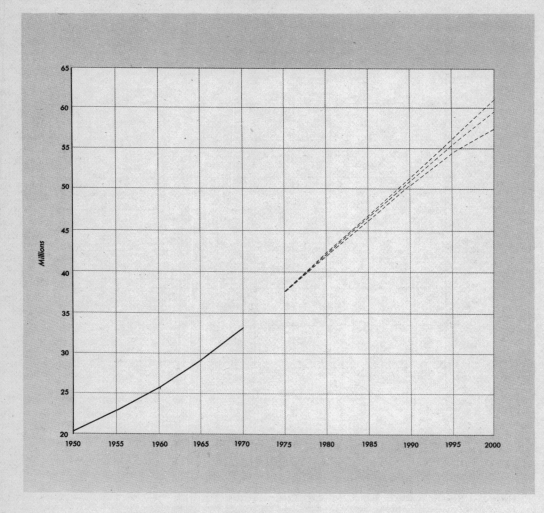

**Figure 15-3.** Egyptian population growth, 1950–2000, Chicago projections.
Figures for 1950–70 are from *World Bank Atlas, 1976.*

Target life expectancies at birth for each country are developed in one of two ways. For some countries, a target life expectancy at birth is chosen for the year 2000, with life expectancies for the intervening years obtained by assuming a reasonable pattern of change in mortality. For other countries, the pattern and degree of change in mortality from year to year is projected, with the eventual life expectancy in the year 2000 falling out of this process.

The choice of method depends on the nature of available data and the judgment of the demographer. For example, where trends in mortality change can be detected, they are judgmentally extrapolated. Where projections of life expectancy in the year 2000 are made by the country concerned and judged reliable, those projections are used. In fact, consideration is always given to national projections and those made by international organizations and to analyses of mortality trends that have occurred in similar countries in the same region that have already experienced that portion of the mortality transition relevant to the countries under consideration.

POPULATION 513

The Chicago mortality projections are derived in part from U.N. studies of trends in mortality decline and projections of future declines in mortality, assuming that national and international efforts to provide health and medical care to the population continue. They are also derived from World Bank adjustments to the U.N. projections, which are based on the observation that in recent years declines in mortality have not been as great as those anticipated by the United Nations in certain countries, especially LDCs. In most cases, these revisions have been reviewed by the United Nations, and future U.N. projections are expected to reflect the slower progress in mortality reduction encountered in recent years. In developing its projections, Chicago accepted the World Bank adjustments of U.N. mortality projections without further change. The Census Bureau, in developing its projections, used the World Bank adjustments as points of departure for further adjustments or as points of reference for independently developed projections.

### Mortality Rates: Egyptian Example

In the case of Egypt, for example, the Census and Chicago projections are based on slightly different exogenous estimates of life expectancies at birth in 1975 and on slightly different exogenous estimates of increase in life expectancies at birth to the year 2000. These differences are based on the different professional judgments of demographers at the Bureau of the Census and at the World Bank (the Bank's mortality projections are used by Chicago). These exogenous projections are considered by their authors to be roughly consistent with the comparable past experience of other representative LDCs that have moved through levels of economic and social development that the Census and Chicago projections assume will be applicable to Egypt in the future (in contrast to the lower economic growth projections presented in Chapter 2).

In general, projections of future life expectancies at birth are judgmental and are often extrapolated directly on graph paper by a hand-drawn curve or line, as shown in Figure 15–4, based on the results of the analysis previously discussed. They are not based on any explicitly defined quantitative relationships involving factors other than life expectancies or increases in life expectancy. It should be noted, incidentally, that when life expectancies at birth are projected for subsequent use by the cohort-component methodology, they are projected separately for males and females and are not averaged for summary presentation as they are in Figure 15–4.

Usually, life expectancies at birth are projected to rise more or less continuously, and related crude death rates are similarly projected to decline more or less continuously. Thus, although Egyptian crude death rates appeared to reach a plateau in the early 1970s, as shown in Table 15–2, future plateaus of this sort are not generally anticipated in either set of projections for any country or region.

Once target life expectancies for males and females at birth are projected for a given region or country, they are translated into survival ratios for 5-year male and female cohorts of all ages using four sets of Coale-Demeny regional model life tables[3] labeled West, East, North, and South. Each set contains 24 tables, calculated for males and females separately, with equal spacing of the values of life expectancy at birth for females, ranging from 20 years (level 1) to 77.5 years (level 24). The mortality levels in the male tables differ from those in the female tables with which they are paired, reflecting the typical relationship between male and female mortality in particular populations.

These tables are used to translate life expectancies at birth to survival ratios for the variously aged cohorts. Although in some cases the Census Bureau used these survival ratios without alteration, for most of the individual projections prepared for the Global 2000 Study, the pattern of change in survival ratios (as life expectancy changes) implied by the Coale-Demeny tables is used to adjust the empirical life tables available for the base date. The East tables are based mainly on Central European experience, whereas the North and South tables were derived from life tables of Scandinavian and South European countries, respectively. The West tables, on the other hand, are representative of a broad residual group, including Canada, the United States, Australia, New Zealand, South Africa, Israel, Japan, and

### TABLE 15–2
### Egyptian Crude Death Rates, 1950–75

| | Death Rate per Thousand |
|---|---|
| 1950–54 | 21.6 |
| 1955–59 | 19.9 |
| 1960–64 | 18.0 |
| 1965–69 | 15.8 |
| 1970–74 | 13.7 |
| 1972 | 13.2 |
| 1973 | 13.8 |
| 1974 | 13.0 |
| 1975 | 12.2 |

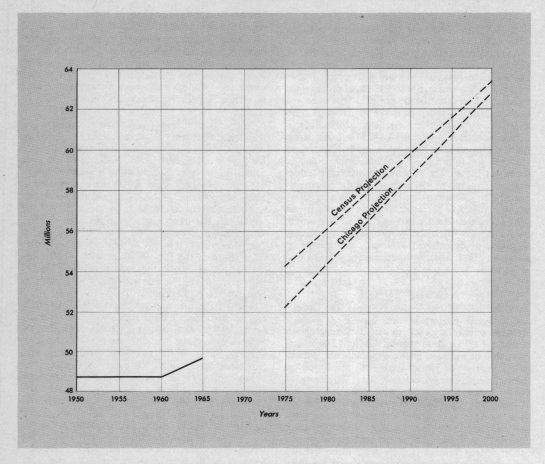

**Figure 15-4.** Projected Egyptian life expectancies, 1950–2000, medium growth case. Figures for 1950–65 are from V. G. Valaorgs, *Population Analysis of Egypt, 1950–70 (with Special Reference to Mortality)*, Cairo Demographic Centre Occasional Paper No. 1, Cairo, 1972, Tables 18–21.

Taiwan, as well as a number of countries from Western Europe.

The differences in the age and sex patterns of mortality in the four regional models are slight in some respects, pronounced in others, and vary in character with levels of mortality. Thus, no simple rules can summarize the extent to which the use of one set instead of another will affect the outcome in any particular application.

Thus, in the case of Egypt, the Census and Chicago projections are based on slightly different disaggregations of slightly different life expectancies at birth. The Census projections are disaggregations developed from the North model life tables (corresponding to Scandinavian experience

of the early and mid-20th century), whereas the Chicago projections developed from the South tables (corresponding to South European experience of the early and mid-20th century). Infant mortality levels are higher in the South than in the North tables. These differences, based on the differing professional judgments of demographers at the Bureau of the Census and the World Bank, are summarized in Table 15–3.

**Exogenous Fertility Rates: Census**

As already noted, the Census and Chicago projections are based on exogenous fertility pro-

## TABLE 15–3

### Age-Specific Egyptian Mortality Estimates, 1975

*(Probability of survival between 5-year cohorts)*

| 5-Year Cohorts | Males | | Females | |
|---|---|---|---|---|
| | Census | Chicago | Census | Chicago |
| 0–4 to 5–9 | .95130 | .92858 | .97729 | .93971 |
| 5–9 to 10–14 | .97991 | .98542 | .98968 | .98601 |
| 10–14 to 15–19 | .98338 | .98751 | .98999 | .98720 |
| 15–19 to 20–24 | .97709 | .98119 | .98509 | .98270 |
| 20–24 to 25–29 | .97242 | .97729 | .98207 | .97937 |
| 25–29 to 30–34 | .97085 | .97588 | .98110 | .97751 |
| 30–34 to 35–39 | .96797 | .97278 | .97922 | .97554 |
| 35–39 to 40–44 | .96255 | .96700 | .97558 | .97252 |
| 40–44 to 45–49 | .95437 | .95770 | .96955 | .96831 |
| 45–49 to 50–54 | .94122 | .94345 | .95843 | .95955 |
| 50–54 to 55–59 | .92249 | .92133 | .94288 | .94390 |
| 55–59 to 60–64 | .89358 | .88682 | .91865 | .91506 |
| 60–64 to 65–69 | .84662 | .83434 | .87763 | .86544 |
| 65–69 to 70–74 | .77613 | .75282 | .81600 | .78531 |
| 70–74 to 75–79 | .67664 | .63614 | .72546 | .66586 |
| Thereafter | .42108 | .42065 | .46330 | .44643 |

jections developed very differently. However, as in the case of mortality projections, both make use of a two-step procedure in developing exogenous projections of fertility. First, total fertility rates are projected over the period for which the forecast is to be made (at 5-year intervals in the case of the Census projections and yearly in the case of the Chicago projections). These total fertility rates are then disaggregated into age-specific fertility rates for each 5-year cohort of famales in the fertile ages (for example, females aged 15–19).

In the case of the Census projections, no mathematical model of fertility change was used in developing the total fertility rate projections. Instead, the projections were made on a judgmental basis by demographers who have worked with the demographic and related socioeconomic data for the individual countries for a number of years. For the less developed countries for which individual projections were made, the demographer set the target fertility levels and paths of fertility decline by taking into consideration the following major factors:

- Current levels and recent trends in fertility;
- Recent fertility trends in countries with similar cultural, social, and economic conditions and prospects;
- Current levels and recent trends in socioeconomic development;
- Current status and past performance of family planning and public health programs;
- Government policy on population matters;

- Expressed desired family size in the population; and
- Fertility assumptions made by international agencies such as the U.N. and the World Bank.

In determining the assumed range of total fertility rate levels in the year 2000, the guideline followed was: the higher the level of fertility at the base date and the greater the uncertainty about current fertility levels and trends, the wider the range.

Three assumptions about future trends in total fertility rates were made for each country or subregion, generally by setting the most likely rate, in the judgment of the Bureau of the Census, for the year 2000. This served as the assumed total fertility rate level for the Census Bureau's medium series. Assumed levels and trajectories for the year 2000 were also selected for the high and low series.

Virtually every industrialized country has made its own official national projections, and the assumptions in these projections were used with, in some instances, slight modification. The populations of Eastern and Western Europe were projected on the basis of the 1975 populations as shown in the U.N. medium series, adjusted slightly by the U.S. Bureau of the Census to take into account later fertility data. Trends in total fertility (as well as mortality) rates for 1975 to 2000 were borrowed from the U.N. projections, which were based on national projections made by the individual countries.

After the Census analysts developed their assumptions on fertility levels and paths, the assumptions for all countries and regions were compared for general consistency and reviewed within the Bureau. Next, the individual country and regional base data and fertility assumptions were discussed with a group of demographers familiar with less developed countries, drawn from universities, federal agencies, an international agency, and a research institute. Appropriate adjustments were then made by the Bureau.

In general, therefore, Census projections of future total fertility rates are judgmental—as are Census and Chicago mortality projections—and are also often extrapolated directly onto graph paper in hand-drawn curves, based on the results of the analysis previously discussed.

### Exogenous Fertility Rates: Chicago

In contrast, the Chicago projections of total fertility rates are based on an explicit quantitative methodology, whose underlying philosophy has

already been described. It is based primarily on
Table 15–4, which relates declines in crude birth
rates of a region or country to its current birth
rate and the strength of its current family planning
programs. The extreme right-hand ("None") column of the table gives the estimated annual
decline in the crude birth rate expected on the
basis of modernization alone, with no special
efforts at providing family planning information
and services. The anticipated downward trend is
almost linear, with a one-point decline in the
crude birth rate every four or five years (shown in
the table as a decline of .20 or .25 per year).
Under this set of conditions, it would require
about 135 years for a population to make the
demographic transition from a crude birth rate of
45 to the replacement level of about 15 per
thousand, which is applicable to many nations.

The "Strong" column of Table 15–4 gives the
annual decline in the crude birth rate that may be
expected in the presence of a strong, sustained,
well-financed, well-organized, and well-administered family planning program reaching the entire
urban and rural population. Under these conditions, it is estimated that the annual rates of
decline are two to four times those that would
occur in the absence of a program—an acceleration able to bring about a complete demographic
transition from a crude birth rate of 45 to one of
15 in about 38 years, or about one-fourth the time
required in the absence of a family planning
program.

The table was based in part on two regression
equations developed to measure a nation's fertility
change as affected by its current fertility level and
family planning program status. The first equation
determined the total fertility rate (TFR) of a region
or country in 1975 ($TFR_{75}$) as a function of its
TFR in 1968 ($TFR_{68}$), its crude birth rate in 1975
(CBR), the strength of its family planning program

## TABLE 15–4

### Assumed Annual Declines in Crude Birth Rate,[a] Chicago Projections

| Crude Birth Rate | Strength of Family Planning Effort | | | |
|---|---|---|---|---|
| | Strong | Moderate | Weak | None |
| 45 and over | .40 | .333 | .25 | .20 |
| 40–44 | .60 | .50 | .30 | .20 |
| 35–39 | .80 | .667 | .40 | .25 |
| 30–34 | 1.00 | .75 | .50 | .25 |
| 25–29 | 1.00 | .667 | .40 | .25 |
| 20–24 | .20 | .50 | .30 | .20 |
| 15–19 | .60 | .333 | .25 | .20 |
| 13–14 | .40 | .25 | .15 | .15 |

[a] Used indirectly in all three growth cases, as explained in the text.

in 1975 (FP), and its per capita GNP in 1975, as
follows:

$$TFR_{75} = 1741.255 + 0.559 \,(TFR_{68})$$
$$119.274 \,(CBR \geq 40)*$$
$$+ 301.053 \,(30 \leq CBR \leq 39)$$
$$- 587.635 \,(strong\ FP)* - 86.437 \,(median\ FP)$$
$$+ 0.028 \,(per\ capita\ GNP).$$

In order to compare empirically the annual
crude birth rate change observed with what was
projected, an equation to convert TFR decline
into CBR decline was used:[4]

$$CBR = 0.007 \,(TFR) + .2453$$

The results indicated that the amounts of decline initially projected (approximately twice the
rates of decline used in the final projections and
presented in Table 15–4) were too optimistic.
About one-half the projected decline was observed
in the data and because additional uncertainty was
implicit in the estimating procedures, simple
rounded values, about twice the originally estimated values, were inserted in the original version
of Table 15–4.

Because TFR is the unit of measure usually
employed in the population projection procedure,
and in order to escape several methodological
difficulties pertaining to age composition, sex
ratios, and interaction between fertility and mortality, this table was then translated into another
table, which related declines in total fertility rates
in a region or country to its current total fertility
rate and the strength of its current family planning
program. The following slightly different regression relationship was used, based on estimating
total fertility rates as a function of crude birthrates:[5]

$$TFR = 137.94 \,(CBR) + 106.16†$$

This basic TFR table was then transcribed into
sets of tables to facilitate the projection of a region
or country's total fertility rates, based solely on
its total fertility rate and the strength of its family
planning program in 1975 (each country was
classified as Strong, Moderate, Weak, or None,
according to the level of its family planning effort).
Three sets of tables were developed for high,
medium, and low fertility projections. (The medium growth set of tables is presented in Table
15–5.) The three sets of tables were based on the
following assumptions:

---

*These variables assume a value of 1 if the condition within
the parentheses is applicable, 0 if it is not.

†According to Chicago demographers, a transposition of
the earlier equation expressing CBR as a function of TFR
cannot be used here, given the separate error terms.

## TABLE 15–5

**Projected Annual Declines in Total Fertility Rates, Chicago Projections, Medium Growth Case**

| Family Planning Program in 1975 | Total Fertility Rate in 1975 | 1976–80 | 1981–85 | 1986–90 | 1991–95 | 1996–2000 |
|---|---|---|---|---|---|---|
| Strong | ≥ 6245 | 55.18 | | | | |
| | 5556–6244 | 82.76 | | | | |
| | 4866–5555 | 110.35 | | | | |
| | 4176–4865 | 137.94 | | Same as 1976–80 | | |
| | 3487–4175 | 137.94 | | | | |
| | 2797–3486 | 110.35 | | | | |
| | 2107–2796 | 82.76 | | | | |
| | 1899–2106 | 55.18 | | | | |
| Moderate | ≥ 6245 | 45.52 | 48.28 | 51.04 | 55.18 | 55.18 |
| | 5556–6244 | 68.97 | 73.11 | 77.25 | 82.76 | 82.76 |
| | 4866–5555 | 92.42 | 97.94 | 103.46 | 110.35 | 110.35 |
| | 4176–4865 | 103.46 | 114.49 | 125.53 | 137.94 | 137.94 |
| | 3487–4175 | 92.42 | 107.59 | 122.77 | 137.94 | 137.94 |
| | 2797–3486 | 68.97 | 82.76 | 96.56 | 110.35 | 110.35 |
| | 2107–2796 | 45.52 | 57.93 | 70.35 | 82.76 | 82.76 |
| | 1899–2106 | 34.49 | 41.38 | 48.28 | 55.18 | 55.18 |
| Weak | ≥ 6245 | 34.49 | 38.62 | 42.76 | 45.52 | 51.04 |
| | 5556–6244 | 41.38 | 49.66 | 59.31 | 68.97 | 75.87 |
| | 4866–5555 | 55.18 | 67.59 | 80.00 | 92.42 | 100.70 |
| | 4176–4865 | 68.97 | 80.00 | 91.04 | 103.46 | 120.00 |
| | 3487–4175 | 55.18 | 67.59 | 80.00 | 92.42 | 114.49 |
| | 2797–3486 | 41.38 | 49.66 | 59.31 | 68.97 | 89.66 |
| | 2107–2796 | 34.49 | 38.62 | 42.76 | 45.52 | 64.83 |
| | 1899–2016 | 20.69 | 24.83 | 28.97 | 34.49 | 44.14 |
| None | ≥ 6245 | 27.59 | 31.73 | 34.49 | 45.52 | 51.04 |
| | 5556–6244 | 27.59 | 34.49 | 41.38 | 68.97 | 75.87 |
| | 4866–5555 | 34.49 | 45.52 | 51.18 | 92.42 | 102.08 |
| | 4176–4865 | 34.49 | 52.42 | 68.97 | 103.46 | 120.01 |
| | 3487–4175 | 34.49 | 45.52 | 55.18 | 92.42 | 114.49 |
| | 2797–3486 | 27.59 | 34.49 | 41.38 | 68.97 | 89.66 |
| | 2107–2796 | 27.59 | 31.73 | 34.49 | 45.52 | 78.63 |
| | 1899–2016 | 20.69 | 20.69 | 20.69 | 34.49 | 44.14 |

*High fertility* projections assumed that each country would follow the schedule of changes indicated for its status by Table 15–4.

*Medium fertility* projections (deemed most likely to take place) assumed that, in addition to the schedule of fertility declines shown in Table 15–4, the nations would strengthen their family planning programs as follows:

• Nations with no programs will remain in that status until 1980, then trend toward a weak program by 1985, a moderate one by 1990, and a strong program by 2000.

• Nations with weak programs will remain in that status until 1980, then trend toward a moderate program by 1990, and a strong one by 2000.

• Nations with moderate programs will trend toward a strong program by 1990 and remain in that status until 2000.

• Nations with strong programs will remain in that status through 2000.

*Low fertility* projections (deemed less likely but possible) assumed that strengthening of family planning programs would take place as follows:

• Nations with no present programs will trend toward a weak program by 1985, a moderate one by 1990, a strong program by 1995.

• Nations with weak programs will trend toward a moderate program by 1985, toward a strong one by 1995, and will remain in that status until 2000.

• Nations with moderate programs will trend toward a strong program by 1980 and will remain in that status until 2000.

• Nations with strong programs will remain in that status through 2000, but the efficacy of their programs will improve from the present 38-year transition time to half that amount (19 years), equivalent to doubling the coefficients in Table 15–4, for the strong program.

If carried out without special adjustments, some of these assumptions (especially those used for the low projections) would produce absurdly low birth rates. It is therefore assumed that when birth rates approach replacement levels (considered roughly equivalent to a crude birth rate of 14 or a total fertility rate of 2.1), there is no strong resistance to further fertility decline, and the birth rates are allowed to sink to a minimum level and remain at this level for the rest of the century. These minimum levels per 1,000 females in the fertile-age groups are:

High-projection TFR = 2000 (CBR of about 14)
Medium-projection TFR = 1900 (CBR of about 13.5)
Low-projection TFR = 1800 (CBR of about 13)

Thus, the medium and low projections permit fertility levels in a few countries to fall somewhat below projected replacement levels in the year 2000. The nations of Western Europe and North America are already below these levels. The projections assumed that they will remain in this state for 10 years and will then trend linearly toward replacement by the year 2000; for medium and low projections, the rates trend linearly toward 1900 and 1800 respectively. As these countries reach a stage of absolute zero growth, it is expected that systems of subsidies and other inducements will be launched to encourage fertility in order to prevent declines in population size.

### Fertility Rates: Egyptian Example

Not unexpectedly, the use of different total fertility rate projection procedures by the Census and Chicago demographers led to somewhat different total fertility rate projections for most countries and subregions. For example, in the case of Egypt, the Chicago fertility projections are 30 percent lower than the Census projections, as shown in Figure 15–5.

In the Census Egyptian fertility projections, the estimated 1975 fertility rate of 5.8 was assumed to have declined by the year 2000 to 4.6 in the high series, to 3.6 in the medium series, and to 2.6 in the low series. In the medium series, the rate for the year 2000 was based on the ideal family size in Alexandria in the mid-1960s and in Cairo in 1970, adjusted downward 10 percent to allow for infertility and for an expected decline in the desired family size as the actual level of fertility declines. The 3.6 figure is also the same as that for 1995–2000 in the U.N. medium variant projections. The total fertility rate for the year 2000 in the high and low series was assumed to be plus or minus one child from the rate for the medium series. A large range between the high and low

series was chosen because of the great uncertainty in future fertility trends in Egypt.

The Census Egyptian fertility projections also take into account the large fertility decline that took place in Egypt since the mid-1960s, but that ended abruptly in 1972. Fertility has been rising sharply ever since. Although all three series assumed this fertility rise will abate, they differ as to the time it will take to return to 1972 levels. The high series assumes it will take 16 years, the medium series 8 years, and the low series 4 years. With this constraint, TFRs for the intermediate years were obtained by graphic interpolation between the 1975 and 2000 levels on the assumption that fertility will change according to a logistic or S-curve pattern.

The Chicago fertility projections for Egypt were developed according to Chicago's unique fertility projection methodology, described above, which would produce identical projections for any region or country with a 1975 total fertility rate estimated at 5.2 and a current family planning program of "moderate" strength.

In assessing these fertility projections for Egypt, two apparently countervailing phenomena not necessarily unique to Egypt need to be pointed out. First, in Egypt in 1975, higher household expenditure levels were apparently correlated with larger numbers of children per household, as shown in Table 15–6. Second, although the Egyp-

### TABLE 15–6

### Egyptian Personal Expenditure Distributions, 1974–75

*(Egyptian pounds)*

| House-hold Expendi-ture | Rural | | Urban | |
|---|---|---|---|---|
| | Expendi-tures per Person | Per-sons per House-hold | Expendi-tures per Person | Per-sons per House-hold |
| 0–50 | 28.7 | 1.3 | 33.0 | 1.1 |
| 50–75 | 32.1 | 1.9 | 45.8 | 1.4 |
| 75–100 | 29.2 | 3.0 | 38.9 | 2.2 |
| 100–150 | 34.3 | 3.7 | 43.9 | 2.9 |
| 150–200 | 38.5 | 4.5 | 46.8 | 3.7 |
| 200–250 | 42.7 | 5.3 | 48.4 | 4.6 |
| 250–300 | 45.9 | 6.0 | 57.6 | 4.8 |
| 300–350 | 49.3 | 6.6 | 64.0 | 5.1 |
| 350–400 | 55.4 | 6.7 | 64.9 | 5.8 |
| 400–500 | 61.5 | 7.1 | 72.3 | 5.9 |
| 500–600 | 69.9 | 7.7 | 87.6 | 6.3 |
| 600–800 | 81.4 | 8.5 | 105.4 | 6.5 |
| 800–1000 | 98.0 | 9.0 | 147.1 | 6.0 |
| 1000–1400 | 149.8 | 8.0 | 168.0 | 6.8 |
| 1400–2000 | 150.8 | 10.6 | 261.9 | 6.7 |
| 2000– | 418.7 | 9.2 | 358.6 | 6.9 |
| Average | 63.0 | 6.0 | 99.8 | 5.6 |

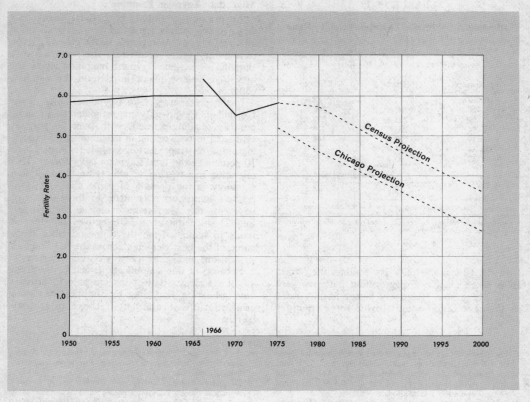

**Figure 15-5.** Projected Egyptian total fertility rates, 1950–2000, medium growth case. Figures for 1950–66 are from A. R. Omran, ed., *Population Problems and Prospects: Egypt*, Chapel Hill, N.C.: Carolina Population Center, 1971, Table 4. Figures are unadjusted register data. Real fertility rate declines may be masked by increasingly complete registration during the 1950–66 period.

tian Government has promoted family planning programs for several years, few expert observers with experience in Egypt believe that these programs have yet had much impact on Egyptian fertility levels. These factors raise questions as to the extent to which higher per capita incomes and a continuation or intensification of family planning programs are likely to lead to lower fertility rates.

Just as the Census and Chicago mortality projections used different procedures for disaggregating a summary statistic (life expectancy at birth) into age-specific statistics (survival ratios for 5-year cohorts), so too the Census and Chicago fertility projections used different procedures for disaggregating total fertility rates into age-specific fertility rates. As a result, significant differences may be observed in Table 15–7 regarding Census and Chicago estimates related to the fertility of younger, as compared to older, Egyptian women.

In the Census Egyptian fertility projections, the age pattern of fertility in 1975 was based on the age pattern of fertility in 1973, the latest year for which such data are available. For the Egyptian low series in the year 2000 the age pattern of fertility was assumed to be that of Cyprus in 1975. Cyprus was selected because its current age-specific fertility rates (ASFR) are known and because it currently has a total fertility rate very close to the low series target rate for Egypt for the year 2000 and is in the same region as Egypt. Cyprus is also part Moslem and therefore was also considered a reasonable proxy for Egypt in the year 2000 for purposes of disaggregating fertility rates. All other ASFRs, including the medium and high series patterns in the year 2000, were linearly interpolated between the 1975 ASFRs and year 2000 low ASFRs, on the assumption that ASFRs were linearly related to total fertility rates.

## TABLE 15-7

## Estimated Age-Specific Egyptian Fertility Rates, 1975

*(Births per thousand females)*

| Age Group | Census | Chicago |
|-----------|--------|---------|
| 15–19 | 27.1 | 88.6 |
| 20–24 | 192.6 | 240.4 |
| 25–29 | 293.3 | 259.9 |
| 30–34 | 263.6 | 218.5 |
| 35–39 | 230.3 | 148.2 |
| 40–44 | 105.9 | 72.0 |
| 45–49 | 50.8 | 14.3 |
| *Total Fertility Rate* [a] | | |
| 5.8 | 5.2 | |

[a] Per woman. The total fertility rate in a given year basically represents the average number of children each woman would have over her lifetime, assuming the age-specific fertility rates for that year applied to her lifetime. It is five times the sum of the age-specific fertility rates, divided by 1,000.

In the Chicago fertility projections, the World Bank's age-specific disaggregation patterns were used. These show relatively higher fertility rates in younger females and lower rates in older females.

### Migration: Egyptian Example

As previously noted, both the Census and Chicago projections assume zero net migration for all countries and subregions. In the case of Egypt (and many other countries) this is a serious simplification, since Egyptian migration levels are high and have a major impact on the nation's economy.

In the preliminary 1976 Egyptian census, over 1.4 million Egyptians were estimated to be temporarily residing abroad, with over 20 percent estimated to be working in neighboring oil-exporting countries (representing anywhere from 2.5 to 10 percent of the total Egyptian labor force). This migration has two major effects on the Egyptian economy in the opinion of some analysts: (1) a positive contribution is made to the balance of payments through foreign exchange remittances, but (2) since migration is selective and since it tends to remove from the domestic labor force some of the best elements across the full range of professions and skills, a heavy cost is incurred.

Because of this simplification, neither the Census nor Chicago projections are able to provide any indication regarding the implications of a continuation or change in these migratory trends.

## REFERENCES

1. For a comparison of Census Bureau estimates with those of other organizations, see R. Kramer and S. Baum, "Comparison of Recent Estimates of the World Population Growth," paper to be presented at the 1978 meetings of the Population Association of America.
2. J. Spitler and N. Frank, "The Feasibility of Measuring Population Growth in Developing Countries," Bureau of the Census, 1977 (mimeo).
3. A. Coale and P. Demeny, *Regional Model Life Tables and Stable Populations*, Princeton: Princeton University Press, 1966.
4. Donald J. Bogue, *Demographic Techniques of Fertility Analysis*, Family Planning Research and Evaluation Manual No. 2, Chicago: Community and Family Study Center, 1971.
5. Ibid., p. 16.

# 16  Gross National Product

The Agency for International Development (AID) in the Department of State is responsible for administering most of the U.S. Government's foreign assistance activities and economic assistance programs. In carrying out this responsibility, the Agency must analyze the probable future economic growth of countries throughout the world. Because of recent budget cuts, AID relies almost entirely on data and projections developed by other, largely international agencies. For information on world GNP (gross national product), the Agency depends largely on the World Bank.

The World Bank Group, an international cooperative organization associated with the United Nations, consists of three institutions: the International Bank for Reconstruction and Development (IBRD), the International Development Association (IDA), and the International Finance Corporation (IFC). The common objective of these institutions is to help raise standards of living in less developed countries (LDCs) by channeling financial resources from industrialized countries to the developing world.

The Bank's projections of the likely future economic growth of its LDC member countries, summarized in its annual *Prospects for Developing Countries,* are developed in the Comparative Analysis and Projections Division of the Bank's Economic Analysis and Projections Department. Ordinarily, these projections would not meet the needs of the Global 2000 Study because they do not extend beyond 1985, are not disaggregated by individual countries, and do not project economic growth in terms of GNP. Instead, projections are presented for three regional groups of industrialized countries and for six groups of less developed countries (representing about 87 percent of the population and national income of all LDCs). These projections are made in terms of GDP (gross domestic product) rather than GNP, but the difference is minor. GDP represents the total value of the net outputs of all units of production physically located within a country. GNP represents the total value of the flow of goods and services becoming available to the citizens and enterprises associated with a country, without regard to whether the income sources or recipients

are physically located within or outside of that country. In most less developed countries, GDP and GNP differ by only a few percent and grow at about the same rate. Therefore, presenting GNP growth rates as equivalent to GDP growth rates for LDCs is a reasonable procedure. Industrialized GNP growth rates were projected directly and therefore did not require conversion from GDP.

Fortunately, GNP projections to the year 2000 on a country by country basis that are roughly consistent with official World Bank projections have recently been published. Although these projections have not been officially endorsed by the Bank, they were prepared with the assistance of members of its staff and were accepted for use by a blue-ribbon panel of international energy experts. In early 1976, the MIT-sponsored Workshop on Alternative Energy Strategies (WAES) asked members of the Bank's Development Policy Staff for assistance in making GNP projections of likely economic growth to the year 2000 for all LDCs, and a report making such projections was published in 1977.*

Two sets of GNP growth projections for the LDCs were developed for the WAES study: a high-growth and a low-growth scenario for 1976–85 and 1985–2000. The high-growth case, in general, projects a continuation of 1960–72 growth patterns, whereas the low-growth case projects a continuation of the pattern characteristic of the 1973–75 period and just sufficiently above that period's population growth to allow an advance in real global GNP per capita. In both scenarios, all GNP growth rates were reduced by roughly 10–30 percent for the period 1985–2000 by WAES analysts to take into account the future impact of declining population growth rates on GNP growth.

Because the two WAES projections cover virtually all countries outside of communist areas on a country by country basis and extend to the year 2000, they serve as the source for the high and low GNP figures presented in Chapter 3 of this volume. A third set of medium-growth projections was developed for Global 2000 Study by averaging

* *Energy: Global Prospects, 1985–2000.* New York: McGraw-Hill, 1977.

the growth rate used in the high and low projections. It should be noted that the WAES high-growth case corresponds approximately to World Bank midlevel projections* for the 1976–85 period.

Projections for GNP growth in communist areas were provided to the Global 2000 Study by CIA regional economic specialists.†

## Key Analytic Methodology

The CIA projections for the various Soviet bloc countries and the People's Republic of China were developed using a combination of professional judgment and basic econometric techniques, including simple trend extrapolations and production-function calculations.‡

The WAES projections for the industrialized countries were developed on an independent, country by country basis by panels of experts assembled by WAES. The panels' projections were based on the use of available econometric models, official government forecasts, and the judgment of government experts.§ They preceded the development of the GNP projections for LDCs. Official World Bank projections for the industrialized countries are developed in much the same way but tend to be higher because they give more weight to official national forecasts.

The GNP projections for the LDCs in the WAES study, which complemented those made earlier for the industralized countries, were developed by the World Bank staff in much the same way as official global World Bank projections—as part of a three-step process: (1) Projections were developed by analysts on an independent, country by country basis, relying on a combination of professional judgment and the use of specialized country or regional models. (2) Using a computer-based model, the various country projections were aggregated and adjusted on a globally consistent basis to reflect probable economic growth constraints due to likely limitations in the availability of foreign trade earnings and foreign investment capital. (3) The projections were further judgmentally adjusted by Bank and WAES analysts.

World Bank projections for individual countries, generally based only on the completion of step one, reflect Bank's optimistic but realistic assessment of growth rates that could be achieved under optimal circumstances (including high economic growth rates for the Western industrialized nations). Thus, they are not necessarily forecasts. However, in preparing global reports that aggregate individual LDCs into groups, the Bank staff has in the past completed steps two and three in order to ensure that the aggregate projections are realistic in view of expected total LDC export earnings and the expected availability of foreign investment capital. It is thus assumed that not all LDCs could experience optimal circumstances simultaneously. For the WAES study, following completion of these three steps, these aggregate projections were then disaggregated for individual LDCs, extended to the year 2000, and further adjusted to reflect the views of the WAES staff regarding the impact of energy shortages and unspecified declines in population growth rates.

Step two has been performed in the past for the World Bank and for the WAES study with the assistance of a World Bank econometric model known as SIMLINK (SIMulated trade LINKages).* This model performs the calculations which, on an explicit quantitative basis, adjust initial economic growth rates to correspond to the projected availability of foreign trade earnings and foreign investment capital, taking into account the growth rates of the industrialized countries and the LDCs simultaneously. It was during this step that the lower WAES GNP projections for the industrialized countries were substituted for the higher World Bank projections.

Development of the SIMLINK model was begun by the World Bank in early 1974 in order to analyze trade linkages and growth prospects for

---

* As contained in "Prospects for Developing Countries 1977–85," World Bank Staff Study, Sept. 1976.

† Some confusion resulted from this process because the base-year (1975) figures used by the CIA and the World Bank were derived using different conversion methodologies. The net result is that the low-growth rate of 2.5 percent for China and 1976 GNP figure for the U.S.S.R. are regarded by the CIA as being too low. It should be noted, however, that the World Bank model used for the WAES study to develop the GNP projections for the LDCs assumed a 6 percent growth rate for the socialist bloc for all growth cases, which significantly exceeds current CIA estimates.

‡ The methodology currently used by the CIA to make Soviet economic projections, which is representative of the methodologies underlying the other CIA projections, is briefly described in *Soviet Economic Problems and Prospects,* Joint Economic Committee, Aug. 8, 1977, pp. 29–30.

§ These are described in some detail in Workshop on Alternative Energy Strategies, *Energy Supply-Demand Integrations to the Year 2000: Global and National Studies,* Cambridge, Mass: MIT Press, 1977.

*Described officially in *The SIMLINK Model of Trade and Growth for the Developing World,* World Bank Staff Working Paper—No. 220, October 1975 and also in Norman L. Hicks et al., "A Model of Trade and Growth for the Developing World," *European Economic Review 7,* 1976.

LDCs under alternative scenarios of development and inflation in the industrialized world. By the end of April 1974, a working version of SIMLINK was available and was used as the basis for the first annual issue of *Prospects for the Developing Countries*. One of the first analyses to be produced by SIMLINK was the effect on LDC economic growth rates of potential changes in the international price of oil. The model supported the view that the direct impact of changes in the price of oil on LDC growth would be minor. However, the same analysis also indicated that the impact of changes in the growth rates of the industrialized nations on LDC growth would be major. Subsequently, the WAES study examined in greater detail the extent to which the economic growth rates of the industrialized nations might be significantly reduced by changes in the international price of oil. The WAES study established that such impacts could be significant, in which case the indirect impact of changes in the international price of oil on LDC growth would be major.

Since its development, SIMLINK has undergone a series of major enhancements and has been adapted to meet changing economic perceptions and World Bank needs. Version V (1975–76) served as the basis for the WAES study. Version VI (1976–77), the most recent version, was utilized by the Bank's Development Policy Staff until mid-1977 and thus, indirectly, by AID and other federal agencies. For this reason, and because the SIMLINK V runs supporting the WAES study are no longer available, a set of three SIMLINK runs based on Version VI was developed by the World Bank staff for the Global 2000 Study as the basis for this methodological discussion. These runs correspond to the high, medium, and low GNP growth scenarios and do not incorporate the subsequent judgmental adjustments customarily performed by Bank and WAES analysts (step 3).

At the time of its development, SIMLINK was neither considered nor intended to represent a theoretical breakthrough in econometric modeling. It combined several existing modeling techniques in a comprehensive system intended to furnish information for policy decisions on a timely basis. Comprehensive in nature, the model was simple enough to be calculated quickly.

Previous modeling efforts involving LDCs consisted largely of parallel, but often unconnected, work along three broad lines: country models that concentrated on one country and assumed the rest of the world as exogenously given; commodity models that examined market equilibrium conditions for a single commodity; and world trade models that used a static share-relationship to balance world exports and imports. Another effort had been made to combine large econometric models and world trade relationships (Project LINK), but it had not proven useful for studies of the less developed world, since most of the models were short-term forecasting models of the industrialized world without the dynamics of the commodity markets and without adequate LDC models. In addition, the LINK system was considered by the World Bank staff to be too unwieldy to provide timely analyses of policy alternatives.

SIMLINK was developed by a team of eight professionals with expertise in economics and econometrics. It has always been a part-time project for those involved with it, so that the cumulative resources invested in it to date are equivalent to roughly three years of one person's full-time effort. Major enhancements since 1974 have included the development of more detailed commodity specifications, more meaningful country aggregations, and improved trade dynamics. It contains over 200 econometric structural equations, not counting definitional equations and identities. It is written in approximately 1,500 lines of FORTRAN, including extensive comments and is run on the Bank's Burroughs 7700 computer.

Before developing SIMLINK, World Bank economists generally used simple calculations and judgment in adjusting regional economic growth projections to be consistent with the likely availability of foreign investment capital and foreign exchange earnings. While SIMLINK has allowed the Bank to make these adjustments on a more explicit, consistent, and sophisticated basis, many members of its Development Policy Staff have become uncomfortable with SIMLINK's simplicity relative to econometric models used for other purposes and have been developing larger, more detailed and sophisticated regional and global econometric models to take the place of SIMLINK. These new models are expected eventually to be more capable structurally of simulating LDC internal investment processes, reciprocal trade linkages between LDCs and the industrialized countries, technological change, resource depletion, and structural change within LDC economies. In particular, the new models are expected to produce acceptable results for a wider range of variation in economic indicators and structure than is possible with SIMLINK. No major enhancements to SIMLINK are currently planned.

While it is clear that the SIMLINK approach has many limitations, it must be emphasized that SIMLINK was not explicitly designed for the purposes to which Global 2000 has put it. According to World Bank analysts, if more time had been available for the completion of the Global 2000 Study, most, if not all of the model's major shortcomings could in fact be remedied. In any event, they note, imperfect as it is, SIMLINK is vastly superior to any model or system that could have been used for World Bank purposes. However, they feel that should the Global 2000 analysis be continued somewhere in the U.S. government, it is clear that a high priority must be given to the development of a much more sophisticated and suitable global economic model.

## Basic Principles

The purpose of SIMLINK is to aggregate and adjust, as appropriate, the economic growth projections developed for individual LDCs by World Bank analysts, so as to take explicit account on a consistent basis of likely limitations in the world-wide availability of foreign trade earnings and foreign investment capital. If individual Bank projections were aggregated without these adjustments, total world trade and foreign investment would exceed plausible levels.

Those 1975–85 projections were adjusted (generally downward) for the WAES study to reflect judgmental estimates by World Bank and WAES analysts of the likely impact of additional factors (particularly changes in energy prices and availabilities) on real GNP growth (Table 16–1). SIMLINK projections for most LDCs were roughly 5 percent lower than the Bank's initial individual

projections and roughly 10 percent higher than the 1975–85 judgmental final projections used by the WAES study and the Global 2000 Study.

In order to perform its calculations, SIMLINK requires exogenous projections of four major sets of variables, which must be separately specified for each year being projected. Projections of these sets of variables were developed by various World Bank country and commodity specialists, largely on an independent basis, and then aggregated as appropriate for SIMLINK. They are the major sets of variables changed in creating new scenarios and include the following:

- Real economic growth rates for the Western industrialized nations (aggregated into three groups).
- Real prices for the 25 primary commodities and commodity groups exported by the LDCs
- Four separate inflation indices.
- Estimates of the maximum potential gap between export earnings and import expenditures, on current account, which the LDCs (aggregated into six groups) are likely to be able to sustain. These estimates act as a surrogate for estimates of likely foreign capital flows into the LDCs.

Other exogenous projections are also required by SIMLINK but are almost never varied in creating different SIMLINK scenarios. For example, for each LDC group, SIMLINK requires exogenous projections of the proportional mix of exported primary commodities and other goods

### TABLE 16–1

#### Projected Average Annual Real GNP Growth, by Adjustment Steps, Medium Growth Case, 1975–85

*(Percent)*

|  | Step 1 Individual Countries[a] | Step 2 SIMLINK[a] | Step 3 Judgmental Final[b] | SIMLINK vs. Individual Countries | SIMLINK vs. Judgmental Final |
|---|---|---|---|---|---|
| Western industrialized nations | 4.1 | 4.1 | 4.0 | 0.0 | 0.1 |
| Socialist nations | 6.0 | 6.0 | 3.0[c] | 0.0 | 3.0 |
| LDC Groups[d]: |  |  |  |  |  |
| India | 3.1 | 3.6 | 3.6 | 0.5 | 0.0 |
| Other South Asian countries | 4.9 | 4.9 | 3.6 | 0.0 | 1.3 |
| Low-income Africa | 4.8 | 4.6 | 3.6 | −0.2 | 1.0 |
| Lower-middle income | 6.4 | 5.8 | 5.4 | −0.6 | 0.2 |
| Middle income | 5.0 | 4.9 | 5.6 | −0.6 | 0.6 |
| Upper-middle income | 5.5 | 5.1 | 4.4 | −0.4 | −0.6 |

[a] Calculated using estimates of 1975 levels of economic activity, which differ from those presented in Chapter 3. Analysts at the World Bank, which developed both sets of 1975 estimates (using different methodological assumptions), recommended that the Global 2000 Study make use of them in this way.
[b] As presented in the WAES study and in Chapter 3 of this volume.
[c] The WAES study did not publish this figure, which summarizes the projections for the U.S.S.R. and Eastern Europe presented in this study.
[d] Constituent countries are identified subsequently in the discussion, under the heading "Basic Components."

and services for each year being projected; as a result, the proportional mix of exports for each LDC group can be and is specified to change over time, although the specifications themselves, once made, are rarely changed. In contrast, the proportional mix of imports for each LDC group is not exogenously specified but is incorporated in the model's structure in the form of linear equations whose constants and coefficients do not change.

Other examples of variables requiring exogenous projections that are rarely changed include: economic growth rates of the socialist nations; elasticities of demand for manufactured goods from the LDCs (as a single aggregate) with respect to economic growth rates in the Western industrialized and socialist nations (four aggregates)*; and proportional compound growth rates in exports of manufactured goods for each of the six groups of LDCs. A single set of demand elasticities with respect to LDC exports of manufactured goods is used for all years being projected. The proportional compound growth rates in exports of manufactured goods for each group of LDCs are separately specified for each year being projected.

SIMLINK then calculates:

- World trade volumes for the various primary commodities.
- Export earnings (in dollars) associated with these trade volumes adjusted for inflation and terms of trade.
- Allocations of these export earnings to each of the six groups of LDCs.
- Total balances available to pay for imports into each LDC group (export earnings plus the maximum potential gap between export earnings and import expenditures, a surrogate for foreign capital flows into the LDCs).
- Real growth rates for each of the six groups of LDCs, based on their capacity to pay for imports from export earnings and foreign capital flows.

The relative efficiency of SIMLINK is achieved through simplicity. LDC economic growth rates are projected solely as a function of internal investment rates, capital flows from the industrialized nations, and trade with the Western industrialized and socialist nations (as projected by SIMLINK, based on differential inflation rates, industrialized economic growth rates, and exogenous price projections). Trade between LDCs is

excluded.* LDC economic growth rates have no impact on the growth rates of the industrialized nations, which, in turn, are not projected to have any impact in the ability of the industrialized nations to invest in the LDCs.

Commodity price projections are exogenously estimated and generally updated by Bank analysts every six months. These projections are consistent with the Bank's current projections of economic growth rates in the industrialized nations. However, in developing separate high, medium, and low growth scenarios, a single set of exogenous commodity price projections is used. The prices are thus independent of changes in the Study's specification of economic growth rates in the industrialized nations, as well as independent of trade volumes and LDC economic growth rates calculated by the model.

Each LDC group contains countries with per capita incomes falling into certain predesignated ranges. Thus, countries as diverse as Bolivia, Thailand, and Morocco—or Argentina, Jamaica, and Yugoslavia—are grouped together on the assumption that they behave economically in structurally equivalent ways, despite their obvious sociopolitical and geographic differences. Earlier versions of SIMLINK had far more homogeneous regional and income groups. The present country groups were subsequently created by Bank analysts to ensure that SIMLINK would not appear to be analyzing country-specific policies.

SIMLINK is also premised on the common assumption used in short-term econometric models that no major structural changes will occur within the groups or the international economic order during the period for which it generates projections. It cannot be used to produce meaningful results based on exogenous inputs that assume that such changes will take place, and it cannot project such changes endogenously. Individual country models developed by World Bank analysts may, to some extent, incorporate assumptions regarding structural change, which are in turn reflected in the exogenous assumptions used by SIMLINK. But except for these adjustments, SIMLINK implicitly assumes, for example, either (1) that significant resource or environmental contraints will not be encountered, major technological change will not take place, the LDCs will not succeed in raising the relative prices of primary commodities through cartelization, the industrialized nations will not implement

---

*According to Bank analysts, these elasticities have proved to be one of the weaker parts of SIMLINK. Final results turn out to be extremely sensitive to the assumptions made here.

*Bank analysts note that any existing trade between LDCs is implicit in the model's parameters, which cover the behavior of the past.

increasingly protectionist policies, rising LDC debt levels will not significantly impede LDC economic growth, and major military, political, or cultural change will not occur; or (2) that such events will have no net impact on present patterns of economic behavior and hence may be disregarded.

The model thus implicitly also assumes (1) that the existing economic system and associated financial institutions and facilities are fundamentally sound, (2) that the industrial nations and the LDCs have a reciprocal interest in maintaining and developing the existing system, and (3) that this reciprocal interest is based on the unavoidable dependence of the poor on the prosperity of the rich.

These assumptions may seem to imply that recent demands of the LDCs for a "new economic order" will not be met; SIMLINK, however, was not designed to analyze this issue. Such a new economic order would involve major changes in the structure of world industry, a new international division of labor, and a dramatic shift in the relative influence of the Western world on the international economic system. As set forth in the 1975 Declaration and Plan of Action on Industrial Development Issues,* these various demands are given concrete form in a single goal: by the year 2000, LDCs should account for at least 25 percent of the world's industrial production.

SIMLINK is structurally incapable of simulating the major changes implied by this 25 percent goal.†In fact, according to the GNP projections developed for the Global 2000 Study using SIMLINK (see Chapter 3), several LDCs are likely to experience negligible per capita economic growth and possible decreases in per capita consumption over the 1985–2000 period. This would be in contrast to recent historic trends, as well as to LDC expectations and might produce severe social and political tensions, which are also not represented in the model.

Because of many of these structural limitations, World Bank analysts are reluctant to use SIMLINK to make projections beyond 1985. While the Bank's new regional and global models have been designed to take into account many more near-term structural variations than SIMLINK,

the Bank still lacks a formal analytic methodology for projecting future GNP growth of LDCs beyond 1985. SIMLINK was extended through the 1985–90 period for the WAES study, but simple GNP trend extrapolations, judgmentally adjusted downward, were used to provide projections for the remaining 1990–2000 period. This procedure was felt to be sounder and less misleading than attempting to run this medium-term model well beyond the time span it was designed to simulate. Judgmental analysis was also used to extend the results of the adjusted formal modeling analysis to countries not explicitly included in the country groups represented in the model.

## Basic Components

In terms of the objectives of the Global 2000 Study, SIMLINK has been used to provide the economic growth projections required to develop the Study's food and energy projections, and the same projections have been used as a point of reference in discussing economic growth issues in relation to population, resource, and environmental trends to the year 2000. SIMLINK itself does not take explicit account of population growth, resource depletion, or environmental impacts. However, some of these factors are taken into account prior to running the model (in developing some of the exogenous projections required for SIMLINK) and after running the model (in judgmentally adjusting SIMLINK's calculations). The assumptions made regarding these factors in many cases are not explicit and, because they involve the Bank's politically sensitive individual country models, were not made available to the Global 2000 Study by the Bank. SIMLINK does, however, take explicit account of a range of projected commodity prices and volumes in international trade. These were made available by the Bank and will be discussed later.

Although global SIMLINK-developed World Bank projections are a primary source of GNP projections used by AID and other federal agencies, alternative growth projections have also been used by these agencies. AID, for example, tends to rely more on the Bank's individual country analyses than on the Bank's aggregate global analyses developed using SIMLINK. The Department of Agriculture's Economics, Statistics, and Cooperatives Service uses projections made by the Food and Agriculture Organization (FAO). The Energy Information Administration of the Department of Energy uses projections made by

---

* At the meeting of the U.N. Organization for Industrial Development at Lima in 1975.

†Bank analysts disagree; in their view, such changes could be built into SIMLINK fairly easily. They explain that these adjustments have not been made to SIMLINK because a new system capable of looking into such issues is now being designed and implemented, as previously mentioned.

the U.N. and the Organization for Economic Cooperation and Development (OECD). The Bureau of Mines relies on international economic projections developed by Wilfred Malenbaum, as described in Chapter 22. The FAO, U.N., and OECD projections tend to be higher than those of WAES or the World Bank; Bureau of Mines projections tend to be lower.

In terms of internal structure, SIMLINK is essentially a block recursive model representing three groups of industrialized nations, the socialist bloc, and six representative groups of LDCs. It covers trade in 25 primary commodities, projected roughly 10 years into the future. "Block recursive" refers to the fact that each major component of the model is solved for all years projected before the next major component is solved. This means, for example, that LDC commodity export projections are calculated for all years to be simulated in one subprogram block, based on unadjusted LDC growth projections (which are adjusted later in a separate subprogram block).

This computational approach reflects the assumption that LDC commodity export levels are essentially independent of LDC economic growth. Although many of SIMLINK's commodity submodels are specified in part as functions of economic growth rates in the Western industrialized nations (excluding the socialist bloc), changes in these rates have only very limited effect in changing LDC commodity export levels. The constant dollar value of LDC exports of primary commodities varies by less than 10 percent. This is because commodity price levels are exogenously specified, and the specification is not varied with changes in the exogenous specification of the economic growth rates of the industrialized nations. However, changes in economic growth rates of the Western industrialized and socialist nations have a major effect in changing levels for LDC exports of manufactured goods and services. The constant dollar value of these exports varies by more than 30 percent.

Within SIMLINK, the Western industrialized nations are grouped geographically into North America, Western Europe, and Japan-Oceania. A socialist country group is also represented but interacts with other components of the model to a lesser extent than the Western industrialized nations. An OPEC importing market for LDCs has been represented in the model for certain specialized World Bank analyses but not for the WAES analysis.

The six representative groups of less developed countries have been defined differently in the various versions of SIMLINK.* In SIMLINK VI, grouped primarily by per capita income, they are:

1. *India.*

2. *Other South Asian Countries:* Bangladesh, Pakistan, Sri Lanka.

3. *Low-income Africa:* Ethiopia, Kenya, Madagascar, Tanzania.

4. *Lower-middle income:* Bolivia, Cameroon, Egypt, Ghana, Ivory Coast, Liberia, Morocco, the Philippines, Senegal, Sudan, Thailand.

5. *Middle income:* Brazil, Chile, Colombia, Guatemala, Korea, Malaysia, Mexico, Peru, Syria, Tunisia, Turkey, Zambia.

6. *Upper-middle income:* Argentina, Jamaica, Yugoslavia.

The less developed OPEC countries are not represented. A geographic perspective on the methodology underlying these projections is provided in one of the colored maps used to illustrate the discussion in Chapter 14.

The 25 primary export commodities and commodity groups represented in SIMLINK were chosen because each accounts for more than 3 percent of the total export earnings for each LDC group (or, in a few cases, for particular countries). These include: 11 commodities or commodity groups involving food exports; 9 involving nonfood agricultural exports; and 5 involving minerals and metal exports. Eleven endogenous submodels containing from 3 to 25 equations are incorporated within SIMLINK for projecting export volumes (or total production) of beef, cocoa, coffee, copper, fats and oils (including coconut oil, copra, groundnuts, groundnut oil, and palm oil), iron ore, rice, rubber, sugar, tea, and tin.

Ten commodities are projected using simple compound growth formulas (generally derived from the results of the World Bank's independently run commodity models). These include: cotton, jute, maize, petroleum, timber, tobacco, wheat, miscellaneous food exports, miscellaneous nonfood agricultural exports, and miscellaneous mineral and metal exports.

*The discussion that follows is based on the current version of SIMLINK, Version VI. The tables are based on SIMLINK VI, run under the same exogenous assumptions that the WAES study used to run SIMLINK V. Complete documentation and runs associated with the original WAES study and SIMLINK V are not presently available, and in any event would not represent the current methodology used (indirectly) by AID and other federal agencies in projecting GNP.

All commodity price forecasts are exogenous and are not changed for the high-, medium-, and low-growth cases. For this reason, the endogenously projected commodity quantities are also very similar for all three cases, regardless of changes to the GNP growth rates of industrialized countries. Trade volumes of other LDC exports to the industrialized nations (i.e., manufactured goods and services), however, do change significantly.

World Bank estimates of potential GDP growth and foreign capital needs for individual LDCs are politically sensitive and therefore confidential. It would not be unusual, however, for an LDC member of the World Bank to forecast its official average annual economic growth rate at 10 percent, for World Bank country experts to project it more realistically at a maximum of, for example, 7 percent under optimal circumstances, and for aggregate forecasts to be between 5 and 6 percent. More common is the relatively poor country, whose plan calls for 6 percent, where Bank analysts are likely to project 4.5 percent, and where aggregate forecasts would decrease it to 3 percent.

In many cases, these internal Bank projections are based on detailed econometric models maintained by the Bank, though the results of those models are subject to extensive heuristic adjustments before being used by SIMLINK. In other cases, they are developed using less formal procedures. The exogenous commodity prices are generally also derived from detailed econometric models for individual commodities and, like all of the exogenous inputs, are subject to judgmental adjustment before being entered into SIMLINK.

SIMLINK internal coefficients and exogenous inputs are derived from data covering the period 1960–75, collected by the World Bank or the United Nations. In general, most available economic data on LDCs are at least two years old, although more current data are available on LDC debt balances and regarding overall economic activity within the Western industrialized countries. The quality of most LDC data is not good, as economic definitions vary across countries and across time. Sampling and reporting error is great, and data are generally collected only on an annual basis. Because of changes in the basic economic structure of most LDCs, data preceding 1960 in general have no validity for projections, so that no more than 10–15 annual observations are generally available. Moreover, in many LDCs an industry sector consists of one or two principal companies, so that data changes over time are

likely to reflect microeconomic rather than macroeconomic determinants.

## Basic Procedures

The sequential operation of the SIMLINK model is shown in Figure 16–1.

The exogenous GNP growth assumptions for the Western industrialized nations and the socialist nations used in the Global 2000 Study medium-growth projections (as run on SIMLINK VI) are summarized in Table 16–2. In this analysis, the North American economic growth rate is projected to be high relative to that of the past 20 years, while economic growth in Western Europe and Japan-Oceania is quite low relative to the same period. Because North America's elasticity of demand for LDC manufactured goods with respect to North America's GNP growth is projected within SIMLINK, at 3.5, to be more than twice that of Western Europe, at 1.7, or Japan-Oceania, at 1.5, these differences should not be thought of as balancing each other.

Based on economic experience of the past 2–3 years, World Bank analysts suggested (after the Global 2000 Study was well underway) adjusting the GNP growth rates of the Western industrialized nations somewhat upward. This would have led to corresponding upward adjustments to projected growth rates under SIMLINK (due to increased LDC export purchases by the Western industrialized nations). CIA experts, on the other hand, suggested that lower average annual growth rates would be more likely over the next decade for both the Western industrialized nations and

### TABLE 16–2

**Historical and Projected Average Annual Real GNP Growth for the Western Industrialized and Socialist Nations**

*(Percent)*

| Country Group | Historical | | | Projected[a] | |
|---|---|---|---|---|---|
| | 1955–60 | 1961–70 | 1971–75 | 1977–80 | 1980–85 |
| North America | 3.2 | 4.2 | 2.4 | 4.4 | 4.0 |
| Western Europe | 4.9 | 4.7 | 2.9 | 3.7 | 3.7 |
| Japan-Oceania | 7.3 | 9.5 | 5.0 | 4.9 | 4.9 |
| Total Western industrialized | 4.1 | 4.9 | 2.7 | 4.2 | 4.0 |
| Socialist countries[b] | | | | 6.0 | 6.0 |

*Note:* Actual rates used in the SIMLINK model are specified for each year being projected and change more gradually than the average annual rates specified in the table.

[a] Medium-growth case.
[b] Historical rates are not readily available on a comparable basis.

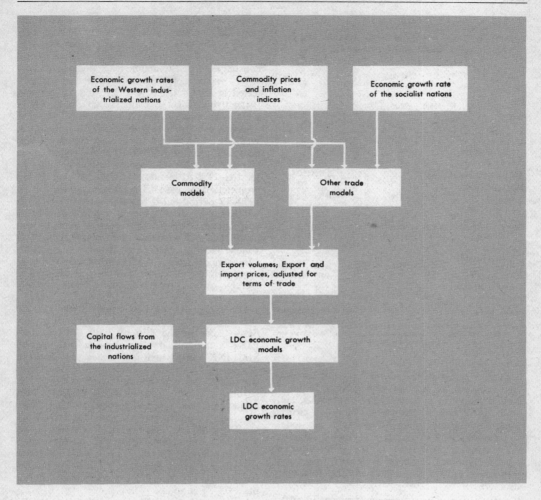

Figure 16-1. Sequential operation of the SIMLINK model.

the LDCs.* Because these recommended adjustments were not consistent, and because the focus of the Global 2000 Study was not directed toward GNP analysis, the original WAES projections were not adjusted for purposes of the Study.

The degree of sensitivity of LDC economic growth rates in SIMLINK to changes in assumptions regarding Western industrialized growth rates is shown in Table 16–3. These changes arise

---

* The CIA also felt that the Study's GNP growth rate figures for the People's Republic of China and for a few other socialist countries were understated, as previously noted.

from the model's key assumed linkage between LDC economic growth and LDC foreign trade earnings, based entirely on trade with the Western industrialized and socialist nations. SIMLINK is incapable of projecting the implications of the alternative internal LDC developmental strategies that are based on factors other than the economic growth rates of the Western industrialized and socialist nations. As previously noted, these growth rates affect only export volumes and not export prices or capital flows.

In its first major programming block, SIMLINK calculates world trade volumes for a wide range of primary commodities for all years to be pro-

## TABLE 16–3

### Projected Average Annual Real GNP Growth for the High, Medium, and Low Growth Cases, 1977–85

*(Percent)*

|  | High (1) | Med. (2) | Low (3) | Med. vs. High (2)−(1) | Med. vs. Low (2)−(3) |
|---|---|---|---|---|---|
| Western industrialized countries | 4.8 | 4.1[a] | 3.3 | −0.7 | 0.8 |
| Socialist countries | 6.0 | 6.0[a] | 6.0 | 0.0 | 0.0 |
| LDC Groups | | | | | |
| India | 4.3 | 3.8 | 3.4 | −0.5 | 0.4 |
| Other South Asian countries | 5.8 | 5.0 | 4.0 | −0.8 | 1.0 |
| Low-income Africa | 5.3 | 4.8 | 4.5 | −0.5 | 0.3 |
| Lower-middle income | 7.6 | 5.6 | 4.5 | −2.0 | 1.1 |
| Middle income | 8.3 | 6.4 | 4.8 | −1.9 | 1.6 |
| Upper-middle income | 5.8 | 4.5 | 3.4 | −1.3 | 1.1 |

[a] These figures are consistent with the figures in Table 16–1 that were calculated for 1975–85 to correspond to the presentation of GNP projections made in Chapter 3. Because SIMLINK, Version VI, projections are not actually made for 1975 and 1976 (because historical estimates were available), those years are omitted in this table and the several tables that follow.

jected, based in many cases on exogenous projections of Western industrialized economic growth, on elasticities of demand with respect to these growth rates, on exogenous price forecasts, and on other variables. However, in other cases, commodity trade volume projections are independent of changes in any exogenous variable. For example, projections of the production of several significant commodities involve only basic compound growth formulas with the following structure.

Quantity$_t$ = Quantity$_{t-1}$ (1+ compound interest rate)

Thus, trade volumes in many minerals and metals (namely, bauxite, lead, phosphate rock, silver, and zinc) are collectively projected to increase at an average annual rate of 6.3 percent, regardless of variations in price or in economic growth rates projected for the industrialized nations or the LDCs. Similarly, timber trade volumes are compounded at 4.1 percent annually, petroleum at 2.8 percent, wheat at 2.5 percent, and cotton 1.7 percent, regardless of changes in any variables.

While these projections are often merely summary representations of more complex interactions simulated on the Bank's commodities models (which are confidential) in advance of running SIMLINK, they are markedly different

from many of the growth trends in trade for the same commodities reflected in the Global 2000 Study's other federal agency projections. For example, average annual growth rates in world consumption of aluminum, lead, phosphate rock, silver, and zinc for the 1973–85 period are projected at only 4.4, 3.6, 4.4, 2.1, and 3.4 percent, respectively, for the Global 2000 Study, all of which are significantly below the 6.3 percent average used in SIMLINK. Crude oil export volumes are projected to increase roughly 4 percent each year for the 1976–85 period (significantly above SIMLINK's 2.8 percent annual growth rate for the 1977–85 period), and wheat exports are projected to increase 4.1 percent each year for the 1970–85 period (also significantly above SIMLINK's 2.5 percent for 1977–85). Since most LDCs tend to be net exporters of minerals and metals and net importers of food and fuel, these volume growth adjustments, if made in the SIMLINK model, might significantly lower the projected foreign exchange earnings of the LDCs, thereby lowering their projected economic growth rates.

The exogenous SIMLINK price projections are also significantly different from other price projections used by the Global 2000 Study. SIMLINK's mineral and metal prices are higher; SIMLINK's food and fuel prices are lower. If adjustments were also made to the exogenous commodity price projections used in SIMLINK so that they corresponded to the project's other projections, the projected foreign exchange earnings and resulting growth rates for the LDCs would be lowered still further. For example, the SIMLINK projections are based on the exogenous assumption that real prices for copper and tin will increase by roughly 5.2 and 2.5 percent per year (in constant dollars) respectively, during the 1975–85 period.

In contrast, the projections developed for the Global 2000 Study regarding the same metals assumed that their real prices will remain constant or decline over the same period. Conversely, the SIMLINK projections are based on the exogenous assumption that petroleum prices will remain constant in real terms,* while the projections developed for the Global 2000 project assumed an increase in real prices of 5 percent per year beginning in 1980. The SIMLINK projections are also based on the assumption that projected wheat prices will decrease by roughly 0.6 percent per

* Bank analysts point out that this assumption was made because the Bank did not wish to appear to take a position with regard to the likelihood of potential changes in petroleum prices, it was not necessarily intended as a forecast.

year (in constant dollars, calculated using a 5-year base period), whereas the projections prepared for the Global 2000 project assumed an increase of roughly 2.1 percent per year during the 1970–85 period.

In its next major programming block, after calculating world trade volumes for the major primary commodities and commodity groups, SIMLINK calculates the demand of the industrialized nations and the socialist bloc for LDC manufactured goods and services. These calculations are based on exogenous, historically derived estimates of the income elasticities of demand of each group of industrialized nations for manufactured LDC goods; they are in turn used with adjustments to calculate demand for all LDC exports other than primary commodity exports and are the same for all three growth cases. These assumed elasticities, in conjunction with the projected economic growth rates, imply that the Western industrialized and socialist nations will, compared to 1975, almost double their imports of LDC manufactured goods by 1980 and almost triple those imports by 1985, as shown in Table 16–4. What this would imply for the year 2000 is an open question. Projected growth in export volumes of manufactured goods for each LDC group is shown in Table 16–5.

A complex set of additional calculations, which interact as part of the same programming block, is then used to project growth rates for other LDC exports, which are individually allocated to each group of LDCs and adjusted to reflect terms of trade. Growth rate projections for each of the various classes of LDC exports for all three scenarios as calculated by SIMLINK, are shown in Table 16–6. Projected growth in export earnings

for each of the six LDC groups for the medium growth case are shown in Table 16–7. Export growth projections for each of the various classes of LDC exports for a representative LDC group (the lower-middle income group for the medium growth case) are presented Table 16–8.

In its final block of programming, SIMLINK iteratively on a year by year basis (1) calculates the level of imports necessary to sustain a given level of GDP growth, (2) compares this figure with endogenously projected available export earnings, plus an allowable gap (exogenously specified) between import and export earnings (reflecting the extent to which projected foreign investment capital will be permitted to be used to offset the gap), and (3) adjusts the initially given level of GDP growth as necessary and returns to step 1 until a stable solution is reached within the acceptable range of the gap.

In a strict economic sense, the "allowable gap" just referred to represents an estimate of projected "excess" demand rather than of the projected availability of foreign capital. Nevertheless, World Bank analysts believe these estimates are roughly consistent with projected flows of official and private capital for the industrialized nations. This might seem to imply that such capital flows are assumed by SIMLINK never to be higher or lower for any LDC group than the LDC group's gap on current account between import expenditures and export earnings. However, bank analysts note that many of the other parameters used in SIMLINK are derived from historical experience or individual country models which, in many cases, may have incorporated other capital flow assumptions. Representative projections for the

## TABLE 16–4

### Projected Demand for LDC Exports of Manufactured Goods

*(Percent)*

| Country Group | Elasticity[a] | Average Annual Economic Growth[b] | | Average Annual Growth in Demand for LDC Manufactured Goods[b] | | Index of Imports of LDC Manufactured Goods[b,c] | | |
|---|---|---|---|---|---|---|---|---|
| | | 1977–80 | 1980–85 | 1977–80 | 1980–85 | 1975 | 1980 | 1985 |
| North America | 3.5 | 4.4 | 4.0 | 15.4 | 14.0 ⎫ | | | |
| Western Europe | 1.7 | 3.7 | 3.7 | 6.3 | 6.3 ⎬ | 1.000 | 1.715 | 2.848 |
| Japan-Oceania | 1.5 | 4.9 | 4.9 | 7.4 | 7.4 ⎪ | | | |
| Socialist | 1.5 | 6.0 | 6.0 | 9.0 | 9.0 ⎭ | | | |

[a] Elasticity (of demand for LDC exports of manufactured goods) with respect to economic growth. This elasticity is projected not to change over the 1977–85 period and remains unchanged for the high, medium, and low growth cases.
[b] Medium growth case.
[c] SIMLINK makes use of an aggregate index rather than regional indices. This index is derived from the regional elasticities and growth rates presented in this table, through complex calculations involving, in addition, other LDC exports and terms of trade. Thus, according to Bank analysts, it would be misleading to present in this table the changes in regional shares of total demand for LDC exports of manufactured goods implied by just these regional elasticities and growth rates, since such calculations are not made by SIMLINK.

## TABLE 16–5

### Projected Average Annual Growth of Export of LDC Manufactured Goods, by LDC Group,[a] Medium Growth Case

*(Percent)*

| LDC Group | 1975–80 | 1980–85 |
|---|---|---|
| India | 6.3 | 7.1 |
| Other South Asia | 6.2 | 7.0 |
| Low-income Africa | 5.4 | 7.5 |
| Lower-middle income | 13.6 | 10.8 |
| Middle income | 12.7 | 11.3 |
| Upper-middle income | 7.2 | 5.4 |

[a] As measured in constant dollars, including adjustments to reflect the effects of projected terms of trade.

lower-middle income group are presented in Table 16–9.

Crucial to this sequence of calculations is the iterative computation of LDC import expenditures, as shown in Table 16–10.

The relationships expressed in Equations 1–6 in Table 16–10 were separately estimated for each LDC group, based on historic data from the 1965–75 period, using least-squares linear regression techniques. They are based on the assumption that the ratio of incremental units of each kind of import per incremental unit of GNP is fixed. This necessarily means that the mix of incremental imports of capital goods, intermediate goods, fuel, services, food, and consumer goods (as measured in constant 1975 dollars) is assumed to remain constant for each group of LDCs as industrialization progresses. The various equations shown in

## Table 16–6

### Projected Average Annual Growth of All LDC Exports, by Type of Export[a]

*(Percent)*

| | 1975–80 | | | 1980–85 | | |
|---|---|---|---|---|---|---|
| | High | Med. | Low | High | Med. | Low |
| Food | 2.3 | 2.3 | 2.3 | 3.4 | 3.3 | 3.3 |
| Nonfood agricultural | 2.2 | 2.0 | 2.1 | 2.3 | 2.1 | 2.0 |
| Minerals and metals | 4.4 | 3.9 | 4.0 | 4.5 | 4.2 | 4.0 |
| Petroleum and fuels | 2.8 | 2.8 | 2.8 | 2.8 | 2.8 | 2.8 |
| Manufactured goods | 12.6 | 11.4 | 10.1 | 12.5 | 10.7 | 8.8 |
| Services | 9.6 | 8.5 | 7.4 | 9.6 | 8.1 | 6.4 |
| Total Primary Commodities[b] | 2.9 | 2.7 | 2.7 | 3.5 | 3.3 | 3.2 |

[a] Adjusted to reflect the effects of projected terms of trade.
[b] Includes food, nonfood agriculture, and minerals and metals.

## TABLE 16–7

### Average Annual Growth of All LDC Exports, by LDC Group,[a] Medium Growth Case

| LDC Group | 1977 | 1980 | 1985 | Average Annual Growth in Earnings 1977–85 |
|---|---|---|---|---|
| | *billions of constant 1975 dollars* | | | *percent* |
| India | 5,979 | 6,625 | 8,970 | 5.2 |
| South Asia | 2,417 | 2,856 | 3,744 | 5.6 |
| Low-income Africa | 2,923 | 2,899 | 3,508 | 2.3 |
| Low-middle income | 18,358 | 21,600 | 29,683 | 6.2 |
| Middle income | 49,856 | 58,317 | 89,167 | 7.5 |
| Upper-middle income | 13,009 | 15,576 | 21,338 | 6.4 |

[a] Adjusted for projected terms of trade.

Table 16–10 can, in fact, be collapsed into the following single linear equation:

Total required imports = $872.4 + (.2824 \times \text{GDP})$.

While SIMLINK thus assumes that each of each LDC group's import components will be a constant linear function of each LDC group's GDP, SIMLINK, as previously noted, does not assume that each of each LDC group's export components will be a constant linear function of each LDC group's GNP. The import component assumptions thus appear to imply a static internal economic structure within each LDC, whereas the export component assumptions appear to imply internal dynamic change.

Especially critical with the sequence of LDC import calculations shown in Table 16–10 is the calculation of required gross investment associated with a given level of total GDP. Although it is expressed in SIMLINK as a constant linear function of total GDP, a variable incremental capital output ratio (as if investment were expressed in this model as a function of incremental GDP) can be inferred from the model's results.[*] Such an incremental capital ratio provides a measure of the implied assumptions regarding changes in the productivity of investment capital. Specifically, the ratio indicates the units of new investment capital associated with one unit of

---

[*] World Bank analysts note that the investment relationships in SIMLINK for the 1965–75 period were generally estimated using distributed lag formulations. However, these formulations were transformed into constant linear functions for insertion into SIMLINK, Version VI. Prior versions of SIMLINK incorporated distributed lag formulations directly, but they were found to be somewhat unstable for projections beyond 1980 and so were taken out.

## TABLE 16–8

## Projected Exports for LDC Lower-Middle Income Group, by Type of Export, Medium Growth Case

| Type of Export | Proportional Mix | | | Value [a] | | | Average Annual Growth in Value[a] 1977–85 |
|---|---|---|---|---|---|---|---|
| | 1977 | 1980 | 1985 | 1977 | 1980 | 1985 | |
| | *percent* | | | *billions of constant 1975 dollars* | | | *percent* |
| Food | 27 | 26 | 24 | 5.0 | 5.6 | 7.1 | 4.5 |
| Nonfood Agricultural | 16 | 15 | 13 | 2.9 | 3.2 | 3.9 | 3.8 |
| Minerals and Metals | 16 | 17 | 16 | 2.9 | 3.7 | 4.8 | 6.5 |
| Petroleum and Fuels | 5 | 6 | 6 | .9 | 1.3 | 1.8 | 9.1 |
| Manufactures | 14 | 16 | 19 | 2.6 | 3.5 | 5.6 | 10.1 |
| Services | 22 | 22 | 22 | 4.0 | 4.8 | 6.5 | 6.3 |
| TOTAL | 100 | 102[b] | 100 | 18.4 | 21.6 | 29.7 | 6.2 |

[a] Does not include adjustments to reflect the effects of projected terms of trade.
[b] Does not sum to 100 due to rounding.

## TABLE 16–9

## SIMLINK Calculations for the Low-Middle Income LDC Group, Medium Growth Case, 1977–85

*(Millions of Constant 1975 U.S. dollars)*

| | Allowable Gap Between Imports and Exports[a] | Unadjusted Export Earnings[b] | Terms of Trade Adjust-ment[c] | Adjusted Export Earnings[d] | Import Expendi-tures[e] | Gross Domestic Product[f] | Gross Domestic Income[g] | Required Gross Invest-ment[h] | Required Gross Domestic Savings[i] |
|---|---|---|---|---|---|---|---|---|---|
| 1977 | 4,325 | 18,304 | 54 | 18,358 | 22,683 | 77,698[j] | 77,751 | 17,749[j] | 13,424 |
| 1978 | 4,806 | 19,524 | −634 | 18,890 | 23,696 | 82,338 | 81,704 | 19,002 | 14,196 |
| 1979 | 4,734 | 21,075 | −1,125 | 19,950 | 24,684 | 85,831 | 84,706 | 19,899 | 15,164 |
| 1980 | 4,509 | 22,863 | −1,263 | 21,600 | 26,109 | 90,882 | 89,619 | 21,195 | 16,686 |
| 1981 | 4,572 | 24,621 | −1,522 | 23,099 | 27,671 | 96,418 | 94,896 | 22,615 | 18,044 |
| 1982 | 4,763 | 26,171 | −1,693 | 24,478 | 29,241 | 101,973 | 100,280 | 24,041 | 19,278 |
| 1983 | 4,842 | 28,039 | −1,965 | 26,074 | 30,915 | 107,900 | 105,935 | 25,561 | 20,720 |
| 1984 | 4,923 | 29,844 | −2,195 | 27,649 | 32,572 | 113,767 | 111,573 | 27,067 | 22,144 |
| 1985 | 4,805 | 32,087 | −2,404 | 29,683 | 34,488 | 120,547 | 118,144 | 28,806 | 24,002 |
| Average annual growth | | | | | | | | | |
| 1977–80 | 1.4% | 7.7% | — | 5.6% | 4.8% | 5.4% | 4.9% | 6.1% | 7.5% |
| 1980–85 | 1.3% | 7.0% | 13.7% | 6.6% | 5.7% | 5.8% | 5.7% | 6.3% | 7.5% |

[a] Exogenously specified. Although the allowable gap technically represents an estimate of projected "excess" demand rather than of the projected availability of foreign capital flows, World Bank analysts believe it is roughly consistent with projected flows of official and private capital from the industrialized nations.
[b] Calculated by SIMLINK, using exogenous price projections and endogenous trade models.
[c] Calculated by SIMLINK, applying different inflation indices to different components of LDC imports and exports.
[d] Calculated by SIMLINK, by adding terms of trade adjustments to unadjusted export earnings.
[e] Calculated by SIMLINK, in conjunction with calculating gross domestic product, and including adjustments for projected terms of trade. A GDP growth rate is determined which equates important expenditures to adjusted export earnings plus the allowable gap between imports and exports (representing foreign investment flows).
[f] Calculated by SIMLINK, as part of the process of calculating import expenditures.
[g] Calculated by SIMLINK, by adding terms of trade adjustment to GDP.
[h] Calculated by SIMLINK, using a formula in the following form: Required gross investment = a constant + a coefficient × GDP. Part of this investment is assumed to come from foreign sources, as represented by the allowable gap between imports and exports.
[i] Calculated by SIMLINK, by subtracting foreign investment (as represented by the allowable gap between imports and exports) from required gross investment.
[j] Exogenously specified for 1977.

additional GDP. In the case of the lower-middle income group, it falls slightly (from 4.6 to 4.3) between the periods 1977–79 and 1983–85, indicating that a given investment can be thought of as producing about 7 percent more incremental GDP in 1985 than in 1977 (in constant dollars). For the other LDC groups, it is projected to decline

anywhere from roughly 5 to 40 percent over the same period, indicating that major increases in the productivity of investment capital are assumed for all LDC groups. For example, the GNP projections assume that, in the case of the other South Asian LDC group (with an incremental capital output ratio declining from roughly 2.9 to 1.8), a

## TABLE 16–10

### Representative LDC Import Calculations,[a] Lower-Middle Income Group, Medium Growth Case

| | | | | | | | | | |
|---|---|---|---|---|---|---|---|---|---|
| *Equation 1:* | Required Gross Investment | | = | a constant | + | (a coefficient) | + | (gross domestic product) | |
| | 1977 Estimate | 17,749[b] | | −2,122.09 | | .25656 | | 77.698[b] | |
| | 1985 Targeted[c] | 30,575 | | −2,122.09 | | .25656 | | 127,446 | |
| | 1985 Probable | 28,805 | | −2,122.09 | | .25656 | | 120.547 | |
| *Equation 2:* | Imports of Capital Goods | | = | a constant | + | (a coefficient) | + | (required gross investment) | |
| | 1977 Estimate | 5,423 | | 186.6 | | .2960 | | 17,749 | |
| | 1985 Targeted[c] | 9,140 | | 186.6 | | .2960 | | 30,595 | |
| | 1985 Probable | 7,911 | | 186.6 | | .2960 | | 28,805 | |
| *Equation 3:* | Imports of Intermediate Goods | | = | a constant | + | (a coefficient) | + | (gross domestic product) | |
| | 1977 Estimate | 5,654 | | −2,170.3 | | .1007 | | 77.698 | |
| | 1985 Targeted[c] | 10,664 | | −2,170.3 | | .1007 | | 127.446 | |
| | 1985 Probable | 9,969 | | −2,170.3 | | .1007 | | 120.547 | |
| *Equation 4:* | Imports of Fuel | | = | a constant | + | (a coefficient) | + | (gross domestic product) | |
| | 1977 Estimate | 2,561 | | 129.2 | | .0313 | | 77.698 | |
| | 1985 Targeted[c] | 4,118 | | 129.2 | | .0313 | | 127.446 | |
| | 1985 Probable | 3,902 | | 129.2 | | .0313 | | 120.547 | |
| *Equation 5:* | Imports of Services | | = | a constant | + | (a coefficient) | + | (gross domestic product) | |
| | 1977 Estimate | 3,967 | | 703.7 | | .042 | | 77.698 | |
| | 1985 Targeted[c] | 6,056 | | 703.7 | | .042 | | 127.446 | |
| | 1985 Probable | 5,767 | | 703.7 | | .042 | | 120,547 | |
| Equation 6: | Imports of Food and Consumer Goods | | = | a constant | + | (a coefficient) | + | (sum of 2–4, above) | |
| | 1977 Estimate | 5,171 | | 3039.3 | | .1563 | | 13,638 | |
| | 1985 Targeted[c] | 6,793 | | 3039.3 | | .1563 | | 24,019 | |
| | 1985 Probable | 6,569 | | 3039.3 | | .1563 | | 22,584 | |
| *Equation 7:* | Total Required Imports | | = | sum of 2–6, above | | | | | |
| | 1977 Estimate | 22,776 | = | 22,776 | | | | | |
| | 1985 Targeted[c] | 36,868 | = | 36,868 | | | | | |
| | 1985 Probable | 34,920 | = | 34,920 | | | | | |

[a] Does not include adjustments to reflect the effect of projected terms of trade.
[b] Exogenously estimated; not calculated by SIMLINK.
[c] The "targeted" figures represent the calculations that would be made if there were no limit to the extent to which import expenditures could exceed export earnings.

given investment can be thought of as producing about 60 percent more incremental GDP in 1985 than in 1977 (in constant dollars).[†]

It was previously pointed out that one major component of gross investment, namely foreign investment, was exogenously estimated for each LDC group in terms of an allowable gap, on current account, between export expenditures and import earnings. In the case of the lower-middle income LDC group, as can be seen in Table 16–9,

_____

[†] World Bank analysts note that the uncertainties surrounding future incremental capital output ratios are compounded by the fact that for several middle-income LDCs, technological change is likely to affect productivity of investment capital in ways not readily deducible from historical experience. To this extent, projections of future incremental capital output ratios must necessarily incorporate significant subjective judgment.

this gap represents roughly 20 percent of annual gross investment and accumulates over the 1977–85 period to about 35 percent of 1985 GDP. The other major component of gross investment, gross domestic savings, is calculated as a residual figure, as can also be seen in Table 16–9. Its calculation as a residual is a necessary consequence of the structure of the model, which considers foreign exchange, rather than savings, capital, or labor, as the binding constraint limiting growth in the developing world. While Bank analysts view this as a serious simplification, since the model is being used to develop projections for a period during which deteriorating terms of trade and suboptimal export volume growth are generally projected to squeeze foreign exchange earnings, they consider it to be acceptable in the context of the types of analysis for which the model was designed.

# 17   Climate

Several government agencies have existing research programs on climate (National Oceanic and Atmospheric Administration, National Aeronautics and Space Administration, National Science Foundation); others fund or conduct special observation and analysis programs or maintain a substantial level of research because their operations are affected by variations in climate (Department of Defense, Department of the Interior, Energy Research and Development Administration). Another group of federal agencies are user or policy agencies with interests or concerns for climate and climatic fluctuations but little or no climate research effort (Department of Agriculture, Department of Health, Education, and Welfare, Department of State, Department of Transportation, Environmental Protection Agency).

There was, therefore, no logical place to turn for climate predictions for the Global 2000 Study. Moreover, it soon became clear that there is a great deal of disagreement among climatologists about what changes are likely in global climate and even about how to predict such changes.

One attempt to quantify the likelihood of significant changes on the basis of the opinions of leading climatologists is being made in an interdepartmental research project conducted by the Research Directorate of the National Defense University (NDU) in Washington, D.C. The study is sponsored jointly by the Department of Defense, the Department of Agriculture, and the National Oceanic and Atmospheric Administration. Technical assistance is provided by the Institute for the Future, Menlo Park, California. The project is guided by an Advisory Group drawn from a cross section of government and civilian agencies and institutions. The major objectives of the NDU study are embodied in four tasks:

*Task I:* To define and estimate the likelihood of changes in climate during the next 25 years, and to construct climate scenarios for the year 2000.

*Task II:* To estimate the likely effects of possible climatic changes on selected crops in specific countries, and to develop a methodology for combining crop responses and climate probabilities into climate/crop scenarios for the year 2000.

*Task III:* To evaluate the domestic and international policy implications of the climate/crop scenarios, and to identify climatic variables of key importance in the choice of policy options.

*Task IV:* To transfer the climate/crop research results and generalized climate response methodology to individuals and organizations concerned with the consequences of climatic changes in fields other than agriculture, and to identify areas of research that might refine or extend the findings of the first three tasks.

In February 1978 work on the first task was completed, and the results were published as a report, *Climate Change to the Year 2000.* The climate scenarios developed in the NDU study have already been described in Chapter 4. The methodology used, as described in the NDU report, is as follows.

## Key Analytic Methodology

The study is based on the perceptions of future climate made by a panel of 24 experts from the United States and six other countries. Panelists were selected both for their competence in climatology and for their diversity of views. Each panelist was asked to respond to a set of questions about climatic factors, including variability, over the next 25 years, to assign probabilities to specific climate changes, and to give the rationale for their answers. Individual responses were weighted by each panelist's expertise as rated by himself and his peers.

This was a first attempt to have a group of experts address a common set of questions and express their judgments of climate changes in terms of quantitative probabilities, rather than on a "what if" basis. The responses were aggregated into five possible scenarios, which indicate some broad measure of the likelihood of climate change over the next 25 years.

## Basic Principles and Components

Atmospheric models, actuarial experience, and existing theories of climate are inadequate to meet the needs of policymakers for information about future climate. For the present, there is no choice but to rely on expert judgments—subjective and contradictory though they may be—about future world climate and its effects on agriculture and other sectors of the economy.

The survey method (described in more detail in Chapter 4) was chosen as the best means of quantifying such judgments. Its purpose is not to forecast climate change nor to reach a consensus on the issue of how climate will change by the year 2000, but to portray reasonable, coherent, and consistent possibilities for world climate at the end of the century and to put plausible bounds on the likelihood of the occurrence of these possibilities.

The questionnaire to which the panelists responded dealt with 10 climatic variables or geographic regions of interest:

1. Average global temperature change
2. Average latitudinal temperature change
3. Carbon dioxide and turbidity
4. Precipitation change
5. Precipitation variability
6. Midlatitude drought and persistence of drought
7. Outlook for 1977 crop year
8. Asian monsoons
9. Sahel drought
10. Length of growing season

Each of the 10 involved three elements: probabilistic (or equivalent) forecasts of a particular climatic variable; reasons for quantitative estimates; and self and peer expertise rating.

## Basic Procedures

Most respondents, as well as some of the invited panelists who declined to participate, voiced some degree of apprehension or concern about the questionnaire and the use (and possible abuse) of the information derived from their responses. These concerns centered on the following issues:

• The lack of sufficient actuarial experience, comprehensive theories, or adequate models to support the quantitative estimates given in the questions;
• The possible suppression of the full range of uncertainty accompanying responses; and
• The risk of being an unwitting party to "science by consensus."

the NDU project team gave considerable attention to the foregoing concerns in analyzing the data and aggregating the range of views—and the expressed qualifications—provided by the respondents.

The following comments by panelists reflect these concerns:

To the best of my knowledge, there exist, in general, no techniques for making climate forecasts that have demonstrated skill in the sense that the forecasts are better than a forecast of the long-term average statistics. Knowledge of even the long-term average statistics (means, variances, extremes, conditional probabilities, etc.) would be most useful for some purposes, but even this data is not readily available.

I think that the strongest message to come from your questionnaire will be that we lack the basis for predicting even the grossest aspects of climate.

We possess no skill for forecasting beyond a short period, other than that which probabilities based on a frequency distribution can provide. Only a deterioration of climate will fire the imagination of the experts. Prophets become known for their prophecies of doom. A prophecy of status quo or improvement would not be interesting.

There is a good deal of guesswork involved, due to uncertainties about feedback mechanisms, the importance of aerosols, the general circulation in the atmosphere and oceans, and many other factors.

I feel that one of the most important outcomes of your study could be a clear statement of our present ignorance. That in itself should clearly indicate the need for contingency plans.

### Self and Peer Ratings

An interesting and useful feature of the questionnaire was the concept of self and peer ratings. The following is an excerpt of the instructions provided at the end of each question and designed to assess the respondents' expertise:

Using the self-ranking definitions provided in the instructions, please indicate your level of substantive expertise on this major question.

5 - 4 - 3 - 2 - 1

Again using the self-ranking guide, please identify those other respondents whom you would rate as "expert (5)" or "quite familiar (4)" in their answer to this particular question.

The categories from 5 to 1 (expert, quite familiar, familiar, casually acquainted, and unfamiliar) were carefully defined in the questionnaire. Table 17–1 shows a sample of the degree of correlation between self and peer ratings for five respondents on Question I. The general agreement between self and peer ratings is fairly evident by a scan of the two right-hand columns in the table. A detailed analysis of the correlation between self ratings and the mean of peer ratings shows it to

## TABLE 17-1

### Correlation Between Self and Peer Ratings (Examples from Question I)

| | | Frequency of Peer Ratings | |
|---|---|---|---|
| Respondent | Self Rating | Expert | Quite Familiar |
| A | Epert | 10 | 3 |
| B | Expert | 4 | 3 |
| C | Quite familiar | — | 3 |
| D | Quite familiar | 1 | 2 |
| E | Familiar | — | — |

have a value of 0.52 at a significance level of 0.007. This is considered a fairly high correlation.

A simple averaging of self and peer ratings for each respondent on each question, rounded to the nearest integer value, provided a weighting that was subsequently used in aggregating responses. The particular weighting scale that was used is shown in Table 17-2. Levels of expertise falling below "familiar" ("casually acquainted" and "unfamiliar") were not used in the processing. Of the three levels shown in Table 17-2, the "expert" category was weighted twice as heavily as the "quite familiar" category and the "quite familiar" was weighted twice as heavily as "familiar." In effect, this reflects the largely empirical and intuitive notion that an expert's opinion is worth about twice as much as one who is "quite familiar," which in turn is worth twice as much as an individual who is ranked as "familiar" with a topic.

### Processing of Responses

The general schema for processing the information from the questionnaires was as follows:

- Tabulate each respondent's probability density function with respect to change about a particular variable at a given time, or derive the probability density function from graphical information provided by the respondent.
- Multiply each probability density function by the appropriate expertise weight (as described earlier).
- Add the weighted density functions of respondents.
- Divide the weighted and aggregated density functions by the sum of expertise weights to normalize the group response.
- Combine the panel's responses on each climatic variable into a set of scenarios spanning the range of uncertainty or range of conditions described by the respondents.

Question I, dealing with possible changes in global mean temperature (used here as equivalent to annual mean temperature between 0° and 80° north latitude), was a pivotal question because perceptions of global mean temperature greatly influence perceptions with respect to the climate variables treated in subsequent questions. The question is based on Figure 17-1 a plot of historical changes in annual mean temperature during the past century. Each respondent was asked to provide three estimates of the future course of possible changes in global temperature to the year 2000. The first estimate was to be a temperature path to the year 2000 such that there was only 1 chance in 10 that the actual path could be even lower. The second estimate was to be a path with an even chance that temperature could be either lower or higher; and the third was a path based on 1 chance in 10 that it could be even higher.

Figure 17-2 shows a sample response to Question I by a single respondent. Each of the three estimates could be drawn in any functional form desired. Percentiles of 10, 50, or 90 can be read off for any year between the "present" (the end of the plot in Fig. 17-1) and the year 2000.

The processing of responses will be illustrated using the answers to this question by a single respondent. Figure 17-3 is a plot of the information shown in Figure 17-2 for the year 2000, converted to a cumulative probability function, in which the ends of the function have been extended beyond the 90th percentile and below the 10th percentile in a linear approximation. For example, the respondent has indicated a 10 percent chance that the temperature will change by 0.04° C or less, a 50 percent chance that it will change by 0.2° C or less, and a 90 percent chance that it will change by 0.47° C or less. (These temperature changes are in relation to the zero reference base period, 1880–84, as shown in Fig. 17-1.) Similar values can, of course, be obtained for any other year from Figure 17-2.

The next step is to convert the cumulative probability function into an equivalent density function by taking the first derivative of the plot in Figure 17-3. Since the plot consists of two straightline segments, we have basically two de-

## TABLE 17-2

### Conversion of Expertise Ranking to Weighted Scale

| Expertise | Weight |
|---|---|
| Expert | 4 |
| Quite familiar | 2 |
| Familiar | 1 |

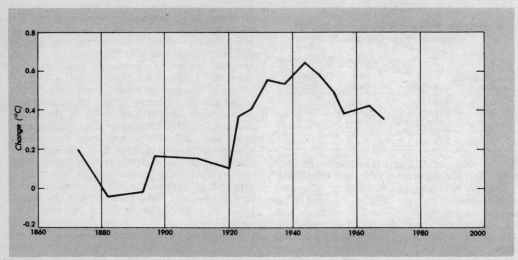

**Figure 17-1.** Global temperatures; historical record of changes in annual mean temperature during the past century for the latitude band 0°–80°N. The period 1880–84 is the zero reference base. *(Mitchell, National Oceanic and Atmospheric Administration)*

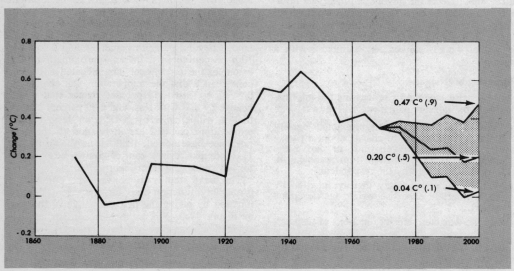

**Figure 17-2.** Sample response to Question I; actual example of a single response to the instructions. The period 1880–84 is the zero reference base.

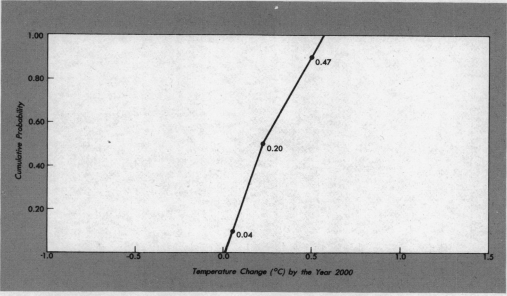

**Figure 17-3.** Cumulative probability function for Question I. The period 1880–84 is the zero reference base.

grees of freedom, or two levels in the density function, which is shown in Figure 17–4. The area under the curve intercepted by any particular temperature range is equal to the probability of occurrence of that particular temperature range, and the total area under the curve in Figure 17–4 is unity.

Figure 17–5 shows unweighted density functions from each of two respondents. The two functions are next weighted by the appropriate expertise weights, added, and then divided by the sum of the weights to obtain the combined and normalized density function for the two respondents. Again, the area under the curve of this combined and normalized density function, shown in Figure 17–6 is equal to unity.

The procedure outlined above was repeated for the responses of each of the other panelists. Figure 17–7 is a plot of the aggregated normalized responses of the full panel for the year 2000. An analogous procedure yields probability density functions of mean global temperature change for the years 1975, 1980, and 1990. The information contained in the probability density functions is shown in Figure 17–8 as extensions to the curve in Figure 17–1. The extensions on the curve show the 10th, 50th, and 90th percentiles for each year from the "present" to the year 2000. Intermediate percentiles are also plotted. Thus, Figure 17–8 is

a summary of the aggregated responses of the panelists with respect to global temperature.

In aggregating the responses by the method of weighted averages, it has been assumed that the respondents are drawing from the same general information base and, therefore, that their information is highly dependent. In such cases of information dependence among respondents, it is customary to use the method of weighted averages to aggregate responses. All responses are used and weighted by the respondents' expertise as perceived by themselves and their peers. The shape and range of the aggregated curves are not acutely sensitive to the weighting system used. The method is "conservative" in the sense that the derived probability curves tend to be broad and to overstate uncertainty as a result of the additive treatment of the individual subjective probabilities. Had the responses been based on independent information, a multiplicative treatment of the individual probabilities would have been more appropriate, and the derived probability curves would have shown less dispersion.

## Climate Scenarios

A convenient procedure for dealing with a range of uncertainty when it is not possible to construct quantitative models is through the use of scena-

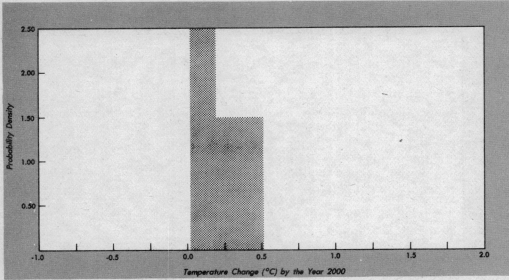

**Figure 17-4.** Equivalent density function for Question I. The period 1880–84 is the zero reference base.

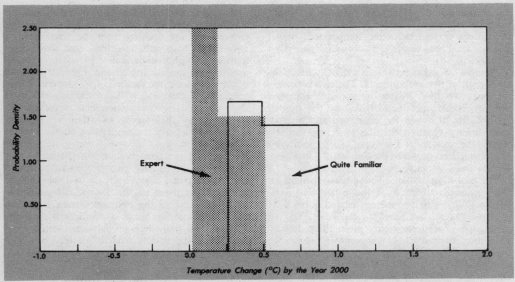

**Figure 17-5.** Adding two density functions for Question I. The period 1880–84 is the zero reference base.

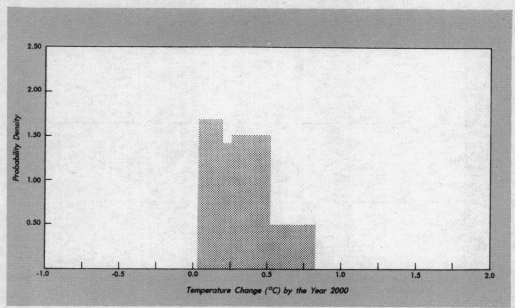

**Figure 17-6.** Normalized density function for two respondents to Question I. The period 1880–84 is the zero reference base.

rios, which may be considered plausible sequences of events or trends. Scenarios describe interconnections—perhaps even causal processes—and highlight, where possible, decision points. In a sense, a scenario is a possible "slice of future history."

### Constructing Scenarios

In the present instance, since responses on global temperature are pivotal in setting the stage for other climate variables, the plot in Figure 17–7 can be used as a basis for dividing the perceived temperature range into a number of categories. These categories then become the bases for constructing scenarios. The number of categories (and scenarios) is, in a sense, arbitrary and can be three or five or even a larger number, if desirable. Table 17–3 shows the perceived temperature range divided into five categories. They range from large global cooling to large global warming. Associated with each temperature range is a probability of occurrence where, in fact, the temperature ranges were selected to make these probability ranges symmetrical.

In order to process information with respect to other climate variables, it is useful to group respondents with respect to these five temperature

### TABLE 17–3

#### Definition of Temperature Categories

| Temperature Category | Change in Mean Northern Hemisphere Temperature from Present[a] by the Year 2000 | Probability |
|---|---|---|
| Large cooling | 0.3°C to 1.2°C colder | 0.10 |
| Moderate cooling | 0.05°C to 0.3°C colder | 0.25 |
| Same as last 30 years | 0.05°C colder to 0.25°C warmer | 0.30 |
| Moderate warming | 0.25°C to 0.6°C warmer | 0.25 |
| Large warming | 0.6°C to 1.8°C warmer | 0.10 |

[a] "Present" temperature is defined as the end point on the graph in Figure 17, the average temperature for the 5-year period ending in 1969.

ranges, according to where the bulk of each respondent's probability density function lies. Table 17–4 is a matrix showing each of the five temperature categories arrayed as rows and the 19 respondents in five groups arrayed as columns of the matrix. Note in the table that the bulk of each group's probability density functions lies along the diagonal element of the 5×5 matrix (one respondent at each end, three and four at the intermediate ranges, and 10 in the middle range).

The results of the information collected under Task I have been embodied in a set of five

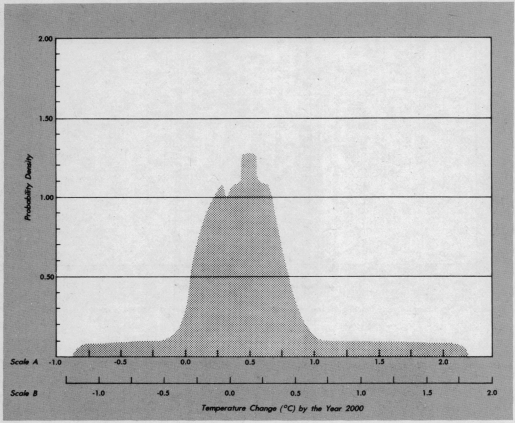

**Figure 17-7.** Probability of mean Northern Hemisphere temperature change by the year 2000 as determined by the panel of climatic experts. Scale A is based on the period 1880–84 as the zero reference base (see Fig. 17-1). Scale B is based on the period 1965–69 as the zero reference base (see the end point on Fig. 1-1).

scenarios described in Chapter 4 of this volume.* The scenarios are labeled in accordance with the global temperature categories in Table 17–3. One purpose is to provide an integrated summary of perceptions of climatologists on climate change and variability to the year 2000. An equally important purpose is to provide a point of departure for structuring questions in Task II and to trace the impact of such possible climatic changes on food production and on the choice of policy options.

The procedure for creating scenarios corresponding to the five global temperature categories is as follows:

- Each respondent is first assigned to a global temperature category, as described in Table 17–4.
- Responses within each temperature category are combined for all other climatic variables (except for precipitation and precipitation variability, where all responses were available†).
- Responses are integrated into a narrative, supported by summary tables.

The processing steps for Questions II through X are identical to those for Question I except that, of course, in these other instances, density func-

*The responses to Question VII, "Outlook for 1977 Crop Year," are not included in the scenarios.

†For questions on precipitation and precipitation variability only, information was obtained from each respondent based on conditional assumptions with respect to global temperature.

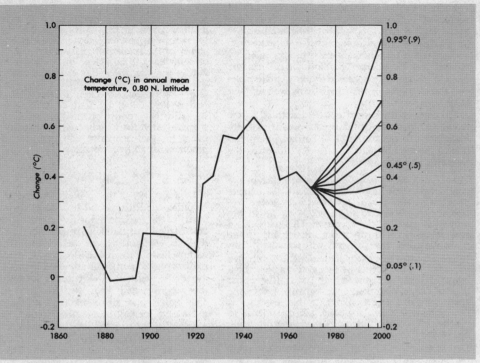

**Figure 17-8.** Probability of mean Northern Hemisphere temperature change to the year 2000 as determined by the panel of climatic experts. The period 1880–84 is the zero reference base.

### TABLE 17–4

**Percentage of Grouped Probability Densities Lying in Each Temperature Category**

| Temperature Categories | Number of Respondents | | | | |
|---|---|---|---|---|---|
| | 1 | 3 | 10 | 4 | 1 |
| Large cooling | 99 | 12 | 2 | — | — |
| Moderate cooling | 1 | 68 | 24 | 10 | — |
| Same as last 30 years | — | 20 | 52 | 31 | — |
| Moderate warming | — | — | 22 | 44 | 20 |
| Large warming | — | — | — | 15 | 80 |

tions or equivalents are provided directly by the respondents and need not be derived through the use of cumulative probability.

The sequence of steps is illustrated by using Question VI, which concerns midlatitude drought. Table 17–5 illustrates how responses for one of the time periods (i.e., 1991 to the year 2000) were weighted and aggregated in the Moderate Warming scenario. The process outlined for Question VI is repeated for each of the other questions.

### TABLE 17–5

**Frequency of Drought in U.S. in 1991–2000**

| Respondents Assigned to Moderate Warming | Expertise | Frequent | Average | Infre-quent |
|---|---|---|---|---|
| A | 3 | 0.25 | 0.50 | 0.25 |
| B | 3 | 0.60 | 0.20 | 0.20 |
| C | 5 | 0.60 | 0.20 | 0.20 |
| Weighted average | | 0.54 | 0.25 | 0.21 |

### Nature of Scenarios

Each scenario seeks to describe average climatic conditions as they might exist in a period of years around 2000 AD. The conditions do not refer specifically to that year; its climate is likely to differ from the scenario projection to an extent consistent with normal year to year climate variability. Some indication of the course of climate changes between the present time and the end of the century is also given in the narrative and in the tables appended to each scenario.

Each scenario is assigned a "probability of scenario." This probability is a derived value based on the panelists' probabilistic temperature forecasts and a weighting scheme to take into account each respondent's expertise as rated by himself and his peers. Therefore, it reflects the range of judgments expressed by the climate panel and the strengths of their beliefs, as well as their level of expertise.*

This probability should not be construed as the likelihood that the total scenario will actually materialize in the future. The correct interpretation of the "probability of scenario" involves the following considerations:

The "probability" is essentially a measure of the confidence, expressed collectively by the climate panel, that *the global temperature change between circa 1970 and circa 2000 will lie in the range indicated by the scenario.* This measure of confidence bears an unknown relationship to the probability that the scenario will actually occur.

It was assumed that the global temperature change indicated by the scenarios has a negligible probability of being greater than $+1.8°$ C (the upper limit of Large Warming) or less than $-1.2°$ C (the lower limit of Large Cooling). In this respect, the five scenarios, taken together, are considered to bracket all realistic outcomes—i.e., the probabilities of the five scenarios sum to unity.

Details are given in each scenario which elaborate on the scenario in respects other than stipulated global temperature change. These are considered by the climate panel to be reasonable inferences about future climatic developments that are consistent with the global temperature change. These details by no means exclude other possible developments. Hence, they are not necessarily to be construed, individually or in combination, as hav-

ing a probability as high as that indicated for the scenario as a whole. Conditional probability information, given in the tables included with each scenario, can be combined with the overall probability of the scenario to assess the absolute level of confidence to be placed in future events specified in the scenarios. For example, one can find the overall "probability" of a specified event (e.g., "frequent" drought in the U.S. for the period 1991–2000) by first calculating for each scenario the product of the "probability" of the scenario and the conditional probability of the event for that scenario, and then summing the products for all five scenarios.

## Validation

In June 1977, the project Advisory Group recommended that an ad hoc panel review early drafts of the five scenarios for internal and mutual consistency. Accordingly, project staff met in July with six climatologists at the National Center for Atmospheric Research at Boulder, Colorado. The reviewers paid particular attention to the large and moderate warming and cooling scenarios, i.e., those constructed from the smaller data bases. The details and the conditional probabilities of these end scenarios, therefore, reflect the judgments of more people than the limited number of panelists who responded to the questionnaires along the lines of these scenarios. The review process, which essentially strengthened the data bases of the end scenarios, resulted in significant changes to only one of them, the Large Global Cooling scenario.

## Documentation

The NDU study is described in detail in its report on the results of Task I, *Climate Change to the Year 2000,* from which the above description of the methodology used in analyzing responses to the questionnaire was taken. The NDU report also includes the questions used, a discussion of the scenarios and climatic probabilities, and a summary of the number of responses and average expertise ratings for each of the questions.

---

*A "probability" of 0.25, for example, does not mean that there was universal agreement that the scenario in question would occur with probability 0.25. Nor does it mean that 25 percent of the panelists "voted" for that particular temperature change to the exclusion of other changes. Roughly speaking, the "probability 0.25" is an amalgam of the proportion of panelists who gave some credence to that particular temperature change, the strength of their individual "beliefs" in the change (their individual probabilities of occurrence) and their individual expertise.

# 18  Food and Agriculture

The Foreign Demand and Competition Division of the Department of Agriculture's Economics, Statistics, and Cooperatives Service is responsible for preparing the federal government's projections of long-term food supply and demand throughout the world, in order to assist in the formulation and execution of U.S. agricultural and trade policy.

## Key Analytic Methodology

Department of Agriculture projections of long-term world food production, consumption, and trade are made with the assistance of a computer-based static equilibrium model known as GOL (because it deals with the world's grain, oilseed, and livestock economy). Although the GOL model is viewed by the Department as merely one mathematical model among several available for analyzing future agricultural prospects, it is the only Departmental model capable of analyzing broad issues regarding world food prospects in relatively detailed commodity and regional terms. For the purposes of the Global 2000 Study, three additional submodels were used by the Department to provide projections of arable area, total food production and consumption, and fertilizer use.*

## The GOL Model

The present GOL model, developed in 1974 by a team of economists and requiring the equivalent of about seven years of full-time effort, was one of the first static equilibrium models to take into account the broad range of feed-livestock relationships at the regional and world level. It was specifically designed to link the grain-oriented food economies of the developing regions with the livestock-oriented food economies of the industrialized regions in a more complete and consistent manner than had been done in the past.†

In the fall of 1974, an early draft of 1985 regional projections produced by the GOL model was made available to the World Food Conference in Rome. Formal publication of the projections followed in December. These projections showed that over the next decade, the world could produce enough grain, oilseed, and livestock products at reasonable prices to supply the largely cereal diet of the developing world and meet a moderately rising feed demand in the industrialized nations. They were used (in conjunction with other projections and analyses) by the Secretary of Agriculture to support his views favoring the limiting of government intervention in the domestic and world food markets and questioning the need for an extensive system of international reserves.‡

*The various Department of Agriculture projections prepared for the Global 2000 Study are not necessarily the same as the projections published by the Department for specific food products or regions, which are often developed utilizing different assumptions and incorporating output from other, more detailed models. However, because the parameters used in the GOL model are based in large part on the outputs of those other models, adjusted judgmentally by commodity and regional specialists within the Department, the GOL projections are considered by Department analysts to be essentially consistent with projections developed using other Departmental models. Because the additional projections developed using the three submodels were derived directly from the GOL model's projections, and especially because they were subsequently reviewed and adjusted (as appropriate) by Department experts, they are also considered by the Department to be essentially consistent with other Departmental projections.

†The Department's Economics, Statistics, and Cooperatives Service has prepared extensive, official documentation of the GOL model under the title, *Alternative Futures for World Food in 1985* by Anthony Rojko, et al. Volume 1, entitled *World GOL Model Analytic Report*, was published in April 1978 as Foreign Agricultural Economic Report Number 146. Volume 2, entitled *World GOL Model Supply-Distribution and Related Tables*, and Volume 3, entitled *World GOL Model Structure and Equations*, were published, respectively, in May and June, 1978, and given report numbers 149 and 151. Volume 4, the final volume, is expected to be published in the fall of 1978 under the title, *World GOL Model Users Manual*.

‡The U.N. Food and Agriculture Organization (FAO) continues to express concern (e.g., in a recent press release issued by the FAO in conjunction with its 1977 Biennial Conference), that the world food situation remains fragile, and that there are no grounds for complacency. According to the Conference, world food production appeared to have risen by only 1.5 percent during 1977, or by less than the population growth of nearly 2 percent. The Conference was especially concerned that progress in production had been slowest in Africa and, in general, in the poorest developing regions, where food needs are the greatest. The Conference noted that this had widened the gap not only between the industrialized and developing countries but also between the better and worse-off developing countries.

Since then, the region-specific models that provide parameter estimates used by the GOL model and the GOL model itself have been significantly enhanced, and the GOL model has been used to examine a broad range of issues for various federal agencies. For example, the model has been used to analyze the potential impact on international food trade of various U.S. agricultural parity pricing policies and to analyze the potential impact of alternative assistance programs for the U.S. Agency for International Development.

In its present form, the GOL model consists of 930 econometric equations (embodying economic, physical, and policy variables), which are solved simultaneously. A matrix generator facilitates data input and a report writer presents results. The equations are specified and solved using the MPS–3 programming language, and all programs are executed on an IBM 370/168 computer. The program produces approximately 30 tables containing basic data on supply and distribution, prices, per capita production and consumption, and growth rates, as well as special summary tables.

Plans to incorporate major improvements into the model are currently under review. A second-generation model has been planned, and some sections are currently under development (e.g., market studies of the British, Iranian, and Venezuelan economies). Areas targeted for improvement over the next 3–4 years include:

• Expanding coverage of the world's agricultural economy (e.g., livestock specifications are abbreviated for many developing countries; water, fertilizer, pesticide, and herbicide are treated exogenously; products such as tropical fruit and vegetables, starches, fish for human consumption, and certain other products are completely omitted in the first-generation model).

• Endogenizing to a greater extent measures of macroeconomic feedback (e.g., the potential impact of changes in foreign exchange positions on commodity trade and economic growth, which are now treated exogenously).

• Building in recursive, dynamic behavior (e.g., because this is a static equilibrium model, output is limited to measuring net long-term adjustments; the model can say little about the year to year adjustments needed to reach the solutions calculated for 1985 or 2000).

## The Three Submodels

The three submodels (related to arable area, total food production and consumption, and fertilizer use) were developed in late 1977 for use in

the Global 2000 Study. They were not programmed for automated execution. Because they were developed rapidly (in approximately three weeks) to meet specific needs, there are no present plans to refine or extend their use, although alternative approaches to projecting the same variables are under consideration by the Department of Agriculture.

The arable area submodel was based on equations for each of 27 regions with reliable historical data. These equations define total arable area as a function of GOL and non-GOL product prices, trend growth in the extent of arable area, and estimates of maximum potential arable area. The arable area equations were solved independently of each other, using projections developed by the GOL model.

The total food production and consumption submodel was based on region-specific, supply and demand equations for products not covered in the GOL model. These equations defined the production and consumption of non-GOL products in terms of historical relationships between GOL and non-GOL products. The production levels calculated for non-GOL products (using the non-GOL supply equations) were checked against the production levels implied by the residual arable area for non-GOL crops (calculated as the difference between total arable area and arable area used for GOL crops) times trend growth in non-GOL product yields. The consumption levels calculated for non-GOL products (using the non-GOL demand equations) were checked against historic income and price relationships and changing taste, and in all cases were found to be within one standard error of the trends in the historic data. Each set of region-specific, supply and demand equations was solved independently of the other sets using projections developed by the GOL model

The fertilizer use submodel was based on region-specific equations defining fertilizer use in relation to total food production and on combined time-series and cross-sectional input-output relationships. These were also solved independently of each other using projections from both the GOL model and the total food production submodel.

## Basic Principles

### The GOL Model

As previously noted, the purpose of the GOL model is to generate projections of world production, consumption, trade, and prices of grain, oilseed, and livestock products to 1985 and 2000. The model's emphasis is on capturing the interaction of the predominantly cereal economies of the developing world with the livestock economies of the industrialized world as they compete for the world's agricultural resources. The calculations of the three submodels that expand this analysis to consider arable area usage, total food production and consumption, and fertilizer use are made subsequent to executing the GOL model and thus do not influence its calculations.

The GOL model's main strength lies in its scope, coupled with its level of commodity, regional, and price detail. For example, the model includes variables that simulate competition for resources across the crop sector and competition among consumers for different crops for food and feed use. It incorporates physical input-output rates in its feed and livestock sector and crop sectors. It differentiates in its regional detail between producing and consuming regions as well as between regions at different economic growth and income levels. However, because the GOL model draws heavily on earlier models that focused more exclusively on grain, the model tends to emphasize grains, while livestock products receive less coverage.

One of the GOL model's main weaknesses is that it is a static equilibrium model. Changes over time in such dynamic factors as population and income growth are calculated exogenously in advance of running the model and are thus not influenced by the calculations of the model. Moreover, the model's static equilibrium projections for a given year are independent of its projections for any other year and may be inconsistent with those projections. In addition, static equilibrium models are incapable, by their very nature, of capturing aspects of market behavior that are fundamentally in a state of dynamic disequilibrium.

The 930 equations in the GOL model reflect not only physical variables and economic behavioral patterns, but also reflect institutional settings, policy constraints, and changes in consumption preferences. The model's region-specific equations may be thought of as constituting 28 interactive regional submodels of widely varying size and complexity ranging from as few as 40 to over 100 equations. Economic activity between regions is related by explicitly incorporating international trade quantity and price variables, which must be consistent for each commodity, and by requiring world production and consumption volumes for each commodity to balance. For the Global 2000 Study, stock adjustments were assumed to equal zero for all commodities, i.e., world grain reserves do not increase to keep pace with changes in world population.

A wide range and large number of assumptions are incorporated into the 28 interactive regional submodels. These assumptions are clearly distinct from conclusions based on the GOL model's calculations. Some of the most critical or representative assumptions are cited below:

• No major wars, natural disasters, or changes in the existing international economic system are assumed to occur (other than petroleum price increases). This is because such changes could only be arbitrarily projected and would completely overshadow the historical relationships on which the GOL model is based. While optimistic and pessimistic weather assumptions are included in the Global 2000 Study's high and low projections, no climatic change is projected, nor is large-scale land degradation assumed to occur due to environmental or human factors other than urbanization.

• Technology—measured in terms of growth in yields, and ultimately dependent largely on the producer prices generated under a particular-scenario—is assumed to continue to evolve at rates comparable to the rapid growth of the last two decades; it is assumed that the industrialized nations and, to a lesser extent, the less developed countries, will take advantage of technology—depending on the incentives supplied by changes in factor-and-product prices.

• Aspects of the international food system related to food processing, distribution, and merchandising (which would also be affected by changes in factor and product prices) are not explicitly represented in the model.

• The countries of Western Europe are assumed to continue to maintain somewhat protectionist agricultural and trade policies aimed at greater self-sufficiency. It is also assumed that price policies of other Western European countries will result in price levels similar to those in the European Economic Community.

• The level of U.S. trade with the U.S.S.R., the People's Republic of China, and Eastern Europe is assumed to be affected more by political than economic factors in the long run. Though no specific long-range multicommodity trade agreements have been assumed between the United States and the centrally planned countries, the levels of trade projected are in line with the quantities outlined in recent bilateral agreements.

• Each region's import or export prices are assumed to be related to the region's demand or supply price through generally constant margins.

# THE GOVERNMENT'S GLOBAL MODEL

548

**EQUATION 1(A):** As estimated prior to use in GOL model

| Dependent variable | Terms and variables treated as independent of each other |
|---|---|
| Total grain area under cultivation | = 22,766.5 + 125 (years since 1970) + 15.34 (wheat supply price) |

**EQUATION 1(B):** As used in GOL model

| Endogenous variables, treated as independent | Exogenous expressions |
|---|---|
| Total grain area under cultivation − 15.34 (wheat supply price) | = 22,766.5 + 125 (years since 1970) |

**EQUATION 1(C):** As subsequently presented in this chapter

| | Exogenous expressions |
|---|---|
| Total grain area under cultivation = | 22,766.5 + 125 (years since 1970) + 15.34 (wheat supply price) |

It should also be recognized that the reports produced by the GOL model are reviewed by the Department's commodity and country specialists to ensure that the model's calculations correspond to their professional judgment regarding the future prospects of world grain, oilseed, and livestock trade. *In many cases, this means that coefficients ultimately used within the GOL model are based on the judgment of country and commodity analysts as well as on statistical analysis.*

The 930 equations of the GOL model are solved simultaneously after they have been coded in matrix form. Prior to being coded, each equation's structure and coefficients are separately estimated, using standard statistical techniques with subsequent review by commodity and country analysts. In many cases this review leads to reevaluation and adjustment of the original equations by Department analysts prior to running the GOL model as a unit. A simple representative equation thus estimated (for the low-income North Africa and Middle East region) has the structure and coefficients of Equation 1(A).

In preparing such an equation for simultaneous solution with the other GOL equations, it is rewritten so that the endogenous variables (those solved simultaneously within the model) are all on the left-hand side of the equation and the exogenous variables (those which are projected prior to running the model) are all on the right-hand side. Thus, Equation 1(A) would be rewritten as Equation 1(B).

When all equations are thus transposed, the left-hand side contains 930 expressions with 930 variables whose values must be determined. The equations can then be thought of as having the form

$$A X = D$$

where $A$ is a square matrix of all the coefficients (exogenously estimated) of the endogenous variables, $X$ is a vector of all the endogenous variables (to be solved by the model), and $D$ is a vector of expressions of exogenous variables and associated coefficients and exponents.

For ease of computation, a standardized computer programming package, developed to execute linear programming calculations, is used to solve this set of relationships. First, the vector of expressions, $D$, on the right-hand side of the equation is solved using exogenously projected values for the exogenous variables, collapsing them into a vector of values, $S$. Then $X$ is solved according to the following formula, using linear programming algorithms to obtain the unique solution to the familiar problem of solving $n$ equations for $n$ unknowns:

$$X = A^{-1}S$$

Matrix $A$ and vector $X$, the endogenous (simultaneous) part of the model, must express only linear relationships, since linear programming algorithms are used to solve the 930 equations. However, in many cases, linear formulations tend to misrepresent real-world relationships, either understating or overstating them. For example, at high price levels, linear equations tend to generate exaggerated price responses. Thus, nonlinear relationships must be and have been simulated by reestimating coefficients and rerunning the model with modified coefficients in cases of initially extremely high or low prices. Such adjustments have been made, for example, to represent the different impacts of very high food prices due to rising energy prices and the impact of support price and acreage restrictions in the U.S. at very low prices.

The exogenous expression vector $D$ is not limited to expressing only linear relationships, since it is solved using exogenously projected variable values prior to making use of the linear programming algorithms. The form of each of the various expressions in vector $D$ depends on the assumptions made with respect to the kind of impact expected from the exogenous variables, and may include, for example, exponential relationships to express compound growth rates.

Although an objective function is technically specified in the case of the GOL model,* the model solves for the unique solution for its 930 equations. Hence, no minimization or maximization takes place. The model also does not currently have a transportation matrix. A transportation matrix could theoretically be added, but there are no current plans to do so.

To simplify further discussion of the model, its matrix-related characteristics will henceforth be disregarded, and equations will be shown in the form of Equation 1(C), even though all endogenous variables are in fact solved simultaneously. Thus, endogenous variables which appear on the right-hand side of the equals sign for the purposes of discussion, should be understood to be no more computationally "independent," as mathematical convention might otherwise suggest, than those appearing on the left-hand side.

The GOL model includes supply, demand, and trade sectors for most commodities. Within the crop supply sector, the key endogenous variable is total harvested area, defined as a function of the prices for the region's most important crops, trend growth, constraining potential arable area maxima, and historical and physical data on the share of GOL crops in the arable area total. Individual GOL crops compete for total area based on historic shares, physical limitations on land allocation among crops, and projected relative prices. Production is determined from total harvested area and an endogenous yield projection based on absolute and relative prices, levels of input usage, and trend growth included to account for wider adaptation of existing technology.

Grain supply equations for a region typically have been constructed in the following form:

Total area = f (wheat and other crop prices; trend growth in arable area, subject to physical constraints defining maximum arable area).
Wheat area = f (total area; price of wheat and other food crops competing for arable area).
Wheat production = f (wheat area; base wheat yields; changes in wheat yields due to changes in wheat prices; other product prices; changes in input usage; trend growth).

Demand for grain for direct use of food by people is a function of grain prices, other food

product prices, income, and population. The price elasticities allow variance in both total food demand for grain and the relative shares of individual grains. Demands for meats and dairy products are modeled similarly. Consumer preferences are reflected in the product's own price and cross-price elasticities and income elasticities. Equations in this sector typically have been constructed in the following form:

Demand for wheat for use as food = f (price of wheat, corn, rice; per capita income; population; changes in taste).
Demand for beef = f (price of beef, pork, and poultry; per capita income; population; changes in taste).

The sector that represents livestock production and demand for grain used as food for livestock is more complex. Meat production is a function of meat prices, feed prices, and productivity. The incorporation of individual meat prices allows competition between the meats. Grain and oilseed feed prices influence the cost of producing meats. Equations in this sector have typically been constructed in the following form:

Beef production = f (price of beef, pork, corn, and oilseed meal; changes in productivity).

Feed demand is a function of appropriate grain prices, oilseed prices, meat prices, and livestock production. Crop prices allow competition between feeds. The coefficients for livestock products are largely physical input-output rates—that relate the tons of grain fed to produce a ton of livestock product. Livestock product prices are used to adjust feed demand, essentially modifying the feeding rate, which forms a second set of relations between crop prices and livestock prices. Equations in this sector have typically been constructed in the following form:

Demand for oilmeal for use as feed = f (production and price of beef, pork, poultry, eggs, and milk; price of corn and meal).

Supply and demand prices for crops and meats are usually related through constant margins. As previously noted, however, price margins fluctuate in the few selected regions where historical data indicate that margins widen or narrow as price levels change.

### The Three Submodels

The three submodels — arable area, total food (production and consumption), and total fertilizer use — were extremely simple, but they can be described only approximately because the Department was unwilling or unable to provide documen-

*Ordinarily, a linear programming model would include such a function, to allow the program to find a solution which would maximize or minimize the value of a specified variable. For example, a linear program might be used to determine the best way to utilize a farm's resources in order to maximize its profits.

tation. The descriptions that follow are based largely on oral responses to questions about the submodels.

The submodels have a few common characteristics. They were all specified seperately for each region in the GOL model for which reliable historical data were available. The submodels were all executed after the GOL model and were dependent on the GOL model in various ways. The function of the submodels and their various assumptions must be described separately.

The arable area submodel supplements the GOL model by providing projections of arable area. The availability of arable land depends on many trends, including urbanization and land reclamation. It is assumed in this submodel that there is a finite amount of land that is potentially arable, and projections are not allowed to exceed this constraint. Up to this constraint, arable area is projected to increase on the basis of time trends and an index of GOL food prices (intended to reflect economic incentives). It is assumed that there will be no large-scale loss or degradation of arable land due to mismanagement or environmental deterioration.

The total food submodel augments the GOL projections (of grains, oilseeds and livestock) to arrive at total food projections. The procedures involved were extremely simple. Growth in total food was in most cases projected as a function of growth in the GOL commodities (grain, oilseeds and livestock) based on historic trends. Their relationship was almost always assumed to be constant over time and linear. Sugars, starches, tropical products and other livestock were taken into account, as appropriate, in the various regions. Fish catches for human consumption were not explicitly taken into account for any region (except Japan), but were included in the analysis of a miscellaneous category. This miscellaneous category was assumed to provide the same percentage of the food supply in the future as in the past. This in turn means that (for all regions except Japan) the fraction of food needs met by fish consumption will be constant, unless substituted by another food in the miscellaneous category (e.g., bananas, goats, camels, etc.). Since food consumption is projected to grow dramatically in all regions, it follows that (in the absence of major shifts to other foods in the miscellaneous category) there will be dramatic growth in the global fish catch. Such growth in fish catch contradicts the Global 2000 Study's fisheries projections.

The fertilizer use submodel supplements the GOL model by providing projections of total fertilizer use. The projections are highly aggregated. The relative amounts of nitrogen, phosphorous and potassium are not given. The aggregate projections are based on regional time-series and cross-sectional relationships involving yields per hectare and growth in crop production. The relationship between fertilizer use and crop production levels is generally assumed to be linear, but the coefficients are adjusted by Departmental analysts (depending on the length of the projection being developed) to reflect assumptions of decreasing return to scale. Decreasing returns to scale are thus specified indirectly (as a function of time) rather than directly (as a function of fertilizer use).

## Basic Components

In terms of the Global 2000 Study's objectives, the GOL model and derivative submodels use population and income growth rates to project worldwide food production, consumption, and trade. Little account is taken of environmental factors, except to the extent that they are implicitly projected to influence the costs of production.

Specifically, the GOL model is a formal econometric model which includes 11 principal commodities—wheat, rice, coarse grains, oilmeal, soybeans, beef and veal, pork, poultry, milk, butter, and cheese. A more detailed listing is presented in Table 18–1.

### TABLE 18–1

#### Food Commodities Specified in the GOL Model

TOTAL WHEAT
    Wheat for human demand
    Wheat for livestock feed
TOTAL RICE
    Rice for human demand
    Rice for livestock feed
TOTAL COARSE GRAINS (including corn, barley, rye, oats, sorghum, millet, and mixed grains)
    Coarse grains for human demand
    Coarse grains for livestock feed
TOTAL OILSEEDS (meal equivalent, including principally soybeans but also cotton seed, linseed, rapeseed, fishmeal, sunflower meal, groundnuts, and copra)
    Oilseeds for human foods
    Oilseeds for livestock feed
TOTAL MEAT
    Beef (including veal)
    Pork
    Poultry
    Mutton (including lamb)
TOTAL MILK AND DAIRY PRODUCTS
    Fluid Milk
    Butter
    Cheese
    Eggs

## TABLE 18–2

### GOL Model Regions

| Regions | Countries |
|---|---|
| | INDUSTRIALIZED COUNTRIES |
| United States | United States |
| Canada | Canada |
| Western Europe | |
| European Community | |
| Euro Six | Belgium, Luxembourg, Netherlands, France, Germany, Italy |
| Euro Three | Denmark, Ireland, United Kingdom |
| Other Western Europe | Austria, Finland, Greece, Iceland, Malta, Norway, Portugal, Spain, Sweden, Switzerland |
| Japan | Japan |
| Oceania | Australia, New Zealand |
| South Africa | Republic of South Africa, Botswana, Lesotho, Namibia, Swaziland |
| | CENTRALLY PLANNED COUNTRIES |
| Eastern Europe | Albania, Bulgaria, Czechoslovakia, East Germany, Hungary, Poland, Romania, Yugoslavia |
| Soviet Union | Soviet Union |
| China | China |
| | LESS DEVELOPED COUNTRIES |
| Middle America | Mexico, Bahamas, Bermuda, Costa Rica, Dominican Republic, El Salvador, Guatemala, Haiti, Honduras, Belize, Jamaica, Nicaragua, Panama, Trinidad and Tobago, other Caribbean isles |
| South America | |
| Argentina | Argentina |
| Brazil | Brazil |
| Venezuela | Venezuela |
| Other South America | Bolivia, Chile, Colombia, Ecuador, French Guiana, Guyana, Paraguay, Peru, Surinam, Uruguay |
| North Africa Middle East | |
| North Africa Middle East—high income | Algeria, Bahrain, Cyprus, Iran, Iraq, Israel, Kuwait, Libya, Oman, Qatar, Saudi Arabia, United Arab Emirates |
| North Africa Middle East—low income | Egypt, Jordan, Lebanon, Morocco, Sudan, Syria, Tunisia, Turkey, Yemen (Sana), Yemen (Aden) |
| Other Africa | |
| East Africa | Kenya, Madagascar, Malawi, Mozambique, Rhodesia, Tanzania, Uganda, Zambia |
| Central Africa | Angola, Burundi, Cameroon, Central African Empire, Chad, Congo, Benin, Ethiopia, Afars and Issas, Gabon, Gambia, Ghana, Guinea, Equatorial Guinea, Ivory Coast, Liberia, Mali, Mauritania, Mauritius, Niger, Nigeria, Reunion, Rwanda, Senegal, Sierra Leone, Somalia, Togo, Upper Volta, Zaire |
| South Asia | |
| India | India |
| Other South Asia | Afghanistan, Bangladesh, Bhutan, Nepal, Pakistan, Sri Lanka |
| Southeast Asia | |
| Thailand | Thailand |
| Other Southeast Asia | Burma, Cambodia, Laos |
| East Asia | |
| Indonesia | Indonesia |
| Other East Asia—high income | Hong Kong, Singapore, South Korea, Taiwan, Brunei |
| Other East Asia—low income | Malaysia, Philippines |
| Rest of World | North Korea, Vietnam, Mongolia, Cuba, Pacific Islands, Papua-New Guinea[a] |

[a] "Rest of World" is also comprised of those regions and countries not yet explicitly modeled.

Within the GOL model, 28 regions are represented—8 regions of industrialized (noncommunist) countries, 3 regions of centrally planned countries, and 17 regions of less developed countries (LDCs). Table 18–2 lists the countries included under each of the 28 regions. A geographic perspective on the methodology underlying these projections is provided in one of the colored maps used to illustrate the discussion on the Government's Global Model in Chapter 14.

The GOL model relationships are said by Department analysts to involve approximately 70–80 percent of total world food production and consumption, and an even larger share of trade. All regions have some crop equations, but not all regions have livestock equations. The centrally planned regions have collapsed international trade equations only; production levels are determined exogenously, with consumption based on the interaction of the production and trade projections. These relationships are summarized in Table 18–3.

## Basic Procedures

While there is no simple way to illustrate all the complex interactions involved conceptually in solving a square matrix of 930 equations simultaneously or in solving the many derivative submodel equations, some representative equations that focus on a particular food product in a particular region can suggest the nature of many of these interactions. For the purpose of illustration, this section will briefly review the equations pertaining to wheat in the low-income North Africa and Middle East region, as projected in the medium-growth, rising-energy-price scenario.

### The GOL Model

The three GOL equations and associated calculations directly related to domestic wheat production are presented in Table 18–4. As can be seen in the table, roughly 80 percent of the increase in "grain area under cultivation" between 1970 and 1985 is due to an exogenous time trend estimate involving a judgmentally adjusted coefficient. Since roughly 45 percent of the increase in "wheat area under cultivation" over the same period is due to increases in "grain area under cultivation" and roughly 45 percent due to another exogenous time trend, about 80 percent of the increase in "wheat area under cultivation" can be attributed to the influence of exogenous time trends and judgmental adjustments.* Similar reasoning shows that about 85 percent of the projected increase in "domestic wheat production" over the 1970–85 period is attributable to similar exogenous influences (roughly 90 percent for the 1985–2000 period).

This means that 85–90 percent of the increase in wheat production included in the model's projections is essentially an exogenous input to the model—a premise rather than a conclusion of the modeling exercise. Other "projections" of the model also incorporate significant, directly exoge-

nous components. These are largely based on the judgment of Department analysts regarding future prospects for world grain, oilseed, and livestock products. However, since the endogenous variables are mutually interdependent, this analysis is suggestive only. In the case of wheat production in the low-income North Africa and Middle East region, the factors contributing to the exogenous variable projections, as determined by Departmental analysis, are noted in Table 18–4. The importance of exogenous area and production variables varies widely by region, depending on the extent to which the agricultural sector is commercialized and on the extent to which resource availability —i.e., constrained arable area in low income North Africa and the Middle East—limit the impact of market factors on future growth.

The equation and associated calculations that project domestic wheat consumption are presented in Table 18–5. Again, changes in the exogenous variables account for over 90 percent of the increase in production between 1985 and 2000 for this region.* Given the importance of these exogenous projections, it should be noted in passing that while the GOL model's population figures were adjusted to be consistent with the population projections provided by the Bureau of the Census, the adjustment was not exact (Table 18–6). Other minor discrepancies between the GOL exogenous projections and other Global 2000 Study projections are also to be found in the per capita GNP growth rate projections.

The equations used to estimate price relationships for the low-income North Africa and Middle East region are presented in Table 18–7. As can be seen, these relationships are not projected to change over the 1970–2000 period. The apparently anomalous phenomenon of a demand price substantially below a supply price is explained by Department analysts as due to historic food subsidy programs in several of the largest countries of the region. Egypt, a major wheat consumer, imports wheat concessionally and disposes of it domestically at subsidized prices. Turkey, the major producer in the region, provides its farmers with a substantial subsidy for wheat production. The negative margin between the region's supply and demand prices points up one of the many problems inherent in breaking the world down into multicountry regions. Regional projections are highly aggregated and consequently should be seen as broad parameters rather than precise

---

*Departmental analysts note that these exogenous trends and adjustments are estimated on the basis of the Department's analysis of regional arable area potential and regional cropping patterns, developed prior to running the GOL model.

---

*Departmental analysts point out that this region is not one of the detailed GOL regions and that market interaction is more important in most other regions

## TABLE 18-3

### Variables Used in the GOL Model

| | Total Grain | | | | Total Meat | | | | | Total Dairy Products | | |
|---|---|---|---|---|---|---|---|---|---|---|---|---|
| | Wheat | Rice | Coarse Grain | Oilseed Meal | Beef Cuts | Beef Products | Pork | Poultry | Mutton & Lamb | Milk | Cheese | Eggs |
| **Industrialized countries** | | | | | | | | | | | | |
| United States | DF PA | D PA | DF PA | F PA | D P | D P | D P | D P | D | D S | D S | P |
| Canada | DF PA | D | DF PA | F PA | | D P | D P | D P | | D S | D S | P |
| Euro Six | DF PA | D | DF PA | F PA | | D P | D P | D P | D P | D S | D S | P |
| Euro Three | DF PA | D | DF PA | F PA | | D P | D P | D P | D P | D S | D S | P |
| Other Western Europe | DF PA | D | DF PA | F PA | | D P | D P | D P | D P | D S | D S | |
| Japan | D PA | DF PA | DF PA | DF PA | | D P | D P | D P | D P | D S | D S | |
| Australia/New Zealand | DF PA | D | DF PA | F PA | | D P | D P | D P | D P | D S | D S | P |
| South Africa | D PA | D | DF PA | F S | | D P | D P | P | D P | D S | D S | P |
| **Less developed countries** | | | | | | | | | | | | |
| Middle America | DF PA | D PA | DF PA | F PA | | D P | D P | | | | | |
| Argentina | D PA | D PA | DF PA | F PA | | D P | D P | | D P | | | |
| Brazil | D PA | D PA | DF PA | F PA | | D P | D P | | | | | |
| Venezuela | D PA | D PA | DF PA | F PA | | | | | | | | |
| Other South America | D PA | D PA | DF PA | F PA | | | | | | | | |
| High-income North Africa and Middle East | D PA | D PA | DF PA | F | | | | | | | | |
| Low-income North Africa and Middle East | D PA | D PA | DF PA | | | | | | | | | |
| East Africa | D PA | D PA | D S | | | | | | | | | |
| Central Africa | D S | D S | D S | T | | | | | | | | |
| India | D PA | D PA | DF PA | F PA | | | | | | | | |
| Other South Asia | D PA | D PA | D PA | | | | | | | | | |
| Thailand | D | D PA | DF PA | | | | | | | | | |
| Other Southeast Asia | D | D PA | DF S | | | | | | | | | |
| Indonesia | D | D PA | D PA | D PA | | | | | | | | |
| High-income East Asia | D PA | D PA | DF PA | F PA | | | | | | | | |
| Low-income East Asia | D | D PA | DF PA | S | | | | | | | | |
| **Centrally planned countries** | | | | | | | | | | | | |
| Eastern Europe | T | T | T | T | | T | T | | | | | |
| Soviet Union | T | T | T | T | | T | T | | | | | |
| China | T | T | T | T | | | T | | | | | |
| **Rest of world** | | | | | | T | T | | T | | T | |

D = Demand, total or nonfeed  
F = Derived demand for feed  
P = Production  
A = Area  
S = Supply  
T = Foreign trade, net

## TABLE 18-4

## Representative Supply Equations: Wheat, Low-Income North Africa and Middle East (Medium-Growth, Rising Energy Price Case)

**Functional form**

Exogenous expressions

$$\text{Total grain area under cultivation} = 22{,}766.5 + (\text{coefficient}^a)\,(\text{years since } 1970) + 15.34 \, (\text{wheat supply price})$$

**Variable values in 1970**

| | | | |
|---|---|---|---|
| 23,965.0 | 0 | 0 | 78.13 |

**Variable values projected for 1985**

| | | | |
|---|---|---|---|
| 26,292.4 | 125 | 15 | 101.50 |

**Variable values projected for 2000**

| | | | |
|---|---|---|---|
| 28,475.6 | 110 | 30 | 144.52 |

**Functional form**

Exogenous expressions

$$\text{Wheat area under cultivation} = -1257.53 + 81 \,(\text{years since } 1970) + .549 \left\{ \begin{array}{c} \text{total grain area} \\ \text{under cultivation} \end{array} \right\} + 25.26 \,(\text{wheat supply price}) - 11.11 \,(\text{coarse grain supply price})$$

**Variable values in 1970**

| | | | | |
|---|---|---|---|---|
| 13,155.0 | 0 | 23,965.0 | 78.13 | 64.61 |

**Variable values projected for 1985**

| | | | | |
|---|---|---|---|---|
| 15,970.1 | 15 | 26,292.4 | 101.50 | 82.63 |

**Variable values projected for 2000**

| | | | | |
|---|---|---|---|---|
| 18,911.2 | 30 | 28,475.6 | 144.52 | 128.10 |

**Functional form**

Exogenous expressions

$$\text{Domestic wheat production} = -15{,}194.09 + 13{,}815 \left[ 1 + .875 \left\{ \begin{array}{c} \text{index of} \\ \text{cost of} \\ \text{physical} \\ \text{inputs}^b \end{array} \right\} \right]^{\left( \begin{array}{c} \text{years} \\ \text{since} \\ 1970 \end{array} \right)} + \left\{ \begin{array}{c} \text{coefficient} \\ \text{for increase} \\ \text{in yields}^c \end{array} \right\} \left\{ \begin{array}{c} \text{years} \\ \text{since} \\ 1970 \end{array} \right\} + 1.05 \left\{ \begin{array}{c} \text{wheat area} \\ \text{under} \\ \text{cultivation} \end{array} \right\} + 17.68 \left\{ \begin{array}{c} \text{wheat} \\ \text{supply} \\ \text{price} \end{array} \right\}$$

**Variable values in 1970**

| | | | | | | |
|---|---|---|---|---|---|---|
| 13,815.0 | 0 | 1$^b$ | 0 | 0 | 13,155.0 | 78.13 |

| | Variable values projected for 1985 | | | | | |
|---|---|---|---|---|---|---|
| 21,309.1 | 0 | J[15] | 275 | 15 | 15,970.1 | 101.50 |
| | Variable values projected for 2000 | | | | | |
| 38,840.9 | −.01 | J[III] | 700 | 30 | 18,911.2 | 144.52 |

[a] This coefficient provides for trend growth in arable area. The coefficient was estimated on the basis of multiple regression analyses defining changes in area as a function of time as well as investment and changes in real food product prices and input costs. The coefficient declines beyond 1985 to 2000 due to provision for absolute constraints on arable area.

[b] This index is ordinarily used by the Department of Agriculture to evaluate policies involving accelerated growth in fertilizer usage. According to Department of Agriculture analysts, the downward adjustment of this index for the year 2000 projection is due to the need to intensify the effects of declining returns to scale for fertilizer user. However, for other regions, a similar adjustment is made to reflect rising energy prices. No such adjustment was made for this region, since its agricultural methods are not considered to be energy intensive. The effects of increasing energy prices are thus assumed to be (and are treated as) negligible for this function for this region.

[c] This coefficient combines the effects on yield of (1) trend growth and (2) technological growth. The effect of these two factors influencing yield is further combined with the effect of changes in area, to calculate changes in production. In 1985, the 275,000-ton annual increase is based on a 10 kilogram per hectare trend increase in yields, plus the equivalent of 165,000 tons of annual increase in production due to trend increase in yields on base and expanded area. The respective figures to 2000 are 20 kilograms per hectare and 410,000 tons of annual increase due to area change.

## TABLE 18–5

## Representative Demand Equations: Wheat, Low-Income North Africa and Middle East (Medium-Growth, Rising Energy Price Case)

| | Exogenous expressions | Functional form | | | | | |
|---|---|---|---|---|---|---|---|
| Domestic wheat consumption[a] | $= -988.07 + 19{,}771 \left[1 + .05 \left\{ \begin{array}{c}\text{per capita GNP growth rate}^b\end{array}\right\} + \left\{ \begin{array}{c}\text{population growth rate}\end{array}\right\}\right] \left(\begin{array}{c}\text{years since 1970}\end{array}\right) - 61.62 \left\{\begin{array}{c}\text{wheat demand price}\end{array}\right\} + 31.31 \left\{\begin{array}{c}\text{case gain demand price}\end{array}\right\} + 23.72 \left\{\begin{array}{c}\text{rice demand price}\end{array}\right\}$ | | | | | | |
| | | Variable values in 1970 | | | | | |
| 19,771.0 | | 0 | 0[b] | | 64.17 | 63.15 | 125.00 |
| | | Variable values projected for 1985 | | | | | |
| 29,599.0 | | .0330 | .0235 J[15] | | 87.54 | 82.63 | 198.21 |
| | | Variable values projected for 2000 | | | | | |
| 42,696.2 | | .0429 | .0290 J[III] | | 130.56 | 128.10 | 274.88 |

[a] All wheat consumed in this region is assumed to be used directly as food for humans and not as food for livestock.

[b] Average annual growth rate since 1970. The relationship of these per capita GNP growth rate assumptions (as reported in the GOL model output) to those developed for the Global 2000 Study (see Chapter *) is problematical and could not be readily resolved by Department analysts.

## TABLE 18-6

### Comparison of Average Annual Projected Population Growth Rates, Medium Series

| Region/Country[a] | 1975–85 | | | 1975–2000 | | |
|---|---|---|---|---|---|---|
| | Agri-culture[b] | Census Bureau[c] | Dif-ference | Agri-culture[b] | Census Bureau[c] | Dif-ference |
| Industrialized countries | 0.69 | 0.59 | −.12 | 0.52 | 0.63 | −.11 |
| United States | 0.70 | 0.75 | 0 | 0.55 | 0.60 | −.05 |
| Western Europe | 0.33 | 0.38 | 0 | 0.43 | 0.38 | +.05 |
| Japan | 0.87 | 0.76 | +.01 | 0.59 | 0.70 | −.11 |
| Centrally planned countries | 1.25 | 1.17 | 0 | 1.21 | 1.22 | −.01 |
| Eastern Europe | 0.68 | 0.65 | 0 | 0.57 | 0.62 | −.05 |
| U.S.S.R. | 0.92 | 0.89 | +.01 | 0.68 | 0.78 | −.10 |
| People's Republic of China | 1.41 | 1.31 | +.01 | 1.42 | 1.41 | +.01 |
| Developing countries | 2.49 | 2.49 | +.01 | 2.37 | 2.41 | −.04 |
| Latin America | 2.87 | 2.84 | +.04 | 2.61 | 2.69 | −.08 |
| Africa and Asia | 2.40 | 2.39 | +.10 | 2.30 | 2.33 | −.03 |
| World | 1.78 | 1.78 | +.01 | 1.77 | 1.76 | +.01 |

[a] Categories are those of the Department of Agriculture. Comparable Census Bureau Categories are:

| Agriculture | Census Bureau |
|---|---|
| Industrialized countries | = United States, Canada, Australia, New Zealand, Japan, Western Europe |
| Centrally planned countries | = U.S.S.R., Eastern Europe, People's Republic of China |
| Developing countries | = Developing countries, excluding People's Republic of China |
| Africa and Asia (North Africa/Middle East, other developing African countries, South Asia, Southeast Asia, East Asia) | = Africa and Asia, excluding People's Republic of China |

[b] As summarized by Department of Agriculture analysts for this chapter; not perfectly consistent with Table 6–1, also prepared by the Department.
[c] As summarized, on a comparable basis, by Census Bureau analysts.

## TABLE 18-7

### Representative Wheat Trade and Price Equations: Low-Income North Africa and Middle East (Medium-Growth, Rising Energy Price Case)

| Functional form: | Wheat imports | = Domestic wheat consumption | − Domestic wheat production |
|---|---|---|---|
| 1970 | 5378.0 | 19771.0 | 13815.0 |
| 1985 | 8289.9 | 29599.0 | 21309.1 |
| 2000 | 4138.3 | 42969.2 | 38830.9 |
| Functional form: | Wheat supply price | = 13.96 + Wheat demand price | |
| 1970 | 78.13 | 64.17 | |
| 1985 | 101.5 | 87.54 | |
| 2000 | 144.52 | 130.56 | |
| Functional form: | Wheat demand price | = 1.27 + Wheat trade price | |
| 1970 | 64.17 | 62.90 | |
| 1985 | 87.54 | 86.27 | |
| 2000 | 130.56 | 129.29 | |

projections to be broken down into individual country totals.

No single equation or subset of equations in the model sets the international trade price of wheat. The trade price is determined by the solution of the model's multiple wheat production and consumption equations. However, the export prices of the major surplus producers and the import prices in the deficit regions of the world are linked to allow the use of a major trading country's price as a world price proxy. Thus, the U.S. price serves as a proxy for the world market wheat price, while Thai export prices and Australian-New Zealand export prices play the same proxy roles for rice and livestock products, respectively.

The continuing projected role of the United States as the world's largest exporter of wheat can be seen in Table 18–8, which shows the U.S.

## TABLE 18–8

### Projected Net Exporters of Wheat (Medium-Growth, Rising Energy Price Case)[a]

*(Million metric tons)*

| | 1970 | | 1985 | | 2000 | | Average Annual Growth Percent | |
|---|---|---|---|---|---|---|---|---|
| | Exports | % Share | Exports | % Share | Exports | % Share | 1970–85 | 1985–2000 |
| United States | 17,881 | 39 | 48,838 | 58 | 58,226 | 57 | 7 | 1 |
| Australia-New Zealand | 8,300 | 18 | 12,165 | 15 | 16,084 | 16 | 3 | 2 |
| Argentina | 1,640 | 4 | 6,410 | 8 | 13,974 | 14 | 10 | 5 |
| Canada | 11,750 | 26 | 15,288 | 18 | 7,311 | 7 | 2 | −1 |
| South Africa | 60 | — | 839 | 1 | 4,108 | 4 | 19 | 11 |
| U.S.S.R. | 4,799 | 11 | 127 | — | 1,995 | 2 | −22 | 20 |
| India | — | — | — | — | 166 | — | — | — |
| Euro Six | 1,170 | 3 | — | — | — | — | — | — |
| Total | 45,600 | 101[b] | 83,667 | 100 | 101,862 | 100 | 4 | 1 |

[a] These figures are representative of the lowest level of disaggregation within the GOL model and are cited to illuminate the GOL methodology. While Department analysts are reasonably confident of the GOL model's computations at the higher levels of aggregation presented in Chapter 6, they would prefer that these more disaggregated projections not be cited as Global 2000 Study projections.
[b] Does not sum to 100 due to rounding.

share of international wheat exports growing from 39 percent in 1970 to 57 percent in the year 2000. This growth is based on a 109 percent increase in total U.S. wheat production between 1970 and 2000. Argentina's total wheat production is projected to increase even more—222 percent—over the same period, and South Africa's total wheat production is projected to increase 406 percent.*

These projected increases in total wheat production lie behind the projected 123 percent increase in world wheat exports which is associated with the projected 106 percent increase in the real trade price of wheat over the 1970–2000 period. Similar increases are also projected for some countries that are not net exporters. For example, total wheat production in East Africa is projected to grow 128 percent* and in Brazil, 277 percent.‡

### The Three Submodels

The arable area submodel's functional variables and variable values for the same case and the same region are shown in Table 18–9. Because of

---

* Department analysts point out that because of interannual variation in food production levels, the selection of 1970 as a base year for the purpose of discussion (because it was used originally to calibrate the GOL model) may be somewhat misleading, since 1970 tended to be a year of relatively low food production levels. For example, the U.S. share of world wheat exports was roughly 45 percent in 1973–75. Similarly, the 109 percent increase in U.S. wheat production to the year 2000, using 1970 as a base, represents only a 45 percent increase in production over the levels of the 1973–75 period. This should be remembered in evaluating all 1970–2000 comparisons.

the rapidity with which the submodel was developed, Department of Agriculture analysts were reluctant to provide the exact form of the function for publication. But they noted that the function assumed a 0.05 price elasticity with respect to area (that is, a 1 percent increase in real returns to farmers after costs) was projected to generate a 0.05 percent increase in arable area—area in crops as well as area in less intensive uages, including pasture — in the absence of binding constraints. They also noted that positive time trends generally represented improvements in land and crop technologies as well as investment in reclamation, development of improved soil management practices, and other improvements. Negative time trends, in contrast, incorporated variables such as urbanization, which work to contract rather than expand arable area over time.

The projections for this region are not, in fact, calculated by this function but instead represent binding constraints affecting the maximum arable area assumed to be available. The maximum arable area is assumed to decline by 3 percent over the 1971–2000 period, from 94 million to 91 million hectares. This decline reflects increased urbanization and its claim on land in a region with a number of countries with severe area problems. Because the total grain area under cultivation is projected to grow by 19 percent, from 24.0 to 28.5 million hectares over the same period—and since only part of the increase can be expected to be in the form of multiple cropping—the projections imply the gradual switch of pasture and other low intensity land uses toward more intensive crop cultivation. Although the Global 2000 Study's

## TABLE 18–9

### Arable Area Submodel, Low-Income North Africa and Middle East

*Medium-Growth, Rising Energy Price Case*

| Functional form: | Arable Area | $= f$ | (GOL aggregate food price index,[a] years since 1971–75) | |
|---|---|---|---|---|
| 1970 | 91.5 million hectares[b] | | 100.0 | 0 |
| 1985 | 92.5 million hectares[c] | | 112.12 | 12 |
| 2000 | 91.0 million hectares[c] | | 129.27 | 27 |

[a] An index of grain, oilseed, and livestock producer prices, weighted by quantities produced from the GOL model results.
[b] The maximum potential area for this region was exogenously estimated for 1970 to be 94.0 million hectares, but the potential was not reached in 1970.
[c] Exogenously estimated maximum potential area for this region for the year specified. Calculations developed using the function on the right-hand side of the equation exceeded this value and as a result the maximum potential area was used instead.

## TABLE 18–10

### Total Food Submodel, Low-Income North Africa and Middle East

*Medium-Growth, Rising Energy Price Case*

| Functional Form: | Total food production index[a] | = | coefficient[b] | × | GOL food production index[c] |
|---|---|---|---|---|---|
| 1970 | 102 | | 1.02001 | | 100 |
| 1985 | 146 | | 1.02001 | | 144 |
| 2000 | 253 | | 1.02001 | | 248 |
| Functional Form: | Total food consumption index[a] | = | coefficient[b] | × | GOL food consumption index[d] |
| 1970 | 102 | | 1.02001 | | 100 |
| 1985 | 167 | | 1.02001 | | 164 |
| 2000 | 276 | | 1.02001 | | 271 |

[a] Weighted caloric index.
[b] Relationship estimated based on historic data.
[c] A caloric index of grain, oilseed, and livestock production, weighted by quantities produced from GOL model results.
[d] A caloric index of grain, oilseed, and livestock consumption, weighted by quantities produced from GOL model results.

## TABLE 18–11

### Fertilizer Submodel, Low-Income North Africa and Middle East

*Medium-Growth, Rising Energy Price Case*

| Functional form: | Fertilizer Usage[a] | = | coefficient[b] | × | weighted caloric value of crop products[c] |
|---|---|---|---|---|---|
| 1971–75 | 1,950 | | 0.13 | | 15,000 |
| 1985 | 4,250 | | 0.17 | | 25,175 |
| 2000 | 8,750 | | 0.24 | | 35,875 |

[a] In thousands of nutrient tons.
[b] Estimated, based on the historic relationship for the region combined with cross-sectional relationships involving the physical response of crops to increasingly intense fertilizer application. The increase in the coefficient represents the effect of declining returns to scale.
[c] Caloric value of crop production calculated using the results of the total food production submodel (excluding livestock production).

environmental analysis indicates that additional large-scale land degradation is occurring for reasons other than urbanization, this was not taken into account in the submodel.

The total food submodel's functional form and variables for the same case and region with regard to total food production are shown in Table 18–10. As can be seen from the first half of the table, GOL food production is projected to increase an average 2.5 percent per year during the 1970–1985 period and to increase to an average 3.7 percent per year during the 1985–2000 period. During the same periods, total food production is expected to increase at roughly the same rates, suggesting

increased multiple cropping and increased cultivation of land previously used for pasture. Total food consumption is projected to increase even faster, using a function similar to that for total food production, as may be seen in the second half of Table 18–10.

The fertilizer use submodel's functional form and variables for the same case and region are shown in Table 18–11. Fertilizer use (for food crops) for this region is projected to increase at about 5 percent per year throughout the 1970–2000 period.

Summaries of the key GOL model and submodel projections for this region are presented in

## TABLE 18–12

### Summary Supply Statistics: Low-Income North Africa and Middle East[a]

*Medium-Growth, Rising Energy Price Case*

| | 1970 | 1985 | 2000 | Average Annual Percent Growth | |
| --- | --- | --- | --- | --- | --- |
| | | | | 1970–85 | 1985–2000 |
| POPULATION AND PER CAPITA GNP | | | | | |
| Population *(millions)* | 116.5 | 165.1 | 229.8 | 2.4 | 2.2 |
| Per Capita GNP[b] *(constant 1970 dollars)* | 188 | 306 | 663 | 3.3 | 5.3 |
| ARABLE AREA | | | | | |
| Total arable area *(million hectares)* | 91.5 | 92.5 | 91.0 | 0.1 | – 0.1 |
| Total grain area under cultivation[c] *(million hectares)* | 24.0 | 26.3 | 28.5 | 0.6 | 0.5 |
| Wheat area under cultivation *(million hectares)* | 13.2 | 16.0 | 18.9 | 1.3 | 1.1 |
| Rice area under cultivation *(million hectares)* | 0.6 | 0.8 | 1.0 | 1.9 | 1.5 |
| Coarse grains area under cultivation *(million hectares)* | 10.3 | 9.5 | 8.6 | – 0.5 | – 0.7 |
| FERTILIZER USE AND YIELDS | | | | | |
| Fertilizer use for food crops *(million nutrient tons)* | 2.0 | 4.3 | 8.8 | 5.2 | 4.9 |
| Total grain yield[c] *(tons per hectare)* | 1.2 | 1.6 | 2.3 | 1.9 | 2.4 |
| Wheat yield *(tons per hectare)* | 1.1 | 1.3 | 2.1 | 1.1 | 3.2 |
| Rice yield *(tons per hectare)* | 3.4 | 3.5 | 3.6 | 0.2 | 0.2 |
| Coarse grain yield *(tons per hectare)* | 1.3 | 1.9 | 2.6 | 2.6 | 2.1 |
| PRODUCTION | | | | | |
| Total food production *(1970 = 100)* | 100 | 144 | 248 | 2.5 | 3.7 |
| GOL food production *(1970 = 100)* | 100 | 144 | 248 | 2.5 | 3.7 |
| Total grain production[c] *(million metric tons)* | 29.0 | 41.9 | 64.7 | 2.5 | 2.9 |
| Wheat production *(million metric tons)* | 13.8 | 21.3 | 38.8 | 2.9 | 4.1 |
| Rice production *(million metric tons)* | 1.9 | 2.7 | 3.5 | 2.4 | 1.7 |
| Coarse grain production *(million metric tons)* | 13.3 | 17.9 | 22.4 | 2.0 | 1.5 |
| PERCENT OF WORLD SUPPLY | | | | | |
| Percent of world total grain production[c] | 2.7 | 4.2 | 4.7 | – | – |
| Percent of world wheat production | 4.3 | 8.2 | 11.6 | – | – |
| Percent of world rice production | 0.9 | 1.4 | 1.2 | – | – |
| Percent of world coarse grain production | 2.4 | 3.3 | 2.9 | – | – |

[a] These figures are representative of the lowest level of disaggregation within the GOL model and are therefore cited to illuminate the GOL methodology. While Department analysts are reasonably confident of the GOL model's computations at the higher levels of aggregation presented in Chapter 6, they would prefer that these more disaggregated projections not be cited as Global 2000 Study projections.
[b] The relationship of these exogenous growth rate assumptions (as reported in the GOL model output) to those developed for the Global 2000 Study (see Chapter 3) is problematical and could not be readily resolved by Department analysts.
[c] Total grain includes wheat, rice, and coarse grains but excludes pulses. As shown in Table 18–3, there are no equations in the GOL model that represent pulses, meat, or meat and dairy products on a disaggregated basis for this region.

Tables 18–12 and 18–13. Since GOL meat projections are generally not computed for individual LDC regions (but for LDCs as an aggregate, instead), they are summarized separately in Table 18–14. Over the 1970–2000 period, the percentage of total grain consumption (including pulses) used for livestock food in the LDCs is relatively constant at roughly 10 percent, whereas it grows from roughly 70 percent to roughly 80 percent in the industrialized nations over the same period.

## TABLE 18–13

### Summary Demand and Trade Statistics: Low-Income North Africa and Middle East[a]

*(Medium-Growth, Rising Energy Price Case)*

| | 1970 | 1985 | 2000 | Average Annual Percent Growth 1970–85 | Average Annual Percent Growth 1985–2000 |
|---|---|---|---|---|---|
| POPULATION AND PER CAPITA GNP | | | | | |
| Population *(millions)* | 116.5 | 165.1 | 229.8 | 2.4 | 2.2 |
| Per Capita GNP[b] *(constant 1970 dollars)* | 188 | 306 | 663 | 3.3 | 5.3 |
| CONSUMPTION | | | | | |
| Total food consumption *(1970 = 100)* | 100 | 164 | 271 | 3.4 | 3.4 |
| GOL food consumption *(1970 = 100)* | 100 | 164 | 271 | 3.4 | 3.4 |
| Total grain consumption[c] *(million metric tons)* | 35.3 | 52.8 | 77.5 | 2.7 | 2.6 |
| Wheat food usage *(million metric tons)* | 19.8 | 29.6 | 43.0 | 2.7 | 2.5 |
| Rice food usage *(million metric tons)* | 1.5 | 2.2 | 3.7 | 2.6 | 3.5 |
| Coarse grains food usage *(million metric tons)* | 9.4 | 14.3 | 21.2 | 2.8 | 2.7 |
| Coarse grains feed usage *(million metric tons)* | 4.6 | 6.7 | 9.6 | 2.5 | 2.4 |
| NET TRADE | | | | | |
| Total grain imports[c] *(million metric tons)* | 5.3 | 11.0 | 12.8 | 5.0 | 1.0 |
| Wheat imports *(million metric tons)* | 5.4 | 8.3 | 4.1 | 2.9 | – 4.6 |
| Rice imports *(million metric tons)* | – 0.4 | – 0.4 | 0.2 | 0.0 | – |
| Coarse grains imports *(million metric tons)* | 0.3 | 3.2 | 8.5 | 17.1 | 6.7 |
| REAL PRICES | | | | | |
| Wheat trade price *(constant 1970 dollars per metric ton)* | 62.90 | 86.27 | 129.29 | 2.1 | 2.7 |
| Rice trade price *(constant 1970 dollars per metric ton)* | – | 204.21 | 280.85 | – | 2.1 |
| Coarse grain trade price *(constant 1970 dollars per metric ton)* | – | 80.03 | 125.50 | – | 3.0 |

[a] These figures are representative of the lowest level of disaggregation within the GOL model and are cited to illuminate the GOL methodology. While Department analysts are reasonably confident of the GOL model's computations at the higher levels of aggregation presented in Chapter 6, they would prefer that these more disaggregated projections not be cited as Global 2000 Study projections.

[b] The relationship of these exogenous growth rate assumptions (as reported in the GOL model output) to those developed for the Global 2000 Study (see Chapter 3) is problematical and could not be readily resolved by Department analysts.

[c] Total grain includes wheat, rice, and coarse grains but excludes pulses. As shown in Table 18-3, there are no equations in the GOL model that represent pulses, meat, or meat and dairy products on a disaggregated basis for this region.

## TABLE 18–14

### Summary Meat Statistics: Less Developed Countries and Industrialized Nations[a]

*(Medium-Growth, Rising Energy Price Case)*

| | 1970 | 1985 | 2000 | Average Annual Percent Growth | |
|---|---|---|---|---|---|
| | | | | 1970–85 | 1985–2000 |
| MEAT PRODUCTION *(million metric tons)* | | | | | |
| Less developed countries | 6.5 | 10.5 | 19.6 | 3.2 | 4.2 |
| Industrialized nations | 46.6 | 63.1 | 75.2 | 2.0 | 1.2 |
| MEAT CONSUMPTION *(million metric tons)* | | | | | |
| Less developed countries | 5.6 | 9.3 | 16.1 | 3.4 | 3.7 |
| Industrialized nations | 47.3 | 63.2 | 77.1 | 2.0 | 1.3 |
| PER CAPITA MEAT CONSUMPTION[b] *(kilograms)* | | | | | |
| Less developed countries | 3.2 | 3.7 | 4.6 | 1.0 | 1.5 |
| Industrialized nations | 67.6 | 82.9 | 94.3 | 1.4 | 0.9 |
| PER CAPITA GRAIN CONSUMPTION FOR FOOD[c] *(kilograms)* | | | | | |
| Less developed countries | 155.9 | 181.7 | 188.6 | 1.0 | 0.2 |
| Industrialized nations | 172.5 | 170.2 | 163.4 | − 0.1 | − 0.3 |
| PER CAPITA GRAIN CONSUMPTION FOR FEED[c] *(kilograms)* | | | | | |
| Less developed countries | 17.0 | 19.4 | 23.8 | 0.9 | 1.4 |
| Industrialized nations | 362.0 | 440.1 | 585.6 | 1.3 | 1.9 |

[a] As shown in Table 18–3, there are no equations in the GOL model that represent meat supply and demand for the centrally planned countries. However, meat products are disaggregated within the GOL model for the less developed countries and industrialized nations, also as shown in Table 18–3.
[b] Not perfectly consistent with Tables 6–6 and 6–8, due to discrepancies noted in footnote b of Table 18–6.
[c] Total grain includes wheat, rice, and coarse grains but excludes pulses. As shown in Table 18–3, there are no equations in the GOL model that represent pulses, meat, or meat and dairy products on a disaggregated basis for this region.

# 19  Renewable Resources

There is at present no adequate, formal and precise means of projecting world trends for renewable resources such as water, forestry, fisheries, soil, and the environment. In some cases (fisheries and forestry), agency experts have humored the staff of the Global 2000 Study by developing world forecasts of renewable resources to the year 2000, but with one exception,* none has presented the Study with a forecast based on an explicit mathematical model. In fact, all were convinced that in their areas of expertise descriptive and judgmental analyses were more accurate, objective, and illuminating than projections based on mathematical models, given the present state of the art.

Description and judgmental analyses are sometimes depreciated as "unscientific." However, it is just as possible to be scientific without being mathematical as it is to be mathematical without being scientific. Indeed, applying mathematical techniques (e.g., regression analysis) prior to the development of an adequate conceptual theory or hypothesis leads to pseudo-scientific reasoning—and often to precise but incorrect conclusions. Therefore, the renewable resource projections should not be considered less credible or less scientific because they are not mathematical. In fact, it might be more appropriate to respect the analysts for applying tools appropriate to present limitations of knowledge in the areas in which they are working.

This chapter will discuss the methods by which the renewable resource projections in this volume were made. All such forecasts were derived from verbal models, and each description of the method used will be preceded by a few generalizations as to why verbal models were preferable and why good quantitative forecasts could not be made for that particular resource.

What do water, forestry, fisheries, soil, and the environment have in common that make them difficult to forecast? For one thing, in the United States all have historically been considered "free

goods." No agents keep track of free goods, and the incentive for the systematic monitoring of renewable resources, particularly on a world level, has been almost nonexistent. Thus firm concepts and data bases for making forecasts are lacking. As free goods in our economic system, renewable resources have been the dependent variables of commodities with higher priorities. The fate of forest lands is apt to be determined by agricultural or grazing needs; water, as it flows from one use to another, becomes laden with wastes; estuaries are wiped out in the course of urbanization. All these circumstances baffle attempts at measurement, thwart record keeping, and make precision difficult, so that the exact future of things tends to become "anybody's guess."

In the last decade, local scarcities have wrought a few changes in the free goods mentality. The inclination to keep track of water, forest, fish, and soil resources has grown stronger. New technologies have made the keeping of accounts easier. Satellite photography has proved useful in gathering global data, and computer-based data processing has expedited the storing, sorting, and digesting of information. The primary bottleneck to effective analysis at this moment is insufficient institutional recognition of ecological concepts and the absence of stable analytic institutions and coordination of efforts. Work is being done at universities scattered throughout the country and in various departments of government, and concepts have been developed, but there is often no consensus—and in some cases, no communication—among experts working on the same resource problem. Where there *is* consensus, the means for implementing findings about effective resource management are often lacking.

A second trait of renewable resources that thwarts projection is the tendency for one resource problem to become inextricably intertwined with another. Consequently, problems are difficult to examine in isolation. Hydrologic regimes and soil problems are greatly influenced by watershed management, which often is a forestry matter. Forestry, in turn, is influenced by attempts to extend agricultural production and by institutional questions, such as what cutting prac-

---

*The Brookhaven National Laboratory developed the mathematical model of the the energy sector's impacts on the environment described at the end of this chapter.

tices are permitted and how much grazing is permissable in forest lands. Where wood is used as a fuel, the prices and availabilities of alternative fuels is also critical in predicting the future of forestry.

Lastly, renewable resources are difficult to forecast because their dynamics frequently include circumstances where cause and effect are widely separated, in time, space, or in both. Trees planted now will not become harvestable timber until after the year 2000. Gradual increases in intensity of exploitation of soil systems may have no noticeable effect until a severe drought sets in. Toxins can be carried through the food chain for long periods of time until they become sufficiently concentrated in the higher predators and cause severe damage. In such situations, it is often not quite clear what is happening until after it has happened, and the chances of subtle changes in renewable resource systems being overlooked are high.

## Water

The institutional history of water projections is an interesting contrast to those of other resources. The U.S. Geological Survey has taken an interest in predicting water supply since the time of Theodore Roosevelt, and national assessments have taken place on a regular basis since the 1950s. The net experience of these years of forecasting has turned the Survey somewhat against attempting to make forecasts of a general nature over broad regions, using simple quantitative measures. They have found local inquiries and "problem identification" approaches more useful. The reason, as described in an early draft of the water forecast for the Global 2000 Study, is that:

There is really no such thing as a global water economy in the same sense as for example, minerals and fuels. A surplus in one place is of little use elsewhere. Cost limits the transport of water. Water problems are usually local, rather than global.

Thus, while in other areas there has been mounting pressure in the government to keep national inventories—and global inventories where there is reason to—the trend in water forecasting has been one of increasing emphasis on problem-specific studies. Nevertheless, the Water Resources Division of the U.S. Geological Survey provided the Global 2000 Study with some global water forecasts, describing how they were constructed and adding commentary for the purpose of identifying the problems involved.

Water is a fluid substance in more ways than one. On the supply side, it slips through all attempts to achieve a uniform definition of "supply." Does one inventory surface water? Groundwater? What about multiple usage? How does one take into account water that would be available if the transportation system were adequate? A different answer to any of the above questions could halve or double "water supply."

On the demand side, it is difficult to hold water to fixed relationships. Where water has been considered a "free good," the pattern of water utilization is the product of complex forces of cultural and technological evolution. The amounts of water required for specific industrial processes often vary by a factor of two or more, without significant cost savings associated with the more water-intensive process. Per capita consumption in national cross sections does not closely follow per capita incomes. In short, there is very little to hang onto in making predictions; water use patterns are highly variable and could assume forms quite different from those we observe today should water scarcity become a problem.

Given this nebulousness, the methodology of global water forecasts is quite arbitrary, and the forecasts themselves not especially meaningful—which is why Chapter 9, "Water Projections," confined itself largely to descriptions of the nature of water as a resource and explanations of why meaningful forecasts are not possible. The two forecasts of global water demand for the year 2000 were chosen not for their excellence but because other global water forecasts could not be found. The two estimates differ by more than an order of magnitude, and the assumptions on which they were based are not publicly documented.

The water forecast chapter concludes with a statement to the effect that local water shortage problems will be much more common by 2000 than they are now, but that quantitative forecasts on a global basis are simply not possible.

## Fisheries

No U.S. government agency is vested with the responsibility to make long-term global forecasts of the fish catch, but the Global 2000 Study turned to the one agency capable of producing such forecasts: the National Marine Fisheries Service of the Commerce Department's National Oceanic and Atmospheric Administration. It was decided that, given the present state of the art of fisheries modeling, a verbal description of the operational characteristics of marine resource behavior combined with inferences drawn from historical data on the fish catch would better serve the Study's purposes than output from a formal model. Thus, the fisheries forecasts (Chapter 7) are based on empirical evidence and on ecological reasons why certain outcomes can or cannot be expected.

Ecological analysis can provide statements about potential supply but not about demand. In the marine resources forecast, statements of demand were synopsized from FAO sources and from the work of Frederick W. Bell and his colleagues at the National Marine Fisheries Service. Both demand forecasts were based on assumptions about population and income growth and income elasticities of demands for marine products. The Bell analysis also took into account supply constraints and the pressure on prices generated by inelastic supplies.

The concepts, precepts, and methodologies of ecology and economics are fundamentally different and stand at odds with one another. This disagreement appears clearly in the fisheries resource forecast. The ecologically derived supply estimates state that it will be reasonable to expect a global catch of around 60 million metric tons in the year 2000—if environmental degradation does not reduce the basic productivity of the oceans. The economically derived FAO projection states that demand for marine harvests in 1985 will have reached 106.5 million metric tons with the implication that it will probably increase thereafter. The economic estimate by Bell projects that demand in the year 2000 will have reached 83.5 million metric tons. It is left to the reader to reconcile the difference between supply and demand forecasts.

## Forestry

No U.S. government agency keeps records or does analysis of forestry on a worldwide basis. The Global 2000 Study turned to the CIA's Environmental and Resources Center for assistance. The projections provided by the Center were based on a review of the literature of forest economics and ecology, combined with informed judgment. Where sources were in conflict—as, for example, when ecologic and anthropologic forecasts came to different conclusions about sustainability of slash-and-burn agriculture—the source with the stronger empirical evidence was preferred.

The focus of the projections presented in Chapter 8 is the anticipated supply and demand for forest products and the costs incurred in supplying them. These variables were considered separately for each of the major forest regions of the world. A separate section is devoted to the problems of the humid tropics.

The strongest structural concept developed was the distinction between forest usage patterns in the industrialized countries and in the less developed countries. The former countries have substantially more wood per capita and use their forest resources primarily in forest products industries, while the latter, with less wood per capita, use a large portion of their wood as fuel. The two patterns are expected to lead to very different consequences by 2000. No formal mathematical structure was developed.

## Environment

As the Global 2000 Study was originally designed, each agency forecast was to include an analysis of the environmental ramifications of its projections. As forecasts were received, the Study team began to realize that the original design was unrealistic. While most agencies have some capacity to do environmental analyses, that capability can seldom be adapted to making long-term forecasts on a global basis. The analyses of environmental implications appended to most of the forecasts were minimal or nonexistent. As a result it was necessary for the Global 2000 Staff to contract out part of the environmental analysis and undertake part of this work itself. On the basis of recommendations made by the staffs of the Environmental Protection Agency and the Council on Environmental Quality, the water-environment forecast was contracted to Threshhold, Inc., a Washington, D.C., environmental consulting company; the marine-environment section was contracted to the Marine Laboratory at Duke University and to George Woodwell at Woods Hole Marine Biological Laboratory; and the section on habitat loss and species extinction was produced by the World Wildlife Fund, Washington, D.C.

The energy-environment forecast was alone in proceeding more or less according to the original plan. The Department of Energy contracted to have Brookhaven National Laboratory prepare an analysis of the environmental implications of the energy projections. This was interpreted by the Global 2000 Study Staff after receiving comments and criticisms from analysts at the Environmental Protection Agency.

The energy-environment forecast was based on a computer analysis of the energy use figures forecast by the energy model. The methodology, focus, and structure of that model is described below. Other sections of the environmental forecasts were made using the normal, judgmental techniques of scholarly research.

Environment was defined for this study as "ability to support life," and emphasis was placed on qualitative and quantitative aspects of the ability to support human life and to stabilize and sustain environmental systems. Particular attention was given to situations where large portions of the world's population or surface areas would be affected, or where widespread irreversible damage might be incurred by changes affecting the environment.

Environmental forecasts followed the basic structure of the other forecasts. For each main forecast, an environmental forecast was made. Both the ways in which the environment might be expected to be influenced, according to the forecast, and the ways in which environmental changes might influence the forecast were discussed. Where there was a clear overlapping of subject matter, as with agriculture, forestry, and water, the subject matter was apportioned according to the analyst's best judgment.

### Energy-Environment Model

The Energy Systems Network Simulator (ESNS) was developed at Brookhaven National Laboratory in 1974. The model is designed to permit highly detailed analyses of the environmental impacts of energy flows in the U.S. energy system. It feeds on data from the Brookhaven Energy Data Base and other data bases.

Through a process of aggregation of disaggregated categories, simplification of mathematical structure, and replication of the simplified structure for various regions, the U.S. ESNS model has been adapted to interface with the International Energy Evaluation System (IEES) described in Chapters 10 and 20.

The adaptation was not made without difficulty. The International version required assumptions about emissions control standards on a worldwide basis. Without estimates of pollution control measures to be taken in other regions of the world, the Brookhaven analysts assumed that U.S. regulatory practices would be adopted on a global basis. While a few countries may adopt more stringent regulatory policies than the U.S., most will probably apply lower standards. Thus the model tends to understate emissions.

The output from the IEES model, in particular the estimates for fuel consumption by end uses for the LDCs, the OPEC regions, and the centrally planned economies, were far too aggregated for use in the ESNS model. The required degree of disaggregation for the LDCs and OPEC countries was developed using estimates for end-use distribution of fuel types from the WAES (Workshop on Alternative Energy Strategies) study.* The WAES scenarios used in both these cases for IEES low, medium, and high rates of growth were, for 1985:

| low | WAES scenario D |
| medium | Weighted average of high and low |
| high | WAES scenario C |

and for 1990:

| low | WAES scenario D7 |
| medium and high | Scaled from 1985 figures in proportion to total fuel use |

Estimates for the centrally planned economies were based on the estimates for Eastern Europe and China presented in the 1977 *Annual Review of Energy*.†

Finally, the IEES estimates included neither base-case figures nor estimates for years after 1990, which limited the Brookhaven analysis to projections for 1985 and 1990.

### Mechanics of the ESNS Model

Mechanically, the IEES adaptation of the ESNS model is simply an accounting device that calculates annual emissions inventories. Basically, it entails no more than repeated use of the following formula and summations across end-use (sectoral) categories and across fuel-type categories:

Total regional energy end use (by fuel type)
  × Emissions generated (by emission type) per unit of energy end use (by fuel type)
= Total regional emissions generated (by emission type).

Mathematically, the operations are carried out using matrix algebra; thus the multiplier, multiplicand, and product in the above formula are all tabular blocks of numbers (matrices) when the actual operations are carried out. Sample values for one of the 187‡ matrix multiplications performed by the model matrices are shown in the accompanying example.

Identical calculations were performed for each of the 17 regions considered in the model. Similar

---

*Energy: Global Prospects 1985–2000*, New York: McGraw-Hill, 1977.

†Jack M. Hollander, ed., *Annual Review of Energy*, vol. 2, Palo Alto, Calif., 1977.

‡Eleven emissions categories are estimated for each of 17 regions.

## Sample Calculation Performed by the ESNS Model

### Fuel Use, Canada, 1985 ($10^{15}$ Btu per year)

| | Electric Utilities | Synthetic Fuels | Industrial | Transportation | Household and Commercial | Raw Materials | Energy Sector |
|---|---|---|---|---|---|---|---|
| Coal | −0.55 | −0.11 | 0.14 | 0 | 0.01 | 0 | 0 |
| Oil | −0.11 | 0 | 0.65 | 2.55 | 1.34 | 0.44 | 0.55 |
| Gas | −0.06 | 0.11 | 0.82 | 0 | 0.74 | 0 | 0.40 |
| Electric | 1.48 | 0 | 0.64 | 0 | 0.66 | 0 | 0.18 |
| Nuclear | 0 | 0 | 0 | 0 | 0 | 0 | 0 |
| Hydro-geothermal | 0 | 0 | 0 | 0 | 0 | 0 | 0 |

### MULTIPLIED BY

### Sulfur Dioxide (in short tons) per $10^{12}$ Btu of Fuel*

| | Coal | Oil | Gas | Electric | Nuclear | Hydro-Geo-thermal |
|---|---|---|---|---|---|---|
| Electric utilities | 202.0 | 320.0 | 0.293 | 0 | 0 | 0 |
| Synthetic fuels | 31.7 | 0 | 0 | 0 | 0 | 0 |
| Industrial | 603.0 | 393.0 | 0.291 | 0 | 0 | 0 |
| Transportation | 0 | 15.0 | 0 | 0 | 0 | 0 |
| Household and commercial | 1,240.0 | 113.0 | 0.276 | 0 | 0 | 0 |
| Raw materials | 603.0 | 393.0 | 0.291 | 0 | 0 | 0 |
| Energy sectors | 603.0 | 393.0 | 0.291 | 0 | 0 | 0 |

### EQUALS

### Sulfur Dioxide Generation (in $10^5$ short tons) per Year, Canada, 1985

| | Coal | Oil | Gas | Electric | Nuclear | Hydro-Geo-thermal |
|---|---|---|---|---|---|---|
| Electric utilities | 78.78 | 35.20 | 0.018 | 0 | 0 | 0 |
| Synthetic fuels | 3.80 | 0 | 0 | 0 | 0 | 0 |
| Industrial | 84.42 | 235.8 | 0.230 | 0 | 0 | 0 |
| Transportation | 0 | 41.4 | 0 | 0 | 0 | 0 |
| Household and commercial | 12.40 | 136.7 | 0.209 | 0 | 0 | 0 |
| Raw materials | 0 | 169.0 | 0 | 0 | 0 | 0 |
| Energy sector | 0 | 220.1 | 0.116 | 0 | 0 | 0 |

* The same matrix is used for all regions, all years.

calculations were performed for each of the following 11 classes of environmental effects:

Carbon dioxide
Carbon monoxide
Sulfur dioxide
Oxides of nitrogen
Hydrocarbon emissions
Particulate emissions
Land use associated with fuel combustion (e.g., powerplants)
Solid waste
Tritium emissions
Population exposure to ionizing radiation
Solid high-level (nuclear) wastes

Given the uncertain nature of the IEES outputs, these calculations are only first approximations. As the model's structure is static and linear, the quality of outcomes are totally dependent on the quality of the input and the emissions coefficients. The model's structure will shed no insight into the dynamics of the question being asked. Much of the data used for fuel-specific end-use estimates of energy consumption for the centrally planned economies has had to be guessed at or inferred. The reliability of the IEES inputs used to drive the model is not above question (as described in Chapter 20).

And it is almost certain that the emissions estimates for many regions—because they anticipate the adoption of U.S. new-source emission-standards—are too low.

The ESNS results produced for the Global 2000 Study are little more than a demonstration of how global emissions inventories could be developed if time, money, and data were made available to undertake the calculations. Beyond this, the model does provide a first-cut approximation of environmental effects of the energy sector. For all its arbitrary assumptions, this estimate may be more realistic than the intuitive guesses that most experts would make without a mathematical calculating device.

# 20 Energy

The Energy Information Administration of the U.S. Department of Energy has lead responsibility within the federal government for collecting and disseminating energy information and performing energy forecasting. The agency produces short-, mid-, and long-range forecasts both of individual fuels and of integrated multifuel, multisector balances. The international forecasts, which make use of both domestic and international work done by several divisions of the agency, are the responsibility of the International Analysis Division.

The International Analysis Division in the Office of Integrative Analysis of the Energy Information Administration produces forecasts of international energy statistics for use within the Department of Energy. To reflect the range of uncertainty in basic assumptions, the forecasts are usually made in multiple sets, each based on different policy or scenario assumptions. As in most forecasting exercises, the Division feels more confident of its methods in performing relative impact analyses than in making single point estimates. Analyses are focused on the industrialized countries and are done in less detail for the entire world. The only documented set of forecasts produced by the Division to date are those contained in *World Energy Prospects*, a report prepared in what was then the Federal Energy Administration (FEA) and released for limited official use in mid-1977.

To make its forecasts for the Global 2000 Study, the International Analysis Division recalculated all data dependent on population or GNP as inputs (this is much of the demand sector data), using the Global 2000 forecasts for these variables. Since the demand sector forecast is based on an econometric analysis of past behavioral response to relative fuel prices and GNP, the Division did not think it appropriate to extend the forecasts beyond 15 years and chose to stop at 1990. Since the Energy Information Administration is currently developing a long-run forecasting capability, it was unwilling to reproduce any other single forecast as an official government projection. Instead, the division surveyed competing views on the international energy market in the year 2000 (see Chapter 10).

## Key Analytic Methodology

All of the international quantitative forecasts provided by the Energy Information Administration are based on the International Energy Evaluation System (IEES). IEES is a mathematical representation of the world energy market and is therefore only a partial equilibrium model. The heart of IEES is a linear programming matrix that combines large amounts of international energy market data to make the final forecasts. The linear programming model approximates the workings of a competitive economic market. Supplying the data to the matrix are six IEES "submodels," which may themselves be forecasting computer models maintained by the International Analysis Division or may be simply procedures for obtaining and adapting data from outside sources. The six submodels are named for the type of data they yield for use in the linear programming matrix: demand; supply; transportation; electric utilities; refining; and miscellaneous conversions.

The methods used to produce the input data to the linear program vary with the submodel. Each of the six submodels relies on considerable outside data; even the submodels that consist primarily of computer models require input data from outside the International Analysis Division. How (and how much) each submodel processes its input data to produce data for the linear program varies, however. The demand submodel produces original econometric forecasts on the basis of certain economic and demographic input data. The electric utilities submodel uses computer programs to convert international industrial statistics into estimates of regional electric production capacities, technologies, and costs. The supply, transportation, refining, and miscellaneous conversions submodels simply collect data from outside sources, for the most part, making adjustments where necessary.

The creation of the IEES model was part of the federal government's response to the exporters' oil embargo of 1973–74. The embargo aroused concern within the U.S. over the nation's extensive reliance on imports for its energy supply. That winter, President Nixon expressed the intention of the government to help make the country energy independent by the year 1980. Activities to this end were designated "Project Independence." The Federal Energy Administration was created in May of 1974 to handle many of the government's energy-related activities. Within it, several divisions as a group were to handle all energy data management and forecasting. Of these, the Supply and Integration Division was responsible for combining the information compiled by the other divisions to evaluate both the ability of the nation to attain its Project Independence goal and the impact of alternative policies and scenarios on this ability.

To this end, it organized the quantitative data produced by the various divisions into a single body according to an accounting framework, which it developed, called the Project Independence Evaluation System (PIES). The staff of the Supply and Integration Division, consisting primarily of economists and operations researchers, developed PIES into a single linear programming model of the U.S. national energy system that draws on the data banks and quantitative forecasting procedures developed by the other divisions for its input data.

Meanwhile the FEA International Division, responsible for the same types of estimates and forecasts on a worldwide basis, began development of a parallel model called the International Energy Evaluation System, which has been briefly described above. IEES is, in effect, an adaptation of PIES. The International Division staff, also primarily economists and operations researchers, reproduced the PIES methods and structure almost exactly for the sake of consistency. Data limitations required a few deviations. The modeling capability behind PIES and IEES has survived several reorganizations of the federal energy agencies. The maintenance and running of PIES is now the responsibility of the Office of Analytic Methods within the Energy Information Administration, and, as already mentioned, updating and running IEES is the function of the International Analysis Division (IAD).

To make the energy forecasts for the Global 2000 project, IAD carried through the standard IEES analysis with the project's forecasts of population and GNP. The Global 2000 forecasts replaced the population and GNP estimates IAD usually relies on. Otherwise the special run of IEES used the input data IAD has compiled for its standard runs of IEES.

When all of the necessary data of the six types have been supplied, the IEES linear program matrix contains approximately 2,000 rows and 6,000 columns. It is solved by the WHIZARD

linear programming package on an IBM 370/168 computer. Solving the matrix itself takes about 30 minutes of computer (CPU*) time, but arranging the large volume of input data for the run and printing out the results in an understandable format takes another hour of computer (CPU) time. The model is principally written in GAMMA, a matrix generation code, while the econometric demand submodel utilizes TSP.†

## Basic Principles

IEES forecasts international energy market variables by mathematically representing the world energy system as a competitive market. Demand and supply are assumed to equilibrate through the price mechanism. In addition, the IEES organizes the energy flows that equilibrate supply and demand so that the total cost of the processes that convert primary fuels to delivered consumable energy products—transportation, refining, conversion, and electrical generation—is minimized, under the assumption that this is approximately how a real competitive market operates. The data quantifying world energy supply, demand, and the costs necessary for these calculations are supplied by the six IEES submodels, which act largely independently of one another and draw on their own outside data sources. The data are arranged into a single linear programming matrix, which is solved to meet the world's final energy demands at the minimum cost. If supply and demand do not balance in the solution, the matrix is rerun iteratively with adjustments in the input data until the two are nearly equal.

The final forecasts made by IEES consist of an "energy balance" for each separate world region. This is a table that includes the quantities of each primary fossil fuel the region will produce and the quantities of each final energy product it will consume. Prices are also determined by the IEES but, to an extent, these are not forecasts unless some constraint is placed on OPEC production. The demand and supply quantities are forecasted initially from an exogenously assumed set of prices. These prices are adjusted in the process of equilibrating supply and demand, and the adjusted prices are output by IEES. Thus the price forecasts are partially dependent on the assumption of price used as input in the IEES analysis.

Like PIES, IEES is meant to simulate a modern competitive energy market that deals primarily in fossil fuels. Member countries of the Organization for Economic Cooperation and Development (OECD), which consume 80 percent of the

* Computer processing unit.    † Time series processor.

world's oil production and are generally the world's most industrialized nations, are treated most extensively in the submodel analyses, though the submodels produce data for every part of the world. (The different treatment IEES gives to various regions of the world is depicted graphically in the color map section in the map entitled "Energy Projections: International Energy Evaluation System Methodology.") Petroleum, natural gas, and coal are the only fuels explicitly modeled in IEES. Estimates of electrical capacity from nuclear, hydro, and geothermal power made by outside sources are entered into the calculations for any one year as constants. The model does not forecast their growth, but by making multiple runs with different nuclear and hydro capacity assumptions IEES can evaluate the impact of different growth patterns of these energy sources. Because the so-called soft energy sources—wood, solar and wind—are not traded internationally, they are not explicitly represented in IEES; nor are they ordinarily the subject of impact analyses made with IEES.

Actual market perturbations are included in IEES wherever possible. There are two ways in which the actions of the OPEC countries are represented. In any one run it is assumed either (1) that OPEC sets its oil production at a definite amount and takes whatever price for oil prevails, or (2) that OPEC sets a price on all of its oil and sells as much at that price as is needed. In the first case, IEES assumes that the world buys all of the OPEC oil, then resorts to other sources for the rest of its needs. The market sets oil price. In the second case, the OPEC oil price is automatically assumed to be the price for all oil in the world. To meet demand, the world buys as much OPEC oil as it needs to supplement other production. In neither type of run is OPEC assumed to have any direct control over the natural gas or coal markets. U.S. price controls are represented extensively. There is also some average pricing of natural gas and electricity throughout the world. In the case of electricity, the cost of electrical generation in IEES depends on the marginal cost of its fuel inputs, but the price of electricity depends on the average cost of generation. Price controls in foreign countries are also included, but less comprehensively than those in the U.S. because information on them is less complete.

The assumptions of supply-demand equilibrium and cost minimization are what justifies calling IEES a model of a "competitive" energy market. As explained later, the IEES linear programming matrix is solved several times until supply and demand are equal (or, technically, until the sum of consumers' and producers' surplus is maxi-

mized). In each solution, including the final one used as the basis for the forecasts, the linear program selects the fuel sources, transportation routes, and processing procedures that make the total world cost of all of these things together an absolute minimum. This formulation follows classical micro-economic theory in that demand and supply quantities at the point in time under analysis are assumed to balance exactly, and the human actors involved are assumed to act so as to minimize cost (they are implicitly assumed not only to want to keep energy-related costs at a minimum, but to actually have the knowledge, ability, and motivation to do so). The IEES formulation differs from classical economics in that individuals or firms are not necessarily assumed to be minimizing their own costs or maximizing profits. All choices of production, transportation, and conversion are made and coordinated around the world to minimize the total global cost of these activities. The profits and costs of individual persons or firms are not explicitly modeled.

Issues not directly related to the international market for fossil fuels are generally neglected by IEES. It does not include political factors or evaluate the social or environmental effects of the energy industry. Nor is resource depletion modeled. Gross national product (GNP), is included as one of the major determinants of energy demand, but within IEES no energy market variables influence it in turn; GNP is implicitly treated as independent of the energy market. IEES does include energy conservation, which is represented as a reduction in energy demand.

The six submodels that supply data to the linear program operate largely independently. Each works under its own set of assumptions about how the sector it models operates. Data are not typically passed between the submodels while they are making forecasts that will go into the integrating linear program.

The demand submodel yields one forecast of quantity demanded for each final fuel product and each region. For each OECD region except the U.S., it also produces one estimate of the price elasticity of demand for each final fuel product; these elasticities are not entered into the linear programming matrix but are used later in the equilibration of supply and demand. The data are all forecasted for the year under analysis. If the run of the linear program is to produce forecasts for 1985, the demand data must pertain to 1985 also. The methods used to obtain the demand forecasts differ significantly between regions and fuels, with by far the more extensive analysis devoted to the OECD countries and the major fuels. The energy demand quantities of noncommunist, non-OECD regions are simply assumed to be a constant fraction of GNP; the modelers estimate this ratio from historical consumption and GNP data. For the U.S. and the communist regions, the IAD staff collects forecasts of net imports from outside sources. These are interpreted as the amounts of energy fuels the regions will export or import; their demand is not explicitly modeled. No demand elasticities are calculated for the U.S. or the non-OECD countries; these regions are assumed to consume a quantity of energy that is fixed relative to price.

The non-U.S. OECD demand data come from an iterative econometric forecasting model. The model itself forecasts only demand quantities, but by varying the price inputs to the model and comparing the resulting quantity forecasts, the model is used to estimate price elasticities, too. The quantities of major fuels demanded by important economic sectors (iron and steel, other manufacturing, residential/commercial) are forecasted by "budget" equations, the most sophisticated type used in the demand model. In the budget formulation, regions determine first how many British thermal units (Btu) of fuel per capita they want to buy based on an energy price index, on gross domestic product (GDP) per capita, and on last year's BTU per capita fuel budget. Then they decide what fraction of the total budget to devote to each fuel, based on individual fuel prices and last year's purchase of the fuel. The budget formulation allows for product substitution by consumers. For less important fuels and other sectors, quantity demanded is generally forecasted by a single equation in which demand is a function of time or GDP, and substitution is not modeled.

Because it uses the lagged variables mentioned above (last year's BTU budget, last year's fuel purchase), the demand model must forecast iteratively from a base year. The base year forecasts are made with historical data. For the Global 2000 Study run, 1975 price, GDP, and population data were used to make 1976 demand forecasts. From these 1976 forecasts the model made 1977 forecasts, and from these, 1978 forecasts, and so on out to 1990. The demand forecasts are driven largely by the input forecasts of price, GDP, and population. These data all come from outside sources, including nongovernment computer forecasting models and from experts both inside and outside the federal government working from judgment. None of the input data sources refer routinely to the IAD econometric demand model or to the data of the other IEES submodels in making their forecasts. The U.S. demand quantities are taken from the output of PIES.

The econometric model captures behavioral response to prices but not policy-mandated conservation strategies. Conservation per se is represented by exogenous adjustments of the demand data to reflect estimates of the savings in energy fuels resulting from specific OECD policies.

The supply data passed to the IEES linear program also consist of a quantity for each region and each primary energy product and of a price elasticity for some regions and each primary product, but the method of their derivation is generally simpler. The U.S. and communist region quantities, like demand, are taken from forecasts of net import positions. But for all other regions, outside experts are asked for estimates of 1975 regional energy production. With historical wellhead prices, these establish a single point on each supply curve. The elasticities of supply for these regions are assumptions of the IAD; for most energy types and regions, the elasticity is assumed to be 0.1 when forecasts are made for 1985 and 0.26 when forecasts are made for 1990.

The transportation costs are actual current costs as reported by outside sources. They must be adjusted slightly because the IEES does not represent every major port in the world; instead, each region has one location, called a centroid, to and from which all fuels are assumed to be shipped. Real transportation costs are assumed constant regardless of how far in the future the forecasts are made.

The electric utilities submodel includes a computer program to convert outside plant data into estimates of regional generation capacities and costs. Nuclear and hydro capacities are then added; they are not variable. These data are given to the linear program, which then interprets them as a description of the limitations on the consumption of electricity: The data tell the program that getting more electricity from an oilburning plant means taking more oil; total consumption within a region cannot exceed total plant capacity; and so on. Included in these data are limits on the permissible rates of retirement of generation capacity; generally, plants cannot be removed at a rate faster than 3 percent per year. There is no limit on the creation of new productive capacity in the data. The absolute amount of productive capacity that can be removed and created in one run thus varies with the time period of the forecasts. The utilities data do not vary from IEES run to IEES run otherwise. Hence average electrical generation costs vary in real terms only as the mix of new and old plants varies.

The refining and miscellaneous conversions data are similar to the utilities data. They describe the processes by which raw fuels are converted to various refined, derivative, and synthetic fuels. No upper bound is put on refining capacities, but the miscellaneous conversions data include limits on the volume of conversions the LP (linear program) matrix can select to achieve its lowest cost solution, to make sure it does not become unreasonably high. In a run of the IEES to make forecasts for 1985, miscellaneous conversions are allowed to be no more than twice their historical 1975 level; for forecasts of later years, the conversions are given a higher limit. All other data in the submodels, including costs and technology specifications, remain the same for each IEES run.

When the final LP matrix is filled with the data from each of the submodels and solved for the first time, supply and demand probably will not match. Supply and demand quantities are determined by the exogenously estimated future prices. The chances that the quantities so derived will match exactly after the LP matrix works out the details of transportation and conversions are slim. So prices are adjusted and demand and supply quantities are recalculated with the new prices and the supply and demand elasticities. The demand model is not rerun with the new prices to get the new demand quantities; presumably the elasticities derived from it are a sufficiently accurate representation of its response to price changes. The LP matrix is then resolved with the new supply and demand quantities replacing the old. This process is repeated until supply and demand in the solved matrix are acceptably close.

## Basic Components

The focus of the IEES model makes it extremely useful to the Global 2000 Study in some international energy issues, especially those dealing with the developed world, but less so in other issues. The IEES forecasts are for international fossil fuel production and trade, and to that extent are most valuable for assessing the future market energy position of industrialized regions. The implications of the forecasts for nonenergy global sectors, such as environment and agriculture, must be made judgmentally. The level of detail contained within the model varies; it is generally finer for the OECD countries and the economically more important fuels. The detail of the output (the forecasts) is roughly the same for all regions of the world and all energy forms represented in the IEES.

To describe the variables used in the IEES, it is most convenient to group them by submodel. Though the submodels need be run in no particular order, it is easiest to catalogue the variables of the IEES by going through the submodels as energy fuels actually flow through the market: from supply to transportation, through the various conversions, to demand.

The supply submodel yields one quantity—the estimated quantity that will be supplied in the forecast year—for each of 33 world regions and the primary energy fuels the region produces, as listed in Tables 20–1 and 20–2. In addition, an estimate of the price elasticity of supply to pertain to all fuels and regions is made by the IAD supply staff. Where there is evidence that the elasticity for a particular fuel and a particular region is likely to be quite different from this world estimate, a separate estimate is made. All of the data produced by the submodel are thus judgmental estimates either from outside agencies or the IAD.

The transportation submodel yields one vector of descriptive data for each ordered pair of the world's 33 regions and each of some 13 modes of transportation that apply to the region pair. For example, for any two regions in Europe there are two vectors: one corresponding to rail and one to barge transport. Each vector consists of one code number for each of the two regions, one for the mode of transport, and an estimate of the unit cost of shipping fuel by that mode from the "centroid" of the originating region to that of the terminating region. Each mode of transport is available in the model to ship only certain fuel

### TABLE 20–1

### The 33 IEES Regions, Grouped According to Energy Position Classification

OECD Region:

| | |
|---|---|
| U.S. East Coast | United Kingdom/Ireland |
| U.S. Gulf Coast | Benelux/Denmark |
| U.S. West Coast | West Germany |
| Puerto Rico/Virgin Islands | France |
| Canada | Australia/Switzerland |
| Japan | Spain/Portugal |
| Australia/New Zealand | Italy |
| Scandinavia | Greece/Turkey |

OPEC Region:

| | |
|---|---|
| Venezuela/Ecuador | Indonesia |
| Libya/Algeria | Iran |
| Nigeria/Gabon | Persian Gulf—Arab |

LDC Oil Exporters Region:

| | |
|---|---|
| Bolivia/Peru | Angola/Congo/Zaire |
| Egypt/Syria/Bahrain | Asian Exporters |

Other Regions:

| | |
|---|---|
| Latin America | Sino-Soviet |
| Africa | Sumed Pipeline |
| Mexico | Caribbean |
| Asia | |

## TABLE 20-2

### The 59 Primary Fuel Types in the IEES Supply Submodel

| Fuel Type | Applicable Region[a] |
|---|---|
| **CRUDE OIL** | |
| **Arab OPEC and OAPEC Crudes:** | |
| Algeria | Libya/Algeria |
| Egypt/Syria/Bahrain | Egypt/Syria/Bahrai |
| Iraq | Persian Gulf—Arab |
| Kuwait | Persian Gulf—Arab |
| Libya | Libya/Algeria |
| Qatar/United Arab Emirates | Persian Gulf—Arab |
| Saudi Arabia light | Persian Gulf—Arab |
| Saudi Arabia heavy | Persian Gulf—Arab |
| **Non-Arab OPEC Crudes:** | |
| Ecuador | Venezuela/Ecuador |
| Indonesia | Indonesia |
| Iran light | Iran |
| Iran heavy | Iran |
| Nigeria/Gabon | Nigeria/Gabon |
| Venezuela | Venezuela/Ecuador |
| **Other Export Crudes:** | |
| Angola/Congo/Zaire | Angola/Congo/Zaire |
| Bolivia/Peru | Bolivia/Peru |
| Canada | Canada |
| China | Sino-Soviet |
| Mexico | Mexico |
| Norway | Scandinavia |
| Russia | Sino-Soviet |
| South Asia mix | Asian Exporters |
| Trinidad | Caribbean |
| United Kingdom | United Kingdom/Ireland |
| **Nonexport Crudes:** | |
| Australia | Australia/New Zealand |
| Tar Sands | Various[b] |
| Japan | Japan |
| Denmark | Benelux/Denmark |
| West Germany | West Germany |
| France | France |
| Austria | Austria/Switzerland |
| Spain | Spain/Portugal |
| Italy | Italy |
| Turkey | Greece/Turkey |
| **U.S. Domestic Crudes:** | |
| Alaska North Slope | U.S. West Coast |
| Alaska South | U.S. West Coast |
| Pacific offshore | U.S. West Coast |
| Wyoming mix | U.S. Gulf Coast |
| Shale oil | U.S. Gulf Coast |
| Louisiana onshore | U.S. Gulf Coast |
| Louisiana offshore | U.S. Gulf Coast |
| Texas Gulf Coast | U.S. Gulf Coast |
| East Texas mix | U.S. Gulf Coast |
| West Texas mix | U.S. Gulf Coast |
| Padd II, indigenous | U.S. Gulf Coast |
| Oklahoma mix | U.S. Gulf Coast |
| Padd I, indigenous | U.S. East Coast |
| Heavy crude, V | U.S. West Coast |
| Heavy crude, IV | U.S. Gulf Coast |
| Heavy crude, III | U.S. Gulf Coast |
| Heavy crude, II | U.S. Gulf Coast |
| NPR-1 | U.S. West Coast |
| Synthetic crude | U.S. Gulf Coast |

| Fuel Type | Applicable Region[a] |
|---|---|
| San Joaquin Valley | U.S. West Coast |
| Los Angeles Basin | U.S. West Coast |
| **COAL** | |
| Metallurgical coal | Various[b] |
| Steam coal | Various[b] |
| Lignite | Various[b] |
| **NATURAL GAS** | |
| Natural gas | Various[b] |

[a] "Applicable Region" is the IEES region from which the fuel type is supplied.
[b] "Various" indicates that the fuel is supplied from more than one region within the IEES.

types; the 13 modes and the fuels they can be used to ship are listed in Table 20–3. Because no limit on shipping capacity is assumed in most cases, the vectors include no capacity entry. The input data to the transportation submodel are themselves estimates of transportation costs of different modes between ports; the IAD staff adjusts them to account for the difference in distance between the routes for which they were made and the hypothetical centroid to centroid routes used in IEES.

The refining submodel produces data vectors distinguished according to 43 types of crude oil refined, 8 regions, 6 final product types, and 10 markets. The 43 crude oil types are a subset of those listed in Table 20–2. The eight regions are the regions that actually do significant refining, including some OECD regions and some others. The six product types modeled are liquid gas, gasoline, jet fuel, distillate fuel, residual oil, and "other refined products." The vector for any one type of refining within a region includes data on the technology used (quantities output per unit input), the productive capacity forecasted to exist, and the costs of building and operating plants. No

## TABLE 20-3

### The 13 IEES Transport Modes and the Fuels Carried

| Mode | Fuel |
|---|---|
| Medium tanker | Crude oil |
| Medium tranship | Crude oil |
| U.S. tanker | Crude oil |
| Large tanker | Crude oil |
| VLCC (supertanker) | Crude oil |
| Product tanker | Refined products |
| Crude pipeline | Crude oil |
| Product pipeline | Refined products |
| Bulk carrier | Coal |
| Liquid natural gas carrier | Natural gas |
| Gas pipeline | Natural gas |
| Rail | Coal |
| Barge | Coal |

limit on the creation of new capacity is included, so it can increase in any IEES run to meet refining demand, albeit at a cost. The data necessary to construct the refinery data vectors are, as in the case of transportation, the same types of data actually in the vectors; they require for the most part only compilation and adjustment to be ready for use in IEES.

The miscellaneous conversions submodel produces a data vector for each OECD region and conversion process contained within the region. The four conversion processes treated are metallurgical coal to coke, lignite to briquettes, liquid oil fuels and coal to synthetic gases, and coke to blast furnace gas. Each vector includes data that quantifies the technology used within the region in the process (physical input-output ratios) and the estimated 1975 productive capacity. In addition, an upper limit on increases in productive capacity is supplied in lieu of any other restrictions on new capacity construction; costs of the plants or production are not included in the data. The input data to the miscellaneous conversions submodel are international statistics from outside sources; they are collected and adjusted for use in the IEES linear program.

The electric utilities submodel produces a vector for each OECD region and fossil fuel plant type found within the region. The generation plant types are residual oil, crude oil, distillate, hard coal, lignite, blast furnace gas, and natural gas. Each vector includes data on generation efficiency, capacity, and cost. A maximum capacity retirement amount, usually corresponding to a 3 percent per year retirement of total plant capacity, is also included. No limit on increases in electrical generation capacity is made. In addition, estimates of nuclear and hydro generation capacity are produced. No variations in these capacities are allowed. The data sets corresponding to one generation type are also assigned a load type or load types. Nuclear plants are always base load plants; distillate plants are always peak load; hydro and existing oil and coal plants can be base, intermediate, or peak, depending on cost considerations in the running of the linear program; new oil and coal plants can be base or intermediate.

One set of three numbers—one for base load, one for intermediate load, and one for peak—are also produced to tell what percentage of each region's total generation capacity must come from each load type. The data for the electrical utilities submodel comes from various outside sources and consists primarily of powerplant statistics for the OECD countries. They are adapted for IEES

linear program use by a separate computer program.

The demand submodel produces one demand quantity forecast and demand elasticity for each non-U.S. OECD region and final energy product, and one demand quantity for each product for all other regions. The final energy products included in the demand forecasts used in the IEES linear program are listed in Table 20–4. The input data required to produce these differ widely from region to region. The U.S. demand quantities are output of a run of PIES that uses price and GNP inputs consistent with those used in the IEES run. The U.S. demand quantities require no other data collection by the IAD, but ultimately depend on all of the input data to PIES. The other OECD regions' data are estimated econometrically for the major fuels from energy prices, population, GNP, and historical demand quantities. For other fuels the input data are usually time or GNP. Demand for non-OECD regions is generally taken directly from outside sources with adjustments made as necessary. Because refining, miscellaneous conversions, and electrical generation are not modeled for non-OECD regions, the demands for such converted products from these regions are changed to their primary fuel equivalents.

## Basic Procedures

A run of the IEES begins with the collection of the input data to the six submodels. Much of this actually remains the same from run to run and so need not be redone for each; data already compiled can be used. These data must then be adjusted for use in the linear programming matrix. Again, much of this does not change between runs and so can draw on past work. Lastly, the linear program is run iteratively until a world energy market solution with demand and supply nearly equal is reached. By virtue of the way the

### TABLE 20–4

### Final Energy Products in the IEES Linear Program

Petroleum Products:

|  | Residual oil |
|  | Gasoline |
|  | Distillate |
|  | Liquid propane gas |
|  | Jet fuel |

Coal:

|  | Hard coal |
|  | Lignite |

Natural Gas
Electricity

linear programming problem is set up, the energy flows between supply and demand that the IEES relies on to equilibrate the two are the flows that minimize the costs of transportation and conversion. The entire process is depicted diagrammatically in Figure 20–1.

The demand data for the U.S. are taken from the PIES output. In the case of the IEES runs made for the Global 2000 Study, the PIES runs from which demand data were taken were done with standard PIES assumptions, except that the U.S. GNP forecasts and fuel price forecasts provided by the Global 2000 project were used in place of the standard PIES data for those variables. The OECD demand data are estimated from GNP, population, and price forecasts. The GNP and population forecasts for the Global 2000 runs were those supplied by the Study, as listed in Chapter 3 of this volume. For large countries, IEES normally uses GNP forecasts taken from DRI (Data Resources, Incorporated) econometric projection service. DRI is a Boston-based firm that provides economic data and forecasts to a broad business and research clientele. The GNP forecasts for the remaining OECD regions are taken from official OECD publications. The population forecasts are normally taken from United Nations estimates. The price forecasts are typically an assumption rather than something estimated from detailed background information. The Global 2000 Study runs of the IEES incorporated two different oil price assumptions. The first had OPEC holding the world oil price constant at $13 per barrel indefinitely. The second assumed that world oil prices would start at $13, then rise at a rate of 5 percent annually beginning in 1981. In both cases, as is customary in IEES runs, the prices of non-oil fossil fuels were assumed to start at about present levels and then to vary according to market forces, as represented in the linear program.

The communist region demand data are taken from forecasts made by the International Affairs Office of the Department of Energy, (or sometimes from CIA forecasts), of the regions' net import positions. If a region is cited by these sources as being a net importer of a fuel, its imports are entered into the IEES as its demand for fuel on the world market. Demand quantities for the noncommunist non-OECD regions are calculated from the GDP forecasts by assuming that energy demand is a constant fraction of GDP. Because refining, conversions, and electrical generation are not modeled for the non-OECD countries, their demands must be expressed as demands for primary fuels, not final products. Once

all demand data are in hand, the demand quantities are reduced by standard percentages to reflect the effects of conservation. To establish these percentages, the IAD commissioned a study by the private consulting firm Resource Planning Associates.

The supply quantity estimates for oil and natural gas are taken from the Department's Office of International Affairs and from the International Coal Federation for coal. The estimates apply to 1975 and so must be adjusted to give an initial supply quantity for the forecast year with which the linear program can begin its iterations. This is done with price elasticities (assumed for almost all fuels and regions to be 0.1 for a forecast year of 1985 and 0.26 for 1990) and with forecasted prices. The prices are the ones used in econometric demand forecasting, with estimated average transportation and refinery costs subtracted. This is meant to yield "wellhead" primary fuel prices that correspond to the final product prices used in the demand submodel.

Transportation costs are taken mostly from the rates published by the Association of Ship Brokers and Agents. Like the costs for electric utilities, refining, and miscellaneous conversions, they are assumed to be constant in real terms in the future and so need not be recalculated for separate IEES runs. The data from these four submodels, as well as the supply data, were nearly identical in all runs made for the Global 2000 Study.

The plant data necessary for the electric utilities submodel comes primarily from publications of the European Economic Community. These are entered into a computer model that compiles them into IEES regional data, and adds data describing load types and load type distributions.

The refining data come primarily from two major sources. The capital expenditure and yield (input-output) data are taken from the RPMS* oil industry computer model developed by Bonner and Moore of Houston. Capacity and operating cost data are from the *Oil and Gas Journal*. These are adjusted for use in the IEES linear program.

Miscellaneous conversion data for fuel gas, blast furnace gas, etc., come from 1975 OECD statistics. Costs for the processes are assumed to be at U.S. values when data from outside sources are not available.

Once it contains all necessary data, the IEES linear program is solved. However, in the solution demand and supply may not match. This is not something that can be foreseen because of the

* Refinery Petrochemical Modeling System.

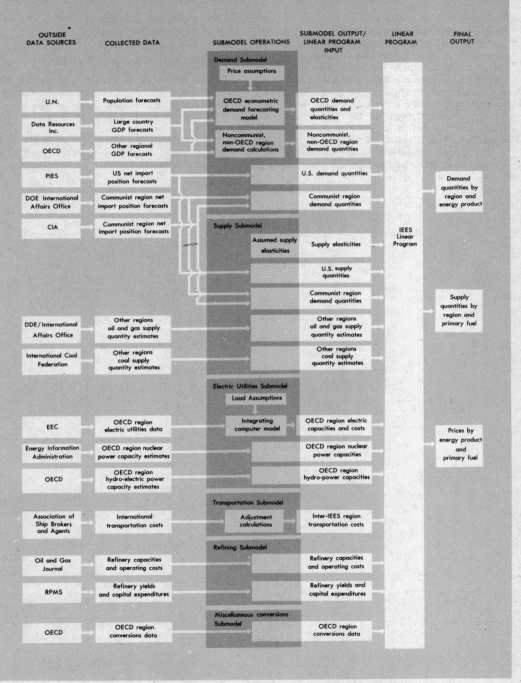

**Figure 20-1.** Structure of the International Energy Evaluation System (*IEES*). (*In all runs made for the Global 2000 Study, population and GNP data came from Study sources, not the customary IEES data sources described in the text; supporting PIES runs made for the Study used the Study's U.S. GNP forecasts.*)

complications of transportation and conversion processes that lie between primary fuel production and final product sale. So prices are adjusted in a fashion that is expected to bring the two quantities closer together. Supply and demand quantities for the OECD regions are then recalculated from the old quantities, new prices, and price elasticities.

The PIES and the econometric demand model, which originally produced the OECD demand data, are not rerun to get the new demand quantities. The IEES linear program is resolved with the new demand and supply quantities. The process of estimating new quantities and resolving the linear program is repeated until supply and demand are acceptably close.

## Documentation and Validation

The Department of Energy has engaged a private firm to completely document the International Energy Evaluation System. The documentation was published in 1978 in two volumes.

The econometric demand model estimates have been compared to actual historical data with generally satisfactory results.

# 21  Fuel Minerals

No one federal agency has exclusive responsibility for producing estimates of world fuel mineral reserves and resources. Parts of this task have been handled in the past by the Bureau of Mines and the United States Geological Survey (both in the Department of the Interior) and by the Department of Energy. In addition, some private organizations, most notably the World Energy Conference, publish estimates widely regarded as authoritative. The Geological Survey estimates the resources of the United States. The Department of Energy is responsible for U.S. reserve estimates. The World Energy Conference periodically estimates both world reserves and world resources.*

Estimates of the energy production potential from renewable sources, such as solar radiation, tides, and waterways, are not as frequently made by established agencies or organizations, and so must be gathered from diverse sources.

To compile, compare, and interpret the data from all of the above sources, the Global 2000 Study engaged Walter G. Dupree (formerly in the Department of Energy and presently with the Bureau of Mines) as an independent expert.

## Key Analytic Methodology

The methods used to derive fuel resource and reserve estimates differed to some extent, depending on the organization that gathered the estimates. Actual field estimates come from a combination of sample drilling and expert judgment. However, the organizations cited here did not generally do this geologic research themselves. Rather, they surveyed corporations and other organizations to obtain size estimates of various mineral deposits and totaled them, or adapted the estimates that other organizations had derived in this manner.

An exception is the United States Geological Survey, which, in addition to conducting surveys, has been doing its own original geological research

---

* The estimates of resources and reserves used in the nonfuel minerals analysis appear in various official publications, as referenced in Chapter 22 ("Minerals and Materials").

to make U.S. resource estimates for decades. Since before World War II, the World Energy Conference (WEC) has done world resource and reserve estimation by survey and published complete sets of estimates periodically. The Congressional Research Service in the Library of Congress commissioned a similar set of resource and reserve estimates, which were released in 1977, because no recent WEC figures were available at the time, although new ones have since been published. The estimates were commissioned after the Congressional Research Service had received a request for a set of such estimates from the House Subcommittee on Energy and Power and the Senate Committee on Energy and Natural Resources. When the Department of Energy (DOE) was formed out of various other federal agencies, it inherited the U.S. reserve estimate responsibilities of those agencies. DOE makes its own estimates of U.S. coal reserves. For oil and natural gas reserve figures, it relies largely on estimates made by the American Petroleum Institute and the American Gas Association.

## Basic Principles

Though mineral resources and reserves are physical quantities that can, theoretically, be measured at any point in time, there is no one standard and infallible method of measuring them. Because the organizations providing resource and reserve estimates in Chapter 11 do not completely coordinate their data, assumptions, and procedures, they have obtained different results. Furthermore, refinements in procedure over time may result in significant revision of previous estimates, as, for example, when the Geological Survey in 1975 reduced its estimate of U.S. oil resources by over one-half (in the publication cited in "Documentation and Validity," below). Nonetheless, some general description of the geological testing methods and other techniques on which the estimates presented in Chapter 11 are based is possible.

*Oil and Gas.* The primary oil and gas resource numbers used were complied by M. King Hubbert for the Congressional Research Service. As Hubbert pointed out, potential oil-bearing regions may be classified according to their degree of exploration into three groups:

1. Regions in a mature state of exploration. For these regions, reasonable estimates of ultimately recoverable oil can be made by use of the statistics on the quantity of drilling and the corresponding oil discoveries per well or per foot. This is basically the macroanalytical approach, which models empirical relationships in aggregated discovery or production data.

2. Regions in an early stage of exploration. For these regions, estimates of ultimately recoverable oil can be based on early successes or failures in drilling. Early successes imply significant quantities of oil (or gas) and vice versa.

3. Virgin undrilled territories. According to Hubbert, the only basis for judgment as to resources is geological analogy. If the virgin area is found by geological and geophysical surveys to be very similar to a productive mature area, then the virgin area is expected to yield comparable quantities of oil and gas per unit of area or volume. This is basically the microanalytic approach, which models structural relationships in the exploration process.

*Solid Fuels*. The resource figures for solid fuels used in this study are based on World Energy Conference estimates. The WEC sends questionnaires to the participating countries, requesting information on reserves, resources, maximum depth of deposit, minimum seam thickness, and the like. How each country estimates its reserves and resources will differ—and in some instances the resulting differences in data may be significant; hence, it is impossible to describe the methodology used. It should be pointed out, however, that the geology of coal is relatively simple and uniform over wide areas, and most coal deposits are closer to the surface than oil or gas. Thus, data on solid fuels are, in general, based on more accurate geological data than oil and are less subject to revision.

*Uranium*. The resource figures for uranium used in this study are also based on WEC estimates. As with solid fuels, questionnaires are sent to the participating countries, and the returns tabulated. Differences in methodology make generalizations difficult.

*Hydro, Geothermal, and Solar Power*. Procedures for estimating the energy potential of these power sources are less well established, and resource and reserve estimates tend to be less certain than those made for fuel minerals. In general, estimates of potential are derived from spot measurements of the relevant variables, such as streamflow for hydropower, tide volume for tidal power, subsurface temperature for geothermal power, and solar insolation for solar power. Discussions of these power sources in this study take their estimates of potential from other publications, which base their estimates on such spot measurements.

## Basic Components

Chapter 11, "Fuel Minerals Projections," focuses on world resources and reserves of fuel minerals and on power potential estimates of the renewable energy sources competing with them. Fine regional disaggregations of the data, which are not consistently available, were generally not presented. Consideration of energy production, consumption, and trade was left to the energy analysis in Chapter 10.

## Basic Procedures

Aside from general geological considerations, the relevant assumptions for the estimation of the reserves of a mineral are the current product price and extraction technology within the industry. Assessing these items is left primarily to the geologist making the estimates. Resource estimation theoretically depends on assumptions of potential future prices and technology. The U.S. oil and gas estimates (made by the U.S. Geological Survey) assume a continuation of price-cost relationships and technological trends generally prevailing in recent years prior to 1974. Price-cost relationships and production since 1974 were not taken into account, nor was an explicit assumption about future prices made. The price and technology assumptions underlying the world resource estimates have not been made explicit by their various authors.

## Documentation and Validation

The U.S. Geological Survey discusses its resource estimation methods in USGS Circular 725, *Geological Estimates of Undiscovered Recoverable Oil and Gas Resources in the United States*, published in 1975. The World Energy Conference outlines its data collection methods in *WEC Activities in the Field of Surveying World Energy Resources*, published in M. Grenon, ed., *First IIASA Conference on Energy Resources*, International Institute for Applied Systems Analysis, Laxenburg, Austria.

The Bureau of Mines, USGS, DOE, and the WEC have made no formal tests of the reliability of their respective resource and reserve estimation methods.

# 22  Nonfuel Minerals

The Bureau of Mines of the U.S. Department of the Interior is responsible for helping to ensure the continued strength of the domestic minerals and materials economy and the maintenance of an adequate minerals and materials base. In carrying out this responsibility, the Bureau develops forecasts of future trends in the supply and demand of minerals and materials on a global basis for the purpose of identifying changes that might affect the national interest. These forecasts, published in the Secretary of the Interior's annual report to Congress, assist the Secretary in carrying out his responsibilities under the Strategic and Critical Materials Stock Piling Act, which directs him to investigate the production and utilization of minerals and materials.

Projections of future consumption, referred to by the Bureau as demand forecasts, are published every 5-years in detail in the Bureau's *Mineral Facts and Problems* and in summary form in its *Mineral Trends and Forecasts*. The last complete set of these forecasts was published in 1975. Recent forecasts for selected minerals and materials are published in an interim report series entitled *Mineral Commodity Profiles*.

The official Bureau forecasts provide high, low, and most probable projections of minerals and materials consumption for 1985 and 2000 in (1) the United States and (2) the rest of the world as a whole. The latter forecasts are based in large part on a study prepared in November 1972 for the U.S. Commission on Materials Policy by Professor Wilfred Malenbaum of the University of Pennsylvania's Wharton School of Finance and Commerce.*

This study (known as the 1972 Malenbaum Report) divided the world into 10 regions and projected trends in overall economic growth, population growth, and growth in primary consumption of 11 minerals and materials for each region.

It presented a single set, rather than a range, of forecasts. In October 1977 Malenbaum updated his 1972 study at the request of the National Science Foundation,* dropping some of his original commodities and adding others.

Current Bureau of Mines forecasts are loosely based on the 1972 Malenbaum Report, judgmentally adjusted and extrapolated by members of the Bureau staff, using basic arithmetical procedures. Members of the Bureau staff expect that future official Bureau projections will be based on the 1977 Malenbaum Report. Therefore, on the recommendation of Bureau staff members, the Global 2000 Study projections in Chapter 12 substitute the latest Malenbaum figures in place of current Bureau figures where this is feasible.†

A comparison of the projections in the 1972 Malenbaum Report, used in current Bureau of Mines publications, with those in the 1977 Malenbaum Report is presented in Table 22–1. The table shows that the 1977 Malenbaum projections are significantly lower than earlier projections made by Malenbaum or the Bureau of Mines for a few commodities (aluminum, cobalt, copper, and nickel) and significantly higher for a few others (manganese, tin, and tungsten).‡

## Key Analytic Methodology

Prior to 1968, the Bureau of Mines did not make long-range projections of minerals and materials consumption, either for the U.S. or on a global basis. In 1968, using 1966 data, the Bureau began making projections internally, relying on the judgment of Bureau analysts and simple rule-

---

*"Materials Requirements in the United States and Abroad in the Year 2000," National Commission on Materials Policy, Mar. 1973 (the original report was submitted Nov. 30, 1972). The Bureau of Mines' use of this report is briefly discussed in the Introduction to the Bureau's *Mineral Facts and Problems*, 1975 edition (p. 21, as preprinted in the Bureau's *Bulletin* 667).

* "World Demand for Raw Materials in 1985 and 2000," Philadelphia, Oct. 1977.

† Malenbaum's latest projections cover 12 minerals and materials; 10 of these 12 are considered in Chapter 12.

‡ An extensive comparison between the methods used by Malenbaum in making regional forecasts and the methods used by the Bureau in making "rest of the world" forecasts, with respect to projecting copper and aluminum consumption, is contained in a paper presented to the Eighth World Mining Congress in Lima, Peru, by the Bureau's Sheldon Wimpfen and Alvin Knoerr, entitled "World Resources vs. Copper and Aluminum Demand to the Year 2000," Nov. 1974.

## TABLE 22–1

## World Consumption of 14 Minerals and Materials in the Year 2000

| | Malenbaum '72 | Bureau of Mines Current | Malenbaum '77 | Percent Change Malenbaum '77 vs. Malenbaum '72 | Percent Change Malenbaum '77 vs. Bureau of Mines |
|---|---|---|---|---|---|
| | | *(thousands of metric tons)* | | | |
| Primary aluminum | 46,761 | 54,160[b] | 36,516 | −22 | −33 |
| Chrome ore | — | 17,600[c] | 16,018 | — | −9 |
| Cobalt | — | 72 | 58 | — | −19 |
| Refined copper | 19,693 | 22,113[d] | 16,839 | −14 | −24 |
| Fluorspar | 15,870 | 14,797 | — | — | — |
| Iron ore | 1,086,000 | 1,025,000 | 919,000 | −15 | −10 |
| Manganese | — | 41,770[e] | 48,060 | — | 15 |
| Nickel | — | 1,546 | 1,314 | — | −15 |
| Platinum group (thousand troy ounces) | — | 13,113[f] | 14,030 | — | 7 |
| Crude steel | 1,332,000 | 1,279,000[g] | 1,315,000 | −1 | 3 |
| Sulfur | 100,424 | 112,000[h] | — | — | — |
| Tin | — | 352[i] | 393 | — | 12 |
| Tungsten | — | 79[j] | 93 | — | 18 |
| Zinc | 13,448 | 11,200[k] | 12,022 | −11 | 7 |

[a] To facilitate comparisons, all Bureau of Mines data (with one exception) have been converted to metric tons: 1 short ton = 0.9072 metric tons; 1 long ton = 1.016 metric tons. The single exception is the platinum group data, which is specified in thousands of troy ounces.
[b] Includes only primary (not nonmetallic) aluminum.
[c] This figure converts the Bureau of Mines figure for contained chromium metal in ore to units of ore as specified in the Malenbaum Report, assuming an average grade of chrome ore to be 27.4 percent chromium.
[d] Bureau of Mines data excludes old copper, whereas refined copper in the Malenbaum Reports includes secondary old copper. Therefore, based on the traditional ratio between refined copper and old copper, and the Malenbaum data, the Bureau of Mines forecasts have been increased by 25 percent to be comparable with Bureau of Mines forecasts (i.e., 17,690 × 1.25 = 22,113 thousand metric tons).
[e] The Malenbaum data must be for manganese ore rather than manganese. To be comparable to Malenbaum data, the Bureau of Mines data on contained manganese has been converted to metric tons of manganese ore, averaging 48 percent manganese: (20,049 metric tons of contained Mn)/0.48 = 41,770, which is comparable to the Malenbaum figure.
[f] Data includes secondary metal.
[g] Data includes iron and steel foundry products and steel mill products.
[h] Customarily specified in long tons; converted here to metric tons.
[i] Includes only primary tin, converted from long tons to metric tons.
[j] Includes only primary tungsten, converted from 1,000 pounds to metric tons.
[k] Includes only primary zinc.

of-thumb relationships. These relationships were based on leading U.S. economic indicators and historic patterns of global minerals and materials production and consumption. Presented in the 1970 edition of *Mineral Facts and Problems* (and summarized in the 1970 edition of *Mineral Trends and Forecasts*), they included price as well as consumption projections. Supply was assumed to equal demand at the prices specified.

The methodological procedures on which these initial 1970 projections were based were severely criticized, particularly those used in developing price projections. As a result, different procedures were followed in the 1975 edition of *Mineral Facts and Problems*. For U.S. consumption forecasts, reliance was placed on the use of leading U.S. economic indicators in elaborate linear regression equations. For consumption forecasts for the rest of the world (treated as an aggregate), reliance was placed on making use of trends in world economic growth, population growth, and growth in consumption of selected minerals and mate-

rials, as projected in the 1972 Malenbaum Report; however, arithmetic relationships were estimated using procedures less complex than those used to project U.S. consumption. No explicit price projections were used in making forecasts either for U.S. consumption or consumption in the rest of the world, and no price forecasts were published.

Both the 1972 Malenbaum Report and its 1977 revision are based on a methodology known as intensity-of-use (IOU) analysis.* This methodology produces lower projections of growth in global minerals and materials consumption by the year 2000 than the simple trend extrapolations used previously by the Bureau of Mines. It also tends to produce lower projections for U.S. mineral consumption than most other methodologies, as they have been used to date by groups outside

---

*The development and several applications of the IOU methodology are briefly discussed in D. B. Brooks and P. W. Andrews, "Mineral Resources, Economic Growth, and World Population," *Science*, July 5, 1974, p. 13.

the Bureau (for example, the input-output techniques used by Resources for the Future in its 1972 report to the U.S. Commission on Population Growth and the American Future†).

Although the Bureau has made extensive use of the 1972 Malenbaum Report in revising its own projections and plans to make future use of the 1977 Malenbaum Report, the Bureau did not commission either report. The earlier report was prepared for the U.S. National Commission on Materials Policy, which was responsible for examining the feasibility of striking a balance between the national need to produce goods on the one hand and to protect the environment on the other. The Malenbaum projections helped the Commission demonstrate the feasibility of striking such a balance, since IOU analysis assumes that increasing economic growth in the industrialized nations requires increasingly less intensive consumption of minerals and materials per unit of economic growth. The long-term environmental implications of the other major assumption of IOU analysis—that increasing economic growth in the less developed countries (LDCs) requires increasingly more intensive consumption of minerals and materials per unit of economic growth—were not examined by the Commission. The environmental impacts of such increasingly intensive use of minerals and materials by the LDCs could rapidly escalate in the period beyond the year 2000, if recent rates of LDC economic growth are sustained into that period.

Events surrounding the 1973 oil embargo called forth energy analyses that differ significantly some of the projections contained in the 1972 Malenbaum Report. For example, according to that report, U.S. energy consumption in the year 2000 was projected to reach levels almost three times as great as those of the 1966–69 period, including a doubling of U.S. natural gas consumption. Japan's energy consumption was projected to increase by a factor of six over the same period. Most subsequent energy studies project much lower rates of growth for energy consumption, based on considerations involving limited supplies, increasing prices, and strategic and balance-of-payment positions. These factors are not explicitly taken into account in Malenbaum's methodology, although the basic principles of IOU analysis could be adapted to methodologies that do take those factors into account. It was against the

background of the changes taking place in the energy sector and the intensifying debate regarding potential limits to economic growth that the National Science Foundation asked Malenbaum to revise his original report.

The 1977 Malenbaum Report did not re-examine the former projections regarding solid fuels, liquid fuels, natural gas, and other energy sources, but it did re-evaluate projections regarding the consumption of aluminum, copper, iron, steel, and zinc. All were revised downward, as shown in Table 22–1, using the same procedures that were used in the 1972 Report. As Malenbaum pointed out in his revised report, these lower projections were in no way based on the arguments advanced by the limits-to-growth proponents, since both the 1972 and 1977 Reports assume that the commodities whose consumption is being forecast will essentially be inexhaustible and available at current real prices throughout the period of the forecast. Instead, the revised report reflects lower exogenous projections of economic growth rates in both the industrialized nations and LDCs and lower exogenous projections of the intensity with which minerals and materials are likely to be used by nations in both categories.

The exogenous economic and population growth rates used in the 1977 Malenbaum Report differ from those provided to the Global 2000 Study. The Global 2000 Study's economic growth rates are significantly higher for Africa, Asia, and Latin America and significantly lower for Eastern Europe, Japan, and the U.S.S.R., as shown in Table 22–2. The economic growth rates used in these two studies are not strictly comparable, however, since they are applied to different historic base estimates, with somewhat different proportionalities (see Table 22–3). The population projections also differ, but the differences appear to be less significant (Table 22–4).

The 1977 Malenbaum Report cites the following sources for historical gross domestic product (GDP) data: United Nations, *Statistical Yearbook* (annual); U.N., *Yearbook of National Account Statistics* (annual); International Bank for Reconstruction and Development, *World Bank Atlas,* 1975. The 1977 Malenbaum Report, in addition, cites the following sources for historical population data: U.N., *Demographic Yearbook,* various issues (1948–1974); U.N., *Population by Sex and Age for Regions and Countries, 1950–2000 as Assessed in 1973: Medium Variant* (1976); U.N., *World Population Prospects as Assessed in 1968* (1973). Chapter III of the 1977 Malenbaum Report explains in some detail how "the projected growth rates reflect the judgment of the principal investi-

† Leon Fischman and Hans H. Landsberg, "Adequacy of Nonfuel Minerals and Forest Resources," in Commission on Population Growth and the American Future, *Population Resources and the Environment,* Washington, 1972.

# THE GOVERNMENT'S GLOBAL MODEL

584

## TABLE 22-2

### Average Annual Economic Growth to the Year 2000

*(Percent)*

| | Malenbaum '72 | Malenbaum '77 | Global 2000 Study | Global 2000 Study Minus Malenbaum '77[a] |
|---|---|---|---|---|
| | GDP 1970–2000 | GDP 1975–2000 | GNP 1975–2000 | |
| Africa | 3.4 | 3.4 | 4.9 | 1.5 |
| Asia | 3.5 | 3.2 | 4.8 | 1.6 |
| China[b] | 4.2 | 3.3 | 3.7 | .4 |
| Eastern Europe | 3.5 | 3.5 | 2.9 | −.6 |
| Japan | 5.0 | 4.1 | 3.5 | −.6 |
| Latin America | 3.7 | 3.6 | 5.0 | 1.4 |
| U.S.[c] | 3.8 | 3.2 | 3.5 | .3 |
| U.S.S.R. | 4.0 | 3.4 | 2.9 | −.5 |
| Western Europe | 3.5 | 3.2 | 3.5 | .3 |
| Other industrialized nations | 3.7 | 3.3 | 3.5 | .2 |
| World | 3.8 | 3.3 | 3.6 | .3 |

[a] Not a precise comparison, due to different base years, base year estimates, and statistics measuring economic growth.
[b] Including Mongolia, North Korea, and North Vietnam.
[c] Including Puerto Rico and other overseas U.S. islands.

## TABLE 22-3

### Base Year National Income

*(Billions of dollars)*

| | Malenbaum '72 | | Malenbaum '77 | | Global 2000 Study | |
|---|---|---|---|---|---|---|
| | GDP[a] | % | GDP[b] | % | GNP[c] | % |
| Africa | 65 | 2 | 71 | 2 | 128 | 2 |
| Asia | 236 | 6 | 201 | 5 | 348 | 6 |
| China[d] | 137 | 4 | 144 | 4 | 301 | 5 |
| Eastern Europe | 195 | 5 | 227 | 6 | 330 | 5 |
| Japan | 240 | 7 | 258 | 7 | 495 | 8 |
| Latin America | 202 | 6 | 200 | 5 | 319 | 5 |
| U.S.[e] | 1,025 | 28 | 1,122 | 28 | 1,516 | 25 |
| U.S.S.R. | 510 | 14 | 617 | 16 | 666 | 11 |
| Western Europe | 900 | 25 | 936 | 24 | 1,634 | 27 |
| Other industrialized nations | 160 | 4 | 183 | 5 | 288 | 5 |
| World | 3,670 | 101[f] | 3,960 | 102[f] | 6,025 | 99[f] |

[a] 1970 figures in 1971 dollars.
[b] An average of 1971–75 figures in 1971 dollars.
[c] 1975 figures, in 1975 dollars.
[d] Including Mongolia, North Korea, and North Vietnam.
[e] Including Puerto Rico and other overseas U.S. islands.
[f] Does not sum to 100, due to rounding.

gator, with full regard to other research and appraisals available on the current scene with respect to world economic development."

## TABLE 22-4

### Representative Population Projections

*(Millions)*

| | Malenbaum '72 | | Malenbaum '77 | | Global 2000 Study | |
|---|---|---|---|---|---|---|
| | 1971 | 2000 | 1971–75 | 2000 | 1975 | 2000 |
| U.S. | 210 | 300 | 214 | 281 | 216 | 248 |
| U.S.S.R. | 245 | 375 | 250 | 336 | 254 | 309 |
| Japan | 105 | 140 | 108 | 133 | 112 | 133 |
| All other nations | 3,224 | 5,615 | 3,276 | 5,608 | 3,508 | 5,661 |
| World | 3,784 | 6,430 | 3,848 | 6,358 | 4,090 | 6,351 |

The methodology and assumptions underlying the Global 2000 Study's GNP projections are presented in Chapter 16, which notes, regarding the LDCs, that in most cases, GNP and GDP are virtually equivalent and, therefore, used interchangeably by the Global 2000 Study. The methodology and assumptions underlying the Study's population projections are presented in Chapter 15.

The Global 2000 staff investigated the feasibility of recalculating the minerals and materials consumption forecasts of the 1977 Malenbaum Report on the basis of the Study's economic growth and population projections. Because Malenbaum's historical GDP data are not consistent with the GNP figures obtained by the Global 2000 Study from the *World Bank Atlas* of 1976, because the IOU methodology requires consistent figures, and because the differences could not be reconciled in the time available for the Global 2000 Study, a new set of consumption projections for minerals and materials, consistent with the project's economic growth and population projections, could not be developed.

## Basic Principles

The purpose of intensity-of-use analysis is to project the consumption of a given mineral or material within a given region in a given year. The analysis considers only primary use and disregards subsequent shipments of processed or manufactured minerals or materials to other regions. Hence, Japan, for example, is represented as having exceptionally high consumption levels, since Japanese exports are disregarded.

Total world consumption of a given mineral or material is calculated as the sum of the consumption levels for that commodity projected for each region. Calculations regarding future consumption levels are independent of similar calculations involving that region's consumption of any other mineral, material, or commodity, and independent of any other region's consumption levels of any commodity. They are also independent of any explicit considerations regarding potential changes in supply levels, prices, or strategic or balance-of-payment positions.

According to the principles of IOU analysis, consumption of a given mineral or material within a given year can be reliably calculated on the basis of just three components:

- An exogenous projection of the level of overall economic activity (GDP) within a given region in a given year.

- An exogenous projection of the total population within the same region in the same year.

- An "IOU table" showing the quantity of a given mineral or material likely to be consumed within that region per unit of that region's total GDP (a ratio known as the commodity's intensity of use) at various levels of regional per capita GDP.

A relatively high IOU statistic for a particular commodity (in a given region at a given level of per capita GDP) indicates that a relatively large quantity of that commodity is projected to be consumed per unit of total GDP (in that region at that level of per capita GDP). According to IOU theory, LDCs that are industrializing require increasing amounts of minerals and materials per unit of total GDP as their economies expand and per capita incomes grow (that is, their IOU statistic increases as a function of increasing per capita GDP). However, industrialized nations that are moving toward postindustrial service economies require decreasing amounts of minerals and materials per unit of total GDP as their economies expand and per capita incomes grow (that is, their IOU statistic decreases as a function of increasing per capita GDP). Thus, mineral and metal consumption levels within a region whose economy is moving from industrialization to postindustrialization are projected using IOU statistics at various levels of per capita GDP that form the inverted U-shaped curve shown in Figure 22–1.

Mathematically, the computations used to project worldwide consumption of a given mineral or material in a given year, according to IOU analysis, can be summarized by the following three equations, where $m$ represents a particular material, $r$ represents a particular region, and $y$ represents a particular year:

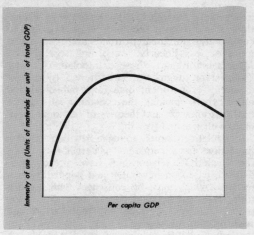

**Figure 22-1.** Intensity-of-use curve of a nation whose economy is moving from an industrializing economy to a post-industrialization service economy.

$$IOU_{mry} = f_{mr}(GDP_{ry}/population_{ry})$$
$$Consumption_{mry} = GDP_{ry} \times IOU_{mry}$$
$$Worldwide\ consumption_{my} = \sum consumption_{mry}$$

According to the 1977 Malenbaum Report, the IOU statistic has several noteworthy aspects:

First, it is readily available over past years, given [reliable] statistics on a nation's use of [the commodity in question].

Second, the very concept of an input and output relationship has a technological dimension. It must reflect changes in use and efficiency of inputs to yield outputs, with account taken of changes in techniques (for input or output) and changes in market relationships associated with supply, demand, and public policy bearing on inputs and outputs.

Third, and of particular interest, the historical evidence on intensity of use suggests there are patterns of behavior of the measure. And these patterns be identified with underlying theory and empirical time observation. Indeed, it is this systematic behavior of the measure that indicates its potential usefulness in demand analysis for raw materials.

However, the 1977 Malenbaum Report also points out that application of IOU analysis is still preliminary and that "there remain further and additional tasks to pursue, particularly with respect to the specific causes of differences in intensity-of-use measures over time and among regions."

The actual estimation of IOU statistics to be associated with future levels of per capita GDP (for various commodities within various regions) is based on historic data but is highly judgmental.* Historic IOUs are plotted as a function of per capita GDP for each region and commodity, and apparent trends are extrapolated more or less linearly. According to the 1977 Malenbaum Report, these extrapolations reflect "consistent judgments, conditioned by a vast assembly of pertinent data (and published and other expert opinion), the economic rationale of past performance, and theories of economic equilibrium change and growth."

It is relatively simple to make new consumption projections for minerals and materials for regions for which IOU relationships have already been defined, based on new GDP and population projections, which must be consistent with the historic GDP and population data used to develop the IOU tables. Considerably more effort and sophistication are needed to make new projections that require the formulation of new IOU tables. A representative IOU table from the 1977 report (showing the IOU relationships for refined copper for 10 regions) is reproduced graphically in Figure 22–2.

The somewhat different curves for each mineral or material in each region are explained by the unique economic characteristics of each region, influenced by three economic determinants peculiar to each mineral and material. The three determinants cited by Malenbaum are:

1. *Demand forces.* These change the composition of GDP. In rich lands, the tendency toward relative expansion of the services component of GDP will persist, perhaps increase; materials use per unit of GDP will on the whole tend to decline. In poor lands, modernization will continue and with it the creation of a higher proportion of total output in industrial sectors. Both considerations suggest the persistence of a relationship in which IOU first increases with per capita income—perhaps rapidly—and sooner or later decline with per capita income—perhaps slowly.

2. *Technological progress.* This plays an important role in intensity of use, serving to lower it. On the whole, throughout the world we can expect continuation of a trend where the net effect

is that smaller inputs of material accomplish essentially what larger inputs did earlier—more efficient fuel utilization, development in alloys, precision designing, and the like, as the U.S. experience has demonstrated.

3. *Substitution.* The substitution of one material for another and of synthetic for natural materials will continue to characterize economic growth. These forces will proceed as technology, demand, and supply bear upon relative market prices and public policy. These are probably universal forces, although special circumstances (relative importance of domestic production, for example) may govern the timing if not the direction of the shift pattern in some parts of the world. In the past, this substitution process contributed to marked downward movements in IOU in some materials and to decisive upward movements in others. Broadly speaking, these trends are projected to continue, although at more moderate rates.

One fundamental premise underlies the way the 1977 Malenbaum Report takes these determinants into consideration, namely:

The growth of nations has an *internal dynamic.* That is, long-term growth is not governed by supply limitations of any specific input materials nor is it limited by any inelasticity of total output imposed by supply or demand of materials. This assumption [has] made it possible to project national and world economic growth in one part of the research effort without regard to the material needs appraised in the other part of the study.

The existence and independence of this internal dynamic, as described by Malenbaum, is thus clearly identified as a premise rather than a conclusion of Malenbaum's study. The theory of IOU analysis also assumes that (1) the countries comprising a region for which each IOU function is developed have historically had comparable economies with respect to the mineral or material for which the function is developed, (2) the same countries have also had comparable per capita GDP levels and will maintain roughly identical growth rates during the forecast period, and (3) their various commodity consumption rates can be projected independently of each other, without explicitly accounting for interregional competition or commodity substitution.

In addition Malenbaum assumes that environmental constraints will not limit the future availability of minerals and materials. Thus, the 1977 Malenbaum Report observes:

The fact that the present [projections] represent a 15 percent reduction [from the projections made in the 1972 Malenbaum Report] must be attributed

---

*Malenbaum cites a wide range of sources for his historical data regarding minerals and materials consumption: Metal Bulletin Limited, *Metal Bulletin Handbooks* (1909–76); National Commission on Materials Policy; Overseas Geological Surveys, Mineral Resources Div., *Statistical Summary of the Mineral Industry: Production, Exports, and Imports,* (1934–71); and the following annuals: Metalgesellschaft Aktiengesellschaft, *Metal Statistics*; United Nations, *The Steel Market*; United Nations, *World Trade Annual and Its Supplement* (1971–74); U.S. Bureau of Mines, *Minerals Yearbooks* (1934–74).

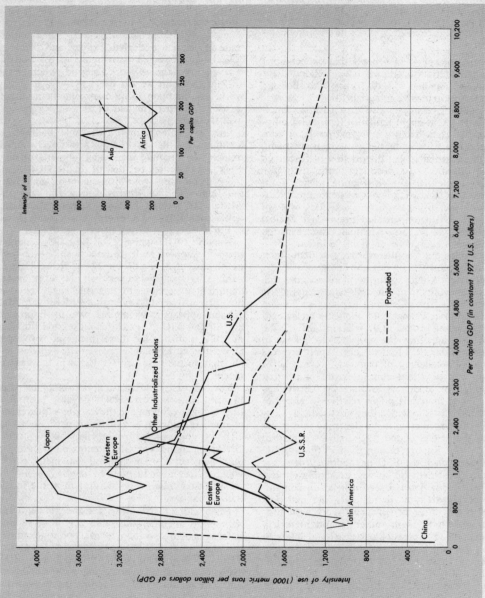

**Figure 22-2.** Graphic representation of the 1977 Malenbaum Report's intensity-of-use table for refined copper. Solid lines indicate historic experience; broken lines indicate projections. ("China" includes Mongolia, North Korea, and North Vietnam.)

to a judgment on man's aspirations for progress and the skills he employs to that end; the fact cannot be attributed to the weight of imminent materials resource exhaustion or of environmental deterioration.

However, the report also notes that expectations of basic materials scarcities have "undoubtedly encouraged man and society to cope with shortage through more intensive materials use."

Malenbaum's analysis also disregards sociopolitical factors that might influence future consumption levels. Thus, factors involving producer control (for example, potential cartelization arising from the irregular global distribution of resources among countries) or producer impotence (for example, potential civil disruption arising from resistance to increasing levels of pollution associated with increasing extraction activities or from resistance to uncompensated boom-bust cycles) are ignored, as are any potential changes in the international economic or political order. Economic cycles are also disregarded (including their destabilizing impacts on demand and prices).

Malenbaum's analysis furthermore assumes that future consumption of minerals and materials is independent of price, except to the very limited extent that price changes are implicitly considered in extrapolating historic IOU relationships. To the degree they are, they are projected to decline in real terms. The 1977 Malenbaum Report projects "a gradual weakening of demand forces relative to supply forces" and concludes, therefore, that "the long term tendency, 1985 and 2000, may thus be for lower materials prices relative to prices of the final products in which they are used."

This price prediction is a judgmental interpretation of the results of the IOU analysis contained in the 1977 Report rather than a direct IOU calculation, since the IOU methodology does not project prices, demand curves, or supply curves. The price prediction is based instead on comparing past growth rates in minerals and materials consumption (5–10 percent per year) with projected growth rates in minerals and materials consumption (3–4 percent per year) and inferring a reduction in demand pressure relative to supply, calculating these rates as the sum of non-U.S. demand and U.S. net imports.

This price projection directly contradicts the price projections for minerals and materials that were used in projecting worldwide GNP growth rates for the Global 2000 Study. These assumed, for example, that average prices for copper and tin will increase by roughly 5.2 and 2.5 percent per year, respectively, in constant dollars, during the 1975–1985 period. However, this difference

may be explained in part because the GNP projections also assumed higher annual growth rates in world trade in most minerals and materials than the 1977 Malenbaum Report. For example, trade in bauxite, phosphate, silver, and zinc was collectively projected to increase at 6.3 percent per year over the 1975–1985 period, whereas the 1977 Malenbaum Report projects average annual world consumption of primary aluminum to increase at 4.2 percent and of zinc at 3.3 percent over the same period.

One of Malenbaum's two most basic IOU assumptions—that as LDCs progressively industrialize, they require increasing amounts of minerals and materials per unit of total GDP—seems to be inconsistent with an assumption underlying the Department of Energy's projections for the Global 2000 Study. The Study's energy methodology assumed that LDC energy imports (measured in Btu's) would be a fixed percentage of GDP.

Historical IOU statistics for the LDCs generally seem to support Malenbaum's position—at least in the case of Africa (Table 22–5). However, past African IOU statistics for cobalt and tin represent important exceptions to this rule since they did not increase steadily over time. Moreover, Malenbaum appears to violate his own rule in projecting African IOU statistics for nickel and tin since the IOU statistics for these metals are projected to decline rather than increase. He explains this anomaly in the case of tin but not in the case of nickel.

The other basic IOU assumption—that as industrialized nations progressively develop postindustrial service economies, they require decreasing amounts of minerals and materials per unit of total GDP—is contradicted by the Global 2000 Study's GNP projections. The GNP methodology assumed that, in general, LDC mineral and metal export volumes to the industrialized nations would increase faster than economic growth in the industralized nations.

Historical IOU statistics for the industrialized nations do not offer the same degree of support for Malenbaum's position, at least not, for example, in the case of U.S. refined copper consumption. Table 22–6 presents U.S. refined copper IOU statistics on both an average and incremental basis (incremental IOU can be defined as incremental mineral consumption divided by incremental GDP growth—i.e., the amount of additional mineral consumption associated with an additional unit of GDP growth). While average IOU values have generally declined, supporting Malenbaum's position, incremental IOU values have not exhibited a continuous pattern of decline. Thus, at least in the case of U.S.

## TABLE 22-5

### Intensity of Use Statistics: Africa (excluding South Africa), 1951–2000

(units per billion dollars GDP, in constant 1971 dollars)

|                                              | 1951–55 | 1961–65 | 1971–75 | 1985  | 2000  |
|----------------------------------------------|---------|---------|---------|-------|-------|
| Primary aluminum (metric tons)               | 36.7    | 163.2   | 559.2   | 600.0 | 900.0 |
| Chrome ore (metric tons)                     | 346.0   | 416.0   | 486.0   | 750.0 | 800.0 |
| Cobalt (metric tons)[a]                      | 13.3    | 12.0    | 9.9     | 10.5  | 11.0  |
| Refined copper (metric tons)                 | 217.8   | 266.7   | 291.4   | 350.0 | 400.0 |
| Iron ore (thousand metric tons)              | 46.4    | 57.9    | 53.2    | 70.0  | 80.0  |
| Manganese (thousand metric tons)             | 3.8     | 4.9     | 6.7     | 7.5   | 8.5   |
| Nickel (thousand metric tons)[b]             | 3.9     | 16.0    | 49.4    | 55.0  | 50.0  |
| Platinum group (troy ounces)                 | 11.0    | 95.0    | 534.0   | 600.0 | 725.0 |
| Crude steel (thousand metric tons)           | 49.3    | 57.6    | 68.9    | 75.0  | 85.0  |
| Tin (metric tons)[c]                         | 46.6    | 64.2    | 21.6    | 60.0  | 55.0  |
| Tungsten (metric tons)                       | 2.3     | 1.7     | 9.6     | 10.0  | 10.2  |
| Zinc (metric tons)                           | 22.9    | 122.0   | 327.5   | 350.0 | 400.0 |

[a] Historic pattern contradicts IOU theory; extrapolation supports IOU theory.
[b] Historic pattern supports IOU theory; extrapolation contradicts IOU theory. Data includes South Africa.
[c] Historic pattern is ambiguous; extrapolation contradicts IOU theory; 1971–75 figure is tentative.

refined copper consumption, the general decline in average IOU values since 1936 can be accounted for arithmetically as due solely to the high-IOU composition of the U.S. industrial base prior to 1936, since the average value always incorporates this dominating component. It clearly does not decline arithmetically because of a consistent, continuing trend of lower and lower IOU increments to that base.

This naturally raises questions regarding the extent to which continuing declines in average IOU values for the industrialized nations can be projected indefinitely into the future with any confidence. It may well be, for example, that even though gains in technological efficiency can significantly reduce mineral consumption (as industrialization progresses), the increasing use of technology by an industrialized society (in more and more areas of human activity from which it was previously excluded) at some point more than compensates for gains in technological efficiency. Under these circumstances, the average IOU statistic for an industrialized nation might well begin to increase (in the absence of supply constraints or price restraints). But, of course, this is merely a speculation neither confirmed nor denied by Malenbaum's analysis, since Malenbaum did not provide extensive analytic support for the basic premises of his methodology.

## TABLE 22-6

### Intensity of Use Statistics: United States, Refined Copper, 1934–75

| Average Values[a]              | 1934–38 | 1951–56 | 1956–61 | 1961–65 | 1966–70 | 1971–75  |
|--------------------------------|---------|---------|---------|---------|---------|----------|
| Refined copper consumption[b]  | 581.38  | 1298.12 | 1258.64 | 1681.26 | 1891.06 | 1886.08  |
| GDP[c]                         | 213.396 | 557.108 | 640.160 | 773.222 | 942.137 | 1122.094 |
| Intensity of use[d]            | 2724.0  | 2330.1  | 1966.1  | 2174.4  | 2006.8  | 1680.9   |

| Incremental Values[e]          | 1936–53 | 1953–58 | 1958–63 | 1963–68 | 1968–73 |
|--------------------------------|---------|---------|---------|---------|---------|
| Refined copper consumption[b]  | 716.74  | −39.48  | 422.62  | 209.80  | −4.98   |
| GDP[c]                         | 343.712 | 83.052  | 133.062 | 169.095 | 179.777 |
| Intensity of use[d]            | 2085.3  | −475.4  | 3176.6  | 1240.7  | −27.7   |

[a] Figures are specified with the same precision as in the 1977 Malenbaum Report.
[b] Millions of metric tons.
[c] Billions of 1971 constant dollars.
[d] Metric tons per billions of 1971 constant dollars.
[e] The 1936–53 incremental value, for example, equals the difference between the 1951–56 average value and the 1934–38 average value.

Although the IOU methodology assumes that the intensity and rate of consumption of various minerals and materials within a region will change over time (in response to changes in the region's rates of GDP and population growth), it does not assume that these intensities and rates will change in the same way for all minerals and materials. This may be seen, for example, in the projections developed for Africa, which are presented in Table 22-7. In these projections the average annual economic growth rate for Africa declines during the 1975-2000 period to only 70 percent of the rate during the 1951-1975 period. Also during the 1975-2000 period, the average annual population growth rate declines to 90 percent of the rate during the 1951-1975 period. Associated with these decreases is a wide range of changes in consumption growth rates for minerals and materials. Some new rates are over 80 percent below previous rates (aluminum and platinum); one is over 500 percent higher than previous rates (tin,

which is clearly an exception). In all cases, as shown in the same table, the African share of world mineral and material consumption is projected to change very little.

## Basic Components

In terms of the requirements of the Global 2000 Study, IOU analysis produces explicit estimates of future resource consumption related to minerals and materials, based on exogenous estimates of economic and population growth. As already stated, resources are generally assumed to be inexhaustible and available at constant real prices. No explicit account is taken of environmental factors.

Specifically, IOU analysis is an uncomplicated arithmetic procedure for using IOU tables (which estimate the intensity with which minerals or

### TABLE 22-7

### Minerals and Materials Consumption: Africa, (excluding South Africa), 1951-2000

| | Average Annual Growth (percent) | | | Share of World Total (percent) | | | |
|---|---|---|---|---|---|---|---|
| | 1951-75 | 1975-85 | 1985-2000 | 1953[a] | 1973[b] | 1985 | 2000 |
| Commodities: | | | | | | | |
| Primary aluminum | 20.5 | 4.0 | 6.2 | — | .3 | .3 | .4 |
| Chrome ore | 8.8 | 4.2 | 3.7 | .3 | .7 | .8 | .9 |
| Cobalt | 3.6 | 3.9 | 3.7 | 3.8 | 3.0 | 3.1 | 3.4 |
| Refined copper | 6.7 | 4.9 | 4.3 | .2 | .3 | .3 | .4 |
| Iron ore | 6.0 | 6.2 | 3.8 | .8 | .9 | 1.3 | 1.5 |
| Manganese | 8.2 | 4.4 | 4.2 | 1.1 | 2.4 | 2.7 | 3.1 |
| Nickel[c] | 19.8 | 4.3 | 2.7 | — | .7 | .8 | .8 |
| Platinum group | 27.4 | 4.3 | 4.7 | — | .7 | .7 | .9 |
| Crude steel | 6.9 | 4.0 | 4.3 | .6 | .8 | .9 | 1.1 |
| Tin | 1.2[d] | 12.9[d] | 7.0 | .8 | .7[d] | 2.3 | 2.5 |
| Tungsten | 12.8 | 3.8 | 3.4 | .3 | 1.7 | 1.8 | 2.0 |
| Zinc | 20.4 | 3.6 | 4.3 | 0 | .4 | .5 | .6 |
| Economic Growth: | | | | | | | |
| Malenbaum '77 (GDP) | 5.1 | 3.5 | 3.3 | 1.6 | 1.8 | 1.8 | 1.8 |
| Global 2000 Study (GNP) | — | 5.5 | 4.6 | — | 2.1[e] | 2.4 | 2.9 |
| Population Growth: | | | | | | | |
| Malenbaum '77 | 2.4 | 2.7 | 2.2 | 8.4 | 9.2 | 10.0 | 10.7 |
| Global 2000 Study | — | 2.9 | 2.9 | — | 9.1[e] | 10.2 | 12.0 |

[a] An average of 1951-55 figures.
[b] An average of 1971-75 figures.
[c] Includes South Africa.
[d] Malenbaum notes that the 1971-75 figure for tin is tentative.
[e] 1975.

materials will be consumed within a given country or region relative to per capita GDP levels) to translate exogenous GDP and population projections into minerals and materials consumption projections. Such tables could be developed for any mineral or material with respect to any given country or region. However, the only IOU tables currently considered to be timely and useful by members of the Bureau of Mines staff are those contained in the 1977 Malenbaum Report. That report contains IOU tables for the following 12 minerals and materials, which are said in the report to account collectively for 80–90 percent of the value of total world mineral production:

| aluminum | copper | nickel | tin |
| chrome | iron | platinum | tungsten |
| cobalt | manganese | steel | zinc |

Each IOU table presents separate IOU curves for each of the following 10 countries or groups of countries, as did the IOU tables contained in the 1972 Malenbaum Report:

- Africa (except South Africa)
- Asia (except Israel, Japan, China, and the countries listed with China below)
- China, Mongolia, North Korea, and North Vietnam
- Eastern Europe (Soviet bloc countries plus Albania and Yugoslavia)
- Japan
- Latin America
- United States (including Puerto Rico and other overseas U.S. islands)
- U.S.S.R.
- Western Europe (that is, Western European members of the Organization for Economic Cooperation and Development)
- Other industrialized nations (Australia, Canada, Israel, New Zealand, and South Africa)

A geographical perspective on the methodology underlying these projections is provided in one of the colored maps used to illustrate the discussion in Chapter 14 on the Government's Global Model.

## Basic Procedures

Given an existing table of IOU relationships, the following sequence of steps is followed in executing an IOU analysis based on new, exogenous GDP and population projections:

1. Obtain an existing IOU table that relates the quantity (per unit of regional GDP) of a mineral or material likely to be consumed within that region to the per capita GDP of the region.

2. Obtain, for the year in which the projection is to be made, exogenous regional (a) GDP and (b) population projections and calculate regional per capita GDP for that year. These exogenous projections must be consistent with the historical GDP and population data used in developing the IOU table.

3. Determine from the IOU table the appropriate IOU value (expressed in terms of commodity units per unit of total GDP) for the regional per capita GDP level just calculated, interpolating or extrapolating as necessary.

4. Multiply this IOU value by the exogenously estimated total regional GDP for that year, in order to calculate the estimated regional mineral or material consumption for the year for which the projection is being developed.

An example of how the 1977 Malenbaum Report projected African copper consumption for the year 2000 is provided below:

1. Refer to the IOU table for copper in Figure 22–2.

2. Assume an annual African GDP growth rate of 3.4 percent and an annual African population growth rate of 2.4 percent for 1975–2000. This yields a total African GDP in the year 2000 of $178 billion (denominated in constant 1971 dollars) and an African population of 680 million in the year 2000. Per capita GDP is thus $262.*

3. From Figure 22–2, assuming an African per capita GDP of $262, it can be determined that the appropriate IOU value for this per capita GDP level is approximately 400 metric tons per billion dollars of GDP.†

4. Multiply the exogenously estimated total African GDP level ($178 billion) by the converted IOU value (400 metric tons per $1 billion of GDP)

---

* The actual calculation in the 1977 Malenbaum Report estimated that average annual African GDP was $71 billion during the period 1971–75; economic growth at 3.4 percent per year was then calculated for 27.5 years; the same calculation was made with respect to population. Roughly comparable calculations using the Global 2000 project's medium projections would forecast an African GNP level of $427 billion in constant 1975 dollars, a population level of 497 million, and a resulting per capita GNP of $859 by the year 2000.

† It would be misleading to apply the Global 2000 Study's per capita GNP projections to the chart in the figure, since, as previously noted, the historical figures used in developing the chart could not be made consistent—in the time available—with the GNP figures used by the Global 2000 project.

in order to obtain estimated African refined copper consumption in the year 2000 (71 thousand metric tons).*

In the absence of an existing table of IOU relationships, there are apparently no explicit rules to follow in developing new IOU tables, other than to begin by plotting historical experience and then to use judgment in proceeding. In the case of the copper IOU table shown in Figure 22–2, several factors are cited in the 1977 Malenbaum Report as influencing the way the historical relationships have been extrapolated for the various industrialized nations and LDCs. These factors do not explain, however, why the extrapolated IOU curves are linear, why they have the particular slopes shown, or why particular variations exist among the industrialized nations or among the LDCs. The primary explanatory factors cited in the 1977 Malenbaum Report are:

Mostly, copper use has been affected by the substitution potential of other metals, notably aluminum, for use in producer durables, construction, motor vehicles and especially in electrical transmission. . . . For the most part, these displacements are irreversible in a given installation. Prices of aluminum and plastics have been adversely affected by energy and especially petroleum costs. . . . For these and perhaps other reasons not yet clear, copper use seems to have stabilized.
[Projected] declines [in the IOU of copper] in rich lands are moderate.
There is as yet little evidence of rapid shifts away from copper that [would] impede the growing [IOU of copper] of poor lands.

The explicit application of IOU theory in developing IOU tables is even less clear in the case of some other metals and materials. For example, in the case of the steel IOU table presented in the 1977 Malenbaum Report, the projected IOU relationships depart sharply from historical experience in many cases, as shown in Figure 22–3.

As in the case of copper, several factors have been cited to explain the way the historical IOU relationships for steel have been extrapolated for the various industrialized nations and LDCs. However, these factors do not explain why an abruptly lowered IOU relationships (with rising per capita GDP) as estimated for China. Nor do

they explain why sudden somewhat less abrupt downturns were estimated for the U.S.S.R., and "Other Industrialized Nations," in sharp contrast to historical experience in those regions. As in the case of copper, they also do not explain why the extrapolated IOU curves are linear, why they have the particular slopes shown, or why particular variations exist among the industrialized nations or among the LDCs. The explanatory factors cited in the 1977 Malenbaum Report are:

Substitution and displacement forces have . . . had an important [role in reducing the IOU of steel in developed nations], probably from the early 1950s. On the one side there was continuous technical innovation from mining (agglomeration and beneficiation of iron ore) through processing (basic oxygen converters, electric-arc furnaces) and final goods production (alloying, light steel). On the other side, there are inroads from substitute materials, notably concrete, plastics and particularly aluminum.
These technological forces are expected to be present but with less weight in the poor-nation world than in today's rich lands. While open hearth processes have become of much smaller importance everywhere and while hydro power and low capital costs encourage electric-arc and direct reduction processes in some poor nations, the prospect of parallel application of new methods remain much smaller over the next decade and generation. Alternative products are less competitive, steel scrap is less available, iron ore is often mined directly: such considerations weigh in favor of a lower technological horizon in many poor nations over the years to 1985 and 2000. [IOU relationships are] thus projected at higher levels in these years.

The most difficult case for the application of IOU theory is in the development of IOU tables for aluminum. Aluminum is the one major commodity whose historical IOU relationships do not exhibit the inverted-U pattern found for other minerals and materials. However, in accordance with IOU theory, the extrapolated IOU relationships for aluminum in the 1977 Malenbaum Report have been estimated to exhibit significantly lower slopes than historical experience alone would suggest (see Figure 22–4).

As in the cases of copper and steel, several factors are cited to explain the way the historical IOU relationships for aluminum have been extrapolated for the various industrialized nations and LDCs. However, there is no explicit quantitative accounting of the extent to which the higher energy prices mentioned (though how much higher is unspecified) are expected to affect aluminum prices. Nor is there a quantitative accounting of the extent to which higher aluminum prices are

---

* This represents 0.4 percent of world copper consumption in the year 2000, as compared to 0.3 percent in 1973—but a 76 percent increase in African per capita copper consumption over the period 1973–2000 (to 0.1 kg per person, as compared to 0.3 kg per person as a world average in the year 2000).

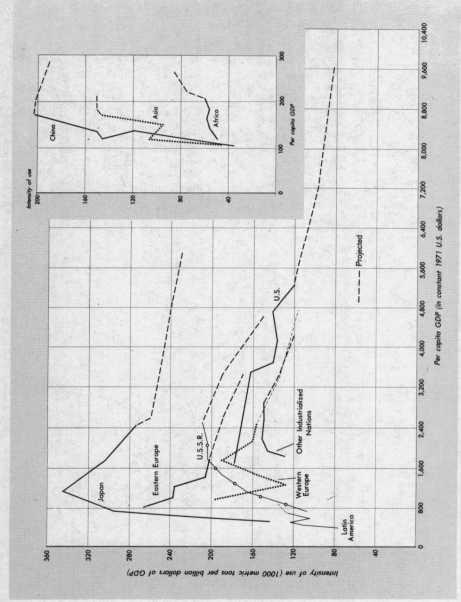

**Figure 22-3.** Graphic representation of the 1977 Malenbaum Report's intensity-of-use curve for crude steel. Solid lines indicate historic experience; broken lines indicate projections. ("China" includes Mongolia, North Korea, and North Vietnam.)

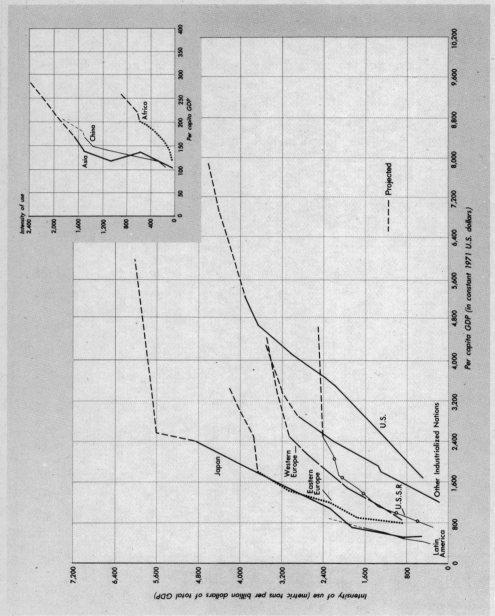

**Figure 22-4.** Graphic representation of the 1977 Malenbaum Report's intensity-of-use table for primary aluminum. Solid lines indicate historic experience; broken lines indicate projections. ("China" includes Mongolia, North Korea, and North Vietnam.)

expected to moderate consumption levels, either through abstinence, improved efficiency of use, or substitution of other materials. An explicit quantitative accounting is also missing with regard to the extent to which decreasing IOU values for copper and steel in the industrialized nations are more properly explained by aluminum substitution (which could account for the increasing IOU values for aluminum in the industrialized nations) rather than by the transition of industrialized nations to postindustrial service economies (which is a basic premise of IOU theory). These more general assumptions are not discussed in detail in the 1977 Malenbaum Report, although the following points, among others, are made:

There remains an impressive and still widening technical scope for further displacement by aluminum of iron ore, nickel, tin, and zinc in metal production, and of steel and copper metal goods

. . . [especially with regard to] the expanding role of aluminum in transmission. Construction and transportation equipment (automobiles particularly) and an expanding array of consumer goods have become greater users of aluminum in most parts of the world.

The rapid growth in [the intensity of use of aluminum] in poor lands combines a high income effect as the economies develop (or at least industrialize), supplemented by what is generally a positive substitution effect. [However,] . . . there is as yet little evidence of rapid shifts away from copper [in the less developed nations]. . . . The copper prospect and especially the uncertain price prospect for aluminum over the next decades of energy shortage are consistent with [the extrapolation].

For the rich world negative income effects are more than offset by substitution. It is hard to visualize a turning point for [the IOU of aluminum].

# 23   Technology

No government agency is uniquely responsible for developing consistent assumptions regarding future rates of technological change for use in official forecasts. The Office of Science and Technology Policy and the Office of Technology Assessment are responsible for advising the President and the Congress, respectively, on particular aspects of technology and for assessing probable social and economic impacts. No federal agency routinely assists other agencies in preparing consistent assumptions about future rates for technological change to be used in official quantitative projections. As a result, the agencies contributing to the present study made their own assumptions regarding rates of technological change, as necessary, when they developed their projections.

While each agency has made technological assumptions over the years in forecasting other variables of interest, there is no well-delineated history of technological forecasting, nor is any well-established methodology in widespread use. Several methodologies, of course, are in use by federal agencies for projecting rates of technological change, based on rates of public and private expenditure for research and development, past rates of technological change, and other factors, but because such projections do not make use of a consistent set of assumptions, their methodologies cannot be used collectively to evaluate the relative impact of different levels of public and private investment in research and development.

## Key Analytic Methodologies

Four basic methods of determining the directions and rates of the development and adoption of technology were used by the agencies contributing to the Global 2000 Study: implicit and explicit endogenous calculations and implicit and explicit exogenous calculations.

### Implicit Endogenous Calculations

Almost all Global 2000 Study projections are based to a considerable extent on historic relationships (e.g., in the form of regression equations), which implicity incorporate historic rates of tech-

nological change. In projecting the future based on a continuation of these historic relationships, the agencies implicitly assume that technological change will continue to contribute to the correlation of variables in the future as it has in the past.

Four explicit quantitative methodologies used in developing the Global 2000 Study projections make particularly extensive use of historic relationships: the SIMLINK (SIMulated trade LINKages) model in the GNP projections; the IEES (International Energy Evaluation System) model in the energy projections; the GOL (grain, oilseed, livestock) model in the food and agricultural projections; and the regression equations used by the Bureau of Mines in the nonfuel minerals projections. The projection of historic rates of technological change is also implicit in the less systematic procedures, for example, those used to develop the environmental projections.

An example of how a more systematically specified model makes implicit endogenous calculations of rates of technological change is provided by the way the GNP projections incorporate assumptions regarding the productivity of new capital investment—assumptions that implicitly incorporate factors related to technological change. Within SIMLINK, the model used to develop the GNP projections, linear equations are used to relate new gross investment to total GDP for each LDC group. A variable incremental capital output ratio (as if new investment were related to incremental GDP instead of total GDP) can be inferred from the model's results. Such an incremental capital output ratio provides a measure of the implied assumptions regarding changes in the productivity of investment capital associated with one unit of additional GDP. These changes are due to many factors, including, implicitly, projected rates of technological changes.

For almost all LDC groups, the incremental capital output ratio is projected to decline anywhere from roughly 5 to 40 percent over the 1977–85 period, indicating major increases in the productivity of investment capital. For example, the GNP projections assume that, in the case of the "Other South Asian LDC" group (with an incremental capital output ratio declining from roughly

4.1 to 2.5), a given investment can be thought of as producing 60 percent more incremental GDP in 1985 than in 1977 (in constant dollars).

## Explicit Endogenous Calculations

Some projections make use of explicitly specified cost factors, in conjunction with explicitly specified maximum market penetration rates. The IEES energy model, in particular, makes extensive use of endogenous calculations involving the development and deployment of various energy technologies not currently in widespread use. For example, with the IEES model, the deployment rate for technologies capable of producing synthetic gas from coal is explicitly modeled endogenously.

First, a maximum level of deployment is specified exogenously for each year for which a projection is developed. For 1985, this maximum level is twice the 1975 production level and, for 1990, three times the 1975 production level in the case of coal and gasification technologies.

Then the model calculates endogenously the economic competitiveness of this synthetic gas in relation to alternative fuels in each region represented in the model.

Those electrical generation plants represented in the model that can burn synthetic gas can also use natural gas and sometimes other fuels. The model projects them to use the fuel that adds the least cost to the global energy production system. This is only rarely coal-derived gas because of the efficiency losses and extra transportation involved in the process. Demand for the gas from other sectors cannot always be satisfied with other fuels, but it is likely to be small, though growing. As a result, the deployment of synthetic gas technologies rarely reaches the maximum levels specified.

## Implicit Exogenous Calculations

All the methodologies used in developing the Global 2000 Study projections make extensive use of judgmental adjustments to information entered into the model. Often these adjustments implicitly incorporate projections of future rates of technological change. For example, the population projections incorporate input data (mortality and fertility assumptions) based on demographers' expectations regarding the development and deployment of medical and birth control technologies. These assumptions are then reflected numerically in the model's calculation procedures.

In the case of the Census Bureau's population projections, for example, these projected fertility rates are based on the assumption that the LDCs will continue to make moderate progress in social and economic development during the 1975–2000 period. As the LDCs progress in social and economic development, the fertility level is expected to decline more or less continuously but with some temporary plateaus. This decline is due to many factors, including the increasingly widespread deployment of birth control technologies, as methods of family limitation become better known and are accepted by couples wishing to reduce their fertility.

As a result of these implicit assumptions involving the rates at which technological change is adopted over the 1975–2000 period, fertility rates in Bangladesh are projected to decline 39 percent. In Mexico, the projected decline is 37 percent over the same period and in the People's Republic of China, 38 percent. Projected fertility declines are generally even greater in the case of the projections made by the Community and Family Study Center of the University of Chicago.

## Explicit Exogenous Calculations

A few projections make use of exogenous time-trend variables to capture explicitly the impact of technological change. Coefficients for these variables are generally derived from the statistical measurement of historical data, although they are also subject to major judgmental adjustment. The GOL model, in particular, makes extensive use of this approach to explicitly modeling technological change in making the food projections.

Unexplained variations in historic yields from those implied by the model's regression equations are assumed to be attributable to technological change regarding both the development and deployment of the technologies. These historically derived rates then serve as the basis for projecting future change. To project future technological change, analysts enter coefficients for time-dependent variables into the model's yield equations. Major adjustments to the historically regressed coefficients are made by expert analysts to ensure that the model produces results that they consider reasonable.

In the case of wheat production in low-income North Africa and the Middle East, for example, a coefficient is applied to a time-trend variable to project growth in wheat production due to the combined influence of trend growth and technological growth. Over 50 percent of the growth in wheat production in this region over the 1970–85 period is due to this factor, and an even larger percentage over the 1985–2000 period.

## Basic Principles

Although many different methods are used by the agencies in developing their technological assumptions, a few generalizations can be made about philosophical approach.

In general, the agencies assume a continuation of past technological trends with no surprise developments. For example, the rapid rates of change associated with the Green Revolution of the 1960s are projected to continue unabated to the year 2000. None of the projections assumes that any technologies not now conceived will be available and in widespread use by 2000. All the projections assume that currently acceptable technologies will continue to be acceptable in 2000 (e.g., birth control pills will not be found to cause cancer, nor will insects develop further immunities to pesticides).

The many factors that directly influence the rate at which technological change and its concomitant effects take place are usually not given explicit consideration. For example, the various resource, environmental, economic, social, and institutional conditions necessary for the development and widespread deployment of major technological change are rarely explicitly analyzed. Instead, the projections simply assume, implicitly, that these conditions will not represent a future barrier to a continuation of past rates of change. Similarly, the resource, environmental, economic, and social consequences of developing and deploying emerging technologies are also rarely explicitly analyzed. However, most projections implicitly assume that the impact of technological change on whatever variables are represented in the projection models will be similar to such impacts in the past.

## Basic Components

The procedures used to choose the indicators and variables representing technological change are not consistent. In the case of the more explicit quantitative methodologies, the procedures chosen tend to focus on variables of traditional interest rather than on variables likely to be of concern in the future. For example, in developing the food projections, the technological variables chosen primarily focus on yield per acre (and do not address technological indicators related to the energy and water required per unit of production). In contrast, the nonquantitative projections were able to take into account more recently proposed measures of technological progress.

The geographic focus of the technological projections varies with the particular projection. Most of the mathematical projections (energy, food, population, GNP, and nonfuel minerals) adjust their measures of technological progress for each geographic region considered. However, the model used in the Global 2000 Study to make global projections of the residuals and pollutants associated with energy conversion processes assumes the complete adoption of U.S. new-source emission-standards uniformly throughout the world by 1985.

## Documentation and Validation

No published documentation of the methods used by the agencies to project rates of technological change is currently available. No formal validity tests of the technological projections have been made by the agencies.

Part III

# Analysis of the Projection Tools:
# Other Global Models

# 24   Introduction

The Global 2000 Study utilizes the following standard institutional means of problem-solving. A policymaker needing information gives a question to an analyst (referred to as the primary analyst). The question is either too large for the primary analyst to answer personally, or else the analyst feels that it would be politic to involve other analysts in whose jurisdictions parts of the question fall. The question is therefore divided into subquestions tailored to fit the bureaucratic framework. These are handed over to secondary analysts in various bureaus whose fields are appropriate to the subquestions. Some ground rules are set forth to avoid inconsistencies. If the primary analyst is worried about consistency, he may provide opportunities and incentives for the secondary analysts to receive input from each other's analyses. However, the secondary analysts are not likely to be enthusiastic about incorporating inputs from other secondary analysts into their own analyses, so the gain in consistency is often minimal.

When the secondary analysts have completed their work, they deliver their results to the primary analyst, who then pieces together the responses to subquestions. In the process, he will have to edit out much of what has been said, fill in things that have not been said, and stretch meanings here and there so as to bring the subanalyses into a cogent whole.

This approach works reasonably well for normal, short-term problem-solving and gives the overbusy policymaker a reasonably concise analysis based on a broad spectrum of information. However, it has two serious shortcomings for long-term analysis.

First, over the long term, the relationships between subquestions become increasingly important to the whole question. For example, the linkage between energy questions and economic questions is critically important to agriculture, (because of increased input prices and, if economies are adversely affected, reduced demand for agricultural products) and environment (inflation in the commercial system causes the world's poor rural communities to lean more heavily on their natural environment for fulfillment of basic needs, resulting in increased grazing and firewood gathering and more overall pressure on the land). Environmental degradation caused by economic and population pressures have serious consequences for agriculture and water availability. Food shortages and environmental degradation have significant effects on human health, and thus on population dynamics. By the year 2000 this crisscrossing of influences may have put the globe into a state quite different from that predicted by the separate answers to subquestions on population, GNP, energy, agriculture, water, and environment. After 2000, the effect will be even more profound.

Second, piecemeal bureaucratic analysis tends to understate difficult but critical questions—such as technological change, attitude shifts, and institutional change—that do not fall into someone's tidy jurisdiction but affect the outcomes of all secondary analyses. The primary analyst tries to fill in the gaps as best he can but seldom has time to do a thorough job and is likely to understate the importance of the intangibles. In the long-term, these factors will be critical. If in the next decade the nations of the world make a commitment to decentralized renewable energy supply systems, we or our descendents will live in quite a different world 20 or 100 years hence. Which way the energy system goes will be determined by public opinion and technological and institutional factors that the Global 2000 Study has not been able, for the reasons given above, to incorporate into its analysis in a consistent and integrated fashion.

One way of circumventing these shortcomings is to supplement the piecemeal, subquestion analyses with an integrated analysis, performed by a single analytic group using appropriate inputs from related analytic groups. There are obvious dangers in this approach. If used as a primary mode of analysis, it would concentrate political power by giving the integrated analysis group a direct line to the policymaker, while making it only marginally answerable to outside analyses. However, the need for integrated analysis in long-term planning does justify the experimental use of such an approach. It may err due to deficiencies in analytic methodology or to the analysts' personal biases. But the system of divided analysis is almost certain to err due to its neglect of system linkages. Moreover, it too will be subject to the biases of the primary analyst's personal judgment.

The next five chapters will be devoted to long-term global models that look at the world on an integrated basis. The models represent a variety of analytic approaches for making integrated forecasts and serve as case studies to highlight some of the problems encountered in managing integrated forecasting groups. The case study analyses will be followed by cross-section analyses of what the models reveal about trends in population, resources, and the environment to the year 2000. The discussion will be prefaced by a review of ecological concepts, because ecology is the science that deals with the relationships among populations, resources, and environments. (It is assumed that most readers are already familiar with the economic concepts introduced into the discussion.) Some of the ecological concepts will be manifested in the models to be analyzed. Others will be conspicuous by their absence, and their absence should be considered as a significant deficiency in the integrated models.

## Carrying Capacity

If a population requires resources in proportion to its numbers, and if resources are limited, then the population cannot grow beyond the size established by the resource limit. Economists refer to this "carrying capacity" as Malthusian logic; biologists think of it as commonsense. Population biologists have developed the concept in many directions and subjected it to empirical and experimental testing. The basic theory has been extended to include cases with more than one resource, with different sorts of resources, and more than one population—competition models and predator-prey models being common instances of multiple population forms.

In simplified terms, the insights shed on the question of population, resources, and environment by the carrying capacity concept are as follows.

First, three basic patterns of population growth can evolve in populations operating within the confines of a finite carrying capacity: stabilization at or below the carrying capacity; oscillation around or below capacity; and overshooting the capacity, which is followed by extinction or incomplete recovery. Stabilization is likely when the resource is self-renewing and the population is kept in check by predation, parasitism, or species behaviors that limit reproduction, such as territoriality. Oscillation results when the dynamics of interdependent populations—particularly predator-prey systems—put them out of phase with one another. When predators overexploit their prey, they bring on the demise of their own populations and create an opportunity for the prey to recover its numbers and restart the cycle. Human interference commonly disrupts the checks and balances that control such interdependent populations. Prey whose predators have been eliminated by man commonly increase to the point where they become pests in managed ecosystems (e.g., eruptions of insect populations in agricultural crops) or to the point where they overexploit the environment that supports them and starve in great numbers (e.g., grazing mammals when large carnivores are exterminated). In the latter situation, oscillations are converted to overshoot and collapse. The overshoot mode will also be observed when a population depends on a resource that cannot be replenished—as in the bloom and bust of a test-tube yeast culture.

Second, many populations are limited by multiple resource constraints. For plants, light, water, and a number of soil nutrients are limiting. Often one resource is much more limiting than another (in desert environments it is usually water). The availability of this most limiting resource will determine the system's carrying capacity. Should the most limiting resources become suddenly available, as when phosphorus is made available to fresh water algae cultures, the population will grow until it encounters some other resource limitation. In the process, it may seriously disrupt other populations that share its local environment—as happens in the case of an algal bloom produced by phosphorus infusion into a phosphorus-limited fresh water system.

Simple mathematical models of population dynamics based on carrying capacity concepts have been around since the 1920s. These are as familiar to the ecologist as supply-demand curves are to the economist. Many ecologists will put human population into a carrying capacity model just as readily as they will any other specie and, at least in conversation, many will express the opinion that we are in danger of exceeding the global carrying capacity for our species.

Carrying capacity concepts will show up in all models discussed in the next five chapters, except the U.N. world model, and will be responsible for virtually all of the pessimistic outcomes generated by the model set. In two cases—the Latin American world model and MOIRA (model of international relations in agriculture)—carrying capacity will be reduced to a curve showing diminishing returns to investment and labor in the agricultural sector. World 2 and World 3 and the Mesarovic-Pestel world model have much more complex formulations of the concept, including interdependent populations (human and machine), multiple constraints (particularly the World 2 and 3 models), and the function of interregional trade in allowing regions to extend their local carrying capacities (Mesarovic-Pestel only).

## Stability and Diversity

In ecology the relationship between stability and diversity tends to generate a philosophical argument—one that can go in many directions depending on how one defines stability and diversity. Both terms are elusive, but there is some consensus among ecologists that genetic simplification, either through reduction of the number of species in a community or through reduction of the genetic diversity of a population, is prone to make the community less stable. Extended, this line of reasoning leads to some of the prevalent ecological nightmares. It gives theoretical credibility to the fear of a crop plague decimating the genetically simplified stands of high-yielding variety grains that support an increasing fraction of the world's population, as well as to the fear that a virulent, drug-resistent disease will develop and take heavy tolls in human lives. On a less dramatic level, the stability-diversity relationship suggests that the difficulty of controlling insects and other crop pests is likely to increase as cultivation practices become more intensive, extensive, and standardized throughout the world. Thus the reduction of crop losses anticipated in many analyses, including the Latin American world model and MOIRA may never mature.

The potential effects of simplification of biological systems on long-term interrelationships between population, resources, and environment have been excluded from all global models under consideration and are either extremely rare or completely absent in regional models as well. The barrier to inclusion appears to be representational, combined with absence of data. The absence of operational definitions and precise conceptualization of how the system is influenced by genetic simplification make it impossible to build a credible model of the effects of biological simplification. Thus quantitative models take no account of the problem. Rather, biological simplification manifests itself as an ill-defined fear, which makes the matter hard to deal with in a rational fashion.

## Ecological Buffering

Closely related to the concept of stability and diversity is the notion of ecological buffering—basically a notion that living growing things, as well as dead organic matter, cushion the interface between the air and the geologic surface of the earth. Plants hold soil in place and protect it from the impact of falling rain. Soil absorbs rain and prevents it from running off in a great flood. Living things bind up nutrients, which will reduce the environment's carrying capacity if they are not present in sufficient quantities and prevent them from being leached out by rain or from seeping down and forming a hard pan below the upper layers of soil surface. In general, the buffering role of biological matter is thought to be more critical in warmer climates where chemical reactions and decomposition of organic matter (i.e., reduction of the sponge-like nature of soil to pure clay, silt, or sand) are more rapid.

While the particulars are complex, as a general rule simplification of an ecological system tends to reduce its capacity as an ecological buffer. Thus, overgrazing, overcutting of timber, and various forms of overcultivation play havoc with ecological systems and greatly reduce their ability to support life.

In principle, the maintenance and destruction of ecological buffers is fairly straightforward and could be easily modeled. In practice, however, modelers experience great difficulty in doing this. The way an ecological buffering system works is often site-specific. For any given location there are often critical points beyond which a system cannot be simplified without extensive and possibly irreversible damage. The location of critical points varies according to factors of climate and geography. A region of steep slopes in the humid tropics is apt to be much more susceptible to damage via disruption of its buffers than a temperate-zone flatland region. Thus it is difficult to come up with a global or large-region representation of the ecological buffering problem. Of the models to be examined, only World 3 attempts to capture the dynamics of ecological buffering.

# 25   Worlds 2 and 3

Man has skyrocketed from a defensive position, largely subordinated to Nature's alternatives, to a new and dominant one. From it, he not only can and does influence everything else in the world but, voluntarily or unwittingly, can and indeed does determine the alternatives of his own future—and ultimately must choose his options for it. In other words, his novel power condition practically compels him to take up new regulatory functions that willy-nilly he has had to discharge with respect to the world's mixed natural-human systems. Having penetrated a number of the erstwhile mysteries and being able to sway events massively, he is now vested with unprecedented, tremendous responsibilities and thrown *into the new role of moderator of life on the planet—including his own life.*

The above words[1] were written by Aurelio Peccei, who commissioned the models known as Worlds 2 and 3. He describes his own state of mind previous to the time at which he commissioned those models as "perplexed and worried by the orderless, torrential character of this precipitous human progress." Perceiving the world's problems as highly interconnected and global in nature, he was convinced that something fundamental should be done before it was too late.[2] Though he found no difficulty finding people to agree with him that there was a problem, he found it difficult to translate that agreement into action. In order to push ahead to actual programs, he founded the Club of Rome, a loose association of businessmen, intellectuals, and nonelected government officials from many countries. The Club was conceived not as a debating society but as an action-oriented organization with two main objectives: (1) "to promote and disseminate a more secure in-depth understanding of mankind's predicament" and (2) "to stimulate the adoption of new attitudes, policies and institutions capable of redressing the present situation."[3]

Jay Forrester, the developer of the system dynamics method of computer simulation, was invited to a Club of Rome meeting in June 1970. He pointed out some of the interactions he saw among problems of interest to Peccei—problems such as rapid population growth, resource depletion, pollution, and hunger—and explained how the system dynamics method could help sort out and clarify these problems. To demonstrate, he constructed during the following month a small model called World 1, linking five basic variables—population, capital, resources, pollution, and food. He presented World 1 to the Club, one of whose members, Eduard Pestel, subsequently arranged for the Volkswagen Foundation to fund elaboration of the model. Forrester completed and published World 2,[4] a more polished version of the first simple model, and simultaneously assembled an international team of researchers under the direction of Dennis Meadows to make a still more detailed and carefully quantified version. This final version, called World 3, took a year to construct and was the basis for the book *The Limits to Growth.*[5]

Peccei and other members of the Club of Rome looked on computer simulation models World 2 and World 3 as means to their ends. It was hoped that by making the human predicament quantitative and clear, the models would wake people up and set them to looking for solutions. As Peccei put it, "We wanted to start a world-wide debate as soon as possible."[6]

Modelers have motives as often as model commissioners, and Forrester probably had an interest in promoting the system dynamics methodology, which he strongly believes is a useful tool for understanding complex, interrelated problems of the sort that concerned the Club of Rome.

The members of the Meadows team, which produced *The Limits to Growth*, probably had less well-defined aspirations. They were relatively young (average age below 30) and for the most part at the start of their careers. Meadows and his wife had just returned from a year in Asia, during which they had become concerned about problems of development and the environment, and were eager to explore the causes and possible cures of such problems. Most of the team members were formally trained in science, engineering or system dynamics, rather than the social sciences.

## The Models and Their Limitations

Worlds 2 and 3 are models of the long-term relationships between population, resources, and environment. They outline the general patterns of causation by which these three factors interact and feed back on one another. Worlds 2 and 3 are the only models considered in the Global 2000 Study that include the study's three major focal variables on an equal footing. The other models considered either omit environmental factors or give them only cursory treatment. Two of the models—the U.N. world model and MOIRA (model of international relations in agriculture)—include population only as an exogenous variable, and two—the Latin American world model and MOIRA—take no account of the depletion of mineral resources and fossil fuels.

Worlds 2 and 3 do have limitations, despite the appropriateness of their focus. They are general, strategy-oriented models and make no attempt to develop specific, detailed analyses. They familiarize one with basic tendencies in population-resource-environment systems but do not speak to the problems of specific regions. As stated in *The Limits of Growth*:

We can say very little at this point about the practical, day-by-day steps that might be taken to reach a desirable, sustainable state of global equilibrium. Neither the world model nor our own thoughts have been developed in sufficient detail to understand all the implications of the transition from growth to equilibrium. Before any part of the world's society embarks deliberately on such a transition, there must be much more discussion, more extensive analysis, and many new ideas contributed by many different people. If we have stimulated each reader of this book to begin pondering how such a transition might be carried out, we have accomplished our immediate goal.[7]

Further problems with the World models include (1) the fact that they are based on a series of controversial assumptions, including the inability of technology to alleviate natural limits to growth and thus cannot be employed without generating debate; (2) their focus on metal resources and inattention to fossil fuels; (3) omission of social factors, such as income distribution and the international order, which may pose limiting problems well before actual physical limits are encountered; (4) weakness of data base and aggregation of items with dissimilar behavior in the pollution sector; and (5) failure to allow for qualitative changes in the nature of economic growth that could make it less demanding on limiting resources.

The breadth of focus and coherent conceptual development of the World models ensure their utility for clarifying the nature of long-term global problems. However, their limitations render them unsuitable as primary tools of analysis or as tools for detailed analysis of global problems and their solutions.

## Method

World 2 and World 3 are both system dynamics models. System dynamics is a form of simulation modeling that incorporates a well-articulated philosophy, precepts about how models should be constructed, and a set of symbolic representational tools (including the DYNAMO computer language and various diagrammatic formats used in model formulation and description), all of which embody the system dynamics methodology. Jay Forrester was the primary developer of the system dynamics methodology. The team that constructed World 3 was made up of people who had studied under Forrester at MIT. Both models can therefore be considered pure system dynamics models, and their methodological bases can best be described by quoting extracts from the system dynamics literature. The following description has been extracted from a paper written by Nathaniel Mass, a senior member of the MIT System Dynamics Group, and Richard Day, Chairman of the Department of Economics at the University of Southern California.

A system dynamics model is, most fundamentally, a theory of how change occurs in a social or economic system. The means for describing the process of change is a set of simultaneous first-order differential or integral equations. Underlying this representation is the assumption that change in social systems occurs through the process of integration. The form of system dynamics models thus differs intrinsically from that of simultaneous-equation models which describe equilibrium rather than intertemporal relationships, and in which change in internal system variables can only occur as a result of change in exogenous variables.

System dynamics assumes that all variables in a system can be subdivided into two fundamental categories: levels and rates. This dichotomy corresponds closely to the distinction between stocks and flows in economics or the distinction between balance-sheet and income-statement variables in accounting. Level variables describe the state of the system at any point in time. In contrast, rate variables are instantaneous rates of flow, which alter the system levels.

Characteristics of the rate-equation structure of a system dynamics model include:

(a) Rate equations are formulated on the basis of observation of the underlying real-life decision processes. All information inputs to a rate equation are information sources actually available to the decision-maker and employed in decision-making. Rate equations should not be based on a theory of equilibrium or optimal economic behavior.

(b) In a well-formulated model, parameters will each have clear and independent real-life meaning. . . . A typical parameter might represent "The average length of time orders for capital equipment are planned and negotiated internally before an actual order is placed with suppliers." Parameters should have operational significance to actors in the real system, not just abstract statistical meaning. Parameters should never be inserted just to correct units of measure or to increase equation fit with data.

(c) Proper rate-equation formulations should incorporate all influences on the corresponding real-life action, including intangible or non-measured variables. Non-measured variables or variables for which little data exist should be formulated and incorporated into the model in as reasonable a way as possible, given data limitations. Simulation experiments should then be performed at a later stage to assess the sensitivity of model behavior and policy outcomes to the exact measurement and specification of intangible or non-measured influences. Such simulation experiments can guide further data-collection and parameter-specification efforts.

(d) Rate-equation formulations should be robust and not break down at extreme conditions or outside the range of observed system behavior. Such robustness of rate equations is important because it can seldom be presumed *a priori* that future behavior or behavior resulting from application of a new policy will fall only within the range of past behavior.[8]

The rate-level structure of system dynamics models has important consequences. For one thing, it makes them effective tools for representation of dynamic feedback processes. System dynamicists are almost unique among social science modelers because they routinely analyze the behavior of their models in terms of positive and negative feedback loops.* For another, it makes

them well suited for representation of problems where time phasing of cumulative events has important ramifications for system behavior, as, for example, in the delayed effects of toxins on biological systems.

The emphasis on inclusion of nonmeasured variables, on operational (as opposed to abstract or statistical) meaning, and on robustness under extreme conditions often make system dynamics models seem strange, if not heretical, to conventional analysts who base their models on existing theory and rely on statistical validation as a test of empirical truth. The same constellation of attributes, however, tends to make system dynamics models attractive to nonacademic audiences by freeing them from the artificiality of abstract theory and imbuing them with the realism that comes of including familiar terminology and processes that interact in a recognized fashion.

An essential part of using operational variables and constructing models that will not break down under extreme conditions or outside the range of observed system behavior is the use of nonlinear functional relationships. It is common in any functional relationship for extreme conditions to lead to increasing or diminishing returns. Hence the gut feeling that one cannot, in many situations, "push things too far" without facing a change in the way the system responds. System dynamicists freely transpose descriptive information of such situations into nonlinear functional relationships. For example, upon being told by a person familiar with a system that past a certain point not much happens when you increase this or that input, the modeler will be likely to draw a curve of diminishing returns that levels off around the point indicated. The system dynamicist's tools make this sort of representation simple to incorporate, thus encouraging its use. As all mathematician's know the inclusion of nonlinearities tends to make systems on equations intuitively unpredictable. Thus, when system dynamics models are made to operate in extreme value regions for critical parameters—or when their own structural tendencies drive them into extreme regions over the course of time—they often manifest unfamiliar modes of behavior. From this arises the "coun-

---

* Positive feedback loops are self-reinforcing behavioral trends, such as "vicious circles" or "snowball effects," where increases in a stock result in increases in the volume of a flow that increases that stock. Growth in population leading to increases in the number of births per unit time is a familiar example. Positive feedback results either in exponential growth or exponential decline. Negative feed-

back is equilibrating or goal-seeking behavior, in which changes in a variable that move it away from the value at which it finds equilibrium will stimulate forces that drive the variable back toward its equilibrium value. A negative feedback loop can also be called a control mechanism. A thermostat is a classic example of a negative feedback system. However, negative feedback will be found controlling many things that stay in balance and are not completely inert.

terintuitive behavior" that system dynamicists see as one of the most insight-generating contributions of their models—the place where computer analysis, at least theoretically, can surpass the analyzing power of the human brain.

## Structure

World 3 is a structural analog of World 2, with a higher degree of detail and further substantiated through parameterization and structural justifications taken from scholarly literature. Increase in detail leads to an increase in size. World 2 contains around 40 equations and 5 levels while World 3 contains closer to 150 equations and 21 state variables.* Table 25–1 shows the lines along which World 2 has been expanded to arrive at World 3.

A full description of either model's structure would be impractical to include here. Those seeking such a description should refer to the modeler's own documentation of their work.[9] The present analysis entails some conceptual distortion by describing the two models as representations of ecological carrying capacity.

As carrying capacity models, Worlds 2 and 3 can be seen as systems including two populations, both of which have carrying capacities partially determined by the other population and partially

## TABLE 25–1

### A Comparison of Levels in World 2 and World 3

| World 2 | World 3 |
|---|---|
| Population | Ages  0–14 |
| | 15–44 |
| | 45–64 |
| | 65+ |
| | 5 delays[a] |
| Natural resources | Nonrenewable resources |
| Capital investment | Industrial capital |
| | Service capital |
| | 7 delays |
| Fraction of capital investment in agriculture | Arable land |
| | Potentially arable land |
| | Urban-industrial land |
| | Land fertility |
| | 2 delays |
| Pollution | Persistant pollution |
| | 7 delays |

[a] A delay is a commonly used structural unit in system dynamics models that serves to delay the effects of changes happening in the system. Structurally, delays are levels. A single delay may be made of one, two, three, or more levels.

---

* Technical definitional problems for "equation" and "state variable" make it impossible to assign exact numbers without careful stipulation of terms.

determined by environmental factors of other sorts. The two populations, human population and machine population (called in the models capital investment or industrial and service capital) are by nature tied into positive feedback loops and thus inclined to expotential growth. Increases in population lead to increases in the number of births per year, which leads to further growth of population. Increases in machines lead to increases in output, which produces more funds for investment and thus more machines. Both growth trends will tend to be exponential.

The basic relationship between human and machine populations might be termed symbiotic. There are functional relationships in the models whereby increases in population tend to increase the growth of the industrial infrastructure and whereby growth industrial infrastructure tends to hasten population growth rates. Structural observations could lead a modeler to deduce that the relationship between capital growth and population growth is quite strong (increased industrial capacity can greatly extend the carrying capacity for human beings), while the relationship between population growth and industrial growth is relatively weak (increase in human population does not greatly increase the carrying capacity for machines). Observation of model behavior will confirm these deductions: In model runs industrial growth tends to continue even when population growth has equilibrated, while collapses of the industrial structure result in similarly large collapses of population.

The apparent symbiosis is not straightforward. In some ways, machine and human populations are antipathetic and retard one another's growth. The machine population generates pollution, which can raise death rates for the population of human beings. If human population increases out of proportion to its food supply, investment becomes diverted from the industrial to agricultural use, which in effect reduces the rate at which industrial capital grows.

Beyond the system of mutual constraints and stimuli and between the human and machine populations are a set of constraints created by natural systems. Primary among these are the limitation on agricultural production created by the limited resources of arable and potentially arable land and the limitations brought about by a finite supply of nonrenewable natural resources. In both cases, these are modeled not as absolute limits but as situations wherein the costs of resource development increase expotentially as the total available supply begins to be exhausted.

As modeled, a further difficulty is embedded in the structure of the agricultural sector. Its carrying capacity is erodable. Overly intensive use of agricultural resources leads to a decline in soil fertility and to decreased agricultural production. Declines in agricultural production will stimulate increased investment in the agricultural sector and further intensification of agricultural production. These, in turn, will hasten the decline in soil fertility. Unless strong forces counteract these trends, their net effect will be an exponential decline in agricultural production and massive starvation of the human population for which the agricultural production has established a carrying capacity.

Worlds 2 and 3 also tend to be structurally unstable and prone to collapse because the man-machine symbiosis permits and encourages both populations to grow beyond the natural limits of land and natural resources. The inertia inherent in the levels representing human and machine populations (neither human population nor stocks of machinery will respond quickly to changes in their outside environment) prevents them from responding quickly when they approach their respective natural limits. Thus both are inclined to overshoot their carrying capacities. This overshoot, in conjunction with the overshoot resulting from erosion of agricultural carrying capacity, is responsible for the crash in human population and industrial infrastructure that makes the World models so startling and so sobering in their prognostications.

## Conclusions

The conclusions the modelers themselves draw from their models are perhaps best stated in their own words from *Dynamics of Growth in a Finite World*, the technical report on World 3:

The dominant behavior mode of World 3 is caused by three basic assumptions about the population-capital system:

1. The prevailing social value system strongly favors the growth of population and capital. Therefore, these quantities tend to grow unless severely pressed by physical limitations. Their growth is exponential because of the inherent positive feedback nature of industrial production and human reproduction.
2. Feedback signals about the negative consequences of growth are generated by the environmental systems that support population and capital. These signals take the form of pressures against growth, such as diminishing returns to investment in agricultural inputs, the buildup of harmful pollutants, increased development costs for new land, increased resource

costs, and less food per capita. The negative feedback signals become stronger as population and capital grow toward environmental limits.
3. Delays in the negative feedback signals arise for two reasons. First, some delays, such as those inherent in population aging, pollution transfers, and land fertility regeneration, are inescapable consequences of physical or biological laws. Second, some delays are caused by the time intervals necessary for society to perceive new environmental situations and to adjust its values, institutions, and technologies in response.

A system that posses these three characteristics—rapid growth, environmental limits, and feedback delays—is inherently unstable. Because the rapid growth persists while the feedback signals that oppose it are delayed, the physical system can temporarily expand well beyond its ultimately sustainable limits. During this period of overshoot, the short-term efforts required to maintain the excess population and capital are especially likely to erode or deplete the resource base. The environmental carrying capacity may be so diminished that it can support only a much smaller population and lower material standard of living than would have been possible before the overshoot. The result is an uncontrollable decline to lower levels of population and capital.

With this understanding of the system characteristics that lead to instability, it becomes relatively easy to evaluate alternative policies for increasing stability and bringing about a sustainable equilibrium. For example:

1. Short-term technologies designed to mask the initial signals of impending limits and to promote further growth will not be effective in the long term. Rather, they will disguise the need for social value change, lengthen the system's response delays, and increase the probability, the speed, and the magnitude of the eventual overshoot and collapse.
2. Policies that combat the erosion of the earth's resource base will certainly reduce the severity of decline after an overshoot. However, so long as growth is still emphasized and feedback delays persist, resource conservation will not in itself prevent overshoot. Furthermore, the overstressed system may not be able to afford the costs of conservation during a period of overshoot.
3. Social value changes that reduce the forces causing growth, institutional innovations that raise the rate of technological or social adaptation, and long-term forecasting methods that shorten feedback delays may be very effective in reducing system instability.
4. A judicious combination of policies designed to prevent the erosion of resources, foresee the effects of approaching limits, and bring a

deliberate end to material and demographic growth can circumvent the overshoot mode altogether and lead to a sustainable equilibrium.

Although these conclusions seem to be simple and self-evident, most economic and political decisions made today are based implicitly on a world view very different from the one presented here. The dominant contemporary model contains the assumptions that physical growth can and should continue; that technology and the price system can eliminate scarcities with little delay; that the resource base can be expanded but never reduced; that the solution of short-term problems will yield desirable long-term results; and that population and capital, if they must ever stabilize, will do so automatically, and at an optimal level. [10]

The conclusions reached by readers of The Limits to Growth vary with the sophistication of the reader. People who have not previously been confronted with the set of problems the World models deal with often react emotionally and find the work depressing. The following comment is typical: "Basically the prediction is that mankind has perhaps 40 or 50 years left. . . . The human race will be wiped out—mostly or completely—by the year 2100." [11] People to whom the problem of limits is not a novelty tend to react less emotionally. Others have such readymade defenses against the limits argument as the following: "Yes, but they do not include technology." "You can rig a model to say anything you want." Or "I don't believe their numbers are correct." Others are favorably predisposed to the concept that material growth must cease and so are inspired to work for global equilibrium.

Worlds 2 and 3 are probably among the most tested computer models ever developed. Not only have they been extensively tested by the modelers themselves, they have also been subjected to extensive testing by the models' critics, by sympathetic academics, and by students at various universities. There are two principal reasons why the World models have undergone so much testing: (1) They are highly visible and present a challenge to users who attempt to get the system to produce different outcomes, and (2) they are easily tested by anyone having access to the appropriate computer hardware. Their computer programs are published and are sufficiently short that they can be transferred without difficulty onto any system with a DYNAMO compiler. Once on the system, they are easy to test, for DYNAMO was written in a way that deliberately encourages testing.

People testing the models have come to differing conclusions about the way the models function. Forrester and members of the Meadows team are generally impressed by how robust the models' behaviors are. They find that the overshoot and collapse behavior persists in the face of many measures that seem certain to eradicate it. Strong measures to curb population and resource growth and extensive industrial growth are the only measures that they found effective in averting the famed collapse mode. On the other hand, after testing the model's sensitivity to parameter changes, a team of investigators from the Science Policy Research Institute at Sussex University concluded: "The model appears to be very sensitive to input parameters which have a wide margin of error and in fact it would appear that according to World 3, high rate of growth is just as likely as a catastrophic collapse." [12] For the most part, the Sussex group's parameter changes were based on the expectation that technological change would constantly extend global limits over time and that the main constraining factor would be the rate at which technology could progress. In particular, they found that flattening the cost curves (which relate costs of resource extraction and cost of agricultural development of new land to the respective fractions of these factors remaining undeveloped or unused) makes continued economic growth much less of a problem than it was shown to be in the Forrester and Meadows studies. The reader who would like to assess for himself the relative merits of these two arguments is referred to Chapter 9 of Models of Doom [13] and to Chapter 7 of Dynamics of Growth in a Finite World. [14]

Statements are sometimes made to the effect that The Limits to Growth has been disproven and that errors have been found in the World models. In fairness to the World modelers, it must be said that there probably isn't a social system model in existence that could not be disproven by critics who change the model's assumptions or attack its data base. Had the other models described in the following chapters been subjected to the extensive testing lavished on the World models, there is little question but that they, too, would have been "disproven" or found in error.

## Documentation

World 2 and World 3 are clearly and thoroughly documented. The equations on which they are based have all been published, and it is possible for anyone with access to a DYNAMO compiler to reproduce the results without difficulty. The equations have also been explained in two of the works cited below.[15] And, of course, the popular and readable *Limits to Growth* has reached an impressive number of readers—about 4 million copies having been printed to date, in over 20 languages.[16]

The fame achieved by Worlds 2 and 3 probably owes as much to the clear and provocative style of their documentation as to the attention-commanding descriptors applied to the documents themselves: "MIT Study" and "Report of the Club of Rome."

## REFERENCES

1. Aurelio Peccei, *The Human Quality*, Oxford: Pergamon, 1977, p. 2.
2. Ibid., p. 62.
3. Ibid., p.73.
4. Jay W. Forrester, *World Dynamics*, Cambridge, Mass.: Wright-Allen, 1971.
5. Donella H. and Dennis L. Meadows et al., *The Limits to Growth*, Washington: Potomac Associates, 1972
6. Peccei, p. 78.
7. Meadows et al., p. 185.
8. Nathaniel J. Mass and Richard H. Day, "Economics and System Dynamics," undated memo D–2426, circulated in the MIT System Dynamics Group.
9. Dennis L. Meadows et Al., *Dynamics of Growth in a Finite World*, Cambridge, Mass.: Wright-Allen, 1974; Forrester, *World Dynamics*.
10. Meadows et al., 1974, pp. 561–63.
11. Theodor H. Nelson, *Computer Lib*, Chicago: Hugo's Book Service, 1974.
12. H. S. D. Cole, ed., *Models of Doom*, New York: Universe, 1973, p. 130.
13. Ibid., Ch. 9.
14. Meadows et al., 1974, Ch. 7.
15. Forrester; Meadows et al., 1974.
16. Peccei.

# 26 Mesarovic-Pestel World Model

The World 2 and 3 models constructed by Jay Forrester and the Meadows group were prime targets for critics. They were highly publicized and documented in such a way that their assumptions were fairly clear, and it was obvious that their approach contradicted many established techniques of problem analysis, particularly those used by economists. But none of the features of the World 2 and 3 models that came under fire was so widely attacked as the fact that the modelers aggregated all nations of the globe into a single operative unit. This disturbed the modelers' sponsors as well as the critics. In the words of Aurelio Peccei and Alexander King, founders of the Club of Rome:

One of the deliberate limitations of the previous [Forrester and Meadows] research was its adoption of worldwide aggregations. This was a matter of choice, prompted by the objective of completing the project rapidly, providing at the same time an initial overall perspective of the trend and constraints inherent in the dynamics of the total system. We knew, of course, that the heterogeny of the world, with its innumerable cultural and environmental differences, varying levels of development and uneven distribution of natural resources, means the consequences of growth in different places is likewise heterogeneous. Thus the *average* curves and trends, as outlined in the first report, could not be adopted as a guide to detailed policy decisions in any particular country. We appreciated therefore the urgent need to follow up this initial global model with disaggregated studies that could lead to a deeper understanding of the wide range of world, regional and national prospects and to their being coupled with the practical business of politics. And, consequently, we supported the Mesarovic-Pestel Study which aims to do just this. [1]

The data base for Worlds 2 and 3 has also drawn severe criticism. Critics have used such adjectives as "unscientific" and "dubious" to describe the empirical base on which the models rest. Mihajlo Mesarovic and Eduard Pestel have made a deliberate attempt to gain approbation from the skeptical segment of the intellectual community and to disassociate their work from that of Forrester and Meadows. In introducing their models, Mesarovic and Pestel stress that their model is scientific and based on real numbers. [2]

Despite the modelers' attempts to set themselves apart from previous world-modeling efforts, the Mesarovic-Pestel world model was inspired by much the same set of motives as World 2 and World 3. Once again, there was an attempt to consider problems on a global scale, to make sense out of the bewildering interconnections of things that either are currently going wrong or might do so soon, and to seek means of directing the global system toward ends for the betterment of mankind.

Mihajlo Mesarovic and Eduard Pestel were both systems analysts. As original members of the Club of Rome, they watched the World 2 and 3 models develop and apparently concluded that they could improve on those models. They suggested as much, got support from the Club of Rome, and secured financial sponsorship from the Volkswagen Foundation, which also sponsored the World 3 project. Work on the Mesarovic-Pestel model (also known as the world integrated model, or WIM) was begun in Hannover, Germany, and later transferred to Case Western Reserve University in Cleveland, Ohio.

## Method

In system dynamics, there is unity between the modelers' world view and the mathematical constructs used to build the models. Forrester and Meadows see the world as a mechanism—not a clockwork mechanism, but a closed, state-determined system, full of nonlinearities, too complex for the human mind to follow. The Mesarovic-Pestel world model does not incorporate quite the same literal translation of world view into mathematical methodology. Instead, the modelers' world view—which they term "hierarchical systems theory"—determines their conceptualization of the world system, and mathematical and computer-science techniques are used eclectically to capture the essence of their conceptualization.

Both the modelers' world view and their mathematical methods are of interest, the former for its influence on the model's overall conceptualization, the latter because they determine what happens when the model is run through the computer.

### The World View

The modelers' world view is discussed at length—though not in a fashion that will convey a clear understanding of hierarchical systems theory—in the popularization of their work, *Mankind at the Turning Point*. Basically they envision the world as stratified into multiple planes, each of which operates with a degree of autonomy. These strata, as the modelers call them, are hierarchically arranged, as in Figure 26-1. At the top is the individual stratum; below it, in descending order, are the group, the demographic-economic, the technological, and the environmental (ecological and geophysical) strata. The documentation does not inform us how or why these strata are distinct, nor does it explain their ordering.

In practice the strata are not equally represented in the model. The demographic-economic stratum and the environment stratum (apparently a meld of the geophysical stratum and the ecolog-

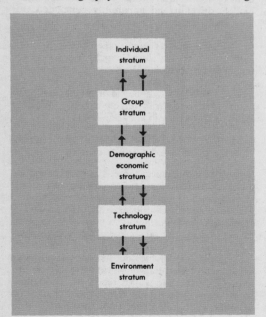

**Figure 26-1.** The five interrelated planes into which the world is stratified in the Mesarovic-Pestel world model.

ical stratum) have been represented in the most explicit terms and take up the bulk of the model's content. The modelers have attempted to allow for the group stratum—that is, political and institutional factors—by making the model interactive and turning over to the model user the function of estimating social group behavior. It is unclear how the technology stratum has been included, although technological influences are implicit in many places in the demographic-economic-model.

Here, a note on the question of "counterintuitive behavior" is in order. As mentioned in the methodological description of Worlds 2 and 3 in Chapter 25, Jay Forrester and most other system dynamicists propound the notion that complex systems are often internally structured in such a way that the human mind is incapable of correctly sensing how they behave. That is, complex systems—which in Forrester's world view means higher-order nonlinear systems—behave in counterintuitive ways. The hypothesized counterintuitive behavior of social systems is not a trivial or an esoteric point; on it rests the basic justification for system simulation modeling—the claim that computer simulation can pull us through the complex logical sequences that baffle or trick our intuitive perceptions.

Like Forrester, Mesarovic and Pestel see social systems as structured in ways beyond the ken of unaided human intuition. However, they offer a different explanation of how such systems exceed our powers of intuitive understanding. The problem, as they see it, arises out of the hierarchical construction of these systems. In normal times different hierarchical strata behave almost independently of one another. However, some conditions can cause the separate strata to become highly interactive. These conditions, the modelers tell us, are what we commonly call "crises"; in such crises the system can adopt modes of behavior so different from those of normal experience that they surpass our intuition.[3] Mesarovic and Pestel's message appears to be that the model they have produced can assist us in fathoming the behavior of both present and future crises.

If we try to place the Mesarovic-Pestel strata among familiar concepts, we find they follow system cleavages that others have followed before. The "environment stratum" seems to correspond to the natural "carrying capacity." The economic and demographic substrata, although combined in a single stratum, coincide with the human and machine populations that coexist in Worlds 2 and 3 in a blend of symbiosis and antipathy. And Mesarovic and Pestel have found the technological and group (social) strata as hard to specify as have other modelers.

Another world-view notion stressed by the modelers is that of organic versus undifferentiated growth. Organic growth they see as internally regulated, integrated, controlled, and sustainable. Undifferentiated growth they see as uncontrolled, unsustainable, and dangerous. Several times in *Mankind at the Turning Point*, they emphasize the desirability of moving toward an organic form of growth for the global system. To illustrate their point, they use as an example of organic growth the leveling off of the growth processes of an oak tree [4]—a disturbing analogy when one reflects that senescence and death are characteristic of all organisms and that a leveling off of organic growth is followed by decline and death. The analogy is not too important, however, since it is not at all clear how—or if—it influences the model structure or shapes its conceptual development.

### The Mathematical Methodology

Mathematically, as opposed to conceptually, the Mesarovic-Pestel model is somewhat like a system dynamics model in which state variables are replaced by matrices of state variables, and the necessary equipment is added to describe interaction between the elements into which the single variables have been disaggregated. (For instance, one can think of the model as having been regionalized through first building a single regional model structure and then replicating it 10 or 12 times, using parameter differences and perhaps computer subroutines to make the individual regional model conform to characteristics of the world's region.) Thereafter it was necessary to link the regions in a trade network. This required more thinking, more equations, and more data.

The same sort of disaggregation process that took place to develop regionalized representation has taken place in many other places in the model. Populations are broken into 85 separate age groups. Energy resources are categorized into five types. Where data permit, regional economics have been disaggregated by sector, each sector having its own capital stock. And so forth.

The net effect (in both senses of the word "net") is hard to follow. There are probably very few people in the world who understand the model well enough to look at an output and say that a given pattern of model behavior was caused by such and such a feature of the model's structure. And because the model's complexity seems to be growing rather than shrinking, the number of people who so understand this model will probably remain small. The model contains feedback loops, but the information streams that control these loops flow through multiple criss-crossing channels. Following these can become quite confusing. And yet if one cannot follow them, it is difficult to say whether model behavior is a faithful representation of world processes or a result of some fluke in the way the model was hooked up.

In short, the Mesarovic-Pestel model is a disaggregated dynamic feedback model. The structure is quite complex. Its complexity requires that one either put in weeks—or months—of effort to understand the structure or else accept it without question and trust that the modelers have faithfully represented the way the world works.

### Relevance

There is no question of the Mesarovic-Pestel model's basic relevance for studying long-term interactions, at least between population and resources. In many ways it seems to come closer than any existing model to the detailed, integrated, policy-oriented planning model that projects like the Global 2000 Study are seeking. It moves toward uniting the equivalents of the models used in making the projections presented in Part II of this volume. That is, it comes close to being GOL, SIMLINK, IEES, and a demographic model all rolled into one. It speaks to the trading between the grain-rich and the oil-rich, as well as to the starvation of those who have neither grain nor oil.

From the environmentalist's point of view, the model leaves much to be desired. It either excludes, or treats in a very superficial manner, forests, fisheries, and resources of soil, water, and air. It makes little attempt to trace the ecological destruction that can be expected as marginal land and mineral resources are brought in to use. It apparently does not even consider the increasing costs of their extraction and development. Thus, it fails to represent what might be called the world's growth pains.

Many of the things the modelers excluded could be put into the model, at least in principle, but not without making the model much larger, more complex, and less easy to understand. As it is, the model's size already poses enough problems that the modelers sometimes find it impractical to run the full system intact. Instead, they drive it in two segments, the one driving the other (hence no feedback) in some cases making off-line adjustments to compensate for the feedback linkages that are severed when running the model in pieces.

In fairness to the modelers, it should be noted that the problems created by complexity are inherent in putting dynamic feedback into a detailed model. Any modeler attempting to build a mathematical structure incorporating similar degrees of detail and interdependence of variables would find himself faced with the same problems in operating, comprehending, and explaining his model. It is to the modelers' credit that they are presently doing what they can to simplify the model's structure and make it more readily comprehensible to conventional analysts. Whether they will succeed remains to be seen.

The many ecological features that one might want to include would present great difficulties. They extend across ecosystems whose boundaries do not conform to the political-regional boundaries defined in the model. Problems peculiar to arid regions, rainforests, tundra, or cornbelts are beyond the model's powers because its regionalization scheme aggregates across major ecological zones. Similarly, problems like the firewood crisis of the Third World would be difficult to represent because the model makes no separate account of the social classes that glean their fuel from the natural environment.

Here again, the modelers cannot be blamed. The world in which they operate is not dominated by concepts of ecological or social class structure. Its data are aggregated in political categories, not by income groups or in ecologically meaningful units. The questions critics have most frequently asked the modelers have probably not been strongly oriented toward ecology or social equity. Under the circumstances one would have to be personally dedicated in an obstinate way to social equity or environmentalism to persist with representations that would speak to questions such as the fate of poor farmers, the firewood crisis, or destruction of agricultural lands through inadequate environmental management.

There are other environmental questions, however, that the model could be adapted to address. These include calculation of amounts of pollutants generated, land disturbance through mining, and effects of climatic change. Presumably, these questions would be incorporated into the model if an interested client were found to support the necessary work.

## Structure

Like World 2 and World 3, the Mesarovic-Pestel world model can be seen as a carrying capacity world model with populations of men and machines. However, World 2 and 3 included one population of men and one or two populations of machines. By contrast, the Mesarovic-Pestel model includes a dozen or so geographically differentiated human population groups (the exact number varies in different versions of the model), each divided into 85 age categories. It also includes about half a dozen categories of machines, two sources of agricultural capital, capital for producing fish, mineral extracting capital, and so on. Most of these are geographically differentiated and some are disaggregated again into usage categories. For example, in each region five varieties of energy capital are recognized and as many as 19 varieties of industrial capital.

Correspondingly, the model's carrying capacity is much more complex than that of World 2 or World 3. Its most binding resources appear to be oil (petroleum), the availability of oil substitutes, and agricultural land. The model allows for the market to make adjustments between use of one source of energy and another and to allow for transfer of energy and agricultural products between regions. Thus one region's carrying capacity can, if it had something to trade, be extended beyond the bounds imposed by its own resource base.

Though more complex, the carrying capacity constraints in the Mesarovic-Pestel model are less diverse than those in World 3, and probably less potent as well. Pollution, in the model, does not decrease agricultural productivity, intensive cultivation does not erode agricultural potential when unmatched by investment for land maintenance, energy seems to be more seriously constrained by the speed at which new reserves can be developed than by absolute scarcity, and shortages of natural resources other than energy cannot feed back into the economic sector in a way that alters growth patterns. Moreover, the man-machine symbiosis appears to be more strongly represented in the Mesarovic-Pestel model. Labor and machinery are figured as complementary inputs in economic production (i.e., as described below, a Cobb-Douglas production function is used). However, Mesarovic and Pestel have added one new way in which biological limits can constrain human-economic systems—one that becomes pernicious in less developed countries. High rates of starvation reduce the capital-output ratio. Where agricultural production is inadequate and there is little to trade, therefore, an increase in population will precipitate reduction of industrial output—to the detriment of investment and capital accumulation. Thus the model can be expected to be sensitive when it comes to striking a balance between population, industrialism, and agriculturalism (and some of the sensitivity may be a reflection of the real world situation).

Carrying capacity concepts, however, are not the terms in which the model has usually been viewed. More commonly, it is looked at through the economist's eyes. From that point of view, the model is a collection of regional models. Each represents economic production using a Cobb-Douglas production function.* The capital for use in the Cobb-Douglas function is generated endogenously through investment processes. The population that provides labor is also generated endogenously. Labor force participation is a function of population age structure. In the regions for which they could be produced, input-output tables have been used to allow a more detailed representation of economic production. This detail allows greater precision in estimating resource usage patterns. For example, the models are made more complete by breaking gross regional products into such groupings as more energy-intensive, more labor-inventive, less labor-intensive, etc.

Broadly put, agricultural investment in the model comes as a spin-off of economic growth—with the rate of investment regulated by the price of agricultural products. Investment in agriculture, through encouraging land development and fostering mechanized and fertilizer-intensive practices, increases agricultural output and food per capita. So in the long run, agricultural supply is a function of capital investment as constrained by land resources.

Demand for agricultural products is a function of income per capita. The balance between supply and demand for agricultural products determines price, which in turn can induce or discourage investment in agriculture.

Energy production and resource production, like economic output in general, are driven by accumulations of capital stock. Here again, investment is partially controlled by price—the higher the resource price, the greater the investment in resource capital. And again the price is determined by the forces of supply and demand. Demand for energy in resources is a function of economic output.

In both the agricultural and resource structures, capital accumulation and the dispersion of unused resource supplies eventually put the system up against natural constraints. In the agricultural system, investment eventually brings the system

to a state in which the results of further investment are subject to rapidly diminishing returns. This stifles further agricultural growth. In the energy and resource submodels, production uses up reserves. While reserves may be replenished by further resource discoveries, a time comes when there are no more undiscovered reserves to be developed. Actually, as formulated, undiscovered reserves will never be totally exhausted, for the model is structured in such a way that the resource discovery rate is proportional to the fraction of the original total of stock of reserves remaining undiscovered. Thus discoveries will approach zero as all of the undiscovered reserves come to be discovered.

Falling off of the discovery rate means that reserves are not replenished and supply shortfalls drive up price. Because the model accounts for substitution between fuel types governed by cross-price elasticities, when resource depletion causes escalation of energy prices, the price mechanism will cause the system to shift to the use of sources of energy other than the one that was depleted. Shortfalls in energy supply also curtail economic growth, so that in the event of an energy shortage, the capital ratio of the model goes up. Higher capital output ratios obviously reduce output.

Much of what has just been described is mitigated by international trade. In most cases, supply and demand shortfalls and excesses stimulate international trade. Goods will then flow from region to region, as constrained by trade-policy barriers and limitations of balances of payments. Adjustments are added as appropriate to compensate for the cost of transport and to allow for regional differences in price.

In addition to being viewed in carrying capacity terms and in economic terms, the model structure can be viewed as a computational sequence, as in Figure 26–2. The sequence might be expected, perhaps, to follow the hierarchical order. However, this does not seem to be the case.

## Conclusions

It is hard to summarize the conclusions to be drawn from the Mesarovic-Pestel world model. The modelers have reported their conclusions in many places, but the styles of reporting, if not the conclusions themselves, vary greatly, depending on the uses to which they are put.

In *Mankind at the Turning Point*, it's very difficult to tell which conclusions were built into the model and which were drawn from it. Many of the concepts stressed in that book appear to be

---

* In its standard form,

$$\text{Output} = \text{labor}^\alpha \times \text{capital}^{1-\alpha} \times \text{factor}^r.$$

$\alpha$, the time factor, and $r$ are statistically estimated constants. The time factor is often equated with technological advance.

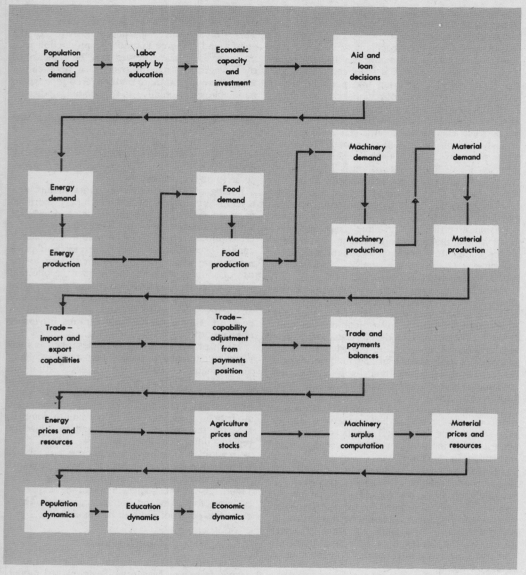

**Figure 26-2.** Computational sequence of the Mesarovic-Pestel world model.
*(Case Western Reserve University, Systems Research Center)*

a priori conclusions. For example, in the italicized* portion of the Prologue to the book, the authors conclude: "*It is this pattern of unbalanced and undifferentiated growth which is at the heart of the most urgent problem facing humanity—and a path which leads to its solution is that of organic growth.*"[5] . . . "*The analyses in this book extend over a period of 50 years. If, during this coming half century a viable world emerges,*

* The passages in italics here and in what follows were italicized in the original.

*an organic growth pattern will have been established for mankind to follow thereafter. If a viable system does not develop, projections for the decade thereafter may be academic."* [6]

Then in the Epilogue, they draw such conclusions as *"Underlying these limits 'crises' is a gap between man and nature which is widening at an alarming rate. To bridge that gap man has to develop a new attitude to nature based on harmonious relationships rather than conquests."* [7] The Epilogue continues:

Mankind cannot wait for a change to occur spontaneously and fortuitously. Rather, man must initiate on his own changes of necessary but tolerable magnitude in time to avert intolerable and massive and externally generated change. A strategy for such change can be evolved only in the spirit of truly global cooperation, shaped in free partnership by the world's diverse regional communities and guided by a rational master plan for long-term organic growth. All our computer simulations have shown quite clearly that this is the only sensible and feasible approach to avoid major regional and ultimate global catastrophe, and that the time that can be wasted before developing such a global world system is running out. *Clearly the only alternatives are division and conflict, hate and destruction.* [8]

Unfortunately, only a little of the computer output used to generate these conclusions is shown in the book, and that little is not identified in a manner that allows the reader to determine which sections of the model were involved in generating the output.

Elsewhere, the modelers are more prosaic and literal-minded in reporting conclusions about their model. In a document prepared for the U.S. Association of the Club of Rome Systems Research Center in June 1977, they report conclusions such as:

*Historical Scenario* [Fig. 26–3] indicates two disturbing eventualities in the world food situation: (a) severalfold increase in world food prices (in real terms) that would most certainly drive domestic food prices unbearably high. (b) A strong possibility of periods of food shortages in various regions of the world which would lead to starvation on a disastrous scale. [9]

*Scenario Two* isolationist [Fig. 26–4]: Domestic food prices could be kept down by restricting food exports. Consequences of such an *Isolationist Scenario* would be truly disastrous. Additional tens of millions could starve (under favorable but feasible conditions of food supply) because of failure of USA to produce or export food. [10]

The modelers have used the model to test a large number of policies, and the list of conclusions goes on and on. The model is versatile, and the conclusion list could be extended almost indefinitely, as long as the modelers were funded for research.

Like the conclusions extracted from *Mankind at the Turning Point*, those above are not supported by clear references to the model form used to generate them. The problem seems to be one of money and priority. Adequate specification would be an expensive and time-consuming process, and the number of people that would read the specifications would be very small.

Presumably the exact specifications used to produce all published model output are on file somewhere, so that it would be possible for a highly motivated person with appropriate status to examine them to see what has been assumed in the process of reaching the conclusions. And it is always possible to ask the modelers, personally, what was assumed. But neither arrangement permits the sort of active peer review necessary to guarantee quality in scientific work, much less to open it to public scrutiny.

The matter of making assumptions available for examination is politically as well as intellectually critical. There are a multitude of ways that a model like the Mesarovic-Pestel world model can, deliberately or accidentally, be rigged to produce an outcome. It isn't, for example, pointed out in the available documentation that the version of the model used in making runs for the U.S. Association for the Club of Rome assumed that raw materials for nucleur power were available in unlimited quantities, or that its use posed any significant problems. Yet these assumptions must have influenced the energy self-sufficiency, fast-nuclear scenario presented in Figure 26–5. It could lead to politically serious misconceptions if this run were interpreted without an understanding of the assumptions behind it. And it is entirely conceivable that a half dozen equally controversial assumptions exist, unidentified, in the model's computer program.

The modelers have also begun to put themselves in direct competition with other futurists by using their models to test scenarios and assumptions made by others. In a Systems Research Center paper of September 1977, prepared for the U.S. Association for the Club of Rome, the modelers reported testing scenarios from Herman Kahn's book, *The Next Two Hundred Years*. They found the Hudson Institute's conclusions full of errors. For example:

*It is impossible to design any energy program in Western Europe or Japan which could, over a*

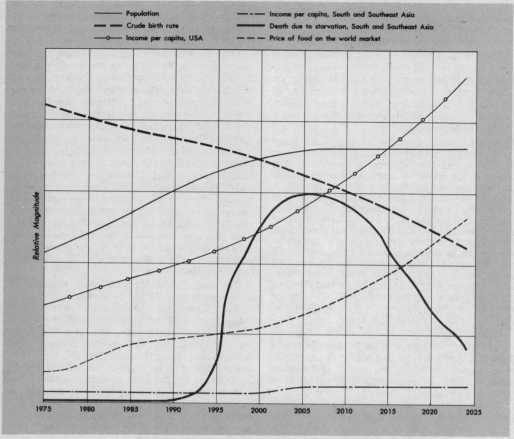

**Figure 26-3.** Historical-pattern no-change scenario, 1975–2020.
*(Case Western Reserve University, Systems Research Center)*

*ten-year period, reduce energy demand and in-crease production of energy from non-petroleum sources sufficiently to compensate for the loss of the Persian Gulf by 1987. The Hudson report statement regarding the ease of adjustment to a quick disappearance of oil reserves is therefore erroneous.*[11]

Scenarios of MIT's Workshop on Alternative Energy Strategies were similarly tested and documented in a Systems Research Center paper in November 1977.[12]

## Testing and Validation

That the Mesarovic-Pestel world model has been extensively used for policy testing has al-ready been made apparent. In addition to policy testing, the modelers state that their model has undergone appropriate historical validation. How-ever, the available model documentation presents little or no evidence of the model's validity. Neither statistical test results nor evidence of the model's ability to replicate historical patterns of behavior are presented in the ordinary documen-tation.

This is not to say that the model has not undergone validity testing. Gholamreza Mirzak-hani, a graduate student, working under Mesa-rovic at Case Western Reserve University, de-voted his M.S. thesis to historical validation of the economic and trade model.[13] Mean errors and standard deviations for percentages of forecast

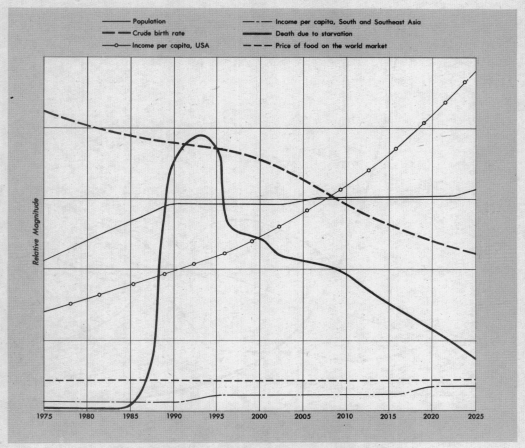

**Figure 26-4.** Isolationist Scenario, 1975–2020. *(Systems Research Center)*

error for model forecasts vs. historical data were calculated for key model parameters. A few fairly high (10–30 percent) rates of mean error were identified. The greatest difficulties seemed to arise in predicting investment imports, exports, and, in some regions, values-added in sectors 2 and 4 (unfortunately, not identified in the text). Aside from these troublesome areas, most mean errors were under 10 percent, and many were under 5. In graphical output of actual versus predicted, the two fit into each other, hand in glove, at some times, while at others the divergence was significant and the model seemed to show an entirely different sort of behavior than the historical trend (Figs. 26–6 and 26–7).

If there are subjects on which the model makes significant errors in replicating historical trends, it is important that these be shown. Otherwise intelligent criticism of the model is blocked. Displays of the model's empirical strengths and weaknesses have not been a priority item in the modeler's tight schedules and budgets. Thus the public is left to judge the model without display of its validity.

## Documentation

Documenting the Mesarovic-Pestel world model in a thorough fashion would be a Herculean, not to say an unrewarding, task. Much of the material that would be needed, such as descriptions of how the various parameters were constructed from the flimsy data sources available would be tedious, both to read and to write. The documen-

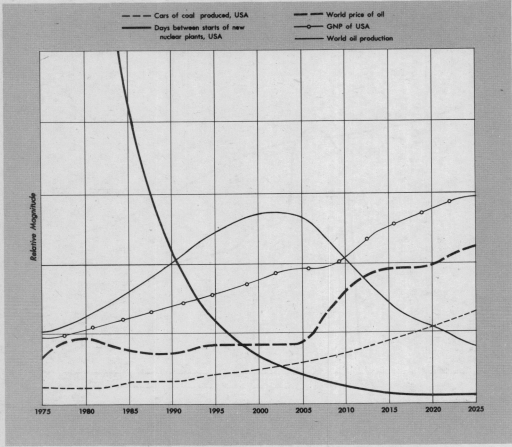

**Figure 26-5.** Energy self-sufficiency fast-nuclear scenario, 1975–2020. *(Systems Research Center)*

tation task is further complicated by the fact that the model has not attained a finalized form. Things written about the model today may be inaccurate tomorrow and outright misleading two years from now. Worse still, no one has been willing to pay the cost involved in careful, thorough, organized documentation.

Existing documentation includes numerous short papers, such as scenario analyses and model summaries, geared to presentation to specific audiences; a fairly complete, though somewhat out of date, description of model equations[14]; and manuals designed for various users at various times.

The Mesarovic-Pestel world model is hard to keep track of. It is not a single entity but an evolving stream of integrating concepts. As with most large models, neither the pressures nor the incentives exist to document this stream in a fashion to make it easy of access and understandable to anyone other than those involved in the model-building process.

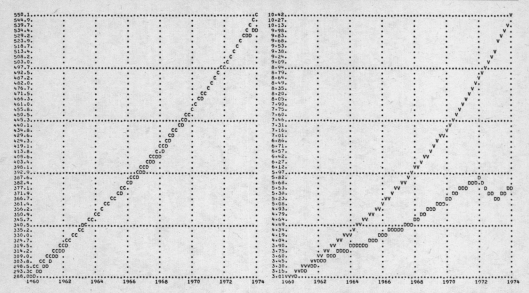

**Figure 26–6.** Actual (D's) vs. predicted (C's) consumption for Western Europe; one of the model's best predictions. (*G. Mirzakhani, Case Western Reserve University thesis*)

**Figure 26–7.** Actual (D's) vs. predicted (V's) value added in the Japanese extractive industries; one of the model's worst predictions. (*G. Mirzhakhani*)

## REFERENCES

1. Quoted in Mihajlo D. Mesarovic and Eduard Pestel, *Mankind at the Turning Point*. New York: Dutton, 1974, p. 202.
2. Ibid., pp. vii, viii, and x.
3. Ibid., p. 53.
4. Ibid., p. 8.
5. Ibid., p. 7.
6. Ibid., p. 17.
7. Ibid., p. 153.
8. Ibid., p. 156–57.
9. "A Computer Based Policy Analysis Tool (The API System) and Its Use for U.S. Policy Evaluation in a Global Context," Case Western Reserve University, Systems Research Center, June 3, 1977 (summary of demonstration at meeting of the U.S. Association for the Club of Rome).

10. Ibid., p. 29.
11. Barry B. Hughes and Mihajlo D. Mesarovic, "Testing the Hudson Institute Scenarios," Washington: U.S. Association for the Club of Rome, Sept. 1977 (mimeo), p. 22.
12. Barry B. Hughes and Patricia Strauch, "Scenario Analysis Using WIM System," Case Western Reserve University, Systems Research Center, Nov. 1977.
13. Gholamreza Mirzakhani, "Historical Validation of the World Economic and Trade Model," M.S. Thesis, Case Western Reserve University, June 1977.
14. Ram Dayal, "Equation-Specifications for the World Integrated Model (WIM)," Case Western Reserve University, Systems Research Center, Jan. 1977 (mimeo).

# 27 MOIRA: Model of International Relations in Agriculture

In 1972 Aurelio Peccei and the Club of Rome, upon the recommendation of Jan Tinbergen, commissioned a team headed by Hans Linnemann at the Free University of Amsterdam to conduct a study of the effect on the global food system of a doubling of world population. The resulting model applies mature analytic techniques to the age-old problem of the world's poor and the world's hungry. The modelers were motivated by the sentiment that human suffering is morally wrong and by a desire to minimize world hunger. Their forthcoming study, which incorporates the model, opens with a quote from Mahatma Gandhi:

*To the poor man God dare not appear except in the form of bread and the promise of work.*

Persons harboring such sentiments in the early 1970s could only have been distressed by the bleak outlook for the future. The bad harvests of '72 and '73 intensified the forebodings of famines emanating from the Club of Rome models and broadcast in such popular works as *Famine 1975* and *The Population Bomb*. The modelers observe in their study: "The historical record suggests that hunger and malnutrition have remained with us throughout the decades, affecting more and more people as time passes." The observation is followed by questions: Why is it so? Is it true that the world is dangerously close to the limits of its capacity to produce food? Or is it a problem of distribution? Are there ways open to the poorer nations to improve their food situation in a stable, self-sufficient way?[1]

These are the questions that are addressed by the Linnemann team's MOIRA (model of international relations in agriculture). In the modelers' words, "It attempts, firstly, to describe the world situation in terms of its underlying causal factors . . . [and secondly] to provide considered judgments regarding the policy measures that may redirect future developments toward improvements of the world food situation, with special emphasis on international policy measures."[2]

MOIRA was supported by the government of the Netherlands through the Dutch university

system. As of 1973, more copies of the Club of Rome's *Limits to Growth* had been sold in Dutch than in any other language,[3] and the sponsorship of the MOIRA project seems to have originated from the genuine interest of the Dutch people and government in the fate of the world and its people. The project, which started early in 1973, was not lavishly endowed. Funds and manpower were tight, and the work progressed slowly. The study was substantially completed by the end of 1976, but due to manpower problems was not scheduled to appear before 1978.

## Method

If all the computers in the world were to break down, MOIRA, of all the models reviewed in the Global 2000 Study, is probably the only one that would remain a useful analytic tool. The modelers themselves call it an algorithmic model. The fabric of the model is a series of interconnected, commonly nonlinear mathematical relationships, statistically estimated from such data as the modelers could find. Documentation of the modelers' work is interspersed with analytical approaches not found in other Global 2000 Study models, such as taking partial derivatives of nonlinear functions. Many of the functions used come straight out of economic theory. Standard graphical techniques used in economics, such as supply and demand curves and figures relating profit curves to cost curves are used freely to elucidate the text.

The computer is used in the model as a device to permit disaggregation and iteration of functional relationships that were postulated before the computer era. Instead of the one- or two-nation models developed in pre-computer economics, 106 nations or groups of nations are considered. Within each of these (except for the three centrally planned economies), 12 income-occupation classes are considered. Thus, when the classical relationship—consumption as a function of income—is modeled, instead of being used once, twice, or three times as it might be in a manual model, it is replicated more than 1,200 times. As the modelers put it, the model is also "disaggregated in time." It is solved by yearly increments, so that in a 50-year simulation, these 1,200 curves will expand into solutions of about 60,000 equations—obviously not a task to be undertaken manually.

In modeling, there seems to be a trade-off between amount of detail and degree of closure. Analysts who attempt to close highly detailed models and to forgo exogenous variables usually wind up in rather large messes. In this trade-off, the Linnemann group has opted for detail. They make it quite clear that their model is meant as a partial model—a model of the agricultural sector. Critical variables such as growth of nonagricultural gross domestic product, population growth, and the price of fertilizer are left as exogenous variables. The values input for those variables are critical factors in determining model behavior. Thus the model outcome can be looked at as an exploration of what the agricultural sector of the world might do in the event the world economy took this or that hypothetical turn. The modelers' discussion of methodology places a premium on detail. Its tone implies that they would have built a more detailed model were it not for the constraints placed on them by the lack of data. One senses, however, from the effort they have taken to overcome the data constraint in the case of income distribution, as contrasted to the ease with which they have aggregated all agricultural output into units of vegetable protein, despite the existence of voluminous fine-grained data on individual crops, that the modelers are much more discriminating in their use of disaggregation than the methodological description implies. The implicit message is: Disaggregate if it's important to your focal problem; if not, don't bother.

Some attempt at statistical verification seems to have been made for almost every equation in the model. In this process, cross-sectional data has consistently been used.

A strong attempt has been made to avoid extensive use of monetary units and to incorporate use of physical units wherever possible. Yield functions are based on analysis of photosynthetic relationships. Food consumption is measured in units of vegetable protein.

In sum, MOIRA is an attempt to link together all the pieces of the global agricultural scene, using old-fashioned tried and true methods. The modelers make no pretense of discovering anything counterintuitive or of developing a new methodology for looking at the world. Rather they have set for themselves the more humble (and

perhaps more realistic) goal of setting the books straight on the subject of global agriculture.

## Relevance

Taken at face value MOIRA appears irrelevant for purposes of the Global 2000 Study. Certainly it is not the ideal model of long-term relationships between population resources and environment. Population is exogenous; resources by and large are omitted; and the model says nothing directly about environment. Problems such as erosion, desertification, salinization, and pollution are completely excluded. But despite these omissions, the model is far from irrelevant. It is based on what appears to be the most careful analysis of global agriclutural carrying capacity ever to have been conducted. The modelers began their project by developing—from up-to-date 1974 UNESCO/FAO soil maps—a detailed estimate of how much biomass growth the nations of the world could support and of the capital costs that would be required to develop lands for cultivation. As may be recalled from the discussion of the World 2 and 3 models in Chapter 29, agricultural capacity and the cost at which it can be extended is critical in evaluation of probable world futures; the analyses on which previous studies had depended for their estimates were highly conjectural.[*]

The estimates of potential biomass production and land development costs produced by the MOIRA study are, admittedly, necessarily rough. For estimating potential biomass production, a formula for photosynthetic potential was used, with appropriate modifications to account for regional differences in soil quality, climate, availability of irrigation, and similar factors. The data for making such approximations is rough, not to mention scarce. Much of the earth's land surface has not been subjected to careful soil surveys. Numerous assumptions must be made in specifying how much land can be irrigated. The quantitative relationship between photosynthetic potential and potential to produce foodstuffs that human beings can consume can only be guessed at. Furthermore, as the modelers themselves state, "The ecological implications of such a massive expansion of agricultural production remain rather uncertain."[4] No attempt has been made to take into account the ecological problems associated with monocultures or the problems of maintaining

---

[*]A study of this type was conducted in conjunction with the GOL (grains, oilseeds, livestock) model described in Chapter 18. Similarities and differences between MOIRA and GOL are pointed out in the *Note* at the end of this chapter.

agricultural production in ecologically frail environments.

Nonetheless, the estimates produced are based on the best available data, using consistent techniques, and could be replicated and altered systematically if one disagreed with the assumptions on which they are based.

The model could also prove highly useful in that conclusions could be drawn from it by inference. A geographical biologist, operating from data the model generates on intensities of cultivation, could probably construct a fairly graphic image of where and when environmental problems such as desertification, erosion, and other symptoms of overexploitation of land resources, can be expected to break out.

## Structure

MOIRA, according to its modelers,

is a model of international relations in the field of food and agriculture which is developed as a linkage of national models. It describes the food sector of individual countries, and links these sectors by means of an equilibrium model of international trade in food. At the national level, two sectors are distinguished: agriculture and nonagriculture; the rate of development of the latter sector is (largely) exogenous. The conflict of interest between the agriculture and nonagriculture population is explicitly taken into account. The agricultural production decision is described for the agricultural sector [of a nation] as a whole; the food consumption decision is modeled for twelve income classes per country, six classes for each sector. Average food consumption per income class is compared with a country-specific food consumption norm, from which the extent of hunger and malnutrition follows. At the international level, the role of policies in developed countries receives special attention.[5]

The production function, which is repeated for each nation in the model, is based on the assumption that the agricultural sector as a whole will operate in a manner that maximizes its expected income. However, actual income may deviate from expected income through unanticipated changes in crop prices or abnormal weather.

Sectoral income maximization, of course, is a mathematically convenient assumption, for the calculus is quite effective in determining maxima. In real-world terms, however, income maximization is a strong and optimistic assumption. Implicitly it assumes that (1) producers have perfect knowledge of the situation—barring possible miscalculations about the weather and prices; (2) that

producers are free, willing, and able to act on the basis of their perfect information—that is, no institutional barriers cause farmers to fall into economically inopportune modes of behavior, and the agricultural sector does not feel the effective influence of social values in conflict with profit-maximizing tactics (e.g., preference for leisure over profit, taste and/or religious sanctions operating against the most profitable cropping pattern); and (3) that individuals will operate in a way that maximizes sectoral (not individual) profits, despite the fact that the two are frequently in conflict.

Putting aside the question of whether sectoral profit maximization is a realistic assumption, the next question is: How is sectoral optimum calculated? Maximum expected profits occur when the difference between production costs and income (price × output) is greatest. The costs tallied in the model are fertilizer costs and capital costs. Prices of both are exogenous in the model. The quantities used are determined via the optimization procedure and take into account a yield response function, to be described shortly. Labor and land are considered fixed means of production. Rents and agricultural wages, therefore, are not counted as costs but are considered part of farm sector income.

Expected income is the product of expected producer price and sectoral output minus production costs. Expected producer price is the average of the prices actually received over the last two years. Production costs are not assumed to decrease due to disembodied technical progress. Output is a nonlinear function of capital employed (CE), labor employed (LE), available land (A), and four coefficients—one (YASY) indicating the region's maximum photosynthetic potential and three ($\alpha$, $\beta$, $\gamma$) describing the shape of the curve by which it will approach that potential with the application of proper inputs.* Because labor and land are considered fixed inputs, capital is the only factor that the producers may vary in quest of maximum incomes. (Fertilizer usage is determined in the model as a dependent function of

---

*The equations used are:

$$Y = \frac{YASY\ Z}{YASY + Z}$$

$$Z = \alpha\left(\sqrt{\frac{CE}{A} + \beta} - \sqrt{\beta}\right) + \gamma\frac{LE}{A}$$

where Y = yields, Z = yield response factor, $\alpha$, $\beta$, and $\gamma$ are coefficients, A = land available, CE = capital employed, LE = labor employed, and YASY = maximum photosynthetic potential (national average).

yield; by varying capital, one automatically varies fertilizer usage.)

Coefficient values for the function have been statistically estimated, but the desired data was not always available and some rather sketchy proxies had to be used. For example, data on tractors had to be used to represent capital employed.[6]

Output, as determined by the producer's production function is further modified by weather. The modifications made are based on the assumption that future weather patterns are likely to resemble those of the past. The assumption is implemented by the use of exogenous data inputs that impose—on the production functions—variabilities in yield that replicate historically observed (mostly weather-induced) annual variations in yield.

In the usual fashion of market models, MOIRA, after calculating supply, balances it against demand. But the modelers are not so naive as to do this directly. They recognize that there is often a great difference between agricultural crop products—the output that their model calculates—and the real-world demand for food. For one thing, much of the vegetal output of many regions is used to feed livestock. For another, the amount of economic activity that food-processing sectors in developed economies put into food processing is comparable to the economic activity taking place on the farm. Thus, they model demand in two stages: demand for vegetal protein, and demand for processing. Both are functions of real income per capita. Since real income is a function of food and nonfood prices, demand (itself a function of real income) is partially a function of food prices. Food-processing demand functions have been estimated separately for agricultural and nonagricultural populations in 103 nations. Protein demands are modeled, in addition, for each of the six income groups in agricultural and nonagricultural populations, which leaves the model with over 1,000 food demand equations.

In the formulations used, consumption demand is static, processing demand is dynamic. Consumption, measured in units of vegetable protein, is determined by the real income at the time for which it is to be estimated. The extent to which food is processed is constrained by the speed at which food processing can grow. Thus, the amount of processing per unit of food consumed in one year is a function of the amount of processing per unit of food in the previous year, plus the amount of additional processing brought on by demand changes associated with changes in

incomes. Increases in the degree of processing along with the forces of supply and demand create changes in food price. Increases in food price feed back to lower real income and thus decrease food demand. Quadratic equations are used to relate consumption of food to income in all the functions described above.

Supply and demand for vegetal protein confront each other through the following model mechanism. The six agricultural income groups in each country remove from the total amount they have produced the amounts their incomes imply they should consume. The remaining product is placed on the market. National markets buffer themselves from the international markets by tariffs or price subsidies, which are determined in the model by a combination of a set of structural constants and variables indicating per capita income in the agricultural sector, the share of agriculture, and GDP. However, the buffering is incomplete, partly because imported food is priced at world prices and partly because the modelers have allowed for a "seepage" effect that tends to drive domestic prices toward world prices. The world market balances the sum of surplus production figures from all nations against the sum of unfilled demand figures. The balance determines world market price, which in turn influences domestic prices. All this has been accomplished through simultaneous equations. Thus, it cannot be said that one factor feeds back upon another, rather that all are simultaneously determined and interrelated.

Price information, in turn, becomes an input into the producer's production decision, which, in turn determines supply. This entails genuine dynamic feedback, as production decisions are made on the basis of the previous year's prices.

The product market is augmented by a labor-migration mechanism that responds to the difference between agricultural and nonagricultural incomes. In effect, this mechanism, in the way that it links the agricultural labor supply in one year to the agricultural labor supply in the next year completes a negative feedback loop. If agricultural labor becomes too scarce, it affects a decrease in agricultural production and thus an increase in crop prices. Increased prices will generate higher agricultural incomes, and these will tend to decrease the outflow of labor from agriculture and so tend to stabilize the agricultural labor force and keep agricultural incomes on par with other incomes. However, in the fashion in which the model is normally run—with exogenously introduced income growth of 4 percent in the developed world and 7 percent in the less developed nations—the loop would need to be very powerful to achieve the equilibrium it seeks. The loop is strongest when the return on labor inputs is quite high—i.e., in labor-scarce agricultural sectors. Therefore, it will come closest to achieving balance between agricultural and nonagricultural incomes and to stopping outflow of labor from the agricultural sector in less populated and less intensely farmed regions of the world.

The modelers' schematic of the main variables in their model is shown in Figure 27–1. Superimposed upon their diagram is this study's own sweeping generalization of the causal flows implicit in the structure.

What modes of operation does the structure fall into? When the model is run, demand is regularly pushed upward by population growth and by increases in income (both exogenously generated). Rising demand leads to rising prices, which stimulate added supply; however, due to the costs associated with added supply, supply increases more slowly than demand. Because the model takes income distribution into account, the rise in prices is reflected across a spread of people, some of whom can—and many who cannot—purchase food at the going market price. This situation results in many people "demanding" less food than they actually need. In more meaningful terms, high food prices relative to people's incomes, result in people going hungry. The model tallies up the total amount by which demands fall short of needs and thus arrives at an index of the magnitude of hunger in separate nations and in the world at large.

## Testing and Validation

Much of MOIRA is constructed around statistically estimated parameters. These are often presented in the text, along with parameters such as $R^2$ and $t$ statistics that give some indication of statistical validity, but they are scattered throughout the text—at least in the draft available for this Study—and not systematically set forth in any one place. Therefore, anyone attempting to assess the model as a whole for its statistical validity would find himself confronted with a painstaking task. In the case of estimates for maximum agricultural potential, which was calculated more or less deductively through theoretical models of photosynthetic potential rather than inductively through observed data, validation takes place through presentation of crop yield statistics from various regions showing that the yield calculated on a theoretical basis is reasonable on the basis of

observed facts. The following passage is representative: "Simpson (1967) reports a maximum yield of wheat in northwestern United States of 14.5 tons per hectare, for which we calculated 15 to 18 tons of grain equivalent."[7] In the draft reviewed for this Study, the model is not validated through comparison of model outputs to historical behavior. That is, there are no assurances of the model's ability to replicate historical behavior other than the fact that it has been calibrated for critical variables using 1965–72 time series data.

No information has been available on the total extent to which the model has been tested. In the available documentation, two sorts of testing are reported. First, there is testing of model sensitivity to assumed exogenous changes—specifically, to different rates of income growth in the nonagricultural population and varying rates of population growth, as well as alteration of income distribution.[8] Secondly, there is testing with a normative intent—specifically, looking for policy measures that would be appropriate to alleviating world hunger problems. Policies tested in these simulations include reductions of food consumption in the rich countries, food aid on a large scale, market stabilization, trade liberalization, and world food market price policies.

The modelers' presentation of these sensitivity and policy tests is admirably clearheaded on two points where many modelers go astray in interpreting their model results. First, precision is not confused with accuracy. Indeed, the modelers vehemently warn their readers:

In view of the imperfections of MOIRA as a model of the real world, the numerical results should not be taken too *literally*. The seemingly *hard* numbers and their variations over time may be interpreted only as indicating tendencies that will manifest themselves in the world food situation under specific assumptions—and the reader will notice that many *ad-hoc* assumptions had to be made.[9]

Second, verbal descriptions of model results show acute consciousness of the extent to which model behavior is a function of model structure. The common tendency of confusing the model with the real world is refreshingly absent. For example, in discussing why, in a particular simulation, high prices do not stimulate greater production increases in Latin America, the modelers give as their reason: "Under the assumptions of the standard run . . . the Latin American production growth rate comes close to the upper limit of production growth of four percent per annum built into MOIRA. This constraint . . . prevents addi-

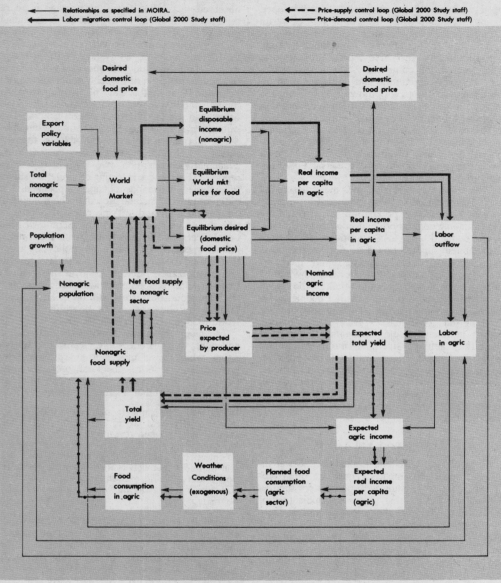

**Figure 27-1.** Channels of causal influence and major feedback controls in MOIRA. *(Hans Linnemann, MOIRA: A Model of International Relations in Agriculture, forthcoming)*

tional effects from further increases to production growth."[10]

In some cases, analytic mathematical techniques, have also been used to test model sensitivity. Specifically, partial derivatives of some of the model's functions have been taken in order to derive information on multiplier effects. This work is done sporadically throughout the chapters describing model structure and is not presented systematically in a fashion that allows the reader to make easy comparisons or draw systematic conclusions.

## Assumptions and Conclusions

When transposed onto the real world, MOIRA assumes that the world possesses the following attributes:

- Agriculture operates independently of the rest of the world except for the outside influences of nonagricultural GDP growth and population growth. In particular, debts, surpluses, and trade imbalances resulting from oil imports and exports do not influence agriculture; no ecological problems are encountered other than those already reflected in historical yield response statistics; and no radical shift in agricultural technology takes place.

- World prices for food are established on a competitive equilibrium basis. National prices are modified by tariff policy but also reflect the world market price.

- Food consumption is a function of price and income. Implicitly, if the poor get richer, they will repeat the pattern of increasing consumption of meat observed in the currently wealthy nations. Further, the rich will continue to prefer meat to vegetable protein.

- The schedule of technical relationships, i.e., the constant production parameters assumed by the modelers, is correct and will remain unchanged until the year 2010, or whichever year the model is run to.

- The agricultural sector as a whole operates in a way that maximizes expected sectoral profits.

MOIRA has been tested in two ways, resulting in two types of conclusions. Sensitivity tests lead to conclusions about the behavior of the agricultural sector under different patterns of nonagricultural income growth, population growth, and income distribution. Policy tests lead to conclusions about the ways in which various instruments of policy tend to influence agricultural prices and production and, more importantly, the alleviation of world hunger.

The standard run, to which all other runs are compared, assumes a "relatively high" rate of growth for nonagricultural GDP. This run shows somewhat more than a doubling of food production by the year 2000 and an increase in average food consumption per capita from 50 kg consumable protein in 1975 to 68 kg in 2000. However, as the modelers emphasize, these seemingly advantageous outcomes are coupled with a marked increase in the number of people suffering from hunger (defined as eating less than two-thirds of the biological requirement for protein). The number of hungry people in the world will have increased from 350 million in 1975 to 740 million in 2000 and to 1160 million in 2010. Likewise, over the 1975–2000 period the total food deficit, measured in protein required but not consumed, will have increased from 2.9 billion to 6.2 billion kilograms. The above trends are accompanied by a substantial increase in the role of North America as a food exporter and a decrease in agricultural self-sufficiency in most other regions.[11]

Sensitivity tests were conducted by alternately reducing the rates of nonagricultural GDP growth and population growth by half. Under slower nonagricultural income growth, the quantities of food demanded, and hence food prices, rose more slowly. Amid many other ramifications this scenario resulted, on the average, in 35 percent more hunger than did the standard run.[12] Halving population growth rates while holding GDP growth to its previously assumed rate resulted in substantially lower food prices than in the standard run, and hence to relative depression in the agricultural, as opposed to the nonagricultural, sector. However, it did reduce hunger. In this scenario, the average amount of hunger over the 1975–2010 period was around 30 percent lower than in the standard run.

Another sensitivity test was conducted by gradually reducing income inequality in the nonagricultural sector in such a way that income inequality was reduced by about half over the 1975–2010 period. This change greatly increased demand for food. Thus it increased prices, stimulated production in regions with significant reserve agricultural production capacity, and increased the need for food imports in regions such as South Asia where the costs of increasing production would be extremely high. In this scenario in the years after 1990 (by which time incomes had undergone considerable leveling), world hunger was reduced to less than half what it was in the standard run.[13]

In the policy tests, four basic policy measures were tried and evaluated for their success in alleviating world hunger.[14] These included two measures intended to achieve a redistribution of available food in the world:

- A reduction of food consumption by the rich countries;
- Food purchases by an international food aid organization (financed by the rich countries) that would distribute this food to the underfed population groups.

The other two measures were intended to stimulate food production in the less developed countries:

- Regulation of the world food market in order to stabilize international prices (the price target pursued on the world market was a policy variable whose influence had been tested);
- The effect that liberalization of international trade would have on developments in the world food situation.

Based on the findings of the individual policy tests, combinations of policy measures were devised to find the package that would best help the world food supply over the simulation period.

To make a long story short, it was found that both reduction of food consumption by the rich countries and liberalization of international trade would result in lowered food prices, decreases in incentives to agricultural production, and increases in total world hunger. On the other hand, it was found that food aid, at a level requiring about 0.5 percent of the rich nations' GNPs, could completely eliminate hunger, provided the food was purchased at prevailing market prices and then given away.[15] It was also concluded that maintaining high and stable agricultural market prices could stimulate production in the poor countries to an extent that would reduce, but not eliminate, world hunger. Logically, high food prices tended to reduce agricultural poverty but to increase hunger in nonagricultural sectors.

The policy package the modelers find most effective includes three policy elements—price stabilization, food aid, and price level policy. It is clear from the documentation that the modelers are sensitive to the fact that they are contradicting widely accepted notions by concluding that food aid will not depress agricultural prices but that trade liberalization will. They conclude a lengthy discussion of the operative effects of food aid with the following qualifying remarks:

As long as the rich countries are able and willing to provide the funds needed for buying food for aid purposes and provided that these transactions do not constitute a large part of the total world market transactions, there is little possibility of conflict between the objective of a stable and relatively high world market food price on one hand and international food aid (actually given to people under the food norm only) on the other.[16]

## Documentation

MOIRA has undergone two bouts of documentation. The first occurred during the preparation of a paper to be presented at a September 1975 symposium on the models sponsored jointly by the United Nations Environment Programme and the International Institute for Applied Systems Analysis.[17] Thereafter, documentation on MOIRA was expanded and revised and should appear in book form sometime in 1978. The MOIRA study has faced an additional problem: In order to be accessible to more than the relatively small number of people who read Dutch, it has had to be translated out of the language in which it was written.

The MOIRA manuscript made available to the Global 2000 Study is in various stages of preparation, ranging from first to third drafts. For the most part, it comprises factual reporting of the model's contents, assumptions, and outputs. Attempts to interpret, dramatize, or construct a MOIRA philosophy are relegated to the Introduction in the manuscript but may eventually be incorporated into the final chapter. The bulk of the work is oriented toward the specialist. Nevertheless, it includes considerable elementary economic theory with which most readers will already be familiar.

Although the text provides a good basic understanding of the model's operation, it is far from adequate for the purpose of reconstructing the model and testing its output. For that, one would presumably have to secure computer programs from the modelers, and it is uncertain whether the programs so obtained would be documented in such a way as to make them usable to anyone other than their creators. At least in manuscript form, the model documentation is not well arranged for users' convenience. For example, there is no complete listing of equations and variable definitions, and the reader must leaf back through pages of text to find the definitions for variables whose meanings he has forgotten.

*Note*: MOIRA bears a strong structural resemblance to the GOL (grains, oilseed, livestock) model described in Chapter 19. The most significant difference between the two models is in what they have disaggregated. GOL has disaggregated crops, whereas MOIRA has measured all agricultural output in terms of vegetal proteins. MOIRA has disaggregated consumers into 12 income groups, whereas GOL aggregates all consumers into a single income class. In effect, MOIRA is more concerned with human welfare, and GOL with the specifics of agricultural trade. MOIRA also differs from GOL in that it considers more geographical units—106 to be exact.

Aside from these differences, the two models are alike in that both are world models disaggregated into multiple geographical regions. Both are agricultural sector models. Both began from estimates of maximum production potential for the geographical units they encompassed. Both lean heavily on traditional economic theories for their formulations, and both see the world as being controlled through market supplies, demands, and prices. Likewise, both consider nonagricultural income growth and population growth as exogenous variables.

## REFERENCES

1. Hans Linnemann, *MOIRA: A Model of International Relations in Agriculture,* forthcoming (probably Amsterdam: North Holland Publishing Co.), Ch. 1, pp. 2, 3. (Chapter and page references are to the drafts supplied to the Global 2000 Study by the Food for a Doubling World Population Project, Institute for Economic and Social Research, Free University, Amsterdam.)
2. Ibid., Ch. 1, p. 3.
3. Potomac Associates, Inc., Memorandum, June 20, 1973. Subject: Foreign editions of *The Limits to Growth.*
4. Linnemann, Ch. 1, p. 9.
5. Ibid., Ch. 1, p. 4.
6. Ibid., Ch. 4.
7. Ibid., Ch. 2, p. 51.
8. Ibid., Ch. 10.
9. Ibid., Ch. 10, p. 10.
10. Ibid., Ch. 10, p. 9.
11. Ibid., Ch. 1, appendix, p. 10a, run 111.
12. Ibid., Ch. 10, p. 4.
13. Ibid., Ch. 10, p. 10.
14. Ibid., Ch. 11, p. 5.
15. Ibid., Ch. 11, p. 8.
16. Ibid., Ch. 11, p. 21.
17. Gerhart Bruckmann, ed., "MOIRA: Food and Agriculture Model," *Proceedings,* Third IIASA Symposium on Global Modelling, Sept. 22–25, 1975, International Institute for Applied Systems Analysis, Laxenburg, Austria, Feb. 1977.

# 28 The Latin American World Model

One of the most perturbing questions that came out of the work of Donella and Dennis Meadows and Jay W. Forrester was this: "What will happen to the poor people and the poor nations of the globe if natural constraints put the brakes on economic growth?" The Meadows group was clearly troubled by this problem. In the final chapter of *The Limits to Growth,* they say that equilibrium may not be so bad for the poor. "It is possible in the steady state economy that new freedoms might also arise—universal and unlimited education, leisure for creativity and inventiveness, and, most important of all, the freedom from hunger and poverty enjoyed by such a small fraction of the world's people today."[1] The Mesarovic-Pestel world model leaves less hope for the poor. In it, rich and poor nations are grouped separately. Using this representation and the model's structural assumptions, there appears to be no realistic means of preventing massive starvation in South Asia.

The Latin American world model had its origin in the refusal of many third world persons to accept scenarios that suggest that the very growth they hoped might save them from their poverty is about to be curbed by natural limits. Basically, the model says that Forrester, Meadows, and Mesarovic-Pestel were asking the wrong questions. The focal questions in the eyes of the persons who created the Latin American world model is not "What will happen when the structures in place in the world have advanced in time by 20 or 100 years?" but rather "How can the resources of the world be used most effectively to improve the lots of all people?"

The model assumes that a well-run, ideal, human-oriented society will be wise enough in its management of resources not to be constrained by natural limits. In the modelers' views, the ecological and resource problems that the world presently faces are not inherent in the process of fulfilling the needs of a growing population but are the result of western materialism. In the modelers' words:

The major problems facing society are not physical but sociopolitical. These problems are based on the uneven distribution of power, both between nations and within nations. The result is oppression and alienation, largely founded on exploitation. The deterioration of the physical environment is not the inevitable consequence of human progress, but the result of social organization based largely on destructive values.[2]

The origin of the Latin American world model is described in the Preface to the documentation of that work:

The idea of building this model emerged at a meeting sponsored by the Club of Rome and the Instituto Universitario de Pesquisas de Rio de Janeiro in Rio de Janeiro in 1970. The meeting had been held to analyze and discuss "Model World III," which had been built by a group directed by Dennis L. Meadows at the Massachusetts Institute of Technology. Out of that meeting came the decision by the Latin Americans present to commit the Fundación Bariloche in Argentina to building a model based on the points of view expressed during the debate.

A committee composed of Carlos A. Mallmann, Jorge Sábato, Enrique Oteiza, Amílcar O. Herrera, Helio Jaguaribe, and Osvaldo Sunkel was established to outline the general aims of the project and to effect its implementation. The first four members of the committee then produced a document stating the hypotheses and variables to be used in the model by the end of 1971. At a later meeting attended by all committee members and some specialists, the general features of the model to be built were established.

Thus, the type of society—egalitarian, fully participatory, nonconsuming—, the concept of basic needs and its central role in the model, the use of a production function with substitution between capital and labour, the criteria with which the problems of natural resources, energy, and pollution would be treated, and the division of the world into regions, were defined.[3]

## Method

In modeling, it is desirable that the methods match the purpose. It is appropriate that the Latin American world model, which attempts to chart an effective route by which to work for fulfillment of basic human needs, should use different methods than its predecessors, which were investigations of a behavioral tendencies inherent in the current world order. The Latin American model uses optimal control techniques, that is, it is a mathematical device that seeks the "best" way of advancing toward a goal—in this case the extension of life expectancy.

Conceptually, optimization is a simple methodology. In the Latin American world model, it is quite complex. The mathematics that the modelers have used to describe the world's operating mechanisms render the task of locating the optimum solution next to impossible. The normal mode of solving an optimization problem involves setting up analytic equations for a surface map of possible solutions and using a computer to trace the slopes and ridges of this map to find its highest or lowest point. However, the modelers have formulated their representation of the world in a way that is neither differentiable nor even expressible in analytic terms. They have conceived of a surface on which one cannot always find slopes. Moreover, the surface, which contains within its specifications a linear optimization routine, cannot be mapped using a set of analytic equations.

Indeed, the modelers have come dangerously close to defining a problem that they themselves cannot solve. In order to calculate a solution the modelers have had to reformulate the problem in different terms, and there is reason to believe that their redefinition of the problem altered its solution. Even after making simplifications, the modelers found it necessary to use sophisticated and esoteric mathematical techniques to work the calculations.

Optimal control techniques have been used to parameterize the model as well as to solve it. Instead of using regression techniques, such as ordinary least squares, the modelers postulated a set of functional relationships between several variables, plugged into the scattered data available to them (for example, data from 1960 and 1970 censuses), and devised an optimization routine to find the set of parameter values that would establish the closest fit when the included variables were estimated simultaneously. This technique has the advantage over standard econometric techniques of requiring less data and is not so susceptible to incorrect estimations due to inaccurate data. It also avoids some of the statistical difficulties encountered in estimating relationships of highly interrelated systems of variables by examining one functional relationship at a time.

On the other hand, the technique has a disadvantage: If the functional relationship postulated in making the estimation is incorrect, the method may lead one astray. For example, if a Cobb Douglass production function is assumed, the method may give reasonable estimates for the labor, capital, and technological coefficients from only a few data points—assuming the system possesses the sort of substitutability and the complementarity of labor and capital assumed by a Cobb Douglass function. Or, if fertility and life expectancy are hypothesized to be an interrelated function of several economic and social indicators, the method can estimate parameters that will establish excellent statistical fits through whatever data points are available for the hypothesized indicators. However, if real world demographic change does not follow the hypothetical rules used for making the estimation, this procedure will not generate reliable forecasts.

In summary, the Latin American group has used optimal control technique as its leading methodology. They have used optimization both in seeking a normative optimal solution and in seeking to optimize the statistical fittings of their parameters. The technique is well suited to the problem. Optimization is appropriate to a normative model, and optimal fitting techniques are appropriate to the sparse data situations that are frequently encountered in dealing with Third World problems. These advantages are not without cost. The mathematics involved are fairly esoteric. It would require at least a couple of courses of graduate-level mathematics to understand completely the model's mathematical routine. At a minimum, understanding requires a bit of control theory and some topology. The technical side of the model may well escape criticism for the reason that critics cannot comprehend the mathematics used in the model.

## Relevance

The most important way in which the Latin American world model is relevant to the question of population, resources, and environment is the spirit in which it was conceived, namely, that the world should seek to manage its resources and environment in a way that will fulfill the basic needs of all its people and that the model should be directed toward achieving that end.

Whereas the other models considered in this study all ask the question "Whither are the mechanisms of the world economy carrying us?" the Latin American world model asks the more positive question "What is the most effective way of getting where we want to go?" Instead of examining the forces that seem most likely to bring about massive economic deprivation and starvation, the Latin American world model explores procedures that would optimize the well-being of the world's poor.

The model is also of interest because it sets forth and parameterizes an explicit and fairly detailed hypothesis on the forces that govern fertility, mortality, and life expectancy. The postulation of this hypothesis is important because the absence of a dependable theory of demographic change is one of the major bottlenecks to accurate forecasts of population, resources, and environment. If the Latin American group's hypothesis holds, it will mark a great advance in global modeling—but unfortunately, the only apparent way of testing the hypothesis will be to follow global demographic variables for another decade or two to see if the model's behavior is reproduced.

Aside from the spirit in which the Latin American world model was constructed and the theory behind its demographic sector, the model is almost the antithesis of what the Global 2000 Study is seeking. Rather than dealing with the problems of resources and environment, the modelers began with an assumption of no problems—particularly no serious resource problems. Their analysis much resembles that presented by Herman Kahn in *The Next 200 Years*.

Some elementary physical constraints have been introduced into the agricultural sector. Land development costs approach a limiting value as all of the arable land becomes cultivated.* Yield response to agricultural inputs levels off at a given maximum output level. Otherwise potential physical problems are excluded or played down. The costs of erosion control and soil maintenance are included in the costing functions for the agricultural sector, but since their payment is automatic, the model excludes any possibility of soil loss or deterioration. Energy resources, minerals, pollution, ecological destabilization, deforestation, desertification, and other biological or physical resource problems in the present world situation are not considered in the model's formulation.

This exclusion is unfortunate. It would be quite desirable if a model concerned with the normative, human needs like the Latin American world model were combined with a realistic representation of some of today's critical and pressing resource and environmental problems.

*There is some question on this point. The conventions used for mathematical operators in the model documentation are not defined in the text, and the land development cost equations are therefore not clearly defined.

## Structure

The general structural features of the Latin American world model have been introduced indirectly in the preceding text. The model's basic construct is an optimization problem in which life expectancy at birth is optimized. The control variables, whose allocations are altered in finding the formula that maximizes life expectancy, are labor and capital. These two inputs are divided between five economic production sectors, each of which directly or indirectly influences the life expectancy. Three of the sectors are associated with basic human needs: food, housing, and education. The remaining two are capital goods, which are required for economic growth, and other goods and services, which have only minor and indirect effects on the system's behavior. Production, consumption, and demographic functions are considered separately for four regions: the industrialized countries, Latin America, Africa, and Asia.

The basic production function used for all sectors and in all regions is the Cobb Douglass production function, written in a fashion that assumes automatic growth through technological progress. On a sector by sector basis, the assumed annual rates of technology-induced growth are as follows: capital goods, 1.5 percent; food, 1 percent; housing, 1 percent; education, 0.5 percent; other goods and services, 1 percent.

Because the controls in the model are used to maximize life expectancy at birth, the mechanisms by which capital and labor allocations impact upon life expectancy (in other words, the mechanisms of the demographic sector) are critical to the way the model behaves.

The web of causal influences assumed in the model's demographic structure is shown in Figure 28–1. This seemingly complex formulation represents one straightforward hypothesis. In the modelers' words: "The only truly adequate way of controlling population growth is by improving basic living conditions."[4]

The way that this hypothesis works itself into the model's structure can be seen in the figure by examining the variables that affect birth rates and life expectancy. Pronounced among these are levels of basic needs satisfaction—food, housing, and education. Increases in any of these variables will increase life expectancy and/or decrease birth rates. Factors relating to employment conditions have also been taken into consideration. The higher the percentage of the population in agriculture, the lower the life expectancy; the more

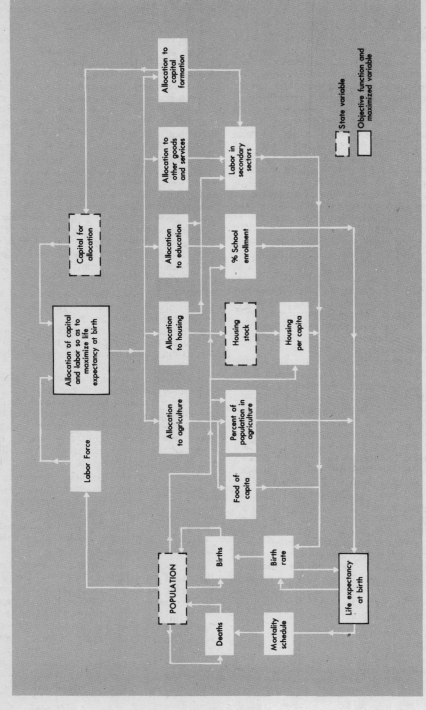

**Figure 28-1.** The demographic sector and objective function of the Latin American world model.

labor in secondary sectors, the greater life expectancy at birth.

These flows of influence are compounded in that increases in birth rate lead to increases in life expectancy; and increases in life expectancy decrease the birth rate. Furthermore, decreases in the birth rate (through slowing population growth) eventually lead to increases in per capita availability of the output of the basic need sectors. Thus, they lead to further decreases of birth rates in stabilization of population with higher life expectancy.

In sum, investment in any of the basic need sectors and shifts toward industrialized production leads to higher life expectancy with lower birth rates. The mathematical problem of the model is calculation of the distribution of resources among the sectors that works most effectively toward that end. However, direct allocations to fulfill needs are not the only variables in the equation. There is also the need and the possibility of allocating labor and capital to the capital goods sector, where they will increase the capital available for production in all sectors. Thus capital, too, competes for resources in the model's allocation decision.

Clearly, the manner in which the model allocates resources will be greatly influenced by the shapes and slopes of the curves relating life expectancy to each of the variables influencing it. For example, if all were linear functions, it would always be most effective to allocate resources to the variable whose effect on life expectancy had the steepest slope. But this approach would be ridiculous, for it would allow life expectancy to be extended indefinitely so long as there were more resources to be invested. The system of equations that the models have used[5] is shown below:

$$LE = -0.052492531\ E^{2.5693255} + 0.054749165\ E^{2.5607114} - 0.006852093\ B^{1.8622645} - 0.096324172\ AG^{1.1816027} + 55.153412.$$

$$B = -0.39895642.10^{-12}\ TK^{3.725411} - 0.16189216\ PS^{1.251819} - 0.17435076\ E^{0.838319} + 366.18269\ LE^{-0.695212} - 0.62262631\ HR^{0.981753} + 29.0057.$$

where

$LE$ = Life expectancy at birth

$E$ = Enrollment, defined as 100 × (Matriculated children 6–18 years old)/ (Total population 6–18 years old).

$B$ = Birth rate defined as number of live births per 1,000 inhabitants

$AG$ = Percentage of the labor force in agriculture

$TK$ = Total caloric intake per person per day

$PS$ = Percentage of the labor force in the secondary sector

$HR$ = Housing rate defined as 100 × (Number of houses)/(Total population).

The notable thing about the above equation set is its use of exponentials, which provides that each factor's contribution of life expectancy or birth rates will be subject to diminishing returns. This creates a condition where the efficacies of different allocation patterns will shift in rather complex fashion as the model works through simulated time, as well as making it impossible, under the most ideal conditions, for life expectancy to extend much beyond 70 years.

The operations of the allocation procedure are somewhat more complicated. In many places the model is constrained so as to permit only so much increase in output of a sector in a given time period. The constraint situation is further complicated by the fact that the program allows the model to violate some of its constraint in the process of finding optimal solutions.

In the course of simulated time, resource allocation will shift back and forth between sectors as one or another sector shows higher returns per unit of labor or capital added to its production processes. The model's parameterization will determine the relative importance of labor and capital to its five economic sectors as well as to the situations in which each sector becomes a priority area for allocation of labor and capital. The modelers state that "the results of the runnings of the Model show that education is one of the most important factors on demographic evolution and particularly on life expectancy."[6] From this, we infer that the estimated model parameterization has given great weight to education as a factor influencing life expectancy.

Though the education sector may be the most important sector of the model in terms of its operation, the food and agriculture sector is generally considered more important by observers. It is by far the model's most complicated sector. It contains three subsectors: agriculture, livestock, and fisheries. Of these, agriculture is the most important and the most complex, containing within itself an optimization routine that allocates resources available to agriculture between land development and production of agricultural input. It also contains mechanisms to account for the process of new land brought into cultivation through investments in land development. The land development mechanisms include what amounts to an assumption of diminishing return to investment as more land is brought into cultivation. The cost of land development is an S shaped curve between $1,200 and $6,000 per hectare as the fraction of arable land under cultivation ranges from zero to one.*

The alternative use for agricultural capital, however, is also subject to diminishing returns. Additional funds spent on agricultural input lead to increasing input per hectare, but incremental yield responses, after increasing exponentially, turn to zero past a given level. Beyond that level, further investment in agricultural inputs will be nonoptimal, and the incentive to invest further will be nil. As both land development and investment in agricultural input are subject to diminishing returns, there will be states in the model's behavior where agricultural investment yields no significant returns. When this happens, the optimizing mechanism will find it profitable to put its money elsewhere—in the livestock or fishery sector, or away from the food sector entirely.

Two optimistic assumptions are included in the formulations of the agricultural sector. First, the model assumes that the cost of fertilizer will remain constant over the optimization period. Second, it assumes that food processing losses in the developing regions will automatically decrease every year through the optimization procedure until they reach the rates found in developed regions.

The fisheries and livestock subsectors are relatively simple. Both allow for investment in production to increase yields up to a maximum carrying capacity figure. The livestock sector also allows for some of the inedible waste portions of the agriculture sector to be used for livestock fodder. It also allows for excess agricultural products to be used as feed for livestock after the dietary needs of the human population have been met. Food wastes and foods are then transformed into measures of meat consumption, using a biological conversion efficiency ratio.

Note, in passing, that the maximum potential fish catch used in the model, one taken from FAO (Food and Agriculture Organization) data, is considerably higher than the maximum catch figure presented in Chapter 7 (120 million metric tons per year, as opposed to 60 million). It is also of interest that the model does not account for problems that might arise from overgrazing.

The housing and education sectors are straightforward and similar. The costs of new housing and education both begin to rise when basic needs

*This seems to be what the documentation means, but it is difficult to see how it works. If the S curve is used and costs do level at $6,000 per hectare, it would seem to be possible in the model for more than 100 percent of the total arable land to be brought into cultivation.

are fulfilled. The building of new houses is defined in the model as urbanization. Education is defined as providing schooling to the 6–18 age group. Higher education is not included in the education sector but is assumed under the category of other goods and services.

The structure of the capital sector and the sector producing other goods and services is not discussed in the documentation. It is, however, stated in the documentation of model output that, in the standard run, the percentage of GNP allocated to other goods and services is constrained so that it cannot fall below 45 percent of total production or increase with respect to the 1970 level until basic needs have been satisfied.[7] In the same text passage, it is stated that the maximum rate of investment, i.e., allocation to the capital sector, is fixed at 25 percent. These constraints would seem to have been imposed to prevent the model from allocating all funds away from other goods and services (which contribute very little in the model to increasing life expectancy) and to prevent the model from allocating unrealistically large sums of investment in capital (which drive economic growth through the Cobb Douglass production function). For want of other information, one assumes that the model uses a standard Cobb Douglass production function in the capital sector and the sector producing other goods and services.

The model also includes a simplistic international trade sector. The modelers' fundamental assumptions used for international trade in the model are as follows:

(a) As the data for 1960 are not complete, it is assumed that the global level of trade of each block for that year is proportional to its total GNP, taking 1970 as the base year. The volume of trade for each sector in 1960, as well as for the years after 1970, is assumed to be proportional to its contribution to the total GNP, taking also 1970 as the base year.

(b) The disequilibrium in the balance of payments of the regions is gradually reduced, until equilibrium is reached in 20 years from the time of implementation of the policies proposed (1980).

Although, as already stated, the model is an optimization model, in practice it has two modes of operation. Over the historical period, the modelers use it as a simulation model, running it at the outset of a run without use of the optimization routine and substituting the assumption of conformance to of observed trends for the assumption of optimalizing behavior over the first 20 or so years of the model run. This is done essentially as a check on model accuracy.

Briefly, the model's most important structural features from the prospective of population resources and environment are: (1) The model envisions a society that allocates its capital and labor in such a way as to maximize life expectancy; (2) life expectancy is a function of satisfaction of basic needs and various other social indicators; (3) economic output is a function of complementary inputs of labor and capital and of (exponentially increasing) growth induced by technological advance by sector; and (4) agricultural yield and investments in land development are subject to diminishing returns.

Other resources are assumed available in unlimited quantities and at constant cost: (5) Forms of environmental maintenance such as forest management, soil conservation, and pollution abatement, are automatic and not subject to mismanagement (soil maintenance has an attached cost; other forms of environmental maintenance are implicitly free); (6) technological improvements contribute, at no cost, to economic production at a rate of 0.5–1.5 percent growth per year, with the magnitude of the contribution varying with the economic sector; and (7) within an economic region, income is divided with complete equality.

## Testing

How does one test the validity of a normative model? One can conceptually test it by observing the assumptions implicit in its structure and passing judgment on those assumptions. One can also perform a sort of experiential testing by running the model under varied assumptions to see if it behaves reasonably.

To some extent, the modelers have circumvented testing difficulties by creating a model that can run both in a normative, optimizing mode and in a mode that supposedly simulates past system behavior. They routinely run the model from 1960 to 1980 using the history-simulating mode before they perform the optimization run. As the model has been calibrated using 1960–70 data, it would be seriously amiss if it failed to reproduce observed behavior over that time period, so the 1960–70 run does not constitute a meaningful test. The 1960–70 simulation seems to be mainly a safety check to establish that nothing in the model has gotten into disorder through accidental changes of the computer program or through other mishaps that bedevil computer modelers. On the other hand, the 1970–78 phases of historical simulation, being outside the calibration period, do constitute a meaningful test of the model's ability to operate accurately in the historical simulation mode.

Since the basic operational structure of the model is altered as the model shifts from historical simulation to optimization mode, it is not totally clear how the model's ability to predict in simulation mode attests to the validity of its findings when operating in optimization mode.

The model is run from 1960 to 2060 in most of the runs. Even if the same mode of model operation were to be applied throughout this period, it is not clear how well an ability to predict 8 years in the future can serve as a basis for judgment of ability to predict 90 years in the future, especially when the model does not consider energy problems and limitations, ecological viability, or other problems encountered in maintaining economic growth within our fixed natural resource space.

Though there are difficult questions as to how to validate a normative model, there is no difficulty about its use for policy testing. The Latin American world model has been so used for at least four tests. Three of the tests shown in the available documentation include (1) a standard run, (2) a technological stagnation run (in which the technological growth, instead of increasing economic production by a steady 0.5, 1.0, or 1.5 percent per year,* diminishes to zero between the years 1980 and 2000—and stays at zero thereafter), and (3) a run in which industrialized countries transfer capital (aid) to Asia and Africa beginning at a rate of 0.2 percent of GNP in 1980 and increasing thereafter at a rate of 0.2 percent per year until a rate of capital transfer of 2 percent of GNP is achieved. The model has also been restructured in order to make one additional policy test (4) namely, the effect of income distribution on economic growth. In this reformulation, the model was run separately for 15 regions, each of which had its population disaggregated into six income groups. In these runs, basic needs were assumed to have been satisfied when the income level of the poorest group reached the level that would allow satisfaction of basic needs. The parameter used as an indicator of the satisfaction of basic needs is the GNP per capita at which basic needs were met in the standard run.[8] Findings from these four policy tests will be described below.

---

*Different rates apply for different sectors.

## Conclusions

The standard run of the model for the industrialized countries is shown in Figure 28–2. Runs for Latin America closely resemble those of African countries. The findings in these simulations correspond to surprise-free projections similar to those given in Herman Kahn's *The Next 200 Years*. GNP growth is steady, basic material wellbeing rises to a level at which all basic needs are satisfied, and the economy steadily moves toward producing more economic frills (other goods and services). Once basic needs are satisfied, population growth rates begin to stabilize, leaving more of everything for everyone. The only thing in these runs that does not look like something that Kahn's Hudson Institute might have forecast is

the very high rate of investment needed in Latin America and Africa to maintain the rates of growth shown. Both regions move rapidly toward the maximum investment rate that the model will allow, once it begins using the optimization mode, and stays at that rate (25 percent per year) throughout the entire simulation.

However, in Asia, as can be seen from Figure 28–3, even optimal resource allocation does not allow sustained improvement of human welfare. The modelers describe the run:

The problem in Asia arises in the food sector. By 2010, all available land is being cultivated. Thereafter, economic effort in the sector is devoted to increasing livestock and fisheries. This, however, is not enough to feed the growing population

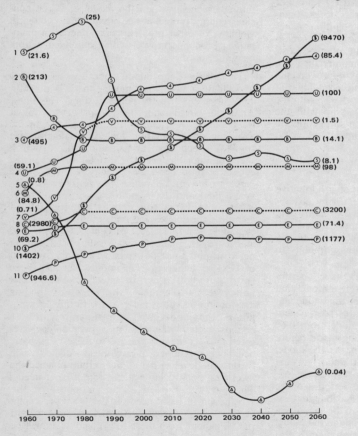

**Figure 28–2.** Latin American world model standard simulation for developed countries. *(Catastrophe or New Society? p. 84)*

Key:

| | | |
|---|---|---|
| 1 | (5) | Percent GNP allocated to sector 5 |
| 2 | (B) | Birth rate |
| 3 | (4) | Percent GNP to other goods and services |
| 4 | (U) | Urbanization |
| 5 | (Δ) | Population growth rate |
| 6 | (M) | Enrollment |
| 7 | (V) | Houses per family |
| 8 | (C) | Total calories per capita |
| 9 | (E) | Life expectancy |
| 10 | ($) | GNP per capita |
| 11 | (P) | Total population |

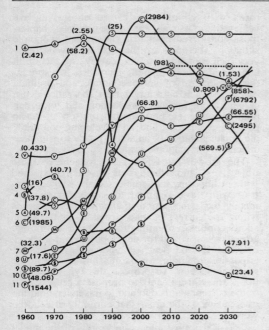

**Figure 28–3.** Latin American world model standard simulation for Asia. (*Catastrophe or New Society? p. 92*)

Key:

1  (Δ)  Population growth rate
2  (V)  Houses per family
3  (5)  Percentage of GNP allocated to Sector 5
4  (B)  Birth rate
5  (4)  Percentage of GNP to other goods and services
6  (C)  Total calories per capita
7  (M)  Enrollment
8  (U)  Urbanization
9  ($)  GNP per capita in 1960 dollars
10 (E)  Life expectancy
11 (P)  Total population

adequately, and consumption drops rapidly to below the minimum needed for survival.

The rapid increase in the cost of producing food, due to the development of new land for agriculture, takes resources from the rest of the economy, causing backwardness and also hindering the satisfaction of the other basic needs. In summary, the delay in reaching adequate levels of well-being leads to a sustained high population growth rate, and a vicious circle develops: increased population and the increased cost of producing food make it more and more difficult to satisfy basic needs.[9]

In short, the economy of Asia collapses in a fashion reminiscent of the way the world economy collapses in the food-system constrained runs of Worlds 2 and 3 and in the way in which South Asia's economy typically collapses in the Mesarovic-Pestel world model. In testimony to the strong effect education has on life expectancy (the variable optimized in the model), school enrollment stays high throughout the run (98 percent). Housing improves steadily but quite slowly throughout the run until about the year 2040, at which time the run is terminated. A severe decline in food per capita begins in the year 2008. Meanwhile, due to the sustained high investment rate of 25 percent, economic growth continues. The last 20 years of the optimization run for Asia are not shown: "The runs were stopped at the year 2040 because after that date the indicators (particularly life expectancy) ceased to have any meaning."[10] Also, the modelers state, "The life expectancy function is meaningful only when food intake is adequate to keep a person alive and to allow levels of physical activity that currently exists in the poorer societies." Apparently, food consumption drops in the model to levels that one would expect to create rising death rates, at which point the model, which lacks mechanisms by which starvation can increase mortality, starts to behave in a very unrealistic fashion.

The results of simulations showing stagnation of technological progress are disastrous for every place except the industrialized countries. In Latin America "the basic needs can be satisfied though only over a longer period than in the standard run, particularly in the cases of food and housing."[11] However, "in Africa, as in Asia, the minimum objectives cannot be achieved if technological progress stops; the economic system finally collapses. . . . Of the basic needs, only food reaches the target level, and then only for a brief period."[12] In a technological stagnation simulation for Africa, for instance, investment in capital formation falls off and GNP per capita actually declines rather than grows exponentially as it did in the collapse of the standard run for Asia. Population increases relentlessly. All of the basic needs sectors, including education, begin a nose dive somewhere between 1990 and 2020. Life expectancy peaks around 2015 and declines thereafter.

The tests considering capital transfer from the industrialized countries to Asia and Africa have the following results: The industrialized countries grow faster because they maintain higher investment rates. They end with markedly higher per capita income than in the standard run—$14,250 as opposed to $9,670 (in U.S. dollars). This aid doesn't have much impact on human welfare in Asia and Africa. While it leads to higher GNP growth (an infusion of capital obviously will), it has very little effect on infant mortality or life expectancy and not a great deal of influence on the amount of time needed for fulfillment of basic needs. The unstated implication is that capital transfer will have a negligible effect on the biggest upcoming human welfare problem in the world— food shortages in Asia.

The tests on income distribution show that egalitarian distribution leads to much more rapid fulfillment of basic needs. ("As can be seen, in the under-developed countries, the GNP per capita needed to satisfy the basic needs in egalitarian conditions is something between 3 to 5 times less than that required if current income distribution structures are maintained." [13])

The conclusions the modelers draw from the modeling exercise are somewhat different from those in the above description. Here, we quote the modelers' conclusions in full:

The results of the model . . . demonstrate that, if the policies proposed here are applied, all of humanity could attain an adequate standard of living within a period a little longer than one generation. The satisfaction of the most essential physical and cultural needs, which has been one of the central objectives of man from his beginnings, could be fulfilled for most of the countries of the Third World toward the end of the century, or in the first years of the next.

The only problem of physical limitation that arises, and which is of a local nature, is the exhaustion of the supply of cultivatable land in Asia in the middle of the next century. However, the large reserves of cultivatable land in other regions could easily cover this deficit. Since the effects of this limitation would only begin to be felt in 80 years, Asia has enough time to look for its own solutions to the problem, such as increasing the yield of crops, which has been assumed to be well below the theoretically possible levels; producing food from nonconventional sources; the application of an effective family planning policy that would enable the population to achieve a balance within a shorter period than predicted by the model; etc.

The model also shows that it is possible to control population growth to the point of equilibrium by raising the general standard of living, particularly with relation to basic needs. This equilibrium could be achieved on a global scale well before the earth's capacity to produce food— the only foreseeable physical limitation within the time horizon of the model—is fully exploited even if food production continues to be based on currently available technology.

The obstacles that currently stand in the way of the harmonious development of humanity are not physical or economic in the strict sense, but essentially sociopolitical. In effect, the growth rates with which the desired objectives are achieved are, as was seen in the previous chapter, those considered normal in the current economic situation. The goals are therefore achieved not by very high economic growth, but by a reduction in nonessential consumption; increased investment; the elimination of socioeconomic and political barriers, which currently hinder the rational use of land, both for food production and for urban planning; the egalitarian distribution of basic goods and services; and, in developing countries, the implementation of an active policy to eliminate deficits in international trade.

The growth rates necessary to achieve these objectives, and which can be easily attained without imposing intolerable social sacrifice, contrast with those required to satisfy, in approximately the same period of time, the basic needs within the current income structure, or the same socioeconomic organization. These economic growth rates, which for developing countries, vary between 10 and nearly 12 percent, are in fact impossible to attain, for the reasons set out in the previous section. To propose this type of "solution," therefore, is only to propose a preservation of the current status quo and to misunderstand the true causes of the crisis that currently affects the world.

One of the most interesting results of the model is the light it sheds on the effect that possible international aid, in particular the transfer of resources from the industrialized countries to the poor countries, would have. Even if a greater level of international aid than that advised by the United Nations is implemented, it may contribute to raise the level of well-being at the time of transfer, but in no way decisively. What has been seen with regard to income distribution clearly demonstrates that international aid, in the conditions currently prevailing in most developing countries, would only contribute to increasing spending by privileged sectors, and would have little or no effect on the living conditions of the majority of the population. The effect of the transfer of capital is only significant for the general well-being if there are conditions of social equality similar to those proposed in the model.

International solidarity can take forms other than the net transfer of resources from rich to poor countries. The model shows the recovery that developing countries can achieve in economic growth precisely at the decisive stage of attaining the satisfaction of basic needs, through the elimination of a negative balance of payments. The developed countries can help to bring forward the attainment of this objective by fixing fair prices for the products of underdeveloped countries to replace present prices that, rather than representing a just distribution between the factors of production of the two production sectors into which the world is divided, are the consequence of an unequal distribution of economic, political, and military power. Moreover, with a reduction in their growth rates, as proposed in the model, the rich countries could contribute to relieving the pressure on available resources, helping the poor countries indirectly in this way.

. . . It was shown that in the year 2060 (at which the computer runs were terminated) there would still be inequalities, expressed in economic indicators, between the levels of well-being in the developed and poor countries, particularly with respect to Asia. To evaluate correctly the significance of this remaining gap, it should be borne in mind that the results of the model over such a long period of time could change considerably with relatively small fluctuations in some of the variables used; a moderate increase in the rate of technological progress, for example, could easily close the gap.

Lastly the model shows, within the obvious limitations of this type of work, that the fate of man does not depend, in the last instance, on insurmountable physical barriers but on social and political factors that man must modify. Their solution is not at all easy, because to change the organization and values of society, as history has shown, is much more difficult than overcoming physical limitations. To attempt the task, however, is the only way open to an improved humanity.

It could possibly be said that this proposal is utopian, and that it would be more realistic to propose solutions that involve less radical modifications to the sociopolitical structure of the world. Those who hold this position should be reminded of the words of John Stuart Mill more than a century ago:

*"For a great evil, a small remedy does not produce a small result; it simply does not produce any results at all."* [14]

## Documentation

The available documentation on the Latin American world model is quite good. There exists both the nontechnical *Catastrophe or New Society? A Latin American World Model* [2] and the 1977 technical *Handbook of the Latin American Model,* distributed on a limited scale by UESCO. [5] The former publication does not present model equations but does a very respectable job of conveying conceptually how the model works, as well as presenting model output and numerous theoretical arguments supporting positions taken in the model. Descriptions of complex mathematical models are inevitably confusing. However, this book is written in such a way that, for a non-technically oriented reader, it almost always helps to clarify the model without confusing the issues.

The modelers are humanistic socialists, and their values are quite apparent throughout the documentation. Often one senses that they are interpreting things through the bias of their value system. However, these biases are sufficiently overt and clearly stated so that a reader who does not share the modelers' values can easily reinterpret their normative statements.

The technical handbook is appropriate for mathematicians, computer programmers, and mathematical economists. It describes some (not all) of the model equations and goes a long way toward documenting the model's data base and presenting references for its conceptual premises—except for occasional problems with undefined equations and poorly identified symbols. It has an orderly arrangement of subjects and a consistency of usages that spares the reader many of the frustrations frequently associated with large sets of equations. The computer program is published along with the model documentation and is well annotated. Apparently, it would allow a person desiring to do so to transfer the model to another system and use it without outside help from the modelers. This, however, is a subjective impression.

Documentation describing an application of the model to Brazil and a criticism of it by the Science Policy Research Unit at the University of Sussex have also been prepared for UNESCO and distributed on a limited scale. [15]

### REFERENCES

1. Donella H. and Dennis L. Meadows et al., *The Limits to Growth,* Washington: Potomac Associates, 1972, p. 184.
2. Amilcar O. Herrera et al., *Catastrophe or New Society? A Latin American World Model,* Ottawa: International Development Research Center, 1976, p. 8.
3. Ibid., p. 5.
4. Ibid., p. 8.
5. *Handbook of the Latin American World Model,* Paris: UNESCO, July 1977, p. 25.
6. Ibid., p. 117.
7. Herrera, p. 85.

8. Ibid., p. 104.
9. Ibid., p. 93.
10. Ibid., p. 93.
11. Ibid., p. 97.
12. Ibid.
13. Ibid., p. 104.
14. Ibid., pp. 107–108.
15. H. S. D. Cole, "The Latin American World Model as a Tool of Analysis and Integrated Planning at a National and Regional Level in Developing Countries," UNESCO, Aug. 1977; Carlos Ruiz, Irene Louisean, and Hugo D. Scolnik, "Adaptation of the Banloche Model to Brazil," Paris: UNESCO, Oct. 1977.

# 29   U.N. World Model

The conclusions drawn from the World 2 and World 3 models and the Mesarovic-Pestel world model were obviously unpalatable to poor nations of the world operating under the hope that growth would eventually extricate them from their poverty. Likewise, the notion that resources for growth were beginning to run out was unsettling to those U.N. agencies involved in formulation strategies for improving the condition of the world's poor.

The U.N. world model can be considered a manifestation of this discomfort. In late 1972, in conjunction with the International Development Strategy adopted by the General Assembly of the U.N. in 1970, Wassily Leontief was asked to construct a model of the world economy to assess whether physical limitations to economic growth would pose a significant obstacle to the economic targets set forth in the Strategy. Funding for the project was provided by the Netherlands. The work had an auspicious beginning: Leontief was awarded a Nobel Prize in economics in 1973. In his acceptance speech, he described the structural concepts on which the model was to be constructed.[1] The task of transforming the basic structure into a working model was undertaken by Anne Carter, Peter Petri, and others at Brandeis University. Joseph J. Stern of Harvard served as coordinator for the project.

## Method

The U.N. world model sets forth an input-output view of the world economy. The basic elements of this view are:

1. We cannot predict the future of the world economy. However, we can rule out of our expectations future scenarios that are internally inconsistent and thus impossible.

2. To rule out internally inconsistent expectations we need to construct a model that guarantees internal consistency. This we can do by visualizing the world as a system of interdependent processes in which

Each process, be it the manufacture of steel, the education of youth or the running of a family household, generates certain output and absorbs a specific combination of input. Direct interdependence between two processes arises whenever the output of one becomes an input of the other: Coal, the output of the coal mining industry, is an input of the electric power generating sector. The chemical industry uses coal not only directly as a raw material but also indirectly in the form of electrical power. A network of such length complicates the system of elements which depend upon each other directly, indirectly, or both.[2]

3. If it is the world we want to model, we can enhance the above visualization by dividing the world into regions and representing, separately, flows within a region and flows between regions.

Mathematically, the structure that has been used to represent the above visualization is quite simple, albeit immense. It is one vast system of simultaneous linear equations with more unknowns than equations. This system is solved using exogenously specified values for key variables to make the number of equations equal to the number of unknowns. To obtain a glimpse of the systems unfolding over time, the exogenous variables as well as some of equations' coefficients are projected forward—in this case by 5-year increments to the year 2000—and the system is solved again. The system provides latitude as to which variables are to be treated as endogenous and which as exogenous in any given simulation.

Probably the most demanding part of constructing such a model is gathering the data and filling in where data don't exist. If one counts time-updates for structural coefficients, the model's number of coefficients is in excess of 10,000. A large portion of these were adapted from other data bases. Many of them, most importantly the input-output ratios (technical coefficients) for some of the world's less developed regions, have had to be estimated by means of cross-section inferences from known data for other regions. Statistical techniques have been used extensively to work over data and to ensure that data from one source are consistent with data from another.

Many of the coefficients going into the model are based on the informed judgment of others. For example, estimates for input-output coefficients for future years have been borrowed from the works of many technological forecasters.

Although in some ways highly empirical, the method also requires a good deal of judgment. Many important decisions about how to employ statistics—for example, deciding how to forecast trade matrices for the People's Republic of China—involve a large amount of subjective judgment. Likewise, construction of scenarios is sufficiently dependent on a "feel" for what is important in the real world and for the model's capabilities that it is more of an art than a science.

## Relevance

The U.N. world model can speak to the following sorts of questions: For a given scenario of population growth and GNP growth with a specified standard of pollution abatement, how much of what mineral resources would have been used by 1980, 1985, 1990, or the year 2000? How much pollutant of various sorts would have been generated by those same years? The model also tells us what to expect in the way of changing sectoral compositions of output for growing economies; it tells us the magnitudes of anticipated trade flows under a set of simplifying assumptions about the mechanisms governing international trade. The model's strongest claim is that it will give consistent forecasts. That is, it will not allow one to forecast the growth of one segment of the economy without taking account of the demands that that segment places on other sectors of the economy. Nor will it allow users to forecast the imports and exports of a given region without making sure that these are balanced against the imports and exports of other regions—that is, for each product, global imports equal global exports for all regions. It also can go into questions of economic development in great detail—detail that brings attention to the explicit structural details of economic development. In a sense, the model prepares a sort of global and national-economic shopping list for all of the elements that will be required for the world to grow.

Such exercises are quite relevant to planning for long-term interrelationships between population resources and environment. There is great need for internal consistency in our forecasting. And it is important that we do look at things on a matter-of-fact, item by item basis in concrete real terms. Unless someone keeps careful and detailed

accounts, it is difficult to avoid double counting and omissions.

But the model does not answer all the relevant questions. When asked about the model's treatment of the environment, Anne Carter replied frankly that it was quite superficial.[3] She made no pretense that the tallying of pollutants and mineral and fossil fuel resources by the model provides adequate indices of the state of the environment. The model does not speak to the way ecological systems will be affected by the development that it forecasts. It does not keep track of the states of forests, grasslands, bodies of water, soil, and other natural systems. It cannot address the firewood crisis.

Carter was of the opinion that the model could be made much more relevant for some of these purposes by distinguishing between urban and rural economies. This, she indicated, would result in better inferences about stresses on land produced by intensive agriculture and other land uses as well as a better means of attacking problems, such as concentration of pollutants, that are primarily urban affairs.

## Structure

The model consists of 15 regional models, which taken together represent the whole world. In structure, these 15 submodels are identical. Each has 175 equations and 229 variables. The 15 regional submodels are linked interface through world trade equations. In the following text the structure of the regional submodels is described first, then the manner in which they are linked. The entire world system of equations is solved simultaneously, however, so no causal sequence should be inferred from any of the descriptions.

Each regional model (Fig. 29–1) can be thought of as a device that first calculates the economy's entire demand for the products of each of 40 economic sectors (total demand) and then, from total demand, estimates resource usage, pollution generated, labor employed, and capital employed. In fact, it is more complicated than that, for pollution generates abatement activities, which in turn add to total demand. Likewise, capital requirements generate investments, and this too adds to total demand.

Total demands for the products of each sector are calculated in the normal fashion of summing up the national income accounts. First, the final demands are calculated by adding up consumption, government spending, and investment. To final demands are added those demands generated

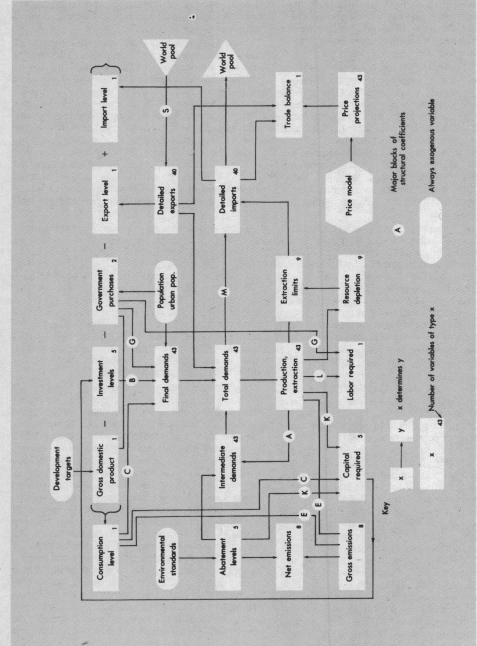

**Figure 29-1.** Internal structure of a region. Major structural coefficients; A, interindustry inputs; B, composition of investment of consumption; E, generation of gross pollution; G, composition of government purchases; K, capital inputs; L, labor in import-dependence ratios; S, shares of world export markets. *(Peter A. Petri, "An Introduction to the Structure and Application of the United Nations World Model," Applied Mathematical Modeling, June, 1977)*

in the process of filling final demands (intermediate demands) and the net of export demands minus import demands. (The input-output matrix is used to calculate the intermediate demand from the final demand.)

The model permits two fundamentally different ways of looking at income determination. One can specify, exogenously, target rates of GNP growth for the model's various regions and let the model calculate consumption endogenously as the residual of what would be left over after the indicated investments, government expenditures, etc., took place. Alternatively, one can specify specific developmental constraints (limits on balance-of-payment deficits, available savings, or labor force) and have the model determine what rates of economic growth would be possible within the specified constraints.

The model computes the investment rates that will be required, either to create the industrial capacity needed for target GNP growth rates or to allow the growth rates determined by the specified development constraints. Investment is divided into the following categories: plant, equipment, irrigation, and land. The amount invested in each category is determined by a set of technical coefficients that relate investment needs to final demand for all of the model's sectors.

Imports and exports, the remaining categories contributing (or deducting) from final demand, comprise the bridge that connects regional economies to the world trade model. The modelers have kept their representations of imports and exports simple, almost artificially so, in order to render the complex problem of international trade as transparent as possible and to allow for changing of assumptions at a later date. Most regional imports are determined via import-dependence ratios, which are exogenously varied over time, relating imports required to output produced on a sector by sector basis. "Import requirements are then summed across regions and the resulting world demands are allocated to the regions as exports. The allocations are accomplished by export-share coefficients specific to each traded commodity. These regional export shares are presently projected with regression studies based on historical and cross section data." In the case of manufactured imports, dependency ratios are constant and estimated by regression analysis. For exhaustible resource commodities such as minerals, "importing regions are assigned output levels consistent with the amount of regional resource reserve still available, and imports are used to fill all the remaining unsatisfied demands."[4]

Thus depletion of mineral reserves induces increased importing of minerals and increased international trading in minerals.

Minerals, pollutants, and agricultural products are treated in real terms. Manufactured goods and services are treated in price terms. The use of physical units, as opposed to monetary units, has advantages for the modeler. It permits utilization of physical data, such as mineral reserve estimates, while at the same time letting the modeler take advantage of physical realities, such as the laws of preservation of matter and biological facts about nutritional needs. Moving in the direction of these advantages, the modelers have departed from the purely monetary flows found in most input-output models and have substituted a mixed accounting system, using both real and physical units.

Prices are generated in a separate model. Basically the price of sectoral output is equated to sectoral production costs. Production costs change with changing interindustry structure (input-output structures). These take into consideration such matters as changes in production efficiencies, input substitution (e.g., plastics for wood and metals), and higher input requirement for production of mineral resources as resource reserves become depleted. For some simulations, resource prices are projected outside the model and set exogenously. Consistent prices for all other sectors are then computed.

Exogenous forecasts of technological change in each of the regions are also fed into the main model. These forecasts were made using cross-section studies of the relationship between per capita income and interindustry structure to derive estimates of how interindustry flows would change as regions undergo economic growth. Technological forecasts were superimposed on these. Numerous assumptions are unavoidably put into these technological forecasts, including controversial issues, such as assumptions about the extent to which nuclear power will substitute for conventional energy sources. The huge number of the assumptions made in estimating time trends for input-output matrices makes for confusion when it comes to considering the model as whole. There are so many assumptions that one is hard put to evaluate the reasonableness of the total picture. Though the modelers tell us they have been moderate in their choice of assumptions and have consistently utilized what seems to be the best guess of accepted experts, it would still seem desirable to have an easy way of checking the assumptions used.

## Testing

The U.N. world model needs a lot of parameter testing and could be utilized for a wide range of policy testing. The modelers' limited time and limited budgets have barely allowed them to scratch the surface of the testing that could and should be done. The model contains a huge number of somewhat arbitrary parameters. One would have a lot more confidence in the model if it had been determined through testing that these parameters were not unduly sensitive. It would also be useful to have identified which parameters *are* sensitive in order to ascertain areas of greatest uncertainty. This knowledge would serve as a basis for determining priorities for further data collection and research. That is, it is much more important that a careful job be done researching parameters to which the model is sensitive than researching things that don't much matter.

The policy tests for which the model has been used have generally conformed to the interests of organizations commissioning use of the model. In real terms, this means that the model has been used to: (1) test economic and—to the extent that the model can show environmental happenings—environmental consequences of the growth targets established by the International Development Strategy; (2) examine the ramifications of resource conservation strategies for the Canadian government's Economic Council of Canada; (3) investigate for the U.S. Department of Commerce the consequences of energy conservation on global economic development; and (4) examine a few scenarios that the modelers themselves felt were useful and meaningful. The results of the Canadian study have yet to be publicly documented; results of the other three tests follow.

The documented work done for the U.N. operates around eight policy scenarios.[5] As prescribed by the International Development Strategy, most of these are based on exogenously given forecasts of population growth and growth of income per capita. The three population and income growth alternatives considered are shown in Table 29–1. The base case, or standard forecast, denoted UN/B in the table, is the case with medium population growth and high gross domestic product (GDP) per capita growth in developing regions and moderate growth in developed regions. Further tests were conducted by altering this base case by changing assumptions, e.g., by assuming more optimistic estimates of resource endowments, as well as increased foreign aid, constraints on balance-of-payment deficits, and faster agricultural investment in the low-income Asian countries. In one final scenario, investment, instead of being driven by targeted GDP growth, was presumed to follow past trends, and GDP growth was generated endogenously according to several constraints: apparently realistic balance of payments, the labor available, and the monies available for investment after consumption had spent its share. The constraints used varied from region to region. (This last test, by the way, produces dim economic prospects for the developing world, and is downplayed in the U.N. documentation.)

In the process of working out the above policy scenarios, the modelers found that the minimum targets for growth set by the International Development Strategy, if implemented, would barely suffice to keep the gap between rich and poor nations from growing, much less to narrow the gap. Accordingly, the growth rate per capita income in less developed countries (LDCs) was adjusted upward in such a way that the income gap between LDCs and industrialized countries would just about halve its proportionate size by the year 2000. Consistent with the objective of evening out income levels, growth rates across the board were adjusted so as to be inversely related to present income per capita. The richer regions were assumed to grow slowly, the poorer regions to grow most rapidly. The growth rate for the basic scenarios used in the model are shown in Table 29–2.

In the work conducted for the U.S. Department of Commerce, the modelers compared a business-as-usual constrained growth run with one in which all regions of the world adopt the highest reasonable curtailment of fossil fuel consumption over the next 20 years. Their conservation maximum was adopted from the most extreme of the energy conservation scenarios prepared by Cavendish Laboratories of Cambridge University for the World Energy Conference of October 1977. They assumed that energy conservation would be ac-

### TABLE 29–1

**Alternative Assumptions Concerning Income Targets and Future Population Growth**

| | Population Growth | | Per Capita GDP Targets | |
|---|---|---|---|---|
| | Developed Regions | Developing Regions | Developed Regions | Developing Regions |
| UN/B | medium | medium | high | high |
| UN/A–1 | low | low | low | high |
| UN/A–2 | high | high | low | high |

*Source:* Wassily Leontief et al., *The Future of the World Economy.* New York: Oxford, 1977, p. 26.

## TABLE 29–2

**Growth Rates and Income Gap Under the Assumptions of Basic Scenarios X and C in the United Nations Model**

| Scenario | Indus-trialized Countries | Less Developed Countries |
|---|---|---|
| | *Percent* | |
| *Growth rate* | | |
| Gross product | X | 4.0 | 7.2 |
| | C | 3.6 | 6.9 |
| Population | X | 0.7 | 2.3 |
| | C | 0.6 | 2.0 |
| Gross product | X | 3.3 | 4.9 |
| per capita | C | 3.0 | 4.9 |
| | | *LDCs =100* | |
| *Income gap in the year 2000* | | |
| Gross product | X | 769 | 100 |
| per capita | C | 715 | 100 |

Source: Wassily Leontief et al., *The Future of the World Economy*. New York: Oxford, 1977, p. 31.

complished by substituting labor and capital for energy.[6]

## Conclusions

The tests described above tend to the conclusion that economic prospects for the LDCs are not in general optimistic. For such countries to meet the targeted growth rates, investment ratios of unprecedented magnitude would have to be maintained, and consumption for private use kept at very low levels. For example, if target growth rates were kept up in the year 2000, none of the developing regions would have a level of personal consumption in excess of 63 percent of income, and none would have a level of private investment of less than 20 percent. It was also found that in order to meet food requirements in a standard scenario, agricultural production in the year 2000 would have to be increased to about four times present figures. In many places, higher rates of increase were called for. In low-income Latin America and low-income Asia, it was found that agricultural output would have to increase by more than 500 percent; in an arid and tropical Africa and centrally planned Asia, increases of 400 to 500 percent were indicated; in the Middle East, the output showed that a 950 percent increase in agricultural output would be required to keep economic growth patterns on target. In currently high-income regions, most of the indicated agricultural growth rates were below 200 percent.[7]

The findings on minerals were more optimistic. In general, it was found that mineral resource limitations would not prove to be a binding constraint on economic growth by the year 2000. With the exception of lead and zinc, the model did not show the world running out of any minerals by 2000.

In view of that the fact that the model produces use estimates for nine critical geologic resources—copper, bauxite, nickel, zinc, lead, iron, crude petroleum, natural gas, and coal—the forecast that only lead and zinc are in danger of being used up by 2000 is significant, although it becomes somewhat less significant if one considers that World 3, which has generally been called a pessimistic model, indicates that in the aggregate 70 percent of our mineral resources will remain in the year 2000. In that model shortages do not become critical until around 2020.[8]

Furthermore, it is not immediately clear what is behind the conclusion that resources are ample enough to last to 2000. It is known that the model does assume to some unspecified extent that nuclear power and gasified coal will be used to substitute for petroleum by 2000, also that the model assumes active recycling of minerals.[9] The "no running out" finding can, thus, only be interpreted to mean that we can avoid running out through appropriate technical solution. The modelers also conclude that the resources that will be available to us will probably be at a higher cost. Price, however, as described earlier, is not determined within the main model. This conclusion, therefore, must stem from either our off-line analysis or from a supplementary model.

Leontief's analysis of the model concludes that "although pollution is a great problem for humanity, it is a technologically manageable problem" and that the economic cost of keeping pollution within manageable limits is not unbearable.[10] Model output implied that if fairly stringent abatement standards were to be applied to all the pollutants now regulated in the United States, abatement costs would come to about 1.4–1.9 percent of gross product. Under less stringent standards—and in the model it was assumed that less stringent standards would be applied in countries with lower income per capita than the U.S.—the total cost of abatement activities would come to about 0.5–0.9 percent of gross product.

In the energy conservation tests conducted for the Department of Commerce, the following tendencies were noted: In the developed regions, which were modeled as having labor-constrained growth rates, energy conservation's greatest effect was to reduce balance-of-payment deficits. In the

LDCs, where GDP growth was constrained by balance-of-payment deficits, energy conservation, in reducing balance of payment deficits, lessened the main constraint to economic growth and thereby resulted in increased GDP growth as well. In all regions, the capital requirements for energy conservation caused the energy conservation scenario to require more savings, and thus less consumption. The required change in savings rates was large enough to imply the need for an appreciable change in distribution of money between savings and consumption—an increase in savings of about 17 to 23 percent.[11]

In policy tests of the modelers' own design, the modelers constructed scenarios to compare the economic consequences for LDCs of adopting standard patterns of development instead of pollution-intensive export strategy. The purpose of the test was to ascertain whether LDCs would be dimming their prospects for economic growth if they avoided becoming specialized hosts for the dirtier industries, which, presumably, industrialized nations might like to exclude from within their boundaries. From these tests, the modelers concluded that

the pollution-intensive approach is found to be more expensive in terms of capital, and requires more input. This approach would also imply sizable shifts in the output mix of the developing economy and might create non-negligible environmental repercussions. . . . In sum, several economic criteria mitigate in favor of the conventional and against the pollution-intensive strategy—provided, and this is quite important—that a choice exists at all.[12]

Other conclusions emanating from the model study centered on consequences of accelerated development in the less developed countries. Most important among these were: (1) Accelerated development would probably require faster growth of heavy industry than of other industrial sectors; (2) high income-elasticities of demand for imports would likely create severe balance-of-payment problems for LDCs under accelerated development strategies; and (3) "to insure accelerated development general conditions are necessary: first, far-reaching internal changes of a social, political and institutional character in the developing countries, and second, significant changes in the world economic order. Accelerated development leading to a substantial reduction of the income gap between the developing and the developed countries can only be achieved through a combination of both these conditions."[13]

## Documentation

The publicly available documentation of the U.N. world model is adequate to give an informed reader a good basic understanding of the model's structure and how it operates. However, to gain an understanding of its particulars, how it is parameterized, where data came from, and what sorts of statistical measures are to be associated with which estimated parameters, one would almost have to personally discuss the question with the modelers themselves. Anne Carter informed the Global 2000 Study staff that the modelers have kept careful records and that technical documentation is being supplied to the United Nations. Resources are not available for documenting the work for a wider audience. Furthermore, the modelers view their work in current form as incomplete and would like it to undergo considerable further testing, refinement, and development before preparing detailed documentation for public circulation.[14]

**REFERENCES**

1. Wassily Leontief, "Structure of the World Economy: Outline of a Simple Input-Output Formulation" (Nobel Memorial Lecture), *American Economic Review*, Dec. 1977, pp. 823–34.

2. Ibid, p. 823.

3. Anne Carter, verbal communication to the Global 2000 Study staff, Nov. 14, 1977.

4. Peter A. Petri, "An Introduction to the Structure and Application of the United Nations World Model," *Applied Mathematical Modeling*, June 1977, p. 263.

5. Wassily Leontief et al., *The Future of the World Economy*, New York: Oxford, 1977.

6. Anne P. Carter and Alan K. Sin, "An Energy Conservation Scenario for the World Model," prepared for the U.S. Department of Commerce, Bureau of International and Economic Policy, at Brandeis University, Nov. 1977, p. 2.

7. Leontief et al., *The Future of the World Economy*.

8. Dennis L. Meadows et al., *Dynamics of Growth in a Finite World*, Cambridge, Mass.: Wright-Allen, 1974, p. 500.

9. Anne Carter, verbal communication.

10. Leontief et al., *The Future of the World Economy*, p. 7.

11. Anne P. Carter and Alan K. Sin.

12. Petri, p. 267.

13. Leontief et al., *The Future of the World Economy*, p. 11.

14. Anne Carter, verbal communication.

Part IV

# Comparison of Results

# 30   Introduction to Model Comparisons

The Global 2000 Study seeks answers to two questions: What are probable trends for global population, resources, and environment to the year 2000? and How does the complex institutional structure of the U.S. federal government derive its expectations about these matters? The latter question is examined to assess the projection capabilities of agencies of the executive branch, to describe their strengths and weaknesses, and to examine alternative methodologies that might overcome weaknesses that are found to exist.

The methodological question has been pursued in this volume as follows: First, the implications of projection by means of a collection of separately developed and operated models have been discussed in Chapter 14. That discussion emphasized the distorting effect of making fragmentary projections of a highly integrated world. Second, specific projection tools developed and utilized in federal agencies—or elsewhere in cases such as GNP projections—have been described in Chapters 15 through 23. Third, in Chapters 25 through 29, five case studies of nongovernment global models that are more integrated than the government's model have been discussed.

The following chapter brings together loose ends in the discussion of modeling methodology through two exercises. First, a comparison will be made of the five nongovernment integrated models. This comparison will stress the ways that models' conceptual and mathematical structures affect their findings and conclusions and the ways that institutional factors affect model conceptualization. A model's idea content is at least coequal with its parameterization in shaping the model's projections. The text is deliberately weighted to show that there is more to modeling than the "garbage in, garbage out" cliché implies. In fact, if this cliché has an appropriate application, it is to characterize models having static, linear structures without endogenous feedback.

Finally, an attempt will be made to answer the question "How would the conclusions of the Government's Global Model be different if the model were more integrated?" A conceptually attractive experimental approach has been used to tackle this question. Two of the integrated models previously described (the World 3 and the World Integrated Model) were selected on the basis of their availability for the experiment and were restructured by breaking the internal feedback loops so that they bore some resemblance to the Government's Global Model, as described in Chapter 14. Comparison of the output from the original integrated versions of the models with the results from the less integrated modified versions was then used as a basis for determining how government projections would differ if the government's model were more integrated.

# 31  The Comparisons

## Comparison of Integrated Global Models

Global modeling is not yet on solid footing. Most of the funding for the world models described in this volume has come from private sources. None of the models is linked to the governmental decision-making process in a stable fashion. The Mesarovic-Pestel world model and the U.N. world model have been used as analysis tools by government decision-making bodies, but as marginal information inputs only, not as primary tools of analysis. The absence of regular clients is a serious constraint to the further development of global models. A fairly large portion of the human capital developed for the construction of global models is currently devoted to the search for funding to permit further development of existing models. Some global modelers have moved on to greener pastures.

The difficulties encountered in adapting global modeling to the political structure appear to be inherent in the institutional structure of the political decision-making process. The only people empowered to deal with global problems on an integrated basis are highly placed and generally lack the time required to learn how to utilize inputs from global models. No agency has a sufficiently broad mandate to justify commissioning and supporting a model with a broad interagency focus. Existent interagency bodies are already swamped with information and constrained in their actions by political necessities.

Integrated modeling, if it is to make a positive contribution to government, must build a style of operation that (1) simplifies information flows (i.e., results in lighter work inflows through inboxes, fewer meetings and telephone calls, and more concise and compact discussion of the issues) and (2) receives the cooperation and political support of the agencies whose independent jurisdictions operate together in the model.

## Structure

Integrated global models tend to expand into several broad questions the traditional question of economics: How are scarce resources allocated among alternative uses? These questions are: Where will resource demands come from? How will they evolve over time? How will the growth of demand interface with changes in the economic structures and natural resource stocks required to create supply?

The two basic forms of growing needs that show up in integrated models are basic human needs associated with population growth and economic needs associated with growth and maintenance of economic systems. This expansion of the model domain has marked effects on the results of analysis. The effects in terms of population and resources will be observed below, and the general failure of even the expanded approach to adequately incorporate environment will be discussed.

### Population and Basic Human Needs

When population dynamics are introduced into models of the global system, physical needs as well as economic demands compete for recognition. If population's needs are not met, people die, migrate, or alter their basic patterns of economic behavior so that their needs can be filled (e.g., by substitution of one type of goods for another or by alteration of the system of production). In other words, it becomes necessary to observe system adjustment processes other than that of the price mechanism.

The real-world linkages between need fulfillment and population behavior are tenuous. Modelers approach them in various ways. In MOIRA (Model of International Relations in Agriculture), unfulfilled food needs are counted, and relative welfare between rural and urban locations is used as a drive mechanism for the model's migration function. In the World 2 and 3 models and the Mesarovic-Pestel model, the extent of fulfillment of economic and food needs effects birth and death rates. In some versions of the Mesarovic-Pestel model, nonfulfillment of needs results in reduction of economic production. Need fulfillment is the heart of the Latin American world model, and attention to human needs is the motive for the model's adoption of an allocation mechanism in which capital and labor are allocated in the fashion that maximizes life expectancy at birth. No feedback from need fulfillment to economic performance is included in the U.N. world model; instead, apparent problem areas are identified off-line and taken to indicate places where the model is unrealistic.

## Resources and Economic Needs

Many resource inputs, including land, water, minerals, energy, and renewable biological resources are important in the global system. Any of these could be locally, if not globally, limiting. How binding the limits posed by such resources become, depends on what substitutions are made, how successfully limits are overcome by technology and how well growth is channeled into patterns that do not conflict with resource limits.

Only one of the models in our study set does not include endogenous natural resource limits—the U.N. world model. (It does, however, include labor and capital constraints in some of its modes of operation, and the capital constraint could become an implicit natural resource constraint if the exogenous resource pricing function makes minerals and energy very expensive.) All of the other models include a land constraint—in each case, a function formulated so as to make the costs of expanding agricultural production rise as the system exhausts its supply of unused arable land. In all of the models examined, this constraint can potentially become a dominant feature of system structure by constricting the expanse of agriculture and thus creating food deficits. The models exhibit great difference in their formulations of where the land constraint manifests itself. In the World 2 and 3 models, it is encountered as a global aggregate, and the land's productive capacity has two dimensions capable of constraining food production: soil fertility and land under cultivation. Because the other models considered here use geographically disaggregated land constraints that recognize only land availability (i.e., they disregard soil fertility), which puts the World 2 and 3 models in the paradoxical position of using, simultaneously, the most complex, least detailed formulation of the land constraint.

MOIRA, in comparison, is highly detailed and conceptually simple. It includes 106 separate agricultural production functions. In each, the investment in land within a given geopolitical region leads to increased food production, subject to diminishing returns. Trade, through a market formulation, moves food from areas with less heavily utilized land resources to areas with tight land constraints. Simular formulations with re-

gional representations of land constraints interlinked by trade are used for the Latin American world model and for the Mesarovic-Pestel model. None of the other models attempts MOIRA's amount of detail, however, and the Latin American model de-emphasizes the role of trade. The land resource constraint indirectly affects the model's nonagricultural economy in both the World 2 and 3 models and the Mesarovic-Pestel model. When the demand for food is high and returns on investment low, the models divert significant amounts of capital away from other economic sectors and invest it in agriculture. This often cramps economic growth outside the agricultural sector. In the Mesarovic-Pestel model, this is particularly apt to occur in the South Asian regional model.

Mesarovic-Pestel, the World 2 and 3 models, and the U.N. world model, all include mineral and/or energy resources. In the U.N. model, the representation is little more than an accounting device that tabulates resources used. The World models and the Mesarovic-Pestel model use formulations wherein depletion of reserves slows production, raises prices, and dampens the basic processes of economic growth. The Mesarovic-Pestel model includes multiple energy and resource categories and makes substitution among energy sources explicit by permitting the relative prices of substitutable resource groups to govern the direction of investment in resource development—i.e., investment goes to the energy type showing the highest returns on investment. In operation, energy deficits in the Mesarovic-Pestel model generally come about because investment in energy capital has not been rapid enough to create supplies rather than because of actual resource shortages. In the World 2 and 3 models, extraction costs rise as the fraction of reserves remaining gets very low. Cost rises feed back to slow economic growth.

The combination of finite, depletable and/or erodable resource stocks and exponentially growing economies and populations makes all the global models considered here, with the exception of the U.N. world model, susceptible to economic collapse. The collapse mode's persistence depends on how severe the modelers have made the resource constraints on growth. Where the model has been parameterized with large amounts of undeveloped arable land with low development costs, then agricultural growth will proceed unhindered to 2000, and perhaps well beyond. Growth may also proceed unimpaired by resource constraints where energy and mineral sectors have been initialized as having large reserves, where substitution to an unlimited resource base is permitted in model formulations (as in the Mesarovic-Pestel model, in which the raw materials for nuclear energy are presumed to be available in unlimited supply, though at fairly high cost), or where technology has been empowered to increase production exponentially with no resource cost (as in some of the runs conducted by the University of Sussex group on World 3).* Where such saving assumptions are not built into global models, they almost invariably simulate economic collapse.

**Environment**

With the exception of the World 2 and 3 models, which allow for both land degradation and biological destruction caused by pollution, none of the models studied accounts for the (highly likely) possibility that human manipulations of physical systems will influence biological systems in ways that affect economic, agricultural, or population dynamics. Virtually all of the possible environmental problems discussed in the environmental forecast are thereby ignored.

The basic way in which information is organized in most models seems to preclude effective environmental modeling. To date, the primary unit for collecting data is the nation. The focus of most data collection is economic or demographic. However, increasing quantities of environmental data—sometimes in forms that are not aggregated by political units—are coming to us through environmental monitoring and satellite scanning.

So long as global models are organized around the concepts implicit in older data sources, their treatment of environmental problems will remain superficial. Ecological systems do not conform to political boundaries. Attempting to keep track of ecological developments through use of national data bases makes only slightly more sense than attempting to perceive political relationships by arranging nations in alphabetical order—or attempting to understand chemical reactions by classifying chemicals by color rather than atomic structure.

Before modelers can build meaningful environmental models capable of deriving realistic forecasts for environmental problems such as desertification, erosion, water management, forest management, and fisheries, it will be necessary for them to think of environmental problems in terms of aggregates of similarly functioning ecological units. In understanding how environmental

problems are likely to unfold, it makes more sense to consider groups of similarly behaving systems, such as industrial cities, grasslands, rice paddies, estuaries, and tropical rain forests, than to group such units according to the national boundaries within which they are found.

Usually the response to the suggestion that environmental analysis should proceed through aggregation of similar ecological systems is met by, "Yes, it's a nice idea, but we simply don't have the data." But is the absence of data a binding constraint? Given good organization, a small amount of data can be made to go far. Think, for instance, of all that an archeologist infers from a few jaw fragments. Or recall the labors of the macro-economists in the 1930's when National Accounts data were just beginning to be collected. There should be a way to weld together the fragments of ecological studies, satellite data, environmental monitoring data, climatological records, and soil studies currently available into a plausible framework for study of the global environment—one that could be used to identify what data ought to be collected in the future in order to provide better indices of environmental developments.

It is clear that the real world, with its high degree of interconnectedness and strong system interlinkages is not going to behave as the independently developed agency forecasts suggest. It is not clear, however, wherein the differences between the real world and the modeled world will lie. In order to gain insight into this question, the Global 2000 Study has commissioned use of the World 3 model (see Chapter 25) and the World Integrated Model (the latter day version of the Mesarovic-Pestel world model described in Chapter 26) to examine the effects of cutting system linkages on model simulation results.

## The Government's Global Model vs. the World 3 Model

The World 3 model consists of five interactive sectors: population, capital, agriculture, nonrenewable resources, and persistent pollution.* In the simulations undertaken for the Global 2000 Study, all linkages between sectors were broken and exogenous data inputs were substituted for the information that had previously been passed between sectors. Thus the model's intersectoral linkages were changed from the highly interactive

---

* H. S. D. Cole, ed., *Models of Doom*, New York: Universe Books, 1973, pp. 117–18.

* For a full description of the sectors, see Dennis L. Meadows et al., *Dynamics of Growth in a Finite World*, Cambridge, Mass.: Wright-Allen Press, 1974.

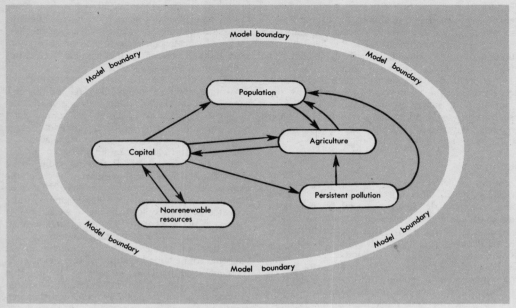

**Figure 31-1.** World 3 model sector linkages *before* linkage breaking.

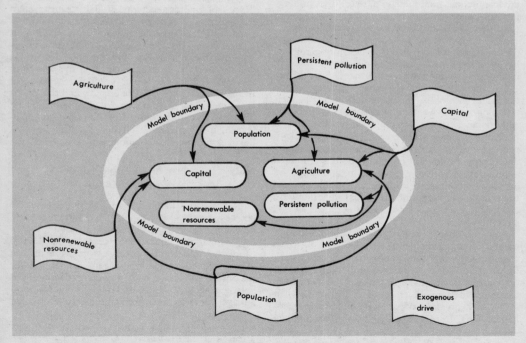

**Figure 31-2.** World 3 model *after* breaking of sectoral linkages and introduction of exogenous drives.

## TABLE 31–1

### Exogenous Inputs and Assumptions in World 3 Simulations for the Global 2000 Study

| Input | Assumption |
|---|---|
| Industrial capital | Continued exponential growth at 3.7 percent per year. |
| Industrial output | Same pattern as industrial capital (exponential growth at 3.7 percent per year). |
| Service output | Continuation of historical trend, growth at 3.0 percent per year. |
| Arable land | Decreasing rate of increase until an equilibrium figure of 27 billion hectares is reached by 2010.[a] |
| Food | Growth of output at 2.0 percent per year (historic rate). |
| Population | Exponential growth at historic rate of 1.2 percent per year, reaching 5.3 billion by 2000 and 17.6 billion by 2100. |
| Pollution | Level of persistent pollution held constant at zero value. |

[a] This figure is unrealistically high, but in the context in which it is used its magnitude does not appear critical.

structure shown in Figure 31–1 to the exogenously programmed structure shown in Figure 31–2. The exogenous inputs used to drive the nonlinked version are specified in Table 31–1.

As can be seen in Figure 31–3, in the open loop simulation, several variables are exogenously fed into one sector of the model at the same time as they are endogenously calculated in another sector. For example, population is exogenously fed into the capital sector while it is endogenously calculated in the population sector. If this dual appearance of variables is not noted, interpretation of the simulation outputs that appear in the following pages will become quite confusing.

The progress of exogenously driven variables over time is shown in Figure 31–3. The modelers chose to extend the simulation period until 2100 because marked difference between the more and less integrated model structures does not become fully visible until well into the 21st century.

The arrangement created by the cutting of linkages is such that the exogenous inputs used in one unlinked sectoral forecast will be endogenously calculated in another. For example, the population estimates calculated in the population sector are different from the population forecasts fed into the capital sector. If this dual appearance of variables is not noted, interpretation of the simulation outputs that appear in the following pages will become quite confusing.

### Results

*Population*. The results of the standard integrated version of World 3 are shown in Figure 31–4.

The results of open-loop simulations will be compared to these. In the open-loop simulation, population was driven by the exogenous data inputs for industrial output, service output, food, and pollution shown in Table 31–1. Thus driven, population was transformed by the dynamics of the population sector from a fast-growing population with a very high fertility and moderately high mortality to a slowly growing population with low fertility and low mortality. Population did not completely stabilize by 2100; however, it was reduced to about 13.5 billion—about 4 billion less than the 17.6 billion calculated for 2100 under the assumption of a constant growth rate of 1.2 percent per year. On the other hand, the resulting population was higher by about 8.5 billion than that of 2100 in the standard run of World 3.

The marked differences in output result, of course, from model structure. Unlike simulations with the fully linked model, the simulation from the population sector with exogenous inputs was not linked to industrial and agricultural structures that collapse in the process of attempting to maintain continued exponential growth in a context of finite land and mineral resources. Rather, it is faced with input assumptions of continued material growth.

It should be observed that while the differences between the closed-loop and open-loop forecasts have become acute by 2100, they are not greatly noticeable by 2000. (Compare Figs. 31–4 and 31–5.) This suggests that on the basis of global aggregates, the effects of system interlinkages on population dynamics will not be terribly significant by 2000.

*Capital*. In the open-loop simulation, the capital sector was driven by the exogenous inputs for population, food, and arable land (Fig. 31–6). In addition, the fraction of capital allocated to obtaining resources was held constant at 5 percent (the rate of investment observed in the World 3 model in times when there are no resource shortages), and the fraction of industrial output allocated to agriculture was held constant at 10 percent (the fraction allocated used in World 3 in "normal" times, when the system is not straining against the limits of availability of agricultural land).

Formulated in this fashion, the capital sector was freed from the resource constraints that cause its decline in the standard version of World 3. Decreasing returns on investment and declining food availability per capita do not shift investment away from the capital sector to the agricultural sector as they do in the standard version, and increasing cost for resource extraction do not cut

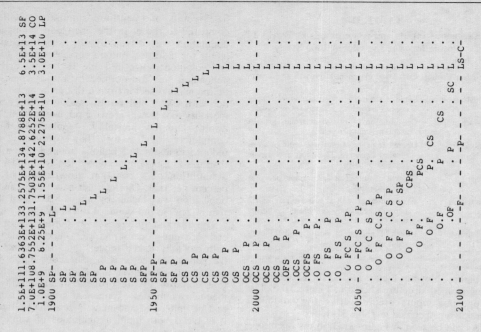

**Figure 31–3.** Exogenous inputs to different sectors of the World 3 model.
*Key to Figures 31–3 through 31–5*

B = Birth rate
C = Industrial capital
D = Death rate
F = Food per capita (vegetal equivalent) in kilograms per year*
I = Industrial output per capita in dollars

L = Arable land in hectares
O = Industrial output in dollars
P = Population (persons)
R = Fraction of resource remaining
S = Service output in dollars per year
X = Index of persistent pollution (dimensionless)

* Calculated by adding kilograms of vegetable food consumed plus 7 times the kilograms of animal food consumed (i.e., if one eats 1 kg of rice and 1 kg of beef, one has consumed the equivalent of 1 + 7 kg of vegetable food).

NOTE to FIGURES 31–3 through 31–11
If the page is turned clockwise so that the letters in these figures can be read in their normal position, the numbers at the top (above the ''1900'' axis) give the scale used for the variables plotted in the output. The variables associated with each scale are indicated to the right (in the direction of reading).

the effective returns on investment in the capital sector. Thus, industrial output per capita, instead of growing until about 2020 and then declining as in the standard version of World 3, grows exponentially at a rate higher than that observed even during the growth phase of the standard run. (Compare Figs. 31–4 and 31–6.).

*Agriculture.* In the agriculture sector, linkages from industrial output, population, and the fraction of output allocated to agriculture were cut (Fig. 31–7). The first two inputs were replaced by

the exogenous data inputs described in Table 31–1. The last was held constant at 10 percent. With intersectoral linkages thus severed, the agricultural sector gives a more optimistic forecast than in the standard run. Nevertheless, agricultural output continues to peak and crash—the difference being that the peak in food per capita is half again as high in the unlinked forecast as it is in the standard run, and the decline begins around 30 years later. (Compare Figs. 31–4 and 31–7.)

Decline occurs in the unlinked forecasts for two reasons:

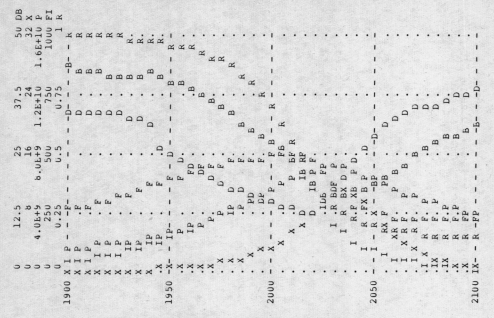

**Figure 31–4.** World 3 model standard run (integrated version).

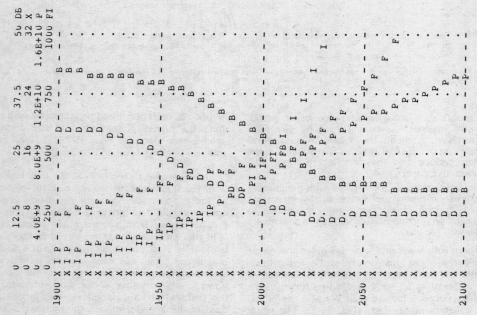

**Figure 31–5.** Four-level population sector with exogenous inputs.

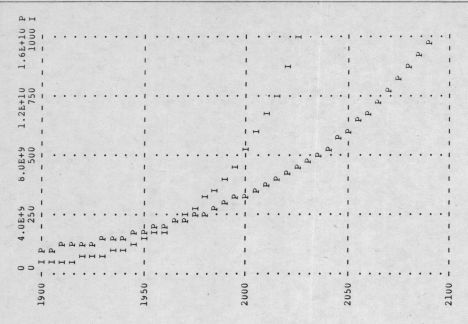

**Figure 31–6.**   Capital sector with exogenous inputs.

*Key to Figures 31–6 through 31–8*

F = Food per capita (vegetal equivalent) in kilograms   P = Population (persons)
    per year *                                             X = Index of persistent pollution (dimensionless)
I = Industrial output per capita in dollars

* Calculated by adding kilograms of vegetable food consumed plus 7 times the kilograms of animal food consumed (i.e., if one eats 1 kg of rice and 1 kg of beef, one has consumed the equivalent of 1 + 7 kg of vegetable food).

• Intensification of agricultural production, particularly when it has been forced by dire food shortages, leads in the World 3 agricultural sector to insufficient rates of investment in soil maintenance and thus decline of basic soil productive capacity.

• The agricultural sector is faced with diminishing returns on inputs and exponentially increasing costs on land development. Thus, it is unable to expand production in pace with an exponentially growing population.

The mechanisms involving soil deterioration are not included in the government's agricultural model and have been deleted in a further run of the unlinked agricultural sector to strengthen the analogy between the unlinked World 3 model and the government forecasts (Fig. 31–8). The result was a change in timing and magnitude, though not

in mode of behavior: Food per capita peaked later and at a higher plateau than in the previous unlinked run (compare Figs. 31–7 and 31–8), but it still rose to a high level and declined.

*Nonrenewable Resources.* In the unlinked version, the nonrenewable resource sector is driven by the exponentially growing population and industrial capital data inputs described in Table 31–1. The linkage from nonrenewable resources to industrial production was preserved in this simulation (Fig. 31–9) and the performance of industrial output per capita has been used as an index of system performance. Two variants of the isolated nonrenewable resource sector were simulated: In the first, which corresponds to the formulation used in the World 3 model, the marginal cost of resource extraction rises very rapidly as the

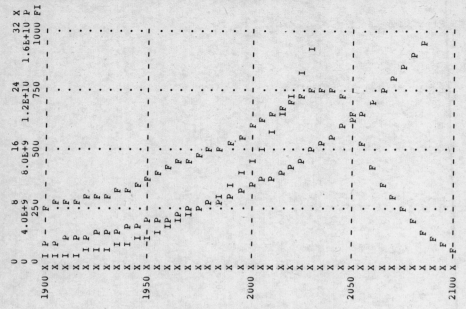

**Figure 31–7.** Agriculture sector with exogenous inputs.

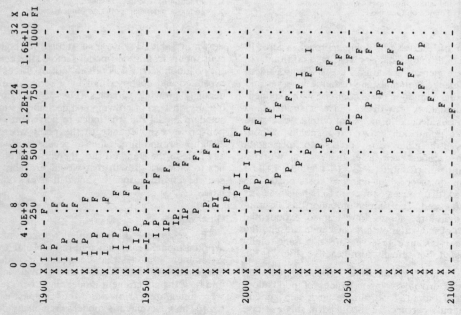

**Figure 31–8.** Agriculture sector with exogenous inputs assuming no erosion or urban-industrial use.

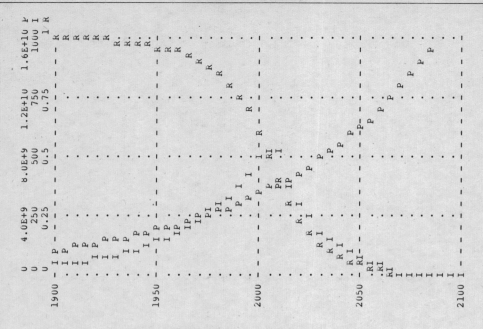

**Figure 31–9.**    Renewable resource sector with exogenous inputs.
*Key to Figures 31–9 through 31–11*

I = Industrial output per capita in dollars.          R = Fraction of resources remaining
P = Population (persons)                               X = Index of persistent pollution (dimensionless)

fraction of reserves remaining approaches zero. In the second, marginal costs were held constant.

Where increasing marginal costs were included, the influence of diminishing resource reserves and increasing extraction costs combine with exponential population growth to cause a sudden and percipitous decline in industrial output per capita. Because population grows exponentially without checks in the unlinked resource sector, per capita growth declines even faster than in the World 3 standard run. (Contrast Figs. 31–4 and 31–9.) The assumption of constant marginal costs breaks the feedback that causes extraction to halt as reserves are exhausted. The simulation under this assumption, therefore, shows unrestrained exponential growth of industrial output per capita, despite the fact that resource reserves are not only totally exhausted, but actually turn negative (Fig. 31–10).

*Persistent Pollution.* The persistent pollution sector is driven by input indices of population, industrial output, food, arable land, and agricultural inputs per hectare (assumed in this exercise to grow exponentially). When the growth rates

shown in Table 31–1 were substituted for endogenous inputs from other model sectors, the persistent pollution sector was driven, not by forces that expanded and collapsed but by a series of exponentially growing variables (Fig. 31–11). Consequently, instead of growing and declining as in the standard model run, the index of persistent pollution grows exponentially to the point where by 2030 it is around three times as severe as it was at any time in the standard run; thereafter, it continues to grow—a growth that would probably poison the entire biosphere should it ever come to pass.

## Observations

The sectorally disassembled version of the World 3 model bears sufficient resemblance to the government's model that comparing it with the integrated version of World 3 may provide insight into how the government model might behave if it were integrated. However, the analogy is not tight. The government's model is regionally disaggregated. World 3 is not. The government's model

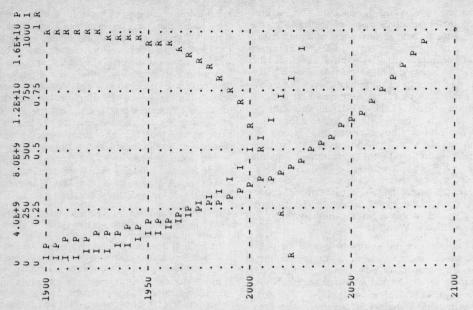

**Figure 31–10.**   Nonrenewable resource sector with exogenous inputs assuming constant marginal cost of the resource.

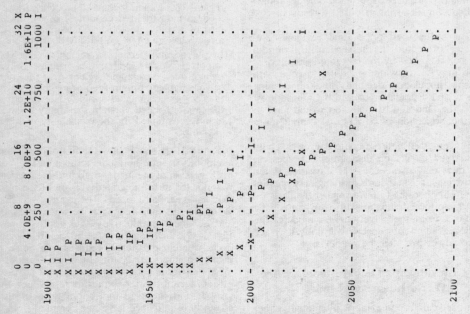

**Figure 31–11.**   Persistent pollution sector with exogenous inputs.

stresses energy, World 3 omits it. The government's model perceives many of the mechanisms of economic growth in much less straightforward terms than those shown in World 3. (For example, few government analysts would agree to the specification that industrial output is simply the product of the capital output ratio and the industrial capital stock.) The assumed schedule of exogenous inputs (Table 31–1) doesn't entirely coincide with present official expectations, and there are probably some strong but explicit assumptions about technological solutions and resource substitution in the government's model that do not figure in World 3.

Keeping these differences in mind, however, the exercise suggests that the following consequences might be expected, were the government's model to include some linkages such as those specified in World 3:

1. Competition for available capital between maintenance and expansion of the agricultural sector, development of new energy reserves, and investment in service and industrial sectors would lead to significant decreases in real GNP growth. Barring major technological advances, the presence of increasing costs (diminishing returns) for investment in minerals extraction and in agricultural development will increase the amount of economic activity needed for each unit of product produced, thus causing a sort of resource-cost inflation.

2. The rising food prices and regional food shortages projected in the agricultural model would be intensified by the fact that agriculture is not the only sector wanting capital to cope with increasing population demands and diminishing returns. Land degradation caused by intense pressure on the land and by pollution would tend to make the projection of agricultural output more gloomy.

3. Slower GNP and agricultural growth could have marked effects on demographic processes. Death rates may rise because of starvation. Lack of improvement in standards of living may prevent people from choosing to have smaller families.

4. Despite these indications of overly optimistic projections from the government's models, the possible transition into decline will not take place for a decade or two after the year 2000.

## The Government's Global Model vs. the World Integrated Model

A model can become more integrated, either through integration of the mechanisms determin-

ing previously exogenous variables (i.e., closing of feedback loops through exogenous variables) or through including more of the details of system interaction between the variables endogenous within a model. Conversely, a model can be made less integrated either by cutting internal feedbacks and replacing the formerly fed-back information with fed-in, exogenous information—as was done in the just described exercises using the World 3 model—or by cutting out internal feedbacks in such a way that former variables become constants—as was done in the exercises with the World Integrated Model.

The internal linkages that were severed in the less integrated version of the World Integrated Model (WIM) include the following:

• In the normal model version, energy deficits arising in the energy sector cause a drop in economic productivity in the economic sector. In the less integrated version, there is no change in the economic sector when energy supplies are insufficient (i.e., response is constant).

• In the normal version, mortality increases when available calories and/or protein are insufficient, particularly in the oldest and youngest age categories. In the less integrated version, mortality is not influenced by food availability.

• In the normal version, fertility patterns change with changes in income in such a way that, as a region's per capita income approaches those of modern industrialized countries, so will its pattern of fertility. In the less integrated version, income has no effect on fertility distributions.

• In the normal version, a region's capacity to import is constrained by its balance of payments; thus, developing regions may find themselves unable to import food or machinery when they have accumulated sizable trade deficits. In the less integrated version, the ability to import is not constrained by the availability of foreign exchange.

Figure 31–12 shows how the first three of these alterations fit into the model structure. The "normal" version of the model used in these exercises was not the most integrated version of the model that has been developed. There are versions of WIM that include feedback between starvation and economic productivity thus (dotted line in Fig. 31–12), building into the model the vicious cycle wherein destitution reduces a region's capacity to improve its lot. In other versions of WIM, environmental degradation may adversely effect agricultural production and economic growth and increase mortality. Both of these channels of influence have been omitted from the version of the model used in these exercises due

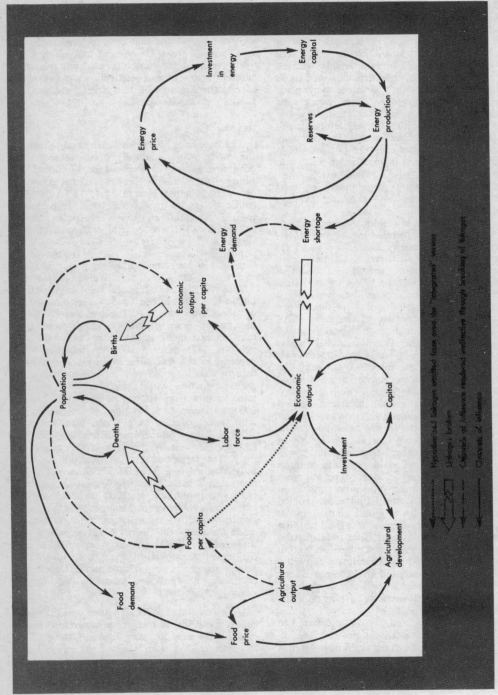

**Figure 31-12.** Major linkages in the World Integrated Model with designation of linkages broken in model-integration experiment. Trade linkages—and broken feedback from balance of payments to ability to import—not shown.

to the difficulty of substantiating them with precise quantitative information.

It should be noted that in most cases considered in this exercise, the omission of a linkage is *prima facie*, an optimistic act. It is a roseate depiction of the world that assumes energy deficits will not slow economic growth, food deficits won't cause starvation, starvation won't harm economic progress, shortages of foreign exchange won't stifle growth in the less developed countries, and abuse of the environment won't adversely effect agricultural production and human health. The only way that cutting linkages has removed optimism is in severing the tendency of increased income to lead to decreased family sizes. Naive though they seem, these assumptions are implicit in most nonintegrated global models—including the government's.

For further contrast of results, other versions of the "normal," more integrated model were developed using less optimistic assumptions about (1) the growth of fossil fuel supplies, (2) the growth of agricultural production, and (3) the amount of capital made available to the LDCs by the industrialized nations. In the optimistic normal case, it was assumed that annual global oil discoveries would grow above the base of the early 1970s until the early 1990s and reach a peak approximately 50 percent higher than the annual discoveries of the early 1970s—an optimistic forecast when contrasted to the forecasts made by the Workshop on Alternative Energy Strategies and the World Energy Conference, both of which projected near stable annual discoveries of oil resources. In the pessimistic version (which many would still call optimistic) it was assumed that the discovery rate would not increase above that of the early 1970s. In another pessimistic run, it was assumed that agricultural yields would be reduced roughly 20 percent on an average by the year 2000—a change that the modelers considered might be anticipated if the world is confronted with significant changes in global climate and/or serious ecological disturbances. In a third test, the amount of capital transfered from industrialized countries to LDCs was reduced to an extent where the LDCs would not accumulate unreasonably large (over 50 percent of GDP) foreign debts, and, in a final test, all three pessimistic hypotheses were introduced simultaneously. Here, only the combined-problems version of the more pessimistic runs will be considered. It will be referred to as the integrated-pessimistic version.

In most of the simulations performed for this study, the model was run only to the year 2000. As will be evident in the material showing model outputs, a 25-year simulation is sufficient to produce sizable differences between the more and less integrated versions of the model. Differences are even more significant on a regional basis, for some regions are at the present time quite sensitively balanced and can be brought into markedly different states over a relatively short period by altering the structure of the system pressures that control their development.

### Results

The outcomes of the less integrated version of the model were generally comparable to the government forecasts prepared for the Global 2000 Study. In the Study's forecasts, global economic production had grown to 17.4, 14.7, and 12.4 trillion dollars by the year 2000 in, respectively, the high, medium, and low forecasts. In the less integrated WIM, the equivalent figure for 2000 was 14.8 trillion dollars. In the Global 2000 Study population forecasts made by the Bureau of the Census high, medium, and low population estimates for 2000 were, respectively, 6.8, 6.4, and 5.9 billion. The less integrated WIM calculated 6.2 billion for 2000. In the Study's agricultural forecasts made by the U.S. Department of Agriculture, world grain production grows from 1,109 mmt (million metric tons) in the 1969–1971 base year to 2,175 mmt in 2000, an increase of 96 percent. In the less integrated model simulation, using a somewhat different scheme for measuring grain production, world grain production is calculated to grow from 1,278 mmt in 1975 to 2,647 in 2000, an increase of 107 percent. In conjunction with these gains in output, the less integrated WIM calculates an increase of fertilizer use from 88.6 to 227 mmt by the year 2000; correspondingly, the Department of Agriculture forecasts project an increase from 80 to 199 mmt. The less integrated WIM's energy projection—with global energy consumption in 2000 standing at 94.5 billion barrels of oil equivalent per year (about 550 quadrillion Btu) is consistent with projections made by the World Energy Conference and with those of the Workshop on Alternative Energy Strategies. Comparison with the Global 2000 Study estimate is not possible as the Department of Energy has provided estimates only for the years 1985 and 1990.

*More Integrated WIM.* The outcomes of simulations using the normal, more integrated version of the WIM were less sanguine than those of the less integrated version. The aggregate global economic product was 21 percent lower than that of the less integrated version: $11.7 billion instead of

$14.8 billion. Economic growth was fastest in the earlier years of the simulation and slowed considerable after 1990 when the energy situation began to put a serious drag on economic growth. Population grew to only 5.9 billion in 2000, as contrasted to 6.2 billion in the less integrated versions. Part of the lower growth was due to starvation (a cumulative total of 158 million starvation deaths were projected by 2000). Another part was due to lower fertility rates brought about by increasing incomes in those areas where economic growth surpassed population growth over the simulation period. Instead of the 107 percent increase in agricultural production projected in the less integrated WIM, the integrated version showed only an 85 percent increase. This led, however, to an increase of less than 85 percent in the grain available for human consumption due to the fact that global meat production, much of it

grain-fed, increased by 57 percent over the 25 year simulation.

In the test in which all three pessimistic assumptions were included in the more integrated model, outcomes were considerably worse than in the optimistic-integrated or less integrated simulations. Aggregate global income reached only 10.4 trillion dollars by 2000, and cumulative starvation deaths totaled 291 million people. World grain production reached only 2,032 mmt instead of 2,367 in the optimistic-integrated version and 2,647 in the less integrated case. The year 2000 world grain price reached $415 per metric ton, as opposed to $245 in the optimistic-integrated and $240 in the less integrated version. The three simulations can be compared (Figs. 31–13 and 31–14).

*Extension of Time Horizon.* In World 3 significant change in the model's mode of behavior does

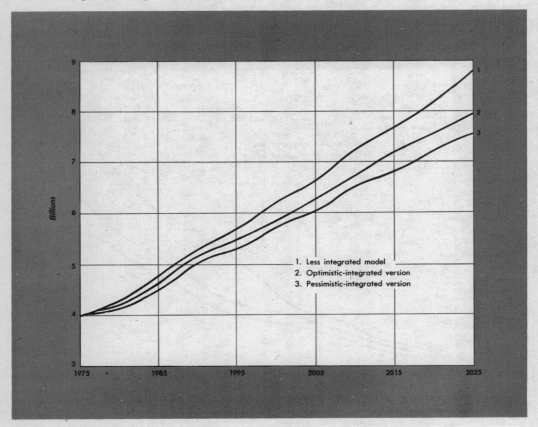

**Figure 31-13.** Global population projections for three versions of the World Intergrated Model.

not set in until after the year 2000. Many demographic changes have much stronger effects in the second generation than in the first. Growth rates on the order of 1–5 percent a year, with doubling times of 70 to 14 years—as experienced for the population and economic growth rates in most long-term models—will lead to significantly different balances and disturbances of balance after 50 years than after 25 years. Thus, it can be expected that the differences between the pessimistic-integrated, optimistic-integrated and less integrated versions of the World Integrated Model will become much more acute if the model's time horizon is extended.

This proves indeed to be the case. As can be seen in Figures 31–13 and 31–14, differences in global GNP and population in the year 2000 appear small by contrast to those of the year 2025. Moreover, by 2025 it begins to look as though the less integrated and optimistic-inte-

grated versions of the model are operating in a continued growth mode, while the pessimistic-integrated version appears to have slackened its rate of economic growth to the point where per capita income will begin to decline.

*Regional Differences.* The 12 regions considered in the World Integrated Model begin with differing initial conditions, which leave them balanced in states that vary in their ability to withstand stress. Thus, different regions undergo different patterns in their internal readjustment to system stresses as simulations progress over time. For example, regions such as South Asia, where large and fast growing human needs are coupled with poor endowments of economic or natural resources required to fill human needs, are likely to undergo more stress than regions such as North America, which still have untapped resources and whose rates of population growth are relatively slow. Thus, they are more likely to experience

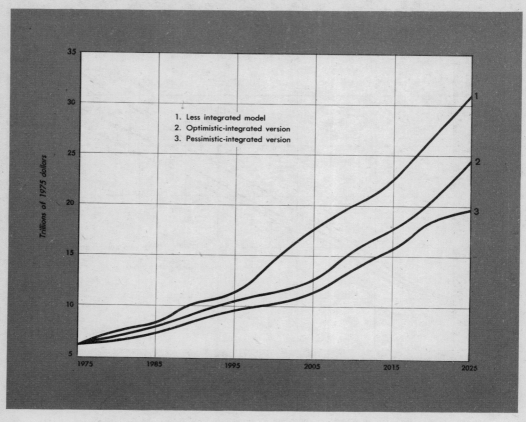

**Figure 31-14.** Global GNP projections for three versions of the World Integrated Model.

declines of previously growing variables and real-locations of economic resources.

Much of what has been termed "stress" in the preceding paragraph is, in abstract terms, infor-mation passed through the feedback loops that integrate the World Integrated Model. It follows, then, that differences between the more and less integrated versions of the model (i.e., versions with more and less feedback) would be greater for regions under severe stress and that the more stressful pessimistic-integrated version of the model would show more signs of basic shifts in model balance than would the optimistic-inte-grated version.

This inference is confirmed by model simula-

tions. As may be seen for GNP per capita by comparing Figures 31–15, 31–16, and 31–17, the three model versions behave similarly for North America, while producing wide divergence in behavior for Latin America and South Asia. In the less integrated version, Latin American GNP grew faster than did that of North America, though differences in population growth rates caused incomes in Latin America capita to grow more slowly than those in North America.

The model's behavior does not entirely corre-spond to our reasoned expectations, however. In the South Asian region, GNP per capita in 2000 is higher in the pessimistic-integrated case than it does in the optimistic-integrated case. This ap-

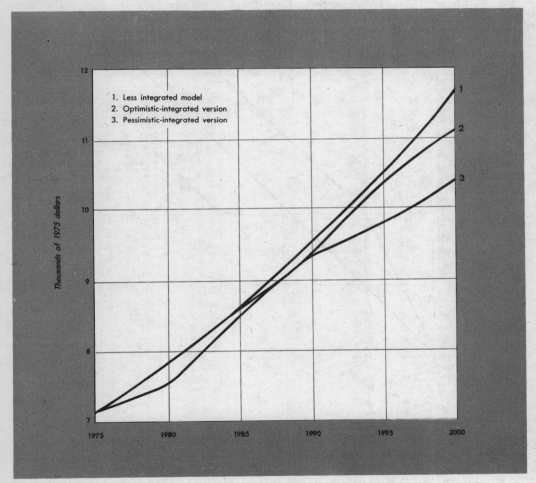

**Figure 31-15.** Projections of North American GNP per capita for three versions of the World Integrated Model.

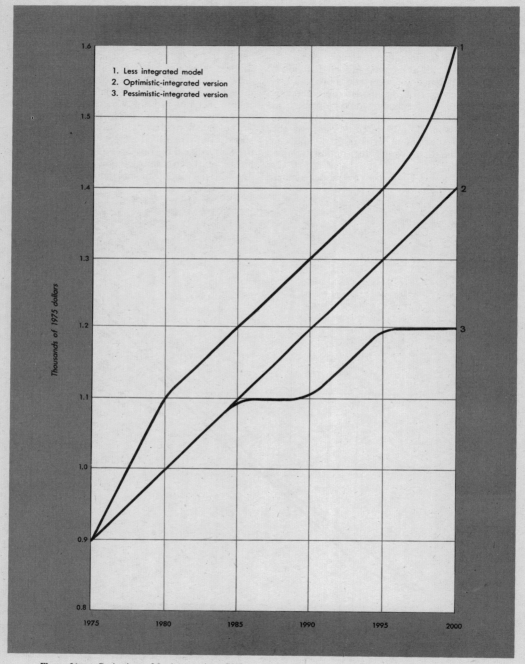

1. Less integrated model
2. Optimistic-integrated version
3. Pessimistic-integrated version

*Thousands of 1975 dollars*

**Figure 31-16.** Projections of Latin American GNP per capita for three versions of the World Integrated Model.

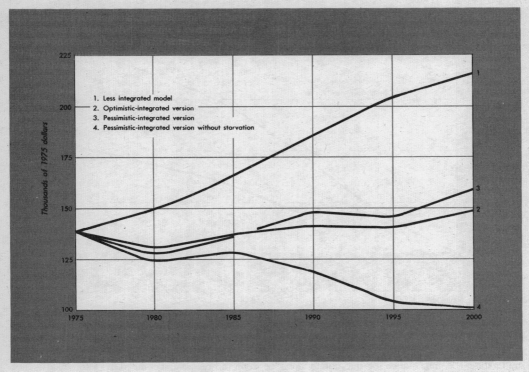

**Figure 31-17.** Projections of South Asian GNP per capita for four versions of the World Integrated Model.

pears to happen because starvation becomes so powerful in reducing population that income per capita begins to rise. In the pessimistic-integrated WIM, cumulative starvation has reached a value that amounts to about 20 percent of the living population by the year 2000 (Fig. 31–18).

(The apparent gain in average income per capita brought about by starvation need not be taken as indicative of the way the real system is likely to behave. It may well be an aberration of the model's structure. Had the linkage by which starvation conditions detract from economic productivity been included into the model's structure, it is quite likely that the pessimistic-integrated simulation would have ended with far lower income per capita in Figure 31–17 than did its optimistic counterpart. Here, clearly, the model's conceptual structure is more than the parameterization that shapes its behavioral tendencies.)

**Observations**

What can be inferred from the experimentation with the World Integrated Model about the distor-

tion imposed on government forecasts by the lack of integration in the methodology by which they are produced? The question is not easily answered. Before it can be approached, a decision must be made as to how much one is to believe the outputs of the World Integrated Model. Should one take seriously the differences in timing and magnitude in the spurts of growth and recession brought about by different formulations of the model in Figure 31–11? Should it be taken seriously that China and the Middle East are relatively unaffected by differences in model formulation while Eastern Europe and South Asia are quite sensitive? Should we believe the estimated magnitudes—for example, should the estimates for starvation be taken literally?

Behind these questions lie other, more important questions: Do the linkages in the model correspond sufficiently well to those in the real world to make the model credible? Are important linkages, such as the linkage that causes economic deterioration under famine conditions omitted even from the more integrated version of the

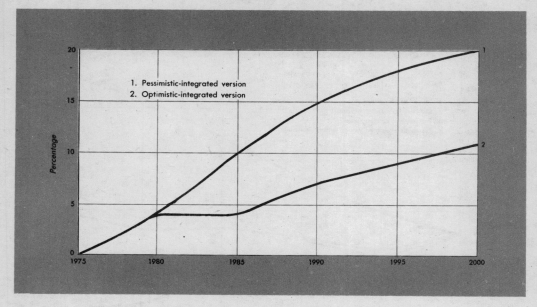

**Figure 31-18.** Projections of South Asian cumulative starvation as a percentage of population for two versions of the World Integrated Model.

model? Do the specified linkages exaggerate or understate the importance of interconnections? Will the real world follow the rules written into the model's structure when it has to choose between agriculture, energy, and other sectors in allocating scarce capital resources? (Investment functions are uncertain ground in modern economics. No formula has been found that can explain observed long-term investment behavior with good statistical results.) Will energy shortages curtail economic production in the fashion that the model describes? Will they have more or fewer lasting effects? More or fewer severe effects? Will the fuel type substitutions described in the model be possible?

If the questioning becomes too insistent, the model—and most other social system models with it—retreats behind a thick hedge of debatable assumptions. The response to most of the questions asked can only be "I don't know."

Despite the uncertainty surrounding specific findings from experiments investigating the effects of eliminating linkages in the World Integrated Model, a few generalizations can be made:

1. With a 25-year simulation interval, economic growth is more subject to alteration of its simulated behavior through addition of linkages than is population growth. A value difference of 50 percent for regional income (GNP) for 2000 is not uncommon among different model structures, while differences of 20 percent would be extreme for population. This stands to reason. Human reproductive patterns are biologically constrained; within a culture, they can be expected to change over the course of generations, whereas economic patterns appear to be relatively vulnerable to short-term perturbations.

2. The effects of breaking linkages depend on the linkages that are broken. In this exercise, the broken linkages involve trade, human birth and death rates, and the effect of energy shortages on economic growth. Consequently, the regions most affected were those modeled as deficient in energy supplies, as dependent on foreign trade for economic development, or as operating at levels of income where differences in income can be expected to have relatively large influences on rates of childbearing and mortality. Had another set of linkages been broken—for example, had the level of investment in agriculture not been responsive to the price of food—linkage breaking would have had different effects with different geographical distributions.

3. *It is every bit as arbitrary to omit linkages—*

and, thereby, implicitly assume that they have no effect on system behavior—as it is to include linkages of which one is unsure. There are, for example, many valid guesses about the effect of energy deficits on economic growth. "No effect" is one of the least likely outcomes in the set, but by default it seems to be the most commonly made assumption. While the art of global modeling is still at a stage where one must take the output of an integrated model with a great deal of skepticism, understanding of system linkages has progressed to the state where one must be even more skeptical of models that do not consider the probable effects of system interactions on long-term system behavior.

## Conclusions

Exercises cutting feedback within integrated world models reveal that the omission of system linkages greatly influences the results of forecasts, which suggests that the Government's Global Model, in that it leaves out important system feedbacks, is presenting a distorted picture of the probable future. The predictive error incurred by omissions of feedback is cumulative over time: in most cases it is not highly significant over a 5-year period but becomes important in a 20-year period and may become paramount over a 50-year span. Error is likely to be greater for regional forecasts than for the global aggregate.

Experiments with both the World 3 and the World Integrated Model suggest that omissions of linkages has made the government's forecasts overly optimistic. The experiments with the World Integrated Model suggest that the collective GNP forecasts for the year 2000 derived on a nonintegrated basis for the Global 2000 Study might have been 15–20 percent lower if a more integrated model specification had been used. For some regions the extent of overestimation may have been well over 50 percent.

However, the problem is not a simple question of integrated vs. nonintegrated models. The manner in which models are integrated is critical. Markedly different results could have been derived from both the World 3 Model and the World Integrated Model if different linkages had been included in the original models, or if different linkages had been severed in the experiments performed with model closure. It is therefore important that various schemes of model integration be used in analyses of global problems and that the schemes used are documented and maintained in a fashion that makes them available for criticism—and improvement.

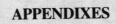

**APPENDIXES**

# Appendix A

# Lessons from the Past*

A survey of some of the commissions, studies, and task forces of the past 70 years whose experiences might be helpful to those now attempting to provide methods and instructions in support of decision-making for international efforts in population, resources, and the environment.

## Introduction

A study of the world's population, natural resources, and environment, made at this juncture, must be viewed in historical perspective. If the study is to serve as a foundation for the nation's longer-term planning, as directed by the President, it must take cognizance of the similar major efforts that have gone before and consider their strengths and weaknesses. Experiences of the past have much to teach us about what arrangements will and will not lead to quality analysis, decisions, and actions addressed to important long-term issues. This appendix will briefly examine studies, commissions, and institutional efforts conducted during this century on population, natural resources, environment, and related subjects to see what lessons can be learned from these experiences that might be applicable today. Commissions reviewed in this appendix have in common high-level governmental connections and include for the most part presidentially appointed or designated groups looking into national and international issues concerned with population, natural resources, or the environment.

There has never been an organized, continuing effort in the federal government to take a holistic approach toward consideration of probable changes in population, natural resources, and the environment. Yet a number of attempts to tackle parts of the problem have been undertaken during the last 70 years. Starting with the second Theodore Roosevelt Administration, continuing through 10 years of Franklin D. Roosevelt's Administration, and during the 25 years from Truman to Ford, temporary presidential and congressional

committees, commissions, and boards have flowered and wilted from time to time. For the most part, this futures work covered the nation's natural resources and materials and produced results that have proved helpful in some measure. Rarely, however, did such groups consider global potentials and problems, and then only superficially.

Over the years, government has tended to wait until crises occur and then has reacted to them—rather than study and analyze issues beforehand. On those occasions when groups have addressed problems with an eye to the future, a President—and others who initiate such studies—have seldom sustained the original level of interest, although much valuable data has been developed, alternative choices have been explored, and options have been presented in the form of recommendations. In most cases, suggestions or recommendations have been made for the formation of an institution to carry on the work of looking at future problems, but none of the recommendations has led to establishing a permanent group. Thus decision-makers and the public have never had the benefits that would accrue if a long-range study group at a high level of government, free from pressures for immediate results, had been in existence to offer alternatives that might help avert or solve future difficulties.

## Historical Perspective, 1908–1967

### The Theodore Roosevelt Administration

*National Conservation Commission (1908).* Even as far back as the first decade of the 20th century, when natural resources seemed virtually inexhaustible, a few conscientious conservationists were looking into the future to a time of scarcities and shortages. "The Nation is in the position of a man, who, bequeathed a fortune, has

*As noted in the acknowledgments, this appendix is the commissioned work of Robert Cahn and Patricia L. Cahn. The opinions expressed are those of the authors and are not necessarily endorsed by the participating agencies or their representatives.

gone on spending it recklessly, never taking the trouble to ask the amount of his inheritance, or how long it is likely to last." That picture, probably overly grim for its time, was painted at the initial meeting in 1908 of the executive committee of the newly appointed National Conservation Commission. The group promptly agreed to have a study made to estimate the existing available natural resources, the proportion that had already been used or exhausted, the rate of increase in their consumption, and the length of time these resources would last if the present rate of use was to continue. Thus began the first national inventory of natural resources.

President Theodore Roosevelt created the Commission as an outgrowth of the May 1908 White House Conference on Natural Resources. He appointed 49 members, with about equal representation among scientists, industry leaders, and public officials, but when the President requested funds of Congress to carry out the inventory, the Senate voted down the bill. Nevertheless, by presidential order Roosevelt directed the heads of several bureaus to make investigations as requested by the Commission in the areas of minerals, water resources, forests, and soils.

The full Commission met on December 1, 1908, to hear the reports of experts, which were later transmitted to the President in three volumes. This first inventory of the nation's natural resources was "but an approximation to the truth," wrote resource expert Charles Richard Van Hise in 1911. "But it is an immense advance over guesses as the natural wealth of the nation . . . [and] furnishes a basis for quantitative and therefore scientific discussion of the future of our resources." The Commission's report was published as a Senate document in a limited edition. (The Commission's recommendation for a popular edition had been turned down by the House Committee on Printing.)

Before leaving office, President Theodore Roosevelt sought to broaden interest in the conservation of resources beyond U.S. boundaries. He invited the governors of Canada and Newfoundland and the President of Mexico to appoint Natural Resource Commissioners and send representatives to a meeting with his National Conservation Commission. At this first North American Conservation Conference, held in Washington, D.C., in February 1909, a Declaration of Principles was issued, and the founding of permanent conservation commissions in each country was recommended.

In a separate action, President Roosevelt requested all the world powers to meet at The Hague for the purpose of considering the conservation of the natural resources of the entire globe. Efforts to institutionalize concern for preservation of natural resources faded, however, after William Howard Taft became President in March 1909, and the international conference was never held.

The intense congressional opposition accorded these efforts resulted not so much from objections to the subject matter as from reaction to what the legislators regarded as the President's attempt to bypass Congress by appointing too many presidential commissions. The opposition prevented the National Conservation Commission and its inventory of resources from becoming a congressionally mandated effort. Gifford Pinchot, whom Roosevelt had appointed as head of the National Conservation Commission, did keep the Commission alive, but without President Taft's approval and at his own expense, and the Commission evolved into a kind of private lobby for conservation.

## The Hoover Administration

*President's Research Committee on Social Trends (1929).* The first organized effort in the area of social reporting was made in the autumn of 1929, when President Herbert Hoover appointed a President's Research Committee on Social Trends. The six-member committee, chaired by Wesley C. Mitchell, included Charles E. Merriam (who, with Mitchell, was to become a member of Franklin D. Roosevelt's original three-man National Planning Board) and William F. Ogburn, who was designated director of research. The Committee was called upon "to examine and report upon recent social trends in the United States with a view to providing such a review as might supply a basis for the formulation of large national policies looking to the next phase in the Nation's development." The Committee issued annual reports, under the editorship of Ogburn, for five years—until the end of the Hoover Administration in 1933.

Ogburn then published a book, *Recent Social Trends,* comprising a report by the Committee, to which a group of papers by experts had been added. In a Foreword, dated October 1932, Hoover wrote: "It should serve to help all of us to see where social stresses are occurring and where major efforts should be undertaken to deal with them constructively." The Committee claimed that the importance of their reports and of the book was in the effort to interrelate the disjointed factors and elements in the social life of America and to view the situation as a whole.

Many government organizations and private citizens contributed to the study, but the work received its major funding from the Rockefeller Foundation. The book did not take up war, peace, or foreign policy, nor did it mention the economic situation that was developing into the Great Depression, and there was no chapter devoted to social science research itself. The topics discussed were population, utilization of natural wealth, the influence of invention and discovery, communication, shifting occupational patterns, the rise of metropolitan communities, the status of racial and ethnic groups, the family and its functions, the activity of women outside the home, childhood and youth, the people as consumers, health and medical practice, public welfare activities, and government and society.

In a 1969 article, social scientist Daniel Bell, harking back to *Recent Social Trends,* commented on the report's chapter on medicine, which dealt with the rise of specialized medical practice, the divergence between research and general practice, and the consequences of geographical concentration. If the signposts in that chapter had been heeded, he wrote, they "would have gone far to avert the present crisis in the delivery of health care." Bell also claimed that the chapter on metropolitan communities was an accurate foreshadowing of postwar suburban problems.

### The Franklin D. Roosevelt Administration

*National Planning Board; National Resources Board; National Resources Planning Board 1933–43.* For the first 10 years of Franklin D. Roosevelt's Presidency, the availability of natural resources to meet future needs for at least six years ahead was a primary consideration of the National Resources Planning Board and its two predecessor organizations. Two special commitments of the President—conservation of natural resources and government planning to achieve social goals—were linked in Roosevelt's use of this Board.

The effort started in 1933 when a National Planning Board was established under Interior Secretary Harold Ickes' Public Works Administration to coordinate the planning of public works projects. The President's uncle, Frederick Delano,* was a Board member along with political

* Delano had been chairman of a privately funded citizens study of the Joint Committee on Bases of Sound Land Policy, which in 1929 issued a 168-page report *What About the Year 2000?* This was an economic summary of answers to the questions: "Will our land area in the United States meet the demands of our future population?" and "How are we to determine the best use of our land resources?"

scientist Charles Merriam and economist Wesley Mitchell. The following year, when Congress by joint resolution asked the President for a comprehensive plan for the development of the nation's rivers, Roosevelt sought to make the Planning Board a part of the White House and to give it the lead role in the river-planning project. Ickes, aided by other Cabinet officers, fought the President's idea, and a compromise resulted in the so-called National Resources Board, its six Cabinet officers under Ickes, as Chairman, outnumbering the three members of the former Planning Board.

In December 1934, the new Board produced an extensive report. Its almost 500 pages, the Board claimed, "brings together for the first time in our history, exhaustive studies by highly competent inquirers of land use, water use, minerals, and related public works in their relation to each other and to national planning." The report addressed itself to such problems as "Maladjustments in Land Use and in the Relation of Our Population to Land, and Proposed Lines of Action." It also included an inventory of water resources, a discussion of policies for their use and control, recommendations for a national mineral policy and a discussion of its international aspects.

The December 1934 report to the President pointed to the significance of the recommendations from the two technical committees that had assisted in preparing the report—one on land-use planning and one on water planning. Both committees recommended the need for a permanent planning organization. The report repeated a recommendation of the former Planning Board that a permanent national planning agency be established. In defense of planning, the report stated:

It is not necessary or desirable that a central system of planning actually cover all lines of activity or forms of behavior. Such planning overreaches itself. Over-centralized planning must soon begin to plan its own decentralization, for good management is local self-government under a central supervision. Thus wise planning provides for the encouragement of local and personal initiative.

Bills to institutionalize a national planning agency were defeated in Congress during the next four years, with opposition coming from antiplanners in Congress, from within the Administration (notably the Army Corps of Engineers, the Forest Service, the Tennessee Valley Authority, and the Bureau of Reclamation), and from a powerful lobbying group known as the Rivers and Harbors Congress.

Finally, in 1939, after Roosevelt had succeeded in getting his executive reorganization plan through Congress and establishing an Executive Office of the President (without the planning agency, of which Congress unrelentingly disapproved), he reconstituted his planning group into the National Resources Planning Board and placed it in his Executive Office by presidential order. Although this action was unpopular with Congress, Roosevelt used his personal influence to get about $1 million a year appropriated for the Board's activities.

From 1934 to 1939, Delano, Merriam, and Mitchell had continued to serve as a planning board and as planning advisers to the President. As members of the revised National Resources Planning Board, the three established a number of technical committees and a field organization. By 1943 the Board had 150 full-time Washington employees, 72 field employees, and 35 per diem consultants. As its staff proliferated, however, it lost much of the influence it had gained as a coordinating body and became merely one agency among many. It met formally with the President more than 50 times, and held many informal meetings for discussion of long-range problems. Its proposals, however, did not ordinarily include detailed recommendations for implementation, and the Board did not strive for action. In 1939, when World War II began, the Board shifted its priority to postwar planning. After the 1940 election, President Roosevelt instructed the Board "to collect, analyze, and collate all constructive plans for significant public and private action in the post-defense period insofar as these have to do with the natural and human resources of the Nation."

Although Roosevelt had been the Board's chief (and sometimes its only) power base, he finally became resigned to the fact that it could not be permanently established and in 1943 signed an appropriations bill directing that the National Resources Planning Board be abolished and that its functions not be transferred to any other agency.

During the 10 years of their existence, the Board and its predecessors issued numerous research publications, including extensive data collections and studies of many national problems. They conducted statistical and analytical studies on subjects such as river basin development and frequently aided some federal agencies in getting their ideas up to the President. More than 300 publications reveal how Roosevelt's boards had expanded from natural resource studies and planning into other futures efforts and subjects that had largely been neglected.*

Part of the Roosevelt boards' poor relations with Congress derived from the members' belief that as a staff arm of the President they should not develop close relationships with Congress. The National Resources Planning Board gave little encouragement to members of Congress who were sympathetic, and its work (some Congressmen thought) enhanced the power of the Presidency unduly and contributed to loss of power by Congress.

## The Truman Administration

*President's Materials Policy Commission (1951).* After the high rate of consumption of natural resources, especially minerals, during World War II, potential scarcities of industrial materials threatened the nation. Then the Korean War caused prices of materials to rise sharply, and the fact that the nation's resources strength was indeed limited became increasingly recognized. On the recommendation of W. Stuart Symington, then chairman of the National Security Resources Board, President Harry S. Truman created the President's Materials Policy Commission in January 1951. He charged the new Commission to "make an objective enquiry into all major aspects of the problem of assuring an adequate supply of production materials for our long-range needs and to make recommendations which will assist me in formulating a comprehensive policy on such materials." In a letter to Commission Chairman William S. Paley (Columbia Broadcasting System Board Chairman), President Truman wrote: "We cannot allow shortages of materials to jeopardize our national security nor to become a bottleneck to our economic expansion."

When the President called Mr. Paley and the four other members of the blue-ribbon citizen Commission to his office late in January 1951, he included in his directions the need to make their study international in scope and to consider the needs and resources of friendly nations. The 18-month study was the most comprehensive of its

---

* Significant titles include: *Economics of Planning of Public Works; Human Resources; Trends in Urban Government; Rural Zoning; Our Cities, Their Role in the National Economy; Technology and Planning; Consumer Incomes; Problems of a Changing Population; A Plan for New England Airports; Urban Planning and Land Policies; Housing Progress and Problems; War-Time Planning in Germany; Rates and Rate Structure; Transportation Coordination; Railroad Financing; After Defense—What?; The Future of Transportation; The Framework of an Economy of Plenty;* and *Post-War Problems of the Aircraft Industry.*

type ever done. Seven Cabinet departments and 25 federal agencies or commissions made special investigations, loaned personnel, and gave consulting help. Research assistance was provided by 20 universities, as well as by experts from more than 40 industries, the International Materials Conference, the International Bank for Reconstruction and Development, and the International Monetary Fund.

The resulting 5-volume report, *Resources for Freedom*, published in June 1952, contained some far-reaching recommendations, but it did not create any great public splash, nor did it have an immediate effect on national policy. It was, however, the first major study to perceive the resources situation as a problem not of absolute shortages but of dealing with rising "real costs," which would be at least as pernicious than shortages. In retrospect, it is easy to see that the Commission neglected several areas now perceived as vital, such as population trends and environmental factors relating to the new technological developments that the Commission assumed would alleviate many future shortage problems. While the report emphasized the danger of increased U.S. dependence on foreign sources of raw materials, it saw as the main problem the technical difficulties of obtaining materials from less developed countries without first considering the trade or political factors that might block access to the resources.

The Commission's inventory of resources, its studies, and its projections for the ensuing 25 years were extremely valuable, and a number of its recommendations were prescient. In projecting materials availability a quarter of a century ahead, it proved remarkably accurate in several areas. The Commission recommended that the nation should have "a comprehensive energy policy and program which embraces all the narrower and more specific policies and programs relating to each type of energy and which welds these pieces together into a consistent and mutually supporting pattern with unified direction."

The concluding chapter of the Commission's first volume addressed the problem of "Preparing for Future Policy." It stated that no single study by a temporary group can deal adequately with the immensely complicated situation "cutting across the entire economy, persisting indefinitely, and changing from year to year."

The report recommended that a single agency— not an operating agency—should survey the total pattern of activities in the materials and energy field, make periodic reports to industry, the public, and to the legislative as well as executive branches of government and be an advisory body located in the Executive Office of the President, framing recommendations for long-range policy (as much as 25 years ahead). The Commission somewhat perfunctorily recommended as a possible solution that the existing National Security Resources Board (NSRB) in the Executive Office of the President serve this function. The NSRB could, if given funds and authority, collect in one place the facts, analyses and program plans of other agencies on materials and energy problems. The Board could also evaluate materials programs and policies in all these fields; it could recommend appropriate action for the guidance of the President, the Congress, and the Executive agencies, and report annually to the President on the long-term outlook for materials, with emphasis on significant new problems, major changes in outlook, and necessary modifications of policy or program. The Paley Commission suggested that to the fullest extent consistent with national security, the annual reports should be made public.

The Paley Commission report reached President Truman in June 1952. By then the resources scarcity issue had lost its political priority and failed to arouse public's concern. Truman took the logical step of directing the NSRB to review the report and its recommendations and to advise him of follow-up actions deemed appropriate. He wrote to NSRB Chairman Jack Gorrie on July 9, 1952, asking the Security Resources Board to

initiate a continuing review of materials (including energy) policies and programs within the executive branch, along the lines recommended by the Commission, and report annually to the President on the progress of materials programs and policies and the long-term outlook for materials, with emphasis on significant new programs.

The NSRB had been established within the Executive Office of the President under the National Security Act of 1947, and its function was to advise the President on the coordination of military, industrial, and civilian mobilization. Thus, many of its activities were concerned with materials. Serving on the Board were the Secretaries of Agriculture, Commerce, Interior, and Labor and the heads of the National Security Agency, the Defense Materials Procurement Agency, and the Defense Production Administration.

NSRB Chairman Gorrie submitted his report to President Truman in 1953, six weeks before Truman left office. It included a recommendation for the President to "ask the Congress to provide the NSRB with adequate funds to enable the Board to develop policy designed to improve the national position with respect to resources affecting the Nation's security, and to carry out the directives in the President's memorandum of July 9, 1952."

Truman left office without taking any action on this recommendation. The new Eisenhower Administration, committed in the election campaign to a lessening of federal intervention and a cutting back of government agencies, ignored the Commission's recommendations, and NSRB eventually faded out of existence.

*Resources for the Future* (1952). William Paley, foreseeing the problem posed by lack of a continuing body to carry out recommendations of the President's Materials Policy Commission, set up an office with his own funds to respond to questions about the Commission's report, to keep some of the statistics up to date, and to keep public interest alive. He established his small office in 1952 as a nonprofit corporation with the name Resources for the Future.

About this time, a group of conservationists, led by former National Park Service Director Horace M. Albright (who was also prominent in the mining industry) were trying to interest the Ford Foundation in establishing a fund to provide financial assistance to conservation organizations. Among Albright's 25 cosponsors was Paley, who also served on a Ford Foundation program development committee on natural resources. This committee recommended establishment of an independent resources center to provide up-to-date information in conservation and natural resources and a continuous evaluation of the long-range programs of the federal government. The committee also recommended a White House National Resources Conference, patterned after Theodore Roosevelt's 1908 Conference on Natural Resources.

As a result of these recommendations, the Ford Foundation agreed to back the conference and to set up a research center—for which purpose Paley then turned over his nonprofit corporation, Resources for the Future. At a December 1952 meeting in New York, Albright succeeded in getting President-Elect Dwight D. Eisenhower to agree to sponsor the White House Conference. But shortly after inauguration, the President's Chief of Staff Sherman Adams sought to kill the Conference because, according to Albright, Adams thought he detected a strong odor of "ex-New Dealers," idealists, and planners on the staff and board of directors of Resources for the Future. After Albright and Paley persuaded Lewis W. Douglas, former director of the Bureau of the

Budget and a conservative critic of the New Deal, to serve as Conference chairman, Adams compromised. He agreed that Eisenhower would be the Conference keynote speaker but insisted that the Conference should not be sponsored by the White House. The resulting 3-day Mid-Century Conference on Resources for the Future drew 1,600 participants in December 1953. Although it endorsed no legislative or political proposals, the Conference did call attention to the need for policy changes and continuing research in resources management.

Resources for the Future carried on some of the work of the Paley Commission. Although it could not directly influence government policy and was not ordinarily international in scope, it continued to make long-range projections of the national economy based on population, the labor force, productivity, and other factors. It then tried to predict from these findings the probable resource requirements, and match them against possible supply, with attention to prices. Paley continued to serve on the board of directors and was partly responsible for the inauguration of a major study, published in 1963, *Resources in America's Future, 1960–2000.*

### The Eisenhower Administration

*Outdoor Recreation Resources Review Commission* (1958). One of the most successful presidential commissions in recent times—in terms of getting its major recommendations implemented— was the Outdoor Recreation Resources Review Commission, which spanned two administrations. Congress passed the Act establishing the Commission in June 1958 after many years of lobbying by conservation groups. Although the Commission was not established by presidential request, Eisenhower readily signed the law and, after a delay of several months, appointed the respected philanthropist and conservationist Laurance S. Rockefeller Chairman. Eight congressmen and six public figures representing widespread interests in outdoor recreation rounded out the Commission.

Although the timing of the Commission's report of its study violated one of the basic axioms of presidential commissions (don't start a study in one Administration and present the results to a new Administration—especially an Administration of the other political party), almost everything else about the Commission was a perfect example of how a presidential commission can operate to achieve its ends. The law establishing the Commission was carefully drawn so as to involve members of Congress who could later sponsor legislation to carry out the Commission's recommendations. The law provided for the appointment of two majority and two minority members of both the Senate and House Interior Committees. This provision ensured stability in case of changes in congressional assignments.

The law also provided for an Advisory Council composed of the Secretaries of federal departments and the heads of independent agencies with a direct interest and responsibility in outdoor recreation, as well as 25 citizen members covering most interests and geographic areas.

Chairman Rockefeller had national stature and an aptitude for working with Congress, the executive branch, and citizen groups. He attracted a bright, capable staff with administrative abilities (it included the future Governor of Massachusetts and the first head of the National Endowment for the Arts).

The research undertaken by the Commission gave a solid base to its recommendations and was valuable as well as newsworthy. The recommendations included an institution through which Commission goals could be carried out. A follow-on citizen lobbying and information activity was organized by the Commission chairman to stimulate continuous press and public interest and to work for implementation of the recommendations.

The Act creating the Commission set forth three basic goals. They were to determine: (1) the outdoor recreation wants and needs of the American people at that time and for the years 1976 and 2000; (2) the recreation resources of the nation available to satisfy those needs—for the same three periods; and (3) policies and programs that would ensure that present and future needs would be adequately met.

The Commission staff, working with federal agencies and private groups, devised a system of classifying outdoor recreation resources so as to provide a common framework and serve as a tool in recreation management. Particular types of resources and areas would be managed for specific uses such as high density recreation, unique natural areas, wilderness, or historic and cultural sites.

Five joint two-day meetings were held by the Commission with the Advisory Council, during which they made on-site inspections of the various types of federal and state recreation areas, including some where they camped out overnight. When the Commission adopted a draft of its recommendations, they submitted the recommendations to the Advisory Council for additions or changes.

The major items among the 53 recommendations of the Commission were:

- Establishment of a Bureau of Outdoor Recreation in the Department of the Interior to coordinate the recreation activities of the federal agencies, to assist state and local governments with technical aid, to administer a grants-in-aid program for acquisition planning for development and acquisition of needed areas, and to act as a clearinghouse for information.

- Development of a federal grants-in-aid program with initial grants to states of up to 75 percent of the total costs for planning and 40–50 percent of acquisition costs.

- Provision of guidelines for managing areas, with a common system of classifying recreation lands.

When the Commission report was submitted to President Kennedy by Chairman Rockefeller in January 1962, it had the unanimous approval of the 15 commissioners. The timing of its release was propitious. The popularity of outdoor recreation was booming. Federal and state land-management agencies were finding it difficult to cope with the growing numbers of visitors, and Congress welcomed help in devising solutions.

Rockefeller did not leave implementation of the recommendations to chance or political whim. With private funds and the cooperation of the other citizen members of the Commission, he immediately established the Citizens Committee for the Outdoor Recreation Resources Review Commission Report. Two full-time coordinators were hired, both experienced conservationists familiar with congressional procedures. Working principally through citizen groups, the organization concentrated in 1963–64 on acquainting citizens with the Commission's report and stimulating discussion and resolution of public policy issues in the light of its findings and recommendations. A booklet, "Action for Outdoor Recreation for Americans," was widely circulated and served as a follow-up to the report. Leaders of the Senate and House Interior Committees who had served on the Commission introduced legislation to implement its major recommendations.

Congress created the Bureau of Outdoor Recreation in the Department of the Interior to serve as a focal point for outdoor recreation at the federal level and as a liaison point for similar state and local agencies. A Land and Water Conservation Fund was established by Congress to assist states and local governments and federal agencies to acquire land for recreation. The fund was generously endowed with a share of the income from federal offshore oil revenues. In 1964, Congress passed the National Wilderness Act, provid-

APPENDIX

ing for a national wilderness system, as recommended by the Commission.

*President's Commission on National Goals (1960).* A year before leaving office, President Eisenhower appointed the President's Commission on National Goals "to develop a broad outline of coordinated policy and programs to set up a series of goals in various areas of national activity." This privately financed activity was sponsored by the American Assembly (Eisenhower had requested that the effort be nonpartisan and have no connection with the government). The 10 members of the Commission were all from the private sector; Henry M. Wriston served as chairman and William P. Bundy as director of the Commission's staff. Approximately 100 people took part in discussions sponsored by the Commission, and 14 individuals submitted essays, which were subsequently published in 1960, just before Eisenhower left office.

The publication's two major sections covered U.S. domestic goals and the U.S. role in the world. There were chapters on education, science, the quality of American culture, and technological change, but there were no formal recommendations, and no follow-up activity took place.

## The Kennedy Administration

*National Academy of Sciences Committee on Natural Resources (1963).* At the suggestion of Presidential Science Adviser Jerome Weisner, President John F. Kennedy announced in a Special Message on Natural Resources, February 1961, that he would be asking the National Academy of Sciences to undertake

a thorough and broadly based study and evaluation of the present state of research underlying the conservation, development, and use of natural resources, how they are formed, replenished and may be substituted for, and giving particular attention to needs for basic research and to projects that will provide a better basis for natural resources planning and policy formulation.

Since Detlev W. Bronk, then President of the National Academy of Sciences, lacked a background in natural resources, he appointed a Committee on Natural Resources to lead the study. The Committee consisted of 13 Academy members, one of whom also represented government, Roger Revelle, then Science Adviser to the Secretary of the Interior. Bronk did not appoint a Committee chairman but convened the organizing sessions himself and gave most of the responsibility for preparing the summary report to John S. Coleman of the Academy staff.

The Committee held a number of seminars led by members of the Committee and each bringing together 20 to 30 experts from government, industry, and academia to discuss issues to be covered in seven reports: Renewable Resources, Water Resources, Environmental Resources (never completed), Mineral Resources, Energy Resources, Marine Resources, and Social and Economic Aspects of Natural Resources. After each seminar, the Committee convened for a week to revise its papers and discuss preparation of a summary document. Although Frank Notestein of the Population Council was a Committee member, no major population-related studies were undertaken. Two of the six completed reports are of special interest here. "Energy Resources" by M. King Hubbert, then employed by the Shell Development Company, estimated the nation's crude oil reserves at about 175 billion barrels. He predicted that production would peak in the late 1960s and that thereafter domestic production and reserves would decline (an estimate that has proved highly accurate). However, Interior's then Assistant Chief Geologist Vincent E. McKelvey, had authored a study for the U.S. Geological Survey which estimated that total domestic oil reserves were on the order of 590 billion barrels. McKelvey predicted that production would not peak for many years and that scarcities would not occur for 30 years or so. As a result of this disagreement, the committee's summary report did not base its recommendations on Hubbert's projections and did not present the oil-depletion issue in a form that made clear the consequences and the course of action that should be taken if Hubbert was correct.

Gilbert White's report "Social and Economic Aspects of Natural Resources" considered the worldwide effects of population growth and distribution on natural resources and also identified the many natural resource areas that required coordination between resource development and the overall welfare of society. White stressed the need to compare demand with supply in both energy and mineral production, to determine who would bear the costs of meeting future energy requirements.

The Committee's summary report to the President made 11 major recommendations, of which the last stressed the need for a small central natural resources group within the federal government. Such a group should be capable of conducting a continuing overall evaluation of research problems related to resources, of bringing to public attention evaluations of natural resources research needs, and of initiating and supporting research that falls outside the interests and competencies of existing agencies. The group should also provide support for international cooperation in resources research.

Submitted to the President in November 1962, the Academy report was referred to Presidential Science Adviser Wiesner, who in turn referred it to the President's Science Advisory Council and the Federal Council for Science and Technology. Whatever interest Wiesner had been able to generate at the presidential level at the beginning of the project had evaporated by the time the report was completed. Although the Academy was eventually asked to design specific programs to implement two of the 11 recommendations, no new research programs were undertaken, and no continuing institution was established.

In the opinion of John Coleman, who was responsible for the summary report, a temporary body such as the Academy's Committee on Natural Resources had little opportunity to build a constituency for its recommendations in Congress or among the public. And without supporters in positions of power or influence, there was no way to implement the findings. The Academy did, however, involve more than one hundred experts in the course of preparing the reports, and Coleman suggests that uncounted benefits came from the attention given to future research problems by these experts.

### The Johnson Administration

*National Commission on Technology, Automation, and Economic Progress (1964).* In the course of its work, the National Commission on Technology, Automation, and Economic Progress (established by Congress in 1964 with 14 members appointed by President Lyndon B. Johnson) considered national goals and a system of social reporting. The Commission's report to the President early in 1966 stated that formation of a national body of distinguished citizens representing diverse interests and constituencies and devoted to a continuing discussion of national goals would be valuable. "Such a body would be concerned with 'monitoring' social change, forecasting possible social trends, and suggesting policy alternatives to deal with them," the report stated. "Its role would not be to plan the future, but to point out what alternatives are achievable and at what cost." Five of the Commission members insisted on including a footnote expressing regret that the report did not explicitly recommend establishing such a national body, but nothing was done about the matter by the President or by Congress.

*Public Land Law Review Commission (1965).* Many observers believe that inclusion of powerful members of Congress on a commission leads to a high rate of implementation, as in the case of the Outdoor Recreation Resources Review Commission. Perry R. Hagenstein, who was appointed senior staff member of the Public Land Law Review Commission in 1965, believes that having members of Congress on a commission is no guarantee that legislative proposals may ensue.

In a paper "Commissions and Public Land Policies: Setting the Stage for Change" (presented at an April 1977 Denver Conference on the Public Land Law Review Commissions), Hagenstein wrote:

Being party to a commission's report does not bind a member to support its recommendations. Within 48 hours of the release of the [1970] Public Land Law Review Commission report, one of the Commission's influential congressional members had already denounced the report roundly and disassociated himself from some of its major recommendations. In addition, members of Congress face the realities of change too. Although only one of the 13 congressional members of the Public Land Law Review Commission failed to serve in the Congress following release of the Commission's report, six more, including the Chairman, had dropped by the wayside in the next Congress, the 93rd. Today (seven years later) only two members of the PLLRC, the Chairmen of the Senate Energy and Natural Resources Committee and the House Interior and Insular Affairs Committee, remain in Congress.

Hagenstein notes that the Public Land Law Review Commission, although structured along the lines of the Outdoor Recreation Resources Review Commission, was actually not a presidential commission. Twelve of its members, plus the chairman, were chosen by Congress from Congress; there were only six presidential appointees. Hagenstein added:

Participation by the Executive Branch in this predominately congressional effort was necessary to give the Commission credibility with recreation and preservation interests and to gain a semblance of commitment to its recommendations from the Executive Branch itself. Some congressional members found it difficult to separate their public posture in committee hearings and with constituents from the private deliberations at the Commission meetings.

Timing and the political atmosphere also played a part in hampering follow-up to the Public Land Law Review Commission:

It was conceived during President Kennedy's

term, the public members were appointed by President Johnson, and it reported to President Nixon. It had no home in the White House, and its recommendations, many of which were based on criticism of the way in which the laws were being administered, did not have the enthusiastic support of the public land management agencies.
. . .

Chairman [Wayne] Aspinall stated at various times that once the Commission finished its work, the next step would be up to the Congress. . . . Some three months after the 92nd Congress convened and nine months after the Commission's report had been filed, H.R. 7211, a bill that put a number of the Commission recommendations in a cumbersome package, was introduced by Chairman Aspinall. The bill in its entirety had a constituency of one, although that one, Aspinall, was in a position as Chairman of the Interior and Insular Affairs Committee to make the bill move. . . . Power in the Congress accumulates slowly, but erodes rapidly, and Aspinall was unable to bring H.R. 7211 to a floor vote following his defeat in a primary some weeks before the 92nd Congress adjourned. Faced with its own problems of timing, elections and politics, the Congress is not the place to center responsibility for follow-up.

*Toward a Social Report (1967) and Other Studies of the Mid-1960s.* Johnson's Secretary of Health, Education, and Welfare John Gardner became interested in social indicators and persuaded the President to assign to his Department the task of developing "the necessary social statistics and indicators to supplement those prepared by the Bureau of Labor Statistics and the Council of Economic Advisers. With these yardsticks we can better measure the distance we have come and plan the way ahead." Johnson so directed in his Message to Congress on Domestic Health and Education.

Under prodding from HEW Under Secretary Wilbur J. Cohen, Assistant Secretary for Planning William Gorham hired Mancur Olson in 1967 as Deputy Assistant Secretary for Social Indicators, to lead in preparing a social report. With the help of a panel cochaired by social scientist Daniel Bell and HEW Assistant Secretary Alice M. Rivlin, Olson sought to devise a system of social indicators—which he defined as measures of the level of well-being in a society—for measuring the social progress or retrogression of the nation. The study was scheduled to be completed in mid-1969, but when President Johnson announced he would not run again and Richard M. Nixon was elected, Olson rushed the study to completion ahead of schedule so it could be published before Johnson left office. The document, "Toward a Social

Report," was submitted to the President by HEW Secretary Wilbur Cohen nine days before Johnson left office.

Three of its seven chapters were titled: "Health and Illness" (Are we becoming healthier?); "Our Physical Environment" (Are conditions improving?); and "Public Order and Safety" (What is the impact of crime on our lives?) A final chapter discussed the need for continuing studies of social indicators and how to apply them in formulating policy.

Although no institutional apparatus for policymaking resulted from "Toward a Social Report," one of the members of the Panel on Social Indicators, Daniel Patrick Moynihan, continued to advocate social reporting when appointed Counselor to President Nixon in 1969. Also, the Census Bureau representative to the Social Indicators Panel, Julius Shiskin, went on to the Office of Management and Budget (OMB), where he headed the staff that produced the OMB report "Social Indicators of 1973." (An updated version, "Social Indicators of 1976," was issued by OMB in December 1977.)

The mid-1960s saw two other efforts in the social area. In 1967, Senator Walter G. Mondale, supported by 10 other senators, introduced "The Full Opportunity and Social Accounting Act," which proposed a Council of Social Advisers in the Executive Office of the President, and the publication for transmittal to Congress of an annual Social Report by the President, similar to the yearly Economic Report of the Council of Economic Advisers. The Mondale bill twice passed the Senate (in 1970 and 1972), but no action was ever taken by the House.

In the private sector, Daniel Bell organized the Commission on the Year 2000, funded by the Carnegie Corporation and run by the American Academy of Arts and Sciences. About 30 prominent social scientists and other experts concerned about preparations for the future and alternative policy choices held working sessions for three days in 1965 and for two days in 1966. During 1967 they contributed papers and participated in the discussions of eight working parties. The Commission's 350-page report, "Toward the Year 2000: Work in Progress," was widely distributed after publication as the entire Summer 1967 issue of *Daedalus,* the journal of the American Academy of Arts and Sciences.

This private-sector commission made no formal recommendations, however. According to Bell, the Commission avoided issues related to natural resources, environment, and population because there were too many variables. Instead, the Commission tried to identify technological trends in terms of a 10-year lead time. And they also looked at changes in social frameworks, such as those in a postindustrial society.

## The Last Decade

### National Environmental Policy Act of 1969

Improving the quality of the environment has been the objective of a number of laws passed by Congress and executive orders issued by Presidents in the last two decades. Only one law, however, served to provide for a long-range, holistic approach to decision-making throughout the government and established an institution that had the potential, on paper at least, for advising the President on how to prepare for some of the problems of the future. This law, the National Environmental Policy Act of 1969, required "environmental impact statements" by the responsible official for all major federal actions "significantly affecting the quality of the human environment." It also provided for establishing in the Executive Office of the President a three-member Council on Environmental Quality.

The legislation was developed by congressional committees without assistance from the Nixon White House. While Congress was considering the legislation, President Nixon had established by executive order his own Cabinet-level Environmental Quality Council in May 1969.

Nixon's Council consisted of the President as Chairman, the Vice President (serving as Chairman in the President's absence), the Secretaries of six Departments—Agriculture; Commerce; Health, Education, and Welfare; Housing and Urban Development; Interior; and Transportation—and the Science Adviser to the President, who was named Executive Secretary. The general purpose of the Council was to "assist the President with respect to environmental quality matters." One of its specific duties was to "review the adequacy of existing systems for monitoring and predicting environmental changes so as to achieve effective coverage and efficient use of facilities and other resources." The Cabinet-level Council met only a few times and accomplished very little.

Congress ignored White House opposition and passed the National Environmental Policy Act in December 1969. The Act was signed into law on January 1, 1970, by the President, who subsequently dropped his Cabinet-level council and appointed three members to the new Council on Environmental Quality required by the Act.

## Council on Environmental Quality

As a declaration of national environmental policy, Section 101 (b) of the 1969 Act provided that:

it is the continuing responsibility of the Federal Government to use all practicable means, consistent with other essential considerations of national policy, to improve and coordinate Federal plans, functions, programs, and resources to the end that the Nation may—

(1) fulfill the responsibilities of each generation as trustee of the environment for succeeding generations;

(2) assure for all Americans safe, healthful, productive, and esthetically and culturally pleasing surroundings;

(3) attain the widest range of beneficial uses of the environment without degradation, risk to health or safety, or other undesirable and unintended consequences;

(4) preserve important historic, cultural, and natural aspects of our national heritage, and maintain, wherever possible, an environment which supports diversity and variety of individual choice;

(5) achieve a balance between population and resource use which will permit high standards of living and a wide sharing of life's amenities;

(6) enhance the quality of renewable resources and approach the maximum attainable recycling of depletable resources.

In preparing environmental impact statements, responsible federal officials were required to include:

• The environmental impact of the proposed action;

• Any adverse environmental effects which cannot be avoided should the proposal be implemented;

• Alternatives to the proposed action;

• The relationship between local short-term uses of man's environment and the maintenance and enhancement of long-term productivity;

• Any irreversible and irretrievable commitments of resources which would be involved in the proposed action should it be implemented.

The Council on Environmental Quality was specifically given the duty "to develop and recommend to the President national policies to foster and promote the improvement of environmental quality to meet the conservation, social, economic, health, and other requirements and goals of the Nation" and also to assist and advise the President in the preparation of an annual Environmental Quality Report.

The annual report was to set forth such things as

• Current and foreseeable trends in the quality, management and utilization of such environments and the effects of those trends on the social, economic, and other requirements of the Nation; and

• The adequacy of available natural resources for fulfilling human and economic requirements of the Nation in the light of expected population pressures.

Another section of the National Environmental Policy Act required that all agencies of the federal government should

recognize the worldwide and long-range character of environmental problems and, where consistent with the foreign policy of the United States, lend appropriate support to initiatives, resolutions, and programs designed to maximize international cooperation in anticipating and preventing a decline in the quality of the environment.

While there have been efforts over the past seven years to carry out these basic provisions of the Act, its implementation has been far less than its framers intended. Federal officials have in most cases followed the letter of the law's requirement that they consider the environmental impact of major decisions and alternative courses of action that might be better for the nation. However, only rarely have officials submitted such statements *before a decision is made,* as the law requires.

While President Nixon did not include the Council on Environmental Quality among his foremost advisers, he relied on it to prepare his environmental legislative program. The Council performed other useful functions in developing major new studies, reviewing international environmental activities, coordinating domestic environmental activities, and overseeing the environmental impact statement process.

## National Goals Research Staff (1969)

In July 1969, President Nixon established a National Goals Research Staff in the White House. The impetus came largely from Daniel Patrick Moynihan, then counselor to the President and head of the newly created Urban Affairs Council, operating out of the White House basement.*

The National Goals Research Staff consisted of a small group of experts, whose primary task was to prepare a report annually, at least until 1976, setting forth some of the key policy choices facing the nation, together with the consequences of those choices. The goals group was not a planning agency; it was to provide information and analysis so that those making decisions "might have a better idea of the direction in which events are moving, the seeming pace of those movements, and alternative directions and speeds that possibly could be achieved, were policies to be shifted in one direction or another." That statement, by Moynihan, prefaced the first report of the Goals Research Staff, published on July 4, 1970, under the title "Toward Balanced Growth; Quantity with Quality."

Moynihan had conceived of the report as a social report, rather than an inventory of natural resources or collection of statistics. In the announcement of July 1969, President Nixon said the new Goals Staff would for the first time create within the White House "a unit specifically charged with the long perspective; it promises to provide the research tools with which we at last can deal with the future in an informed and informative way." The President also said the Goals Staff would provide for "new mechanisms which can enable government to respond to emerging needs early enough so that the response can be effective."

The functions of the National Goals Research Staff were to include

forecasting future developments, and assessing the longer-range consequences of present social trends; measuring the probable future impact of alternative courses of action, including measuring the degree to which change in one area would be likely to affect another; estimating the actual range of social choice—that is, what alternative sets of goals might be attainable, in light of the availability of resources and possible rates of progress; developing and monitoring social indicators that can reflect the present and future quality of American life, and the direction and rate of its change; summarizing, integrating, and correlating the results of related research activities being carried on within the various Federal agencies, and by State and local governments and private organizations.

The President announced that the first assignment of the new group would be to assemble data

---

*Moynihan had been aiming at such a futures study since his first days in office, when he had appointed an Urban Affairs Research Committee to develop projections and forecasts with a comprehensive, long-range perspective on

trends and to study the most probable longer-range consequences of major policy alternatives, as well as to anticipate developments for "an improved assessment of current priorities . . . useful in articulating feasible national goals."

that could help illumine the possible range of national goals for the nation's 1976 Bicentennial. The public report to be delivered by July 4, 1970—and annually thereafter— would make possible discussion of key choices and their consequences

while there still is time to make the choices effective. . . . Only shortly beyond the 200th anniversary lies the year 2000. These dates, together, can be targets for our aspirations. Our need now is to seize on the future as the key dimension in our decisions, and to chart that future as consciously as we are accustomed to charting the past.

Even before release of the President's statement, a power struggle had arisen within the White House over who would direct this goals research: Would it be Moynihan as Executive Secretary of the Council for Urban Affairs? Or would it be Arthur Burns, also a Counselor to the President and head of the Office of Program Development? Nixon solved the controversy by naming his Special Consultant, Leonard Garment, director of the National Goals Research Staff. Garment found out about his new "job" shortly before leaving on a long trip to the Soviet Union to set up a cultural exchange program. When he returned, he brought in some futures experts, including the Hudson Institute's Herman Kahn, the Harvard Business School's Raymond Bauer, and Brookings Institution's Director Charles Schultz, to assist him in setting up the group.

Garment soon encountered difficulties in implementing his task, as funds for the project were limited, and it was necessary to borrow some of the 10 members of the staff from federal agencies. He hired Bauer as senior consultant and staff report coordinator and appointed Charles Williams of the National Science Foundation as staff director. Garment, who modestly claimed "my main job was to protect the work," had the President's ear and was able to maintain Mr. Nixon's support, although he had to bypass the normal channels to keep the President informed of the Goals Staff's activities.

One of the early ideas was to build a network among state, regional, and local planning groups in order to obtain ideas about national goals through interaction with citizens. This effort was discontinued after one public hearing because of opposition from the White House staff. The Goals Staff, however, was able to bring in consultants in various fields.

Some work was done with the Bureau of the Budget's Office of Statistical Policy in developing

regularly published social statistics using available data, but this work was not published in the 1970 report. No efforts were made to include foreign policy issues, as in the Eisenhower Commission on National Goals.

The Goals Staff worked instead on a relatively few issues; it tried to define the questions, analyze the "emerging" debates, and examine the alternative sets of consequences. Garment believes that the main strength of the goals work was its bringing forward for debate some issues which were ahead of their time, such as national growth policy, revenue sharing, and technology assessment. Civil rights, the Vietnam war, and other issues with which the public was already preoccupied were entirely ignored.

Even with the program's shortcomings, the July 4, 1970, "Toward Balanced Growth" provided a springboard for national debate on a number of vital issues. The report concentrated on population growth and distribution, environment, education, basic natural science, technology assessment, consumerism and economic choice, and balanced growth:

Confronted with the trend toward ever greater concentration of a growing population in already crowded metropolitan regions, should we accept the present trend? Or, if not, to what extent should the focus of public policy be on encouraging the spread of population into sparsely populated areas, fostering the growth of existing middle-sized cities and towns, or experimenting with the development of new cities outside of existing metropolitan areas? Given the present threat to our natural environment, how should we balance changes in patterns of production and consumption with new means of waste disposal or recycling—and how should be allocate the costs? Should they be borne by producers, by consumers, by the general public—or by what combination of these? How can consumer protection best be advanced without so interfering with the market mechanism as to leave the consumer worse off in the long run?

The report, published without White House or Bureau of the Budget interference, made some bold statements. For instance:

FHA and VA mortgage insurance, the interstate highway system, Federal and State tax policies, State and local land use programs, all contributed to the massive suburbanization of the last 25 years.

Defense contract awards have accelerated the population booms in Southern California and along the Gulf Coast.

Agricultural research and support programs have accelerated depletion of the rural population.

These policies make individually positive contributions to society, but their collective impact may not be desirable from the standpoint of distribution of population and economic opportunity.

The discussion in the population section was even more bold:

A considerable number of population experts strongly endorse the goal of a zero rate of increase—that is, a stationary population—as soon as we can achieve it. This means that in the interest of society, all American families should have an average of two children. Even many of those who do not see the problem as pressing see this as a desirable goal.

This choice implies a significant change in public policy. It calls for a deliberate government effort to promote the reduction in the growth rate until population stability is achieved. It also implies that we must not leave the possibility of population stability to chance. It means we may have to do more than rely upon liberalized abortion laws in the States, and upon the distribution of free contraceptives to the poor, who are the focus of most U.S. family-planning programs. We may also have to devise ways of changing individual and social attitudes, governmental policies and incentives, and through these, the motivation of young people and adults in all socio-economic groups.

Even if the country elects the goal of arresting the growth of U.S. population by the end of the century, it is not at all clear whether or not the Government can bring about a societal consensus voluntarily to control the growth of the U.S. population within a generation. More active public policies might be required than "moral encouragement." Changes in tax laws and health insurance programs might help. An extreme form of an active public policy would be to regulate family size by fiat. Some persons have even gone so far as to suggest enforced sterilization when each family reaches its maximum allowance. Less drastic forms of coercion could be devised. But whatever the form, coercion in the regulation of family size is likely to be unacceptable to the American people."

Several months before publication of the report, Garment and Williams formed an ad hoc committee to evaluate the possibilities for setting up an institute or organization in the private sector that would be the equivalent of the governmental goals effort. Williams discovered that the Senior Executive Council of the Conference Board was already considering something along similar lines. At a White House meeting chaired by Garment in March 1970 and attended by a half dozen private sector leaders, the Conference Board's Executive Council agreed to study the possibility of putting together a Center for National Goals. White House officials said that President Nixon would announce formation of the institution when he issued the first National Goals Report on July 4, 1970. The private sector representatives did not believe that they could get a structure ready in so short a time. The timing problem did not develop, however, because no presidential statement was issued on July 4.

In June, a month before the Goals Research Staff's report was due to be published, the staff found out that its first report would also be its last. The President had decided to create a Domestic Council under John Ehrlichman, who felt the Domestic Council could carry on any additional goals and alternatives work. (In fact, however, it did not perform truly long-range policy analysis.)

The National Goals Research Staff was disbanded when the July 4, 1970, report was completed. Moynihan had prepared an introductory statement for the President to sign, but the President decided he should not be so directly associated with the report, and the Moynihan introduction appeared as a "statement of the Counselor to the President." The document emerged, finally, as a report from the National Goals Research Staff to the President.

The report was published just before the Fourth of July, while the President was in California, and no presidential statement was issued. Press coverage was accordingly light.

## Proposal for a Center for National Goals and Alternatives (1970)

With the White House goals mission apparently ended, the Senior Executives Council, an advisory group to the Conference Board (an independent nonprofit business research organization) nevertheless decided to continue its investigation of the possibilities for a private sector effort for establishing national goals. The Council is composed of 36 chief executives, 25 of them from business and the rest from universities, foundations, and public institutions. They finance their own studies and activities and operate independently of the Conference Board. Board President H. Bruce Palmer was interested in the subject, having been one of the sponsors for the formation of the Institute for the Future. The Senior Executives Council put up $60,000 to study the best design for such an organization, and the National Endowment for the Humanities contributed $9,800 for the study. Willis W. Harman of the Stanford Research Institute was selected to do a 4-month analysis, assisted by representatives from Arthur D. Little Company, the Institute for the Future, the Center for a Voluntary Society, the Senior Executives Council, and Anthony Wiener of the Hudson Institute, who had been a research consultant for the National Goals Research Staff.

In December 1970, the Harman group submitted its report to the steering committee of the Senior Executives Council. The report proposed forming a Center for National Goals and Alternatives. The essential function of the proposed Center would be to address four basic issues: (1) how to understand the processes of social change, interpret the present moment in history, and anticipate the consequences of alternative actions; (2) how to explore the range of attainable social choices; (3) how best to clarify bases for value choices and goals selection; and (4) how to identify, evaluate, and implement alternative policies and strategies. The Center, at least in theory, would be free of domination by any power group; it would foster an interdisciplinary approach and would have a permanent staff as well as visiting fellows, scholars, and interns. Joint involvement of public, private, and voluntary sectors would be provided through the mechanism of a Forum that would give a broad representational base for steering the Center and would ensure objectivity and promote credibility. Forum members would select a third of the members of the Board of Trustees. The estimated budget was $7.5 million for the first three years, and $5 million per year after that. Two-thirds of the budget would be obtained from nongovernment sources, one-third from the federal government.

The Conference Board's Senior Executive's Council asked Erik Jonsson of Texas Instruments, former Mayor of Dallas and head of Goals for Dallas, to assess the viability of the proposal for a Center. In answer to questions raised by Jonsson's assessment, Harman prepared a paper justifying the need to discover whether the future would be more or less an unbroken extrapolation of the past, or whether, after a tumultuous period of a few decades, radical societal change would be required.

In the absence of any solid knowledge on which the nation could base its choice of a course to follow, Harman felt the Center should formulate means with which to examine national goals, priorities, and policies in both contexts. In support of the need for approaches to meet radical societal changes, he presented a table showing how "successes" of the technological era had resulted in

problems for the future because they had been "too successful," inferring, that we had not prepared in advance to cope with the results. For instance:

Prolonging the life span had resulted in overpopulation and problems of the aged.

Weapons for national defense had resulted in the hazard of mass destruction through nuclear and biological weapons.

Replacement of manual and routine labor by machines had exacerbated unemployment; efficiency had resulted in dehumanization of the world of work.

Growth in the power of systematized knowledge produced threats to privacy and freedom, and erected a knowledge barrier to the underprivileged.

Affluence had increased per capita environmental impact, pollution and energy shortages.

Satisfaction of basic needs had produced a worldwide revolution of rising expectations, rebellion against nonmeaningful work, and unrest among affluent students.

Although Jonsson's review of the Harman proposal approved the technical basis of the proposed organization, some members of the Senior Executives Council raised questions, and further study was ordered in 1971 under the guidance of Robert O. Anderson, chairman of the Board of the Atlantic Richfield Company and new head of the Senior Executives Council. The proposal was accordingly refined to create an Institute for National Objectives—A Center for Integrative Studies of National Policies, Priorities, and Alternatives. Its 12- to 30-man Board of Trustees would include representatives from the Administration, Congress, and the National Science Foundation, and perhaps one or more governors or mayors. Involvement of public, private, and voluntary sectors would be reinforced through an Advisory Council of up to 50 members elected for 3-year terms, plus about 20 members elected by the Advisory Council itself. Business, foundations, and labor and voluntary organizations would be asked to participate in funding; half the initial $10 million would be sought from the National Science Foundation, the National Institutes of Health, Congress, and other federal sources.

Robert O. Anderson and Erik Jonsson presented the proposal for the new Institute to the President in January 1972. Nixon agreed that something should be done. He felt that a government effort would be viewed as political, but if the Institute originated as a private organization, he would see that government funds were made available. He put John Ehrlichman in charge of Administration cooperation for the project. Nixon said that the Institute's sponsors would have to be credible and outside of politics, and that the money would have to come from several pockets.

Although some members of the Senior Executives Council still expressed reservations, $115,000 was raised initially. Robert Anderson placed the project under Joseph Slater, head of the Aspen Institute for Humanistic Studies (Anderson serves as board chairman of the Institute), but Slater was unable to get the necessary additional funding from foundations, and the project, as proposed by the Senior Executives Council, was terminated. However, the Aspen Institute developed the concept in its own way, proposing an Institute for Analysis of Public Choices, free of all federal ties. The proposal was submitted to Nelson Rockefeller in 1973 and, according to Slater, influenced the direction Rockefeller took when he started his Commission on Critical Choices for Americans. The Aspen Institute is now seeking to turn many of its own programs toward developing analysis of choices in decision-making.

## Commission on Population Growth and the American Future (1970)

In July 1969 President Nixon sent to Congress a historic first population message, recommending the establishment by legislation of a blue-ribbon commission to examine the growth of the nation's population and the impact it will have on the American future. John D. Rockefeller III, who had started the Population Council, had been urging since the early days of the Eisenhower Administration that such a commission be established. Lyndon Johnson had refused to see Rockefeller in 1964, but by 1968, he was ready to yield to pressure and established the President's Committee on Population and Family Planning, co-chaired by Rockefeller and HEW Secretary Wilbur Cohen.

The Committee established by President Johnson was not a full-blown commission. Its report, sent to the President at the end of 1968, "Population and Family Planning: The Transition from Concern to Action," suggested the establishment of a presidential commission to give the problem further study. It recommended that family planning services be extended to every American woman unable to afford them. It also recommended an increase in the budgets of HEW and the Office of Economic Opportunity for the purpose of population research. The report was released without publicity in January 1969, just before Johnson left office. He did not meet with the Committee to receive the report, nor make a statement on it.

In early 1969, Rockefeller's pressure for a presidential commission was abetted by presidential Counselor Moynihan, who convinced Nixon that the time had come to face the problems of population. The President asked in his message to Congress that a Commission be assigned to develop population projections and estimate the impact of an anticipated 100 million increase in U.S. population by the year 2000. For the interim, the President called for more research "on birth control methods" and for the establishment, as a national goal, of "the provision of adequate family planning services within the next five years for all those who want them but cannot afford them." In his message to Congress, Nixon stated:

One of the most serious challenges to human destiny in the last third of this century will be the growth of the population. Whether man's response to that challenge will be a cause for pride or for despair in the year 2000 will depend very much on what we do today. If we now begin our work in an appropriate manner, and if we continue to devote a considerable amount of attention and energy to this problem, then mankind will be able to surmount this challenge as it has surmounted so many during the long march of civilization.

When the Congress passed a bill in March 1970 creating the Commission on Population Growth and the American Future, President Nixon named John D. Rockefeller III chairman of the 24-member group, which included four women, two college students, three blacks, two senators, and two representatives. About 20 full-time professionals and 10 consultants supervised a 2-year effort which resulted in the release of a controversial final report in March 1972, plus seven volumes of research papers. More than 100 research projects were conducted, and more than 100 witnesses testified at public hearings in Washington, Los Angeles, Little Rock, Chicago, and New York. Additional information concerning public attitudes was obtained through a special detailed public opinion poll.

The Commission's conclusion was that no substantial benefits would result from continued growth of the nation's population:

The population problem, and the growth ethic with which it is intimately connected, reflect deeper external conditions and more fundamental political, economic, and philosophical values. Consequently, to improve the quality of our existence while slowing growth, will require nothing less than a basic recasting of American values.

The more than 60 Population Commission recommendations included:

- Creation of an Office of Population Growth and Distribution within the Executive Office of the President;
- Establishment, within the National Institutes of Health, of a National Institute of Population Sciences to provide an adequate institutional framework for implementing a greatly expanded program of population research;
- Legislation by Congress establishing a Council of Social Advisers, with one of the main functions the monitoring of demographic variables;
- The addition of a mid-decade census of the population; and
- National planning for a stabilized population.

These recommendations were overshadowed, at least in the publicity given them, by the recommendations that states adopt legislation permitting minors "to receive contraceptive and prophylactic information and services in appropriate settings sensitive to their needs and concerns" and "that present state laws restricting abortion be liberalized along the lines of the New York statute, such abortion to be performed on request by duly licensed physicians under conditions of medical safety." The Commission also recommended that abortion be covered by health insurance benefits, and that federal, state, and local governments make funds available to support abortion in states with liberalized statutes.

President Nixon was unhappy with the Commission report, released in March 1972 at the beginning of his re-election campaign, largely because of the recommendations on liberalized abortion and the furnishing of contraceptives to teen-agers (which in 1972 was a bigger issue than abortion). The President met only a few minutes with Mr. Rockefeller. He perfunctorily received the Commission report, but issued a statement repudiating it. No word of support was forthcoming for the stabilized population concept that he had backed in 1969.

Although all members of the Commission showed their support for the report by signing it, several members wrote minority statements about certain recommendations, especially the one on abortion. The Commission debated whether to finesse the two controversial issues, since these recommendations were not of major demographic importance. But Chairman Rockefeller felt it was only right that the majority of the Commission be able to state an opinion on all relevant issues.

"We went ahead, realizing we would get our heads cut off," said the staff director, Charles Westoff. "But we hadn't quite appreciated how much these recommendations were going to dominate the response to the report."

The timing of the report was unfortunate in that during the three years since Nixon's population message, the public had come to agree on stabilizing population growth, and the goal of the two-child family was already being achieved in the statistics.

No recommendations were made by the Commission in the resources and environment areas.

The Commission staff chose a basis methodology for its extensive research efforts, which were published in six large volumes. The research was organized basically around one simple question: What difference will it make if the U.S. population grows at a two-child per family rate, or if it grows at a three-child per family rate? This approach was adopted in all research efforts except where it was not appropriate, as in migration studies. The research documents used U.S. Bureau of the Census statistics in its projections, and extensive new data on these assumptions was supplied by the Bureau of Economic Analysis of the Department of Commerce.

Volume III, *Population, Resources and the Environment*, contained extensive research on the relative impacts of the two growth scenarios on resources and the environment. Chapters were devoted to: the economy; resource requirements and pollution levels; energy; outdoor recreation and congestion; agriculture, population, and the environment; future water needs and supplies; urban scale and environmental quality; and ecological perspectives.

The other volumes covered: *Demographic and Social Aspects of Population Growth* (Vol. I); *Economic Aspects of Population Change* (II); *Governance and Population: The Governmental Implications of Population Change* (IV); *Population Distribution and Policy* (V); *Aspects of Population Growth Policy* (VI). Research on global population and resources was not a part of the Commission mandate.

Despite the lack of White House support, Commission members and staff sought ways to disseminate to the public the findings of the report and the research materials. Chairman Rockefeller testified before congressional hearings. A privately financed Citizens Committee on Population and the American Future, formed after release of the report, took the leading role in spreading the findings; it tried to create a dialogue on the issues and lobbied in Congress for passage of some of the recommendations. It also sponsored two large conferences.

A privately financed film version of the Population Commission report, which had been in preparation for more than a year, was issued about six months after the Commission made its report and received wide distribution. It was shown over the National Educational Television network, a number of individual TV stations, and by many schools. A set of teaching materials was prepared for the classroom use. The film stressed the impacts of too much population and did not dwell on the Commission's recommendations.

The deputy director of the Population Commission staff, Robert Parke, felt that the report and the research volumes made a strong base for future efforts at meeting population growth problems. And he believed the Commission and its staff had learned at least one valuable lesson: A commission studying a controversial subject should not publish its report during a presidential campaign.

### National Commission on Materials Policy (1970)

Congress legislated a new National Commission on Materials Policy in the fall of 1970 as a part of the Resources Recovery Act. Although the chief sponsor of the Commission was a Republican, J. Caleb Boggs, of Delaware, the White House did not look with favor on the Commission, and President Nixon delayed almost a year before appointing the five public members to join the Secretaries of Interior and Commerce. There were three Secretaries of Commerce during the term of the Commission. Only the first, Maurice Stans, attended Commission meetings; the last, Frederick Dent, issued a separate statement disagreeing with many of the Commission's major recommendations. Secretary of the Interior Rogers Morton did not personally attend meetings.

Commission Chairman Jerome Klaff was head of a secondary materials processing company; Staff Director James Boyd was a former director of the Bureau of Mines and, at the time, head of a mining company. A full-time staff of 25 was hired.

The Materials Policy Commission did not attempt a materials resources inventory and update of the Paley Commission but rather concentrated its attention on the policy area and emphasized the environmental aspects of resources problems, an area which the Paley Commission had ignored. The new Commission contracted for a study of the estimated demand for 10 commodities to the year 2000. A report was made on basic mineral stocks, reserves, production data, consumption, and exports for selected foreign countries, including the People's Republic of China, the Soviet Union, and the East European countries, none of which had been considered by the Paley Commission of 1951. A number of other reports were prepared by independent contractors.

Advisory panels from industry participated by submitting information and assisting with more than a dozen meetings and hearings conducted around the nation. Federal agencies also supplied data and analysis.

The summary report of the National Materials Policy Commission and its special publications have proved useful to a number of federal agencies and to industry. As with earlier studies, the involvement of several hundred public officials and industry participants helped to educate a sizable cadre in the need for forward-looking analyses.

The major recommendations of the Commission, when it reported to the President and Congress in June 1973, were mostly general policy directives:

Strike a balance between the "need to produce goods" and the "need to protect the environment" by modifying the materials system so that all resources, including environmental, are paid for by users. Strive for an equilibrium between the supply of materials and the demand for their use by increasing primary materials production and by conserving materials through accelerated waste recycling and greater efficiency-of-use of materials. Manage materials policy more effectively by recognizing the complex interrelationships of the materials—energy—environment system so that laws, executive orders, and administrative practices reinforce policy and not counteract it.

More specific recommendations of the Commission included creation of a comprehensive Cabinet-level agency for materials, energy, and the environment, and the formation of a joint committee of Congress having legislative jurisdiction roughly parallel to the proposed new agency.

By the time the Commission report was completed, the Commission's chief sponsor in the Senate had been defeated in a bid for re-election, and the White House, for its part, showed no interest in publicizing the report.

After release of the report in June 1973, Staff Director Boyd set up a small office on his own (with some financial help from his company) to follow through on the Commission study and to try to get some of the recommendations implemented. Much of the follow-up was done by working with members of Congress, congressional staffs, and federal agencies, with Boyd testifying at congressional hearings on the usefulness of the report and the need for implementation of some of the recommendations.

Because the report had appeared after passage of the Federal Advisory Committee Act, the Administration was required by law to at least respond to the findings. A task group and subcommittee of the President's Domestic Council drafted an executive branch response which noted that some of the recommendations were simplistic and subjective, that some were inappropriately worded or did not reflect ongoing activities in the executive agencies, and that there was no clear ordering of priorities in the report. The White House position was that regular program activities of the Department of the Interior and the Environmental Protection Agency would accomplish most of the actions recommended by the Commission, and that a separate mechanism to insure their implementation was unnecessary. An Interior Department spokesman pointed out at a congressional hearing that many of the Commission's 177 recommendations were encompassed by nine broader recommendations in the Secretary of the Interior's June 1973 Second Annual Report under the Mining and Minerals Policy Act of 1970.

A report by the General Accounting Office (GAO) entitled "Better Followup System Needed to Deal with Recommendations by Study Commissions in the Federal Government" (RED–76–33, Dec. 4, 1975), used the Materials Policy Commission as one of its four examples.

GAO criticized the White House response document for not being specific regarding the nature and timing of the action to be taken "and therefore it cannot be considered an effective vehicle for implementing the recommendations." It pointed to one recommendation in the Commission report calling for "improved utilization and conservation of groundwater through early completion of surveys of the Nation's major aquifers, using them for planning the optimum management of ground and surface supplies, and monitoring aquifers from which substantial withdrawals are being made." The executive branch response, according to GAO, was confined to its concurrence in principle and stated that "Interior and Agriculture are working toward these ends. Increased activity will be required."

GAO added that other responses to recommendations with which the executive branch expressed concurrence or concurrence in principle described the actions to be taken in general language such as "current efforts are under way," "efforts are being made," or "interested agencies

are fully involved in the question," but gave no further particulars. GAO concluded:

We believe that the results of the study on a national materials policy could have been more beneficial if it had been directed to more specific problem areas and had specified recommended actions. Also, preparation of an executive branch response, as required by the Federal Advisory Committee Act, is not enough to insure successful implementation of a study commission's report. Effective machinery for implementation and follow through must be established and monitored at the highest level in the executive branch.

One of the Commission members, University of Indiana political scientist Lynton K. Caldwell, disagreed that this Commission, or any other, should try to be too specific or try to dictate legislation. "Anyone who has been around Government knows that the surest way to kill something is to make it so specific that no one else can ever adopt it as his own," Caldwell has said. "People feel inclined to reject specific recommendations so they can come up with something that reflects exactly what they want to do."

Some observers felt that the report would have been more influential if the Commission's chairman had been more nationally prominent. The general problem of a commission having been imposed on the President by legislation without his concurrence also worked against its effectiveness. The stated disagreements of Commission member Frederick Dent (the Secretary of Commerce) were detrimental.

## National Growth Policy Reports (1972, 1974, and 1976)

Section 703(a) of the 1970 Housing and Urban Development Act directed the President, "in order to assist in the development of a National Urban Growth Policy, to prepare every even-numbered year beginning with 1972 a 'Report on Urban Growth.'" The Act called for the report to include identification of significant trends and developments, a summary of significant problems facing the nation as a result of these trends, a statement of current and foreseeable needs in the areas served by policies, plans, and programs designed to carry out an urban growth policy, and recommendations for programs and policies for carrying out the urban growth policy.

Members of the Nixon Administration opposed this part of the legislation, claiming they were working out policy for urban and national growth in their own way, chiefly through the Cabinet Committee on National Growth Policy, appointed by President Nixon and chaired by the Secretary of Housing and Urban Development (HUD) and including the Secretaries of Agriculture, Commerce, Labor, and Transportation, the Chairman of the Council of Economic Advisers, and the Director of the Office of Economic Opportunity. The Administration also disliked the Act's specific provision that the Domestic Council was to be "adequately organized and staffed for the purpose [of carrying out the legislative mandate]."

John Ehrlichman, as head of the Domestic Council, decided early in 1971 that the biennial report should be assigned to the Department of Housing and Urban Development. The resulting draft report featured a number of new housing and urban initiatives that HUD Secretary George Romney hoped to institute, with a budget-busting price tag. Ehrlichman rejected the report and had the Domestic Council revise it completely. The report the President submitted to Congress in February 1972 bore little resemblance to what Congress had envisioned. It was called a "Report on National Growth." The introductory statement explained that the term "national urban growth policy" was too narrow. Instead, the report would cover national growth policy, "recognizing that rural and urban community development are inseparably linked." The report also interpreted the 1970 Act narrowly, pointing out that the statute required only that the report "assist in the development" of national policy; it was not required to "enunciate" such policy.

Most of the 1972 report featured Census Bureau statistics about population growth and distribution, a recitation of the Nixon Administration's achievements in its first two years, and promotional descriptions of White House proposals then before Congress, including a proposed Department of Community Development, general and special revenue sharing, national land use planning, powerplant siting, and welfare reform.

Before the 1974 report was prepared, Ehrlichman sent a detailed questionnaire to the Secretaries of HUD, Transportation, HEW, and Commerce. Among the 135 questions were these:

Is there any reliable estimate of alternative futures for the country in the absence of a national growth policy?

Are there growth objectives which can safely be said to have widespread or universal support which are not being promoted by present Federal policy?

How do we define the national interest—how do we balance the relative weights of economic, social, and other considerations?

To what extent should a national growth policy attempt to achieve welfare and social goals?

The small group at HUD preparing the 1974 report was never furnished the answers to this questionnaire. They were told by the White House, only to avoid putting in any new policy recommendations. The draft went from HUD to the White House late in 1973, but no action was taken for almost a year. Then the Domestic Council under President Gerald Ford revised the draft and submitted it to Congress under the title "Report on National Growth and Development." It came out early in 1975, almost a year late, and contributed little to any analysis of future national growth problems or preparations to meet them. It listed 13 "national goals related to growth" (one sentence per goal), and stated that the policymakers' task was to understand how and whether present and proposed actions would affect these goals. This would require "systematic review in the course of decision-making of the possible effects, not just on the mission goal of each decision-maker, but on other national goals as well; and improved evaluation of existing activities with emphasis on both attainment of the mission goal and effects on other goals."

The report concluded that such evaluation was "much easier said than done." It then suggested developing an agreed-upon set of guidelines for the decision-making process. It did not, however, produce any such guidelines.

The 1976 report, without measuring up to congressional expectations, was a decided improvement over the two earlier reports. HUD convened a technical research program and selected a 25-member federal interagency task force to help delineate growth trends, identify problems and present broad policy options. For the first time, public participation was permitted through seminars on regional growth and development held in Washington, D.C., Kansas City, and San Francisco. Also, HUD received funding with which it let a number of contracts for preparation of technical materials as the basis for public and interagency discussion. A draft report was circulated for review and comment to 35 public-interest groups, trade groups, state and local government representatives, areawide organizations and Congress, and HUD publicized the comments in a separate volume.

The 1976 report was subtitled "The Changing Issues for National Growth." While the report identified ongoing problems, it did not offer detailed analyses of their relation to the future, nor did it adequately identify the options and alternatives available. The principal recommendations for addressing the issues, the report stated, "can be found in the Budget Message, the State of the Union Message and legislative proposals now before the Congress."

The report did, however, make suggestions for increased public participation "to provide for orderly and direct communication to the President and the Congress of a wide range of perceptions of national growth issues," and "to increase public awareness of future implications of the present policies and of the necessity to plan for the future." The report also suggested that, because federal assistance for state and local growth planning efforts is fragmented and uncoordinated, "a designated element of the Executive Branch under the auspices of the Domestic Council should accomplish the rationalization of Federal planning assistance programs and requirements across department and agency lines."

The first four chapters of the 1976 report described national trends and the changes that were appearing in the national economy and society. Another nine chapters examined broad policy alternatives in several areas of growth (such as energy impacts and promises and problems of alternative energy sources), growth consequences of environmental regulations and environmental impacts on the location of growth, choices in natural resources, transportation policy, housing policy, and balanced economic growth.

The National Forum on Growth Policy, a private organization, comprising over 40 organizations involved in business, the design professions, public interest matters, public affairs, the environment, civil rights, banking, and state and local government, sponsored a critique of the 1976 report, pointing out that the report did "not contain recommended national goals, policy or programs." It was said that the report lacked a "theoretical framework needed to interpret the meaning of the analytical information" and that it failed "to clearly articulate its assumptions and define its terms." The Forum recommended that the 1978 report should evaluate and recommend new institutions to improve the process of policy development and should focus on revitalization of the central city, national housing policy, environmental quality, and growth policy.

Hubert Humphrey, as cochairman of the Senate Joint Economic Committee's Subcommittee on Economic Growth and Stabilization, submitted to HUD a detailed critique of the 1976 report, which was longer than the report itself. Although he saw it as an improvement over the 1972 and 1974 reports, Senator Humphrey wrote that it had two great flaws:

First, even though it contains considerably more information than earlier reports, it does not really help us to understand the meaning of the information it presents.

Second, as in the past the report does not confront the high priority problem presented by the structure of decisionmaking processes that impede the formulation of growth and development policy for the United States.

Humphrey recommended that the timing of the report be changed so that it would be ready for each new Congress, that future reports contain important research findings and relevant policy recommendations presented elsewhere by the Administration, that the growth report receive wider distribution, and that future reports give increased attention to the problem of improving public access to the growth policy planning process.

"The fundamental issue in growth policy today is that the Federal Government, in both its legislative and executive branches, is not structured in such a way that it can systematically assess long-range policy and program questions or estimate long-range impacts of current decisions," stated Humphrey and Senator Jacob Javits in a Joint Economic Committee document that reviewed the 1976 report. They added: "There is growing public concern about the performance of Government, in part because of Government promising more than it can deliver. We believe that this public concern is the result of an awareness on the part of the public that the Federal Government has failed to develop the capacity to make public policy decisions in a rational, informed, future-oriented, and coherent way."

One HUD official involved in the biennial reports said that such one-shot studies were highly inadequate. An institution vested close to the President, he believed, should be created for long-range studies and planning. The institution should be in a position to cycle major presidential initiatives, like the state of the union address and the budget, through its members for response and policy suggestions. The group should also be in a position to consult with state and corporate leaders and with members of Congress.

For the 1978 report, the Democratic Administration recommended a revision of the 1970 Housing and Urban Development Act in order to convert the biennial urban *growth* report into a national urban *policy* report. This change was made to reflect the patterns of population and job movements and the continuing decline of some older established cities since the 1970 Act.

The President appointed the HUD Secretary in March 1977 to head a federal working group that would formulate the urban policy and recommendations for national government action. Participating agencies included HUD, The Departments of Treasury, Labor, Transportation, and Commerce, The Environmental Protection Agency, Community Services Administration, ACTION, and The Law Enforcement Assistance Administration. Involvement of nonfederal groups was extensively sought and encompassed the views of state and local officials, civil-rights, labor, and corporate leaders, public-interest and volunteer groups, businessmen and businesswomen, and private citizens.

The President announced on March 27, 1978, a comprehensive urban policy, based on the working group's recommendations and extensive White House discussion with many interest groups, congressional representatives, and the public.

The urban policy set forth a framework of concern for urban areas with special emphasis on remedial actions to help the older, more distressed communities as well as preventative actions to avoid hurting them in the future.

### Workshop on Alternative Energy Strategies (1974)

The Workshop on Alternative Energy Strategies (WAES) was a private sector initiative that included government and business decision-makers from 15 countries. It is included here as one of two nongovernmental examples of such a group because it offers some valuable insights into organizing for effectiveness on an international scale.

Over a 3-year period ending in 1977, the Workshop produced the first energy assessment to the year 2000 on a nearly global scale (communist countries were not included). The project was led by Carroll L. Wilson of the Massachusetts Institute of Technology and supported by a number of private philanthropic foundations, three corporate foundations, and the National Science Foundation.

Wilson had, in recent years, initiated and led a number of other studies such as the "Study of Critical Environmental Problems" (1969) and "Man's Impact on Climate" (1970). He concluded, however, that while these and similar studies received recognition in academic circles, they were not adequately presented to decision-makers.

The Workshop on Alternative Energy Strategies was born of Wilson's belief that more effective mechanisms were needed for the study of critical global problems. He selected energy as the study topic because he felt the world was moving steadily, and with little apparent concern, toward a new and massive energy crisis. The catalytic ingredient of this new study was its use of people who had major standing in their own communities and who had access to a network of influence in their own country.

Wilson assembled people who, rather than being technical experts in energy, were high-level representatives of large energy users or producers or government officials having some responsibility for energy policy. Participants were from Canada, Denmark, Finland, France, Germany, Iran, Italy, Japan, Mexico, the Netherlands, Norway, Sweden, the United Kingdom, the United States, and Venezuela. One-third of all the participants were from government.

Each participant was required to choose and provide funding for at least one associate who could work nearly full-time for the Workshop and secure the necessary data and technical expertise for his country. Associates met 13 times for 1–2 week sessions over a period of 28 months. Participants met seven times, 2–4 days at a time. The goals of the study were:

- To develop a useful method of projecting national supply and demand for energy;

- To study supply and demand to 1985 and 2000 for the countries participating in the Workshop, which, together, consume most of the world's energy;

- To develop a method for estimating global production of oil, gas, coal and nuclear power; and

- To determine whether and when prospective global shortages of certain fuels are likely to occur and how rapidly they might grow.

The report, published in a book, *Energy: Global Prospects 1985–2000*, contained conclusions but did not make recommendations.

From the start, the project participants kept in mind the need for adequate dissemination of the findings. Most members briefed the editorial boards of the leading newspapers in their countries in advance of the release of the report. Press conferences were held on the same day in the capitals of the countries. Wilson testified before energy hearings in Congress, and participants from several other countries communicated the information to their governments or to the private sector.

## International Institute for Applied Systems Anaylsis (1972)

A unique institution with a holistic approach to common problems that cannot be solved by any single country alone is the International Institute for Applied Systems Analysis (IIASA). The Institute is situated near Vienna, Austria, and supports about 100 research scientists. It is considered nongovernmental because its members are scientific institutions from the participating nations and not the political entitites of the governments themselves. It was founded in October 1972 on the initiative of the academies of science or equivalent institutions in 12 industrial nations, both East and West (institutions from five other countries have since joined the the institute). The Academy of Science of the U.S.S.R. and the U.S. National Academy of Sciences (funded through the National Science Foundation) contribute the largest part of the financial support, and private sources such as philanthropic or corporate foundations contribute about $1 million a year.

IIASA's programs are classified as either "global" (programs that affect and can be resolved only by the actions of more than one nation) and "universal" (those that affect and can be resolved by actions of individual nations but which all nations share). As the name of the Institution indicates, its scientific research and study concentrate on applying modern methods of analysis to contemporary problems of society, using the tools of modern management, such as systems theory, operations research, and cybernetics. Emphasis is placed on attempting to bridge the gap between scientists and decision-makers. The results of studies are widely communicated through publications distributed by member scientific institutions, and an effort is made to inform the nonexpert of the results of studies of international problems.

Two current major global projects are on energy systems and on food and agriculture. The energy project is concentrating on finding strategies for the transition over the next 15 to 50 years from an energy economy based on oil, gas, and conventional coal to an economy based on the virtually inexhaustible resources—solar, nuclear, and geothermal—as well as to some extent on new sources of coal. Research activities include studying systems implications of the exploitation of scarce energy resources; energy demand studies, such as one that projects global energy demand with regard to the development of regions, world population growth, and changes in lifestyle; and a study of strategies relating the nuclear-risk prob-lem to decision-making. The final energy project report is expected in 1979.

Although IIASA is composed of scientific representatives from industrial nations, the food and agriculture program is concerned also with a number of less developed countries (LDCs) that have agricultural economies. The program objectives are to evaluate the nature and dimensions of the world food situation, to study alternative policy actions at the national, regional, and global level that may alleviate existing and emerging food problems, and to determine how to meet the nutritional needs of the growing global population.

Typical projects include developing a model of the dynamic interdependence between migration and human settlement patterns and agricultural technology, identifying and measuring the environmental consequences of water use in agriculture as constraints on agricultural production, and modeling the agricultural structures of some pilot LDCs—describing their agricultural policy objectives and devising planning models suitable for estimating the consequences of alternative national policies.

## National Commission on Supplies and Shortages; Advisory Committee on National Growth Policy Processes (1975)

Another Nixon-Ford era initiative in the materials field with a major institutional objective was the National Commission on Supplies and Shortages and its separate Advisory Committee on National Growth Policy Processes. These activites, like the 1971–73 National Commission on Materials Policy, were conceived by Congress. During 1974 Senate Majority Leader Mike Mansfield pushed for legislation that resulted in creation of the National Commission on Supplies and Shortages. He drew support from other members of Congress concerned with the 1973–74 oil crisis as well as shortages of other materials in the early 1970s. They believed that the shortages were a symptom of inadequate preparation by government and that existing institutions were not doing enough to identify and anticipate such shortages. They were also concerned that the data on materials being collected in various agencies of the government, were not being systematically coordinated and transmitted to the appropriate agencies and to Congress.

However, Senator Mansfield's concern reached beyond shortages of materials. As Majority Leader, he had become increasingly troubled and frustrated over the inability of government to identify resource availability problems in a timely fashion and to suggest alternatives for dealing with them. Mansfield felt so strongly about this that he worked with Republican Senate leader Hugh Scott to get cooperation from the White House for the legislation and to work out an arrangement for making appointments to the Commission in a way that would be satisfactory to President Nixon, who was not enthusiastic over the new Commission. After a number of meetings, the White House agreed to back the bill, which would give the President the opportunity to appoint 9 of the Commission's 14 members, 4 to be senior officials from the executive branch and 5 private citizens selected in consultation with the Majority and Minority Leaders of the Senate.

The original idea was for a 6-month study using existing data but focusing on institutional changes that could aid in examination and anticipation of shortages. When the enabling legislation went to the floor for passage, however, it provided for a one-year study. On the day the bill was to be voted on in the Senate, Hubert Humphrey introduced an amendment to add a Citizens Advisory Committee and expand the list of study areas beyond materials and into almost all parts of the Government. Humphrey's purpose was to develop recommendations for establishing a more adequate economic policymaking process and structure within the executive and legislative branches.

For years, Humphrey had been interested in getting better institutional arrangements for developing economic policies and alternatives to deal with future problems. Earlier in 1974, as part of a Humphrey legislative proposal for a Balanced National Growth and Development Act, the Senator had proposed a National Citizens Council on the American Future.

When Humphrey introduced his amendment to the Mansfield bill, the Majority Leader opposed the surprise amendment because he thought it would unnecessarily burden his bill. But Humphrey was insistent, and Mansfield eventually agreed to a watered-down version of the amendment. When the amended bill was approved by the Senate, many observers believed the Humphrey-proposed Advisory Committee would be eliminated in a Senate-House Conference.

For several weeks a good deal of political maneuvering took place as presidential support for the Mansfield bill waned. White House officials felt that another presidential commission was unnecessary. Late in September, however, Mansfield used the tactic of offering the entire bill, which already had passed the House, in the form of an amendment to another bill to change the

Defense Production Act of 1950. The strategy worked, and the Congress approved the Mansfield-proposed National Commission on Supplies and Shortages, along with its Advisory Committee on National Growth Policy Processes, as part of the defense bill. President Ford signed the legislation in September 1974, a few weeks after taking office.

After almost a year's delay, resulting from the inability of the White House to come up with selections for the five private-sector members, the Commission finally got under way in September 1975. Donald Rice, president of the Rand Corporation (a former assistant director of the Office of Management and Budget), became chairman.

Many of the administration and congressional members of the Commission did not personally attend Commission meetings, which were held every six weeks or so; they sent delegates instead. The early Commission meetings were not announced in the *Federal Register,* although ostensibly they were open to the public. Later meetings, at which decisions were made, were open only to Commission members.

The Commission did not attempt any new data collection or make supply-and-demand projections into the future. Instead it analyzed available information, concluding that "we see little reason to fear that the world will run out of natural resources during the [next] quarter century."

Nine case studies were prepared that examined the causes of shortages in certain materials during the 1973–74 period. The Commission's major recommendations were for improvement of data collection and analysis in specific government agencies, with emphasis on line agencies. On the subject so important to Senator Mansfield—a new institution for policymaking—the Commission wound up recommending the creation within the Office of Management and Budget of a unit of 20–30 "sectoral and industry specialists" to monitor key materials industries and sectors, to develop a framework for analyzing the comprehensive effects of proposed major federal policy actions, and to monitor the basic data collection, data analysis, and policy analysis activities of the line agencies and departments. They also recommended adding 10 senior staff positions to to the President's Council of Economic Advisers to build up sectoral and industry analysis capabilities in the materials area.

The Commission's report, "Government and the Nation's Resources," was released the first week of 1977. The timing could not have been worse. Not only had Senator Mansfield left office, but both of the senators who served on the

Commission had been defeated, and one of the two House members had left office. The Administration was changing, and the mining industry was upset over one of the recommendations concerning the U.S. Bureau of Mines. Staff Director George Eads spent January 1977 working at the Council of Economic Advisers, seeking to get some of the Commission's ideas implemented. The only bright spot was a hearing held by the Senate Subcommittee on Science, Technology, and Space (of the Commerce Committee), which gave some visibility to the report's findings and recommendations.

While the National Commission on Supplies and Shortages was making its year-long study and preparing its report, its Advisory Committee on National Growth Policy Processes had been at work along separate and sometimes conflicting lines. The Advisory Committee's 19 members all came from outside Government and included a former Cabinet member and a noted presidential historian. Industrialist Arnold A. Saltzman was named Advisory Committee Chairman. The staff director, James E. Thornton, had been the author of the Humphrey amendment that establishe J the Committee, and while working on the Senate Agriculture and Forestry Committee, had helped Humphrey on his proposal for achieving balanced national growth and development.

The legislation authorizing the Advisory Committee provided a wide-ranging mandate ("to develop recommendations as to the establishment of a policymaking process and structure within the executive and legislative branches of the Federal Government as a means to integrate the study of supplies and shortages of resources and commodities into the total problem of balanced national growth and development"). The Advisory Committee, however, had a sparse budget that supported only a staff director and one assistant, and many of the Committee members paid their own expenses when attending monthly meetings. Members wrote their own papers and worked up proposals between meetings. The issue that received most attention was the attempt to determine how to improve the long-range policymaking processes of government in both the executive and legislative branches.

In its report to the President and Congress, the Advisory Committee urged that the nation become not a *planned* society, but a *planning* society. Adequate and open planning for the future would result in less governmental interference, and the necessary government intervention would be more considered, more timely, and less heavy-handed. The report's prime recommendation was for the institutionalization of the planning process in an independent executive branch agency to be created by Congress and called the National Growth and Development Commission. The new Commission would have the mandate "to examine emerging issues of middle- to long-range growth and development, and to suggest feasible alternatives for the Congress, the President, and the public." The Commission would provide an early warning system that would identify and examine policy issues before they surfaced as crises. It would have no executive, legislative, or judicial powers. The Advisory Committee recommended that enabling legislation to establish the National Growth and Development Commission should require the President and Congress to respond in some fashion to the Commission's reports. The proposed Commission would conduct its affairs openly and hold public hearings. It would submit an annual report to Congress and the President, setting forth its proposed research agenda, the status of ongoing work, and a summary of the reaction from Congress, the President, and the public to previous reports. The new Commission would receive an initial budget authorization for eight years to ensure its continuity. To balance presidential and congressional influence, the chairman of the Commission would be appointed by the President, but the President would be required to consult with the congressional leadership before making Commission appointments. The Advisory Committee report also suggested that the new Commission consist of nine people, five full-time and four part-time (allowing for participation by those not able to accept full-time appointments). Terms of office would run for five years. No member could be removed except for cause, and all appointments would require Senate confirmation.

The Advisory Committee was not unanimous on this recommendation. One Committee member argued that it would give too much power to "the group of wise men," as the Committee members informally referred to the members of the proposed Commission.

Another institutional recommendation of the Advisory Committee was the creation of a Center for Statistical Policy and Analysis to coordinate statistical support for the work of the President and Congress. The Center would be an independent agency in the executive branch, but outside the Executive Office of the President.

Among recommendations of the Advisory Committee that dealt with Congress was one that would require each congressional committee report accompanying proposed legislation to include an outline of the bill's foreseeable indirect middle-to long-range effects, as well as a concise statement of the general goals and specific objectives of the bill.

Reflecting one of the major differences of approach between the parent National Commission on Supplies and Shortages and its Advisory Committee, the Commission in its report expressed doubts concerning creation of an independent new National Growth and Development Commission, as recommended by the Advisory Committee. In the formal letter to the President and to Congress submitting the Advisory Committee's report, Commission Chairman Rice stated that the Commission believed that the proposed new institution "fails the test of feasibility and that the aims sought would be better met by the proposals we have made in our own report for improving the analytical capabilities of existing agencies and departments." The impact of the two groups' reports was marred by this disagreement.

## Conclusions

### Some Observations

1. For the past 70 years the nation's leadership has perceived periodically a need for long-term analysis of problems relating to natural resources, population, or the environment. For the most part, these issues have been addressed on an ad hoc basis by appointing presidential commissions or other temporary groups to study the situation, make their reports, and then disband. As a result, decision-makers continue to deal primarily with immediate problems, while consideration of how to prepare for conditions that might exist 10, 20, or 30 years in the future is postponed for lack of adequate and systematic information on the options available and on the social, economic, and environmental impacts of alternate choices.

2. Future-oriented commissions or study groups have generally studied natural resources problems separately from problems related to population and the environment. There has been insufficient recognition of the interrelation of these three issues. Each succeeding year, as the problems become more complex and the interrelationships more involved, the need for a holistic approach to decision-making becomes more urgent.

3. Most analyses of future problems in population, natural resources, and the environment have been made only on a national basis. President Truman recognized the need for assessing global implications of natural resources when he instructed his Materials Policy Commission in 1951 to make its study of materials policy international in scope, at least to the extent of considering the needs and resources of friendly nations. But while the harmful effects of population growth, resource consumption, and pollution spread across borders and oceans, the international approach to long-range planning for solutions to these problems continues to be neglected.

4. When commissions or other bodies have been formed to consider long-term problems in population, natural resources, and the environment, their effectiveness has been hampered by lack of provisions for following up on their recommendations. In several cases the heads of commissions felt so strongly about the need for ongoing institutions that they set up private organizations on their own to follow up with their group's recommendations, which have led to some efforts of ongoing analysis.

5. One recommendation has been made by virtually every presidential commission on population, natural resources, or the environment: the establishment of a permanent body somewhere high in the executive branch for performing continuous futures research and analysis. Although ideas for location of such a permanent group have varied, proposals have generally indicated that a statutorily created institution with access to the President could explore potential goals, watch for trends, and look at alternate possibilities for accomplishing stated objectives.

### Lessons from the Past

The recommendation of President Truman's Materials Policy Commission for an advisory body in the Executive Office of the President to frame recommendations for policy up to 25 years ahead went unheeded. The National Goals Research Staff was terminated by President Nixon after completing only one of its scheduled annual reports on goals, and before it could complete its work of setting up in the private sector a National Center for Goals and Alternatives to work with the governmental efforts at decision-making for the future. The National Materials Policy Commission (appointed by President Nixon in 1971), recommended creation of a comprehensive Cabinet-level agency for looking at the future in terms of materials, energy, and the environment, but the recommendation produced no results. And the 1976 recommendation of the National Commission on Supplies and Shortages' Advisory Committee on National Growth Policy Processes, calling for a permanent National Growth and Development Commission, was submitted in the last few weeks of the outgoing Ford Administration, too late to be acted upon. The Advisory Committee had urged that a permanent institution for planning conduct its affairs openly, hold public hearings, and submit an annual report setting forth its proposed research agenda, the status of ongoing work, and a summary of reactions from Congress and the President to previous reports.

In the one case in which a President did establish—without congressional authorization—a mechanism for long-range planning and advice, the institution was often at odds with other agencies and with the Congress and was finally legislated out of existence by Congress. This was Franklin D. Roosevelt's National Resources Planning Board and its earlier entities. When the Board helped to coordinate activities of some Cabinet agencies and to get their ideas before the President, it had some success. But when it tried to establish its own field staff and do its own planning, it incurred hostility from regular line agencies. Roosevelt's Board also did most of its work in secret, which aroused further antagonism.

On the other hand, in the one case in which Congress enacted legislation (the National Environmental Policy Act of 1969) to establish a permanent Council on Environmental Quality to advise the President regularly on long-term national environmental policies, the results were indecisive and the Council has not yet been used to its statutory potential.

A permanent advisory group could provide early warning of problems so that public officials and private citizens would have time to prepare contingency plans. As demonstrated by the presidential commissions, research and analysis of long-term impacts can have a significant educational influence, even if no actions are taken immediately as a result of recommendations. Truman's Materials Policy Commission and the 1961–62 National Academy of Sciences Committee on Natural Resources brought large numbers of scientists and other experts together to work on future problems and thus formed a cadre of individuals who continued to enlighten others. The study groups also helped to coordinate research efforts among government, universities, and industry. An unmeasurable educational factor was present in the activity of the Commission on Population Growth and the American Future (1970–72) through Commission-sponsored seminars with experts, public hearings, a film, and brochures. The research work directed by the Commission also resulted in extensive new knowledge and its dissemination through publication of its research papers. The same has been true of all the other commissions and groups dealing with future problems.

Involvement of the private sector in the activities of a permanent future-oriented high-level advisory group would serve both to educate citizens and build a constituency for carrying out recommendations. This was demonstrated by the 1958 Outdoor Recreation Resources Review Commission when it formed an advisory council that included 25 citizen leaders representing varied citizen organizations. The Commission held joint meetings and field trips with the advisory council, and Commission recommendations were submitted in draft form to the advisory council for consideration. A Citizens Committee that was formed after completion of the Commission report helped obtain support for implementing the recommendations. The seminars and public hearings held by the 1970 Commission on Population Growth and the American Future served an educational purpose. And the Commission's Citizens Committee, which promoted a film and an education program on the Commission's work, provided new avenues for dissemination of the findings. Public participation in the 1976 National Growth and Development report through seminars in San Francisco, Kansas City, and Washington, provided advisory assistance to the HUD team preparing the report. A draft of the report was circulated for review and comment to 35 public groups and Congress. These activities proved helpful to a report which previously had inputs only from a few people in the White House Domestic Council and the Department of Housing and Urban Development.

### The Matter of Timing

A permanent institution would have much more freedom in choosing the moment to present new ideas, and thus avoid the timing and politics-related problems that have often hindered activities of temporary presidential commissions. The interest of a President or Congress or the public proved to be much greater at the time a study is started than when it is completed. The Materials Policy Commission was appointed by President Truman in January 1951, when military involvement in Korea had reintroduced fears of shortages that were still fresh in the minds of administrators and the public following World War II. But when the Commission's report went to the President in June 1952, the scarcity issue had lost its priority and public concern. When President Nixon sent a Message to Congress in 1969 asking for creation of a commission to study population growth, the subject was politically attractive inasmuch as people were concerned about rising birthrates. But by the time the Population Commission's report was submitted, statistics showed that the birthrate in the nation had already declined to a stability rate—two children per family—and the subject had less political importance. Another unfavorable timing factor was that the report was sent to the President at the start of his 1972 re-election campaign; some of the Commission's recommendations raised controversy, causing the President to repudiate the Commission's work. On the other hand, the release of the report of the Outdoor Recreation Resources Review Commission came at a time when the popularity of outdoor recreation was booming, and Congress welcomed help in devising solutions to the problems connected with the growing recreation use of public lands, national parks, and national forests.

Another problem of timing was the frequent long delays between the request for a commission and its creation, or between the time the law was passed and the President appointed the public members. Sometimes the period allowed for a study was too short, as with the preparation of "Toward a Social Report." That study also ran into a frequent timing problem: having been started by one President, the study is then submitted either at the end of his term or to his successor.

For all of these reasons, many observers have urged the establishment by law of a permanent group in the Executive Office of the President to institutionalize the coordination of long-term global and holistic considerations of population, resources, environment, and their related issues.

# Appendix B

# Advisory Views: A Critique of the Study

The agency experts who prepared the Global 2000 Study projections were assisted by the counsel of two groups of advisers. These advisers, whose names and affiliations are given in the Preface to this volume, provided the agency experts with counsel, insights, and criticisms from the perspectives of corporations, foundations, national and international governmental organizations, and the academic community.

The first group consisted of over one hundred informal advisers who received early drafts of sections of the Study related to their areas of expertise. Throughout the course of the Study, they provided a flow of marginal comments, correspondence, supporting materials, and direct discussions, which greatly enhanced the final quality of the Study.

The second group consisted of seven experts with unique experience in analyzing—on a coherent, interrelated basis—long-term global trends involving population, resources, and the environment. These "outside" experts (so called to distinguish them from the agency experts preparing the projections) participated in extended discussions with the agency experts on two occasions during the course of the Study. The first occurred immediately after the first drafts of the projections were developed. This meeting of the two groups of experts lasted two days and led to several key revisions in the initial drafts. The second meeting took place after the final projections had been developed. It lasted one day and provided many additional interpretative insights.

The wisdom and expertise that these two groups shared with the Global 2000 Study has influenced the Study in innumerable ways. Perhaps the single most dramatic instance of this influence was the collective decision of the agency and outside experts, during their first meeting, to include the assumption that real petroleum prices will rise 5 percent annually from 1980 to 2000 as a basic component of the Study's most likely projections, wherever feasible. Previously, all of the Study's projections had been based on the assumption that real petroleum prices would be constant throughout the 1975–2000 period.

Although many of the insights and criticisms of these two groups have been previously taken into account throughout this report, numerous insights and criticisms which they provided could not be taken into account because of the particular focus of the Study, because of time and resource constraints, and because of basic limitations in the current ability of the government to develop long-term global projections. A summary of a representative selection of these comments is presented in this appendix in the hope that it will provide additional perspectives on ways of improving the government's foundation for longer-term planning.

The somewhat diffuse summary that follows consolidates the views of many individual advisers. It does not necessarily represent a consistent set of positions supported by any single person or organization associated with the Global 2000 Study. In fact, many advisers of both groups as well as other participants in the Study would probably disagree with many of these criticisms.

## Characteristics of the Recent Past

Many advisers were concerned that the Study's projections were based to a large extent on the extrapolation of trends and relationships characteristic of the past two or three decades only. They asserted that data pertaining to the past two or three decades is often misleading and that quite different trends or relationships can be perceived when a longer past period is taken into consideration.

With respect to weather, for example, they pointed out that the three decades preceding 1970 were unique in recorded history in three respects: (1) There were no major global geophysical perturbations; (2) on balance, crop-growing weather worldwide was not only remarkably close to optimal conditions, but was also remarkably non-

713

variable; and (3) at no time was there a global, as opposed to local, depression of crop production traceable to a global perturbation.

Most advisers felt that the Global 2000 Study should have used a much longer past period of weather history as its basis for projecting the potential impacts of weather variability over the next 22 years. Many felt that the use of a shorter, anomalous period has given the Study's projections an unduly optimistic bias—for instance, with regard to the likely impact of weather on future crop yields. They speculated that other anomalies of the past two to three decades involving variables other than weather may also have distorted the projections.

Many advisers were concerned also that the Study tended to project only those characteristics of the recent past for which "hard" quantitative data were readily available. For example, they noted that the GNP projections ignored the major segments of LDC economies that were not cash economies, that the energy projections ignored firewood consumption (a major fuel in the LDCs), and that the food, energy, and mineral projections ignored water consumption. They felt, in addition, that the available hard data was often used in ways that implied that it was of higher quality than was in fact the case.*

These advisers asserted that, in general, a more extensive attempt should have been made—on a best-effort basis—to project those characteristics of the recent past for which hard data were not readily available. Specifically, they felt that the Study should have first attempted to identify important issues related to population, resources, and the environment, and only thereafter should have proceeded to (1) identify the trends that must be projected in order to analyze those issues on a balanced basis, and (2) develop projections of those trends in the best way possible under the constraints of the Study, with explicit notes included regarding ranges of potential error.

## Beyond the Year 2000

Many advisers were concerned that, in general, the Study's projections do not extend beyond the year 2000. They asserted that some of the most

important trends over the 1978–2000 period are not likely to be adequately identified, described, or interpreted unless longer-term future perspective is taken into account.

One adviser provided the following examples of events in the past that might have been more favorably influenced if their longer-term implications had been better understood at the time of their incidence:

- The dysfunctional use of new chemical agents produced from the bonding of halogens and hydrocarbons (e.g., DDT and PCBs).
- The low nonmarket pricing of natural gas and underpricing of oil that caused many industrial processes to be unsuitably fueled and many power-plants to be converted from coal to these fuels in recent decades.
- The failure to balance the benefits of subsidizing family farms at modest levels against the socioeconomic costs of driving the rural poor into city slums and endless welfare problems.

Another adviser, looking to the longer-term future, suggested that the uncritical development of energy resources (which she perceives to be taking place today) might have similarly dysfunctional consequences in the future—consequences might be avoided or ameliorated if they were properly perceived and responded to today. In her view, the greatest problem is not, as most think, how to obtain what we need, but that we will use too much of it. Most energy projections for developed countries are far too high—but not because we might not actually use that much if it were available. The danger is that we would—with disastrous results for the ecosphere and, inevitably, for ourselves. Such rapidly rising energy use would also put enormous pressure on other resources.

Still other advisers, also looking to the longer-term future, suggested that the most important changes currently taking place—changes that are likely to produce major unforeseen dysfunctional consequences if they are not properly perceived and responded to—are socioeconomic and cultural rather than biophysical. The pervasive fragmentation they perceive to be taking place in Western industrialized society has been particularly well outlined, according to one observer, by Bertram Gross:

From the broader point of view, [there are] many forms of fragmentation in the emerging service society:
—in technology, the fragmentation of knowledge,
—in macrosystems, the fragmentation of responsibility and accountability,
—in extended professionalism, the fragmentation of social role, skills, and culture,

*One adviser felt that the population projections were particularly unbalanced. He observed that, on the one hand, inappropriately elaborate computational procedures were applied to what are essentially very rough estimates of future fertility, mortality and migration (taken to be zero) rates, while, on the other hand, no explicit relationships were used to relate social, economic, and cultural (as opposed to "demographic") factors into the projection of fertility, mortality and migration rates.

—in extended urbanism. the fragmentation of community life.
To this, [must be added] the fragmentation of the family and the individual.*

Some even suggested that this fragmentation ought to be examined in the context of the Decline-of-the-West perspective adopted by some scholars and statesmen. One adviser quoted André Malraux:

We are living at the end of a quite unprecedented era. the end of the 1450–1950 cycle, which was a model of complete civilization. 1450 marked the beginning of the great discoveries, and the conquest of the world by the Europeans. Within two or three years of 1950, we had Mao in Peking and Nehru's speech—in other words the liberation of China and India.

We are more or less aware that we live in a world that is dying, and we find it very difficult to imagine another one. There was also, I suppose, the end of Rome, but by the time people became aware of the fact it was already well and truly dead. We, on the other hand, are actually living out the process.*

Another adviser commented that projecting trends only to the year 2000 reminded him of the story about the man falling from a very tall building who, when asked how he was doing as he passed the 10th floor, responded, "Things are great so far!" Many severe supply constraints, increases in demand, and socioeconomic and ecological changes may well occur shortly after 2000—and be completely overlooked by the Study's projections because the projections do not extend beyond 2000. Other severe changes that do occur prior to 2000 may also be disregarded because, in the absence of a post-2000 perspective, they may not be perceived or their significance may not be understood.

### Absence of Shocks

Many advisers were concerned that the focus of the Global 2000 Study on projecting foreseeable trends necessarily excluded projecting shocks whose incidence, severity, and specific impacts could only be arbitrarily specified. They asserted that assuming a complete absence of such shocks was unrealistic and produced an overly optimistic assessment of the future.
One adviser provided the following taxonomy to suggest the range of potential "surprises" that had been excluded from the Study's projections:

*Bertram M. Gross, "Planning in an Era of Social Revolution", *Public Administration Review*, May/June 1971, p. 281.

*"Interview with André Malraux", *The Guardian*, Apr. 13, 1974, p. 14.

## NATURAL SURPRISES

I. Disasters
   1. Weather
      a. Large scale crop or livestock destruction (e.g., due to frost, drought, flood, or snow)
      b. Societal disruption (e.g., due to floods or blizzards)
   2. Earthquake
   3. Disease
      a. Crop or livestock epidemic (e.g., corn blight)
      b. Severe flu or other human diseases on the same scale (e.g., Legionnaire's disease and similar epidemics)
II. Other
   1. Resources—unexpected discoveries (e.g., huge petrochemical resources on continental margins or in marine basins)
   2. Food—extraordinary growing seasons resulting in food surpluses.

## TECHNOLOGICAL SURPRISES

I. Distribution failures
   1. New York City-type blackout—longer or wider area
   2. Water system failure (e.g., Trenton in 1976)
   3. Gas or oil pipeline failure
   4. Toxic leak—(e.g., chlorine or ammonia in a population center)
   5. Nuclear mishap—generation, transport, or waste
   6. Prolonged temperature inversion causing serious air pollution incidents
II. Design or concept failures
   1. Chemicals appearing in unpredicted places (e.g., PCBs)
   2. Chemicals with long lasting and/or highly toxic degradation products
   3. Bridge, building, or dam failure
III. Advances
   1. Solution to clean fusion
   2. Water recycling technology or acceptance breakthrough
   3. Tide or ocean thermal power breakthrough
   4. Cancer or heart disease cure
   5. Development of self fertilizing crops

## SOCIAL SURPRISES

I. Overthrow of government
II. Widespread social disorder
III. Collapse of a social system

In many cases, the Study's advisers believed the transient effects of such shocks would be far more severe than their long-term impacts. For example, many felt that the shock of the 1973 quadrupling of the international price of oil was far more damaging to most countries than the anticipated long-term impact of the price rise was likely to be.

Many advisers also believed that the projected emergence of increasing international and national economic interdependencies and other trends (e.g., increasing agricultural reliance on monoculture production) is likely to increase the severity of such shocks when they do occur. For example, even simple variations in weather patterns similar to those experienced in the past may create impacts disregarded in the Study. According to one adviser:

The U.S. economy is increasingly moving in the direction of very tight coupling between importing fuel and paying for fuel imports by exporting crops. America's ability to purchase fuel will thus be increasingly influenced by its crop-growing weather (which will affect U.S. production) and crop-growing weather in the countries that import most of America's exported crops (which will affect foreign demand for U.S. crops). As a result, the American energy supply and demand situation will be increasingly sensitive to a variety of types of weather perturbation, which collectively have a probability close to one of occurring at 22-year intervals. Other, less expected perturbations (e.g., blights, the discovery of unacceptable side effects associated with fertilizer, herbicide, or pesticide use, the politicization of international food production or distribution, climatic change, or civil or international disruption) could have far more severe impacts.

Many advisers also believed that many current U.S. policy alternatives would be likely to have different potential impacts in increasing or decreasing America's future vulnerability to such shocks. One adviser thought that this was particularly true with regard to choosing to emphasize nuclear or alternative energy sources:

Once the choice has been made—especially if the choice is to put all our eggs in one nuclear basket—future options may be foreclosed. If the first choice proves disastrous, it may not be possible to abandon it and start over because of resource contraints, including energy. In contrast, many advantages would accrue to a strategy based on a diverse decentralized mix of energy sources designed to minimize waste and match source to end use. Among the advantages would be efficiency in the use of energy (reducing environmental impacts), probably a lower overall pressure on resources per unit of energy (because a wider variety would be needed for various types of development and because of efficiency), and flexibility in the energy economy. If one mode proves unsatisfactory, its loss could be made up from several others without disrupting the entire system. Which direction is chosen will

have profound effects on the kinds and amounts of environmental impact from energy use and mobilization, on economic systems, on politics (local to international), and on social values such as personal liberty.

Many advisers were concerned that the Global 2000 Study, by ignoring potential shocks, might encourage policymakers to disregard impacts on system resilience—i.e., a system's ability to withstand different types of potential future shocks—in evaluating alternative policy options, when in fact this should be an important evaluative criterion. They were also concerned that the Study tended to disregard the differential impact of shocks (and more gradual change) on smaller groups, disaggregated by region, income, race, religion, and other factors.

### Potential Discontinuities

To a large extent, the Global 2000 Study's projections were based on extrapolations of past trends and relationships, although minor adjustments to such trends were incorporated in many cases. This was an area of concern to many advisers who considered that the future is likely to be fundamentally discontinuous with the past in significant ways.

They pointed out, for example, that real energy prices have been declining for most of the past century, encouraging the use of energy-intensive products (e.g., aluminum, automobiles, high-yield varieties of grain), and in general facilitating the substitution of capital for labor. Real food and mineral prices have also generally been declining. They felt that the reversal of these basic trends indicated in the Study's projections was likely to severely alter domestic and international socioeconomic systems so that in the future they would behave in ways not at all characteristic of the past.

Many advisers insisted that this is not only possible but probable, in view of what they perceive to be the following general trends:

- Approaching exhaustion of the world's inexpensive fluid fuel reserves.
- Approaching limits to the environmental absorptive capacity and agricultural productive capacity of the planet—which may be prevented only by massive capital investment (which is either not likely to be made or which is likely to be characterized by increasingly high marginal costs).
- Shifts in international strategic goals from ensuring access to markets to ensuring access to raw materials.
- Shifts in power from countries with large industrial resources to countries with large raw material resources.

• Shifts in economic goals from stimulated supply and demand to stimulated conservation.

• Shifts in social goals from growth to equity.

Some advisers were particularly concerned that the following specific political factors (and policy changes which might be associated with them) were not taken into account in most of the Study's projections:

• Negotiations over a new international economic order, which may affect the availability and price of many raw materials.

• Other North-South disputes (e.g., those involved in the Law of the Sea negotiations), which may make international environmental cooperation increasingly difficult.

• The new shift in development models toward meeting basic human needs, which may lead to new pressures on available resources.

• Increasing poverty in the poorest LDCs, which may lead to significant political unrest.

They felt that the Study should have explicitly taken such factors into account by making major rather than minor adjustments to variables involving the supply and demand for resources, and by making major adjustments to all models to reflect projected severe environmental impacts.

## Absence of Normative Analysis

All of the Study's projections assumed, in general, a continuation of past policies or past policy trends (in part because policy changes are difficult to project and in part because debate regarding projected policy changes can attract attention away from underlying problems). Nevertheless, many of the Study's advisers noted that policies are likely to change in response to changing circumstances, and that not taking such change into account produces trend projections that are likely to be severely biased.

They pointed out, moreover, that people often look ahead and change their current behavior in order to achieve their future goals, just as people often change their current goals to take into account anticipated future circumstances. Thus, they felt, it may be seriously misleading to project the future, as the Study has done, without taking into consideration that behavior and goals can change well in advance of changing circumstances.

By not explicitly projecting potential changes in goals and goal-seeking behavior, the Study missed an important opportunity to identify a broad set of alternative future scenarios which might well be significantly different from those identifiable by

merely projecting past trends and relationships. According to some advisers, many of these scenarios might appear to be more desirable than those likely to be attained through incremental decision-making practices, which they believed would be implicitly encouraged by the Study's lack of normative analysis. In their view, the Study neither (1) presents an array of goals to strive for (while demonstrating the feasibility of attaining these goals), nor (2) indicates which present policy decisions are the most critical in defining the future. They viewed these as the two most important objectives of future-oriented research and considered the Study seriously deficient for disregarding them.

Some advisers argued that the absence of normative analysis from the Study has probably led to irrelevance and bias. One adviser submitted the following quote to support his points:

A few decades ago the view prevailed that demographic "stagnation" was bad; yet today many people favor a stable, or nearly stable population. Economic stagnation, on the other hand, is still felt to be bad. Perhaps in the year 2000, more of us will favor John Stuart Mill's "stationary state," not only in the demographic sphere but also in much of the economic sphere (though not in culture). If this happens, economic growth will be smaller than we now project on the basis of the current trade-off between more goods and more leisure. By the same token, people will *care* less about economic growth. Thus, our predictions regarding economic growth will not only be rather inaccurate, but they will describe what, by the year 2000, will be quite an uninteresting feature.*

As a result of these and other considerations, many advisers regretted that the Study did not incorporate normative analyses of the following types of issues:

*Political issues*—e.g., whether the Western industrialized nations are likely to encourage or even permit faster growth of energy use in the LDCs while curbing their own growth (or, more generally, whether resource competition will lead to international conflict).

*Ethical issues*—e.g., whether investment in pollution control in the U.S. (assuming minor health benefits) is ethically acceptable, given the much higher returns in health that the same investment might produce in the LDCs.

*Budgetary issues*—e.g., whether current U.S. budgetary decisions affecting, for example, de-

---

*Fred Charles Ikle, "Can Social Predictions Be Evaluated?" *Daedalus,* Summer 1967, p. 750.

fense, energy, food, and welfare programs conflict with U.S. long-term international goals regarding population, resources, and the environment.

Many advisers emphasized, in particular, their feeling that problems related to the unequal distribution of population and resources are likely to be more significant in the future than problems related, for example, to potential physical limits to growth. But because of the absence in the Study of normative analyses of political, ethical, budgetary, and other issues, they felt that an adequate foundation had not been established, in the context of the Study, for commenting extensively on these distributional problems.

Many also regretted that the Study's focus (as well as time and resource contraints) did not permit more penetrating economic analysis—especially one taking potential normative change into consideration. One adviser noted, in particular, that

the assumptions of formal economics are not inexorable laws of nature, like the laws of thermodynamics. Their truths are, in part, fiction—that is to say, made truths. They are true as long as people believe in and act in accordance with them; their validity is a function of their acceptance. As values change, some of the assumptions of formal economics and the behavior of economic systems are also likely to change in ways that might be anticipated or even guided.

Many advisers were concerned that the Study, by not incorporating normative analysis, might encourage policymakers to debate issues only at the instrumental level (i.e., how best to accomplish well-understood and widely accepted goals) without evaluating alternative goals or even assessing whether, in many cases, presumed existing goals are in fact well understood or widely accepted.

## Hidden Premises

All the Study's projections were developed making use of available data and were structured and manipulated according to existing theory, as represented in the methodological tools used by the various agencies. This was an object of concern to several advisers. They asserted that various hidden premises, missing variables, and inadequate data and methodologies inherent in this approach may have created projections that disseminate misconception and error rather than knowledge.

One adviser commented that, for example, many of the Study's projections are in effect tautologies—premises masquerading as conclusions. He felt that, in many cases, the projections merely provide a framework for making prejudices consistent. In his view:

Many of the projection tools that will be used to make the resource and food projections require GNP projections as inputs. But how can we predict GNP? Economic models can do so only by assuming some appropriate algorithm and investing future habits with current mores. Moreover, such models almost certainly require such inputs as the capital and energy requirements for resource exploitation and population growth. But where are those data to be found, or elucidated? Thus, the Study's projections must remain essentially pious hopes in which "high" economic growth may be attractive to a politician, but unattractive to an environmentalist.

Some advisers observed that in many cases even this limited form of consistency was not achieved within a given set of projections. To paraphrase one of their criticisms with regard to the energy projections:

In one instance the assertion is made that the past wide availability and low price of petroleum have allowed Americans and consumers to substitute energy for labor and other inputs on an unprecedented scale. Such an assertion is in accord with a conceptual model that assumes that low energy prices (relative to the cost of labor) stimulate an energy-for-labor substitution, which, by implication, would tend to increase unemployment, increase rates of resource depletion, pollution, and crime, increase government expenditures, decrease capital availability for other purposes, and decrease the rate of economic growth. In fact, every step of that causal pathway can be documented in longitudinal and cross-sectional analyses of all available data.

In contrast, in another instance, the assertion is made that apart from the very real possibility of a supply disruption for political or other reasons, the major problem faced by the United States and other energy consuming countries is the threat of large increases in real energy prices and the associated reduction in economic growth and aggravation of unemployment and inflation. In fact, the causal pathway postulated here is the opposite to that postulated previously, and there is no support for it in longitudinal or cross-sectional analysis of national or international data.

This logical inconsistency raises important misgivings regarding the usefulness of the energy projections. The establishment of a realistic, consistent conceptual model of the relationship between energy prices and other economic variables is an absolute prerequisite to making any kind of credible projection of energy supply or energy demand.

## Missing Variables

Many advisers felt that crucial variables and variable linkages were omitted from the projections. A small representative sampling is provided below:

### The population projections omit health factors.

Unfortunately, none of the Study's population scenarios assumes increased mortality rates, although these are a real possibility in poor countries, especially the poorest and hungriest. The projections' unanimous rises in life expectancy in industrialized nations I also find dubious. Have you noticed the soaring cancer rate in the U.S. and Europe? It is believed that at least 80 percent of cancers are environmentally induced, and exposure of the public to environmental carcinogens has increased enormously in the last few decades. Other environmentally related diseases (particularly respiratory ones) are also increasing in frequency.

### The fisheries projections omit pollution factors.

My review draft contains the rather surprising statement that "it is probable that the amount of pollution will peak in the next 10 years and decline thereafter." There is no indication of where this surmise comes from. I consider this assumption highly unlikely for several reasons: (a) we will remain in an oil economy till the year 2000; transportation of oil by tanker will increase during this period, with an inevitable increase in barrels of oil spilled; (b) as terrestrial sources of energy increase, aerial fallout of released pollutants will fall predominantly in the sea; (c) the preceding point is simply a corollary of the larger point that as long as we assume an increase in GNP between now and 2000, there will be an increase in the volume of toxic material released to the environment and an increase in thermal pollution, there being no historical basis for assuming otherwise. These considerations imply a lower fish harvest in the decades ahead than one based on an assumption that pollution will decrease.

### No consistent accounting is made of land, labor, and capital deployment.

A lot of people are talking about growing biomass (e.g., grains) specifically to make alcohols, but one must keep in mind that this would be in direct competition to growing food. If we are assuming all available arable land will be used for food production, then there won't be any available for energy plantations. I suspect that in the competition between food and fuel, we will usually be willing to pay more for food. Since the calorie conversion efficiency of grain to alcohol fuel is even worse than that of grain to livestock feed, growing grain (or other biomass) in the use for fuel raises the same ethical questions regarding the needs of the LDC's that feeding our grain to cattle for meat raises.

Similar concerns related to consistent accounting (and ethics) are likely to arise with regard to the deployment of labor and capital. For example, entry-level labor, at least for the next 20 years, will decline in the United States and increase rapidly in Mexico (and in many Caribbean countries). Wages, however, are variously estimated at up to 10 times greater in the United States than in Mexico. In the foreseeable future, at entry-level employment, migrants—legal and illegal—could be adding more new workers to the U.S. labor force than entry-level U.S. citizens.

In contrast, in the developing world the unskilled worker population is growing at an unprecedented rate. By the 1980s, industries relying heavily on a large entry-level labor force—for example, fast-food chains—will face a shrinking labor pool. (U.S. high school graduating classes are beginning to decline now.) U.S. industries, then, must consider at least (1) whether this type of needed labor will be available where and when a new plant is built, and (2) whether some types of plants and industries should be located outside the United States because of the large pool of available entry-level labor.

## Inadequate Data and Methodologies

Regarding weak data and methodologies, one adviser provided three thoughtful quotations concerning the limitations and opportunities inherent in making projections. They are presented at some length at the conclusion of this appendix because of the critical insights they provide into the kinds of understanding that can realistically be expected of a study of this nature.

### Our information regarding reality is limited.

Numerical operations with economic data . . . impose their own requirements. Without knowledge of errors, the feeding of economic data into high-speed computers is a meaningless operation. The economist should not believe that "correct" solutions of many linear equations and of other computations, such as multiple correlations, are necessarily meaningful. This is true even when only two linear equations in two unknowns are involved. The following example, which could of course be generalized, shows what enormous differences very slight errors of observations . . . will produce in the solution.

The equations

$$x - y = 1$$
$$x - 1.00001\, y = 0$$

have the solution $x = 100,001$, $y = 100,000$, while the almost identical equations

$$x - y = 1$$
$$x - 0.999999\, y = 0$$

have the solution $x = -99,999$, $y = -100,000$. The coefficients in the two sets of equations differ by at most two units in the fifth decimal place, yet the solutions differ by 200,000.

If one recalls how easily equations are sometimes written down purporting to show economic relationships and how shaky is our determination of the parameters, it will be realized what difficulties have to be overcome in constructing and applying an empirically significant theory. If the number of equations is even moderately large, it becomes far from trivial to find out whether or not the determinant actually vanishes.*

**Our ability to make effective use of our information is limited.**

The difficulties of parameter estimation are not the most serious problems in the study of complexity. Suppose that we did know the interrelations among all parts of a system and could describe the rate of change of each variable as a function of the others. Then we would have a very large set of simultaneous non-linear equations in a vast number of variables . . . depending on so many parameters, the estimation of each of which may take a lifetime.

These equations [would probably] be insoluble. They would be likely to be too numerous to compute. If we could compute [them], the solution would be simply a number. If we could solve the equations, the answer would be a complicated expression in the parameters that would have no meaning for us. Therefore the only way to understand a complex system is to study something else instead.

That something else is a model. A model is a theoretical construction, a collection of objects and relations some, but not all of which correspond to components of the real system. In one sense it is a simplification of nature. . . . We replace the universal but trivial statement "things are different, interconnected, and changing" with a structure that specifies which things differ in what ways, interact how, change in what directions. . . .

Models differ in the aspect of reality preserved, in the departures from reality, and in their manipulative possibilities. They can therefore give different results. Since it is not always clear which consequences derive from the properties of nature, it is often necessary to treat the same problem with different models. A theorem is then called robust if it is a consequence of different models, and fragile if it depends on the details of the model itself. The search for robustness leads to the proposition that truth is the intersection of independent lies.*

**Many effective approaches do exist for making use of our information.**

If one presumes to say anything at all about the future of a social system, he must assume that there

---

*Oskar Morgenstern, *On the Accuracy of Economic Observations*, 2nd ed., Princeton, N.J.: Princeton University Press, 1963, pp. 109–110.

*R. Levins, "Complex Systems," in C. H. Waddington, ed., *Towards a Theoretical Biology*, vol. III, Chicago: Aldine, 1970, pp. 75–76.

is something dependable about the behavior of that system. There are relatively few distinct ways in which social systems are dependable. The different methods of futures research are based essentially on various combinations of six principles that characterize complex, highly interconnected social systems.

*One: Continuity.* First of all, societies exhibit continuity. Social systems change smoothly from one state to another; generally they do not change in discontinuous jumps. (Even during relatively disruptive and seemingly discontinuous periods, such as the American Civil War or the French Revolution, much of the culture, social roles, and institutional framework of a society persists without fundamental change.) Thus, in making forecasts we commonly and reasonably extrapolate from past experience. This principle of continuity is used in all sorts of projections of trends and cycles—for forecasting demographic trends, economic cycles, and annual energy consumption; for anticipating future attitudes from polling data; for estimating future financial performance—to mention only a few. . . .

*Two: Self-consistency.* A second guiding principle underlying futures research is that societal systems tend to be internally self-consistent. That is, the behavior of one sector of society does not generally contradict that of another. For instance, basic research is not likely to be well supported and flourishing when the economy is depressed.

The principle of self-consistency underlies one of the popular, if less systematic, techniques for examining the future—namely, scenario-writing. The purpose of writing scenarios about the future is to insure that the characteristics asserted, whether arrived at from trend projections or other methods, "hang together" and make a reasonable story. A plausible future has to feel like it might be lived in. Familiar examples of scenario-writing include Edward Bellamy's *Looking Backward*, Aldous Huxley's *Brave New World*, and George Orwell's *1984*.

*Three: Similarities among social systems.* Because the individuals making up varied social systems have fundamental characteristics in common, the systems themselves inevitably exhibit certain similarities. Accordingly, one group will tend to behave somewhat like another under similar circumstances. This observation of similarities across groups is used in anthropological approaches to the study of the future, in gaming methods where an individual assumes the role of a group or a nation, and in cross-cultural comparisons (e.g., of stages of economic development).

Historical analogies in particular, if not carried too far, can be useful in suggesting possible future scenarios. For example, studies of historical occurrences of revolutionary cultural and political transformations suggest possible parallels today.

*Four: Cause-effect relationships.* Social systems exhibit apparent cause-effect connections or statistical correlations that imply cause and effect relationships. For instance, when making economic projections we assume that if scarcities occur, prices will rise, or that if the rate of inflation is lowered by manipulating the money supply, unemployment will increase. Such presumed cause-effect linkages underlie much economic and simulation modeling. They are the basis for the models in the Club of Rome's study *The Limits to Growth* which has generated much controversy since its publication in 1972. They form the basic principle in the widely used method of cross-impact analysis (in which aspects of the future are studies through the presumed interactions of contributing events on one another).

*Five: Holistic trending.* In their process of evolving and changing, social systems behave like integrated organic wholes. They have to be perceived in their entirety; thus there is no substitute for human observation and judgment about the future state of a system. To overcome the problem of bias of an individual observer, collective opinion can be sought in various ways. One of these is the so-called Delphi technique wherein the opinions of a number of judges are systematically processed and the results fed back to each of the judges as additional input, the object

being to obtain refined judgments (but not necessarily consensus).

*Six: Goal-seeking.* Societies have goals. They act with apparent intentionality, although the goals that might be inferred from observation are not necessarily declared ones. Just as individuals have aims of which they are but dimly aware, so do societies seek destinies that they have never explicitly proclaimed. In short, social change is not aimless, however obscured the goal. Modern industrialized society is confronted with a set of dilemmas that it seeks to resolve. Goals that once inspired commitment and loyalty no longer have the same power, and new priorities are being formed. The possible futures are distinguished, as much as anything, by the ways society seeks resolution of its dilemmas, and by the kinds of new goals that emerge.*

* Reprinted with permission of The Portable Stanford, Stanford Alumni Association, from *An Incomplete Guide to the Future* by Willis W. Harman, Stanford, Calif.: Stanford Alumni Association, 1976 (New York: W. W. Norton, forthcoming).

# Appendix C

## Embassy Reports on Forestry and Agricultural Trends

In preparation for the Global 2000 Study, a request was made to a number of countries via U.S. Embassies to supplement the meager information available on forestry and agricultural trends. The hope was that new, but as yet unpublished, data might exist which would be useful in assessing global conditions. The following questions were asked of a score of Embassies in African, Asian, and Latin American countries:

**Forestry.** How much deforestation (land units per year) is taking place? Are good forestry practices being used? Is there any effective reforestation? To what extent are existing forests showing signs of stress from forest grazing, firewood gleaning, expanded or accelerated slash-and-burn agriculture, etc.? To what extent does disruption of watershed cover appear to be causing problems downstream (erratic stream flow, dam siltation, etc.)? What institutional programs are in effect to improve forestry practices? Are these adequate?

**Soil.** If agricultural land is being lost to cultivation through problems such as erosion, salinization, waterlogging, desertification, laterization, etc., please specify cause and magnitude (units per time period). Specify problems either currently visible or foreseeable concerning maintenance of fertility in currently used crop land. What institutions exist to promote soil conservation? Are these adequate?

**Land Development.** How much does it cost to bring an additional hectare of land into cultivation? How are costs distributed between public and private costs (e.g., for irrigation projects)? What addition to crop production can be anticipated as a result of expansion of arable land?

**Yield Gains from Technological Change.** What estimates of yield gains attained by technological change are available? Has any effort been made to quantify the inputs and capital costs necessary to achieve such gains?

The following sections are abstracted from the Embassy responses.

## BANGLADESH

**Summary.** Deforestation and land degradation are not considered significant problems in Bangladesh at present. However, the country's modest forest resources could be exhausted by the end of the century if not effectively managed. Loss of forest cover in Bangladesh itself does not pose a significant threat to agricultural land, but deforestation in neighboring areas could cause flooding problems here. In its development efforts the government of Bangladesh has focused on improving the productivity of existing arable land. Forestry management has received considerably less attention. Data generated in the planning process is not invariably consistent, and the projections based on them involve assumptions of limited reliability. In light of this, the following responses to questions are suggestive rather than conclusive.

**Forestry.** Some deforestation as a result of illegal cutting and "slash and burn" agriculture is evident from aerial observation, but the amount has not been quant'fied. About 15 percent of the country is covered by forest, mainly in the Sunderbans area in the southwest and in the hilly, less densely populated border areas of the Chittagong hill tracts and Sylhet. Forest cover in these areas has not decreased significantly, but village groves scattered throughout the country are disappearing as the population (and thus the demand for agricultural land and fuel) increases.

There is no concerted reforestation program at present. Some forest areas (e.g., the mangrove forests of the Sunderbans and bamboo groves elsewhere) regenerate fairly quickly if left alone, but the large hardwood forests of the Chittagong hill tracts are slow to recover from cutting.

Cultivation of products such as pineapples in previously uncultivated areas of the Chittagong hill tracts has caused some soil erosion and increased runoff. The acreage involved at present is small but could pose future problems as the amount of land under such cultivation increases. The major watershed disruption problem facing Bangladesh concerns deforestation in the regions upstream, from which an immense volume of water flows to the Bay of Bengal through the Brahmaputra and Meghna River systems. Observable removal of forest cover has occurred in the areas bordering Sylhet; increased deforestation could exacerbate flooding problems in Bangladesh.

The government is undertaking, with FAO assistance, to develop programs for a systematic survey of forestry resources and reforestation through its Forestry Research Institute in Chittagong. These programs are just getting under way.

**Soil.** Some land is being lost for cultivation through expansion of the large urban centers of Dacca-Naray-Anganj (combined population over 2 million) and Chittagong (population 889,000). Otherwise the amount of land under cultivation has remained relatively constant.

The Bangladesh Agricultural Research Council and Horticulture Development Board both have programs designed to promote good cropping practices. Traditional cropping practices have not significantly damaged the soil. However fertility and thus crop yields could be greatly improved by increased application of fertilizer.

**Land Development.** The cost of bringing an additional hectare of land into production has not been quantified, as nearly all available arable land is now being cultivated and there is little potential for adding significantly to acreage presently devoted to agriculture. Even so, the Bangladesh Water Development Board has been directed to prepare a master plan for reclamation in the coastal areas and offshore islands. No cost figures have been developed yet and in any case the increase in acreage will not be great. Rather than stretching the total acreage the government has concentrated its efforts on increasing cropping intensity and food production. The costs and quantity of inputs involved in this effort are discussed below, under "Yield Gains."

Gains in production attributable to increased acreage are not expected to be significant. However, the potential for gains in yield is considerable, as discussed below.

**Yield Gains.** Various estimates of the potential increase in food production have been made. All of them emphasize that increased use of high-yielding varieties (HYVs) of rice, fertilizer, and irrigation could greatly increase crop yields, cropping intensity, and consequently overall output. USAID has calculated that the addition of one pound of fertilizer per acre of paddy increases the yield by about 3.5 pounds. The Bangladesh government, in its 1973–78 five year plan, projected

that increased use of HYVs in conjunction with fertilizer application and irrigation could generate rice yields of .898 tons per acre compared to .582 tons per acre for traditional varieties. The Asian Development Bank, using assumptions leading to a higher production growth rate, estimated that foodgrain production could rise to 26.22 million long tons by 1985 in a "high growth" scenario, or 21.35 million long tons in a "low growth" scenario.

In its 1973–78 five year plan, the government of Bangladesh proposed to supply agricultural inputs (HYV seeds, fertilizer, and plant protection) worth 6.4 billion taka ($426 million at 15 taka equal to one U.S. dollar) to farmers, for which the latter would pay 5.2 billion taka, leaving a subsidy of about 1.2 billion, approximately 19 percent of the total. In addition, the plan proposed to spend 5.8 billion taka ($387 million) for irrigation facilities of which 1.5 billion taka would be paid for by the users. However, due to a variety of circumstances, neither the expenditure targets or the anticipated foodgrain output of 15.4 million long tons have been achieved.

The World Bank has developed a scenario for increasing foodgrain production by 500,000 tons per year (the increase necessary to achieve the projections discussed above). It envisages the following yearly increases in inputs: (1) installation of 1,000 low lift pumps, 5,000 shallow tubewells, 1,000 deep tubewells, and 30,000 hand tubewells to provide irrigation to an additional 158,000 acres of paddy and 60,000 acres of wheat; (2) application of 74,000 tons of fertilizer; and (3) use of an additional 2,400 tons of HYV wheat seeds, 1,400 tons of HYV Aman rice seeds, 800 tons of HYV AUS and 400 tons of HYV Boro. The World Bank has not projected cost figures for these inputs.

**Comment.** By the end of the century Bangladesh is expected to have a population of 150 million. In the face of this prospect, the government has bent its resources toward increasing food production by enhancing the output of existing agricultural land. Assuming an adequate supply of necessary inputs, land degradation does not loom as a serious problem. However pressure on forested areas, both to increase cultivated areas and to provide fuel, could result in the destruction of the country's extractable timber by the year 2000. The environmental impact of this in terms of increased runoff and erosion would be most significant in the Chittagong hill tracts. Elsewhere most deforested areas would be relatively level and would subsequently be cultivated.

Should population pressures lead to large-scale removal of forest cover in Nepal and Assam, Bangladesh as a whole would be adversely affected by the increased runoff. Under present conditions the country is subject to periodic severe flooding and the prospect of more frequent and damaging floods would threaten both the productivity of the land and large portions of the population. This may be the most significant environmental problem facing Bangladesh by the year 2000.

## BOLIVIA

**Forestry.** Deforestation has increased in the last few years and is estimated to total 250,000 to 300,000 hectares in 1978. Approximately 90 percent of the ground cover is destroyed, and very little timber is cut for later uses. Overgrazing and slash and burn agriculture have changed river flows and have also stripped off top soils exposing the underlying clay of sandy soils.

Reforestation plans are limited. Forestry organizations have some plans for the future. Various government organizations have prepared programs and studies concerning forestry practices. Budget limitations and lack of trained personnel have hampered these efforts.

**Soil.** Problems of erosion, salinization, desertification, and laterization are increasing and are caused by the following: improper use of the land, overgrazing, colonization, and destruction of ground cover either by slash and burn methods or by using machinery which not only destroys the jungle but also the physical composition of the soil.

On the Altiplano, grazing animals remove virtually all plant life. Most grazing, however, occurs on the fallow fields that are maintained as grazing areas by the small communities that control land areas.

Estimates as to the extent and rate of erosion are difficult to make. The silt composition of the rock formations and the steep terrain lead to substantial rates of natural erosion. Human activity also has an important impact, but no data exists about its relative magnitude.

## BRAZIL

**Summary.** Notwithstanding the decrease in resources for reforestation in the last three years, Brazilian experts unanimously state that the fiscal incentive program adopted by the Brazilian government has not only alerted Brazilians to their enormous forestry potential but has also enabled them to adapt foreign technology in this sector to Brazilian conditions of climate and soil. Evidence of this is the fact that Brazil had reportedly managed to obtain average productivity of 45 cubic meters per hectare-year in the last 10 years, as opposed to an average of 18 cubic meters before the fiscal incentive program started. The European average (particularly in the planting of eucalyptus and pinus) is, according to Brazilian experts, between 4 and 10 cubic meters per hectare-year.

**Forestry.** Most of the following data were taken from an article on the subject that recently appeared in the *jornal do Brasil*. Material for the article was collected through research and interviews with Brazilian officials and businessmen from the 500 Brazilian private companies that operate in the area of reforestation in Brazil.

Brazil had originally about 5.2 million square kilometers of natural forest area. It now has less than 3.5 million. Eighty percent of Brazil's current forests are concentrated in the Amazon area, and the most deforested areas are located in the southern and southeastern regions of the country. The Amazon region has lost 840,000 square kilometers of forests, which corresponds to 24 percent of its original reserve. Experts have reportedly estimated that if current deforestation rates continue, the Amazon forest will disappear in less than 30 years.

Sources in the Brazilian Institute for Forest Development have reportedly stated that tree cutting in Brazil had totaled about 160 million cubic meters, 120 million of which were used as firewood or in the production of charcoal. Only 40 million cubic meters were used in the production of higher-valued materials, such as lumber, essential oils, and pulp.

Deforestation figures in some states in Brazil are as follows. Parana: 370,000 hectares per year; the state has lost 70 percent of its native reserves in the last 10 years. Rio Grande do Sul: In the last 20 years the state's original reserves have decreased from 43.3 percent to 1.8 percent. Minas Gerais: In the last 15 years the state has lost 3 million hectares of dense forest and 6.5 million hectares of savannas (*cerrados*). São Paulo: 80 percent of state territory was covered by forest a century ago; that percentage is now reduced to 7 percent.

In view of seriousness of the deforestation picture in Brazil, the government in 1966 decided to adopt a reforestation program through which it delegated to the private sector the task of providing the raw material necessary to meet the demand for wood in all its varied applications. The law creating the program (No. 5,106 of 1966) provided that investments in companies that operated in the area of reforestation could be deducted from income tax to be paid both by corporation and private individuals. This fiscal incentive program was highly successful until three years ago, when resources for reforestation started to decrease. The following figures show the success of the program in the 12 years of its existence. Before the program, the annual nationwide planting rate was less than 40,000 hectares per year. Current rate is of the order of 300,000–400,000 hectares per year. Five hundred private companies are currently engaged in reforestation in Brazil. The reforested area has practically doubled since 1966; 2.5 million hectares, representing 5.6 million trees have been planted. Brazil is now surpassed in reforestation practices only by three countries—China, the Soviet Union, and the United States. Investments in the primary sector of reforestation have totaled 26 billion cruzeiros (1.6 billion U.S. dollars) since 1966.

Leading states in reforestation are: Minas Gerais, with 690,000 hectares; São Paulo, with 570,000 hectares; Parana, with 520,000 hectares; and Mato Grosso, with 240,000 hectares. Most planted trees are eucalyptus (1.3 million hectares) and pinus (865 thousand hectares)—both non-natives.

Brazilian experts and companies involved in reforestation have expressed concern about the decrease in the reforestation rate in the last three years, due to changes in legislation, which have resulted in a decrease in resources allocated to private companies. Those sources estimate that Brazil will face a deficit of 1.7 million hectares by 1980, since internal demand for wood by that time will be on the order of 2.9 million hectares, and Brazil would not be able to reforest more than 1.2 million hectares at present rates.

## CHAD

Virtually no statistical data are available with regard to the questions raised. Deforestation throughout the country has been significant during the past decade and is likely to continue through the year 2000 with aggravated results. The common perception of most observers in Chad is that the demand for cooking fuel is the primary and unabated cause of unquantified but significant level of deforestation. The secondary causes are uncontrolled expansion of slash and burn agricultural practices and forage demands for livestock. While the forestry service is making an effort, along with a few aid donors, to maintain existing reserves and develop new ones, these efforts are, on a national scale, inadequate. A requirement for alternative fuel sources is indicated. However, no economically feasible solution is presently anticipated. Furthermore, it is believed that deforestation, along with traditional livestock management practices, is having a serious effect on soil fertility levels. This is certainly true in the Sahelian portion of the country. One portion of Chad, which has been the site of considerable observation, is the rangelands located southeast of Lake Chad. In this area, food crop production is only marginal and range management experts have determined that, due to overgrazing, the range is in a state of rapid decline. There has been no evidence observed regarding changes in watershed due to forestry practices. However, one might suspect that the impact of human populations is contributing to long-term changes in the water levels of Lake Chad. The final conclusion is that unless the trend is reversed, severe land degradation over much of Chad will be evident by the year 2000.

No data are available regarding land development and crop yields.

## COLOMBIA

**Forestry.** As a result of many processes, such as farming practices, erosion, and colonization settlements, it is estimated that approximately 908,000 hectares of natural forest land are being lost each year. Forestry practices are being used on only a small portion of the land.

At the present time, only approximately 5,000 hectares are being reforested each year. Plans are in effect, however, that would bring a total of approximately 540,000 hectares into reforestation during the period 1965–95. Significant portions of existing forests are showing stress for all the reasons indicated.

Tremendous watershed problems result from the disruption of the watershed cover, although they cannot be documented. One institutional program to improve forestry practices involves paying campesinos 2 pesos (5 U.S. cents) for each seedling planted. All programs of this type are recognized as inadequate and in need of expansion. One measure of hope is the recent creation of the Forestry Fund by the Colombian government.

**Soil.** No specific data are available on maintenance of cropland fertility, but fertilizers are widely used on commercial crops. The major institution to promote soil conservation is the Instituto Colombiano Agropecuario, under the

Ministry of Agriculture. It is efficacious, but not fully adequate.

A study entitled "Land Erosion in Colombia," published in 1977 by the Ministry of Agriculture's National Institute of Renewable Natural Resources and the Environment, printed the following table:

### Type of Erosion and Intensity Area

|  | Square Kilometers | Percent of Country |
|---|---|---|
| Areas without serious erosion processes | 282,000 | 24.8 |
| Areas affected principally by surface water erosion | 586,000 | 51.4 |
| Minor to light intensity | 415,000 | 36.4 |
| Light to medium intensity |  | 12.8 |
| Medium to strong intensity | 7,000 | 0.6 |
| Strong to very strong intensity | 18,000 | 1.6 |
| Areas affected principally by mass earth movements | 268,000 | 23.5 |
| Minor to light intensity | 28,000 | 2.5 |
| Light to medium intensity | 233,000 | 20.4 |
| Medium to strong intensity | 7,000 | 0.6 |
| Areas affected principally by wind erosion | 3,000 | 0.3 |
| Strong to very strong intensity | 3,000 | 0.3 |
| Total country area | 1,139,000 | 100.0 |

**Land Development.** The variables involved in answering these questions of land development are tremendous. No data are available at present.

# EGYPT

The principal published data source for the questions raised is the 1975 USAID/USDA study "Egypt: Major Constraints to Agricultural Productivity." Little new information is available. While the Egyptian Ministry of Agriculture has several technical people familiar with data collection, the Ministry lacks full resources for compilation, integration, and analysis of such information.

**Soil.** Salinity and waterlogging have become unexpectedly urgent problems in the past few years due to the farmers' traditional overuse of the available water supply, which was increased with the completion of the Aswan High Dam and the subsequent introduction of widespread irrigation. Traditional methods of the seasonal soaking/flooding of crops contributed to the sudden, unanticipated increase in the incidence of problems due to the rise in water tables. The Ministry of Agriculture estimates that 50,000 to 60,000 acres (roughly 1 percent of the cultivable land area) have been lost to production due to these complications over the last five-year period. With donor assistance, however, the government is taking steps to rectify the problem through the installation of a tile drainage system in the delta and other irrigated areas. Extensive projects, principally financed by IBRD, will provide drainage for approximately one-fifth of the total cultivable land areas by 1981 and prevent further loss due to salinity. If projects are fully implemented on schedule, the Ministry foresees no increase in lands lost to salinity and waterlogging. Furthermore, existing losses should be restored to production.

An even greater threat to cultivable lands is the rapid urbanization in Cairo and Alexandria, which annually claims highly productive acres in the river valley or delta. Fertility maintenance on existing land is becoming increasingly difficult with absence of the annual resilting due to construction of the Aswan High Dam. The Egyptian Ministry of Agriculture, however, has a program underway to increase the use of chemical fertilizers and to rotate certain crops to replenish soils.

**Land Development.** The Aswan High Dam has contributed to reclamation of approximately 1 million feddans (one feddan equals slightly more than one acre) since its construction. The cost of reclamation has not been matched by significantly increased productivity. Virtually all reclamation costs have been borne by the government. The peculiar circumstances of Egypt make it impossible to project production increases from the expansion of arable lands, because the costs of desert reclamation (averaging about $2,000 per acre) are far in excess of the projected potential returns during the short or medium term. Moreover, reclaimed lands reach optimum production levels 7–10 years after they are brought into production; only then can increased productivity be evaluated. The majority of the reclaimed Egyptian lands have not yet attained optimum production levels. This factor understandably contributes significantly to the high cost of reclamation.

**Yield Gains.** The principal impact of technological advance has been the introduction of new varieties of existing crops—e.g., rice, cotton, and wheat. In this area, measured gains have been impressive, but widespread application of technological advances has been slow. The Ministry of Agriculture, in a recent submission for the 1978–82 five year plan, made the point that the agricultural sector's principal problem is the failure to implement widespread technical changes rapidly. Consequently, many potential gains in productivity are lost.

## INDIA (Calcutta)

**Forestry and Soil.** Forestry is certainly an important subject in eastern India. There are regional forestry officials of the government of India located in Calcutta and in West Bengal, a central and populous but not territorially extensive state of the region.

West Bengal technicians offered the following information for the state area.

A. Area Under Forests in West Bengal (in square kilometers)

|  | Total Forest Area |
|---|---|
| 1901 | 13,491 |
| 1951 | 12,225 |
| 1974 | 11,837 |

B. River (in hectares per 100 km²)

|  | Annual Rate of Siltation |
|---|---|
| Teesta | 98.40 |
| Mayurakshi | 16.43 |
| Panchet | 10.00 |
| Kangsabati | 3.76 |

C. Areas Under Shifting Cultivation

| State | 1,000 Hectares | Percentage of Net Shown Area Where Shifting Cultivation Is Practiced |
|---|---|---|
| Assam | 498.3 | 3 |
| Meghalaya | 416.0 | 46 |
| Manipur | 100.0 | 43 |
| Tripura | 220.9 | 9 |
| Nagland | 608.0 | 72 |
| Mizoram | 604.0 | 90 |
| Andhra Pradesh | 248.6 | 80 |
| Total | 2,695.7 | |

In West Bengal approximately 1.7 million hectares of agricultural land suffers from different kinds of soil erosion/land deterioration, and approximately 148,000 hectares of barren land under the administration of the Forest Department require rejuvenation. The table below gives tentative estimates of the different types of deterioration of agricultural land and the areas affected:

| Type of Deterioration | Area (in hectares) |
|---|---|
| Waterlogging | 500,000 |
| Sheet, rill, and gully | 600,000 |
| Flood-prone | 400,000 |
| Salinity | 150,000 |
| Landslides and landslips | 16,000 |
| Total | 1,666,000 |

Officials who are working in this field also made more general observations:

Forest in eastern India are gradually being denuded. One of the main causes is illegal cutting of trees, especially saplings, for fuel and the construction of homes by the poor people. This problem is most acute in the tribal areas of West Bengal. There is an acute shortage of land both for cultivation and for grazing cattle, and intense overgrazing of forest areas. The overgrazing has led to the loss of the porosity of the soil, which has retarded the development of humus. This in turn has caused widespread soil erosion.

The indiscriminate cutting of trees in the watershed areas, especially in hilly regions, has affected the flow of rivers and streams. The flow is becoming more seasonal instead of being relatively constant through the year. The disruption of the watershed cover has also caused a general lowering of the ground-water table. The downstream effects of this are an increase in the frequency and intensity of flooding during the monsoon and a reduction of the water flow during the dry season. This in turn has led to a silting up of not only agricultural land in the flood plains but also a silting up of the reservoirs of river valley projects and an alarmingly high rate of sedimentation in the rivers.

Slash and burn farming is widely practiced in most parts of northeastern India. The area affected by shifting cultivating is estimated at about 2.7 million hectares. (A similar system prevails in the hill forests of Orissa and Andhra Pradesh over an area of about 0.3 million hectares.) Owing to the growing pressure of population on land, the cycle of slash and burn agriculture, which formerly covered a period of 20–30 years, now occurs every 4–6 years. Consequently, despite official activities to curb slash and burn agriculture and encourage settled cultivation, forests are being denuded very rapidly, and soil erosion in these areas is intense and widespread. Inadequate terracing of areas under permanent cultivation is also a problem.

The central and state governments are aware of the importance of preserving forests, but they are handicapped by a shortage of funds and trained personnel and by the poverty of the people, who cannot afford to buy fuel or shelter and consequently have no alternative but to encroach on the forests. In recent years the funding of the government of West Bengal for development of forests has increased. In U.S. dollar equivalents, the budget for 1977 was $1.5 million, while the estimated budget for 1978 is $1.8 million. The government has reportedly also finalized a $2.6 million program for rehabilitating more than 1,000 hectares of degraded forests and over 2,500 hectares of plantations. This program is scheduled to begin in Fiscal Year 1978.

According to officials of the West Bengal Forestry Department, the plans prepared by it for the protection and the development of forests are very comprehensive, but there is often a shortage of funds and the gap between the preparation of plans and their execution is often very wide. Soil officials stressed the lack of trained and experienced personnel, which often means that the financial resources available cannot be properly used.

Significant areas in North Bengal (adjoining Nepal and Bangladesh) are adversely affected by changes in the courses of the rivers. Statistics are not readily available on the population or the total areas affected by this problem, but it is considered serious. Countermeasures required extensive research and planning, interstate and international cooperation, and very large financial investments, which are probably beyond any current capacities of the state.

## INDIA (New Delhi)

**Forestry.** The combination of both overgrazing and stripping of trees for fuel is making a serious impact on the Himalayan watershed. Effects are seen in landslides, flooding in the Gangetic Plain, lowering of the ground-water table, and reservoir siltation. No studies have been made to estimate the total environmental and economic cost of deforestation. Resolving the sociological problems of forestry management would appear to be as problematical as finding the resources for reforestation. Supplying an alternate means for the economic survival of the people currently using the forests for their livelihood must proceed simultaneously with good forestry practices. A summary of some of the more important data points is given below.

#### Land Use Classification as of 1973

|  | Millions of hectares |
|---|---|
| Total geographical area | 328.05 (100 %) |
| Agriculture or cultivated land | 152.27 (45.4) |
| Forests | 74.57 (22.7) |
| Other uncultivated land | 42.18 (13.0) |
| Nonagricultural uses | 16.25 ( 5.0) |
| Barren and uncultivated land | 42.78 (12.9) |
| Manmade forests in India created up to 1969 | 1,546,400 ha |

#### Forest Areas, 1970–73

|  | Millions of hectares | Loss of Forests (deforestation) |
|---|---|---|
| 1970 | 74.89 | — |
| 1971 | 74.83 | 0.05 |
| 1972 | 74.60 | 0.23 |
| 1973 | 74.57 | 0.03 |
| Average loss of forests per year, 1970–73 | | 106,700 ha* |

*Actual deforestation is expected to be more because of some increase by reforestation.

Sedimentation data for 23 selected reservoirs have been collected. The trend of the sedimentation in the reservoirs varies from 2.5 to 18 hectare-meters per square kilometer (54 to 382 acre-feet per 100 square miles) of the catchment per year. For example the sediment rate for the period 1965–70 (five years) is 7,358 acre-feet per year for Mayurakshi Reservoir, which is three times the expected rate of siltation.

**Soil.** Agricultural land loss through:

| Gully erosion (total) | 2.3 million ha (1974) |
|---|---|
| Ravages of water and wind erosion | 80,000 ha/year (estimate) |
| Salinity (total) | 7 million ha (estimate) |
| Deserts | No data collected |

Land recovered:

| Ravines | 70,000 ha in 15 years |
|---|---|
| Alkali soil | 20,000 ha in 3 years |

Over a 25-year period, 22 million ha were recovered for agriculture use by various soil conservation programs.

Several good institutions are concerned with soil conservation, notably.

Central Soil and Water Conservation Research and Training Institute (ICAR), Dehra Dun
Central Arid Zone Research Institute, Jodhpur
Central Soil Salinity Research Institute, Karnal
Indian Grassland and Fodder Research Institute, Jhansi
Soil Conservation Directorate, Faridabad.
Forest Research Institute and Colleges, Dehra Dun

Their budgets are too small, however, to make dramatic impacts.

**Land Development.** Approximate cost per hectare of development of land for agriculture in 1970 was:

|  | Rupees |
|---|---|
| Ravines | 6,000 (including cost of irrigation) |
| Alkali soil | 5,000–6,000 (including cost of irrigation) |
| Terracing | 3,000–5,000 |

Anticipated crop production for each additional hectare of land recovered is 2–3 tons of food grains.

## INDONESIA

**Forestry.** Total land area in Indonesia is 190.5 million hectares. Of this, about 122.2 million hectares are in forests. The most common estimate of the current rate of deforestation is 400,000 hectares per year. The most important cause, accounting for at least half of the total, is slash and burn agriculture on islands other than Java, Madura, and Bali. The next most important cause of deforestation is considered to be unwise land use, i.e., cultivating too high up mountain slopes.

No data on whether good forestry practices are being used was obtained. About 50 million hectares of forest cutting concessions have been granted. The concession agreements include regulations regarding methods and rates of cutting, size of trees that can be cut, replanting, etc. However, enforcement of the regulations is difficult. Therefore, forestry practices vary greatly from concession holder to concession holder.

River and dam siltation, flooding, etc., are serious problems, especially on Java, but no quantitative data on this problem were uncovered.

The government has two programs for returning land to forest or agricultural productivity: the reforestation program and the "greening" program. The reforestation program is carried out by the Directorate General of Forestry on government-owned land; 1,600 trees (usually pine species) per hectare are planted. Costs for this program are from 30,000–60,000 rupiah (415 rupiah equal one U.S. dollar) per hectare in the first year, 15,000–30,000 rupiah in the second year, and 7,500 in the third year. The greening program is carried out by the Department of Public Works with Inpres C (presidential instruction) money and in cooperation with the Department of Interior. Under this program 600 trees per hectare are planted, usually agricultural species such as fruit trees, cloves, oil palm, etc. The government subsidy is 16,250 rupiah per hectare when terracing is required, and 5,250 rupiah without terracing.

The amount of land rehabilitated under these programs since 1972 is shown below (in thousands of hectares):

|  | Reforestation | Greening | Total |
|---|---|---|---|
| 1972/73 | 82.7 | 42.3 | 125.0 |
| 1973/74 | 78.8 | 40.0 | 118.8 |
| 1974/75 | 84.3 | 57.0 | 141.3 |
| 1975/76 | 25.3 | 37.8 | 63.1 |
| 1976/77 | 162.8 | 302.6 | 465.4 |
| 1977/78 (Projected) |  |  | 800 |
| 1978/79 (Projected) |  |  | 1000 |

One source stated that probably only about 60 percent of the total figure for 1976/77 was actually achieved. Shortages of trained field workers is one of the main limiting factors to expansion of the program. The Directorate General of Forestry is training about 2,500 new field workers a year to attempt to overcome the problem. The effectiveness of the greening program is highly variable.

The objective of the two programs is to eventually rehabilitate a total of 42 million hectares of land classified as follows (in millions of hectares):

|  | Critical Condition | Other | Total |
|---|---|---|---|
| Dry agricultural land | 3 | – | 3 |
| "Alang-alang" grassland, abandoned land, and other | 13 | 3 | 16 |
| Deforested land | 4 | 19 | 23 |
| Total | 20 | 22 | 42 |

**Soil.** While agricultural land is being lost, very little data exist to describe the extent of the problem. One study of the upper Solo River Basin in central Java, one of the most intensely cultivated areas in the country shows erosion in some places of as much as 4 cm annually.

**Land Development.** No data were located on what it costs to bring an additional hectare of land into development. However, the Minister of Research estimates that a total of 41 million hectares of land could be brought into cultivation in Indonesia.

**Yield Gains.** The Central Research Institute for Agriculture in Bogor has estimated yields that could be otained by farmers using already available technology for the following crops:

|  | Current | Potential |
|---|---|---|
|  | (metric tons) | |
| Corn | 1.2 | 4 |
| Rice | 1.3 | 5 |
| Soybeans | .76 | 2 |
| Cassava | 9 | 30 |
| Sweet potatoes | 8.1 | 30 |

## LIBERIA

**Forestry.** In an attempt to diversify its economy from dependence on iron ore and rubber, the government of Liberia has started to implement a 1976 feasibility study on oil palm and coconut plantations. The study calls for the establishment of 22,500 acres of industrial oil palm estates, 15,000 acres of smallholder oil palm plantations, and 20,000 acres of smallholder coconut plantations in eastern Liberia. The total cost of the project is estimated at $89.8 million, and the average rate of return is projected at about 6.5 percent. Foreign loans and grants have been or will be obtained to finance the project. Its implementation has been delayed by failure to get the target acreage of 2,500 acres cleared at one of three sites in 1977. There is some apprehension that the 1978 goal of clearing 5,000 acres of land may not be attained.

## MALAYSIA

The embassy has collected as much data as possible on areas concerned. In many cases the data is "unofficial," and many of the comments are subjective in nature.

**Forestry.** Over the past 10 years Malaysian forests, primarily in the States of Sabah and Sarawak, have been logged at the rate of 500,000 acres per year. Malaysia is, however, starting to become more conservation conscious, and small-scale replanting programs have been started in various parts of the country.

**Soil.** While agricultural land is presently being lost due to deforestation, exhaustion of soil fertility, and shifting cultivation, it is not possible to quantify the amounts of land involved. The Malaysian Agricultural and Research Development Institute, the Rubber Research Institute, and the Forest Department are involved in soil conservation efforts.

**Land Development.** Malaysia has a unique land development approach, operated by the Federal Land Development Authority (FELDA). FELDA's approach is to provide all necessary infrastructure, i.e., housing, roads, schools, etc., as well as to open new land and plant it, usually with rubber and oil palm. This approach is more expensive than many others, and FELDA reports that they spend $3,000 per acre for developing rubber land and $2,800 per acre for developing palm oil land. The government of Malaysia plans to develop 1 million acres in this manner during the third Malaysia plan (1976-80).

**Yield Gains.** Yield gains through technological change are difficult to estimate. Malaysia's corporate agriculture is very progressive and quick to take advantage of changes in technology. Past experience has shown that smallholders are more conservative in their acceptance of changes, but they did readily accept new rice varieties when twin yield, disease resistance, and pest resistance were demonstrated. Government estimates on where the country will be in 1981 are contained in the third Malaysia plan.

## MAURITANIA

**Forestry.** Inquiries confirm that problems of deforestation and land degradation are indeed acute here, but no meaningful data exist on rate of loss. Officials concerned with the problem cite the rapid loss already of small-tree population here as due to the practice of breaking instead of cutting branches to enable small animals to feed and to the use of live trees for charcoal production. The extent of the concern about reforestation is best illustrated by the fact that the 325 hectare project run by the Lutheran Federation outside of Nouakchott is the only known reforestation effort in Mauritania.

**Soil and Land Development.** Information is limited to the visible evidence that desertification is an active process.

## MEXICO

Soil erosion is one of Mexico's greatest problems. The government has recently launched a National Reforestation and Social Betterment Program in the state of Jilotepec as part of the Portillo Administration's "Alliance for Production." The intent of the new program is to halt erosion, protect the environment, and promote forestation. Various government agencies will be involved in this effort.

The following analysis is based largely on "unofficial" data and observations of key personnel in soil and water conservation at the Agriculture and Water Resources Secretariat (SARH).

**Forestry.** We have no estimate of total deforestation in Mexico, but have a partial estimate showing that, in tropical zones only, some 80,000 hectares annually are being subjected to slash and burn techniques, which leads at best to two good harvests. Then the land is lost. Good forestry practices have not been used until now (with some exceptions). As noted above, a major reforestation program is just beginning. Whether the new program will prove adequate has yet to be determined.

**Soil.** We have no figures but are convinced that all the processes [mentioned in the questions on soil] are occurring here and contributing to significant loss of agricultural land to cultivation. SARH is concerned with the problem, but efforts to date have not markedly reduced the deterioration.

**Land Development.** It is estimated that it costs 50,000 to 60,000 pesos to develop an additional hectare of irrigated land (22.6 pesos equals one U.S. dollar). Seasonal land can be developed, with drainage, for 25,000 to 30,000 pesos per hectare. Some 12 million hectares have a potential for irrigated cultivation, and some 18 million hectares for seasonal cultivation. An eightfold increase in crop production is said to be theoretically possible by the year 2000, though there are doubts that this could really be brought about in practice.

**Yield Gains.** No data were available on yield gains attainable from technological change.

## PAKISTAN

Reliable data on the questions posed are rare.

**Forestry.** The Himalayan region of Pakistan has never been heavily forested. Only 3.4 percent of Pakistan's 200 million acre land area is generally reported as forested. This compares with 1965 estimates that 9.8 percent of West Pakistan's land was forested at the time of partition. Available data are insufficient to permit estimating the net rate of deforestation taking place or to test the high rate suggested by the two figures above, but nearly all estimates are that there is a net loss.

The *Pakistan Statistical Yearbook* of 1976 cites a 21.45 million cubic feet total out-turn from forests, of which 7.8 million cubic feet were used as timber and 13.6 million cubic feet for fire wood, a nearly 2:1 ratio of firewood to timber. The importance of firewood as a fuel was confirmed from a 1975 Survey of Households and Establishments, which showed firewood as the principal source of energy for both urban and rural households in all strata sampled. There is no apparent public or private concern over these practices. Plans to limit forest gleaning were stymied by "grandfather clauses" permitting families engaged in the timber business at the time of the legislation to retain their means of livelihood.

Pakistan's high rate of population growth (3 percent plus) amplifies the pressure of the rural and landless poor on the resources of the land, and a steady depletion of woodland has been the result. Many landless poor have minor livestock such as goats, which destroy ground cover. According to Erik P. Eckholm,* both the needy and the entrepreneurs are forced to poach for fuelwood in the protected (and economically and ecologically essential) national forest reserves.

The scale of the problem overwhelms scattered attempts to reverse the negative trends. Good forestry practices are not implemented, and no one really knows how much, if any, effective

reforestation is taking place. Disruption of watershed cover is responsible for declining soil fertility, accelerated soil erosion, and increasingly severe flooding.

The silt load in the Indus Basin, the principal hydrological system of Pakistan, is high, particularly on the upper reaches of the Indus River itself before it joins with the other less heavily silted major rivers of the system. At Tarbela, the silt load has been estimated at 440 million tons a year. The forestry institutes, which direct the few programs, have proven to be inadequately financed and unable to meet either the immediate or long-term needs of forest preservation.

**Soil.** Data on soil conservation efforts in response to problems of erosion, salinity, and waterlogging is also impressionistic. There is some concern, and work on the problem is being carried out, but a comprehensive, quantitative picture is not yet available. Quantifiable data are being gathered by a World Bank-managed study on the Indus Basin, with soil salinity surveys over a very wide area. Data are now being processed by computer, and preliminary results on rate of soil loss through salinity may be available from the World Bank. The low values of output per capita in Pakistan, whether measured in terms of value or of nutritional content, reflect the fact that agricultural yields in the area are among the lowest of all countries where agriculture is practiced on a large scale. Not only are farm yields low in Pakistan, but their growth continues to be constrained by a low rate of investment in both inputs and infrastructure in comparison to need.

As to waterlogging, the water table represents a dynamic equilibrium among evaporation, infiltration of river, rain, and irrigation water, and underground flows. This equilibrium has been upset by leakage from the new water courses and overwatering of fields. By some estimates, at least a third of the water diverted to the canals percolates downward to the water table, greatly increasing the overall rate of infiltration. Most serious is the capillary rise and evaporation of the underground water that occurs whenever the water table is within 10 feet of the surface. In an area where underground water has a salinity of 1,000 parts per million, evaporation at a rate of 2 feet per year (a typical value where the water table is only a few feet deep) will raise the salt content of the top 3 feet of soil to about 1 percent in 20 years. This is said to be too high for even the hardiest crops.

Ground-water evaporation is only one of the causes of high salinity in the soils of the Punjab.

---

* "The Other Energy Crisis: Firewood," Washington: Worldwatch Institute, 1975.

Irrigation practices have also contributed to salt accumulation. Percolation through the silt soils is slow; consequently, some of the irrigation water washes down very far beneath the root zone before it evaporates, and the residue of salt left by evaporation remains in the upper soil layers. In the Indus Plain, according to a special IBRD study, an estimated 18 million acres should be reclaimed. This is roughly 20 percent of the canal-irrigated area and 15 percent of the cultivated area in the Punjab District within the Indus Plain.

Fifteen years ago, waterlogging and salinity damage in the Punjab reached serious proportions. Investigators were convinced it could be cured or arrested in areas of relatively fresh and usable ground-water by constructing a system of large wells to provide vertical drainage. This program continues and is having success, but a consensus is growing that sizable investments on surface drainage will also be required. A further problem is that, as drainage is used to reduce the rate of salinization in the upper Indus irrigation system, the salt content of water used by farmers on the lower Indus in the Sind increases.

A critical area for research and analysis is finding the extent and significance of soil deterioration as a consequence of the salt or of the conjunctive use of marginal quality ground-water. What are the forms of deterioration? It is difficult to obtain a firm quantitative measure of the effect that waterlogging and salinity have had on agricultural production, and shifts in cropping patterns have occurred in response to other factors as well. However, the costs in human terms have been substantial.

**Land Development.** This question is too general and the problem it addresses contains too many interdependent variables for a reasonable estimate to be given. There are too many mixed costs, depending on whether it is hill land that needs to be terraced or irrigated land in which salts must be leached out—or if there is an extension of an irrigation system to previously unirrigated land. Regarding additions to crop production, there is the generally acknowledged dilemma of resolving uncertain yield potentials of present agricultural technology and feasible methods by which this new technology can be communicated to farmers.

**Yield Gains.** Agricultural output in Pakistan is limited by adverse physical conditions and other factors. The total cultivated area is increasing at about 1.3 percent a year and agricultural production methods hold the output per acre virtually constant in a situation of rapid population growth. The traditional practices governing the timing and amount of distribution of water among farmers are often inappropriate but difficult to change. In addition to such physical constraints as salinity and waterlogging (and financial ones like a lack of resources to invest in the use of fertilizer, high-yield varieties, and pesticides) farmers are often reluctant to risk trying new methods of cultivation. These factors all hold agricultural production down.

## SENEGAL

The following sketchy information was obtained from local sources, the few studies available, and the government's fifth quadrennial plan.

**Foresty.** The Department of Eaux et Forêts reports show that approximately 100,000 tons of charcoal are consumed annually for fuel in Senegal. Of this, 80 percent is used in the Cap Vert region. This represents 500,000 tons of wood, or all the wood produced on 10,000 ha of unclassified forests. At present, Eaux et Forêts reports, all unclassified forests in the Cap Vertathies area are depleted. Eaux et Forêts defines an unclassified depleted forest as one where all first growth wood has been removed and shrubs have taken over. This type growth will yield 0.5 to 0.7 tons of charcoal per hectare per year, whereas a properly managed forest under average Senegal conditions will yield 5.5 to 7 tons. Eaux et Forêts further estimates that all unclassified forests in Senegal will be depleted in 30 years at the present rate.

Indications in reports are that, in addition to the heavy fuel requirement for wood, extensive burning and uncontrolled grazing are doing as much damage as rapid harvest for charcoal and other wood products. The government of Senegal recognizes the problem as reflected in their fifth four year plan (i.e., planned expenditures of more than $40 million through Eaux et Forêts for such projects as forest seedling nurseries, forest reserve management, new forest preserves, fire protection, and windbreak and village woodlot plantings).

**Soil.** Data with respect to soil are weak. Of the approximately 2,300,000 hectares of land classed as permanent cropland, 822,000 are badly eroded from wind. On the erosion scale of USDA's Soil Conservation Service, this would probably be classed as a level 3 erosion. Based on a 1 to 5 scale, with 1 being slight, this erosion is critical. An additional 1,000,000 hectares would be classed as a level 2 erosion. The remaining approximately 500,000 hectares would actually gain some soil from windblown deposits and water-eroded sediment. Reports and studies done by USAID in project planning indicate the practice of allowing land to lie fallow is the exception rather than the rule, thus indicating very strong pressure on the land. The fifth four year plan (1977–81) recognizes the need for improvements: $45 million in projects affecting basic food crops (i.e., cereals, crop rotation, fertilizers, etc.). Additionally, approximately $50 million are planned for irrigation projects during this same period.

**Land Development.** Little information exists that would show that additional land, other than through irrigation, is available to bring into production. Estimates of new land that could be irrigated with water available or water that could be developed would not exceed 300,000 hectares at a cost of $5,000 per hectare. This would represent an investment requirement of $1.5 billion dollars.

**Yield Gains.** Yield gains under proper management of rainfed agriculture (i.e., crop rotation, water conservation measures, weed control, fertilizer, and better varieties) could double yields on traditional crop lands. Again, some effort is being made by the government and outside donors.

## SUDAN

We do not have a high degree of confidence in the data, but the consensus is that desertification and deforestation problems in the Sudan are very serious.

**Forestry.** Annually, about 3 million acres are cleared—2 million for mechanized crop production and 1 million for traditional agriculture and forest products. Only inside forestry reserves (0.5 percent of the total area of the Sudan) are good forestry practices followed. Expansion of forestry reserves is planned to cover 15 percent of the Sudan by 2000. Within reserves reforestation is taking place at the rate of 50,000 acres per year. Existing forests are showing severe signs of stress. Overgrazing is common, and 500,000–800,000 square kilometers are burned each year, removing about 300 million tons of foliage. Fuel wood consumption is estimated at 30 million stacked cubic meters. (Nomadic tribes uproot about 550 million acacia trees annually for firewood.) Deforestation has caused a pronounced problem in many water courses in central Sudan. Desertification is moving southward at a rate of 5–6 kilometer per year, according to a 1975 study of the National Council of Research. Other sources think the movement may be faster—perhaps 8–10 kilometer per year. Institutional programs to improve forestry generally are inadequate.

**Soil.** As indicated by the above desertification statistics, substantial agricultural land is being lost. About 600,000 acres in northern Sudan are affected by salinity problems. Sheet and gully erosion are common problems. No unit per time estimates are available of loss of agricultural soil. Current rainfed mechanized agricultural techniques generally require abandonment of cultivation after about five years. Introduction of different technologies perhaps could have a major impact. Various institutions exist to promote soil conservation, but they are inadequately staffed.

**Land Development.** Land development costs vary substantially. Irrigated land can be developed for about $2,000 per acre. These have been almost entirely public costs. However, in terms of new private sector agriculture developments, Sudan has started some concessionary assistance for infrastructure (pumps, canals) whereas at the time of project inception all of these costs were to be borne by the project. Costs of development of mechanized rainfed areas are about 10 percent of irrigated costs and generally are private costs. Expansion of arable land will have substantial impact on crop production. About 500,000 additional acres of irrigated land will be added in the next two to three years, and other projects to irrigate more than 1 million acres may be started in the next five years. Cultivation of 3–4 million additional rainfed acres is also projected in the next six years.

**Yield Gains.** Scattered estimates are available of what changes a particular technology would produce. However, in isolation these statistics are not very useful. Concerning the 2.3 million acre Gezira scheme, several agronomists have commented that they believe that, with modest capital inputs and some new technologies and incentives, production could be doubled or tripled within five years. Changes in rainfed technology also probably could achieve great increases in yields, particularly for acreage that has been cultivated for more than two years.

## THAILAND

**Summary.** The rate of deforestation in Thailand is accelerating and far outstrips efforts to control it. Less than 39 percent of the total land area remains in forests; at the present rate, this will drop to 17 percent by 1981 and effectively to zero by the end of the decade. Agricultural land expanded by 20 percent from 1971 to 1975 at the expense of the forests, but problems of water control remain more significant than land availability. Only 5.6 million hectares of land are irrigated or irrigable, and 12 percent of this land is in the northeast, the region most susceptible to drought and flooding. High costs of irrigation and technological innovation preclude rapid dissemination of more modern services and facilities to the majority of Thai farmers.

**Forestry.** One of the more significant problems facing Thailand now and in the immediate future is the excessive rate of deforestation. Based on satellite imagery from the Earth Resources Technology Satellite ERTS–1 in 1973, it was reported that the area of forest in Thailand totaled 20,074,900 hectares, or 39 percent of the country. An earlier study (1970) demonstrated that the annual consumption of wood and wood products in Thailand averaged 63.5 million cubic meters (mcm), of which 12.0 mcm was sawnwood, 1.5 mcm poles, and 50.0 mcm fuelwood requirements. A survey of Thai forests determined that 532,000 hectares of forest were required to satisfy such needs with an additional 255,000 hectares of forest also lost annually for shifting cultivation, or a total of 1.14 million hectares of forest cleared in 1970. Assuming that the rate of consumption will increase in proportion to the rate of population growth, or 2.55 percent per year, it is estimated that there will remain less than 9 million hectares of forest in Thailand in 1981, or 17 percent of the country, and by 1987 the entire forest area of Thailand will be effectively cleared.

The Royal Thai government has recognized the seriousness of the deforestation problem and has enacted measures to control it. There is already an established system of national parks and game preserves covering 2.26 million hectares, or 4.39 percent of the country. In addition, all areas above 600 meters elevation are protected by law against any logging or clearing for cultivation. These laws hold little relevance for the hill tribes system of shifting cultivation. The government reforestation program claims some success to date: 94,000 hectares of new forest have been replanted in the 10 years ending in 1976. Plans call for an additional 320,000 hectares of forest to be replanted each year over the next five years. While this target falls far short of the yearly rate of deforestation and is far beyond the present rate of reforestation, it does represent an increasing official awareness of the seriousness of the problem. However, despite all efforts to preserve the remaining forests and to replant those already cleared, illegal log poaching and subsequent illegal cultivation of forest land persists. A very rough estimate of the cost to a log poacher to clear a single hectare of forest with modern equipment is $600. Squatters moving into the cleared area can cultivate the land for one to two years, but by the third year it has been taken over by imperata and penisetum grass—pest grass that effectively prevents further cultivation. The pest grasses are particularly vulnerable to fire in the dry seasons and frequent grass fires destroy any chance for natural reforestation of the area. The result is that without some assistance by man, nature in Thailand cannot arrest or reverse the destruction of the forest once begun by the perpetrator, man himself. Present government reforestation programs do not balance the present rate of deforestation and even the most optimistic estimates of the rate of destruction offer no hope of significant forest stands in Thailand beyond 1993.

**Land Development.** Although by consensus it is agreed that agricultural land is being lost to cultivation through problems relating generally to water control, the direct correlation has not been quantified to date. A study completed by the Ministry of Agriculture and Agriculture Cooperatives (MAAC) in 1972 reveals that of the total area of land in Thailand, 51.4 million hectares, only about 29.7 million hectares are suitable for agricultural production. A later study, in 1975, revealed that from 1971 to 1975 the land area devoted to farm holdings had increased from 15.5 million to 18.6 million hectares, or by about 20 percent, and that most of this expansion was at the expense of forested areas. During the same period, the MAAC and other government agencies noted increasing problems of alternate flooding and drought in the north and northeast, the regions most seriously denuded of their past extensive and protective forest areas. Controlled water availability is a problem at least as significant in agricultural production as land scarcity, and MAAC estimates "irrigable land" at about 3.2 million hectares and "irrigated land" at about 2.4 million hectares, although irrigation is primarily supplemental during an adequate rainy season. Less than a third of a million hectares represent areas with adequate water control to permit double cropping. It is of interest to note that the northwest region, the region in which virtual total deforestation has been achieved, contains only 12 percent of the total irrigable land.

**Yield Gains.** Given the close correlation that exists between controlled moisture availability, crop yields, and return on investments in purchased inputs, it is quite understandable that the poorest farmers are found in those areas with limited irrigation facilities and unpredictable rainfall distribution patterns. These are also the groups facing the greatest risks in terms of technological innovation, and they are thus prone to follow low-yield, low-risk, traditional methods of production. The high costs of irrigation have precluded sufficiently large scale projects that might benefit significant numbers of poor farmers, and without adequate technology adapted to the prevailing rainfed conditions of the majority of Thai farmers, little relief can be expected in the foreseeable future.

## UPPER VOLTA

**Forestry.** Deforestation and degradation of agricultural land cannot be readily quantified because it is an ongoing process. People do recognize its extent and importance because they feel its consequences. Rather than attempt to quantify it in terms of area of deforested land (which depends on the definition of "deforested" and which has meaning only in relation to the prior equilibrium density of forest cover), one can argue that deforestation and degradation are better measured in terms of their impact on people: the number of people made hungry by declining crop yields, the number of people made poorer by loss of livestock, and the loss of revenue from agricultural and forestry activities in general as a result of decreased productivity of the resource base. It is not presently feasible to add up from year to year the area of "deforested land." At best, one can systematically sample the density and composition (species present and their relative frequency) of the vegetative cover, in order to document the condition and trend of the vegetation, and list the formerly abundant species that have become scarce. Many species that play crucial roles in protecting agricultural harvests, in maintaining soil fertility (and thus crop yields), and in forage production for livestock are being lost through deforestation and land degradation processes. Similarly, one cannot document the number of hectares "lost to the desert" from year to year, as there is no advancing boundary (from east to west below the Sahara) between desert and savanna pasture or farmland. Rather, desertification is also a process reflecting the fact that land has been exploited beyond its capacity to regenerate itself and to sustain its productivity. Declines in the productivity or in the biomass of the vegetation can be documented. There are, however, such tremendous variations within small areas that regional generalizations are of doubtful value. For example, several hectares in the forested lowland may be more productive and remain so in spite of increased use, while several adjacent hectares of eroded uplands are much less productive and may lose 50 percent of their potential productivity as a result of small increases in the intensity of use.

Regarding forestry practices, the government's Forest Service personnel play a protective role exclusively—i.e., they attempt to regulate the cut on essentially unmanaged forestland by prohibiting the taking of live wood. There are less than 500 hectares of plantations more than 20 years old. These have not been managed, that is, there has been no fire protection, no thinning, no planned harvesting. Since 1970, several hundred hectares of plantations have been established, but again there is little in place (personnel, operating budgets, equipment, marketing outlets) that would permit their long-term management. Some natural forest stands have been inventoried. However, no treatments have been prescribed or implemented except on an experimental scale. In brief, forest management and forestry in general have yet to be practiced in Upper Volta on a significant scale. Before this can be done, much more must be learned about regenerating local species and natural stands, about the silviculture of mixed—species/savanna forestland, and about the concepts of planned harvests and regeneration.

Regarding effective reforestation, only several hundred hectares, mostly eucalyptus and gmelina arborea, had been planted prior to 1974. Between 1974 and 1977, 2693 hectares have been planted in four different projects. By 1980 the government plans to establish over 5,000 hectares of mechanized plantations for firewood production. In summary, we can conclude that population growths in Upper Volta, lack of firewood plantations in the face of growing demand, misuse or overuse of existing resources, and climatic disasters have led to a condition where forest resources in Upper Volta must be characterized as "severely stressed."

The government has initiated or attempted to initiate programs to improve its institutional capacity to improve forest management practices. It has undertaken programs to increase the forestry school student capacity and has developed training programs to enable the forest service to absorb and manage larger-scale reforestation and forest management programs. Programs and initiatives have suffered from lack of operating funds and lack of qualified personnel, particularly at the village level.

**Soil.** Productivity of agricultural land is being lost annually on a large scale from erosion, laterization, and desertification. Since only 6,700 hectares are under irrigation in Upper Volta, there has been little damage from salinization or water-logging.

Soil fertility has been maintained primarily through sparse and sporadic spreading of manure in fields close to homesteads and through a system of crop rotation that is frequently violated by the exigencies of pressures to meet food production necessities.

**Land Development.** Under the auspices of the government's Authority for the Development of the Volta Valleys (AVV), a program has been established to facilitate settlement and development of areas cleared of the black fly, which transmits onchocerciasis (river blindness). Using the program as an example of bringing an additional hectare of land into cultivation, we estimate the costs to be about $1,450 per hectare. This figure represents an AVV program that costs about $14,500 to settle a family into a river basin (the family brings about 10 hectares into production). This AVV family settlement program is a costly method of bringing new land into production in Upper Volta, the costs of which are borne as a public expenditure. In contrast with the government-sponsored AVV program are spontaneous settlement, resettlement, and expansion of arable land. Although reliable figures are not available, the cost per hectare associated with spontaneous settlement would be significantly lower than the AVV example cited and the cost would represent private rather than public expenditure.

**Yield Gains.** Reliable data in Upper Volta are not readily available that would allow us to state with authority how much of crop production yield gains are attainable from or attributed to technological change. One reason is the absence of baseline information and uneven data collection procedures. Another reason is that production yields have fluctuated widely over the past 15 years, with declines registered in the early and mid-1970s because of the drought. Our best estimate is that over the past 15 years about a 20 percent crop production yield gain can be attributed to technological changes such as introduction of, or improved use of, fertilizers, pesticides, animal traction, irrigation, and timing and density of production.

Planning projections to the year 2000 by the government calls for doubling crop production. Government strategy to double production would be brought about by increased productivity, new and improved technology, reducing the vulnerability of agriculture production to drought, and by opening new lands to cultivation.

## ZAIRE

None of the government agencies queried has quantitative data with projections through the year 2000. Individual studies exist for certain areas of Zaire, but given the immense variety of terrain, soil, vegetation, and climate, it is impossible to extrapolate and generalize for the entire country. For example, AID/Zaire is preparing a study on land usage, soils, and agricultural yields in the region of northern Shaba, where AID is commencing a large-scale maize project. However, conditions there are completely different from mountainous regions in Kivu or the tropical rain forests of the Zaire River Basin. The information given below is drawn from conversations with knowledgeable officials and advisers of the government.

**Forestry.** With about 1 million square kilometers of forests (about 45 percent of the land area), deforestation was not considered a problem until recently. Lumber companies have done relatively little harm over the previous decades, since they cut only 12 varieties of the approximately 100 kinds of trees that grow in Zaire. Currently about 500,000 cubic meters of wood per year are cut for commercial purposes, and about one-third of that is exported. However, with the rapid population increase of the cities, deforestation around urban areas is becoming increasingly evident. Six percent of the population has electricity, and the majority cannot afford kerosene. Consequently, the government estimates that about 20 million cubic meters of wood per year are consumed for heat and to make charcoal for cooking. In the relatively heavily populated region of Bas Zaire, 60 percent of the forests have already been cut and the remaining major forest of 100,000 hectares at Mayombe is being heavily exploited.

The government began planting trees (mainly eucalyptus) around Kinshasa and in Bas Zaire in 1968. The goal is to expand the activity to deforested areas around other cities. The replanting brigade is currently under control of the Bureau de Préservation de Terre in the Department of Environment, Conservation of Nature, and Tourism. Previously, lumber companies paid a tax to Zaire to cover reforestation costs. However, the government's reforestation efforts in logged areas proved inadequate, and in a speech on November 25, 1977, President Mobutu repealed the tax and asked lumber companies to assume responsibility for replanting.

**Soil.** Although erosion has been accelerated by mining and slash and burn land clearing, especially on the Biano Plateau in southeastern Zaire, laterization and leaching of soil is endemic to most of Zaire due to extremely heavy rain and heat, which breaks down humus. In the areas of sandy type soil, there is more siltation due to increased land utilization. Ironically, the biggest natural problem on rivers is caused by rapidly spreading water hyacinth, which was introduced in the early 1960s and is now clogging rivers and lakes. The previously mentioned Bureau and a division within the Department of Agriculture promote soil conservation, but their efforts are inadequate.

**Land Development.** In a country where 50 percent of the territory is potentially arable but only 1 percent is actually cultivated, farmers can increase yield more rapidly and more cheaply by cultivating new land rather than by investing in technological change. Subsistence farmers traditionally clear new land every three years, allowing used land to lie fallow for 12 years or so. Commercial farmers are well aware that yield increases dramatically, especially for palm oil and certain other crops, when fertilizer is added to leached soil, but no fertilizer is manufactured locally and the current shortage of foreign exchange has made fertilizer very scarce. With completion of the Inga Dam, Zaire will have tremendous electrical production, which could be used for manufacturing fertilizer, but this is far in the future. The costs of bringing additional hectares into production differ enormously for subsistence farmers who slash and burn, and commercial, mechanized farmers. Costs to commercial farmers rise dramatically the further the land is located from highways, railroads, and navigable rivers. Fuel is currently very scarce in the interior, which greatly adds to the cost of cultivating new land far from Kinshasa or Lubumbashi.

# Appendix D: **Metric Conversion Factors**

It was intended that all units used in this study would be metric. Unfortunately, in the rush to prepare the manuscript, it was not possible to maintain uniformity of metric units. To help the reader convert units as necessary, it was decided to include an appendix of conversion factors. The best table of conversion factors that the Global 2000 Study was able to locate was the following alphabetical list, prepared jointly by the American Society for Testing Materials and the Institute of Electrical and Electronic Engineers in a short report "Metric Practice." Copies of the complete report (no. IEEE Std 268–1976) can be obtained from the Institute of Electrical and Electronic Engineers, 395 East 45th St., New York, N.Y. 10017.

**General:** The following tables of conversion factors are intended to serve two purposes.

To express the definitions of miscellaneous units of measure as exact numerical multiples of coherent "metric" units. Relationships that are exact in terms of the base unit are followed by an asterisk. Relationships that are not followed by an asterisk are either the results of physical measurements or are only approximate.

To provide multiplying factors for converting expressions of measurements given by numbers and miscellaneous units to corresponding new numbers and metric units.

### Notation.

Conversion factors are presented for ready adaptation to computer readout and electronic data transmission. The factors are written as a number greater than one and less than ten with six or less decimal places. This number is followed by the letter E (for exponent), a plus or minus symbol, and two digits which indicate the power of 10 by which the number must be multiplied to obtain the correct value. For example:

3.523 907 E−02 is $3.523\,907 \times 10^{-2}$

or                     0.035 239 07

Similarly:

3.386 389 E+03 is $3.386\,389 \times 10^{3}$

or                     3 386.389

An asterisk (*) after the sixth decimal place indicates that the conversion factor is exact and that all subsequent digits are zero. All other conversion factors have been rounded to the figures given in accordance with 4.4. Where less than six decimal places are shown, more precision is not warranted.

### Further example of use of tables:

| To convert from: | to: | Multiply by: |
|---|---|---|
| pound-force per square foot | Pa | 4.788 026 E+01 |
| inch | m | 2.540 000*E−02 |

means          $1\ \text{lbf/ft}^2 = 47.880\,26$ Pa
                    1 inch = 0.0254 m (exactly)

### Organization:

The conversion factors are listed in two ways—alphabetically and classified by physical quantity. Both lists contain those units which have specific names and compound units derived from these specific units. The classified list contains the more frequently used units for each physical quantity.

The conversion factors for other compound units can easily be generated from numbers given in the alphabetical list by the substitution of converted units, as follows:

EXAMPLE: To find conversion factor of lb·ft/s to kg·m/s:

first convert          1 lb to 0.453 592 4 kg

and                         1 ft to 0.3048 m

then substitute:

(0.453 592 4 kg)·(0.3048 m)/s

= 0.138 255 kg·m/s

thus the factor is 1.382 55 E−01

EXAMPLE: To find conversion factor of oz·in$^2$ to kg·m$^2$:

first convert          1 oz to 0.028 349 52 kg

and                         1 in$^2$ to 0.000 645 16 m$^2$

then substitute:

(0.028 349 52 kg)·(0.000 645 16 m$^2$)

= 0.000 018 289 98 kg·m$^2$

thus the factor is 1.828 998 E−05

739

## Alphabetical List of Units

### (Symbols of SI units given in parentheses)

| To convert from | to | Multiply by |
|---|---|---|
| abampere | ampere (A) | 1.000 000*E+01 |
| abcoulomb | coulomb (C) | 1.000 000*E+01 |
| abfarad | farad (F) | 1.000 000*E+09 |
| abhenry | henry (H) | 1.000 000*E−09 |
| abmho | siemens (S) | 1.000 000*E+09 |
| | | |
| abohm | ohm ($\Omega$) | 1.000 000*E−09 |
| abvolt | volt (V) | 1.000 000*E−08 |
| acre foot (US survey)[12] | meter$^3$ (m$^3$) | 1.233 489 E+03 |
| acre (US survey)[12] | meter$^2$ (m$^2$) | 4.046 873 E+03 |
| ampere hour | coulomb (C) | 3.600 000*E+03 |
| | | |
| are | meter$^2$ (m$^2$) | 1.000 000*E+02 |
| angstrom | meter (m) | 1.000 000*E−10 |
| astronomical unit[13] | meter (m) | 1.495 979 E+11 |
| atmosphere (standard) | pascal (Pa) | 1.013 250*E+05 |
| atmosphere (technical = 1 kgf/cm$^2$) | pascal (Pa) | 9.806 650*E+04 |
| | | |
| bar | pascal (Pa) | 1.000 000*E+05 |
| barn | meter$^2$ (m$^2$) | 1.000 000*E−28 |
| barrel (for petroleum, 42 gal) | meter$^3$ (m$^3$) | 1.589 873 E−01 |
| board foot | meter$^3$ (m$^3$) | 2.359 737 E−03 |
| | | |
| British thermal unit (International Table)[14] | joule (J) | 1.055 056 E+03 |
| British thermal unit (mean) | joule (J) | 1.055 87 E+03 |
| British thermal unit (thermochemical) | joule (J) | 1.054 350 E+03 |
| British thermal unit (39°F) | joule (J) | 1.059 67 E+03 |
| British thermal unit (59°F) | joule (J) | 1.054 80 E+03 |
| British thermal unit (60°F) | joule (J) | 1.054 68 E+03 |
| | | |
| Btu (International Table)·ft/h·ft$^2$·°F (k, thermal conductivity) | watt per meter kelvin (W/m·K) | 1.730 735 E+00 |
| Btu (thermochemical)·ft/h·ft$^2$·°F (k, thermal conductivity) | watt per meter kelvin (W/m·K) | 1.729 577 E+00 |
| Btu (International Table)·in/h·ft$^2$·°F (k, thermal conductivity) | watt per meter kelvin (W/m·K) | 1.442 279 E−01 |
| Btu (thermochemical)·in/h·ft$^2$·°F (k, thermal conductivity) | watt per meter kelvin (W/m·K) | 1.441 314 E−01 |
| Btu (International Table)·in/s·ft$^2$·°F (k, thermal conductivity) | watt per meter kelvin (W/m·K) | 5.192 204 E+02 |
| Btu (thermochemical)·in/s·ft$^2$·°F (k, thermal conductivity) | watt per meter kelvin (W/m·K) | 5.188 732 E+02 |

---

[12] Since 1893 the US basis of length measurement has been derived from metric standards. In 1959 a small refinement was made in the definition of the yard to resolve discrepancies both in this country and abroad, which changed its length from 3600/3937 m to 0.9144 m exactly. This resulted in the new value being shorter by two parts in a million.

At the same time it was decided that any data in feet derived from and published as a result of geodetic surveys within the US would remain with the old standard (1 ft = 1200/3937 m) until further decision. This foot is named the US survey foot.

As a result all US land measurements in US customary units will relate to the meter by the old standard. All the conversion factors in these tables for units referenced to this footnote are based on the US survey foot, rather than the international foot.

Conversion factors for the land measure given below may be determined from the following relationships:

1 league = 3 miles (exactly)
1 rod = 16½ feet (exactly)
1 section = 1 square mile (exactly)
1 township = 36 square miles (exactly)

[13] This value conflicts with the value printed in NBS 330 (17). The value requires updating in NBS 330.

[14] This value was adopted in 1956. Some of the older International Tables use the value 1.055 04 E+03. The exact conversion factor is 1.055 055 852 62*E+03.

| To convert from | to | Multiply by |
|---|---|---|
| Btu (International Table)/h . . . . . . . . . | watt (W) . . . . . . . . . . . . . . . . . . | 2.930 711 E−01 |
| Btu (thermochemical)/h . . . . . . . . . . . . | watt (W) . . . . . . . . . . . . . . . . . . | 2.928 751 E−01 |
| Btu (thermochemical)/min . . . . . . . . . | watt (W) . . . . . . . . . . . . . . . . . . | 1.757 250 E+01 |
| Btu (thermochemical)/s . . . . . . . . . . | watt (W) . . . . . . . . . . . . . . . . . . | 1.054 350 E+03 |
| | | |
| Btu (International Table)/ft$^2$ . . . . . . . | joule per meter$^2$ (J/m$^2$) . . . . . . . | 1.135 653 E+04 |
| Btu (thermochemical)/ft$^2$ . . . . . . . . . | joule per meter$^2$ (J/m$^2$) . . . . . . . . | 1.134 893 E+04 |
| Btu (thermochemical)/ft$^2$·h | watt per meter$^2$ (W/m$^2$) . . . . . . . . | 3.152 481 E+00 |
| Btu (thermochemical)/ft$^2$·min . . . . . . | watt per meter$^2$ (W/m$^2$) . . . . . . . . | 1.891 489 E+02 |
| Btu (thermochemical)/ft$^2$·s . . . . . . . . | watt per meter$^2$ (W/m$^2$) . . . . . . . . | 1.134 893 E+04 |
| | | |
| Btu (thermochemical)/in$^2$·s . . . . . . . . | watt per meter$^2$ (W/m$^2$) . . . . . . . . | 1.634 246 E+06 |
| Btu (International Table)/h·ft$^2$·°F | | |
|   (C, thermal conductance) . . . . . . . . | watt per meter$^2$ kelvin (W/m$^2$·K) . . | 5.678 263 E+00 |
| Btu (thermochemical)/h·ft$^2$·°F | | |
|   (C, thermal conductance) . . . . . . . . | watt per meter$^2$ kelvin (W/m$^2$·K) . . | 5.674 466 E+00 |
| Btu (International Table)/s·ft$^2$·°F . . . . | watt per meter$^2$ kelvin (W/m$^2$·K) . . | 2.044 175 E+04 |
| Btu (thermochemical)/s·ft$^2$·°F . . . . . . | watt per meter$^2$ kelvin (W/m$^2$·K) . . | 2.042 808 E+04 |
| | | |
| Btu (International Table)/lb . . . . . . . . | joule per kilogram (J/kg) . . . . . . . . | 2.326 000*E+03 |
| Btu (thermochemical)/lb . . . . . . . . . | joule per kilogram (J/kg) . . . . . . . . | 2.324 444 E+03 |
| Btu (International Table)/lb·°F | | |
|   (c, heat capacity) . . . . . . . . . . . . | joule per kilogram kelvin (J/kg·K) . . | 4.186 800*E+03 |
| Btu (thermochemical)/lb·°F | | |
|   (c, heat capacity) . . . . . . . . . . . . | joule per kilogram kelvin (J/kg·K) . | 4.184 000 E+03 |
| | | |
| bushel (US) . . . . . . . . . . . . . . . . . | meter$^3$ (m$^3$) . . . . . . . . . . . . . . | 3.523 907 E−02 |
| caliber (inch) . . . . . . . . . . . . . . . | meter (m) . . . . . . . . . . . . . . . . . | 2.540 000*E−02 |
| calorie (International Table) . . . . . . . | joule (J) . . . . . . . . . . . . . . . . . . | 4.186 800*E+00 |
| calorie (mean) . . . . . . . . . . . . . . . | joule (J) . . . . . . . . . . . . . . . · . | 4.190 02 E+00 |
| calorie (thermochemical) . . . . . . . . . . | joule (J) . . . . . . . . . . . . . . . . . . | 4.184 000*E+00 |
| | | |
| calorie (15°C) . . . . . . . . . . . . . . . | joule (J) . . . . . . . . . . . . . . . . . . | 4.185 80 E+00 |
| calorie (20°C) . . . . . . . . . . . . . . . | joule (J) . . . . . . . . . . . . . . . . . . | 4.181 90 E+00 |
| calorie (kilogram, International Table) . . | joule (J) . . . . . . . . . . . . . . . . . . | 4.186 800*E+03 |
| calorie (kilogram, mean) . . . . . . . . . . | joule (J) . . . . . . . . . . . . . . . . . . | 4.190 02 E+03 |
| calorie (kilogram, thermochemical) . . . . | joule (J) . . . . . . . . . . . . . . . . . . | 4.184 000*E+03 |
| | | |
| cal (thermochemical)/cm$^2$ . . . . . . . . . | joule per meter$^2$ (J/m$^2$) . . . . . . . . | 4.184 000*E+04 |
| cal (International Table)/g . . . . . . . . . | joule per kilogram (J/kg) . . . . . . . . | 4.186 800*E+03 |
| cal (thermochemical)/g . . . . . . . . . . . | joule per kilogram (J/kg) . . . . . . . . | 4.184 000*E+03 |
| cal (International Table)/g·°C . . . . . . . | joule per kilogram kelvin (J/kg·K) . | 4.186 800*E+03 |
| cal (thermochemical)/g·°C . . . . . . . . . | joule per kilogram kelvin (J/kg·K) . | 4.184 000*E+03 |
| | | |
| cal (thermochemical)/min . . . . . . . . . . | watt (W) . . . . . . . . . . . . . . . . . . | 6.973 333 E−02 |
| cal (thermochemical)/s . . . . . . . . . . . | watt (W) . . . . . . . . . . . . . . . . . . | 4.184 000*E+00 |
| cal (thermochemical)/cm$^2$·min . . . . . . | watt per meter$^2$ (W/m$^2$) . . . . . . . . | 6.973 333 E+02 |
| cal (thermochemical)/cm$^2$·s . . . . . . . | watt per meter$^2$ (W/m$^2$) . . . . . . . . | 4.184 000*E+04 |
| cal (thermochemical)/cm·s·°C . . . . . . . | watt per meter kelvin (W/m·K) . . . | 4.184 000*E+02 |
| | | |
| carat (metric) . . . . . . . . . . . . . . . . | kilogram (kg) . . . . . . . . . . . . . . . | 2.000 000*E−04 |
| centimeter of mercury (0°C) . . . . . . . . | pascal (Pa) . . . . . . . . . . . . . . . . . | 1.333 22 E+03 |
| centimeter of water (4°C) . . . . . . . . . | pascal (Pa) . . . . . . . . . . . . . . . . . | 9.806 38 E+01 |
| centipoise . . . . . . . . . . . . . . . . . . . | pascal second (Pa·s) . . . . . . . . . . | 1.000 000*E−03 |
| centistokes . . . . . . . . . . . . . . . . . . | meter$^2$ per second (m$^2$/s) . . . . . . . | 1.000 000*E−06 |
| | | |
| circular mil . . . . . . . . . . . . . . . . . | meter$^2$ (m$^2$) . . . . . . . . . . . . . . | 5.067 075 E−10 |
| clo . . . . . . . . . . . . . . . . . . . . . . . | kelvin meter$^2$ per watt (K·m$^2$/W) . . | 2.003 712 E−01 |
| cup . . . . . . . . . . . . . . . . . . . . . . . | meter$^3$ (m$^3$) . . . . . . . . . . . . . . | 2.365 882 E−04 |
| curie . . . . . . . . . . . . . . . . . . . . . . | becquerel (Bq) . . . . . . . . . . . . . . | 3.700 000*E+10 |

| To convert from | to | Multiply by |
|---|---|---|
| day (mean solar) | second (s) | 8.640 000 E+04 |
| day (sidereal) | second (s) | 8.616 409 E+04 |
| degree (angle) | radian (rad) | 1.745 329 E-02 |
| | | |
| degree Celsius | kelvin (K) $t_K = t_{°C} + 273.15$ | |
| degree centigrade | [see 3.4.2] | |
| degree Fahrenheit | degree Celsius $t_{°C} = (t_{°F} - 32)/1.8$ | |
| degree Fahrenheit | kelvin (K) $t_K = (t_{°F} + 459.67)/1.8$ | |
| degree Rankine | kelvin (K) $t_K = t_{°R}/1.8$ | |
| | | |
| $°F \cdot h \cdot ft^2$ /Btu (International Table) | | |
|   ($R$, thermal resistance) | kelvin meter$^2$ per watt (K·m$^2$/W) | 1.761 102 E-01 |
| $°F \cdot h \cdot ft^2$ /Btu (thermochemical) | | |
|   ($R$, thermal resistance) | kelvin meter$^2$ per watt (K·m$^2$/W) | 1.762 280 E-01 |
| denier | kilogram per meter (kg/m) | 1.111 111 E-07 |
| dyne | newton (N) | 1.000 000*E-05 |
| dyne·cm | newton meter (N·m) | 1.000 000*E-07 |
| dyne/cm$^2$ | pascal (Pa) | 1.000 000*E-01 |
| electronvolt | joule (J) | 1.602 19    -19 |
| | | |
| EMU of capacitance | farad (F) | 1.000 000*E+09 |
| EMU of current | ampere (A) | 1.000 000*E+01 |
| EMU of electric potential | volt (V) | 1.000 000*E-08 |
| EMU of inductance | henry (H) | 1.000 000*E-09 |
| EMU of resistance | ohm ($\Omega$) | 1.000 000*E-09 |
| | | |
| ESU of capacitance | farad (F) | 1.112 650 E-12 |
| ESU of current | ampere(A) | 3.335 6    E-10 |
| ESU of electric potential | volt (V) | 2.997 9    E+02 |
| ESU of inductance | henry (H) | 8.987 554 E+11 |
| ESU of resistance | ohm ($\Omega$) | 8.987 554 E+11 |
| | | |
| erg | joule (J) | 1.000 000*E-07 |
| erg/cm$^2$·s | watt per meter$^2$ (W/m$^2$) | 1.000 000*E-03 |
| erg/s | watt (W) | 1.000 000*E-07 |
| faraday (based on carbon-12) | coulomb (C) | 9.648 70   E+04 |
| faraday (chemical) | coulomb (C) | 9.649 57   E+04 |
| faraday (physical) | coulomb (C) | 9.652 19   E+04 |
| fathom | meter (m) | 1.828 8    E+00 |
| fermi (femtometer) | meter (m) | 1.000 000*E-15 |
| fluid ounce (US) | meter$^3$ (m$^3$) | 2.957 353 E-05 |
| | | |
| foot | meter (m) | 3.048 000*E-01 |
| foot (US survey)$^{12}$ | meter (m) | 3.048 006 E-01 |
| foot of water (39.2° F) | pascal (Pa) | 2.988 98   E+03 |
| ft$^2$ | meter$^2$ (m$^2$) | 9.290 304*E-02 |
| ft$^2$/h (thermal diffusivity) | meter$^2$ per second (m$^2$/s) | 2.580 640*E-05 |
| ft$^2$/s | meter$^2$ per second (m$^2$/s) | 9.290 304*E-02 |
| | | |
| ft$^3$ (volume; section modulus) | meter$^3$ (m$^3$) | 2.831 685 E-02 |
| ft$^3$/min | meter$^3$ per second (m$^3$/s) | 4.719 474 E-04 |
| ft$^3$/s | meter$^3$ per second (m$^3$/s) | 2.831 685 E-02 |
| ft$^4$(moment of section)$^{15}$ | meter$^4$(m$^4$) | 8.630 975 E-03 |
| | | |
| ft/h | meter per second (m/s) | 8.466 667 E-05 |
| ft/min | meter per second (m/s) | 5.080 000*E-03 |
| ft/s | meter per second (m/s) | 3.048 000*E-01 |
| ft/s$^2$ | meter per second$^2$ (m/s$^2$) | 3.048 000*E-01 |
| footcandle | lux (lx) | 1.076 391 E+01 |
| footlambert | candela per meter$^2$ (cd/m$^2$) | 3.426 259 E+00 |

---

[15] This is sometimes called the moment of inertia of a plane section about a specified axis.

| To convert from | to | Multiply by |
|---|---|---|
| ft·lbf | joule (J) | 1.355 818 E+00 |
| ft·lbf/h | watt (W) | 3.766 161 E−04 |
| ft·lbf/min | watt (W) | 2.259 697 E−02 |
| ft·lbf/s | watt (W) | 1.355 818 E+00 |
| ft·poundal | joule (J) | 4.214 011 E−02 |
| free fall, standard ($g$) | meter per second$^2$ (m/s$^2$) | 9.806 650*E+00 |
| | | |
| gal | meter per second$^2$ (m/s$^2$) | 1.000 000*E−02 |
| gallon (Canadian liquid) | meter$^3$ (m$^3$) | 4.546 090 E−03 |
| gallon (UK liquid) | meter$^3$ (m$^3$) | 4.546 092 E−03 |
| gallon (US dry) | meter$^3$ (m$^3$) | 4.404 884 E−03 |
| gallon (US liquid) | meter$^3$ (m$^3$) | 3.785 412 E−03 |
| gal (US liquid)/day | meter$^3$ per second (m$^3$/s) | 4.381 264 E−08 |
| gal (US liquid)/min | meter$^3$ per second (m$^3$/s) | 6.309 020 E−05 |
| gal (US liquid)/hp·h (SFC, specific fuel consumption) | meter$^3$ per joule (m$^3$/J) | 1.410 089 E−09 |
| | | |
| gamma | tesla (T) | 1.000 000*E−09 |
| gauss | tesla (T) | 1.000 000*E−04 |
| gilbert | ampere (A) | 7.957 747 E−01 |
| gill (UK) | meter$^3$ (m$^3$) | 1.420 654 E−04 |
| gill (US) | meter$^3$ (m$^3$) | 1.182 941 E−04 |
| | | |
| grad | degree (angular) | 9.000 000*E−01 |
| grad | radian (rad) | 1.570 796 E−02 |
| grain (1/7000 lb avoirdupois) | kilogram (kg) | 6.479 891*E−05 |
| grain (lb avoirdupois/7000)/gal (US liquid) | kilogram per meter$^3$ (kg/m$^3$) | 1.711 806 E−02 |
| | | |
| gram | kilogram (kg) | 1.000 000*E−03 |
| g/cm$^3$ | kilogram per meter$^3$ (kg/m$^3$) | 1.000 000*E+03 |
| gram-force/cm$^2$ | pascal (Pa) | 9.806 650*E+01 |
| hectare | meter$^2$ (m$^2$) | 1.000 000*E+04 |
| horsepower (550 ft·lbf/s) | watt (W) | 7.456 999 E+02 |
| | | |
| horsepower (boiler) | watt (W) | 9.809 50 E+03 |
| horsepower (electric) | watt (W) | 7.460 000*E+02 |
| horsepower (metric) | watt (W) | 7.354 99 E+02 |
| horsepower (water) | watt (W) | 7.460 43 E+02 |
| horsepower (U.K.) | watt (W) | 7.457 0 E+02 |
| | | |
| hour (mean solar) | second (s) | 3.600 000 E+03 |
| hour (sidereal) | second (s) | 3.590 170 E+03 |
| hundredweight (long) | kilogram (kg) | 5.080 235 E+01 |
| hundredweight (short) | kilogram (kg) | 4.535 924 E+01 |
| | | |
| inch | meter (m) | 2.540 000*E−02 |
| inch of mercury (32°F) | pascal (Pa) | 3.386 38 E+03 |
| inch of mercury (60°F) | pascal (Pa) | 3.376 85 E+03 |
| inch of water (39.2°F) | pascal (Pa) | 2.490 82 E+02 |
| inch of water (60°F) | pascal (Pa) | 2.488 4 E+02 |
| | | |
| in$^2$ | meter$^2$ (m$^2$) | 6.451 600*E−04 |
| in$^3$ (volume; section modulus)[16] | meter$^3$ (m$^3$) | 1.638 706 E−05 |
| in$^3$/min | meter$^3$ per second (m$^3$/s) | 2.731 177 E−07 |
| in$^4$ (moment of section)[15] | meter$^4$ (m$^4$) | 4.162 314 E−07 |
| | | |
| in/s | meter per second (m/s) | 2.540 000*E−02 |
| in/s$^2$ | meter per second$^2$ (m/s$^2$) | 2.540 000*E−02 |
| kayser | 1 per meter (1/m) | 1.000 000*E+02 |
| kelvin | degree Celsius | $t_{°C} = t_K - 273.15$ |

[16] The exact conversion factor is 1.638 706 4*E−05.

| To convert from | to | Multiply by |
|---|---|---|
| kilocalorie (International Table) . . . . . . | joule (J) . . . . . . . . . . . . . . . . . | 4.186 800*E+03 |
| kilocalorie (mean) . . . . . . . . . . . . . | joule (J) . . . . . . . . . . . . . . . . . | 4.190 02   E+03 |
| kilocalorie (thermochemical) . . . . . . . . | joule (J) . . . . . . . . . . . . . . . . . | 4.184 000*E+03 |
| kilocalorie (thermochemical)/min . . . . . | watt (W) . . . . . . . . . . . . . . . . | 6.973 333 E+01 |
| kilocalorie (thermochemical)/s . . . . . . . | watt (W) . . . . . . . . . . . . . . . . | 4.184 000*E+03 |
| kilogram-force (kgf) . . . . . . . . . . . . . | newton (N) . . . . . . . . . . . . . . . | 9.806 650*E+00 |
| kgf·m . . . . . . . . . . . . . . . . . . . . . | newton meter (N·m) . . . . . . . . . . | 9.806 650*E+00 |
| kgf·s$^2$/m (mass) . . . . . . . . . . . . . . | kilogram (kg) . . . . . . . . . . . . . . | 9.806 650*E+00 |
| kgf/cm$^2$ . . . . . . . . . . . . . . . . . . . | pascal (Pa) . . . . . . . . . . . . . . . | 9.806 650*E+04 |
| kgf/m$^2$ . . . . . . . . . . . . . . . . . . . . | pascal (Pa) . . . . . . . . . . . . . . . | 9.806 650*E+00 |
| kgf/mm$^2$ . . . . . . . . . . . . . . . . . . . | pascal (Pa) . . . . . . . . . . . . . . . | 9.806 650*E+06 |
| km/h . . . . . . . . . . . . . . . . . . . . . . | meter per second (m/s) . . . . . . . . | 2.777 778 E-01 |
| kilopond . . . . . . . . . . . . . . . . . . . . | newton (N) . . . . . . . . . . . . . . . | 9.806 650*E+00 |
| kW·h . . . . . . . . . . . . . . . . . . . . . . | joule (J) . . . . . . . . . . . . . . . . . | 3.600 000*E+06 |
| kip (1000 lbf) . . . . . . . . . . . . . . . . | newton (N) . . . . . . . . . . . . . . . | 4.448 222 E+03 |
| kip/in$^2$ (ksi) . . . . . . . . . . . . . . . . | pascal (Pa) . . . . . . . . . . . . . . . | 6.894 757 E+06 |
| knot (international) . . . . . . . . . . . . . | meter per second (m/s) . . . . . . . . | 5.144 444 E-01 |
| lambert . . . . . . . . . . . . . . . . . . . . | candela per meter$^2$ (cd/m$^2$) . . . . . | 1/$\pi$        *E+04 |
| lambert . . . . . . . . . . . . . . . . . . . . | candela per meter$^2$ (cd/m$^2$) . . . . . | 3.183 099 E+03 |
| langley . . . . . . . . . . . . . . . . . . . . . | joule per meter$^2$ (J/m$^2$) . . . . . . . | 4.184 000*E+04 |
| league . . . . . . . . . . . . . . . . . . . . | meter (m) . . . . . . . . . . . . . . . . | [see footnote 12] |
| light year . . . . . . . . . . . . . . . . . . . | meter (m) . . . . . . . . . . . . . . . . | 9.460 55   E+15 |
| liter[17] . . . . . . . . . . . . . . . . . . . . . | meter$^3$ (m$^3$) . . . . . . . . . . . . . . | 1.000 000*E-03 |
| maxwell . . . . . . . . . . . . . . . . . . . . | weber (Wb) . . . . . . . . . . . . . . . | 1.000 000*E-08 |
| mho . . . . . . . . . . . . . . . . . . . . . . | siemens (S) . . . . . . . . . . . . . . . | 1.000 000*E+00 |
| microinch . . . . . . . . . . . . . . . . . . . | meter (m) . . . . . . . . . . . . . . . . | 2.540 000*E-08 |
| micron . . . . . . . . . . . . . . . . . . . . . | meter (m) . . . . . . . . . . . . . . . . | 1.000 000*E-06 |
| mil . . . . . . . . . . . . . . . . . . . . . . . | meter (m) . . . . . . . . . . . . . . . . | 2.540 000*E-05 |
| mile (international) . . . . . . . . . . . . | meter (m) . . . . . . . . . . . . . . . . | 1.609 344*E+03 |
| mile (statute) . . . . . . . . . . . . . . . . | meter (m) . . . . . . . . . . . . . . . . | 1.609 3    E+03 |
| mile (US survey)[12] . . . . . . . . . . . . | meter (m) . . . . . . . . . . . . . . . . | 1.609 347 E+03 |
| mile (international nautical) . . . . . . . . | meter (m) . . . . . . . . . . . . . . . . | 1.852 000*E+03 |
| mile (UK nautical) . . . . . . . . . . . . . | meter (m) . . . . . . . . . . . . . . . . | 1.853 184*E+03 |
| mile (US nautical) . . . . . . . . . . . . . . | meter (m) . . . . . . . . . . . . . . . . | 1.852 000*E+03 |
| mi$^2$ (international) . . . . . . . . . . . . . | meter$^2$ (m$^2$) . . . . . . . . . . . . . | 2.589 988 E+06 |
| mi$^2$ (US survey)[12] . . . . . . . . . . . . | meter$^2$ (m$^2$) . . . . . . . . . . . . . | 2.589 998 E+06 |
| mi/h (international) . . . . . . . . . . . . . | meter per second (m/s) . . . . . . . . | 4.470 400*E-01 |
| mi/h (international) . . . . . . . . . . . . . | kilometer per hour (km/h) . . . . . . | 1.609 344*E+00 |
| mi/min (international) . . . . . . . . . . . . | meter per second (m/s) . . . . . . . . | 2.682 240*E+01 |
| mi/s (international) . . . . . . . . . . . . . | meter per second (m/s) . . . . . . . . | 1.609 344*E+03 |
| millibar . . . . . . . . . . . . . . . . . . . . | pascal (Pa) . . . . . . . . . . . . . . . | 1.000 000*E+02 |
| millimeter of mercury (0°C) . . . . . . . | pascal (Pa) . . . . . . . . . . . . . . . | 1.333 22   E+02 |
| minute (angle) . . . . . . . . . . . . . . . . | radian (rad) . . . . . . . . . . . . . . . | 2.908 882 E-04 |
| minute (mean solar) . . . . . . . . . . . . | second (s) . . . . . . . . . . . . . . . . | 6.000 000 E+01 |
| minute (sidereal) . . . . . . . . . . . . . . | second (s) . . . . . . . . . . . . . . . . | 5.983 617 E+01 |
| month (mean calendar) . . . . . . . . . . . | second (s) . . . . . . . . . . . . . . . . | 2.628 000 E+06 |
| oersted . . . . . . . . . . . . . . . . . . . | ampere per meter (A/m) . . . . . . . | 7.957 747 E+01 |
| ohm centimeter . . . . . . . . . . . . . . . . | ohm meter (Ω·m) . . . . . . . . . . . | 1.000 000*E-02 |
| ohm circular-mil per ft . . . . . . . . . . . | ohm millimeter$^2$ per meter<br>(Ω·mm$^2$/m) . . . . . . . . . . . . . . | 1.662 426 E-03, |

---

[17] In 1964 the General Conference on Weights and Measures adopted the name liter as a special name for the cubic decimeter. Prior to this decision the liter differed slightly (previous value, 1.000 028 dm$^3$) and in expression of precision volume measurement this fact must be kept in mind.

| To convert from | to | Multiply by |
|---|---|---|
| ounce (avoirdupois) . . . . . . . . . . . . . | kilogram (kg) . . . . . . . . . . . . | 2.834 952  E-02 |
| ounce (troy or apothecary) . . . . . . . . | kilogram (kg) . . . . . . . . . . . . | 3.110 348  E-02 |
| ounce (UK fluid) . . . . . . . . . . . . . . | meter$^3$ (m$^3$) . . . . . . . . . . | 2.841 307  E-05 |
| ounce (US fluid) . . . . . . . . . . . . . . | meter$^3$ (m$^3$) . . . . . . . . . . | 2.957 353  E-05 |
| ounce-force . . . . . . . . . . . . . . . . | newton (N) . . . . . . . . . . . . . | 2.780 139  E-01 |
| ozf·in . . . . . . . . . . . . . . . . . . . . | newton meter (N·m) . . . . . . . . . | 7.061 552  E-03 |
| oz (avoirdupois)/gal (UK liquid) . . . . . | kilogram per meter$^3$ (kg/m$^3$) . . . | 6.236 021  E+00 |
| oz (avoirdupois)/gal (US liquid) . . . . . | kilogram per meter$^3$ (kg/m$^3$) . . . | 7.489 152  E+00 |
| oz (avoirdupois)/in$^3$ . . . . . . . . . . . | kilogram per meter$^3$ (kg/m$^3$) . . . . | 1.729 994  E+03 |
| oz (avoirdupois)/ft$^2$ . . . . . . . . . . . | kilogram per meter$^2$ (kg/m$^2$) . . . . | 3.051 517  E-01 |
| oz (avoirdupois)/yd$^2$ . . . . . . . . . . | kilogram per meter$^2$ (kg/m$^2$) . . . . | 3.390 575  E-02 |
| parsec[13] . . . . . . . . . . . . . . . . . . | meter (m) . . . . . . . . . . . . . . | 3.085 678  E+16 |
| peck (US) . . . . . . . . . . . . . . . . . . | meter$^3$(m$^3$) . . . . . . . . . . . . | 8.809 768  E-03 |
| pennyweight . . . . . . . . . . . . . . . . | kilogram (kg) . . . . . . . . . . . . | 1.555 174  E-03 |
| perm (0°C) . . . . . . . . . . . . . . . . . | kilogram per pascal second meter$^2$ (kg/Pa·s·m$^2$) . . . . . . . . . . . . | 5.721 35   E-11 |
| perm (23°C) . . . . . . . . . . . . . . . . . | kilogram per pascal second meter$^2$ (kg/Pa·s·m$^2$) . . . . . . . . . . . . | 5.745 25   E-11 |
| perm·in (0°C) . . . . . . . . . . . . . . . . | kilogram per pascal second meter (kg/Pa·s·m) . . . . . . . . . . . . | 1.453 22   E-12 |
| perm·in (23°C) . . . . . . . . . . . . . . . | kilogram per pascal second meter (kg/Pa·s·m) . . . . . . . . . . . . | 1.459 29   E-12 |
| phot . . . . . . . . . . . . . . . . . . | lumen per meter$^2$ (lm/m$^2$) . . . . . | 1.000 000*E+04 |
| pica (printer's) . . . . . . . . . . . . . | meter (m) . . . . . . . . . . . . . . | 4.217 518  E-03 |
| pint (US dry) . . . . . . . . . . . . . . . | meter$^3$ (m$^3$) . . . . . . . . . . . | 5.506 105  E-04 |
| pint (US liquid) . . . . . . . . . . . . . . | meter$^3$ (m$^3$) . . . . . . . . . . | 4.731 765  E-04 |
| point (printer's) . . . . . . . . . . . . . . | meter (m) . . . . . . . . . . . . . . | 3.514 598*E-04 |
| poise (absolute viscosity) . . . . . . . . . . | pascal second (Pa · s) . . . . . . . . | 1.000 000*E-01 |
| pound (lb avoirdupois)[18] . . . . . . . . . | kilogram (kg) . . . . . . . . . . . . | 4.535 924  E-01 |
| pound (troy or apothecary) . . . . . . . . | kilogram (kg) . . . . . . . . . . . . | 3.732 417  E-01 |
| lb·ft$^2$ (moment of inertia) . . . . . . . . | kilogram meter$^2$ (kg·m$^2$) . . . . . . | 4.214 011  E-02 |
| lb·in$^2$ (moment of inertia) . . . . . . . . | kilogram meter$^2$ (kg·m$^2$) . . . . . . | 2.926 397  E-04 |
| lb/ft·h . . . . . . . . . . . . . . . . . . . | pascal second (Pa·s) . . . . . . . . . . | 4.133 789  E-04 |
| lb/ft·s . . . . . . . . . . . . . . . . . . . | pascal second (Pa·s) . . . . . . . . . . | 1.488 164  E+00 |
| lb/ft$^2$ . . . . . . . . . . . . . . . . . . . | kilogram per meter$^2$ (kg/m$^2$) . . . . | 4.882 428  E+00 |
| lb/ft$^3$ . . . . . . . . . . . . . . . . . . . | kilogram per meter$^3$ (kg/m$^3$) . . . . | 1.601 846  E+01 |
| lb/gal (UK liquid) . . . . . . . . . . . . . | kilogram per meter$^3$ (kg/m$^3$) . . . . | 9.977 633  E+01 |
| lg/gal (US liquid) . . . . . . . . . . . . . | kilogram per meter$^3$ (kg/m$^3$) . . . . | 1.198 264  E+02 |
| lb/h . . . . . . . . . . . . . . . . . . . . | kilogram per second (kg/s) . . . . . . . | 1.259 979  E-04 |
| lb/hp·h (SFC, specific fuel consumption . . . . . | kilogram per joule (kg/J) . . . . . . . | 1.689 659  E-07 |
| lg/in$^3$ . . . . . . . . . . . . . . . . . . . | kilogram per meter$^3$ (kg/m$^3$) . . . . | 2.767 990  E+04 |
| lb/min . . . . . . . . . . . . . . . . . . . | kilogram per second (kg/s) . . . . . . . | 7.559 873  E-03 |
| lb/s . . . . . . . . . . . . . . . . . . . . | kilogram per second (kg/s) . . . . . . . | 4.535 924  E-01 |
| lb/yd$^3$ . . . . . . . . . . . . . . . . . . . | kilogram per meter$^3$ (kg/m$^3$) . . . . | 5.932 764  E-01 |
| poundal . . . . . . . . . . . . . . . . . . | newton (N) . . . . . . . . . . . . . | 1.382 550  E-01 |
| poundal/ft$^2$ . . . . . . . . . . . . . . . . | pascal (Pa) . . . . . . . . . . . . . | .1488 164  E+00 |
| poundal·s/ft$^2$ . . . . . . . . . . . . . . . | pascal second (Pa·s) . . . . . . . . . . | 1.488 164  E+00 |
| pound-force (lbf)[19] . . . . . . . . . . . . | newton (N) . . . . . . . . . . . . . | 4.448 222  E+00 |
| lbf·ft . . . . . . . . . . . . . . . . . . . | newton meter (N·m) . . . . . . . . . | 1.355 818  E+00 |
| lbf·ft/in . . . . . . . . . . . . . . . . . . | newton meter per meter (N·m/m) . . . . | 5.337 866  E+01 |
| lbf·in . . . . . . . . . . . . . . . . . . . | newton meter (N·m) . . . . . . . . . | 1.129 848  E-01 |
| lbf·in/in . . . . . . . . . . . . . . . . . . | newton meter per meter (N·m/m) . . | 4.448 222  E+00 |
| lbf·s/ft$^2$ . . . . . . . . . . . . . . . . . | pascal second (Pa·s) . . . . . . . . . . | 4.788 026  E+01 |

---

[18] The exact conversion factor is 4.535 923 7*E-01.

[19] The exact conversion factor is 4.448 221 615 260 5*E+00.

| To convert from | to | Multiply by |
|---|---|---|
| lbf/ft | newton per meter (N/m) | 1.459 390  E+01 |
| lbf/ft$^2$ | pascal (Pa) | 4.788 026  E+01 |
| lbf/in | newton per meter (N/m) | 1.751 268  E+02 |
| lbf/in$^2$ (psi) | pascal (Pa) | 6.894 757  E+03 |
| lbf/lb (thrust/weight [mass] ratio) | newton per kilogram (N/kg) | 9.806 650  E+00 |
| quart (US dry) | meter$^3$ (m$^3$) | 1.101 221  E-03 |
| quart (US liquid) | meter$^3$ (m$^3$) | 9.463 529  E-04 |
| rad (radiation dose absorbed) | gray (Gy) | 1.000 000*E-02 |
| rhe | 1 per pascal second (1/Pa·s) | 1.000 000*E+01 |
| rod | meter (m) | [see footnote 12] |
| roentgen | coulomb per kilogram (C/kg) | 2.58        E-04 |
| second (angle) | radian (rad) | 4.848 137  E-06 |
| second (sidereal) | second (s) | 9.972 696  E-01 |
| section | meter$^2$ (m$^2$) | [see footnote 12] |
| shake | second (s) | 1.000 000*E-08 |
| slug | kilogram (kg) | 1.459 390  E+01 |
| slug/ft·s | pascal second (Pa·s) | 4.788 026  E+01 |
| slug/ft$^3$ | kilogram per meter$^3$ (kg/m$^3$) | 5.153 788  E+02 |
| statampere | ampere (A) | 3.335 640  E-10 |
| statcoulomb | coulomb (C) | 3.335 640  E-10 |
| statfarad | farad (F) | 1.112 650  E-12 |
| stathenry | henry (H) | 8.987 554  E+11 |
| statmho | siemens (S) | 1.112 650  E-12 |
| statohm | ohm ($\Omega$) | 8.987 554  E+11 |
| statvolt | volt (V) | 2.997 925  E+02 |
| stere | meter$^3$ (m$^3$) | 1.000 000*E+00 |
| stilb | candela per meter$^2$ (cd/m$^2$) | 1.000 000*E+04 |
| stokes (kinematic viscosity) | meter$^2$ per second (m$^2$/s) | 1.000 000*E-04 |
| tablespoon | meter$^3$ (m$^3$) | 1.478 676  E-05 |
| teaspoon | meter$^3$ (m$^3$) | 4.928 922  E-06 |
| tex | kilogram per meter (kg/m) | 1.000 000*E-06 |
| therm | joule (J) | 1.055 056  E+08 |
| ton (assay) | kilogram (kg) | 2.916 667  E-02 |
| ton (long, 2240 lb) | kilogram (kg) | 1.016 047  E+03 |
| ton (metric) | kilogram (kg) | 1.000 000*E+03 |
| ton (nuclear equivalent of TNT) | joule (J) | 4.184        E+09[20] |
| ton (refrigeration) | watt (W) | 3.516 800  E+03 |
| ton (register) | meter$^3$ (m$^3$) | 2.831 685  E+00 |
| ton (short, 2000 lb) | kilogram (kg) | 9.071 847  E+02 |
| ton (long)/yd$^3$ | kilogram per meter$^3$ (kg/m$^3$) | 1.328 939  E+03 |
| ton (short)/h | kilogram per second (kg/s) | 2.519 958  E-01 |
| ton-force (2000 lbf) | newton (N) | 8.896 444  E+03 |
| tonne | kilogram (kg) | 1.000 000*E+03 |
| torr (mm Hg, 0°C) | pascal (Pa) | 1.333 22    E+02 |
| township | meter$^2$ (m$^2$) | [see footnote 12] |
| unit pole | weber (Wb) | 1.256 637  E-07 |
| W·h | joule (J) | 3,600 000*E+03 |
| W·s | joule (J) | 1,000 000*E+00 |
| W/cm$^2$ | watt per meter$^2$ (W/m$^2$) | 1.000 000*E+04 |
| W/in$^2$ | watt per meter$^2$ (W/m$^2$) | 1.550 003  E+03 |

---

[20] Defined (not measured) value.

| To convert from | to | Multiply by |
|---|---|---|
| yard | meter (m) | 9.144 000*E-01 |
| yd$^2$ | meter$^2$ (m$^2$) | 8.361 274 E-01 |
| yd$^3$ | meter$^3$ (m$^3$) | 7.645 549 E-01 |
| yd$^3$/min | meter$^3$ per second (m$^3$/s) | 1.274 258 E-02 |
| year (calendar) | second (s) | 3.153 600 E+07 |
| year (sidereal) | second (s) | 3.155 815 E+07 |
| year (tropical) | second (s) | 3.155 693 E+07 |

# INDEX

# INDEX

Guatemala, 249, 509
Guinea, 223
Guyana, 509
Guzman, Raphael, 280

Häfele, Wolf, 342
Hagenstein, Perry R., 693
Haiti, 95, 280, 298
Halogenated hydrocarbons, 307
Handler, Philip, 275–276, 292
Hardeman County, Tenn., 254
Hardin, Garrett, 233, 240, 332
Harlan, Jack, 291
Harman, Willis W., 699
Hawaii, 304
Hayes, Earl, 389
Hennemuth, Richard, 498
Herbicides. See Pesticides.
Hexachlorobenzene, 306, 307
Holdren, John P., 348
Hoover, Herbert, 686–687
Housing and Urban Development Act of 1970, 703, 705
Housing and Urban Development, Department of (U.S.), 704
Hubbert, M. King, 191, 579, 692
Hudson Institute, 621–622, 699
Humphrey, Hubert, 705, 708
Hungary, 197
Hunt, Larry, 333

Iceland, 301
Ickes, Harold, 687
IEES. See International Energy Evaluation System.
Illinois, 281
Iltis, Hugh H., 290
India
  Bio-gas, 378
  Charcoal smelting, 389
  Chipko Andolan tree hugger movement, 322–323
  Climate trends and, 259
  Deforestation, 280, 320–325
  Dung fuel, 377, 378
  Embassy reports from, 728–729
  Forests, 133
  Fuelwood shortage, 406
  Loss of agricultural land, 282
  Mangrove communities, 304
  Migration and, 33–34, 36
  Pesticide use in, 285
  Population data, 509
  Radioactive pollution by, 309
  Water use, 148, 151
  Water withdrawals, 150
  Wood fuel, 375, 376
Indians, American, 233
Indonesia, 129, 130, 166, 280, 321, 323, 729–730
Industrialized nations
  Causes of death, 249–250
  Energy and environmental prospects, 373—374
  Energy development in, 421–422
  Energy projections, difficulties with, 348
  Environment and GNP, 422
  Environment and health issues in, 249–251
  Environment and population projections, 426–427
  Food consumption statistics, 274
  Land deterioration in, 415
  Life expectancies in, 249

Loss of agricultural lands, 1960–2000, 282
Population and environment of, 238–241
Resource consumption in, 238
Shift to coal, 405
Shift to nuclear energy, 405–406
Urbanization and, 244–246, 408
Water pollution, 2000, 404
Institute for the Future, 535, 698, 699
Intensity of use analysis. See Malenbaum.
Interior Department (U.S.) model, 462
International Bank for Reconstruction and Development. See World Bank Group.
International Board for Plant Genetic Resources, 291
International Coal Federation, 576
International Conference on Water for Peace, 492
International Development Association. See World Bank Group.
International Energy Evaluation System (IEES)
  Assumptions of, 70
  Components of, 573–575
  Described, 493
  Emissions projections, 181, 183
  Energy market forecasts, 165
  Energy projections, 180
  Final energy products in linear program, 575
  Interface with Energy System Network Simulator (ESNS), 566
  Level of investment for pollution control assumed, 469
  Level of water availability assumed, 469
  Limitations of, 567, 571
  Primary fuel types in supply submodel, 574
  Principles of, 570–573
  Procedures, 575–578
  Rate of resource consumption in LDCs, 469
  Regional classifications, 573
  Structure of, 577
  Submodels of, 573–575
  Transport modes and fuels carried, 574
International Federation of Institutes of Advanced Study, 370
International Finance Corporation. See World Bank Group.
International Institute of Applied Systems Analysis, 267, 634, 707
International Institute for Environment and Development, 371
International Labor Office, 32
International Maritime Consultative Organization, 429
International Materials Conference, 689
International Monetary Fund, 689
International Rice Research Institute, 417
International Seabed Resource Authority, 224
International Union for the Conservation of Nature and Natural Resources, 316, 344
International Whaling Commission, 314
IOU. See Malenbaum reports, Intensity of use analysis.
Iowa, 281
Iran, 148, 169, 248, 322, 706
Iraq, 152, 343
Ireland, 289
Irish Sea, 305
Irrigation. See Water.
Ismir, Turkey, 242
Israel, 298
Italy, 31, 706
IUCN. See International Union for the Conservation of Nature and Natural Resources.
Ivory Coast, 128, 280

Jakarta, 426
Jamaica, 33, 223, 509